The New Film Index

The New Film Index

A Bibliography of Magazine Articles in English, 1930–1970

By RICHARD DYER MacCANN and EDWARD S. PERRY

with special editorial assistance by Mikki Moisio

E. P. DUTTON & COMPANY, INC. | NEW YORK | 1975

10 9 8 7 6 5 4 3 2 1

Published simultaneously in Canada by
Clarke, Irwin & Company Limited, Toronto and Vancouver
ISBN: 0-525-16554-1

Library of Congress Cataloging in Publication Data

MacCann, Richard Dyer.
    The new film index.

    1. Moving-pictures—Bibliography.   I. Perry,
Edward S., joint author.   II. Title.
Z5784.M9M29   1974   011   74-16218

Contents

CONTENTS

To the Reader

For many years, the only existing English-language bibliography of motion picture materials was *The Film Index,* edited by Harold Leonard in 1941 for the Museum of Modern Art Film Library and the H. W. Wilson Company. It emphasized the silent period, with some entries up to about 1936.

The present bibliography is intended to stand on the shelf beside that pioneering work. The two indexes differ, however, in certain important ways.

The earlier volume covered films as well as articles and books. We have left the films to the American Film Institute: its exhaustive, multivolume catalog of all American motion pictures, begun about the same time as our project, promises to be the final word on that subject.

We have chosen, also, to deal only with magazine articles. A parallel index of film books was part of the original plan, but turned out to be more than we could accomplish and still carry on our academic duties. Ideally such a list should be given extensive annotation and evaluation and should be categorized and cross-categorized for the benefit of students new to the field. For the time being, George Rehrauer, professor in the Graduate School of Library Service at Rutgers University, has helped us out with his *Cinema Booklist* (1972), which is alphabetical, selective (1,505 entries), and annotated primarily for librarians.

The 1941 *Index* also appears to have been quite selective, with lengthy descriptions of items deemed especially important. The present work is intended to be more exhaustive, with brief annotations. We have in fact omitted any descriptive note when the title seemed self-explanatory (or in a few cases, when we could not find and check the article itself). We have tried to hold to the goal of a simple informational tool, avoiding evaluative words in favor of straight reporting. Occasionally a longer citation may suggest that the item deserves greater attention, and in the general effort for brevity and simplicity, we have not felt it obligatory to be dull.

From the first, the main objective has been to provide teachers, students, writers, librarians, and general readers with a quick and easy guide to a great deal of material heretofore inaccessible, unevaluated, and often unknown. Film magazines are seldom adequately indexed. Furthermore, a high proportion of valuable writing about motion pictures occurs in magazines of general circulation—important and thoughtful accounts of individual directors, foreign films, Hollywood's economic conditions, social aspects of cinema, and similar matters. These often escape the attention of the teacher of film studies because (1) they are not in the few film magazines he manages to read and (2) they are inevitably lost in the chronology gap—that is, he must go through each of the many biennial volumes of the *Readers Guide* even to find that they exist.

COVERAGE AND LIMITATIONS

We began with the *Readers Guide.* The 150 members of the first class in American motion picture history at the University of Kansas were asked to help by turning in small projects—selected bibliographic reports from 1930 to 1967. These became the nucleus for a five-year task: full coverage of all cinema materials in all magazines in every index we could find, decade by decade, 1930–1970, including the *Art Index* and the *International (Social Science and Humanities) Index.* To this we added extensive scanning of literary and other "little" magazines, especially over the last ten years, scrutiny of existing bibliographies, and of course a page-by-page study of every issue of all the major film periodicals in the English language.

Nevertheless, we make no claim to completeness. We are sure that many valuable items have slipped through our nets. We hope to hear about this from you.

We soon became aware, for example, of the limitations of published magazine indexes—delays of several years in selecting certain magazines for listing, changes in categorizing policies from issue to issue, unexplained omissions of various kinds. These limitations became most apparent in the Biography section. There was not only no way to be complete but no way to tell how complete we might be. For a number of years, the *Readers Guide,* under "moving pictures," tried to cross-index directors and actors by name. Eventually, the reader was simply instructed to look up all actors and actresses by name. We did not undertake to do that.

The Biography section does include all material of this sort from all major film magazines, and there is sufficient annotation for many of the auteur-oriented pieces to give some direction to scholars. Fortunately Mel Schuster was working simultaneously on the magazines available in the Lincoln Center Library and Museum of the Performing Arts in New York City (including *Photoplay*) and his 1971 book is warmly recommended for those who seek 27 quick listings on June Allyson or Danny Kaye (*Motion Picture Performers: A Bibliography of Magazine and Periodical Articles 1900–1969*). His book on directors is also a useful reference work.

In keeping with the subtitle of the earlier *Index,* "The Film as Art," we restricted our attention primarily to theatrical, documentary, and experimental films and ruled out

1. the utilization of films as audiovisual aids in classrooms and in business;
2. amateur film making;
3. strictly technical subjects, such as the mechanics of laboratory, camera work, editing, sound, projection, special effects, etc.

We did include the impact on the industry of sound and of three-dimensional and widescreen projection.

We were not concerned at all with book reviews or film reviews, including those reported from film festivals. Reviews can be found quite easily by year of appearance and by title in the *Readers Guide,* the *Book Review Index, The New York Times,* or other similar sources. Reviews in film magazines are not always close to release dates, but they are not hard to track down. Here again, we have already been assisted by another reference book, published in 1971. *A Guide to Critical Reviews* (Part 4), by James M. Salem, offers a two-volume listing of film reviews from many sources.

We have, on the other hand, accommodated those special articles (usually in film magazines) appearing outside the regular review columns, which closely analyze or compare single films.

The relationship of television and motion pictures offered special difficulties. Wherever industrial or financial analyses seemed to deal with both television and motion picture companies, our policy was to include them. But critical, social, technical, and historical articles about moving images intended to be seen first on TV have been generally omitted. Technology may bring the chemistry of film and the electronics of TV much closer together in the 1970s; other bibliographers will then be compelled to deal with this question.

Starting with 1972, the *International Index to Film Periodicals* is preparing comprehensive article bibliographies for 60 or more magazines on an annual basis. It is to be hoped that they will be able to pick up the year 1971 as well, now that we have done the 40-year retrospective. Meanwhile Vincent Aceto and Fred Silva have done a *Film Literature Index* for 1971 based on 28 periodicals.

There are certain fine-mesh checks we couldn't afford to do. We don't always have both date and issue number, for example. Sometimes hard-pressed editors of film magazines don't want to admit they let a year go by without publishing, so they don't even put a date on the issue. In other cases, the numbering was so bewildering we chose to use dates only. Page numbers? We didn't try to count all the back pages, especially of general magazines, because so many advertising columns intervene that there is no way to tell how long the article really is. Illustrations? Over the years, our annotation process failed to be consistent on this, so we determined to leave out any reference to it at all. Certain magazines, such as *Sight and Sound* and *Life,* can be expected to offer pictures; others, such as *Atlantic,* won't.

ACKNOWLEDGMENTS

Annotations for the articles in general magazines have been written, for the most part, by film students. The major contributors have been John Tibbetts, Richard Geary, and Mikki Moisio at the University of Kansas; Timothy Lyons, Donald Fredericksen, and Linda Provinzano at the University of Iowa; Diane Policy, Kathleen Condray, and Dennis Giles at the University of Texas; and Dennis Dillon and Barbara Lund at New York University.

Other part-time assistants at Kansas were Gary Shivers, Thomas Swale, Ronald Parker, Leigh Clark, and Curtis Waugh; at Iowa, Marylaine Block, James Beranek, J. J. Murphy, Susan Lewis, William Gilcher, Philip Rosen, Kristin Thompson, and Mark Johnson; at Texas, Pamela Corn; at New York, Miriam Perry, Elena Simon, John Hanhardt, Judith Trojan, Jenifer Millstone, Sam McElfresh, Larry Collins, David Packman, Madeline Warren, Caroline Baum, Joel Zuker, Ricki Twersky, and Brenda McElnea; in California, Steven Mamber and Janey Place.

Three indexes prepared by graduate students in cinema at the University of Southern California have been incorporated with considerable revision: a catalogue of articles in the *Hollywood Quarterly* (later the *Quarterly of Film, Radio, and Television*) by Douglas Menville, covering the years 1945–1957; a master's thesis analyzing articles in *Sight and Sound,* 1949–1959, by Russell McGregor; and a master's thesis analyzing articles in *Films in Review,* 1950–1959, by Frederick Carpenter.

If we remember that Harold Leonard's historic work in 1941 was originally financed by federal relief funds (WPA), it is especially fitting to acknowledge that this continuation of *The Film Index* was assisted at first by the work-study program of the U.S. Office of Economic Opportunity at the University of Kansas. Later, graduate assistantships in the Radio-Television-Film programs at Kansas, Iowa, and Texas made it possible for some of the students listed above to give extended time to the project.

Private enterprise also took part: Commonwealth Theaters of Lawrence, Kansas, provided a scholarly grant of $1,000 for each of two years. "End money," to use the familiar movie production term, has been provided by E. P. Dutton and Company, administered by Cyril Nelson, editor of their long and distinguished line of paperback books about film.

CATEGORY CONFLICTS

> I was just out of college and still believed in classifications and categories.—Jean Renoir "A Modern Parable," *JSPG* (March 1964). See 3b(4).

May we encourage the users of this *Index* to approach it in some degree as collaborators—to browse a little, as active participants in the search for information? We urge this because we know the limitations of our work—and of all such attempts to classify the humanities and the arts.

In the first place, we had to decide to make the annotations brief, partly to keep the volume to a convenient size. Then we had to decide to put each article as nearly as possible in a single category. This was not easy in many cases, and we did do some cross-indexing. Perhaps one item in ten has a brief reference in a second place, and a few are triple-listed. But our primary assumption was that one entry is enough. Since no system of categories is ever adequate, there may be times when a useful article will be missed because we haven't listed it in the place you first looked for it. The notes at the top of each category are intended to help the reader cross over to other sections which may contain related material.

Our categories have been developed inductively from the materials—the articles we actually found in general magazines and film magazines. We studied alternatives, including the Dewey decimal system. We found the present arrangement more to our liking. It is not very different from the one used by the editors of *The Film Index.* We feel that any such system of classification can be quickly grasped by an alert reader in search of specific subjects.

The order within subheadings is *chronological,* not alphabetical by author. In this way, even though a good deal of trivia crops up in some categories, the effect is surprisingly close to a documentary history of each subject.

Exceptions were made to this chronological order when we thought the reader would want it that way. Biography (Part 5) is in *alphabetical* order by name. Case Histories of Film Making (Part 9) is in alphabetical order by title of film, and two smaller sections are also alphabetical by title: Extended Analysis of Single Films (3c) and Case Studies of documentary films, 8c(4).

Some special problems:

1. Most of the discussion over the years in English-language magazines about censorship, audiences, and the industry has been connected with the American film and with Hollywood. Therefore the Film and Society and the Motion Picture Industry categories are primarily American in content and items are placed there which might equally well be placed under U.S. history. Censorship policies of other countries than the U.S. will usually be found under the history of those countries. Censorship actions taken by one country against the films of another will be found in the "international relations" section, 7e(3).

2. Similarly, almost everything about the films, the industry, and the social aspects of production in Europe, Asia, and Latin America is placed under a country name rather than a topical category. We have assumed that this is where the reader is most likely to look. We have cross-referenced when the item seemed to have broader application.

3. Biography no doubt belongs under history, but we felt that many readers would want to look for particular directors, actors, producers, writers, and executives by name. There is a large bulk of material of this sort, and since some prominent directors have moved from one country to another, it seemed sensible to give individuals separate billing. Instead of cross-indexing each name entry under national histories, we have listed the names at the head of each country category (except for the American biography entries, which were simply too numerous).

4. A large number of items have had to be consigned to "general" categories. For the most part, all headings are used. Entries placed under subheadings are *in addition to* the general headings above them. When an article deals with both Italy and France, for example, it moves up naturally to the overall designation "Europe." But where can one put the kind of trend story that is about the film industry and its films and is also about film and society and the audience? We have sometimes cross-referenced, but if you are interested in these general critical studies, look at a wide range of categories, as indicated in the sectional cross-references.

5. Certain other classifications have been separated from national histories. Most of Part 1, for example, including such matters as film societies, film study, archives, and so on, is international in scope and will not be found elsewhere. Similarly, the sections on writers and writing and on animation in Part 2 are not cross-referenced by country. This is true of most of the technical categories and also of Nonfiction Film (Part 8).

6. The final Index to the Index (Part 10) is not just a convenient way of looking up an item by author's name. It is also a way of filling out what you want to know about a film maker or critic or writer. We wanted to feel free to put an article written by Josef von Sternberg under cinematography and lighting—or one by Sergei Eisenstein under editing. We have not put every one of these items under Biography, too. We have assumed that you would consult Part 10 in addition to Part 5. In fact, the persistent scholar will look up the titles of films in 3c, Extended Analysis of Single Films, and in 9, Case Histories of Film Making, to round out his study of a particular director.

We are sure our readers will not be so incautious as to trust the annotations to tell all about the articles. They are only partial guides, at best, and we know that many mistakes must have crept in. Even more important: don't always trust the articles themselves, just because they are in print. Obviously some magazines and some authors are more reliable than others. Show business is notoriously fanciful, forgetful, and foolish —and this rubs off on journalists, critics, and historians as well. If the article is "by Samuel Goldwyn," such a by-line is a historical fact, but he usually had one of the best press agents in town doing this kind of work for him. It is also true that many subjects and people were written about only for publicity reasons—over and over again. Other important subjects may have been ignored, and of course they can't be put in an index. Future critics and historians have the opportunity to redress that balance.

It is our hope that the provision of these

references will have a strengthening effect on the development of film study. Students of film theory and of film and society may find a few things written long ago that are still worthy of respect. Students of film history and criticism may develop a richer sense of detail about the way things were. Some may think that our labors in preparing this bibliography have made it too easy for the graduate students and teachers of the 1970s and 1980s. We would rather think that we have enabled them to turn their attention from the drudgery of searching to the delights of selecting, comparing, evaluating, theorizing, debating, elaborating, and predicting.

RICHARD DYER MAC CANN
EDWARD S. PERRY

BRIEF GUIDE

1. *The New Film Index* is essentially a subject index, with each entry arranged in chronological order by publication date. This provides, in effect, a history of what has been written about each of the categorized aspects of motion pictures.

2. The technical (2), economic (6), and social (7) categories relate primarily to American film history. The same subjects for other countries will be found under the geographical headings under history (4).

3. There is also a name index, Biography (5), consisting primarily of directors, producers, and actors, in alphabetical order.

4. Film reviews are not included, but articles devoted to extended analysis of one or two films appear under 3c, alphabetically by title. Further articles about films in production appear in Part 9, alphabetically by title.

5. Comparative studies of similar films, sometimes described as "genres," can be found in section 4k, Types of Fiction Films.

6. About 10 percent of the entries are cross-indexed—that is, they appear under a second category without page numbers or annotations. Broader cross-references to related subjects may be found before the first entry in many categories.

7. The Index to the Index (Part 10) is simply an alphabetical list of the authors of the 12,000 or more articles annotated under the 278 categories in Parts 1 to 9.

Abbreviations of Magazines Indexed

FILM MAGAZINES INDEXED

	Action (Directors Guild, Hollywood)	1 (No. 1, Sep–Oct 66) to 5 (No. 6, Nov–Dec 70)
	Afterimage	(No. 1, Apr 70) to (No. 2, Autumn 70)
CdC in Eng	*Cahiers du Cinéma in English*	(No. 1, Jan 66) to (No. 12, Dec 67)
	Cinéaste	1 (No. 1, Fall 67) to 4 (No. 3, Winter 70–71)
	Cinema (California)	1 (No. 1, 1962) to 6 (No. 2, 1970)
	Cinema (Cambridge, England)	(No. 1, Dec 68) to (Nos. 6–7, Aug 70)
CJ	*Cinema Journal* (since 1966— earlier title: *Journal of Society of Cinematologists*)	1 (1961) to 10 (No. 1, Fall 70)
	Cinema Studies (Journal of Society for Film History Research, England)	1 (No. 1, 1960) to 2 (No. 5, 1967)
	Close Up	1930–1933
	Experimental Cinema	(No. 1, Feb 30) to (No. 4, Feb 33)
	Film (Federation of Film Societies in Britain)	(No. 1, Oct 54) to (No. 60, 1970)
F Com	*Film Comment* (first two issues titled *Vision*)	1 (No. 1, Spring 62) to 6 (No. 4, Winter 70–71)
F Cult	*Film Culture*	(No. 1, Jan 55) to (No. 49, 1970)
F Her	*Film Heritage*	1 (No. 1, Autumn 65) to 6 (No. 2, Winter 70–71)
F Lib Q	*Film Library Quarterly*	1 (No. 1, Winter 67–68) to 3 (No. 4, Fall 70)
FQ	*Film Quarterly* (formerly *Hollywood Quarterly* and *Quarterly of Film, Radio, and Television*)	12 (No. 1, Fall 58) to 24 (No. 1, Fall 70)
	Films (U.S.)	1 (No. 1, Nov 39) to 1 (No. 4, Summer 40)
F&F	*Films and Filming*	1 (No. 1, Oct 54) to 17 (No. 1, Dec 70)

FILM MAGAZINES INDEXED
(Cont.)

FIR	Films in Review	1 (No. 1, Feb 50) to 21 (No. 10, Dec 70)
F Soc Rev	Film Society Review (U.S.)	1 (No. 1, Sep 65) to 6 (No. 4, Dec 70)
Hwd Q	Hollywood Quarterly (later Quarterly of Film, Radio, and Television; later Film Quarterly)	1 (No. 1, Oct 45) to 5 (No. 4, Summer 51)
	Image (Journal of Photography of George Eastman House)	1 (No. 1, Jan 52) to 12 (No. 6, Jan 65)
J Soc Cin	Journal of Society of Cinematologists (see Cinema Journal)	
JUFA JUFPA	Journal of University Film (Producers) Association	6 (No. 2, Winter 53) to 22 (No. 4, 1970)
JSPG	Journal of Screen Producers Guild (Producers Guild of America—Hollywood)	2 (No. 2, Aug 54) to 12 (No. 3, Sep 70)
	Medium	Summer 67 to Fall 70
	Motion	(No. 1, Summer 61) to (No. 6, Autumn 63)
	Movie (England)	(No. 1, June 62) to (No. 18, Winter 70–71)
	Moviegoer	(No. 1, Winter 64) to (No. 3, Summer 66)
NY F Bul	New York Film Bulletin	Series 1, No. 1, to 3 (No. 5—issue No. 46). Some missing.
Penguin F Rev	Penguin Film Review	(No. 1, Aug 46) to (No. 9, May 49)
QFRTV	Quarterly of Film, Radio, and Television (previously Hollywood Quarterly; later Film Quarterly)	6 (No. 1, Fall 51) to 11 (No. 4, Summer 57)
	Screen (England)	10 (No. 1, 1969) to 11 (No. 6, 1970)
	Screen Writer (Hollywood)	1 (No. 1, June 45) to 4 (No. 1, Oct 48)
	Sequence (England)	(No. 1, Dec 46) to (No. 14, 1952)
S&S	Sight and Sound	1 (No. 1, Spring 32) to 39 (No. 4, Autumn 70)
	Silent Picture	(No. 1, Winter 68–69) to (No. 8, Autumn 70)
	Take One (Canada)	1 (No. 1, Sep 66) to 2 (No. 12, Dec 70)

OTHER MAGAZINES INDEXED

We have made no attempt to list or even count the general, specialized, and scholarly magazines covered by our researchers. Special efforts were made to scan *New Masses* 1935–1945 and *Playboy* 1962–1970, and this is a fair indication of the range of our coverage. In general, all periodicals (from *Good Housekeeping* to the two incarnations of *Show Maga-*

zine) are here, *if they were indexed* in *Readers Guide, Art Index* and *International* (later called *Social Science and Humanities*) *Index* 1930–1970. The following are titles frequently encountered and abbreviated:

AV Com Rev	*Audio-Visual Communication Review*
Bus Wk	*Business Week*
Chris Cent	*Christian Century*
CSMM	*Christian Science Monitor Magazine*
Esq	*Esquire*
J Pop Cult	*Journal of Popular Culture*
Lit Dig	*Literary Digest*
New Rep	*New Republic*
New S&N	*New Statesman and Nation*
Newswk	*Newsweek*
NYTM	*New York Times Magazine*
Pop Mech	*Popular Mechanics*
Pop Photog	*Popular Photography*
Pop Sci	*Popular Science Monthly*
Pub Opin Q	*Public Opinion Quarterly*
Rdrs Dig	*Reader's Digest*
SRL	*Saturday Review of Literature* (U.S.)
Sat Rev	*Saturday Review* (U.S.)
SEP	*Saturday Evening Post*
Th Arts	*Theatre Arts*
TDR	*Tulane Drama Review*

Other titles are generally spelled out (*Atlantic, America, American, Harper's, Reporter, Nation, Look, Life, Time, Fortune, Holiday, Collier's, Commonweal, Commentary,* etc.) but the following words are abbreviated:

Am	*American*		*Lib*	*Library*
Bul	*Bulletin*		*Q*	*Quarterly*
Educ	*Education; Educational*		*Rev*	*Review*
Hist	*History*		*Sci*	*Science; Scientific*
J	*Journal*			

The New Film Index

Motion picture specialist Paul Spehr views an early film from the paper positive collection, one of more than 50,000 moving pictures in the U.S. Library of Congress.

1. Introduction and Reference

1a. Education About Films

[See also 7b(1).]

Grundy, C. Reginald. "Cinema and Culture." *Connoisseur* 86 (No. 351, Nov 30) 277–278. Proposals for establishing the film as art.

Blakeston, Oswell. "Can Cinema Be Taught?" *Close Up* 8 (No. 2, June 31) 100–107. Theoretical comments.

Blakeston, Oswell. "Film Inquiry." *Arch Rev* 69–71 (July, Aug, Oct, Nov 31; Jan, Feb, Mar 32). A series of eight short essays on various aspects of film theory and production.

Richardson, Dorothy M. "Continuous Performance." *Close Up* 8 (No. 4, Dec 31) 304–308. The need for educating the film audience.

Hoare, F. A. "Progress in Film Appreciation." *CQ* 1 (No. 4, Summer 33) 219–222. Film societies, not lectures by pedagogues.

Lambert, R. S. "How to Get the Films You Want." *S&S* 3 (No. 9, Spring 34) 5–9. Suggestions for creating a more critical audience which will in turn demand better films.

"Course in Film Art at Museum of Modern Art." *Museum News* 15 (1 Oct 37) 1. Report on a course in the history, aesthetics, and technique of the motion picture held at the Museum of Modern Art Film Library in New York.

Dyer, Ernest. "Training Film Taste in America." *S&S* 7 (No. 28, Winter 38–39) 179–181. What is being done to develop film appreciation.

Smith, Brian. "The Next Step." *S&S* 9 (No. 36, Winter 40–41) 69–70. The need for a manual on film appreciation.

"A Course in Cinema." *S&S* 11 (No. 43, Winter 42–43) 65–67. Description of a film-appreciation course.

Beresford, Warden M. W. "Teaching Film Analysis." *S&S* 13 (No. 50, July 44) 40–41. One man's methods.

Neilson-Baxter, R. K. "F.A. or f.a." *S&S* 14 (No. 56, Winter 45–46) 124–126. Film appreciation for social purposes is better than discussion of technique.

Nichtenhauser, Adolf. "The Tasks of an International Film Institute." *Hwd Q* 2 (No. 1, Oct 46) 19–24. Plea for coordination of film preservation, film schools, etc.; historical precedents.

Grierson, John, Herbert Edwards, and Richard Griffith. "Notes on 'The Tasks of an International Film Institute.'" *Hwd Q* 2 (No. 2, Jan 47) 192–200. Response to an article by Adolf Nichtenhauser.

Wollenberg, H. H. "Legislation and Film." *S&S* 16 (No. 63, Autumn 47) 122–123. The importance of legislation to help support films and film appreciation internationally.

Oakes, Vanya. "Family Guide to Movies." *Horn Book* 25 (Mar 49) 144–149. Guiding children's taste in motion pictures, including the Green Sheet.

Dickinson, Thorold. "The Filmwright and the Audience." *S&S* 19 (Mar 50). See 2d.

Pratley, Gerald. "Furthering Motion Picture Appreciation by Radio." *Hwd Q* 5 (No. 2, Winter 50) 127–131. Some Canadian programs; interviews, talks, and a series on film music.

Marsh, W. Ward. "1,372 Students." *FIR* 3 (Apr 52) 175–178. A Cleveland movie critic tells of his experience teaching a course entitled "History, Enjoyment, and Criticism of the Movies."

Marsh, W. Ward. "The TV Yegg and I." *FIR*

Readers are advised to acquaint themselves with the range of categories throughout the bibliography in the search for specific subjects. In some cases, cross-categorical comparisons are directly suggested. In general, however, each article is placed under one category only. Cross-references on individual articles have been kept to a minimum.

Entries are in chronological order of publication under each category. Exceptions are: Part 5, Biography, in which the order is alphabetical by name; Part 9, Case Histories of Film Making, which is alphabetical by film title; and 3c and 8c(4), also alphabetical by title.

4 (Nov 53) 465–466. Difficulties the author, a Cleveland film critic, encountered in getting and keeping his half-hour television program about film history.

Hurd, Reggie, Jr. "Re-issues." *FIR* 4 (Dec 53) 519–522. An argument for the regular re-releasing of superior films of the past.

Tilton, Roger. "The Moving Picture: A Case of Criminal Neglect." *College Art J* 12 (No. 2, Winter 53) 153–157. A criticism of American education for ignoring the motion picture as a major art form.

Peters, J. M. L. "The Necessity of Learning How to See a Film." *AV Com Rev* 3 (No. 3, Summer 55) 197–205. Film is an important, separate visual language.

"The Problem of the Movie Still." *Image* 5 (No. 3, Mar 56) 64–65. To be used for a study of films, a still photograph must be a representation of the film and an aesthetically satisfying photograph.

Pratley, Gerald. "Take Yourself Seriously." *JSPG* (Nov 56) 11, 14–15. CBC film commentator suggests film promotion not by advertising but by educating the public in film appreciation.

Miller, Don. "Televiewing Movies." *FIR* 8 (Feb 57) 54–59. An appraisal of the cultural potentiality of the study of the motion pictures available on television to students of the cinema and the general public.

Scully, William. "Movies: A Positive Plan." *America* 96 (30 Mar 57) 726–727. Chairman of Episcopal Committee on Motion Pictures discusses work of National Legion of Decency and proposes study groups to educate film viewers.

Marcorelles, Louis. "Journées du Cinema." *S&S* 27 (Winter 57–58) 114. Publicly financed film showings in French towns.

Lean, David. "What You Can Learn from Movies." *Pop Photog* 42 (Mar 58) 108–109+. An interview, edited by C. Reynolds: "To really study a film you should have reached the point where you are no longer involved in the dramatic action."

Poole, Victor. "The Cinema Today." *Film* (No. 25, Sep–Oct 60) 8–10. Producer of BBC series *The Cinema Today* discusses the program.

Peters, J. M. L. "Art of Seeing a Film." *UNESCO Courier* 15 (Mar 62) 4–9. Introduction to the author's recent UNESCO book *Teaching About the Film*; analysis of film form.

Knight, Arthur. "The Ripple Effect." *Sat Rev* 46 (12 Oct 63) 60–61. First annual Aspen Film Conference has as theme "The American Film: Its Makers and Its Audience."

Taylor, Stephen. "Notes on the Fordham Film Conference." *F Com* 2 (No. 3, Summer 64) 50–53. Analysis of speeches by Marshall McLuhan, Judith Crist, Robert Rossen, Paul Newman, Bosley Crowther.

Knight, Arthur. "Aspen experience." *Sat Rev* 47 (3 Oct 64) 27–28. The second annual Aspen Film Conference.

"Hollywood Changes Script on Sightseers." *Bus Wk* (10 July 65) 30–31. Report on studio tours for tourists.

Forsdale, Joan R., and Louis Forsdale. "Film Literacy." *JUFPA* 18 (No. 3, 1966) 9–15+. Specific forms of film "illiteracy," such as lack of understanding of film conventions; teaching of rich and complex films is recommended.

Barry, L. "Super 8 on the Back Lot." *Pop Photog* 59 (Aug 66) 36+. Report on third year of Universal Studio tour for public.

Amberg, George. "Cinevision." *F Cult* (No. 42, Fall 66) 25–28. Film professor avers that most people don't know how to look at films; discussion.

"Rubberneck Rush." *Newswk* 70 (21 Aug 67) 52–53. Tours of Hollywood studios.

Rapf, Maurice. "Can Education Kill the Movies?" *Action* 2 (No. 5, Sep–Oct 67) 10–11+.

Knight, Arthur. "In Conference." *Sat Rev* 51 (29 June 68) 32. Recent film conferences sponsored by Associated Councils of the Arts.

"If You Want to Visit a Hollywood Studio." *Good Housekeeping* 167 (July 68) 153.

Whannel, Paddy. "The Problem of Film Availability." *Screen* 10 (No. 1, Jan–Feb 69) 67–73.

Whannel, Paddy. "Film Education and Film Culture." *Screen* 10 (No. 3, May–June 69) 49–59. Part of Education Department Report, British Film Institute; problems of definition and method in film studies.

Jewison, Norman. "Tuning In on Salzburg." *Action* 4 (No. 4, July–Aug 69) 15–16. American director talks at an international film seminar held at Salzburg.

Arrowsmith, William. "Film as Educator." *J Aesthetic Educ* 3 (No. 3, July 69) 75–83. The ability of film study to become the new liberalizing force in the curriculum.

Dworkin, Martin S. "Seeing for Ourselves: Notes on the Movie Art and Industry, Critics and Audiences." *J Aesthetic Educ* 3 (No. 3, July 69) 45–55. A plea for intelligent film study.

Bolas, Terry. "Developments in Film Education." *Screen* 11 (No. 3, Summer 70) 96–111. Annual Report, 1969–1970, of nineteenth year of Society for Education in Film and Television, followed by section reports by various authors.

Callahan, M. A. "Confrontation in Cinema City." *America* 122 (11 Apr 70) 392–394. Report on film conference, held in USC's film school, concerning such topics as changing patterns in the industry, unions, audiences, film content.

Crowther, Bosley. "The Entertainment Film in Education." *Lib J* 95 (15 Apr 70) 1555–1557. From the author's address to the New York State Educational Communication Association.

McArthur, Colin. "Problems of Providing Film Study Materials." *Screen* 11 (No. 2, 1970) 16–21.

Whannel, Paddy. "Servicing the Film Teacher." *Screen* 11 (No. 4–5, 1970) 48–55. The apparent development, past and future, of film study.

Katz, John. "An Integrated Approach to the Teaching of Film and Literature." *Screen* 11 (No. 4–5, 1970) 56–65.

Knight, Roy. "Film in English Teaching." *Screen* 11 (No. 6, 1970) 67–74.

1a(1). FILM SOCIETIES

[See also 8d.]

Bond, R. "A True Story." *Close Up* 7 (No. 6, Dec 30) 418–422. Problems of censorship in film societies in England.

Hughes, Glenn. "Making the Film Pay for the Theatre." *Th Arts* 16 (July 32) 561–565. Discusses development and workings of university film series.

Montagu, Ivor. "The Film Society, London." *CQ* 1 (No. 1, Autumn 32) 42–50. How it started in 1925; other societies from Oxford to Edinburgh.

"Film Forum and Film Society." *Th Arts* 17 (Feb 33) 93. Notice about film series in New York City, one experimental, the other for features.

"Little Cinema." *Time* 21 (6 Feb 33) 24. New York City has a film society sponsored by George Gershwin, Nelson Rockefeller, and others, plus a film forum headed by Sidney Howard.

Davy, Charles. "Eisenstein's *October*; and the Film Society Movement." *Bookman* 86 (Apr 34) 37. Discussion of the film-society movement and praise for London Film Society's screening of uncut *October*.

Buchanan, Donald. "For the Intelligent Filmgoer." *Canad Forum* 15 (Feb 36) 15. Review of the formation of film clubs for the appreciation of the motion picture as a fine art in Canada.

Dickinson, Thorold. "Why Not a National Film Society?" *S&S* 7 (No. 26, Summer 38) 75–77. Such a society would help to determine production decisions.

Lindgren, Ernest H. "Nostalgia." *S&S* 9 (No. 35, Autumn 40) 49–50. A theoretical statement about the nature of film and some comments on the function of the film-appreciation movement.

"Film Forums Grant." *Lib J* 66 (15 May 41) 460. Grant from the Carnegie Foundation will permit the use of films to promote discussion across the country.

Hardy, Forsyth. "An Open Letter to the Film Societies." *S&S* 10 (No. 38, Summer 41) 29–31. The problems of film supply and program building.

Hardy, Forsyth. "Testing Time." *S&S* 11 (No. 43, Winter 42–43) 62–64. Challenges to the film-society movement.

"Children's Cinema Clubs." *S&S* 12 (No. 45, Summer 43) 21–22. Organized by J. Arthur Rank for the Odeon Theatres.

Spencer, T. L. "A Local Authorities Experiment." *S&S* 13 (No. 49, May 44) 14–15. The Bury Film Society, its programs, and the response of audiences.

"Motion Picture Series." *Museum News* 22 (15 Oct 44) 2. Information on film programs at various museums in the United States.

Grayson, Dorothy. "Films and Youth Clubs." *S&S* 13 (No. 52, Jan 45) 104–106. Guidelines.

Wilson, Norman. "Film Societies: The Next Days." *S&S* 14 (No. 54, July 45) 37–38. Still ahead: the tasks of lifting taste and creating a small audience for experimental films.

Hawley, C. J. "The Tyneside Cinema Appreciation Club." *S&S* 14 (No. 56, Winter 45–46) 123–124.

Thompson, Kenneth L. "Film Progress in Hastings." *S&S* 14 (No. 56, Winter 45–46) 128. Clubs and societies.

Bean, Keith. "Towards an Imperial Film Society." *S&S* 15 (No. 58, Summer 46) 41–42. A federation could more easily get films.

Hoffman, E. "Movies for Hire." *Woman's Home Companion* 73 (Dec 46) 62. 16mm prints of Hollywood films for club or private showings.

Ansell, Gordon B. "Cinema for the Few." *Hwd Q* 2 (No. 2, Jan 47) 179–183. The Cambridge Film Society shows films and has plans for making some.

Gerrard, John. "Film Societies in Ireland." *S&S* 17 (No. 67, Autumn 48) 133–134.

"Educational Films Promoted in Many Communities." *Am City* 63 (Dec 48) 113. A grant from the Carnegie Corporation to the Film Council of America has enabled them to begin many new community film councils.

Hardy, Forsyth. "Target for Film Societies." *Penguin F Rev* 8 (Jan 49) 86–91. Older films should be shown as well as the latest releases to give minority audiences a chance to study them.

Harper, Mr. "Only Path." *Harper's* 199 (July 49) 101–102. Cinema 16: nonprofit organization for screening films neglected by commercial theatres.

Vogel, Amos. "Film Do's and Don'ts." *Sat Rev* 32 (20 Aug 49) 32–34. How to operate a film society.

"Film Societies: The Other Side." *S&S* 19 (Jan 50) 45. Some comments by the secretary of a film society in a small town (60,-000).

Vogel, Amos. "Cinema 16: A Showcase for the Nonfiction Film." *Hwd Q* 4 (No. 4, Summer 50) 420–422. Origin and operation of society in New York City.

Burch, Glen. "The FCA and the Film Council Movement." *Hwd Q* 5 (No. 2, Winter 50) 138–143. Executive director of Film Council of America, which supplanted the U.S. government's wartime 16mm Advisory Committee, urges formation of local councils.

Hardy, Forsyth. "20 Years of World Cinema." *FIR* 2 (Apr 51) 11–17. Films shown by the Edinburgh Film Guild in 280 programs for its members.

Wilson, Norman. "Edinburgh's Film Guild." *FIR* 2 (Apr 51) 6–11. Its history and activities; films shown at the first four International Festivals of Documentary Films in Edinburgh (1947–1950).

Stevenson, Grace T. "Seattle's Film Enthusiasts." *FIR* 2 (May 51) 14–18. Film appreciation advanced by Public Library, Film Society, and University of Washington.

Levenson, Minnie G. "Movies and the Community." *FIR* 3 (Mar 52) 105–111. The Worcester (Massachusetts) Better Films Council supports good films, obtained by them for public showing in five different kinds of programs, growing out of programs at the Worcester Art Museum.

MacKenzie, N. "Sixteen Mill." *New S&N* 45 (3 Jan 53) 8. Increase in "art houses" and film societies.

Everson, William K. "Film Societies Should Federate." *FIR* 4 (Mar 53) 28. Survey of the British Federation of Film Societies history and achievements; the author proposes federation of the approximately 300 American film societies.

Anderson, Joseph L. "Antioch's Film Activity." *FIR* 4 (May 53) 215–219. The Antioch Motion Picture Advisory Council, students and faculty members of Antioch College at Yellow Springs, Ohio.

Watson, J. Blair, Jr. "The Dartmouth Film Society." *FIR* 4 (Nov 53) 467–470. Its history, activities, policies, and films.

Nelson, William. "The Wichita Film Society." *FIR* 5 (Feb 54) 78–81. Five hundred members may be too many.

Hine, Al. "Cinema 16." *Holiday* 15 (Mar 54) 26–27+. A cultural, nonprofit organization begun in October 1947.

Kraft, Richard. "Audience Stupidity." *FIR* 5 (Mar 54) 113–114+. The ignorant reception of silent-film classics; some suggestions.

Caras, Roger A. "Film Society Hints." *FIR* 5 (Apr 54) 184–186.

Lee, Walter W., Jr. "Films at Cal-Tech." *FIR* 5 (May 54) 232–235. Activities of the Film Society at California Institute of Technology.

Lucas, Colin. "Film Preview Centers." *Lib J* 79 (1 Sep 54) 1482–1483. Review of this 1953–1954 16mm film project conducted by the Film Council of America.

Healy, Paul W. "New Mexican Cinemaddicts." *FIR* 5 (Oct 54) 413–417. University of New Mexico's film society.

Seton, Marie. "Taking Eisenstein to France." *Film* (No. 2, Dec 54). See 4e(2).

Oliver, R. C. B. "The Film Society Versus Marilyn Monroe." *Film* (No. 3, Feb 55) 27–28. One film society finds that its members are almost all middle-aged or elderly.

Caulfield, Peggy. "They Started Something." *Mlle* 40 (Mar 55) 106. Cinema 16, begun by Amos and Marcia Vogel, is the largest film society in the world.

Dickinson, Thorold. "Some Notes on the Way." *Film* (No. 5, Sep–Oct 55) 7–9. Comments on the future and function of film societies.

Seton, Marie. "Italian Cine-Clubs." *Film* (No. 5, Sep–Oct 55). See 4e(3).

Road, Sinclair, et al. "New Directions for Film Societies." *Film* (No. 8, Mar–Apr 56) 12–18. Various authors discuss the relationship between film societies and film makers, film study, film sponsorship, and the schools.

O'Laoghaire, Liam. "Film Society Conference." *S&S* 26 (Summer 56) 7. First such national meeting in England.

Card, James. "The Fifth Anniversary of the Dryden Theatre Film Society." *Image* 5 (No. 6, June 56) 136–137.

"Craze for the Oldies." *Newswk* 49 (20 May 57) 116–118. Report on "friends of old films" and sources for renting them.

Aquin, Mary. "Are We Ready for Movie Clubs?" *America* 97 (6 July 57) 385–386.

Tennant, Sylvia. "Miss Mitford Goes to the Pictures." *Film* (No. 14, Nov–Dec 57) 26–27. A satirical piece on the codes of behavior for film-society viewers.

Gandin, Michele, et al. "Why Film Societies?" *Film* (No. 16, Mar–Apr 58) 4–8. Various authors discuss the state of film clubs in several countries.

Bachmann, Gideon. "The American Federation." *Film* (No. 17, Sep–Oct 58) 24–26. Film-society movement in the U.S.

Jenkinson, Philip. "In the Film Pen." *Film* (No. 18, Nov–Dec 58) 15–17. Film societies must help film distributors and help create markets for the exhibition of good films.

Evans, Jon. "The Pattern of Programming." *Film* (No. 20, Mar–Apr 59) 4–9+. Survey of British film societies.

Road, Sinclair. "Fifteen Years." *Film* (No. 24, Mar–Apr 60) 6–9. The British Federation of Film Societies.

Bachmann, Gideon. "Change or Die." *Film* (No. 28, Mar–Apr 61) 17–18. A plea for changes in film-society roles.

Dent, Maggie. "A Film Society Takes Root in Chapel Hill." *F Com* 1 (No. 2, Summer 62) 46–49.

Chamberlin, Philip. "What About Film Societies?" *JSPG* 11 (No. 5, Sep 63) 35–38. Types of groups in American Federation of Film Societies.

"Meanwhile . . . Action." *Film* (No. 39, Spring 64) 20–25. The film society at the London School of Film Technique.

Stewart, David C. "Movies on the Campus." *Sat Rev* 48 (20 Feb 65) 82–83. Campus film series and courses: will it all lead to dusty scholarship?

Parker, David L. "Projection Room—A University Film Series." *JUFPA* 19 (No. 1, 1967) 26–29. Describes a classic-film series on Ohio State's educational TV station.

Hodgkinson, Anthony. "What Is a Film Society For?" *F Soc Rev* (Apr 67) 24–29. A film society defined as an educational organization.

Lynes, Russell. "Flicks for the Fastidious." *Harper's* 236 (June 68) 24–28. The growth of film societies in America.

Dickinson, Thorold. "Film Societies." *J Aesthetic Educ* 3 (No. 3, July 69) 85–95. Historical overview of the movement and its function.

Archer, Fred. "Erotophobia in the Film Society." *Film* (No. 58, Spring 70) 33–34. Satirical view.

Hill, Derek. "New Cinema Club." *Film* (No. 58, Spring 70) 10–11. A brief history of the club and its attempt to show specialist films.

1a(2). INSTITUTES, MUSEUMS, ACADEMIES

[*See also* 1a(3b), 2a(5), 2b(5).]

Cameron, A. C. "The Case for a National Film Institute." *S&S* 1 (No. 1, Spring 32) 8–9. Principal questions dealt with by the Commission on Educational and Cultural Films.

Lambert, R. S. "Experiment with a Film Institute." *New S&N* 4 (16 July 32) 70–71. Plan for formation of a British Film Institute. Discussion (8 Oct) 402–403, (15 Oct) 443–444, (29 Oct) 510.

"Proposed British Film Institute." *School and Society* 36 (16 July 32) 76–77; 37 (7 Jan 33) 4–5; 38 (18 Nov 33) 681–682.

Defeo, Luciano. "Documentation and Research." *CQ* 1 (No. 3, Spring 33) 159–162. International Institute of Educational Cine-

matography in Rome proposes studies on the uses of film.

Lambert, R. S. "The British Film Institute." *CQ* 1 (No. 4, Summer 33) 212–215. Film trade and representatives of education agree on plans.

"What the British Film Institute Is Doing." *S&S* 2 (No. 8, Winter 33–34) 134–36; 3 (No. 9, Spring 34) 21–24; (No. 10, Summer 34) 84–85.

Noxon, G. F. "Italy's 'International' Institute." *CQ* 3 (No. 1, Autumn 34) 12–14. Educational film institute sponsored by League of Nations is controlled by Mussolini's money. See defense of I.I.E.C. in *CQ* 3 (No. 2, Winter 1935) by Rudolf Arnheim.

"Film Archives." *CQ* 3 (No. 4, Summer 35) 220–222. Museum of Modern Art in New York.

"Film Museum." *Time* 26 (1 July 35) 34. Museum of Modern Art's Film Library.

Troy, W. "Film Library, Museum of Modern Art." *Nation* 141 (24 July 35) 112.

Arnheim, Rudolf. "I.C.E.—A Reply to G. F. Noxon." *CQ* 3 (No. 2, Winter 35) 95–97. Mussolini's League of Nations institute has promise and is not merely for propaganda.

"Sanctuary for Film Art." *Lit Dig* 121 (11 Jan 36) 22. Report on the creation of the Museum of Modern Art Film Library in New York and the beginning of the circulation of its visual history of film.

"Infancy of an Art." *Nation* 142 (29 Jan 36) 118. Beginnings of the library of motion pictures at New York's Museum of Modern Art; early films.

Adams, Ward. "Heirlooms from Hollywood." *Country Life* 69 (Mar 36) 83+. Formation of New York's Museum of Modern Art Film Library.

Peet, C. "Film Library for Posterity." *Rdrs Dig* 28 (Mar 36) 81–82. At Museum of Modern Art.

"Film Library of the New York Museum of Modern Art." *School and Society* 43 (2 May 36) 591.

"Films Reborn." *Lit Dig* 121 (16 May 36) 23. Review of recent programs by Museum of Modern Art in New York.

Barry, Iris. "The Museum of Modern Art Film Library." *S&S* 5 (No. 18, Summer 36) 14–16. Its founding, goals, and work.

Buttles, Bruce. "Films of Auld Lang Syne." *CSMM* (26 Aug 36) 5+. New York's Museum of Modern Art film-preservation program.

"Third Annual Report." *School and Society* 44 (5 Dec 36) 733. Of the British Film Institute.

Barry, Iris. "Last Year and This." *Mag of Art* 30 (No. 1, Jan 37) 40–44. A brief survey of the films in the Museum of Modern Art Film Library in New York.

"Film Library of the Museum of Modern Art." *School and Society* 47 (16 Apr 38) 500. Acquisition of D. W. Griffith memorabilia.

Hartung, Phillip. "We Look Before and After . . ." *Commonweal* 30 (23 June 39) 240. Old film screenings by the Museum of Modern Art.

Holmes, Winifred. "The Danes Have a Word for It." *S&S* 8 (No. 31, Autumn 39) 117–118. New Danish Film Institute, Statens Filmcentral.

Bell, Oliver. "The First Ten Years." *S&S* 12 (No. 47, Oct 43) 56–58. Of the British Film Institute.

Brass, William. "The B.F.I." *S&S* 14 (No. 53, Apr 45) 10–11. Comments on the eleventh annual report of the British Film Institute.

Barry, Iris. "Why Wait for Posterity?" *Hwd Q* 1 (No. 2, Jan 46) 131–137. How the Museum of Modern Art set about collecting old films and what remains to be done.

"Museum Film Library." *Time* 48 (28 Oct 46) 103. A rundown on what films the Museum of Modern Art has and does not have for nonprofit showings.

Barry, Iris. "In Search of Films." *S&S* 16 (No. 62, Summer 47) 65–67. Her search for films for New York's Museum of Modern Art; some prints exist only in Europe; responses to other film activities in Europe.

Smith, G. Buckland. "The German Film Institute." *S&S* 16 (No. 62, Summer 47) 83–84.

Hersholt, Jean. "The Academy Speaks." *Atlantic* 181 (May 48). *See 3d.*

Manvell, Roger. "The British Film Academy." *FIR* 3 (Jan 52) 28–33. Its history, function, membership, and awards, 1947–1950.

Harris, Louis. "The Academy of Motion Picture Arts and Sciences." *FIR* 3 (Feb 52) 71–76. Its publications, monthly screenings, library and film library, together with a list of its charter members.

Dent, Alan. "Dream Come True." *Illus London News* 221 (15 Nov 52) 822. Membership and programs of the British Film Institute's National Film Theatre.

Brackett, Charles. "A Letter from Charles Brackett." *FIR* 5 (Feb 54) 49–50. President of the Academy of Motion Picture Arts and Sciences lists activities of organization apart from awards.

Forman, Denis. "The Work of the British Film Institute." *QFRTV* 9 (No. 2, Winter 54) 147–158. Director since 1949 describes BFI from 1948 to 1954; also printed in Roger Manvell, *The Film and the Public* (Penguin, 1955).

"Latin American Educational Film Institute." *School and Society* 85 (16 Mar 57) 93.

"The Front Page." *S&S* 27 (Autumn 57) 57. Editorial on policies for the now permanently established National Film Theatre in London.

"The Front Page." *S&S* 27 (Autumn 58) 269. Editorial on 25 years of BFI, its relation to "the trade" and minority audiences.

Lindgren, Ernest, and John Huntley. "Films from the BFI." *Film* (No. 20, Mar–Apr 59) 25–27+. The work of the National Film Archive and the Film Distribution Library.

Luft, Herbert G. "Hollywood Has Come of Age." *JSPG* (Sep 60) 19–20. Plans for Hollywood Motion Picture and Television Museum (which did not come to pass).

Young, Colin. "An American Film Institute: A Proposal." *FQ* 14 (No. 4, Summer 61) 37–50. A wide range of archival, cataloguing, educational, publishing, producing, and distributing activities: a blueprint.

Knight, Arthur. "Curator's Choice." *FQ* 15 (No. 3, Spring 62) 35–39. The curator of film and tape for the proposed Hollywood Motion Picture and Television Museum outlines his program.

Johnson, Albert. "Prelude to a Palace." *S&S* 32 (Winter 62–63) 14. On the old site of Hollywood's Garden of Allah Hotel is the Lytton Savings and Loan building with the Center of the Visual Arts, devoted to the history of the movies.

Kuper, Theodore F. "The Los Angeles County Hollywood Museum." *JUFPA* 16 (No. 1, 1964) 7+. Description of its goals, its staff, and its proposed audience.

Hodgkinson, Tony. "The British Film Institute." *F Com* 2 (No. 4, Fall 64) 31–34. Lecturer at Boston University gives details on archives, theatre, publications, and education department of BFI.

Paine, Frank R. "The American Film Institute." *JUFPA* 18 (No. 3, 1966) 3–4. The most useful function AFI could serve is as funding source for decentralized training and scholarship in film; statement by current president of University Film Producers Association.

Hodgkinson, Anthony W. "Some Observations on the Foundation and Functions of an American Film Institute." *F Soc Rev* (Apr 66) 5–8.

Knight, Arthur. "Why We Need a Film Institute." *Sat Rev* 49 (13 Aug 66) 50–52. Review of film institutes in Europe.

Hutchinson, Tom. "Wogs Begin at Hampstead." *20th Century Studies* 174 (Winter 66) 43–44. Recollections of the difficulties of trying to organize a film society; comments on "A Report to the Governors of the British Film Institute" for extending the National Film Theatre to the provinces.

Van Dyke, Willard. "Film at the Museum of Modern Art." *Arts in Soc* 4 (No. 1, Winter 67) 34–45. Description of the functions and history of the Museum.

Alpert, Hollis. "Onward and Upward with the Institute." *Sat Rev* 50 (24 June 67) 50. Review of the beginnings of the AFI in the month of its birth.

Knight, Arthur. "Rising Sun in Film's Firmament." *Sat Rev* 50 (26 Aug 67) 37. The AFI after the first meeting of the board of trustees outlines its future plans: training of film makers, development of audiences, preservation of film history.

"Show of Concern." *Newswk* 70 (4 Sep 67) 74. The birth of the AFI.

Steele, Robert. "AFI, Cinema, Egg Salad and Omelets." *Cinéaste* 1 (No. 3, Winter 67–68) 5–8+. Initial reaction to the AFI, suggestions on its goals.

Van Dyke, Willard. "The Role of the Museum of Modern Art in Motion Pictures." *F Lib Q* 1 (No. 1, Winter 67–68) 36–38. The vigorous sponsorship of film as an art form; the programs of the museum: acquisition, circulation and research.

MacCann, Richard Dyer. "To Bridge the Gap." *JUFA* 20 (No. 1, 1968) 3–5. The structure and intended programs of the American Film Institute, including "bridging the gap" between film training at universities and first jobs in professional film making.

Peck, Gregory. "Background of the American Film Institute." *JUFA* 20 (No. 1, 1968) 8–10. Congressional legislation regarding AFI; research conducted to decide what the AFI should do; programs it is considering supporting.

"Remarks of George Stevens, Jr. on his appointment as Director of the American Film Institute." *JUFA* 20 (No. 1, 1968) 6. American film history to be preserved; the future of American films to be supported by AFI.

Peck, Gregory. "The American Film Institute: An Answer to Public Demand." *Action* 3 (No. 1, Jan–Feb 68) 11–13. The goals of the AFI are to develop new film makers and refine film tastes.

Eisenstadt, David. "The Canadian Film Institute." *JSPG* (Mar 68) 27–30.

Kahlenberg, Richard S. "The American Film Institute—Programs in Work." *JUFA* 20 (No. 4, 1968) 99–100+. Film projects, seminars, archives, and fellowships supported by the AFI.

Coe, Richard L. "Support for New Talent." *Sat Rev* 51 (28 Dec 68) 22+. The programs of the American Film Institute. Part of *Saturday Review* report "The Now Movie."

Barry, Iris. "The Film Library and How It Grew." *FQ* 22 (No. 4, Summer 69) 19–27. The first film curator of New York's Museum of Modern Art tells how she began the collection, with trips to Hollywood and to Europe.

Geller, Robert, and Sam Kula. "Toward Filmic

Literacy: The Role of the American Film Institute." *J Aesthetic Educ* 3 (No. 3, July 69) 97–111. The education, production, and critical contribution of the AFI.

Montagu, Ivor. "Birmingham Sparrow: In Memoriam: Iris Barry 1896–1969." *S&S* 39 (Spring 70). *See 3b(1)*.

Hermetz, Aljean. "The American Film Institute." *Show* (20 Aug 70) 16–19. Its projects.

1a(3). FILM STUDY IN UNIVERSITIES

1a(3a). U.S. Theory and Practice

[See also 4a(1).]

"The University Film Foundation of Harvard University." *Science* 71 (11 Apr 30) 381. Rockefeller grant used to build film studio.

Brandon, Tom. "A New Film School." *New Rep* 77 (22 Nov 33) 49–50. Announcement of Harry Alan Potamkin Film School by its director.

Troy, William. "An Academy of the Film." *Nation* 137 (22 Nov 33) 605–606. Announces opening of Harry Alan Potamkin Film School in New York.

"Harvard University Film Service and the Fine Arts Theatre of Boston." *School and Society* 40 (6 Oct 34) 438–439. Adult-education committee plans college of motion pictures.

"A Course in the Artistic, Educational and Social Aspects of the Motion Picture." *School and Society* 42 (5 Oct 35) 461. New course offered at New York University School of Education.

"Film Study at Columbia University." *School and Society* 46 (17 July 37) 78.

"Fourth Annual Convention of Cinema Appreciation League of University of Southern California." *Wilson Lib Bul* 12 (Sep 37) 40.

Goodman, Ezra. "Hollywood in Cap and Gown." *S&S* 7 (No. 25, Spring 38) 29–30. The universities are at last taking film seriously.

"Bachelors of Pix Biz." *Newswk* 25 (2 Apr 45) 86. NYU's Robert Gessner is profiled as the only professor of film in the country in 1945.

Barry, Iris. "Motion Pictures as a Field of Research." *College Art J* 4 (No. 4, May 45) 206–209. Proposals for research in film history.

Beranger, Clara. "Cinema Is Ready for College." *Th Arts* 31 (Jan 47) 61–63. A plea for expanded film study in colleges: trained film makers would make better films.

"Books into Films; Movies' Acceptance as Integral Part of American Culture." *Publishers Weekly* 151 (15 Feb 47) 1138. Colleges are beginning to adopt motion-picture study programs and workshops.

Margolis, Herbert F. "The American Scene and the Problems of Film Education." *Pen-*

7

guin *F Rev* 2 (Jan 47) 54–63. Experimental film courses at the American University Centre in Biarritz, France; the establishment in the U.S. of a Motion Picture Foundation for colleges and universities headed by Robert Gessner of NYU; the Actor's Laboratory.

Margolis, Herbert F. "An Experiment at Biarritz." *Hwd Q* 2 (No. 3, Apr 47) 273–279. Report on courses in film appreciation at U.S. Army University Center in France.

Fulton, A. P. "A University Course in the Moving Picture." *Hwd Q* 3 (No. 2, Winter 47–48). Teacher describes his "comparative study of narration" at Purdue University.

Macgowan, Kenneth. "Teaching the Young Idea How to Feel." *Screen Writer* 4 (Aug 48) 9–10+. Goals and courses at UCLA, where author is chairman of theatre arts (including film): "No university should be a trade school."

Spottiswoode, Raymond. "Ideas on Film." *Sat Rev* 32 (8 Jan 49) 36. New approaches to film at universities.

Gessner, Robert. "Motion Pictures at the University." *FIR* 1 (May–June 50) 16–18+. Various academic approaches proposed by chairman of department of motion pictures at NYU.

Hart, Henry. "An Educational Scandal." *FIR* 2 (Aug–Sep 51) 1–2. An editorial against the misuse of NYU's facilities through the presentation of *Trilogy,* by Gregory J. Markopoulos.

Ellis, Jack C. "Work Print: A College English Department and Films." *QFRTV* 6 (No. 1, Fall 51) 37–47. Graduate student at Columbia University relates vicissitudes of film-series program at small college, financial problems incurred, lists of films used.

Adams, William B. "A Definition of Motion Picture Research." *QFRTV* 7 (No. 4, Summer 53) 408–421. UCLA lecturer in cinema says it has four aspects: theatrical, nontheatrical, social science, historical.

Ellis, Jack C. "Teaching the Film." *FIR* 5 (Aug–Sep 54) 352–356. English teacher describes his experience in giving a course in cinema for the first time at a junior college in western Michigan.

Kellich, Martin, and Malcolm M. Marsden. "Teaching Film Drama as Literature." *QFRTV* 11 (No. 1, Fall 56) 39–48. Film drama has been taught as literature at South Dakota State College and deserves to be given this kind of importance.

Lusa, Daniel. "Learning the Film at UCLA." *F Cult* 3 (No. 11, 1957) 21.

Weales, Gerald. "Teaching Film Drama as Film Drama." *QFRTV* 11 (No. 4, Summer 57) 394–398. Response to article (Fall 56) by Martin Kallich and Malcolm Marsden on film drama as literature; author contends

it should be taught using the films themselves and as a separate form.

MacCann, Richard Dyer. "USC Cinema—Practice and Purpose." *JUFPA* 11 (No. 2, Winter 59) 5–6. The production workshop is the center of things at the University of Southern California; professional training in film communication is a university responsibility similar to that in law or medicine.

Strevey, Tracy E. "Cinema and the Communication Arts." *JUFPA* 11 (No. 2, Winter 59) 4+. Dean of the College at USC relates cinema to other departments there.

Wagner, Robert W. "Cinema Education in the United States." *JUFPA* 13 (No. 3, Spring 61) 8–10+. Journal editor provides Society of Motion Picture and TV Engineers with history and proposed scope of university film teaching.

"Film at Boston University." *JUFPA* 13 (No. 4, Summer 61) 4–5. Statement about the teaching program.

Steele, Robert. "Film Curriculum." *JUFPA* 13 (No. 4, Summer 61) 10–11. Courses at Boston University.

Leyda, Jay. "Waiting Jobs." *FQ* 16 (No. 2, Winter 62–63) 29–33. His proposed objectives for film scholarship: how films are paid for; international film history; studies of "enclosed" periods of national film history; more concern about the screenwriter.

Toeplitz, Jerzy. "Film Scholarship: Present and Prospective." *FQ* 16 (No. 3, Spring 63) 27–37. Some leading books of theory and history appraised; centers for research, including archives; encyclopedias, screenplays, directorial studies; needed are bibliographies, a book on directing, cooperation among scholars, archives, and film makers.

Young, Colin. "University Film Teaching in the United States." *FQ* 16 (No. 3, Spring 63) 37–48. The schism between university training and professional practice; programs reported by Columbia, NYU, Northwestern, Ohio State, Iowa, USC, UCLA. See *FQ* 16 (No. 4, Summer 63) 63–64 for City College of New York.

Goldman, Freda. "Some Forms of Cinema Appreciation Programs." *Arts in Society* 2 (No. 3, Spring–Summer 63) 195–201. Description of university courses.

Benton, Charles. "Film Study: At What Profit?" *JSPG* 11 (No. 5, Sep 63) 3–8. Executive of Encyclopaedia Britannica Films reports on meeting of film teachers and critics he convened to propose next needs in the field.

Knight, Arthur. "Coals for Newcastle." *JSPG* 11 (No. 5, Sep 63) 25–28. Teaching film at USC; how the planned Hollywood Museum might help.

Gessner, Robert. "On Teaching Cinema in College." *F Cult* (No. 31, 1963–1964) 47–50. In place of literary, dramatic, and sociological approaches, the NYU professor would put simply history, script analysis, and production.

Fischer, Edward. "How to Develop a Discerning Film Audience." *JUFPA* 16 (No. 3, 1964) 23–25. An orderly approach to learning about film is as necessary as an orderly approach to science; author describes in some detail his own course in film criticism.

Kantor, Bernard R. "A New Approach to Film Education." *JUFPA* 16 (No. 3, 1964) 12–15. Describes new course titles in the required program for a cinema major at the University of Southern California as well as some of the optional courses.

Kuiper, John. "The First Step: The Beginning Course in Film." *JUFPA* 16 (No. 3, 1964) 7–9+. The "appreciation" course and the production course is each an incomplete approach; a beginning film course must include both.

Lamont, Austin F. "Boston University Film School." *F Com* 2 (No. 2, 1964) 42–44.

Staples, Don. "The Teaching of Film at Northwestern." *JUFPA* 16 (No. 3, 1964) 16–18.

Young, Colin. "Teaching Film at UCLA." *JUFPA* 16 (No. 4, 1964) 14–22. History, résumé of faculty, undergraduate, and graduate curricula.

Steele, Robert. "Film Scholars at the New York Film Festival." *F Com* 2 (No. 4, Fall 64) 41–45. Professor at Boston University has grave doubts about the value of the national meeting sponsored by American Council on Education to organize leadership for film teaching.

Byrne, Richard B. "Stylistic Analysis of the Film: Notes on a Methodology." *Speech Monographs* 32 (No. 1, Mar 65). *See 3b.*

Fischer, Edward. "Film Studies Are Coming—Ready or Not." *JUFPA* 17 (No. 4, 1965) 25–26. Two approaches to film teaching: to "academicize" it into dullness, or to avoid any rigorous intellectual approach at all in fear of putting students off; the need is to impose at least some form on the material.

Gessner, Robert. "An Approach to the Basics in Cinema." *J Soc Cin* 5 (1965) 90–95. The first film course should train students to notice changes in movement, size, and light in films; after that can come advanced grammar, script analysis, production, and contemporary cinema.

Steele, Robert. "A Personal Reaction." *JUFPA* 17 (No. 4, 1965) 20–23. The Dartmouth Film Study Conference struck him as mostly "canned academism," but Burchard, Kael, and Stoney were stimulating.

Wagner, Robert W. "Conference at Dartmouth." *JUFPA* 17 (No. 4, 1965) 19–20. List of speakers and others at Dartmouth Film Study Conference in October.

Hodgkinson, Anthony. "That Meeting at Dartmouth." *F Com* 3 (No. 14, Fall 65) 54–55. Report on conference of film teachers called by American Council on Education.

Stewart, David. "Celluloid Syllabus." *Am Educ* 1 (No. 8, Sep 65) 29–32. A report on the current status of film education in the colleges.

Young, Colin. "The UCLA Film School." *F Her* 1 (No. 1, Fall 65) 35–41. Successes and problems; graduate program; faculty.

Dronberger, Ilse. "The Foreign Film: Student Discussions with a View Toward International Encounter." *JUFPA* 18 (No. 1, 1966) 11–15+. A lengthy checklist for a systematic study of film content proposed by certain German scholars.

Huss, R., and N. Silverstein. "Film Study: Shot Orientation for the Literary-Minded." *College English* 27 (No. 7, 1966) 566–568. Film study should concentrate on cinematic qualities.

Hammond, Robert M. "Foreign Language by Feature Film." *F Her* 1 (No. 3, Spring 66) 29–34. Review of a course given at Harvard Summer School: French by film.

Stewart, David C. "Men and Movies at Dartmouth." *JUFPA* 18 (No. 3, 1966) 5–8. History of the college's support of film activities, from viewings to production and academic study.

Staples, Donald E. "An Approach to Cinema at the Graduate Level." *JUFPA* 19 (No. 1, 1967) 8–12. The program at Ohio State University.

Wagner, Robert W. "A Department of Photography and Cinema—An Environment for Seeing." *JUFPA* 19 (No. 1, 1967) 3–5. Chairman of department at Ohio State University suggests importance of understanding the photographic image.

Kantor, Bernard, Colin Young, David Mallery, David Stewart, Jack Ellis, Haig Manoogian, Arthur Mayer. "The Journal Looks at College Films and Hollywood." *JSPG* (Mar 67) 3–28. College teachers of film and others report on expanding field of film study.

Suber, Howard. "A New Approach to the Teaching of Film History." *JUFPA* 19 (No. 2, 1967) 40–43. The teacher should concentrate on the films themselves and what they have to communicate, as opposed to antiquarianism, pigeonholing, technological jargon, and other time-wasting approaches.

Kantor, Bernard R. "Film Study in Colleges—How to Help the Film Industry Despite Itself." *Cinéaste* 1 (No. 2, Fall 67) 3–5.

Young, Colin. "Films Are Contemporary: Notes on Film Education." *Arts in Soc* 4 (No. 1, Winter 67) 23–33. The teacher should begin with contemporary film experiences instead of "classics" and show earlier films as social documents; courses at UCLA.

9

Fielding, Raymond. "Film Study and History Research at the University of Iowa." *Cinéaste* 1 (No. 3, Winter 67–68) 14–15+.

Fell, John. "Dear Dean Korzybski." *JUFPA* 20 (No. 3, 1968) 70–74. A lighthearted report by a knowledgeable "consultant" on how a university film program should be set up.

Prince, Barry. "But I Couldn't Get a Job." *Cinéaste* 1 (No. 4, Spring 68) 9–11+. A call for an industry-run trade school to prepare young technicians; objections to stressing the aesthetics of film as taught in the university.

Williams, Raymond. "Film and the University." *Cinema* (Cambridge) (No. 1, Dec 68) 24–25. Interview by Noel Purdon. Williams was preparing to lecture on film for the English faculty at Cambridge.

Mueller, Henry L. "Film As Art." *J Aesthetic Educ* 3 (No. 1, Jan 69). *See 3b.*

Davis, Robert E. "New Cinema: New Problems." *JUFA* 21 (No. 2, 1969) 35–39+. Today's cinema students have less reverence for film conventions, more willingness to experiment, and film teaching should make allowances for this.

Rose, Ernest D. "Problems and Prospects in Film Teaching." *JUFA* 21 (No. 4, 1969) 95–101+. A new generation already sophisticated in film is a problem for a tradition-minded faculty; how to plan for the future when technology may be completely altered in 25 years?

Worth, Sol. "The Relevance of Research." *JUFA* 21 (No. 3, 1969) 81–84. Film research is relevant to those who want to know how film communicates.

Jameson, Richard T. "Manhandling the Movies." *FQ* 22 (No. 3, Spring 69) 4–11. A lengthy attack on some of the articles in W. R. Robinson's anthology *Man and the Movies* (Baton Rouge: 1967) as inadequate scholarship.

O'Grady, Gerald. "The Preparation of Teachers of Media." *J Aesthetic Educ* 3 (No. 3, July 69) 113–134. They should have broad and encompassing concerns with image making.

Wegner, Hart. "The Literate Cinema." *Western Humanities Rev* 24 (1970) 279–282. On the need for scholarly research techniques in film study.

Simon, Bill. "NYU Cine-Strike." *Cinéaste* 3 (No. 4, Spring 70) 21. New York University's film students strike for peace.

Nichols, Bill. "The Film School and Political Action." *Cinéaste* 4 (No. 1, Summer 1970) 26–28+. The UCLA strike and a critique of political theory in film schools.

Harcourt, Peter. "In Defence of Film History." *Screen* 11 (No. 6, 1970) 75–86. A personal memoir suggests the value of being guided by one's own enthusiasms in teaching; analysis of *Bonnie and Clyde*.

"New Ph.D. Program in Cinema." *School and Society* 98 (Dec 70) 460–461. Courses at New York University.

1a(3b). Production Training and Student Films

[*See also 1a(2), 2a(5), 2b(5), 7f(3).*]

"Hollywood Training." *Art Dig* 12 (1 Mar 38) 27. Founding of the Chouinard School of Motion Picture Arts, Los Angeles.

Stern, E. M. "Denver Students Learn Movie-Making in the Classroom." *Pop Sci* 138 (Apr 41) 77–80+. Same abridged: "These Students Make Their Own Movies." *Rdrs Dig* 38 (Apr 41) 69–72.

Rozsa, Miklos. "University Training for Motion Picture Musicians." *Etude* 64 (June 46). *See 2g(2).*

Sternfeld, Frederick W. "Preliminary Report on Film Music." *Hwd Q* 2 (No. 3, Apr 47). *See 2g(2).*

Zimmer, Andrew. "Undergraduate Film-making." *FIR* 3 (May 52) 224–228. Member of Ivy Films reports on student extracurricular production at Harvard and on the films *A Touch of the Times* and *Much Ado About Studying*.

Howard, Jack. "The Film Gains a Dimension." *QFRTV* 7 (No. 1, Fall 52) 77–86. UCLA student film on housing offered as combining both instruction and research functions in university; portion of script using subjective camera.

Katz, Robert. "Teaching Film on Half a Shoestring." *QFRTV* 7 (No. 2, Winter 52) 178–190. Director of film workshop and seminar at California School of Fine Arts in San Francisco describes school's history, methods, sponsor problems, and financial accounts.

"Movies with a College Education." *Th Arts* 37 (Jan 53) 16. Screen Producers Guild establishes Intercollegiate Film Award for student film makers.

Pichel, Irving. "College Courses on Film-Making: At UCLA." *FIR* 4 (Dec 53) 523–525.

Wald, Malvin. "College Courses on Film-Making: At USC." *FIR* 4 (Dec 53) 525–529.

Finn, James D., and Fred F. Harcleroad. "The Professional Training of the Non-Theatrical Film Worker in the University." *JUFPA* 7 (No. 2, Winter 54) 4–8. Professors of education propose liberal background, production training, and some other specialization (business, communication, etc.); professional ethics in news and documentary should also be taught.

Blume, Wilbur, Mendell Sherman, Warren Stevens, and John Nugent. "The Training and Future of the Non-Theatrical Film Worker."

JUFPA 7 (No. 2, Winter 54) 9–11. A symposium commenting on paper by Finn and Harcleroad.

Rose, Ernest D. "University Thesis Films: A Step Across the Barrier." *QFRTV* 9 (No. 4, Summer 55) 333–340. UCLA Theater Arts faculty member praises M.A. thesis film program, relating problems encountered in making his own film about Southern California water resources.

"*Look* Applauds." *Look* 19 (27 Dec 55) 10. *Look* joins the Screen Producers Guild in its Intercollegiate Film Awards.

Luft, Herbert G. "Students on a Set." *FIR* 9 (Mar 58) 130–132. A report on the visit of three USC cinema students, Barry M. Kirk, John Morrill, and Erik Daarstad, throughout the production of *Witness for the Prosecution*.

Stenholm, Katherine. "Thespis in a Christian Frame." *JUFPA* 11 (No. 4, Summer 59) 10–12. The training of film actors at Bob Jones University in Greenville, South Carolina.

Sloan, Melvin. "The 'Why' and 'How' of Cinema Education." *JUFPA* 11 (No. 2, Winter 59) 7–8. The production teaching sequence at the University of Southern California.

Noxon, Gerald F. "A Scholar in Indecision." *JUFPA* 13 (No. 4, Summer 61) 6–7. About the student writer-director at Boston University: a dialogue in which the professor helps him select his own subject for filming.

Neyman, Michael. "*Off the Highway*." *S&S* 31 (Autumn 62) 177–178. Report on a film of this title made by USC cinema students under the supervision of Fred Zinnemann.

Rawlinson, Dustin. "A World Survey of Training Programs in Cinema." *JUFPA* 14 (No. 4, 1962) 3+. Professional technical training institutes abroad compared with academically oriented programs affiliated with American universities; author finds greater potential and freedom of choice in the university training programs.

Tyo, John H. "Film Production Courses in U.S. Universities." *JUFPA* 14 (No. 4, 1962) 8–13+. Statistical analysis of the course offerings of the ten schools offering the largest number of film courses; tabulation of results of interviews with production personnel.

Williams, Don G. "Teaching Programs in Film Production in the U.S." *JUFPA* 14 (No. 4, 1962) 4–7+. A school-by-school account of degrees and credit hours offered in film, numbers of students enrolled, and numbers of films produced.

Worth, Sol. "Student Film Workshop." *F Com* 1 (No. 5, Summer 63) 54–58. Description of author's teaching at Annenberg School of Communication, University of Pennsylvania.

Hawkins, Richard C. "A Primer for Motion Pictures." *JSPG* 11 (No. 5, Sep 63) 9–12+. List of needs for film production teaching at a university, written by head of motion-picture division at UCLA.

"Film Makers at Northwestern." *JUFPA* 16 (No. 2, 1964) 18–19. Describes specific professional film projects by Northwestern's students, aims of the film program, and award-winning student films.

Goggin, Richard J. "The Theatrical Tradition and Cinema and Television Training in American Universities." *JUFPA* 16 (No. 3, 1964) 4–6+. Most university film programs and film students are tending away from the traditional dramatic framework of movies; a paper given at the International Congress of Schools of Cinema and Television.

Mercer, John. "Teaching Film Production— One Approach and One Problem." *JUFPA* 16 (No. 3, 1964) 19–21. The approach at Southern Illinois University is crew-work production rather than individual student projects; the problem is how to grade.

Stenholm, Katherine. "The Philosophical Approach to Film Training." *JUFPA* 16 (No. 3, 1964) 10–11. Describes cinema production training at Bob Jones University.

Wagner, Robert W. "Beyond Teaching." *JUFPA* 16 (No. 3, 1964) 3+. Once trained to make films, the students need to be given practical opportunities to use their knowledge.

Krasney, Phillip. "The Responsibility of the University to the Photographic Profession." *JUFPA* 16 (No. 4, 1964). *See 7f(1a)*.

Hitchens, G. "*Sunday on the River*." *Pop Photog* 54 (May 64) 134–135+. Story of author's collaboration with Ken Resnick on student film about Harlem outing.

Gessner, R. "Handwriting on the Screen." *Sat Rev* 47 (10 Oct 64) 36. In Europe the cinema academies train and place young talent in the studios of their countries, whereas Americans cannot get comparable training here.

Clarke, Shirley. "Teaching Film Making Creatively." *JUFPA* 17 (No. 3, 1965) 6–14. The university is valuable for film because it allows time enough to experiment in film making, an atmosphere in which films are taken seriously, and a place where new kinds of films may be seen and appreciated.

Stewart, David C. "The Movies Students Make: New Wave on Campus." *Harper's* 231 (Oct 65) 66–72.

"Student Filmmakers." *Newswk* 66 (25 Oct 65) 114+. UCLA's festival.

Jackson, Burgess. "Student Film-Making: First Report." *FQ* 19 (No. 3, Spring 66) 29–33. Certain trends among UCLA student films; fiction dominant, a tendency toward *weltschmerz* and gloom, lack of experimentalism.

11

72070

Rubin, Joan Alleman. "Student and Film." *Mlle* 62 (Mar 66) 172. Study of motion-picture production in college.

Sargent, Ralph. "8mm at UCLA." *FQ* 19 (No. 4, Summer 66) 39–41. Its use in film classes.

Capp, Al, and Roberta Reisig. "Are These Films Offensive? Al Capp vs. the Modern Young Ladies of Wellesley." *Pop Photog* 59 (Dec 66) 168–171. Prizes given at Wellesley festival for student films from 48 schools; Capp was a judge but didn't like two of the choices.

Dart, Peter. "The Importance of Structure in Teaching Film Production." *JUFPA* 19 (No. 2, 1967) 49–52. Structured film-production courses can best guide students toward mastery of the medium and therefore to the freedom they want.

Perry, Ted. "A Liberalized Concept of the Teaching of Film Production." *JUFPA* 19 (No. 2, 1967) 44–48. More important than technical data is training in visual perception.

Lester, Elenore. "Shaking the World with an 8-mm Camera." *NYTM* (26 Nov 67) 44–45+. On student film making, especially at NYU.

Dart, Peter. "Student Film Production and Communication." *English J* 57 (Jan 68) 96–99. The logistics of student film-production classes and their rationale.

"Student Movie Makers." *Time* 91 (2 Feb 68) 78–79. Report on the nationwide interest in film schools and on the annual National Student Film Festival.

Braverman, Robert. "The Chicken or the Egg." *Cinéaste* 2 (No. 1, Summer 68) 19–20. A teacher of film making at School of Visual Arts (New York City) criticizes the film student for not becoming more involved in his immediate community.

McCarty, Robert J. "The Evening Course in Basic Film Production at the School of Visual Arts." *Cinéaste* 2 (No. 1, Summer 68) 22–23.

Schnitzler, Peter. "UFA, Denver, and Revolution." *JUFA* 20 (No. 4, 1968) 89–90+. UFA conference reveals university film training as years behind in techniques and in awareness of social responsibility.

Schuth, H. Wayne. "Techniques of Teaching Film Production." *JUFA* 21 (No. 3, 1969) 85–87. Brief description of teaching techniques at Stephens College; author also relays reports at conference by Hugh Grauel for UCLA and Peter Rodis for NYU.

Childs, Richard B. "A Place for the Young Filmmaker." *Cinéaste* 2 (No. 4, Spring 69) 6. Explanation of goals behind Genesis program to distribute films of student and independent film makers.

Peavy, Charles. "The Films of Richard Mason." *Cinéaste* 2 (No. 4, Spring 69). *See 5, Richard Mason.*

Yellen, Linda. "Campus, Camera and Me: Filming of *Come Out, Come Out*." *Seventeen* 28 (May 69) 154–155+. The director explains how she made the first student-made full-length commercial film about the 1968 Columbia University strike.

Genelli, Thomas J. "Basic Guides for Student Film Production." *F Com* 5 (No. 3, Fall 69) 58–59. Producer of documentaries and teacher at New School sizes up available books.

Riegel, O. W. "Some Thoughts on Student Films." *F Com* 5 (No. 4, Winter 69) 64–69. Professor at Washington and Lee University in Virginia, who introduced motion-picture history courses in the 1930s and production courses in 1947, comments on "what kinds of students make films."

Monaco, R. J. "You're Only as Young as They Think You Are." *Sat Rev* 52 (27 Dec 69) 15–17. Young film makers and university courses.

Steele, Robert S. "Down with 8mm—Even Super 8." *JUFA* 22 (No. 2, 1970) 43–47. It is not an adequate medium for academic film training because it is associated with amateurism and does not encourage technical finesse or meticulous editing.

"Results of *Esquire*'s First College Film Festival." *Esq* 74 (Aug 70) 6+. Winners described with editorial comment.

1a(3c). International Film Schools

"A People's Cinema University in London." *School and Society* 36 (13 Aug 32) 201–202. Plans for film school.

"A Sound-Film University." *School and Society* 36 (15 Oct 32) 504–505. Reprint from *British Medical Journal* about People's Cinema University, London.

Eisenstein, S. M. "Detective Work in the GIK." *Close Up* 9 (No. 4, Dec. 32) 287–294. Eisenstein describes the detective work necessary to find youthful talent as students for the Moscow State Institute of Cinematography (GIK).

Eisenstein, S. M. "Cinematography with Tears." *Close Up* 10 (No. 1, Mar 33) 3–17. The problems involved in teaching film students at the GIK (Moscow State Institute of Cinematography).

Potamkin, Harry Alan. "A Proposal for a School of the Motion Picture." *Hound & Horn* 7 (No. 1, Oct–Dec 33) 140–143. An outline for a program of film study in a university—includes curriculum, library, and faculty.

Philipson, Aldo. "Italian Experiment." *S&S* 8 (No. 31, Autumn 39) 118–119. A description of the Centro Sperimentale di Cinematografía and its work.

Boyer, Charles. "Advanced Training for Film Workers: France." *Hwd Q* 1 (No. 3, Apr 46) 287–290. Courses and admission policies of Institut des Hautes Études Cinématographiques (IDHEC).

Leyda, Jay. "Advanced Training for Film Workers: Russia." *Hwd Q* 1 (No. 3, Apr 46) 279–286. Program and publications of Soviet Institute of Cinematography compared with failure of U.S. to do anything comparable.

Willis, E. "French Film Institute." *Th Arts* 31 (May 47) 68–69. Faculty of four-year-old French Institut des Hautes Études Cinématographiques (IDHEC) includes Mitry, Sadoul, Carné, Spaak, and others.

Margolis, Herbert F. "UNESCO and a Film Student Exchange Plan: A Symposium of Hollywood Opinion." *Screen Writer* 2 (Apr 47) 1–13. Asks for UNESCO-organized film-student exchanges (U.S., England, France, Russia) as one way to upgrade and encourage the serious study of film as an art form.

Institut des Hautes Études Cinématographiques. *"Le Silence est d'or:* A Student Film Analysis." *Hwd Q* 3 (No. 3, Spring 48). See *3c.*

De La Roche, Catherine. "The State Institute of Cinema and the Film Actors' Theatre in Moscow." *S&S* 17 (No. 66, Summer 48). See *4e(8).*

Verdone, Mario. "Italian Experiment." *S&S* 18 (Summer 49) 86–87. Experimental Center (film school) in Rome.

Verdone, Mario. "The Experimental Cinema Center in Italy." *Hwd Q* 4 (No. 1, Fall 49) 65–68. Editor of *Bianco e Nero* describes facilities, courses, and objectives of Italian film school, its relationship with the industry; its graduates, including DeSantis, Zampa, Germi, Antonioni, Alida Valli, Girotti.

Fong, Monique. *"Shoe-Shine:* A Student Film Analysis." *Hwd Q* 4 (No. 1, Fall 49). See *3c, Shoe-Shine.*

Lane, John Francis. "On Studying the Film." *S&S* 19 (Apr 50) 93–94. L'Institut des Hautes Études Cinématographiques in Paris.

Lerman, L. "Something to Talk About: Centro Sperimentale di Cinematografía." *Mlle* 39 (May 54) 112–114.

Wagner, Robert. "Report on Cannes." *JUFPA* 8 (No. 4, Summer 56) 3–4. Greetings and summary of activities at third International Congress of Schools of Cinema and Television, held at the same time as the film festival.

Williams, Don. "Report on Venice." *JUFPA* 8 (No. 4, Summer 56) 12. "The Entrance of Students into the Profession" was the theme of second meeting of International Congress of Schools of Film and Television.

Hauff, Eberhard. "The German Institute for Film and Television." *JUFPA* 10 (No. 1, Fall 57) 7–8. Director of Munich school tells its history and courses.

Rauch, Robert J. "An American in a European Film School." *JUFPA* 10 (No. 1, Fall 57) 9–11. English instructor at Notre Dame reports on the daily routines and yearly projects he worked on at the Centro Sperimentale di Cinematografía in Rome.

Tessoneau, Rémy. "The French Institute of Cinema (IDHEC)." *JUFPA* 10 (No. 1, Fall 57) 4–6. Administrator-general tells about admission and examination policies, courses, and production.

Wagner, Robert. "Report from Latin America." *JUFPA* 10 (No. 1, Fall 57) See *4h.*

Anderson, Joseph L. "The Department of Cinema at Nihon University." *JUFPA* 10 (No. 4, Summer 58) 3–9. Required and elective courses at this private university in Japan.

"Film Lectureship." *S&S* 29 (Winter 59–60) 23. Sir William Coldstream, Slade Professor of Fine Art, University of London, announces grants for a film lecturer in graduate studies and two film fellowships.

Medvedev, A. "Birth of a Film-Maker." *F&F* 5 (No. 4, Jan 59). See *4e(8).*

"Film Study at London University." *S&S* 30 (Spring 61) 70–71. Note on Thorold Dickinson's plans for relating film making and film criticism.

Guroshev, Alexander. "Giving Youth Its Chance." *F&F* 7 (No. 6, Mar 61). See *4e(8).*

Dickinson, Thorold, and Michael Orrom. "The Start at the Slade." *Film* (No. 28, Mar–Apr 61) 22–25. The need for national support for film making and the establishment of a national film school are discussed in terms of the current offerings at the Slade School, London University.

Stone, Margaret. "Five Years and Then?" *Motion* (No. 1, Summer 61) 21–22+. Thorold Dickinson and the beginning years of film teaching at the Slade School in London.

Brandt, George W. "And at Bristol." *Motion* (No. 1, Summer 61) 23–25. Comments on the film program in the drama department of the University of Bristol.

Anderson, Joseph L. "The Search for International Standards." *JUFPA* 14 (No. 1, Fall 61) 4–7. Report on speeches by delegates and the proceedings of the International Liaison Center of Schools of Cinema and Television held at Berkeley in conjunction with the annual meeting of the University Film Producers Association.

Robinson, David. "Better Late than Never." *S&S* 31 (Spring 62) 67–70. Apart from a private institution, the London School of Film Technique, and the Royal College of

Art, with its small department of film and television design, there is no training school for future film makers in England; suggestions made.

Fruchter, Norman. "Two Hours a Week." *S&S* 31 (Autumn 62) 198–200. Evaluation of the film courses the writer, a young American novelist, has been teaching at Kingsway Day College in London.

Fischer, Edward. "The Salzburg Seminar in American Studies." *JUFA* 15 (No. 2, 1963) 12–15. Visiting lecturer tells about his audience and lists the films he used, including some made by students.

Lorentz, Pare. "The University, the Film, and the Community." *JUFPA* 15 (No. 2, 1963). *See* 7f(3).

Patterson, Oscar E. "Congress in Vienna." *JUFPA* 15 (No. 4, 1963) 12–17. Similarities and differences between American and European (especially Italian and Spanish) film training programs; student films turned out by these programs and screened at the Congress of Schools of Cinema and Television.

Gessner, Robert. "Report from Lodz." *S&S* 32 (Spring 63) 66–67. Training program of Polish film school.

Ellis, Jack C. "Does the Screen Need Education?" *JSPG* 11 (No. 5, Sep 63) 17–19. Professor at Northwestern University reports on meeting in Norway about film and TV appreciation: the British stress character motivation, not "anatomized lists of questions about camera work, acting, sets, music."

Murari, Jagat. "Film Institute of India." *JUFPA* 17 (No. 1, 1965) 3–5+. Training film makers.

Farmer, Herbert. "Russian and Polish Film Schools." *F Soc Rev* (May 66) 21–25. A brief account of the film schools in the two countries.

Schein, Harry. "Film School in Sweden." *S&S* 36 (Autumn 67) 199–200. Director of the Swedish Film Institute reports on Sweden's three-year-old film school; some of its problems of talent, emotions, and discipline.

Wright, Ian. "National Film School." *S&S* 36 (Autumn 67) 197–198. Summary of the published report of Lord Lloyd's committee of Great Britain's Department of Education and Science calling for an autonomous national film school "at the earliest possible moment," paid for by the government or by Eady fund money from the box office.

Dickinson, Thorold. "Film Study in British Schools." *JSPG* (Mar 67) 29–31. Former film maker, now lecturer on film at Slade School of Fine Art, University College, London, reports on limited production training, expanding courses in film art, and the future development of university studies in all subjects aided by the moving image.

Daniel, Frantisek. "The Czechoslovakian Academy of Arts." *JUFA* 20 (No. 1, 1968) 11–14. Describes principally the training program for cameramen, editors, scriptwriters, directors of film and TV.

Symonds, Elfreda. "The Development of Film Study at Hammersmith College for Further Education." *Screen* 10 (No. 1, Jan–Feb 69) 42–66. Responses of students to study of film medium.

Watkins, Roger. "Film and Television: A Main Subject Course at Bulmershe College of Education." *Screen* 10 (No. 1, Jan–Feb 69) 34–41. Separation from the English department: "It is no good deciding by the standards of (say) literature what film should be; it is a matter of finding out what it is."

Hudson, Roger. "Camera Adventure: An Experiment in Hornsey." *Screen* 10 (No. 2, Mar–Apr 69) 56–68. English art students do interviews, improvisations, and observations with film.

"The London School of Film Technique." *Cinéaste* 3 (No. 1, Summer 69) 4–7+. Analysis of the school by an American student.

Maben, Adrian, and Gerlad Jacobson. "The Centro Sperimentale di Cinematografía." *Cinéaste* 3 (No. 1, Summer 69) 8–10+. A description of the school in Rome by two American students.

Millar, Daniel. "The Use of Extracts in Film Teaching." *Screen* 10 (Nos. 4–5, July–Oct 69) 67–79. At Bede College, Durham, they can be "worked in several ways," including auteur, genre, and thematic approaches, which have pretty much supplanted the "grammar of film" and chronological approaches. Reprinted from *English in Education* (Spring 68).

Williams, Don G. "CILECT—The Early Years." *JUFA* 22 (No. 4, 1970) 100–102. Founding and early history of the congress of film schools.

Goggin, Richard J. "A View of Many Seasons." *JUFA* 22 (No. 4, 1970) 103–105. Discusses past meetings of CILECT (Congress of Schools of Cinema and TV)—what was done, how it was done, and how valuable it was.

Rose, Ernest D. "Postscripts from Prague and Vichy." *JUFA* 22 (No. 4, 1970) 108–111. Recent meetings of CILECT; the activities of the International Film and Television Students and Graduates Association; international exchange of ideas in film generally; is there new vitality and challenge?

Wagner, Robert W. "UFA Goes to Latin America." *JUFA* 22 (No. 4, 1970) 112–113. Film viewing and film making in Latin America; visits by university film teachers.

Kelly, Terence. "Teaching Film." *S&S* 39 (Autumn 70) 185. Colin Young, appointed director of new National Film School in London, says students want to see films, work with other students, and get their hands on equipment, not learn dogmas from teachers.

Wilson, David. "London Film School." *S&S* 39 (Autumn 70) 187. Note on student films recently shown.

Crofts, Stephen. "Film Education in England and Wales." *Screen* 11 (No. 6, 1970) 3–22.

1a(4). HIGH SCHOOLS AND GRADE SCHOOLS

"An Experiment in Appreciation of Motion-Picture Plays." *School Rev* 41 (Apr 33) 249–250. Reports study by National Council of Teachers of English.

"Motion Pictures in the Schools." *School and Society* 42 (12 Oct 35) 498–499. Literary films contributed to schools.

"Motion Picture Films for the Schools To Be Selected from Hollywood Vaults." *School and Society* 46 (24 July 37) 107–108. Committee from the Motion Picture Producers and Distributors of America working to effect a union between education and the film industry.

Mason, J. B. "Grant to the Committee on Motion Pictures in Education." *School and Society* 46 (18 Dec 37) 793. Grant from the General Education Board for a three-year program.

Thrasher, F. M. "Sociological Approach to Motion Pictures in Relation to Education." *Education* 58 (Apr 38) 467–473. An analysis of the educational implications of film; ways in which schools can participate.

Potamkin, Harry Alan. "The Cinematized Child." *Films* 1 (No. 1, Nov 39) 10–18. Film study and production by children proposed as counterbalance for excessive influence of the screen; studies by Lasker and Mitchell cited.

Lewis, A. B. "Scholastic Hollywoods." *Design* 41 (Dec 39) 14–17. Students at Central High School, Newark, study motion-picture technique.

Finch, H. R. "Motion Picture Study, A Credit Course." *Scholastic* 35 (22 Jan 40) 5T–6T.

Allen, D. "Cartoon Movie Project." *School Arts* 41 (Sep 41) 24.

Gillett, Bernard E. "Second Thoughts." *S&S* 11 (No. 42, Autumn 42) 47–49. The role of popular films in school education.

O'Dwyer, Kelvin. "The Child and the Cinema in Eire." *S&S* 15 (No. 58, Summer 46) 68. Irish activities designed to increase children's appreciation of films.

Llewelyn, Michael G. "The New Schools Must Have Cinemas." *S&S* 15 (No. 58, Summer 46) 72. Cinema auditoriums must be designed into new school buildings.

"Libraries Licensing Educational Films." *Lib J* 72 (1 Apr 47) 538. Teaching Films Custodians has agreed to distribute extracts from feature films as well as nonprofit educational films of the Motion Picture Association to libraries for educational use.

Jones, Ceinwen, and F. E. Pardoe. "Film Study." *S&S* 18 (Summer 49) 91–93. Detailed report on course introduced in modern urban secondary school for girls in Oldbury (England) to provide them "with some means of resisting the cinema's all-powerful appeal."

Jensen, Amy E. "Our Animated Movie of 'Peter and the Wolf.'" *School Arts* 49 (Jan 50) 178+. Wisconsin pupils' own creation of a script.

Wachtel, Lillian. "Good Features Never Die." *FIR* 1 (Dec 50) 28–32. They're cut apart and used in schools, thanks to a corporation called Teaching Films Custodians.

Williamson, May Gordon. "Film Appreciation in Scottish Schools." *QFRTV* 10 (No. 3, Spring 56) 273–280. Scottish children go to the movies more than those of any other country; "the whole approach to film must be switched from the purely emotional level to a more intellectual plane."

Hodgson, Lena. "Children as Film-Makers." *S&S* 26 (Autumn 56) 100–102. A report on a number of successful attempts to get children to make their own films as a class project, and to teach them to form critical opinions.

Lewin, William. "Film Appreciation in Schools." *FIR* 8 (Nov 57) 453–458. By the author of the monograph *Photoplay Appreciation in American High Schools*.

Hodgkinson, Tony. "Children's Films and Screen Education." *F Com* 2 (No. 2, 1964) 14–18. History of the Society for Education in Film and Television by one of its founders; course approaches; films made by children.

"Talent Under Twenty." *JUFPA* 16 (No. 2, 1964) 13–15. Descriptions of winning films in the Kodak teenage movie competition. Trend toward greater visual awareness and technical sophistication discussed.

Luke, Sister Mary. "Shouldn't We Teach Them the Movies?" *Education* 84 (Jan 64) 310–312. General suggestions for teaching film appreciation in high schools.

Eisler, Michael. "Moving Art." *School Arts* 64 (Dec 64) 34–36. Outline for a first film-production course.

Selby, Stuart. "Screen Education for American Schools." *Teachers College Rec* 116 (Feb 65) 446.

Craig, Donald. "Why Aren't We Teaching Film?" *Educ Forum* 29 (No. 4, May 65) 399–405. Films that can be labeled art are available in many cities yet there is no extensive study of film in our schools.

Johnson, W. "When the School Desk Is a Theatre Seat; Courses in Movie Appreciation." *Senior Scholastic* 86 (6 May 65) 26.

Sullivan, Sister Bede. "Headstart in Film Appreciation." *F Her* 1 (No. 2, Winter 65–66) 28–33. Review of a film-appreciation course for high-school-level students.

Lipton, L. "My Son, the Film-maker." *Pop Photog* 58 (Apr 66) 128–129. Children draw on film at Yellow Ball Workshop near Boston.

DePaul, Brother. "Teaching the Screen Arts." *Cath World* 203 (May 66) 109–112.

Johnson, William. "They Found It at the Movies." *Senior Scholastic* 88 (6 May 66) sup. 6. Seminar for 50 teachers in Philadelphia sees *The Hustler,* hears Pauline Kael, debates symbolism.

Culkin, John M. "I Was a Teen-Age Movie Teacher." *Sat Rev* 49 (16 July 66) 51–53+. *Discussion* 49 (20 Aug 66) 48. On film study in the high school.

Wright, G. S. "Teaching About the Screen Arts; Place in the School Art Program." *Scholastic Arts* 66 (May 67) 41–43.

Andersen, Yvonne. "Film Animation at the Yellow Ball Workshop." *Design* 69 (Fall 67). *See 2h.*

Lenk, Marjorie. "Amateurs and Animation." *Cinéaste* 1 (No. 2, Fall 67) 18. Report on animated films made by children in Lexington, Massachusetts.

Sheratsky, Rodney E. "Film Education in High School: Who's Kidding Who(m)?" *F Soc Rev* (Sep 67) 40–45. Criteria for meaningful screen education.

Foster, Joanna. "Film Happening at Fordham University." *Senior Scholastic* 91 (21 Sep 67) sup. 11. Report on the Fordham Film Study Conference.

Kinzer, S. "Mr. Pierson's Brainstorm." *Pop Photog* 61 (Dec 67) 132+. Film appreciation at Brookline High, near Boston.

Brehm, Randi. "Film as Film." *Take One* 1 (No. 10, 1968) 19–22. An approach to the study of cinema exemplified through a study guide for *Billy Liar,* a film directed by John Schlesinger.

Bigby, John. "Fade to Black." *Take One* 1 (No. 12, 1968) 20–21. Seeing Harlem through 8mm films made by third graders.

"Filmmaking Can Be Child's Play." *Senior Scholastic* 92 (29 Feb 68) sup. 10–11. On the Capistrano, California, 8mm film festival.

Andersen, Yvonne. "Yellow Ball Workshop." *F Lib Q* 1 (No. 2, Spring 68) 15–17. The programs offered for children in film animation in Lexington, Mass.

Holzman, S. "Film-in: To Turn Vidiots into Seeing-eye People; Montclair, N.J., High School." *Senior Scholastic* 92 (21 March 68) sup. 13.

Glennon, Michael L. "Small Groups and Short Films." *English J* 57 (May 68) 641–645. Plans used for high-school English seminars emphasizing film art.

Poteet, G. Howard. "Film as Language: Its Introduction into a High School Curriculum." *English J* 57 (Nov 68) 1182–1186. Outline of a four-year high-school program.

"Take 1 Scene 1." *Senior Scholastic* 94 (7 Feb 69) sup. 7. List of towns receiving AFI grants for investigations of film as a teaching vehicle.

Scheufele, Kirk. "Making Films with Students." *English J* 58 (Mar 69) 426–427+. Outline of a high-school program in California.

Robertson, George. "Film in English Teaching." *Screen* 10 (Nos. 4–5, July–Oct 69) 80–87. At Abbey Wood Comprehensive School, "with children of restricted experience and real poverty of reading," the purpose is to "feed a dialogue between teachers and pupils and creative artists about matters of common concern—not to be 'portentously "academic." ' " Reprinted from *English in Education* (Spring 69).

Matzkin, M. "Teaching Film-making to First-graders." *Mod Photog* 33 (Sep 69) 34+.

Franza, August. "Liveliest Art in the Classroom." *English J* 58 (Nov 69) 1233–1237. Outline of a high-school program in New York.

"Film Study in the Secondary School." *English J* 58 (Nov 69) 1259–1267. Discussion of books and periodical literature dealing with high-school film study.

Buscome, Ed. "Compiling a Study Unit." *Screen* 11 (No. 6, 1970) 61–66.

"Approaches to Film Teaching." *Screen* 11 (No. 1, Feb 70) 14–26. Seminar discussion, August 1969, at British summer school of Society for Education in Film and TV.

1a(5). SPECIAL PROJECTS IN FILM EDUCATION

[See also 7a(3).]

"Insiders' Watts." *Newswk* 69 (1 May 67) 84+. Mafundi Institute supervises film project in Watts, black section of Los Angeles.

Hitchens, Gordon. "How the Other Half Makes Movies." *F Soc Rev* (Feb 68) 31–34. Comments on film making by slum children.

Dart, Peter. "The San Quentin Film Workshop." *JUFA* 21 (No. 2, 1969) 40–45. How inmates are allowed to make movies.

Hofer, Lynne. "Young Film Makers." *F Lib Q* 2 (No. 2, Spring 69) 4–7. Film clubs in New York City under the direction of the Young Film Maker's Foundation for the production of films by teenagers.

Peary, Charles D. "Cinema from the Slums." *Cinéaste* 3 (No. 2, Fall 69). *See 8c(4)*.

"Belafonte Plays Angel On and Off the Screen." *Ebony* 24 (Oct 69). *See 5, Henry Belafonte*.

"Teenagers Make Movies." *Top of the News* (Nov 69) 54–56. List of librarians of films made by members of Young Film Makers Foundation and others from inner city.

Fransecky, Roger. "Visual Literacy and the Teaching of the Disadvantaged." *Screen* 11 (No. 6, 1970) 23–32.

1b. Reference Resources

1b(1). BIBLIOGRAPHIES

Stenhouse, Charles E. "Cinema Literature." *Close Up* 7 (No. 5, Nov 30) 335–340. Comments on film books published in France.

Pottinger, M. C. "Literature of the Film." *Lib Assoc Rec* 38 (June 36) 228–237. A call to equip libraries with a "nucleus" of literature on film, with reviews of important works and a bibliography.

Block, M. "Aids to Motion Picture Appreciation." *Wilson Lib Bul* 11 (June 37) 693. Bibliography of sources for movie stills and film books.

Ellis, P., and Jay Leyda. "A Guide to the Social Study of the Film." *Theatre Workshop* 1 (No. 2, Apr–July 37) 73–79. Annotated booklist prepared for *A Guide to Marxist Studies* in various fields.

"A Bibliography of the Film Writings of Harry Alan Potamkin (1900–1933)." *Films* 1 (No. 1, Nov 39) 19–24. As prepared for *The Film Index*.

Leyda, Jay. "Movie Jubilee." *Publishers Weekly* 136 (9 Dec 39) 2144–2147. A survey of recent books on all phases of American film; deals extensively with Lewis Jacobs' *Rise of the American Film*.

Leyda, Jay. "Full Year of Film Literature." *Publishers Weekly* 140 (16 Aug 41) 450–454. A guide to current film books and pamphlets.

Rubsamen, Walter H. "Literature on Music in Film and Radio—Addenda (1943–1948)." *Hwd Q* 3 (No. 4, Summer 48–Summer 49) 403–404. Supplement to a supplement to Volume I of *Hollywood Quarterly*.

Richmond, N. W. "Reference Collection on the Moving Picture." *NY Pub Lib Bul* 53 (June 49) 263–273. An annotated guide to printed sources.

Zuckerman, John V. "A Selected Bibliography on Music for Motion Pictures." *Hwd Q* 5 (No. 2, Winter 50) 195–199.

Pratley, Gerald. "Film Music on Records." *QFRTV* 6 (No. 1, Fall 51) 73–97; 7 (No. 1, Fall 52) 100–107; 8 (No. 2, Winter 53) 194–205; 9 (No. 2, Winter 54) 195–208. Original orchestral scores; discography by composer; index by film title.

"Books in French on the Cinema." *Yale French Studies* (No. 17, 1956) 109–110.

Kuiper, John B. "A Selected and Annotated Bibliography of Books and Articles on Pictorial Composition in the Cinema." *JUFPA* 10 (No. 4, Summer 58) 10–17.

"Course in Motion Picture Reading." *Pop Photog* 44 (Feb 59) 86–87+. Bibliography for film makers.

MacCann, Richard Dyer. "Recent Theses at USC." *JUFPA* 13 (No. 3, Spring 61) 4–5+. List, with descriptions, of the first two Ph.D. dissertations in cinema (communication) and twenty-five M.A. theses.

Mirams, Gordon. "How the Cinema Affects Children." *UNESCO Courier* 14 (Mar 61). *See 7b(3)*.

"Library Resources." *FQ* 16 (No. 2, Winter 62–63) 45–49. Reports on printed film materials from New York Public Library Theatre Collection, University of Southern California, UCLA, and the Academy of Motion Picture Arts and Sciences.

Steele, Robert. "The Library Organization of Printed Materials Having to Do with Cinema." *J Soc Cin* 3 (1963) 45–71. Proposal for new Library of Congress subheadings.

Fielding, Raymond. "Motion Picture Technique: A Basic Library." *FQ* 16 (No. 3, Spring 63) 49–50.

Fielding, Raymond. "Theses and Dissertations on the Subject of Film at U.S. Universities, 1916–1967: A Bibliography." *JUFA* 20 (No. 2, 1968) 46–53.

Perry, Ted. "The Aesthetics and Criticism of the Motion Picture: A Selected Bibliography." *JUFA* 21 (No. 2, 1969) 52–61.

Fielding, Raymond. "Second Bibliographic Survey of Theses and Dissertations on the Subject of Film at U.S. Universities, 1916–1969." *JUFA* 21 (No. 4, 1969) 111–113.

Corliss, Richard. "Leni Riefenstahl: A Bibliography." *F Her* 5 (No. 1, Fall 69). *See 5, Leni Riefenstahl*.

Fell, John L. "A Film Student's Guide to the Reference Shelf." *CJ* 9 (No. 1, Fall 69) 43–48. A bibliographic essay.

Genelli, Thomas J. "Basic Guides for Student Film Production." *F Com* 5 (No. 3, Fall 69). *See 1a(3b)*.

Weiss, Naomi. "The Film Library's Book Collection." *F Lib Q* 3 (No. 3, Summer 70) 17–21. Basic reference books.

Allard, Pierre. "Godard: A Select Bibliography." *Take One* 2 (No. 11, 1970). *See 5, Jean-Luc Godard.*

1b(2). FILM PERIODICALS

"Cinema Corner." *Time* 16 (22 Dec 30) 17. Martin Quigley has acquired five motion-picture trade papers.

Wilson, Norman. "The Spectator." *CQ* 1 (No. 1, Autumn 32) 3–6. Editorial statement of policy for *Cinema Quarterly,* which proposes to deal with film "as a medium for the communication of ideas and the exposition of ideals."

Arnold, Kenneth. "Current Periodicals: *Motion Picture Herald.*" *Films* 1 (No. 2, Spring 40) 81–94. Contemporary profile of content and style of the trade weekly edited by Martin Quigley.

Catling, Darrel. "Ourselves and Our Contemporaries." *S&S* 9 (No. 33, Spring 40) 16–17. A critique of film magazines.

Macgowan, Kenneth. "Keep the Lines Open." *Screen Writer* 1 (Feb 46) 21–24. A defense of the periodical the *Hollywood Quarterly* against charges that it is Communistic.

Shaw, Robert. "New Horizons in Hollywood." *Pub Opin Q* 10 (Spring 46) 71–77. The establishment of the *Hollywood Quarterly* seen as a uniting of industry and education.

"Report from the Editors." *Hwd Q* 2 (No. 2, Jan 47) 220–224. *Hollywood Quarterly* looks at its subscribers and its subject matter statistically and proposes to do better.

"Report on the *Screen Writer* Questionnaire." *Screen Writer* 3 (June 47) 29–33. Writers Guild magazine editor Gordon Kahn gets replies from 450 members and 260 others on content and goals of magazine.

Rosenheimer, Arthur, Jr. "A Survey of Film Periodicals, I: The United States and England." *Hwd Q* 2 (No. 4, July 47) 338–352. Categorized and annotated.

L'Institut des Hautes Études Cinématographiques. "A Survey of Film Periodicals, III: France (as of Nov. 1, 1947)." *Hwd Q* 3 (No. 2, Winter 47–48) 153–154.

Noble, Peter. "A Survey of Film Periodicals, II: Great Britain." *Hwd Q* 3 (No. 2, Winter 47–48) 140–151. Annotated list of thirty-six, plus list of fan magazines; see also Appendix in 3 (No. 4, Summer 48–Summer 49) 445–446.

Hursley, Frank. "An Evaluation of *The Screen Writer.*" *Screen Writer* 4 (June–July 48) 14–15+. Wisconsin English professor praises the magazine.

Grierson, John. "Welcome, Stranger!" *S&S* 18 (Spring 49) 51. Praise for new English film magazine, *Sequence.*

Whitebait, William. "New Precision in Film-Reviewing." *New S&N* 39 (21 Jan 50). *See 3b.*

Vorontzoff, Alexis N. "French Film Publications (August 1944–December 1948): A Preliminary List to a Basic Bibliography—Part I." *Hwd Q* 5 (No. 2, Winter 50) 208–212. Partially annotated.

Vorontzoff, Alexis N. "French Film Publications (August 1944–December 1948): A Preliminary List to a Basic Bibliography—Part III." *QFRTV* 6 (No. 1, Fall 51) 98–99.

Lambert, Gavin. "A Last Look Round." *Sequence* (No. 14, 1952). *See 4a(3).*

Anderson, Joseph L. "Japanese Film Periodicals." *QFRTV* 9 (No. 4, Summer 55) 410–423.

Bachmann, Gideon (ed.). "1,151 Film Periodicals." *Cinemages* Special Issue No. 2 (15 Apr 57) 1–80. An attempt to list all the world's film periodicals, alphabetically and by nationality, with the address of each.

Rotha, Paul, *et al.* "The Critical Issue." *S&S* 27 (Autumn 58). *See 3b.*

Frankel, Tobia. *"Sovietski Ekran." NYTM* (15 Mar 59). *See 4e(8).*

Hill, Steven. "Soviet Film Criticism." *FQ* 14 (No. 1, Fall 60). *See 4e(8).*

Armitage, Peter. "The War of the Cults." *NY Film Bul* 2 (Nos. 12, 13, 14, 1961) 22–24. The battle in English film criticism between the "social-consciousness" critics of *Sight and Sound* and the *Cahiers du Cinéma*–influenced critics of *Oxford Opinion.*

Cameron, Ian. "Purely for Kicks?" *NY Film Bul* 2 (Nos. 12, 13, 14, 1961) 25–27. A defense of the *Oxford Opinion* critics and their use of the auteur theory against the sociological approach of *Sight and Sound.*

Franci, R. M. "A Bibliography for the 'Critical Debate.'" *NY Film Bul* 2 (Nos. 12, 13, 14, 1961) 30. Articles centered around the debate over the influence of *Cahiers du Cinéma* on English film criticism.

Wood, Robin. "New Criticism." *NY Film Bul* 2 (Nos. 12, 13, 14, 1961) 27–29. An attack on *Sight and Sound,* which (the author claims) sees the content of a film as its script; a call for a new criticism founded on an analysis of *mise-en-scène.*

Stoller, James. "Trackings." *NY Film Bul* 2 (No. 15, 1961) 5–8. An attack on *Cahiers du Cinéma*–based criticism with attention to several recent films.

Armitage, Peter. "The War of the Cults." *Motion* (No. 1, Summer 61) 4–6. An overview of the critical positions taken by several British journals, critics, and theorists.

"A Checklist of World Film Periodicals." *FQ* 17 (No. 2, Winter 62–63) 49–50.

Shipman, David. "Against the Critics." *F&F* 9 (No. 5, Feb 63). *See 3b.*

"Literate Filmgoer." *Times Lit Supplement* (No. 3244, 30 Apr 64) 374. The rise of serious cinema journals and activity in the publishing world.

Sarris, Andrew. "The Farthest-Out Moviegoers." *Sat Rev* 47 (26 Dec 64) 14–15. Sixteen movie publications, such as *Cahiers du Cinéma, Sight and Sound, Film Quarterly,* assessed; part of *Saturday Review* report "The Movies and the Critics."

"Letters from Readers." *F Com* 3 (No. 3, Summer 65). *See 5, Leni Riefenstahl.*

Levy, Alan. "Voice of the Underground Cinema." *NYTM* (19 Sep 65). *See 5, Jonas Mekas.*

Sarris, Andrew. "*Cahiers* in Context." *CdC in Eng* (No. 1, Jan 66) 5–7. Prospectus for the translated version: the problem of words and of "delicious anarchy"

Sarris, Andrew. "Editor's Eyrie." *CdC in Eng* (No. 2, 1966) 79–80. Sarris answers questions about the first two issues of *Cahiers du Cinéma in English* and attempts the definition (translation) of some French technical terms, such as *cinéaste* and *mise-en-scène.*

Steele, Robert. "More Film Magazines." *Cinéaste* 1 (No. 4, Spring 68) 27–29. Film publications and how to subscribe to them.

Carreno, Richard D. "French Film Magazines: Biased But Fun." *Cinéaste* 2 (No. 2, Fall 68) 13–14+. Sketchy review of the major French film magazines; special emphasis on *Cahiers du Cinéma.*

Callenbach, Ernest. "Looking Backward." *FQ* 22 (No. 1, Fall 68). *See 4d.*

1b(3). FILM ARCHIVES

"British Empire Film Institute." *Museums J* 29 (Apr 30) 349–351. Its first acquisition was the film of the Scott Antarctic expedition; preservation and space problems.

Rotha, Paul. "A Museum for the Kinema and the Collecting of Films." *Connoisseur* 86 (No. 347, July 30) 34–37. Proposal for a museum devoted to the aesthetic and technological development of the cinema.

Lindgren, E. H. "A National Film Library for Great Britain." *S&S* 4 (No. 14, Summer 35) 66–68. Argument for its establishment.

"National Film Library." *School and Society* 42 (17 Aug 35) 237–238.

"Motion Picture Films of the National Archives of the United States." *Science* 82 (6 Sep 35) 214–215.

"Empire Film Library." *School and Society* 44 (12 Sep 36) 335–336.

Lindsay, H. "Visual Instruction at the Imperial Institutes: The Cinema and Empire Film Library." *Museums J* 36 (Oct 36) 289–293. British Library, which now contains 1,000 films, was begun by the Empire Marketing Board.

"A National Film Library." *S&S* 6 (No. 21, Spring 37) 48–49. Recent additions to the British collection.

Lindgren, E. H. "The National Film Library."
S&S 6 (No. 23, Autumn 37) 167. A brief statement about the British library and its recent acquisitions.

"Organization and Purpose." *School and Society* 48 (16 July 38) 79; (5 Nov 38) 582–583. Foundation of the International Federation of Film Archives.

Lindgren, Ernest H. "Cataloguing the National Film Library." *S&S* 9 (No. 35, Autumn 40) 50–51. British selection processes.

Walls, H. "Film Archive." *Wilson Lib Bul* 18 (Nov 43) 244–245. Proposed Library of Congress collection.

Deming, Barbara. "The Library of Congress Film Project: Exposition of a Method." *QJ Lib Congress* 2 (Nov 44) 3–37. Criteria for selection of films to serve the student of history.

"Motion Picture Repository." *Lib J* 70 (12 Sep 45) 813. Library of Congress has instituted a motion-picture repository for the preservation of American films.

Evans, Luther. "Library of Congress Plans Large Film Collection." *Lib J* 71 (1 May 46) 634–635. Portion of an address by the Librarian of Congress.

Page, Charles A. "A Guild's Film Library." *Screen Writer* 2 (July 46) 34–38. A proposal to set up a library funded by five Hollywood guilds plus local universities to include classic films, reference books, and research materials; Motion Picture Academy president Jean Hersholt responds.

Bradley, John. "Library of Congress Plans Its Film Program." *Lib J* 71 (15 Nov 46) 1592–1597+. Talk given before the Washington Visual Workers, April 24, 1946.

Langlois, Henri. "The Cinémathèque Française." *Hwd Q* 2 (No. 2, Jan 47) 207–209. Brief history of this private-enterprise film library which has some support from the state.

Lindgren, Ernest. "The Importance of Film Archives." *Penquin F Rev* 5 (Jan 48) 47–52.

Batlett, Norman. "Film Library Idea Catches on in Australia." *Lib J* 75 (15 Jan 50). *See 4j.*

"Historic Motion Pictures." *CSMM* (9 Sep 50) 15. Details of George Eastman House in Rochester, New York.

Stone, Dorothy T. "The First Film Library." *FIR* 2 (Aug–Sep 51) 29–35. A history of the oldest commercial library dealing in stock footage sales, first promoted in 1908 by Abram Stone.

"The International Federation of Film Archives." *Image* 1 (No. 9, Dec 52) 3. George Eastman House becomes a member.

Hart, Henry. "Preserving the Film Past." *FIR* 4 (Aug–Sep 53) 321–324. Collections at Eastman House in Rochester, N.Y.

Mitchell, George. "The Library of Congress." *FIR* 4 (Oct 53) 417–421. Its little-known film collection; its methods of acquisition and systems of cataloguing; Italian and German films as well as early American and paper prints.

"The Front Page." *S&S* 26 (Summer 56) 3. Editorial on the archive problem; some films are destroyed when remakes are filmed.

"Index to the Motion Picture Study Collection." *Image* 6 (No. 2, Feb 57) 43. In this and following issues are listed, and briefly described, a selection of materials from the George Eastman collection in Rochester, New York; through 6 (No. 7); also 6 (No. 9); 7 (Nos. 1–3, 5, 7–10).

Lauritzen, Einar. "The Swedish Film Archive." *QFRTV* 11 (No. 4, Summer 57) 326–336.

Card, James. "Film Archives." *Image* 7 (No. 6, June 58) 137–141.

Lindgren, Ernest. "A Film *and* TV Archive." *F&F* 6 (No. 1, Oct 59) 32–33. Argument for including television films in the National Film Archives.

Lindgren, Ernest. "Film Archives." *Cinema Studies* 1 (No. 1, Mar 60) 5–9. Problems of selection; list of members of international federation.

Culver, James H. "The Library of Congress and the American Film Heritage." *JUFPA* 12 (No. 4, Summer 60) 15–16. Status of collection described by head of motion-picture section.

"The Front Page." *S&S* 29 (Summer 60) 107. Editorial on the twenty-fifth anniversary of the National Film Archive; preservation should also lead to exhibition.

Robinson, David. "The Players' Witness." *S&S* 29 (Summer 60) 148–151. Notes on some early acting performances preserved in the National Film Archive in London.

McMurry, Glenn D. "Film Cataloguing with IBM." *JUFPA* 14 (No. 3, 1962). See *4a(1)*.

"Our Resources for Scholarship." *FQ* 16 (No. 2, Winter 62–63) 34–45. The sad state of America's film archives; representatives of the Museum of Modern Art, Eastman House, and Library of Congress discuss their facilities and needs. See 17 (No. 4, Summer 64) 60–61 for Canadian Film Institute.

Anderson, Jack. "Towards a Dance Film Library." *Dance Mag* 39 (Sep 65). See *4k(6)*.

Wallace, Sarah L. "Scholar and Screen." *JUFPA* 17 (No. 4, 1965) 7–11. Brief description of the kinds of films owned by the Library of Congress, the history of their acquisition, and the changing purposes of the library in preserving them; reprinted from *Quarterly Journal of the Library of Congress.*

Hill, Steven P. "Film Archive Work in the USSR." *F Soc Rev* (Jan 66). See *4e(8)*.

Deneroff, Harvey. "The Accidental Archive."

F Soc Rev (Nov 66) 20–23. A brief description of the Library of Congress Archive and Motion Picture Division.

Hunnings, Neville. "Copyright." *S&S* 36 (Summer 67). See *7c(5)*.

Fielding, Raymond. "Archives of the Motion Picture: A General View." *Am Archivist* 30 (No. 3, July 67) 493–500. Acquisition goals and problems for the motion-picture archive; the many kinds of materials, description of the major American collections.

Kuiper, John B. "Opportunities for Film Study at the Library of Congress." *F Lib Q* 1 (No. 1, Winter 67–68) 30–32. The motion-picture collection available for use by the film librarian.

"National Film Collection Planned for LC." *Lib J* 93 (15 Jan 68) 134.

"Film Lovers of the World Unite." *Economist* 226 (24 Feb 68) 32. Demonstrations against Malraux for firing Henri Langlois from Cinémathèque.

Genet. "Letter from Paris." *New Yorker* 44 (2 Mar 68) 98+. Dismissal of Henri Langlois, his contribution to the Cinemathèque Française.

Knight, Arthur. "L'Affaire Langlois." *Sat Rev* 51 (27 Apr 68) 51. Report on Henri Langlois' work at the Cinemathèque Française and on the uproar his dismissal has caused.

Houston, Penelope. "Statutory Deposit." *S&S* 38 (Spring 69) 74. Note on proposal for a print of all films exhibited in England to be placed in National Archive.

Zilletti, Ugo. "Destroyed American Film Collection in Florence, Italy." *F Com* 5 (No. 2, Spring 69) 4–7. Appeal for replacement of list of documentaries collected since 1965 and lost in the Arno flood.

Goodman, Rhonna. "A 20th Century Visual Encyclopedia." *F Lib Q* 3 (No. 2, Spring 70). See *8b*.

"The Movie Saver." *Newswk* 76 (24 Aug 70) 64. Henri Langlois, director of Cinemathèque Française; his series of films arranged for the Metropolitan Museum in New York.

1b(4). PUBLIC LIBRARY FILM COLLECTIONS

Pottinger, M. C. "Cinema and the Library; With Discussion." *Lib Assoc Rec* 39 (June 37) 303–307. An analysis of the ways that two important means of communication can cooperate, with some dispute over the type of film apparatus a library should acquire. Reply (Sep 37) 503 and rejoinder (Nov 37) 608.

Howard, Paul. "Libraries, War and 16mm." *Lib J* 69 (1 Jan 44) 2. The use of 16mm films by libraries to promote understanding of war problems.

Rahbek-Smith, E. "Library's Place in Film Distribution." *Wilson Lib Bul* 18 (June 44) 743.

"Libraries and Films." *Wilson Lib Bul* 19 (Oct 44) 124.

Ress, E. "Motion Pictures in Libraries." *Wilson Lib Bul* 19 (Apr 45) 561–563.

Gregory, William. "Motion Pictures for the Technical Library." *Lib J* 70 (15 Nov 45) 1060–1062. Films for the college library: guidelines for selection.

Croughton, Amy. "Scanning the Screen." *Lib J* 71 (15 June 46) 908. Hollywood should appreciate support given to film by librarians.

Brown, Karline. "What Libraries Are Doing in the Audio-Visual Field." *Lib J* 72 (1 Jan 47) 39–44.

"To Study Libraries as Non-Commercial Film Centers." *Lib J* 72 (1 Sep 47) 1170. The Public Library Inquiry in cooperation with the Twentieth Century Fund is to undertake a study of the role of public libraries in promoting the use of noncommercial films.

"Does Your Library Own or Rent Its Films?" *Lib J* 73 (15 Sep 48) 1293. List of libraries which own films.

Blair, Patricia. "Film Service in Public Libraries." *Lib J* 73 (1 Nov 48) 1549–1551. List of public libraries which have film services.

Mathews, Mildred. "Supplies Film Information." *Lib J* 74 (15 Mar 49) 473–475. The New York Public Library has initiated a film information service without a film collection of its own.

Blair, Patricia. "Ideas on Film." *Sat Rev* 32 (11 June 49) 34–36. Report on films circulated by public libraries.

Stevenson, Grace. "Library Film Service." *Lib J* 76 (15 Jan 51) 128–130. It is the responsibility of library film departments to maintain and extend standards of quality and services.

Starr, Cecile, and Lillian L. Wachtel. "Ideas on Film." *Sat Rev* 34 (10 Mar 51) 28+. Report on film libraries around the nation.

Tollefson, Horace. "Why Preview Centers?" *Lib J* 78 (Aug 53) 1316–1318. The need for the opportunity for all Americans to view and utilize educational and informational films for adults.

Jones, Emily. "Getting Started with Films." *Lib J* 81 (15 Feb 56) 493–494. Pointers on how to obtain films for library programs and how to arrange showings.

Cipperly, G. "Films in the Public Library." *Wilson Lib Bul* 30 (Mar 56) 547.

McClean, Frederick. "Survey on Use of Films in the Library." *Lib J* 82 (1 Jan 57) 40–41. Review of report prepared by the U.S. Office of Education: statistics on circulation of films, especially Southern California Film Circuit.

"Film Librarians Form Independent Council." *Lib J* 92 (July 67) 2498.

Wheeler, H. "Films for the Community College Library." *Wilson Lib Bul* 42 (Dec 67) 411–414.

Peltier, Euclid J. "Toward Total Media Librarianship." *F Lib Q* 1 (No. 2, Spring 68) 19–21. The expanding "salesman" role of the film librarian

Aceto, Vincent J. "Opening New Doors to Film Literacy." *F Lib Q* 1 (No. 3, Summer 68) 36–37. A program for training in film education for librarians at the School of Library Science of the State University of New York at Albany.

Limbacher, James L. "Focusing in on Features." *F Lib Q* 1 (No. 4, Fall 68) 35–36. Why libraries should move into the showing of feature films.

Spehr, P. "Feature Films in Your Library." *Wilson Lib Bul* 44 (Apr 70) 848–855. A discussion of film collecting in libraries with lists of distributors, cinema periodicals, and outstanding films.

A crane shot for a 20th Century-Fox picture called *There's No Business Like Show Business* (1954).

2. Motion-Picture Arts and Crafts

2a. General

Williams, Ben Ames. "The Arduous Art." *SEP* 202 (3 May 30) 6–7+. General production details of Hollywood film making.

Williams, Ben Ames. "Lets and Hindrances." *SEP* 202 (14 June 30) 10–11+. More production details.

Adams, Mildred. "Talkies in the Making." *Woman's J* 15 (June 30) 16–17+. Impressions of Hollywood production methods.

Condon, Frank. "Not a Lady in Sight." *SEP* 205 (13 Aug 32) 26+. On assistant directors, makeup men, and other personnel.

Golden, John. "Have You Any Jokes?" *SEP* 205 (27 May 33) 14–15+. Production details of Hollywood film making; it's profitable if the scenario (the jokes) is acceptable to the public.

"Movie Magic in the Making." *Pop Mech* 62 (Dec 34) 801–808+; 63 (Jan 35) 1–8+. Photo essay on production details of movie making.

Nichols, Beverly. "They Shot Me in Hollywood." *Golden Book* 22 (Aug 35) 142–145. British journalist summarizes experiences in Hollywood.

Stuart, I. "Script Girl." *Collier's* 99 (13 Feb 37) 15+.

Martyn, H. "Motion Picture Art." *Canad Forum* 16 (Mar 37) 12–13.

"Strange Lingo of the Movies." *Pop Mech* 67 (May 37) 722–726+. Vocabulary of film production.

"Sound Stages of Hollywood Hum with Work on Movies for 1938." *Life* 3 (27 Dec 37) 39–46. Crews, sets, props.

Ripley, R. "Don't Say I Didn't Tell You." *Pictorial Rev* (June 38) 25+. The working world of Hollywood; its special tricks and terminology.

Thomas, F. "Script Girl's Story." *Woman's Home Companion* 66 (May 39) 18.

Isaacs, Edith (ed.) "Artists of the Movies." *Th Arts* 23 (June 39) 424–428. Why a film cannot always rely only on technical correctness to ensure success.

Mulvey, K. "Keeping Up with Hollywood." *Woman's Home Companian* 67 (Aug 40) 8. Technical slang used on the set.

Johnston, Eric. "Super Movie for a Super Age." *Look* 12 (No. 16, 3 Aug 40) 84–85. The president of the Motion Picture Association of America predicts what films will be like in 1975: screens which surround audience, and photographs from satellites.

"Slang Rules the Movies." *Pop Sci* 138 (Apr 41) 96–97. Vocabulary of film production.

March, J. M. "One Minute on the Screen or Two Days on the Lot." *NYTM* (28 Sep 41) 6–7+. Behind-the-scenes look at the average day in making a picture.

Farber, Manny. "Movie Art." *New Rep* 107 (26 Oct 42) 546. Reply to Elmer Rice, who had objected to "technological paraphernalia" and "synthetic construction" of film.

Lejeune, C. A. "Film as an Art Form." *Fortnightly Rev* 159 (Jan 43) 43–49; (Feb 43) 127–133; (Mar 43) 194–199. Trends, technical developments, and a look ahead.

"Miracles in Slow Motion." *Newswk* 26 (22 Oct 45) 104. Future developments of film— 3D, stereophonic sound, 16mm educational films.

Weldon, Marvin. "The Script Supervisor." *Hwd Q* 1 (No. 3, Apr 46) 331–333. Brief description of his job on the set.

Grinde, Nick. "Pictures for Peanuts." *Penguin F Rev* 1 (Aug 46) 40–51. How "B" pictures are put together.

Readers are advised to acquaint themselves with the range of categories throughout the bibliography in the search for specific subjects. In some cases, cross-categorical comparisons are directly suggested. In general, however, each article is placed under one category only. Cross-references on individual articles have been kept to a minimum.

Entries are in chronological order of publication under each category. Exceptions are: Part 5, Biography, in which the order is alphabetical by name; Part 9, Case Histories of Film Making, which is alphabetical by film title; and 3c and 8c(4), also alphabetical by title.

Ludwig, Emil. "The Seven Pillars of Hollywood." *Penguin F Rev* 1 (Aug 46) 90–95. Actors, musicians, screenwriters, cameramen, directors, producers, and distributors: all conform to a mold which is about to crack from internal dissatisfactions.

"Movies . . . Industry or Art?" *Senior Scholastic* 52 (22 Mar 48) 13–16. Introduction for laymen: the technique of film making.

Jones, Andrew Miller. "Television and Cinema." *Penguin F Rev* 6 (Apr 48) 45–52. A comparison of television and film: production, quality, and audience.

Shearman, John. "Who Are Those Technicians?" *Penguin F Rev* 6 (Apr 48) 87–90. The production crew deserves critical recognition.

Morgan, Henry. "I'm What's Wrong in Hollywood." *NYTM* (13 June 48) 66–67. Radio comedian is impressed by the professionalism of the film industry after appearing in his first movie, *So This Is New York*.

Baxter, R. K. Neilson. "The Man with the Box Brownie." *Penguin F Rev* 9 (May 49) 82–87. It takes more than one man to make a film.

Moskowitz, Gene. "Ephemeral Heartbreak." *Sequence* (No. 11, Summer 50) 32–35. Author describes his background in film and his progress toward the shooting, in Paris, of *The Ephemeral Coward,* which was never completed.

Steinbart, Kurt O. "Alas, Poor Dialogue Director." *FIR* 2 (Jan 51) 29–31.

"Speaking of Pictures." *Life* 36 (17 May 54) 20–22. Al Hirschfeld caricatured seventy-five great names of the movies for a mural in New York's Cinema Theatre.

Abramson, Albert. "A Motion Picture Studio of 1968." *QFRTV* 9 (No. 2, Winter 54) 137–146. Television engineer and former teacher prophesies that TV and film techniques will have merged and all cutting will be electronic; he also proposes a camera without lenses, operating on the same principle as radar.

Day, Tilly. "Continuity." *F&F* 3 (No. 12, Sep 57) 36. Work of continuity girl in film making.

Alcott, Arthur. "Production Controller." *F&F* 4 (No. 4, Jan 58) 28.

Ardmore, Jane K. "Home Is a Movie Set." *Parents Mag* 33 (Apr 58) 50–51+. Andrew Stone and his wife, Virginia, make movies at home for MGM.

Yoakem, Lola G. "Casting." *FQ* 12 (No. 2, Winter 58) 36–41. Type casting, face casting, casting directors—all may be outdated; recent changes in movies and TV; some new procedures proposed.

Alpert, Hollis, and Arthur Knight. "The Film, Survey of the Craft and Its Problems." *Sat Rev* 41 (20 Dec 58) 6. The fixed skills

which no "transition" can change in the movie industry.

"People at the Top of Entertainment's World." *Life* 45 (22 Dec 58) 160–161. A gallery of top stars, directors, writers, etc. in film, theatre, music.

"Gang Girl." *Time* 76 (22 Aug 60) 58+. Sally Perle, casting agent for *West Side Story*.

"Lonely Art of Film Making." *Sat Rev* 45 (29 Dec 62) 10. Editorial introduction to annual report on movies.

Compton, Gardner. "Film Dance and Things to Come." *Dance Mag* 42 (Jan 68) 34–37. Choreo-cinema, multimedia, and holography.

2a(1). PRODUCERS AND PRODUCTION MANAGERS

[See also 6c(1), 6c(3).

[See 5, Biography: Michael Balcon, Hall Bartlett, Georges de Beauregard, Mag Bodard, Benedict Bogeaus, Samuel Bronston, Merian Cooper, John Davis, Anatole De Grunwald, Dino De Laurentiis, Louis De Rochemont, Walt Disney, Robert Evans, William Fox, Arthur Freed, Samuel Goldwyn, Oscar Hammerstein, Leland Hayward, W. R. Hearst, Harold Hecht, Mark Hellinger, John Houseman, Howard Hughes, Ross Hunter, Arthur P. Jacobs, Sam Katzman, Alexander Korda, Stanley Kramer, Carl Laemmle, Jesse Lasky, Michael Laughlin, Joseph Levine, David Loew, Goffredo Lombardo, Kenneth Macgowan, L. B. Mayer, Stuart Millar, Harold and Walter Mirisch, Robert O'Brien, Harriet Parsons, Joseph Pasternak, Charles Pathé, William Pine, Erich Pommer, Carlo Ponti, J. Arthur Rank, Martin Ransohoff, Michael Relph, Hal Roach, Harry Saltzman, Dore Schary, Nicholas Schenck, B. P. Schulberg, David Selznick, Walter Seltzer, Mack Sennett, Spyros Skouras, Sam Spiegel, David Susskind, Mike Todd, Lawrence Turman, Ray Wagner, Jerry Wald, Hal Wallis, Walter Wanger, Jack Warner, Lazar Wechsler, Robert Young, Darryl Zanuck, Adolph Zukor.]

Noxon, G. F. "Purposeful Direction." *S&S* 2 (No. 5, Spring 33) 15–17. The need for a close cooperative effort between director and producer.

Balcon, Michael, and John Grierson. "The Function of the Producer." *CQ* 2 (No. 1, Autumn 33) 5–9. The Gaumont-British chief describes the studio producer, and Grierson, the documentary producer.

"Getting Ready to Shoot." *Pop Mech* 65 (Feb 36) 228–231+. How the production manager gets ready for a sound film at 20th Century-Fox; one of a series.

Boone, A. R. "Modern Movie Magic Brings Realistic Scenes and Sounds to Your Theater." *Pop Sci* 128 (May 36) 29–32+. Production management controls costs; the process of production.

Beatty, Jerome. "The Props Under Hollywood." *American* 122 (Nov 36) 46–47+. How assistant directors "keep the machinery running."

Lewis, Albert. *"Peccavi!" Th Arts* 25 (Sep 41) 659–665. Subtitled "True Confessions of a Movie Producer."

Farber, Manny. "Writers as Producers." *New Rep* 108 (26 Apr 43). *See 2d.*

Pichel, Irving. "Creativeness Cannot Be Diffused." *Hwd Q* 1 (No. 1, Oct 45) 20–25. Directors used to be the only creators, then writers became more important and collaboration often worked; but "umpires" were needed, hence producers; some writers have become producers; almost always one of the three is dominant.

Sistrom, Joseph. "The Writer-Producer Relationship." *Screen Writer* 3 (No. 8, Jan 48) 8–10. A producer is like a magazine editor.

Blakeston, Oswell. "The Producer's Credit." *S&S* 18 (Summer 49) 69–70. "He must sustain the director as a human being" (David Lean).

Brown, Clarence. "The Producer Must Be Boss." *FIR* 2 (Feb 51) 1–3+. Others, of course, are involved, but "the idea that efficiency and creative achievement are incompatible is absurd."

Beute, Christopher A. "The Production Manager." *FIR* 2 (Mar 51) 5–8.

Youngstein, Max E. "How to Be a Movie Executive—Without Thinking." *FIR* 3 (Feb 52) 49–54. A satire on motion-picture executives: how to ad-lib (1) the first screening, (2) the staff meeting, (3) the advertising agency, (4) the boss; by the vice-president of United Artists in charge of advertising and publicity, as reprinted from *Variety.*

Knight, Arthur. "Hollywood's Multiple Geniuses." *Th Arts* 36 (Apr 52) 41–42+. Examples: Ben Hecht and Joseph Mankiewicz.

Wilson, Carey. "The Producer Is Necessary." *FIR* 4 (Mar 53) 133–136. How the role came about historically; how dangerous it is to use authority too often; how wrong the author was in holding out for a "pet scene" in *The Postman Always Rings Twice.*

"The Old and the New." *S&S* 22 (Apr–June 53) 163–164. Brief biographies of a number of the old hands in Hollywood and of some of the relative newcomers, both producers and directors.

Schary, Dore. "Executive Responsibility." *FIR* 5 (Aug–Sep 54) 321–326. Obligations of the motion-picture executive to the film industry and the public.

Lasky, Jesse. "The Birth of the Producer: Hollywood." *JSPG* (Nov 54) 4+.

Weingarten, Lawrence. "The Birth of the Producer: Culver City." *JSPG* (Nov 54) 5+. Irving Thalberg's "supervisors" at MGM.

Hammerstein, Oscar, II. "Getting to Know You." *JSPG* (Nov 54) 10+. Theatrical producer becomes film producer.

Selznick, David O. "Time for Retooling." *JSPG* (Nov 54) 11+. Screen producer turned TV producer tells of inflexible deadlines he encountered.

Shulman, Max. "The Silver Scream." *Good Housekeeping* 141 (Nov 55) 38. Amusing anecdotes about such producers as L. B. Mayer, Samuel Goldwyn, Cecil B. DeMille, and Howard Hughes.

St. John, Earl. "Executive Producer." *F&F* 3 (No. 4, Jan 57) 15.

MacQuilty, William. "The Producer." *F&F* 3 (No. 4, Jan 57) 15–16.

Crowther, Bosley. "End of a Hollywood Legend." *NYTM* (7 Sep 58) 51+. The changing role of the film producer.

O'Donnell, R. J. "The Producer." *JSPG* (Mar 59) 14. General manager of interstate circuit discusses the expansion of the producer's role in the modern world into distribution and public relations.

Montague, A. "The 'Competitive' Producer." *JSPG* (Mar 59) 15–16. Executive vice-president of Columbia Pictures discusses new responsibilities of producers toward exploiting every possible market value of a picture.

Ferguson, H. N. "Operations Worldwide." *FIR* 9 (Dec 59) 598. Letter to editor about information exchange program on facilities abroad sponsored by Unit Production Managers Guild's eighty-five members.

Mirisch, Walter M. "Where We Stand." *JSPG* (June 60) 1–2+. President of the Screen Producers Guild discusses the accomplishments of the guild during the past year.

Vale, Eugene. "The Daring Conviction." *JSPG* (June 60) 13–16. Novelist and screenwriter argues that producers and investors as well as artists need "daring conviction" to create where there are no guidelines or formulas for success.

Lancaster, Burt. "Hollywood Drove Me to a Double Life." *F&F* 8 (No. 4, Jan 62). *See 5, Burt Lancaster.*

Laughlin, Michael. "Confessions of a Young American Producer." *F&F* 14 (No. 7, April 68) 18–19.

Subotsky, Milton. "The Work of the Film Producer." *Screen* 10 (No. 6, Nov–Dec 69) 24–32. Transcript of talk by film producer at Hornsey College of Art; budgets, completion guarantees, etc.

2a(2). AGENTS

[See also 2b(4).]

"Hollywood Middleman." *SEP* 208 (16 May 36) 14–15+; (27 June 36) 16–17+; 209 (29 Aug 36) 16–17+. A talent agent tells how he does his work.

"Hollywood Agents." *Ken* 4 (No. 10, 8 June 39) 19–26. Myron Selznick, Leland Hayward, William Morris, H. N. Swanson, and others; thumbnail sketches and photographs.

"Beverly Hills Building of Myron Selznick and Co." *Calif Arts and Arch* 56 (Aug 39) 22–23. Views and floor plan for offices of leading talent agency.

"Office Building for Myron Selznick, Beverly Hills; G. B. Kaufmann, Architect." *Arch Forum* 72 (May 40) 358–359.

March, J. M. "Nemesis, Alias Hollywood Agent." *NYTM* (7 Dec 41) 14+. "No actor can ever be sure what his agent can do for him—if anything."

Johnston, Alva. "Hollywood's Ten Per Centers." *SEP* 215 (8 Aug 42) 9–10+; (15 Aug 42) 26–27+; (22 Aug 42) 23+. Profiles of the agents who represent stars, writers, and directors.

Martin, P. "Forty Shirley Temples Every Week." *SEP* 216 (12 Feb 44) 35. Shirley Temple's agent finds a new star.

Wittels, D. G. "Star-Spangled Octopus." *SEP* 219 (31 Aug 46) 23–24+. The history, the hassles, and the stars of the Music Corporation of America, the world's largest talent agency.

Swanson, H. N. "An Agent Speaks Up." *Screen Writer* 3 (No. 9, Feb 48) 1–3. Instances (no names given) of top writers who have adjusted to change and some who haven't; marginal people should go back to selling insurance.

Siegel, Sol. "The Day of the Package." *JSPG* (Nov 54) 12. The agent, with both script and stars, should not replace the staff producer.

Davidson, Bill. "MCA: The Octopus Devours the World." Part I: *Show* 2 (Feb 62) 50–53. "MCA: A Case Study in Power." Part II: *Show* 2 (Mar 62) 68–71. Powerful talent agency and its influence.

Heller, Joseph. "Irving Is Everywhere." *F&F* 9 (No. 12, Sep 63). *See 5, Irving Lazar.*

Brakhage, Stan. "A Moving Picture Giving and Taking Book." *F Cult* (No. 41, Summer 66) 40–56. About shutters, splicing, and lighting for the beginning film maker.

Wolfe, B. "Ten Percenters of Hollywood." *NYTM* (18 June 67) 26–33. Talent agents and how they work.

2a(3). WOMEN PRODUCERS, DIRECTORS, TECHNICIANS

[*See 5, Biography: Dede Allen, Mary Ellen Bute, Shirley Clarke, Storm De Hirsch, Ida Lupino, Ruth Orkin, Harriet Parsons, Leni Riefenstahl, Leontine Sagan, Agnès Varda, Mai Zetterling.*]

Condon, Frank. "Not a Lady in Sight." *SEP* 205 (13 Aug 32). *See 2a.*

Sagan, Leontine. "Courage in Production." *CQ* 1 (No. 3, Spring 33). *See 2c.*

Dunn, Reina Wiles. "Off-Stage Heroines of the Movies." *Nat Bus Woman* 13 (July 34) 202–203+. Surveys production personnel.

Sarthe, Jean. "She Makes Movies." *Nat Bus Woman* 13 (Oct 34) 315+. Profile of woman director Vyvyan Donner.

Muir, Florabel. "They Risk Their Necks for You." *SEP* 218 (15 Sep 45). *See 2j(3).*

Level, Hildegard. "Women Behind the Screen." *Independent Woman* 27 (June 48) 170–172. Costume designer, film producer, script girl, and several others introduced.

Evans, Ernestine. "Films Tell Your Story Better." *Independent Woman* 27 (Dec 48) 350–352+. Women urged to do nontheatrical films about the world they live in.

Feldman, Joseph and Harry. "Women Directors." *FIR* 1 (Nov 50) 9–12. Short career sketches of Dorothy Arzner (United States), Margarita Barskaya (Russia), Leni Riefenstahl (Germany), Leontine Sagan (Germany), Germaine Dulac (France), Wanda Jakubowska (Poland), Ida Lupino (United States).

Lupino, Ida. "New Faces in New Places." *FIR* 1 (Dec 50). *See 2b(4).*

Tildesley, A. L. "She Stepped Down to Step Up." *Independent Woman* 32 (Nov 53) 402–403. Dorothy Arzner, director.

Parsons, Harriet. "What Producers Do." *FIR* 5 (Oct 54) 404–408. Introduction to the role of the producer, with some references to the author's function in that capacity for *I Remember Mama* and *The Enchanted Cottage*.

Ford, Charles. "The First Female Producer." *FIR* 15 (No. 3, Mar 64) 141–145. Alice Guy-Blaché, still alive at age ninety-one.

Clarke, Shirley, and Storm De Hirsch. " 'Female' Film-Making." *Arts Mag* 41 (Apr 67) 23–24. The woman as film maker "transcends subjectivity."

Lupino, Ida. "Me, Mother Directress." *Action* 2 (No. 3, May–June 67). *See 5, Ida Lupino.*

Bucher, Felix. "Women, Film Direction and Vocation." *Camera* 46 (No. 9, Sep 67) 46. Various women film directors.

Dewey, Langdon. "Three Lady Iconoclasts." *Film* (No. 58, Spring 70) 20–21. A brief discussion of the work of three directors: Agnès Varda, Vera Chytilová, and Mai Zetterling.

2a(4). PRODUCERS AND DIRECTORS FROM MINORITY GROUPS

"Breakthrough in Hollywood." *Ebony* 19 (Dec 63) 82–84+. Story of Wendell Franklin and Otis Greene, highest-ranking blacks in Hollywood film production.

Kagan, Norman. "Black American Cinema." *Cinema* (Calif) 6 (No. 2, 1970) 2–7. A survey of the history of black film making in America, especially in the period before 1940.

Moore, Walter. "Needed: A Negro Film Movement." *Negro Dig* 15 (Jan 66) 45–48. Calls for feature film making by blacks; obstacles to creating black film industry.

2a(5). DEVELOPMENT OF NEW TALENT

[*See also 1a(2), 1a(3b), 2b(5).*]

Corwin, Norman. "Careers in Screen and Radio." *Th Arts* 25 (July 41) 513–516.

Cocteau, Jean. "Focus on Miracles." *NYTM* (24 Oct 48) 38–39. Cocteau argues that the high cost of film making poisons the art by prohibiting youth from freely participating; he urges widespread experimentation with 16mm.

Bard, Ben. "Finding What They've Got." *F&F* 4 (No. 9, June 58) 10+. By director of talent school for 20th Century-Fox.

Lassally, Walter. "The Dead Hand." *S&S* 29 (Summer 60) 113–115. Union die-hards, distributor apathy, and production rigidity— so many things prevent a young director from having his chance; written by a British cameraman.

Wald, Malvin. "All You Need Is Talent." *JSPG* (June 60) 21–23. Screenwriter urges apprenticeship system in the U.S. film industry.

Perlberg, William. "A Call for New Blood." *JSPG* (Sep 61) 29–30. Producer argues that the film industry is committing suicide by not opening up jobs for talented newcomers.

Lazarus, Paul N., Jr. "Of Images and Kings." *JSPG* (June 62) 11–12. Hollywood's image isn't so important as training future leadership.

Perlberg, William, Mervyn LeRoy, Malvin Wald, John Stembler, Hall Bartlett, David Harmon, Herbert Aller, Robert Ford, Michael Neyman, Harris Dienstfrey, William Ludwig, A. Martial Capbern. "The Journal Looks at the Need for New Blood." *JSPG* (Sep 62) 3–38. Issue devoted to the problem of training new talent for film production, including article by Wald on Kent Mac-

kenzie (independent film maker of *The Exiles*), by Aller defending the restrictive practices of the cameramen's union, and by Ford on screenwriting.

Muhl, Edward. "New Film Horizons." *JSPG* (June 63) 29–30. Universal executive explains limits of "new talent" program at studio.

Taylor, Jay. "Interview with David Wise." *F Cult* (No. 35, 1964–1965) 57–61. An eight-year-old film maker.

Knight, Arthur. "Where Is the New Talent?" *Sat Rev* (24 Dec 66) 20–22. Survey of channels available for new talent; they don't work very well. Part of *Saturday Review* report "The American Motion Picture: 1966."

"The DGA-Producers' Training Program." *Action* 2 (No. 2, Mar–Apr 67). See 2c.

Mallery, David. "The Young Film Makers Explosion." *JSPG* (Dec 68) 29–31.

Murphy, A. D. "New Room at the Top." *Sat Rev* (28 Dec 68) 21+. The youth craze makes possible openings for youth, acting, writing, and even producing and directing. Part of *Saturday Review* report "The Now Movie."

Monaco, R. J. "You're Only as Young as They Think You Are." *Sat Rev* (27 Dec 69) 15–17. Problems which hinder the entrance of young student film makers into the industry. Part of *Saturday Review* report "The Art That Matters."

Knight, Arthur, *et al.* "Special Report: Film Student/Film Director." *Action* 5 (No. 2, Mar–Apr 70) 21–33. An analysis of the positive and negative aspects of the film student emerging into the professional world.

Corman, Roger. "The Young Filmmakers." *JSPG* (June 70) 5–6+. They may be too "conceptually ambitious"; a list of the young people Corman has helped.

Champlin, Charles. "Bright New Day?" *JSPG* (June 70) 7–9. Is the "ideational content inadequate to the skill of the images" in the new young film maker's films?

Gillette, Don Carle. "Whither Goest, New Blood?" *JSPG* (June 70) 11–13. Some of the old rules are worth keeping.

2b. Actors and Acting

Beaton, Welford. "High-Hatting Little Brother." *SEP* 202 (24 May 30) 62+. Stage actors moving to Hollywood.

Hale, Louise Closser. "The New Stage Fright: Talking Pictures." *Harper's* 161 (Sep 30) 417–424. Personal experience in small movie roll.

Hale, Louise Closser. "Tragedy and Comedy in

the Talkies." *Woman's J* 15 (Oct 30) 18–19+. Actress discusses her profession.

"Beauty Routed by the Talkies." *Lit Dig* 112 (5 Mar 32) 18. English critic suggests beauty is a curse, especially to silent-film acresses.

Collins, Frederick L. "Unstarred Stars." *Pictorial Rev* 33 (May 32) 16–17+.

Collins, Frederick L. "Four Women Who Suffered." *Good Housekeeping* 95 (July 32) 40–41+. On Barbara LaMarr, Olive Thomas, Alma Rubens, Mabel Normand—actresses who ended tragically.

Shawell, J. "You Think They're Beautiful." *Pictorial Rev* 34 (Oct 32) 22–23.

Shawell, J. "Movies Need a Romeo." *Pictorial Rev* 34 (May 33) 15+.

"Casting 91,000 Film Actors a Year." *Lit Dig* 122 (19 Dec 36) 21–23. Billy Grady, casting director at MGM; biography and activities.

"Starlets Are World's Most Envied of Girls." *Life* 8 (29 Jan 40) 37–39. A listing of the facts and "figures" concerning typical Hollywood actresses.

Hoffmann, G. W. "Crashing Hollywood at Sixty." *SEP* 212 (4 May 40) 39+. The trials and tribulations of a freelance actress.

"Girls of Hollywood." *Life* 13 (3 Aug 42) 42–47. Color photographs and statistics of ten favorites.

Graffis, H. "All in for Victory." *Collier's* 111 (6 Feb 43) 17+. Hollywood stars, on entertainment and bond-selling tours.

"Stagestruck." *Time* 54 (8 Aug 49) 59. Hollywood actors do summer stock at the La Jolla Playhouse.

Chaplin, J. "Hollywood on Broadway." *Th Arts* 35 (Aug 51) 24–25. Actors come to New York.

Downing, Robert. "The Movie That Changed a Life." *FIR* 3 (Aug–Sep 52) 335–341. Actor tells how his close watching of *The Guardsman* got him fired as an usher in Cedar Rapids, Iowa, but took him into the movies.

"Three Girls in a Tub." *Collier's* 130 (25 Oct 52) 19. Betty Grable, Rhonda Fleming, Jan Sterling in bathtubs for *The Farmer Takes a Wife* and *Pony Express*.

McDonald, Gerald D. "Authors as Actors." *FIR* 5 (Dec 54) 519–521. Instances of authors who became film actors and film actors who were authors.

"Three Miffed Misses Frame Frustrations." *Life* 40 (23 Apr 56) 22–23. Young Hollywood actresses photographed as they are cast and as they think they should be.

"Discovery: British Women Are Beautiful." *Look* 20 (21 Aug 56) 26–30+. A picture essay about theatre and movie actresses.

"Greatest Stars; Timeless Stars; Glamour in Our Time; Star System in 1956; Newcomers." *Cosmopolitan* 141 (Oct 56) 28–39. A gallery of portraits and biographies; on pp. 38–39, "Hollywood Tragedies," Jean Harlow, James Dean, Wallace Reid, John Gilbert.

Hume, Rod. "Gentlemen in England." *F&F* 3 (No. 12, Sep 57) 12–13. Young actors in Great Britain.

"Cast of Characters." *Time* 72 (17 Nov 58) 74. A roundup of six diverse bits of industry gossip about actors.

"Fame That Was All Too Brief." *Life* 46 (2 Mar 59) 69–70+. Young German actress is dismissed as female lead in *Spartacus*.

Bohm, Karlheinz. "The World Before Us." *F&F* 6 (No. 5, Feb 60) 11+. German actor writes of his experiences in film making.

Robinson, David. "The Players' Witness." *S&S* 29 (Summer 60). See *1b*(3).

"Abundance of Beauties." *Life* 49 (26 Dec 60) 46–50+. Gallery of screen actresses of the 1940s and 1950s.

Williams, Tennessee. "Five Fiery Ladies." *Life* 50 (3 Feb 61) 84–89. Williams appreciates actresses in the Hollywood versions of his dramas: A. Magnani, V. Leigh, G. Page, E. Taylor, and K. Hepburn.

Peck, Seymour. "Europe's New Symbols of Femininity." *NYTM* (24 Sep 61). See *4e*.

Fleischer, Richard. "Case for the Defense." *F&F* 9 (No. 1, Oct 62). See 5, *Orson Welles*.

Peck, Seymour. "Leading Men, European Style." *NYTM* (18 Nov 62). See *4e*.

"Taken for Granite." *Show* 3 (June 63) 52–55. Pictorial comparisons of ancient statues and popular "star" personalities (i.e., Loretta Young and Greek statue from the Archaic period, 520–510 B.C., *et al.*).

Scott, V. "Stars, Second Generation." *McCall's* 90 (July 63) 68–69+. Children of the stars appearing in the movies.

"Idols Junior Grade." *Time* 82 (26 July 63) 47. Children of stars going into show business.

"The Cast: The First Principles of Film Acting and the Stars of Three New Films." *Cinema* (Calif) 1 (No. 6, Nov–Dec 63) 24–30.

Newman, David, and Robert Benton. "The Late Late Ladies." *Mlle* 61 (July 65). See *4a*(3).

"Me? A Movie About Me? Manny, It's a Natural." *Esq* 65 (Jan 66) 48–49. Thirty celebrities (actors and others) answer a question: Whom would you want to play you in the story of your life?

"Pictorial: Trio Con Brio." *Playboy* 13 (No. 3, Mar 66) 105–113. Shirley Anne Field, Rossana Podesta, Christiane Schmidtner.

Stewart, James. "That's Enough for Me." *F&F* 12 (No. 7, Apr 66). See 5, *James Stewart*.

Whitehall, Richard. "The Face of the Vampire." *Cinema* (Calif) 3 (No. 3, July 66) 11–15. Article on vamps; focus on Theda Bara.

Braun, Eric. "Where Have All the Stylists Gone? *F&F* 13 (No. 8, May 67–No. 12, Sep 67). See *4d*.

"Have Nymphet, Will Travel." *Time* 89 (12 May 67) 49–50. On Romina Power, the fifteen-year-old daughter of Linda Christian.

Heston, Charlton. "Actors and Other Minority Groups." *JSPG* (Mar 68) 35–37. Discrimination is less than it used to be.

Hallowell, John. "In My Day We All Had Faces." *Life* 64 (24 May 68) 109–110. Beauty is out of fashion in Hollywood; comments by former stars and producers.

Au Werter, Russell, *et al.* "Special Report: The Director-Actor." *Action* 5 (No. 1, Jan–Feb 70) 11–26. Actors who direct and vice versa: John Cassavetes, Paul Henreid, and others.

2b(1). THEORY, PRACTICE, AND STYLES OF ACTING

[See also 3f(1a).]

Potamkin, H. A. "The Personality of the Player." *Close Up* 6 (No. 4, 1930) 290–297. Notes on a theory of film acting.

"Our 'Wild-Flower' Talkie Actresses." *Lit Dig* 110 (1 Aug 31) 19. Analyses of acting styles of Greta Garbo, Nancy Carroll, Marlene Dietrich, Tallulah Bankhead, Ruth Chatterton.

Young, Stark. "Note: Moving Picture Acting." *New Rep* 72 (21 Sep 32) 150–151. Some talentless actors are interesting on the screen; some actors gain a freedom suited to them, like Charlie Chaplin; Lionel Barrymore, through technique and sometimes genuine feeling, is worth special attention.

Coxhead, Elizabeth. "A Film Actor." *Close Up* 10 (No. 1, Mar 33) 47–49. Toward a theory of film acting.

Parry, Florence Fisher. "Are Movie Stars Actors?" *Delineator* 123 (Sep 33) 4+. On film acting, especially Greta Garbo, Katharine Cornell, Lillian Gish, and *The Birth of a Nation*.

Griffith, Richard. "The Function of the Actor." *CQ* 3 (No. 3, Spring 35) 139–142.

Graham, Charles. "Acting for the Films in 1912." *S&S* 4 (No. 15, Autumn 35). *See 4b.*

Suckow, Ruth. "Hollywood Gods and Goddesses." *Harper's* 173 (July 36) 189–200. Descriptions of film idols from Tom Mix through Garbo to Mae West; they have made American movies "an unconscious social document rather than an art." Same condensed *Lit Dig* 121 (27 June 36) 18–19.

Pudovkin, V. I. "Film Acting: Two Phases." *Theatre Workshop* 1 (No. 1, Oct 36) 53–67. Cinema actors lack both the excitement of the presence of the audience and its reaction.

Howard, Leslie. "My Movie Lot Is Not a Happy One." *Rdrs Dig* 31 (Sep 37) 41–42. An actor tells of the delays and confusions on the sound stage.

Arliss, George. "Where Authors Become Writers—How Actors Are Broken and Writers Made." *Sat Rev* 21 (30 Mar 40). *See 2d.*

Davis, Bette, and David Chandler. "Acting in Films." *Th Arts* 25 (Sep 41) 633–639.

Knox, Alexander. "On Playing Wilson." *Hwd Q* 1 (No. 1, Oct 45) 110–111. Too many people remember President Wilson well.

Knox, Alexander. "Acting and Behaving." *Hwd Q* 1 (No. 3, Apr 46) 260–269. While not discounting altogether the kind of performance in many popular films which he calls "behaving," the man who played the title role in *Wilson* feels that a versatile actor can contribute imagination and nobility to drama on the screen.

Curtiss, Thomas Quinn. "Movie Acting." *S&S* 16 (No. 62, Summer 47) 68. Its difference from the stage, its seemingly accidental quality.

Knox, Alexander. "Performance Under Pressure." *Hwd Q* 3 (No. 2, Winter 47–48) 159–168. Noted actor objects to interruptions and technical difficulties that make Hollywood film work unattractive; British film makers "seem to value acting, to some extent at least, for its own sake."

Martin, Pete. "Gable Can Have It." *SEP* 221 (14 Aug 48) 17+. The author's own experience as a bit player in MGM's *Command Decision* with Clark Gable.

Cronyn, Hume. "Notes on Film Acting." *Th Arts* 35 (June 49) 45–48. A stage actor talks of the values in his craft for the film actor.

Hope-Wallace, Philip. "Acting." *S&S* 19 (Dec 49) 22. See additional articles 19 (Mar 50) 30–31; 19 (June 50) 167; 19 (Nov 50) 289; 19 (Jan 51) 375; 19 (Mar 51) 443; 20 (June 51) 51.

Laver, James. "Some Thoughts on Pulchritude." *S&S* 19 (Mar 50) 19. It is the curse of American pictures.

Zetterling, Mai. "Some Notes on Acting." *S&S* 21 (Oct–Dec 51) 83, 96. Essentials for creative acting are not fulfilled by cinema; some suggestions.

Pudovkin, V. "Stanislavsky's System in the Cinema." *S&S* 22 (Jan–Mar 53) 115–118+. Pudovkin recalls that Stanislavsky first realized his method in a small theatre, with the actors close to the audience; he taught subtleties and nuances, the restrained gesture; his methods were ideally suited to the cinema.

Redgrave, Michael. "I Am Not a Camera." *S&S* 24 (Jan–Mar 55) 132–137. An autobiographical account of Mr. Redgrave's career, with comments about some of the directors under whom he has worked, the work of other actors, and the theory of acting.

Prouse, Derek. "Notes on Film Acting." *S&S* 24 (Spring 55) 174–180. A long discussion of the problems directors face in getting the kind of performance they want from actors, and comments about the actors' relationship with other actors.

Cole, Clayton. "The Brando Boys." *F&F* 1 (No. 8, May 55) 9. New names and styles of acting in Hollywood.

Arletty. "Performing Sartre for the Screen." *F&F* 2 (No. 1, Oct 55) 7. *Huis-Clos* just completed; comments on acting.

Mulock, Al. "School for Actors." *F&F* 3 (No.

1, Oct 56) 17. On London Actor's Studio.

Genschow, Gustov. "They Put Talent Before Publicity." *F&F* 3 (No. 3, Dec 56). *See 4e(4).*

Richardson, Tony. "The Method and Why." *S&S* 26 (Winter 56–57) 132–136. An account of the Actor's Studio, New York, led by Lee Strasberg and inspired by the method of Konstantin Stanislavsky; dangers of individual mannerism, self-consciously offered, as in the cases of Brando and Dean.

Steiger, Rod. "The Truth About 'The Method.' " *F&F* 3 (No. 7, Apr 57) 7+. Reflections on acting taught by Lee Strasberg's New York Actor's Studio.

Quayle, Anthony. "Society and the Actor." *F&F* 3 (No. 10, July 57) 6+. Comparison of British and American economics and acting opportunities.

Ciampi, Yves, *et al.* "Film Acting." *Film* (No. 13, Sep–Oct 57) 5–9. Symposium; the use of nonprofessionals.

"Busy Star at Work." *Newswk* 50 (28 Oct 57) 104–105. William Holden tells about actor's tensions while filming *The Key* in London.

"Half-Dozen Displays of Fine Acting." *Life* 43 (25 Nov 57) 127–128+. Six fine performances in current films.

Stanbrook, Alan. "Towards Film Acting." *Film* (No. 17, Sep–Oct 58) 15–18. Overview; the "method."

Cobb, Lee J. "Take My Advice . . ." *F&F* 5 (No. 2, Nov 58) 7. Actor's general comments on acting.

Luchting, Wolfgang. "Profound Banality in the Film." *J Aesthetics and Art Criticism* 17 (Dec 58) 208–213. Recent movie acting stresses everyday, casual behavior and colloquial speech.

"Private Lives." *F&F* 5 (No. 6, Mar 59) 27–28. Anonymous psychiatrist examines hazards of acting.

Smith, Frank Leon. "Trade Secrets." *FIR* 10 (June–July 59) 381–382. Stolid actors are best for close-ups.

Rogosin, Lionel. "Interpreting Reality." *F Cult* (No. 21, 1960) 20–28. "Notes on the esthetics and practices of improvisational acting" by the director of such documentaries as *Come Back, Africa* and *On the Bowery.*

Quinn, Anthony. "The Actor and His Mask." *F&F* 6 (No. 12, Sep 60) 7–8. Interview.

Marcorelles, Louis. "Talking About Acting: Albert Finney and Mary Ure." *S&S* 30 (Spring 61) 56–61. A tape-recorded discussion between two actors who have worked for stage, screen, and TV.

Ivanov, Boris. "Our 'Method.' " *F&F* 7 (No. 6, Mar 61). *See 4e(8).*

Janowska, Alma. "Truth Behind a Mask." *F&F* 8 (No. 2, Nov 61) 10+. The Polish actress discusses acting and explains some basic dif-

ferences in approach to acting between East and West.

Hayakawa, Sessue. "Nazis and Japs." *F&F* 8 (No. 5, Feb 62) 21+. The actor's reflections about the acting of Von Stroheim and Alec Guinness.

Christiansen, Arthur. "Should Mrs. Christiansen Have Allowed Her Husband to Be Put on the Stage, Mr. Christiansen?" *F&F* 8 (No. 12, Sep 62) 21. Reflections of a nonprofessional actor on his part in a film.

Sarris, Andrew. "Acting Aweigh." *F Cult* (No. 38, 1965) 47–60. Sarris' own personal selection of the best film-acting performances from the silent days to the present.

Durgnat, Raymond. "On Getting Cinema on the Right Wavelength." *F&F* 11 (No. 5, Feb 65) 46–50. Physical actions, gesture, and acting as important in judging style in film.

McVay, Douglas. "The Art of the Actor." *F&F* 12 (No. 10, July 66) 19–25; (No. 11, Aug 66) 36–42; 13 (No. 1, Oct 66) 27–33.

McVay, Douglas. "The Art of the Actor." *F&F* 12 (No. 12, Sep 66) 44–50. The relationship between acting and music.

Steiger, Rod. "On Acting." *Cinema* (Calif) 3 (No. 6, Winter 67) 18–19+.

McKenna, Pat. "Camera, Action, Let's Pretend!" *Cinéaste* 1 (No. 3, Winter 67–68) 18–19. Relationship between actor and director.

McArthur, Colin. "The Real Presence." *S&S* 36 (Summer 67) 141–143. It is not fashionable to talk about actors' contributions to the cinema, but "valid critical points can be made about movies in terms of the physical attributes of the actors and the 'feedback' that occurs from one role to another."

Blue, James. "Satyajit Ray." *F Com* 4 (No. 4, Summer 68). *See 5, Satyajit Ray.*

2b(2). STARS AND THE STAR SYSTEM

[See also 7b(1c), 7d.]

Condon, Frank. "Little Things They Save." *SEP* 204 (14 Nov 31) 30+. On stars' eccentricities.

Collins, Frederick L. "A Motion Picture Roll of Honor." *Good Housekeeping* 95 (Aug 32) 62–63+. Nominates John Bunny, Theodore "Daddy" Roberts, Lon Chaney, Louis Wolheim.

Collins, Frederick L. "Some Stars That Have Set." *Good Housekeeping* 95 (Sep 32) 78–79+. On Valentino, Harold Lockwood, Wallace Reid.

Arvey, V. "How Music Has Helped the Stars." *Etude* 50 (Oct 32) 693–694+.

Shawell, J. "Garbo or Dietrich?" *Pictorial Rev* 34 (July 33) 16–17+.

Muir, Jean. "How to Become a Movie Star." *American* 119 (May 35). *See 5, Jean Muir.*

Blank, A. H. "Whozinnit?" *American* 121 (Jan 36). *See 6e(1)*.

"Fortune Survey: Movies and Movie Stars." *Fortune* 16 (July 37). *See 7b(1b)*.

"Unpopularity Contest." *Current Hist* (Sep 37) 73–74. How American film stars rate in England.

Pitkin, W. B. "Stars of Yesterday." *Woman's Home Companion* 64 (Nov 37) 13–14. Francis X. Bushman runs a hot-dog stand, according to the author of *Life Begins at 40*.

"Glamour Under Fire." *Bus Wk* (14 May 38). *See 6e*.

"Fortune Surveys Movies' Favorite Actors and Actresses." *Fortune* 20 (Nov 39) 67–76.

Churchill, D. W. "Hollywood Span of Life." *NYTM* (7 July 40) 6–7. How a star's popularity is measured and how long it may last.

Powell, Dilys. "Variable Stars." *S&S* 9 (No. 36, Winter 40–41) 66–67. The star system and its relation to film realism.

Crowther, Bosley. "Male Movie Stars Outshine the Female." *NYTM* (16 Feb 41) 10–11+.

March, J. M. "Star-Gazing in Hollywood." *NYTM* (12 Oct 41) 10–11+. Hunt for new stars more feverish with curb on block booking.

"Some Film Actors Who Have Made Themselves Known This Year." *Th Arts* 26 (Mar 42) 184–189. Including Van Heflin, Lana Turner, and Victor Moore.

Crowther, Bosley. "Movies Without Gables." *NYTM* (13 Sep 42) 14–15. With romantic heroes off to war, Hollywood faces a dilemma; it's not easy to build male stars.

Stoddard, Frank. "Top Ten Western Stars." *Good Housekeeping* 116 (Mar 43). *See 4k (2)*.

Pryor, Thomas. "Stars in New York." *NYTM* (1 Apr 45). *See 6d(1)*.

"Who Is Your Favorite Star?" *Woman's Home Companion* 72 (June 45) 12+; 73 (June 46) 7–8. Popularity poll selects four top male and female stars.

Crowther, Bosley. "Hollywood's New Fair-Haired Boys." *NYTM* (15 July 45) 14–15. A comparison of the screen's leading men before and after the war.

Sisk, John P. "The Timeless Tales of Hollywood." *Commonweal* 44 (4 Oct 46) 595–596. How the audience (a kind of irony) projects onto a screen characterization its own knowledge of the star; future viewers may derive out of today's movies something quite different.

"Star on the Door." *Woman's Home Companion* 74 (Mar 47) 146–147. A look at Hollywood's new portable dressing rooms.

De La Roche, Catherine. "That 'Feminine Angle.'" *Penguin F Rev* 8 (Jan 49). *See 7a(2)*.

"Big Deal: Selznick Stars to Warner Bros."

Time 53 (7 Mar 49) 98. Selznick's practice of loaning his stars to other companies.

Klonsky, Milton. "Along the Midway of Mass Culture." *Partisan Rev* 16 (Apr 49) 356–359. Hollywood stars as gods and goddesses whose lives make up the national folklore.

"Big Dig." *Time* 54 (22 Aug 49) 48–50+. The fading stable of superstars; a look at newcomer Elizabeth Taylor.

"Star Turn: Judy Garland." *S&S* 20 (June 51). *See 5, Judy Garland*.

Lord, Daniel A. "Movies Cost Too Much." *Cath World* 176 (Nov 52) 92–95. Evaluation of the price paid by entertainers who sacrifice their lives for the amusement of audiences.

"Which Is Glamor?" *Collier's* 131 (3 Jan 53) 34–35. Italian actresses Silvana Mangano and Rossi Drago: Do they have more appeal when they are disheveled?

"America's Favorite Movie Stars." *Look* 17 (13 Jan 53) 14–16. Picture essay.

Huff, Theodore. "40 Years of Feminine Glamour." *FIR* 4 (Feb 53) 49–63. Identifying characteristics of each era's most beautiful feminine stars.

De La Roche, Catherine. "Stars." *S&S* 22 (Apr–June 53) 172–174. The star system, how it thwarts or recognizes talent.

"Stars' Favorite Photos." *McCall's* 80 (July 53) 14+.

McDonald, Gerald D. "Origin of the Star System." *FIR* 4 (Nov 53) 449–458. Florence Lawrence, Maurice Costello, Mary Pickford, and others.

"Glamour-Imported." *NYTM* (15 Nov 53) 26–27. A portfolio of European actresses, including Anna Magnani and Gina Lollobrigida.

"Stronger Sex Makes Strong Box Office." *Life* 36 (31 May 54) 93–96. The "muscles of the industry" are found in its male stars: Holden, Lancaster, Cooper, and Wayne.

Lerman, L. "Indestructibles." *Mlle* 39 (June 54) 74–75.

Bell, B. "Hollywood Discovers the Natural Look." *McCall's* 81 (July 54) 43–46. A picture essay on actresses who used to look like stars and new stars who look like people.

"Beauty Abroad." *Coronet* 36 (Aug 54) 125–132. Picture story about foreign movie actresses.

Jamison, Barbara B. "Bonanza in Beards." *NYTM* (24 Oct 54) 78–79. For such stars as Kirk Douglas and Gregory Peck, beards seem to enhance their box-office image.

"What Is Sex Appeal?" *Look* 19 (25 Jan 55) 52–53+. A tribute paid to the stars from Theda Bara to Ava Gardner.

Viotti, Sergio. "Vogues in Vamps." *F&F* 1 (No. 5, Feb 55) 5. The changing fashions in American screen personalities.

Britannicus, Cato. "Why the Stars Shine." *FIR* 6 (Oct 55) 369–376. An anonymous opinion about the qualities that have made stars out of actors and actresses.

Launder, Frank, and Sidney Gilliat. "What's in the Stars?" *F&F* 2 (No. 3, Dec 55) 7. Two British producers write about the star system.

Franklin, R. "What Future for Young Stars?" *NYTM* (11 Dec 55) 28–29.

McPherson, Mervyn. "Hollywood Gave Them a Chance." *F&F* 2 (No. 9, June 56). *See 4d.*

Billard, Ginette. "Les Boys of French Cinema." *F&F* 2 (No. 12, Sep 56). *See 4e(2a).*

Peck, Seymour. "Hollywood's Search for New Faces." *NYTM* (7 Oct 56) 28–29. Among the possibilities: Paul Newman, Anthony Perkins, and Sophia Loren.

"Amour and the Man." *Sat Rev* 39 (13 Oct 56) 29. Small gallery of the "kings of movieland" from Bushman to Brando.

"Top Ten." *Time* 68 (17 Dec 56) 100. The most popular movie stars according to *Box Office* magazine.

Harris, T. "The Building of Popular Images: Grace Kelly and Marilyn Monroe." *Studies in Pub Com* 1 (1957) 45–48.

Eisner, Lotte. "The Passing of the First Film Star." *Film* (No. 11, Jan–Feb 57). *See 4b.*

"Yesterday's Pin-Ups Re-created." *Life* 43 (8 July 57) 4–5. Pin-up pictures as in World War I for use in *A Farewell to Arms.*

Whitcomb, John. "Speed Record for Stardom." *Cosmopolitan* 143 (Aug 57) 18–19. Introduction of Australian Victoria Shaw.

"Queens of the Foreign Hollywoods." *NYTM* (10 Nov 57) 36–37. Photographs.

Dyer, Peter John. "When the Stars Were Born." *F&F* 4 (No. 3, Dec 57) 10–12+. History of the stars from the early days of film.

Norman, D. C. "What Makes the Stars Shine?" *Ladies' Home J* 74 (Dec 57) 58–59+. Hollywood beauties tell about their tricks.

Pryor, Thomas M. "Their Past Recaptured." *NYTM* (8 Dec 57) 96–97. Stars react to seeing their early films on television.

Brooks, Louise. "Gish and Garbo." *S&S* 28 (Winter 58–59). *See 4b.*

"Ring-A-Ding Girl." *Time* 73 (22 June 59) 66–70. Portrait of Shirley MacLaine, notes on other young actresses.

Donen, Stanley. "What to Do with Star Quality." *F&F* 6 (No. 11, Aug 60) 9. A director talks about working with film stars.

Wilkinson, Stephan. "Men." *Cosmopolitan* 149 (Nov 60) 56–61. Stills of top stars, with short introductions.

Grant, Cary. "What It Means to Be a Star." *F&F* 7 (No. 10, July 61) 12–13+. Reflections on advantages and disadvantages of acting.

Harris, Jack. "A Sudden Surge of Magnetic Males." *Life* 51 (15 Sep 61) 140–148. Gallery of European leading men: Horst Buchholz, Peter O'Toole, Alain Delon, and Jean Paul Belmondo.

Kazan, Elia. "What Makes a Woman Interesting?" *Vogue* 139 (15 Jan 62) 26–29. Observations on star quality by a director.

"Ladies Who Came to Stay." *Life* 52 (9 Feb 62) 136–139+. Short summaries of female stars who have been public favorites for twenty years or more.

Gehman, Richard. "Indestructibles." *McCall's* 89 (Mar 62) 78–81+. Story of great "immortal" stars, such as Cary Grant, Ingrid Bergman, Mae West.

"Kicking, Cooking—Casting *Nothing Like a Dame.*" *Life* 52 (9 Mar 62) 71–74+. The many talents of five foreign actresses.

Johnson, Ian. "The Reluctant Stars." *F&F* 8 (No. 8, May 62) 24+. Stars discovered by the British realist films of the late 1950s and early 1960s.

LaBadie, Donald W. "The Last Roundup." *Show* 2 (Sep 62) 74–77. Pictorial survey with caption comments on the cowboy movie star; includes Broncho Billy Anderson, Tom Mix, W. S. Hart, Ken Maynard, William Boyd.

Peck, Seymour. "They Still Find Room at the Top." *NYTM* (28 Oct 62) 44–45. Production stills from recent films of older stars.

Haas, Bert, Robert Lippert, Joan Crawford, Henry King, Barbara Stanwyck, Richard MacCann, Frank Whitbeck, Charles Schnee, Irwin Allen. "The Journal Looks at Hollywood's Star System." *JSPG* (Dec 62) 3–28. Articles by producers, actresses, theatre men, and others, pro and con.

Lewis, Richard Warren. "Hollywood's New Breed of Soft Young Men." *SEP* 235 (1 Dec 62) 73–77. Beymer, Donahue, Hamilton—players of immature, misunderstood characters.

Slavitt, David. "Who'll Be the Next Goddess?" *Newswk* 60 (10 Dec 62) 96–97. Introduction of Sue Lyon, Jane Fonda, and Lee Remick.

Lewis, Richard Warren. "Fair Young Hollywood Girls." *SEP* 236 (7 Sep 63) 22–27. The careers of Carol Lynley, Stella Stevens, Yvette Mimieux, and Suzanne Pleshette.

Odets, Clifford. "The Transient Olympian—The Psychology of the Male Movie Star." *Show* 3 (Nov 63) 106–107+. Fictional account of "Bob Farrar" as the prototype of the Hollywood "star" and how he became famous.

Rhode, Eric. "The Day of the Butterfly." *S&S* 33 (Winter 63–64) 44–47. Comments on some new popular films and on Richard Schickel's book *The Stars* (Dial Press, 1962); as an art of the present tense, film may depend heavily on the dynamism of star energy, the trappings of landscape, and momentary fashion.

Greene, M. "Some Very Winning Europeans." *Life* 55 (20 Dec 63) 132–143. Picture gallery of popular European stars.

"Portraits in Nostalgia." *NYTM* (5 Apr 64) 32–33. Photos of older stars.

Bean, Robin. "Will There Be Film Stars in 1974?" *F&F* 10 (No. 10, July 64) 9–14. Yes: recent promising new actors and actresses.

"More Chips Off the Old Block." *Show* 4 (Oct 64) 62–63. Pictorial comparing the similarities between ancient sculptures and current "star" personalities (i.e., Mel Ferrer and King Amenophis IV of Egypt).

McVay, Douglas. "The Goddesses." *F&F* 11 (No. 11, Aug 65) 5–9; (No. 12, Sep 65) 13–18. The legendary sex symbols of the film; second article is on those of the last decade.

Davis, Bette. "What Is a Star?" *F&F* 11 (No. 12, Sep 65). *See 5, Bette Davis.*

"Ages of Man." *Time* 86 (1 Oct 65) 90. A report on aging Hollywood stars.

"Pictorial: The Playboy Portfolio of Sex Stars." *Playboy* 12 (No. 12, Dec 65) 180–193.

Knight, Arthur, and Hollis Alpert. "The History of Sex in the Cinema—Part 8: Sex Stars of 30's." *Playboy* 13 (No. 4, Apr 66). *See 4k(8).*

"If You Flunked the 2-S Test, Nice Going." *Esq* 66 (Sep 66) 110–113. Pin-ups from World War II and for Vietnam war.

Knight, Arthur, and Hollis Alpert. "The History of Sex in the Cinema—Part 11: Sex Stars of the 40's (U.S.A.)." *Playboy* 13 (No. 10, Oct 66). *See 4k(8).*

McVay, Douglas. "The Art of the Actor." *F&F* 13 (No. 2, Nov 66) 26–33. On the notion of the "star."

Knight, Arthur, and Hollis Alpert. "The History of Sex in the Cinema—Part 13: Sex Stars of the 50's." *Playboy* 13 (No. 12, Dec 66). *See 4k(8).*

Bart, Peter. "$upercollossaliti$." *Sat Rev* 49 (24 Dec 66). *See 6c(1).*

Knight, Arthur, and Hollis Alpert. "The History of Sex in the Cinema—Part 14: Sex Stars of the Fifties." *Playboy* 14 (No. 1, Jan 67). *See 4k(8).*

Alpert, Hollis. "The Falling Stars." *Sat Rev* (28 Dec 68) 15–17. Decline of the star image in Hollywood. Part of the *Saturday Review* report "The Now Movie."

Knight, Arthur, and Hollis Alpert. "The History of Sex in the Cinema—Part 20: Sex Stars of the 60's." *Playboy* 16 (No. 1, Jan 69). *See 4k(8).*

"New Ones: Fresh and Independent." *Time* 93 (7 Feb 69) 50a–50f. Picture essay about new stars and anti-stars.

Goldstein, Richard. "Why the Young Killed Movie Superstars." *Vogue* 154 (1 Aug 69) 128–129+.

Knight, Arthur, and Hollis Alpert. "Sex Stars of 1969." *Playboy* 16 (No. 12, Dec 69) 206–219. Raquel Welch, Faye Dunaway, Vanessa Redgrave, Jim Brown, Paul Newman.

Ehrlich, H. "Zanuck: Last of the Red Hot Star-Makers." *Look* 34 (3 Nov 70). *See 5, Darryl Zanuck.*

Hamilton, J. "Where, Oh Where Are the Beautiful Girls?" *Look* 34 (3 Nov 70) 62–67. The stars of Hollywood's past as they are today: Mary Pickford, Rita Hayworth, Dorothy Lamour, Jane Russell, Donna Reed, Janet Gaynor.

Mothner, I. "Now Faces." *Look* 34 (3 Nov 70) 72–77. New favorites: Barbara Hershey, Donald Sutherland, Elliott Gould, Jacqueline Bissett: short interviews and pictures.

Knight, Arthur, and Hollis Alpert. "Sex Stars of 1970." *Playboy* 17 (No. 12, Dec 70) 200–211. Mainly pictures: including Raquel Welch, Elliott Gould, Robert Redford, as the Big Three.

2b(3). ACTORS' SALARIES AND WORKING CONDITIONS

[See also 6c(2).]

Wagner, Bob. "Anchors to Windward." *Collier's* 87 (6 June 31) 20–21+. On business investments by stars.

Condon, Frank. "Some Make a Living." *SEP* 204 (4 July 31) 25+. On Hollywood acting jobs.

Croy, Homer. "Are Hollywood Salaries Due for Paring?" *Lit Dig* 116 (9 Dec 33) 30. NRA investigates star wages.

"Stars and Salaries." *Time* 24 (30 July 34) 26. NRA administrator's report (not by name).

"Movie Actors Win Long Fight." *Newswk* 5 (26 Jan 35) 26–27. Establishment of Screen Actors Guild.

"Congressional Committee Finds More Facts on Film's Fancy Fees." *Newswk* 7 (28 Mar 36) 26. Salaries of stars.

Ellis, Peter. "The Screen: On Calling Names." *New Masses* 20 (28 July 36) 29. Actors can't be blamed for appearing in reactionary film since they are exploited and have limited choice in their work.

"Star Rebels." *Lit Dig* 122 (8 Aug 36) 19. They want out of contracts.

"Frantic Stars." *Lit Dig* 123 (15 May 37) 12. Screen Actors Guild faces a decision regarding a strike.

Ryskind, M. "It Happened One Night; Motion Picture Producers Have Granted Screen Actors a Closed Shop." *Nation* 144 (15 May 37) 563.

Thompson, M. "Hollywood Is a Uniontown." *Nation* 146 (2 Apr 38) 381–383. The history, struggles, and successes of the Screen Actors Guild.

Reynolds, Quentin. "Man with a Union Card:

R. Montgomery." *Collier's* 103 (1 Apr 39). *See 5, Robert Montgomery.*

Kaufman, W. "The Wages of Cinema." *Am Mercury* 47 (July 39) 300–301. Actors, actresses, and extras; their wage scales.

Daugherty, Frank. "Hollywood Goes to the Ant." *CSMM* (8 July 39) 7. Players put their money into business.

Lehman, Harvey C. "Chronological Ages of Some Recipients of Large Annual Incomes." *Social Forces* 20 (Dec 41) 196–206. Actors, actresses, and directors when they were receiving their largest incomes (1915–1939).

Brown, Louis M., and Morris E. Cohn. "The Palette and the Revenuer." *Hwd Q* 3 (No. 4, Summer 48–Summer 49) 368–371. An author or actor is taxed unfairly because of the erratic highs and lows of income; a plan based on bond-buying is suggested.

"Dangerous Thoughts, This Property Is Condemned." *Nation* 171 (25 Nov 50). *See 7c (2d).*

"Six Times and Out." *Time* 66 (29 Aug 55) 37. The Screen Actors Guild votes to end strike, accepting a new contract.

"Hollywood Actors Win $80 Day for Now." *Bus Wk* (24 Mar 56) 170. A new contract, including a five-day week.

"Box-Office Appeal, After Tax, Is Not What It Seems." *U.S. News & World Report* 42 (8 Feb 57) 128–131. Concerning the Internal Revenue Service and the salaries of film stars.

Knight, Arthur. "Stranglehold of the Stars." *Sat Rev* 42 (28 Feb 59) 24. High cost of talent; established stars are incorporating; statements by Cary Grant and Tony Curtis.

"When Millionaires Go on Strike." *US News & World Report* 48 (21 Mar 60) 89–92. Screen Actors Guild wants a percentage of the sale of movies to TV.

"Monroe Doctrine." *Time* 79 (22 June 62) 56. Studios begin to get angry over star salaries, demands, and delays.

"Something's Got To Give?" *Newswk* 60 (2 July 62) 78–79. Costs of star system discussed by Richard Brooks and Stanley Kramer; problems at Fox and M-G-M.

Scott, Vernon. "Why Barbara Stanwyck Grinned All the Way to the Bank." *McCall's* 92 (Mar 65) 82. Stars in TV commercials.

Sarne, Mike. "How to Handle Directors." *F&F* 11 (No. 7, Apr 65) 41–43. The difficulty actors have in finding employment.

"On the Vine in Hollywood." *Newswk* 74 (20 Oct 69) 116+. Actors' unemployment.

2b(4). DISCOVERING ACTING TALENT

[See also 2a(2).]

Pickford, Mary. "Stay Away from Hollywood." *Good Housekeeping* 91 (Oct 30) 36–37+.
Ed. by Campbell MacCulloch. Star discourages would-be actresses.

Collins, Frederick L. "Where Are Those Second Mary Pickfords?" *Good Housekeeping* 96 (Apr 33) 20–21+. Suggests Mary Miles Minter, Bessie Love, Vivian Martin, Janet Gaynor and others.

Parry, Florence Fisher. "Mary and the Movies." *Delineator* 122 (May 33) 12+. On would-be actresses.

Cantor, Eddie, and David Freedman. "You Oughta Be in Pictures." *SEP* 207 (20 Oct 34) 29+. Star discusses difficulty of becoming successful in movies.

Young, Helen Schermerhorn. "Movie Mother." *Delineator* 124 (Feb 34) 4+; (Mar 34) 25+. Account of young actress' entry into movies.

Smith, H. H. "So You Want a Screen Test!" *Pictorial Rev* 37 (Dec 35) 10–11+.

Bucquet, Harold S. "Have You a Screen Personality?" *CSMM* (15 Jan 36) 5+. Director of screen tests explains what the camera reveals.

"Hollywood Now Looks For You." *Ladies' Home J* 52 (Nov 35) 12–13+. Inside story of talent scouting. See also *Lit Dig* 121 (14 Mar 36) 26.

Hinsdell, Oliver. "What It Takes to Get into the Movies." *American* 122 (July 36) 20–21+. Acting coach recommends determination, talent, warmth, and a little reading.

Francis, Kay. "Don't Try Your Luck Out Here!" *Pictorial Rev* 38 (Jan 37) 16–17+. Working as an extra is not much better than no work at all, and certainly not the way to begin a movie career.

Johnston, Alva. "Quest for New Stars." *Woman's Home Companion* 64 (Oct 37) 21–22+.

Crichton, K. "Movie Entrance." *Collier's* 100 (25 Dec 37) 14+. Harry Evans, movie talent scout, talks about how and how not to get into movies.

Eddy, D. "Hollywood Spies on You." *American* 130 (July 40) 24–25+. Talent scouts.

Palmer, Greta. "Screen Appeal: Our Highest Priced Commodity." *Rdrs Dig* 47 (Oct 45) 93–95. Studio efforts to find new screen personalities.

"Life Visits Nine Hopeful Starlets." *Life* 20 (18 Feb 46) 123–126+. The typical aspiring actress, her chances for success, her daily routine.

"Stars of Tomorrow." *Newswk* 30 (8 Sep 47) 78. The exhibitors' selections.

Porter, A. "Four Cinderellas." *Collier's* 119 (1 Feb 47) 18–19+. Current Hollywood favorites and their rise to fame.

Hyer, Martha. "What It Takes to Be a Starlet." *American* 145 (Feb 48) 136–140. Actress describes movie tests and contracts, and gives some advice to hopefuls.

"Hollywood's New Generation." *Life* 24 (24 May 48) 93–94.

Eunson, Dale. "We Let Our Daughter Go To Hollywood." *American* 146 (Nov 48) 32–33+. Personal account of the "big break": fourteen-year-old Joan Evans succeeds in Hollywood.

"Speaking of Pictures." *Life* 25 (6 Dec 48) 22–24+. Hollywood's promising young actors include Montgomery Clift and Richard Basehart.

Winge, John H. "Star Manufacture." *S&S* 17 (No. 68, Winter 48–49) 192–193. Discovering them in America.

"Quintet of Beauties; Photographs." *Life* 27 (15 Aug 49) 63–67. A portfolio of Hollywood starlets.

"Eight Girls Try Out Mixed Emotions." *Life* 27 (10 Oct 49) 95–98. Starlets, including Marilyn Monroe, are given an acting test.

"Steps to Stardom." *Coronet* 27 (Dec 49) 16.

Lupino, Ida. "New Faces in New Places." *FIR* 1 (Dec 50) 17–19. They're needed behind the camera too, according to actress-director-producer, who tells about new people discovered by her own production company.

"Another Garbo?" *Coronet* 32 (July 52) 14–15. Stills about the newest foreign candidates for stardom.

Gipson, G. "ABC's of Movieland." *Our World* 7 (Sep 52) 60–64. "So you want to crash the movies and be a star?"

Lerman, L. "Most Likely to Succeed." *Mlle* 39 (Sep 54) 134–135.

Pryor, Thomas. "Hollywood's Search for Stars." *NYTM* (12 June 55) 14–15+. As accomplished stars reach middle age, the studios feverishly look for young talent.

Godley, John. "In the Wake of the Whale: John Huston." *Vogue* 126 (15 Nov 55). *See 5, John Huston.*

Arnow, Max. "When You Take a Screen Test." *Good Housekeeping* 142 (Jan 56) 38+. A Columbia "talent executive" discusses the screen tests he gave Susan Strasberg and Kim Novak.

Curtiz, Michael. "Talent Shortage Is Causing Two-Year Production Delay." *F&F* 2 (No. 9, June 56) 9. Plea for gambling on new talent.

Nicholas, M. "Foreign Accent in Starlets." *Coronet* 40 (Aug 56) 44–55. Picture story and short introduction.

"Nine Girls Trying to Get the Big Break." *Cosmopolitan* 141 (Oct 56) 40–45. Photo essay on the life of the starlets.

Peck, Seymour. "Up-and-Coming in Movies." *NYTM* (26 Jan 58) 28–29. Photos of rising young actresses.

"Hollywood's Hidden Beauties." *Look* 22 (4 Feb 58) 39–43. New actresses.

Nicholas, M. "Six Girls in Search of Success." *Coronet* 44 (Sep 58) 75–87.

Wallis, Hal. "New Talent—Old Problem." *JSPG* (Sep 59) 15–16. Responsibility of the independent producer to present new talent on the screen.

Weales, Gerald. "Star Is Born." *Atlantic* 205 (Apr 60) 90–91. Story inspired by Joshua Logan's search for an unknown actor for *Parrish.*

"Small Rumble." *New Yorker* 36 (2 Apr 60) 34–35. Testing actors for *West Side Story.*

Whitcomb, J. "New French Movie Stars." *Cosmopolitan* 149 (Aug 60) 10–13. Beauties of the New Wave since Brigitte Bardot.

Peck, Seymour. "Hollywood's Script Calls for Youth." *NYTM* (20 Nov 60) 48–49. Photos of young actors and actresses.

"How to Get into Films." *F&F* 7 (No. 8, May 61) 7–9+. The editors ask film makers and actors about British films.

Wintle, Julian. "Finding Our Own Talent." *F&F* 7 (No. 9, June 61) 28. Producer writes about encouraging new talent.

"People Are Talking About the Men in the Theatre." *Vogue* 138 (1 Oct 61) 116–117. New faces in film and theatre.

"Windfall of New Beauties." *Life* 52 (13 Apr 62) 113–117+. Gallery of new young actresses.

"Bouquet of Blossoming Blondes." *Life* 53 (17 Aug 62) 85–89. A gallery of young Hollywood actresses.

Weaver, John D. "Instant Portrait of the Hollywood Starlet." *Holiday* 33 (Mar 63) 76–77. Quotes and statistics.

Ornitz, D. "Ah, What Sights! Water Sprites!" *Life* 54 (26 Apr 63) 58–67. A picture gallery of Hollywood beauties.

"Sex Shortage." *Time* 82 (13 Dec 63) 66+. Young actresses are reluctant to become sex goddesses.

"Les Girls." *Time* 84 (21 Aug 64) 72–73. A gallery of new European actresses.

"End of the Great Girl Drought." *Life* 57 (2 Oct 64) 136–139. Photos of current Hollywood starlets.

"Common Market's Glamour Stock." *Life* 60 (28 Jan 66) 40–51. Beauties of Europe.

"Pictorial: Jocelyn Lane: Heiress Apparent." *Playboy* 13 (No. 9, Sep 66) 118+. Starlet of *Tickle Me.*

Gordon, Dr. George M., and Irving A. Falk. "You Oughta Be in Pictures." *Cinéaste* 2 (No. 3, Winter 68–69) 3–9. Excerpt from a book entitled *Your Career in Film-Making* (Messner, 1969) by Gordon and Falk; advice to the young actor/actress breaking into the business.

Uselton, R. "The Wampas Baby Stars." *FIR* 21 (No. 2, Feb 70) 73–97. History of the organization promoting the young stars of tomorrow; what happened to the "baby stars."

Lurie, D. "Actresses Who Are Real People."

Life 68 (29 May 70) 40–47. Pictorial essay and interviews with ten starlets.

2b(5). ACTORS' TRAINING

[See also 1a(2), 1a(3b), 2a(5).]

Mack, Grace. "You at Center Stage." *Ladies' Home J* 50 (Dec 33) 23+. How screen stars overcome self-consciousness.

"Training Talent for the Movies." *Lit Dig* 123 (30 Jan 37) 23–24. Sam Briskin of RKO and his methods for training young actors.

Ergenbright, E., and J. Smalley. "Star Factory." *Ladies' Home J* 54 (July 37) 14–15+.

"Young Starlets Learn to Act at Fox Drama School." *Life* 3 (13 Nov 37) 36–39.

"Terry Hunt's Job Is to Keep Movie Stars Lean and Healthy." *Life* 9 (15 July 40) 55–57.

Haynes, H. "Terrible Terry, Hollywood's Leading Physical Trainer." *Collier's* 108 (22 Nov 41) 13+.

Wallace, Irving. "Smorgasbord Circuit." *Collier's* 118 (21 Dec 46) 11+. A dramatic school that nurtures Sweden's gifts to Hollywood.

"Big Build-Up." *Life* 25 (30 Aug 48) 77–81+. Subtitle: Hollywood starts to turn "a pretty girl from next door" into a star.

Heflin, Van. "Actor Goes to School." *Th Arts* 34 (Oct 50) 36–37+. The importance to the screen actor of knowledge of technical aspects of the medium, especially direction.

"Apprentice Goddesses." *Life* 30 (1 Jan 51) 36–41.

Tregaskis, Richard. "Prep School of the Stars." *Nation's Business* 41 (Mar 53) 43–45+. Pasadena's Playhouse, Hollywood's biggest single supplier of talent.

"New Gestures for Old." *Life* 37 (8 Nov 54) 73–74+. Universal's talent-school students are asked to portray standardized emotions of early silent films.

"Strange Doings of Actress at Practice." *Life* 42 (28 Jan 57) 96–98+.

Zolotow, Maurice. "The Stars Rise Here." *SEP* 229 (18 May 57) 44–45+. The New York Actors' Studio.

Dickens, Homer. "The AADA." *FIR* 10 (Dec 59) 596–616. A report on the American Academy of Dramatic Arts, which in seventy-five years has had 35,000 students, among whom are William Powell, Edward G. Robinson, Joseph Schildkraut.

2b(6). SPECIALIZED PERFORMERS

[See also 7a(5).]

Collins, Frederick L. "Homely Heroes of Hollywood." *Good Housekeeping* 94 (June 32) 44–45+. On Gable, Chevalier, Will Rogers, Wallace Beery, George Arliss, and Edward G. Robinson.

Collins, Frederick L. "Sweethearts of the Film." *Good Housekeeping* 96 (May 33) 36–37+. On movie married couples: George Burns and Gracie Allen, Marie Dressler and Wallace Beery, among others.

Sterling, Eloise. "Face Is Familiar." *American* 126 (Dec 38) 61+. S. S. Hinds, once a wealthy lawyer, now is a lawyer before the camera.

Hamman, M. "You Know Their Faces, But Do You Know Their Names?" *Good Housekeeping* 111 (Aug 40) 13+. A tribute to character actors.

Durant, J. "Tough On and Off." *Collier's* 106 (31 Aug 40) 24+. The movies' professional "tough guys."

"Axis Villains Fill Hollywood's Rogues Gallery." *Life* 13 (23 Nov 42) 12–13+. Photos of Hollywood actors as Axis badmen.

Robinson, F. "The Hiss-s-s-s Through the Years." *NYTM* (15 Aug 43) 16–17. Pictures of villainous types, from Hun through gangster to Japanese.

"Presidential Stars." *NYTM* (20 Oct 46) 36–37. Pictorial history of stars who have portrayed American presidents.

Frank, S. "Knockouts to Order." *SEP* 220 (3 Jan 48) 12. Mushy Callahan teaches Hollywood movie tough guys.

Hine, Al. "Siren Song." *Holiday* 9 (Mar 51) 6. Screen vamps, past and present.

"New High in Movie Heels." *NYTM* (18 Apr 54) 78–79. New movie bad guys, including Jack Palance and Richard Widmark, are confusing mixture of charm and evil.

Connor, Edward. "The 6 Charlie Chans." *FIR* 6 (Jan 55) 23–27. A survey of the role as portrayed by George Kuwa, Kamiyama Sojin, E. L. Park, Warner Oland, Sidney Toler, and Roland Winters; a complete list of the Charlie Chan pictures made 1926–1949.

Connor, Edward. "Multiple Roles." *FIR* 6 (May 55) 232–236. A survey of the films in which one or more of the actors assume two or more roles, including *Seven Faces* (1929), in which Paul Muni played seven parts.

Connor, Edward. "The 12 Bulldog Drummonds." *FIR* 7 (Oct 56). See 4k(10).

Talese, Gay. "Pugs in Pix." *NYTM* (24 Feb 57) 68+. Prizefighters who have acted in the movies.

Connor, Edward. "The Genealogy of Zorro." *FIR* 8 (Aug–Sep 57). See 4k(10).

Connor, Edward. "The 9 Philo Vances." *FIR* 9 (Mar 58). See 4k(10).

Peck, Seymour. "It Must Be More Than Sex." *NYTM* (14 Sep 58) 34–36+. On sex appeal in the movies.

"Anatomy of an Amateur." *Newswk* 53 (20 Apr 59) 114. Joseph Welch—lawyer turned actor in Preminger's *Anatomy of a Murder.*

"Pictorial: Europe's New Sex Sirens." *Playboy* 10 (No. 9, Sep 63) 136–149.

Guy, Rory. "The Character Actors: Going, Going, Gone." *Cinema* (Calif) 2 (No. 2, July 64) 14–18. Article and pictures of 95 character actors.

Winick, Charles. "The Face Was Familiar." *F&F* 11 (No. 4, Jan 65) 12–17. Study of the character actor.

Beaumont, Charles. "The Heavies." *Playboy* 12 (No. 2, Feb 65) 132–135. Stroheim, Robinson, Bogart, Cagney, Karloff.

Moore, Thomas F. "Long Reign as King of the Apes." *Sports Illus* 26 (2 Jan 67) 48–54. The history of film Tarzans.

Goldstein, Richard. "Season of the Witch: Excerpts." *Vogue* 152 (Oct 68) 170–171+. On the ugly-beautiful actress.

"Which Man Would You Pick as the New James Bond?" *Life* 65 (11 Oct 68) 120–124. New contenders for the role.

Clein, Harry. "The Reel People." *Show* (9 July 70) 14–19. Comments on the character actor's return to prominence in the cinema (i.e., Brenda Vaccaro, Alice Ghostley, Stacy Keach) and the deemphasis on perfect ("star") types.

2b(7). ACTORS FROM MINORITY GROUPS

[*See also 7a(2), 7a(3).*]

Noble, George. "Black and White: The Negro in Hollywood." *S&S* 8 (No. 29, Spring 39) 14–16. The nature of the roles assigned to Negroes in current films.

Harrison, William. "Black and White: The Negro and the Cinema." *S&S* 8 (No. 29, Spring 39) 16–17. The dearth of good film roles for Negro actors.

Denton, J. F. "Red Man Plays Indian." *Collier's* 113 (18 Mar 44). See 9, *Buffalo Bill.*

Moten, Etta. "Negro Actors Put on the Spot." *New Vistas* 1 (No. 8, Mar 46) 61–64. Protest against stereotyping of Negro actors on stage and screen; Negroes should organize to fight the patterns of stereotyping they dislike; constructive suggestions.

Norford, G. "On Stage: Negro in Theater, Radio, and Screen." *Opportunity* 25 (July 47) 167+.

Norford, G. E. "The Future in Films. . . ." *Opportunity* 26 (1 July 48) 108–110. For black actors.

"Do You Remember . . . Our Gang?" *Negro Digest* 9 (Dec 50). See 4k(1).

"Movie Musicals." *Ebony* 6 (Aug 51) 51–53. Ranking Negro performers given musical bits in half-dozen coming Hollywood productions.

"Boycott in Hollywood?" *Time* 70 (2 Dec 57) 90. Boycott planned among black actors of the Goldwyn film *Porgy and Bess.*

Razaf, A. "Passing Years." *Negro Hist Bul* 22 (Jan 59) 93–94. *Show Biz,* a book recently published by *Variety,* contains very little mention of Negro show people; such histories must be written by blacks.

Harmon, Sidney. "How Hollywood Is Smashing the Colour Bar." *F&F* 5 (No. 6, Mar 59) 7+. Negroes in American films.

Nash, Johnny. "My Way to Escape." *F&F* 5 (No. 12, Sep 59) 7. Black actor writes about his getting into acting.

"Hollywood and the Negro." *JSPG* (Mar 62) 3–4. Editorial suggests writing scripts with parts for blacks is harder than providing more jobs for them behind the camera.

"Teen-agers in Movie Roles." *Ebony* 18 (May 63) 150–152+. Story of Judy Pace, a young black girl with a part in a new espionage film, *The Candy Web.*

"Yank Movie Man of Japan." *Ebony* 18 (July 63). See 4f(1).

Killens, John Oliver. "Hollywood in Black and White." *Nation* 201 (20 Sep 65) 157–160. Negro writers and performing artists can't get jobs.

Cambridge, Godfrey. "Godfrey Cambridge's Open-Door Policy." *Look* 33 (7 Jan 69). See 5, *Godfrey Cambridge.*

"The Tenth Cavalry Rides Again." *Ebony* 24 (Feb 69) 92–97. Black equestrian unit available as Old West black fighters for films.

"Paula Adds Zip to *Sweet Charity.*" *Ebony* 24 (June 69). See 5, *Paula Kelly.*

"Football Heroes Invade Hollywood." *Ebony* 24 (Oct 69) 195–197. Black athletes go to Hollywood: Jim Brown, "Woody" Strode, O. J. Simpson, Rafer Johnson, and others.

2b(8). DANCERS AND SINGERS

[*See also 4k(6), 8a(4).*]

Carrick, E. "Film, Theatre, and Ballet in the United States." *London Studio* 20 [*Studio* 120] (Spring 40). See 3f(1).

"They Dance: It's Murder!" *Look* 17 (5 May 53) 90–91.

Knight, Arthur. "From Dance to Film Director." *Dance Mag* 28 (Aug 54). See 2c.

Joel, L. "Open Letter to the Academy of Motion Picture Arts and Sciences." *Dance Mag* 30 (May 56) 14. A suggestion that the "dance arts be included in the categories of the Academy Awards."

Knight, Arthur. "Interview with Jack Cole in New York." *Dance Mag* 30 (May 56) 20–23.

Nelson, Gene. "Working in Hollywood." *Dance Mag* 30 (May 56) 24–27.

Clark, Roy. "So You Want to Dance in Movies?" *Dance Mag* 31 (Oct 57) 24–26+. The mechanics of getting a film job.

Lane, John Francis. "Mr. Volare Finds He's Become an Actor." *F&F* 6 (No. 4, Jan 60)

10+. On Domenico Modugno, a popular Italian singer who recorded the song "Volare," now making a film based on that song.

Clark, Roy. "Have Shoes, Will Travel." *Dance Mag* 34 (Oct 60). See 2k(4).

McVay, Douglas, and Tom Vallance. "Gotta Sing! Gotta Dance!" *Film* (No. 40, Summer 64) 7–11. Brief comments on great musical performers: Fred Astaire, Gene Kelly, Judy Garland, Ann Miller.

Kelly, Gene. "Some Notes for Young Dancers." *Dance Mag* 39 (Sep 65) 49. Gene Kelly on film dancing.

Swisher, Viola Hegyi. "Toumanova in Hollywood." *Dance Mag* 40 (Mar 66) 26–27. Tamara Toumanova and Hitchcock's *Torn Curtain*.

Joel, Lydia. "Dancer-Choreographer-Show-Doctor Now Film Director, Herb Ross Talks Shop." *Dance Mag* 41 (Dec 67) 42–49+.

"Dancers Go Dramatic." *Ebony* 24 (Sep 69) 38–40+. Story of Lola Falana and Fayard Nicholas, black dancers who star in *Liberation of L. B. Jones*.

Robin, S. "On Location with Edvard Grieg." *Dance Mag* 44 (Jan 70) 50–59. The choreography of *Song of Norway* by Lee Theodore through illustrations.

2b(9). EXTRA PLAYERS AND STAND-INS

Beatty, Jerome. "Movie Star Nobody Knows." *American* 110 (July 30) 30–32+. Profile of Jane Arden, with remarks about other screen extras, known as the Big Eight of Extradom.

"Stand-ins for Stars." *Lit Dig* 116 (4 Nov 33) 35.

Strand, Edith. "You Ought to Be in Pictures." *American* 119 (June 35) 24–25+. Hollywood extra relates why she dropped out of movies for work as cashier.

Mainwaring, D. "Hollywood Nobodies: Stand-ins." *Good Housekeeping* 106 (Apr 38) 40–41. Sally Sage, Bette Davis' stand-in.

Jones, G. "Star Shadows." *Collier's* 101 (30 Apr 38) 18+. Hollywood stand-ins: their work and growing status.

Beatty, Jerome. "Your Chance in the Movies." *American* 125 (May 38) 30–32+. The Hollywood "extra" and Central Casting.

Wallace, I. "Robin Hood's Double." *Collier's* 102 (6 Aug 38) 17+. An interview with Archer Howard Hill, Errol Flynn's double in Warners' *The Adventures of Robin Hood*.

Bower, Anthony. "Screen Actors: Class B, Extras." *Nation* 152 (12 Apr 41) 453–454; 152 (7 June 41) 676. The inequities of wages, living, and classification of actors through Central Casting.

Ferguson, Otis. "Hollywood Footnote." *New Rep* 105 (17 Nov 41) 670. The willfulness or incompetence of extras.

"Movies Stand-ins for Hollywood's Most Glam-orous Stars." *Life* 16 (26 June 44) 49–51. An unglamorous and poorly paid job.

"Movie Tempest: Screen Extras Drive for Own Union." *Bus Wk* (29 July 44) 104+.

"Screen Extras Win." *Bus Wk* (23 Dec 44) 106+. Union is formed.

"Hollywood Extras." *Look* 11 (No. 4, 18 Feb 47) 28–31. The life of two extras in the Hollywood motion-picture industry.

"Pearl's Big Moment." *Life* 29 (3 July 50) 71–75. "Movie-struck waitress gets a second of glory on the screen."

"Happy Little Wittlingers." *Life* 35 (17 Aug 53) 102+. Three sisters in Hollywood play bit parts in films which allow them the life of leisure they enjoy.

"Central Caster." *Good Housekeeping* 145 (Oct 57) 13. Central Casting, Hollywood's official clearinghouse of extras, explained by its manager, Arthur Bronson.

Edson, Lee. "So You Want to Be a Hollywood Extra?" *SEP* 231 (24 Jan 59) 26–27+. On the Central Casting Bureau.

"You Call Us." *Newswk* 53 (18 May 59) 118. Casting of "extras" and what an extra does.

2b(10). CHILD ACTORS

"Children in the Talkies." *Commonweal* 13 (26 Nov 30) 88. The effect of the talkies on the moral and intellectual development of child actors.

Collins, Frederick. "Truth About Those Baby Stars." *Good Housekeeping* 96 (June 33) 38–39. Discussion of the effect of being a film star.

"Children at Work: School for Actor Children." *New Outlook* 162 (Nov 33) 58.

Johnston, A. "Baby Leroy: Mechanics of a Wonder Child." *Woman's Home Companion* 61 (Aug 34) 10–11.

Willson, D. "Child Stars of Hollywood." *Delineator* 126 (Jan 35) 14–15.

Temple, Gertrude. "Bringing Up Shirley." *American* 119 (Feb 35). *See 5, Shirley Temple*.

Courtney, W. B. "Mother's Little Darlings." *Collier's* 96 (12 Oct 35) 14–15+. The problems director Norman Taurog has with child actors and their mothers.

"Children of the Celluloid: Portraits." *Lit Dig* 120 (9 Nov 35) 51. Pictures of child actors such as Shirley Temple, Jane Withers, Jackie Cooper, and "Our Gang."

Clark, F. "School on Location." *CSMM* (4 Nov 36) 12. Child actor has to go to school even on location.

Crichton, Kyle. "Actor at 8." *Collier's* 98 (21 Nov 36) 22+. The life of Spanky McFarland, child actor.

"Quintupling Assets." *Lit Dig* 122 (22 Aug 36) 26. 20th Century-Fox buys story by Bruce

Gould about country doctor and quintuplets, signing them to three-picture contract.

Lowenstein, Harold. "Can Children Act?" *S&S* 6 (No. 21, Spring 37) 17.

Orcutt, E. "And Their Mamas." *SEP* 209 (24 Apr 37) 16–17+. Children in films: their working conditions.

Joseph, R. "Your Child's Chances in Hollywood." *Parents Mag* 12 (Oct 37) 22–23.

McNichols, C. L., and H. M. Nelson. "Mother, May I Make a Million?" *Ladies' Home J* 55 (Jan 38) 30–31+. Children in Hollywood films.

"Boom in Child Stars: Shirley Temple Still Leads in Box-Office Lure." *Newswk* 12 (25 July 38) 25.

Foster, C. "Mrs. Temple on Bringing Up Shirley." *Parents Mag* 13 (Oct 38) 22–23.

Kutner, Nanette. "Box-Office Babies." *Collier's* 103 (25 Mar 39) 74–77. The life of child actors: Freddie Bartholomew, Jane Withers, and Shirley Temple.

Hersholt, Jean. "Five Little Stars." *Woman's Home Companion* 66 (June 39) 20–21. Anecdotes in movie making with the Dionne quintuplets.

"Made-to-Order Punks." *Collier's* 104 (29 July 39) 13+. The "Dead-End Kids" take a bow.

Singer, F. "Where and How Movie Children Go to School." *School and Society* 50 (14 Oct 39) 499–501. The lengths studios go to in order to bring education to their juvenile stars.

Hamman, Mary. "Adventures of a Baby Star." *Good Housekeeping* 109 (Nov 39) 42–43+. Story of child actress Sandra Lee Henville.

Churchill, Douglas. "Youthful Stars That Mostly Wane." *NYTM* (26 May 40) 8–9+. Survey of child stars as Shirley Temple contemplates retirement at eleven.

Condon, Frank. "No Mothers Wanted." *Collier's* 106 (17 Aug 40) 20+. Zanuck has chosen the successor to Shirley Temple and closed his gates to ambitious mothers.

MacKaye, M. "Rooney, Garland, Durbin: Mighty Atoms of Hollywood." *Ladies' Home J* 57 (Sept 40) 19+.

"Three Little Movie Girls." *Life* 18 (26 Feb 45) 71–77. Brief biographies of three child actresses: Margaret O'Brien, Elizabeth Taylor, and Peggy Ann Garner.

White, Magner. "Starlet School." *Collier's* 115 (30 June 45) 22–23. School for child actors.

Albert, Dora. "Children's Year in Hollywood." *American* 140 (July 45) 122–123. Picture story on five child actors: Jackie Jenkins, Ted Donaldson, Margaret O'Brien, Joan Carroll, and Elizabeth Taylor.

Busch, N. "Margaret O'Brien." *Life* 19 (10 Dec 45) 106–108+. Story of child actress.

Eddy, Don. "Babes in Hollywood." *American* 142 (Sept 46) 38–39+. How children get to be Hollywood stars.

"Film Star Family." *Life* 22 (10 Mar 47) 133–136. Clifford Brill Severn of Hollywood raises a family of eight child actors.

Levison, Francis. "A Staggering Performance." *Life* 25 (13 Dec 48) 105–108. Bobby Henrey, child actor, who was in Carol Reed's *The Fallen Idol*.

"Youngest Generation of Movie Stars." *NYTM* (17 Apr 49) 18–19. Pictures of Bobby Henrey, Natalie Wood, and others.

Chandler, David. "Bringing Up a Movie Moppet." *Collier's* 124 (13 Aug 49) 17+. Child actress Gigi Perreau.

"My Boy and I." *Parents Mag* 24 (Nov 49) 38–39+. Hollywood diary of father of sixteen-year-old star of MGM's *Intruder in the Dust*.

"Black Angel." *Life* 28 (20 Mar 50) 137–138+. Story of German child actress Anna Caroline Mueller.

"Hot Tots." *Newswk* 51 (13 Jan 58) 58.

Bester, Alfred. "Princess of Pretend." *Holiday* 25 (Mar 59) 111–112+. What happened to child stars Margaret O'Brien and Roddy McDowall.

"Tomorrow's Stars Show Their Stuff." *Life* 28 (27 Feb 50) 107–108+. Picture story of the benefit for the March of Dimes put on by the Professional Children's School in memory of Mary MacArthur.

Melick, Weldon. "Young Rebel." *American* 148 (Dec 49) 50–51+. Interview with child star Dean Stockwell.

"Stars A-Growing." *Coronet* 36 (May 54) 141–148. Picture story about child stars.

Marks, Louis. "All About Kids." *F&F* 1 (No. 6, Mar 55) 4. Jonathan Ashmore, a new child actor in the British tradition.

"Baby Who Plays Moses." *McCall's* 84 (Nov 56) 20+. Picture essay: Charlton Heston's son plays infant Moses in *The Ten Commandments*.

Nichols, Mark. "Child Stars Who Came Back." *Coronet* 43 (Mar 58) 79–89. Jackie Coogan, Roddy McDowall, Margaret O'Brien, Jackie Cooper, and Shirley Temple.

Donner, Clive. "These Are the Most Selfish Actors of All." *F&F* 4 (No. 7, Apr 58) 7. Problems of directing children.

"Bright Chips off Old Blocks." *Life* 45 (4 Aug 58) 39–40. Stars' children get roles in their parents' movies.

Shavelson, Melville, and Jack Rose. "Children— Why Shouldn't We Hate Them?" *F&F* 5 (No. 8, May 59) 12+. Problems with children in making *Five Pennies*.

Wright, C. "How Not to Direct Children!" *Pop Photog* 48 (Jan 61) 90–91. For amateurs, but useful pointers for all new directors.

Peck, S. "Not Dolls But Actors." *NYTM* (21 Jan 62) 14–15. Child actors who work hard.

"Children Caught in Adult Dramas." *Life* 54

(8 Feb 63) 97–100+. Child actors in current movies.

Zierold, N. "Where Are They Now? Child Stars." *Good Housekeeping* 165 (Sep 67) 154.

Godfrey, Lionel. "Because They're Young." *F&F* 14 (No. 1, Oct 67) 42–48; (No. 2, Nov 67) 40–45. On child stars in the films.

2b(11). ANIMAL ACTORS

Shipman, Nell. "This Little Bear Went Hollywood." *Good Housekeeping* 92 (Jan 31) 30–31+. A bear's screen life.

"How Animals 'Talk' for the Movies." *Pop Mech* 55 (May 31) 722–726. Hidden cameras record sight and sound of animals.

"Truth About Wild Animals in the Movies." *Pop Mech* 57 (Feb 32) 194–199.

"Two Kinds of Childishness." *Commonweal* 15 (23 Mar 32) 565. The low level of taste and decency reached by films employing the torture of animals.

"Big Animals Shot for Movies in California Jungle." *Pop Sci* 120 (Apr 32) 38–39.

"Working the Big Cats in the Kleig Lights." *Lit Dig* 115 (22 Apr 33) 24+. Clyde Beatty comments on the filming of *The Big Cage,* in which he handles 43 lions and tigers; excerpted from *The Detroit Sunday News.*

Boone, R. "Wild Actors of the Movie Jungles." *Travel* 61 (May 33) 23–25.

"Dumb Actor Gets a Break; Dogs in a Movie." *Nature* 22 (July 33) 39.

Boone, A. "Animal Movie Actors Trained by Strange Tricks." *Pop Sci* 123 (Sep 33) 30–31.

McNichols, C. L. "Picture Horse; Styles in Movie Mounts." *Rev of Reviews* 95 (Feb 37). See *4k(2).*

Rogers, S. N. "Hollywood Horses." *Rev of Reviews* 95 (June 37) 54–55. How they are supplied to the studios.

Pringle, Henry. "In Character." *Collier's* 100 (20 Nov 37) 11+. Stories on the suppliers of animals for the movies.

Stuart, Isobel. "Shooting Pains." *Collier's* 101 (1 Jan 38) 19–20+. A script girl's diary of the months spent in making a wild-animal picture.

"Barnyard Wizards of the Films." *Pop Mech* 70 (Sep 38) 392–395+. Animals in movies.

Robinson, E. Keith. "Wild Animals and the Films." *S&S* 8 (No. 29, Spring 39) 8–9. Many films do violent and cruel injury to animals.

"Hollywood's Dog Stars." *CSMM* (20 July 40) 15.

"Cruelty for Profit." *Collier's* 106 (14 Dec 40) 82. Endorsement of William Randolph Hearst's crusade against cruelty to animals in the making of motion pictures.

"Hollywood's Animal Actors." *Pop Mech* 79 (June 43) 28–33.

Sharritt, G. "Motion Picture Animals Have a Champion." *Nature* 38 (June 45) 293–295.

"Horse Glamour." *Life* 19 (22 Oct 45) 137–138+. Animal actors get movie makeup.

Stimson, Thomas, Jr. "Smart Actors." *Pop Mech* 86 (Sep 46) 97–104. Hollywood's animal actors.

Muir, F., and B. Morgan. "Lassie Did Come Home, Rich." *SEP* 219 (19 Oct 46) 32–33.

Kent, J. "Animal Stars of *The Yearling.*" *Nature* 39 (Nov 46) 465–468.

Albert, Dora. "Zoo's Who in Hollywood." *American* 143 (Jan 47) 36–37. A picture story on animals in Hollywood films.

Jensen, Oliver. "Persecuted Lion." *Life* 22 (3 Mar 47) 19–20+. Story of Jackie the lion in pictures.

"Speaking of Pictures." *Life* 23 (28 July 47) 14–16. Birds star in new film, *Bill and Coo.*

Sharritt, G. "Dog Pound to Kleig Lights." *Nature* 41 (Jan 48) 24.

Crocker, Harry. "Assignment in Hollywood." *Good Housekeeping* 126 (May 48) 10–11+. Animals in Hollywood pictures.

Colton, H. "Top Dog in Hollywood: Lassie." *NYTM* (27 Feb 49) 20–21.

"Safety First for Movie Animals." *American* 147 (June 49) 117. The American Humane Association makes certain that animals are not mistreated while making films.

"Animals Enact Aesop's Fables." *Pop Mech* 92 (July 49) 132–133.

Hine, Al. "How Hollywood's Most Amiable Stars Barked, Heehawed and Whinnied Their Way to Success." *Holiday* 8 (Sep 50) 20+.

"A Star Is Born." *Time* 57 (30 Apr 51) 104. A new chimpanzee for the Jungle Jim series.

Duncan, R. "Beasts in Your Backyard." *Holiday* 10 (Nov 51) 82+. Thousand Oaks, California, is the home of many animals and their trainers.

"Smash Menagerie." *Time* 59 (7 Apr 52) 102. The annual "Patsy" awards.

Kerr, C. "Mel Koontz Twists Tigers' Tails." *Pop Mech* 101 (Mar 54) 81–85.

Harvey, Evelyn. "Kirk Gets a Seal of Approval." *Collier's* 134 (20 Aug 54) 22–23. Kirk Douglas and a seal star in *Twenty Thousand Leagues Under the Sea.*

De La Roche, Catherine. "Animals and the Cinema." *S&S* 25 (Summer 55) 44–47. Animals in fiction films from *Rescued by Rover* (1905) through *Black Beauty,* the animated cartoon, and the documentary.

Sayre, Joel. "Four Lives of Rin Tin Tin." *McCall's* 82 (July 55) 32–35+. The story of the dog star's series.

Reese, J. "Movie Horses Are Real Hams!" *SEP* 228 (30 June 56) 42–43.

"It's a Dog's Life." *McCall's* 84 (Jan 57) 20+. Picture story of Hollywood's newest dog star, Kelly, in *Kelly and Me.*

"Million-Dollar Mutt, Spike." *Look* 22 (21 Jan

58) 75. Picture story of the star of Walt Disney's *Old Yeller*.

Adelman, Benjamin. "Lights, Camera, Animals." *Am Mercury* 88 (Mar 59) 141–144. The work of the American Humane Society with animals used in Hollywood movies.

"Shaggy Sheep Dog's Social Life." *Life* 46 (25 May 59) 135–136. Pictures of the star of the film *The Shaggy Dog*.

"The Horse in Hollywood." *Newswk* 56 (10 Oct 60) 104–106. The activities of the American Humane Society in Hollywood.

"Some Remarkable Animals Pace a Brace of Films." *Life* 53 (16 Nov 62) 120–123.

"Cross-Eyed Lion." *Life* 57 (25 Sep 64) 71–72. Clarence the Lion gets a Hollywood contract.

"King of Beasts." *Newswk* 67 (21 Feb 66) 96. Ivan Tors supplies 90% of all animals used in films and TV.

"*Born Free.*" *Look* 30 (19 Apr 66) 106. True story of the lioness in *Born Free* found orphaned in the Kenya bush.

"King of the Beasties." *Time* 89 (16 June 67) 67–68. Ivan Tors uses "affection training" for animals in his pictures.

Helfer, Ralph. "The DGA's Own Bwana Simba." *Action* 3 (No. 1, Jan–Feb 68) 22–25. Animal trainer discusses his work.

2c. Directors and Directing

[*See also* 2a(3), 2a(4), 3a(3), 3b(2).]

"René Clair Indicts the Film 'Industry.' " *Lit Dig* 114 (20 Aug 32) 14–15. French director condemns bigness of Hollywood and praises Chaplin, Sennett, Ince, and Griffith.

Asquith, Anthony. "Rhythm in Sound-Films." *CQ* 1 (No. 3, Spring 33) 144–147. Scenario, directing, and cutting should be related to meaning and to sound; examples.

Sagan, Leontine. "Courage in Production." *CQ* 1 (No. 3, Spring 33) 140–143. Thoughts on directing films after years of work in the theatre.

MacDonald, Dwight. "Notes on Hollywood Directors." *Symposium* 4 (Apr 33). *See 4d.*

Troy, William. "Values Once Again." *Nation* 136 (10 May 33). *See 3b(2).*

Viertel, Berthold. "The Function of the Director." *CQ* 2 (No. 4, Summer 34) 206–210. The studio machinery.

Reynolds, Quentin. "Shooting Stars." *Collier's* 95 (9 Feb 35) 12+. Von Sternberg, De Mille, LeRoy, and other directors with "technical know-how."

"Ace Director at Pinnacle in Films." *Lit Dig* 121 (15 Feb 36) 24. Cornelia Penfield article in *Stage* lists top directors, describes their work.

Rosson, R. "No Fooling! Modern Movie Thrills Are Real." *Pop Sci* 129 (Nov 36) 38–40. Dangers of second-unit directing on locations.

"It All Depends on the Director." *Scholastic* 29 (21 Nov 36) 8–9.

"Speaking of Pictures . . . These Show How Movie Directors Act." *Life* 3 (18 Oct 37) 16–17. Lubitsch, Curtiz, Cukor, and others presumably demonstrating for their performers.

Hitchcock, Alfred. "Directors' Problems." *Living Age* 354 (Apr 38) 172–174. An analysis of his own directorial style coupled with a defense of the English film.

McEvoy, J. P. "Tricked into Acting." *Rdrs Dig* 36 (Feb 40) 71–73. How far directors go to achieve desired acting quality; examples.

Nathan, George Jean. "Mal de Hollywood." *Newswk* 16 (1 July 40) 41. The position of movie directors in Hollywood just before the war.

Jacobs, Lewis. "Film Directors at Work." *Th Arts* 25 (Jan, Mar 41) 40–48, 225–232. The on-the-set personalities and techniques of Alfred Hitchcock, Frank Capra, Garson Kanin, and Fritz Lang; two-part article.

Isaacs, H. R. "Citizen Kane and One-Man Pictures in General." *Th Arts* 25 (June 41) 427–434. The advantages and drawbacks of the "one-man picture" with Welles, Capra, and Sturges principal examples.

Kanin, Garson. "I Direct." *Th Arts* 25 (Sep 41) 640–644. The role of the director, with emphasis on relation of director to writer as an interpretive artist.

Busch, Niven. "Myth of the Movie Director." *Harper's* 193 (Nov 46) 452–456. A writer's view of the contrast between the silent-era director and the modern director.

Blakeston, Oswell. "In Search of a Director." *S&S* 16 (No. 63, Autumn 47) 96–97. Aesthetic criteria and qualifications for being a great director.

Siodmak, Curt. "Medium-Close Shot in Bel-Air." *Screen Writer* 3 (Nov 47) 5–7. Dialogue between writer and director: Why doesn't the director try putting down actual words on paper instead of simply saying "no" to what is written?

Nugent, Frank S. "Writer or Director, Who Makes the Movie?" *NYTM* (21 Dec 47). *See 2d.*

Seril, William. "The Camera's Bright Eye Is Lowered Becomingly." *Hwd Q* 3 (No. 2, Winter 47–48). *See 3a.*

Hartman, Don. "Two Heads Are Worse Than One (Especially If They're on You)." *Screen Writer* 3 (Feb 48) 21–22. Writer becomes director, and is scared half to death; author later became head of production at Paramount.

Leonard, Harold. "New Directors—Where From?" *S&S* 17 (No. 6, Summer 48) 103. Some of the people who have directed recent films; their backgrounds.

"New Wigwag Signals Direct Movie Scenes." *Pop Sci* 156 (Mar 50) 142–143. Arm movements for giving orders during shooting.

Macgowan, Kenneth. "Film Director's Contribution to the Screen." *English J* 40 (Mar 51) 127–134.

"Behind That Camera." *Coronet* 30 (July 51) 16–17. Stills of directors at work.

Sidney, George. "The Director's Art." *FIR* 2 (June–July 51) 9–10. He should not be intrusive, this director believes.

Newman, Joe. "Directors Are Businessmen." *FIR* 2 (Aug–Sep 51) 24–28. They should give up the notion of art, shoot master scenes, show them to test audiences, then expand the best ones.

Pichel, Irving. "In Defense of Virtuosity." *QFRTV* 6 (No. 3, Spring 52) 228–234. Film is young yet and has not produced many virtuosi such as Méliès, Chaplin, Welles, Hitchcock, who exhibit "an overflow of competence which is plainly visible and which gives pleasure for its own sake."

Henreid, Paul. "The Actor as Director." *FIR* 3 (June–July 52) 270–273. He makes the best director because he can "act it out" for his performer or at least anticipate his needs.

von Sternberg, Josef. "On Life and Film." *FIR* 3 (Oct 52) 383–392. Artists, writers, actors, emotions, and the spectacle of life: these must be understood by a director.

Samuels, Gertrude. "The Director—Hollywood's Leading Man." *NYTM* (26 Oct 52) 22–23. Short profiles of Ford, Zinnemann, Curtiz, and Koster.

"The Old and the New." *S&S* 22 (Apr–June 53). *See 2a(1).*

Everson, William K. "The Gentle Art of Borrowing." *FIR* 4 (Aug–Sep 53) 349–353. Sometimes a copied scene is a tribute to another director (*Henry V* from *Alexander Nevsky*); stories that were made over and over.

Welles, Orson. "The Third Audience." *S&S* 23 (Jan–Mar 54) 120–122. Edited version of a lecture delivered by Welles at the British Film Institute Annual Summer Film School in 1953; the creative artist *must* address sixty million people; the answer is to find a middle ground between 16mm avant-garde and the big commercial production; some comments on his work in *Macbeth* and *Othello*.

Houston, Penelope. "The Ambassadors: Americans in Europe." *S&S* 23 (Apr–June 54) 176–180. Reversal of the usual trend: directors are leaving Hollywood to make pictures in foreign countries and with foreign companies; Lewis Milestone, John Huston, Anatole Litvak, and others.

Knight, Arthur. "From Dance to Film Director." *Dance Mag* 28 (Aug 54) 21–23+. Charles Walters, Gene Kelly, and Stanley Donen.

Richardson, Tony. "The *Metteur en Scène*." *S&S* 24 (Oct–Dec 54) 62–66+. Some of the "showier" directors in cinema: Becker, Max Ophuls, Visconti, Kazan, Welles.

Symposium. "The Director and the Public." *F Cult* 1 (No. 2, 1955) 15–18. Some of the leading Hollywood directors (John Ford, Elia Kazan, George Stevens, etc.) answer questions regarding their attitudes toward their general public.

Oughton, Frederick. "Man with a Roving Eye." *F&F* 1 (No. 5, Feb 55) 13. Interview with British casting director Robert Lennard.

Johnson, Albert. "The Tenth Muse in San Francisco." *S&S* 24 (Jan–Mar 55) 152–156. Selected portions of lectures given at a San Francisco film festival by a number of directors, and Johnson's comments on films which were shown there; Rouben Mamoulian speaks of D. W. Griffith, Mitchell Leisen about Cecil B. De Mille.

Spears, Jack. "2nd-Unit Directors." *FIR* 6 (Mar 66) 108–112. Survey of the work of the better-known men in this field, such as B. Reeves Eason (*Ben-Hur*), Yakima Canutt, Paul Mantz, Andrew Marton.

"Actor as Director." *Newswk* 46 (26 Sep 55) 114. Some film actors who have tried their hand at it.

Zebba, Sam. "Casting and Directing in Primitive Societies." *QFRTV* 11 (No. 1, Winter 56) 154–166. Producer of *Uirapuru* in Brazil and *Fincho* in Nigeria describes problems working with native actors and nonactors.

Anderson, Lindsay. "Notes from Sherwood." *S&S* 26 (Winter 56–57) 159–160. Documentary director reflects on the experience of directing five episodes of *Robin Hood* for TV.

Dreyer, Carl. "Thoughts on My Craft." *S&S* 25 (Winter 55–56) 128–129. "We must use the camera to create a new language of style, a new artistic form."

Hurst, Brian Desmond. "The Director." *F&F* 3 (No. 5, Feb 57) 27+. The role of the director in film making.

Patrick, Nigel. "Directing My First Film." *F&F* 3 (No. 8, May 57). *See 9, Uncle George.*

Cotes, Peter. "Cinema Has the Edge on TV." *F&F* 4 (No. 6, Mar 58) 9–10. Comparison of the two media by television director turned film director.

Davidson, Bill, and Joshua Logan. "Fear Is My Enemy." *Look* 22 (22 July 58) 70–74+. Logan tells of his experiences as director and the common fears among actors, writers, and producers. See also *Look* 22 (5 Aug 58).

Cartier, Rudolph. "A Foot in Both Camps." *F&F* 4 (No. 12, Sep 58) 10. Film and TV directing compared.

Robson, Mark. "The Director's Way." *Sat Rev* 41 (20 Dec 58) 12. Technique is not an end in itself, the big thing is the emotion between actors. Part of *Saturday Review* report "The Film: Survey of the Craft and Its Problems."

"A Free Hand." *S&S* 28 (No. 2, Spring 59) 60–64. British directors indicate what projects they'd like to do: Jack Clayton, Clive Donner, Robert Harner, Seth Holt, Pat Jackson, John Krish, Jack Lee, Tony Richardson, Paul Rotha.

Moskowitz, Gene. "The Tight Close-Up." *S&S* 28 (Nos. 3, 4, Summer, Autumn 59). *See 4d.*

Marton, Andrew. "*Ben-Hur's* Chariot Race." *FIR* 11 (No. 1, Jan 60). *See 9, Ben-Hur.*

"Three Directors." *F&F* 7 (No. 1, Oct 60) 12+. Three directors present their views on film: Jacques Dupont, Jacques Doniol-Valcroze, and Edouard Molinaro.

Truffaut, François. "Tomorrow—The Artists." *F&F* 7 (No. 1, Oct 60) 17. The problems of the director.

Antonioni, Michelangelo. "Reflections on the Film Actor." *F Cult* (Nos. 22–23, 1961) 66+. "The director owes no explanations to the actor . . . he must not compromise himself by revealing his intentions."

Hill, Steven P. "Evaluating the Directors." *FIR* 12 (No. 1, Jan 61) 7–13. Listing of the thirty-six best directors. Numerical ranking of directors by pictures on National Board of Review's *Thirty Years of the Ten Best.*

Wright, C. "How Not to Direct Children!" *Pop Photog* 48 (Jan 61). *See 2b(10).*

"Shop Talk in Hollywood." *Sat Rev* 44 (23 Dec 61) 34–36. Arthur Knight leads a panel discussion with directors Otto Preminger, Denis Sanders, Fred Zinnemann, Michael Gordon, John Frankenheimer, and Stanley Kramer. Part of *Saturday Review* report "Film Directors at Work."

"The Director Is the Star." *NYTM* (18 Feb 62) 24–25. Photographs of top foreign directors.

"How Would You Make a Film About the H-Bomb?" *Show* 2 (June 62) 78–81. Film directors respond to the above question: Antonioni, Bergman, Zinnemann, Cocteau, *et al.*

Signoret, Simone. "On Being Under the Director's Spell." *F&F* 8 (No. 9, June 62) 11–12. Interview on some of the directors she has worked with.

Sarris, Andrew. "The American Cinema." *F Cult* (No. 28, 1963) 1–67. Critical judgments on "pantheon directors" and a host of others; later revised and expanded for his book of the same title.

Silke, James R. "The Best Directors and 20 on Their Way." *Cinema* (Calif) 1 (No. 4, June–July 63) 19–20. List of twenty-two top directors, twenty new ones, and some of their films.

Coughlan, R. "The Directors." *Life* 55 (20 Dec 63) 156–158+. Many directors give views of their art.

"Ten Questions to Nine Directors." *S&S* 33 (Spring 64) 62–67. Stanley Kubrick, Jean-Luc Godard, Ermanno Olmi, Clive Donner, Roger Corman, and Joseph Losey, among others considered "independent," answer questions about their films: Was the original idea your own? How was the film financed? What was the production cost? Did you have an assurance of distribution?

"*Show* Selects 100 Directors." *Show* 4 (Apr 64) 88–90. Survey of 156 films in progress by noted directors from 16 countries with brief content breakdown of each film.

Godard, Jean-Luc. "Bergmanorama." *CdC in Eng* (No. 1, Jan 66). *See 5, Ingmar Bergman.*

Ophuls, Max. "My Experience." *CdC in Eng* (No. 1, Jan 66) 63–68. "The *métier* advances only when there is an opening, when experience can no longer help us"—as when Chaplin and Rossellini worked, without precedent to go on.

Spears, Jack. "Mary Pickford's Directors." *FIR* 17 (No. 2, Feb 66). *See 5, Mary Pickford.*

Sarne, Mike. "On the Other Side of the Camera." *F&F* 12 (No. 10, July 66) 36–37. Director on making films.

George, George L. "The Merger Has Passed the Test." *Action* 1 (No. 1, Sep–Oct 66) 5. Comments on the success of the merger of the Directors Guild of America with the Screen Directors International Guild.

Marvin, Ira. "The Directors' Bill of Rights." *Action* 1 (No. 1, Sep–Oct 66) 20. Directors Guild of America statement on the rights of the director.

Christie, Julie. "Maybe It Is a Sort of Sado-Masochistic Relationship." *Action* 1 (No. 2, Nov–Dec 66) 12–13. The actress discusses working with directors.

Windeler, Robert. "Youngerman of the DGA." *Action* 1 (No. 2, Nov–Dec 66) 9–10. Biographical sketch of the man who is secretary of the Directors Guild of America.

Heston, Charlton. "What I Want, and Don't Want, from My Director." *Action* 2 (No. 1, Jan–Feb 67) 19–20. The American actor discusses working with directors, giving special consideration to his relationship with William Wyler.

von Sternberg, Josef. "Fun in a Chinese Laundry." *F&F* 13 (No. 4, Jan 67) 14–18. Excerpt from his book; on film directing.

"The DGA-Producers' Training Program." *Action* 2 (No. 2, Mar–Apr 67) 16–19. A report on the Directors Guild program to train young directors.

Pratt, James C. "The Assistant Director's Dilemma." *Action* 2 (No. 2, Mar–Apr 67) 14–15. His shifting, changing role.

Flatley, Guy. "And for Best Director." *NYTM* (19 Mar 67) 174. Comments about, and by, film directors.

Knight, Arthur. "Three Missing Minutes." *Sat Rev* 50 (8 Apr 67). See 3b.

"The Great Giveaway." *Action* 2 (No. 3, May–June 67) 11. Reaction against changes in the way producers and directors are listed in the credits, as dictated by the Writers Guild of America West and the Association of Motion Picture and Television Producers.

Madsen, Axel. "A Cinematic Love Affair: European Style." *Cinema* (Calif) 3 (No. 6, Winter 67) 9–13. Article on young directors of Europe and themes of love.

Sarris, Andrew. "Movers." *Sat Rev* 50 (23 Dec 67) 10+. Biographical sketches of Milos Forman, Sergei Bondarchuk, Dusan Makavejev, and Istvan Szabo.

"Winners All in a Vintage Year." *Action* 3 (No. 2, Mar–Apr 68) 8–9. Description and account of the Directors Guild Awards of the year.

Crist, Judith, *et al.* "Directors Meet Critics." *Action* 3 (No. 3, May–June 68) 15–17. Excerpts from a New York forum in which directors and critics met and discussed their work.

Brady, Robert. "Directing Actors for Film." *Cinéaste* 2 (No. 1, Summer 68) 21. Brief report on one method of teaching directors to work with actors.

Goldwasser, Noe. "Film Diary for a Film Version of Shakespeare's *Macbeth*." *Cinéaste* 2 (No. 2, Fall 68) 9–12. A fictitious re-creation of a "director's" notebook; spoof on Welles.

"Image Breakers: New Film Directors." *Harper's Bazaar* 101 (Sep 68) 316–317. Introduc-tion to Peter Whitehead, Bo Widerberg, Dusan Makavejev, and John Korty.

Lindsay, Michael. "An Interview with Jeanne Moreau." *Cinema* (Calif) 5 (No. 3, 1969). See 5, Jeanne Moreau.

Panama, Norman, *et al.* "Why Directors Criticize Critics." *Action* 4 (No. 1, Jan–Feb 69). See 3b.

Dmytryk, Edward. "The Director and the Editor." *Action* 4 (No. 2, Mar–Apr 69). See 2f.

"Film Maker as Ascendant Star." *Time* 94 (4 July 69) 46–51. Hollywood system long denied the directors complete authority over their creations; the auteur theory has given new power to American directors.

Pierson, Frank. "Through the Looking Glass." *F&F* 15 (No. 12, Sep 69). See 2d.

AuWerter, Russell, *et al.* "Special Report: The Director-Actor." *Action* 5 (No. 1, Jan–Feb 70). See 2b.

Lerman, Leo. "The Movie Makers." *Mlle* 70 (Jan 70) 69–73+. Short paragraphs on fifteen current film makers from around the world.

Nogueira, Rui. "*Psycho*, Rosie and a Touch of Orson." *S&S* 39 (Spring 70). See 5, Janet Leigh.

Steiger, Rod. "The Director: An Actor's View." *Action* 5 (No. 4, July–Aug 70) 27–29.

"First Feature." *Action* 5 (No. 5, Sep–Oct 70) 4–30. A special issue in which the following directors discuss making their first feature: Michael Ritchie, Hal Ashby, Gilbert Cates, Jack Haley, Jr., Harold Prince, Cy Howard, Paul Williams, Stuart Hagmann, Richard Colla.

Hamilton, J. "Movies: And Everybody's Doing It." *Look* 34 (3 Nov 70) 41–47. Sketches on current directors: Dennis Hopper, Russ Meyer, Andy Warhol, Paul Morrissey, Robert Aldrich, Jean Renoir, Francis Ford Coppola, Glenn Brown.

2d. Writers and Writing

[See also 3a, 3f(1b), 3f(2).

[See 5, Biography: Edward Anhalt, Antonin Artaud, George Axelrod, Samuel Beckett, Robert Benton, Charles Brackett, Bertolt Brecht, Jacques Brunius, Truman Capote, Borden Chase, I. A. L. Diamond, F. Scott Fitzgerald, Carl Foreman, Barney Fradkin, Jules Furthman, Paul Green, Graham Greene, Ben Hecht, Buck Henry, William Inge, Christopher Isherwood, Alexander Jacobs, Garson Kanin, Ring Lardner, Jr., Vincent S. Lawrence, Ernest Lehman, Anita Loos, Norman Mailer, Wolf Mankowitz, Abby Mann, Frances Marion, Carl Mayer, David Newman, Dudley Nichols, Harold Pinter, Jacques Prévert, Alain Robbe-Grillet, William Rose, Damon Runyon, Stanley Shapiro, G. B. Shaw, Irwin Shaw, Terry Southern, Charles Spaak, Donald Ogden Stewart, Lamar Trotti, Dalton Trumbo, Jim Tully, Peter Ustinov, Salka Viertel, Edgar Wallace, Nathanael West, Tennessee Williams, Eugene Zamiatin, Cesare Zavattini.]

Rotha, Paul. "The Art Director and the Composition of the Film Scenario." *Close Up* 6 (No. 5, 1930). See 2k.

Stuart, Michael. "Scenario-Writer." *Close Up* 6 (No. 3, 1930) 198–204. Comments on the career of Jimmy Perkins.

Pudovkin, Vsevolod. "Film Direction and Film Manuscript." *Experimental Cinema* 1 (No. 1,

Feb 30) 5–6; (No. 2, June 30) 7–10; (No. 3, Feb 31) 16–18.

Wylie, Philip. "Writing for the Movies." *Harper's* 167 (Nov 33) 715–726. Tongue-in-cheek précis of scriptwriting.

Legg, Stuart. "The Film on Paper: Planning the Production." *CQ* 2 (No. 2, Winter 33–34) 131–134. Finding the visual ways to express a theme.

Dukes, Ashley. "The English Scene." *Th Arts* 18 (Nov 34). *See 4e(1b).*

Nairne, Campbell. "The Writer's Approach to Cinema." *CQ* 3 (No. 3, Spring 35) 134–138.

Metfessel, M. "Personal Factors in Motion Picture Writing." *J of Abnormal Psych* 30 (Oct 35) 333–347. Film writers are not more neurotic than other people.

"Hollywood Story Conference." *SEP* 209 (10 Oct 36) 14–15+. "Transcript" of Gene Fowler, Nunnally Johnson, Grover Jones, and Patterson McNutt trying to adapt a story to the screen.

McCall, Mary. "Hollywood Close-Up." *Rev of Reviews* 95 (May 37) 44. Writer decides she likes working on movies. Reprinted from *Vassar Alumnae Magazine.*

Eustis, M. "Additional Dialogue: Scribblers in Hollywood." *Th Arts* 21 (June 37) 443–452. Three kinds of writers: the script girl, the publicity writer, the scenarist.

Law, Robert, and J. Carlyle Benson. "Boy Meets Girl." *Cinema Arts* (1 No. 2, July 37) 76. A discussion between Larry Toms, who wrote *Boy Meets Girl,* and Robert Law and J. Carlyle Benson, a Hollywood writing team, about scriptwriting.

"Story Conference: A Hollywood Document." *Cinema Arts* 1 (No. 2, July 37) 84. Four screenwriters—Nunnally Johnson, Patterson McNutt, Gene Fowler, and Grover Jones—discuss a story for a screenplay.

"Scene-setters: Cinema's Writers Set the Stage for from $300 to $3,500 Weekly." *Lit Dig* 123 (10 July 37) 19–20. The importance and the problems of the scenario writer; how scripts are written.

Patterson, Frances Taylor. "The Author and Hollywood." *North Amer Rev* 244 (No. 1, Autumn 37) 77–89. As the cinema comes into its own, it needs developed writers working within the medium not just "adapting" from the novel and the stage.

Fuchs, Daniel. "Dream City, or the Drugged Lake." *Cinema Arts* 1 (No. 3, Sep 37) 41. The problems of scenarists.

"Speaking of Pictures . . . These Are Hollywood Shakespeares." *Life* 3 (No. 20, Dec 37) 4–5. Screenwriters, including John Lee Mahin and Jerry Wald, in gag pictures.

Arliss, George. "Where Authors Become Writers—How Actors Are Broken and Writers Are Made." *Sat Rev* 21 (30 Mar 40) 14–

15+. An actor discusses the relation of the film writer to his medium.

Kanin, Garson. "I Direct." *Th Arts* 25 (Sep 41). *See 2c.*

Nichols, Dudley. "Film Writing." *Th Arts* 26 (Dec 42) 770–774. Screenwriting as a distinct literary form.

Farber, Manny. "Writers as Producers." *New Rep* 108 (26 Apr 43) 566. Writer-produced movies are based on intellectual idiom of writers, not visual idiom of film; still they are a "necessary wedge of integrity and earnestness."

Nichols, Dudley. "The Writer and the Film." *Th Arts* 27 (Oct 43) 591–602. The aesthetic problems of cinema described by a prominent screenwriter.

Maddow, Ben. "Reconstruction of the Truth." *Calif Arts and Arch* 61 (No. 1, Jan 44). *See 8c.*

Curtiss, Thomas Quinn. "The Movie Writer." *S&S* 13 (No. 52, Jan 45) 93–94. His role; praise for a few.

Nugent, Frank S. "How Long Should a Movie Be?" *NYTM* (18 Feb 45). *See 3a(1).*

Duggan, Pat. "Casting Writers." *Screen Writer* 1 (July 45) 28–30. Story editor for Samuel Goldwyn says the job of the producer is to "cast" the writer so well for his story that he doesn't need to bring in a lot of rewriters.

Turmell, K. "So You'd Like to Write a Scenario." *Writer* 58 (July 45) 209–210. Discouraging the hopeful scenarist; advice from a professional.

McNulty, John. "Dear Me." *Screen Writer* 1 (Aug 45) 30–34. Humorous approach to the notes a writer writes himself but can't decipher after he turns sober.

Presnell, Robert R. "The Great Parenthesis." *Screen Writer* 1 (Sep 45) 12–16. On the problems of the writer returning to find a job in Hollywood following World War II; work in the service has meant years of growth and Hollywood should realize this.

Buchman, Sidney. "A Writer in VIP's Clothing." *Screen Writer* 1 (Oct 45). *See 7e.*

Chandler, Raymond. "Writers in Hollywood." *Atlantic* 176 (Nov 45) 50–54. "That which is born in loneliness and from the heart cannot be defended against the judgment of a committee of sycophants." See response in *Screen Writer* (Dec 45) by Philip Dunne.

Rose, Tony. "So I Went to a Doctor." *S&S* 14 (No. 56, Winter 45–46) 121–122. Opinions about the structure of films, especially the importance of beginnings.

Kibbee, Roland. "Two Men on a Vehicle." *Screen Writer* 1 (Dec 45) 9–14. A satirical article on how to achieve one-upmanship with any collaborator you may be working with on a screenplay.

Nathan, Robert. "A Novelist Looks at Hollywood." *Hwd Q* 1 (No. 2, Jan 46) 146–147.

Film is like "a novel to be seen, instead of told"; screenwriting offers many disappointments but it is also a worthwhile challenge.

Strawn, Arthur. "The Case for the Original Story." *Screen Writer* 1 (Jan 46) 24–29. Despite the low status of original screenplays with producers, author lists five "precepts" for the "benefit of those who would write originals."

Herman, Lewis. "Dialect Dialectics." *Screen Writer* 1 (Mar 46) 1–8. The need for study of speech patterns and dialects as well as authentic costuming and architecture; the writer should "hear" it that way.

Herman, Lewis. "The Gift of Tongues." *Screen Writer* 1 (Apr 46) 26–32. How to present characters of different nationalities authentically in terms of speech by using words "with similar universal pronunciation."

Delehanty, Thornton. "Let Them Become Directors!" *Screen Writer* 2 (June 46) 31–34. Former critic, now Hollywood correspondent for *New York Herald Tribune,* notes inadequate recognition for writers because the critic can't watch every step of a picture's evolution.

Simonov, Konstantin. "The Soviet Film Industry." *Screen Writer* 2 (June 46) 17–30. An interview with this Soviet screenwriter in a seminar chaired by Dalton Trumbo; writer's rights, unions, wages.

Kirkley, Donald. "Credits Are Not Enough." *Screen Writer* 2 (Aug 46) 23–26. This film critic for *The Baltimore Sun* argues that most original screenplays are such "morally crooked, deliberate and egregious fakes" that the writer would do better to hide behind anonymity than to demand public credit by reviewers.

De La Roche, Catherine. "The Moscow Script Studio and Soviet Screenwriting." *Penguin F Rev* 2 (Jan 47). *See 4e(8a).*

Goldsmith, I. G. "Made in England." *Screen Writer* 2 (Jan 47) 1–6. Argues that the improvement of the British film stems from the fact that producers now "look upon the work of the writer as the axis upon which the talents and labor of all . . . others revolve."

Gibney, Sheridan. "What Is Screenwriting?" *Screen Writer* 2 (May 47) 10–14. Film is a specialized art form and a film belongs artistically to the screenwriter as much as an opera belongs to (is the creation of) a composer.

Clarke, T. E. B. "Screenwriter and Director in a British Studio." *Screen Writer* 3 (June 47). *See 4e(1).*

Lyon, Sumner. "Other End of the Rainbow." *Screen Writer* 3 (June 47). *See 8a.*

Gibney, Sheridan. "The Future of Screenwriting." *Screen Writer* 3 (July 47) 22–24. Commercialism keeps writers from presenting

honestly their perceptions of truth; all real art, like religion, evaluates, purges, corrects or resolves the inner life of man (*Brief Encounter* an example).

Levin, Meyer. "Writing and Realization." *Screen Writer* 3 (July 47) 4–7. Making the "fact-drama" *Survivors;* how the author (a writer) worked with Herbert Kline, the director, in Palestine with equal production responsibility on this kind of film.

Paxton, John. "Coffee in a Teacup: Notes on an English Adventure." *Hwd Q* 3 (No. 1, Fall 47). *See 4e(1).*

Seaton, George. "One-Track Mind on a Two-Way Ticket." *Screen Writer* 3 (Sep 47) 10–12. Writer-director (for four years) gives advice to screenwriters: make many visits to sets and judge script by the way it works "on its feet"; 20th Century-Fox and RKO actually will let you do it.

Nichols, Dudley. "Film Dollars from Lean Pockets." *Screen Writer* 3 (Oct 47) 19–21. Argues that the 75% British tax and other marketing problems would dissolve if Hollywood made better movies; writers should be allowed to work with directors, not producers.

Nugent, Frank S. "Writer or Director, Who Makes the Movie?" *NYTM* (21 Dec 47) 16–19. A collection of opinions from directors on the relation of the writer to film making.

Natteford, Jack, and Luci Ward. "The Economics of the Horse Opera." *Screen Writer* 3 (No. 8, Jan 48). *See 4k(2).*

Bull, Donald. "Screenwriter Versus Film." *Screen Writer* 3 (Feb 48) 11–13. The new hybrid, the literary-pictorial film, tempts us to believe that the screenwriter really makes the film.

Englund, Ken. "Quick! Boil Some Hot Clichés." *Screen Writer* 3 (No. 9, Feb 48). *See 3b(4).*

Lee, Norman. "Hollywood! You've Been Warned." *Screen Writer* 3 (No. 9, Feb 48). *See 4e(1).*

Swanson, H. N. "An Agent Speaks Up." *Screen Writer* 3 (No. 9, Feb 48). *See 2a(2).*

Seff, Manuel. "The Original Story." *Screen Writer* 3 (Mar 48) 1–5. Some advice on elements that sell.

Field, Martin. "Type-casting Screen Writers." *Penguin F Rev* 6 (Apr 48) 29–32. Is a writer good for only certain types of films?

Leech, Clifford. "Dialogue for Stage and Screen." *Penguin F Rev* 6 (Apr 48) 97–103. The film maker must avoid the appearance of artifice.

Field, Martin. "Type-casting Screen Writers." *Screen Writer* 4 (June–July 48) 11–12+. Some people get to be known as experts on certain subjects.

Zinnemann, Fred. "The Story of *The Search.*" *Screen Writer* 4 (Aug 48) 12–13+. Director of this film pays tribute to Richard Schweizer, the writer, and to Paul Jarrico, who "subtracted" some dialogue.

Krims, Milton. "*Iron Curtain* Diary." *Screen Writer* 4 (Sep 48) 14–15+. Writer's active part in research, production, and editing of *The Iron Curtain*.

Wald, Malvin. "Cops and Writers." *The Writer* 61 (Sep 48) 287–290. Screenwriter of *The Naked City* urges truth as a basis for detective stories.

Pagnol, Marcel. "Rx for Hollywood." *NYTM* (21 Nov 48) 37+. All the "equipment" which Hollywood possesses is incomplete without the force and direction of a dramatist.

Smith, D. C. "The Heart of the Business." *S&S* 17 (No. 68, Winter 48–49) 180–181. The inspired writer is the most important contributor.

Smith, D. C. "Words and Meanings." *S&S* 18 (Spring 49) 33+. A film writer needs inspiration.

Kahan, J. H. "Scripting." *S&S* 19 (Apr 50) 80; 19 (May 50) 128–129.

Dickinson, Thorold. "The Filmwright and the Audience." *S&S* 19 (Mar 50) 20–25. Address to a film society, emphasizing need to develop audiences receptive to innovations; comments on the historical role of directors and writers.

Koch, Howard. "A Playwright Looks at the Filmwright." *S&S* 19 (July 50) 210–214. Commenting on a previous article in *Sight and Sound* by Thorold Dickinson, Koch says an attempt to revitalize film making by stressing anew the role of the director is not valid; films were less complicated in silent days; the screenplay must be accorded the same centrality and protection guaranteed on stage by a Dramatists Guild contract.

"Twice-Told Tales." *Good Housekeeping* 131 (Nov 50) 16. Disguising movie remakes.

Hinsdale, Harriet. "Writing for Stage and Screen." *FIR* 2 (Jan 51) 25–28. Character and idea are still paramount.

Houston, Penelope. "Scripting." *S&S* 19 (Jan 51) 376; (Mar 51) 442. *All About Eve* (Mankiewicz) and *Sunset Boulevard* (Brackett-Wilder): the values and weaknesses of the films and their scripts; *Union Station* an example of taut melodrama.

Dowling, Allan. "Scenarios Are an Art Form." *FIR* 2 (Mar 51) 9–10. They should be developed by offering large cash prizes.

Wilder, Thornton, and Sol Lesser. "*Our Town:* From Stage to Screen." *S&S* 19 (Mar 51) 433–438. Letters exchanged between Wilder and Lesser, dealing with the script written from Wilder's play *Our Town*. Reprinted from *Theatre Arts*.

Seril, William. "Narration vs. Dialogue." *FIR* 2 (Aug–Sep 51) 19–23+. Ironic images contrasted with narration; many other examples.

Vidor, King. "The Story Conference." *FIR* 3 (June–July 52) 266–269. An account of a story conference with Irving Thalberg conducted on the way to and from the funeral of Mabel Normand; from Vidor's forthcoming autobiography.

Vidor, King, and Richard Brooks. "Two Story Conferences." *S&S* 22 (Oct–Dec 52) 85–88. The first story conference is repeated from Vidor's autobiography, not then published, and the second from a novel by Richard Brooks entitled *The Producer*.

Zavattini, Cesare. "Some Ideas on the Cinema." *S&S* 23 (Oct–Dec 53). See *4e(3b)*.

Reinhardt, Gottfried. "Sound Track Narration." *FIR* 4 (Nov 53) 459–460. Producer of *The Red Badge of Courage* emphasizes some of the values of using narration.

Purvis, Harry. "Sure-Fire Dialogue." *FIR* 6 (June–July 55) 278–283. A collection of time-worn phrases used in the class "B" film: mysteries, safaris, pioneers, army life, private eyes, monsters, etc.

Carew, Jim. "Right for the Screen." *F&F* 1 (No. 11, Aug 55) 4. The problems facing the film scriptwriter.

Freund, P. "Write Before You Shoot." *Pop Photog* 37 (Nov 55) 134+.

Kracauer, Siegfried. "The Found Story and the Episode." *F Cult* (No. 7, 1956). See *3a(2)*.

Seaton, George. "A Comparison of the Playwright and the Screen Writer." *QFRTV* 10 (No. 3, Spring 56) 217–226. Hollywood writer-director comments on his and others' work at educational theatre conference in New York; rules for the writer adapting a play to the screen; how theatre now imitates film.

Freed, Edward. "Pre-planning the Documentary Film." *JUFPA* 9 (No. 3, Spring 57). See *8c*.

Mix, Hugh. "Telling the Story—On Film." *JUFPA* 9 (No. 3, Spring 57) 11–12. Suggestions for planning and writing newsreel and documentary programs in educational broadcasting.

Estridge, Robin. "The Screen Writer." *F&F* 3 (No. 6, Mar 57) 13.

Ardrey, Robert. "Hollywood: The Toll of the Frenzied Forties." *Reporter* 16 (21 Mar 57). See *7c*.

Balcon, Sir Michael. "An Author in the Studio." *F&F* 3 (No. 10, July 57) 7+. How clash between actors and film makers might be worked out.

Willis, Ted. "Society and the Writer." *F&F* 3 (No. 12, Sep 57) 15+. This writer's personal approach to scriptwriting.

Chayefsky, Paddy. "Art Films—They're Dedicated Insanity." *F&F* 4 (No. 8, May 58) 7+. On the problems of film writing.

Stonier, G. W. "The Intimate Screen." *S&S* 27

(Autumn 58) 323–325. Film critic writes for television just to gain some experience with the medium; frustrations described.

Russell, Ken. "Ideas for Films." *Film* (No. 19, Jan–Feb 59). *See 5, Ken Russell.*

Wald, Malvin. "The Making of a Bio-Pic." *FIR* 10 (Apr 59) 193–197. A case study of the research and writing for the film *Al Capone,* by one of its writers.

Gotfurt, Frederick. "Where Credit's Due." *F&F* 5 (No. 8, May 59) 8+. The importance of the writer in making good films.

Odets, Clifford. "The Hard Truth About a Writer's Life." *F&F* 6 (No. 4, Jan 60) 27.

Hill, Derek. "A Writers' Wave?" *S&S* 29 (Spring 60) 56–60. John Osborne, Alan Sillitoe, Arnold Wesker, and other new film writers are interviewed on status, adaptation compromises, the possibility of British contributions to film history.

James, T. F. "Man Who Talks Back to John Wayne." *Cosmopolitan* 149 (Aug 60) 60–65. Screenwriter Jimmy Grant's dream of filming *The Alamo* comes true.

Dunne, Philip. "The Animal Called a Writer." *F&F* 7 (No. 12, Sep 61) 33.

Project 20 Staff. "The Anatomy of a Documentary." *JUFPA* 14 (No. 2, Winter 62) 5–7+. Basic lessons learned by NBC-TV documentary film makers, including Richard Hanser, narration writer, Robert Russell Bennett, composer, and Silvio d'Alisera, editor; also notes on recording and mixing sound.

Rose, Ernest D. "Screen Writing and the Delicate Art of Persuasion." *JUFPA* 14 (No. 2, Winter 62) 8–10+. Most of the films produced in universities are persuasive as well as educational; terms and techniques; the special responsibility of the educator.

MacCann, Richard Dyer. "Memorandum for Scriptwriters." *JUFPA* 14 (No. 2, Winter 62) 11. A checklist of questions for scriptwriters to ask themselves about structure, visuals, narration, and dialogue; brief bibliography.

Snyder, Luella. "Are Technical Advisors People?" *JUFPA* 14 (No. 2, Winter 62) 12–14. An essential quality of the university film maker is the ability to pick the brains of the technical advisor and at the same time retain his responsibility for writing and making the film; can this be taught somewhere in the curriculum?

Swain, Dwight V. "Ten Traps." *JUFPA* 14 (No. 2, Winter 62) 3–4+. If the scriptwriter lacks a strong sense of the purpose and audience of a film, he may produce an incoherent and unconvincing film by succumbing to some of these pressures.

Oren, Uri. "Carl Foreman in Israel." *F Com* 2 (No. 3, Summer 64) 40–43. Government information officer reports on a course in screenwriting Foreman gave to eighty in

lectures and to thirty-five others in a workshop.

Hammond, Robert M. "Luis Alcoriza and the Films of Luis Buñuel." *F Her* 1 (No. 1, Fall 65). *See 5, Buñuel.*

Moore, Noel. "The Script Conference." *Take One* 1 (No. 2, 1966) 18–20. A humorous account of what happens at an industry script conference.

Truffaut, François. "A Certain Tendency of the French Cinema." *CdC in Eng* (No. 1, Jan 66). *See 3b(2).*

Mayersberg, Paul. "The Great Rewrite." *S&S* 36 (Spring 67) 72–77. From his *Sight and Sound* book *Hollywood, The Haunted House* (Penguin, 1967) the work of the screenwriter in Hollywood, extracted from various published accounts: Richard Brooks, Dudley Nichols, Frank Gruber, Raymond Chandler, Daniel Taradash.

Heller, Joseph. "How I Found James Bond." *Holiday* 41 (June 67) 123–125+. Humorous report of experiences author had when temporarily assigned to script rewrite on *Casino Royale.*

"Visualizing." *Times Lit Supplement* 3405 (1 June 67) 487. An examination of screenwriting, with emphasis on Frederic Raphael's introduction and script of *Two for the Road.*

Richler, Mordecai. "Writing for the Movies." *Take One* 1 (No. 12, 1968) 15–19. Personal account.

Vogel, Nancy. "Television and Film Writing." *Writer's Dig* 48 (Mar 68) 60–65; (Apr 68) 12+; (June 68) 34–35; 49 (Feb 69) 24–29; 50 (Apr 70) 42–44. How to write for television and film; a practical guide with examples and rules.

Bragg, Melvyn. "Writing for Films." *Times Lit Supplement* 3474 (26 Sep 68) 1076–1077.

Wald, Malvin. "Who Is the Film Author?" *Cinéaste* 2 (No. 3, Winter 68–69) 11–12. Negative view of auteur theory stressing the importance of the scriptwriter.

Foreman, Carl. "The Changing Role of the Film Writer." *JSPG* (Dec 68) 17–19.

Serling, Rod. "The Challenge of the Mass Media to the 20th Century Writer." *JSPG* (Dec 68) 9–12.

Pierson, Frank. "Through the Looking Glass." *F&F* 15 (No. 12, Sep 69) 29–31. On the role of writer and director in films.

Carriere, J.-Claude. "The Buñuel Mystery." *Show* (Apr 70). *See 5, Luis Buñuel.*

Dempsey, Michael. "They Shaft Writers, Don't They?—James Poe Interviewed." *F Com* 6 (No. 4, Winter 70–71) 65–73. Differences among the novel, the Poe screenplay, and the film of *They Shoot Horses, Don't They?* What happened to film, cast, and writer (who was to have been the director) when the production company was taken over by a former agent.

"Screenwriters Symposium." *F Com* 6 (No. 4, Winter 70–71) 86–100. Responses to questionnaires about careers and conflicts from Harry Brown, Delmer Daves, Philip Dunne, John Michael Hayes, Howard Koch, Norman Krasna, Arthur Laurents, Ernest Lehman, Ben Maddow, John Lee Mahin, Daniel Mainwaring, John Paxton, Morrie Ryskind, Stirling Silliphant, Michael Wilson, George Zuckerman. Filmographies.

2d(1). WRITERS' STATUS IN THE INDUSTRY

[See also 3a(3).]

Patterson, Frances Taylor. "Descent into Hollywood." *New Rep* 65 (14 Jan 31) 239–240. Autobiographical sketch of novelist's Hollywood experience: he was pushed aside and his book changed almost beyond recognition.

"Why Playwrights Leave Hollywood." *Lit Dig* 108 (21 Mar 31) 16. Burlesque dialogue by disillusioned Hollywood writer.

"Wodehouse in a Golden Daze." *Lit Dig* 109 (27 June 31) 18. Humorist relates experience as nonwriter in Hollywood.

Simon, Bernard. "Scenarios to the Office Boy." *North Am Rev* 232 (July 31) 76–82. Humorous article on Hollywood screenwriting.

"Mr. Wodehouse Told." *Lit Dig* 110 (25 July 31) 18. Personal experiences of screenwriting.

Howard, Clifford. "Jabberwocky." *Close Up* 9 (No. 1, Mar 32) 55–57. The plight of the author in Hollywood.

Cain, James M. "Camera Obscura." *Am Mercury* 30 (Oct 33) 138–146. Novelist-screenwriter complains of conditions writing for movies.

Upson, William Hazlett. "Why Hollywood Drives You Crazy." *SEP* 208 (21 Dec 35) 5–7+. Disillusioned writer reports unpleasant experience.

Stong, Phil. "Writer in Hollywood." *SRL* (10 Apr 37) 3–4+. Also *Rev of Reviews* (June 37) 43–44. Hollywood's improved attitude toward writers and stories.

Nathan, G. J. "What Hollywood Does to Playwrights." *Scribner's* 102 (Nov 37) 66+. Scathing attack on Hollywood and its allurement for playwrights.

Saroyan, William. "Hollywood Hacks." *Lit Dig* 124 (18 Dec 37) 24.

Fenton, F. "Hollywood Literary Life." *Am Mercury* 45 (Nov 38) 280+. Writing screenplays: getting the job, doing the writing and the rewriting.

Trivers, Paul. "Hollywood Writers Move Up." *New Masses* 48 (14 Sep 43) 20–21. They are making a contribution to the nation.

Trumbo, Dalton. "Samuel Grosvenor Wood: A Footnote." *Screen Writer* 1 (June 45) 22–31. Answer to Sam Wood's attack on writers

which appeared in *The Los Angeles Times* 25 Feb 45 with a Bob White byline.

McCall, Mary. "Facts, Figures on Your Percentage Deal." *Screen Writer* 1 (June 45) 32–35. A rare example of 57% of producer's share paid to this writer ($18,000) for script on *The Sullivans*.

Cole, Lester. "Unhappy Ending." *Hwd Q* 1 (No. 1, Oct 45) 80–84. Screenwriter reports in detail on substitute ending which destroyed the meaning of his script for *Blood on the Sun,* about Japanese imperialism.

Chandler, Raymond. "Writers in Hollywood." *Atlantic* 176 (Nov 45) 50–54. The screenwriter, his status, problems, future.

Dunne, Philip. "An Essay on Dignity." *Screen Writer* 1 (Dec 45) 1–8. Response to Raymond Chandler article in November *Atlantic;* status of the writer in Hollywood; the need for him to be able to control his material; the price the writer would have to pay for such freedom.

Leberthon, T. "Writers Who Were Once Men: Hollywood Continuity Writers." *Cath World* 162 (Dec 45) 219–222. Attack on Hollywood's misuse of the writer.

Herbert, F. Hugh. "The Boys in the Front Room." *Screen Writer* 1 (Jan 46) 11–15. Why attack Sam Wood (June 45) and Cecil B. De Mille (Nov 45) in *Screen Writer*? It is better to achieve greater status in the industry than to be envious of the power of individuals.

Lawson, John H. "Hollywood—Illusion and Reality." *Hwd Q* 1 (No. 2, Jan 46) 231–233. Screenwriter defends Hollywood writers from some stereotyped accusations by Raymond Chandler in the November *Atlantic.*

Scully, Frank. "The Battle of Billing." *Screen Writer* 1 (Mar 46) 27–31. On the status of the writer in Hollywood—the need for better recognition, more money, and the name above the title.

"Movie Companies Look to Detective Story Writers for the New Psychological Film." *Publishers Weekly* 149 (9 Mar 46) 1515–1516.

Harari, Robert. "Book Review—*Hollywood Reporter* Style." *Screen Writer* 2 (June 46). See 3b(4).

McCall, Mary C., Jr. "The Unlick'd Bear Whelp." *Screen Writer* 2 (Aug 46) 27–30. Argues against economic security for screenwriters and for more concern with film as a medium of artistic expression.

Mealand, R. "Are Writers Authors?" *Publishers Weekly* 150 (3 Aug 46) 464–466. The Hollywood screenwriter, his problems, position, and technique.

Cole, Lester. "Re: '. . . Coming of Age . . .' " *Screen Writer* 2 (Oct 46) 20–24. Argues in favor of the proposed annual minimum wage for writers; opposes article by Mary McCall in August issue.

Sherwood, Robert. "They're Film Writers, Not Juke Boxes." *NYTM* (1 Dec 46) 15+. A plea for more authority for the screenwriter.

Kahn, Gordon. "Letter from Mexico." *Screen Writer* 3 (June 47). See 4h(1).

Box, Sydney. "A New Deal for Film Writers." *Penguin F Rev* 3 (Aug 47) 49–52. Their current position; what should be done.

Gangelin, Paul. "What's Happening to Our Jobs?" *Screen Writer* 3 (Aug 47) 26–27. Unemployment is bound to increase as "B" picture production decreases.

Stevenson, Philip. "Where Credit Is Due." *Screen Writer* 3 (Aug 47) 31–33. Condemns the Hollywood system of screenwriting piece-work—giving credit to all the writers on a project, he argues, will expose this faulty system.

Rodell, John S. "Authority and the Screen Writer." *Screen Writer* 3 (Nov 47) 8–10. The writer should recognize that in films his authority must be limited.

Vargas, A. L. "The Future of the British Film Writer." *S&S* 16 (No. 64, Winter 47–48). *See 4e(1).*

Clarke, T. E. B. "British Writers Speak Out." *Screen Writer* 3 (No. 8, Jan 48) 11–13. Grievances: too many writers on one script and lack of reference to writers by critics or in publicity.

Morgan, Guy. "Cash Down and No Credit." *Penguin F Rev* 6 (Apr 48) 15–28. Grievances of British screenwriters revealed in answers to questionnaire.

Pascal, Ernest. "What IS a Screen Writer?" *Screen Writer* 3 (Apr 48) 2–4. He should not be an employee but an independent contractor.

Herczeg, Geza. "What's Wrong with Hollywood." *UN World* 2 (June 48) 44–45. Screenwriter says: It kills originality—but cannot do otherwise.

Field, Martin. "Hollywood Report on a 'Trend.'" *Penguin F Rev* 9 (May 49) 100–102. At first it was artistic for writers to become directors, now it's economical.

Hine, Al. "Movies." *Holiday* 6 (Oct 49) 21. "Screen writers now trust their own imaginations and tell their own stories instead of picking other people's brains."

Read, Jan. "'Pregnant with Jeopardy.'" *Hwd Q* 4 (No. 4, Summer 50) 354–359. Screenwriter reports on low estate of screenwriters in England, except for Ealing Studio under Michael Balcon.

Sheldon, Sidney. "The Hollywood Writer." *Th Arts* 35 (Aug 51) 31. According to this screenwriter, now the story's the thing.

Algren, Nelson. "Hollywood Djinn." *Nation* 177 (25 July 53) 68–70. Hilarious account of a writer's introduction to Hollywood.

Lambert, Gavin. "Shadow upon Shadow upon Shadow." *S&S* 23 (Oct–Dec 53) 78–83. The coming of English author Hugh Walpole to Hollywood during the mid-1930s to help adapt *David Copperfield, Vanessa,* and *Little Lord Fauntleroy.*

Bronner, Edwin. "Old Wine in New Bottles." *FIR* 6 (June–July 55) 260–263. List of writers from the East who came to Hollywood after 1928.

Gray, Hugh. "When in Rome . . . (Part II)." *QFRTV* 10 (No. 4, Summer 56) 344–353. Writer who worked on *Ulysses* tells problems and why there are so many writing credits on such films. See also "When in Rome (Part I)." *Hwd Q* 10 (No. 3, Spring 56) 262–272.

Kazan, Elia. "Writers and Motion Pictures." *Atlantic* 199 (Apr 57) 67–70. From introduction to published version of Budd Schulberg's *A Face in the Crowd;* the writer should not have such a subordinate role in Hollywood.

Kazan, Elia. "The Writer and Motion Pictures." *S&S* 27 (Summer 57) 21–24. Preface to Budd Schulberg's script *A Face in the Crowd,* published in America after this article was written: "There cannot be a fine picture without a fine script. There cannot be a fine script without a first-class writer, and a first-class writer won't do first-class work unless he feels the picture is his."

Wesley, I. P. "How Writers Work: Hollywood." *Cosmopolitan* 145 (Aug 58) 30–31.

Schulberg, B. "Writer and Hollywood." *Harper's* 219 (Oct 59) 132–137. Historical changes in attitude in Hollywood toward the job of the writer.

Tunberg, Karl. "Uncle Tom's Cabin Cruiser." *JSPG* (Mar 60) 11–13. Increased importance of the screenwriter as he begins to direct and produce his own scripts.

Fadiman, William. "Unread Writers of Hollywood." *Sat Rev* 43 (4 June 60) 10–12+. Screenwriters should be better known to the public.

Fadiman, William. "The Typewriter Jungle." *F&F* 7 (No. 3, Dec 60) 8+. The executive story editor of Columbia Pictures discusses the position of Hollywood writers.

Knight, Arthur. "Make It True." *Sat Rev* 44 (2 Sep 61) 28. Playwright William Inge objects to recent "remakes."

Mortimer, John. "Life in Celluloid." *Spectator* 207 (24 Nov 61) 741–743. Personal recollections of a scriptwriter in Great Britain and his opinions about the cinema.

Fuchs, Daniel. "Writing for the Movies." *Commentary* 33 (Feb 62) 104–116. Personal recollection of the Hollywood of the 1940s.

"Shaw Strikes Back." *Newswk* 60 (5 Nov 62)

110+. Author Irwin Shaw explains troubles of a Hollywood screenwriter and why he turned producer.

Alpert, Hollis. "The Joys of Uncertainty." *Sat Rev* 45 (29 Dec 62) 16–17. The difficulties a screenwriter faces in attempting to protect what he's written from the hands of members of the production studio.

"Great Ideas That Never Got Filmed." *Show* 3 (Aug 63) 59–62+. Poll of top screenwriters about unproduced scenarios; includes responses from Ben Hecht, Joseph L. Mankiewicz, Ring Lardner, Jr., I. A. L. Diamond, *et al.*

Knight, Arthur. "The Big Novel Syndrome." *Sat Rev* 46 (31 Aug 63) 18. Position of the screenwriter in Hollywood.

Reynolds, P. R. "Hollywood Screen Writers: Who Are They and How Do They Work?" *Sat Rev* 49 (9 July 66) 52–53+.

Yafa, Stephen H. "My, How Fast They Learn." *Playboy* 14 (No. 5, May 67) 84. Neophyte screenwriter in Hollywood works with producer Harold Hecht; how original scripts are conceived.

Silliphant, Stirling. "The Word Is Symbiosis." *Action* 3 (No. 1, Jan–Feb 68) 16–18. A Hollywood writer discusses the virtues of working closely with directors Norman Jewison, Ralph Nelson, and John Sturges.

Farber, Stephen. "The Writer in American Films." *FQ* 21 (No. 4, Summer 68) 2–13. "The main problem in American films is still with material"; interviews with Robert Benton and David Newman, screenwriters for *Bonnie and Clyde,* and John Boorman, director of *Point Blank.*

Adamson, Joseph. "The Seventeen Preliminary Scripts of *A Day at the Races.*" *CJ* 8 (No. 2, Spring 69) 2–9. The problems Robert Pirosh and George Seaton had with Irving Thalberg and the Marx Brothers; descriptions of many changes in the story and the gags.

Alpert, Hollis. "But Who Wrote the Movie?" *Sat Rev* 53 (26 Dec 70) 8–11. The screenwriter's anonymity, his relationship to the film, to the director; part of report on "Writing and the Film."

Corliss, Richard. "The Hollywood Screenwriter." *F Com* 6 (No. 4, Winter 70–71) 4–7. Introduction to entire issue devoted to screenwriters: The auteur of a film may in many cases be the man who wrote it, and this means there is much more research to be done beyond directorial pantheons and filmographies.

Foreman, Carl. "Confessions of a Frustrated Screenwriter." *F Com* 6 (No. 4, Winter 70–71) 22–25. Problems with producer-collaborators and with critics, who either blame the script or praise the director without mentioning the script; filmography of Foreman films.

2d(2). STORY EDITORS, SCRIPT MARKETING, RIGHTS

[See also 7c(5).]

Burford, Roger. "Published Scenarios." *Close Up* 10 (No. 1, Mar 33) 50–53. Problems involved in, and the need for, published film scenarios.

Berchtold, William E. "Men Behind Your Movie Diet." *New Outlook* 164 (Nov 34) 23–31+. Profiles of story editors Samuel Marx, Kate Corbaley, Jeff Lazarus, and others.

Beranger, Clara. "Let Hollywood Discover You." *Delineator* 128 (Apr 36) 4+. By film-writing teacher at USC.

"Twice-Sold Tales." *SEP* 209 (1 Aug 36) 10–11+. How movie stories are found, synopsized, sold.

Croy, H. "Selling Stories to the Movies." *Harper's* 176 (Dec 37) 96–102. Firsthand account of the complexities and exasperations a writer encounters in the movie business.

Porter, V. "Copyright, 1938, by ———; Literary Agent as a Copyright Detective." *SEP* 211 (19 Nov 38) 25+. The problems in tracking down and clearing the rights of a novel or drama to be filmed; case history.

Barber, D. A. "Hollywood Situation: Writing for the Movies." *Writer* 53 (July 40) 205–207. Advice to the writer; what the studios buy, how they buy it, and where it goes from there.

Brown, Ned. "Literary Agent, Hollywood Style." *Publishers Weekly* 139 (28 June 41) 2530–2532. Arranging sales of movie rights on books.

"$500,000 Down; Film Rights for *Life with Father.*" *Time* 40 (14 Sep 42) 40.

Tigrett, J. B., and M. Dawson. "Hey! You Stole My Story." *SEP* 215 (1 May 43) 22+. Irate "authors" claim that what's on the screen is their own brainchild.

Pratt, Theodore. "From the Novel by . . ." *Atlantic* 175 (Mar 45) 109–112. About deals for picture sales by an author who has sold three to Hollywood.

Wood, Audrey. "Too Fast and Too Soon." *Screen Writer* 1 (Aug 45) 35–38. Eastern agent for playwrights advises film writers on Broadway contracts.

Cohn, Morris E. "Author's Moral Rights: Film and Radio." *Hwd Q* 1 (No. 1, Oct 45) 69–79. Counsel for Screen Writers Guild studies European legal doctrine.

Klorer, John. "Writing for Percentage." *Screen Writer* 1 (Feb 46) 7–10. Screenwriters can have royalties or participation, particularly in independent productions.

Harper, Patricia. "Your Minimum Basic Flat Deal." *Screen Writer* 1 (Apr 46) 19–25.

Contracts for screenplays, treatments, first drafts, options, etc.

Wear, David, and Budd Lesser. "Original Syns." *Screen Writer* 1 (Apr 46) 8–13. Two story analysts describe the importance of this work on "synopses," how the writer should adjust to the process.

Cain, James M. "The Opening Gun." *Screen Writer* 1 (May 46) 6–9. About a court action involving plagiarism and a plea for action by the Screen Writers Guild (in such cases) on behalf of writers.

Lavery, Emmet. "A Time for Action." *Screen Writer* 1 (May 46) 1–5. The Screen Writers Guild agreement covers only employment; now is the time to propose copyright protection and percentage licensing arrangements for material sold directly for the screen.

Field, Martin. "Who Works for Nothing?" *Screen Writer* 2 (June 46) 37–40. Condemns the studios' practice of asking for "something on paper" without pay; work "on speculation," Screen Writers Guild notes, violates guild rules.

Cohn, Morris E. "Booby Traps." *Screen Writer* 2 (Sep 46) 34–36. On the screenwriter's rights, contracts, control of material.

Field, Martin. "Independents' Day." *Screen Writer* 2 (Sep 46) 12–17. On the increase of independent film production and its advantages and disadvantages; percentage deals, taxation, and other economic subjects.

Dimsdale, Howard, and Guy Endore. "Want to Buy the Brooklyn Bridge?" *Screen Writer* 2 (Oct 46) 11–14. Unlike an oil well, *Alice in Wonderland* is free for anybody to use after fifty-six years; the concept of public domain can also be used as a threat against the modern writer.

Field, Martin. "Read 'Em and Weep." *Screen Writer* 2 (Dec 46) 14–21. A defense of the proposed American Authors' Authority and several case histories of films made without proper remuneration for the author of the original idea.

Bromfield, Louis, James M. Cain, Taylor Caldwell, and Theodore Pratt. "The Screen Writer's Special Supplement on the American Authors' Authority." *Screen Writer* 2 (Mar 47) 1–63. Pro and con articles on the scheme for leasing instead of selling scripts outright.

Field, Martin. "Twice-Sold Tales." *Screen Writer* 2 (May 47) 1–9. Discusses the losses to writers when their original stories are resold, rather than produced, by a studio.

Lavery, Emmet. "Snowball in the Spring." *Screen Writer* 3 (June 47) 1–4. Favors a quick decision on whether or not an American Authors' Authority should be established and argues in its favor.

Bernstein, Harry. "Reading for the Movies." *Screen Writer* 3 (July 47) 24–27. Exposé of the miserable working conditions and low pay of freelance "readers" who synopsize and recommend novels for movie companies.

Shaw, George Bernard. "Authors and Their Rights." *Screen Writer* 3 (Aug 47) 1–2. Shaw describes the specific conditions and rules that would cause him to join the proposed American Authors' Authority; he urges a strong bargaining union unlike the incompetent Authors' League of America; brief reply by Oscar Hammerstein II.

Lardner, Ring, Jr. "First Steps in Arithmetic." *Screen Writer* 3 (Aug 47) 16–20. The junior writer has to compete against 1,300 others for about 200 steady jobs; minimum guarantees should be increased and apprentices abolished; writers don't get enough of the gross.

Cole, Lester. "A Fundamental Right?" *Screen Writer* 3 (Aug 47) 21–23. Argues that, for the salary received from the producer, writers should sell an option only—that is, "the right *not* to produce"; the right of the producer to make the film should be covered by royalties, like the playwright's.

Field, Martin. "No Applause for These Encores." *Screen Writer* 3 (Aug 47) 24–25. Writers should receive some remuneration for reissues of pictures.

"What of the Market for Originals?" *Screen Writer* 3 (Aug 47) 28–30. It's a lot more profitable to write novels or plays; report of economic subcommittee of Writers Guild.

Cohn, Morris E. "What Is a License of Literary Property?" *Screen Writer* 3 (Sep 47) 27–28. Argues for leasing screenplays for a specific period of time by the writer to the studio, not sold to the studio.

Goldwyn, Samuel, James Hilton, Stephen Longstreet, Irving Pichel, Howard Lindsay, David Selznick, Millen Brand. "The Writer's Share." *Screen Writer* 3 (No. 4, Sep 47) 29–33. Should an increasing percentage of industry gross be received by writers? Producers, writers, and others disagree on actual contribution of writers to finished product and the value of across-the-board increases for all writers.

Fadiman, William J. "Sources of Movies." *Annals Am Acad Polit and Soc Sci* 254 (Nov 47) 37–40. The story departments of the studios (readers and film writers); casting; star making.

Pratt, Theodore. "Kindergarten of Authors' Economics." *Screen Writer* 3 (Nov 47) 13–14. Opposition attitudes to Authors' Authority idea.

Longstreet, Stephen. "Markets for Words." *Screen Writer* 3 (No. 8, Jan 48) 2–7. If you're unemployed, write a novel or an article.

Taylor, Dwight. "The Story-Expert." *Screen Writer* 3 (Mar 48) 35–37. This emissary from the producer has a certain jargon of objections such as "contrived" or "corny" which take the life out of a script—and out of the movie business.

Goldwyn, Samuel. "Where Do You Go from Here?" *Screen Writer* 3 (Apr 48) 19–21. The trouble with the screenwriter is that he thinks too much about money and doesn't act like "a free artist" (quoted from Dudley Nichols); Goldwyn claims he's willing to give a percentage of the profits to writers of originals.

Gangelin, Paul. "The Goldwyn Fallacy." *Screen Writer* 3 (May 48) 14–16. If writers are to be encouraged to express their inner selves as artists, then producers must be willing to reach specialized audiences. See also statement by Samuel Goldwyn in April issue.

Young, Collier. "In Defense of Story Experts." *Screen Writer* 4 (June–July 48) 5+. Response to article by Dwight Taylor in March issue; producer's story assistant may save writer from many aches and mistakes.

MacMullan, Hugh. "Another Vicious Circle." *Screen Writer* 4 (Sep 48) 12–13+. Why do writers' agents dump a deluge of material on a story editor who has clearly explained what kind he wants?

Peck, Seymour. "TV to LA: Plays for Sale." *NYTM* (15 May 55) 26–27. After the success of *Marty,* TV playwrights find an eager market for their work in Hollywood, sometimes before it appears on TV.

Campbell, Kay. "Key to Hollywood." *Writer* 70 (Apr 57) 14–15. Tips for writers who want to sell material to Hollywood.

Campbell, Kay. "Report from Hollywood." *Writer* 71 (June 58) 22–23. About Arthur Kramer, story editor at 20th Century-Fox.

Wald, Jerry. "Writing for Motion Pictures." *Writer* 74 (Feb 61) 5–6+. Tips about the market from a film producer.

Nathan, Paul. "Wonderland of Subsidiary Rights." *Sat Rev* 46 (14 Dec 63) 58–59+. Article on subsidiary rights to literature (novels, biographies, etc.) includes the selling of such rights to film production companies.

Mitgang, Herbert. "Hot Property: A Hilarious Insight into What Happens to a Novel Kissed by Hollywood." *Sat Rev* 48 (2 Oct 65) 39–40. His experience with his novel *The Return* as a Hollywood "property."

2d(3). WRITERS' ORGANIZATIONS

[See also 6c(2).]

Mangold, W. P. "Hollywood Fights Its Writers." *New Rep* 87 (27 May 36) 70–71. The split in the Writers Guild and the formation of a company union.

Broun, Heywood. "Broun's Page." *Nation* 142 (27 May 36) 678. Rupert Hughes leaves the "Soviet system" of the Screen Writers Guild in order to support "Americanism" and his employers; Broun is contemptuous of his action. Response by Rupert Hughes in *Nation* 142 (10 June 36) 755–756.

Cabarus, Stephen. "Hollywood Scribes Strike? Ho! Ho!" *CSMM* (12 Aug 36) 5+. How the producers bought off most of the Writers Guild membership instead of signing an agreement.

"Bad News from Hollywood." *New Rep* 88 (19 Aug 36) 35. The fight to crush the Screen Writers Guild goes on.

Barzman, Ben. "Hollywood Writer Goes to War." *Calif Arts and Arch* 59 (No. 10, Nov 42) 24. The work of the Hollywood Writers Mobilization.

Pomerance, William. "They're Not All Swimming Pools." *Screen Writer* 1 (July 45) 24–27. About unions, "closed shops," the Screen Writers Guild's role in protecting the writer, the "pool" of available writers.

Rapf, Maurice. "Credit Arbitration Isn't Simple." *Screen Writer* 1 (July 45) 31–36. The present Screen Writers Guild procedure for determining who gets credit on the screen.

Rapf, Maurice. "The Credits Question." *Screen Writer* 1 (Feb 46) 25–29. Screen Writers Guild arbitration procedures in settling disputes about credits.

Cain, James M. "An American Authors' Authority." *Screen Writer* 2 (July 46) 1–18. A proposal to establish an agency modeled somewhat after ASCAP, to protect infringed rights of writers, especially copyright; based on Screen Writers Guild committee discussions.

Lindsay, Howard. "The Way Ahead." *Screen Writer* 2 (Sep 46) 7–9. Describes the obstacles that lie in the path of establishing an "American Authors' Authority," as, for example, the need to change the copyright law.

Cain, James M. "Just What Is A.A.A.?" *Screen Writer* 2 (Oct 46) 1–4. Describes how the proposed American Authors' Authority would protect the rights of the writer as "a creator of properties."

Dunne, Philip. "SWG—Trade Union or Writers' Protective Association?" *Screen Writer* 2 (Oct 46) 5–10.

Ring, Frances Kroll. "The Case of the Cream Puffs." *Hwd Q* 2 (No. 1, Oct 46) 30–34. Duties of screen story analysts; comments on strike of their small guild in 1945.

Dunne, Philip. "This Issue of 'Politics.'" *Screen Writer* 2 (Dec 46) 1–9. An argument for keeping pertinent political issues such as the Wagner Act before the Screen Writers Guild, because, like all employees' organizations, the Guild can't avoid being political.

Maltz, Albert. "Authors to Screen Writers: A Guide to Common Action." *Screen Writer*

2 (Dec 46) 34–41. On the nature of the Authors Guild and its activities; and a plea for screenwriters to support it.

Fuller, Samuel. "Joe Loved Everybody." *Screen Writer* 2 (Feb 47) 15–18. An imaginary case of how a writer might be cheated of his rights because he hasn't the protection of the proposed American Authors' Authority.

Dunne, Philip, and Morris E. Cohn. "Absolutely, Rep. Hartley—Positively, Sen. Taft." *Screen Writer* 3 (Sep 47) 1–4. An analysis of the Taft-Hartley Act which emphasizes its detrimental effect upon the Screen Writers Guild.

McCall, Mary. "A Brief History of the Guild." *Screen Writer* 3 (Apr 48) 25–31. From 1933 to 1943, summaries of meetings, officers, actions, and the conflict with the producers' organization of the Screen Playwrights group.

"SWG Takes Court Action Charging Blacklist Conspiracy." *Screen Writer* 4 (June–July 48). See 7c(2d).

Poe, Elisabeth. "Credits and Oscars." *Nation* 184 (30 Mar 57) 267–269. Dispute about Guild credits for blacklisted writers.

"Whose River Kwai?" *Newswk* 51 (24 Mar 58) 104. Dispute over the screenplay for *The Bridge on the River Kwai*.

"Gold in the Reruns." *Newswk* 54 (28 Dec 59) 53. Hollywood writers threatening to walk out on studios in dispute over resale of movies to TV.

Knight, Arthur. "Writers' Dilemma." *Sat Rev* 52 (26 Apr 69) 51. Writers Guild of America conference discusses the question of writer control.

2d(4). SCRIPTS AND EXTRACTS

Eisenstein, S. M. "An American Tragedy." *Close Up* 10 (No. 2, June 33) 109–124. Director discusses his proposed scenario.

Hart, Moss, and George S. Kaufman. *"You Can't Take It with You."* *Cinema Arts* 1 (No. 3, Sep 37) 62. Highlights from the comedy script.

Lawson, John Howard. "Film Sequence: *Blockade.*" *One Act Play Mag* (Oct 38) 405–420. An excerpt from screenplay by Lawson.

Agee, James. *"Man's Fate."* *Films* 1 (No. 1, Nov 39) 51–60. Notes for a film treatment of the Malraux novel.

Gorky, Maxim. *"Descent to the Lower Depths."* *Films* 1 (No. 1, Nov 39) 40–50. Unfinished sketch for scenario of his own play, found by literary executors, translated by Alexander Bakshy.

Rukeyser, Muriel. "Gauley Bridge." *Films* 1 (No. 3, Summer 40) 51–64. Notes for film treatment based on hearings in Washington on the deaths of hundreds of men who drilled a tunnel through a silica hill; the author also wrote a poem about it, "The Book of the Dead."

Saroyan, William. *"Human Comedy."* *Th Arts* 26 (Sep 42) 585–589. Excerpt from the screenplay.

Johnson, N. *"Pied Piper."* *Scholastic* 41 (28 Sep 42) 19–21. Excerpt from the movie scenario of Nevil Shute's novel.

"Journey for Margaret." *Scholastic* 41 (11 Jan 43) 17–19. Excerpt from the screenplay.

Nichols, Dudley, and René Clair. *"It Happened Tomorrow:* Excerpts from the Script." *Th Arts* 28 (June 44) 375–379+.

Butler, Frank. "A Medal for Benny." *Screen Writer* 1 (July 45) 8–14. Extract from screenplay.

Hartman, Don, Melville Shavelson, and Philip Rapp. *"Wonder Man."* *Screen Writer* 1 (Aug 45) 14–22. A short scene from this Goldwyn production starring Danny Kaye.

Eisenstein, Sergei M. *"Ivan the Terrible."* *Life and Letters* 47 (Nov 45) 91–107. Scenario for *Ivan the Terrible,* Parts I and II, translated by Herbert Marshall. Continued Dec–Feb 45–46, May–July 46.

Maddow, Ben. *"Death and Mathematics:* A Film on the Meaning of Science." *Hwd Q* 1 (No. 2, Jan 46) 173–184. Documentary script, with tentative narration, about the atomic bomb, written for Office of War Information overseas branch but never produced; collaborator Irving Lerner adds a director's note.

Lardner, Ring, Jr., Maurice Rapf, John Hubley, and Phil Eastman. *"Brotherhood of Man:* A Script." *Hwd Q* 1 (No. 4, July 46) 353–359. Animation documentary based on book, *Races of Mankind,* with thirty-two frames reproduced. See also note on use of film by occupation government in Germany, *Hwd Q* 2 (No. 3, Apr 47) 305.

"Brotherhood of Man." *Arts & Arch* 63 (Dec 46) 22–25. A script of animation film for armed forces as an antidote to racial prejudice.

Phillips, James E. "Adapted from a Play by W. Shakespeare." *Hwd Q* 2 (No. 1, Oct 46) 82–90. Analysis of Laurence Olivier's cutting of *Henry V* for film and of *Richard III* for radio.

Shakespeare, William, and Laurence Olivier. *"Hamlet:* The Play and the Screenplay." *Hwd Q* 3 (No. 3, Spring 48) 293–300. Parallel printing of "nunnery scene" in *Hamlet* as Shakespeare wrote it and as Olivier interpreted it in the screenplay for his film by Allan Dent.

Newport, Raymond. "Why Not Miniature Scripts?" *S&S* 18 (Spring 49) 52. Plea for publishing original screenplays.

Akutagawa, Ryunosuke. *"San Sebastian:* A Scenario." (Tr. by Arthur Waley.) *Horizon*

20 (No. 115, Sep 49). Japanese author who died in 1927 wrote brief visual shot-list about a converted Christian forced to hide in the mountains.

Dickinson, Thorold. "*The Mayor of Casterbridge.*" *S&S* 19 (Jan 51) 363–371. In 1949, Associated British Picture Corporation told Wolfgang Wilhelm and Thorold Dickinson to write a screenplay for the Thomas Hardy novel; it seemed doubtful that the picture would ever be made; story stills drawn by John Howell, excerpts from the screenplay, and notes about the adaptation.

Mackendrick, Alexander, *et al.* "In the Script: *The Man in the White Suit, Kind Hearts and Coronets, David,* and *No Highway.*" *S&S* 21 (Oct–Dec 51) 57–59+. Excerpts from shooting scripts of British pictures.

Agee, James, *et al.* "The African Queen." *Sequence* (No. 14, 1952) 39–47. Excerpts from the screenplay.

Clarke, T. E. B. "In the Script: *Encore.*" *S&S* 21 (Jan–Mar 52) 112–114+. An excerpt from *The Ant and the Grasshopper,* one of the episodes in *Encore;* the excerpted portion (three pages) occupied only eight lines of Somerset Maugham's original story.

Williams, Tennessee. "In the Script: *A Streetcar Named Desire.*" *S&S* 21 (Apr–June 52) 173–175. An excerpt from the final scenes of Kazan's shooting script; Williams also worked on the film version. Two slightly different endings to the final scene are presented together with the last five speeches of the play.

Natanson, Jacques, and Max Ophuls. "In the Script: *Le Plaisir.*" *S&S* 22 (July–Sep 52) 32–34. A three-page excerpt from the script of *La Maison Tellier,* one of three short stories by Guy de Maupassant released under the title *Le Plaisir.*

Houseman, John. "*Julius Caesar:* Mr. Mankiewicz' Shooting Script." *QFRTV* 8 (No. 2, Winter 53) 109–124. Producer shows how writer-director prepares shooting script from play; two excerpts from script—the assassination and the scene leading up to Antony's oration.

Houston, Penelope. "Cukor and the Kanins." *S&S* 24 (Spring 55) 184–191+. Director George Cukor and writer team Garson Kanin and Ruth Gordon (Mrs. Kanin) are the hope for the future of good screen comedy; their careers and some of the films they made together; included is a sequence from the script of *The Marrying Kind.*

von Stroheim, Erich. "Two Synopses." *F Cult* 1 (No. 1, 1955) 33–35. The "original and unaltered" summary plots of *Walking Down Broadway* and *Queen Kelly.*

Pegge, C. Denis. "*Caligari:* Its Innovations in Editing." *QFRTV* 11 (No. 2, Winter 56). *See 2f.*

Gance, Abel, and Nelly Kaplan. "*The Kingdom of the Earth.*" *F Cult* 3 (No. 15, 1957) 10–13; 4 (No. 16, 1958) 14–16. Excerpts from a script for their planned first Polyvision production about the peaceful uses of nuclear force; two parts in successive issues.

Wilder, Billy. "*Love in the Afternoon.*" *F&F* 3 (No. 5, Feb 57) 8–10. An extract from the film script.

Agee, James, Salvador Dali, Maxim Gorki, Henry Miller, Romain Rolland, Dylan Thomas. "Unfilmed Scenarios." *Cinemages* 9 (Aug 58) 1–86. With brief biographical notes on each author.

Cornelius, Henry. "*Next to No Time!*" *F&F* 5 (No. 1, Oct 58) 27–28. Extract from this film.

Brunius, Jacques. "Ideas for Films." *Film* (No. 18, Nov–Dec 58) 12–14. An analysis of the unfilmed screenplays published in *Cinemages* No. 9.

DeLaurot, Edouard. "*Vive la Guerre!*" *F Cult* (No. 20, 1959). See *4k(12).*

Murnau, F. W., and Robert J. Flaherty. "Turia, an Original Story." *F Cult* (No. 20, 1959) 17–26. More nearly Flaherty's conception for *Tabu,* according to Richard Griffith.

Murnau, F. W., and Robert J. Flaherty. "*Tabu* (Taboo), a Story of the South Seas." *F Cult* (No. 20, 1959) 27–38. This version is close to F. W. Murnau's completed film.

Zavattini, Cesare. "First Outline for a Film on Peace." *F Cult* (No. 20, 1959). See *4k(12).*

Castellani, Renato. "*Nella Citta l'Inferno.*" *F&F* 5 (No. 7, Apr 59) 9+. Extracts from the script *Hell in the City.*

Bergman, Ingmar. "*Wood Painting.*" *TDR* 6 (No. 2, 1961) 140–152. A morality play written as an exercise for Bergman's acting classes which formed the basis for the film *The Seventh Seal.*

Lane, John Francis. "The Intellectuals of *La Dolce Vita.*" *F&F* 7 (No. 4, Jan 61) 14+. Translation of a scene from Fellini's *La Dolce Vita.*

Chukhrai, Grigori, and Valentine Yezhov. "*Ballad of a Soldier.*" *F&F* 7 (No. 10, July 61) 22–23+. Extract from the script.

Odets, Clifford. "*Wild in the Country.*" *F&F* 7 (No. 11, Aug 61) 17–18. Extract from the script.

Visconti, Luchino. "*Rocco and His Brothers.*" *F&F* 7 (No. 12, Sep 61) 19–21+. Extract.

Williams, Tennessee. "*The Roman Spring of Mrs. Stone.*" *F&F* 8 (No. 1, Oct 61) 20–21+. Extract.

Andrzejewski, Jerzy, and Jerzy Skolimowski. "*The Innocent Sorcerers.*" *F&F* 8 (No. 2, Nov 61) 16–17+. Extract.

Jennings, Humphrey. "Working Sketches of an Orchestra." *FQ* 15 (No. 2, Winter 61–62). *See 5, Humphrey Jennings.*

"The Innocents." F&F 8 (No. 3, Dec 61) 14–15+. Extract.

Godard, Jean-Luc. "Scenario of *Vivre Sa Vie.*" F Cult (No. 26, 1962) 52.

"Billy Budd." F&F 8 (No. 4, Jan 62) 16–18+. Extract.

Inge, William. *"Splendour in the Grass."* F&F 8 (No. 5, Feb 62) 22–23+. Extract.

Wilder, Billy, and I. A. L. Diamond. *"One, Two, Three."* F&F 8 (No. 6, Mar 62) 13–15+. Extract.

Moffat, Ivan. *"Tender Is the Night."* F&F 8 (No. 7, Apr 62) 18–19+. Extract.

"No Method: Vincente Minnelli." *Movie* (No. 1, June 62). See 5, Vincente Minnelli.

Rae, John. *"Reach for Glory."* F&F 8 (No. 9, June 62) 24–25+. Extract.

Sillitoe, Alan. *"The Loneliness of the Long-Distance Runner."* F&F 8 (No. 12, Sep 62) 10–13. Extract.

Cameron, Ian. "Chris Marker: *Cuba, Si! Censor, No!"* *Movie* (No. 3, Oct 62). See 8c(4).

"Cleo from 5 to 7." F&F 9 (No. 3, Dec 62) 22–23. Extract from Agnès Varda's screenplay.

Smith, Jack, and Ken Jacobs. "Soundtrack of *Blonde Cobra.*" F Cult (No. 29, 1963) 2+. From the authors' film.

Mailer, Norman. *"The Last Night."* Esq 60 (Dec 63) 151+. A treatment for a proposed movie; with a bang, not a whimper—is that the way the world ends?

Rossellini, Roberto, and Federico Fellini. "*Paisan,* Sixth Episode." F Cult (No. 31, 1963–1964) 61–67. Scenario for the episode on the Po River.

"The Movie That Shocked the French." *Show* 4 (Sep 64) 68–74+. Condensed shooting script (in English) of *Les Amitiés Particulières (Special Friendships),* written by Pierre Bost and translated by Harold Salemson.

"The Narration of *The River.*" F Com 3 (No. 2, Spring 65) 57–60.

" 'The Future Is Entirely Ours'—the Sound-and-Picture Outline for Leni Riefenstahl's *Triumph of the Will.*" F Com 3 (No. 1, Winter 65) 16–23. Description in full is followed by Marshall Lewis' program notes for the New Yorker Theatre when the film was shown there 27 June 1960.

Lynch, Dennis. "The Evolution of a Film Script." JUFPA 17 (No. 1, 1965) 10–15. Changes from outline to script to film in University of Iowa production about hearing tests.

"Years of Lightning, Day of Drums." F Com 4 (Nos. 1–2, Fall–Winter 67). See 7f(1b).

Godard, Jean-Luc. "*A Woman Is a Woman:* Scenario." CdC in English (No. 12, Dec 67) 34–37. Summary of script based on idea by Geneviève Cluny.

Lyons, Timothy. *"The Gold Rush."* Cinema (Calif) 4 (No. 2, Summer 68) 17–44. Transcript of the shots and titles of the Chaplin film.

Elkin, Stanley. *"The Six-Year-Old Man."* Esq 70 (Dec 68) 142–145+. Text of the screenplay.

Segal, E. *"R.P.M."* Yale Lit Mag 140 (1970) 13–16. A short screenplay about student/administration conflict in a fictional university.

Burgess, Anthony. "To Be or Not to Be in Love with You." *Show* (Jan 70) 75–80+. His script on the life of Shakespeare for Warner Brothers (working title: *The Bawdy Bard*); excerpts from script included.

Schulberg, Budd. "Back to the Enemy." *Show* (June 70) 26–29+. Comments by author on the screenplay for Robert Kennedy's *The Enemy Within,* including excerpts from the screenplay.

Richie, D. "I Read the Movie." *Nation* 210 (22 June 70) 757–758. A review of the problem of publishing film scripts, with a selected checklist of published scripts.

Jodorowsky, Alexandre. *"Mole."* TDR 14 (Winter 70) 56–69. Excerpts from a film script entitled *Mole:* metaphor for man's seeking nature.

2d(5). TITLES AND SUBTITLES

[See also 2g(3), 2h(7), 7e(1).]

Weinberg, Herman G. "The Language Barrier." Hwd Q 2 (No. 4, July 47) 333–337. Difficulties of translating foreign nuances of dialogue into printed subtitles in English; also a proposal for various national versions of films intended for the world market, to be passed on by an international committee.

Weinberg, Herman G. "I Title Foreign Films." Th Arts 32 (Apr 48) 50–51. Amusing brushes with the censors in translating dialogue.

Everson, William. "Movie Titles." FIR 4 (Dec 53). See 7e.

Spinrad, Leonard. "Titles." FIR 6 (Apr 55) 168–170. Factors a producer must consider in choosing a title for his film; examples of titles that were changed, *An American Tragedy* to *A Place in the Sun* and *Everybody Comes to Rick's* to *Casablanca.*

Gunston, David. "Eyes and Ears of the World." F&F 3 (No. 5, Feb 57) 15. Mai Harris, leading titler in Great Britain for foreign films.

"Words by Weinberg." *Good Housekeeping* 147 (Sep 58) 14. Herman Weinberg provides English subtitles for foreign films.

"Those English Subtitles." *Newswk* 56 (8 Aug 60) 76. Report on the work of subtitler Herman G. Weinberg.

Minchinton, John. "What the Eye Does Not Hear." *Film* (No. 35, Spring 63) 39–40. The problems involved in subtitling.

Minchinton, John. "Subtitles." *Film* (No. 37, Autumn 63) 42–43.

Halliwell, Leslie. "What's in a Name?" *F&F* 12 (No. 12, Sep 66). *See 3f.*

Halliwell, Leslie. "Gone with *What* Wind?" *F&F* 14 (No. 8, May 68) 12–18; (No. 9, June 68) 48–54. On getting the right name for a film; two articles.

2e. Cinematography and Lighting

[*See also 2m.*

[*See 5, Biography: Lucien Ballard, Billy Bitzer, William Clothier, Raoul Coutard, Gianni di Venanzo, Arnold Eagle, Gabriel Figueroa, Karl Freund, Lee Garmes, James Wong Howe, Boris Kaufman, Laszlo Kovacs, Walter Lassally, Herbert Ponting, Douglas Slocombe, Gregg Toland, Haskell Wexler, Robert Young.*]

Wayne, Palma. "Aces of the Camera." *SEP* 206 (22 July 33) 16–17+. On cameramen Hal Rosson, Charles Lang, Lee Garmes, and others.

Courant, Curt. "The Function of the Cameraman." *CQ* 3 (No. 1, Autumn 34) 22–24.

"Little Fraternity Which Grinds Hollywood's Cameras." *Time* 36 (2 Dec 40) 77. Brief description of the Hollywood cameraman, his abilities and duties; short vignettes of Tony Gaudio, Gregg Toland, Ernest Haller, and Joseph Valentine.

Argent, Sidney, and Muriel Argent. "The Camera's Share." *S&S* 12 (No. 48, Jan 44) 94–96. Comments on several films and the role of perception of camera movement in the viewer's response.

Streeter, Victor. "The Disciples of Pan." *S&S* 13 (No. 51, Oct 44) 63–65. The virtues of panning versus the static camera.

Farber, Manny. "The Case of the Hidden Camera." *New Rep* 112 (1 Jan 45) 19. After seeing Billy Wilder's *Lost Weekend*, Farber urges further use of this technique to restore a sense of reality in Hollywood films.

Howe, James Wong. "The Cameraman Talks Back." *Screen Writer* 1 (Oct 45) 32–37. Argues against Stephen Longstreet's contention that "brilliant cameramen are the curse of the business"; the cameraman's role and his relationship with the writer and the director.

Pichel, Irving. "Seeing with the Camera." *Hwd Q* 1 (No. 2, Jan 46) 138–145. How the camera can be used for different purposes; but it is fundamental that the content is "more important than the manner in which it is transmitted."

Van Dyke, Willard. "The Interpretive Camera in Documentary Films." *Hwd Q* 1 (No. 4, July 46). *See 8c(1).*

Rahtz, Robert. "The Traveling Camera." *Hwd Q* 2 (No. 3, Apr 47) 297–299. Brief brief in favor of moving camera shots.

Salemson, Harold J. "The Camera as Narrator —Technique or Toy." *Screen Writer* 2 (Mar 47) 38–41. On making films in the first person, and how Robert Montgomery's *Lady in the Lake* used the technique unsuccessfully and obscured its potential.

Brinton, Joseph P., III. "Subjective Camera or Subjective Audience?" *Hwd Q* 2 (No. 4, July 47). *See 3c, Lady in the Lake.*

Mascelli, Joseph V. "Cinemacraft Then and Now." *Photo Arts* (Spring 48).

Hepworth, Cecil. "Those Were the Days." *Penguin F Rev* 6 (Apr 48). *See 4e(1a).*

Debrix, Jean R. "Camera Dramaturgy." *FIR* 3 (May 52) 233–237; (June–July 52) 281–288. Translated by David A. Mage. The principal camera movements and their complex action on the psychology of the spectator—two articles.

Moreno, Julio L. "Subjective Cinema and the Problem of Film in the First Person." *QFRTV* 7 (No. 4, Summer 53). *See 3a.*

von Sternberg, Josef. "More Light." *S&S* 25 (Autumn 55) 70–75+. A commentary on light, its use in film and by painters; some comments about techniques, composition, mood; by a director noted for his lighting.

Courant, Curtis. "Cameraman in the Golden Age of Cinema." *F Cult* 2 (No. 9, 1956) 17–19. Reminiscences of the early silent days of film by the cameraman for *Quo Vadis?* (1924) and *Le Jour Se Leve* (1939).

Mitchell, George. "The Cameraman." *FIR* 7 (Jan 56) 7–18; (Feb 56) 67–76. The role of the cinematographer as both technician and artist with a description of his camera crew; a history of cameras and outstanding directors traced through the silent-film era; developments since sound; two articles.

Unsworth, Geoffrey. "The Director of Photography." *F&F* 3 (No. 7, Apr 57) 15+.

"Popular Photography Analyzes an Outstanding New Film: *Bridge on the River Kwai*." *Pop Photog* 42 (Apr 58) 114. Ten questions (plus detailed applications) about sound, color, light, and camera movement.

Kuiper, John B. "A Selected and Annotated Bibliography of Books and Articles on Pictorial Composition in the Cinema." *JUFPA* 10 (No. 4, Summer 58). *See 1b(1).*

Almendros, Nestor. "Neorealist Cinematography." *F Cult* (No. 20, 1959). *See 4e(3b).*

Estes, Oscar G. "Aerial Photographer Perry." *FIR* 9 (No. 3, Mar 60) 145–159. The career of Harry Perry.

Durgnat, Raymond. "Alexander and the Greats."

F&F 11 (No. 6, Mar 65) 18–22. How content is "created" by the film's style, especially lighting style and camera movements.

Hudson, Roger. "The Secret Profession." *S&S* 34 (Summer 65) 112–117. Interview with two cameramen on their artistic contribution to film making; Douglas Slocombe explains in detail the technical decisions that have to be taken, and how they found expression in a particular film, *The Servant;* Walter Lassally discusses his contributions to the films of Tony Richardson, with whom he has worked on several occasions.

Solomon, Stanley J. "Modern Uses of the Moving Camera." *F Her* 1 (No. 2, Winter 65–66) 19–27. An increase in contemporary use of the moving camera is seen as an expression of disoriented or unstable society, the suspension of intellectual judgment.

Hartley, William, and Ellen Hartley. "Adventures of an Underwater Cameraman." *Pop Mech* 126 (Sep 66) 92–95. The story of Lamar Boren, top cameraman of Hollywood's deep-sea sagas.

Mitchell, George J. "The ASC." *FIR* 18 (No. 7, Aug–Sep 67) 385–397. Describes the history and present significance of the American Society of Cinematographers.

Higham, Charles, and Joel Greenberg. "North Light and Cigarette Bulb." *S&S* 36 (Autumn 67) 192–196. Conversation with veteran cameramen: Lee Garmes, James Wong Howe, and William Daniels; special emphasis on natural sources of light.

Surtees, Bob. "Using the Camera Emotionally." *Action* 2 (No. 5, Sep–Oct 67) 20–23. Cameraman discusses his work in *The Graduate.*

Surtees, Robert L. "*The Graduate*'s Photography." *FIR* 19 (No. 2, Feb 68) 89–111.

Durgnat, Raymond. "Colours and Contrasts." *F&F* 15 (No. 2, Nov 68) 58–62. Lighting, sets, color in older films.

Durgnat, Raymond. "The Restless Cinema." *F&F* 15 (No. 3, Dec 68) 14–18. On camera movement in film.

Durgnat, Raymond. "Images and Individuals." *F&F* 15 (No. 4, Jan 69) 62–67. On picture composition in films.

2e(1). TECHNICAL ASPECTS OF CAMERA WORK

Irwin, Theodore D. "Camera!: Feeding the News Reels." *Pop Mech* 53 (May 30) 794–799. Surveys difficulties in photographing newsreels.

"New Film Gives Night to Movie." *Pop Sci* 118 (June 31) 40. Supersensitive camera and high-powered incandescent lamps add realism to movies.

"Camera Tricks in the Talkies." *Pop Mech* 57 (Feb 32) 227–228. Details method of multiple images and other trick photography.

Metzner, Erno. "The Travelling Camera." *Close Up* 10 (No. 2, June 33) 182–187. Problems in various films which Metzner worked on with Pabst.

"A Movie Lot on the Sea Bottom." *Pop Mech* 60 (Oct 33) 546–549. Filming on ocean floor requires construction of diving bell for camera.

Schnurmacher, Emile C. "The Cameraman Foretells Disaster." *Pop Mech* 60 (Dec 33) 836–841. Cameramen risk lives to photograph movie stunts.

"Girl Fights Octopus for Underwater Movie." *Pop Sci* 123 (Dec 33) 27. Periscope-like camera films underwater.

Lodge, John E. "Portable Equipment Makes Whole World a Movie Studio." *Pop Sci* 124 (May 34) 32–33+.

Weir, Hugh. "Have You a Camera Face?" *Ladies' Home J* 51 (July 34) 12+. Camera does strange things to beautiful faces.

Chamberlin, F. T. "A Movie Camera Gun Stock." *Sci Am* 151 (Nov 34) 266. Inventor details invention.

"Multiplane Camera Developed to Give Depth Illusion." *Sci Newsletter* 33 (14 May 38) 321.

Daugherty, Frank. "Movies' Own Land of Make-Believe." *CSMM* (25 Jan 39) 8–9. Camera tricks and techniques.

"Daylight Made to Order." *Pop Mech* 75 (Mar 41) 376–379+. Lighting for the movies —the materials, problems, terms, and the results.

"Rolling Forward." *Bus Wk* (11 July 42) 68. New method of timing stops visual effect of wheels going backward.

"Seeing History Through American Achievements." *Scholastic* 50 (17 Feb 47) 25. The hundredth anniversary of Edison's birth spurs a pictorial look at the early history of the movie camera.

O'Brien, Brian. "Faster Than You Think." *Sci Dig* 25 (May 49) 16–18. High-speed photography.

Pichel, Irving. "Stills in Motion." *Hwd Q* (No. 1, Fall 50). *See 8a(3).*

Shamroy, Leon. "Evolution of a Cameraman." *FIR* 2 (Apr 51) 23–28. Advance of the techniques of lighting, photography, and composition over the past three decades.

Mascelli, Joseph V. "Nice Work If You Can Get It." *Photog* 32 (Mar 53) 64–69+.

Shamroy, Leon. "Shooting in Cinemascope." *FIR* 4 (May 53) 226–228. From the viewpoint of director of photography on *The Robe.*

"Crazy Wide-Screen Camera." *Photog* 33 (Nov 53) 96.

Stobart, T. "Movie Camera's Role in Conquering Everest." *Photog* 34 (Apr 54) 112+.

Everson, William K. "Additions and Corrections." *FIR* 10 (June–July 59) 374. Letter about D. W. Griffith and the much earlier uses of moving camera and iris.

Steele, Robert. "Report on a Study of Light Variables Measured as a Function of Time in the Cinema." *J Soc Cin* 4 (1964) 37–57. Recording variations in light intensity from the screen for a number of feature and short films, the investigator only rarely discovered what might be called "light rhythm."

"A Lot to Learn." *Newswk* 65 (31 May 65) 83+. Electronovision used to film W. Sargent's *Harlow*.

Wexler, Haskell. "It's Time We Scrapped the Ancient Iron." *Action* 2 (No. 3, May–June 67) 16–17. A plea for a new kind of portable equipment for film making.

Phillips, Dale. "Flicks Afloat." *Motor Boating* 121 (May 68) 37–38+. Techniques for taking movies on the water.

Cousteau, Jacques. "How We Film Under the Sea." *Pop Sci* 194 (Feb 69) 65–69+.

Matzkin, Myron. "Just Where Does Super 8 Stand Five and a Half Years After Its Introduction?" *Mod Photog* 34 (Feb 70) 36+. A review of the development of the super 8 camera and film.

2e(2). COLOR

Peck, A. P. "Movies Take on Color." *Sci Am* 142 (Apr 30) 285. Details of color processes.

Hughes, Pennethorne. "The Colour of It." *CQ* 2 (No. 1, Autumn 33) 16–18. Color doesn't necessarily make film more realistic and its use may lead to "injudicious monstrosities."

Elliott, Eric. "Wither Colour?" *CQ* 2 (No. 3, Spring 34) 161–165. Technical problems; mental effects.

"La Cucaracha Uses Technicolor's Latest Process." *Newswk* 4 (21 July 34) 16–17. Brief history of color in movies.

Boone, Andrew R. "Pictures in Full Color Open New Era in Movies." *Pop Sci* 126 (May 35) 13–15+. On the color filming of *Becky Sharp*.

Hardy, Forsyth. "The Colour Question." *CQ* 3 (No. 4, Summer 35) 231–234.

Mamoulian, Rouben. "Colour and Emotion." *CQ* 3 (No. 4, Summer 35) 225–226.

"Technicolor May Revolutionize the Screen." *Lit Dig* 119 (8 June 35) 24–25. Background of Technicolor discovery.

"*Becky Sharp* in Color May Open Movies' Third Era." *Newswk* 5 (22 June 35) 22–23.

Chumley, Allen. "The Screen: Movies in Motley." *New Masses* 16 (2 July 35) 49. Economic background of the new Technicolor process; pessimistic prediction as to its use, from a Marxist viewpoint.

Arnheim, Rudolf. "Remarks on the Colour Film." *S&S* 4 (No. 16, Winter 35–36) 160–162. A plea for more artistic use.

"Technicolor." *Fortune* 13 (June 36) 40+. Walter Wanger's *Trail of the Lonesome Pine* was a success in color and suggests that the Technicolor Corporation will soon stop losing money.

Boone, A. R. "Movie Cartoons in Color." *Sci Am* 156 (Jan 37). *See 2h.*

"Color Film Increase." *Bus Wk* (22 May 37) 49. History of Technicolor.

"Celluloid Rainbow for Hollywood." *Lit Dig* 123 (29 May 37) 35. Samuel Goldwyn "goes color"; a look at the history and processes of color in film.

Kuhn, Irene. "Rainbow 'Round the Screen." *Cinema Arts* 1 (No. 1, June 37) 28–32. McClelland Barclay, a Hollywood color consultant, discusses the possibility of color in film, its use and misuse.

Holden, Lansing C. "COLOR! The New Language of the Screen." *Cinema Arts* 1 (No. 2, July 37) 64. The color designer for Selznick International contends color in motion pictures is as revolutionary as sound was in 1927.

Lye, Len. "The Man Who Was Colour Blind." *S&S* 9 (No. 33, Spring 40) 6–7. Color would be an asset to any film scripted to make positive use of it.

Catling, Darrel. "Colour in the Mud." *S&S* 11 (No. 43, Winter 42–43) 72–74. Plea for the artistic use of color in films.

Taylor, F. J. "King and Queen of Color: Dr. and Mrs. H. T. Kalmus." *Rdrs Dig* (Aug 44) 62–64. Story of Technicolor, Inc.

Harley, Basil. "Concerning Colour." *S&S* 13 (No. 52, Jan 45) 97–98. Complexity of ideas and emotions require more aesthetic use.

Powell, Dilys. "Colour and the Film." *S&S* 15 (No. 58, Summer 46) 56. A plea for imaginative use.

"Profits Through Loss." *Time* 48 (23 Sep 46) 88–90. Technicolor's new rival, Cinecolor.

Ball, J. Arthur. "Quality in Color Reproduction." *Hwd Q* 2 (No. 1, Oct 46) 45–49. Nontechnical explanation of processes used in 1946.

Biberman, Edward. ". . . in Glorious Technicolor." *Hwd Q* 2 (No. 1, Oct 46) 50–56. Plea for artistic use of color.

"Polaroid Unveils New Movie Color Method." *Bus Wk* (27 Dec 47). "Polacolor"—a time-saving, economical way of printing films in full color.

"Revolution in Color? Rouxcolor." *Time* 51 (7 June 48) 94. Used by Marcel Pagnol.

Coote, J. H. "A Technician's View of the Colour Film." *Penguin F Rev* 9 (May 49) 73–81. Difficulties with both Technicolor and Agfacolor, but the advantage with the former.

"Dupont in Color." *Bus Wk* (11 June 49) 22. What sort of competition will it give to Kodak and Ansco materials?

Taylor, F. J. "Mr. Technicolor." *SEP* 222 (22 Oct 49). *See 5, Herbert Kalmus.*

Meyer, Bernard. "Color Can Mar or Make." *FIR* 2 (June–July 51) 30–33. Kinds of color film; examples of uses.

Gagliardi, Gio. "Lenticulated Film." *FIR* 2 (Nov 51) 29–33. It makes color possible for even the cheapest pictures; condensed from *Better Theatres* (Sep 51).

"Fictional Color of *Moulin Rouge*." *New Yorker* 29 (14 Mar 53) 23–25. Some French reactions.

Limbacher, James L. "A Color Chronology." *FIR* 5 (Dec 54) 527–529. A chronological list that briefly describes the more important events in the history of color and the motion picture and some of the names for the processes.

Hillier, Erwin. "Are You Colour Conscious?" *F&F* 2 (No. 5, Feb 56) 11. Technical comments by a cameraman.

"Technicolor Buys Out Pavelle to Strengthen Film Processing." *Bus Wk* (18 Aug 56) 146.

Dreyer, Carl Th. "Color and Color Films." *FIR* 6 (Apr 58) 165–167. Only three or four films have made an aesthetic use of color; a possible solution is a color script and a painter who would control the color composition of a film.

Limbacher, James L. "Color's an Old Device." *FIR* 10 (June–July 59) 346–350. Diverse processes discussed and indexed chronologi-

cally; representative motion pictures tinted in whole or part from 1900 to 1956; films with natural color sequences from 1920 to 1958. See also letters to editor, *FIR* 10 (Aug–Sep 59) 435+.

Mamoulian, Rouben. "Colour and Light in Films." *F Cult* (No. 21, 1960). *See 3a(1).*

Eisenstein, Sergei. "One Path to Colour." *S&S* 30 (Spring 61) 84–86. An autobiographical piece in which Eisenstein recalls his early theories about color, and how he planned to utilize it in his films.

McCoy, E. P. "Influence of Color on Audience's Rated Perception of Reality in the Film." *AV Com Rev* 10 (Jan 62) 70–72.

Behlmer, Rudy. "Technicolor." *FIR* 15 (No. 6, June–July 64) 333–351. History of Technicolor.

Kurosawa, Akira. "Why Mifune's Beard Won't Be Red." *Cinema* (Calif) 2 (No. 2, July 64) 40. Statement on color.

Dewey, Lang. "The Colours in *Cherbourg*." *Film* (No. 42, Winter 64). *See 3c.*

Sharits, Paul J. "Red, Blue, Godard." *FQ* 19 (No. 4, Summer 66). *See 5, Jean-Luc Godard.*

Johnson, William. "Coming to Terms with Color." *FQ* 20 (No. 1, Fall 66) 2–22. A comprehensive critical essay on how color affects us and how certain color schemes are used in films.

2f. Editing

[*See also 2m, 3a(1), 3a(5), 4a(4b).*]
[*See 5, Biography: Aram Avakian, Anthony Harvey, Carl Lerner.*]

"Film Technique Revolutionized." *Living Age* 342 (May 32) 269–270. Pudovkin theory of filming at varying speeds.

Bond, Kirk. "Léger, Dreyer, and Montage." *Creative Art* 11 (No. 2, Oct 32) *See 5, Fernand Léger.*

"Snip, Snip, Film Editors Can Make or Break Stars and Pictures." *Lit Dig* 122 (12 Sep 36) 18.

Massingham, Richard. "Continuity." *S&S* 8 (No. 30, Summer 39) 64. Too much attention is paid to this.

Cross, Elizabeth. "The Pace That Kills . . . ." *S&S* 11 (No. 42, Autumn 42) 36–37. In contemporary films.

Reisz, Karel. "Editing." *S&S* 19 (Jan 50) 32. See additional articles 19 (Apr 50) 79; 19 (July 50) 209; 19 (Dec 50) 335; 19 (Feb 51) 415; 19 (Apr 51) 476.

Seton, Marie, Karel Reisz, and Lewis McLeod. "Editing Unfair to Eisenstein." *S&S* 20 (June 51) 54–55+. Seton objects to Reisz article

in *Sight and Sound* (Feb 51) to the effect that Eisenstein had surprisingly little influence on film making.

Shipp, Cameron. "Hollywood Cutup." *Collier's* 130 (22 Nov 52) 17–19. About film editors, especially Harry Gerstad, who won Academy Award for *Champion*.

Everson, William K. "Stock Shots." *FIR* 4 (Jan 53) 15–20. A review of particular films that, in part, contain footage from previous films: from a single scene to as much as 80% of the film.

Debrix, Jean R. "Film Editing: I.—Theory." (Tr. by David A. Mage.) *FIR* 4 (Jan 53) 21–24. Spatial rhythms, time rhythms, and their components.

Mayer, Gerald. "Film Editing: II.—Practice." *FIR* 4 (Jan 53) 24–27. The editor's relationship with the director; the account of an editing problem in Monta Bell's *The Letter*.

Everson, William K. "The Stock Shot Habit." *S&S* 22 (Apr–June 53) 183–184. Humorous exposé listing a number of films partially made from shots from old films. Reprinted from *Films in Review*.

Gerstlé, Ralph. "Optical Effects." *FIR* 5 (Apr

54) 171–174. Examples the author considers imaginative.

Connor, Edward. "Ruining Re-issues." *FIR* 5 (May 54). *See 4a(4b).*

Murphy, William B. "Film Editing." *FIR* 6 (Feb 55) 70–72. Human relations are important; the film editor's role as a member of a production unit.

Harris, Louis. "Editing TV Films." *FIR* 6 (Apr 55) 158–164. The pressures, uncertainties, and problems under which a television film editor must work.

Everson, William K. "Movies out of Thin Air." *FIR* 6 (Apr 55) 171–180. A complementary article to "Stock Shots" (Jan 53) that further discusses the fabrication of new features from older footage; features made from shorts and shorts from features.

Card, James. "Which Cut Do You Prefer?" *Image* 5 (No. 2, Feb 56) 38–39. The problem of editing in determining the "true" version of a film.

Pegge, C. Denis. "*Caligari:* Its Innovations in Editing." *QFRTV* 11 (No. 2, Winter 56) 136–148. Teacher and film maker analyzes effects achieved by German silent film *The Cabinet of Dr. Caligari;* lengthy, annotated excerpt from screen transcript.

"The Front Page." *S&S* 26 (Spring 57). *See 7c(5).*

Wilson, Frederick. "The Film Editor." *F&F* 3 (No. 10, July 57) 8–9.

Williams, Elmo. "Genius in the Cutting Room." *FIR* 8 (Nov 57) 443–452. A survey of the career of Merrill G. White, with a profile of his personality and career written by the assistant he took to England in 1933 to work with Herbert Wilcox; Williams, who later became the editor of *High Noon* and a producer at 20th Century-Fox, tells of White's hot temper and great talent.

Miller, Don. "The Visual Chronicle." *FIR* 8 (Dec 57) 513–518. The use of film clips by television to relate history visually in such shows as *The Twentieth Century;* brief biographies of producer Burton Benjamin and his associate, Isaac Kleinerman.

Foss, Brian. "Below the Threshold." *S&S* 27 (Spring 58) 208–209. A report on subliminal advertising; some experiments in visual and auditory perception; some possible uses and dangers of this technique.

Gillett, John. "Cut and Come Again." *S&S* 27 (Summer 58) 258–260. An account of the regrettable reediting done to so many old films reissued or run on television, as well as the censorship which various countries or cities impose; sometimes they are given new titles.

Knight, Arthur. "The Lost Art of Editing." *Sat Rev* 41 (20 Dec 58) 7–11. Historical survey from Griffith and the Russian directors of the 1920s through the coming of sound

and of the wide screen; the editing practices of George Stevens. Part of *Saturday Review* report "The Film: Survey of the Craft and Its Problems."

Knight, Arthur. "Editing: the Lost Art." *F&F* 5 (No. 9, June 59) 12+. Editing styles of the great masters of film.

Mascelli, Joseph V. "Directional Continuity." *FIR* 10 (Nov 59) 513–517. An introduction to the concept of screen direction and its axis of the action, the stage line, with reference to different kinds of camera angles, and the problem that results for the editor.

Colpi, Henri. "Debasement of the Art of Montage." *F Cult* (Nos. 22–23, 1961) 34–37. The disappearance of the art of montage in the sound film, with the exception of its use in the short film. Originally published in *Cahiers du Cinéma.*

Godard, Jean-Luc. "*Montage, Mon Beau Souci.*" *F Cult* (Nos. 22–23, 1961) 37–39. The problems of editing and direction. Originally published in *Cahiers du Cinéma.*

Colpi, Henri. "On *Last Year at Marienbad.*" *NY F Bul* 3 (No. 2, 1962) 14–15. Editor's account of his editing of *Last Year at Marienbad.*

Gessner, Robert. "Faces of Time: A New Aesthetic for Cinema." *Th Arts* 46 (July 62) 13–17. Discussion of how film juggles time through editing.

"Vandals." *Time* 80 (10 Aug 62) 45. The process of editing films for TV.

Brakhage, Stan. "Letter from Brakhage: On Splicing." *F Cult* (No. 35, 1964–1965) 51–56. Reprint of a Brakhage letter to Gregory Markopoulos detailing his "splicing" technique, when it should be visible, etc.

"Reasons of the Eye." *New Yorker* 40 (13 Feb 65) 25–27. Description of editing course at Museum of Modern Art taught by Slavko Vorkapich.

Jaffe, Patricia. "Editing Cinéma Vérité." *F Com* 3 (No. 3, Summer 65). *See 8c(3).*

Williams, Elmo. "The Editor's Skill." *F&F* 11 (No. 9, June 65) 55. 20th Century-Fox production head writes on European and American editing.

Colpi, Henri. "Debasement of the Art of Montage." *CdC in Eng* (No. 3, 1966) 44–45. A brief history of the use of montage, nearly destroyed by the coming of sound. (See *Film Culture* [Nos. 22–23, 1961].)

Godard, Jean-Luc. "*Montage, Mon Beau Souci.*" *CdC in Eng* (No. 3, 1966) 45–46. Directing and editing are inextricably intertwined. (See *Film Culture* [Nos. 22–23, 1961].)

Knight, Arthur. "Fighting Back." *Sat Rev* 49 (19 Feb 66) 64–65. The battle of Otto Preminger and George Stevens to retain full artistic control over their films, including the right to determine how it is to be shown on TV.

Hudson, Roger. "Putting the Magic in It." *S&S* 35 (Spring 66) 78–83. Editors describe how they work and their relationship with directors; Anthony Harvey with Kubrick and Ritt; James Clark with Schlesinger and Clayton.

"Emasculation? Inserting Commercials." *Newswk* 67 (7 Mar 66) 65. The problem of the cutting of films for the insertion of commercials on television.

Vas, Robert. "Meditation at 24 Frames per Second." *S&S* 35 (Summer 66) 119–124. Reflections on editing in the 1960s; Godard, Lester, Antonioni, especially Resnais, and also *cinéma vérité*.

Gessner, Robert. "Studies in Past and Decelerated Time." *CJ* 6 (1966–1967) 33–45. Examples, including script excerpts of flashbacks and slow-motion scenes in feature films.

Falkenberg, Paul. "The Editor's Role in Film Making." *CJ* 7 (1967–1968) 22–28. Equipment, traditions, and relation with the director; thinking about images; working with sound and mixing.

Daynard, Don. "Spectacle Out of the Can." *Take One* 11 (No. 1, 1968) 14–15. Mechanical use of stock footage in many films, especially after the advent of TV.

Lassally, Walter, *et al.* "Multiscreen." *Film* (No. 51, Spring 68) 14–21. Various opinions about its value and function including reference to the Labyrinth presentation at Expo '67.

Siegler, Robert. "Masquage." *FQ* 21 (No. 3, Spring 68). *See 3a(5).*

Falkenberg, Paul. "The Editor's Role in Film Making." *F Lib Q* 1 (No. 4, Fall 68) 20–27. The nature and importance of film editing. Reprinted from *Cinema Journal*.

Di Franco, Philip. "Past, Present, Future in Cinema." *CJ* 8 (No. 1, Fall 68) 42–45. Six types of time in editing.

"Special Report: The Multi-Image Screen." *Action* 3 (No. 6, Nov–Dec 68) 20–39. Articles by Arthur Knight, Don W. Weed, and viewpoints expressed by Richard Fleischer, Norman Jewison, and Ralph Nelson, who are working with multi-image effects.

Rabe, Andreas J. "Multiple-Image Techniques." *JUFA* 21 (No. 1, 1969) 20–22. A brief history and rationale for the use of multiple images.

Gladwell, David. "Editing Anderson's *If . . .*" *Screen* 10 (No. 1, Jan–Feb 69) 24+. Some wry comments on Lindsay Anderson followed by technical data and work with specific scenes.

Dmytryk, Edward. "The Director and the Editor." *Action* 4 (No. 2, Mar–Apr 69) 23–25. An editor turned director discusses some of the problems of the editor and communication between director and editor.

Blasi, Ralph. "Dede Allen—The Force on the Cutting Room Floor." *Show* (Jan 70) 62–67. How film editor Allen works, with special emphasis on the editing of *Alice's Restaurant*.

2g. Sound

[*See also 4c.*]

Denbo, Doris. "He's the Big Noise Behind the Talkies." *American* 111 (June 31) 82+. See also *Lit Dig* 105 (28 June 30) 37. Profile of Count Cutelli, sound-effects artist for Disney and others.

Ogden, Ronald. "Art of René Clair." *Bookman* 82 (Apr 32). *See 5, René Clair.*

Grierson, John. "Pudovkin on Sound." *CQ* 2 (No. 2, Winter 33–34) 106–110. His "asynchronism" is fairly simple; his pictures are better than his textbook.

Borneman, Ernest J. "Sound Rhythm and the Film." *S&S* 3 (No. 10, Summer 34) 65–67. Recent research points up their intimate relationship.

Grierson, John. "Introduction to a New Art." *S&S* 3 (No. 11, Autumn 34) 101–104. Theoretical treatise about the role of sound in cinema, asking for a break with theatrical dialogue.

Hardy, Forsyth. "Developing Sound." *CQ* 3 (No. 1, Autumn 34) 39–43. In documentary, animation, and features.

Read, Herbert. "Experiments in Counterpoint." *CQ* 3 (No. 1, Autumn 34) 17–21. Sound in British documentaries.

Beatty, J. "Norma Shearer's Noisy Brother." *American* 123 (May 37) 26–27+. Extensive account of sound engineer Douglas Shearer and the problems and techniques in making a sound picture.

Cavalcanti, Alberto. "Sound in Films." *Films* 1 (No. 1, Nov 39) 25–39. Principles and practice in the use of speech, music, and noise: "The picture is the medium of statement, the sound is the medium of suggestion."

Keen, Stuart. "Must We Always Have Dialogue?" *S&S* 15 (No. 60, Winter 46–47) 145. A plea for some films with just music and sound effects.

Williams, Martin T. "The Audible Image." *FIR* 5 (Aug–Sep 54) 371–373. George Stevens' *A Place in the Sun* put dogs and sirens on a background soundtrack long before the scene in which they appeared.

Robson, Mark. "Why You Hear What You

Hear at the Movies." *Good Housekeeping* 141 (July 55) 99–102. Director discusses art and technique of using sound in films.

McCullum, Gordon. "The Sound Department." *F&F* 3 (No. 11, Aug 57) 30–31+.

Brakhage, Stanley. "The Silent Sound Sense." *F Cult* (No. 21, 1960). *See 3a(1).*

2g(1). TECHNICAL ASPECTS OF SOUND

"Talking Motion Pictures." *Science* 71 (17 Jan 30) supp 10+. Reports development of synthetic resin to produce cheap, unbreakable phonograph records.

"Accuracy in Talkie Equipment." *Sci Am* 143 (Aug 30) 102–103. Details of sound processes.

Draper, John. "Sound Tricks in the Talkies." *Pop Mech* 55 (Feb 31) 236–240. Details methods of reproducing sounds for movies.

"The New Magic Movies." *Pop Mech* 55 (Apr 31) 539–541. Reviews technical advances: sound and color.

Boone, Andrew R. "Canning Nature's Noises for the Talkies." *Pop Sci* 119 (Nov 31) 54–55+.

Lane, Jerry. "The Voice of the Film." *SEP* 205 (11 Mar 33) 10–11+. Details of sound on film.

Boone, Andrew R. "Prehistoric Monsters Roar and Hiss for Sound Film." *Pop Sci* 122 (Apr 33) 20–21+.

Kegl, Zoltan J. "Crackup of Mighty Glacier Caught for First Time by Sound Camera." *Pop Sci* 123 (Dec 33) 24–26. Recording at Rink Glacier, Greenland.

Boone, R. "Shooting Sound from Arctic to Equator." *Travel* 64 (Feb 35) 32–34.

"Sounder Sounds: RCA Demonstrates Ultra-Violet Ray Recording for Movies." *Bus Wk* (29 Feb 36) 27.

Shearer, Douglas. "Hollywood's Tin Ear: An ABC of Sound." *Cinema Arts* 1 (No. 3, Sep 37) 32–35. A recording engineer discusses the intricacies of sound in basic terms.

Coldby, J. "Electronic Technique of Making Talking Pictures." *Radio News* 25 (Jan 41) 8–10+. How sound is reproduced on film.

Isaacs, H. R. "New Horizons: *Fantasia* and Fantasound." *Th Arts* 25 (Jan 41). *See 2h(3).*

"Voomp, Clank, Bonk: Name Your Noise and the Movies' Sound Makers Will Give It to You." *Pop Sci* 138 (Mar 41) 106–109.

"Manufacturing Quiet for the Movies." *Pop Sci* 139 (Dec 41) 98. Devices developed by the industry to kill stray noise.

"Sound Tricks of the Movies." *Pop Mech* (Sep 44) 56–61. The problems of preparing battle noises for movies.

MacDougall, Ronald. "Sound—and Fury." *Screen Writer* 1 (Sep 45) 1–7. Objections to the unrealistic mixing of sound and music in films.

Oboler, Arch. "Look—Then Listen!" *Screen Writer* 1 (Dec 45) 26–30. Author agrees with Ronald MacDougall (Sep 45) that realistic sound is important but doubts if audiences care; mixing is the only economical way.

"Hen Tracks on Sound Tracks." *Pop Mech* 91 (Apr 49) 168–169. Norman McLaren's methods of drawing the sound directly on movie film.

Ebel, Fred E. "That Old Regenerative Set of Mine." *Pop Electronics* 28 (Jan 68) 50–51. A story about film sound effects.

Kingery, R. A., and others. "The Man Who Taught the Movies How to Speak." *Sat Rev* 51 (6 Apr 68) 56–58. The career of Joseph Tykocinski-Tykociner, researcher in sound engineering.

2g(2). MUSIC FOR FILMS

[*See also 4k(6).*

[*See 5, Biography: Harold Arlen, Irving Berlin, Elmer Bernstein, Aaron Copland, Ken Darby, Hugo Friedhoffer, George Gershwin, Jerry Goldsmith, Victor Herbert, Bernard Herrmann, Jerome Kern, Arthur Kleiner, Erich Korngold, Alfred Newman, Alex North, David Raksin, Richard Rodgers, Leopold Stokowski, Herbert Stothart, Virgil Thomson, Dimitri Tiomkin, Franz Waxman, Frank Zappa.*]

Arvey, V. "How Music Has Helped the Stars." *Etude* 50 (Oct 32). *See 2b(2).*

Hackenschmied, Alexander. "Film and Music." *CQ* 1 (No. 3, Spring 33) 152–155.

"Music in the Movies Wins New Place." *Musician* 40 (Jan 35) 14. Establishment of Academy Award for movie music.

Calvocoressi, M. D. "Music and the Film." *S&S* 4 (No. 14, Summer 35) 57–58. Understanding and cooperation are needed between producer and composer.

Leigh, Walter. "The Musician and the Film." *CQ* 3 (No. 2, Winter 35) 70–74.

Garden, Mary. "Music Comes to Hollywood." *Cinema Arts* 1 (No. 1, June 37) 19. "Talent scout" chats about the importance of singers to film.

"Movie Mirrors Music-Mindedness." *Musician* 43 (Apr 38) 75.

Daugherty, F. "Music for the Millions." *CSMM* (27 Apr 38) 8–9.

"Music in Films: A Symposium of Composers." *Films* 1 (No. 4, Winter 40) 5–24. Answers to questions by Marc Blitzstein, Benjamin Britten, Aaron Copland, Dmitri Shostakovich, Virgil Thomson, and others; their film credits; bibliography of articles by composers on film music.

Cameron, Ken. "Sound Recordist Ken Cameron Protests." *S&S* 10 (No. 40, Spring 42) 75–76. A reaction against previous articles in *Sight and Sound* which made improper statements about film music.

Zissu, Leonard. "The Copyright Dilemma of the Screen Composer." *Hwd Q* 1 (No. 3, Spring 46). *See 7c(5)*.

Rozsa, Miklos. "University Training for Motion Picture Musicians." *Etude* 64 (June 46) 307+.

DeVore, N. "Film Music Attains Artistic Stature." *Musician* 51 (Nov 46) 150–151.

Keller, Hans. "Film Music—Some Objections." *S&S* 15 (No. 60, Winter 46–47) 136. Either film music will corrupt music appreciation or music appreciation will have to demand better film music.

Huntley, John. "Film Music." *Penguin F Rev* 2 (Jan 47) 21–25. Methods of studying film music. (Current reviews of music in films occur in every issue of this magazine.)

Sternfeld, Frederick W. "Preliminary Report on Film Music." *Hwd Q* 2 (No. 3, Apr 47) 299–302. Note on committee seeking deposit of film scores at universities for study.

Hartwell, D. "Masses Go for Music." *Collier's* 119 (24 May 47) 14–15+. Hollywood experiments with "long-hair" music.

Rubsamen, W. H. "Fortunes in Movie Music." *Etude* 65 (July 47) 420. Letter details top-paying positions and personalities in movie music.

Heinsheimer, H. W. "Hollywood's Music Doctors." *Sci Dig* (Aug 47) 52–56. How the music score can correct mistakes on the screen.

Thomas, Anthony. "Hollywood Music." *S&S* 16 (No. 63, Autumn 47) 97–98. Composing for films.

Herrmann, Bernard. "From Sound Track to Disc." *Sat Rev* 30 (27 Sep 47) 42. A film composer discusses the merits of recordings of film music.

Mathieson, Muir. "Developments in Film Music." *Penguin F Rev* 4 (Oct 47). *See 4e(1b)*.

Sternfeld, F. W. "Music and the Feature Film." *Musical Q* 33 (Oct 47) 517–532. Film music acts as a subtle modernizer of the musical taste of the film audience.

Keller, Hans. "Hollywood Music—Another View." *S&S* 16 (No. 64, Winter 47–48) 168–169. Negative view.

Mathieson, Muir. "Music for Crown." *Hwd Q* 3 (No. 3, Spring 48) 323–326. Composers who have worked for British documentaries: Walter Leigh, Benjamin Britten, Maurice Jaubert, Darius Milhaud, Richard Addinsell, Ralph Vaughn Williams, and others.

Rubsamen, Walter H. "Literature on Music in Film and Radio—Addenda (1943–1948)." *Hwd Q* (No. 4, Summer 48–Summer 49). *See 1b(1)*.

Winge, John H. "Cartoons and Modern Mu-

sic." *S&S* 17 (No. 67, Autumn 48). *See 2h(4)*.

Moor, Paul. "Composers and the Music Track." *Th Arts* 33 (July 49) 49. Deploring Hollywood's use of the film composer.

Copland, Aaron. "Tip to Moviegoers: Take off Those Ear-Muffs." *NYTM* (6 Nov 49) 28–32. A film composer explains his craft.

Huff, Theodore. "Chaplin as Composer." *FIR* 1 (Sep 50). *See 5, Charles Chaplin*.

Zuckerman, John V. "A Selected Bibliography on Music for Motion Pictures." *Hwd Q* 5 (No. 2, Winter 50). *See 1b(1)*.

Pratley, Gerald. "Film Music on Records." *QFRTV* 6 (No. 1, Fall 51). *See 1b(1)*.

Asklund, G., and K. Grayson (eds.). "Singing in the Movies." *Etude* 70 (Nov 52) 16+.

Cahn, Robert. "Marilyn Monroe Hits a New High." *Collier's* 134 (9 July 54). *See 5, Marilyn Monroe*.

Lavastida, Bert, Pete Stallings, Norman Phelps, and Glen Gould. "Music for Motion Pictures." *JUFPA* 7 (No. 2, Winter 54) 12–16. Transcript of an elaborate presentation at University Film Producers conference in which Stallings showed films made by the Calvin Company, Phelps described his work as composer for an Ohio State promotional film, and Gould played some of his title music and commented on practical problems of working with musicians.

"Movie Background Music Available for All Moods." *Photog* 37 (Sep 55) 111.

Debnam, R. "Celluloid to Vinylite: The Hollywood LP's." *Sat Rev* 39 (16 June 56) 43–44. The world of LP's derived from movie sound tracks.

Affelder, P. "Sound-Track Favorites on Discs." *Cosmopolitan* 141 (Oct 56) 6. A list of popular, semiclassical, classical musicals; special emphasis on *Pinocchio, Moby Dick,* and *Trapeze*.

Heylbut, Rose. "Disney Fun with Music." *Etude* 74 (Oct 56) 23+. The musical background of Walt Disney productions carefully analyzed.

Green, Philip. "The Music Director." *F&F* 3 (No. 9, June 57) 12–13.

McCarty, Clifford. "Filmusic Librarian." *FIR* 8 (June–July 57) 292–293. A brief description of the responsibilities and duties of a motion-picture studio film librarian; George G. Schneider, music librarian for MGM for twenty-five years.

"Pop Records." *Time* 71 (24 Feb 58) 46+. The popularity of movie sound-track albums.

Hentoff, N. "Movie Music Comes into Its Own." *Reporter* 18 (12 June 58) 28–30. The causes and effects of the rise of the sound-track album.

Alwyn, William. "Composing for the Screen." *F&F* 5 (No. 6, Mar 59) 9+.

Gold, Ernest. "Notes from the Cutting Room." *Opera News* 26 (26 Nov 61) 8–13. The job of the film composer.

"Never Too Much Music." *Time* 79 (25 May 62) 70+. Henry Mancini and "Moon River."

Jennings, C. Robert. "Cahn & Van Heusen: Hollywood's Tin Pan Aladdins." *Show* 3 (July 63) 76–77+. Songwriting team; songs cited with biographical comments.

Schiffer, George. "The Law and the Use of Music in Film." *F Com* 1 (No. 6, Fall 63). *See 7c(5).*

"To Touch a Moment." *Time* 83 (17 Jan 64) 70. A survey of current composers of film music.

Hauduroy, Jean-François. "Interview with Betty Comden and Adolph Green." *CdC in Eng* (No. 2, 1966) 43–50. The two scenarists discuss their careers writing for musicals; filmography by Patrick Brion.

"Aboard the Bandwagon." *Time* 87 (14 Jan 66) 62+. A look at composer John Barry.

Hanson, Curtis Lee. "Three Screen Composers." *Cinema* (Calif) 3 (No. 3, July 66) 8–9+. Interview with Henry Mancini, Maurice Jarre, and Dmitri Tiomkin.

Uselton, Roi. "Opera Singers on the Screen." *FIR* 18 (No. 4, Apr 67) 193–206; 18 (No. 5, May 67) 284–309; 18 (No. 6, June–July 67) 345–359. Individual biographies of opera stars who also worked in silent and sound films.

Lees, Gene. "New Sound on the Soundtracks." *High Fidelity* 17 (Aug 67) 58–61. Current trends in film music.

Ascher, Felice. "An Interview with Teo Macero." *F Lib Q* 2 (No. 2, Spring 69) 9–12. The avant-garde composer discusses his work for films.

Lewis, Michael. "Composing for Films." *Screen* 11 (No. 2, 1970) 80–85. Interview by Peter Amsden.

2g(2a). Theory and Function of Music

Watts, Stephen. "Alfred Hitchcock on Music in Film." *CQ* 2 (No. 2, Winter 33–34) 80–83. The emotional values of music need to be rediscovered; sound brought too much of an obsession with words.

Hussey, Dyneley. "Music in the Cinema." *Spectator* 154 (15 Feb 35) 247. If music is to find a significant place in the cinema, it must disregard conventions used in theatre and opera and free itself to flow with the movement of the camera.

Moore, Douglas. "Music and the Movies." *Harper's* 171 (July 35) 181–188. Summary of use of music in movies with speculations for future.

Pollak, Robert. "Hollywood's Music." *Mag of Art* 31 (Sep 38) 512–513. The importance of the film score composer; many composers cited.

Antheil, George. "Hollywood Composer." *Atlantic* 165 (Feb 40) 160–167. Problems of "background" music; relationship of composer and director.

Milano, Paolo. "Music in the Film: Notes for a Morphology." *J Aesthetics and Art Criticism* 1 (No. 1, 1941) 89–94. Formulation of music-image relationships of three types: (*a*) dominant visuals, (*b*) dominant aurals, (*c*) equal collaboration with specific discussion of filmic uses of music.

Haggin, B. H. "Music for Documentary Films." *Nation* 152 (15 Feb 41) 194. Questions the need for music, citing Aaron Copland for *The City* and Marc Blitzstein for *Valley Town*.

Winter, M. H. "Function of Music in Sound Film." *Musical Q* 27 (Apr 41) 146–164.

Williams, Michael. "Demoralizing Use of Musical Backgrounds with Newsreels of the War." *Commonweal* 35 (6 Mar 42) 485–486.

Frye, Northrop. "Music in the Movies." *Canad Forum* 22 (Dec 42) 275–276. Discussion 22 (Jan 43) 303; 22 (Feb 43) 330–331.

Huntley, John. "Film Music." *S&S* 12 (No. 48, Jan 44) 90–93. Historical and theoretical discussion of the relation of film and music.

Catling, Darrel. "Film Music." *S&S* 13 (No. 49, May 44) 19. Intended as a supplement to article by John Huntley 12 (No. 48, Jan 44).

"Is It Bad to Be Good?" *Newswk* 26 (9 July 45) 93. Aaron Copland and Bernard Herrmann defend the quality of film music; various approaches to film scoring.

Jones, Chuck. "Music and the Animated Cartoon." *Hwd Q* 1 (No. 4, July 46). *See 2h(1).*

Nelson, Robert U. "Film Music: Color or Line?" *Hwd Q* 2 (No. 1, Oct 46) 57–65. Emotional values contrasted with intellectual "line" or "structure" of music in films; devices used by composers; parts of scores reproduced.

Milhaud, Darius. "Music for the Films." *Th Arts* (Sep 47) 27–29. Famous composer writes of film as both accessory and necessity.

Canby, Edward Tatnall. "Music for Background." *SRL* 32 (8 Jan 49) 29. Analysis of movie music as a unique art form.

Tiomkin, Dmitri. "Composing for Films." *FIR* 2 (Nov 51) 17–22. Accompanist for Max Linder has become composer for ballets and film; borrowing is often harder than inventing but sometimes it is better to "telegraph" feelings than to use original themes.

Hendricks, Gordon. "Film Music Comes of Age." *FIR* 3 (Jan 52) 22–27. Successful use of the leitmotif versus musical clichés; the value of the "absence" of film music in "preparation" of the audience; an analysis of George Auric's music for *The Lavender Hill Mob*.

Embler, Jeffrey. "The Structure of Film Music." *FIR* 4 (Aug–Sep 53) 332–335. Theme melody, leitmotif, and music used within the scene; examples.

McVay, Douglas. "The Art of the Actor." *F&F* 12 (No. 12, Sep 66). *See 2b(1).*

Cage, John. "A Few Ideas About Music and Films." *F Cult* (No. 29, 1963) 35–37. "I love the idea of writing for films but when I am doing it it is not so good!"

Johnson, William. "Face the Music." *FQ* 22 (No. 4, Summer 69) 3–19. The uses of music in dramatic films, treated in historical order at first, with some attention to "background" versus "Mickey-Mousing," followed by many detailed examples of music which directly enhances the spectator's involvement in the story.

Gallez, Douglas W. "Theories of Film Music." *CJ* 9 (No. 2, Spring 70) 40–47. By Kracauer and Pudovkin, film theorists; by Jaubert and Eisler, composers; proposed functional taxonomy.

2g(2b). History of Music

Antheil, George. "Hollywood and the New Music." *Cinema Arts* 1 (No. 2, July 37) 28. Composer discusses growth of motion-picture music and persons responsible.

White, E. B. "Mood Men: Playing for Silent Pictures." *Rdrs Dig* 33 (July 38). *See 4b.*

Morros, Boris. "Motion Pictures Turn to Music." *Musician* 43 (Sep 38) 154. The place of music in film from silent days to the present.

Ferguson, Stanley. "Gone with the Sound Track." *New Rep* 106 (30 Mar 42). *See 4b.*

Sobel, B. "Let the Audience Think." *SRL* 28 (10 Nov 45) 30+. A plea for better or less incidental music for the screen; a history of music for stage and screen included.

Kindschi, Lowell. "Twilight Furioso." *Atlantic* 181 (May 48) 95–96. Reminiscences of a theatre organist during the silent days.

Hine, A. "Movie Music Has Plenty of Listeners." *Holiday* 6 (July 49) 22. The evolution of film music.

"Music by the Frame." *New Yorker* 25 (6 Aug 49) 14–15. Talk at the Museum of Modern Art with Arthur Kleiner, who writes original scores for silent pictures.

"Arthur and the Keystone Kops." *American* 148 (Oct 49) 112. Brief profile of Arthur Kleiner, pianist for daily showings at Museum of Modern Art in New York.

Franchère, Lucille. "Rebirth of Music." *Cath World* 174 (Oct 51) 36–39. Impact of the introduction of the vitaphone on movies, radio, studying, and an appreciation of good music.

Winkler, Max. "The Origin of Film Music." *FIR* 2 (Dec 51) 34–42. In an excerpt from his autobiography, *A Penny from Heaven*, the author relates the events and their background that led to his invention of the music cue sheet and the spontaneous acceptance of it by the silent-film industry as a standard.

McNulty, J. "Come Quick: Indians!" *Holiday* 13 (Jan 53) 22–23+. A piano player of the silent movies recalls his work.

Griggs, John. "The Music Master." *FIR* 5 (Aug–Sep 54) 338–342. The days of the piano and the grand organ, recalled by one who played them in the silent-film era in Lombard, Illinois.

McCarty, Clifford. "Filmusic for Silents." *FIR* 8 (Mar 57) 117–118+. A review of the silent films (1908–1927) for which outstanding original scores were composed by such composers as Saint-Saëns, Victor Herbert, Sigmund Romberg, and Deems Taylor.

Fothergill, Richard. "Putting Music in Its Place." *F&F* 5 (No. 6, Mar 59) 10–11+. Evolution of the composition of music for films.

Stang, Joanne. "Making Music, Silent Style." *NYTM* (23 Oct 60) 83–84. Arthur Kleiner, silent-film pianist.

"Allegro, Presto, Whee!" *Newswk* 60 (13 Aug 62) 83. Full-time silent-movie pianist Arthur Kleiner.

Beckley, Paul V. "Divas in Movieland." *Opera News* 29 (19 Dec 64) 8–13. A history of opera singers in Hollywood.

Mann, Margery. "What's a Film Classic Without the Mighty Wurlitzer?" *Pop Photog* 66 (Jan 70) 27–28+. The Avenue Photoplay Society of San Francisco, begun by Vernon Gregory, features silent films accompanied by "the mighty Wurlitzer" originally from the State-Lake Theater in Chicago.

2g(2c). Technical Aspects of Music

"Bringing the Symphony Orchestra to Movie Patrons; Multiple Channel Recordings." *Etude* 55 (Nov 37) 710.

"Latest in Music Add Thrills to Movies." *Pop Mech* 68 (Dec 37) 830–831+. Efforts of Leopold Stokowski in applying sound-"mixing" techniques to the musical background of a film.

Varese, E. "Organized Sound Film." *Commonweal* 33 (13 Dec 40) 204–205. A composer discusses unique sound combinations for film music.

Kleiner, Arthur. "Film Scores." *S&S* 13 (No. 52, Jan 45) 103–104. Brief history and description; they have not changed much since 1908.

Forrest, David. "From Score to Screen." *Hwd Q* 1 (No. 2, Jan 46) 224–229. General view of technical process of music for films.

Potter, Ralph K. "Audivisual Music." *Hwd Q* 3 (No. 1, Fall 47) 66–78. Somewhat technical article on music synchronized and correlated with visual stimuli; examples of author's birdsong films, works by Whitney brothers, Disney, and others.

Epstein, Dave A. "Back Stage with the Film Music Composer." *Etude* 71 (Feb 53) 19+. Technical problems in producing background music; from an interview with Dmitri Tiomkin.

McLaren, Norman. "Notes on Animated Sound." *QFRTV* 7 (No. 3, Spring 53) 223–229. Detailed explanation by well-known artist at National Film Board of Canada; how artificial sounds and music are photographed on the sound track.

2g(2d). Case Studies and Criticism

Josephson, Matthew. "Modern Music for the Films." *New Rep* 66 (1 Apr 31) 183. Review of evening of music by Copland, Sessions, Milhaud, Blitzstein, McPhee, accompanied by movies.

White, Eric W. "The Music to *Harlequin*." *Close Up* 9 (No. 3, Sep 32) 164–171. The musician who worked with Lotte Reiniger discusses the score he created for this film.

London, Kurt. "Film Music of the Quarter." *Films* 1 (No. 1, Nov 39) 76–80. Korngold, Prokofiev, Copland, Honegger; documentary and other films reviewed in later issues (No. 2, Spring 40) 43–48 and (No. 4, Summer 40) 25–29.

Rubsamen, Walter H. "Music in the Cinema." *Arts & Arch* 61 (June 44) 9+. First of regular monthly articles for two years on the function and quality of cinema music.

Deutsch, Adolph. "*Three Strangers*." *Hwd Q* 1 (No. 2, Jan 46) 214–223. Blow-by-blow account by author; how he wrote the music for this film.

Morton, Lawrence. "The Music of *Objective: Burma*." *Hwd Q* 1 (No. 4, July 46) 378–395. Close analysis, with many reprinted themes from Franz Waxman's score.

Dickinson, Thorold. "Search for Music." *Penguin F Rev* 2 (Jan 47). *See 4g.*

Sternfeld, Frederick W. "The Strange Music of Martha Ivers." *Hwd Q* 2 (No. 3, Apr 47) 242–251. Study of relationship between story and music, with themes reproduced, for *The Strange Love of Martha Ivers*.

Morton, Lawrence. "Film Music of the Quarter." *Hwd Q* 3 (No. 1, Fall 47) 79–81. Critique of scores for *Song of Love, Woman on the Beach, Torment*, and others; this feature continues in each issue through *QFRTV* 6 (No. 1, Fall 51) 69–72.

Sternfeld, Frederick W. "Current Chronicle." *Musical Q* 35 (Jan 49) 115–121. The works of Virgil Thomson, composer of screen music; the music of *The River* and *Louisiana Story* explained in musical terms with sections from the scores.

Brown, H. "Two Film Scores." *Partisan Rev* 16 (Feb 49) 193–195. Differences in music tracks of *Louisiana Story* and *Kalpana*.

Hopkins, Anthony. "Music." *S&S* 19 (Dec 49) 23. See additional articles 19 (Mar 50) 32–33; 19 (May 50) 127; 19 (Dec 50) 336; 19 (Feb 51) 416.

"Thriller with a Zither Theme." *CSMM* (25 Feb 50) 14. On Anton Kara, composer of *The Third Man* theme.

Sternfeld, Frederick W. "Current Chronicle." *Musical Q* 36 (Apr 50) 274–276. Gail Kubik's musical score for *C-Man* and for other films.

Sternfeld, Frederick W. "Gail Kubik's Score for *C-Man*." *Hwd Q* 4 (No. 4, Summer 50) 360–369. Dartmouth music teacher tells how composer worked with director; portions of score reproduced. See also Helm, Everett, "Gail Kubik's Score for *C-Man*: The Sequel." *Hwd Q* (Spring 55).

Hopkins, Anthony. "Music: Congress at Florence." *S&S* 19 (Aug 50) 243–244. The setting and discussions of the Congress of Music held in Florence, Italy; objections to Hollywood film music; list of papers read.

Morton, Lawrence, and Anthony Hopkins. "Orchestration Run Riot?" *S&S* 20 (May 51) 21–23+. Rebuttal to an article written by Anthony Hopkins in earlier issue 19 (Aug 50) 243–244, in which he criticized Hollywood film music; Hopkins defends his position.

Morton, Lawrence. "Composing, Orchestrating, and Criticizing." *QFRTV* 6 (No. 2, Winter 51) 191–206. Portions of music as orchestrated by David Raksin (*Carrie*), George Duning, and Hugo Friedhofer (*Broken Arrow*).

Hendricks, Gordon. "*Ivory Hunter*'s Music." *FIR* 3 (Aug–Sep 52) 342–345. The best composers should write the music of films; a critical analysis of the musical score of *Ivory Hunter* by Alan Rawsthorne (in England titled *Where No Vultures Fly*).

Helm, Everett. "Gail Kubik's Score for *C-Man*: The Sequel." *QFRTV* 9 (No. 3, Spring 55) 263–282. Eleven excerpts from the symphony, which won a Pulitzer prize in 1952, contrasted with original score for film. See also Sternfeld, Frederick W., "Gail Kubik's Score for *C-Man*," *Hwd Q* (Summer 50).

Diether, Jack. "*Richard III*: The Preservation of a Film." *QFRTV* 11 (No. 3, Spring 57) 280–293. RCA Victor recorded the complete feature-length sound track of music and dialogue; but film and music by Sir William Walton were cut from three hours to two and a half.

McVay, Douglas. "The Music in *Les Parapluies*." *Film* (No. 42, Winter 64). *See 9, Umbrellas of Cherbourg*.

2g(3). DUBBING

[See also 2d(5), 7e(1).]

Johnston, William A. "The World War of Talking Pictures." *SEP* 203 (19 July 30). See 7e(1).

"New Art Fits Foreign Speech to Any Film." *Pop Sci* 121 (Nov 32) 36–37. German method for dubbing.

Pound, Louise. "Hollywood Slang in Spanish Translations." *Am Speech* 14 (Feb 39). See 4h.

Wolf, Julia. "The Continental Film in Britain." *Penguin F Rev* 4 (Oct 47) 89–94. The problems in subtitling and dubbing of foreign films; examples.

Blakeston, Oswell. "Synthetic Stars." *S&S* 16 (No. 64, Winter 47–48) 158. Positive case for dubbing foreign-made films.

Summers, Walter. "No! Mr. Blakeston." *S&S* 17 (No. 65, Spring 48) 14–15.

Crocker, Lester G., and Guardiola E. Cardellach. "Movie Dubbing? Does Redialogued Film Aid World Understanding?" *Rotarian* 72 (May 48) 22–24. Technique explained; a debate on the point of view of Latin America.

Volmar, Victor. "The Babel of Tongues." *FIR* 2 (Mar 51) 11–16. Current methods of dubbing and subtitling; problems imposed by foreign preferences and foreign governments' restrictions; a unique list of the major foreign governments and their usual official reasons for rejection of a film by the censor.

Guernsey, Otis L. "Ghosts in the Reel." *Sat Rev* 38 (30 Apr 55) 27. How dubbing links beautiful voices with the stars.

"Dubbing in the Voices, Also a Big Production." *Life* 46 (15 June 59) 79–80+. The dubbing for *Porgy and Bess*.

Iker, Sam. "Hollywood *Spricht Deutsch*." *Pop Mech* 112 (Dec 59) 65–69+. The process of dubbing English films into German.

Hatch, Robert. "Films." *Nation* 191 (3 Sep 60) 119–120. Answer to *New York Times'* Bosley Crowther concerning subtitles versus English-dubbed dialogue.

Knight, Arthur. "The Great Dubbing Controversy." *Sat Rev* 43 (29 Oct 60) 28. Dubbing differences in Jules Dassin's films.

Lane, John Francis. "*La* (The) *Dolce* (Sweet) *Vita* (Life)." *F&F* 7 (No. 9, June 61) 30+. On dubbing *La Dolce Vita* by the man who dubbed it.

Pratley, Gerald. "Now Entirely in English!" *Take One* 1 (No. 10, 1968) 8–9. Against the dubbing of foreign films.

"Labials and Fricatives." *New Yorker* 44 (9 Mar 68) 32–33. An interview with Lee Kresel, who works for a dubbing company, while he was dubbing Russian *War and Peace* in English.

Nowell-Smith, Geoffrey. "Italy *Sotto Voce*." *S&S* 37 (Summer 68). See 4e(3d).

2h. Animation

[See also 3f(3), 8d.

[See 5, Biography: Alexandre Alexeieff, Saul Bass, Walerian Borowczyk, Walt Disney, John Hubley, Norman McLaren, George Pal, Lotte Reiniger, Ladislas Starevitch, Jirí Trnka.]

"Again, Boop." *Time* 23 (30 Apr 34) 20. Helen Kane claims *Betty Boop* (a cartoon) steals her phrases and style.

"All-Cartoon Theater." *Newswk* 4 (20 Oct 34) 40.

Miller, J. "Army's Animated Cartoons Make Better Soldiers." *Pop Sci* 126 (June 35) 30–31.

Boone, A. R. "Movie Cartoons in Color." *Sci Am* 156 (Jan 37) 16–17. The innovation of color in animation techniques.

"Movie Cartoons Show How an Antitank Gun Works." *Pop Sci* 141 (Oct 42) 62–63.

Jones, Chuck. "Music and the Animated Cartoon." *Hwd Q* 1 (No. 4, July 46) 364–370. Potentialities for matching movements and music in musical education, folklore, abstractions, etc.; visual correlatives drawn for abstract words "tackety" and "goloomb."

Halferty, Guy. "Famous But Unknown." *CSMM* (9 Aug 47) 6. Mel Blanc does the voice of Bugs Bunny, and Clarence Nash, the voice of Donald Duck.

"Censor in the Barnyard." *Time* 58 (29 Oct 51) 83. The rules of cartoon censorship; *Red Hot Riding Hood* case.

Turner, G. A. "Artists Behind the Animated Cartoon." *Design* 54 (May 53) 190. How an illustrator applies for a job in animation with a major studio.

"Return of the Animals." *Newswk* 57 (22 May 61) 94. Problems of movie cartoons.

Halas, J., and R. Manvell. "Animated Cartoon." *Design* 64 (Sep 62) 33–36.

Crockwell, Douglas. "A Background to Free Animation." *F Cult* (No. 32, 1964) 30.

"Film Makers." *New Yorker* 39 (15 Feb 64) 25–27. Visit with David Wise, nine-year-old cartoonist of *Short Circuit*.

Andersen, Yvonne. "Film Animation at the Yellow Ball Workshop." *Design* 69 (Fall 67) 7–11. Techniques used by children and adults in a Lexington, Massachusetts, program.

Gough-Yates, Kevin. "The 'Mouvart' Group." *Studio Inter* 175 (Jan 68) 47. Artists working in animation.

Burns, Dan. "Pixillation." *FQ* 22 (No. 1, Fall

68) 36–41. New kinds of human movement make pixillation the perfect vehicle for integration of fantasy and reality.

2h(1). HISTORY AND THEORY OF ANIMATION

De Mille, William. "Mickey vs. Popeye." *Forum* 94 (Nov 35) 295–297. Cartoons' child appeal: Is Mickey Mouse a "New Dealer" and Popeye a "fascist"?

Grinde, N. "Whimsy by the Mile." *Rdrs Dig* 28 (Jan 36) 61–63. Survey of animated films in the U.S.

Wilson, H. "McCay Before Disney." *Time* 31 (10 Jan 38) 4.

Wright, Lawrence. "Barking Up the Wrong Tree." *S&S* 7 (No. 27, Autumn 38) 99–100. A plea for cartoon films to try more experiments, especially nonrealism.

Charlot, J. "But Is It Art? A Disney Disquisition." *Am Scholar* 8 (No. 3, July 39) 260–270. A look at animation, its history, its significance as an art form, parallels with painting.

Fleury, Gene. "Whimsy Has Growing Pains." *Calif Arts and Arch* 59 (No. 2, Feb 42) 18. The potentials of the animation film.

"Enter Private Snafu." *NYTM* (25 July 43). *See 7f(1a)*.

Hubley, John, and Zachary Schwartz. "Animation Learns a New Language." *Hwd Q* 1 (No. 4, July 46) 360–363. Because the armed services needed technical and orientation films, "pigs and bunnies have collided with nuts and bolts."

Grinde, Nick. "Greasepaint, Inkwell and Co." *Screen Writer* 2 (Sep 46) 18–26. Surveys the history of film making in which cartoon characters and human beings are combined.

Palmer, Charles. "Cartoon in the Classroom." *Hwd Q* 3 (No. 1, Fall 47) 26–33. How the animated film can put over ideas compared with live-action; examples from Disney's *Jet Propulsion, Reason and Emotion, Fantasia,* and others.

Schwerin, Jules. "Galloping Mirror of Nature." *Th Arts* 33 (Oct 49) 34–37. Was the genesis of animation in folk art and cave drawings?

Algar, James. "Animated Film: Fantasy and Fact." *Pacific Spectator* 4 (No. 4, 1950) 4–20. Reflections on the "coming of age" of the American animated cartoon by a Disney director.

Schwerin, Jules. "Drawings That Are Alive." *FIR* 1 (Sep 50) 6–9. Probable examples of art and sculpture that foreshadowed the development of animation; contemporary history from the one-dimensional dinosaur named "Gertie" in 1909 to Walt Disney; other countries' work.

Pratley, Gerald. "The Cartoon's Decay." *FIR* 2

(Nov 51) 34–36. Both British and American cartoons are hackneyed.

Culshaw, John. "Violence and the Cartoon." *Fortnightly Rev* 170 (Dec 51) 830–835. Comparison between early Disney cartoons and the newcomers.

Starr, Cecile. "Animation: Abstract and Concrete." *Sat Rev* 35 (13 Dec 52) 46–48. Disney's entrance into 16mm field; recent animation by Mary Ellen Bute and Norman McLaren.

Orna, Bernard. "Cartoons Before Films." *F&F* 1 (No. 3, Dec 54) 12. The inventions of Emile Reynaud, father of the cartoon.

Coates, Robert M. "Contemporary American Humorous Art." *Perspectives USA* (No. 14, 1956) 113–115. Humorous art in the animated cartoon with reference to Winsor McKay, Norman McLaren, Walt Disney, Paul Terry, Mary Ellen Bute, and others.

Bosustow, Stephen, and John C. Mahon, Jr. "American Animation Films Today." *JUFPA* 8 (No. 4, Summer 56) 5–6. A paper read at the Third International Congress of Schools of Cinema and Television.

Halas, John. "Not for Fun!" *F&F* 3 (No. 2, Nov 56) 6+. Serious purposes of animated films.

Manvell, Roger. "Giving Life to the Fantastic: A History of the Cartoon Film." *F&F* 3 (No. 2, Nov 56) 7–9+.

Rosenberg, Milton J. "Mr. Magoo as Public Dream." *QFRTV* 11 (No. 4, Summer 57) 337–342. Yale psychology professor suggests how the public identifies with this "adult" cartoon character; how his antics reflect general anxieties.

"Mousetrap." *Newswk* 52 (7 July 58) 72. Brief history of cartoons.

Mussen, Paul, and Eldred Rutherford. "Effects of Aggressive Cartoons on Children's Aggressive Play." *J of Abnormal & Social Psych* 62 (1961). *See 7b(4)*.

Martin, Pete. "20—Cartoons—20." *Kulchur* 2 (No. 5, Spring 62) 65–69. On the cartoon Saturday matinee.

Alexeieff, Alexandre. "Reflections on Motion Picture Animation." *F Cult* (No. 32, 1964) 28+.

Polt, Harriet. "The Death of Mickey Mouse." *F Com* 2 (No. 3, Summer 64) 34–39. Survey of animation studios around Hollywood.

Williams, S. "Animation." *Contemp Rev* 211 (Aug 67) 98–104. Many animated films influenced by modern art and its interest in science.

Arnall, Richard. "The Future of Animation." *Film* (No. 52, Autumn 68) 39–42.

Martarella, F. D. "Animated Cinema." *America* 120 (8 Mar 69) 271–273. Cartoons are a separate art form, and should not imitate live-action films.

Halas, John. "Tomorrow's Animation." *FIR* 20 (No. 5, May 69) 293–296.

2h(2). TECHNICAL ASPECTS OF ANIMATION

"Making of a Sound Fable." *Pop Mech* 54 (Summer 30) 353–355. How animated films are made.

"With the Unpaid Stars of the Movies." *Pop Mech* 56 (July 31) 8–12. How artificial voices are given to film cartoons.

"Slow Movies Aid Mickey Mouse." *Pop Mech* 57 (Sep 32) 434–435. Animators study film to reproduce exact animal movements in cartoons.

Boone, Andrew R. "When Mickey Mouse Speaks." *Sci Am* 148 (Mar 33) 146–147. Profile of Disney animation techniques.

"Breathing Life into Cartoon Characters." *Pop Mech* 63 (Mar 35) 386–389.

Garity, W. E. "Latest Tricks of the Animated Film Makers." *Pop Mech* 69 (May 38) 712–715+. *Snow White* affords a look at new animation techniques, particularly the multiplane camera; a summary of how a typical animated film is conceived and made.

Trotter, C. "Animating Art." *School Arts* 38 (Jan 39) 151–152.

"Boo to You." *American* 129 (Feb 40) 118. Pinto Colvig, cartoonist, draws facial expressions using himself as a model.

Halas, John. "Cartoon Films in Commerce." *Art and Industry* 29 (Nov 40) 170–176. How an animation film is made; its effectiveness in advertising.

"New Cartoon Camera Combines Drawings and Photographs." *Pop Sci* 137 (Dec 40) 98–99.

"How Disney Combines Living Actors with His Cartoon Characters." *Pop Sci* 145 (Sep 44) 106–111. Rear-screen projection.

Halas, John, and Joy Batchelor. "European Cartoon." *Penguin F Rev* 8 (Jan 49) 9–15. The methods of animation; some mention of Trnka and other Europeans.

Turner, G. A. "Artists Behind an Animated Cartoon." *Design* 54 (May 53) 190+.

Turner, G. A. "New Horizons in Animated Cartooning." *Design* 55 (Jan 54) 128–129.

Kimball, Ward. "Cartooning in Cinemascope." *FIR* 5 (Mar 54) 118–119. Animation director for Walt Disney estimates benefits and problems.

Verrall, Robert. "Making an Animated Film: *The Romance of Transportation.*" *Canad Art* 9 (No. 4, Summer 54) 148–150.

Hulett, R. "Artist's Part in the Production of an Animated Cartoon." *Am Artist* 19 (May 55) 33–39.

Kiesling, Barrett. "They Paint a Million Cats." *F&F* 3 (No. 2, Nov 56) 10–11. Making "Tom and Jerry" cartoons.

"Cheaper Cartoons." *Bus Wk* (4 May 57)

192–193. Artiscope transforms live human performers into cartoon characters.

"Designers in Film." *Print* 11 (Mar–Apr 58) 33–38. Description and development of a sales film created by designer Morton Goldsholl and his associates.

"Making Cartoons Out of People." *Sci Dig* 53 (Feb 63) 27–34.

"Animated Movies Made by Computer." *Sci Newsletter* 85 (2 May 64) 287. Review of a recent film by Professor Kenneth Knowlton of Bell Laboratories.

Knowlton, Kenneth C. "Computer-Produced Movies." *Science* 150 (26 Nov 65) 1116–1120. Computer-generated animated films and their use in education. Reply 151 (18 Feb 66) 839–840.

Knowlton, Kenneth C. "Computer-Generated Movies, Designs and Diagrams." *Design Q* (Nos. 66–67, 1966) 58–63. A demonstration of the feasible use of programmed languages for the production of animated films.

Halas, John, and Roger Manvell. "Animated Cartoon." *Design* 70 (Winter 68) 25–27. A general introduction to animation technique.

2h(3). DISNEY STUDIO

[See also 5, Walt Disney.]

"Mickey Mouse's Miraculous Movie Monkeyshines." *Lit Dig* 106 (9 Aug 30) 36–37. Story about the character of Mickey Mouse with excerpts of an "interview" by Dick Hyland in *The New Movie Magazine* and comments by Creighton Peet from *The Outlook and Independent.*

"Mickey Mouse and His Playmates." *Rev of Reviews* 83 (Apr 31) 81.

"Europe's Highbrows Hail Mickey Mouse." *Lit Dig* 110 (8 Aug 31) 19. Mickey Mouse seen as the birth of a new art of cinema; quotations from French periodicals.

Seldes, Gilbert. "Disney and Others." *New Rep* 71 (8 June 32) 101–102. Critic reviews animation development of Disney, Max Fleischer, and Hollywood in general.

Disney, Walt. "Merry Christmas from Mickey and Minnie Mouse." *Delineator* 121 (Dec 32) 15.

"Profound Mouse." *Time* 21 (15 May 33) 37–38. Description of Mickey Mouse's doings on screen, his career, and the career of Walter Disney.

Disney, Walt. "Cartoon's Contribution to Children." *Overland Monthly and Outwest Mag* (No. 91, Oct 33) 138. "If Mickey were to say or do one thing to hurt the child audience in any way, he would die of shame."

"Mickey Mouse, Financier." *Lit Dig* 116 (21 Oct 33) 41. On Mickey Mouse's fifth birthday: a report from *Forbes* on his financial success—where the profits go.

"Mechanical Mouse." *SRL* 10 (11 Nov 33) 252. Mickey Mouse attacked by the Nazis, who apparently wish to return to the folk tales of a simpler time.

Schwab, Mack W. "The Communalistic Art of Walt Disney." *CQ* 2 (No. 3, Spring 34) 150–154. How the studio works together.

Jamison, J. "Around the World with Mickey Mouse." *Rotarian* 44 (May 34) 22–24.

Bragdon, C. "Mickey Mouse and What He Means." *Scribner's* 96 (July 34) 40–43.

Johnston, A. "Mickey Mouse." *Woman's Home Companion* 61 (July 34) 12–13.

Rim, Carlo. "French Cartoonist on Mickey Mouse." *Living Age* 346 (July 34) 461. Excerpt from article in *Marianne*.

"Walt Disney and Mickey Mouse." *S&S* 4 (No. 14, Summer 35) 64–65. Disney, his cartoon character, and the cartoon process.

Burnet, D. "Rise of Donald Duck, Mickey Mouse's Enemy." *Pictorial Rev* 37 (Oct 35) 19.

"Mickey Mouse Is Eight Years Old." *Lit Dig* 122 (3 Oct 36) 18–19.

"Mouse and Man." *Time* 30 (27 Dec 37) 19–21. The story of Walt Disney and Mickey Mouse.

Boone, A. R. "*Snow White and the Seven Dwarfs:* First Full-Length Cartoon Movie." *Pop Sci* 132 (Jan 38) 50–52+. Behind the scenes; technical aspects.

"*Ferdinand the Bull.*" *Scholastic* 33 (12 Nov 38) 10–11. High spots from Walt Disney's Technicolor movie short.

Robins, S. "Disney Again Tries Trailblazing: *Fantasia.*" *NYTM* (3 Nov 40) 6–7+.

Daugherty, F. "How Donald Comes Out of the Paint Pots." *CSMM* (14 Dec 40) 6.

Isaacs, H. R. "New Horizons: *Fantasia* and Fantasound." *Th Arts* 25 (Jan 41) 55–61. The innovations and problems in *Fantasia,* both technical and aesthetic; detailed look at "Fantasound."

LaFarge, Christopher. "Disney and the Art Form." *Th Arts* 25 (Sep 41). See *3a(1).*

"South American Caravan." *Calif Arts and Arch* 59 (No. 7, July 42) 20+. "Silly Symphonies" by Walt Disney on Latin-American themes.

"Walt Disney: Great Teacher." *Fortune* 26 (Aug 42) 90–95+. Subtitles: "His films for war are revolutionizing the technique of education."

"Walt Disney Goes to War." *Life* 13 (31 Aug 42) 61–69. Disney's animated war-training films.

Hallet, R. "Trail of *Bambi.*" *Collier's* 110 (3 Oct 42) 58+. Drawings for Walt Disney's *Bambi* made from photographs taken of Maine forests.

Delehanty, Thornton. "Disney Studio at War." *Th Arts* 27 (Jan 43) 31–39. Training, instruc-

tional, morale, and mobilization films from "the industry's prime realist."

"Mickey Mouse and Donald Duck Join the Colors." *Sch Arts* 43 (Sep 43) 7–8.

Disney, Walt. "Mickey as Professor." *Pub Opin Q* 9 (No. 2, 1945) 119–125. Animated cartoons as instructional devices.

"Saga of Pablo." *NYTM* (4 Feb 45) 28–29. "The Cold-blooded Penguin" in Disney's *Three Caballeros:* drawings from continuity.

Nugent, F. "That Million-Dollar Mouse." *NYTM* (21 Sep 47) 22+. History of Mickey.

Wallace, J. "Mickey Mouse and How He Grew." *Collier's* 123 (9 Apr 49) 20–21.

Disney, Walt. "How I Cartooned 'Alice.' " *FIR* 2 (May 51) 7–11. Why characters were left out; how test audiences responded.

"New Art Medium for 'Alice' . . . Animated Cartoons." *Design* 53 (Oct 51) 10–11. How Disney studio creates a feature-length animated cartoon.

"*Peter Pan:* Real Disney Magic; Real Animals Also Make Money." *Newswk* 41 (16 Feb 53) 96–99. History and analysis of Walt Disney Productions.

Jamison, Barbara B. "Of Mouse and Man; or Mickey Reaches Twenty-five." *NYTM* (13 Sep 53) 26–27.

Whitcomb, Jon. "Girls Behind Disney's Characters." *Cosmopolitan* 136 (May 54) 50–55. Disney's cartoon heroines (Snow White, Wendy, etc.) and how real people are used as models.

Disney, Walt. "Animated Mr. Disney." *Cosmopolitan* 141 (Oct 56) 56–57. Brief pictorial survey of the different kinds of animation Disney does.

Heylbut, Rose. "Disney Fun with Music." *Etude* 74 (Oct 56). See *2g(2).*

Whitaker, F. "Day with Disney." *Am Artist* 29 (Sep 65) 44–48+. The process involved in making Disney films.

Sayers, Frances. "Walt Disney Accused." *Horn Bk* (Dec 65) 602–611. Misuse of children's books.

"Magic Kingdom." *Time* 87 (15 Apr 66) 84.

MacFadden, Patrick. "Letting Go." *F Soc Rev* 4 (No. 1, 1968) 22–25. Comments on Walt Disney's works as possible psychological manifestations.

Tucker, N. "Who's Afraid of Walt Disney?" *New Society* 11 (1968) 502–503.

Schickel, R. "Bringing Forth the Mouse." *Am Heritage* 19 (Apr 68) 24–29. History of Disney's Mickey Mouse.

Bayer, A. "Happy 40th, Mickey." *Life* 65 (25 Oct 68) 57–58.

Hicks, Jimmie. "*Fantasia*'s Silver Anniversary." *FIR* 16 (No. 9, Nov 68). See *9, Fantasia.*

Grove-Baxter, Grange. "Snow White Meets the Blue Meanies." *Film* (No. 54, Spring 69) 27–31. A discussion of Walt Disney's career and a comparison of his work with that in *The Yellow Submarine.*

2h(4). UPA AND OTHER AMERICAN STUDIOS

"Cuckoo Rampant." *Newswk* 31 (9 Feb 48) 75. The creation of Impossible Pictures, Inc., by Leonard L. Levinson to produce new cartoons.

Winge, John H. "Cartoons and Modern Music." *S&S* 17 (No. 67, Autumn 48) 136–137. MGM's "Tom and Jerry" series and those made by Tex Avery seem to have musical ambitions.

"Speaking of Pictures, These Show Film Star McBoing-Boing." *Life* 30 (15 Jan 51) 8–9. A preview of the UPA production with eleven drawings.

"Boing!" *Time* 57 (5 Feb 51) 78. United Productions of America make *Gerald McBoing-Boing.*

Hine, A. "McBoing-Boing and Magoo." *Holiday* 9 (June 51) 6. Some of UPA's ambitious and imaginative animated cartoons.

Knight, Arthur. "Up From Daisy." *Th Arts* 35 (Aug 51) 32–33. The UPA organization as a conscious reaction to Disney; imagination as opposed to technical realism in animation.

Sagar, Isobel C. "The UPA Cartoons." *FIR* (Nov 51) 36–37. Short note on *Gerald McBoing-Boing* and others.

Knight, Arthur. "UPA, Magoo and McBoing-Boing." *Art Dig* 26 (1 Feb 52) 22. UPA's attempt to challenge Disney's domination of the animation field by shunting Disney's anthropomorphic approach.

Seldes, Gilbert. "Delight in Seven Minutes." *Sat Rev* 35 (31 May 52) 27. The animated cartoons of United Productions of America are a return to the first principles of the animated cartoon: a drawing that deliberately distorts.

Farber, Manny. "Films: Kinesis Films." *Nation* 175 (11 Oct 52) 337. Jordan Belson and Storm de Hirsh: experimental animation.

Crowther, Bosley. "McBoing-Boing, Magoo, and Bosustow." *NYTM* (21 Dec 52) 14–15+. A report on the rise of UPA, makers of unconventional animated cartoons.

Oerl, G. "UPA, A New Dimension for the Comic Strip; with German and French Texts." *Graphis* 9 (No. 50, 1953) 470–479+.

Fisher, David. "Disney and UPA." *S&S* 23 (July–Sep 53) 40–41. A discussion of two animated cartoons, Disney's *Peter Pan* and UPA's *The Dog Catcher,* starring Mr. Magoo, with some added comments on the development of more sophisticated animated films.

Turner, G. A. "New Horizons in Animated Cartooning: UPA Cartoons." *Design* 56 (Jan 54) 128–129.

Weinman, M. "Just Call Him Howdy Dude-Y, Pardner." *Collier's* 134 (23 July 54) 64–65. Introduction to a new cartoon, called *Howdy Doody's Magic Hat.*

Langsner, Jules. "UPA." *Arts & Arch* 71 (Dec 54) 12–15. An appraisal of the UPA animation films.

Sullivan, Catherine. "United Productions of America." *Am Artist* 19 (Nov 55) 34–39+.

Harbert, Ruth. "Mr. Tom and Mr. Jerry." *Good Housekeeping* 142 (Mar 56) 44+. The work of cartoonmen Bill Hanna and Joe Barbera.

Larkin, Thomas. "Art Films." *Scholastic Arts* 55 (May 56) 44. The influence of UPA cartoons.

Fisher, David. "UPA in England." *S&S* 26 (Summer 56) 45. Fisher, an animator himself, sees the UPA decision to go into production in England as a hopeful sign.

"Up from Bugs." *New Yorker* 37 (5 Aug 61) 18. Animated *Children of the Sun,* made for UNICEF by John Hubley, uses only sounds of the children to make the point that children are hungry.

Callenbach, Ernest. "Auguries?" *FQ* 17 (No. 3, Spring 64) 28–31. Visual experiences created and reproduced electronically; new directions seen from the work of John Whitney, Jordan Belson, Bill Risdon.

MacDonald, Dwight. "Complete Works of Ernest Pintoff." *Esq* 61 (Apr 64) 16+.

Crick, Philip. "Notes on Jimmie Murakami." *Film* (No. 43, Autumn 65) 34–37. The work of the American animator.

"Put a Panther in Your Tank." *Time* 86 (1 Oct 65) 90. "Cartoon Renaissance" by the Pink Panther and his creators.

Armitage, Peter. "Animation." *Film* (No. 45, Spring 66) 24–29. A critical overview since 1940, with special emphasis on UPA.

Wilson, John. *"Archy and Mehitabel."* *Cinema* (Calif) 5 (No. 2, 1969) 36–37. "Animated film is a legitimate art form"; comments by the director on the making of this feature.

Jones, Chuck. "The Roadrunner and Other Characters." *CJ* 8 (No. 2, Spring 69) 10–16. In an interview with Robert Benayoun of *Positif,* retranslated into English, the American director of animation films tells how characters are created and developed.

Rieder, Howard. "Memories of Mr. Magoo." *CJ* 8 (No. 2, Spring 69) 17–24. Based on interviews with UPA animation artists and directors for an M.A. thesis at the University of Southern California; development of the character, the drawing style, the philosophy for this series of cartoon shorts.

Adamson, Joe. "You Couldn't Get Chaplin in a Milk Bottle." *Take One* 2 (No. 9, 1970). *See 5, Tex Avery.*

2h(5). INTERNATIONAL DEVELOPMENTS

[See also 4i.]

Weaver, Randolph T. "Prince Achmed and Other Animated Silhouettes." *Th Arts* 15 (June 31) 505–509. Animation techniques by Frau Reiniger Koch.

"Etchings for the Movies." *Living Age* 347 (Oct 34) 174. Russian painter Alexeiev discovers new animation technique.

Reiniger, Lotte. "Scissors Make Films." *S&S* 5 (No. 17, Spring 36) 13–15. Her methods for making silhouette films.

White, E. W. "Lotte Reiniger and Her Art." *Horn Bk* 15 (Jan 39) 45–48. Silhouette films.

Mackay, James. "Animation in the Canadian Film." *Studio* 129 (Apr 45) 115. About the National Film Board of Canada.

Barty-King, Hugh. "Italy's First Sound Cartoons." *S&S* 16 (No. 61, Spring 47) 4–5.

Halas, John. "Animated Film." *Art and Industry* 43 (July–Aug 47) 2–7+. Two articles reviewing the technical and aesthetic development of the British animated film.

Wilson, John. "Cartoons in the Countryside." *CSMM* (31 Dec 48) 8–9. Profile of British Animation Company.

"Battle of Wonderland." *Time* 58 (16 July 51) 90. French-made puppet and live-action versus Disney's animated *Alice in Wonderland*.

Imamura, Taihei. "Japanese Art and the Animated Cartoon." *QFRTV* 7 (No. 3, Spring 53) 217–222. Critic and editor of motion-picture magazine *Movie Culture* describes several traditional picture-scrolls, urges animators to draw on this tradition rather than imitating Western styles.

Martin, Geoffrey. "The Designer and the Cartoon Film." *Art and Industry* 55 (Sep 53) 94–99. The author describes his work on the production of George Orwell's *Animal Farm*.

Rosner, C. "Halas and Batchelor: Artists and Film-makers; with German and French Texts." *Graphis* 10 (No. 53, 1954) 194–201. The British animation team.

Borshell, Allan, *et al.* "The Animated Film." *Film* (No. 4, Mar 55) 12–18. Its history, the work of Halas and Batchelor, UPA, *Animal Farm*, etc.

Orna, Bernard. "Little Studio of Arcady." *F&F* 2 (No. 1, Oct 55) 13. Animation film maker Arcady works in south Paris.

Orna, Bernard. "Trnka's Little Men." *F&F* 3 (No. 2, Nov 56) 12. Influence of Jiří Trnka's animated films on Polish and Rumanian film makers.

"Cinema Cold War in Asia: Animated Cartoons." *America* 99 (12 July 58). *See 7b(5)*.

Williams, Richard. "Animation and *The Little Island*." *S&S* 27 (Autumn 58) 309–311. By the artist who made this half-hour film.

Martin, André. "Animated Cinema: The Way Forward." *S&S* 28 (No. 2, Spring 59) 80–85. International survey, including UPA, McLaren, Bass, and East Europe.

Knight, Derrick. "Berthold Bartosch." *Film* (No. 23, Jan–Feb 60) 26. Brief comments on the French film maker who made the animated film *L'Idée*.

Manvell, Roger. "A Festival for Animation." *F&F* 6 (No. 11, Aug 60) 31. At Annecy, France.

Richie, Donald. "Yugoslav Short Films." *FQ* 14 (No. 4, Summer 61) 31–36. Emphasis on animation studio, which is self-supporting.

Halas, John. "Introducing Hamilton." *F&F* 8 (No. 9, June 62) 18–19. On his new animation character, Hamilton the elephant.

Hill, Derek. "The Unknown Cartoonists." *S&S* 31 (Autumn 62) 186–188. During the second Animated Film Festival held at Annecy, all the best cartoons were British.

Weinstock, N. "Fourth International Cartoon Film Conference, Annecy, 1962; with German and French Texts." *Graphis* 18 (Sep 62) 534–539.

Hill, Derek. "Cartoons and Commercials." *S&S* 32 (Spring 63) 67. Richard Williams supports his animated films for theatres by making TV commercials.

"East Meets West in Cartoon Venture." *Bus Wk* (11 May 63) 104–105. Japanese animated cartoon features and commercials for the United States.

Benayoun, Robert. "Animation: The Phoenix and the Road-Runner." *FQ* 17 (No. 3, Spring 64) 16–25. Whether autonomous art form or cinematic extension, animation develops too fast to be subject to definition; a survey of leading artists in various countries; reprinted from *Positif* (July–Aug 63).

"Cinéastes Associés." *Film* (No. 39, Spring 64) 36. A description of the Parisian animation group which includes, among others, Walerian Borowczyk.

Hill, Derek. "Animation Amid the Animators: A Report from the Annecy Festival." *FQ* 17 (No. 3, Spring 64) 25–28. Recent work by Hubley, Alexeieff, Lenica, Vukotic.

Polt, Harriet R. "The Czechoslovak Animated Film." *FQ* 17 (No. 3, Spring 64) 31–40. Its history; techniques and descriptions of animated and puppet films; Trnka, Pojar, and Zeman—the "big three."

Crick, Philip. "The Need to Draw 80,000 Bug-Eyed Men." *Film* (No. 40, Summer 64) 16–20. An interview with Richard Williams, the British animator.

Crick, Philip. "The Freelance Vision of Stan Hayward." *Film* (No. 42, Winter 64) 10–13. British writer and animated-film maker.

"K is for Kuri and Kristl." *Film* (No. 42,

Winter 64) 36–37. Brief comments on the animated shorts of Yoji Kuri and Vlado Kristl.

Junker, Howard. "Art of Animation." *Nation* 202 (28 Feb 66) 249–250. Festival sponsored by the Museum of Modern Art with foreign entries.

Weinstock, N. "Seventh International Cartoon Film Festival in Annecy, 1967; with German and French Texts." *Graphis* 23 (No. 133, 1967) 466–473.

Rider, David. "Animation." *Film* (No. 49, Autumn 67) 14–15. An overview of recent animation in Britain and America.

Holloway, Ronald. "Animation from Zagreb." *F Com* 5 (No. 11, Fall 68) 80–87. Several films and film makers in Yugoslavia; list of films shown by Museum of Modern Art in New York; program notes for the showing by Adrienne Mancia.

Osborn, Elodie. "Animation in Zagreb." *FQ* 22 (No. 1, Fall 68) 46–51. History and characteristics of Yugoslav school; many titles discussed.

Eason, Patrick. "Cambridge Animation." *S&S* 38 (Winter 68–69) 22. Report on a festival, including French retrospective.

Taylor, Richard. "Animation Limited." *Film* (No. 57, Winter 69–70) 16–17. Problems of making animated films in Great Britain: sponsorship, technique, theory.

Glover, Guy. "Nine Film Animators Speak: Introductory Note." *Arts Canada* 27 (Apr 70) 28–34. The work at the National Film Board of: Laurent Lodevre, Ryan Larkin, Sidney Goldsmith, Derek May, Bernard Longpré, Norman McLaren, Kar Liang, Ritchard Raxlen, Donald Winxler.

Gelder, Paul. "Lotte Reiniger: Figures in Silhouette." *Film* (No. 59, Summer 70) 9–10. An overview of the work of the German silhouette-film maker, now living in England.

Reiniger, Lotte. "The Adventures of Prince Achmed, or What May Happen to Somebody Trying to Make a Full-Length Cartoon in 1926." *Silent Picture* (No. 8, Autumn 70) 2–4.

2h(6). PUPPETS AND OTHER TECHNIQUES

"Create Movie Characters in Clay." *Pop Sci* 121 (Dec 32) 43.

Brenon, Aileen St. John. "Three Thousand Puppets in Motion Pictures." *Design* 38 (May 36) 22–23. Production of A. Ptushko's *The New Gulliver* (USSR).

Hutchins, Patricia. "Puppets on Parade." *S&S* 5

(No. 19, Autumn 36) 69–71. Brief historical and critical statements on puppet films.

"Puppet Movies: George Pal's Puppetoons, Combining Puppets with Actual Sets." *Pop Sci* 138 (Apr 41) 82–84.

Oppenheim, B. "Propaganda Puppets." *NYTM* (20 Feb 44). *See 7e(2)*.

"Six-Inch Wax Dolls Are New Stars in Filmland." *Pop Sci* 148 (May 46) 108–110.

Gorney, Sondra. "The Puppet and the Moppet." *Hwd Q* 1 (No. 4, July 46) 371–375. Russian puppet films; George Pal's Puppetoons.

"Putting Life in Puppets." *Pop Mech* 88 (Sep 47) 156–159.

Broz, Jaroslav. "The Czech Puppet Films." *FIR* 3 (Mar 52) 112–117. Karel Dodal, Hermína Tyrlová, Karel Zeman, and Jiří Trnka, and their work.

Ford, Charles. "Ladislas Starevitch." *FIR* 9 (Apr 58) 190–192+. Translated by Anne and Thornton K. Brown. The Russian-born puppet-film maker has worked in Russia, France, and Czechoslovakia.

Bocek, J. "Czechoslovak Puppet Films; with German and French Texts." *Graphis* 16 (Sep 60) 416–421.

2h(7). TITLE DESIGN

[See also 2d(5).]

Haan, E. R. "Easy to Make Movie Titles." *Pop Mech* 107 (Apr 57) 191–193.

Bass, S. "Film Titles—A New Field for the Graphic Designer; with German and French Texts." *Graphis* 16 (May 60) 208–215.

"Man with a Golden Arm." *Time* 79 (16 Mar 62) 46. A look at Saul Bass and his title designs.

Oswald, J. R. "Backlight Your Movie Titles." *Pop Mech* 119 (Jan 63) 168–169.

Gid, R. "Saul Bass: New Film Titlings and Promotional Films; with German and French Texts." *Graphis* 19 (Mar 63) 150–159.

Zeitlin, David. "What a Way to Start." *Life* 56 (7 Feb 64) 99–101+. A report on movie-title sequences.

Aison, Everett. "The Current Scene: Film Titles." *Print* 19 (July–Aug 65) 26–30. Historical review of development of opening credit (title) design, the wide interest generated by Saul Bass and the James Bond (007) films.

"Titles: Coming on Strong." *Newswk* 72 (8 July 68) 64–65. Saul Bass and other creators of credit-title sequences.

Kane, Bruce, and Joel Reisner. "A Conversation with Saul Bass." *Cinema* (Calif) 4 (No. 3, Fall 68) 30–35. How he works on film-title designs; examples.

2i. Actors' Services

2i(1). COSTUMES

Mount, Laura. "Designs on Hollywood." *Collier's* 87 (4 Apr 31) 21. On Gabrielle Chanel and star fashions.

Pretzfelder, Max. "The Film Costumer's Problems." *Close Up* 9 (No. 4, Dec 32) 275–280. Pabst's costumer discusses his work.

Adrian. "Setting Styles Through the Stars." *Ladies' Home J* 50 (Feb 33) 10–11+. Costumer suggests impact of movie clothing.

Luick, Earle. "Costuming the Movies." (Ed. by Mary Brush Williams.) *SEP* 206 (9 Sep 33) 18–19+.

"Movie Costumes Worth Millions." *Pop Mech* 65 (Jan 36) 82–84.

Churchill, L. "Modes *à la* Movies." *NYTM* (7 Jan 40) 8–9. Costume films bring back fashions of long ago.

Valentina. "Designing for Life and Theatre." *Th Arts* 25 (Feb 41) 139–145. Theatrical costumes.

"Costume Design." *Th Arts* 25 (Feb 41) 163–166. A gallery of designers and their creations.

"Gown Goes to Town." *Collier's* 111 (15 May 43) 18–19. About costume designer for 20th Century-Fox.

Head, Edith. "A Costume Problem: From Shop to Stage to Screen." *Hwd Q* 2 (No. 2, Oct 46) 44. Paramount costume specialist explains female costumes in several recent films; captions only.

"Movie Mermaid." *Life* 24 (9 Feb 48) 91–92+. The construction and fitting of a tail for Ann Blyth, in *Mr. Peabody and the Mermaid*.

Harbert, Ruth. "Assignment in Hollywood." *Good Housekeeping* 137 (July 53) 199. The handweaving of the fabric for *The Robe*.

Harbert, Ruth. "Hollywood's Storehouse." *Good Housekeeping* 137 (Oct 53) 17+. Western Costume Company is the storeroom for six major film companies.

Whitcomb, Jon. "He Makes the Stars Look That Way." *Cosmopolitan* 137 (July 54) 42–45. Hollywood Svengali Don Loper, who redesigns personalities as well as clothes for the stars.

Furse, Roger. "A Wardrobe for Richard." *F&F* 1 (No. 7, Apr 55) 8–9. Costume designer reports on his part in the production of Olivier's *Richard III*.

Furse, Roger. "Middle Ages Through Modern Eyes." *F&F* 1 (No. 8, May 55) 10–11. Costumes and sets for *Richard III* must be acceptable to modern audiences.

Woulfe, Michael. "Costuming a Film." *FIR* 6 (Aug–Sep 55) 325–327. Motion-picture costume designer describes his duties and problems.

Laitin, J. "Up in Edie's Room." *Collier's* 136 (2 Sep 55) 26–31. A portrait of costume designer Edith Head.

"An Unrumpled Rest in Ruffles." *Life* 41 (24 Sep 56) 96+. Actresses prevent elegant dresses from wrinkling between takes by resting on "leaning boards."

Harris, Jake. "Costume Designing." *F&F* 4 (No. 2, Nov 57) 17.

Beaton, Cecil. "On Making *Gigi*." *Vogue* 131 (June 58) 88–91. By the fashion designer of the film.

Head, Edith, and Jane K. Ardmore. "I Dress the World's Most Glamorous Women." *Good Housekeeping* 148 (Mar 59) 64–67+. Story by the fashion designer of Paramount Pictures.

Silke, James R. "The Costumes of George Stevens' *The Greatest Story Ever Told*." *Cinema* (Calif) 1 (No. 6, Nov–Dec 63) 17–19.

Beaton, Cecil. "*My Fair Lady*." *Ladies' Home J* 81 (Jan 64) 56–65. Excerpts from Cecil Beaton's diary; costumes for film.

"New Zing in Style for Starlets." *Life* 65 (16 Aug 68) 72–75. Background for photographs: Century City, L.A.

"Those 'Damned' Fashions Are Turning Up Everywhere." *Show* (May 70) 52–55. Piero Tosi's costumes for Visconti's *The Damned*, sketches and movie stills.

Head, Edith. "Honesty in Today's Film Fashions." *Show* (6 Aug 70) 14–15. Why today's screen fashions no longer set trends.

2i(2). MAKEUP

Peak, M. O. "Hollywood Tells How to Make Up." *Ladies' Home J* 49 (Feb 32) 16–17.

Wagner, Rob. "You'd Never Know Me Now." *Collier's* 89 (14 May 32) 10+. On makeup man's ability to transform actresses.

Albert, Katherine. "Remodel—Hollywood Fashion." *Good Housekeeping* 97 (Oct 33) 60–61+. Shows before/after of movie queens Joan Crawford, Greta Garbo, Norma Shearer.

"Mysteries of Movie Make-Up." *Sci Am* 149 (Nov 33) 220–221.

"Actor's Rubber Masks to Replace Make-Up." *Pop Sci* 125 (Oct 34) 44.

"Rubber Make-Up Gives Actors Many Faces." *Pop Sci* 132 (Mar 38) 58–59.

"How Faces Are Made to Order for the Movies." *Pop Mech* 71 (Jan 39) 82.

"Eye for a Cyclops." *Life* 35 (21 Sep 53) 173–174. Makeup crew for Polyphemus, in the Italian version of *The Odyssey*.

Westmore, Wally, and Pete Martin (ed.). "I Make Up Hollywood." *SEP* 229 (4 Aug 56) 17–19+; (11 Aug 56) 30+. Reminiscences by top Hollywood makeup man.

Conrad, Derek. "Laboratory for Faces." *F&F* 3 (No. 11, Aug 57) 18–19. Makeup work of Charles Parker.

Partleton, Billy. "The Make-Up Artist." *F&F* 4 (No. 3, Dec 57) 26.

"Make-up Job in Reverse." *Life* 47 (26 Oct 59) 128. Deglamorizing Rita Hayworth for her new film, *They Came to Cordura*.

Kehoe, U. "Basic Rules for Movie Make-Up." *Pop Photog* 48 (Jan 61) 96–97.

"Funnyman Changes Face." *Life* 55 (18 Oct 63) 139–141. Tony Randall makes up for *The Seven Faces of Dr. Lao*.

"Planet Gone Ape." *Life* 63 (18 Aug 67) 82–83. Million dollars' worth of makeup obliterates some famous faces in *Planet of the Apes*.

2j. Special Technical Services

Dunn, H. H. "The World's Queerest Jobs." *Pop Mech* 54 (Sep 30) 434–439. Movie making has work for sculptors, blacksmiths, hairdressers.

Lodge, J. E. "World's Craziest Jobs Add Realism to Modern Movies." *Pop Sci* 128 (Mar 36) 36–38.

"Odd Jobs in Hollywood." *Pop Mech* 68 (Sep 37) 364–367+. The prop men, the collectors, the character actors.

"Packing Drama in the Films." *Pop Mech* 69 (Jan 38) 72–75. Behind the scenes with stunt men and special effects.

Beatty, Jerome. "Strange Ways to Make a Living." *American* 126 (June 38) 42–43+. Prop men, stunt artists, and others.

Lloyd, Frank. "Millions for Movie Ideas." *Pop Mech* 70 (Oct 38) 514–517+. Some of the technical problems of movies that have been overcome, and some that haven't.

"Movies That Mimic Life." *Pop Mech* 76 (Dec 41) 66–69+. Technical advances and professional tricks add realism.

"Side Show: Master Craftsmen of Illusion." *American* 134 (Sep 42) 55. Behind-the-scenes effects.

Wharton, Mel. "Feudal Craftsmen of the Movies." *Pop Mech* 89 (May 48) 163–165. Techniques used in turning out authentic copies of historic costumes, settings, arms.

2j(1). SPECIAL EFFECTS

"Models and Photographs in Motion Picture Studios." *Science* 71 (31 Jan 30) supp 12. Reports use of mirrors in Schüfftan process.

"Explosions in the Movies." *Lit Dig* 105 (12 Apr 30) 28. Special effects for war movies.

"Giant Movie Sets Now Built from Tiny Models." *Pop Sci* 119 (Oct 31) 25. On miniatures used for *The Greene Murder Case*.

Boone, Andrew R. "Startling Movie Stunts with Toy Planes on Strings." *Pop Sci* 121 (Nov 32) 18–19+. Filming *Air Mail*.

"The Latest Movie Magic." *Pop Mech* 59 (Apr 33) 586–588. On Dunning process of background shooting.

Boone, Andrew R. "On the Battlefields of Make-Believe." *Travel* 62 (Nov 33) 23–25+. Special effects for war films.

"Does the Camera Ever Lie?" *Pop Mech* 61 (Feb 34) 234–238+. Use of miniatures.

"Earthquake Is Made to Order for the Movies." *Pop Mech* 62 (Aug 34) 193.

"The Master of Movie Thrills." *Pop Mech* 63 (Mar 35) 348–351+. Kenneth Strickfaden, movie electrician on *Frankenstein*.

Lodge, John E. "Odd Machines Put Fun in Movies." *Pop Sci* 126 (Mar 35) 26–27+.

"Latest Stunts of the Movie Magicians." *Pop Mech* 63 (Apr 35) 540–543+. Devised by John P. Fulton and Frank Williams for *The Invisible Man*.

"Explosion Experts Add Thrills to Movies." *Pop Mech* 64 (Oct 35) 530–533+. Battle sequences.

"Remaking the World for the Movies." *Pop Mech* 65 (Apr 36) 546–549+. Special-effects department at Warners; one of a series.

Wharton, M. "Indoor Blizzards Produced in Refrigerated Movie Stage." *Pop Sci* 128 (June 36) 20–21.

"Secrets of Movie Weather." *Pop Mech* 66 (Sep 36) 356–359. One of a series on production.

"Weather Made-to-Order for the Movies." *Pop Mech* 66 (Nov 36) 706–709.

"Battlefield in Miniature." *Pop Sci* 130 (June 37) 31. How sets are used to create illusions of depth and size.

"Latest Movie Thrills." *Pop Mech* 69 (June 38) 818–821+. A gallery of special effects and how they are done.

"Better Hurricanes." *Sci Newsletter* 34 (12 Nov 38) 311. The new trick of motion pictures—movie storms must be noiseless, treadmills silent.

Lodge, J. E. "Fighting Wars for the Movies." *Pop Sci* 136 (May 40) 84–88+. Planning and technical effects.

"Mechanical Monsters of the Movies." *Pop Mech* 74 (Sep 40) 376–379+. Behind the scenes with J. M. Schleisser, head technician of the Hollywood Museum; how the special effects are achieved.

"Cashing in on a Fantasy." *Pop Mech* 75 (Apr 41) 568–569+. Special effects by Ray Harryhausen.

Miller, R. Dewitt. "Blizzards Made to Order." *Pop Mech* 75 (May 41) 696–698+. Technicians who create realistic snow effects for movies.

"Movie Make-Believe Made to Order." *Pop Mech* 79 (Apr 43) 89–92+. Staging battle scenes on Hollywood sound stages.

"Table-Top War Movies." *Pop Mech* (June 44) 57–61. Behind the scenes of George Pal Productions and how they utilize special effects for training films.

"Making Up the Monsters." *Pop Mech* 83 (May 45) 33–37.

Marshall, Jim. "Catastrophe Maker." *Collier's* 118 (10 Aug 46) 28. Reeves Eason arranges chariot races and train crashes.

Hoffman, W. "Blowing Up Hollywood." *Pop Mech* 88 (Aug 47) 154–157. The methods, problems, risks, results of Hollywood's "smoke and powder men" and their simulations of disasters.

Molyneux. "Technical Notes." *Penguin F Rev* 3 (Aug 47) 18–20. The work of the special-effects department. (Comments on current technical aspects occur in nearly every issue of this magazine.)

"Speaking of Pictures." *Life* 24 (19 Apr 48) 24–26+. Movie trick helps Bob Hope fly without moving in a scene from *The Paleface*.

Woodson, W. "Movie Dragons." *Nature Mag* 41 (Nov 48) 461–463.

Simon, A. L. "Hollywood Tricksters Who Fool You." *Coronet* 26 (Oct 49) 57–60.

Hochman, Louis. "Come-Apart Cars Let Camera In." *Pop Sci* 155 (Oct 49) 153–156. "The Studio Process Body Company" provides jigsaw-puzzle cars.

"Giant Transparencies Bring World Indoors." *Pop Sci* 156 (Jan 50) 161–163. Photographs for backgrounds.

"Death on the Movie Lot." *Life* 28 (30 Jan 50) 29. A live bomb explodes during the shooting of an Italian battle scene.

Boone, Andrew R. "How Movies Take You on Trip to the Moon." *Pop Sci* 156 (May 50) 124–129. Special effects.

"How Invisible Rabbits and Other Miracles Are Born." *Good Housekeeping* 131 (Aug 50) 216–217. Special effects in *Harvey*.

Hamilton, A. "Mastermind for Hollywood's Wars." *Pop Mech* 96 (Aug 51) 65–69. Louis Witte, Hollywood explosives technician.

Norton, Paul. "Train Wrecks Made to Order." *Sci Dig* 34 (Aug 53) 56–60.

Fleischer, Richard. "Underwater Filmaking." *FIR* 5 (Aug–Sep 54) 333–337. Problems encountered by the director in Disney's *20,000 Leagues Under the Sea*.

Laitin, J. "Monsters Made to Order." *Collier's* 134 (10 Dec 54) 52–53. The manufacture of the Gill Man, Frankenstein, and others at Universal-International.

Griswold, Wesley S. "He's Hollywood's Kindest Killer." *Pop Sci* 167 (Dec 55) 128–129. Special effects by Ross Taylor.

"Fanciful Flights." *Life* 40 (28 May 56) 22–23. Huge movie backdrops, spread flat on a pavement, provide an opportunity for photographic illusions.

Stimson, Thomas E. "Movie Magic and Illusions Take You *Around the World in 80 Days*." *Pop Mech* 106 (Aug 56) 65–69.+ Technical problems involved in special effects.

Franchey, J. "Gettysburg in Miniature." *Pop Mech* 106 (Sep 56) 102–104.

Sale, Richard. "They Built the Sea." *F&F* 3 (No. 5, Feb 57) 14. Creating a shipwreck in a studio.

Randall, James. "Playing at War!" *F&F* 4 (No. 7, Apr 58) 26. Battlefield effects in Douglas Sirk's *A Time to Live and a Time to Die*.

"Golden Gate Going." *Life* 49 (28 Nov 60) 53. Japanese film crew blows up a scale-model bridge.

"Almost the Real Thing." *Newswk* 57 (30 Jan 61) 76. Dummies in moving pictures.

"Up Anchor! Otto's Navy." *Life* 58 (5 Mar 65) 73–74. Filming a scale-model sea battle for *In Harm's Way*.

Zeitlin, David. "Great General Slays 'Em Again." *Life* 60 (27 May 66) 93–95+. Yakima Canutt stages the battles in *Khartoum*.

Jenkinson, Philip. "Camera Magic." *Film* (No. 54, Spring 69) 19–25. Special effects in the cinema from 1893 to the present.

Freeland, Nat. "Special-Effects Expert Dour Trumball: A Cinematic Peter Max." *Show* (23 July 70) 44–45. Comments on the making of the "star-gate" sequence of *2001,* and simulated computer printouts, microphotography and X rays used in *The Andromeda Strain;* both designed by Trumball Film Effects Co.

2j(2). PROPERTIES

Condon, Frank. "No Such Word as No." *SEP* 204 (16 Apr 32) 47+. Property men.

Magee, H. W. "The Magician of the Movies: Property Man." *Pop Mech* 59 (Jan 33) 50–55.

"The Aladdin of the Movies." *Pop Mech* 64 (Dec 35) 850–853+. Irving Sindler, property man for Goldwyn.

"Master Craftsmen of the Movies." *Pop Mech*

65 (May 36) 706–709+. The property department at Paramount; one of a series on production techniques.

Boone, A. R. "Aladdins of Hollywood Create Realistic Effects for Movies." *Pop Sci* (Jan 37) 30–31+. Problems of property departments in major studios.

"Styles and Railings: Errors in the Properties of *Rembrandt*." *Antiques* 31 (No. 2, Feb 37) 90. A criticism of the English historical film *Rembrandt* with respect to its seventeenth-century period properties.

"Prop Shops: Movies Run Department Stores, Factories, and Gardens." *Lit Dig* 123 (29 May 37) 20–22. Warner Brothers' property department.

Crichton, K. "Property Man." *Collier's* 100 (27 Nov 37) 14+.

Boone, A. R. "They Never Say No." *Sci Am* 160 (June 39) 370–371. The property men who furnish the thousands of odd items that make motion pictures more realistic.

"Props." *American* 128 (Aug 39) 90–91.

Beatty, J. "Hollywood's Fabulous Fakirs." *American* 141 (Apr 46) 48–49+. The adventures of the indispensable property men.

Wechsberg, J. "It Pays to Be Crazy: Prop Men Work Hard to Whip Up Gags." *SEP* 219 (18 Jan 47) 30–31+.

Lewis, M. D. S. "Jewelry and the Period Film." *S&S* 16 (No. 63, Autumn 47) 99–101. A description of certain pieces of period jewelry and the best methods for creating facsimiles.

Martin, Pete. "Hollywood's Box of Miracles." *SEP* 220 (21 Feb 48) 12. The property man.

Finnerman, S. "Hollywood's Antique Auto Livery: Pacific Auto Rentals." *Pop Mech* 95 (Feb 51) 133–137.

Boone, Andrew R. "His Death Rays Only Tickle Your Spine." *Pop Sci* 163 (July 53) 109–111. Top inventor of fantastic props.

Gaiters, Albert. "Property Master." *F&F* 4 (No. 1, Oct 57) 26.

Sandler, C. "In Hollywood, Even the Food Must Perform." *Am Mercury* 88 (Jan 59) 89–90. The commissary department of Warners prepares outlandish foods.

Shuldiner, Herbert. "James Bond's Weird World of Inventions." *Pop Sci* 188 (Jan 66) 60–63+. Gadgets for Bond movies displayed.

"Dick Van Dyke Drives the Zany *Chitty Chitty Bang Bang*." *Pop Sci* 192 (Mar 68) 74–75. Car used in film of that title.

"Season of Fun Arrives with a Bang!" *Good Housekeeping* 167 (Dec 68) 44+. Pictures of gadgets in *Chitty Chitty Bang Bang*.

Freeman, David. "Lights, Camera, Auction." *On Film* (1970) 15–20. Properties sold at MGM.

Bellamy, V. H. "W.W.II Revisited; Flying Restored Planes." *Flying* 86 (Mar 70) 56–64.

An airman's story of the planes he flew for the making of the film *The Battle of Britain*.

2j(3). STUNTS

Dunn, H. H. "Today's War Postponed—Wet Ground." *Pop Mech* 53 (June 30) 962–967. On stunt flyers and movie tricks.

Boone, Andrew R. "With the Movie Circus." *Pop Mech* 55 (Apr 31) 610–613. On staging circus parades and stunts. See also *Lit Dig* 109 (18 Apr 31) 17.

"Dynamite in the Talkies." *Pop Mech* 55 (May 31) 748–751. Movie explosives experts.

Boone, Andrew R. "Thrilling Air Battles Fought for Movies." *Pop Sci* 121 (July 32) 26–28+.

Dyer, Elmer. "Riding the Wings of Death." *Travel* 59 (Sep 32) 27–29+. Stunt flyers.

Boone, Andrew R. "Wild Horses in Stampede for Movies." *Pop Sci* 122 (Jan 33) 32–34. Production details for *The Wild Stampede*.

"Fake Movie Jungle Fights." *Lit Dig* 115 (14 Jan 33) 37–38. A. H. Fisher describes wild-animal photography.

Rose, Bob. "Cheating Death for a Living." *Pop Mech* 63 (Feb 35) 226–229+. Stunt man tells of dangers in profession.

Lodge, John E. "Movie Stunt Men." *Pop Sci* 127 (Nov 35) 22–23+. Cliff Lyons, Yakima Canutt, Bob Rose, and friends.

French, W. F. "Double's Troubles." *SEP* 209 (25 July 36) 16–17+. Stunt men.

"Three Seconds from Death." *Pop Mech* 70 (Nov 38) 674–677+. The importance of timing to a stunt man; examples offered by Cliff Lyons.

May, George. "Stunt Men of the Movies." *Life & Letters Today* 22 (July 39) 109–113.

Muir, Florabel. "They Risk Their Necks for You." *SEP* 218 (15 Sep 45) 26–27+. The dangers faced by stunt women.

"They Die a Thousand Deaths: Stunt Actors." *Pop Mech* 86 (Aug 46) 131–135.

"Hollywood's Extra-Specialists." *American* 145 (Jan 48) 106–107. Expert ropers, fencers, riders teaching the stars.

Johnson, Gladys. "Bashful Ben of the Bang-Bangs." *Collier's* 124 (22 Oct 49) 28–29+. On stunt rider Ben Johnson.

"He Is a Stunt Man." *Life* 32 (5 May 52) 89–90+. About Dave Sharp.

Itria, Helen. " 'Idiots' for Hire." *Look* 17 (No. 12, 16 June 53) 86–91. Hollywood stunt men; examples of work.

"Skewered Extra." *Life* 37 (11 Oct 54) 189–190. An Italian actor, in *Helen of Troy*, demonstrates how death from a spear is simulated.

Infield, G. "Cinerama Wings." *Flying* 56 (June 55) 22. Paul Mantz, a skilled stunt pilot: his special equipment for *This Is Cinerama*.

Everson, William K. "Stunt Men." *FIR* 6 (Oct

55) 394–402. Categories of stunts and the men who do them. See also letters 6 (Dec 55) 537–538.

Thruelsen, R. "Hollywood's Plane Crasher." *SEP* 228 (14 Apr 56) 50+. The life of stunt pilot Paul Mantz.

Peters, Andrew. "Playing Safe—With Danger." *F&F* 2 (No. 9, June 56) 7+. British stunt men.

"Danger for a Living." *Newswk* 48 (13 Aug 56) 94–95.

"Action Man's Action." *Action* 1 (No. 1, Sep–Oct 66) 14–15. A brief description of the work of a famous stunt man, Yakima Canutt.

2j(4). RESEARCH AND TECHNICAL ADVICE

Kennedy, John B. "Hits and Errors." *Collier's* 92 (1 Apr 33) 18+. Authenticator forestalls anachronisms and continuity errors.

Bonner, Amy. "Sleuths of Cinema-land." *CSMM* (10 July 35) 8–9. On the RKO research department.

Boone, Andrew R. "Ancient Battles in the Movies." *Sci Am* 153 (Aug 35) 61–63. Research by De Mille for *The Crusades*.

Hyatt, R. M. "Movies as Historians." *Rev of Reviews* 95 (Apr 37) 56. The historical contributions of Hollywood's research departments.

"Sea Lore Kept Alive by Films." *Pop Mech* (June 37) 874–877+. The marine technical adviser.

"Making Movies True to Life." *Pop Mech* 68 (Nov 37) 706–709. Tribute to the technical adviser; examples, movies cited.

"Film Facts versus Fancy." *CSMM* 101 (20 Apr 38) 12. Increasing use of authentic historic and geographic detail in Hollywood films.

Richardson, F. C. "Previous to Previews." *Wilson Lib Bul* (May 39) 589–592. The work of the research department at 20th Century-Fox Studios.

Carter, M. D. "Film Research Libraries." *Lib J* 64 (15 May 39) 404–407. A look at the research departments of the various studios.

Wayne, P. "What's Wrong with This Picture? Work of the Technical Adviser." *SEP* 211 (3 June 39) 14–15. Efforts and value of the technical adviser—from films such as *Emile Zola* and *Gunga Din*.

Martin, J. "Librarian to Walt Disney." *Wilson Lib Bul* 14 (Dec 39) 292–293.

Percey, H. G. "*Union Pacific*: Use of Western History in Creative Work." *Oregon Hist Q* 41 (June 40) 128–132. The production of *Union Pacific*; Paramount and Cecil B. De Mille; production research.

Percey, H. "Historical Research in a Motion Picture Library." *Wilson Lib Bul* 16 (Dec 41) 315.

Martin, Pete. "The Movies Must Mislead You." *SEP* 220 (31 Jan 48) 12. On a studio's necessary legal research.

Van Den Ecker, Louis. "A Veteran's View of Hollywood Authenticity." *Hwd Q* 4 (No. 4, Summer 50) 323–331. Technical director on more than forty films tells of his role and the special care required in military films.

Hartmann, Cyril Hughes. "The Technical Expert in British Films." *Hwd Q* 4 (No. 4, Summer 50) 332–337. Historical adviser on many features observes that care about settings is easier to achieve than suitable dialogue and reactions to situations.

"Indian Sign for Hollywood." *American* 151 (Mar 51) 57. Brief profile of Nipo Strongheart, his work as an "Indian expert" from De Mille on.

Nathan, P. S. "Books into Films." *Publishers Weekly* 162 (27 Sep 52) 1445. *Viva Zapata* as an example of research work.

Pasinetti, P. M. "*Julius Caesar*: The Role of the Technical Adviser." *QFRTV* 8 (No. 2, Winter 53) 131–138. UCLA professor of Italian literature describes his research on dress, dialogue, etc., for the Houseman-Mankiewicz film.

"New Role for Rafer." *Ebony* 21 (Dec 65) 181–184. Rafer Johnson, 1960's Olympic decathlon champion, is adviser to United Artists comedy *Billie*.

2k. Production Design and Art Direction

[See 5, Biography: *Piero Gherardi, Cedric Gibbons*.]

Rotha, Paul. "The Art-Director and the Composition of the Film Scenario." *Close Up* 6 (No. 5, 1930) 377–385.

Rosse, Herman. "Cinema Design." *Th Arts* 16 (June 32) 467–470. Collection of designs for *Frankenstein*, *The King of Jazz*, and *The Murders in the Rue Morgue*.

Blakeston, Oswell. "The Films in Pictorial Review." *Arch Rev* 73 (No. 436, Mar 33) 127. Recent work by motion-picture art directors.

Korda, Vincent. "The Artist in the Film." *S&S* 3 (No. 9, Spring 34) 13–15. Elements of design in the cinema and the role of the designer.

Grey, E. "Breaking into the Movies: Harbor of Refuge for Architects During the Depression." *Arch and Eng* 120 (Feb 35) 39–42.

Cavalcanti, Alberto. "The Function of the Art Director." *CQ* 3 (No. 2, Winter 35) 75–78.

Eustis, M. "Designing for the Movies: Gibbons

of MGM." *Th Arts* 21 (Oct 37) 782–798. Detailed look at the significance of the art director in films; examples of planning, procedure, results.

"Lazare Meerson." *S&S* 7 (No. 26, Summer 38) 68–69. An important art director for both British and Continental films.

Daugherty, Frank. "Art on the Screen." *CSMM* (7 Sep 38) 8–9+. The role of the art director.

Cutts, Anson Bailey. "Homes of Tomorrow in the Movies of Today." *Calif Arts and Arch* 54 (No. 5, Nov 38) 16–18.

Dawe, Cedric. "The Artist's Job in Making a Film." *Studio* 119 (Jan–June 40) 38–41. The art director's role in film making.

Horner, Harry. "Designing for the Screen." *Th Arts* 25 (Nov 41) 794–799. Horner, set designer for William Wyler's *The Little Foxes,* discusses his craft.

"Scenery for Cinema at Baltimore Museum." *Art Dig* 16 (No. 10, 15 Feb 42) 7. Duties of the art director.

Junge, A. "Art Director and His Work." *Artist* 27 (Mar–June 44) 9–11+.

Gorelik, Mordecai. "Hollywood's Art Machinery." *S&S* 15 (No. 59, Autumn 46) 90–91. Hollywood's use of film settings reveals its generally inferior approach to reality.

Gorelik, Mordecai. "Hollywood's Art Machinery." *Hwd Q* 2 (No. 2, Jan 47) 153–160. Famous stage designer has found bureaucratic insistence on glamorized realism a bar to style and originality in settings; examples of conflicting views.

Ferguson, Russell. "Crisis in Fairyland." *S&S* 18 (Spring 49) 20–21. Commentary on the status of the art director on basis of new book by Edward Carrick, *Art and Design in British Film* (Dobson, 1948).

Isaacs, J. "The Visual Impact." *S&S* 19 (Apr 50) 81–82. Film design is more like architecture because the actor must move through the scene.

Horner, Harry. "Designing *The Heiress.*" *Hwd Q* 5 (No. 1, Fall 50) 1–7. How Horner worked with director William Wyler to "translate the style and conception of the story into a practical motion picture setting"; what a good art director does.

Field, Alice Evans. "The Art Director's Art." *FIR* 3 (Feb 52) 60–66. Extract from her book *Hollywood, U.S.A.* (Vantage, 1952); appraisal of work by such men as William Cameron Menzies, Cedric Gibbons, and William Pereira.

"Loudon Sainthill." *F&F* 1 (No. 1, Oct 54) 10–11. Designer of sets for theatre and film: *The Man Who Loved Redheads.*

Carter, Maurice. "Life Class." *F&F* 3 (No. 6, Mar 57) 7+. Veteran art director recounts experiences in his career.

Dillon, Carmen. "The Art Director." *F&F* 3 (No. 8, May 57) 12–13.

Kuter, Leo K. "Art Direction." *FIR* 8 (June–July 57) 248–258. An illustrated introduction to the role of the art director in the motion-picture industry, giving some of the history of art direction in films.

Gray, Martin. "The Shape of Things Past." *F&F* 5 (No. 5, Feb 59) 11+. History of British art directors.

Luft, Herbert G. "Production Designer Horner." *FIR* 10 (June–July 59) 328–335. Career of Harry Horner; drawings of sets.

Hudson, Roger. "Three Designers." *S&S* 34 (Winter 64–65) 26–31. The function of the film designer; interviews with Ken Adam, whose credits include *Goldfinger* and *Dr. Strangelove;* Edward Marshall, the designer of *Tom Jones* and *Room at the Top;* and Richard Macdonald, who has worked with Losey for about twelve years.

Durgnat, Raymond. "Movie Eye." *Arch Rev* 137 (Mar 65) 186–193. Architecture's visual and emotional overtones in the making of films.

Taylor, John Russell. "Larking Back." *S&S* 37 (Spring 68) 68–71. Some observations on popular aesthetics in films, television and commercial design; it's dangerous for a film to be modish because the attention-catching sets may be out of style by the time it's released.

Barry, Jonathan. "The Art of the Art Director." *Film* (No. 59, Summer 70) 15. Author discusses his own work.

2k(1). SET DESIGNS

Carrick, Edward. "Moving Picture Sets, a Medium for the Architect." *Arch Rec* 67 (May 30) 440–444. Surveys *Dr. Caligari, Thief of Bagdad, Woman of Paris,* and many others.

Metzner, Ernö. "A Mining Film." *Close Up* 9 (No. 1, Mar 32). See 9, *Kameradschaft.*

Laing, A. B. "Designing Motion Picture Sets." *Arch Rec* 74 (July 33) 59–64. In-depth survey of current design methods.

Stuart, Betty Thornley. "Movie Set-Up." *Collier's* 92 (30 Sep 33) 20+. On Hollywood set decorating.

Blakeston, Oswell. "The Architect at the Movies." *Arch Rev* 75 (No. 446, Jan 34) 21. A brief proposal for set construction outside of the studio.

"The Influence of Motion Pictures on Interiors." *Calif Arts and Arch* 50 (Nov 36) 26. A brief commentary on art director Duncan Cramer's design for *Star for a Night.*

Winter, A. A. "Pictures You'll Like." *St. Nicholas* 64 (Feb 37) 34. Behind the scenes in several pictures—a look at some set designs.

"Drawings for Film Sets: The Work of Anton

Grot." *London Studio* 16 (Dec 38) 302–303. Designer for Warner Brothers.

Platt, J. B. "Decorating for Scarlett O'Hara." *House and Garden* 76 (Nov 39) 36–40+. Design of interiors for *Gone with the Wind*.

Capps, McClure. "Architectural Gimracks: Architectural Horrors of the American 80's Set the Scene for a Modern Motion Picture." *Calif Arts and Arch* 59 (No. 1, Jan 42) 18–19. Art director Perry Ferguson's design for *Ball of Fire*.

De La Roche, Catherine. "Scenic Design in the Soviet Cinema." *Penguin F Rev* 3 (Aug 47). *See 4e(8)*.

"Art of the British Film Designer." *Illus London News* 212 (6 Mar 48) 273. Exhibition held at Victoria and Albert Museum.

Verk, S. "Designer for the Screen: Cedric Gibbons Interview." *American Artist* 12 (Nov 48) 9+.

Sullivan, Catherine. "The Artist in Hollywood." *Am Artist* 14 (No. 7, Sep 50) 42–46. The role of the artist in Hollywood studios.

Carrick, Edward. "Designing for the Motion Pictures." *Design* 52 (Nov 50) 14–17.

Gueft, O. "Interiors for the Camera." *Interiors* 112 (Feb 53) 80–81. Gianni Polidori designs sets for stage and cinema, including Renoir's *The Golden Coach*.

Adam, Ken. "Designing Sets for Action." *F&F* 2 (No. 11, Aug 56) 27. Sets for *Child in the House*.

Gray, Martin. "Design for Living." *F&F* 3 (No. 4, Jan 57) 8–9. Set designing by Alexandre Trauner.

2k(2). SETS AND SCENERY

Boone, Andrew R. "Planting the South Pole in Sunny California." *Pop Sci* 118 (Mar 31) 22–23+. Movie set reproduces "frigid wastes of ice."

"What's New in the Movies." *Pop Mech* 64 (Aug 35) 169–176+; (Sep 35) 329–336+. On technical aspects of movie scenery.

"Wonders of the Scenic Engineers." *Pop Mech* 65 (Mar 36) 354–357+. Van Nest Polglase at RKO; one of a series on production techniques.

Williams, Dorothy Doran. "Backstage Scene in the Movies." *Th Arts* 20 (Dec 36) 961–965. Sketches made "on the lot."

"Landscapes from the Screen." *Landscape Arch* 27 (Apr 37) 145–149. A review of landscape representation in three films: *Lloyd's of London, Quality Street*, and *The Good Earth*.

Boone, A. R. "Behind the Scenes with the Men Who Build Giant Movie Sets." *Pop Sci* 130 (May 37) 36–38+.

"Robin Hood." Landscape Arch 28 (July 38) 200–201. Ingenuity of certain effects.

Palmer, E. L. "Substitutes: Natural History in Moving Pictures." *Nature* 33 (May 40) 302.

Where the movies go wrong in their settings; *Northwest Passage* cited as a particularly bad example.

"Why the Movies Are Influencing American Taste." *House Beautiful* 84 (July 42) 36–37. Movie sets often contain valuable ideas for decorations.

"Movie Illusions: Hollywood Technicians Create Reality Inside Studios." *Life* 17 (7 Aug 44) 71–79. Pictorial essay on the creation of artificial exterior sets.

Marshall, J. "Folding Tree." *Collier's* 115 (21 Apr 45) 61. Hollywood greenery expert procuring trees for films.

Crocker, H. "Assignment in Hollywood." *Good Housekeeping* 122 (Mar 46) 12–13. The extent to which sets and set dressings affect the public.

Shearer, L. "The Three Most Popular Movie Sets of the Last Twenty Years and What They Mean." *House Beautiful* 88 (Dec 46) 218–221. They seem to be an odd blend of past and present.

"Hollywood Cuts Cost of Make-Believe Worlds." *Pop Sci* 158 (Feb 51) 118–119. Motion Picture Research Council's experiments.

"Hollywood Sunset." *Life* 31 (6 Aug 51) 73. Man painting backdrop at MGM.

"How to Fly a Saucer." *Collier's* 130 (4 Oct 52) 50–51. Technicolored *War of the Worlds*; pictures of settings.

Peck, Seymour. "Mr. Smith Goes to Hollywood." *NYTM* (9 Oct 55) 28–29. Oliver Smith, a Broadway set designer, creates backgrounds for two filmed musicals: *Oklahoma!* and *Guys and Dolls*.

"Why Hollywood Builds Plastic Log Cabins." *Pop Sci* 168 (May 56) 148–149.

"Rome: Part of the New Jerusalem Being Constructed for a Film Set." *Illus London News* 238 (4 Mar 61) 341. Two photos of papier-mâché Roman gate for De Laurentiis' *Barabbas*.

"Model City on Old Movie Lots." *Bus Wk* (22 Apr 61) 123–124.

"Hollywood: An Archaeologist's View." *Show* 1 (Oct 61) 70–79. Photo essay by Saul Leiter on Hollywood studio sound stages and back lots as monuments to old movie illusions.

"Happy Inventions." *House and Garden* 121 (Jan 62) 102–105. Sets from the movie *El Cid* adaptable to the private home.

Erengis, George P. "20th's Backlot." *FIR* 13 (No. 4, Apr 62) 193–205. Famous sets at 20th Century-Fox; pictures.

Erengis, George P. "MGM's Backlot." *FIR* 14 (Jan 63) 23–37. Historical study of MGM's lots 2 and 3 containing towns, villages, lakes, rivers, etc., used in shooting that studio's films.

Freeland, Nat. "Yonkers in Los Angeles. Portobello Road in Burbank." *Show* (20 Aug 70). *See 6c(2)*.

2k(3). SHIPS

Dunn, H. H. "Stately Ships Wrecked for Movies." *Pop Sci* 120 (Jan 32) 38–39+.

"Old Sailing Vessels Made Up as Famous Ships for the Movies." *Pop Sci* 128 (Jan 36) 20–21.

"Secrets of the Movie Ships." *Pop Mech* 66 (July 36) 74–78. At Fox, RKO, and MGM.

"Replica of Columbus' Ship in a British Film, *Christopher Columbus.*" *Illus London News* 213 (7 Aug 48) 159. Models of the *Santa Maria.*

Hamilton, Andrew. "Hollywood Boatman." *Pop Mech* 91 (Apr 49) 156–160+. Benton Roberts, nautical equipment supplier for epics; anecdotes about films using his boats.

"Admiral of the Hollywood Fleet." *American* 153 (Jan 52) 55. Ed Cunningham has a navy that he rents to movie and TV studios.

McCarthy, Frank. "I Borrowed the British Navy." *Look* 17 (25 Aug 53). *See 9, Sailors of the King.*

Marienhoff, Jim. "*Disco Volante,* the Saucer That Flies." *Motor Boating* 116 (Dec 65) 32–33+. Re: the yacht used in the James Bond film *Thunderball.*

2k(4). LOCATIONS

[See also 6c(4).]

Reid, C. L. "Filming a Volcano." *Cornhill* (new series) 71 (July 31) 16–26. An adventurous account of on-location shooting in Java (no film title given).

Wagner, Rob. "When the Movies Tell the Truth." *Collier's* 88 (22 Aug 31) 18–20+. On movies' use of locations, especially in Southern California.

Condon, Frank. "Many Miles Away." *SEP* 204 (24 Oct 31) 29+. On-location shooting.

Laing, A. B. "Bookshops as Atmosphere." *Publishers Weekly* 123 (4 Mar 33) 833–834. Paramount uses local bookstore for *No Man of Her Own.*

"The World in Hollywood." *Pop Mech* 64 (Nov 35) 712–715+. Surrounding areas of Southern California used for just about anywhere in the world.

Jones, Grover. "On Location." *Collier's* 98 (5 Dec 36) 24+. Screenwriter reports on various location troubles.

Boone, A. R. "Hollywood Improves on Nature in Making Outdoor Movies." *Pop Sci* 130 (Feb 37) 58–59+. The set designer's use of natural settings.

"Around the World for Realism." *Pop Mech* 68 (Dec 37) 872–875.

Shellaby, R. K. "World at Their Feet." *CSMM* (1 June 38) 6. "Foreign" backgrounds are no problem to location scouts in California.

"Hollywood Visits Virginia." *Arts and Decoration* 52 (Oct 40) 12–13. On-location filming.

Albright, A. "City Gets a Screen-Test." *Scho-lastic* 50 (3 Mar 47) 29. The trend toward location shooting.

"Coordination: Shooting a Movie on the Sidewalks of New York." *New Yorker* 23 (3 Jan 48) 16–17.

Lochridge, P. "Look Who's in the Movies Now: Urge to Make Movies in New York." *Woman's Home Companion* 75 (May 48) 7–8.

Foster, Inez Whitely. " 'Shooting' Manhattan." *CSMM* (11 Sep 48) 11. Opportunities and difficulties of location shooting.

"Location New York." *Newswk* 33 (25 Apr 49) 92+.

"Utah's Hollywood." *Life* 27 (19 Sep 49) 156–158+. Small Utah town supplies locale, extras, and props for Westerns.

"Make a Movie and See the World." *Woman's Home Companion* 77 (Jan 50) 12.

Smith, H. Allen. "Just Like a Movie—Pioneertown, California." *SEP* 222 (28 Jan 50) 32–33+. A community built to provide a permanent set for the movies.

"Scenery Scout." *American* 151 (Jan 51) 57.

Gordon, Gordon. "Towns for Rent." *Nation's Business* 40 (Dec 52) 84+. Communities offer locations, scenery, and character types to Hollywood.

"Moab Gets Rich on Three-D Scenery." *Bus Wk* (5 Sep 53) 80–84. Hollywood filming Westerns in Moab, Utah.

"Location Loafing." *Look* 17 (20 Oct 53) 150+. Stills of the stars in the Canadian Rockies.

Mitchell, George. "Sidney Olcott." *FIR* 5 (Apr 54). *See 5, Sidney Olcott.*

"Hollywood Discovers Egypt." *Look* 18 (5 Oct 54) 124–125. Stills from different movies, including *The Ten Commandments.*

"Adventurama: Eggert-Hatch Green and Colorado Rivers Expedition." *New York* 31 (11 June 55) 24–26. Location perils.

Peck, Seymour. "Join Hollywood and See the World." *NYTM* (5 May 57) 30–31. Film productions on foreign locations.

Mankiewicz, Joseph L. "Shoot It in Tanganyika." *Sat Rev* 40 (21 Dec 57) 14–15. Movies with authentic backgrounds.

Lasky, Jesse L. "No Business Like Snow Business: Filming *The Alaskan.*" *Rdrs Dig* 72 (Jan 58) 187. Quoted from Lasky's autobiography, *I Blow My Own Horn.*

Jennings, Dean. "The Movies' Modern Marco Polo." *SEP* 232 (23 Apr 60) 36+. The career of Stanley Goldsmith, 20th Century-Fox's troubleshooter for pictures filmed overseas.

Clark, Roy. "Have Shoes, Will Travel." *Dance Mag* 34 (Oct 60) 16–17+. Dancing on movie and television locations.

Cullen, Tom A. "Letter from London." *Nation* 191 (12 Nov 60) 374–375. 20th Century-Fox filming in England; Hollywood's sudden rush to film abroad.

Foreman, Carl. "Of Peregrinating Producers." *Sat Rev* 43 (24 Dec 60) 52–53. Defense of location shooting abroad.

Alpert, Hollis. "Far-off Tents of Hollywood." *Th Arts* 45 (June–July 61) 11–15+. Hollywood is filming everywhere in the free world.

"The Locationers." *Time* 78 (14 July 61) 72. Around the world.

Alpert, Hollis. "New York Renaissance?" *Sat Rev* 44 (18 Nov 61) 33. Films being made in New York City.

Moore, John. "Art Director Moore on Making a Plastic Revolt." *F&F* 8 (No. 8, May 62) 38. The sets he made for Bronson films in Spain.

"The Runaways." *Time* 80 (14 Sep 62) 53+. U.S. and European companies on location everywhere.

"Old Tucson, A Step into the Past." *Sunset* 129 (Nov 62) 48. Report on a still-existing set for a whole town used in the 1940 film *Arizona*.

Peck, Seymour. "Exotic Stages for the Movies." *NYTM* (4 Nov 62) 60–61. Photo from recent films shot around the world.

Shavelson, Melville. "Viva Italian Film Flam!" *Life* 53 (9 Nov 62) 19. Troubles of American companies shooting in Italy.

"Four on Location." *Time* 81 (17 May 63) 78+. Four films under production: *Of Human Bondage*, *Zulu*, *Act One*, and *From Russia with Love*.

Knight, Arthur. "Meanwhile, Back in Hollywood." *Sat Rev* 48 (25 Dec 65) 21. Some reasons for the current neglect of Hollywood by many important directors and producers.

"Muddle in Puddleby." *Newswk* 68 (11 July 66) 40+. Protests by villagers in Castle Combe, England, against making *The Adventures of Doctor Doolittle* there.

"A Beginning." *New Yorker* 42 (13 Aug 66) 22–23. Talk with special consultant to the mayor about simpler procedure for permits to shoot on location in New York.

"Manhattan Towers Become a Set Again." *Bus Wk* (10 Sep 66) 178–180. Resurgence of film making in New York City due to Mayor Lindsay's red carpet treatment.

Smith, Desmond. "On Location in Rostov; Filming the New Revolution." *Nation* 204 (27 Feb 67) 268–272. On the filming of *Ivan Ivanovich*, an American documentary made in Russia.

Golden, David. "Praise Be the Mayor." *Action* 2 (No. 3, May–June 67) 20–21. Praise for Mayor John Lindsay's streamlining of procedure for filming in New York City, and particularly how it has helped the filming of *You're a Big Boy Now*.

"New York, The Big Set." *Newswk* 69 (29 May 67) 86–87. New York welcomes film makers for location shooting.

"Multi-Gadget Movie Van Rolls into Hollywood." *Bus Wk* (15 Mar 69) 152–154. Fouad Said's cinemobile slashes costs of location shooting.

Chaplin, Patrice. "Malta Dog." *London Mag* (new series) 9 (No. 1, Apr 69) 79–90. On filming a war story on Malta; a "B" picture, no title given.

"New Mexico: Dollars in the Desert." *Newswk* 76 (26 Oct 70) 78. The movie boom in on-location shooting in New Mexico; courting an industry.

2m. Projection Techniques

[See also 2e, 2f, 6b(4).]

Caldwell, O. H. "Realism in the Movies." *Scribner's* 9 (Apr 41) 95–98. Sound projection and "odorated" films herald a new realm of audience appeal.

"How Hollywood Hopes to Hit Comeback Road." *Newswk* 41 (12 Jan 53) 66–67. Cinerama, 3-D, closed circuit, etc.

"The 3-D's." *Time* 61 (9 Feb 53) 96. Moviemakers' plans.

Klonsky, M. "From Cinema to Cinerama." *Am Mercury* 76 (Mar 53) 14–18.

"New Dimensions Perk Up Hollywood." *Bus Wk* (14 Mar 53) 122+. A short history.

Crowther, Bosley. "Three-Dimensional Riddle." *NYTM* (29 Mar 53) 14–15+. The writer questions 3-D and wide-screen innovations.

"How They Make Movies Leap at You." *Pop Sci* 162 (Apr 53) 97–99. From 3-D techniques to CinemaScope and Cinerama.

"Movies with Depth: The Answer to TV?" *U.S. News & World Report* 34 (10 Apr 53) 77–79.

Keller, Reamer. "That Third Dimension." *NYTM* (12 Apr 53) 40. Cartoon sketches spoofing 3-D film effects.

"Speaking of Pictures." *Life* 34 (13 Apr 53) 18–19. Scenes from the new 3-D films.

"The New Industry." *Time* 61 (4 May 53) 102. Opinions of the experts about the age of 3-D.

Crowther, Bosley. "Picture of Hollywood in the Depths." *NYTM* (14 June 53) 17+. Anxiety about new screen techniques.

Morrison, Chester. "Three-D High, Wide and Handsome." *Look* 17 (30 June 53) 27–33. A thorough explanation of three basic systems of 3-D cinematography and speculation on its future.

"Many Dimensions." *S&S* 23 (July–Sep 53) 2.

Notes on 3-D and wide screen in Hollywood.

Hochman, L. "On the Three-D Bandwagon: Stereo and Non-Stereo Wide-Screen Processes." *Photog* 33 (Aug 53) 92.

"Making the Decisions on 3-D Movies." *Bus Wk* (15 Aug 53) *See 5, Dore Schary.*

"Smellies." *Newswk* 42 (31 Aug 53) 74.

"Third Dimentia Takes Over in Hollywood." *Rdrs Dig* 63 (Sep 53) 49–53. "Natural Vision" and "CinemaScope": effects on box office.

"2-D or Not 2-D?" *Scholastic* 63 (7 Oct 53) 7–8.

"Birthday of the Revolution." *Time* 62 (12 Oct 53) 110. Evaluation of one-year-old 3-D.

"The Front Page: Waiting and Seeing." *S&S* 23 (Oct–Dec 53) 63. Curtis Harrington reports on 3-D and wide screen in Hollywood; editorial comment doubts if it's progress.

"4-D." *Time* 62 (16 Nov 53) 100+. Fourth dimension: the future of gloomy movie industry.

"New Dimension." *Time* 64 (6 Sep 54) 78+. VistaVision, CinemaScope, and a new brand of films, including *On the Waterfront, From Here to Eternity.*

Manvell, Roger. "The Battle of the Systems." *F&F* 1 (No. 1, Oct 54) 8. Cinerama, Cinema-Scope, VistaVision, 3-D.

"Big Screen." *Fortune* 51 (Feb 55) 158. The various processes—Cinerama, VistaVision, 3-D, Todd-AO.

Lerman, L. "Experiment: Theatre, Movies; Todd-A.O. Wideangle, Large-Screen Process." *Mlle* 40 (Mar 55) 112–113.

"Dynamic Frame." *S&S* 25 (Autumn 55) 64. Glenn Alvey making *The Door in the Wall* with new screen technique that changes in size.

Lipton, N. C. "Disneyland's Circarama." *Pop Photog* 37 (Dec 55) 96–97+.

Prouse, Derek. "Dynamic Frame." *S&S* 25 (Winter 55–56) 159–160. An account of the film *The Door in the Wall*, by Glenn Alvey, an experiment with a variable frame done through composition when filming and through the use of movable mats.

Fernstrom, Ray. "Movies in the Round." *FIR* 9 (Apr 58) 161–165. Report on Circarama, which utilizes eleven 16mm cameras and eleven projectors; how it is used by Disney cameramen.

"Behind the Scenes." *Newswk* 51 (14 Apr 58) 116–117. Giant picture techniques developed during the 1950s.

"The First Sniff?" *Newswk* 54 (9 Nov 59) 106. Contest between scented movies.

Kruse, B. "Seattle World's Fair Film Takes Public Way Out in Space; 360°-Dome Screen!" *Pop Photog* 50 (Apr 62) 105.

Lapham, Lewis H. "The Feely Is Here." *SEP* 237 (18 Apr 64) 28–29. A new machine

offers 3-D films that provide sounds, smells, and sensations.

"Movie You Feel and Smell as Well as See." *Pop Sci* 187 (July 65) 44–45. Borg-Warner's Science Hall in Chicago houses a "smell-o-cinema."

Day, Barry. "Beyond the Frame." *S&S* 37 (Spring 68). *See 3d.*

Thomsen, P. "Movies by Hologram." *Sci News* 95 (10 May 69) 460–461.

2m(1). HISTORY AND THEORY

Elliott, Eric. "Stereoptimism." *Close Up* 6 (No. 5, 1930) 344–351; (No. 6, 1930) 442–449. Pros and cons of 3-D films.

Vessello, A. "Stereoscopy." *S&S* 3 (No. 12, Winter 34–35) 157–159. An argument against Arnheim's view that stereoscopic film is antithetical to film art.

Knight, Arthur. "Film of the Future?" *Sat Rev* 35 (4 Oct 52) 40–41. A review of Cinerama as a new process.

Alpert, Hollis. "The Big Switch." *Sat Rev* 36 (14 Mar 53) 37–38. New 3-D processes will not save Hollywood from having to make good pictures.

Lambert, Gavin. "Report on New Dimensions." *S&S* 22 (Apr–June 53) 157–160. A description of 3-D and Cinerama; basic theory and some comments on the possible outcome.

Tyler, Parker. "Era of the Three-D's." *New Rep* 128 (18 May 53) 22–23. The phenomena of 3-D and Cinerama in terms of the audience's sensory experience as opposed to the experience in watching TV.

Hawkins, Richard C. "Perspective on 3-D." *QFRTV* 7 (No. 4, Summer 53) 325–334. UCLA film teacher describes systems, history going back to 1861, films produced (especially in Russia); other depth illusions.

Knight, Arthur. "Hollywood's Defense in Depth." *Reporter* 8 (9 June 53) 32–34. Speculation on 3-D techniques; comparison with other countries and early days of the movies.

Farber, Manny. "Films." *Nation* 177 (8 Aug 53) 117–118. Wide screen doesn't seem to improve the films.

Sisk, J. P. "Passion in a New Dimension." *Commonweal* 59 (23 Oct 53) 63–65. New projection systems such as 3-D simply extend the violence, involvement, and privacy invasion Hollywood has been pursuing since 1903.

Lindgren, Ernest. "CinemaScope." *S&S* 23 (Jan–Mar 54) 114. Brief comment on history of screen shapes.

Tyler, Parker. "Movie Note: The 3-D's." *Kenyon Rev* 16 (No. 3, 1954) 468–472. Third dimension reinforces unreality of the cinema; kinesthetic sensations challenge content.

Whitebait, William. "Cinerama." *New S&N* 48

(9 Oct 54) 437. Cinerama as *trompe l'oeil* in action.

Kohler, Richard, and Walter Lassally. "The Big Screens." *S&S* 24 (Jan–Mar 55) 120–126. Kohler presents the aesthetic objections to wide screen and Lassally gives the technical limitations and disadvantages of the "new" processes.

Malcolm, Donald. "Films." *New Rep* 133 (14 Feb 55) 19. Negative view of CinemaScope.

"The Big Screens." *S&S* 24 (Spring 55) 209–212. *Sight and Sound* sent out a questionnaire to a number of film directors: Cavalcanti, Clair, Dickinson, Dreyer, Gance, King, Milestone, De Mille, Renoir, Sternberg, Vidor, and Wilder; a surprising degree of acceptance of new screen sizes.

Limbacher, James L. "Widescreen Chronology." *FIR* 6 (Oct 55) 403–405. Current competitive forms.

Lassally, Walter. "Cult of Bigness." *Film* (No. 8, Mar–Apr 56) 6–8. Cameraman deplores wide-screen trend.

"Wide Screen or Vision?" *America* 95 (7 Apr 56) 8. Concern over losing conventional "small" pictures when "vulgar" spectacles are made.

Bluestone, George. "In Defense of 3-D." *Sewanee Rev* 64 (Fall 56) 683–689.

Macgowan, Kenneth. "The Screen's 'New Look' —Wider and Deeper." *QFRTV* 11 (No. 2, Winter 56) 109–130. Wide screen and 3-D are not new; history of film frame sizes; Abel Gance and other users of big screens.

Macgowan, Kenneth. "The Wide Screen of Yesterday and Tomorrow." *QFRTV* 11 (No. 3, Spring 57) 217–241. From Magnascope (1924) to dynamic frame.

Macgowan, Kenneth. "Screen Wonders of the Past—and to Come?" *QFRTV* 11 (No. 4, Summer 57) 381–393. Stereo sound—1881, 1929, 1940; video processes.

Tyler, Parker. "Reply with Rejoinder." *Sewanee Rev* 66 (Spring 58) 359–362. Takes issue with Bluestone's assessment of 3-D 64 (Fall 56).

"Something for the Nose: Smellovision." *America* 102 (12 Dec 59) 338. There was a Renaissance counterpart.

Barr, Charles. "CinemaScope: Before and After." *FQ* 16 (No. 4, Summer 63). *See 3a(1).*

Connor, Edward. "3-D on the Screen." *FIR* 17 (No. 3, Mar 66) 159–182. History, present and future of 3-D.

Shapps, Tony. "What Do We Mean by Widescreen?" *Cinéaste* 1 (No. 2, Fall 67) 10–11+. A question-and-answer essay on problems and advantages of shooting for wide screen.

Dewdney, Keewatin. "The Dream Machine." *Cinéaste* 2 (No. 4, Spring 69) 7–8. Essay on what the next form of visual technology (screen, projector, etc.) might look like.

Herzog, Milan. "The Language of the Small Screen." *JUFA* 22 (No. 2, 1970) 48–52. It calls for small and short topics and is best for instructing one person at a time.

2m(2). THIRD DIMENSION

"Spoor." *Time* 16 (1 Sep 30) 43. George K. Spoor and two engineers claim invention of 3-D camera with two lenses and a single aperture and also a sound track cut in a groove, like a record.

"Stereoscopic Projection for Motion Pictures." *Science* 72 (7 Nov 30) supp 12+. Projection without use of eyepiece.

"Stereoscopy." *Time* 18 (19 Oct 31) 60. Difficulties with new and old 3-D processes.

"Lifelike Depth Given to Movies." *Pop Sci* 121 (July 32) 22.

"Natural Vision Is Latest Movie Invention." *Pop Mech* 62 (Nov 34) 701. On 3-D movies.

"Flickering Mirrors Give Depth to the Movies." *Pop Mech* 64 (July 35) 92–93. On 3-D movie technique invented by William F. Adler.

Davis, V. "Three-Dimensional Motion Pictures." *Sci Newsletter* 32 (23 Oct 37) 260.

"Movies Soon to Have 3 Dimensions in Both Sight and Sound." *Arch Rec* 83 (Jan 38) 38. The advent of stereophonic sound and stereoscopic viewing at Bell Telephone Laboratories.

Kaufman, Sidney. "Three-Dimensional Films." *New Masses* 26 (15 Feb 38) 28–29. The capitalist nature of the movie industry makes it inevitable that 3-D will be used for shock effect for a long period before its artistic possibilities are exploited.

"Three-Dimensional Movies." *Hwd Q* 1 (No. 2, Jan 46) 237–238. Report from U.S. Embassy in Moscow of 3-D process without using spectacles.

Baxter, R. K. Neilson. "Stereoscopy." *Penguin F Rev* 3 (Aug 47) 68–71. Attempts to create 3-D.

Macleod, Joseph. "Stereoscopic Film." *S&S* 16 (No. 63, Autumn 47) 118–119. Seen in Moscow.

Eisenstein, S. M. "About Stereoscopic Cinema." (Tr. by Catherine De La Roche.) *Penguin F Rev* 8 (Jan 49) 35–45. Proposed uses; the last essay written by the Soviet director and film theoretician.

Gagliardi, Gio. "Movies in 3 Dimensions." *FIR* 2 (Feb 51) 23–24+. Five methods of motion-picture stereoscopy.

Pratley, Gerald. "The Latest 3-Dimensional Films." *FIR* 3 (Apr 52) 171–174. Norman McLaren's short films made in three-dimensional form in color and with strophonic sound as seen at the Festival of Britain.

"Third Dimension: New Bait for Movie Box Offices." *Bus Wk* (8 Nov 52) 132–134+.

"A Lion in Your Lap!" *Time* 60 (15 Dec 52) 108. Natural Vision (3-D) introduced.

"Three-D Day Hits Hollywood in Blinding Flash." *Life* 34 (16 Feb 53) 26–27. All the major studios schedule 3-D films.

"A.B.C. of 3-D." *Newswk* 41 (16 Feb 53) 68–70.

"New Voyagers." *Time* 61 (16 Feb 53) 104. Hollywood's excitement over 3-D films.

Lipton, N. C. "Realistic Movies." *Photog* 32 (Mar 53) 22.

"Flash in the Pan." *Time* 61 (2 Mar 53) 90. Reservations about 3-D future.

"Third Dimension." *Time* 61 (18 May 53) 114. Some troubles on the side.

"3-D Bonanza." *Time* 61 (23 Mar 53) 101. Polaroid Corporation production boom.

Brunel, Christopher. "3-D in England." *FIR* 4 (May 53) 228–231. An Englishman's adverse opinion of 3-D, with appraisals of British and Russian stereoscopy.

Kaempffert, Waldemar. "Are 3-D Movies Really New?" *Sci Dig* 33 (May 53) 26–28. Scientific explanation on similar experiments long ago.

"Three-D Movies Find Eye Trouble Never Suspected." *Sci Newsletter* 63 (9 May 53) 291. A doctor's comment on eye troubles caused by 3-D movies.

Hochman, L. "Hollywood Report." *Photog* 32 (June 53) 104.

"Third Dimension: An Industry Changes Its Product." *Bus Wk* (25 July 53) 60–62+.

"Three-D Movies Will Reveal Eye Defects." *Sci Dig* 34 (Aug 53) 30. A vision specialist's comments.

Long, A. "Three-D: A Two-Eyed Wonder." *Sci Newsletter* 64 (1 Aug 53) 74–75. Speculation on its lasting power.

Hochman, L. "Hollywood Report." *Photog* 33 (Sep 53) 92.

Lowe, W. "Screen's Third-Dimensional Round-Up." *Th Arts* 37 (Sep 53) 72–73+. Speculations on attempts to film 3-D directly from the stage.

Haines, Aubrey A. "Hollywood's Reply to Television." *America* 89 (12 Sep 53) 576–577. Three-dimensional movies.

"Three-D Comeback." *Bus Wk* (12 Dec 53) 45–46. *Kiss Me Kate* success revives hopes for 3-D.

"Superior Stereo." *Bus Wk* (30 Jan 54) 72+. New 3-D process of Polaroid and Technicolor introduced.

"Yesterday's Wow." *S&S* 23 (Jan–Mar 54) 115. Note on decline of interest in 3-D.

"Three-D Gets New Screening." *Bus Wk* (7 Sep 68) 56. Report on optical techniques developed by Fairchild Hiller and Tru-D, Inc.

Aigner, Hal. "The Coming 3-D Movie Revolution." *Take One* 2 (No. 9, 1970) 6–8. Possibilities for new way of producing 3-D motion pictures.

2m(3). WIDE SCREEN

Dunn, H. H. "New Giant Movies." *Pop Mech* 53 (May 30) 705–709. Process of "Magnafilm" projects 36mm film through magnifying lenses.

"One for the Aisle Sitters: Nu-Screen." *Newswk* 29 (21 Apr 47) 99. Curved screen eliminates distortion.

Armagnac, Alden P. "Supermovies Put You in the Show." *Pop Sci* 157 (Aug 50) 74–78. Techniques used in Cinerama.

"In Sync." *New Yorker* 27 (5 May 51) 23–25. A preview of Cinerama with stereophonic sound.

"The Third Dimension." *Time* 58 (2 July 51) 94. Cinerama.

Dempewolff, R. F. "Movies on a Curved Screen Wrap You in Action." *Pop Mech* 98 (Aug 52) 120–124.

"Movie Revolution." *Time* 60 (13 Oct 52) 104. Cinerama.

"Speaking of Pictures." *Life* 33 (27 Oct 52) 20–21+. Cinerama's "terrifying realism" provides the "biggest new entertainment event" of the year.

Hart, Henry. "Cinerama." *FIR* 3 (Nov 52) 33–35. Its technique and measurements.

Hartung, Philip. "Better with a Dramamine." *Commonweal* 57 (21 Nov 52) 165. Comment on Cinerama.

"Cinerama, the Broad Picture." *Fortune* 47 (Jan 53) 92–93+.

Kaempffert, W. "Cinerama: Movies in 3 Dimensions." *Sci Dig* 33 (Jan 53) 33–35.

Kempner, M. J. "Cinerama." *Vogue* 121 (Jan 53) 128–129+.

Postal, J. "Cinerama, a Wide Horizon for Dance." *Dance Mag* 27 (Jan 53) 27.

"Primitives on Broadway." *Harper's* (Jan 53) 191–192. Reactions to Cinerama and conjectures as to its importance and the revolutionary aspects involved.

"Cinerama, the Broad Picture." *Fortune* 48 (Feb 53) 92–93+. Historical treatment of Fred Waller's development of the Cinerama system through his contact with Hazard B. Reeves' stereophonic sound system and finally Louis B. Mayer's and Mike Todd's guiding hands.

"Fox's Moves." *Bus Wk* (7 Feb 53) 27. Switch to CinemaScope: threat to Cinerama?

"CinemaScope Upcoming." *Newswk* 41 (9 Feb 53) 61.

Manchester, H. "Fred Waller's Amazing Cinerama." *Rdrs Dig* (Mar 53) 45–48. His work, theoretical and practical, on the development of wide-screen projection.

"Zanuck Drops an Anti-Depth Charge." *Life* 34 (9 Mar 53) 34–35. 20th Century-Fox attacks 3-D with new innovation: CinemaScope.

"More 3-D." *Bus Wk* (4 Apr 53) 30. The Magna System introduced.

"Enter Magna." *Newswk* 41 (6 Apr 53) 92. New company, new screen system.

Knight, Arthur. "Movies Are Wider Than Ever." *Sat Rev* 36 (16 May 53) 32. Doubts about advantages of new wide-screen proportions.

Coughlan, Robert. "Spyros Skouras and His Wonderful CinemaScope." *Life* 35 (20 July 53). *See 5, Spyros Skouras.*

Boone, A. R. "Squeezed Movies Challenge 3-D's." *Pop Sci* 163 (Aug 53) 100–103.

Harper, Mr. "The Big Picture." *Harper's* 207 (Nov 53) 91–93. CinemaScope and *The Robe.*

Kimball, Ward. "Cartooning in CinemaScope." *FIR* 5 (Mar 54). *See 2h(2).*

"VistaVision." *Newswk* 43 (15 Mar 54) 104. Paramount announces its new wide-screen process.

Knight, Arthur. "Another Scope: Superscope." *Sat Rev* 37 (17 Apr 54) 23.

"Half Circle Movies Is Latest Wide-Screen Idea." *Sci Dig* 35 (May 54) 92.

"Hollywood's Future Begins to Take Shape." *Bus Wk* (8 May 54) 42–44. Fox's CinemaScope and Paramount's VistaVision explained and compared with standard systems.

Boone, Andrew R. "Hollywood Now Shoots Movies Sideways." *Pop Sci* 165 (July 54) 62–64. VistaVision.

Brunel, Christopher. "Widescreens, etc., in Britain." *FIR* 5 (Oct 54) 418–421.

"New Systems." *S&S* 24 (Oct–Dec 54) 60. VistaVision and Cinerama.

"Contest in Damascus." *Collier's* 134 (12 Nov 54) 106. Cinerama at the International Trade Fair.

Sayre, Joel. "Mike Todd and His Big Bug-Eye." *Life* 38 (7 Mar 55). *See 5, Mike Todd.*

"American Optical: Yankee in Filmdom's Court." *Bus Wk* (1 Oct 55) 176–178+. Speculation on Todd-AO's future and impact.

Wright, Basil. "The Big Screens." *Film* (No. 6, Dec 55) 7–11. A discussion of the various big-screen formats and how they might affect the film scene and film societies.

Lipton, N. C. "Todd-AO." *Pop Photog* 38 (Jan 56) 10+.

"Another Wide-Screen Filming Technique—Cinemiracle." *Sci Dig* 42 (July 57) 92.

"Cinemiracle." *Pop Photog* 42 (Feb 58) 114–115+. Louis De Rochemont finishes his new film in this new wide-screen form.

Reynolds, C. R. "Wide Screens, Blessing or Curse?" *Pop Photog* 42 (Feb 58) 116.

Hart, Henry. "De Rochemont's *Windjammer.*" *FIR* 9 (May 58) 235–240. A discussion of the Cinemiracle wide-screen process and a survey of the career and abilities of Louis De Rochemont, who is also the producer of its films.

Whitebait, William. "Big Screens and Little." *New S&N* 55 (17 May 58) 634–635. Use of new wide-screen process called Cinemiracle in the film *Windjammer.*

Barr, Charles. "Wider Still and Wider." *Motion* (No. 2, Winter 61–62) 30–33. An argument for CinemaScope, or the wide screen, based upon several films by Nicholas Ray, Don Siegel, Stanley Kubrick, and others.

2m(4). THEATRE TELEVISION

[See also 6a(2).]

Waltz, George H., Jr. "The Big Fight." *Pop Sci* 155 (July 49) 109–113. Five types of video projectors in movie theatres.

"More Theatre TV." *Bus Wk* (13 Aug 49) 26. Experiments of Fabian Theatres, Inc., Paramount and RCA.

McCoy, John E., and Harry P. Warner. "Theater Television Today." *Hwd Q* 4 (No. 2, Winter 49) 160–177; (No. 3, Spring 50) 262–278. History, equipment, programs, costs; relation with FCC; color; financing (two articles).

"Theatre Television." *Good Housekeeping* 131 (Nov 50) 17+. Possibility of closed-circuit television in movie theaters.

Hungerford, E. Arthur, Jr. "Theatre TV Is Ready." *FIR* 1 (Dec 50) 33–36. The two available systems are direct projection and videofilm.

"Bid for Theater TV." *Bus Wk* (10 Feb 51) 40+. FCC hearings.

"Movie Houses Grasp at TV." *Bus Wk* (12 May 51) 44+. Can large-screen presentations of special events help box office?

"Movies Move In on TV's Fights." *Life* 31 (9 July 51) 26–27. The closed-circuit showing of a boxing match seen as a step in winning back theatre audiences.

"Movie Color TV." *Newswk* 38 (30 July 51) 60. 20th Century-Fox's plan to show closed-circuit television broadcasts in movie theatres.

"Fifteen-Foot Weapon Against TV." *Life* 33 (6 Oct 52) 113+. Eidophor picks up the televised signal of live events, and projects it in color onto theatre screens.

"New Kind of TNT." *Time* 60 (6 Oct 52) 56. Growth of Theater Network Television.

"Life Looks In on Closed-Circuit TV." *Life* 34 (5 Jan 53) 100–102. Distorted sound and images in the Metropolitan Opera's *Carmen.*

The film director in Federico Fellini's *8½* fantasizes an order to hang the critic-intellectual. (Courtesy of Rizzoli Film Distributors—Museum of Modern Art.)

3. Film Theory and Criticism

3a. Theory

[See also 2d, 2g(2a), 2h(1), 2m(1), 2b(1), 4k, 8d.]

Segal, Mark. "Filmic Art and Training." *Close Up* 6 (No. 3, 1930) 195–197. An interview with Eisenstein provides information on film theory and education.

Saalschutz, L. "Present Tense." *Close Up* 6 (No. 3, 1930) 204–210. Theoretical argument against the indiscriminate use of sound and the appreciation of film art in terms of present-tense, subconscious experience.

Saalschutz, L. "The Relativity of Transition." *Close Up* 7 (No. 1, 1930) 5–12. Theoretical notes on aspects of cinematic relativity and change.

Braver-Mann, Barnet. "The Modern Spirit in Films: Motion, the Medium of the Movie." *Experimental Cinema* 1 (No. 1, Feb 30) 11–12.

Turin, Victor. "The Problem of the New Film Language." *Experimental Cinema* 1 (No. 3, Feb 31) 11.

Eisenstein, Sergei M. "The Intellectual Cinema." *Left* 1 (No. 2, Summer 31) 75–77. A call for support of the kind of cinema which brings together the emotional, the documentary, and the abstract.

Eisenstein, S. M. "The Principles of Film Form." *Close Up* 8 (No. 3, Sep 31) 167–181.

Richardson, Dorothy M. "Continuous Performance." *Close Up* 8 (No. 3, Sep 31) 182–185. The power of the cinema rests with its ability to raise the viewer to a level of contemplation.

Tonecki, Zygmunt. "The Preliminary of Film-Art." *Close Up* 8 (No. 3, Sep 31) 193–200; (No. 4, Dec 31) 321–324. A theoretical statement about the nature of film.

Richardson, Dorothy M. "Continuous Performance." *Close Up* 9 (No. 1, Mar 32) 36–38. Masculine and feminine tendencies in the cinema.

Eisenstein, S. M. "The Principles of Film Form." *Experimental Cinema* 1 (No. 4, Feb 33) 7–12.

Fairthorne, Robert A. "The Nature of Film Material." *Close Up* 10 (No. 2, June 33) 138–151. A theoretical statement about the nature of film material: visual, expressing duration, spatial extension, and direction in time.

Read, Herbert. "Towards a Film Aesthetic." *CQ* 1 (No. 1, Autumn 32) 7–11. Essentially an "open form," film's only unity is continuity; it must use "the lumbering material of the actual visible world."

Read, Herbert. "The Poet and the Film." *CQ* 1 (No. 4, Summer 33) 197–202. It is not enough to reach for the cliché images of metaphor; the film poet must exercise the true disciplines of imagination before the film can rank with great works of drama, literature, and painting. See *CQ* 2 (No. 1, Autumn 33) 33–36 for an objection by G. F. Dalton and response by Read.

Mullen, S. M. "Following the Films: All Motion Pictures Have a Basic Theme." *Scholastic* 26 (23 Mar 35) 28.

Arnheim, Rudolf. "The Film Critic of Today and Tomorrow." *CQ* 3 (No. 4, Summer 35) 203–209. "The talking-film . . . excludes the possibility of artistic form" and critics should realize this.

Mullen, S. M. "Motion Pictures, A Twentieth-Century Art." *Scholastic* 28 (18 Apr 36) 7–8+.

Vesselo, Arthur. "Love and Death." *S&S* 7

Readers are advised to acquaint themselves with the range of categories throughout the bibliography in the search for specific subjects. In some cases, cross-categorical comparisons are directly suggested. In general, however, each article is placed under one category only. Cross-references on individual articles have been kept to a minimum.

Entries are in chronological order of publication under each category. Exceptions are: Part 5, Biography, in which the order is alphabetical by name; Part 9, Case Histories of Film Making, which is alphabetical by film title; and 3c and 8c(4), also alphabetical by title.

(No. 27, Autumn 38) 102–104. Theoretical statement about the nature of film beauty.

Glendenning, Alex. "Commentary." *19th Century* 124 (Nov 38). *See 4b.*

Knight, Eric. "Moving Picture Goals." *Th Arts* 23 (Jan 39) 57–64.

Isaacs, Edith (ed.). "Artists of the Movies." *Th Arts* 23 (June 39). *See 2a.*

Milne, W. S. "Movies That Move." *Canad Forum* 19 (Dec 39) 287. The merits of "dynamic" movies as opposed to the often "static" films that came with sound; examples.

Hopper, G. M. "Mathecinematics." *Am Math Monthly* 47 (Oct 40) 565–568.

Whitman, E. A. "Film—A Triple Integral." *Am Math Monthly* 49 (June 42) 399–400.

Pratt, J. "Notes on Commercial Movie Techniques." *Inter J Psych* 24 (1943) 185–188. Fantasies of omnipotence, among others.

Lejeune, C. A. "Film as an Art Form." *Fortnightly Rev* 159 (Jan, Feb, Mar 43). *See 2a.*

Nichols, Dudley. "The Writer and the Film." *Th Arts* 27 (Oct 43). *See 2d.*

Montani, A., and G. Pietranera. "First Contribution to the Psychoanalysis and Aesthetics of Motion Pictures." *Psychoanalytic Rev* 33 (1946) 177–196. Uncontrolled stream-of-unconscious feelings would make "pure cinema" with no literary pretensions.

Pichel, Irving. "Seeing with the Camera." *Hwd Q* 1 (No. 2, Jan 46). *See 2e.*

Hammid, Alexander. "New Field—New Techniques." *Screen Writer* 1 (May 46) 21–27. The richness of film's potential; today film's "values are literary rather than cinematographic"; film should express "cinematic thought."

Wollenberg, H. H. "Exploring the Psychology of the Cinema." *S&S* 15 (No. 59, Autumn 46) 99–101. Historical overview of several positions taken on the psychology of the cinema.

Panofsky, Erwin. "Style and Medium in the Moving Pictures." *Critique* 1 (Jan–Feb 47). "Dynamization of space" and "spatialization of time"—an early statement (originally a lecture in 1934) of the aesthetic possibilities of "pictures that move," independent of the written word.

Seril, William. "Film Suspense and Revelation." *Screen Writer* 3 (Oct 47) 7–9. Unique dramatic intensity results from camera movements, animation, montage; many examples from films.

Seril, William. "The Camera's Bright Eye Is Lowered Becomingly." *Hwd Q* 3 (No. 2, Winter 47–48) 185–188. Concise encouragement for camera to be a "brilliant, allusive instrument" and suggest action by indirection and understatement; examples from a number of films.

Hauser, Arnold. "Can Movies Be 'Profound'?" *Partisan Rev* 15 (No. 1, Jan 48) 69–73. Only the novel can probe "psychological complexities," but film can be pleasing, take on tragic forms, show relationships among characters, and reveal through actions and symbols "a hint of depth."

Taig, Thomas. "The Anatomy of Film." *Penguin F Rev* 5 (Jan 48) 30–35. Toward an objective formal analysis of films.

Seril, William. "The Language of the Screen." *S&S* 17 (No. 65, Spring 48) 18–19. A theoretical statement.

Manvell, Roger. "The Poetry of the Film." *Penguin F Rev* 6 (Apr 48) 111–124. The coming of sound has increased the poetic possibilities as the film begins to reach maturity.

Tyler, Parker. "The Elements of Film Narrative." *Mag of Art* 41 (Apr 48) 137–141. Examination of the complex relations of space/time in the arts; Eisenstein's theory of montage brings film to its purest form.

Kennedy, Jay Richard. "Plots and Characters." *Screen Writer* 3 (May 48) 3–4+ Film "has no symbols. It communicates directly . . . plot is the method by which the film medium achieves characterization"; a paper given at NYU motion-picture symposium.

Anderson, Lindsay. "Creative Elements." *Sequence* (No. 5, Autumn 48) 8–12. The elements necessary to a great film.

Reisman, Leon. "Cinema Technique and Mass Culture." *Am Q* 1 (1949). Stars replace face-to-face relationships; other observations.

Rippy, Frazier W. "On Tragedy, Motion Pictures, and Greta Garbo." *Ariz Q* 5 (No. 1, 1949) 29–38. Possibilities inherent in the cinema medium for the enactment of the classic tragedies; Garbo as an actress with great affinity for tragic roles.

Dekeukeleire, Charles. "Towards a Science of Art." *Penguin F Rev* 8 (Jan 49) 77–85. Psychology can help us plan our emotions through film.

Keir, Gertrude. "Psychology and the Film." *Penguin F Rev* 9 (May 49) 67–72. Brief critique of Kracauer's theory of the collective unconscious and Parker Tyler's assumption that horses represent "an extension . . . of sexual power."

Rawnsley, David. "Design by Inference." *Penguin F Rev* 9 (May 49) 32–38. Not colossal sets but design of the thought line of the film, a "continuity of inference," will stir the imagination of the audience; special remarks on effects of changing colors.

Hafeez, M. A. "Psychology of Films." *J of Educ and Psych* 8 (1950) 14–22.

Seril, William. "Irony on the Screen." *FIR* 1 (May–June 50) 3–6. There are dramatic irony, irony of fate, irony of circumstances, and conscious irony.

Lambert, Gavin. "Sight and Sound." *Sequence* (No. 11, Summer 50) 3–7. Too much film theory still looks back to the silent period; *Earth* may be a poem and perhaps silent films more easily meet that description; not "luscious visuals" but truth to character in places and people will make a sound film poetic.

Seldes, Gilbert. "The Magic of the Movies." *FIR* 1 (Sep 50) 10–13+. There is a connection between the images, time, and rhythm of films and the things we live by from infancy; yet "nothing in the nature of the movies prevents the creation of human beings in all their complexities."

Richter, Hans. "The Film as an Original Art Form." *College Art J* 10 (No. 2, Winter 51) 157–161. Especially the experimental film. See also *F Cult* 1 (No. 1, 1955).

Broughton, James. "Odd Birds in the Aviary." *S&S* 21 (Jan–Mar 52) 126–127. The film's neglect of the essence of poetry, the heart and feelings; timing, montage, and the image; a series of short notes.

Manvell, Roger. "Debate with a Past Self." *S&S* 21 (Jan–Mar 52) 108–110+. In the book *Réflexion faite* (Paris, Editions Gallimard, 1951), Clair argues with his younger self by taking quotations from his notes, written in the 1920s, when he was in the advance guard of French film making, and replying to them from his position in 1950; Manvell comments further.

Cocteau, Jean. "Conversation." *S&S* 22 (July–Sep 52) 6–8. André Fraigneau wanted to help Cocteau edit a book on cinema; Cocteau decided he could express his ideas in the freer style of conversation; this article is an excerpt in the form of an extended interview.

Debrix, Jean R. "TV's Effect on Film Esthetics." *FIR* 3 (Dec 52) 504–506. Translated by David A. Mage. TV will save the cinema by forcing it to retreat to its strongest positions.

Moreno, Julio L. "Subjective Cinema: And the Problem of Film in the First Person." *QFRTV* 7 (No. 4, Summer 53) 341–358. Editor of film magazine in Montevideo relates first-person narrative in literature to examples of camera work used in films to suggest a character's dreams or a spectator's point of view: *Los Olvidados, Variety, Le Jour Se Leve, Lady in the Lake,* and others.

Huxley, Aldous. "Film Folio 3: Silence Is Golden." *S&S* 23 (July–Sep 53) 47–48. A reprint from an article written in 1929 in which Huxley lamented the coming of sound with a scathing review of *The Jazz Singer.*

Mann, Thomas. "Film Folio 4: On the Film." *S&S* 23 (Oct–Dec 53) 107. Reprint of an essay published in *Past Masters and Other Papers* (1933); his reaction to the few films he saw, and speculation on the future of this phenomenon.

Bennett, Arnold. "Film Folio 5: The Film Story." *S&S* 23 (Jan–Mar 54) 165–166. Reprint from an article in *Close Up* (Dec 27) by the novelist, who wrote the script for *Piccadilly* in 1929; "while the graphic side of cinema has been satisfactorily advancing, the dramatic side has been most unsatisfactorily lagging behind."

Richter, Hans. "The Film as an Original Art Form." *F Cult* 1 (No. 1, 1955) 19–23. Is the camera used to *reproduce* any object which appears before the lens or to *produce* sensations not possible in any other art medium? Both the documentary and the avant-garde represent original forms, but the former is by nature limited.

Peters, J. M. L. "The Necessity of Learning How to See a Film." *AV Com Rev* 3 (No. 3, Summer 55). See 1a.

Jones, Dorothy B. "The Language of Our Time." *QFRTV* 10 (No. 2, Winter 55) 167–179. History of visual communication, including picture magazines, films, and TV; its promise for world understanding.

Dreyer, Carl. "Thoughts on My Craft." *S&S* 25 (Winter 55–56). See 2c.

Agel, Henri. "Celluloid and the Soul." *Yale French Studies* (No. 17, 1956) 67–74. Cinema appears to possess a "soul" when its inspiration, direction, and interpretation give an impression that the work cannot be reduced to a simple psychological, affective, or aesthetic satisfaction; examples proposed.

Debrix, Jean. "Cinema and Poetry." *Yale French Studies* (No. 17, 1956) 86–104. Nostalgia for the silent film.

Riesman, David. "The Oral Tradition, the Written Word, and the Screen Image." *F Cult* 2 (No. 9, 1956) 1–5. Oral communication keeps people together; books create individualists; perhaps radio and film contribute to psychic mobility, especially in nonliterate societies that may skip the print-oriented stage; the last section of an article later included in *Abundance for What?* (Doubleday, 1964).

Houseman, John. "How—and What—Does a Movie Communicate?" *QFRTV* 10 (No. 3, Spring 56) 227–238. Images of human beings in movies and TV: is there some "weak echo of the American dream"?

Sasaki, Norio. "Current Problem of the Theory of Film Art." *Bigaku* 7 (No. 4, 1957) 30–42.

Tyler, Parker. "A Preface to the Problems of the Experimental Film." *F Cult* 4 (No. 17, 1958). See 8d.

Holland, Norman N. "Aristotle for Filmmakers." *FIR* 9 (June–July 58) 324–328. *The Poetics* applied in some detail: *mimesis* is getting the essential quality, not copying reality; *catharsis* is giving pleasure through teaching; scattered examples from films.

Vorkapich, Slavko. "Toward True Cinema." *F Cult* (No. 19, 1959) 10–17. "Composing visually, but in time," not merely recording a theatrical performance.

Buñuel, Luis. "A Statement." *F Cult* (No. 21, 1960) 41–42. The lack of creativity in film making; the gap between possibility and fact.

Evans, C. "The Cinema and Temporal Aesthetics." *Shenandoah* 11 (No. 3, Spring 60) 21–30. An analysis of Bergman's *Wild Strawberries* is used to explore the ability of cinema to present elements which relate to man's inner, psychic life.

Elster, Michael. "Bodily Distance Mechanism and Loud Noise: Cinema." *20th Century* 168 (Nov 60) 452–456. Criticism of what has been achieved in cinema.

Buñuel, Luis. "The Cinema, an Instrument of Poetry." *NY Film Bul* 2 (No. 2, 1961) 4–6. Buñuel criticizes cinema for not fulfilling its potentialities to express subconscious life.

Connor, Edward. "Of Time and Movies." *FIR* 12 (No. 3, Mar 61) 131–143. How time can be manipulated on film.

Gessner, Robert. "An Introduction to the Ninth Art: A Definition of Cinema." *Art J* 21 (Winter 61–62) 89–92. Concepts of film composition.

Riley, Philip. "Criticizing Criticism." *London Mag* (new series) 1 (No. 10, Jan 62) 66–70. On the British magazine critics' debate over the relative importance of form and content.

Harris, Hilary. "Thoughts on Movement." *Vision* [*Film Comment*] 1 (No. 1, Spring 62) 5–6. The true experimental film is one based on a purely visual experience.

Peters, J. M. L. "Art of Seeing a Film." *UNESCO Courier* 15 (Mar 62). See 1a.

Chabrol, Claude. "Big Subjects—Little Subjects." *Movie* (No. 1, June 62) 12–13. The important thing is the way they are handled.

Price, James. "The Illusion of the Present." *London Mag* (new series) 2 (No. 5, Aug 62) 66–70. On the feeling of spontaneity of action in some films and its absence in others.

Broughton, James. "Film as a Way of Seeing." *F Cult* (No. 29, 1963) 19+. "It is not merely looking. . . . You will never understand art at all if you are too inquisitive. . . . Intellect is incapable of vision"; author's filmography.

Deren, Maya. "The Cleveland Lecture." *F Cult* (No. 29, 1963) 64–68. The text of a lecture given by Maya Deren at the Cleveland Museum of Art, 6 April 1951, in which she discusses the nature of art and the "poetic" film. The focus is on her films *Ritual in Transfigured Time* and *Meditation on Violence*.

Holland, Norman. "The Puzzling Movies: Their Appeal." *J Soc Cin* 3 (1963) 17–28. *Hudson Review* literary and film critic proposes the notion that intellectuals like the mystery of meaning in Bergman, Resnais, and Antonioni films in the same way that audiences used to like the message in De Mille pictures, partly as a justification for eroticism; perhaps it also means we can argue about the puzzle and avoid the emotional problems.

Kelman, Ken. "Film as Poetry." *F Cult* (No. 29, 1963) 22–27. When is it lyric? When does it express an inner world? The opening flashback in Ingmar Bergman's *Sawdust and Tinsel* (*The Naked Night*) is an example.

Lye, Len. "Is Film Art?" *F Cult* (No. 29, 1963) 38+. There are kinesthetic developments in the arts, yet film cannot seem to get support for experiments; incomplete list of author's films.

"Poetry and Film: A Symposium." *F Cult* (No. 29, 1963) 55–63. Transcription of a symposium on the "poetic" film held at Cinema 16 on 28 October 1953, with Parker Tyler, Maya Deren, Dylan Thomas, Arthur Miller, and Willard Maas (as chairman).

Casty, Alan. "On Approaching the Film as Art." *F Com* 1 (No. 5, Summer 63) 29–34. Rejecting "delimiting" approaches, whether auteurist, political, or psychoanalytical, English teacher at Santa Monica City College suggests need for films to convey "a sense of the universal" through synthesis of form and meaning; he analyzes recent films by Ingmar Bergman as having moved toward the Stanley Kramer kind of problem film.

Lassally, Walter. "Communication and the Creative Process." *Film* (No. 37, Autumn 63) 18–24. Emotion is the basis.

Kelman, Ken. "Classic Plastics (and Total Tectonics)." *F Cult* (No. 31, 1963–1964) 44–46. Two major traditions of the classic film: form orientation in *Earth,* plot in *Sunrise.*

Richter, Hans. "From Interviews with Hans Richter During the Last Ten Years." *F Cult* (No. 31, 1963–1964) 26–35. Compiled from previous interviews given to Jonas Mekas, Gideon Bachmann, and Dansk Filmmuseum; Richter discusses the film medium itself, his own work, and that of other avant-garde film makers.

Smallman, Kirk. "Toward Visual Cinema." *F Com* 2 (No. 3, Summer 64) 44–45. Patterns and *phi* effects, in the manner of the Slavko Vorkapich theories.

Allen, W. H., and S. M. Cooney. "Nonlinearity in Filmic Presentation." *AV Com Rev* 12 (Summer–Fall 64) 164–176+.

Kelves, Barbara L. "Slavko Vorkapich on Film as a Visual Language and as a Form of Art." *F Cult* (No. 38, 1965) 1–46. Notes taken from Slavko Vorkapich's series of lectures at the Museum of Modern Art (1965) under the general heading "The Visual Nature of the Film Medium," in which he attempted "to put forth the rules inherent in the visual language of the film." Various interviews with Vorkapich and others who were there.

"Reasons of the Eye: Course at Museum of Modern Art." *New Yorker* 40 (13 Feb 65). *See 2f.*

Lerner, Carl. "The Film Lectures of Slavko Vorkapich." *F Com* 3 (No. 3, Summer 65) 51–52. Portrait. Brief reaction to talks given at the Museum of Modern Art, which seem to have been well-organized, confusing, but stimulating; biographical sketch on p. 53.

Solomon, Stanley J. "Modern Uses of the Moving Camera." *F Her* 1 (No. 2, Winter 65–66). *See 2e.*

McLuhan, Marshall. "Questions and Answers." *Take One* 1 (No. 2, 1966) 7–10. McLuhan discusses some films, film makers, and the medium itself.

Leenhardt, Roger. "Ambiguity of the Cinema." *CdC in Eng* (No. 1, Jan 66) 42–51. The evolution of the cinema, as in the other arts, moves from well-defined genres to more subtle forms "designed for the individual informed spectator."

Cendrars, Blaise. "The ABC of the Cinema." *F Cult* (No. 40, Spring 66) 19–20.

Vanderbeek, Stan. "Re: Vision." *Am Scholar* 35 (Spring 66) 335–340. Metaphoric thoughts on seeing anew, film making as personal dialogue, and picture poetry leading to new areas of human experience.

Doesburg, Theo van. "Film as Pure Form." *Form* (No. 1, Summer 66) 5–11.

Johnson, William. "Coming to Terms with Color." *FQ* 20 (No. 1, Fall 66). *See 2e(2).*

Michelson, Annette. "Film and the Radical Aspiration." *F Cult* (No. 42, Fall 66) 34–42+. The dissociative principle in postwar cinema; the use of new narrative conventions in Godard's *Alphaville;* a lecture at Fourth New York Film Festival.

Silverstein, Norman. "Camera of Ideas." *Salmagundi* 2 (No. 1, Spring 67) 74–87. On ideas that work well on screen, especially the notions of the "peep show" and the "chase."

Earle, William. "Some Notes on the New Film." *Triquarterly* (No. 8, Winter 67) 157–164. Comments on the characteristics of the narrative film.

Day, Barry. "Too Hot Not to Cool Down." *S&S* 37 (Winter 67–68) 28–32. A long discussion of Marshall McLuhan's ideas about "hot" movies and "cool" TV, with many quotations.

Falconer, V. "Films: Prose and Poetry." *Senior Scholastic* 92 (21 Mar 68) supp 20.

Durgnat, Raymond. "Ebb and Flow." *F&F* 14 (No. 11, Aug 68) 12–17. Importance of visual structure in older films.

Ustinov, Peter. "Art and Artlessness." *F&F* 15 (No. 1, Oct 68) 4–8. Film as an art form.

Medjuck, Joe. "Marshall McLuhan Makes a Movie." *Take One* 2 (No. 5, 1969) 15. An interview with the Canadian professor concerning films he might make.

Perry, Ted. "The Aesthetics and Criticism of the Motion Picture: A Selected Bibliography." *JUFPA* 21 (No. 2, 1969). *See 1b(1).*

Vanderbeek, Stan. "Movies: Disposable Art—Synthetic Media—And Artificial Intelligence." *Take One* 2 (No. 3, 1969) 14–16. Theoretical stance and plea for understanding of movies as a way of seeing anew and changing man.

Durgnat, Raymond. "Shapes and Stories." *F&F* 15 (No. 5, Feb 69) 56–60. Stories as they relate to the nature and aesthetic of film.

Durgnat, Raymond. "Plots and Subplots." *F&F* 15 (No. 6, Mar 69) 60–64. How subplots contribute to the shape of a film.

Perry, Ted. "The Seventh Art as Sixth Sense." *Educ Th J* 21 (Mar 69) 28–35. One view of the ontology of cinema reveals it to be constitutive, capable of creating as much as revealing the world.

Durgnat, Raymond. "Epics and Existence." *F&F* 15 (No. 7, Apr 69) 60–66. On plot construction in films.

Harriton, Maria. "Film and Dance." *Dance Mag* 43 (Apr 69). *See 8a(4).*

Falkenberg, Paul. "Notes on Film and Film History." *J Aesthetic Educ* 3 (No. 3, July 69) 57–64. A plea for the uniqueness of film and film-making theory.

Gordon, M. W. "What Film-Making Is All About." *America* 121 (6 Dec 69) 555–557. Discussion of basic film techniques using three recent avant-garde films.

Morgan, Gwen, and Donald Skoller. "Dreyer in Double Reflection." *Cinema* (Calif) 6 (No. 2, 1970). *See 5, Carl Dreyer.*

Cameron, Evan. "On Mathematics, Music, and Film." *Cinema Studies* (Bridgewater, Mass.) (No. 3, Spring 70) 1–103. A theoretical treatise dealing with the functions of mathematics and art, the limits of cinematic space, and suggested procedures for film and music composition.

Currie, R. H. "Film as the Immediate and Reflexive Image and the Reaches of Filmic Encounter." *Language and Style* 3 (No. 4, Fall 70) 293–302.

3a(1). TECHNICAL ASPECTS OF THEORY

[See also 2e, 2f.]

Blakeston, Oswell. "Telecinema." *Close Up* 7 (No. 1, 1930) 38–41. Notes on the coming of television and its relation to film.

Eisenstein, S. M. "The Future of the Film." *Close Up* 7 (No. 2, 1930) 143–144. As paraphrased by Mark Segal in an interview with Eisenstein; comments on new techniques—color, sound, 3-D.

Herring, Robert. "London Looke Backe." *Close Up* 6 (No. 6, 1930) 455–463. A critique of sound versus silent film.

Potamkin, H. A. "Phases of Cinema Unity." *Close Up* 6 (No. 6, 1930) 463–474. An argument for the use of sound in cinema. See also "Playing with Sound," 7 (No. 2, 1930) 112–115.

Richardson, Dorothy. "Continuous Performance." *Close Up* 7 (No. 3, 1930) 196–202. Personal reflections on sound versus silent film.

Bakshy, Alexander. "Dynamic Composition." *Experimental Cinema* 1 (No. 1, Feb 30) 2.

Laird, Donald A. "Our Eyes and the Movies." *Sci Am* 142 (Mar 30) 200–201. Uses Eadweard Muybridge's experiments to explain "persistence of vision."

Bond, R. "Dovjhenko on the Sound Film." *Close Up* 7 (No. 4, Oct 30) 273–275. The Russian director discusses the sound film, in an interview.

Ogino, Yasushi. "Characterisation of Sound Talkies." *Close Up* 7 (No. 5, Nov 30) 340–345. A Japanese writer provides a theoretical statement about the use of sound in motion pictures.

Eisenstein, Sergei. "The Dynamic Square." *Hound & Horn* 4 (No. 3, Apr–June 31) 406–410. The Russian film maker suggests new proportions for the film frame.

Eisenstein, Sergei. "The Dynamic Square." *Close Up* 8 (No. 1, Mar 31) 3–16; (No. 2, June 31) 91–94. An article based on Eisenstein's speech in which he favors new proportions or aspect ratios for the screen.

Kinross, Martha. "The Screen, From This Side." *Fortnightly Rev* 136 (Oct 31) 499–512. Suggests technical elements of film outweigh literal application.

Martyn, Howe. "The New Art Film." *Canad Forum* 11 (Sep 31) 479. Stresses technique and mechanical properties as artistic elements of cinema.

Howard, Clifford. "Symphonic Cinema." *Close Up* 10 (No. 4, Dec 33) 347–350. Theoretical statement about the possibilities of film sound in the future.

Hall, Mordaunt. "Sound, Not Silence, Is Golden." *Cinema Arts* 1 (No. 2, July 37) 46. Defense of the sound film as art.

"The Shadows Find a Voice." *New Masses* 40 (22 July 41) 26–29. An anonymous manifesto by several screenwriters calling for writers to understand the technology of film; the coming of sound made realistic portrayal of people possible.

La Farge, Christopher. "Disney and the Art Form." *Th Arts* 25 (Sep 41) 673–680. Though limited by his stories and use of color, Disney comes closest to achieving an art form in film—by creating in a manner impossible in any other medium.

Davidman, Joy. "Before the Talkies." *New Masses* 43 (5 May 42) 28. Silent films such as *The Gold Rush* had a more effective style than current films because silent cameramen "were forced to explore every possibility of their medium."

Nugent, Frank S. "How Long Should a Movie Be?" *NYTM* (18 Feb 45) 18–19+.

Barbarow, George. "Movies in Limbo." *Th Arts* 29 (Dec 45) 719–724. An attempt to look beyond the "trappings" of films (such as 3-D, color) into the real basis of film—freedom of space and time; how the "trappings" negate this freedom.

Asquith, Anthony. "The Tenth Muse Climbs Parnassus." *Penguin F Rev* 1 (Aug 46) 10–26. The growth of film technique toward artistic status.

Wright, Basil. "Cinema; the New Year." *Spectator* 178 (3 Jan 47) 12. Future developments in cinema not based on dialogue alone but on moving toward a universally intelligible art.

Queval, Jean. "Cinema and Television." *S&S* 19 (May 50) 141–142. What each medium can best do.

Brown, Robert. "Film Myth and the Limits of Film." *Hudson Rev* 4 (No. 1, 1951) 111–117. The cinema's purely mechanical limitations and abilities help create its aesthetic ones.

Clair, René. "Television and Cinema." *S&S* 19 (Jan 51) 372. Direct (live) television is similar to the stage and has some of its disadvantages and advantages; filmed television teaches us nothing the cinema screen cannot show us.

DeKay, James T. "Dark Thoughts on the New." *FIR* 4 (June–July 53) 263–265. A rejection of technical advancements in cinema since sound; greater reality provides less imaginative qualities and more limitations on the mobility of the camera.

Tyler, Parker. "Movies as a Fine Art." *Partisan Rev* 24 (Summer 57) 422–427. Film museums may chart technical progress but not the "art" of the medium.

Brakhage, Stanley. "The Silent Sound Sense." *F Cult* (No. 21, 1960) 65–67. Brakhage argues that certain silent films were able to create a musical or sound sense, an inventiveness he claims was never equaled in the sound film.

Mamoulian, Rouben. "Colour and Light in Films." *F Cult* (No. 21, 1960) 68–79. In two parts—Part One: "The Esthetics of Colour"; Part Two: "The Use of Colour in Films 1946–1956" (*Black Narcissus, Gate of Hell, Moby Dick*, etc.).

Gessner, Robert. "The Parts of Cinema: A Definition." *J Soc Cin* 1 (1961) 25–39.

Borge, Vagn. "The Camera Within Us." *London Mag* 1 (No. 12, Mar 62) 76–82. The camera expresses the inner camera of the imagination of the camera operator.

Barr, Charles. "CinemaScope: Before and After." *FQ* 16 (No. 4, Summer 63) 4–24. A defense of wide screens as taking us away from "literary" montage and increasing "the involvement of the spectator and the physical integration of the characters."

Dickinson, Thorold. "The Maturing Cinema." *J Soc Cin* 4 (1964) 9–19. With the widening of the screen and the deepening of focus has come unification of the documentary and theatrical traditions in that enduring aspect of cinema which reveals human character developing in its environment.

Goodman, Paul. "Griffith and the Technical Innovations." *Moviegoer* (No. 2, Summer–Autumn 64) 51–54. D. W. Griffith's work used to illustrate the aesthetic problem of the relationship between technique and content.

Halas, John. "No Frontiers." *Studio Inter* 176 (Sep 68) 108–109. Animation director tells of his earlier association with the Bauhaus and Moholy-Nagy; the future of "total" theatre through modern technology.

Andrew, J. Dudley. "A Technical Point and Limitation." *Take One* 2 (No. 11, 1970) 19–20. Film criticism must deal with the film as perceived on the screen.

3a(2). PROBLEMS OF REALISM

[See also 7a, 8c(1).]

Hughes, C. J. Penethorne. "Dreams and Films." *Close Up* 7 (No. 2, 1930) 120–124. Film as dream, the adoption of the mechanization of the dream.

Rotha, Paul. "The Revival of Naturalism." *Close Up* 7 (No. 1, 1930) 21–32. Zola as the background for a naturalistic cinema.

Howard, Clifford. "Cinema Psychology." *Close Up* 10 (No. 1, Mar 33) 71–73. Cinema has a true affinity for psychology, fantasy, and idealism.

MacKegg, D. M. "Art in the Cinema? Well . . ." *CSMM* (17 June 36) 9. Cedric Hardwicke says cinema is too realistic to be art; René Clair says art is possible if the public wants it; a critic says it took 200 years for Salisbury Cathedral to get its spire.

"*Snow White* and Escape from Reality." *Chris Cent* 55 (20 July 38) 886–887. Neither this film nor others like it provide an "escape from reality"; a defense of the imaginative film.

Arnheim, Rudolf. "Fiction and Fact." *S&S* 8 (No. 32, Winter 39–40) 136–137. The cinema has only two ways of getting rid of its hybridism—photographic theatre or reproduction of reality.

Ferguson, Otis. "Life Goes to the Pictures." *Films* 1 (No. 2, Spring 40) 19–29. American movies very often reflect "the unaffected and unconscious process of life" itself.

Cross, Elizabeth. "A Little More Nonsense Please!" *S&S* 9 (No. 35, Autumn 40) 45. Films should sometimes provide fantasy and escape.

Sachs, Hanns. "Missions of the Movies." *Life & Letters Today* 26 (Sep 40) 261–268. Mass fantasies and community daydreams.

Powell, Dilys. "Variable Stars." *S&S* 9 (No. 36, Winter 40–41). See *2b(2)*.

Crowther, Bosley. "Reality or Escape." *NYTM* (14 June 42). See *7b(1)*.

Rossen, Robert. "New Characters for the Screen." *New Masses* 50 (18 Jan 44) 18–19. Screenwriters who want to deal with reality will go out and discover the changes engendered by the war.

Farber, Manny. "Theatrical Movies." *New Rep* 110 (14 Feb 44) 211–212. "Preservation of the purity of an event is the reason for being of the camera"; an attempt to define "theatrical" as uncinematic.

Bean, Keith F. "An Open Letter to Oliver Bell." *S&S* 13 (No. 49, 10 May 44) 8–10. The relationship between film and reality in wartime.

Beresford, Maurice. "Realism and Emotion." *S&S* 14 (No. 53, Apr 45) 13–15. Problems arise out of the communal nature of cinema viewing.

Edwards, Tudor. "Film and Unreality." *S&S* 15 (No. 58, Summer 46) 59–61. Given the recent experiences of the war, the cinema should move away from overly realistic statements.

Cairns, Adrian. "We Are Such Stuff as Films Are Made On." *S&S* 15 (No. 59, Autumn 46) 92–93. Arguments against several previous articles which stressed the importance of escape and fantasy in films.

Gundlach, R. H. "The Movies: Stereotypes or Realities?" *J Soc Issues* 3 (No. 3, 1947) 26–32. The movies which are produced do tend to provide outlets for escapism, conventional notions, and dreams, but a small number of realistic movies are created in spite of difficulties.

De Voto, Bernard. "Easy Chair." *Harper's* 194 (Feb 47) 126–129. The movies' mishandling of psychiatry is the springboard for this discussion of reality and fantasy in the film.

Isaacs, Hermine Rich. "The Movies Murder Illusion." *S&S* 16 (No. 61, Spring 47) 27–29. The cinema should not always try to make visible what is invisible.

Kennedy, Jay Richard. "An Approach to Pictures." *Screen Writer* 3 (June 47) 5–11.

Describes the blending of the wartime documentary approach and the prewar Hollywood theatrical technique (which contrived to glorify a central character) in the author's new script about the Bureau of Narcotics.

Gassner, John. "Expressionism and Realism in Films." *Penguin F Rev* 3 (Aug 47) 21–30. Two tendencies: the problem is to raise the level.

Burov, Semyon. "Realism the Basis of Soviet Film Art." *Penguin F Rev* 4 (Oct 47) 76–82. A discussion of the term "realism" as a true description of contemporary life and historic events.

Swallow, Norman. "Social Realism in Film and Radio." *S&S* 16 (No. 64, Winter 47–48) 170–171.

Winge, John H. "Low and High Lustre." *S&S* 16 (No. 64, Winter 47–48) 166–167. Film reality and illusion.

Yerrill, D. A. "The Technique of Realism." *S&S* 17 (No. 65, Spring 48) 23–24. True realism demands that the audience watch and listen intently to what is most true to themselves and the world.

Wald, Malvin. "Cops and Writers." *Screen Writer* 3 (Mar 48) 23–26. Co-writer for *The Naked City* did research with New York City police department and they told him a few things about authenticity.

Tyler, Parker. "Film Form and Ritual as Reality-Principle." *Kenyon Rev* (Summer 48) 528–538.

De La Roche, Catherine. "The Mask of Realism." *Penguin F Rev* 7 (Sep 48) 35–43. Cinema does not reflect the reality of contemporary life.

Tyler, Parker. "Documentary Technique in Film Fiction." *Am Q* 1 (1949) 99–115. The distortion of the documentary idea in American scientific crime-detection films, including *Boomerang*.

Pavitt, Ian. "Set Piece." *S&S* 18 (Spring 49) 14–17. There are more kinds of films than "realistic" ones.

Cranston, Maurice. "The Pre-Fabricated Daydream." *Penguin F Rev* 9 (May 49) 26–31. The audience is unable to use its imagination.

Wollenberg, H. H. "The Return of Romanticism." *Penguin F Rev* 9 (May 49) 103–107. The new realism is already being taken over by commercialism; perhaps the old German romanticism of *The Student of Prague* is due for revival.

Hawkes, Jacquetta. "Space, Time, and the Possible." *S&S* 19 (Apr 50) 67+. Film has the potentiality to go beyond temporal realism.

Grover, Gloria Waldron. "Documentry Values in Fiction Films." *FIR* 1 (May–June 50) 7–8+. Examples she considers outside the boundaries of rigid classification: *The River, The Titan, Nanook, Henry V, Paisan, Oxbow Incident, Grand Illusion, Children of Paradise*, "some" of the Marx Brothers films, and "several" Chaplin films.

Tyler, Parker. "Violating Reality via the Fact-Fiction Film." *FIR* 1 (May–June 50) 9–11+. The documentary style can be pseudoconscientious and often delusive.

Ford, Charles. "Thirty Years of Conscious Realism." *S&S* 19 (Nov 50) 280–282. Early film makers who stuck to reality in their fiction were "unconscious realists"; they were not aware they were following a theory of art; German expressionism brought in fantasy again; the new "conscious realism" is a reaction.

Burke, Kenneth. "Toward a New Romanticism." *FIR* 1 (Dec 50) 25–27+. The terms "romantic," "realistic," and "classical" as used in *A New Romantic Anthology* by Stephen Watts (New York: New Directions, 1950. Stefan K. Schimanski and Henry Treece, eds.); thoughts on scriptwriting.

Kaplan, Abraham. "Realism in the Film: A Philosopher's Viewpoint." *QFRTV* 7 (No. 4, Summer 53) 370–384. UCLA philosophy professor contrasts "propaganda art," realistic but not aesthetic, and "escapist art," which may satisfy the aesthete but not the realist; special study of John Ford's *The Long Voyage Home*.

Zavattini, Cesare. "Some Ideas on the Cinema." *S&S* 23 (Oct–Dec 53). *See 4e(3b)*.

de Laurot, Edouard L. "Towards a Theory of Dynamic Realism." *F Cult* 1 (No. 1, 1955) 2–14. The author indicts the American avant-garde for neglecting "realism," which he defines as "a matter of content dictated by a dynamic perception of reality reflecting the development of the human conscience within its historical context."

Kracauer, Siegfried. "The Found Story and the Episode." *F Cult* (No. 7, 1956) 1–5. Theoretical formulation of two story forms for films.

Renoir, Jean. *"La Chienne." Film* (No. 9, Sep–Oct 56). *See 9, La Chienne*.

Riley, Ronald H., and Philip Leacock. "Fact and . . . Fiction." *F&F* 3 (No. 7, Apr 57). *See 8c(1)*.

Crosby, John. "Romance Comes Back." *Holiday* 21 (June 57) 119+. Realism is on the run in the entertainment world.

Butcher, Maryvonne. "Realism on the Screen." *Commonweal* 67 (22 Nov 57) 202–204. Comparison of the "realistic" techniques of *Gervaise, Le Notti di Cabiria*, and *Baby Doll*.

Gow, Gordon. "The Quest for Realism." *F&F* 4 (No. 3, Dec 57) 13–15+. Six directors, five stars, and two writers discuss realism.

Gerasimov, Sergei. "All Is Not Welles." *F&F* 5 (No. 12, Sep 59) 8. Attack on formalistic film making like that of Orson Welles.

Fielding, Raymond. "The Dearth of Fantasy."

FIR 10 (Nov 59) 534–536. Often we cannot believe commercialized fantasy on the screen because the "realistic style is self-defeating."

Bazin, André. "The Ontology of the Photographic Image." (Tr. by Hugh Gray.) *FQ* 13 (No. 4, Summer 60) 4–9. "For the first time an image of the world is formed automatically." It is "the object itself, the object freed from the conditions of time and space" and the "aesthetic qualities of photography are to be sought in its power to lay bare the realities."

Widem, Allen M. "Why Not Realism?" *JSPG* (Sep 60) 13–14. Theatre editor for *Hartford Times* argues for exploiting motion pictures' potential for realistic studies.

Leacock, Richard. "For an Uncontrolled Cinema." *F Cult* (Nos. 22–23, 1961) 23–25. A proposal for film makers to observe and select, not control their material.

Tyler, Parker. "Declamation on Film." *F Cult* (Nos. 22–23, 1961) 26–32. An aesthetic argument that "art, and not physical reality remains film's most important metier no less than its most challenging problem."

Harkfield, W. "By the Light of the Silvery Screen." *Commentary* 31 (Mar 61) 251–254. Discussion: 32 (Aug 61) 168–170. Discussion of theories of Siegfried Kracauer and Parker Tyler.

Pearson, Gabriel, and Eric Rhode. "Cinema of Appearance." *S&S* 30 (Autumn 61) 160–168. One assumption of the French New Wave is that, in a world of discontinuity, morality is a process of improvisation; the humanist critic, who may believe in a stable reality, should observe there is a shift away from this kind of film "from *Bicycle Thieves* through *L'Avventura* to *Breathless.*"

Munier, Roger. "The Fascinating Image." *Diogenes* (No. 38, 1962) 85–94. The power of the cinema to capture the images of the real world enlarges our world.

Schleifer, Marc. "*La Dolce Vita* and *L'Avventura* as Controversy; *L'Avventura* and *Breathless* as Phenomenalist Film." *F Cult* (No. 26, 1962) 59–62. The various implications of phenomenalism in three films.

Roud, Richard. "Novel Novel: Fable Fable?" *S&S* 31 (Spring 62). *See 3f(2).*

Buñuel, Luis. "Cinema: An Instrument of Poetry." *Th Arts* 46 (July 62) 18–19. On film in the fantastic and realistic modes.

Milne, Tom. "How Art Is True?" *S&S* 31 (Autumn 62) 166–171. The question of improvisation: In such films as *Shadows* and *The Connection* it is faked and becomes an end itself.

Pingaud, Bernard. "The Aquarium." *S&S* 32 (Summer 63) 136–139. One goes to the cinema, not to see the world, but to see images.

Antonioni, Michelangelo. "The Hollywood Myth Has Fallen!" *Pop Photog* 53 (July 63) 94–97+. Preprinting of introduction to book of four screenplays.

"Movies (Non-Escape)." *NYTM* (17 Nov 63) 86+. Pictures from films which deal with reality rather than escapism.

Antonioni, Michelangelo. "The Event and the Image." *S&S* 33 (Winter 63–64) 14. A short article reprinted from *Cinema Nuovo;* an example of the special reality a director has to be able to see; for Antonioni the image remains, and he would try "to remove the actual event from the scene."

Nowell-Smith, Geoffrey. "Through the Looking Glass." *S&S* 33 (Summer 64) 130–135. An inquiry into realism in the cinema; discussion of the Rossellini, Visconti, and De Sica-Zavattini neorealist models, of the sophisticated observation in Resnais' *Muriel;* photographic techniques in the magical fable *Lola.*

Walsh, Moira. "Meaningful Films." *America* 111 (22 Aug 64) 197–198. Discussion of what constitutes a "truthful" film.

Roemer, Michael. "The Surfaces of Reality." *FQ* 18 (No. 1, Fall 64) 15–22. Simplicity, intimate detail, immediacy, ordinary situations, concreteness: film is made from "the stuff of life itself" yet it is "basically an artifact" which forces us to draw conclusions from the structuring of concrete detail.

Durgnat, Raymond. "Truth Is Stronger Than Fiction." *F&F* 11 (No. 4, Jan 65) 44–48. Style is more important than realism in film; experience more central than information.

Antonioni, Michelangelo. "Reality and *Cinéma Vérité.*" *Atlas* 9 (Feb 65) 122–123. There is no such thing as *cinema-vérité;* all reality is subjective.

Durgnat, Raymond. "Expressing Life in Celluloid." *F&F* 11 (No. 8, May 65) 44–48. Expressionism and realism in film.

Broderick, Dorothy. "Confessions of a Purist." *Lib J* 91 (15 Mar 66) 1599–1600. Reply by M. R. Smith (15 Sep 66) 4156+. On authenticity in films.

Casty, Alan. "*The Pawnbroker* and the New Direction in Screen Realism." *F Her* 1 (No. 3, Spring 66) 3–14. The movement of American film from social realism to a symbolic or poetic realism marked by greater complexity of character and resonance of metaphor.

Linder, Carl. "Who's on First, What's on Second?" *December* 8 (No. 1, Spring 66) 117–125. The problem of "believability" in film; reality versus illusion.

Polt, Harriet R. "Notes on the New Stylization." *FQ* 19 (No. 3, Spring 66) 25–29. The films of the 1960s are characterized by something quite different from yesterday's realism —"stylization," so differently handled in *Um-*

brellas of Cherbourg and What's New, Pussycat?

Arnheim, Rudolf. "Art Today and the Film." *F Cult* (No. 42, Fall 66) 43–45. "Using imagery to describe reality" is film's best role, a mental process. Reprinted from *Art Journal* 25 (No. 3, 1966).

Wagenheim, Allan Jay. "On the Necessity for Hollywood." *North Am Rev* 3 (new series) (Sep 66) 28–29. Hollywood has manufactured one of the most valuable substances known to modern man—an antidote for reality poisoning.

Dart, Peter. "Figurative Expression in the Film." *Speech Monographs* 35 (No. 2, 1968) 170–174. Problems involved in a medium that has the literalness of the photographic image at its foundation.

Lumsden, Hugh D. "The Cinema of the Future." *Explorations* (No. 21, Apr 68) 67–86. The nature of cinema; its strengths; it can constitute a new reality.

Harcourt, Peter. "What, Indeed, Is Cinema?" *CJ* 8 (No. 1, Fall 68) 22–28. Bazin and Kracauer are not so far apart in their faith in the objectivity of the real world which affects what happens on film; this is the great tradition to which cinema returns "to renew itself after periods of big-studio artificialities or avant-garde experimentation."

Blake, R. A. "Reality and Structure in Film Aesthetics." *Thought* 43 (Autumn 68) 429–440. The particular vitality of film is born of the tensions between reality and structure.

Earle, W. "Revolt Against Realism in the Films." *J Aesthetics and Art Criticism* 27 (No. 2, Winter 68) 145–151. An attempt to define realism in terms of perception shared with others in a public arena as well as having particular meaning for the self; three methods of destroying it are extreme retinal changes, surrealism, and irony.

Lellis, George. "Cinema and Arti-Facts." *F Her* 4 (No. 2, Winter 68–69) 11–18. Some contemporary films which focus attention on the illusion of their artistic creation: *La Chinoise, Report on the Party and the Guests, Marat/Sade.*

Dowd, Nancy Ellen. "Popular Conventions." *FQ* 22 (No. 3, Spring 69) 26–31. Comparison of *Battle of Algiers*, seen as melodramatically contrived, with *Titicut Follies*, which is said to be nearer the reality we actually experience—the speech which says nothing, the sense of time which goes nowhere, the characters which never develop.

Corliss, Richard. "The Limitations of Kracauer's Reality." *CJ* 10 (No. 1, Fall 70) 15–22. An item-by-item critique of Siegfried Kracauer's *Theory of Film* (Oxford, 1965): it is "not only narrow, it is also obscure, contradictory, and misleading."

3a(3). THE AUTEUR THEORY

[See also 2c, 2d(1).]

Farber, Manny. "The Movie Art." *New Rep* 107 (26 Oct 42) 546–547. Signature of an artist is still possible in spite of the technology of film.

Cole, Lester. "Script and Screen." *New Masses* 47 (20 Apr 43) 28–29. Writers, not the cameras, write stories; Joy Davidman and others who think of technique as more important than the story will lead films away from concern with people to abstractions.

Davidman, Joy. "Miss Davidman Replies." *New Masses* 47 (20 Apr 43) 29–30. Reply to Lester Cole: storytelling about people is the basis of film, but it is done by means of images joined together, not by means of "verbalizations which the director must perspiringly translate into pictures." The writer should work more closely with the director.

Schofield, Stanley. "They Built a Cathedral." *S&S* 14 (No. 56, Winter 45–46) 129. Like the medieval cathedral, a film should represent a communal effort to heighten and purge the emotions.

Delehanty, Thornton. "Let Them Become Directors!" *Screen Writer* 2 (June 46). See 2d.

Mankiewicz, Joseph L. "Film Author! Film Author!" *Screen Writer* 2 (May 47) 23–28. Agrees with Benoit-Lévy that a true film author is a writer-director who envisions the finished film; this is the kind of "authority" writers must have over their work.

Dunne, Philip, Milton Krims, Allen Rivkin, Albert Lewin, Preston Sturges, Niven Busch, Norman Krasna, and Delmer Daves. "Can Screen Writers Become Film Authors?" *Screen Writer* 3 (June 47) 34–37. Brief statements in response to Joseph Mankiewicz article in May issue.

Anderson, Lindsay. "The Director's Cinema?" *Sequence* (No. 12, Autumn 50) 6–11+. An argument for the director as the creative force in the cinema, albeit admitting the role of the playwright; an exchange between Thorold Dickinson and Howard Koch on the same subject.

Armitage, Peter. "The Role of the Director." *Film* (No. 10, Nov–Dec 56) 14–15. A brief account of the problems of defining film authorship.

Arnheim, Rudolf. "Who Is the Author of a Film?" *F Cult* 4 (No. 16, 1958) 11–13. The answer varies according to the actual situation; some films are collaborations, others are dominated by one person; the screenwriter and director actually do the same work.

Sarris, Andrew. "The Director's Game." *F Cult* (Nos. 22–23, 1961). See 3b.

Sarris, Andrew. "Dialogue of a Schizocritic." *NY F Bul* 3 (No. 4, 1962) 10–12. A humorous dialogue which discusses several films in terms of the auteur theory and female stars.

Sarris, Andrew. "Notes on the Auteur Theory in 1962." *F Cult* (No. 27, 1962–1963) 1–8. After considering André Bazin's doubts about *la politique des auteurs,* the American critic prescribes three "premises" for directorial eminence—technical competence, distinguishable personality, and "tension" between his personality and his material.

Kael, Pauline. "Circles and Squares." *FQ* 16 (No. 3, Spring 63) 12–26. Wide-ranging indictment of the auteur theory, especially as postulated by Andrew Sarris; sidelights on New Cinema, Jonas Mekas, and the role of the critic.

Knight, Arthur. "The Auteur Theory." *Sat Rev* 46 (4 May 63) 22. Power and politics behind the scenes in movie making limit the value of this theory about directors as authors.

Sarris, Andrew. "The Auteur Theory and the Perils of Pauline." *FQ* 16 (No. 4, Summer 63) 26–33. Defense of the auteur theory as "the most efficient method of classifying the cinema: past, present, and future"; also, *Cahiers du Cinéma* is a better magazine than *Film Quarterly;* a reply to Pauline Kael's attack in spring issue.

Cameron, Ian, Mark Shivas, Paul Mayersberg, and V. F. Perkins. "*Movie* vs. Kael." *FQ* 17 (No. 1, Fall 63) 57–64. Editors of *Movie* make twenty points in rebuttal to Pauline Kael's article on auteur theory in spring issue; she makes four points in response to theirs.

Magid, M. "Auteur! Auteur! Opposing Camps." *Commentary* 37 (Mar 64) 70–74. *Cahiers du Cinéma, Movie,* Sarris and their respective views on the auteur theory.

Anderson, Thom. "The Controversial Seach for Value." *Sat Rev* 47 (26 Dec 64) 18–19+. Auteur theory reexamined.

Durgnat, Raymond. "Who Really Makes Movies?" *F&F* 11 (No. 7, Apr 65) 44–48. On the auteur theory.

Bazin, André. "On the *Politique des Auteurs.*" *CdC in Eng* (No. 1, Jan 66) 8–18. The difficulties of the auteur approach to film criticism.

"Cinematic Style." *F Cult* (No. 42, Fall 66) 89–95. New York Film Festival symposium by Andrew Sarris, James Stoller, Roger Greenspun.

Staples, Donald E. "The Auteur Theory Reexamined." *CJ* 6 (1966–1967) 1–7. What Truffaut and Bazin said about approaching films from the point of view of their authors —that is, their directors.

Wald, Malvin. "Who Is the Film Author?" *Cinéaste* 2 (No. 3, 1968–1969). See 2d.

Siska, William C. "Movies and History." *F Her* 4 (No. 4, Summer 69) 27–32. The subjective base for auteur theory categories.

Armes, Roy. "A Polemic." *Screen* 10 (No. 6, Nov–Dec 69) 75–79. "Evaluation is not one of the strong points of the auteur theory"— nor is a practical understanding of commercial pressures and collaborative efforts; an extended response to Peter Wollen's book *Signs and Meaning in the Cinema* (Indiana, 1969).

Sobchack, Thomas. " '*Auteur! Auteur!' Oui* or *Non?* Negative Notes on the *Politique des Auteurs.*" *Western Humanities Rev* 24 (1970) 76–77.

Sarris, Andrew. "Notes on the Auteur Theory in 1970." *F Com* 6 (No. 2, Fall 70) 7–9. It was "never a theory at all, but rather a collection of facts, a reminder of movies to be resurrected."

Staples, Donald. "*La Politique des Auteurs—* The Theory and Its Influence Upon the Cinema." *Language and Style* 3 (No. 4, Fall 70) 303–311. An overview of the auteur theory and its development in the United States.

3a(4). ART AND ENTERTAINMENT

[See also 6a, 7b(1).]

Herring, Robert. "Cinema Circus." *Close Up* 6 (No. 5, 1930) 359–368. Cinema as circus, particularly in Laurel and Hardy.

Rowland, Stanley. "The Future of the Cinema." *Quarterly Rev* 258 (Jan 32) 63–78. It should divorce itself from the entertainment tradition of America and of stage plays and work with actuality and the best fictional works.

Sachs, Hanns. "Kitsch." *Close Up* 9 (No. 3, Sep 32) 200–205. Psychoanalytic methods are used to understand kitsch in the film.

Grierson, John. "One Hundred Per Cent Cinema." *Spectator* 155 (23 Aug 35) 285–286. Commercial pressures did not come with sound but were there in silents, too; experimenters, not the industry, will produce artful cinema.

Watts, Richard, Jr. "Films of a Moon-Struck World." *Yale Rev* 25 (Dec 35) 311–320. Cinema's attempt to capture *Midsummer Night's Dream* shows difficulty of trying to please everyone; that goes for attempts at social conscience, too; it's rare for a film to be both artistic and commercial.

Havelock, E. "Merits of Opium." *Canad Forum* 16 (Apr 36) 17–18. Defense of movies, "suffering just now from an acute attack of amateur philosophy," as simple entertainment.

Krutch, J. W. "Not So Hopeless Movies." *Nation* 142 (6 May 36) 585–586. The manager of the Roxy Theater is right in relating movies to mass appeal, but Shakespeare and Chaplin show that they may still be art.

Mamoulian, Rouben. "The World's Latest Fine Art." *Cinema Arts* 1 (No. 1, June 37) 17–18. Argument for film as art rather than industry.

Van Doren, Mark. "Let the Movies Be Natural." *Am Scholar* (Oct 37) 435–444. Movies are placed in a perilous position when they begin to be called "art."

Schoenberg, Arnold. "Art and the Moving Pictures." *Calif Arts and Arch* 57 (No. 4, Apr 40) 12+. The author argues what film requires to establish itself as an art.

Cross, Elizabeth. "Large as Life—Twice as Natural." *S&S* 12 (No. 48, Jan 44) 97–98. More films should present emotional escape.

Farber, M. "Happiness Boys." *New Rep* 110 (28 Feb 44) 280. A defense of film as art against those who go "only for entertainment."

Smith, Brian. "Good Movies Are a Menace." *S&S* 13 (No. 49, May 44) 5–6. Some humorous remarks on the relationship between business needs and making good films.

Isaacs, H. R. "Laugh, and You Laugh Alone." *Th Arts* 29 (Apr 45) 226. Review of the "comic element" in cinema.

Clayton, Bertram. "Cinema: Art or Industry?" *Quarterly Rev* 283 (July 45) 321–334. A casual discussion, including also a survey of the history of British government actions and relations with the American market.

Burke, John A. V. "Films for Humanity." *S&S* 18 (Spring 49) 29–30. Catholic priest urges art instead of commercialism.

Betjeman, John. "The Bored and the Exhausted." *S&S* 19 (Dec 49) 13. "To come out of a picture gallery of great paintings heightens one's appreciation of the ordinary scene . . . to come out into the world after having seen a film is like waking up from a hangover." Films are an art only if entertainment is an art.

Guthrie, Tyrone. "Two Faces Under One Hat." *S&S* 19 (Jan 50) 22+. The necessary separation of industry and art; to be a hit, a film must find wide acceptance: it may have human interest, but it will probably be deficient in subtlety.

Callenbach, Ernest. "The Comic Ecstasy." *FIR* 5 (Jan 54) 24–26. The transmutation of mock-documentary into fantasy; the manipulation of anxiety; the triumphant detachment of Keaton; how long screen comedy has lasted.

Mishkin, Leo. "Escapist Entertainment? . . . Sez Who?" *JSPG* (June 60) 17–18. TV and film critic for *New York Morning Telegraph* argues that TV has taken over the escape and entertainment function of films, and the film industry has gone over to adult dramas, Tennessee Williams, and kitchen-sink realism.

Bachmann, Gideon. "Ustinov." *Film* (No. 30, Winter 61). See 5, Peter Ustinov.

Knight, Arthur. "Art for Whose Sake?" *J Soc Cin* 2 (1962) 14–22.

Dworkin, Martin. "Seeing for Ourselves." *Arts in Soc* 2 (No. 4, Fall–Winter 63–64) 138–144. Comments on the relationship of industry to the art; and the role of the critic.

Vidor, King, Philip Dunne, W. Ward Marsh, David Levy, James Meade, Colin Young, Alan Pakula, Robert Gessner, and John F. Fitzgerald. "The *Journal* Looks at the Film—Is It Art or Industry?" *JSPG* 12 (No. 7, Mar 64) 7–31.

Dunne, Philip. "The Art That's an Industry." *FIR* 15 (No. 5, May 64) 292–308.

Steele, Robert. "Looking at Film and Its Aesthetics." *Motive* 27 (Nov 66) 7–10. "Obsessive repetition of devices" is not enough; "the film that is worthy of being called an art object has content"; the artist is in some degree a communicator, because he "cannot hate people and succeed as an artist."

Garis, Robert. "Art-Movie Style." *Commentary* 44 (Aug 67) 77–79.

Kael, Pauline. "Trash, Art, and the Movies." *Harper's* 238 (Feb 69) 65–83. We should enjoy entertainment films; some of them are better than the ones praised as "art" by academics, and they should be talked about in terms of how audiences enjoy them. Discussion (Apr 69) 6.

Steele, R. "What Do We Mean by Film Art?" *Cath World* 209 (Apr 69) 35–38. A series of questions to be asked about any particular film as a way of answering the question of film art.

Birstein, Ann. "Going to the Movies." *Vogue* 155 (1 Mar 70) 210–211+. Personal reminiscences on the change from entertainment to "art."

3a(5). MONTAGE, SIGNS, AND MISE-EN-SCÈNE

[See also 2f.]

Macpherson, Kenneth. "An Introduction to 'The Fourth Dimension in the Kino.'" *Close Up* 6 (No. 3, 1930) 175–184. An introduction and clarification of the Eisenstein article which follows.

Eisenstein, S. M. "The Fourth Dimension in Kino." *Close Up* 6 (No. 3, 1930) 184–194; (No. 4, 1930) 253–268. A discussion of montage, with particular emphasis on the overtonal type; two articles.

Eisenstein, S. M. "The Cinematographic Principle and Japanese Culture: With a Digression on Montage and the Shot." *Experimental Cinema* 1 (No. 3, Feb 31) 5–10.

Eisenstein, S. M. "Intellectual Cinema." *Left* 1 (No. 2, Summer and Autumn 31) 75–77. In the approaching epoch of art, only *intel-*

lectual cinema is capable of meeting existing challenges; it represents a "synthesis of the emotional, the documentary and the abstract."

Dalton, G. F. "The Misconception of 'Montage.'" *CQ* 1 (No. 2, Winter 32) 81–84. There is no such thing—the director simply puts together what the scenarist proposed.

Brailovsky, Alexander. "A Few Remarks on the Elements of Cine-Language." *Experimental Cinema* 1 (No. 4, Feb 33) 24–26.

Stern, Seymour. "Hollywood and Montage: The Basic Fallacies of American Film Technique." *Experimental Cinema* 1 (No. 4, Feb 33) 47–53.

Vesselo, A. "Camera Movement." *CQ* 3 (No. 2, Winter 35) 97–98+. It is important; how it fits with montage.

Eisenstein, Sergei M. "Montage in 1938." *Life & Letters To-Day* 21 (June 39) 93–101. Montage is inseparable from the cognitive function of film art; the distinction between representation and image. Part 2: (July 39) 99–108.

Tyler, Parker. "The Horse." *S&S* 16 (No. 63, Autumn 47) 112–114. The horse seen as the totem animal of American films.

Harrah, David. "Aesthetics of the Film: The Pudovkin-Arnheim-Eisenstein Theory." *J Aesthetics and Art Criticism* 13 (Dec 54) 63–74. Principles of montage; cinematic devices for economy through inference of sign images.

Bazin, André. "New Meaning of Montage." *F Cult* (Nos. 22–23, 1961) 40–43. Renoir and Rossellini interviewed by Bazin on the subject of montage; brief extract of original in *France Observateur;* English translation in *Sight and Sound* (Winter 1958–1959).

Bazin, André. "The Forbidden Montage." (Tr. by Nell Cox.) *F Cult* (Nos. 22–23, 1961) 43–51. The principles of montage, with a detailed analysis of *The Red Balloon*.

Yutkevich, Sergei. "Montage 1960." *F Cult* (Nos. 22–23, 1961) 51–59. The author attempts to clarify what he feels are misconceptions and simplifications of the theory of montage as presented in Karel Reisz's *The Technique of Film Editing* (Hastings House, 1960).

Astruc, Alexandre. "What Is *Mise-en-Scène?*" *F Cult* (Nos. 22–23, 1961) 63–65+. Praise for Mizoguchi and *Ugetsu;* originally published in *Cahiers du Cinéma*.

Dreyfus, Dina. "Cinema and Language." *Diogenes* (No. 35, Fall 61) 23–33.

Yutkevich, Sergei. "Cutting It to Style." *F&F* 8 (No. 6, Mar 62) 10+. Difference between East and West in montage.

Stephenson, R. "Space, Time and Montage." *Brit J Aesthetics* 2 (No. 3, July 62) 249–258. The artistic use of space/time as the central aesthetic characteristic of film, embodied in the principle of montage.

Kuiper, John B. "Cinematic Expression: A Look at Eisenstein's Silent Montage." *Art J* 22 (Fall 62) 34–39. An analysis of the cinematic tropes which Eisenstein uses as the basic pattern of organization in his four full-length silent films.

Gessner, Robert. "Some Notes on Cinematic Movements." *J Soc Cin* 3 (1963) 1–5. Two types of present and past time; subject movement; frame movement; decelerated edit; other terms.

Markopoulos, Gregory. "Towards a New Narrative Film Form." *F Cult* (No. 31, 1963–1964) 11+. Markopoulos argues for "the fusion of the classic montage technique with a more abstract system."

Astruc, Alexandre. "What Is *Mise-en-Scène?*" *CdC in Eng* (No. 1, Jan 66) 53–55. The means of transforming the world into a spectacle given primarily to oneself; the distancing of the action from the viewer.

Worth, Sol. "Film as a Non-Art: An Approach to the Study of Film." *Am Scholar* 35 (No. 2, Spring 66) 322–334. Communication theory and psycholinguistics seen as models for understanding film as process.

Vanderbeek, Stan. "Culture: Intercom." *TDR* 2 (Fall 66) 38–48. Cinema as nonverbal international language and experience machine.

Pasolini, Pier Paolo. "The Cinema of Poetry." *CdC in Eng* (No. 6, Dec 66) 34–43. From a speech given at the New Cinema Festival in Pesaro, June 1965, by the Italian director; a discussion of cinema as language and the terminology of semiotics.

Pryluck, Calvin, and Richard E. Snow. "Toward a Psycholinguistics of Cinema." *AV Com Rev* 15 (No. 1, Spring 67) 54–75.

Worth, Sol. "Cognitive Aspects of Sequence in Visual Communication." *AV Com Rev* 16 (No. 2, Summer 68) 121–145.

Pryluck, Calvin. "Structural Analysis of Motion Pictures as a Symbol System." *AV Com Rev* 16 (No. 4, Winter 68) 372–402.

Siegler, Robert. "Masquage." *FQ* 21 (No. 3, Spring 68) 15–21. Expands Eisenstein's montage theories to the multi-image film, particularly *A Place to Stand*.

Russell, Lee. "Cinema—Code and Image." *New Left Rev* (No. 49, May–June 68) 65–81. A chapter on the semiology of the film from his book written under his real name, Peter Wollen.

Durgnat, Raymond. "Style and the Old Wave." *F&F* 15 (No. 1, Oct 68) 12–16. On cutting and *mise-en-scène* in older films.

Andrew, J. Dudley. "The Stature of Objects in Antonioni's Films." *Triquarterly* (No. 11, Winter 68). *See 5, Michelangelo Antonioni.*

Pryluck, Calvin. "Motion Pictures and Language." *JUFA* 21 (No. 2, 1969) 46–51. Linguistic analysis is not necessarily applicable to film.

Durgnat, Raymond. "Objects as Ectoplasm." *F&F* 15 (No. 8, May 69) 27–30. Physical objects suggestive of abstractions and how they are used in film.

Durgnat, Raymond. "Spheres of Symbolism." *F&F* 15 (No. 9, June 69) 30–33.

Wallington, Mike. "Pasolini: Structuralism and Semiology." *Cinema* (Cambridge) (No. 3, June 69) 5–10. His contribution to theory.

Durgnat, Raymond. "Time and Timelessness." *F&F* 15 (No. 10, July 69) 62–67. On symbolism in film.

McTaggart, Andrew. "Signs and Meaning in the Cinema." *Screen* 10 (No. 6, Nov–Dec 69) 67–75. An intellectual approach like Peter Wollen's does not help us much with "fundamentally anti-intellectual directors like Hawks and Ford."

Worth, Sol. "The Development of a Semiotic of Film." *Semiotica* (No. 3, 1970) 281–321. An attempt to develop, in a historical and analytical context, a theory of signs for the cinema.

Silverstein, Norman. "Film Semiology." *Salmagundi* (No. 13, Summer 70) 73–80. Toward a theory of cinematic signs which would allow the critic to understand the nature and function of cues which create audience response.

Crick, Philip. "Pasolini: Philosophy of Cinema." *Cinema* (Cambridge) (Nos. 6–7, Aug 70) 13. A summary and critique of Pasolini's view of the nature of cinematic language.

3a(6). SOCIAL AND POLITICAL GOALS

[*See also 4i, 7a, 7b(2), 7c(3), 7f.*]

Balazs, Bela. "The Future of the Films: Movies for the Middle Class." *Living Age* 339 (Nov 30) 294–297. "Romancing is one of the weapons of defense that the middle class has developed."

Stern, Seymour. "A Working-Class Cinema for America?" *Left* 1 (No. 1, Spring 31) 69–73. A call for a rise of people's film makers; comments on the already existing Workers' Film and Foto League of America and the American Prolet-Kino.

Potamkin, Harry A. "Motion Picture Criticism." *New Freeman* 2 (4 Mar 31) 591–593. New young critics will arise with a social ideology; to disparage criticism is a typical bourgeois defense.

Herring, Robert. "Enthusiasm?" *Close Up* 9 (No. 1, Mar 32) 20–24. The works of Vertov and Pabst are discussed, with special attention to the principles of pleasure versus social relevance.

Rotha, Paul. "Approach to a New Cinema." *CQ* 1 (No. 1, Autumn 32) 18–22. Not the "contemplation of beauty" but the shock

effect of ideas upon the public is what the film maker works for.

"Are the Movies Entertainment or Education?" *Chris Cent* 49 (30 Nov 32) 1460–1461. Wry comment on recent discovery by *Film Daily* that movies are educational, therefore should not be taxed.

Walter, Felix. "Hollywood Goes Slightly Pink." *Canad Forum* 13 (May 33) 300–301. Post-Depression years increase Hollywood's social statements.

Taylor, D. F. "In the Service of the Public." *S&S* 2 (No. 8, Winter 33–34) 128–131. Recent films fail to provide social values.

Cavalcanti, Alberto, and Stuart Legg. "Ethics for Movies." *CQ* 2 (No. 3, Spring 34) 166–168. Conversation about collectivism versus individualism; the crew versus the director's "dictatorship"; ritual versus art.

Schrire, David. "The Social Purpose of the Film Director." *S&S* 3 (No. 11, Autumn 34) 107–109. The negative and positive social aspects of the film.

"Politics on the Screen." *S&S* 5 (No. 18, Summer 36). *See 4e(1e).*

"Movies: Entertainment Plus Education." *Chris Cent* 55 (27 Apr 38) 520–521. A plea for the industry to be aware of educational values of film as well as entertainment; a reply to Will Hays.

Kauffman, G. A. "Einstein in Hollywood." *Nation* 147 (6 Aug 38). *See 3b(4).*

Dugan, James. "Public Eudemonist No. 1." *New Masses* 31 (11 Apr 39) 28. Are Movies being forced to meet their democratic responsibilities?

Dugan, James. "Making the Social Film." *New Masses* 31 (23 May 39) 28–30. *Confessions of a Nazi Spy* and *Juarez* represent the birth of a new form—political statements using traditional dramatic convention—and a new critical method is necessary if reviewers are to cope with them.

Vesselo, Arthur. "Theme for Peace." *S&S* 8 (No. 30, Summer 39) 60–61. An interview with Andrew Buchanan, who says that the screen's most vital need is to explore ways to peace.

Pollano, Etta. "The Importance of Being Angry." *S&S* 8 (No. 31, Autumn 39) 112–113. Cinema should interpret the anger and restlessness of society today.

Dunhamel, G. "Modern Methods in Soul-Building." *Cath World* 149 (Sep 39) 736–737. The feasibility of a flourishing culture based on visual and auditory apparatus.

Falk, Sawyer. "Towards a New Ethical Base." *Films* 1 (No. 1, Nov 39) 5–9. There should be neither Protestant codes of "decency" nor art for art's sake but films which "say something" about good and evil, based on a communal morality.

Dugan, James. "Changing the Reel." *New*

Masses 341 (9 Jan 40) 28–30. The movies are beginning a period of reaction with films such as *Ninotchka* and *Gone with the Wind*.

Sterling, Philip. "A Channel for Democratic Thought." *Films* 1 (No. 2, Spring 40) 7–18. Historical study of films of protest.

Wanger, Walter. "Role of Movies in Morale." *Am J of Sociology* 47 (Nov 41) 378–383. The primary role has been as entertainment and recreation; it could become one of clarification and inspiration, if national leaders will first clarify the concepts associated with the democratic way of life. These concepts could then be dramatized and presented in films.

Shaver, Anna Louise. "New Art and the Old Artisans." *Cath World* 154 (Dec 41) 306–310. Assessment of the contributions of film and older arts toward the "perfection of moral personality, which is man."

Wanger, Walter. "Movies with a Message." *Sat Rev* 25 (7 Mar 42) 12. The role of films in creating wartime morale and unity; artistic and political responsibility versus profit.

Vesselo, Arthur. "The Film's Limitations." *S&S* 11 (No. 42, Autumn 42) 45–47. Cinema cannot solve problems, merely explore them.

Davidman, Joy. "The Will and the Way." *New Masses* 45 (27 Oct 42) 28–31. Producers want to make films which will aid in the war effort, but till now have merely stressed sex and death.

Davidman, Joy. "The War Film: An Examination." *New Masses* 45 (24 Nov 42) 29–30. Lowell Mellett, in a recent speech to the National Board of Review, implicitly condemned all escapist movies, but too readily accepted Hollywood's old alibis.

Wanger, Walter. "Hollywood and the Intellectuals." *Sat Rev* 25 (5 Dec 42) 6+. Liberal intellectuals should establish direct contact with large groups through the motion picture.

Solovay, J. C. "Hollywood and the Intellectuals: Reply." *Sat Rev* 26 (6 Feb 43) 13. In a letter to the editor, Solovay replies to Wanger, arguing that Hollywood has not produced films promoting liberal ideals.

Reeves, Joseph. "The Workers' Film Association." *S&S* 11 (No. 44, Spring 43) 106. The creation of an organization to place the worker's social aspirations on the screen.

Hussey, Nancy. "Talkies Set Them Talking." *S&S* 12 (No. 47, Oct 43) 61–63. The use of films to encourage discussion of human values.

Wanger, Walter. "Motion Pictures in the Fight for Freedom." *Free World* 6 (Nov 43) 443–447. Jeffersonian principles behind Hollywood's special war services.

Trivers, Paul. "Town Meeting Comes to Hollywood." *Screen Writer* 1 (Oct 45) 8–16. Describes the debate presented on the radio show *Town Meeting of the Air*, on the question "Should Hollywood make pictures designed to influence public opinion?" Robert Riskin for the affirmative; James McGuinness the negative.

Bessie, Alvah. "Blockade." *Screen Writer* 1 (Jan 46) 16–23. Discusses the film *Blockade* and others that dealt with the Spanish Civil War in the 1930s as distortions of history because they never identified the Fascist enemy.

Dietz, Howard. "Must the Movies Be Significant?" *NYTM* (27 Jan 46) 18+. Protest against the sacrifice of entertainment for messages in films.

Grierson, John. "Film Horizons." *Th Arts* 30 (Dec 46) 698–701. The duty of the film to cope with the changing attitudes and ideas of the times; some promising changes and advances in American and English film noted.

Woelfel, Norman. "The American Mind and the Motion Picture." *Annals of Am Acad of Polit and Soc Sci* (1947) 88–94. Films can bring more unity to the United States by touching on social issues.

"Are Movies the Opium of the People?" *Chris Cent* 64 (8 Jan 47) 36. A call for movies to instruct the people concerning their responsibilities as citizens of the atomic age.

Manvell, Roger. "The Philosopher at the Cinema." *S&S* 16 (No. 61, Spring 47) 18–20. Comments on recent books that deal with the philosophic and social aspects of the cinema.

Yerrill, D. A. "The Still, Small Voice." *S&S* 16 (No. 62, Summer 47) 45–46. A plea for better films, freed from ties to stage or novel, dealing with human problems.

Scott, Adrian. "You Can't Do That!" *Screen Writer* 3 (Aug 47) 4–7. A detailed account of the preparation of *Crossfire* and the opposition to it; a list of other films which have broken political and social taboos.

Benoit-Lévy, Jean. "The Mission of the Cinema." *Penguin F Rev* 4 (Oct 47) 10–11. To create a community among men.

Kracauer, Siegfried. "Those Movies with a Message." *Harper's* 196 (June 48) 567–572. The immediate post-World War II "progressive" films have failed to live up to the purpose of "showing the strength of liberalism."

Burke, John A. V. "Signs of a Renaissance." *S&S* 17 (No. 68, Winter 48–49) 175–178. Recent films indicate less bias against religion in films.

Strand, Paul. "Realism: A Personal View." *S&S* 19 (Jan 50) 23–26. Realism is not the mere recording of things as they are, with dispassionate and objective eyes, nor is it a description, no matter how honest, of the exceptional or sensational in life; we must take sides, as in *Open City, The Grapes of Wrath, The River,* and *Native Land.*

Starr, Cécile. "Film as Education." *FIR* 1 (May–June 50) 1–2+. Deploring "formula" films, the author asks for education by experience: film can interest, inform, and arouse.

Reisz, Karel. "Hollywood's Anti-Red Boomerang." *S&S* 22 (Jan–Mar 53) 132–137+. How Hollywood portrays Communism, and the positive damage it does.

Elkin, Frederick. "Value Implications of Popular Films." *Sociology and Social Research* 38 (May 54) 320–323. Audiences cannot escape Hollywood's messages; significant themes should be analyzed.

Kael, Pauline. "Morality Plays: Right and Left." *S&S* 24 (Oct–Dec 54) 67–73. "Hollywood may well exhaust anti-Communism (*Night People*) before it has gotten near it: the cycle begins by exploiting public curiosity and ends by satiating it"; Communist propaganda, on the other hand, is thoughtful, clever, and subtle: *Salt of the Earth* is the kind of social-realist film the Communists use. See correspondence 25 (Jan–Mar 55) 162 and author's response 25 (Summer 55) 53–54.

Mutzenbecher, Hans E. "Responsibilities of the Film Artist." *F Cult* 1 (Nos. 5–6, 1955) 21–22. An address delivered by the director of Film Department, Ministry of Culture, Saarland, before the International Conference of Film Sciences.

Anderson, Lindsay. "The Last Sequence of *On the Waterfront.*" *S&S* 24 (Jan–Mar 55). *See 3c.*

Hughes, Robert. *"On the Waterfront,* a Defense and Some Letters." *S&S* 24 (Spring 55). *See 3c.*

Rubin, D., and A. Ford (eds.). "Help Your Community." *Pop Photog* 36 (Mar 55) 110–113.

Hunkin, Oliver. "The Cinema Has No Soul." *Film* (No. 5, Sep–Oct 55) 16–17. A negative view of most religious films; a positive view of the possibility of Christian influence in commercial films.

Kazis, Israel J. "If I Were a Movie Producer." *Rotarian* 87 (Dec 55) 18+. Also: Greenlaw, Charles F. "If I Were a Religious Leader." (Dec 55) 19+. Men from religion and entertainment business hypothetically change jobs.

Greenwald, William I. "Substance, Quality, and Social Content of Films." *J Educ Soc* 29 (1956) 330–339. Film's power to shape social ideals.

Houston, Penelope. "Rebels Without Causes." *S&S* 25 (Spring 56) 178–181. Though admittedly most of Hollywood's social-protest films are diluted with melodrama or evasive conclusions, still they criticize with more freedom than is found in films of most other countries; *Trial, The Desperate Hours, The Wild One, Blackboard Jungle, Rebel Without a Cause.*

Anderson, Lindsay. "Stand Up! Stand Up!" *S&S* 26 (Autumn 56). *See 3b.*

Popkin, Henry. "Liberal Unpolitics on Stage and Screen." *Commentary* 23 (Feb 57) 161–166. Deprived of politics as an arena, the popular arts have set forth on a search for other areas where they can go through the necessary liberal motions without being actually controversial.

"Replies to a Questionnaire." *S&S* 26 (Spring 57). *See 4e(1b).*

Boyd, Malcolm. "Theology and the Movies." *Theology Today* 14 (Oct 57) 359–375. The necessity of interpreting film in a Christian way.

Montagu, Ivor. "Politics on the Screen." *F&F* 4 (No. 4, Jan 58) 11–12. Examination of the "political" dimensions of the most ordinary of entertainment films.

McCarthy, Matt. "Free Cinema—in Chains." *F&F* 5 (No. 5, Feb 59). *See 8c(2a).*

Dyer, Peter John. "American Youth in Uproar." *F&F* 5 (No. 12, Sep 59). *See 4d.*

Kramer, Stanley. "The Great Stone Face." *JSPG* (June 60) 11–12. Director argues for the value of films with messages.

Mercey, Arch. "The 1960 Kenneth Edwards Address." *JUFPA* 12 (No. 4, Summer 60). *See 8c(1).*

Dworkin, Martin S. "Dissenting Screen." *Cath World* 191 (Sep 60) 362–367. Films of social protest behind the Iron Curtain and in Italy (Fellini, De Sica).

Karaganov, Alexander. "Once More on the New Generation." *F Cult* (No. 24, 1962) 22–25. Young American film makers "remain socially passive" whereas socialist directors are interested in values and character.

Gans, H. J. "The Rise of the Problem-Film: An Analysis of Changes in Hollywood Films and the American Audience." *Social Problems* 11 (No. 4, 1964). *See 7b(1).*

Sarris, Andrew. "Film Fantasies, Left and Right." *F Cult* (No. 34, 1964) 28–34. Analysis of Otto Preminger's *Advise and Consent* and John Frankenheimer's *The Manchurian Candidate;* the literary origins of these political films; social consciousness in American cinema.

Udoff, Yale. "Cinematic Politics." *F Com* 2 (No. 2, 1964) 37–38. Brief report on symposium in New York by James Blue, Dwight Macdonald, and Alberto Moravia; comments on *Seven Days in May* and other films.

Brodbeck, Arthur J. "Placing Aesthetic Developments in Social Context: A Program of Value Analysis." *J Soc Issues* 20 (Jan 64)

8–25. Social scientists are in a more advantageous position to develop an esthetic for the cinema than the humanists are.

Durgnat, Raymond. "Vote for Britain!" *F&F* 10 (No. 7, Apr 64). *See 4e(1b)*.

Trotter, F. Thomas. "Motion Pictures and Social Problems." *JSPG* (June 64) 31–33. Some films are like sermons, says this Methodist dean of Cleveland School of Theology.

Ustinov, Peter. "The Art of Asking Questions." *Sat Rev* (25 Dec 65) 22. Moral courage and the arts: the film has heavy burden of responsibility to diffuse a picture of life and how it should or should not be lived. Part of *Saturday Review* report "Where the Action Is."

Mardore, Michel. *"Age of Gold* (Buñuel), *Age of Iron* (Rossellini): Notes on Politics and Cinema." *CdC in Eng* (No. 3, 1966) 47–51. Any art form is a substitute for action; the aim of politics in the cinema is not to repeat the action of the combatants but to supply the intelligence with facts.

Trachtenberg, Stanley. "Undercutting with Sincerity: The Strategy of the Serious Film." *Midwest Q* 7 (Apr 66) 281–295. "Everything is all right the way it is, provided there is an appearance of concern"; the misleading documentary realism of *Love with the Proper Stranger, Seven Days in May,* and other films pretending to examine "problems."

Chiaretti, T. "Clear and Explicit." *Atlas* 12 (Aug 66) 56. Leftists favor Bellochio over Godard.

Macklin, F. A. "The New Palatability." *F Her* 2 (No. 3, Spring 67) 1–2. Editorial on softer "problem films," especially from England.

Kustow, Michael. "Without and Within." *S&S* 36 (Summer 67) 113–117. Peter Watkins' *Privilege,* Godard's *Made in U.S.A.* and *Deux ou Trois Choses Que Je Sais d'Elle* grapple with political matters which are somehow related to very personal scenes in the films, as well.

"Engaged Cinema in the United States." *Cinéaste* 1 (No. 3, Winter 67–68) 16–17+. Cinematic art's function is a kind of metaphor on contemporary reality. Reprinted from *Cinéma Engagé.*

Coles, Robert. "Hollywood's New Social Criticism." *Trans-Action* 5 (May 68) 15–21. Critical discussion of *Bonnie and Clyde* and *The Graduate* by a psychiatrist.

Walsh, Moira. "A Civilizing Influence?" *America* (22 June 68) 798–800. Responsibilities of film makers to truth, and audience responsibility to recognize it.

Macbean, James R. "Politics and Poetry in Two Recent Films by Godard." *FQ* 21 (No. 4, Summer 68). *See 5, Jean-Luc Godard.*

Morgenstern, Joseph. "How to Stop Telling It Like It Isn't." *Newswk* 72 (5 Aug 68) 66–67. Some films of social conscience are coming along; additional subjects proposed.

Braudy, Leo. "Newsreel: A Report." *FQ* 22 (No. 2, Winter 68–69) 48–51. Critical report on various releases by this radical film-making group; fifteen films completed.

Fruchter, Norm, Robert Kramer, Marilyn Buck, and Karen Ross. "Newsreel." *FQ* 22 (No. 2, Winter 68–69) 43–48. Statements by radical film makers on their "propaganda of confrontation" as opposed to clarity and exposition (Kramer).

North, Steven. "Notes on an Involved Commercial Cinema." *Take One* 2 (No. 6, 1969) 14–16.

Henaut, Dorothy. "Film as an Instrument for Social Change." *Arts Canada* 26 (Feb 69). *See 4i.*

Bollman, R. W. "Theology and the Moving Picture." *Thought* 44 (Spring 69) 101–121. Cinema may be approached theologically but using the media as a whole, not just its thematic content.

Blum, John M. "Cinema for Whom?" *J Aesthetic Educ* 3 (No. 3, July 69) 13–19. Cinema's relationship to society.

Young, Colin. "Film and Social Change." *J Aesthetic Educ* 3 (No. 3, July 69) 21–27.

Steiner, Shari. "Europe and America: A Question of Self-Image." *Sat Rev* (27 Dec 69) 18–20. Representation of youth's political ideals seen in European films but not so much in American films. Part of *Saturday Review* report "The Art That Matters."

Esnault, Philippe. "Cinema and Politics." *Cinéaste* 3 (No. 3, Winter 69–70) 4–11. The political nature of all cinema.

Gilman, R. "1 + 1." *Partisan Rev* 37 (No. 2, 1970) 274–283. The American "relevance" films, in depicting society as it is, betray themselves as an art form in their failure to explore seriously and to render imaginatively the presuppositions underlying that reality.

Nichols, Bill. "Revolution and Melodrama: A Marxist View of Some Recent Films." *Cinema* (Calif) 6 (No. 1, 1970) 42–47.

Steel, Ronald. "Where's the Relevance?" *F Soc Rev* 6 (No. 2, 1970) 33–39. Brief notes on films which confront or avoid political reality.

"Yves de Laurot Defines *Cinéma Engagé.*" *Cinéaste* 3 (No. 4, Spring 70) 3–15. The director and theorist defines engagement as the possibility of transforming personal anguish into history.

Godard, Jean-Luc. "What Is to Be Done?" *Moviegoer* (Apr 70) n.p. A manifesto for the political film.

Hartog, Simon. "Nowsreel." *Afterimage* (No. 1, Apr 70) 12 pages. The potentialities, present history, and theory of a political cinema—such as Newsreel.

McPherson, Hugo. "The Future of the Moving Image." *Arts Canada* 27 (Apr 70) 2. Head of National Film Board discusses "the most significant events in visual communication in this generation—the invention of the Polaroid camera" and the "discovery that film and T.V. are arts in their own right."

Rocha, Glauber. "The Aesthetics of Violence." *Afterimage* (No. 1, Apr 70) 2 pages. A film aesthetic which functions in a political climate of hunger and oppression.

Watson, Patrick. "Challenge for Change." *Arts Canada* 27 (Apr 70). See 4i.

"From Logos to Lens: From the Theory of Engagement to the Praxis of Revolutionary Cinema." *Cinéaste* 4 (No. 1, Summer 70) 10–23. A discussion of theory with Yves de Laurot and associates of *cinéma engagé*.

de Laurot, Yves. "Production as the Praxis of Revolutionary Film: The Concrete Stages of Realization: Part One." *Cinéaste* 4 (No. 2, Fall 70) 2–17+. The theory and practice of revolutionary cinema.

Farnell, Graeme. "Which Avant-Garde?" *Afterimage* (No. 2, Autumn 70) 64–71. Not the avant-garde film, only the political film seeks to transform the world.

Bromwich, David. "Hollywood Discovers 'The Revolution.'" *Dissent* 17 (No. 6, Nov–Dec 70). See 4k.

de Laurot, Yves. "Composing as the Praxis of Revolution: The Third World and the U.S.A.: The Concrete Stages of Realization: Part 2." *Cinéaste* 4 (No. 3, Winter 70–71) 15–24+.

Sanjines, Jorge. "Cinema and Revolution." *Cinéaste* 4 (No. 3, Winter 70–71) 13–14. Revolutionary cinema proposes to create a consciousness for liberation.

Solanos, Fernando, and Octavio Getino. "Toward a Third Cinema." *Cinéaste* 4 (No. 3, Winter 70–71) 1–10. The two Argentine directors see cinema as a means of subverting capitalistic society.

3b. Criticism

[See also 4k.]

Mayor, H. A. "Film Criticism." *Close Up* 6 (No. 6, 1930) 478–481. Negative opinion of current film criticism.

Potamkin, Harry A. "Film Novitiates, Etc." *Close Up* 7 (No. 5, Nov 30) 314–324. Film criticism suffers from the presence of the perennial novice, as in many of those who discuss Chaplin.

Blakeston, Oswell. "Films and Values." *Close Up* 10 (No. 3, Sep 33) 243–246. Criticism is finally involved in describing the value of the film experience.

"Good Movies Pay!" *Chris Cent* 51 (27 June 34) 852. Current comparison of critics with box office.

Grierson, John. "Art and the Analysts." *S&S* 4 (No. 16, Winter 35–36) 157–159. The appearance of Spottiswoode's *Grammar of Film* (University of California, 1950) suggests the need for principles of film evaluation.

Greene, Graham. "Is It Criticism?" *S&S* 5 (No. 19, Autumn 36) 64–65. The current state of film criticism merely affirms a continuation of mediocre films.

Morgan, Guy. "Critic or Reporter?" *S&S* 7 (No. 26, Summer 38) 53–54. Film reporter of *The Daily Express* attempts to answer attacks on popular-press film critics.

Knight, E. "Moving Picture Goals." *Th Arts* 23 (Jan 39) 57–64. The art of film criticism; also factual and entertainment films, past and future, are discussed.

"Wind Blows: *Commonweal* Misrepresented by *World Telegram*." *Commonweal* 31 (12 Jan 40) 267. A feud between *Commonweal* and *The World Telegram* initiates a look into the nature of movie review writing.

Bulleid, H. A. V. "Film Analysis." *S&S* 10 (No. 39, Autumn 41) 55–57.

Mannock, P. L. "We Critics Have Our Uses." *S&S* 10 (No. 39, Autumn 41) 40–42. Film criticism seems to be dying.

Ferguson, Otis. "Case of the Critics." *New Rep* 106 (2 Feb 42) 147–148. We have developed no standard of film criticism, according to this film critic.

Harman, Jympson. "Don't Smother the Child." *S&S* 10 (No. 40, Spring 42) 67–69. Constructive comments on the role of film criticism.

Mizener, Arthur. "The Elizabethan Art of Our Movies." *Kenyon Rev* 4 (No. 2, Spring 42) 181–194. The need for a critical approach that can deal with a great popular art.

Russell, Evelyn. "Films of 1941." *S&S* 10 (No. 40, Spring 42) 70–72. A discussion of critical criteria, particularly in terms of British and American films released in 1941.

Sewell, J. E. "Considered in Committee." *S&S* 11 (No. 41, Summer 42) 7–9. Criteria for film criticism.

Dent, Alan. "A Critic Criticises." *S&S* 11 (No. 42, Autumn 42) 34–35. The nature of film and film criticism.

Edwards, C. C. "What Does the *Parents Magazine* Movie Guide Say?" *Parents Mag* 17 (Oct 42) 30–31+. "How we appraise films."

Joseph, Robert. "Cinema: Comment and Criticism." *Calif Arts and Arch* 60 (No. 3, Mar 43) 18. A study of film criticism, historically and theoretically.

Grant, Elspeth. "Those Critics!" *S&S* 13 (No. 49, May 44) 12–13. A critique of some decisions made by the New York critics.

"The Critic and the Box-Office." *S&S* 14 (No. 53, Apr 45) 23–24. He should not let it influence him.

Lewis, S. "Some of My Best Friends Are Critics: Reply." *Am Mercury* 60 (June 45) 759. What the role of a critic should be.

Shaw, Robert. "Hearstian Criteria for Movie Critics." *Screen Writer* 1 (Sep 45) 42–50. Former staff writer for Hearst papers tells how William Randolph Hearst dictated policies and censored the material of all Hearst newspaper movie critics, promoted certain films and damned others—such as *Citizen Kane*—and how he harassed Herman Mankiewicz in newspaper stories.

Pardoe, F. E. "Film Critics and Criticism." *S&S* 14 (No. 56, Winter 45–46) 119–120. Suggestions for revising the current role of film critics.

Kaufman, Wolfe. "What Is the Answer?" *Screen Writer* 1 (May 46) 29–34. This newspaper reviewer and sometime publicist details some of his experiences with publicity departments and suggests that writers get more of this publicity.

Winnington, Richard. "Critic's Prologue." *Penguin F Rev* 1 (Aug 46) 27–34. The state of films and film criticism at the "half-centenary" of the cinema.

Hubler, Richard G. "Opinion and the Opinion Picture." *Screen Writer* 2 (Oct 46) 25–28. Argues for a "middle ground" in film criticism, in a "constructivism" which "would not flatter the conceit of the critic nor that of the subject."

Ellis, John. "Film Critics and Film Reviewers." *Now* (No. 7, Feb–Mar 47) 65–69. An attempt to distinguish day-to-day reviewing from criticism, which requires space, time, and a very complete knowledge of all aspects of the film.

Leonard, Harold. "Recent American Film Writing." *S&S* 16 (No. 62, Summer 47) 73–75. Writing about films.

Thompson, Kenneth L. "Criticism and Opinion." *S&S* 16 (No. 62, Summer 47) 71–72. The serious-minded film viewer versus the film fan.

Anderson, Lindsay. "Angles of Approach." *Sequence* (No. 2, Winter 47) 5–8. Criteria of relevance in film appreciation and criticism.

Barbarow, George. "Anesthetic Film Criticism." *Hudson Rev* 1 (No. 1, 1948) 440–448. Criticism dealing with films in terms of their social-economic-political orientation, penetrating as it may be, anesthetizes the larger concern for film as an art form.

"The Critic's Vocabulary." *Senior Scholastic* 52 (8 Mar 48) 28+. Explanation of the terms movie critics use, including "documentary," "satire," "musicals."

Sauvage, Leo. "Open Letter to New York Film Critics." *Nation* 167 (10 July 48) 48–49. A blast at lack of acumen regarding French films, particularly work by Pagnol.

Weinberg, Herman G. "A Return to Reason." *Hwd Q* 3 (No. 4, no date: Summer 48 to Summer 49) 421–424. Critics' factual mistakes about history suggest need for principles: A. B. Walkley's 1903 lectures in London said that criticism "cannot pierce to the artist's inmost self."

Yerrill, D. A. "On Film Critics." *S&S* 17 (No. 66, Summer 48) 98–99.

"Mr. Minney and the Film Critics." *Spectator* 181 (17 Sep 48) 357. Brief note on screenwriter R. J. Minney's bad opinion of film critics; his reply (24 Sep 48) 400.

Smith, Brian. "Rest—and Unrest." *S&S* 17 (No. 68, Winter 48–49) 179–180. Empirical analysis should be used in film criticism.

Houston, Penelope. "Leading the Blind." *S&S* 18 (Spring 49) 42–43. Some standards for the movie critic.

De La Roche, Catherine. "No Demand for Criticism?" *Penguin F Rev* 9 (May 49) 88–94. Critics are expected to be entertaining and to know something about literary sources and acting, but they seldom know much about technique, theory, and film history.

Ustinov, Peter. "Extra Weight." *S&S* 19 (Dec 49) 14–15. The creative output of an artist today is much less than it was in Mozart's time, partly because of "the regiment of critics" who descend like bees on every pollinating flower.

Whitebait, William. "New Precision in Film-Reviewing." *New S&N* 39 (21 Jan 50) 64. Comments on the *Sequence* school of impressionistic film criticism and its influence on *Sight and Sound*.

"What I Look For in a Film." *FIR* 1 (Mar 50) 1–2. A symposium. Pearl Buck, William Saroyan, Tennessee Williams, and others; brief remarks.

"What I Look For in a Film: Our Symposium Continued." *FIR* 1 (Apr 50) 12–13. Margaret Mead: "I look for indications of the way our national dreams are developing and changing."

Pichel, Irving. "Crisis and Incantation." *Hwd Q* 5 (No. 3, Spring 51). See 6d.

England, Leonard. "The Critics and the Box-office." *S&S* 20 (June 51) 43–44. Mr. England catalogues a number of films and shows on which, in many cases, the public and the critics did indeed agree.

Callenbach, Ernest. "U.S. Film Journalism—A Survey." *Hwd Q* 5 (No. 4, Summer 51) 350–362. A survey of film reviewing in the U.S. by one who later became editor of *Film Quarterly* (successor to *Hollywood Quarterly*); content analysis of reviews, mostly judged as stereotyped, from *Nation, Commonwealth, Library Journal, Life, New Republic, New Yorker, Newsweek, Rotarian, Saturday Review, Theater Arts, Time,* together with background information on ten critics not named.

"Replies to a Questionnaire." *S&S* 23 (Oct–Dec 53) 99–104+. Eleven film critics answer questions about critics and criticism, and seven film makers answer questions about their feelings toward critics and criticism. The film makers: Sir Michael Balcon, T. E. B. Clarke, Henry Cornelius, Charles Crichton, John Grierson, Robert Hamer, and Brian P. Hurst. The critics include: Paul Dehn, Catherine De La Roche, Forsyth Hardy, Ernest Lindgren, Roger Manvell, Robert Ottaway, and Dilys Powell.

Grierson, John. "A Review of Reviews." *S&S* 23 (Apr–June 54) 207–208+. Most film critics are a tired lot, bored with film and preoccupied with being journalistically clever; critics should not "sit above the battle" but rather should join in to think up, produce, and create ideas.

Grierson, John. "A Review of Reviews." *S&S* 24 (July–Sep 54) 43–44. An inquiry into the methods and work of some contemporary critics, with quotes from letters he had received in response to his previous articles.

Grierson, John. "A Review of Reviews." *S&S* 24 (Oct–Dec 54) 101–103. Some comments on the status of criticism in Great Britain and about the "box office"; "there was never a time when the opposition had greater need to realize the nature of the changes taking place in the film world, or greater need to understand where the forces of imaginative leadership can be applied."

de Laurot, Edouard L. "On Critics and Criteria." *F Cult* 1 (No. 2, 1955) 4–11. Films must be critically discussed in terms of prevailing ethical and aesthetic values, and ultimately in terms of their broader historical, social, and cultural context.

Jacobs, Lewis. "Preparation for Film." *F Cult* 1 (No. 2, 1955) 2–3. The author argues for the need of explaining new possibilities of film making and for more serious and sophisticated film criticism.

Grierson, John. "A Review of Reviews." *S&S* 24 (Jan–Mar 55). *See 8c(1).*

Emerling, Ernest. "Can Critics Make or Break Them?" *JSPG* (Apr 55) 11+. Director of publicity for Loew's Theaters discusses types of critics and their effect on a picture's success.

Callenbach, Ernest. "A New 'General Line'—for Critics." *QFRTV* 9 (No. 4, Summer 55) 374–379. Most film criticism today is either all in the realm of aesthetics with no regard for social consciousness, or vice versa; the need for a more balanced approach and more understanding of the way the industry operates.

Anderson, Lindsay. "Stand Up! Stand Up!" *S&S* 26 (Autumn 56) 63–69. The critic should be committed, politically and socially, to ideas. See also letter by J. R. Taylor in same issue which takes a different view.

"The Front Page." *S&S* 26 (Autumn 56) 59. Editorial response to letters and articles; should criticism be "committed"?

Maddison, John. "An Open Letter." *S&S* 26 (Autumn 56) 103–104. An article commenting on the editorial policy of *Sight and Sound;* more attention should be paid to the documentary and educational film, and to television.

Lawrie, James, *et al.* "The Critics." *Film* (No. 10, Nov–Dec 56) 16–19. Several film critics discuss film criticism.

Young, Vernon. "Love, Death, and the Foreign Film—1957." *Hudson Rev* 10 (Spring 57) 103–110. Attack on some American critics for sneering at decadence in foreign films, with special reference to Braunberger's *Bullfight.*

Giesler, Rodney. "Too Much Talk." *F&F* 3 (No. 6, Mar 57) 14–15. Plea for more attention to visual aspects of film making.

Farber, Manny. "Underground Films." *Commentary* 24 (Nov 57) 432–439. The hard-boiled, "life-worn" action films made by Howard Hawks, William Wellman, and their successors are in danger of being forgotten in favor of the "candy-coated," sentimental message pictures approved by current movie critics.

De Mille, Cecil B. "How to Be a Critic." *F&F* 4 (No. 6, Mar 58) 11. De Mille criticizes the critics.

Rotha, Paul, Basil Wright, Lindsay Anderson, Penelope Houston. "The Critical Issue." *S&S* 27 (Autumn 58) 270–275+. *Close Up, Sequence, World Film News, Documentary News Letter, Cinema Quarterly,* and *Sight and Sound* helped the advancement of criticism; the authors ask if there is now an overbalance of witty but snobbish criticism written by men who see new films with old eyes; symposium on the occasion of the twenty-fifth year of the British Film Institute.

Albert, Robert S. "The Role of the Critic in Mass Communications: A Theoretical Analysis." *J Soc Psych* 48 (Nov 58) 265–274. He is an important cultural mediator between artists and consumers.

"Mincing a Dead Horse." *Time* 72 (10 Nov 58)

68+. Pressure applied by studios is changing newspaper movie criticism.

Gardiner, H. C. "Avant-Garde Catholic Critics?" *America* 101 (19 Sep 59) 730–732. Attacks on the "lofty disdain" of Catholic critics are countered.

Callenbach, Ernest. "Editor's Notebook." *FQ* 13 (No. 2, Winter 59) 2–8. A magazine concerned with criticism must be aware of the conditions of production, should even propose what kinds of films should be made—that is, realistic, committed, revealing the contemporary human condition.

Roud, Richard. "The French Line." *S&S* 29 (Autumn 60). *See 4e(2).*

Cameron, Ian, and Ian Jarvie. "Attack on Film Criticism." *Film* (No. 25, Sep–Oct 60) 12–14.

Dyer, Peter John. "Counter Attack." *Film* (No. 26, Nov–Dec 60) 8–9. An argument against earlier statements on criticism by Cameron and Jarvie and a plea for a movement away from the *Cahiers du Cinéma* attitude toward directors.

Callenbach, Ernest. "Editor's Notebook: The Critical Question—Another View." *FQ* 14 (No. 2, Winter 60) 2–4. Responding to Penelope Houston's article on film criticism in autumn *Sight and Sound, Film Quarterly* editor wants to go beyond concern with "commitment to ideas" to close analysis of works as unified wholes.

"Religion and Other Things." *Commonweal* 73 (2 Dec 60) 245. Concern about critics who reject films with tenets they don't understand.

Armitage, Peter. "The War of the Cults." *NY F Bul* 2 (Nos. 12, 13, 14, 1961). *See 1b(2).*

Cameron, Ian. "Purely for Kicks?" *NY F Bul* 2 (Nos. 12, 13, 14, 1961). *See 1b(2).*

Franci, R. M. "A Bibliography for the 'Critical Debate.'" *NY F Bul* 2 (Nos. 12, 13, 14, 1961). *See 1b(2).*

Sarris, Andrew. "The Director's Game." *F Cult* (Nos. 22–23, 1961) 68–81. Quick judgments on American directors; comparison of the French film magazine *Cahiers du Cinéma* and *Sight and Sound;* "American criticism has a long way to go."

Stoller, James. "Trackings." *NY F Bul* 2 (No. 15, 1961). *See 1b(2).*

Wood, Robin. "New Criticism." *NY F Bul* 2 (Nos. 12, 13, 14, 1961). *See 1b(2).*

Vaughan, Dai, and Philip Riley. "Letters from the Trenches." *Film* (No. 27, Jan–Feb 61) 9–11. The role of the film critic and the degree of commitment required.

Houston, Penelope. "Critic's Notebook." *S&S* 30 (Spring 61) 62–66. "One unrepentantly stands by content" but of course it can only be defined "through the given form"; literary elements such as character and construction are important but the moment of emotional response is more central to cinema; note the

critical responses to Truffaut and to *L'Avventura, La Dolce Vita,* and *Rocco and His Brothers.*

Jarvie, Ian. "Towards an Objective Film Criticism." *FQ* 14 (No. 3, Spring 61) 19. Neither technical descriptions, subjectivism, nor pseudo-objective social commitment are enough: we need a tradition of discussion and agreement on some negative principles, helped by "clear-cut statements about the way the film works" and an understanding of "the making of the film and the artist responsible for it."

Armitage, Peter. "Free Criticism." *Film* (No. 28, Mar–Apr 61) 8–10. The need for an eclectic approach.

Cameron, Ian. "What's the Use?" *Film* (No. 28, Mar–Apr 61) 10–11. The critic seen as attempting to understand and evaluate the purposes of the director.

Jarvie, Ian. "Comeback." *Film* (No. 28, Mar–Apr 61) 18. A response to Peter John Dyer's criticism of Jarvie's earlier article on criticism.

Cameron, Ian, V. F. Perkins, and Mark Shivas. "Oxford Opinion." *FQ* 14 (No. 4, Summer 61) 64. Letter responding to editorial about criticism (No. 2, Winter 60) says *Sight and Sound* article distorted their view of the importance of textual and stylistic criticism.

Walsh, Moira. "On Movies—Even About Saints." *America* (9 Aug 61) 630–631. A critical look at Catholic responses to film, and a call for more informed film criticism at all levels among Catholics.

Williams, David. "Early Film Criticism in Leicester." *Cinema Studies* 1 (No. 4, Dec 61). *See 4e(1a).*

"Film and Its Critics." *America* 106 (13 Jan 62) 458.

Callenbach, Ernest. "Editor's Notebook: 'Turn On! Turn On!'" *FQ* 15 (No. 3, Spring 62) 2–14. A call for personal criticism that responds to personal films that place individual needs above those of society. See also brief responding letter by William S. Pechter 15 (No. 4, Summer 62) 62.

Baker, Peter. "The Screen Answers Back." *F&F* 8 (No. 8, May 62) 11–18+. Two combined articles on film criticism: (1) listing of major British critics and their backgrounds, (2) answers to questions on criticism from film writers, directors, actors, and producers.

Cameron, Ian. "Films, Directors and Critics." *Movie* (No. 2, Sep 62) 4–7. A plea for more detailed criticism which takes into account the contributions of the American film and the contribution of film form.

Alpert, Hollis. "Are Movie Critics Necessary?" *Sat Rev* 45 (13 Oct 62) 58–59. Excerpt from his book *The Dream and the Dreamers* (Macmillan, 1963).

Stern, Seymour. "Interview with Seymour

Stern." *F Cult* (No. 27, 1962–1963) 66–72. "The proper scope and subject matter of film criticism?"—everything, including the subject matter the film presents.

Alloway, Lawrence. "On the Iconography of the Movies." *Movie* (No. 7, Feb 63) 4–6. Films should be studied in relation to other films which form cycles and genres.

Shipman, David. "Against the Critics." *F&F* 9 (No. 5, Feb 63) 67–68. Reflections on the *Cahiers* critical theory.

Nowell-Smith, Geoffrey. "Movie and Myth." *S&S* 32 (Spring 63) 60–64. About audiences and critics; *Cahiers du Cinéma* cherishes only the mythical image of America; movie-goers are either "humanists" (to whom "the cinema is a mirror of reality") or "movie-manes" (to whom "the very essence of the cinema is illusion"); still some people find it possible to like both *La Terra Trema* and *Funny Face*.

Walsh, Moira. "What Reviewers Have Not Done." *America* 109 (23 Nov 63) 689.

Limbacher, J. "Film Evaluation and Criticism." *ALA Bul* 58 (Jan 64) 43–47.

Alloway, Lawrence. "Critics in the Dark." *Encounter* 22 (Feb 64) 50–55. Review of four books (1958–1960) the basis for essay on critics and audiences.

"Dial-a-Movie: Taped Ratings." *America* 110 (11 Apr 64) 502. Telephone reviews in several states.

Sarris, Andrew. "Pop Go the Movies!" *Moviegoer* (No. 2, Summer/Autumn 64) 25–34. A plea for a more sensible, sophisticated film criticism.

Alpert, Hollis. "The Movies and the Critics." *Sat Rev* 47 (26 Dec 64) 10–12+. Critics and film makers respond to questionnaire regarding the critic's function.

Frankenheimer, John. "Criticism as Creation." *Sat Rev* (26 Dec 64) 12+. Director says film critic should be aware of film maker's intentions, encourage public love of film, and create an atmosphere conducive to better films. Part of *Saturday Review* report "The Movies and the Critics."

Knight, Arthur. "How to Rate a Critic." *Sat Rev* (26 Dec 64) 16–17. Otto Preminger on role of film critics: A critic should be biased, should believe what he is writing, should know something about the cinema, and should be a guide for his readers. Part of *Saturday Review* report "The Movies and the Critics."

Byrne, Richard B. "Stylistic Analysis of the Film: Notes on a Methodology." *Speech Monographs* 32 (No. 1, Mar 65) 74–78. A method proposed for close analysis of films by use of shot-by-shot breakdown of film.

Routt, William, and Richard Thompson. "We Got It at the Movies." *December* 7 (No. 1,

Spring 65) 122–127. General attempts to begin a theory of film criticism.

Baker, Peter. "Know Your Enemy!" *F&F* 11 (No. 8, May 65) 5–6. On the importance of critics.

Sarris, Andrew. "Random Reflections II." *F Cult* (No. 40, Spring 66) 21–23. Miscellaneous film critiques.

Greenspan, Lou, Norman Corwin, George Seaton, Leo Mishkin, Michael Gordon, Paul Lazarus, Chuck Wheat, Thomas Pryor, Kaspar Monahan, Richard Coe, Philip Scheuer, Dick Richards. "The Journal Looks at Critics and Criticism." *JSPG* (Mar 66) 1–41. Six from the industry and six from the press write of their relationship.

Gottlieb, Stephen. "Some New Criticism." *F Cult* (No. 41, Summer 66) 68–82. Andrew Sarris publishes letters he has received from Gottlieb since publication of the Sarris issue on directors; personal reactions to many films.

Tyler, Parker. "Is Film Criticism Only Propaganda?" *F Cult* (No. 42, Fall 66) 29–34. Six propositions about modern criticism and doubts about underground "critics."

"What Are the New Critics Saying?" *F Cult* (No. 42, Fall 66) 76–88. Comments by Ken Kelman, Toby Mussman, P. Adams Sitney, Sheldon Renan in New York Film Festival symposium.

French, Philip. "Goodbye to All What?" *S&S* 35 (Autumn 66) 176–178. Why do film critics such as Wolcott Gibbs (*New Yorker*), Kenneth Tynan (*Observer*), Harry Schein, and John Donner (Sweden) resign their jobs?

Wead, George. "Fear, Games and Virginia Woolf." *America* (24 Sep 66) 325–329. Criteria for judging films.

Sarris, Andrew. "Hollywood Haters: Illusions and Independents." *Sat Rev* 49 (24 Dec 66) 23–25. Since independents have trouble finding backers, a great deal depends upon the role the critic assumes in promoting new works; film distributors and exhibitors should be encouraged to take more risks with new films.

Macklin, F. Anthony. "Editorial: The Accusers." *F Her* 2 (No. 2, Winter 66–67) 1+. Contemporary critics are propagandists.

Pratley, Gerald. "A Lusty, Loveable Brawl . . . Etc." *Take One* 1 (No. 3, 1967) 20–21. How American film criticism is used to influence Canadian cinema.

Knight, Arthur. "Three Missing Minutes." *Sat Rev* 50 (8 Apr 67) 48+. The film critic can't be sure if the director is responsible for the entire film.

Di Franco, Phillip. "In Criticism of Criticism." *Cinéaste* 1 (No. 1, Summer 67) 14–16. Notions of form and content in cinema, as exemplified by the teaching of Robert Gessner.

Macklin, F. Anthony. "Editorial: Return to Meaning." *F Her* 2 (No. 4, Summer 67) 1–2+. Criticism should not end with the immediacy of the experience of the work of art, as Susan Sontag seems to say, but should continue through interpretation to understanding in the manner of John Simon.

Mayne, Richard. "Scrutinising." *Encounter* 29 (July 67) 41–45. Cinema's critical standards and aesthetics are far less rigorous than those of literature.

Callenbach, Ernest. "What Film Critics Don't Do." *Arts in Soc* 4 (No. 1, Winter 67) 4–13. On the various functions the film critic could and should perform.

Jenkinson, Philip. "Whatever Happened to Opinion, or How I Learned to Stop Criticising and Love the Movies." *Film* (No. 50, Winter 67) 7–9. A negative overview of current film criticism.

Dean, William. "Criticism and the Underground Film." *Take One* 1 (No. 9, 1968) 12–14. The need for a criticism based upon the visual nature of the medium, particularly as represented in the underground film.

Ross, T. J. "Of British Critics, American Films, and Puritan Burdens." *December* 10 (No. 1, 1968) 151–155. Some problems of film criticism; a personal, sensual approach to the cinema is best.

Crist, Judith, *et al.* "Directors Meet Critics." *Action* 3 (No. 3, May–June 68). See 2c.

Young, Vernon. "I've Been Reading These Film Critics." *Hudson Rev* 21 (Summer 68) 337–344. Critique of articles in *New American Cinema* (Dutton, 1967), edited by Gregory Battcock, Richard Roud's *Jean-Luc Godard* (Indiana, 1970), and others.

Richard, J. "Foggy Mountain." *Antioch Rev* 28 (Fall 68) 388–392. Film criticism seen as currently a noninterpretation truce between critic and artist; problems of film style; influence of *Bonnie and Clyde* on behavior of young.

Mueller, Henry L. "Film as Art." *J Aesthetic Educ* 3 (No. 1, Jan 69) 69–77. A plea for the development of a specific terminology for the description of film.

Kubrick, Stanley. "Critics and Film." *Action* 4 (No. 1, Jan–Feb 69) 16–18. Kubrick discusses the critics and their response to *2001: A Space Odyssey*.

Panama, Norman, *et al.* "Why Directors Criticize Critics." *Action* 4 (No. 1, Jan–Feb 69) 13–14. Several directors articulate their response to most critics.

Thomas, Kevin, A. D. Murphy, and Arthur Knight. "Why Critics Criticize." *Action* 4 (No. 1, Jan–Feb 69) 11–12. Critics discuss their basis for criticism.

Schickel, Richard. "A Movie Critic on Movie Critics." *Harper's* 240 (Jan 70) 97–99. A discussion of the movie critic in general and Renata Adler and her book *A Year in the Dark* (Random House, 1970) in particular.

Nowell-Smith, Geoffrey. "Cinema and Structuralism." *20th Century Studies* (No. 3, May 70) 131–139. An overview of the way in which thematic and semiological film criticism are derived from structuralism and an attempt to propose a new direction based upon structuralism.

Wanderer, J. J. "In Defense of Popular Taste: Film Ratings Among Professionals and Lay Audiences." *Am J of Sociology* 76 (Sep 70). See 7b(1b).

Koch, S. "The Cruel, Cruel Critics." *Sat Rev* 53 (26 Dec 70) 12–14+. The critic, his role, his effect on audiences; some critics in particular: Judith Crist, Stanley Kauffman, Pauline Kael, Andrew Sarris. Part of *Saturday Review* report "Writing and the Film."

3b(1). INDIVIDUAL CRITICS

Young, Stark. "Screen Version." *New Rep* 72 (19 Oct 32) 259–261. Critic answers letter objecting to review of *Strange Interlude;* answer contains Young's critical assumptions.

"Comment in Memory of Potamkin, 1900–1933." *Hound & Horn* 7 (No. 1, Oct–Dec 33) 3–4. A eulogy on the death of Harry Alan Potamkin.

Wolff, Daniel. "Harry Alan Potamkin." *New Theater* (Feb 36) 28. Review of Potamkin's work as a film critic.

Hutchens, John K. "Heart on Sleeve: A Confession." *Cinema Arts* 1 (No. 3, Sep 37) 25. A former film reviewer nostalgically muses on the critic's role.

Trewin, J. C. "I Hate the Films!" *S&S* 7 (No. 25, Spring 38) 17–18. One viewer details his dislikes.

"A Bibliography of the Film Writings of Harry Alan Potamkin (1900–1933)." *Films* 1 (No. 1, Nov 39). See 1b(1).

Powell, Dilys. "Credo of a Critic." *S&S* 10 (No. 38, Summer 41) 26–27.

Strauss, Theodore. "No Jacks, No Giant Killers." *Screen Writer* 1 (June 45) 1–14. *New York Times* reviewer writes about *Daily News'* Kate Cameron, *Nation's* James Agee, *New Republic's* Manny Farber, *New Yorker's* Wolcott Gibbs, *P. M.'s* John McManus, *New York Post's* Archer Winsten, *Telegraph's* Leo Mishkin, *New York Herald-Tribune's* Howard Barnes, *New York Times'* Bosley Crowther and how they operate as reviewers.

Gibbs, Wolcott. "Kingdom of the Blind: Reviewing Moving Pictures." *SRL* 28 (17 Nov 45) 7–8. *The New Yorker* critic explains why Hollywood movies are bad and why film criticism is all but useless.

"Critic's Goodbye." *Time* 46 (10 Dec 45) 94. The departure of Wolcott Gibbs as film critic for *Saturday Review*.

Lardner, John. "Last Word." *Screen Writer* 1 (Dec 45) 15–18. On film reviewing—its low level and the need for critics with broader film experience; Lardner wrote reviews for *The New Yorker* for a few months.

Manvell, Roger. "A Forgotten Critic." *S&S* 18 (Spring 49) 31–32; (Summer 49) 76–77. The poet Vachel Lindsay was a film enthusiast; two articles giving extracts from *The Art of the Moving Picture* (1915; reprint, Liveright, 1970).

Winge, John. "The Critic's Success." *S&S* 18 (Summer 49) 70–71. Reviewer doubts his influence.

Pegge, C. Denis. "Another Forgotten Critic." *S&S* 18 (Summer 49) 78–80. Brief biography of Hugo Münsterberg, Harvard philosophy professor, and commentary on his 1916 book *The Photoplay: A Psychological Study* (reprint, Dover, 1969).

Isaacs, Hermine Rich. "The Film Critic's Quest." *FIR* 1 (Apr 50) 19–20. Former film critic for *Theater Arts Magazine* wants in films compassion and the driving force of a single intention.

Lambert, Gavin. "Who Wants True?" *S&S* 21 (Apr–June 52) 148–151. Personal notes on the basis for criticism in cinema: a film should be true and "moving"; this is a personal decision and holds only for single films.

Cooke, Alistair. "Film Folio 2: A Critic's Testament." *S&S* 22 (Jan–Mar 53) 112–113. Reprint of an article in *The Listener*, 17 October 1934, about the role of the film critic, his bias, his aims, and his human weaknesses; Cooke's own standpoint.

Turner, Charles L., Gerald McDonald, Kirk Bond, *et al.* "Theodore Huff, in Memoriam." *FIR* 4 (May 53) 209–215. Biography and appreciations of this film scholar, critic, and teacher. See also letters 4 (June–July 53) 312–315, especially quotations from Huff's own letters by George Pratt.

Weinberg, Herman. "Theodore Huff—In Memoriam." *S&S* 23 (July–Sep 53) 53. Brief obituary for American film scholar and critic.

Rotha, Paul, *et al.* "Richard Winnington." *S&S* 23 (Jan–Mar 54) 160–162. Six authors contribute short tributes to Winnington, known for his penetrating reviews and cartoon caricatures.

Everson, William K. "The Films I Missed." *FIR* 5 (Mar 54) 128–134. A personal account of the effect *Stagecoach* and *Of Mice and Men* had on this future critic's life and his subsequent pursuit of one hundred films he felt compelled to see.

Marsh, W. Ward. "The Loneliest Man." *FIR*

5 (Dec 54) 522–523. Too many critics of the cinema are not qualified for reviewing; Marsh, a reviewer himself, suggests some ways of raising the standard.

Leyda, Jay. "James Agee—A Poet Filmwright." *F Cult* 1 (No. 4, 1955) 3. A brief eulogy for the writer, who was also a novelist and critic.

Phelps, Donald. "James Agee as Film Critic." *F Cult* 1 (No. 4, 1955) 17–18.

Beaufort, John. *JSPG* (Apr 55) 8+. *Christian Science Monitor* film critic on reviewing: "We prefer the beautiful and the true to the ugly and the false."

Crowther, Bosley. *JSPG* (Apr 55) 7. "There can no more be rules for reviewing than rules for the making of great films."

Cameron, Kate. *JSPG* (Apr 55) 7+. New York reviewer's function is to "tell the reader where to get the best return on his money."

Cohen, Harold. *JSPG* (Apr 55) 9. Pittsburgh film critic on reviewing: "It is easy to be a movie fan. . . . It is not so easy to be a critic."

Hogan, William. *JSPG* (Apr 55) 10. San Francisco film critic on reviewing: "A critic's function is to protect the public from tired, indifferent film fare."

Knight, Arthur. *JSPG* (Apr 55) 8+. *Saturday Review* film critic talks about reviewing: "Only a fraud would pretend that personal bias doesn't exist."

Marsh, W. Ward. *JSPG* (Apr 55) 9+. Cleveland film critic on reviewing: "We are the bastards in the field of criticism."

Schallert, Edwin. *JSPG* (Apr 55) 10+. Film critic on reviewing: "The Los Angeles critic is in a particularly responsible position."

Costello, Donald P. "G.B.S. the Movie Critic." *QFRTV* 11 (No. 3, Spring 57) 256–275. Ph.D. candidate at University of Chicago traces Shaw's impressions of the cinema from 1914, antagonistic, hopeful, enthusiastic, disappointed, and disillusioned, in turn; excerpts from magazine articles; reactions to the filming of his own plays.

"Harold Leonard." *S&S* 26 (Spring 57) 222. Tribute to the late film scholar and critic who edited *The Film Index* and wrote for *Sight and Sound* from Hollywood.

Landers, Bertha. "New Film Review Source." *Lib J* 82 (15 Apr 57) 1042–1043. The author explains her reviews of short films for educators and librarians.

Lambert, Gavin. "Good-bye to Some of All That." *FQ* 12 (No. 1, Fall 58) 25–29. What happened to this film critic's judgment and outlook when he worked on production in Hollywood as assistant to Nicholas Ray.

Roud, Richard. "Face to Face: James Agee." *S&S* 28 (No. 2, Spring 59) 98–100. Biography of the American critic and essay review of his collected reviews.

Lejeune, C. A. "On Not Being Committed." *F&F* 5 (No. 9, June 59) 9. Film critic of *The Observer* looks at her own criticism.

Roud, Richard. "Face to Face: André Bazin." *S&S* 28 (Nos. 3 and 4, Summer–Autumn 59) 176–179. Biography and evaluation of writings of French critic.

Hinxman, Margaret. "Even a 'Fan' Deserves an Honest Answer." *F&F* 5 (No. 10, July 59) 15. Review editor of *Picturegoer* writes about her own criticism.

Mosley, Leonard. "The Audience Is My Enemy." *F&F* 5 (No. 11, Aug 59) 15. Critic of *The Daily Express* writes about her own criticism.

Carew, Dudley. "A Compromise with Art." *F&F* 5 (No. 12, Sep 59) 15+. Film critic writes about his criticism.

Dehm, Paul. "Both Sides Have a Fence." *F&F* 6 (No. 1, Oct 59) 15+. Film critic of the *News Chronicle* writes about his own criticism.

Harman, Jympson. "All I Demand Is Sincerity." *F&F* 6 (No. 2, Nov 59) 15+. Critic of *The Evening News* reflects on his years of film criticism.

Mallett, Richard. "Honesty Is Best." *F&F* 6 (No. 3, Dec 59) 15+. Film critic for *Punch* looks at his own criticism.

Majdalany, Fred. "In an Age of 'No Time.'" *F&F* 6 (No. 4, Jan 60) 15. Critic of *The Daily Mail* writes about his criticism.

Hardy, Forsyth. "Looking to Reality." *F&F* 6 (No. 5, Feb 60) 15+. Scottish critic looks at his own criticism.

Gow, Gordon. "The Spell of Mere Movement." *F&F* 6 (No. 6, Mar 60) 13+. Film critic for BBC writes about his own criticism.

Dixon, Campbell. "All Criticism Is Prejudiced." *F&F* 6 (No. 7, Apr 60) 15+. Critic of *The Daily Telegraph* writes about his film criticism.

Richards, Dick. "Writing for the Masses." *F&F* 6 (No. 8, May 60) 15+. Critic of *The Daily Mirror* writes about his own criticism.

Baker, Peter. "Without Fear, Favour . . . or Pretention." *F&F* 6 (No. 9, June 60) 15+. Editor of *Films and Filming* writes about his own criticism.

Larrabee, Eric. "Reflections in a Puddle." *Harper's* 222 (Jan 61) 28+ The state of film criticism; Siegfried Kracauer is trying to improve it.

Armitage, Peter. "The War of the Cults." *Motion* (No. 1, Summer 61). See 1b(2).

Tracey, Mike. "Dwight MacDonald." *Motion* (No. 1, Summer 61) 14–17. An interview in which the film critic discusses some of his attitudes about film criticism, Resnais, Bergman, and other subjects.

Stonier, G. W. "Life with Whitebait." *New S&N* 62 (6 Oct 61) 485. What it is like to be a movie critic in London.

Truffaut, François. "It was Good to Be Alive." *NY F Bul* 3 (No. 3, 1962) 3–5. A personal portrait of French critic André Bazin and the role he played in Truffaut's life.

Kael, Pauline. "Is There a Cure for Film Criticism?" *S&S* 31 (Spring 62) 56–64. "Some Unhappy Thoughts on Siegfried Kracauer's *Theory of Film: The Redemption of Physical Reality*" (Oxford, 1965).

Pechter, W. S. "Two Movies and Their Critics." *Kenyon Rev* 24 (Spring 62) 351–362. Norman Holland on *La Dolce Vita* and *L'Avventura* in *Hudson Review:* Pechter critiques Holland's critiques.

Rosenthal, Alan. "The Outlook of C. A. Lejeune." *Cinema Studies* 1 (No. 6, Dec 62) 123–129; (No. 9, June 64) 221–226. *The Observer's* film critic wants compassion and normalcy, according to profesor at San Francisco State college; second article describes her faith in the good sense of the cinema audience.

Anderson, Lindsay. "Sport, Life, and Art." *F&F* 9 (No. 5, Feb 63). *See 5, Lindsay Anderson.*

Dienstfrey, Harris. "Hitch Your Genre to a Star." *F Cult* (No. 34, 1964) 35–37. The film criticism of Robert Warshow [*The Immediate Experience* (Atheneum, 1970)] suggests that the genre itself (not the director) is what makes a picture such as *Casablanca* great.

Pechter, William S. "On Agee on Film." *S&S* 33 (Summer 64) 148–152. Evaluation of James Agee as a critic and screenwriter, based on his two collected volumes, *Agee on Film* (Grosset and Dunlap, 1969).

Phelps, Donald. "Rosencrantz vs. Guildenstern." *Moviegoer* (No. 1, Winter 64) 2+. Discussion of the Andrew Sarris–Pauline Kael controversy, with comments by the editor, James Stoller.

Anderson, Thom. "The Controversial Search for Value." *Sat Rev* (26 Dec 64) 18–19+. Surveys American film critics (Sarris, Kael, and MacDonald) with brief history of auteur criticism. Part of *Saturday Review* report "The Movies and the Critics."

Sarris, Andrew. "Random Reflections." *F Cult* (No. 35, 1964–1965). Comments on films, actors, and his own critical stance.

Sarris, Andrew. "The Movieness of Movies." *December* 7 (No. 1, Spring 65) 114–121. An explanation of his own moviegoing history

Phelps, Donald. "Essays of a Man Watching." *Moviegoer* (No. 3, Summer 66) 17–26. A critique of Robert Warshow's criticism.

Macklin, F. Anthony. "Editorial: The Perils of Pauline's Criticism." *F Her* 2 (No. 1, Fall 66) 1+. Miss Kael as lecturer mocks educators; she praises emotional reactions yet relies for her critiques on logical standards.

McBride, Joseph. "Mr. MacDonald, Mr. Kauff-mann, and Miss Kael." *F Her* 2 (No. 4, Summer 67) 26–34. Review of the state of current film criticism, with particular discussion of these three critics.

Ayers, Richard. "Pauline Kael—Film Critic with a Chip on Her Shoulder." *Cinéaste* 1 (No. 2, Fall 67) 6–9+.

Macklin, F. Anthony. "Editorial: Critic of Honor." *F Her* 3 (No. 1, Fall 67) 1–2. James Agee loved movies; he overrated some of them.

MacDonald, Dwight. "Agee and the Movies." *F Her* 3 (No. 1, Fall 67) 3–11. Comments on James Agee as critic by a longtime friend; includes excerpts of a letter from Agee to MacDonald written in 1927.

Siegel, Joel. "On *Agee on Film*." *F Her* 3 (No. 1, Fall 67) 12–19. Study of James Agee's work of collected criticism.

Simon, John. "James Agee." *F Her* 3 (No. 1, Fall 67) 35. Agee was a good film critic because he was interested in so many things besides film.

Alpert, Hollis. "Case of Crowther." *Sat Rev* 50 (23 Sep 67) 111.

"Rigors of Criticism." *Time* 90 (1 Dec 67) 38. On Bosley Crowther.

Thompson, Richard. "The American Movie Critic: Manny Farber." *December* 10 (No. 1, 1968) 135–141. American critic known for his baroque style and passion for the "B" film.

Roud, Richard. "André Bazin: His Fall and Rise." *S&S* 37 (Spring 68) 94–96. An evaluation of Hugh Gray's English translation of Bazin's book *What Is Cinema?* (University of California, 1967), in which Roud finds numerous errors; also a revaluation of some of Bazin's critical theories.

Michelson, Annette. "Books." *Artforum* 6 (No. 10, Summer 68) 67–71. A detailed analysis of André Bazin's work, his place in film criticism, his philosophical and historical influences and roots.

"The Pearls of Pauline." *Time* 92 (12 July 68) 38+. On Pauline Kael.

Paletz, David. "Judith Crist: An Interview with a Big-Time Critic." *FQ* 22 (No. 1, Fall 68) 27–35. Her background, critical canons, reviewing process, conception of audience, critics' awards, and conflict with Hollywood.

Lovell, Alan. "Robin Wood—A Dissenting View." *Screen* 10 (No. 2, Mar–Apr 69) 42–55. Wood's critical writing stems from F. R. Leavis and is therefore too personal and not schematic enough.

Wood, Robin. "Ghostly Paradigm and H. C. F.: An Answer to Alan Lovell." *Screen* 10 (No. 3, May–June 69) 35–48. Criticism has to be personal, as D. H. Lawrence insisted, and cannot be scientific; it is "a discussion of values. If the values were all agreed there would be little point in discussing them."

MacDonald, Dwight. "After Forty Years of Writing About Movies . . ." *Esq* 72 (July 69) 80–83+. Former film critic for *Esquire* examines his reasons for approving of certain movies and disliking others.

Simon, John. "Let Us Now Praise Dwight MacDonald." *Commonweal* 91 (17 Oct 69) 68–70.

Clarens, Carlos. "Eric Rohmer: L'Amour Sage." *S&S* 39 (Winter 69–70). See 5, Eric Rohmer.

Bach, Margaret. "Parker Tyler Then and Now." *Cinema* (Calif) 6 (No. 2, 1970) 42–44. A review of several Tyler books and an overview of the critic's work; bibliography of his film criticism, and articles not collected in his books.

Lynch, F. Dennis. "Pauline Kael's Critical Theories." *JUFA* 22 (No. 2, 1970) 35–38.

Montagu, Ivor. "Birmingham Sparrow: In Memoriam: Iris Barry 1896–1969." *S&S* 39 (Spring 70) 106–108. The "first film critic employed by any serious British journal, co-founder of the world's first (London) film society, initiator of the first American film archive" at the Museum of Modern Art—her life and her significance for the development of cinema appreciation.

Highsmith, John Milton. "Alexander Bakshy: Pioneering Critic of Drama and Motion Pictures." *J Aesthetics and Art Criticism* 29 (No. 2, Winter 70) 195–202. Brief study of the early American critic and his theories.

Lovell, Alan. "The Common Pursuit of True Judgment." *Screen* 11 (Nos. 4–5, 1970) 76–88. Further on the differences between author and Robin Wood (see Mar–Apr and May–June issues).

3b(2). CONTEMPORARY FILM TRENDS

[See also 2c, 4d, 6a, 7b(4), 7b(6).]

Betts, Ernest. "All-Talking, All-Singing, All-Nothing." *Close Up* 6 (No. 6, 1930) 449–454. A negative view of current cinema.

Pitkin, Walter B. "The Crisis in the Movies." *Parents Mag* 5 (Feb 30) 11. Responsibility for better movies rests on public demands.

Godwin, Murray. "Sociology, Fate, Form and Films." *New Rep* 67 (3 June 31) 72–73. Reviews differences in Russian and American approaches to film stories.

Blakeston, Oswell, and Kenneth Macpherson. "A Manifesto!" *Close Up* 9 (No. 2, June 32) 92–106. For a return to the simpler joys of earlier, primitive films.

Bond, Kirk. "Notes on the Modern Cinema." *Europa* 1 (Oct 32) 32–36.

Troy, William. "Values Once Again." *Nation* 136 (10 May 33) 538–539. Response to opinion by Dwight MacDonald assessing

Griffith, Vidor, Mamoulian, d'Arrast, King, and Lubitsch as technically proficient but without "driving passion."

Watts, Richard, Jr. "The Movies Are Coming!" *Th Arts* 17 (Oct 33) 795–800. Surveys current film production.

Trumbo, Dalton. "Stepchild of the Muses." *North Am Rev* 236 (Dec 33) 559–566. Pleads for new possibilities in movies.

Gooden, Opal. "Wanted: Movies with a Kick." *Chris Cent* 51 (17 Oct 34) 1311–1313. The author denies that what the movie clean-up movement wants is "wishy-washy milk and water kind of pictures"; she then goes on to give examples of what constitutes genuine conflict and artistic truthfulness.

Phelps, William Lyon. "Stories I'd Like to See Screened." *Delineator* 125 (Dec 34) 4+. Prefers novel adaptations, exploration films, and slapstick comedy.

Seldes, Gilbert. "The Movies in Peril." *Scribner's* 97 (Feb 35) 81–86. Reviews past five years of talkies, praising gangster films, explaining Mae West, and making suggestions for better movies.

Greene, Graham. "Movie Parade." *S&S* 6 (No. 24, Winter 37–38) 206–207. Critic reviews the films of 1937.

Ferguson, Otis. "Movies: Not a Lean Year." *Th Arts* 22 (June 38) 412–423. Survey of the best in film, worldwide, and the apparent advances in the medium.

Foelsch, C. B. "Toward Better Motion Pictures." *Lutheran Church Q* 11 (Oct 38) 355–364.

Russell, Evelyn. "Films of 1942." *S&S* 11 (No. 44, Spring 43) 99–101. A critical overview of British and American films released in 1942.

Farber, Manny. "The Trouble with Movies." *New Rep* 108 (19 Apr 43) 508. Characters are traditionally subordinated to plot; camera should tell more about people and situations.

Cross, Elizabeth. "It Won't Last Forever." *S&S* 12 (No. 45, Summer 43) 22–23. Criticisms of the current film fare.

Bean, Keith. "Keith Bean Writes." *S&S* 13 (No. 52, Jan 45) 95–97. A review of the most important films released in 1944.

Edwards, C. C. "Let's Talk About the Movies." *Parents Mag* 20 (Oct 45) 30–31+. Which recent movies are good for the masses; emphasis on the importance of children's movies and music in films.

Houseman, John. "Violence, 1947: Three Specimens." *Hwd Q* 3 (No. 1, Fall 47). See 7b(4).

Yerrill, D. A. "On Carts and Horses." *S&S* 16 (No. 64, Winter 47–48) 153–154. Plea for more experiment and less economic constraints in making new films.

Untermeyer, L. "Why I Like the Movies." *Woman's Home Companion* 75 (Dec 48) 7–8.

"Is the Quality of Motion Pictures Declining?" *Consumers Res Bul* 26 (Nov 50) 16.

Poster, William. "The Death of a Hero." *Am Mercury* 72 (Feb 51) 225–229. A discussion of the decline of the "dream world" of early American films, and the growing penchant for realistic situations, common characters, and drabness.

"Of Note: Movies." *Commonweal* 54 (8 June 51) 216. The "artistic" impetus is necessary to films if they are to be "morally good."

Genauer, E. "Art Film." *Th Arts* 35 (Aug 51) 20–21+. Signs of life with short films and features such as *Henry V* and increased museum attendance.

Farber, Manny. "Movies Aren't Movies Any More." *Commentary* 13 (June 52) 560–566. Lament for the passing of naturalistic films and protest against the current emphasis on "sensational effects reeking with recondite significance"; influence traced to *Citizen Kane*.

Shaw, George Bernard. "The Cinema as a Moral Leveler." *S&S* 22 (Oct–Dec 52). See 7b(6).

Macrorie, Ken. "Movies Don't Move." *English J* 41 (No. 9, Nov 52) 474–479. Recent movies rely on clichéd movement and ignore natural motion; author champions Pudovkin, Eisenstein, Lorentz, and Flaherty.

Farber, Manny. "Blame the Audience." *Commonweal* 57 (19 Dec 52) 280–281. Pictures are bad because the audience, led on by the reviewers, wants prestigious or sophisticated treatment instead of unpolished "B's" with the immediacy of life.

Pratley, Gerald. "The Cult of the Unintelligible." *QFRTV* 8 (No. 3, Spring 54) 302–306. Film commentator for CBC objects to experimental film makers who prefer obscurity to communication, including Cocteau (especially *Orphée*), Deren, and Richter.

Everson, William K. "The Decline of Charm." *S&S* 23 (Apr–June 54) 203–206. In the sound era this quality went out of fashion; *Lili, Genevieve, The Pickwick Papers,* and *Roman Holiday;* examples of this sort of film.

Grierson, John. "The Prospect for Cultural Cinema." *Film* (No. 7, Jan–Feb 56) 20–21+. Extracts from a lecture on the impact of television.

Wald, Jerry. "The Men in the Empty Suits." *JSPG* (Nov 56) 4–5+. Producer declares we have entered the age of nonconformity for picture makers.

Anderson, Lindsay. "Ten Feet Tall." *S&S* 27 (Summer 57) 34–36. The contemporary Hollywood scene; some new directors of talent; a number of films which show encouraging intelligence and serious themes: *A Man Is Ten Feet Tall, Fear Strikes Out, Twelve Angry Men, Bachelor Party.*

Armitage, Peter. "Film Strikes Out." *Film* (No. 13, Sep–Oct 57) 17–19. Recent films based on American television plays.

Kozintsev, Gregory. "Deep Screen." *S&S* 28 (Nos. 3 and 4, Summer–Autumn 59) 157–160. Soviet director responds to round-table discussion in *Sight and Sound,* proposing international meetings with film makers and calling for a new quality of depth in films.

Knight, Arthur. "The New Frankness in Films." *Sat Rev* (19 Dec 59). See *7b(6).*

Houston, Penelope, and Duncan Crow. "Into the Sixties." *S&S* 29 (Winter 59–60) 4–8. Survey of the past decade and speculations for the 1960s; more inward exploration, less social crusading, may follow the French New Wave; Crow considers the reduced size of the audience, and other statistics.

Armitage, Peter. "Film in the Fifties." *Film* (No. 23, Jan–Feb 60) 10–21. An overview of the film scene in the 1950s: genres, directors, countries, etc., attempting to show that one of the dominant themes has been delinquency and the problems of youth.

Bond, Kirk. "Symbolism and the New Cinema." *NY F Bul* 2 (No. 10, 1961) 4–6. An essay on new films by Resnais, Kurosawa, and Antonioni, noting their emphasis on visual elements and symbolism rather than dramatic value.

Kael, Pauline. "Fantasies of the Art House Audience." *S&S* 31 (Winter 61–62) 4–9. "The educated audience often uses 'art' films in much the same self-indulgent way as the mass audience uses Hollywood 'product.'" An attack on *Hiroshima, Mon Amour* and other films.

de Laurot, Edouard. "Reflections on a Theory of World Cinema." *F Cult* (No. 26, 1962) 63–70. The author is critical of the current cinema for its lack of ideas, its negative and unsound philosophical base, as well as its lack of engagement.

Moller, David. "Adventures in the Sin Game." *Vision [Film Comment]* 1 (No. 1, Spring 62) 17–19. The "moral desert" of the rich and the idle cannot be so vital a subject for films as the characters' yearnings in *The Grapes of Wrath* or *La Strada.*

Gilman, Richard. "About Nothing—With Precision." *Th Arts* 46 (July 62) 10–12. Films of today trace the arc of despair that leads to truth.

Farber, Manny. "White Elephant Art Versus Termite Art." *F Cult* (No. 27, 1962–1963) 9–13. Self-conscious attempts to frame masterpieces are never so interesting as the unkempt, beaverish activity that concentrates on "nailing down one moment without glamorizing it"; Truffaut, Richardson, Antonioni rejected.

Fadiman, William. "Blockbusters or Bust?" *F&F* 9 (No. 5, Feb 63). See *4k(4).*

Cameron, Ian, *et al.* "Movie Differences." *Movie* (No. 8, Apr 63) 28–34. The editors of *Movie* discuss their different opinions, especially on recent movies by Godard, Bresson, Antonioni.

Alpert, Hollis. "So Deeply Obscure, So Widely Discussed." *NYTM* (21 Apr 63) 68–69+. On recent "obscure" films.

Young, Colin. "Conventional—Unconventional." *FQ* 17 (No. 1, Fall 63). See *4e(2b).*

Cowie, Peter, and George Fenin. "Two of a Kind." *F&F* 10 (No. 1, Oct 63) 36–38. British critic's view of current U.S. films and American critic's view of current British films.

Lane, John Francis, and Peter Graham. "Two of a Kind." *F&F* 10 (No. 3, Dec 63) 35–37. *Films and Filming's* critic in Italy looks at current French films and their critic in France looks at current Italian films.

Holland, Norman N. "Puzzling Movies: Three Analyses and a Guess at Their Appeal." *J Soc Issues* 20 (Jan 64) 71–96. Analyses of *The Seventh Seal, La Dolce Vita,* and *Last Year at Marienbad.*

Silke, James R. "Attack: An Analysis of the New Cinema and Its Hollywood Beginnings." *Cinema* (Calif) 2 (No. 1, Feb–Mar 64) 4.

Holland, Norman N. "Movies You Are Not Supposed to Dig." *F&F* 10 (No. 11, Aug 64) 32–34. On the new movies that puzzle an audience but still hold their interest.

Didion, Joan. "I Can't Get That Monster Out of My Mind." *Am Scholar* 33 (Autumn 64) 629–630+. In the popular imagination the motion-picture industry has been a mechanical monster which destroys the creative and humane spirit; but even with "independent" production there can only be a few interesting minds at work at any one time; brief critiques of a number of films.

Houston, Penelope. "Keeping Up with the Antonionis." *S&S* 33 (Autumn 64) 163–168. "The Antonioni scene has become a convention in its own right," and the failure of communication has become "a cliché in the whole of contemporary cinema."

Kael, Pauline. "Are Movies Going to Pieces?" *Atlantic* 214 (Dec 64) 61–66. Movies are being stripped of all the "nonessentials"— that is to say, faces, actions, details, stories, places; the feeling for life that moves people is gone. See discussion 215 (Mar 65) 42.

Mitchell, Andrew. "Jump Cuts: Notes on the Mid-Sixties." *Film* (No. 43, Autumn 65) 16–24. Comments on film in the mid-1960s: various directors, acting, comedy, color; women directors, hostile critics.

Silverstein, Norman. "Movie-going for Lovers of *The Wasteland* and *Ulysses.*" *Salmagundi* 1 (No. 1, Fall 65) 37–55. On the new style of film making, especially Antonioni and Godard.

Truffaut, François. "A Certain Tendency of the French Cinema." *CdC in Eng* (No. 1, Jan

66) 31–41. A call for change from "the tradition of quality" and of "psychological realism" dominated by scenarists such as Jean Aurenche and Pierre Bost (who did not even adapt novels faithfully) to a cinema in which directors will help prepare their own stories.

Kael, P. "Movie Brutalists." *New Rep* 155 (24 Sep 66) 23–24. "Automatic writing" with a camera is what the young people who attack Hollywood want to do, but while they seem tough, they don't want to do any preparatory work; praise for Godard, who does improvise with technical control.

Crist, Judith. "Down with Bigness!" *Ladies' Home J* 84 (Jan 67). See *4k(4)*.

Leary, D. J. "Cinema of the Absurd." *Cath World* 204 (Feb 67) 301–306. Discussion of several recent American and English films which are using new modes of communication in treating modern man's uneasiness.

Smith, Peter. "A New Direction." *Medium* 1 (No. 1, Summer 67) 2–8. Museum of Modern Art series of international films.

Kael, Pauline. "Onward and Upward with the Arts." *New Yorker* 43 (3 June 67) 124–134. Movies on television: "an important part of our past . . . jumbled together, out of historical sequence; even the trash contributed to our values because a mass medium has to be on the side of the poor."

Lynch, William F. "Counterrevolution in the Movies." *Commonweal* 87 (20 Oct 67) 77–86. New trend toward words and ideas in modern cinema.

MacCann, Richard Dyer. "A Little More Peripheral Vision, Please." *Arts in Soc* 4 (No. 1, Winter 67) 14–20. Neither social concern nor the recent fascination with technical experiment can broaden our "sympathetic feeling for others" if this motivation is missing in the film maker's creative vision.

Young, Vernon. "Poetry, Politics, and Pornography." *Hudson Rev* 20 (Winter 67–68) 643–649. Recent films by Kluge, Bonheur, Sjöman, Buñuel, and Le Louch indicate that fraud has become the common denominator for the public arts.

Weintraub, William. "Fluxation and Slurrage." *Take One* 11 (No. 2, 1968) 14–15. An ironic view of the latest films.

Alloway, Lawrence. "More Skin, More Everything in Movies." *Vogue* 151 (1 Feb 68) 186–187+. Some current trends in films, especially sexual.

Gilliat, Penelope. "Only Films Are Truly, Deep-Down Groovy." *New Yorker* 44 (8 June 68) 117–118. Comments on the language of grooviness and on the fashionable tendency to consider films as up-to-date and other arts as old-fashioned.

Durgnat, Raymond. "Throwaway Movies." *F&F* 14 (No. 10, July 68) 4–10. A criticism of the new trend in film by an analysis of the old style of films.

Durgnat, Raymond. "The Impossible Takes a Little Longer." *F&F* 14 (No. 12, Sep 68) 12–16. Article on the great diversity of styles and types of current films.

Newman, David, and Robert Benton. "Movies Will Save Themselves." *Esq* 70 (Oct 68) 182–187. Changing attitudes toward movies (by the writers of *Bonnie and Clyde*).

Knight, Arthur. "Engaging the Eye-Minded." *Sat Rev* 51 (28 Dec 68) 17–19+. Style of storytelling in films has changed from revealing depths to suggesting them, which tends to involve the viewer more. Part of *Saturday Review* report "The Now Movie."

Stulberg, Gordon. "Hollywood Transition." *Sat Rev* (28 Dec 68). See *6c*.

Sobchack, Thomas. "Today's Cinema: Form Versus Content." *Western Humanities Rev* 23 (1969) 253–260. Study of the change from older films that stressed narrative to the more recent films with their emphasis on technique and style.

Schickel, Richard. "Movies Are Now High Art." *NYTM* (5 Jan 69) 32–34+. An evaluation of the current film scene.

Claman, Julian. "Spot Check: Some Observations on Films in America." *Harper's Bazaar* 102 (Feb 69) 122+. Summary of the movies of 1968.

Koch, Stephen. "Fiction and Film: A Search for New Sources." *Sat Rev* (27 Dec 69). See *3f(2)*.

Farber, Stephen. "End of the Road?" *FQ* 23 (No. 2, Winter 69–70) 3–16. Is the answer to the downturn in movie receipts the low-budget, "on the road" youth picture? *Alice's Restaurant*, *Medium Cool*, and *The Rain People* offer the sincerest and most revealing picture of America, while *Midnight Cowboy* "coarsens" and *Easy Rider* "idealizes" the recent American past.

Madson, Axel. "Reaching the Tribes." *S&S* 39 (Winter 69–70) 33–35. The author seems to believe that "the war is over," and Hollywood is the Young Man's Burden; an opinion piece written from Los Angeles.

Sarris, Andrew. "Tomorrow's Movies." *Mlle* 70 (Jan 70) 68+. Some thoughts on where movies are going: more noise, youth, fragmentation, combinations of reality and illusion, and do-it-yourself movies.

Wagner, G. "Of Pot and Pigs: The New Cinema." *Nat Rev* 22 (27 Jan 70) 96–97. Analysis of the rhetorical clichés of "the hippie cinema," such as *Easy Rider* and *Putney Swope*.

Mowat, D. "Cinema's New Language." *Encounter* 34 (Apr 70) 62–67. The Continental films of the 1960s, especially the work of Fellini, Antonioni, and Bergman, have led to imitative English-language films which fail because they are woven out of mere technical mannerisms and other failures in depth.

Morgenstern, J. "Bang! Apocalypse for Sale." *Newswk* 75 (27 Apr 70) 97–98. The "sentimental nihilism" of recent films predicting the end of the world are decrepit producers' attempts to con confused youth; needed are films that make allowance for a future.

Vidor, King. "The Old and the New." *JSPG* (June 70) 19–21. No longer is there a mass audience, and today an Irving Thalberg can't allow "experimental" films as part of a program.

Karpel, Craig. "Last Great Show on Earth." *Esq* 74 (Aug 70) 59. How Hollywood has come closer to reality, making films about youth to capture the young audience; introduction to series of articles by film makers.

Hampton, Charles C., Jr. "Movies That Play for Keeps." *F Com* 6 (No. 2, Fall 70) 65–69. Films such as *Bonnie and Clyde, Butch Cassidy,* and *Easy Rider* fulfill the old genre expectation of a "sequential emotional workout" but stories of incompatibility of lifestyles change the genres so that "boy gets girl, boy loses girl, boy and girl are killed by somebody we don't even know."

Kael, Pauline. "Numbing the Audience." *New Yorker* 46 (3 Oct 70) 74–80. New films follow old Hollywood tactics but they don't give the audience anything; new audiences are characterized by susceptibility to emotional manipulation by the new film makers. Attempts in the past year to appeal to youth have misfired; they are sentimental about youth and despairing about America.

Farber, Stephen. "Melodramatic Truths." *Hudson Rev* 23 (Winter 70–71) 685–696. Much of current film tends to be purely visual painting; without the plot dimension no consistent moral view can be developed.

3b(3). CRITICISM AND DEFENSE OF HOLLYWOOD

[See also 7d.]

Beaton, Welford. "In Darkest Hollywood." *New Rep* 63 (23 July 30) 287–289. See also *Lit Dig* 106 (16 Aug 30) 16. Calls for logical plot development.

Lorentz, Pare. "Moral Racketeering in the Movies." *Scribner's* 88 (Sep 30) 256–262. The ways producers pay for protection from critics, such as keeping films at level of children.

"The Reformed Movies." *Chris Cent* 47 (22 Oct 30) 1270–1271. Attacks movies' sentimentality, false views of life, glorification of earthiness, and asks for elimination of block booking.

Howard, Clifford. "Sapient Hollywood." *Close Up* 7 (No. 6, Dec 30) 425–428. Hollywood's attitude toward films and film making.

Peet, Creighton. "A Letter to Hollywood." *Outlook* 156 (17 Dec 30) 612–613+. Reply to letter from Carl Laemmle asking magazine's assessment of movies. Rejoinder by J. R. Metcalf 157 (14 Jan 31) 80.

Root, Edward Tallmadge. "Milliken, Eastman Debate Movies." *Chris Cent* 48 (15 Apr 31) 518. Motion Picture Producers and Distributors of America secretary faces Chicago theologian in Maine debate.

"An Archbishop and Mr. Milliken on the Movies." *Lit Dig* 109 (25 Apr 31) 23. Secretary of Motion Picture Producers and Distributors of America charges "movie pulpiteers" with misrepresentation of religious opinion.

"Dreiser on the Sins of Hollywood." *Lit Dig* 109 (2 May 31) 21. Novelist sees films as "hokum, insincere make-believe."

"The Movie Mail." *Chris Cent* 48 (13 May 31) 640–641. Reports public outrage at movie fare.

Wellesby, Norah. "Temple Rocking in the Movies." *North Am Rev* 232 (Aug 31) 166–172. Claims producers try to fit public to pictures, rather than vice versa.

"A Jew Speaks to the Jews of Hollywood." *Chris Cent* 48 (19 Aug 31) 1036. Laments Jews who have chosen profits over virtue in movie industry.

Howard, Clifford. "The Coming Revolution." *Close Up* 8 (No. 3, Sep 31) 214–218. Certain signs point to a change in Hollywood films and film making.

Bryher. "The Hollywood Code." *Close Up* 8 (No. 3, Sep 31) 234–238; (No. 4, Dec 31) 280–282. Hollywood's insistence on making films according to a formula of sex appeal and eroticism.

Howard, Clifford. "Reflections." *Close Up* 8 (No. 4, Dec 31) 318–320. Hollywood and its role in the world cinema.

"The Movies Are Brought to Judgment." *Chris Cent* 48 (3 Dec 31) 1647–1648. Suggests drop in movie profits indicates moral decay of industry.

Howard, Clifford. "Hollywood in Fact." *Close Up* 9 (No. 2, June 32) 87–91. The nature of the film audience, Hollywood, and the denigration of Hollywood.

Arliss, George. "It's Like the Lawns of England." *Woman's Home Companion* 59 (Aug 32) 19–20+. English actor says American movies are better.

"Money the Movies Miss." *Chris Cent* 50 (8 Mar 33) 318–320. Millions of patrons would come to see a run of good pictures such as *Cimarron* instead of filth.

Knight, Eric M. "The Passing of Hollywood." *CQ* 1 (No. 4, Summer 33) 216–218. Commercial cinema is surely destroying itself.

"In Praise of American Movies." *Living Age* 348 (Mar 35) 85–86. Alastair Cooke suggests viewing U.S. movies by U.S. standards, not those of England.

Rand, Jay. "Hitlerites in Hollywood." *New Masses* 16 (23 July 35) 29–30. Hollywood moguls are fascist chauvinists conducting an anti-radical campaign in their current films.

Forsythe, Robert. "Let It Happen No More." *New Masses* 18 (10 Mar 36) 27–28. Because of censorship and capitalism, Hollywood produces films that are predominantly innocuous or reactionary.

Herring, Robert. "America's Universal Entertainment Service." *S&S* 5 (No. 18, Summer 36) 10–12. About Will Hays' 1935 report: Is American cinema really improving?

Seldes, Gilbert. "Quicksands of the Movies." *Atlantic* 158 (Oct 36) 422–431. Some advice for movie makers: if their loyalty is to be maintained, moviegoers will need more of the lasting satisfaction of rich human characterizations, not just movies made to be forgotten.

Wilson, Edmund. "It's Terrible! It's Ghastly! It Stinks!" *New Rep* (21 July 37) 311–312. Starting from a review of a biography of Samuel Goldwyn, the critic launches into a diatribe against the bigness and emptiness of Hollywood movies.

MacDonald, Dwight. "Correspondence." *New Rep* 92 (8 Sep 37) 133. Support for article by Edmund Wilson attacking Hollywood's tastes in movie production.

North, Joseph. "Renaissance in Hollywood?" *New Masses* 32 (4 July 39) 3–6. Despite Wall Street control, there have been significant works of art.

Dugan, James. "Lost: 65,000,000 Movie Fans." *New Masses* 36 (25 June 40) 30–31. Decreases in the foreign market because of war are causing producers to look for new schemes to draw audiences: war propaganda and the exploitation of sex.

Goodman, E. "Hollywood and the American Scene." *Common Ground* 3 (No. 4, Summer 43) 91–95. A call for a change from the distortion of real life in America created by Hollywood to a more realistic portrayal of American life as exemplified by the protest films of the 1930s.

Farber, M. "Production Line." *New Rep* 109 (2 Aug 43) 142–143. An attack on Hollywood "production values."

Curtiss, Thomas Quinn. "Hollywood Defended." *S&S* 13 (No. 50, July 44) 28–29.

Farrell, James T. "The Language of Hollywood." *Sat Rev* (5 Aug 44) 29–32. The emptiness of daydreams.

Foster, Joseph. "Changing Hollywood." *New Masses* 54 (6 Feb 45) 27–28. The social consciousness of both the Hollywood worker and the audience have progressed because of the war.

Carew, D. "Hollywood Indicted: A British Viewpoint." *NYTM* (23 Sep 45) 22–23. A scathing attack on the superficiality of Hollywood, even when dealing with the tragic themes of war.

Crowther, Bosley. "Hollywood Defended: An American View." *NYTM* (30 Sep 45) 16+. A reply to D. Carew's attack on Hollywood (23 Sep 45), with a discussion of audience values and films in wartime.

Knepper, M. "Is Hollywood Growing Up?" *Forum* 105 (June 46) 880–885. The commercial growth and artistic lag in movies.

Dohm, John. "The Return of a Rationalist." *Screen Writer* 2 (Sep 46) 27–33. A discussion of the low quality of American films and their relationship to public taste.

Edwards, C. "It Shouldn't Happen to the Movies." *Parents Mag* 21 (Oct 46) 26–27+. The decline in Hollywood's film quality— what the causes are and the means to a better film future.

Eisenstein, S. M. "Purveyors of Spiritual Poison." *S&S* 16 (No. 63, Autumn 47) 103–105. American films are contributing to the darkness and oppression which are the fundamental features of imperialist society.

Hunter, A. A. "A Clergyman Looks at the Movies." *Annals of Am Acad of Polit and Soc Sci* 254 (Nov 47) 95–97. An attack on the economic dictates on and false values of movies.

Houston, Penelope. "Hollywood Warning." *Sequence* (No. 2, Winter 47) 15–17. A criticism of declining artistic tastes and standards in Hollywood.

"Thunder from the West." *Harper's* 196 (Feb 48) 190–191. Psychology behind Hollywood attempts at high-brow movies.

Robertson, William. "The World Likes American Films." *S&S* 17 (No. 66, Summer 48) 91–92.

Freeman, Everett. "Hollywood and *The New Yorker*." *Screen Writer* 4 (June–July 48) 3–4+. Defense of movies against Harold Ross' statement that an intellectual couldn't like movies.

Hine, Al. "Movies: For Adults Only." *Holiday* 5 (Mar 49) 23–24+. Why can't Hollywood make mature movies instead?

Kracauer, Siegfried. "The Mirror Up to Nature." *Penguin F Rev* 9 (May 49) 95–99. Hollywood story purchasing and production by their very nature prevent "that adventurous spirit with which alone the screen can capture reality"; *Brief Encounter* and *The Search* are rare exceptions.

Hodgins, Eric (ed.). "Roundtable on the Movies." *Life* 26 (27 June 49) 90–96+. Participants include producers Dore Schary, Jerry Wald, and Hal Wallis, scholar Charles Siepmann, and directors John Huston and Fred Zinnemann. Excerpts: *Time* 53 (27 June 49) 88–89.

Bloomfield, Paul. "Mild Expostulations." *S&S* 19 (May 50) 113. Critic and author suggests less intellectual laziness and more uncommon characters in films.

Klein, Alexander. "The Challenge of Mass Media." *Yale Rev* (July 50) 675–691. A critical study of the problems and ills of mass media, including recommendations on bringing better films to the screen.

Powdermaker, Hortense. "Celluloid Civilization." *Sat Rev* (14 Oct 50) 9–10. How the big business of movie making smothers ideas and creativity.

Rorty, J. "Paradise Enslaved." *Commonweal* 53 (1 Dec 50) 191–192. Attack on Hollywood's love of the dollar rather than art.

Feldman, Joseph and Harry. "Snobbism and Foreign Films." *FIR* 2 (Apr 51) 18–22. The tendency of some critics and reviewers to emphasize the virtues of foreign pictures and the faults of American ones.

Mayer, Arthur L. "Myths and Movies." *Harper's* 202 (June 51) 71–77. A defense of Hollywood and its efforts to reach a varied audience.

Schary, Dore. "Better Than Ever." *Commonweal* 57 (19 Dec 52) 279–280. The limited amount of superior talent is what limits the movies, plus the insecurity of the times.

Mayer, Arthur. "Hollywood Verdict: Gilt But Not Guilty." *Sat Rev* 36 (31 Oct 53) 11–12+. In a time of new techniques a dissenting note on quality.

Bankhead, Tallulah. "Not Three-D, But No-T." *NYTM* (31 Jan 54) 14+. Actress argues that a return to the greatness of the silent era ("no-talking") would solve Hollywood's current woes. Discussion (14 Feb 54) 4.

Lolos, Kimon. "Cinematic Xenophilia." *FIR* 8 (Jan 57) 8–11. A protest against the unfounded opinions that European films are intellectually, politically, and philosophically superior to American films; that American films do not contain realism or naturalism.

Brustein, Robert. "The New Hollywood: Myth and Anti-Myth." *FQ* 12 (No. 3, Spring 59) 23–31. Belated discovery of realism is more like Zola's surfaces, suitable for immature audiences; *Marty, Baby Doll, A Hatful of Rain,* and *The Goddess* merely represent newcomers from Broadway and TV, "swapping their own conventions for the conventions of the romantic film."

Fadiman, William. "In This Corner—Hollywood." *Sat Rev* (19 Dec 59) 9–11+. Factors which hinder the production of higher-quality films; suggestions for getting around these obstacles. Part of *Saturday Review* report "The New Frankness in Films."

Champion, John. "The Headline Hunters."

JSPG (Sep 60) 21–22. Attacks criticisms of Hollywood as anti-intellectual; says the function of the entertainment business is to entertain.

Knight, Arthur. "Creative Films in America?" *Sat Rev* 43 (24 Dec 60) 50–51.

Roemer, M. A. "New Wave and the Old Rock." *Reporter* 25 (26 Oct 61) 45–46. Criticism of American studios for refusing to change their styles.

Belson, Walter W. "No Sad Songs for Hollywood." *JSPG* (Mar 62) 31–32. Hollywood's image is in fine shape.

Boyd, Malcolm. "Images, Fury, and Sound." *JSPG* (Mar 62) 17–18+. Hollywood's image of vulgarity has got to go if people are to understand "that the industry . . . is now taking film-making very, very seriously."

Coe, Richard L. "Hollywood's Many Images and Audiences." *JSPG* (Mar 62) 11–13. Since there are many kinds of audiences there are many kinds of films.

Eden-Green, Alan. "Hollywood's Image in Britain." *JSPG* (Mar 62) 29–30. Advises "less conformity," more willingness to make an original contribution, instead of present image of mere competence.

Golden, L. L. L. "The Answer Is Quality." *JSPG* (Mar 62) 25–27. Better films are the best public relations for Hollywood.

Kennedy, Bishop Gerald. "The Hollywood Image." *JSPG* (Mar 62) 33–35. "Ignoring moral standards in any profession or business will ruin it ultimately."

Lee, Charles. "A Professor Looks at Hollywood." *JSPG* (Mar 62) 19–21. The movies should attract more young people and others who don't come now.

Kamins, Bernard. "The Semantics of Public Relations." *JSPG* (June 62) 19–20. Hollywood has various publics and it must decide what image it wants to convey.

MacCann, Richard Dyer. "Know Thyself, Get to Know the People." *JSPG* (June 62) 11–12. Not short-term publicity goals, but long-term self-respect will lead to a better "image" of Hollywood, and after that the need is to get acquainted with present-day Americans.

Reagan, Ronald. "Here We Go Again!" *JSPG* (June 62) 3–4+. Hollywood has "never tried to research" what public objects to.

Rivkin, Allen. "What Happened to the Firemen?" *JSPG* (June 62) 5–8. Motion Picture Industry Council used to "put out fires" of criticism of Hollywood; response to earlier critical articles.

Youngstein, Max E. "The View from a Hollywood Window." *JSPG* (June 62) 9–10. Responses to *Journal of the Screen Producers Guild* articles in previous issue; defense of movie industry.

"Trumpets and Drums." *Th Arts* 46 (July 62) 5. On the current state of Hollywood.

Sahl, Mort. "It Isn't Even Evil." *Look* 26 (25 Sep 62) 56. Humorist's view of Hollywood, including some comments on the cautious dependence on violence.

De Sica, Vittorio. "What's Right with Hollywood." *F&F* 10 (No. 2, Nov 63) 47. Praise for Hollywood's recent turn toward "serious" themes in films.

Johnson, William. "Hollywood 1965." *FQ* 19 (No. 1, Fall 65) 39–51. Recent Hollywood films may seem bolder and more controversial but upon close scrutiny are still "contrived hokum"; *The Pawnbroker, Lord Jim, Ship of Fools,* and *The Collector* are cited.

Farber, Stephen. "New American Gothic." *FQ* 20 (No. 1, Fall 66) 22–27. A "desperately bizarre tone" is being added, perhaps since *The Manchurian Candidate* and surprisingly in *Inside Daisy Clover.*

Kael, Pauline. "Creative Business." *New Rep* 155 (8 Oct 66) 32–35. Producers nowadays don't even pretend they are merely making bad movies until they have a chance to make a good one; they openly worship success; one of them even offered Kael a chance to write a script.

3b(4). SATIRICAL VIEWS

Blakeston, Oswell. "Super Film." *Close Up* 6 (No. 3, 1930) 210–213. Humorous notes on what constitutes good and bad in a film.

Castle, Hugh. "Geometric Criticism." *Close Up* 6 (No. 5, 1930) 352–358. Sarcastic comments on the state of film criticism.

Knox, E. V. "Cinema English." *Living Age* 338 (1 Apr 30) 187–189. Editor of *Punch* gives humorous account of American slang sound.

"Russia in American Films." *Living Age* 343 (Sep 32) 91–92. Tongue-in-cheek article of wrongful portrayal of prerevolutionary Russia.

"Save the Grown-ups!" *Nation* 138 (28 Mar 34). See *7c.*

Brande, Dorothea. "A Letter on the Movies." *Am Rev* 3 (May 34) 148–160. Tongue-in-cheek look at recent movie fare.

Dyer, Ernest. "Cinema Pests." *S&S* 6 (No. 24, Winter 37–38) 192–193. The plight of the film viewer: a humorous view of stupid exhibition practices, hostile and indifferent audiences, etc.

Kauffman, G. A. "Einstein in Hollywood." *Nation* 147 (6 Aug 38) 128–129. A humorous condemnation of producers and writers who try to work messages into entertainment —the theory of relativity, for instance.

Dick, William E. "Film Clichés." *S&S* 7 (No. 28, Winter 38–39) 172–173.

Catling, Darrel. "The Lighter Side." *S&S* 9 (No. 36, Winter 40–41) 63–64. Humorous

comments on some of the film books published between 1912 and 1914.

Crowther, Bosley. "Possible Formula for a Screen Hit." *NYTM* (22 Mar 42) 12–13. Crowther's prescription based on ten notable money-makers (*Gone with the Wind, Philadelphia Story,* others).

Cross, Elizabeth. "Film Commentary." *S&S* 13 (No. 49, May 44) 7–8. A fictional account of comments that film viewers might make about films they have seen.

Paul, E. "Musical and Low." *Atlantic* 176 (July 45). See *4k(6).*

Kaufman, George S. "Notes for a Film Biography." *New Yorker* 21 (11 Aug 45). See *4k(7).*

Farber, Manny. "Postwar Movies." *New Rep* 113 (20 Aug 45) 223–224. A satire on the movies' future, with predictions of the effects of television.

Kahn, G. "And Selected Short Subjects." *Atlantic* 177 (Feb 46). See *4a(5).*

Harari, Robert. "Book Review—*Hollywood Reporter* Style." *Screen Writer* 2 (June 46) 35–36. Credit given to publisher, illustrator, bookbinder, and paper cutter but not to writer.

Hubler, Richard. "The Last Picture." *Screen Writer* 2 (No. 11, Apr 47) 23–28. Parody of picture making as if last film in history were being produced.

Kibbee, Roland. "Stop Me If You Wrote This Before." *Screen Writer* 2 (May 47) 16–22. Satirical survey of cliché plots, lines, and characters in film scripts.

Diamond, I. A. L. "Darling! You Mean . . . ?" *Screen Writer* 3 (Sep 47) 5–9. A survey of the clichés found in different types of films.

Herbert, F. Hugh. "Subject: Bindle Biog." *Screen Writer* 3 (No. 4, Sep 47) 16–23. Parody on story development for epic biography and publicity about it in Hollywood; see postscript (No. 5, Oct 47) 6.

Chandler, David. "The Corporate Author: An Essay in Literary Criticism." *Screen Writer* 3 (Dec 47). See *7a(2).*

Englund, Ken. "Quick! Boil Some Hot Clichés." *Screen Writer* 3 (No. 9, Feb 48) 4–9. "If you don't see many pictures," the executive said, "where do you get your ideas?" Screenwriters should not constantly use such familiar scenes as are listed here.

Herbert, F. Hugh. "Attention: Grievance Committee." *Screen Writer* 3 (Apr 48) 5–10. Fictional story about a writer of third-rate scripts who even has his publicity gag stolen by a high-salaried writer.

Goldschmidt, Eric. "Come and Join Us!" *S&S* 17 (No. 68, Winter 48–49) 190–191. How to become a film highbrow.

Levin, Martin. "Leopold's Irish Rose." *Sat Rev* 33 (11 Mar 50) 48. Humorous article on the purchase of *Ulysses* by a film producer.

Callenbach, Ernest. "Exhortation to the Trade." *Hwd Q* 5 (No. 2, Winter 50) 115–116. The author, who has studied films at the University of Chicago and Paris, writes mild satire on the habits of the film maker, written in the style of Old English.

Mannes, Marya. "Memo to a Hollywood Producer." *Reporter* 12 (21 Apr 55) 45–46. A humorous script suggestion for a picture about a big symphony orchestra.

Jackson, Michael. "Seventh-Reel Stretch." *Atlantic* 198 (Sep 56) 88–89. Essayist suggests when movie sequences are silent or boring Louella Parsons or Hedda Hopper could fill in with gossip background on the sound track, like sports announcers on TV.

Atkinson, Alex. "The Dusenberg Place." *Atlantic* 199 (Mar 57) 91. Forms picture of typical American family from Hollywood's portrayals.

Holland, Norman N. "Good Bad Movie." *Atlantic* 203 (Jan 59) 90–91. A critic's view of "honest trash" such as Tarzan, space, and monster movies.

Nichols, Mike. "Save My Seat." *New Yorker* 37 (18 Nov 61) 57. Satiric synopses from current Italian movies.

"A Primer of Passion." *Show* 2 (Mar 62). *See 4k(8).*

Capp, Al. "The Roman Spring of Al Capp." *F&F* 9 (No. 1, Oct 62) 16–18. Humorous article on people brought to mind by *The Roman Spring of Mrs. Stone,* i.e., Eddie Fisher, Federico Fellini.

Barthelme, Donald. "L'lapse." *New Yorker* 39 (2 Mar 63) 29–31. A scenario proposal for Michelangelo Antonioni.

Purvis, Harry. "Sure Fire Dialogue: II." *FIR* 14 (Aug–Sep 63) 385–388. Satirical self-help article for writers.

Degnan, James P. "Through a Dark, Glassily." *Atlantic* 212 (Sep 63) 102+. Satirical review of Unferth Mygboor (Ingmar Bergman) film, *Virgin Mermaids.*

Meehan, Thomas. "Friday Night and Saturday Night." *New Yorker* 39 (19 Oct 63) 48–49. Selected moments (script) from the "next" relentlessly realistic British motion picture.

Renoir, Jean. "A Modern Parable." *JSPG* (Mar 64) 3–6. "I was just out of college and still believed in classifications and categories," but Marie Louise was more than a prostitute, she was also an artist; a story of wartime in answer to the question: Are films an art or an industry?

Angell, Roger. "More Film Fun." *New Yorker* 40 (26 Sep 64) 42–43. Tentative program notes for another hypothetical week of cinematic entertainment, drawn up after a study of the festival news.

Field, Edward. "Old Movies." *Evergreen Rev* 8 (No. 34, Dec 64) 18–25. A series of poems based on old film characters or genres.

Seaton, George. "(Un) Solicited Advice to a Budding Critic." *JSPG* 7 (No. 2, June 65) 33–37. Hollywood director, tongue in cheek, suggests strategy for "tough, controversial" role; further extended in March 1966 issue.

"Surfside Sex." *Chris Cent* 82 (1 Sep 65) 1079. Script for sequel to *The Sandpiper.*

Comden, Betty. "To Those of You Who Remember Eric Linden in *Are These Our Children?,* I Say: 'Are These Our Parents?' " *Esq* 65 (Jan 66). *See 7b(6).*

Cotler, Gordon. "Little Kwanda Does It Again." *New Yorker* 43 (8 July 67) 26–27. Film making in the Republic of Kwanda—a spoof.

Marx, Groucho. "Groucho Writes." *Take One* 1 (No. 11, 1968). *See 5, Marx Brothers.*

Russell, Robert. "The Next Medium: Superdoc." *Take One* 2 (No. 2, 1968). *See 8c(1).*

Brown, Jeff. "High Art at Pike's Peak." *SEP* 241 (23 Mar 68). *See 3d.*

Riffe, Ernest. "Bergman: Through a Filmmaker Darkly." *Take One* 2 (No. 3, 1969). *See 5, Ingmar Bergman.*

Degnan, John. "A Boy and a Girl." *F Her* 4 (No. 3, Spring 69) 23–25. "Ultimately . . . it defies analysis"—a parody of excessively intellectual film reviews.

Tullitus, F. P. "Ninety-nine Years Is Not Forever." *New Yorker* 46 (19 July 69) 20–21. Supposed story in *Avant-Garde* magazine: Pennebaker is filming a fight between Rip Torn and Norman Mailer.

Davis, Daniel. "On Film." *NYTM* (13 Sep 69) 60+. Quotes about the movies by famous film people.

3c. Extended Analysis of Single Films

Milne, Tom. *"Accident."* *S&S* 36 (Spring 67) 56–59. Structure and mysteries in Joseph Losey's film "in which nothing is signalled, nothing given away."

Williams, David. *"An Actor's Revenge."* *Screen* 11 (2 Nov 70) 3–15. Close analysis of this Japanese film.

Wood, Robin. "Attitudes in *Advise and Con-* sent." *Movie* (No. 4, Nov 62) 14–17. The Otto Preminger film.

Margolis, John P. *"Alice's Restaurant* and the Search for Amazing Grace." *Western Humanities Rev* 24 (1970) 399–406. On the film's view of contemporary life, especially the revival of a feeling for religion among the young.

Jones, Dorothy B. "War Without Glory." *QFRTV* 8 (No. 3, Spring 54) 273–289. *All Quiet on the Western Front*.

Cutts, John. *"All Quiet on the Western Front." F&F* 9 (No. 7, Apr 63) 55–58. The 1930 Lewis Milestone film.

Roud, Richard. "Anguish: *Alphaville." S&S* 34 (Autumn 65) 164–166. Godard's *Alphaville* is not only "Godard's best film, but one of the most important in recent years"; Godard wanted to call it *Tarzan vs. IBM*.

Manvell, Roger. "Ideas from Britain." *F&F* 1 (No. 7, Apr 55) 11. The tradition of British animated film seen through the first feature cartoon, *Animal Farm*.

Dale, R. C. "Clash of Intelligences: Sound vs. Image in René Clair's *À Nous la Liberté." French Rev* 38 (No. 5, 1965) 637–644. Sound is still subordinated.

Callenbach, Ernest. "Comparative Anatomy of Folk-Myth Films: *Robin Hood* and *Antonio das Mortes." FQ* 23 (No. 2, Winter 69–70). *See 3c, Robin Hood*.

Smith, John M. "Elia Kazan's *The Arrangement." Movie* (No. 18, Winter 70–71) 14–17. An attempt to relate it to the rest of the director's work.

Boultenhouse, Charles. "Stan Brakhage on *The Art of Vision." Kulchur* 5 (No. 18, Summer 65) 16–19. On the film *The Art of Vision*.

Real, Jere. *"Arturo's Island." F Her* 4 (No. 3, Spring 69) 27–32. A reappraisal of the 1962 film by Damiano Damiani.

Manvell, Roger. "Revaluations: *L'Atalante,* 1934." *S&S* 19 (Feb 51) 421–422. The main principle of such realist films as *L'Atalante,* to achieve unity of atmosphere and faithfulness to the kind of life shown, is maintained.

Jacob, Gilles. *"Au Hasard, Balthazar." S&S* 36 (Winter 66–67) 7–9. Robert Bresson's "greatest and most Bressonian" film; references to his other films.

Doniol-Valcroze, Jacques. "The R.H. Factor and the New Cinema." *NY F Bul* 2 (No. 5, 1961) 8–9. A detailed review of Antonioni's *L'Avventura*.

Jarvie, Ian. "Love, Creation, and Destruction." *Motion* (No. 1, Summer 61) 7–10. An analysis of Antonioni's *L'Avventura*.

Aristarco, Guido. "La Notte and L'Avventura." *F Cult* (No. 24, 1962). *See 3c, La Notte*.

Lesser, Simon O. "L'Avventura: A Closer Look." *Yale Rev* 54 (Oct 64) 41–50. A critical study of the film, emphasizing the insights of depth psychology.

Wood, Robin. *"La Baie des Anges." Movie* (No. 14, Autumn 65) 33–35. A detailed analysis of the film by Jacques Demy.

Brown, Kenneth R. "Reality Inside-Out: *The Ballad of Cable Hogue." F Her* 6 (No. 1, Fall 70) 1–6+. Critique of Sam Peckinpah's film.

Cameron, Ian, *et al. "Barabbas:* A Discussion." *Movie* (No. 1, Jan 62) 25–27. Several critics discuss various aspects of the film and its director, Richard Fleischer.

Stein, Elliott. "Buñuel's Golden Bowl." *S&S* 36 (Autumn 67) 172–175. An appraisal of Luis Buñuel's *Belle de Jour,* which the author considers to be a masterpiece; the content of Joseph Kessel's novel from which the film was adapted; comments by other critics.

Durgnat, Raymond, and Robin Wood. *"Belle de Jour." Movie* (No. 15, Spring 68) 27–31. Two critical statements on Buñuel's film.

Oakes, Philip. "A Seat at the Circus." *S&S* 29 (Spring 60) 94–95. *Ben-Hur:* the story, the script, the production, the film; "it encourages no serious criticism."

Weinberg, Herman G. "An Interview with Seymour Stern." *F Cult* (No. 25, 1962) 73–75. Stern dislikes Wyler's *Ben-Hur*.

McKegney, Michael. "Chabrol's Zoo Story." *F Her* 4 (No. 4, Summer 69) 17–26. Critique of *Les Biches*.

Ross, T. J. "Notes on an Early Losey." *F Cult* (No. 40, Spring 66) 35–37. Joseph Losey's 1952 film *The Big Night* examined.

Blades, John. *"The Big Sleep." F Her* 5 (No. 4, Summer 70) 7–15. Reappraisal of Howard Hawks' film.

Brehm, Randi. "Film as Film." *Take One* 1 (No. 10, 1968). *See 1a(3), Billy Liar*.

Potamkin, Harry A. "Reelife." *Close Up* 7 (No. 6, Dec 30) 386–392. Analytical and critical statements on wide-screen format in King Vidor's *Billy the Kid,* and the problems of the short film.

Carter, E. "Cultural History Written with Lightning: The Significance of *The Birth of a Nation." Am Q* 12 (Fall 60) 347–357. Griffith's film seen as classic cinema.

O'Dell, Paul. "The Simplicity of True Greatness: David Wark Griffith and *The Birth of a Nation." Silent Picture* 4 (Autumn 69) 18–20. Emphasis on its innovative techniques.

Harrison, Carey. *"Blow-Up." S&S* 36 (Spring 67) 60–62. The craftsmanship and the appearance-and-reality of Antonioni's film.

Knight, Arthur. *"Blow-Up." F Her* 2 (No. 3, Spring 67) 3–6.

Meeker, Hubert. *"Blow-Up." F Her* 2 (No. 3, Spring 67) 7–15.

Mussman, Toby. *"Blow-Up." Medium* 1 (No. 1, Summer 67) 55–60. Analytic review, more on content than form; parallel between Antonioni and Godard.

Kauffmann, Stanley. "A Year with *Blow-Up:* Some Notes." *Salmagundi* 2 (No. 3, Spring–Summer 68) 67–75. Comments on *Blow-Up*.

Slover, George. "Blow-Up: Medium, Message, Mythos and Make-Believe." *Mass Rev* 9 (Autumn 68) 753–770. An extended gloss on the role of photography in Antonioni's film.

Golaman, Annie. "On *Blow-Up*." *Triquarterly* (No. 11, Winter 68) 62–67. On the powerlessness of the photographer in the dissolving world of the film.

Ferández, Henry. *"Blow-Up."* *F Her* 4 (No. 2, Winter 68–69) 26–32. From Cortázar to Antonioni: study of an adaptation.

Wagner, Geoffrey. *"The Blue Angel:* A Reconsideration." *QFRTV* 6 (No. 1, Fall 51) 48–53. English scholar synopsizes Sternberg's film and discusses the symbolism employed.

Wagner, Geoffrey. "Revaluation: *The Blue Angel.*" *S&S* 21 (Aug–Sep 51) 42–44. "In *The Blue Angel,* in the climate of Berlin at the end of the twenties, Sternberg created Dietrich's first and last real role."

Detweiler, Robert. "The Moral Failure of *Bob and Carol and Ted and Alice.*" *J Pop Cult* 4 (No. 1, Summer 70) 292–298.

Hildebrand, H. P. "We Rob Banks." *Mental Health* 26 (1967) 15–17. Psychoanalytic study of *Bonnie and Clyde.*

Glushanok, Paul. *"Bonnie and Clyde."* *Cinéaste* 1 (No. 2, Fall 67) 14–17. Thematic interpretation of Penn's work.

Geduld, Carolyn. *"Bonnie and Clyde:* Society vs. the Clan." *F Her* 3 (No. 2, Winter 67–68) 1–6.

Macklin, F. A. *"Bonnie and Clyde:* Beyond Violence to Tragedy." *F Her* 3 (No. 2, Winter 67–68) 7–19.

Free, William J. "Aesthetic and Moral Value in *Bonnie and Clyde.*" *QJ Speech* 54 (No. 3, 1968) 220–225. The film is essentially moral but empathy is gained through aesthetic means.

Brode, Douglas. "Reflections on the Tradition of the Movie Western." *Cinéaste* 2 (No. 2, Fall 68) 2–6. Reconsideration of *Bonnie and Clyde* as an outgrowth of the American Western tradition; criticism of Bosley Crowther's view of this film.

Cook, Jim. *"Bonnie and Clyde."* *Screen* 10 (Nos. 4–5, July–Oct 69) 101–114.

William, F. D. "The Morality of *Bonnie and Clyde.*" *J Pop Cult* 4 (No. 1, Summer 70) 299–307. The film exhibits a situational social ethic.

Sarris, Andrew. *"Boudu Saved from Drowning."* *CdC in Eng* (No. 9, Mar 67) 53. Jean Renoir's 1935 film.

Fritscher, John J. "A Look at Derivation Plagiarism in Americanné Aesthetics: But I Didn't Think *Boys in the Band* Was About Incest, for Gosh Sakes!" *J Pop Cult* 3 (No. 4, Spring 70) 833–840. Cultural forefathers of this film.

Pechter, Wm. S. "=Time^2." *Contact* 3 (No. 2, June 62) 74–81. Extended review of *Breathless.*

Ashmore, Jerome. *"The Cabinet of Dr. Caligari* as Fine Art." *College Art J* 9 (No. 4, Summer 50) 412–418.

Pegge, C. Denis. *"Caligari:* Its Innovations in Editing." *QFRTV* 11 (No. 2, Winter 56). See 2f, *The Cabinet of Dr. Caligari.*

Shivas, Mark, and Ian Cameron. "Two Views of Jean Renoir's *Le Caporal Epinglé.*" *Movie* (No. 4, Nov 62) 10–12. See also *The Elusive Corporal* below.

Geist, Kenneth. *"Carrie."* *F Com* 6 (No. 3, Fall 70) 26–27. Retrospective study of the William Wyler film.

Craddock, John. *"The Charge of the Light Brigade:* In Perspective." *F Soc Rev* 4 (No. 7, 1969) 14–34. Tony Richardson's film.

Houston, Penelope. "Ray's *Charulata.*" *S&S* 35 (Winter 65–66) 31–33. It brings together the two characters who have most persistently appeared in his films: the eternal student and the New Woman: "Neither of them is, in Western terms, quite of the present day."

Gough-Yates, Kevin. *"The Chase."* *Screen* 10 (Nos. 4–5, July–Oct 69) 88–100. Film lecturer at Hornsey College of Art analyzes characters in Arthur Penn's films.

Ehrenstein, David. "Room Service (*The Chelsea Girls*)." *F Cult* (No. 42, Fall 66) 8–9. Description of the Warhol film.

Sarris, Andrew. "The Sub-New York Sensibility." *CdC in Eng* (No. 10, May 67) 43–45. Reconsideration of Warhol's *The Chelsea Girls.*

Gavronsky, Serge. "Warhol's Underground." *CdC in Eng* (No. 10, May 67) 46–49. Critique of *The Chelsea Girls* in the context of Warhol's cinematic world.

Mussman, Toby. *"The Chelsea Girls."* *Medium* 1 (No. 1, Summer 67) 9–18.

Crawford, Pamela. "Andy Warhol's *Chelsea Girls.*" *Cinéaste* 1 (No. 3, Winter 67–68) 20–21. A thematic consideration of *Chelsea Girls* as a mirror of our times and of middle-class mores.

Hedges, William L. "Classics Revisited: Reaching for the Moon." *FQ* 12 (No. 4, Summer 59) 26–34. Scene-by-scene analysis of Carné's *Children of Paradise* in terms of motive and symbolic content.

McBride, Joseph. "Welles' *Chimes at Midnight.*" *FQ* 23 (No. 1, Fall 69) 11–20. Analysis of the composite story of Falstaff in the light of Orson Welles' other Shakespearean films.

Simon, John. "Bull in the China Shop: Godard's *La Chinoise.*" *F Her* 3 (No. 3, Spring 68) 35–47. Critique of film: "mitigated trash"; "childishness is all he has got"; "Godard is insignificant as an artist, but highly significant as a disease."

Roud, Richard. "Minimal Cinema: *Chronicle of Anna Magdalena Bach.*" *S&S* 37 (Summer 68) 134–135. Jean-Marie Straub has attempted to make a film about music completely free of all music-film conventions, and in which all movement is held to a minimum.

Bordwell, David. *"The Circus."* F Com 6 (No. 3, Fall 70) 40–41. Retrospective study of the Chaplin film.

Farber, Manny. "Movies Aren't Movies Any More." *Commentary* 13 (June 52). *See 3b(2).* About *Citizen Kane.*

Sarris, Andrew. *"Citizen Kane:* The American Baroque." *F Cult* 2 (No. 9, 1956) 14–16. "An intense vision of American life, distorting and amplifying its materialistic elements at the expense of human potentialities."

Cutts, John. *"Citizen Kane."* F&F 10 (No. 3, Dec 63) 15–19. One of a series of retrospective studies.

McBride, Joseph. *"Citizen Kane."* F Her 4 (No. 1, Fall 68) 7–18. A critical reassessment of Orson Welles' film.

Shivas, Mark. *"Cléo de 5 à 7* and Agnès Varda." *Movie* (No. 3, Oct 62) 32–35. Critical comments and an interview with its director.

Longstreet, Stephen. "Setting Back *The Clock."* *Screen Writer* 1 (Aug 45) 9–13. Criticism of the "set-decorating orgy that resulted" when Vincente Minnelli directed the Paul Gallico story from a screenplay by Robert Nathan and Joseph Schrank.

Mellen, Joan. "Artur London and Costa-Gavras: The Politics of *The Confession."* *Cinéaste* 4 (No. 3, Winter 70–71) 25–32. An analysis of the Greek director's film, based on London's memoir.

Stanbrook, Alan. *"The Covered Wagon."* F&F 6 (No. 8, May 60) 12–14+.

Perry, John. *"The Covered Wagon."* F Her 4 (No. 3, Spring 69) 17–22. James Cruze's film, made in 1923.

Scott, Adrian. "Some of My Worst Friends." *Screen Writer* 3 (Oct 47) 1–6. The producer of *Crossfire* answers charges that it gives a false picture of anti-Semitism; comments by his fellow professional film makers.

McVay, Douglas. *"Crossways."* F&F 6 (No. 9, June 60) 10–12+. Analysis of the 1928 Japanese film.

Bland, Edward. "On *The Cry of Jazz."* F Cult (No. 21, 1960) 28–32. Analysis of *The Cry of Jazz* by its director from the standpoint of its philosophical and aesthetic bases; reactions to it.

Tarratt, Margaret. *"The Damned:* Visconti, Wagner, and the 'Reinvention of Reality.'" *Screen* 11 (No. 3, Summer 70) 44–56. Analysis of the Visconti film.

Fischer, Jack. "Visconti's *The Damned:* Words, Sights, Echoes." *Contempora* 1 (No. 4, Oct–Nov 70) 2–11. Color and narrative; literary sources.

Byron, Stuart. *"Darling Lili."* On Film (1970) 30–34. Analysis of the Blake Edwards film.

Dworkin, Martin. *"The Desperate Hours* and the Violent Screen." *Shenandoah* 11 (No. 2, 1960) 39–48.

Weales, Gerald. "The Police Revolver as *Deus ex Machina."* QFRTV 7 (No. 2, Winter 52) 203–209. English professor at Georgia Institute of Technology examines Wyler's *Detective Story* as to its psychological, philosophical, and sociological implications.

Milne, Tom. "The Two Chambermaids." *S&S* 33 (Autumn 64) 174–178. Comparison of the style and technique of Luis Buñuel's *Le Journal d'une femme de chambre* and Jean Renoir's *Diary of a Chambermaid,* both adapted from Mirbeau's 1900 novel; "Diary becomes one of the normally gentle Renoir's most violent films; while the normally savage Buñuel scales down to meet Renoir in reticence."

Durgnat, Raymond. *"Diary of a Country Priest."* F&F 13 (No. 3, Dec 66) 28–32. Study of the 1950 Bresson film.

Stanbrook, Alan. *"Don Q—Son of Zorro."* F&F 7 (No. 5, Feb 61) 17–19+. Analysis of Donald Crisp's 1925 production.

Shklovsky, Viktor. "The Magnificent Irony of the Don." *F&F* 4 (No. 12, Sep 58) 8. Analysis of Grigory Kozintsev film *Don Quixote* by Russian critic.

Stanbrook, Alan. *"Die Dreigroschenoper."* F&F 7 (No. 7, Apr 61) 15–17+. Analysis of G. W. Pabst's 1931 production.

Connolly, Ray. "Eden Revisited." *Motion* (No. 2, Winter 61–62) 34–35. A reassessment of *East of Eden.*

Bean, Robin. *"East of Eden."* F&F 10 (No. 8, May 64) 36–41. Study of the 1954 film directed by Elia Kazan.

Macklin, F. Anthony. *"Easy Rider:* The Initiation of Dennis Hopper." *F Her* 5 (No. 1, Fall 69) 1–12.

Warshow, Paul. *"Easy Rider."* S&S 39 (Winter 69–70) 36–38. An appraisal of its "quality of truthfulness," which the author sees as "a small triumph of style."

Sullivan, Mary Rose. *"Easy Rider:* Critique of the New Hedonism?" *Western Humanities Rev* 24 (1970) 179–187.

Sullivan, Thomas R. *"Easy Rider:* Comic Epic Poem in Film." *J Pop Cult* 3 (No. 4, Spring 70) 843–850.

Holland, Norman. "Not Having Antonioni." *Hudson Rev* 16 (No. 1, Spring 63) 89–95. In *Eclipse* the director has kept his audience from being able to respond.

Perry, Ted. "A Contextual Analysis of M. Antonioni's Film *L'Eclisse."* Speech Monographs 37 (June 70) 79–100. Visual motifs.

Ehrenstein, David. "Notes on *El Dorado."* Medium 1 (No. 2, Winter 67–68) 15–19. A contrast with *Rio Bravo.*

Bluestone, George. "Adaptation or Evasion: *Elmer Gantry."* FQ 14 (No. 3, Spring 61) 15–19. How the conventions of Hollywood have changed the vision of Lewis' work; the original novel compared to Richard Brooks' film version.

Greenspun, Roger. "Individual Combat." *Moviegoer* (No. 2, Summer–Autumn 64) 11–24. Renoir's *The Elusive Corporal*. See also *Le Caporal Epinglé* above.

Oddie, Alan. "*Elvira Madigan—More Than Beauty*." *F Her* 4 (No. 1, Fall 68) 29–35. Critique of the symbolism in the film.

Schwartz, Allen K. "The Impressionism of *Elvira Madigan*." *CJ* 8 (No. 2, Spring 69) 25–31. Close analysis of the photographic aspects of Swedish director Bo Widerberg's film.

Battcock, Gregory. "Notes on *Empire*: A Film by Andy Warhol." *F Cult* (No. 40, Spring 66) 39–40.

McArthur, Colin. "*Everything for Sale*." *S&S* 38 (Summer 69) 139–141. A critical assessment of Andrzej Wadja's memorial in this film to his leading actor, Zbigniew Cybulski; the author sees it as a departure from his former themes and tortured heroes.

Purdy, Strother. "Existential Surrealism: The Neglected Example of Buñuel's *The Exterminating Angel*." *F Her* 3 (No. 4, Summer 68) 28–34. Critique of Buñuel's 1962 film.

Cameron, Ian. "*Eyes Without a Face*." *Film* (No. 26, Nov–Dec 60) 22–25. Georges Franju's film and how it relates to the rest of his work.

Bluestone, George. "The Fire and the Future." *FQ* 20 (No. 4, Summer 67) 3–10. Analysis of Truffaut's film *Fahrenheit 451*.

Lyle, John. "The Inner Space Project." *Afterimage* (No. 1, Apr 70) 8 pages. Analysis of the film *The Fall* by Peter Whitehead.

Boswell, Peyton. "Wonder of *Fantasia*." *Art Dig* 15 (1 Dec 40) 3.

Genauer, Emily, and Dorothy Thompson. "Art of *Fantasia*." *Art Dig* 15 (1 Dec 40) 10–11. A masterful combination of the visual and aural arts according to Metropolitan art critic; negative comments by Dorothy Thompson, stating that the film was obviously a portrayal of Nazism. See also letter to editor (15 Dec 40) 11.

Winkler, Richard. "*Far from Vietnam*." *Movie* (No. 15, Spring 68) 34–36. Film made by several directors, including Lelouch, Klein, Ivens, Resnais, Godard, and Marker.

French, Philip. "*Une Femme mariée*." *Movie* (No. 13, Summer 65) 2–5. Godard's film and comments on his work.

Hampton, C. C., Jr. "Samuel Beckett's *Film*." *Mod Drama* 11 (Dec 68) 299–305. A philosophical analysis.

Miller, Daniel. "*Fires Were Started*." *S&S* 38 (Spring 69) 100–104. Analysis of Humphrey Jennings' 1943 film about the Auxiliary Fire Service in London in 1941; the distinctive qualities of Jennings' style.

Macklin, Anthony. "*Five Easy Pieces*: An Enigma." *F Her* 6 (No. 2, Winter 70–71) 1–10. Critique of Robert Rafelson's film.

Siegel, Joel. "*Five Easy Pieces*: A Fraud." *F Her* 6 (No. 2, Winter 70–71) 11–13.

Kelman, Ken. "Smith Myth." *F Cult* (No. 29, 1963) 4–6. Praise for Jack Smith's *Flaming Creatures*.

Sontag, Susan. "Feast for Open Eyes." *Nation* 198 (13 Apr 64) 374–376. Discussion 198 (27 Apr 64) inside cover. A defense of the sexuality portrayed in Jack Smith's controversial *Flaming Creatures*.

Steele, Robert. "Arne Sucksdorff's *The Flute and the Arrow*." *J Soc Cin* 1 (1961) 40–54.

"Two Sidney Poitier Films." *F Com* 5 (No. 4, Winter 69). *For Love of Ivy*. See also *Guess Who's Coming to Dinner?* below.

Jensen, Paul. "*Frankenstein*." *F Com* 6 (No. 3, Fall 70) 42–45. Retrospective study of James Whale film.

Strick, Philip. "*The General*." *F&F* 7 (No. 12, Sep 61) 14–16+. Analysis of the 1926 Keaton film.

Mast, Gerald. "*The Gold Rush* and *The General*." *CJ* 9 (No. 9, Spring 70). See *The Gold Rush* below.

Stein, Elliott. "*Gertrud*." *S&S* 34 (Spring 65) 56–58. A reaction to the French public and critical response to Carl Dreyer's *Gertrud*, which was given its world premiere in December 1964 in Paris; writer considers it "Dreyer's finest, most perfect work."

Skoller, Don. "To Rescue *Gertrude*." *F Com* 4 (No. 1, Fall 66) 70–76. Response to Stanley Kauffmann review and to other reactions against the Dreyer film.

Shivas, Mark. "Blondes." *Movie* (No. 5, Dec 62) 23–24. *Gentlemen Prefer Blondes* (1953) as part of Howard Hawks' work.

Phillips, James E., and Thalia Selz. "*The Golden Coach*: Jean Renoir's Latest." *QFRTV* 9 (No. 1, Fall 54) 15–27. UCLA English professor examines the techniques of *commedia dell'arte*; Selz, former film teacher at Chicago Institute of Design, notes symbolism and "fairy tale" atmosphere.

Callenbach, Ernest. "Classics Revisited: *The Gold Rush*." *FQ* 13 (No. 1, Fall 59) 31–37. Synopsis and evaluation; the world as a series of traps and dangers; the problem of sentimentality in the Chaplin character.

Mast, Gerald. "*The Gold Rush* and *The General*." *CJ* 9 (No. 2, Spring 70) 24–30. The differences between the two films; Chaplin's is a comedy of character, Keaton's, a comedy of narrative; extract from author's forthcoming book *A Short History of the Movies* (Pegasus, 1971).

Grossinger, Richard. "Review of a Movie Called *The Graduate*." *Caterpillar* (No. 6, Jan 69) 137–154.

Reck, T. S. "*Graduate* Reclassified." *Commonweal* 90 (2 May 69) 202–204. Analysis of symbols in *The Graduate*, some of them proposed in student papers at Chico State College in California.

Seydor, Paul. "*The Graduate* Flunks Out." *F Soc Rev* 5 (No. 5, Jan 70) 36–44. A reevaluation of the Nichols film; its failings as social document.

Kerans, James. "Classics Revisited: *La Grande Illusion*." *FQ* 14 (No. 2, Winter 60) 10–17. Renoir's antiwar film.

Goodman, Paul. "A Reply." *Moviegoer* (No. 1, Winter 64) 55–62. Reprint of an earlier article by Goodman on *The Great Dictator*; a more recent statement about why he no longer goes to many movies.

Daney, Serge. "Strange Bodies." *CdC in Eng* (No. 3, 1966) 26–27. A critique of Blake Edwards' *The Great Race*.

Fulton, A. R. "Stroheim's *Greed*." *FIR* 6 (June–July 55) 263–268. A short analytical review of Erich von Stroheim's adaptation of the Frank Norris novel *McTeague*, suggesting he did not do it "just as it was originally written."

Newhall, Beaumont. "Miracle of Observation." *Image* 5 (No. 4, Apr 56) 88–91. Commentary on von Stroheim's *Greed*.

Faia, M. A. "Straight with No Cop-Outs." *Social Problems* 16 (Spring 69) 525–527. *Guess Who's Coming to Dinner?* is permeated with the kinds of racist assumptions which are causal factors of America's 300-year interracial nightmare.

"Two Sidney Poitier Films." *F Com* 5 (No. 4, Winter 69) 26–32. Maxine Hall Elliston, film critic of Chicago Organization of Black American Culture, gives her impressions of *Guess Who's Coming to Dinner?* and *For Love of Ivy*; brief biography of Poitier.

Marcus, Robert D. "Moviegoing and American Culture." *J Pop Cult* 3 (No. 4, Spring 70) 755–766. An analysis of the interaction of outward and covert cultural patterns in *A Guide for the Married Man*.

Manvell, Roger. "The Film of *Hamlet*." *Penguin F Rev* 8 (Jan 49) 16–24. Olivier's production.

Tyler, Parker. "*Hamlet* and Documentary." *Kenyon Rev* 11 (No. 3, 1949) 527–532. Documentary approach of Olivier's *Hamlet* displaces view of Hamlet as a suffering individual.

Brook, Peter. "Finding Shakespeare on Film." *TDR* 11 (Fall 66) 117–121. Discussion of style and structure in Kozintsev's *Hamlet* (1964); interview by Geoffrey Reeves.

Perkins, V. F. "*Hatari!*" *Movie* (No. 5, Dec 62) 28–30. Howard Hawks' film.

Manvell, Roger. "Revaluations: *Hearts of the World*, 1918." *S&S* 19 (May 50) 130–132. The D. W. Griffith film.

Koszarski, Richard. "*Hello, Sister*." *S&S* 39 (Autumn 70) 208–210. History of Erich von Stroheim's last film and his only sound picture, *Walking Down Broadway*, which surfaced in 1933 under the title *Hello, Sister*; was reshooting by Al Werker confined to the ending?

O'Laoghaire, Liam. "*Herr Arne's Treasure*." *F&F* 6 (No. 11, Aug 60) 12–14+. Mauritz Stiller's 1919 production.

Burton, Howard A. "*High Noon*: Everyman Rides Again." *QFRTV* 8 (No. 1, Fall 53) 80–86. English instructor at Purdue compares the film with the medieval morality play.

Luchting, W. A. "*Hiroshima, Mon Amour*, Time, and Proust." *J Aesthetics and Art Criticism* 21 (No. 3, Spring 63) 299–313.

Bateson, Gregory. "Cultural and Thematic Analysis of Fictional Films." *Transactions of the NY Acad of Sci* (Ser. 2) 5 (No. 4, 1943) 72–78. An official of Museum of Modern Art film library reports on Nazi film, *Hitler-junge Quex*, and its treatment of family and party loyalties.

Macbean, James Roy. "*La Hora de los Hornos*." *FQ* 24 (No. 1, Fall 70) 31–37. Analysis of Fernando Solanas' film *The Hour of the Furnaces*, which supports Peronism in Argentina.

Wood, Robin. "*Hour of the Wolf*." *Movie* (No. 16, Winter 68–69) 9–12. Ingmar Bergman's film.

Kael, Pauline. "*Hud*, Deep in the Divided Heart of Hollywood." *FQ* 17 (No. 4, Summer 64) 15–23. Lengthy study of the "schizoid" tendencies in the film; how an indictment of materialism turned into a celebration of it.

Davis, Peter. "A Hero of Our Times." *S&S* 30 (Winter 60–61) 39–40. Author criticizes fiction films that masquerade as documentaries, particularly *I Aim at the Stars*, which makes the Nazi Wernher von Braun seem like a friendly neighbor.

Dempsey, Michael. "*If . . .*" *F Her* 5 (No. 1, Fall 69) 13–20. Confusions in Lindsay Anderson's film and its reviews.

McBride, Joseph. "Welles' *Immortal Story*." *S&S* 39 (Autumn 70) 194–195. Review of Orson Welles' first film in color since *It's All True*, relating this shorter film to the rest of Welles' work.

Smith, John Harrington. "Oscar Wilde's Earnest in Film." *QFRTV* 8 (No. 1, Fall 53). *See 3f(1), The Importance of Being Earnest.*

Kozloff, Max. "*In Cold Blood*." *S&S* 37 (Summer 68). *See 7b(4).*

Stanbrook, Alan. "*The Informer*." *F&F* 6 (No. 10, July 60) 10–12+. John Ford's 1935 film.

Joad, C. E. M. "*Intolerance*." *New S&N* 37 (19 Feb 49) 176–177. D. W. Griffith's film illustrates that film can be used to convey lessons.

Trewin, J. C. "Rush Hour in Babylon." *S&S*

127

18 (Spring 49) 37–38. Rediscovering D. W. Griffith's *Intolerance*.

Jones, Dorothy B. "William Faulkner: Novel into Film." *QFRTV* 8 (No. 1, Fall 53) 51–71. History of production of *Intruder in the Dust;* analysis of content; comparison with original Faulkner story.

Minchinton, John. "Home-Spun Superman." *F&F* 1 (No. 3, Dec 54) 13. *The Iron Mask* (Douglas Fairbanks, Sr.) and its place in film history.

Fradier, George. "Dialogue on the film *The Island*." *UNESCO Courier* 16 (Apr 63) 8–13. A Japanese student and a European discuss this Japanese film.

Shadoian, Jack. "Stuart Heisler's *Island of Desire*." *F Her* 5 (No. 4, Summer 70) 16–20. An exercise in the legitimate extraction of pleasure.

Manvell, Roger. "Revaluations: *The Italian Straw Hat*." *S&S* 19 (July 50) 219–227. Manvell feels that, primarily, it is the characters which give this René Clair film the right to be listed among the classics.

Maddow, Ben. "Eisenstein and the Historical Film." *Hwd Q* 1 (No. 1, Oct 45) 26–30. Strengths and weaknesses of *Ivan the Terrible,* Part One.

Garga, B. D. "*Ivan the Terrible,* Part Two." *S&S* 27 (Spring 58) 184–189. Film worker from India gets to see in Moscow the heretofore banned film; description of scenes; Eisenstein's sketches.

Bady, Douglas. "In Defense of Formalism." *NY F Bul* 1 (No. 1, 1960) 4–7. A defense of "formalistic" cinema and its relation to theatre and myth, through an examination of *Ivan the Terrible*.

Gerstein, Evelyn. "*Ivan the Terrible:* A Peak in Darien." *F Com* 5 (No. 1, Fall 68) 52–57. "What a film this is, as pregnant with meanings as the brilliantly painted Russian eggs with their myriads of lesser eggs within."

Armes, Roy. "Resnais and Reality." *F&F* 16 (No. 8, May 70) 12–14. On *Je T'Aime, Je T'Aime*.

Budgen, Suzanne. "*Je T'Aime, Je T'Aime*." *Screen* 11 (No. 3, Summer 70) 88–95. Analysis of the Resnais film.

Homan, Sidney R. "An Unconscious Pearl Among Conscious Swine." *J Pop Cult* 2 (No. 1, Summer 68) 149–153. An aesthetic question raised by *Jolson Sings Again* (1949).

Strick, Philip. "*Jour de Fête*." *F&F* 8 (No. 8, May 62) 19–20+. The 1947 Tati film.

Cameron, Ian. "*Judex*." *Movie* (No. 14, Autumn 65) 36–38. The Georges Franju version.

Greenspun, Roger. "Elective Affinities: Aspects of *Jules et Jim*." *S&S* 32 (Spring 63) 78–82. The circular and triangular structure of Truffaut's film and the relationships among its characters.

Castello, Giulio Cesare. "*Giulietta degli Spiriti*." *S&S* 35 (Winter 65–66) 18–19. A critical review of Fellini's *Juliet of the Spirits,* which the author discusses as "basically another *8½* . . . a repetition of a whole repertoire of effects.

Williams, Forrest. "Fellini's Voices." *FQ* 21 (No. 3, Spring 68) 21–25. Praise for Fellini's *Juliet of the Spirits* as integration of dialogue and imagery.

Manvell, Roger. "Revaluations: *Kameradschaft* (1931)." *S&S* 19 (Nov 50) 298–299. The film has lost some of its original strength; its special virtue is now seen to lie in the integrity of its artistic values, rather than in the oversimple social philosophy that it represents.

Stanbrook, Alan. "*Kind Hearts and Coronets*." *F&F* 10 (No. 7, Apr 64) 17–21. The 1949 Balcon-Hamer-Guinness film.

Archer, Eugene. "*A King in New York*." *F Cult* 4 (No. 16, 1958) 3–6+. Chaplin's film.

Durgnat, Raymond. "The Apotheosis of Va-Va-Voom." *Motion* (No. 3, Spring 62) 30–34. Defense of Aldrich's *Kiss Me Deadly*.

Brinton, Joseph P., III. "Subjective Camera or Subjective Audience?" *Hwd Q* 2 (No. 4, July 47) 359–366. Film student closely analyzes conceptual faults in *Lady in the Lake,* starring Robert Montgomery but photographed from his point of view.

Stanbrook, Alan. "*The Lady Vanishes*." *F&F* 9 (No. 10, July 63) 43–47. The 1938 Hitchcock film.

Grenier, Cynthia. "Explorations in the Unconscious." *Sat Rev* (23 Dec 61) 37–38. Study of *Last Year at Marienbad* by Alain Resnais. Part of *Saturday Review* report "Film Directors at Work."

Melville, Jean-Pierre, *et al.* "*L'Année Dernière à Marienbad*." *Film* (No. 31, Spring 62) 19–21. Various people, including Alain Resnais, comment on the film *Last Year at Marienbad*.

Nowell-Smith, Geoffrey. "*L'Année Dernière à Marienbad*." *New Left Rev* (Nos. 13–14, Jan–Apr 62) 146–150.

Brunius, Jacques. "Every Year in Marienbad." *S&S* 31 (Summer 62) 122–127. Analysis of Resnais' *Last Year at Marienbad* is usually too literary: "the discipline of uncertainty" in the film's structure is the important thing; the content is the form; it is a "mental continuity."

Oxenhandler, Neal. "*Marienbad* Revisited." *FQ* 17 (No. 1, Fall 63) 30–35. There is no "key" to the film; views by both Robbe-Grillet and Resnais reveal surprising differences in interpretation and concept; if "emotion is the guiding principle," *Last Year at Marienbad* is a failure.

Fadiman, Regina K. "*Imagino Ergo Sum:* A Critical Analysis of *Last Year at Marienbad*."

Point of View: An Occasional Publication of the Writers Guild of America, West 1 (Oct 63) 31–41.

Ashmore, Jerome. "Symbolism in *Marienbad.*" *Univ Rev* 30 (Mar 64) 225–233. Interpretation of symbolic narration in *Last Year at Marienbad* as related to modern existentialism.

Alter, J. "Alain Robbe-Grillet and the Cinematographic Style." *Mod Lang J* 48 (No. 6, Oct 64). *See 3f(2), Last Year at Marienbad.*

Bolas, Terry. "*The Left-Handed Gun* of Arthur Penn." *Screen* 10 (No. 1, Jan–Feb 69) 15–23. The childishness and tragic role of Billy the Kid in the film of this title.

Harcourt-Smith, Simon. "A Strange Suppression." *S&S* 19 (Mar 50) 34–36+. Report on seeing *Letter from an Unknown Woman* in the provinces after distributor failed to open it in London; description and praise.

Ilyina, Lydia. "Reality and Fiction at the Crossroads." *F&F* 7 (No. 6, Mar 61) 5. On the Russian film *The Letter That Was Not Sent.*

Gessner, Robert. "Porter and the Creation of Cinematic Motion." *J Soc Cin* 2 (1962) 1–13. Subtitled "An Analysis of *The Life of an American Fireman.*"

Griffith, Richard. "*The Lights of New York:* A Critique." *J Soc Cin* 1 (1961) 55–65.

Farber, Stephen. "*Lilith.*" *F Com* 6 (No. 3, Fall 70) 51–54. Retrospective study of Robert Rossen film.

Clouzot, Claire. "Sons of Kafka." *S&S* 36 (Winter 66–67) 35–37. Czech film *Little Pearls from the Bottom,* made by six promising directors, including Jirí Menzel, Jan Nemec and Evald Schorm, shows characteristic mix of realism and fantasy.

Taylor, Richard. "*The Living Corpse.*" *Silent Picture* (No. 9, Winter 70–71) 22–25. The film directed by Fyodor Otsep of Tolstoy's play—credits, synopsis, and analysis, with a shot breakdown of the opening sequence.

Manvell, Roger. "Revaluations: *The Lodger,* 1927." *S&S* 19 (Jan 51) 377–378. Silent film was more of a fantasy world and therefore this early Hitchcock film is harder to accept today.

Siegel, Joel E. "*Lola.*" *F Her* 1 (No. 4, Summer 66) 26–32. Jacques Demy's directorial debut.

Joss, Gerald. "*Lola Montes.*" *On Film* (1970) 22–27. Analysis of the Max Ophuls film.

Sarris, Andrew. "Second and Third Thoughts on *Lola Montes.*" *December* 12 (Nos. 1–2, 1970) 122–126. Sarris evokes the movie world of 1955 in which *Lola Montes* first appeared and clarifies his own subsequent praise for the film.

Harcourt, Peter. "I'd Rather Be Like I Am." *S&S* 32 (Winter 62–63) 16–19. *The Loneliness of the Long-Distance Runner,* directed by Tony Richardson from Allan Sillitoe's original story, does not succeed in bringing out its best qualities, especially the language of the main character.

Kael, Pauline. "Throwing the Race." *Moviegoer* (No. 1, Winter 64) 35–39. *The Loneliness of the Long-Distance Runner,* its weakness, yet box-office appeal.

Kaplan, Abraham. "Realism in the Film: A Philosopher's Viewpoint." *QFRTV* 7 (No. 4, Summer 53). *See 3a(2), The Long Voyage Home.*

Robinson, David. "*Look Back in Anger.*" *S&S* 28 (Nos. 3–4, Summer–Autumn 59) 122–125+. Comparison of film (written by Nigel Kneale and directed by Tony Richardson) with the play; extract from script.

Bacon, S. D. "A Student of the Problems of Alcohol and Alcoholism Views the Motion Picture *The Lost Weekend.*" *QJ of Studies on Alcohol* 6 (1945) 402–405.

Stoller, James. "After *The 400 Blows.*" *Moviegoer* (No. 1, Winter 64) 12–18. Truffaut's sketch ("Antoine et Colette") for *Love at Twenty.*

Stephenson, Ralph. "*Louisiana Story.*" *F&F* 8 (No. 3, Dec 61) 20–22+. The 1948 Flaherty film.

Rannit, Aleksis. "Was the Artistic World of Van Gogh a Cataclysm?" *F Cult* 2 (No. 10, 1956) 10–13. A piece critical of the portrayal of the artist in *Lust for Life.*

Koszarski, Richard. "*Mad Love.*" *F Her* 5 (No. 2, Winter 69–70) 24–29. A critique of a long unrecognized and unseen film (1935) by Karl Freund.

Milne, Tom. "Love in Three Dimensions." *S&S* 34 (Spring 65) 71–75. Jean Renoir's *Madame Bovary.*

Carreno, Richard D. "*Made in U.S.A.*—The Cliché of French Anti-Americanism." *Cinéaste* 1 (No. 3, Winter 67–68) 3–4. Negative response to Godard's political film.

Goldwasser, Noe. "*Made in U.S.A.:* The Paper Tiger in Your Tank." *Cinéaste* 1 (No. 4, Spring 68) 16–18. Is the Godard film anti-American or a reflection of America to the world?

Kernan, Margot. "*Made in U.S.A.:* Jean-Luc Godard's Walt Disney Movie." *F Her* 3 (No. 3, Spring 68) 31–34.

Macbean, James Roy. "Politics, Painting, and the Language of Signs in Godard's *Made in U.S.A.*" *FQ* 22 (No. 3, Spring 69) 18–25.

Anderson, Joseph L. "When the Twain Meet: Hollywood's Remake of *The Seven Samurai.*" *FQ* 15 (No. 3, Spring 62). *See 3c, The Magnificent Seven.*

Glushanok, Paul. "*Mahanagar*—Ray on Revolution." *Cinéaste* 2 (No. 2, Fall 67) 20–25. Satyajit Ray's film.

Leahy, James. "*Major Dundee.*" *Movie* (No. 14, Autumn 65) 29–32. The Sam Peckinpah film; the relationship between America and the moral ambiguities in the film.

Eyles, Allen. *"The Maltese Falcon." F&F* 11 (No. 2, Nov 64) 45–50. The 1941 Huston Film.

Sarris, Andrew. "Cactus Rosebud or *The Man Who Shot Liberty Valance." F Cult* (No. 25, 1962) 13–15. John Ford's film.

Vaughan, Dai. *"The Man with a Movie Camera." F&F* 7 (No. 2, Nov 60) 18–20+. Dziga Vertov's 1928 production.

Milne, Tom. "Jean-Luc Godard, *ou La Raison ardente." S&S* 34 (Summer 65) 106–111. The structure and imagery of *Une Femme mariée* (*A Married Woman*).

de Laurot, Edouard L. "All About *Marty." F Cult* 1 (No. 4, 1955) 6–9. Paddy Chayefsky's declared intention: to unveil the "world of the ordinary" and to reach the characters "in an untouched moment of life."

Jensen, Paul. *"Metropolis." F Her* 3 (No. 2, Winter 67–68) 22–28. Fritz Lang's film (1927).

Walker, Michael. *"Mickey One." Screen* 10 (No. 3, May–June 69) 60–71. Personal examination of Arthur Penn's film.

Petrucci, Antonia. "De Sica's New Film." *S&S* 19 (Apr 51) 480–481. *Miracolo a Milano:* "the great formal difficulty of combining fantastic and realistic elements."

Hawkins, Robert F. "De Sica Dissected." *FIR* 2 (May 51) 26–30. How much of *Miracle in Milan* is Zavattini?

Maddison, John. "The Case of De Sica." *S&S* 20 (June 51) 41–42. Some reactions to *Miracle in Milan* at Cannes; a number of critics say it is fraught with fake symbols; Maddison feels any tricks he used, even from Clair or Chaplin, were treated in a personal way.

Grinstein, Alexander. "Miracle of Milan: Some Psychoanalytic Notes on a Movie." *Am Imago* 10 (No. 3, Fall 53) 229–245. A detailed explication of one of De Sica's "subtle" films, *Miracle in Milan.*

Fairservice, Donald. *"The Miracle Worker." Screen* 10 (No. 2, Mar–Apr 69) 69–78. Search for symbols in this "melodrama."

Croce, Arlene. *"The Misfits." S&S* 30 (Summer 61) 142–143. A severely critical article on the film written by Arthur Miller and directed by John Huston.

Rowland, Richard. *"Miss Julie." QFRTV* 6 (No. 4, Summer 52) 414–420. Columbia University English professor describes various technical elements of Alf Sjöberg's film in relation to Strindberg's play, says it is "stamped with the unifying mind of an artist."

Davidman, Joy. "Deaths and a Warning." *New Masses* 47 (18 May 43) 30–31. Attacks critics who attacked *Mission to Moscow,* including Manny Farber and Dorothy Thompson.

Davidman, Joy. "Mission of Sabotage." *New Masses* 47 (25 May 43) 29. Reply to a May 9 letter to *The New York Times* written by John Dewey and Suzanne La Follette attacking *Mission to Moscow.*

Davidman, Joy. "Masquerade." *New Masses* 47 (1 June 43) 29–31. Attacks on *Mission to Moscow* demonstrate the Trotskyite-fascist alliance.

Shumiatski, B. "Charlie Chaplin's New Picture" [tr. from *Pravda*]. *New Masses* 16 (24 Sep 35) 29–30. The head of the Soviet film industry interprets early footage for *Modern Times* as antibourgeois.

Newhouse, Edward. "Charlie's Critics." *Partisan Review* 3 (Apr 36) 25–26. An attack on critics who do not see *Modern Times* as a film of social consciousness.

Zukofsky, Louis. *"Modern Times." Kulchur* 1 (No. 4, Winter 61) 75–82. Chaplin's 1936 comedy.

Houston, Penelope. "Losey's Paper Handkerchief." *S&S* 35 (Summer 66) 142–143. Joseph Losey's *Modesty Blaise* and its "snip-snap technique" of the comic strip.

Ross, T. J. "Pop and Circumstance in *Modesty Blaise." F Her* 2 (No. 4, Summer 67) 3–8.

Durgnat, Raymond. "Symbols and *Modesty Blaise." Cinema* (Cambridge) (No. 1, Dec 68) 2–7. Analysis of Joseph Losey's film.

Belton, John. *"Monkey Business." F Her* 6 (No. 2, Winter 70–71) 19–26. A reappraisal of Howard Hawks' film (1952).

Polonsky, Abraham. *"Odd Man Out* and *Monsieur Verdoux." Hwd Q* 2 (No. 4, July 47). *See 3c, Odd Man Out.*

Bentley, Eric. *"Monsieur Verdoux* as 'Theater.' " *Kenyon Rev* 10 (No. 4, Autumn 48) 705–716. A commentary on Chaplin's film with attention focused on comedy and its varying expressions.

Manvell, Roger. *"Monsieur Verdoux." Penguin F Rev* 7 (Sep 48) 77–82. Analysis of philosophy of the film.

Manvell, Roger. "Revaluations: *Mother,* 1926." *S&S* 19 (Aug 50) 259–261. The Pudovkin film.

Rohdie, Sam. "A Structural Analysis of *Mr. Deeds Goes to Town." Cinema* (Cambridge) (No. 5, Feb 70) 29–30.

Houston, Penelope. "Resnais' *Muriel." S&S* 33 (Winter 63) 34–35. This time people are "seen from the outside" (according to Resnais), but still his theme is "the compelling power and the futility of memory."

Sontag, Susan. "On Godard's *Vivre Sa Vie." Moviegoer* (No. 2, Summer–Autumn 64) 2–10. In the U.S., *My Life to Live.*

Gillett, John. *"The Mysterious X." S&S* 35 (Spring 66) 99. Rediscovery of this Danish film, made in 1913 by Benjamin Christensen.

Eyles, Allen. *"A Night at the Opera." F&F* 11 (No. 5, Feb 65) 16–20. The Marx Brothers' film.

Wood, Robin. *"Night of the Hunter:* Novel into Film." *On Film* (1970) 68–71.

Cutts, John. *"Ninotchka." F&F* 8 (No. 6, Mar 62) 21–23+. The 1939 Lubitsch film.

Guillermo, Gilberto Perez. "Shadow and Substance." *S&S* 36 (Summer 67) 150–153. F. W. Murnau's *Nosferatu* (1922).

Bordwell, David. *"Notorious." F Her* 4 (No. 3, Spring 69) 6–10+. Reassessment of the Hitchcock film (1946).

Aristarco, Guido. *"La Notte* and *L'Avventura." F Cult* (No. 24, 1962) 82–83. Two Antonioni films.

Wolfenstein, M., and Nathan Leites. "The Unconscious Versus the 'Message' in an Anti-Bias Film—Two Social Scientists View *No Way Out." Commentary* 10 (1950) 388–391.

Cameron, Ian. *"Now About These Women." Movie* (No. 13, Summer 65) 6–9. How Bergman's film attempts to isolate critic and public from film maker.

Grigs, Derick, and Guy Coté. "Revaluation: *October*, 1928." *S&S* 21 (Oct–Dec 51) 92–94. The overlapping movement, the kinds of montage, the arrangement and cutting of sequences in Eisenstein's film.

Polonsky, Abraham. *"Odd Man Out* and *Monsieur Verdoux." Hwd Q* 2 (No. 4, July 47) 401–407. Extended comparison of two films of different styles which challenge the authority and habits of modern society.

Pratley, Gerald. "Tyrone Guthrie's First Film." *F&F* 2 (No. 11, Aug 56) 6. *Oedipus Rex.*

Barcia, J. Rubia. "Luis Buñuel's *Los Olvidados." QFRTV* 7 (No. 4, Summer 53). *See 5, Luis Buñuel.*

Anderson, Lindsay. "The Last Sequence of *On the Waterfront." S&S* 24 (Jan–Mar 55) 127–130. The violent conclusion "can only be taken in two ways: as hopelessly, savagely ironic, or as fundamentally contemptuous." Anderson believes it is a bad film and compares its "dishonesty of method" with some of America's great social films, such as *The Grapes of Wrath* and *Force of Evil.*

Hughes, Robert. *"On the Waterfront:* A Defense and Some Letters." *S&S* 24 (Spring 55) 214–216. Mr. Hughes objects to Lindsay Anderson's article attacking the last sequence of the film (see [Jan–Mar 55]).

Cowie, Peter. "The Western . . . and Brando." *Motion* (No. 2, Winter 61–62) 8–11. *One-Eyed Jacks* and its relationship to the conventions of the Western.

Shivas, Mark. "Coming Soon: *Ophelia." Movie* (No. 10, June 63) 14–15. Chabrol's film.

Debrix, Jean R. "Cocteau's *Orpheus* Analyzed." *FIR* 2 (June–July 51) 18–23. Translated by Edith Morgan King. Refreshing magic, but outmoded surrealism.

Durgnat, Raymond. *"Orphée." F&F* 10 (No. 1, Oct 63) 45–48. The 1949 Cocteau film.

Long, Chester Clayton. "Cocteau's *Orphée:* From Myth to Drama to Film." *QJ Speech* 51 (No. 3, Oct 65) 311–325. A study of the transition from one medium to another.

Nelson, Harland S. *"Othello." F Her* 2 (No. 1, Fall 66) 18–22. Critique of Laurence Olivier's film.

Plotkin, Frederick. *"Othello* and Welles: A Fantastic Marriage." *F Her* 4 (No. 4, Summer 69) 9–15. Critique with reference to Welles' other films. See 5 (No. 2, Winter 69–70) 29 for editor's apology stating this article is not original.

Kozloff, Max. *"In Cold Blood." S&S* 37 (Summer 68). *See 7b(4).*

Manvell, Roger. *"Paisan:* How It Struck Our Contemporaries." *Penguin F Rev* 9 (May 49) 53–60. A great film to some; technically poor, hasty, and cynical to others; a note on the amateur actors and simplicity of photography.

Johnson, Ian. *"Paisan." F&F* 12 (No. 5, Feb 66) 36–42. The 1946 Rossellini film.

Johnson, Ian. *"The Crossing of the Rhine." Motion* (No. 2, Winter 61–62) 25–29. *Le Passage du Rhin,* directed by André Cayatte.

Harcourt, Peter. "The Interplay of Forces Large and Small." *Cinema* (Calif) 6 (No. 2, 1970) 32–39. Bergman's *Passion of Anna.*

Klingler, Werner. "Analytical Treatise on the Dreyer Film, *The Passion of Joan of Arc." Experimental Cinema* 1 (No. 1, Feb 30) 7–10.

Manvell, Roger. "Revaluations: *La Passion de Jeanne d'Arc*, 1928." *S&S* 19 (Dec 50) 337–339. It needed sound and, in fact, Dreyer said he wished it were a sound film.

Stanbrook, Alan. *"The Passion of Joan of Arc." F&F* 7 (No. 9, June 61) 11–13+. The 1928 Dreyer film.

Sragow, Michael. *"Patton." FSR* 5 (No. 7, Mar 70) 25–32. Patton's biography; lack of a consistent perspective in the film by Franklin Schaffner.

Steele, Robert. *"Patton." F Her* 5 (No. 4, Summer 70) 21–27.

Lyons, Joseph. *"The Pawnbroker:* Flashback in the Novel and the Film." *Western Humanities Rev* 20 (1966) 243–248. How they differ; reply by Graham Petrie 21 (1967) 165–169 says flashbacks are used for the same purpose; reference also to *Tristram Shandy.*

Steele, Robert. "Another Trip to the Pawnshop." *F Her* 1 (No. 3, Spring 66) 15–22. Sidney Lumet's *The Pawnbroker:* a critique.

Farber, Stephen. "The Nightmare Journey: *Performance." Cinema* (Calif) 6 (No. 2, 1970) 16–21. A detailed analysis of the film starring Mick Jagger.

Sontag, Susan. *"Persona." S&S* 36 (Autumn 1967) 186–191. Essay on Ingmar Bergman's

131

film; it might be a "duel between two mythical parts of a single 'person.'"

Comolli, Jean-Louis. "The Phantom of Personality." *CdC in Eng* (No. 11, Sep 67) 30–33. A critique of *Persona*.

Wood, Robin. "*Persona*." *Movie* (No. 15, Spring 68) 22–24.

Boyers, Robert. "Bergman's *Persona*: An Essay in Tragedy." *Salmagundi* 2 (No. 4, Fall 68) 3–31. Compared to *Electra, Oedipus, Lear*, and *Hamlet*.

Cutts, John. "*The Philadelphia Story*." *F&F* 8 (No. 10, July 62) 24–25+. Plot outlines, production, critics' statements, biographies, and "revaluation" of one of "great films of the century."

Ross, T. J. "*Point Blank*." *F Her* 5 (No. 1, Fall 69) 21–26. John Boorman's film is more than an action movie.

Eisenstein, S. M. "Organic Unity and Pathos in the Composition of *Potemkin*." *CdC in Eng* (No. 3, 1966) 36–43. A structural analysis by its director.

Tyler, Parker. "For *Shadows*, Against *Pull My Daisy*." *F Cult* (No. 24, 1962). *See 3c, Shadows*.

Lennig, Arthur. "*Queen Kelly*." *F Her* 2 (No. 1, Fall 66) 24–29. Erich von Stroheim's last directorial effort.

"*Cur Vadis?*" *Chris Cent* 69 (26 Mar 52). *See 4k(5)*. About *Quo Vadis?*

Archer, Eugene. "Generation Without a Cause." *F Cult* 2 (No. 7, 1956) 18–20. Nicholas Ray's *Rebel Without a Cause*.

Roud, Richard, and Penelope Houston. "*The Red Desert*." *S&S* 34 (Spring 65) 76–81. Although Roud feels that Antonioni's film is "great" and "a remarkable achievement," he still finds it essentially abstract; Houston, who adds a study of landscape and color in the film, regards it as "a magnificent failure."

Wood, Robin. "*Deserto Rosso*." *Movie* (No. 13, Summer 65) 10–13.

Eames, Marian. "Gray Thoughts on *Red Shoes*." *FIR* 1 (Dec 50). *See 4k(6)*.

Barr, Charles, and Peter von Bagh. "*Repulsion*." *Movie* (No. 14, Autumn 65) 26–28. Two analyses of the Roman Polanski film.

Landesman, Rocco. "*The Revolutionary*." *F Her* 6 (No. 2, Winter 70–71) 27–32. Critique of Paul Williams' film.

Phillips, James E., and Harry Schein. "*Richard III*: Two Views." *QFRTV* 10 (No. 4, Summer 56) 399–415. UCLA English department chairman analyzes dramatic and filmic values of the adaptation; Schein, Swedish film critic, is more critical of the interpretation of the play and the character.

Brown, Constance. "Olivier's *Richard III*—A Reevaluation." *FQ* 20 (No. 4, Summer 67) 23–32.

Wood, Robin. "*Rio Bravo*." *Movie* (No. 5,

Dec 62) 25–27. Analysis of the Howard Hawks film.

Gollub, Judith. "A Bergman Film for Television." *CJ* 10 (No. 1, Fall 70) 48–50. *The Ritual (Ritorna)*.

Silke, James R. "Douglas Fairbanks' Production of *Robin Hood*." *Cinema* (Calif) 1 (No. 3, 1962–1963) 20–22.

Callenbach, Ernest. "Comparative Anatomy of Folk-Myth Films: *Robin Hood* and *Antonio das Mortes*." *FQ* 23 (No. 2, Winter 69–70) 42–47. Films by Michael Curtiz (1938) and Glauber Rocha; both (seen at San Francisco Festival) strive to be mythic and symbolic.

Armitage, Peter. "Visconti and Rocco." *Film* (No. 30, Winter 61) 28–34. *Rocco and His Brothers*.

Jorgenson, Paul A. "Castellani's *Romeo and Juliet*: Intention and Response." *QFRTV* 10 (No. 1, Fall 55) 1–10.

Cirillo, Albert R. "The Art of Franco Zeffirelli and Shakespeare's *Romeo and Juliet*." *Triquarterly* (No. 16, Fall 69) 69–93.

Houston, Penelope. "*Room at the Top?*" *S&S* 28 (No. 2, Spring 59) 56–59. Critical study of this new British film and speculation on its possible successors.

Pichel, Irving. "A Long Rope." *Hwd Q* 3 (No. 4, Summer 48–Summer 49) 416–420. Detailed study of Hitchcock's film *Rope* as contradicting the director's preference for shooting "bits and pieces"; how other films substitute camera movement for cutting.

Houston, Beverle, and Marsha Kinder. "*Rosemary's Baby*." *S&S* 38 (Winter 68–69) 17–19. Roman Polanski's visual imagery and the acting of Mia Farrow and John Cassavetes.

Bradbury, Ray. "A New Ending to *Rosemary's Baby*." *F&F* 15 (No. 11, Aug 69) 10. A suggestion for an alternate ending to the film.

Lewis, Marshall. "A Masterpiece on 8th Street." *NY F Bul* 2 (No. 1, 1961) 3–5. Renoir's *Rules of the Game*.

Whitehall, Richard. "*La Règle du Jeu*." *F&F* 9 (No. 2, Nov 62) 21–25. The 1939 Renoir film *Rules of the Game*.

Joly, Jacques. "Between Theater and Life: Jean Renoir and *Rules of the Game*." *FQ* 21 (No. 2, Winter 67–68) 2–8. A "collective analysis of a class" and of the character Octave as the "dupe" of his friends; translated from *La Nouvelle Critique* (July–Aug 1965).

Budgen, Suzanne. "*La Règle du Jeu*." *Screen* 11 (No. 1, Feb 70) 3–13. Analysis of Renoir's *Rules of the Game*.

Kelman, Ken. "Thanatos in Chrome." *F Cult* (No. 31, 1963–1964) 6–7. Interpretation of Kenneth Anger's *Scorpio Rising*.

Dempsey, Michael. "The Secrets of *Secret Ceremony*." *F Her* 5 (No. 4, Summer 70) 1–6. Joseph Losey's film.

Ross, T. J. "*The Servant* as Sex Thriller."

December 7 (No. 1, Spring 65) 128–136. Joseph Losey's film.

Anderson, Joseph L. "When the Twain Meet: Hollywood's Remake of *The Seven Samurai*." *FQ* 15 (No. 3, Spring 62) 55–58. Comparisons with the new John Sturges film, *The Magnificent Seven*.

Sarris, Andrew. "*The Seventh Seal*." *F Cult* (No. 19, 1959) 51–61. The 1956 Ingmar Bergman film.

Cowie, Peter. "*The Seventh Seal*." *F&F* 9 (No. 4, Jan 63) 25–29.

Tyler, Parker. "For *Shadows*, Against *Pull My Daisy*." *F Cult* (No. 24, 1962) 28–33. John Cassavetes operates more like Chekhov; the Beat film makers are out for publicity.

Dawson, Ian. "*Shame*." *S&S* 38 (Spring 69) 89–92. Essay on film the author calls "Bergman's *Week-end*"; references to his previous work.

Hoops, Jonathan H. "*Shame*." *F Her* 4 (No. 3, Spring 69) 1–5+. The Bergman film.

Walker, Michael. "*Shame*." *Movie* (No. 17, Winter 69–70) 32–34.

Stanbrook, Alan. "*Shane*." *F&F* 7 (No. 8, May 66) 37–41. The 1953 George Stevens film.

Fong, Monique. "*Shoe-Shine*: A Student Film Analysis." *Hwd Q* 4 (No. 1, Fall 49) 14–27. Intensive analysis of the De Sica film by a student at the French film school, IDHEC, including dramatic and cinematographic techniques.

Sarris, Andrew. "Inside the Piano Player." *NY F Bul* 3 (No. 3, 1962) 12. The "inside" jokes in *Shoot the Piano Player*.

Kael, Pauline. "*Shoot the Piano Player*." *F Cult* (No. 27, 1962–1963) 14–16. Praise for the Truffaut film: anarchistic in style, it is a plea for the right to be left alone.

Greenspun, Roger. "Through the Looking Glass." *Moviegoer* (No. 1, Winter 64) 3–11. *Shoot the Piano Player*; how visual and verbal puns and inversions support theme.

Manvell, Roger. "Revaluations: *Shooting Stars*, 1928." *S&S* 19 (June 50) 172–174. A review of sharp, satiric comedy about the movie world of the late 1920s; story by Anthony Asquith.

Manvell, Roger. "Revaluations: *Siegfried* 1922–1924." *S&S* 19 (Apr 50) 83–85. Lang's film (1924).

Institut des Hautes Études Cinématographiques. "*La Silence est d'or*: A Student Film Analysis." *Hwd Q* 3 (No. 3, Spring 1948) 301–310. Analysis of René Clair film by a student, representative of such work at the French film school; included is information about production and the director, analysis of the script and the dramatic devices, and comments on the "cinegraphic" elements.

Brightman, Carol. "The Word, the Image, and *The Silence*." *FQ* 17 (No. 4, Summer 64) 3–11. This close examination of the latest work of Ingmar Bergman also attacks the technique of critics, especially John Simon, toward this film and Antonioni's *Eclipse*.

Hamilton, J. W. "Some Comments About Ingmar Bergman's *The Silence* and Its Sociocultural Implications." *J Am Acad of Child Psychiatry* 8 (1969) 367–373.

Grabowski, Simon. "Picture and Meaning in Bergman's *Smiles of a Summer Night*." *J Aesthetics and Art Criticism* 29 (No. 2, Winter 70) 203–207. The use of the photographs in the film is seen as a cue to understanding the film's stylization.

Perkins, V. F. "Clive Donner and *Some People*." *Movie* (No. 3, Oct 62) 22–25. Critical comments on Donner's film, including remarks by Donner himself.

Haskell, Molly. "*Stage Fright*." *F Com* 6 (No. 3, Fall 70) 49–50. Retrospective study of the Hitchcock film.

Whitehall, Richard. "*The Stars Look Down*." *F&F* 8 (No. 4, Jan 62) 22–23+. The 1939 Carol Reed film.

Paul, William. "The Two Worlds of *Stolen Kisses*." *F Her* 5 (No. 2, Winter 69–70) 11–16. François Truffaut's film.

Greenspun, Roger. "*Stolen Kisses*." *On Film* (1970) 11–14. Analysis of Truffaut's "best" since *Jules and Jim*.

Swados, Harvey. "*La Strada*: Realism and the Comedy of Poverty." *Yale French Studies* (No. 17, 1956) 38–43. Why *La Strada*'s emotional treatment of poverty has enormous appeal for French audiences.

Culkin, John M. "*La Strada*, A Theological Interpretation." *Motive* 27 (Nov 66) 32–35.

de Laurot, Edouard. "*La Strada*—A Poem on Saintly Folly." *F Cult* 2 (No. 7, 1956) 11–14. The style and substance of Fellini's film.

Korte, Walter. "*The Stranger* as Film." *December* 10 (No. 1, 1968) 159–162. Fidelity to the Camus novel; comparisons with Visconti's other films.

Montagu, Ivor. "Rediscovery: *Strike*." *S&S* 26 (Autumn 56) 105–108. "Such an abundance of trial runs as was never dreamed of in cinema before or since in any single work"; description of the early Eisenstein film.

Cutts, John. "*Strike*." *F&F* 7 (No. 6, Mar 61) 17–19+. The 1924 Eisenstein film.

Kuiper, John. "Eisenstein's *Strike*: A Study of Cinematic Allegory." *J Soc Cin* 3 (1963) 7–15. His "figurative cinema" often used the physical world to evoke mental symbols, as when the workman hung himself from the very belt which represents the power of the factory owners.

Crowdus, Gary. "*Sundays and Cybele*." *Cinéaste* 1 (No. 1, Fall 67) 18–25+. The Serge Bourguignon film.

Jones, Dorothy B. "*Sunrise*: A Murnau Masterpiece." *QFRTV* 9 (No. 3, Spring 55) 238–262.

Davis, Gary L. *"Tabu." F Her* 1 (No. 3, Spring 66) 35–37. Fred W. Murnau's last film (1929).

Henderson, Brian. *"Targets." F Her* 4 (No. 4, Summer 69) 1–8. Critique of film by Peter Bogdanovich.

Tanner, Alain. "Rediscovery: *La Terra Trema." S&S* 26 (Spring 57) 213–216+. The neorealist approach in its most extreme form, surprisingly true to the letter of Verga's novel, *I Malavoglia;* Visconti's "sombre rhythms," Aldo's precise photography.

Farber, Stephen. "The Monster Marathon." *Cinema* (Calif) 6 (No. 1, 1970) 10–15. Analysis of *They Shoot Horses, Don't They?,* including some comparison with novel.

Vas, Robert. "Arrival and Departure." *S&S* 32 (Spring 1963) 56–59. Lindsay Anderson's *This Sporting Life* is a new breakthrough in British cinema, intensely concerned with human feelings.

Milne, Tom. *"Thomas l'Imposteur." S&S* 35 (Spring 66) 87–89. Comparison between Georges Franju's visual adaptation and Jean Cocteau's original novel.

Blumenthal, J. *"Macbeth* into *Throne of Blood." S&S* 34 (Autumn 65) 190–195. "Akiri Kurosawa's *Throne of Blood* is the only work, to my knowledge, that has ever completely succeeded in transforming a play of Shakespeare into a film"; analysis of his cinematic handling of the forest, the horses, and the characters.

Adams, Robert H. *"Through a Glass Darkly:* What Can Be Seen?" *Western Humanities Rev* 18 (1964) 65–66. The theme of the Bergman film is not "God is love" but that the mind is free to create an immanent God of love or hate.

Weinberg, Herman G. *"Thunder in the East:* A Forgotten Masterpiece." *F Her* 4 (No. 1, Fall 68) 19–28. A critique of the first directorial effort by Nicholas Farkas in 1934.

McBride, Joseph. *"Topaz." F Her* 5 (No. 2, Winter 69–70) 17–23. Hitchcock's film.

Grieves, Jefferson. *"Top Hat." F&F* 9 (No. 1, Oct 62) 45–48. The 1935 Astaire-Rogers film directed by Mark Sandrich.

Sarris, Andrew, *et al.* "Defense of *Torn Curtain." CdC in Eng* (No. 10, May 67) 50–61. A collection of short critiques of Alfred Hitchcock's film.

Mayersberg, Paul. *"The Trial of Joan of Arc." Movie* (No. 7, Feb 63) 30–32. The contemplative cinema as realized in Bresson's work, particularly this film.

Haller, Robert. "Tribunal of the Night: Vittorio de Sica and *The Condemned of Altona." F Her* 1 (No. 1, Fall 65) 2–11. Analysis of the film with extracts from dialogue.

Koszarski, Richard. *"Trouble in Paradise." F Com* 6 (No. 3, Fall 70) 47–48. Retrospective study of the Ernst Lubitsch film (1932).

Kelman, Ken. *"Twice a Man." F Cult* (No. 31, 1963–1964) 10–11. Interpretation of the Gregory Markopoulos film.

Haskell, Molly. "Omegaville." *F Her* 3 (No. 3, Spring 68) 23–26+. Critique of Godard's *Two or Three Things I Know About Her.*

Gasser, Mark. *"2001: A Space Odyssey." Cinéaste* 2 (No. 1, Summer 68) 10–11. Plot outline; importance of opening and closing sections.

Crowdus, Gary. "A Tentative for the Viewing of *2001." Cinéaste* 2 (No. 1, Summer 68) 12–14. A point-by-point discussion of some of the major criticisms of Kubrick's work, with the author deploring the film's poor reception by most New York critics.

Barker, Cliff. "Is *2001* Worth Seeing Twice?" *Cinéaste* 2 (No. 1, Summer 68) 15–16. A consideration of Kubrick's *Space Odyssey* as a dramatized documentary.

Becker, Michael. "2004?" *Cinéaste* 2 (No. 1, Summer 68) 17. Strong objection to the cuts (19 minutes' worth) taken from *Space Odyssey.*

Daniels, Don. "2001: A New Myth." *F Her* 3 (No. 4, Summer 68) 1–11.

Hunter, Tim, *et al.* "2001: A Space Odyssey." *F Her* 3 (No. 4, Summer 68) 12–20.

Holland, Norman. "2001: A Psychosocial Explication." *Hartford Studies in Lit* 1, 20–25. See also articles on *2001* in issue No. 2 (1969).

Michelson, Annette. "Bodies in Space: Film as 'Carnal Knowledge.' " *Artforum* 7 (No. 6, Feb 69) 54–63. Kubrick's *2001* as a paradigm of filmic experience; emphasis on phenomenology and epistemology.

"2001: A Space Odyssey." F Com 5 (No. 4, Winter 69) 6–15. Views of the film by Elie Flatto, "The Eternal Renewal" as published in *Orion* (June 1969), and by F. A. Macklin, editor of *Film Heritage,* "The Comic Sense of *2001.*"

Sragow, Michael. *"2001: A Space Odyssey." F Soc Rev* 5 (No. 5, Jan 70) 23–26. A call for an end to fear of technology.

Pohl, Frederik. "2001: A Second Look." *F Soc Rev* 5 (No. 6, Feb 70) 23–27. *Space Odyssey* fails as a science-fiction film.

Mayersberg, Paul. "The Testament of Vincente Minnelli." *Movie* (No. 3, Oct 62) 10–13. His *Two Weeks in Another Town.*

Rhode, Eric. *"Ugetsu Monogatari." S&S* 31 (Spring 62) 97–99. Analysis of Kenji Mizoguchi's film, its style and story, in which Rhode finds similarities with both Greek and Shakespearean drama.

Dewey, Lang. *"Ulysses." Film* (No. 49, Autumn 67) 23–26. A comparison of the novel and the Joseph Strick film.

"Phenomenon of *Les Parapluies de Cherbourg*." *Vogue* 144 (1 Nov 64) 184–185+. Three writers (Virginia Cowles, François-Régis Bastide, and François Nourissier) explore the appeal of *The Umbrellas of Cherbourg*.

Dewey, Lang. "The Colours in *Cherbourg*." *Film* (No. 42, Winter 64) 28–31. A discussion of the use of color in *The Umbrellas of Cherbourg*.

Perkins, V. F. "Unamerican Activities." *Movie* (No. 5, Dec 62) 3–6. Analysis of Samuel Fuller's *Underworld, U.S.A.* in terms of its form.

Hurwitz, H. "High School Principal Looks *Up the Down Staircase*." *Senior Scholastic* 91 (5 Oct 67) supp 16–17.

Visconti, Luchino. "Drama of Non-Existence." *CdC in Eng* (No. 2, 1966) 13–18. The film maker discusses his film *Vaghe Stella dell'Orsa* as an unusual detective story.

Collet, Jean. "The Absences of Sandra." *CdC in Eng* (No. 2, 1966) 18–21. Critique of Visconti's *Vaghe Stella dell'Orsa*.

Cutts, John. "*Vampyr*." *F&F* 7 (No. 3, Dec 60) 17–19+. Carl Theodor Dreyer's 1931 production.

Nevins, Francis M., Jr. "*Vertigo* Re-viewed." *J Pop Cult* 2 (No. 2, Fall 68) 321–322. A study of Hitchcock's film, with emphasis on the theme of reality and illusion.

Madden, David. "*The Virgin Spring*: Anatomy of a Mythic Image." *F Her* 2 (No. 2, Winter 66–67) 2–20. Ingmar Bergman's film as a "supreme aesthetic metaphor" in the mythic mode.

Riera, Emilio G. "*Viridiana*." *F Cult* (No. 24, 1962) 76–82.

Sarris, Andrew. "Luis Buñuel, the Devil and the Nun: *Viridiana*." *Movie* (No. 1, June 62) 14–16.

Robinson, David. "Thank God I Am Still an Atheist." *S&S* 31 (Summer 62) 116–118+. Analysis of Luis Buñuel's themes, symbols, and technique in *Viridiana,* which the author regards as Buñuel's second masterpiece, after *L'Age d'or*.

Dempsey, Michael. "*A Walk with Love and Death*." *F Her* 6 (No. 2, Winter 70–71) 14–18. John Huston's film.

Finler, Joel. "Stroheim's *Walking Down Broadway*." *Screen* 11 (Nos. 4–5, 1970) 89–96.

Zolotussky, Igor. "*War and Peace*: A Soviet View." *London Mag* new series 8 (No. 12, Mar 69) 57–64. Russian view of the Russian film version of the book.

Napier, Alan. "Tolstoy Betrayed." *F Her* 4 (No. 3, Spring 69) 11–16+. An examination of the Soviet film *War and Peace*.

Wood, Robin. "Godard and *Weekend*." *Movie* (No. 16, Winter 68–69) 29–33.

Macbean, James Roy. "Godard's *Weekend,* or The Self-Critical Cinema of Cruelty." *FQ* 22 (No. 2, Winter 68–69) 35–43. Analysis of scenes.

Whitehall, Richard. "*Westfront 1918*." *F&F* 6 (No. 12, Sep 60) 12–14+. Pabst's 1930 film.

Farber, Stephen. "Peckinpah's Return." *FQ* 23 (No. 1, Fall 69). *See 5, Sam Peckinpah. The Wild Bunch.*

Pechter, William. "*The Wild Bunch*." *F Com* 6 (No. 3, Fall 70) 55–57. Retrospective study of Sam Peckinpah film.

McCann, Eleanor. "The Rhetoric of *Wild Strawberries*." *S&S* 30 (Winter 60–61) 44–45. Author suggests that Ingmar Bergman may be ambiguous and fallible in his choice of symbols, and that his viewers "may identify with his suffering characters for the wrong reasons."

Greenberg, H. R. "Rags of Time: Ingmar Bergman's *Wild Strawberries*." *Am Imago* 27 (No. 1, Spring 70) 66–89. A psychological explication. With reply by S. Bach.

Gerard, Lillian N. "Of Lawrence and Love." *F Lib Q* 3 (No. 4, Fall 70) 6–12. The work of D. H. Lawrence adapted to the screen: *Women in Love*.

Giles, Dennis. "The Tao in *Woman in the Dunes*." *F Her* 1 (No. 3, Spring 66) 23–28. Hiroshi Teshigahara's film seen as an expression of the Chinese philosophy known as Taoism.

Weiss, Nathan Norman. "Spiders in His Mind." *Hwd Q* 3 (No. 2, Winter 47–48) 189–191. An attempt to explicate the symbolism, Frenchness, and complexity of Jean Renoir's American film *Woman on the Beach*.

Macklin, Anthony. "*Zabriskie Point*." *F Her* 5 (No. 3, Spring 70) 22–25. A critique of Antonioni's film.

"*Zabriskie*: What's the Point?" *F Her* 5 (No. 3, Spring 70) 26–40. On WBAI-FM in New York: Al Lee, film critic, WBAI; John Simon, *The New Leader*; Joseph Gelmis, *Newsday*; Martin Last, Pacifia Stations; and Harrison Starr, executive producer of *Zabriskie Point*.

Jebb, Julian. "Intimations of Reality: Getting the *Zabriskie Point*." *S&S* 39 (Summer 70) 124–126. The critics' response to Antonioni's first American movie: did they all miss the point?

Handzo, Stephen. "Michelangelo in Disneyland: *Zabriskie Point*." *F Her* 6 (No. 1, Fall 70) 7–24.

3d. Awards, Festivals, and Fairs

Pasinetti, P. M. "66 Films in a Lido Hotel." *CQ* 3 (No. 1, Autumn 34) 14–16. Brief report on first Venice festival.

Ackerman, Carl. "Pulitzer Prizes for the Cinema." *Cinema Arts* 1 (No. 2, July 37) 15–17. Dean of Columbia's Graduate School of Journalism makes a case for it.

Goodman, Ezra. "Neat Pete-Roleum." *S&S* 8 (No. 30, Summer 39) 62–63. A brief discussion of films recently shown at the World's Fair.

Griffith, Richard. "Films at the Fair." *Films* 1 (No. 1, Nov 39). *See 8c(2).*

Bower, A. "Academy Awards." *Nation* 152 (15 Mar 41) 305. Occasioned by President Roosevelt's address to the film industry during the awards presentations, this article gives the history and structure of the Academy of Motion Picture Arts and Sciences.

Elliot, Paul. "Looking Over the Oscars." *Atlantic* 174 (Aug 44) 103–107.

Stanley, F. "Oscar: His Life and Times." *NYTM* (18 Mar 45) 18–19.

Hubler, Richard G. "Pulitzer Prize for Motion Pictures." *Screen Writer* 2 (Jan 47) 7–10. Condemns the Academy of Motion Picture Arts and Sciences for the "inbred praise and exhibitionism" of its Oscar awards, and calls for an impartial agency "to sift the artistic facts and make the proper awards."

Powell, Dilys. "The Importance of International Film Festivals." *Penguin F Rev* 3 (Aug 47) 59–61.

Ray, Cyril. "Film Festivals." *Spectator* 179 (26 Sep 47) 392–393. Remarks on the value of international film festivals and criticism of jury selection and film choices.

Chandler, Raymond. "Oscar Night in Hollywood." *Atlantic* 181 (Mar 48) 24–27. The Academy recognizes quality only in terms of success.

Hersholt, Jean. "The Academy Speaks." *Atlantic* 181 (May 48) 43–45. Report on the work of the Academy of Motion Picture Arts and Sciences on Oscar night and throughout the year.

"Abandoned Oscar." *Newswk* 33 (11 Apr 49) 90. The presidents of the five major film companies in Hollywood announce they will no longer support the Academy Awards ceremony financially.

Lavery, Emmet. "Mr. Shakespeare's Earthquake; Much Ado About the Oscars." *SRL* 32 (16 Apr 49) 13+. Award to Olivier's *Hamlet* caused five major Hollywood studios to refuse to underwrite production expenses of the Academy Awards.

Chandler, Raymond. "Oscar Night in Hollywood." *S&S* 19 (June 50) 157–161. The Oscar awards have little to do with artistic achievement; "the motion picture industry's frantic desire to kiss itself on the back of the neck."

Hardy, Forsyth. "The Edinburgh Film Festival." *Hwd Q* 5 (No. 1, Fall 50) 33–40. History and aims of Great Britain's only festival up to that time and the emphasis on realistic and documentary subjects.

Knight, Arthur. "Film Festivals Aren't All Commercial." *FIR* 1 (Oct 50) 1–2. Venice, Antibes, Biarritz, Edinburgh, for example.

Wilson, Norman. "Edinburgh's Film Guild." *FIR* 2 (Apr 51). *See 1a(1).*

"First Art Film Festival in America Held at the Playhouse in Woodstock." *Am Artist* 15 (Oct 51) 66.

Wald, Jerry, and Norman Krasna. "Oscar Fever." *FIR* 3 (Mar 52) 102–104. Academy Awards should honor genuine creative ability—not adaptations of hit plays and best-selling novels.

Bickerstaff, Isaac. "The Oscars—By Radio." *FIR* 3 (Apr 52) 164–170. The ceremony of the annual awarding of the Oscars of 1951 as heard by radio.

Koegler, Horst. "A Berliner's Reaction." *FIR* 3 (Aug–Sep 52) 321–322. Reasons for the choices of the winning films at the 1952 Berlin Film Festival through a description of the mental makeup of the average Berliner, who does the voting.

Koval, Francis. "Film Festival Juries." *FIR* 4 (Mar 53) 113–118. Political and other biases.

"Oscar on TV." *Life* 34 (30 Mar 53) 39+. Picture story of Academy Award presentations, the first to appear on TV.

Schary, Dore. "Film Awards." *FIR* 4 (Apr 53) 161–163. The desire for them does not increase the cost of production.

Alpert, Hollis. "A Matter of Opinion." *Sat Rev* 36 (11 Apr 53) 55. A review of the Academy Awards presentation; Hollywood has once again revealed a fondness for sentiment and an inability to distinguish between the pretentious and the real.

Parsons, Louella. "What Happens to Oscar Winners." *Cosmopolitan* 136 (Mar 54) 18.

"International Film Festivals." *S&S* 24 (July–Sep 54) 9–11. Chart of British entries 1949–1953; analysis of entry problems and new International Federation of Film Producers ratings of festivals.

Knight, Arthur. "Domestic Film Festival." *Sat Rev* 34 (11 Sep 54) 44–45. The mushrooming of film festivals around the world.

Hurd, Reggie, Jr. "Academy Award Mistakes." *FIR* 6 (May 55) 209–215. Nominees of the past that should have had awards.

Manvell, Roger. "Prize Day." *F&F* 1 (No. 8, May 55) 6. Awards given to films: festivals, critics' awards, American Academy "Oscars," and British Film Academy awards.

"Oscar." *F&F* 1 (No. 9, June 55) 3. History of the Academy Awards.

Knight, Arthur. "The Lesson of the Festivals." *Sat Rev* 38 (8 Oct 55) 26–27. The poor image presented by American movies at European film festivals.

Howard, T. "Whingding of the Movie Queens." *SEP* 229 (18 Aug 56) 21–23. Starlets at Cannes.

Garringer, Nelson E. "Academy Award Nominations." *FIR* 8 (Mar 57) 111–115. Nominations for the best and best-supporting actor and actress, and the best director; who got more than one nomination, who got the most nominations without winning an award, etc.

"Oscars and Good Taste." *America* 97 (13 Apr 57) 32. A review of the Academy Awards of past years in comparison with the National Legion of Decency ratings.

Knight, Arthur. "Films at the Fair." *Sat Rev* 41 (11 Jan 58) 52–55. The Brussels Film Festival.

"Sadder But Braver." *Nation* 188 (24 Jan 59) 62. The Academy of Motion Picture Arts and Sciences has voted to revoke the amendment which forbids the presentation of an Oscar to anyone who declines to swear that he is not a Communist.

"That's Me." *Newswk* 53 (26 Jan 59) 25. Dalton Trumbo, then blacklisted, revealed to be the "Robert Rich" who won a 1957 Oscar for the best original film story, *The Brave One.*

Brunius, Jacques. "The Cinema and the Exhibition." *Film* (No. 19, Jan–Feb 59). *See 4a(3).*

"Focus on Festivals." *F&F* 5 (No. 11, Aug 59) 11+. Directors of five festivals discuss their value.

"Meeting 'La Nouvelle Vague' . . ." *F&F* 6 (No. 1, Oct 59) 7–8. Comments by the New Wave directors at the Cannes festivals.

Ammannati, Floris L. "How Valuable Are Film Festivals?" *JSPG* (Mar 60) 27–28. Director of Venice Festival points out trade advantages.

Le Bret, Robert Favre. "International Film Festival." *JSPG* (June 60) 27–28. Note on beginnings of Cannes festival.

Grenier, Cynthia. "Ill-Starred Thirteenth Festival of Cannes." *FQ* 13 (No. 4, Summer 60) 15–19.

Lynch, W. F. "Let's Have Film Festivals." *America* 104 (11 Mar 61) 753–756. Reply by S. Allen.

Baker, Peter. "Festival Fantasy." *F&F* 7 (No. 9, June 61) 27. An open letter to the president of the Fédération Internationale des Associations de Producteurs de Films about film festivals. Reply by Arthur Watkins 10 (July 61) 19.

Bauer, Jerry. "Festival-Go-Round." *Th Arts* 45 (June 61) 24–27+. European festivals and their role in determining what films are seen in theatres generally.

Skolsky, S. "What Goes on at the Academy Awards." *McCall's* 89 (Apr 62) 74–75.

"Lady, Do You Want to Get in Pictures?" *Life* 52 (15 June 62) 84–89. Natalie Wood and other starlets at Cannes.

Hart, Henry. "NYC's First Film Festival." *FIR* 14 (Oct 63) 449–450+. Account of entries, with comments.

Kauffmann, Stanley. "After the Ball Was Over." *New Rep* 149 (5 Oct 63) 33+. Long comment on the first New York Film Festival as a whole.

"Regulations for International Film Festivals, as Promulgated by the International Federation of Film Producers Associations." *JSPG* 12 (No. 8, June 64) 16–18.

Stevens, George, Jr., Seymour Poe, Stanley Kramer, Irving Levin, Alfred Bauer, Bert Reisfeld, Glenn Ireton, Robert Favre Le Bret. "The Journal Looks at International Film Festivals." *JSPG* 12 (No. 8, June 64) 3–28. USIA Motion Picture chief, 20th Century-Fox executive, film producer, and three directors of festivals write about the problems of participation.

Alpert, Hollis. "Cannes: Cinema and Semantics." *Sat Rev* 48 (6 June 64) 20–21. Best and worst pictures; general problems of the festival.

Hitchens, Gordon. "Survey Among Unsuccessful Applicants for the Ford Foundation Film Grants." *F Com* 2 (No. 3, Summer 64) 10–32. They tell their intended projects and their reaction to the Ford grants; list includes Bruce Baillie, Stan Brakhage, Gordon Hitchens, John Korty, Taylor Mead, D. A. Pennebaker, Michael Roemer.

Hoover, Clara H. "*Film Comment* Announces the Recipients of the 1964 Anniversary Awards." *F Com* 2 (No. 3, Summer 64) 2–3. Allen Downs, Robert Feldman, Ken Lindon, Al Maysles, and Frank Taboas get $500 each for proposed films.

Knight, Arthur. "Films at the Fair." *Sat Rev* 47 (15 Aug 64) 26. New York World's Fair.

Kauffmann, Stanley. "World as a Fair." *New Rep* 151 (19 Sep 64) 31–32. Three films at New York World's Fair: *The Searching Eye, To Be Alive!,* and the IBM film.

Angell, Roger. "More Film Fun." *New Yorker* 40 (26 Sep 64). *See 3b(4).*

Schlesinger, Arthur, Jr. "Annual Rites at Cannes." *Harper's* 230 (Feb 65) 79–84.

Kauffmann, Stanley. "Are We Doomed to Festivals?" *New Rep* 153 (2 Oct 65) 30–32.

Wellington, Fred. "Film '65—Thirteen Panel Discussions." *F Cult* (No. 40, Spring 66) 24–30. Quotations of participants at panels for Third New York Film Festival.

Billard, Ginette. "Tours—and the Salvation of Shorts." *FQ* 19 (No. 4, Summer 66). *See 4a(5).*

Wellington, Fred. "Towards Understanding of 'Subversion.'" *F Cult* (No. 42, Fall 66) 13–25. Personal responses to lectures as well as films at Fourth New York Film Festival.

Tynan, Kenneth. "Our Man at the Film Festivals." *Playboy* 13 (No. 12, Dec 66) 223–224. History of Cannes and Venice festivals, with sardonic comments on today's versions.

Medjuck, Joe. "Films at Expo." *Take One* 1 (No. 5, 1967) 17–18. A description of the films shown at the 1967 Montreal fair.

Heller, Franklin. "Fair Films Are Fantastic." *Action* 2 (No. 4, July–Aug 67) 6–7. Description of, and positive reaction to, the films at Expo 67.

"Magic in Montreal." *Time* 90 (7 July 67) 80–82. The films at Expo 67: *A Time to Play, Labyrinth.*

Alpert, Hollis. "How Useful Are Film Festivals?" *Sat Rev* 50 (8 July 67) 56–58. The nature and history of film festivals.

Kappler, Frank. "A Film Revolution to Blitz Man's Mind." *Life* 63 (14 July 67) 20–28c. Film at Expo 67 in Montreal.

Morgenstern, Joseph. "Expo: The Point Is Pictures." *Newswk* 70 (17 July 67) 88–90.

Knight, Arthur. "Marshaling McLuhanism." *Sat Rev* 50 (12 Aug 67) 41–42+. A review of Expo 67 films.

Shatnoff, Judith. "Expo '67—A Multiple Vision." *FQ* 21 (No. 1, Fall 67). *See 8d.*

Hitchens, George. "Movie Maker's Guide to Foreign Film Festivals." *Pop Photog* 61 (Dec 67) 130+. Service provided by Council on International Nontheatrical Events.

Day, Barry. "Beyond the Frame." *S&S* 37 (Spring 68) 80–85. Some observations about the expansion of cinema possibilities in Montreal Expo 67's mixed-media experiments, and about new innovations in underground cinema and television, such as the use of video tape.

Brown, Jeff. "High Art at Pikes Peak." *SEP* 241 (23 Mar 68) 80–81. Fictional anecdote about the Pikes Peak International Film Festival.

Myers, F. "Almost-Joint Film Awards." *Chris Cent* 85 (3 Apr 68) 427–428. The second annual joint Protestant-Catholic Film Award ceremonies.

Swados, H. "How Revolution Came to Cannes." *NYTM* (9 June 68) 128–131. Radicals, led by Godard, closed down the film festival.

Jacob, Gilles. "The 400 Blows of François Truffaut." *S&S* 37 (Autumn 68). *See 5, François Truffaut.*

Sachs, Charles. "The Days in May." *Cinema* (Calif) 4 (No. 3, Fall 68) 6–12. Report on political uproar that led to collapse of Cannes festival.

Lamont, Austin F. "Films at Expo—A Retrospect." *JUFA* 21 (No. 1, 1969) 3–12. Films made specifically for Expo, especially *A Place to Stand, Earth Is Man's Home, Kaleidoscope,* and *Laterna Magika.*

Barnes, Clive. "From Oscars to Boredom." *Holiday* 45 (May 69) 8+. Questions value of awards such as New York Film Critics Award, Tonys, Oscars and Emmies.

Shaw, Irwin. "Grand Guignol on the Grand Canal." *Playboy* 16 (No. 8, Aug 69) 97. Portrait of contemporary Venice festival.

Knight, Arthur. "What Is a Festival Film?" *Sat Rev* 52 (13 Sep 69) 99. A discussion brought on by the upcoming Seventh New York Film Festival.

Wolfe, Maynard Frank. "Films at Expo 70." *Show* (25 June 70) 26–32. Comments on Japanese fair and pavilion exhibitions of various multilevel film experiments; color photos.

3e. Selective Lists of Films

"Season's Summary." *Time* 17 (15 June 31) 44. *Chicago Times* movie critic made best guesses about box-office success of films 1930–1931.

Lejeune, C. A. "Films You Ought to See." *S&S* 1 (No. 1, Spring 32) 25. A listing, with brief critical comments.

"Favorite Films of Foreign Writers." *Living Age* 347 (Sep 32) 81. Writers choose Chaplin, Clair, Eisenstein's *Potemkin.*

"Motion Picture Classics: Films I Would Like to See Again." *Th Arts* 25 (Sep 41) 621+. Lists selected by John Gielgud, Raymond Swing, Fred Astaire, Samuel Goldwyn, Lillian Gish, Mortimer Adler, *et al.*

Benét, William Rose. "Excursions of a Movie-Goer." *FIR* 1 (Apr 50) 17–18. Poet, author, and associate editor of the *Saturday Review of Literature* praises some favorite films.

"The Front Page: The Big Money." *S&S* 19 (Feb 51) 389–390. Editorial examines trade polls of most popular films with English audiences in 1950.

Ramsaye, Terry. "Films That Sold Tickets." *FIR* 3 (May 52) 209–212. The biggest moneymaking American films 1948–1951 according to *Motion Picture Herald,* with brief descriptions of their entertainment qualities.

Lambert, Gavin. "As You Like It." *S&S* 22 (July–Sep 52) 18–19. A number of film makers were asked to list their favorite films; Lambert discusses some of the choices and omissions.

Koebner, Hans. "The European Taste." *FIR* 3 (Aug–Sep 52) 314–316. Belgian questionnaire asked screenwriters and directors to give the names of the ten films they considered the best ever made.

Stainton, Walter H. "A 60-Year Calendar of Motion Pictures." *FIR* 3 (Aug–Sep 52) 305–316. Cornell professor's opinions as to the best film for each of the 60 years 1893–1952; see also letters 3 (Oct 52) 424–428 by Terry Ramsaye, Theodore Huff, and James Card.

Crowther, Bosley. "The Ten Best of Forty Years." *NYTM* (17 Aug 52) 22–23+. *The New York Times'* critic's choice of foreign films includes *Potemkin, M, Grand Illusion,* and *The Bicycle Thief.*

Lambert, Gavin. "As the Critics Like It." *S&S* 22 (Oct–Dec 52) 58–60. The results of an informal referendum of eighty-five film critics asked to list their ten favorite films.

"Top Draws." *Time* 61 (5 Jan 53) 68. List of the top box-office actors and films for 1952 by *Motion Picture Herald.*

"Two Views of the Hollywood Scene." *S&S* 22 (Apr–June 53) 161–162. Commercial and critical successes compared, with lists of box-office winners, Academy Awards, New York Critics Awards, and *Sight and Sound* choices for best picture 1945–1952.

"This Man Has Seen 5,592 Movies." *Look* 19 (9 Aug 55) 96–98+. Movie fan's own list of the best and worst pictures and performances and all-time superstars.

Starr, Cecile. "Movies and Frank Lloyd Wright." *House Beautiful* 97 (Nov 55) 364–366. His at-home movie showings, especially Flaherty films and some French movies.

Connor, Edward. "Televiewing Movies." *FIR* 8 (Feb 57) 49–54. A survey of those films seen by the author on television since 1941 which he deems either noteworthy or representative.

"The So-Called Greatest." *Newswk* 51 (17 Feb 58) 105. Some longtime observers of Hollywood select their own list of all-time masterpieces (Griffith, John Huston, Frank Capra, etc.).

Reynolds, C. "World's Top Professionals Choose the Ten Greatest Films." *Pop Photog* 42 (May 58) 118+. Gordon Hendricks compares *Sight and Sound* and other polls and comes up with a composite list.

Koval, Francis. "A Dubious Dozen." *FIR* 9 (Nov 58) 481–485. Film events at the Brussels World's Fair; the selection of twelve best films "of all time" (mostly silent) and the failure to select only one from these.

Knight, Arthur. "A Long Way for a Movie." *Sat Rev* 41 (8 Nov 58) 24. Belgian Film Library's showing of the twelve "best films of all time" at the Brussels World's Fair.

Gillett, John. "The Best at Brussels." *S&S* 28 (Winter 58–59) 18–20. At the World's Fair the Belgian Cinémathèque showed "The Best Films of All Times," also a series of subsidiary screenings.

"The Year." *F&F* 5 (No. 4, Jan 59) 7+. Survey of the films of 1958 according to what the public liked, what the critics liked, and what *Films and Filming* liked. This feature continues each year through 1970.

"*Cahiers du Cinéma* Films of the Year: 1955–1960." *NY F Bul* 2 (No. 10, 1961) 1+. Critics' choices for the period.

"Top Ten." *S&S* 31 (Winter 61–62) 10–14. Referendum of seventy film critics: favorite films listed of forty-five of them, the top three: *Citizen Kane, L'Avventura, Rules of the Game.*

Hill, Steven P. "The Popular Directors." *FIR* 13 (No. 7, Aug–Sep 62) 385–389. *Film Daily* and newspaper movie reviewers' "best" list numerically analyzed.

"*Show's* Definitive Poll of World-Famed Moviegoers." *Show* 2 (Aug 62) 56–57. Poll of celebrities asking about their ten favorite films of 1961; responses include Eleanor Roosevelt, Captain Kangaroo, *et al.*

"Ten Best." *Film* (No. 33, Autumn 62) 24–25. A poll of readers reveals a list of best directors and best films.

"Best Performance." *Film* (No. 34, Winter 62) 31–34. A poll of subscribers.

"Desert Island Films." *F&F* 9 (No. 11, Aug 63) 11–13. "What ten films would you take with you to a desert island?" answered by a number of British film people.

"Directors Choose the Best Films." *Cinema* (Calif) 1 (No. 5, Aug–Sep 63) 14. Hubert Cornfield, Julien Duvivier, John Ford, Henry Hathaway, John Huston, Stanley Kubrick, Joshua Logan, Rouben Mamoulian, Daniel Mann, Paul Rotha, George Seaton, Norman Taurog, King Vidor, Fred Zinnemann.

Strickland, Paul. "U.S. Movie Taste." *FIR* 16 (No. 4, Apr 65) 233–236. Compilation of the films (since 1922) that were in the top fifteen every week in *Variety.*

Beresford, Bruce, *et al.* "Critics' Choice." *Cinema* (Cambridge) (No. 4, Oct 69) 2–5. Seventeen contributors to *Cinema* list their ten best directors and ten best films, followed by *Cinema's* pantheon, based on the choices made by the contributors/critics.

3f. Relations with Other Arts

Williams, W. E. "Film and Literature." *S&S* 4 (No. 16, Winter 35–36) 163–165. Suggested by filming of *Midsummer Night's Dream*.

Underhill, Duncan. "Respectfully Submitted." *Cinema Arts* 1 (No. 3, Sep 37) 23+. A self-proclaimed "veteran film addict" fantasizes about ten plays and novels that ought to be produced.

Perkoff, H. L. "The Screen and the Ballet." *S&S* VII (No. 27, Autumn 38) 122–123. Cinema is breaking down a number of restrictions which have thus far paralyzed many art forms.

Freeman, Joseph. "Biographical Films." *Th Arts* 25 (Dec 41) 900–906. *See 4k(7)*.

Boud, John. "Film Among the Arts." *Sequence* (No. 1, Dec 46) 2–4. The varying relationships between form and theme in film make it difficult to assign it a specific relationship to the other arts.

Arnheim, Rudolf. "Epic and Dramatic Film." *F Cult* 3 (No. 11, 1957) 9, 10. The dramatic film undertakes the solution of a particular problem, which may succeed or fail, whereas "the epic style of narration has a preference for stringing episodes in sequences."

"Hollywood Bets on Books and Broadway." *NYTM* (11 Aug 57) 26–27. Production stills from recent adaptations.

Buck, Tony. "Cherkassov's *Don Quixote*." *S&S* 27 (Autumn 58). *See 5, Nikolai Cherkassov*.

Taradash, Daniel. "Into Another World." *F&F* 5 (No. 8, May 59) 9+. Explanation of the work of adaptation from another medium to film.

Durgnat, Raymond. "This Damned Eternal Triangle." *F&F* 11 (No. 3, Dec 64) 15–19. On the aesthetics of literature, theatre, and film.

Fadiman, William. "But Compared to the Original." *F&F* 11 (No. 5, Feb 65) 21–23. On criticizing films as films and not comparing them to their sources.

3f(1). THEATER AND FILM

Prince Henry of Ruess. "The Future of the Films: Talkies and the Stage." *Living Age* 339 (Nov 30). *See 4c*.

Bakshy, Alexander. "New Dimensions in the Talkies." *Nation* 131 (24 Dec 30) 702–703. Comparison of stage and screen.

Wolfe, Humbert. "I Look at the Theatre." *Th Arts* 15 (Jan 31) 49–52. Will film take its place?

Tonecki, Zygmunt. "The Theatre of the Future and the Talking Film." *Close Up* 8 (No. 1, Mar 31) 27–32. The effect of film on the new theatre.

Segal, Mark. "Eye and the Ear in the Theatre." *Close Up* 8 (No. 1, Mar 31) 38–43. The need to appeal to both in theatre and film.

Nathan, George Jean. "The Play Is Still the Thing." *Forum* 86 (July 31) 36–39.

"Talkies Preferred." *Living Age* 340 (Aug 31). *See 4c*.

"Effects of Technological Changes upon Employment in the Amusement Industry." *Monthly Labor Rev* 32 (Aug 31). *See 6c(2)*.

Williams, David P. "Cinema Technique and the Theatre." *19th Century* 110 (Nov 31) 602–612. Contrasts new stagecraft with techniques of film narrative.

Tonecki, Zygmunt. "At the Boundary of Film and Theatre." *Close Up* 9 (No. 1, Mar 32) 31–35.

Carter, Huntly. "Cinema and Theatre: The Diabolical Difference." *English Rev* 55 (Sep 32) 313–320. Cinema evokes primitive urges from the subconscious, while theatre is life-centered, evoking truth.

Hughes, Pennethorne. "The Historical Inception of Stage and Film." *Close Up* 10 (No. 4, Dec 33) 341–346.

Jones, C. R. "Stage People and Film Things." *CQ* 2 (No. 4, Summer 34) 222–227. The struggle against theatricality; the special drama of men and things.

Isaacs, Edith J. R. "Let's Go to the Movies." *Th Arts* 19 (June 35) 399–410. Sees theatre as more effective than movies; reviews current films and plays.

Vesselo, A. "Stage and Screen." *English Rev* 62 (Feb 36) 194–196. Cinema's freedom of passage in time and space.

Dukes, Ashley. "English Scene." *Th Arts* 20 (May 36) 344–348. How *Modern Times* and *Things to Come* challenge the theatre.

Eisenstein, S. M. "Through Theatre to Cinema." *Th Arts* 20 (Sep 36) 735–747. How the Soviet director used montage ideas on the stage; stills from *Bezhin Meadow*, "in preparation."

Hopkins, A. "Hollywood Takes Over the Theatre." *Scribner's* 101 (Mar 37) 14+. History of theatre and film relationships; discussion by Burns Mantle and Brooks Atkinson.

Leyda, Jay. "Theatre on Film." *Th Arts* 21 (Mar 37) 194–207. Discussion of theatrical plays and players preserved on film from earliest days.

Helburn, T. "Theater, Bloody But Unbowed." *North Am Rev* 243 (June 37) 231–242. How the motion picture has affected the theatre; what directions the theatre may take.

Arliss, George. "The Stage and the Screen." *Royal Soc of Arts J* 85 (30 July 37) 862–875. Also remarks on the state of the British film industry.

Seldes, Gilbert. "Good Theatre." *Atlantic* 161 (Jan 38) 82–85.

Daugherty, F. "He Has the Common Touch." *CSMM* (9 Nov 38). *See 5, Frank Capra.*

Paul, Norman. "Artistic Alliance." *S&S* 8 (No. 31, Autumn 39) 116. Cinema and theatre should and can be allied for various purposes.

Carrick, E. "Film, Theatre, and Ballet in the United States." *London Studio* 20 [*Studio* 120] (Spring 40) 80–84.

Poggioli, Renato. "Aesthetics of the Stage and Screen." *J Aesthetics and Art Criticism* 1 (No. 2, 1941) 63–69. Cinema and theatre are almost in opposition to one another; metaphysical distinctions; director as creator and as interpreter; differences in audience and acting.

Dukes, Ashley. "Journey Through Theatre: VIII. Screen Reflections." *Th Arts* 25 (Sep 41) 689–696.

Enters, Angna. "A Mime and the Movies." *Calif Arts and Arch* 58 (No. 10, Oct 41) 18+. The author discusses her theatre of mime and its relation to film.

Nathan, P. S. "Hunting with a Movie Scout." *NYTM* (6 Aug 44) 17+. Hollywood's ambivalent attitude toward the theatre.

Crichton, Kyle (ed.). "Gamble with Music." *Collier's* 117 (23 Mar 46). *See 4k(6).*

Trewin, J. C. "Backs Not Easy Riz." *S&S* 15 (No. 57, Spring 46) 17–18. The stage attacks the cinema, but the latter does not retaliate.

Mamoulian, Rouben. "Stage and Screen." *Screen Writer* 2 (Mar 47) 1–15. They are entirely different; they need to stay apart, but both need profound ideas and deep emotions to rise out of present doldrums; techniques this director has used to gain effects in each.

Laufe, A. L. "Not So New in the Theatre." *South Atlantic Q* 46 (July 47) 384–389. With all the new developments in technique, neither stage nor screen has discarded medieval clichés which hold audience appeal.

Mamoulian, Rouben. "Recommended . . . A Divorce." *Th Arts* 32 (June 48) 22–23. How cinema differs from theatre.

Eisenstein, S. M. "Through Theatre to Cinema." *S&S* 19 (May 50) 133–138. His own experience, a chapter from forthcoming book, *Film Form* (Harcourt Brace Jovanovich, 1969).

Burton, Howard A. *"High Noon:* Everyman Rides Again." *QFRTV* 8 (No. 1, Fall 53). *See 3c, High Noon.*

McDonald, Gerald D. "From Stage to Screen." *FIR* 6 (Jan 55). *See 4b.*

Strauss, Harold. "My Affair with Japanese Movies." *Harper's* 211 (July 55). *See 4f(1a).*

Alpert, Hollis. "Movies Are Better Than the Stage." *Sat Rev* 38 (23 July 55) 5–6. Cinema is an evolving form of theatre; because it possesses certain capabilities that the stage does not, it has been able to proceed further in its evolutionary path and become the better form of theatre.

Costello, Donald P. "G. B. S. the Movie Critic." *QFRTV* 11 (No. 3, Spring 57). *See 3b(1).*

Richie, Donald, and Joseph Anderson. "Traditional Theater and the Film in Japan." *FQ* 12 (No. 1, Fall 58). *See 4f(1a).*

Havemann, Ernest. "Business of Show Business: Riches or Ruin." *Life* 45 (22 Dec 58). *See 6a(1).*

Donehue, Vincent J. "A Man in Three Mediums." *Th Arts* 43 (June 59) 60–62. The author is a theatre, television, and film director.

Robinson, David. *"Look Back in Anger." S&S* 28 (Nos. 3–4, Summer–Autumn 59). *See 3c, Look Back in Anger.*

Morsberger, R. E. "Shakespeare and Science Fiction." *Shakespeare Q* 12 (Spring 61). *See 4k(3).*

Kuiper, John B. "Stage Antecedents of the Film Theory of S. M. Eisenstein." *Educ Th J* 13 (Dec 61). *See 5, Sergei Eisenstein.*

Foreman, Carl, and Tyrone Guthrie. "Debate: Movies vs. Theatre." *NYTM* (29 April 62) 10–11+.

Kauffmann, Stanley. "End of an Inferiority Complex." *Th Arts* 46 (Sep 62) 67–70. Film is no longer inferior to theatre.

Czinner, Paul. "Documenting the Stage." *Opera News* 27 (22 Dec 62) 28–29. A producer describes his method of preserving great theatre.

Laurie, Edith. "Film the Rival of Theatre." *F Com* 1 (No. 6, Fall 63) 51–53. Report on drama round table at Edinburgh.

Kerman, Joseph. "Chase." *Opera News* 28 (28 Dec 63) 8–12. Film as the counterpart of opera a century ago.

Johnson, Ian. "Merely Players." *F&F* 10 (No. 7, Apr 64) 41–48. Impact of Shakespeare on international cinema.

Sontag, Susan, Milton, Cohen, M. Kirby, Robert Blossom, Peter Weiss, Roger Blin, Roger Planchon, Vito Pandolfi. "Film and Theatre." *TDR* 11 (Fall 66) 24+. Issue devoted to mutual influence of stage and screen.

Svoboda, Josef. *"Lanterna Magika." TDR* (Fall 66) 141–149. Excerpts from a pamphlet by the Experimental Studio of the Czechoslovak State Film Industry discussing techniques and performances combining film and live actors.

Meyerhold, Vsevelod. "Two Lectures." *TDR* (Fall 66) 186–195. Notes on Chaplin and the relationship of film and theatre.

Godard, Jean-Luc, and Michel Delahaye. "Two Arts in One: René Allio and Antoine Bourseiller." *CdC in Eng* (No. 6, Dec 66) 24–33. Director and scenarist discuss their move from French theatre to cinema.

Steele, Robert. "The Two Faces of Drama." *CJ* 6 (1966–1967) 16–32. Similarities and differences should not make rivals of cinema and theatre.

Kerr, Walter. "Movies Are Better Than the Theatre." *NYTM* (3 Mar 68) 36–37+.

Madden, David. "Harlequin's Stick, Charlie's Cane." *FQ* 22 (No. 1, Fall 68) 10–26. Parallels between the tradition of commedia dell'arte and the silent comedy: masks, situations, acrobatics.

Steele, Robert. "Screen and Theatre Reality." *JSPG* (Dec 68) 3–7.

Camp, Gerald M. "Shakespeare on Film." *J Aesthetic Educ* 3 (No. 1, Jan 69) 107–120. On the aesthetic problems of filming Shakespeare, with special attention to Olivier's *Henry V.*

Fell, John L. "Dissolves by Gaslight." *FQ* 23 (No. 3, Spring 70) 22–34. Subheading: "Antecedents to the Motion Picture in Nineteenth-Century Melodrama."

Burian, Jarka. "Josef Svoboda: Theatre Artist in the Age of Science." *Educ Th J* 22 (No. 2, May 70) 123–145. Set designer of the Czech *Lanterna Magika* and other stage/film productions.

3f(1a). Stage and Screen Acting

[*See also 2b(1), 2b(2).*]

Jannings, Emil. "Why I Left the Films." *Living Age* 338 (1 July 30) 554–557. German actor finds more value in stage acting.

Bakshy, Alexander. "Concerning Dialogue." *Nation* 135 (17 Aug 32) 151–152. Function of dialogue in talkies should be different from stage.

Pudovkin, V. I. "The Actor's Work: Film Versus Stage." *Close Up* 10 (No. 3, Sep 33) 227–234. The difference between stage and screen acting.

Ervine, John. "Actor and the Cinema." *London Mercury* 33 (Mar 36). *See 4e(1a).*

Washburn, Charles. "Hollywood Goes Broadway." *Cinema Arts* 1 (No. 1, June 37) 24–25. Desire of many stage actors, now film stars, to go back to the stage.

Nathan, George Jean. "Memo to Hollywood." *Newswk* 11 (20 June 38) 24. Hollywood stars on the legitimate stage.

Davis, Bette, and David Chandler. "On Acting in Films." *Th Arts* 25 (Sep 41) 632–639. Bette Davis contrasts film and stage acting, on both technical and creative levels.

Pichel, Irving. "Character, Personality, and Image: A Note on Screen Acting." *Hwd Q* 2 (No. 1, Oct 46) 25–29. Differences between stage and screen acting; problems in adapting after stage experience.

Withers, Googie. "Acting for Stage and Screen." *Penguin F Rev* 4 (Oct 47) 36–40. A comparison by an actress of both mediums.

Kracauer, Siegfried. "Stage vs. Screen Acting." *FIR* 1 (Dec 50) 7–11. Both must project

character but in different degrees; cinema doesn't always need the human figure.

Hatfield, Hurd. "Stage vs. Screen Acting." *FIR* 1 (Dec 50) 11–16+. Practical differences explored in some detail.

Wayne, David. "Acting for the Screen." *Th Arts* 35 (Aug 51) 7+. Theatre acting compared to the screen.

Lewis, Theophilus. "Theatre." *America* 89 (20 June 53) 325. Actors should not forget that theatre is their home.

Wayne, David. "Acting—East Coast and West." *FIR* 4 (Aug–Sep 53) 328–331. The differences are social and psychological as well as technical: the environment in which a Hollywood film actor works in contrast to that of the New York stage actor.

Wayne, David. "Theatre's Creative Spark vs. Hollywood's Deep Freeze." *Th Arts* 38 (Jan 54) 26–29. Whereas Broadway acting is creative, Hollywod acting is passive, frozen.

"Stage Stars Were Screen Pioneers." *Th Arts* 38 (Feb 54) 24–25.

Miles, Bernard. "The Acting Art." *FIR* 5 (June–July 54) 267–282. Its differences on stage and screen; essay written for a joint meeting of the British Kinematograph Society and the British Film Academy.

Mason, James. "Back to the Stage." *FIR* 5 (Aug–Sep 54) 327–332. British star appraises acting for stage and film, including the role the actor lives at home and at work during and between film productions.

Mason, James. "Stage vs. Screen." *F&F* 1 (No. 2, Nov 54) 5. The British actor expresses his opinion.

Mason, James. "Stage vs. Screen." *F&F* 1 (No. 3, Dec 54) 7. Reprinted from *Films in Review.*

Brinson, Peter. "The Real Interpreter." *F&F* 1 (No. 7, Apr 55). *See 5, Laurence Olivier.*

von Sternberg, Josef. "Acting in Film and Theatre." *F Cult* 1 (Nos. 5–6, 1955) 1–4+. German director shows how "the art of acting has to be transformed in order to enter the specific synthesis of the film."

Miles, Bernard. "Acting on Stage and Screen." *Drama* (No. 40, Spring 56) 29–33. Differences in acting techniques for the two media.

Winters, Shelley. "That Wonderful, Deep Silence." *Th Arts* 40 (June 56) 30–31+. The values of stage and movie acting and what can be learned from both.

Bogarde, Dirk. "Stop Calling Me a 'Film' Star." *F&F* 3 (No. 4, Jan 57) 7. Comparison of stage to film acting.

Keating, John. "Broadway Magnet Draws Them Back." *NYTM* (26 Feb 61) 20+. Film celebrities in plays on Broadway.

Meehan, Thomas. "Between Actors—A Conversation." *Show* 4 (Dec 64) 28–29+. Alec Guinness and Robert Redford discuss the differences and similarities between stage and screen acting; difficulties with film comedy; theories about comic acting; films are for money and travel and the stage is for real satisfaction in one's profession.

3f(1b). Plays and Screenplays

[See also 2d.]

Troy, William. *"Ex Cathedra."* Nation 137 (27 Dec 33) 744–745. Playwright Elmer Rice says plays are more effective than talkies.

Bower, Dallas. "Wagner and Film." *CQ* 3 (No. 1, Autumn 34) 27–29. "He needed cinema": like Shakespeare, Wagner was a great scenarist.

"Avon Swan's Classic Brought to the Screen." *Lit Dig* 120 (17 Aug 35) 23. Composer Erich Wolfgang Korngold wants Shakespearean movies; actor Walter Hampden does not.

"Broadway: 'The Dog' of Hollywood." *Lit Dig* 119 (20 Apr 35) 20. Theatre is fast becoming proving ground for film stories.

Krutch, Joseph Wood. "Sweet Swan of Hollywood." *Nation* 142 (22 Jan 36) 107–108. Responding to an article by Charles Kenyon, who wrote the scenario for *A Midsummer Night's Dream,* Krutch suggests Hollywood is "torn beween its arrogance and its inferiority" and awaits someone who dares to adapt Shakespeare ruthlessly and skillfully to the screen.

Patterson, F. T. "Author and Hollywood." *North Am Rev* (Sep 37). *See 2d.*

Milne, W. S. "Shakespeare: Script Writer." *Canad Forum* 19 (Nov 39) 252. Shakespeare was a natural scenario writer; he is still waiting for the right film treatment.

Anstey, Edgar. "Scenes from Shakespeare." *Spectator* 175 (13 July 45) 35. British Film Council stages and films short excerpts from Shakespearean dramas for screening overseas and classroom study.

Phillips, James E. "Adapted from a Play by W. Shakespeare." *Hwd Q* 2 (No. 1, Oct 46). *See 2d(4).*

Gibney, Sheridan. "The Screen Writer's Medium." *Screen Writer* 3 (June 47) 23–24. Comparison with playwriting: "The screenwriter, with no artificial limitations to overcome, is faced with the difficult task of making the most of his freedom" and keeping only those scenes which are relevant.

Nathan, Paul S. "A Man Can Stand Up." *Screen Writer* 3 (Dec 47) 34–35. Compares the quality of films with Broadway plays, defending Hollywood.

"O'Neill on the Screen." *Look* 12 (No. 1, 6 Jan 48) 67. Illustrated list of films adapted from the dramas of the American playwright.

Leech, Clifford. "Dialogue for Stage and Screen." *Penguin F Rev* 6 (Apr 48). *See 2d.*

Shakespeare, William, and Laurence Olivier. "Hamlet: The Play and the Screenplay." *Hwd Q* 3 (Spring 48). *See 2d(4).*

Herzberg, M. "Shakespeare and the Screen." *Scholastic* 49 (14 Oct 46) 6T.

Melnitz, William W., David W. Sievers, Richard J. Goggin, Norman G. Dyhrenfurth. "Four Ways to Drama." *Hwd Q* 4 (No. 2, Winter 49) 114–144. Stage, radio, TV, and motion-picture versions, respectively, of the same material discussed and compared.

Hinsdale, Harriet. "Writing for Stage and Screen." *FIR* 2 (Jan 51). *See 2d.*

Phillips, James E. " 'By William Shakespeare— with Additional Dialogue.' " *Hwd Q* 5 (No. 3, Spring 51) 224–236. UCLA English professor analyzes changes and interpretations in film versions of Shakespeare, concluding that cutting and rearranging is often necessary but his sense of drama is hard to improve.

Raynor, Henry. "Shakespeare Filmed." *S&S* 22 (July–Sep 52) 10–15. There has not yet been a really successful screen version.

Benedek, Laslo. "Play into Picture." *S&S* 22 (Oct–Dec 52) 82–84+. An article by the director of *Death of a Salesman;* the changes dictated by the adaptation from stage to screen.

Asquith, A. "Importance of Being Faithful." *Th Arts* 37 (Apr 53) 72–74. Why some plays (like Wilde's *Importance of Being Earnest*) must suffer from "cinematic" treatment.

Smith, John Harrington. "Oscar Wilde's *Earnest* in Film." *QFRTV* 8 (No. 1, Fall 53) 72–79. English professor gives history of *The Importance of Being Earnest* and compares film and stage versions.

Phillips, James E. *"Julius Caesar:* Shakespeare as a Screen Writer." *QFRTV* 8 (No. 2, Winter 53) 125–130. Approval of Houseman-Mankiewicz version by English professor at UCLA, with comments on visual and dramatic impact of play.

Houseman, John. *"Julius Caesar:* Mr. Mankiewicz' Shooting Script." *QFRTV* 8 (No. 2, Winter 53). *See 2d(4).*

Ball, Robert Hamilton. "Shakespeare in One Reel." *QFRTV* 8 (No. 2, Winter 53–54) 139–149. Survey of early silent versions by professor in English department, Queens College, New York City.

Seaton, George. "A Comparison of the Playwright and the Screen Writer." *QFRTV* 10 (Spring 56). *See 2d.*

Lillich, Meredith. "Shakespeare on the Screen." *FIR* 7 (June–July 56) 247–260. A survey of the sixty-six films that have been adapted from twenty-two of the thirty-three plays by Shakespeare from the 1905 silent version of *Macbeth* to the 1956 British production

Richard III by Laurence Olivier. Condensation of a Cornell University thesis.

Giesler, Rodney. "Shakespeare and the Screen." *F&F* 2 (No. 10, July 56) 7+. Adaptations of Shakespeare in recent films.

Roud, Richard. "The Empty Streets." *S&S* 26 (Spring 57) 191–195. A play such as *The Member of the Wedding* cannot be expanded for the screen to show the social setting; it is not therefore so successful as *Bus Stop* or *Picnic*.

Macgowan, Kenneth. "O'Neill and a Mature Hollywood Outlook." *Th Arts* 42 (Apr 58) 79–81. On the new film version of O'Neill's *Desire Under the Elms*.

Roman, Robert C. "O'Neill on the Screen." *FIR* 9 (June–July 58) 296–305+. Film adaptations of the works of Eugene O'Neill, the actors in them, and some judgments on them.

Mycroft, Walter. "Shaw—and the Devil to Pay." *F&F* 5 (No. 5, Feb 59). *See 5, G. B. Shaw.*

Nichols, Dudley. " 'O'Neill on the Screen.' " *FIR* 9 (Aug–Sep 58) 409. Letter to editor responding to article by Robert Roman 9 (June–July 58); screenwriter comments on tragedy, the public, and *Mourning Becomes Electra*.

Roberts, Meade. "Williams and Me." *F&F* 6 (No. 11, Aug 60). *See 5, Tennessee Williams.*

Peck, Seymour. "The Play's the Thing, for the Movies." *NYTM* (25 Mar 62) 38–39. Production stills of recent films adapted from the stage.

Alpert, Hollis. "In With the New." *Sat Rev* 45 (17 Nov 62) 36. MCA and Seven Arts back Broadway shows to obtain properties for the screen.

Bolt, Robert. "The Playwright in Films." *Sat Rev* (29 Dec 62) 15–16. Part of *Saturday Review* report "The Lonely Art of Film-Making."

Delacorte, Valerie. "GBS in Filmland." *Esq* 62 (Dec 64) 150–151+. The former wife of Shaw's cinema collaborator peppers this memoir with unpublished letters from George Bernard Shaw.

Reeves, Geoffrey. "Shakespeare on Three Screens." *S&S* 34 (Spring 65) 66–70. Interview with Peter Brook about the problems of adapting Shakespeare, including the Orson Welles and Laurence Olivier versions; Kozintsev's *Hamlet* and Kurosawa's *Throne of Blood* are the best Shakespearean screen adaptations to date. Reprinted from the *Tulane Drama Review*.

Long, Chester Clayton. "Cocteau's *Orphée:* From Myth to Drama to Film." *Q J Speech* 51 (No. 3, Oct 65). *See 3c, Orphée.*

Godfrey, Lionel. "It Wasn't Like That in the Play." *F&F* 13 (No. 11, Aug 67) 4–8. On film adaptations.

Hayman, Ronald. "Shakespeare on the Screen." *Times Lit Supplement* 3,474 (26 Sep 68) 1081–1082. An examination of various adaptations of Shakespeare's plays for film.

Potter, Henry C., George Roy Hill, and Gene Saks. "Stage to Film." *Action* 3 (No. 5, Sep–Oct 68) 12–14. Excerpts from a forum discussion of the problems of adapting stage works to the screen.

Sewell, John B. "Shakespeare on the Screen: Part II." *FIR* 20 (No. 7, Aug–Sep 69) 419–441. Continuation of 1956 article.

3f(2). LITERATURE AND FILM

[See also 2d.]

Blakeston, Oswell. "Our Literary Screen." *Close Up* 6 (No. 4, 1930) 308–310.

Rotha, Paul. "The Revival of Naturalism." *Close Up* 7 (No. 1, 1930). *See 3a(2).*

Potamkin, Harry A. "Novel into Film: A Case Study of Current Practice." *Close Up* 8 (No. 4, Dec 31) 267–279. Comparison of Eisenstein's scenario and the novel *An American Tragedy.*

"Making the Movies Sell Books." *Publishers Weekly* 122 (17 Sep 32) 1027–1030. Tie-ups between popular-priced reprints and motion-picture versions.

"Books into Movies." *Publishers Weekly* 121 (18 June 32) 2416. Lists books currently being adapted for movies.

Bond, Kirk. "Film as Literature." *Bookman* 84 (July 33) 188–189. A defense of the film drama as an art comparable to literature.

MacDiarmid, Hugh. "Poetry and Film." *CQ* 2 (No. 3, Spring 34) 146–149. A poet finds cinema close to literature.

Fadiman, William James. "Books into Movies." *Publishers Weekly* 126 (8 Sep 34) 753–755. In 1933 nearly 200 books were purchased for screen rights.

"Books into Movies." *Publishers Weekly* 126 (15 Sep 34) 921–922.

Fadiman, William James. "Selling Books to Movies." *Publishers Weekly* 126 (22 Sep 34) 1085–1087. Recommendations to writers.

Lewin, William. "The Effect of Photoplays on Reading." *Publishers Weekly* 126 (20 Oct 34) 1474–1475.

"Current and Forthcoming Movies from Books." *Publishers Weekly* 127 (23 Mar 35) 1238; (27 Apr 35) 1688.

Gibbon, Lewis G. "A Novelist Looks at the Cinema." *CQ* 3 (No. 2, Winter 35) 81–85. It's preferable to theatre but many things are wrong.

"Current and Forthcoming Movies from Books." *Publishers Weekly* 129 (1 Feb 36) 618.

Block, Maxine. "Films Adapted from Published Works." *Wilson Lib Bul* 10 (Feb 36) 394–395. Classics sought since Legion of Decency campaign; list of books and plays.

Robertson, E. Arnot. "Intruders in the Film World." *Fortune* 145 (No. 139, Feb 36) 194–198. Novelist tries her hand at making a short film after reacting negatively to a Claudette Colbert film based on her book.

Holmes, Winifred. "The New Renaissance." *S&S* 5 (No. 18, Summer 36) 7–9. The pros and cons of filming literary classics.

"Prospero in 1936." *SRL* 14 (18 July 36) 8. Editorial: suggestions for movie versions of literature.

Hurley, R. J. "What About the Movies?" *Lib J* 61 (1 Sep 36) 639–640. Literary sources for films offer opportunity to encourage reading; guides for film study.

Casson, Stanley. "Homer Filmed." *Fortune* 146 (No. 140, Sep 36) 294–301. What a fine movie the story of Odysseus would make!

"Motion Pictures from Books." *Publishers Weekly* 130 (3 Oct 36) 1420; (17 Oct 36) 1611; (21 Nov 36) 2028; (26 Dec 36) 2505; 131 (6 Feb 37) 746.

Seldes, Gilbert. "Vandals of Hollywood." *SRL* 14 (17 Oct 36) 3–4. Why a good movie cannot be faithful to the original novel or play. Same abridged, *Rev of Reviews* 94 (Nov 36) 70–71.

Mullen, S. M. "From Paper to Celluloid." *Scholastic* 29 (17 Oct 36) 17–18.

Seldes, Gilbert. "No More Swing?" *Scribner's* 100 (Nov 36) 71–72. Article on the popular arts concludes with references to writers who use cinematic styles and movies which have drawn on books; *The General Died at Dawn,* written by Odets.

Nicoll, Allardyce. "Literature and the Film." *English J* 26 (Jan 37) 1–9.

"Off the Shelf." *Lit Dig* 123 (12 June 37) 31. Film versions of literary classics cause public-library runs.

Block, M. "Looking Backward and Forward at Films." *Wilson Lib Bul* 12 (Nov 37) 202+. A survey of films past and present that are adaptations of famous literary works.

MacLean, Helen. "Movies, the Radio and the Library." *Lib J* 63 (July 38) 550–551. Use of films to lure public to better reading.

Stephenson, F. "Hollywood Reads." *Publishers Weekly* 134 (10 Sep 38) 844–845. Hollywood's story-department efforts to bring literature to the screen.

Myers, Frederick. "Library-Film Cooperation." *Lib J* 63 (15 Oct 38) 792. Cooperation designed to increase reading and draw more people to the box office; special editions of bookmarks.

Garrison, Gretchen. "Forgetting a Thousand Cares; Library-Film Cooperation." *Lib J* 64 (1 Feb 39) 87–90. Using films to stimulate reading.

Havener, H. "Reader Interest Stimulated." *Lib J* 64 (15 May 39) 408. The film *Wuthering Heights* stimulates reading of the novel.

"Film Stimulates Reading." *Lib J* 64 (1 Nov 39) 866. *Wuthering Heights* as a film stimulates reading of the novel.

Walton, Thomas. "Filming the Masterpiece." *S&S* 8 (No. 32, Winter 39–40) 134–135. Flaubert and Hugo as precursors of cinematic qualities.

Mealand, R. "What Books Do the Movies Want?" *Publishers Weekly* 137 (15 June 40) 2262–2264. A look at film trends and what types of books are appropriate to them.

Mosier, R. D. "Motion Pictures for Story Backgrounds." *Writer* 54 (Nov 41) 338–339. How films can help the young writer with character development and story.

Home, H. "Cooperation That Counts: Promotion of Books Made into Movies." *Publishers Weekly* 144 (4 Sep 43). See 6d.

Sobel, B. "Film Futurities." *Th Arts* 28 (Mar 44) 167–170. A proposal for Hollywood to attempt to become more "literate" by adapting classics such as the works of Balzac and Fielding to the screen.

Pratt, Theodore. "From the Novel by . . ." *Atlantic* 225 (Mar 45) 109–112.

Hilton, James. "A Novelist Looks at the Screen." *Screen Writer* 1 (Nov 45) 30–34. Hollywood's influence on the novelist and the novelist's influence on Hollywood; Hollywood should move beyond "gilt, girls, glamor and goofiness," as it already has in some degree.

Kraft, H. S. "Dreiser's War in Hollywood." *Screen Writer* 1 (Mar 46) 9–13. An account (by a participant) of Theodore Dreiser's battle with Paramount Studios over their treatment of his novel *An American Tragedy,* produced in 1931. He lost the legal case for protection of his "standards" and story.

Mealand, R. "What's a Book Got?" *Publishers Weekly* 150 (9 Nov 46) 2716–2717. Are books better than movies? A humorous discussion.

Hilton, James. "Literature and Hollywood." *Atlantic* 178 (Dec 46) 130–136. Writers are up against a machine of myth making in all media, and the old-fashioned relationship of author and publisher may be disappearing.

"Goldwyn vs. Thurber." *Life* 23 (18 Aug 47). See 9, *The Secret Life of Walter Mitty.*

Hodgins, Eric. "Mr. Blandings Goes to Hollywood." *Life* 24 (12 Apr 48) 110–124+. A lighthearted journal of the author's visit to Hollywood to watch his novel made into a film.

Rippy, Frazier W. "On Tragedy, Motion Pictures, and Greta Garbo." *Ariz Q* 5 (No. 1, 49). See 3a.

Ambler, Eric. "The Film of the Book." *Penguin F Rev* 9 (May 49) 22–25. Fictional spoof of relationship between novelist and film producer; not much is left of the book or the relationship.

Eisenstein, S. M. "Dickens, Griffith, and the Film Today." *S&S* 19 (June 50) 169–171; (July 50) 216–218; (Aug 50) 256–258; (Nov 50) 294–297. From his forthcoming book *Film Form* (Harcourt Brace Jovanovich, 1969).

Brenton, Guy. "Two Adaptations." *Sequence* (No. 12, Autumn 50) 33–36. Reflections on the nature of filmic adaptations from novels as provoked by *All the King's Men* and *Force of Evil*.

Thorp, Margaret. "The Motion Picture and the Novel." *Am Q* 3 (No. 3, 1951) 195–203. The film as an evolving medium could profitably study the novel in areas of major concern shared by each: point of view, a command of space, and the use of symbols.

Asheim, Lester. "From Book to Film: Simplification." *Hwd Q* 5 (No. 3, Spring 51) 289–304. First of four articles based on University of Chicago dissertation; from twenty-four "standard" novels made into films between 1935 and 1946, author finds examples of simplification, often unnecessary.

Asheim, Lester. "From Book to Film: Mass Appeals." *Hwd Q* 5 (No. 4, Summer 51) 334–349. How characters are altered, plots changed, dialogue rearranged, violence and sex emphasized to give novels more appeal on the screen.

Asheim, Lester. "From Book to Film: The Note of Affirmation." *QFRTV* 6 (No. 1, Fall 51) 54–68. The emphasis on romantic love and happy endings, sometimes intelligently accomplished.

Hutchins, Patricia. "James Joyce and the Cinema." *S&S* 21 (Aug–Sep 51) 9–12. Joyce's connections with the cinema as an exhibitor and collaborator; his interest in films; his influence on Eisenstein and others.

Debrix, Jean R. "The Movies and Poetry." *FIR* 2 (Oct 51) 17–22. Translated by Dorothy Milburn. Both help us to see in new ways; both use an irrational language appealing to our primary instincts.

Stern, Seymour. "Griffith and Poe." *FIR* 2 (Nov 51) 23–28. Through an analysis of D. W. Griffith's film *The Avenging Conscience*, Stern shows the specific parts of the film that are adapted from Edgar Allan Poe's stories and poems.

Brooks, Richard. "A Novel Isn't a Movie." *FIR* 3 (Feb 52) 55–59. Hollywood director explains why changes are necessary in the film adaptation of a novel; how the author's own novel, *The Black Foxhole*, was changed, with his approval.

Asheim, Lester. "From Book to Film: Summary." *QFRTV* 6 (No. 3, Spring 52) 258–273. Fourth and last article based on author's dissertation; problems of technology, the star system, deference to the audience and other pressures; film artists should do more than reflect what the audience wants at the moment.

"Hemingway in Hollywood." *NYTM* (14 Sep 52) 58–59. Stills from five of the movies based on his work.

Moreno, Julio L. "Subjective Cinema: And the Problem of Film in the First Person." *QFRTV* 7 (No. 4, Summer 53). *See 3a.*

Jones, Dorothy B. "William Faulkner: Novel into Film." *QFRTV* 8 (No. 1, Fall 53). *See 3c, Intruder in the Dust.*

Shull, William, and Earl Leslie Griggs. "*The Ancient Mariner* on the Screen." *QFRTV* 8 (No. 1, Fall 53) 87–99. Maker of film based on Coleridge poem used Gustav Doré engravings; his problems with adaptations, pacing, and sound; Professor Griggs then reviews the finished film.

Wald, Jerry. "Screen Adaptation." *FIR* 5 (Feb 54) 62–67. Producer praises Dan Taradash for *From Here to Eternity* and quotes Philip Dunne and others on the problem of adapting novels.

Woolf, Virginia. "The Film Folio 6: The Cinema." *S&S* 23 (Apr–June 54) 215–216. Written in 1926 and published in a book in 1950, *The Captain's Deathbed;* she comments on the state of the art at that time (crude but with potential) and the film's dependence on novels for material (unfortunate for both media).

Leyda, Jay. "Tolstoy on Film." *S&S* 24 (July–Sep 54). *See 8a.*

McDonald, Gerald D. "Authors as Actors." *FIR* 5 (Dec 54). *See 2b.*

Wilson, N. Hope. "The Kettles." *FIR* 5 (Dec 54) 524–526. *See 4k(1).*

Minchinton, John. "The Glory Trilogy." *F&F* 1 (No. 4, Jan 55). *See 4e(8a).*

Finch, Hardy. "Hollywood: Our New Book Salesman." *Scholastic* 65 (5 Jan 55) 27T. Movies stimulate interest in reading.

Starr, Cecile. "Film's Cousin, the Book." *Sat Rev* 38 (9 Apr 55) 35–36. A selection of films from famous literary sources.

Schulberg, Budd. "Why Write It When You Can't Sell It to the Pictures?" *Sat Rev* 38 (3 Sep 55) 5–6+. Comparing the novel with the motion picture.

Mankiewicz, Don. "Screenplays, Real and Unreal." *Sat Rev* 38 (22 Oct 55) 9–10. Adapting the novel *Trial*, the author discovers the differences between novel and film.

Houston, Penelope. "The Private Eye." *S&S* 26 (Summer 56). *See 4k(10).*

Wald, Jerry. "The Long Sellers." *Lib J* 81 (1 Oct 56). *See 7b(1a).*

Bluestone, George. "Word to Image: The Problem of the Filmed Novel." *QFRTV* 11 (No. 2, Winter 56) 171–180. Brief history of the filming of novels; how film versions have affected the popularity of novels; comments on *Wuthering Heights, Lost Horizon,* and others; the critic's problem.

Montani, Harold. "Zola Out of Focus." *F&F* 3 (No. 3, Dec 56) 12. Comments on films from Zola's writings.

Todd, Oliver. "Paris Letter." *Hudson Rev* 10 (Spring 57) 101–102. Problems of adaptation in René Clement's *Gervaise,* Astruc's *Les Mauvaises Rencontres.*

"Hollywood Goes Hemingway." *NYTM* (26 May 57) 66–67. Production stills from *A Farewell to Arms, The Old Man and the Sea,* and *The Sun Also Rises.*

Kirschner, Paul. "Conrad and the Film." *QFRTV* 11 (No. 4, Summer 57) 343–353. From his M.A. thesis at University of London, author draws examples of Conrad's "filmic" methods and discusses *Outcast of the Islands* and *The Secret Sharer,* made from Conrad's works.

Riesman, Evelyn T. "Film and Fiction." *Antioch Rev* 17 (Fall 57) 353–363.

"It's Hemingway's Year." *Newswk* 50 (16 Dec 57) 116+. Problems of filming *The Old Man and the Sea* and others. Opinions of Hemingway's work are given by scriptwriter Peter Viertel, director Henry King, and David Selznick.

Brooks, Richard. "On Filming *Karamazov.*" *FIR* 9 (Feb 58) 49–52. Director-writer tells how the novel *The Brothers Karamazov* was dramatized for film; he wanted it faithful, entertaining, profitable, and only ninety minutes in length.

Clarke, T. E. B. "Every Word in Its Place." *F&F* 4 (No. 5, Feb 58). See 9, *A Tale of Two Cities.*

Mason, Ronald. "The Film of the Book." *Film* (No. 16, Mar–Apr 58) 18–20. Problems of transforming book into film reveal the inherent incompatibility of the two media.

Roud, Richard. "Two Cents on the Rouble." *S&S* 27 (Summer 58) 245–247. Disappointing attempts to translate great novels to film: *The Brothers Karamazov, A Farewell to Arms,* and *The Long Hot Summer;* the best American novel-films are made from less intimidating works: *Magnificent Ambersons, Grapes of Wrath,* and *The Ox-Bow Incident.*

MacLaren-Ross, J. "Story-Telling and the Screen." *Times Lit Supplement* 2946 (15 Aug 58) xxviii. Direct forms of storytelling may eventually be superseded by the cinema.

Wald, Jerry. "This Is Why We'll Film James Joyce." *F&F* 4 (No. 12, Sep 58) 9+. Audience is changing and producer must take chances.

"Book Buyer." *Time* 72 (6 Oct 58) 50–51.

Fox producer Jerry Wald finds fortune in turning books into films.

Roman, Robert C. "Dickens' *A Christmas Carol.*" *FIR* 9 (Dec 58) 572–574. Appraisal of ten different films, all of which are based on Charles Dickens' work.

Scott, Kenneth W. "Hawkeye in Hollywood." *FIR* 9 (Dec 58) 575–579. Films based on the works of James Fenimore Cooper, including six versions of *The Last of the Mohicans.*

Wald, Jerry. "From Faulkner to Film." *Sat Rev* 42 (7 Mar 59) 16+. The producer of two Faulkner films discusses the problems of literary adaptations.

Wald, Jerry. "Faulkner and Hollywood." *FIR* 10 (Mar 59) 129–133. He worked there but never on his own books; brief reference to his films and others' films of his books; problems of adaptation in Wald's productions of *The Long Hot Summer* and *The Sound and the Fury.*

Tupper, Lucy. "Dickens on the Screen." *FIR* 10 (Mar 59) 142–152. A survey of the screen adaptations of the novels of Charles Dickens made internationally since 1909.

Lillich, Richard B. "Hemingway on the Screen." *FIR* 10 (Apr 59) 208–218. Film adaptations of his works.

Bates, H. E. "It Isn't Like the Book." *F&F* 5 (No. 8, May 59) 7. Writer criticizes transition from book to film.

Hyams, Joe. "An 'Interview' with 'Pappy' Faulkner." *JSPG* (Sep 59) 17–20. Tribulations of attempting to get an interview with William Faulkner, who has "never seen the pictures" Jerry Wald made of his books.

Linden, M. "Book-Based Oscars." *Lib J* 85 (1 Apr 60) 1346–1347.

Lambert, Gavin. "Lawrence: The Script . . ." *F&F* 6 (No. 8, May 60). See 9, *Sons and Lovers.*

Holland, Norman N. "How New? How Vague?" *Hudson Rev* 13 (Summer 60). See 4e(2b).

Roman, Robert C. "G. B. S. on the Screen." *FIR* 11 (No. 7, Aug–Sep 60) 406–418. Handling of Shaw's plays; his comments on movies.

Fadiman, William. "The Great Hollywood Book-Hunt." *Sat Rev* 43 (17 Sep 60) 27–30+. Hollywood's raw material; what happens once a story has been bought.

Noxon, Gerald. "The Anatomy of the Close-Up." *J Soc Cin* 1 (1961) 1–24. Subtitled "some literary origins in the works of Flaubert, Huysmans, and Proust."

Sidney, George. "William Faulkner and Hollywood." *Colorado Q* 9 (1961) 367–377.

Roman, Robert C. "Mark Twain on the Screen." *FIR* 12 (No. 1, Jan 61) 20–35. How Twain's stories have been adapted for the screen over the years.

Bluestone, George. "Time in Film and Fiction."

J Aesthetics and Art Criticism 19 (No. 3, Spring 61) 311–315. Cinema differs from literature in structuring both time and reality; compression and distention; time flux.

Bluestone, George. "Adaptation or Evasion: *Elmer Gantry.*" *FQ* 14 (No. 3, Spring 61). *See 3c, Elmer Gantry.*

Knight, Arthur. "Hemingway into Film." *Sat Rev* (29 July 61) 33–34. The seeming simplicity of his prose has not turned out to be so cinematic after all; a list of fourteen Hollywod pictures based on his works.

Fadiman, William. "The New-Style Myth Makers." *F&F* 7 (No. 11, Aug 61) 20. Growing phenomenon of books being written specifically with film in mind.

Pasolini, Pier Paolo. "Cinematic and Literary Stylistic Figures." *F Cult* (No. 24, 1962) 42–43. Italian director's theories.

Roud, Richard. "Novel Novel; Fable Fable?" *S&S* 31 (Spring 62) 84–88. The fable may be the art form most suited to our time, because it recognizes the irrational elements in life and frees the film maker "from the obligations of story-telling."

Koningsberger, H. "Not by the Book." *Horizon* 4 (May 62) 116–118. General comments about films from novels; specific comments on Otto Preminger's *Advise and Consent.*

Burke, John. "The Book of the Film." *Film* (No. 33, Autumn 62) 48. A personal account of adapting screenplays into books.

Culkin, J. "When a Book Becomes a Movie." *Senior Scholastic* 81 (10 Oct 62) 24T–26T.

Hammond, R. M. "The Literary Style of Luis Buñuel." *Hispania* 46 (No. 3, 1963). *See 5, Luis Buñuel.*

Scherman, D. "Everybody Blows Up!" *Life* 54 (8 Mar 63) 49–50. Literary antecedents for *Dr. Strangelove* and *Fail Safe.*

Bodeen, DeWitt. "The Adapting Art." *FIR* 14 (June–July 63) 349–356. Description of problems involved in adapting literary works for film.

Knebel, Fletcher. "*Seven Days in May:* The Movie the Military Shunned." *Look* 27 (19 Nov 63). *See 9, Seven Days in May.*

Culkin, John M. "Movies, TV and Paperbacks." *Senior Scholastic* 83 (17 Jan 64) 28T–29T. Differences between print and image listed and discussed.

"Catch $95." *Newswk* 63 (9 Mar 64) 83–84. Novelists William Styron, Joseph Heller, and Terry Southern are invading movies.

Schickel, R. "Big Money Writers: Books Turned into Movies." *Life* 57 (31 July 64) 58–60.

Peck, S. "Based on the Best Seller By . . ." *NYTM* (13 Sep 64) 44–45. Photos of movies from novels.

Alter, J. "Alain Robbe-Grillet and the Cinematographic Style." *Mod Lang J* 48 (No. 6, Oct 64) 363–366 A discussion of the cinema-

novel *Last Year at Marienbad,* compared with his other works.

Price, James. "Words and Pictures." *London Mag* new series 4 (No. 7, Oct 64) 66–70. On adaptations from novels, especially *The Pumpkin Eater* and *Lord of the Flies.*

Noxon, Gerald. "Some Observations on the Anatomy of the Long Shot." *J Soc Cin* 5 (1965) 70–80. Part of a longer work on literary origins of cinema narrative; descriptions of a castle by Stendhal, of a man in the distance by Balzac, and of Paris by Zola.

Nolan, Jack Edmund. "Simenon on the Screen." *FIR* 16 (No. 7, Aug–Sep 65) 419–446. How author Georges Simenon's works have fared on the screen.

Silverstein, Norman. "Movie-Going for Lovers of *The Wasteland* and *Ulysses.*" *Salmagundi* 1 (No. 1, Fall 65). *See 3b(2).*

Sayers, Frances. "Walt Disney Accused." *Horn Bk* (Dec 65). *See 2h(3).*

Lyons, Joseph. "*The Pawnbroker:* Flashback in the Novel and the Film." *Western Humanities Rev* 20 (1966). *See 3c, The Pawnbroker.*

Gow, Gordon. "Novels into Films." *F&F* 12 (No. 8, May 66) 19–22. Comments by three novelists who have written works later made into films: Patricia Highsmith, Rumer Godden, and Alan Sillitoe.

Larson, Lawrence A. "The Cinematic and the Biblical Points of View: A New Correlation." *Religion in Life* 35 (Summer 66) 457–467. The storytelling process offers "a vitalized view of reality."

Sugg, Alfred. "The Beatles and Film Art." *F Her* 1 (No. 4, Summer 66) 3–13. Also J. D. Salinger; the film art and its relation to the art of literature.

Battestin, Martin C. "Osborne's *Tom Jones:* Adapting a Classic." *Virginia Q Rev* 42 (Summer 66) 378–393. Why Osborne's *Tom Jones* is one of the most successful cinematic adaptations ever made, with special reference to the literary modes and methods of the English Augustan Age.

Stone, Irving. "A Novelist Looks at His Movie." *F&F* 12 (No. 12, Sep 66). *See 9, The Agony and the Ecstasy.*

Leonard, Neil. "Theodore Dreiser and the Film." *F Her* 2 (No. 1, Fall 66) 7–16. His experiences in Hollywood (which he wrote about) and his novels transformed into films.

Mailer, Norman. "The Writer and Hollywood." *F Her* 2 (No. 1, Fall 66) 23. Mailer answers the questions: Has Hollywood treated your works justly? Can the serious writer's works survive in Hollywood?

French, Philip. "All the Better Books." *S&S* 36 (Winter 66–67) 38–41. The current European tendency to make mention of books and other arts within films.

"Page and Screen." *Times Lit Supplement* 3390 (16 Feb 67) 127. An examination of film and literature, the differences and theoretical foundations of each.

McCabe, Bernard. "Ulysses in the Reel World." *New Cath World* 204 (Mar 67) 346–351. How the movie might reflect the Joyce novel.

Godfrey, Lionel. "It Wasn't Like That in the Book." *F&F* 13 (No. 7, Apr 67) 12–16. Study of film adaptations from novels.

Madden, David. "James M. Cain and the Movies of the Thirties and Forties." *F Her* 2 (No. 4, Summer 67) 9–25. The cross-fertilization of the tough-guy novel and its movie counterpart: Cain as scriptwriter and as novelist.

Madden, Roberta. *"The Blue Hotel:* An Examination of Story and Film Script." *F Her* 3 (No. 1, Fall 67) 20–34. James Agee's film script of the Stephen Crane story analyzed.

Dewey, Lang. *"Ulysses." Film* (No. 49, Autumn 67). *See 3c, Ulysses.*

Jensen, Paul. "H. G. Wells on the Screen." *FIR* 18 (No. 9, Nov 67) 521–527. How Wells' fiction has survived translation on the screen.

Corbett, T. "Film and the Book: A Case Study of *The Collector." English J* 57 (Mar 68). *See 9, The Collector.*

Baldwin, James. "I Can't Blow This Gig." *Cinema* (Calif) 4 (No. 2, Summer 68) 2–3. Author comments on problems of scripting *The Autobiography of Malcolm X.*

Fuller, Stanley. "Melville on the Screen." *FIR* 19 (No. 6, June–July 68) 358–377. How Herman Melville's works have fared on the screen.

Macklin, F. Anthony. " '. . . Benjamin Will Survive . . .' Interview With Charles Webb." *F Her* 4 (No. 1, Fall 68) 1–6. *The Graduate;* novel and film; interview with the author of the novel.

"Camera Styles." *Times Lit Supplement.* 3474 (26 Sep 68) 1079. The visual style of film juxtaposed to words in literature and film.

Gollub, Judith. "French Writers Turned Film Makers." *F Her* 4 (No. 2, Winter 68–69) 19–25. Robbe-Grillet, Marguerite Duras, Jean Cayrol, and Romain Gary.

Ferández, Henry. *"Blow-Up." F Her* 4 (No. 2, Winter 68–69) *See 3c, Blow-Up.*

Nolan, Jack E. "Graham Greene's Movies." *FIR* 15 (No. 1, Jan 69). *See 5, Graham Greene.*

Koningsberger, Hans. "From Book to Film—Via John Huston." *FQ* 22 (No. 3, Spring 69) 2–4. How the author's novel *A Walk with Love and Death* was adapted for the screen; he was on the set with the director throughout and often had to "explain every word and action to him in precise terms."

Phillips, G. D. "Graham Greene: On the Screen." *Cath World* 209 (Aug 69) 218–221.

Weightman, John. "Outsider Rides Again." *Encounter* 33 (Nov 69). *See 7a.*

Koch, Stephen. "Fiction and Film: A Search for New Sources." *Sat Rev* (27 Dec 69) 12–14+. Neither recent literature nor European films of the 1960s are sufficient stimuli for new film making in the 1970s. Part of *Saturday Review* report "The Art That Matters."

Wood, Robin. *"Night of the Hunter:* Novel into Film." *On Film* (1970). *See 3c.*

Soderbergh, Peter A. "Upton Sinclair and Hollywood." *Midwest Q* 11 (Jan 70) 173–191. How he dealt with Eisenstein, with Hollywood in two novels, and with newsreel attacks on his candidacy for governor.

Rhode, Eric. "Dostoevsky and Bresson." *S&S* 39 (Spring 70) 82–83. Rhode compares Robert Bresson's film adaptation *A Gentle Creature* and Dostoevsky's original story, written in 1876, about the suicide of a young seamstress.

Rosen, Robert. "Enslaved by the Queen of the Night: The Relationship of Ingmar Bergman to E. T. A. Hoffman." *F Com* 6 (No. 1, Spring 1970) 26–32. German professor at New York City College compares *Hour of the Wolf* with Hoffman's story "The Golden Pot."

Buscombe, Edward. "Dickens and Hitchcock." *Screen* 11 (Nos. 4–5, 1970) 97–114.

Miller, Henry. *"Tropic of Cancer* Revisited." *Playboy* 17 (No. 6, June 70) 133+. Shots from film *Tropic of Cancer* (Joseph Strick) with accompanying text by Miller, commenting on his reaction to the film and reminiscences about the book.

Folsom, James K. *"Shane* and *Hud:* Two Stories in Search of a Medium." *Western Humanities Rev* 24 (No. 4, Autumn 70) 359–372. A study of the differences between the novels and the films from these same two stories.

Highet, G. "Whose *Satyricon,* Petronius's or Fellini's?" *Horizon* 12 (Autumn 70) 42–47. Comparison of Fellini's film with Petronius' book; discussion of film's historical authenticity.

Thegze, Chuck. " 'I See Everything Twice': An Examination of *Catch-22." FQ* 24 (No. 1, Fall 70). *See 9.*

Purdy, S. B. "Gertrude Stein at Marienbad." *Pubs Mod Lang Assoc* 85 (No. 5, Oct 70) 1096–1105. The Robbe-Grillet script for *Last Year at Marienbad* echoes Stein's repetition of words and phrases.

Tarratt, Margaret. "An Obscene Undertaking." *F&F* 17 (No. 2, Nov 70) 26–30. On the films that have come from the novels of D. H. Lawrence.

Thomaier, William. "Conrad on the Screen." *FIR* 21 (No. 10, Dec 70) 611–621. How Joseph Conrad's novels have fared in the transition to film.

3f(3). PAINTING, SCULPTURE, GRAPHIC ARTS

[See also 2e, 2h, 8a(3).]

Moholy-Nagy, Laszlo. "The Problem of Modern Cinematography: Its Emancipation from Painting." *Intercine* (*International Review of Educational Cinematography*) 2 (1930) 1363–1368. Film must free itself from pictorial art and create a new art form based on colors and chromatic scales obtained by a bold and imaginative use of light and movement.

Blakeston, Oswell. "Stills and Their Relation to Modern Cinema." *Close Up* 8 (No. 1, Mar 31) 20–26. Theoretical comments on the use of stills.

Blakeston, Oswell. "Prospective Perspective." *Close Up* 9 (No. 2, June 32) 117–118. The interaction between film and culture is easily illustrated in Chinese versus Western painting.

Shearsby, Arthur. "The Artist and the Film." *CQ* 3 (No. 3, Spring 35) 143–146. He can contribute to abstraction and fantasy.

Rotha, Paul, and R. H. Wilenski. "The Poison of 'the Pictures'; Painting v. the Film." *London Studio* 12 (Sep 36) 140–141. The art critic R. H. Wilenski argues that neither photograph nor film ever will be a work of art; Paul Rotha responds that one cannot blame the film or camera for devitalizing painting.

"Mad Enough to Spit." *Art Dig* 12 (Sep 38) 15. Should serious American artists work in the medium of animation instead?

"Motion Pictures." *Design* 41 (Dec 39) 7–31. Issue includes such articles as "Motion Pictures and Art Education," "ABC's of Movie Making," "Scholastic Hollywoods," "Motion Pictures Must Come from a Design," "Early Films," "Artistic Motion Pictures."

Walker, George Graham. "Film and Fine Art." *S&S* 17 (No. 68, Winter 48–49) 173–174. The effects of art, particularly graphic art, upon the form of the film.

Hugo, Ian. "An Artist Makes a Movie." *FIR* 1 (Sep 50) 24–26+. Engraver's views on film making, especially his own *Ai-Ye* (*Mankind*).

Richter, Hans. "Easel-Scroll-Film." *Mag of Art* 45 (Feb 52) 78–86. The artist traces his personal development from the initial problems posed by the cubists to his creation of abstract films.

Davis, James E. "The Only Dynamic Art." *FIR* 4 (Dec 53) 511–515. Painter and sculptor explains why he now works only in film.

Tyler, Parker. "Film Sense and the Painting Sense." *Art Dig* 28 (15 Feb 54) 10–12+.

Tyler, Parker. "Film Sense and the Painting Sense; with an Account of Some Recent American Experimental Films." *Perspectives USA* (No. 11, 1955) 95–106. The interrelationship of film and painting with regard to the works of Griffith, Emmer, Méliès, McLaren, Dreyer, Eisenstein, and others.

Eisenstein, Sergei. "Sketches for Life." *F&F* 4 (No. 7, Apr 58). *See 5, Sergei Eisenstein.*

Noxon, Gerald. "Cinema and Cubism." *J Soc Cin* 2 (1962) 23–33.

Mathews, J. H. "Surrealism and the Cinema." *Criticism* 4 (No. 2, 1962) 120–133. The continuing vitality of surrealism as an influence on film.

Noxon, Gerald. "Pictorial Origins of Cinema Narrative: Chinese Scroll Paintings." *J Soc Cin* 3 (1963). *See 4a(4a).*

Young, Vernon. "Nostalgia of the Infinite: Notes on Chirico, Antonioni, Resnais." *Arts Mag* 37 (Jan 63) 14–21. Antonioni and Resnais related to various issues in art.

"Taken for Granite." *Show* 3 (June 63). *See 2b.*

Hill, Jerome. "Some Notes on Painting and Film-making." *F Cult* (No. 32, 1964) 31–32.

Noxon, Gerald. "Pictorial Origins of Cinema Narrative: Paleolithic Cave Wall Paintings of Lascaux." *J Soc Cin* 4 (1964). *See 4a (4a).*

"More Chips off the Old Block." *Show* 4 (Oct 64). *See 2b(2).*

Durgnat, Raymond. "Fake, Fiddle and the Photographic Arts." *Brit J Aesthetics* 5 (No. 3, July 65).

Arnheim, Rudolf. "Art Today and the Film." *Art J* 25 (Spring 66) 242–244. Aspects of today's art applied to film: "aesthetic demands of our time."

Spears, Jack. "Comic Strips on the Screen." *FIR* 7 (Aug–Sep 56) 317–325+. History of the adaptation of the major comic strips; most successful were *Skippy* (1930), which won its director, Norman Taurog, an Oscar, and the 26 films in the *Blondie* series, which began in 1938 and ran for thirteen years.

Lacassin, Francis. "Dick Tracy Meets Muriel." *S&S* 36 (Spring 67). *See 5, Alain Resnais.*

Noxon, Gerald. "The Bayeux Tapestry." *CJ* 7 (1967–1968). *See 4a(4a).*

Leepa, Allen. "A Painter Looks at Film." *JUFA* 20 (No. 2, 1968) 34–38. Professor of art at Michigan State University compares contemporary approaches to art and cinema: whether existentialist or minimalist, they emphasize problems of subjectivity.

Gessner, Robert. "Erwin Panofsky, 1892–1968." *F Com* 4 (No. 4, Summer 68) 3. Tribute to critic and professor of fine arts who wrote the article "Style and Medium in the Motion Pictures."

Whitford, Frank. "Expressionism in the Cinema." *Studio Inter* 179 (Jan 70). *See 4e(4).*

4. Film History

4a. General

[*See also* 2g(2b), 2h(1), 2m(1), 7b(1a), 7c(1a), 8b(1), 8c(2).]

Ernst, Morris. "Supercolossal: The Movies." *Atlantic* 166 (July 40) 17–28. This outline of film history focuses on the conflict between the business and the artistic considerations of movie making.

Crowther, Bosley. "It's a Far, Far Cry from Valentino Days." *NYTM* (22 June 41) 6–7+. Remakes of film classics dramatize changes in writing and producing films.

Cameron, Anne. "Double Gold Rush: Transition from Stakes to Scripts." *SRL* 26 (30 Oct 43) 10–11. A literary history of California which ends in Hollywood.

Pichel, Irving. "Creativeness Cannot Be Diffused." *Hwd Q* 1 (Oct 45). *See 2a(1).*

Shamroy, Leon. "Evolution of a Cameraman." *FIR* 2 (Apr 51). *See 2e(1).*

"Movies: The Mirror of Our Times." *Image* 3 (No. 2, Feb 54) 11–14. The historic value of feature films and newsreels.

Card, James. "Shooting Off the Set." *Image* 6 (No. 6, June 57) 135–141. Production stills from the scrapbooks of the movie colony.

"Marilyn Monroe in a Remarkable Recreation of Fabled Enchantresses." *Life* 45 (22 Dec 58). *See 5, Marilyn Monroe.*

"Long Remembered." *Newswk* 52 (8 Dec 58) 94. Re-release of *Uncle Tom's Cabin* and *The Birth of a Nation* occasions article about value of old films.

Schulberg, B. "Writer and Hollywood." *Harper's* 219 (Oct 59). *See 2d(1).*

Stern, B. "Topsy-Turvy Flashbacks to Yesterday's Films." *Life* 35 (20 Dec 63) 54–67. Pictures of present-day stars in classic movie roles.

"Portraits in Nostalgia." *NYTM* (5 Apr 64). *See 2b(2).*

De Rome, Peter. "Off-Broadway Cinema." *S&S* 33 (Winter 63–64) 42–43. Discoveries of an unofficial, shabby world of New York's out-of-the-way movie houses, where the genuine Hollywood antique of the 1920s and 1930s is having a renaissance.

Dickinson, Thorold. "The Maturing Cinema." *J Soc Cin* 4 (1964). *See 3a(1).*

Alpert, Hollis. "Retrospective; Fifteen Years of Movie-Going." *Sat Rev* 48 (27 Nov 65) 45.

Ophuls, Max. "My Experience." *CdC in Eng* (No. 1, Jan 66). *See 2c.*

4a(1). HISTORICAL METHOD

[*See also* 1a(3a).]

Pinthus, Kurt. "History Directs the Movies." *Am Scholar* 10 (Oct 41). *See 7a.*

Sadoul, Georges. "Early Film Production in England." *Hwd Q* 1 (No. 3, Apr 46). *See 4e (1a).*

Sisk, John P. "The Timeless Tales of Hollywood." *Commonweal* 44 (4 Oct 46). *See 2b(2).*

Huff, Theodore. "Sadoul and Film Research." *Hwd Q* 2 (No. 2, Jan 47) 203–206. American film historian disputes assertion of French historian Georges Sadoul that Vitagraph films of 1907 had close-ups in them or that American directors learned chases from the "Brighton School" of British film makers. See "Early Film Production in England," *Hwd Q* 1 (No. 3, Apr 46) 249–259.

Sadoul, Georges. "English Influences on the Work of Edwin S. Porter." (Tr. Veronica Templin.) *Hwd Q* 3 (No. 1, Fall 47) 41–50. Examination of early scripts, especially James Williamson's *Fire* compared with Edwin S. Porter's *Life of an American Fireman.*

Card, James. "Problems of Film History." *Hwd*

Readers are advised to acquaint themselves with the range of categories throughout the bibliography in the search for specific subjects. In some cases, cross-categorical comparisons are directly suggested. In general, however, each article is placed under one category only. Cross-references on individual articles have been kept to a minimum.

Entries are in chronological order of publication under each category. Exceptions are: Part 5, Biography, in which the order is alphabetical by name; Part 9, Case Histories of Film Making, which is alphabetical by film title; and 3c and 8c(4), also alphabetical by title.

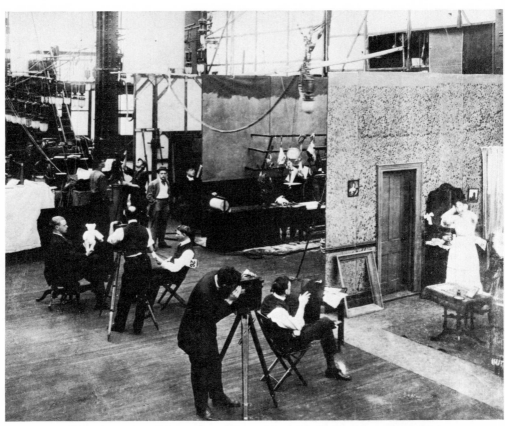

The Thomas A. Edison film studio at Menlo Park, New Jersey, in 1915.

Q 4 (No. 3, Spring 50) 279–288. Official of Eastman House in Rochester deplores "quagmire of gossip and guess" in many film histories and urges student access to more of the old films.

Weinberg, Herman G. "Of Time and the Critics." *FIR* 1 (Nov 50) 4–6. Future historians will reevaluate the first fifty years of cinema; Paul Rotha's *The Film Till Now* is a careless work.

Griffith, Richard. "Richard Griffith's Riposte." *FIR* 1 (Nov 50) 7–8+. Reply to Weinberg article, same issue, on film historians.

Eisner, Lotte. "Film History." *FIR* 2 (Dec 51) 18–21. The historian must appreciate and understand not political issues, but stylistic epochs, in the manner of art history.

Hart, Henry. "Terry Ramsaye (1885–1954)." *FIR* 5 (Oct 54) 885–886. A tribute to the late author of *A Million and One Nights* (reprint Simon and Schuster, 1964), outlining his life and career.

Pratt, George. "A Myth Is as Good as a Milestone." *Image* 6 (No. 9, Nov 57) 208–211. An appraisal of four legends of motion-picture history: Buster Keaton's debut in films, beginning of Sennett's Keystone comedies, etc.

Richter, Hans. "On the Function of Film History." *F Cult* 4 (No. 18, 1958) 25–26. Criticism of most film-history books for simply being an accumulation of facts without interpretation.

"Editorial." *Cinema Studies* 1 (No. 1, Mar 60) 3–4. The present limits of film-history writing; the purpose of this new journal is "to encourage the basic research necessary to enable the history of the cinema, especially in Britain, to be adequately written." Editors: Neville March Hunnings and John Gillett, for the Society for Film History Research.

O'Laoghaire, Liam. "Towards a History of the Movies." *Cinema Studies* 1 (No. 1, Mar 60) 12–15. Pioneer historians must now be followed by researchers; *Films in Review*, in the U.S., offers a model.

Hendricks, Gordon. "A New Look at an Old Sneeze." *F Cult* (Nos. 22–23, 1961) 90–95. Historical examination of *Fred Ott's Sneeze*, which was not "Edison's first film."

Heaword, Rosemary. "Problems Facing a Student of Film History." *Cinema Studies* 1 (No. 5, Sep 62) 94–98. Prejudices, lack of facilities and films.

McMurry, Glenn D. "Film Cataloging with IBM." *JUFPA* 14 (No. 3, 1962) 10–13.

Gessner, Robert. "Cinema and Scholarship." *J Soc Cin* 3 (1963) 73–80. Problems of dating, of comparing versions (e.g., *The Life of an American Fireman*), and of describing a shot.

Siska, William. "Movies and History." *F Her* 4 (No. 4, Summer 69). See *3a(3)*.

4a(2). INDUSTRY AND AUDIENCE

[*See also 6, 7b.*]

Jones, G. "Magic Lantern." *SEP* 209 (23 Jan 37) 16–17+; (6 Mar 37) 17+; (10 Apr 37) 34+. Series of reminiscences of film making and Hollywood life from silent days.

"The Movies Hit a Slump and Turn to Old Pictures to Fill Empty Houses." *Life* 4 (20 June 38) 55–57. One of them is *Son of the Sheik;* photos of Valentino funeral.

Manvell, Roger, *et al.* "Post-War Survey." *S&S* 14 (No. 54, July 45) 43–50. A series of four articles dealing with the film industry in Egypt, Palestine, India, and Greece.

Ramsaye, Terry. "Rise and Place of the Motion Picture." *Annals of Am Acad of Polit and Soc Sci* 254 (Nov 47) 1–11. Brief history of film audience and industry in U.S.

Zierer, C. M. "Hollywood, World Center of Motion Picture Production." *Annals of Am Acad of Polit and Soc Sci* 254 (Nov 47) 12–17. The origins and growth of Hollywood and the studios; the effects on Los Angeles.

Schulberg, B. "Fifty Years of Movies, for What?" *Rdrs Dig* 52 (Jan 48) 125–128. The historical split between business and art; the possibility of audience desire for individual artists' work in future. See *4a(3)*.

Somlo, Josef. "The First Generation of the Cinema." *Penguin F Rev* 7 (Sep 48) 55–60. Former director of German UFA export department doubts if the U.S. can dominate world markets; historical survey.

Schulberg, Budd. "Hollywood: Its Life and Industry Ranging from 'Amazingly Colossal' to 'Ztinks.'" *Holiday* 5 (Jan 49) 34–49+. History and analysis of Hollywood and film people; the conflict between business and art.

Agel, Henri. "What Is a Cursed Film?" *Hwd Q* 4 (No. 3, Spring 50) 293–297. Biarritz festival of films unreleased or inadequately pushed by distributors reminds us also that audiences may be at fault; furthermore, élite critics should beware of admiring "the extravagant" as much as "the authentic."

Morris, L. "Merchants of Dreams." *Th Arts* 35 (Aug 51) 12–13+. The early days of the first producers and exhibitors—Fox, Laemmle, Zukor, Loew.

Lipsky, Roma. "Then and Now." *NYTM* (12 Sep 54) 18. The old Vitagraph studio in Brooklyn is now used to film color TV spectaculars for NBC.

Schulberg, Budd. "It Was Great to Be a Boy in Hollywood." *Holiday* 17 (Jan 55) 70–72+. Schulberg recalls the early days of Hollywood: its people, manners, and mores.

"The Front Page." *S&S* 27 (Spring 58) 165. Editorial on decline of Western cinema production.

MacCann, Richard Dyer. "Hollywood Faces

153

the World." *Yale Rev* 51 (June 62). *See 7e(1)*.

"Movies: The Big Flick Kick." *Look* 29 (9 Mar 65) 17–28+. History of film and audiences in U.S. culture.

Swanson, Gloria. "Hollywood Sunset." *Esq* 66 (Aug 66). *See 7d*.

Crowther, Bosley. "Magic, Myth, and Monotony: Movies in a Free Society." *Television Q* 7 (No. 4, Fall 68) 51–65. Admitting the prime aim of movie makers is to provide escape, we must remember that the cycle of myth carried to monotonous extremes—now emphasizing pointless violence—is seldom interrupted by pictures which deal seriously with war, race relations, or any other complex issue.

4a(3). SURVEYS OF FILMS, U.S. AND OTHERS

Potamkin, Harry A. "The Year of the Eclipse." *Close Up* 10 (No. 1, Mar 33) 30–39. Critical comments on the films of 1932, noting the decline of certain film figures.

Knight, E. "Moving Picture Goals." *Th Arts* 23 (Jan 39). *See 3b*.

Carlisle, C. "The Motion Picture Marks a Milestone." *Parents Mag* 14 (Oct 39) 30–31. A condensed history of the film up to 1939.

"Movies Are Growing Up." *Scholastic* 35 (2 Oct 39) 25E–26E. The fiftieth birthday of Edison's kinetoscope occasions both a look back at early films and a look at the increasing influence of movies of the day.

Daugherty, F. "Fifty Years of Moving Pictures." *CSMM* (6 Jan 40) 8–9.

Reisman, Leon. "From Caligari to Metro-Goldwyn-Mayer." *Kenyon Rev* 158 (Nov 40) 544–549.

Pinthus, Kurt. "History Directs the Movies." *Am Scholar* 10 (Autumn 41) 483–497. The thematic, social, and artistic evolution of the movies.

Wanger, Walter F. "Films: Forward from 1941." *Th Arts* 25 (Sep 41) 622–630. Brief history of American film, with predictions of better films to come.

Crowther, B. "From Peep Shows to Technicolor." *NYTM* (23 Apr 44) 15+.

Wollenberg, H. H. "Round the World's Studios." *Penguin F Rev* 1 (Aug 46) 52–56. Statistics and information on production in various countries; this feature recurs in succeeding issues.

Jensen, O. "Movies." *Life* 21 (25 Nov 46) 65–68+. General survey of the American movie, its experiments, failures, censorship.

Schulberg, Budd. "Movies in America: After Fifty Years." *Atlantic* (Nov 47) 115–121. A writer's perspective, with emphasis on extremes of artistry and banality. *See 4a(2)*.

"Age of Hollywood: A Working Script." *New Rep* 120 (31 Jan 49) 11–24. A look back to the silent days; recent depressions may cause new life in the American film.

Barry, Iris. "Retrospect with Lament and Motto." *SRL* 32 (6 Aug 49) 138–141. A comparison between the period of 1924–1927 and the period of 1949 and a tribute to sound movies.

Arnheim, Rudolf. "From Flickers to Fischinger." *SRL* 33 (18 Feb 50) 34. A brief history of film's first fifty years.

Ford, Charles. "Thirty Years of Conscious Realism." *S&S* 19 (Nov 50). *See 3a(2)*.

"Milestones in Movies." *Coronet* 30 (Sep 51) 109–124. Picture story from *The Birth of a Nation* to *The Informer* and *Going My Way*.

Lambert, Gavin. "A Last Look Round." *Sequence* (No. 14, 1952) 4–8. A personal account of the films and film world during the years of *Sequence*.

Daugherty, Frank. "The Cutting Room Floor." *FIR* 3 (Dec 52) 519–526. Reminiscences of Hollywood: Charlie Chaplin, Joseph von Sternberg, Mary Pickford, and others.

"Old Time Movies." *Look* 17 (19 May 53) 20+. Stills from yesterday's cinematic triumphs.

Whitebait, William. "The First Sixty Years." *S&S* 26 (Summer 56) 9–11. A report about an exhibition held in London depicting the history of cinema.

Gregson, John. "60 Years of Cinema." *F&F* 2 (No. 11, Aug 56) 12+. Star reports on his visit to exhibition of cinemabilia.

Springer, John. "Westhampton's Film Festival." *FIR* 7 (Aug–Sep 56) 305–308. A report on the activities and films of a "Cavalcade of Film Classics" held at Westhampton, Long Island, New York, at which the first five nominees—Mary Pickford, D. W. Griffith, Cecil B. De Mille, Douglas Fairbanks, and Charles Chaplin—were chosen for a proposed motion-picture hall of fame.

McCarthy, J. "Confessions of a Moviegoer." *Cosmopolitan* 141 (Oct 56) 76–81. Cinema history through viewpoint of a knowledgeable fan.

Brunius, Jacques. "The Cinema and the Exhibition." *Film* (No. 19, Jan–Feb 59) 21–24. Brussels exhibition: film values of past and present.

Dyer, Peter John. "An Index." *F&F* 6 (No. 3, Dec 59) 4+. An index for a series of articles by Dyer called "Patterns of the Cinema" which appeared in *Films and Filming* from December 1957 to November 1959.

Gessner, Robert. "Moving Image." *Am Heritage* 11 (Apr 60) 30–35+. Early motion pictures.

Alpert, Hollis. "Show of Strength Abroad." *Sat Rev* (24 Dec 60) 43–45. Compares American films unfavorably with new films from Europe; part of *Saturday Review* report "Are Foreign Films Better?"

Sarris, Andrew. "The Forgotten Film at the New Yorker: Rossellini, Renoir, Ford and Others." *NY F Bul* 2 (No. 4, 1961) 4–7. A reassessment of *The Greatest Love, Strangers, French Can Can,* and *The Wagonmaster* as major examples of cinema art.

Weaver, John D. "Movies: A Capsule History." *Holiday* 29 (Mar 61) 66–67. Memorable quotes from film people.

"A Hundred Up—and a Hundred More to Come." *F&F* 9 (No. 4, Jan 63) 34–36. In the hundredth issue of the magazine, a series of producers, directors, and actors write what they think has been the most important development in the last eight years of film making (the length of the magazine's existence) and where things will go from here.

Johnson, Ian, and Raymond Durgnat (eds.). "Puritans Anonymous." *Motion* (No. 6, Autumn 63) 3–62. The editors summarize the various forms of Puritanism as any attempt at an actual eradication of "unworthy" impulses; a group of articles on Puritanism and/or moral codes in the cinema; Dreyer, Bergman, Bresson, Buñuel, and the epic (especially the Italian).

"A Religion of Film." *Time* 82 (20 Sep 63) 78–82. A major report on the new status of world cinema, with brief characterizations of major directors.

"Moving Mirror of Modern Times." *Life* 55 (20 Dec 63) 4-5. An appraisal of film as international art.

"Universal Magic of the Movies." *Life* 55 (20 Dec 63) 14–27. Picture gallery illustrating movies' global appeal.

Durgnat, Raymond, and Peter Armitage. "Ten Years That Shook an Art." *Film* (No. 40, Summer 64) 22–33. An overview of the films of the 1960s, their concerns and innovations.

Dickinson, Thorold. "Has the Cinema Grown Up?" *F&F* 10 (No. 10, July 64) 44–47. General film history and a look into the future of the art.

Milne, Tom, John Russell Taylor, Penelope Houston, and Richard Roud. "The Tone of Time: Notes on Nostalgia." *S&S* 34 (Spring 65) 86–92. A nostalgic selection of films by each critic, and their brief comments; among the twenty choices are two Keatons, two Feuillades, and Welles' *The Magnificent Ambersons.*

Newman, David, and Robert Benton. "The Late Late Ladies." *Mlle* 61 (July 65) 4. A look at the movies of the 1930s on the *Late Late Show* on TV.

Young, Vernon. "Verge and After: Film by 1966." *Hudson Rev* 19 (Spring 66) 92–100. List of the films of the 1960s exploring the human condition which possess authenticity, style, and rare expositional qualities; predictions about the future films of Torre-Nilsson, Fellini, Bresson, Antonioni, Bergman, Godard and Lester.

Vas, Robert. "Meditation at 24 Frames per Second." *S&S* 35 (Summer 66). See 2f.

Houston, Penelope. "Seventy." *S&S* 39 (Winter 69–70) 3–5. The editor of *Sight and Sound* looks at the sense of instability now, the considerable changes since 1960, and suggests that 1970 may be more the end of something than a beginning.

Kostelanetz, Richard. "Recent Film Reconsidered." *Shenandoah* 21 (No. 4, Summer 70) 70–88. On the 1960s: New Wave, American Independent Cinema, new technical innovations, and *2001.*

Yurenev, R. N. "Cinema." *J World Hist* 12 (Nos. 1–2, 1970), 256–264. Quick overview of world film.

4a(4). SPECIALIZED ASPECTS

Whiting, P. "Movies Become Museum Pieces." *Mag of Art* 28 (Sep 35) 560.

"Narrow Gage Movies; 16mm Movies in TV and Small Theatres." *Pop Mech* 86 (Dec 46) 105–109. Detailed article on the rise of 16mm film in entertainment, industry, education.

Connor, Edward. "Cinemistakes." *FIR* 5 (Oct 54) 409–412. Many boners in films, such as, "No more than two coins are ever cast in *Three Coins in the Fountain."*

"All Summer in a Day." *S&S* 25 (Autumn 55) 62. Note on Paris exhibit of posters and documents about cinema history.

"The Front Page." *S&S* 25 (Spring 56) 167–168. Guest editorial: Anonymous visitor to the Tenth Muse on her sixtieth birthday; written in the manner of *Sunset Boulevard.*

Rotha, Paul. "On Collecting Old Stills." *Film* (No. 15, Jan–Feb 58) 19–21. Personal account of his movie still collection and the problems and rewards involved.

Morris, L. "28mm Movies? Aw C'mon." *Mod Photog* 31 (July 67) 16+.

Collins, E. D. "Silent and Sound Film: A Growing Hobby." *Hobbies* 74 (Aug 69) 113+. Collecting the early heritage of film art.

4a(4a). Prehistory and Inventions

"Early History of the Motion Picture." *School Arts* 30 (Dec 30) 198–199+. Brief sketch of developments leading up to motion pictures.

"First Days of the Movies." *Lit Dig* 108 (10 Jan 31) 18. On French inventor Louis Le Prince.

Blackton, J. Stuart. "An Interview with Thomas Alva Edison." *School Arts* 31 (Dec

31) ix–xii. Account of Edison interview given in a lecture by a pioneer movie director.

Waley, H. D. "The Evolution of Cinematography." *S&S* 3 (No. 13, Spring 35) 47–48; 4 (No. 14, Summer 35) 101–102; 4 (No. 15, Autumn 35) 150–152. Brief statement on the precursors of cinema; development of the camera and projector.

Edison, Thomas A. "How the Movies Got Their Start." *Sci Illus* 3 (July 47) 33–35+. Extract from inventor's diary.

"Mr. Edison's Kinetoscope." *Image* 1 (No. 3, Mar 52) 2. A description of the instrument reprinted from the *Scientific American* of November 10, 1894.

"The Horse in Gallop." *Image* 1 (No. 4, Apr 52) 3. Eadweard Muybridge and a predecessor, Lieutenant L. Wachter, a Frenchman who illustrated correctly how horses run in 1862 with a phenakistoscope.

"The Kammatograph." *Image* 1 (No. 8, Nov 52) 3. The development of a camera and projector using glass plates rather than nitrate film.

Card, James. "From Muybridge to Cinemascope." *Image* 3 (No. 2, Feb 54) 15–16. Basis for new techniques lies in the past.

Freiday, Dean. "The Heyday of the Magic Lantern." *Image* 3 (No. 3, Mar 54) 21.

Macgowan, Kenneth. "The Coming of Camera and Projector—Part I." *QFRTV* 9 (No. 1, Fall 54) 1–14. Early history of film machines.

Macgowan, Kenneth. "The Coming of Camera and Projector—Part II." *QFRTV* (No. 2, Winter 54) 124–136. From Muybridge to Edison's vitascope in 1896.

Ford, Charles. "Film's Basic Fact." (Tr. by Anne and Thornton K. Brown.) *FIR* 5 (Nov 54) 472–473. How a blind Belgian, Joseph-Antoine-Ferdinand Plateau, lawyer and physicist, established the existence of persistence of vision when he built the phenakistoscope.

Newhall, Beaumont. "Muybridge and the First Motion Picture." *Image* 5 (No. 1, Jan 56) 4–11. An extensive account of Eadweard Muybridge's activities, photographic and otherwise, leading up to his films of Stanford's horses.

Card, James. "The Choreutoscope." *Image* 5 (No. 10, Dec 56) 230–231. A description of a pre-motion-picture shutter found on a magic-lantern slide.

Pratt, George. "Around the World by 2 A.M." *Image* 6 (No. 4, Apr 57) 90–93. The Jules Verne play on magic-lantern slides.

Newhall, Beaumont. "How George Eastman Invented the First Kodak Camera." *Image* 7 (No. 3, Mar 58) 59–64.

Coe, Brian. "The Will Day Collection." *Cinema Studies* 1 (No. 5, Sep 62) 91–94.

Exhibitor's collection of cinema apparatus summarized.

Noxon, Gerald. "Pictorial Origins of Cinema Narrative: Chinese Scroll Paintings." *J Soc Cin* 3 (1963) 29–43.

Peet, Creighton. "Grandpa's Cinerama." *Show* 3 (Jan 63) 12+. Painted panoramas of moving canvas were predecessors of wide-screen films.

Stainton, Walter H. "A Neglected Pioneer." *FIR* 14 (Mar 63) 160–166. Historical study of contribution of Louis Le Prince to motion-picture apparatus.

Homer, W. I., and J. Talbot. "Eakins, Muybridge and the Motion Picture Process." *Art Q* 26 (No. 2, Summer 63) 194–216. An extensive criticism of the theory that Eakins played a major role in the invention of the motion-picture process.

Mitchell, George J. "The Malkames Collection." *FIR* 14 (Nov 63) 529–540. Description of the collection of motion-picture apparatus owned by Don Malkames.

Noxon, Gerald. "Pictorial Origins of Cinema Narrative: Paleolithic Cave Wall Paintings of Lascaux." *J Soc Cin* 4 (1964) 20–25.

Stainton, Walter H. "Movie Pre-History." *FIR* 16 (No. 6, June–July 65) 333–342. From 1855 to 1905.

Auer, Michel. "Dr. J. H. Smith's Cinematograph." *Camera* 45 (No. 6, June 66) 52. An appraisal of his work at the turn of the century.

Hill, Roland. "Louis and Auguste Lumière: Paris, 28th December 1895, First Public Film Performance in the Salon Indien du Grand Café 14 Boulevard des Capucines." *Camera* 45 (No. 12, Dec 66) 74–77. Film program for first public show; technical information on the equipment used.

Stainton, Walter. "The Prophet Louis Ducos Du Hauron and His Marvelous Moving Picture Machine." *CJ* 6 (1966–1967) 46–51. On 1 March 1864 this inventor-photographer applied for a French patent for a system (later amended) which closely resembles the flexible film and projection of today.

Noxon, Gerald. "The Bayeux Tapestry." *CJ* 7 (1967–1968) 29–35. One of a series on the origins of cinema narrative.

Noxon, Gerald. "Pictorial Origins of Cinema Narrative." *Cinema Studies* (Bridgewater, Mass.) (No. 2, Spring 68) 3–56. The birth and development of the "scene" in prehistoric and ancient art.

Coe, Brian. "William Friese-Greene and the Origins of Cinematography." *Screen* 10 (No. 2, Mar–Apr 69) 25–41; (No. 3, May–June 69) 72–83; (Nos. 4–5, July–Oct 69) 129–147. Kodak employee examines photographic journals 1885–1896 and concludes the British inventor's work was "interesting but unfruitful." Reprinted from *The Photographic Journal*.

Hamilton, Harlan. "*Les Allures du Cheval*—Eadweard James Muybridge's Contribution to the Motion Picture." *F Com* 5 (No. 3, Fall 69) 16–35. English professor, studying original sources available in the East, describes Muybridge's projection work and his influence on Marey, Edison, Dickson; critique of Terry Ramsaye's history; extensive bibliography.

4a(4b). Problems of Preservation

[See also 2f.]

Abbott, J. E. "Cataloging and Filing of Motion Picture Films." *Lib J* 63 (1 Feb 38) 93–95. Restorative techniques used by the Museum of Modern Art Film Library in New York.

"Library of Congress Unearths First Newsreels." *Life* 15 (20 Sep 43). *See 8b.*

"Preservation of War Films; Resolution Adopted by the National University Extension Association." *School Rev* 53 (Dec 45) 571.

Blair, Patricia. "Treatment, Storage and Handling of Motion Picture Film." *Lib J* 71 (1 Mar 46) 333–336. Review of preservation techniques for storing films.

"Collecting Old Films." *Image* 1 (No. 7, Oct 52) 4. The necessity of preservation.

"Memo to a Foundation." *Harper's* 206 (Apr 53) 97–98. The impending tragedy of film deterioration and the need for transfer of nitrate stock film to acetate; Richard Griffith comments.

"Doomed: A Half Century Film Record of America's Past." *Image* 3 (No. 2, Feb 54) 9–11. Nitrate film stock inevitably destroyed by chemical deterioration (films made 1894–1928).

Connor, Edward. "Ruining Re-issues." *FIR* 5 (May 54) 221–223+. An appeal that the entire original versions of film classics be kept intact; a few films that have been re-issued in shortened versions.

Weinberg, Herman G. "The Legion of Lost Films." *S&S* 31 (Autumn 62) 172–176. Listed by countries and directors, projects by Murnau, Chaplin, Welles, Flaherty, Renoir, and others which were never completed, not released, or mutilated.

Weinberg, Herman G. "The Legion of Lost Films." *S&S* 32 (Winter 62–63) 42–45. This second part gives a brief description of lost or mutilated films mainly in Russia and Germany.

Davies, Brenda. "Can *The Leopard* . . . ?" *S&S* 33 (Spring 64) 99–100. The badly cut and dubbed American version of Visconti's *The Leopard* prompted its director to sue Fox and the writer to ponder over the question: who is the author of a film work? She

lists the cuts from the original version of *The Leopard* and cites other cases of mutilated films.

Niver, Kemp R. "From Film to Paper to Film." *QJ Lib Congress* 21 (Oct 64) 248–264. An account of the restoration onto film of the library's paper-print collection of early films.

Niver, Kemp R. "Paper Prints of Early Motion Pictures." *JUFPA* 17 (No. 4, 1965) 3–6. The problems of restoring old films on the basis of paper prints made for copyright purposes.

Weinberg, Herman G. "Lost Ones." *F Com* 5 (No. 3, Fall 69) 6–12+. Remarks on the twenty-eight lost films from which 130 photographs were exhibited by the Museum of Modern Art; Weinberg's additional list; stills include two by Sternberg, others by Lubitsch, Cruze, Stiller, von Stroheim.

Gerard, Lillian. "The Study and Preservation of Films at the Museum of Modern Art." *F Com* 5 (No. 3, Fall 69) 13–14. Recent acquisitions.

Koszarski, Richard. "Lost Films from the National Film Collection." *FQ* 23 (No. 2, Winter 69–70) 31–37. Von Stroheim's *Merry Widow*, Keaton's *The Cameraman*, Vidor's *The Patsy*, and other rediscovered films evaluated as shown at New York Film Festival under auspices of American Film Institute.

4a(5). SHORTS AND SERIALS

Potamkin, Harry A. "Reelife." *Close Up* 7 (No. 6, Dec 30). *See 3c, Billy the Kid.*

Buchanan, Donald W. "Reflections on the Film." *Canad Forum* 15 (Mar 36) 11. Short films should be programmed to fit the features.

Buchanan, D. W. "Leaven in the Lump." *Canad Forum* 16 (Apr 36) 12. About short films.

Desmond, R. W. "Something to Think About." *CSMM* (17 Aug 38) 4. Short films.

Crowther, Bosley. "Two-Reelers Comeback." *NYTM* (26 Oct 41) 8+. " 'Shorts' are fighting it out with 'second features' for a place on the screen."

Buchanan, Andrew. "Whither the Short?" *S&S* 11 (No. 41, Summer 42) 12–13. History and future of the short film.

Kahn, G. "And Selected Short Subjects." *Atlantic* 177 (Feb 46) 142+. Satirical condemnation of current quality in the short theatrical film.

Hall, David L. "Short Subjects and Shortcomings." *Hwd Q* 1 (No. 4, July 46) 439–440. Brief note on sad state of shorts for theatres, with a pat on the back for MGM.

Marshall, Jim. "The Perils of Pearl White." *Collier's* 118 (6 July 46) 72. Betty Hutton plays in movie about *The Perils of Pauline*.

Rose, Tony. "The 'One Act' Film." *S&S* 15

(No. 60, Winter 46–47) 152. A plea for the British studios to create a new species of film similar to the one-act play.

Trewin, J. C. "One Thing After Another." *S&S* 16 (No. 63, Autumn 47) 106–107. Motion-picture serials.

Reid, Adrian. "The Short Film in Italy." *S&S* 17 (No. 68, Winter 48–49). *See 4e(3a).*

Reid, Adrian. " 'Let's Wait Till the Big Picture Starts.' " *S&S* 19 (May 50) 139–140. Audience attitudes and recommendations on the short subject for theatres.

Reid, Adrian. "Economics: The Supporting Film." *S&S* 19 (June 50) 178–180. The public reaction to theatrical shorts, their value as a training ground for new talent, and their seemingly impossible economic situation.

Hift, Fred. "1950's Shorts." *FIR* 2 (Jan 51) 10–12.

Everson, William K. "Serials with Sound." *FIR* 4 (June–July 53) 269–276. Their history; the causes of their decline.

Connor, Edward. "The Serial Lovers." *FIR* 6 (Aug–Sep 55) 328–332. Walter Miller and Allene Ray as a team made several of the most popular serials produced 1925–1929.

Smith, Frank Leon. "The Man Who Made Serials." *FIR* 7 (Oct 56) 375–383+. A study of the life and career of the late writer, producer, and director of films George Seitz, written by his scenario editor; his work included most of the Pearl White serials, and later features, including thirteen Andy Hardy films.

Geltzer, George. "40 Years of Cliffhanging." *FIR* 8 (Feb 57) 60–67. A survey of the career of a director of fifty-two serials and fifty-four features, Spencer Gordon Bennet.

Smith, Frank Leon. "The First American Serial." *FIR* 9 (Feb 58) 108–109. Letter about earliest stories and forms.

Grenier, Cynthia. "Wild Time in Tours." *FQ* 13 (No. 3, Spring 60) 23–26. Short-film festival had many American entries.

Vas, Robert. "Short—or Documentary." *S&S* 29 (Summer 60) 136–138. Recent short-film festivals, where awards seem to go to animated films; the shortage of the personal social documentary.

Geltzer, George. "Ruth Roland." *FIR* 11 (No. 9, Nov 60). *See 5, Ruth Roland.*

Hill, Derek. "The Short Film Situation." *S&S* 31 (Summer 62) 108–112. The short-film maker in Great Britain can survive only by working for sponsors; facts and figures on the problems faced by Dick Williams and others in making shorts for theatres.

Beach, Stewart. "The Penalty Short." *Harper's* 226 (Mar 63) 26+. Humorous comments

on "avant-garde" shorts and documentaries for theatres.

"The Little Ones That Get Away." *Film* (No. 39, Spring 64) 34–35. Short films are important but often are not seen.

"Service to Shorts." *S&S* 33 (Spring 64) 75. Derek Hill organizes Short Film Service in London to help sell them to critics, distributors, and TV.

Everson, William K. "Continued Next Week." *NYTM* (29 Mar 64) 16–17. Stills from famous film serials.

Tebbel, John. "When Movies Joined the Jet Set." *Sat Rev* 47 (14 Nov 64) 78–79. Non-theatrical and short-subject motion pictures for international festivals.

"Cinematic Mediocrity." *Economist* 213 (21 Nov 64) 879–880. The state of the British short film, as seen at the Fifth International Industrial Film Festival.

Knight, Derrick. "Time for a Change." *Film* (No. 42, Winter 64) 33–35. The problems of making and distributing short films.

Durgnat, Raymond. "The Serial Rides Again." *Cinema* (Calif) 2 (No. 5, Mar–Apr 65) 8–10.

Hoffman, Hilmar. "Trends in the Short Film." *F Com* 3 (No. 3, Summer 65) 41–42. Artistic director of Oberhausen short-film festival comments on a few animated and documentary pictures.

"Short Film Showcase for Talent." *Cinema* (Calif) 3 (No. 1, Dec 65) 46. Interview with James Frawley.

Billard, Ginette. "Tours—and the Salvation of Shorts." *FQ* 19 (No. 4, Summer 66) 16–18. The origins and success of the French short-film festivals at Tours and Annecy.

Robinson, David, and Ian Wright. "Shorts and Cinemas." *S&S* 36 (Spring 67) 63–67. D. Knight and V. Porter's book *A Long Look at Short Films* (Pergamon, 1967) raises questions: the value of a short film, how the cost and price gap can be closed, what directors and shorts are available.

Knight, Arthur. "And Selected Short Subjects." *Sat Rev* 50 (13 May 67) 73. A review of distributors of short films.

Wright, Ian. "Blast and Counterblast." *S&S* 36 (Summer 67) 123. Note on Rank Organization defense of its shorts series *Look at Life* against Monopolies Commission report; will Film Producers Association give money for shorts to head of government action?

Starr, Cecile. "Selected Short Subjects." *F Com* 4 (Nos. 1–2, Fall–Winter 67) 66–67. Where to see them; Brant Sloan's new Kinesis collection.

Zeoli, Nicholas. "The Short Film." *Cinéaste* 1 (No. 3, Winter 67–68) 22+. An opportunity for education and communication; independent film makers should make more of them.

Heller, Caroline. "The Mystery of the Thirteen Vanishing Slots." *Film* (No. 51, Spring 68) 38–41. Problems in the British short-film scene.

4b. Silent Period

[*See also 2g(2b).*]

Blakeston, Oswell. "Check-Up on Technique." *Close Up* 7 (No. 3, 1930) 191–196. Recent technical innovations.

Arthur, Charlotte. "In the Old Days." *Close Up* 6 (No. 4, 1930) 297–303; 6 (No. 5, 1930) 369–377. Remembrances of acting experiences at Inceville; two articles.

"Early History of the Motion Picture." *School Arts* 30 (Dec 30) 198–199+.

"Current Art Notes: Still History." *Connoisseur* 88 (No. 364, Dec 31) 427. Review of and exhibition of film stills assembled by Paul Rotha.

Condon, Frank. "Before Sound." *SEP* 206 (5 May 34) 34+. Reviews silent-film era. Continued in "All Because of the Sunshine." *SEP* 207 (28 July 34) 30+.

Hughes, Rupert. "Early Days in the Movies." *SEP* 207 (6 Apr 35) 18–19+; (13 Apr 35) 30–31+. Personal experiences in silent films.

Graham, Charles. "Acting for the Films in 1912." *S&S* 4 (No. 15, Autumn 35) 118–119. An actor who worked with Vitagraph and Hepworth describes his early experiences.

Vinten, W., and A. S. Newman. "Looking Back." *S&S* 5 (No. 17, Spring 36) 54–46. Two early film-industry figures reminisce.

Cavalcanti, Alberto. "A Pioneer." *S&S* 7 (No. 26, Summer 38) 55–56. Brief remarks on early film pioneers, including Edward Charles Rogers, British expert in trick photography.

White, E. B. "Mood Men: Playing for Silent Pictures." *Rdrs Dig* 33 (July 38) 87–89. Humorist reminisces about those who played the piano down front.

"I Remember." *S&S* 7 (No. 27, Autumn 38) 133–134. Reminiscing about old films.

Glendenning, Alex. "Commentary." *19th Century* 124 (Nov 38) 581–582. A brief tribute to the silent film as opposed to "amplified theatre"—the talkie.

Saroyan, William. "Year of Heaven: 1917." *New Rep* 97 (4 Jan 39) 255–256. A wistful look at the silent-screen days.

Jacobs, Lewis. "Movies and the World War." *One-Act Play Mag* (Mar 39) 830–840. The role of motion pictures in World War I: from pacifism to a pro-war stand. Reprinted from *The Rise of the American Film* (Columbia Teachers College, 1968).

Vesselo, Arthur. "Searchlight on Veterans." *S&S* 8 (No. 31, Autumn 39) 109–111. The author reviews his own selective annotated catalog of the early films of all countries.

Catling, Darrel. "The Lighter Side." *S&S* 9 (No. 36, Winter 40–41). *See 3b(4).*

Trewin, J. C. "Cornish Pasty." *S&S* 9 (No. 35, Autumn 40) 41–42. Reminiscences of the silent period; Special comments on subtitles.

Ferguson, Stanley. "Gone with the Sound Track." *New Rep* 106 (30 Mar 42) 426–427. The days of movie theatre pit orchestras.

Pope, V. "When the Movies Were Young." *Good Housekeeping* 116 (June 43) 30–31. Reproductions of between-reel slides—rules of conduct in theatre, advice, instructions.

Jones, P. "Scarred Veteran of the Screen; Interview with B. Hill." *Forum* 105 (Feb 46) 540–541. A press agent reminisces about the silent film.

"When Movies Were Young: Motion Picture Printed Slides." *NYTM* (5 May 46) 32–33. Pictorial review of the slides.

Busch, Niven. "Myth of the Movie Director." *Harper's* 193 (Nov 46). *See 2c.*

"Seeing History Through American Achievements." *Scholastic* 50 (17 Feb 47). *See 2e(1).*

Dietz, H. "Album 1923: Motion Pictures." *Th Arts* 32 (Aug 48) 46–51. Remembrance of personalities and their work.

Manvell, Roger. "Revaluations: *Shooting Stars* 1928." *S&S* 19 (June 50). *See 3c, Shooting Stars.*

Knight, Arthur. "Dawn Over Hollywood (1919)." *Th Arts* 34 (Sep 50) 21–27. The star system, the star director, and new producing companies in that year.

Huff, Theodore. "Hollywood's Predecessor." *FIR* 2 (Feb 51) 17–22. Fort Lee, New Jersey, was a motion-picture producing center of the silent-film era.

Stainton, Walter R. "Pearl White in Ithaca." *FIR* 2 (May 51) 19–25. Ithaca, New York, was a motion-picture production center of the silent-film era.

Parsons, Louella O. "Essanay Days." *Th Arts* 35 (July 51) 33. Reminiscences of a former scenarist who became the first movie columnist.

Spears, James F. "Birth of the Movies." *Hobbies* 57 (July 52) 39+.

Halper, N., and B. Mandelker. "I Got Two, Who Got Three? When Movies Were Two for a Nickel." *Commentary* 14 (July 52)

60–64. Nostalgic recollections of early theatres and their silent films in New York City.

"The Good Old Silents." *Time* 60 (20 Oct 52) 112. *The Last Laugh, Variety,* and others come back in art houses.

Drum, Dale D. "Silent Movies in Los Angeles." *FIR* 3 (Nov 52). *See 6e(1).*

"Edison's Kinetophonographic Theatre." *Hobbies* 57 (Jan 53) 153+. On method used filming Corbett-Courtney fight.

McDonald, Gerald D. "Origin of the Star System." *FIR* 4 (Nov 53). *See 2b(2).*

Ball, Robert Hamilton. "Shakespeare in One Reel." *QRRTV* 8 (No. 1, Winter 53). *See 3f(1).*

Card, James. "Where Are the Vampire Films?" *Image* 3 (No. 4, Apr 54) 31. Theda Bara, film temptress.

McDonald, Gerald D. "U.S. Filmaking Abroad." *FIR* 5 (June–July 54) 257–262. Pre-World War I foreign locations; the facilities they built, including one American studio in Ireland.

McDonald, Gerald D. "From Stage to Screen." *FIR* 6 (Jan 55) 13–18. A 1903–1912 historical survey of futile attempts to attract stage celebrities to film roles.

Vidor, King. "Gilbert, Garbo, Bea Lillie." *F&F* 1 (No. 5, Feb 55) 6–7. The director describes three personalities of the silent cinema. Reprinted from his autobiography, *A Tree Is a Tree* (Harcourt, 1953).

Bachmann, Gideon (ed.). "Dawn of the American Screen, 1893–1916." *Cinemages* 5 (June 55) 1–48. A compilation of articles by various authors dealing with films by Griffith, Ince, Porter, Sennett, and the early concept of realism.

Crowther, Bosley. "When Movies Were Very Young." *NYTM* (19 June 55) 62–63. A nostalgic look at the era of the nickelodeons, 1905–1915.

Card, James. "Silent Film Speed." *Image* 4 (No. 7, Oct 55) 55–56. There was no specific speed for running the projector during the silent period.

"Festival of Film Artists." *Image* 4 (No. 8, Nov 55) 62–63. Honoring personalities of the period 1921–1925.

Macgowan, Kenneth. "The Story Comes to the Screen—1896–1906." *QRRTV* 10 (No. 1, Fall 55) 64–88. Early stories, theatres, studios, playbills.

Everson, William K. "The Living Past." *FIR* 6 (Dec 55) 503–506+. A report on the First Festival of Film Artists held by the George Eastman House in Rochester, New York, which awarded gold medals for "distinctive" contributions 1915–1925 by five each of actors, actresses, directors, and cameramen through a poll of 500 of their contemporaries.

Walrath, Jean. "First 'George' Awards Presented to Silent Film Stars at Eastman." *Image* 4 (No. 9, Dec 55) 68–69. Account of the festival.

"Film Pioneers' Roll of Their Living Immortals." *Life* 40 (23 Jan 56) 116–123. Pickford, Gish, Keaton, and Chaplin are among the twenty selected by their contemporaries of the silent period (1915–1925) as making "distinctive contributions" to American cinema according to a George Eastman House poll.

McPherson, Mervyn. "The Silent Stars Were Not So Dumb." *F&F* 2 (No. 7, Apr 56) 6–7. Early Hollywood publicity representative to Great Britain recalls silent stars and Griffith.

"A Wistful Reunion at Pickfair." *Life* 40 (16 Apr 56) 163–164. Mary Pickford brings together famous film figures of the 1920s.

McPherson, Mervyn. "Valentino's Career Became a Graveyard Gamble." *F&F* 2 (No. 8, May 56) 15.

Doublier, Francis. "Reminiscences of an Early Motion Picture Operator." *Image* 5 (No. 6, June 56) 134–135. A French photographer remembers his experiences before 1902.

Courant, Curtis. "Cameraman in the Golden Age of Cinema." *F Cult* 2 (No. 9, 1956). *See 2e.*

Debrix, Jean. "Cinema and Poetry." *Yale French Studies* (No. 17, 1956). *See 3a.*

Jackson, Michael. "First Reader: Silent Movies." *Atlantic* 198 (Nov 56) 116. Saturday afternoon at the silent serials.

Eisner, Lotte. "The Passing of the First Film Star." *Film* (No. 11, Jan–Feb 57) 4. A tribute to the wife of Georges Méliès, who sometimes acted in her husband's films under the name Jehanne d'Alcy.

Card, James. "Winners of the Second Festival of Film Artists." *Image* 6 (No. 8, Oct 57) 180–194. Recipients of the George Eastman House Medal of Honor for Distinguished Contribution to the Art of Motion Pictures 1926–1930.

Everson, William K. "The Eastman House Awards." *FIR* 8 (Dec 57) 507–512+. A report on Second Festival of Film Artists, sponsored by the George Eastman House (1957) for the purpose of honoring with gold medals five living actors, five living actresses, and five living directors for their contributions to the cinematic art.

Dyer, Peter J. "When the Stars Were Born." *F&F* 4 (No. 3, Dec 57). *See 2b(2).*

Dyer, Peter John. "When the Stars Grew Up." *F&F* 4 (No. 4, Jan 58) 14–15+. Actors and actresses of the 1920s; part of a series on film history.

Dyer, Peter J. "Some Silent 'Sinners.'" *F&F* 4 (No. 6, Mar 58). *See 7b(6).*

Dyer, Peter John. "Sex, Sin—and Revolution." *F&F* 4 (No. 8, May 58) 13–15+. Scandinavian and Russian silent films; part of a series on film history.

"From What Strange Source." *Image* 7 (No. 8, Oct 58) 178–184. A contemporary account of how motion pictures were made in 1903.

"Old Days, Sixty Cents." *Newswk* 53 (27 Apr 59). *See 6e(1)*.

Brooks, Louise. "Gish and Garbo." *S&S* 28 (Winter 58–59) 13–17+. Hollywood star of the 1920s writes on the early star system.

Everson, William K. "Additions and Corrections." *FIR* 10 (June–July 59). *See 2e(1)*.

Hendricks, Gordon. "A Collection of Edison Films." *Image* 8 (No. 3, Sep 59) 156–163. Description and dates of fourteen films from the Eastman House collection.

Pratt, George. "No Magic, No Mystery, No Sleight of Hand." *Image* 8 (No. 4, Dec 59) 192–211. The first ten years of motion pictures in Rochester, New York.

Everson, William K. "The Silents Are Back." *NY F Bul* 1 (Nos. 12, 13, 14, 1960) 5–9. The re-release of silent films on television and in theatres.

Connor, Edward. "Memories of the Silents." *FIR* 11 (No. 2, Feb 60) 84–90. One man's childhood memories of the silent movies in the 1920s.

Hall, B. M. "The Best Remaining Seats." *Am Heritage* 12 (Oct 61) 42–49+. The movie palace of the 1920s.

Pratt, George. "The Jack-Rabbits of the Movie Business." *Image* 10 (No. 3, 1962) 10–11. The nickelodeon era.

Spears, Jack. "Chaplin's Collaborators." *FIR* 13 (No. 1, Jan 62). *See 5, Charlie Chaplin*.

Stern, Seymour. "An Interview with Seymour Stern." *F Cult* (No. 28, 1963) 82–94. An extended attack on Edward Wagenknecht's book, *The Movies in the Age of Innocence* (Ballantine, 1971); the silent period was just as racked by trade wars and sex scandals as any other.

"Letter from Stan Delaplane." *Today's Health* 42 (May 64) 85. Recollections of silent films.

Carroll, Kevin. "The Cinematograph in the London Music Hall." *Cinema Studies* 1 (No. 9, June 64) 212–221. Theatres, types of projection equipment, and films 1900–1939, especially the silent period.

Munsey, Jack T. "From a Toy to a Necessity: A Study of Some Early Reactions to the Motion Picture." *J Soc Cin* 5 (1965) 96–122. Articles about and editorial reactions to the movies in *Munsey's Magazine, Leslie's Illustrated Weekly,* and *Scribner's Magazine,* 1896–1915, including a period of "apathy" from 1901 to 1908.

Reynolds, C. "Show the World's Greatest Movies." *Pop Photog* 56 (Feb 65) 108–114. Sources and titles of 8mm silent films for collectors.

Crowther, Bosley. "Birth of *The Birth of a Nation.*" *NYTM* (7 Feb 65) 24–25+. On the audience reaction to D. W. Griffith's film.

Slide, Anthony. "Bioscope Shows at Hull Fair." *Cinema Studies* 2 (No. 1, June 65) 7–9. Jugglers attracted the customers 1896–1913.

Aylott, Dave. "Reminiscences of a Showman." *Cinema Studies* 2 (No. 1, June 65) 3–6. Writing and producing 1906–1910 in London.

Callenbach, Ernest. "The State of 8." *FQ* 19 (No. 4, Summer 66) 36–39. Prints of silent films available from various sources.

O'Leary, Liam. "The Importance of the One-Reel Film." *Cinema Studies* 2 (No. 2, June 66) 32–34. It was a prolific and experimental period.

Love, Bessie. "Jokers Mild." *F&F* 12 (No. 11, Aug 66) 21–22. Actress recalls practical jokers from early days of filming.

Whitehall, Richard. "The Flapper." *Cinema* (Calif) 3 (No. 4, Dec 66) 18–22.

Holmes, Marjorie. "Days of Movie Magic." *Today's Health* 45 (Oct 67) 38–41. Recollections of silent films.

"The Early Years." *Arts in Soc* 4 (No. 1, Winter 67) 105–116. Letters from the collection of business papers of the Aitken Brothers, early film producers.

Gibson, Helen. "In the Very Early Days." *FIR* 19 (No. 1, Jan 61) 28–53. Personal recollections of Hollywood.

Luddy, Tom. "Some Neglected Masterpieces." *F Soc Rev* (Feb 68) 24–27. Brief comments on films by Murnau, Griffith, von Sternberg, and Lang.

Weiss, Margaret R. "Film Firsts in Flashback." *Sat Rev* 51 (13 Apr 68) 64–65. Kemp R. Niver's presentation of the restored reels of the formative years of the cinema (1894–1912).

Leyda, Jay. "A Note on Progress." *FQ* 21 (No. 4, Summer 68) 28–33. Kemp Niver's book *Motion Pictures from the Library of Congress Paper Print Collection 1894–1912* (University of California, 1967) reveals years crowded with "imitation and progress," but there are many other sources for probing the mysteries of those early years.

Robinson, David, Tom Milne, and John Russell Taylor. "Twenties Show People." *S&S* 37 (Autumn 68) 198–202. The British National Film Theatre's season "The 20's: How They Roared," inspired this tribute to three of the "faces" of that decade: Clara Bow, Marion Davies, Gloria Swanson.

Madden, David. "Harlequin's Stick, Charlie's Cane." *FQ* 22 (No. 1, Fall 68). *See 3f(1)*.

Fielding, Raymond. "Hale's Tours: Ultrarealism in the Pre-1910 Motion Picture." *Smithsonian J Hist* 3 (1968–1969) 101–124. Historical and descriptive account of travelogue films seen from inside a railroad car.

Slide, Anthony. "The Kalem Serial Queens." *Silent Picture* (No. 1, Winter 68–69) 7–10.

Documentation of the women who starred in the Kalem company serials.

Brownlow, Kevin. "Chasing the Parade." *S&S* 38 (Summer 69) 148–152. Brownlow writes about his lively experiences while looking for Hollywood's silent past for his book *The Parade's Gone By* (Ballantine, 1969).

Fielding, Raymond. "Hale's Tours: Ultrarealism in the Pre-1910 Motion Picture." *CJ* 10 (No. 1, Fall 70) 34–47. History of the rise and fall of George C. Hale's railway-car theatres, which rumbled and shook as if the car were moving; substantially reprinted from *Smithsonian J Hist* 3 (1968–1969) 101–124.

4c. Transition to Sound

[See also 2g.]

Potamkin, H. A. "In the Land Where Images Mutter." *Close Up* 6 (No. 1, 1930) 11–19. Critical comments on recent sound films.

Howard, Clifford. "The Menace Around the Corner." *Close Up* 6 (No. 1, 1930) 59–66. The effect on Hollywood of sound and other possible technologies.

Herring, Robert. "Twenty-three Talkies." *Close Up* 6 (No. 2, 1930) 113–128. Critical notes on the use of sound.

Lanauer, Jean. "In Praise of Simplicity." *Close Up* 6 (No. 2, 1930) 134–140. An argument for the sound film.

Wagner, Rob. "Lend Me Your Ears." *Collier's* 85 (11 Jan 30) 10–11+. Also 86 (13 Dec 30) 16–18. Review of progress made in talkies.

"The Talkies' Future." *Nation* 130 (15 Jan 30) 61–62. Suggests movies could go beyond technique.

Huxley, Aldous, and Robert E. Sherwood. "Do You Like the Talkies?" *Golden Book* 11 (Apr 30) 51–54. Pro and con, with Huxley for silents.

"The Hand of Death on the Screen." *Lit Dig* 105 (5 Apr 30) 19–20. French author Bernard Fay says sound is killing art of the film.

Ahern, Maurice L. "Hollywood Horizons." *Commonweal* 12 (21 May 30) 71–73. Suggests talkies have revolutionized audience viewing and impact.

"New Arbiter of Women's Movie Styles." *Lit Dig* 105 (10 May 30) 23. Predicts tomorrow's cinema styles influenced by demands of microphone.

"Galsworthy on the Talkies." *Living Age* 338 (15 May 30) 349–350. Playwright gives views on coexistence of silents and talkies.

Rose, Donald. "Silence Is Requested." *North Am Rev* 230 (July 30) 127–128. Lauds Chaplin for not making talkies.

Whipple, Leon. "Gone Talkie." *Survey* 64 (1 July 30) 321–322. Assesses power of sound film emotionally and intellectually.

"All-Talking Pictures Are Lost on Japanese Audiences." *Trans-Pacific* 18 (3 July 30) 12.

"Multilingual Talkies." *Lit Dig* 106 (12 July 30) 15. Marie Dressler doubts foreign talkie appeal.

Hale, Louise Closser. "The New Stage Fright: Talking Pictures." *Harper's* 161 (Sep 30). See 2b.

"Paramount's Paris Studio." *Living Age* 339 (Oct 30) 206–207. U.S. firm producing talkies in eleven languages.

Potamkin, H. A. "Movie: New York Notes." *Close Up* 7 (No. 4, Oct 30) 235–252. Comments on recent films and film writing.

Sherwood, R. E. "Renaissance in Hollywood." *World Today* 56 (Nov 30) 564–570.

"Charlie Chaplin and Talking Pictures." *Th Arts* 14 (Nov 30) 908. Speculates on whether *City Lights* will use sound.

Yates, Raymond Francis. "A Technician Talks About the Talkies." *Sci Am* 143 (Nov 30) 384–385. Points out some failings of talkies and ways to overcome these.

Prince Henry of Reuss. "The Future of the Films: Talkies and the Stage." *Living Age* 339 (Nov 30) 298–300. German theatrical director suggests sound film will require theatre to reach for new heights.

Nichols, Robert. "Cinema-To-Be." *Spectator* 146 (24 Jan 31) 103–104. Effects on film form with coming of sound; predictions on use of color, stereoscopic projection, and animation.

"Good Word for the Talkies." *Lit Dig* 108 (21 Mar 31) 17. Suggests *City Lights* cannot bring back silents.

Kent, George. "New Crisis in the Motion Picture Industry." *Current Hist* 33 (Mar 31) 887–891. Coming of sound destroyed internationalism of movies.

Ahern, Maurice L. "An Overseas Headache." *Commonweal* 13 (11 Mar 31) 519–521. Surveys European beginnings in competing with American talkies.

Cousins, E. G. "Talkies Wield a Duster." *Bookman* 80 (Apr 31) 52–53. The coming of sound will revive many forgotten classics.

"Britain's Talkies Come To." *Living Age* 340 (Apr 31) 207–208. John Maxwell, British producer, sees new prosperity in sound film.

Spinola, Helen. "That Terrible Talkie Test." *Delineator* 118 (May 31) 17+. Humorous article on Hollywood activities.

Collins, F. L. "First Year Was the Loudest." *Woman's Home Companion* 58 (May 31) 11.

"Talkies Preferred." *Living Age* 340 (Aug 31) 606–607. Columbia students and Spanish correspondent prefer talkies to theatre and opera.

Ahern, Maurice L. "Diggin' in the Graveyard." *Commonweal* 14 (12 Aug 31) 358–360. Since 1928 over 130 silents remade into talkies.

Johnson, Julian. "Pandora's Chatterbox." *SEP* 204 (23 Jan 32) 10–11+. Reviews development of talkies.

Trumbo, Dalton. "Frankenstein in Hollywood." *Forum* 87 (Mar 32) 142–146. Struggle between those who believe in talkies and those who wait for return of silents.

"Charlie Chaplin and Talkies." *Rev of Reviews* 86 (Aug 32) 49–50. Reprint of *La Revue Mondiale* article by René Fonjallaz suggesting superiority of silents over talkies.

Boone, Andrew R. "Talkie Troubles." *Sci Am* 147 (Dec 32) 326–329. About conditions under which *Trader Horn, Igloo,* and *Eskimo* were filmed by W. S. Van Dyke.

Graves, Charles. "Significant Speech." *CQ* 1 (No. 2, Winter 32) 89–92. Struggles with sound film compared with crude days of theatre before Shakespeare.

Beath, P. R. "Neologisms of the Film Industry." *Am Speech* 8 (Apr 33) 73–74. The coming of sound leads people to coin new words.

Marshall, Norman. "Music in the Talkies." *Bookman* 84 (July 33) 191–192. Cinematic reality is now threatened by the unnatural effects of musical accompaniment.

"Talkies in Three Languages." *Living Age* 344 (July 33) 455–456. Gaumont-British-UFA complete fourth trilingual film.

Delehanty, Thornton. "The Film Cycle from Music to Guns to Music." *Lit Dig* 116 (8 July 33) 27. Patterns of talkies.

Troy, William. "Retrospect: 1933." *Nation* 138 (3 Jan 34) 27–28. Talkie reflects evasion, abandonment, and confusion of period.

Grierson, John. "The G.P.O. Gets Sound." *CQ* 2 (No. 4, Summer 34) 215–221. Documentary uses; examples.

Davy, Charles. "Is There a Future for Talkies?" *Bookman* 86 (Aug 34) 248. Realistic sound and abstract black and white images do not mix well.

Freeland, Matthew. "I Remember." *S&S* 14 (No. 56, Winter 45–46) 126–127. Memories of early uses of sound in films.

"Credit Should Go to Barrymore for First Sound Motion Picture." *Scholastic* 49 (23 Sep 46) 16T. John Barrymore's 1926 *Don Juan.*

Quarry, Edmund. "Midwife to the Talkies." *S&S* 18 (Summer 49) 94. About a sound film made in England as early as 1924–1925.

Knight, Arthur. "All Singing! All Talking! All Laughing! 1929, Year of Great Transition." *Th Arts* 33 (Sep 49) 33–40. Sound movies, the stars who became famous, and those who were ruined.

Huxley, Aldous. "Film Folio 3: Silence Is Golden." *S&S* 23 (July–Sep 53). See 3a.

Vidor, King. "The End of an Era." *F&F* 1 (No. 6, Mar 55) 8–9. The friendship between William Randolph Hearst and Marion Davies; the coming of sound. Reprinted from *A Tree Is a Tree* (Harcourt, 1953).

Bronner, Edwin. "Old Wine in New Bottles." *FIR* 6 (June–July 55). See 2d(1).

Macgowan, Kenneth. "The Coming of Sound to the Screen." *QFRTV* 10 (No. 2, Winter 55) 136–145. From 1906 to 1930.

Macgowan, Kenneth. "When the Talkies Came to Hollywood." *QFRTV* 10 (No. 3, Spring 56) 288–301.

Miller, Don. "Movie History on TV." *FIR* 11 (No. 2, Feb 60) 65–69. Review and discussion of single program in TV's *20th Century* series, dealing with coming of sound to movies.

Halliwell, Leslie. "Merely Stupendous." *F&F* 13 (No. 5, Feb 67) 4–12; (No. 6, Mar 67) 48–56; (No. 7, Apr 67) 33–38; 14 (No. 4, Jan 68) 10–15; 14 (No. 5, Feb 68) 38–44; 14 (No. 6, Mar 68) 42–47; 14 (No. 7, Apr 68) 49–53. Seven articles on the decade when films first learned to talk; the last two are on British cinemas of 1930s.

4d. U.S. Since 1930

[See also 2c, 3b(2), 4k, 6, 7.]

"Movies Build a New Industry Over Night." *Bus Wk* (19 Feb 30) 38–40. Producers prepare to add color and big screen to technical possibilities.

Howard, Clifford. "Hollywood Review." *Close Up* 8 (No. 2, June 31) 112–119. Comments on recent film making in Hollywood.

Herring, Robert. "New German Cinema." *London Mercury* 24 (Oct 31) 539–544. Critique of American treatment of German themes and literature in the cinema.

Boone, Andrew R. "History of the Talkies." *Sci Am* 148 (Feb 33) 70–74. Traces development of sound films.

"Hollyday." *Time* 21 (20 Mar 33) 41. Bank holiday and proposals for pay cuts result in shut-down studios.

MacDonald, Dwight. "Notes on Hollywood Directors." *Symposium* 4 (Apr 33) 159–177; 4 (July 33) 280–300. A discussion in two parts of ten major Hollywood directors viewed as technically resourceful, but aesthetically barren.

Knight, Eric M. "Synthetic America." *CQ* 2 (No. 2, Winter 33–34). *See 7a.*

"Plots and Plans." *Time* 23 (25 June 34) 40–44. Roundup of studio policies and projects for the future.

Angly, Edward. "Boycott Threat Is Forcing Movie Clean-Up." *Lit Dig* 118 (7 July 34). *See 7c(2b).*

"Review of the Year in the Film World." *Lit Dig* 118 (29 Dec 34) 27. Summarizes Legion of Decency drive, rise of English film, and movie highlights.

Seldes, Gilbert. "The Movies in Peril." *Scribner's* 97 (Feb 35). *See 3b(2).*

Klingender, F. D. "The New Deal and the American Film." *CQ* 3 (No. 4, Summer 35). *See 7a.*

Holdom, Courtland. "Filmland Smiles Again." *CSMM* (11 Mar 36) 5. *Romeo and Juliet* and *The Good Earth* in production in "best year" for movie box office since start of Depression.

Suckow, Ruth. "Hollywood Gods and Goddesses." *Harper's* 173 (July 36). *See 2b(1).*

Warner, Jack L. "Talking Pictures: The Tenth Year." *Cinema Arts* 1 (No. 3, Sep 37) 45. The power of the film, how it has grown, and the implications of its growth.

Brogan, D. W. "Screen World: Symposium." *Spectator* 160 (14 Jan–4 Feb 38). *See 4e(1b).*

Weinberg, Herman G. "American Film Directors and Social Reality." *S&S* 7 (No. 28, Winter 38–39) 168–170.

Morrison, Charles C. (ed.). "Liberty Bells in Hollywood." *Chris Cent* 56 (8 Mar 39) 310. The U.S. movie just before the war: government pressures, "Films for Democracy," and the failing box office abroad.

Sterling, Philip. "A Channel for Democratic Thought." *Films* 1 (No. 2, Spring 40). *See 3a(6).*

Werner, M. R. "Yellow Movies." *New Yorker* 16 (14 Sep 40). *See 5, William Randolph Hearst.*

"Hollywood to the Colors." *Newswk* 18 (22 Dec 41) 59. The movie business plans to help the war effort.

Nugent, F. S. "Hollywood Faces Reality." *NYTM* (8 Mar 42) 16–17. The industry and its people react to war.

"Hollywood Swaps Sets and Even Salvages Nails to Comply with $5,000 Ceiling on Film Backdrops." *Newswk* 19 (8 June 42) 54+. War Production Board conservation order limits nonessential construction.

"Retake for War: Reducing Consumption of Film." *Bus Wk* (25 July 42) 38+.

"Hollywood Talks of Pooling and Looting Talent." *Newswk* 20 (24 Aug 42) 58+. Industry reacts to loss of talent as stars are drafted or enlist.

"Walt Disney Goes to War." *Life* 13 (31 Aug 42). *See 2h(3).*

Othman, F. C. "War in the World of Make-Believe." *SEP* 215 (17 Oct 42) 28–29+. Wartime shortages of materials and actors make production difficult.

"Axis Villains Fill Hollywood's Rogue's Gallery." *Life* 13 (23 Nov 42). *See 2b(6).*

Delehanty, Thornton. "Disney Studio at War." *Th Arts* 27 (Jan 43). *See 2h(3).*

Crichton, Kyle. "Hollywood Gets Its Teeth Kicked In." *Collier's* 111 (9 Jan 43) 34–35. Stars go to war; enlistments hampering production.

"Films to Entertain Soldiers." *Th Arts* 27 (Mar 43) 169–176. U.S. Army Motion Picture Service.

Agee, J. "So Proudly We Fail." *Nation* 157 (30 Oct 43) 509. An attack on American complacency and noninvolvement during the war; exceptions are *Battle of Britain* and *Battle of Russia.*

Isaacs, H. "Whistling in the Dark." *Th Arts* 27 (Dec 43) 727–733. Movies for the World War II army camps.

Jones, Dorothy B. "Is Hollywood Growing Up?" *Nation* 160 (3 Feb 45) 123–125. The effects of the war on Hollywood and movies in general.

Crowther, Bosley. "Hollywood's New Fair-Haired Boys." *NYTM* (15 July 45). *See 2b(2).*

"Films Reconvert." *Bus Wk* (1 Sep 45) 28+. The effects on Hollywood of the war: subject matter, film-footage restrictions, etc.

Jones, Dorothy B. "The Hollywood War Film: 1942–1944." *Hwd Q* 1 (No. 1, Oct 45) 1–19. Broad definition; "why we fought"; films about the enemy, the allies, and the home front; selected list with writer credits; see also letter by Arthur Rosenheimer, Jr., 1 (No. 3, Apr 46) 330–331.

Kracauer, S. "Hollywood's Terror Films." *Commentary* 2 (1946) 132–136. Sadism may be a preview of fascism.

Macgowan, Kenneth. "Some Gleams of Hope from Hollywood." *NYTM* (11 Aug 46) 20+. War and the documentary-film influence the Hollywood product; a defense of Hollywood film makers.

Read, Jan. "Box Office or Bust." *Penguin F Rev* 5 (Jan 48) 64–72. An analysis of current trends in Hollywood, including De Rochemont's realistic films and Albert Sindlinger's New Entertainment Workshop, where writers are to work according to formulas chosen by audiences.

Dawson, Anthony H. "Motion Picture Economics." *Hwd Q* 3 (No. 3, Spring 48). *See 6a(1).*

Knepper, Max. "Hollywood's 1948 Line-up." *Penguin F Rev* 7 (Sep 48) 113–116. No renaissance due this year.

Macgowan, K. "And So into the Sunset." *New Rep* (31 Jan 49) 23–24. The situation of the Hollywood movie after the war.

Houston, Penelope. "Mr. Deeds and Willie Stark." *S&S* 19 (Nov 50) 276–279+. Films which might reveal the current feelings America has about itself: *All the King's Men, Mr. Smith Goes to Washington,* and other sociological pictures.

Alpert, Hollis. "Summing Up." *Sat Rev* 33 (30 Dec 50) 23–24. Looking back over the film year of 1950.

Hamilton, Marie L. "1950's Production." *FIR* 2 (Jan 51) 8–9. Eight categories of U.S. features.

Lambert, Gavin. "A Line of Experiment." *S&S* 19 (Mar 51) 444–447. Recent examples of American low-budget subjects produced by Dore Schary unit at MGM.

Crowther, Bosley. "Hollywood Accents the Downbeat." *NYTM* (16 Mar 52) 22–23+. Inspired by the neorealist movement, and challenged by TV and a mature postwar audience, Hollywood turns to grim realism and unhappy endings.

Alpert, Hollis. "Postwar Generation of Arts and Letters." *Sat Rev* 36 (14 Mar 53) 16–17+. "New blood" in Hollywood is scarce—save for Stanley Kramer.

Houston, Penelope. "Rebels Without Causes." *S&S* 25 (Spring 56). *See 6h.*

McPherson, Mervyn. "Hollywood Gave Them a Chance." *F&F* 2 (No. 9, June 56) 17+. Stars discovered in sound period, especially Greer Garson.

Roud, Richard. "Britain in America." *S&S* 26 (Winter 56–57). *See 4e(1c).*

Crowther, Bosley. "Communiqué from Hollywood and Vine." *NYTM* (3 Feb 57) 24–26+. Population flow to suburbia and increasing viewer discrimination may help explain decline in film manufacture.

Houston, Penelope. "Hollywood in the Age of Television." *S&S* 26 (Spring 57). *See 6a(2).*

Carson, Robert. "Haunted Hollywood." *Holiday* 22 (Oct 57) 68–73+. Hollywood old and new.

Pryor, Thomas M. "Their Past Recaptured." *NYTM* (8 Dec 57). *See 2b(2).*

Dyer, Peter John. "The Murderers Among Us." *F&F* 5 (No. 3, Dec 58) 13–15+. Gangster, crime, and prison films between World Wars I and II.

Cassavetes, John. "What's Wrong with Hollywood?" *F Cult* (No. 19, 1959) 4–5.

Croce, Arlene. "Hollywood the Monolith." *Commonweal* 69 (23 Jan 59) 430–433. James Agee and the failure of American cinema as a national tragedy.

Dyer, Peter John. "The Face of the Goddess." *F&F* 5 (No. 9, June 59) 13–15+. Mythic woman in American films of the 1930s.

Lambert, Gavin. "From a Hollywood Note-book." *S&S* 28 (No. 2, Spring 59) 68–73. Vitality in a few little films such as *Hot Car Girl* and *The Party Crashers.*

Moskowitz, Gene. "The Tight Close-Up." *S&S* 28 (Nos. 3–4, Summer–Autumn 59) 126–132. Television directors now working on theatrical films.

Gillett, John. "The Survivors." *S&S* 28 (Nos. 3–4, Summer–Autumn 59) 151–155. Recent work by well-known American directors.

Young, Colin. "The Old Dependables." *FQ* 13 (No. 1, Fall 59) 2–17. Directors Billy Wilder, John Ford, Fred Zinnemann, and Lewis Milestone talk about their recent films.

Dyer, Peter John. "American Youth in Uproar." *F&F* 5 (No. 12, Sep 59) 10–12+. American films with "social" content.

"New Wavelet." *Time* 75 (23 May 60) 69. New American films inspired by the *Nouvelle Vague.*

Houston, Penelope. "After the Strike." *S&S* 29 (Summer 60) 108–112. Both the Actors Guild and the Writers Guild won residual payments; the general mood in Hollywood, and the attempts to end the Hollywood blacklist.

Knight, Arthur. "Visit to a Ghost Town." *Sat Rev* 43 (13 Aug 60) 24. Hollywood studios are nearly empty; on-location production; fewer films.

Franchi, R. M. "Don't-Make-a-Wave." *NY F Bul* 2 (No. 8, 1961) 1–5. Attacking the notion of an "American New Wave."

Sarris, Andrew. "Remembrance of Films Past." *NY F Bul* 2 (No. 5, 1961) 5–9. A review of several old Hollywood films, including ones by Walsh, LeRoy, Huston, and Aldrich.

Young, Colin. "West Coast Report." *S&S* 30 (Summer 61) 137–141. Why there is no new wave in Hollywood; the new projects of John Cassavetes, Denis and Terry Sanders, and Irvin Kershner.

Taylor, John Russell. "The High Forties." *S&S* 30 (Autumn 61) 188–191. Survey of the thrillers, emotional dramas, and *femmes fatales* that, the author complains, nobody seems to remember.

Knight, Arthur. "Shop Talk in Hollywood." *Sat Rev* 44 (23 Dec 61). *See 2c.*

Franchi, R. M. "Don't Make a Wave . . ." *Motion* (No. 2, Winter 61–62) 20–22. An argument against Gideon Bachmann's assertion that there is an American New Wave.

Sarris, Andrew. "The High Forties Revisited." *F Cult* (No. 24, 1962) 62–70. It was a golden age of talented directors—not of producers, genres, or stars (as John Russell Taylor seems to suggest *S&S* [Autumn 61]).

Bogdanovich, Peter. "Talkies: a Conversation Piece in Short Takes, Starring the Last Tycoons." *Esq* 58 (Aug 62) 33–40. Interviews with such people as Alfred Hitchcock, Billy Wilder, Gordon Douglas, William Goetz,

Jerry Lewis, Jack Lemmon, Cary Grant, Laurence Harvey, Walt Disney, Richard Brooks, Jerry Wald, Mark Robson, George Stevens, William Wyler, and Clifford Odets.

Fenin, George. "Son of Uncle Sam." *F&F* 9 (No. 1, Oct 62) 49–54. The past ten years of American film making.

Marcorelles, Louis. "American Diary." *S&S* 32 (Winter 62–63) 4–8. Critic visits the U.S. and Canada; his impressions about the movies he saw and people he met, among others Richard Leacock, Stan Brakhage, and King Vidor; with Robert Florey he takes a look at the supermarkets that have replaced the Chaplin and Griffith studios.

Brightman, Carol. "The Chicago Film Scene." *F Com* 1 (No. 4, 1963) 41–44. Reviewers, censors, art-theatre people, union leaders attend film class at Roosevelt University.

Sarris, Andrew. "The American Cinema." *F Cult* (No. 28, 1963). *See 2c.*

Yoshimaya, Tats. "Film News from the Fiftieth State." *F Com* 1 (No. 4, 1963). Japanese and American films shown; the image of Hawaii in American features; short travel films made by George Tahara.

MacCann, Richard Dyer. "From Technology to Adultery." *F&F* 9 (No. 4, Jan 63) 73–77. From technical innovations of 3-D and CinemaScope to the new trend in more mature themes for films, 1952–1961; chapter from *Hollywood in Transition* (Houghton Mifflin, 1962).

Fenin, George. "The Face of '63: No. 2— U.S." *F&F* 9 (No. 6, Mar 63) 55–63. U.S. actors, directors, and producers likely to make an impact on films of 1963.

Schlesinger, Arthur, Jr. "When the Movies Really Counted." *Show* 3 (Apr 63) 77–78+. Remarks on the decline of Hollywood's influence on American life from fans to the shaping of the American dream; characteristic figures cited, genres discussed.

Young, Colin. "Letter from Hollywood." *S&S* 32 (Autumn 63) 165–167. New language in cinema? *Hud*, perhaps, but not *Lilies of the Field* or *David and Lisa;* Hollywood's trouble is its ignorance of what's happening in other countries and its distance from people Americans know.

Johnson, W. "Movies: Have They Come of Age?" *Senior Scholastic* 83 (25 Oct 63) 11–15. The history of film from *The Jazz Singer* to the 1963 film festival in Philharmonic Hall.

"Everybody Wants to Say It in Films." *Life* 55 (20 Dec 63) 38–45. The rising popularity of cinema as an expressive medium.

Schulberg, Budd. "How Are Things in Panicsville?" *Life* 55 (20 Dec 63) 104–109. Reminiscence of the heyday of the big studios.

Knight, Arthur. "What Golden Years?" *Sat Rev* 47 (29 Aug 64) 169–171. The golden

era of the movies did not necessarily end with the studio system; independent production is like the Mack Sennett days.

Higdon, Hal. "Harlow, Nyoka, Fay Wray and Me." *Show* 5 (May 65) 62–67+. Recollections on the Hollywood pictures of the 1930s (i.e., *Hell's Angels*) and movie serials (i.e., *Nyoka the Jungle Girl*).

Young, Colin. "Letter from Hollywood." *S&S* 34 (Summer 65) 135–137. A survey of current activities and productions in Hollywood, such as Sam Peckinpah's *Major Dundee* and John Cassavetes' *Shadows;* Young also mentions some student projects.

Higham, Charles. "Hollywood Boulevard 1965." *S&S* 34 (Autumn 65) 117–179. A visit to Hollywood: the film capital is full of fears and nostalgia and obsessed with the subject of stars.

Holmes, John C. "15¢ Before 6:00 P.M.: The Wonderful Movies of the 'Thirties.'" *Harper's* 231 (Dec 65) 51–55.

Hagen, Ray. "The Day of the Runaway Heiress." *F&F* 12 (No. 7, Apr 66) 40–43. American films of the 1930s.

Behrman, S. N. "You Can't Release *Dante's Inferno* in the Summertime." *NYTM* (17 July 66) 6–7+. On Hollywood's golden era.

"Happy Movies Are Here Again!" *Good Housekeeping* 164 (Apr 67) 102–105. Comments on increase in "upbeat" family movies; *Dr. Doolittle, Thoroughly Modern Millie,* others.

Markfield, W. "'Play It Again, Sam'—and Again." *SEP* 240 (22 Apr 67) 72–76. TV's *Late Show*—movies from the past.

Braun, Eric. "Where Have All the Stylists Gone?" *F&F* 13 (No. 8, May 67) 50–55; (No. 9, June 67) 38–43; (No. 10, July 67) 12–16; (No. 11, Aug 67) 10–14; (No. 12, Sep 67) 12–16. Five articles on the actresses with style in the films of the 1930s and 1940s.

Sarris, Andrew. "Films of the Thirties: The White Satin Gown and the Working Girl." *Arts Mag* 42 (Sep–Oct 67) 17–18. American cinema of the 1930s.

"Shock of Freedom in Films." *Time* 90 (8 Dec 67) 66–68+. On the current state of film making, emphasizing the making of *Bonnie and Clyde*.

Jacobs, Lewis. "World War II and the American Film." *CJ* 7 (1967–1968) 1–21. Gradual changes in themes from 1939 to 1944.

Geduld, Carolyn and Harry. "From Kops to Robbers: Transformation of Archetypal Figures in the American Cinema of the Twenties and Thirties." *J Pop Cult* 1 (No. 4, Spring 68) 389–394. Comedians of the 1920s become the gangsters of the 1930s, expressing undisguised noncomic aggression.

"Late Show as History." *Time* 91 (28 June 68) 32–33. Essay on TV's movie reruns from the

1930s and 1940s and the changing attitudes and taste of the public.

Madsen, Axel. "Fission/Fusion/Fission." *S&S* 37 (Summer 68) 124–126. Fusion of traditional and revolutionary film making together with European influence may again put American cinema in the forefront; new men at the top in the film companies; some new film makers, such as Francis Ford Coppola, Gordon Parks, and Noel Black.

Callenbach, Ernest. "Looking Backward." *FQ* 22 (No. 1, Fall 68) 1–9. "Personal notes" on the occasion of *Film Quarterly*'s tenth birthday: the decline of narrative in films, the advancement of "film culture," the possibility of more low-budget production, simpler technology.

Farber, Stephen. "The Outlaws." *S&S* 37 (Autumn 68). See *7a(5)*.

North, Christopher. "Industry Highlights." *FIR* 19 (No. 10, Dec 68) 613–617. Important historical dates in film, culled from *Film Daily*.

Schillaci, Anthony. "Film as Environment." *Sat Rev* (28 Dec 68). See *7b(1a)*.

Dawson, Jan. "The Acid Test." *S&S* 38 (Winter 68–69) 49–50. Hollywood's attempts to create an image of American youth more sophisticated and real than in *Pollyanna* and beach-party movies, especially in terms of sex; *The Graduate, Out of It,* and *Wild in the Streets* are discussed.

Astor, Mary. "What It Was Like to Kiss Clark Gable." *Rdrs Dig* 94 (June 69) 49–53. Personal remembrances.

Morgenstern, Joseph. "Hollywood: Myth, Fact and Trouble." *Newswk* 73 (30 June 69) 82. A report on an uneasy period of change.

Reck, T. S. "Come Out of the Shower, and Come Out Clean." *Commonweal* 90 (26 Sep 69) 588–591. Sex and violence were more skillful in the films of the 1940s than in recent imitations.

Cohen, Larry. "The New Audience: From Andy Hardy to Arlo Guthrie." *Sat Rev* 52 (27 Dec 69). See *7b(1a)*.

Madson, Axel. "Reaching the Tribes." *S&S* 39 (Winter 69–70). See *3b(2)*.

Kagan, Norman. "Black American Cinema." *Cinema* (Calif) 6 (No. 2, 1970). See *2a(4)*.

"The Day the Dream Factory Woke Up." *Life* 68 (27 Feb 70). See *6b(2)*.

Friedman, Norman L. "American Movies and American Culture, 1946–1970." *J Pop Cult* 3 (No. 4, Spring 70) 815–823. Study of the relationship of post-World War II films to the cultural changes in America in that period.

Jowett, Garth S. "The Concept of History in American Produced Films: An Analysis of Films Made in the Period 1950–1961." *J Pop Cult* 3 (No. 4, Spring 70) 794–813. A study

of the attitude toward history expressed by films made in those ten years.

Lounsbury, Myron. " 'Flashes of Lightning': The Moving Picture in the Progressive Era." *J Pop Cult* 3 (No. 4, Spring 70) 769–797. A study of the role of motion pictures in the first two decades of the century, especially as seen by writers, reviewers, and critics of the period.

Madsen, Axel. "The Changing of the Guard." *S&S* 39 (Spring 70) 63–65. Changes in big Hollywood film companies, now largely run by young bosses; new productions and costs.

Fleming, K. "Dreams for Sale." *Newswk* 75 (4 May 70). See *6b(2)*.

"Memories on the Block." *Life* 68 (22 May 70). See *6b(2)*.

Madsen, Axel. "California Dreamin'." *S&S* 39 (Summer 70) 127–129. Madsen discusses the projects of George Lucas, Douglas Trumbull, Richard Rush, and Dennis Hopper, all revolutionary film makers of a sort.

Corliss, Richard. "The Radicals Have Occupied the Asylum." *JSPG* (June 70) 15–18. New films about revolution (reprinted from newsletter of Museum of Modern Art).

Stein, Elliott. "New York 1970: The Year of the Foof." *S&S* 39 (Autumn 70) 204–207. Old films have turned up in New York theatres, including Rowland V. Lee's *Zoo in Budapest*, John Ford's *Judge Priest*, Raoul Walsh's *Me and My Gal*; some judgments.

North, Christopher. "Film History for Exhibitors." *FIR* 21 (No. 8, Oct 70) 473–477. Headlines culled from 50 years of *Boxoffice* magazine.

Schickel, Richard. "Good Days, Good Years." *Harper's* 241 (Oct 70) 44–50. The era of the strong men: John Ford, Allan Dwan, and Raoul Walsh.

4d(1). STUDIO HISTORIES

[See also *2h(3), 2h(4), 6b(2), 6c(1)*.]

"North Formosa Novelties." *Time* 26 (21 Oct 35) 46–47. Traces development of United Artists.

"Twentieth Century-Fox." *Fortune* 12 (Dec 35) 85–93+. Surveys studio from its beginnings through the coming of Zanuck.

"Warner Brothers Rode to Success on a Wave of Sound." *Newswk* 8 (26 Dec 36) 23–26.

Johnston, A. "The Great Goldwyn." *SEP* 209 (8 May 37, 22 May 37, 5 June 37, 19 June 37). See *5, Samuel Goldwyn*.

"Warner Brothers." *Fortune* 16 (Dec 37) 110–113+. Extensive history full of statistics, producers, movies, etc.; special emphasis on Warners' role in the "talkie" revolution.

"Disney Productions Occupy New Home." *Arch and Eng* 143 (No. 1, Oct 40) 58. A brief, laudatory description of the Disney plant in Burbank.

"United Artists: Final Shooting Script." *Fortune* 22 (Dec 40) 99–102. A whimsical blend of shooting script and factual history from 1919; a chart of films and producers.

Weber, K. "Walt Disney Studios." *Calif Arts and Arch* 58 (No. 1, Jan 41) 27. A brief discussion, with photographs, of the design of the Disney Studios.

Isaacs, H. R. "Presenting the Warner Brothers." *Th Arts* 28 (Feb 44) 99–101+. Historical analysis.

Goodman, Ezra. "M-G-M: Mammoth of the Movies." *Coronet* 26 (May 49) 172–178.

"MGM Celebrates Its Twenty-fifth Birthday." *Look* 13 (No. 14, 5 July 49) 40–47. Review of the American film studio's twenty-five-year history: famous films, new productions, a collective portrait of top talent.

Poster, William. "Hollywood Caterers to the Middle Class: An Appraisal of M-G-M." *Am Mercury* 73 (Aug 51) 82–91. An analysis of MGM as "a powerful, formidable presence on the American scene" and its formula for success in pleasing the public; discussion of individual films.

"RKO: It's Only Money." *Fortune* 47 (May 53) 122–129+. Account of period of control by Howard Hughes since 1948.

"The Universal Appeal." *Life* 34 (15 June 53) 103–104. Universal-International switches from "distinguished" films (1946) to earthy American adventure movies, which pay the films' stars, notably James Stewart, a percentage of the profits.

"Flare-Up in Hollywood." *Newswk* 43 (1 Mar 54) 79. Ill feelings over Dore Schary's failure to credit certain important people in a television tribute to MGM.

North, Christopher. "UA's 35th Birthday." *FIR* 5 (Apr 54) 65–70. Historical outline of the United Artists Corporation, surveying the films made there since 1919; a recent letter from Max Youngstein to the Motion Picture Association, complaining that other studios get better treatment from the code office.

North, Christopher. "MGM's First 30 Years." *FIR* 5 (May 54) 216–220. Brief summary of the history of Metro-Goldwyn-Mayer Corporation, listing only outstanding personalities and most successful films.

Houston, Penelope. "Lion Rampant: The Record of MGM." *S&S* 24 (July–Sep 54) 21–30. The studio's three production executives, Mayer, Thalberg, and Schary; comments on the beginnings of the star system, the changes of policy, the musicals, and the best films; the article celebrates the thirtieth anniversary of MGM.

Mayer, Arthur L. "The Origins of United Artists." *FIR* 10 (Aug–Sep 59) 390–399. Its founding by Griffith, Pickford, Chaplin, and Fairbanks, whose business and artistic abilities are appraised; the firm's history is

sketched up through 1951, when Robert Benjamin and Arthur Krim took over.

Kraft, Richard. "A Host of Yesterdays." *NY F Bul* 3 (No. 4, 1962) 13–20. Films from Warner Brothers 1930–1948, including *Casablanca* and *The Big Sleep*.

Erengis, George P. "MGM's Backlot." *FIR* 14 (Jan 63). See 2k(2).

"Nostalgia Lifts the Bids." *Bus Wk* (10 Aug 63) 30–31. Report on the auction at bankrupt Hal Roach Studios.

Zeitlin, D. "Meanwhile Back in Hollywood, Efficiency Takes Over." *Life* 55 (20 Dec 63) 46–50. The new face of Universal Pictures.

4d(2). INDEPENDENT PRODUCTION

[See also 6c(3).]

"Hollywood in the Bronx." *Time* 35 (29 Jan 40) 67. The Micheaux Picture Corporation produces Negro films.

"One of the Masters?" *Time* 46 (13 Aug 45) 86+. David Selznick teams up with J. Arthur Rank to form Selznick International Pictures.

Shipp, Cameron. "Hollywood's Million-Dollar Shoestrings." *Collier's* 120 (12 July 47) 28+. Problems and rewards of independent production.

Baum, Frank. "The Oz Film Co." *FIR* 7 (Aug–Sep 56). See 4k(9).

Young, Colin. "The Hollywood War of Independence." *FQ* 12 (No. 3, Spring 59) 4–15. The problems of independent film makers Stanley Kubrick, Martin Ritt, and young Denis and Terry Sanders.

Mekas, Jonas. "New York Letter: Towards a Spontaneous Cinema." *S&S* 28 (Nos. 3–4, Summer–Autumn 59) 118–121. "True independents" in U.S. include Lionel Rogosin, Morris Engel, John Cassavetes, Stanley Brakhage.

Young, Colin, and Gideon Bachmann. "New Wave—or Gesture?" *FQ* 14 (No. 3, Spring 61) 6–14. Current production by some independent film makers: John Cassavetes, Irvin Kershner, Denis and Terry Sanders, Curtis Harrington, and Shirley Clark.

Gehman, Richard. "Hollywood's Independent Spirit." *Th Arts* 45 (June 61) 16–19. The old assembly-line order gives way to actor-producer-director-writers.

Knight, Arthur. "There's Nothing Wrong with the Movies." *Th Arts* 45 (June 61) 8–10+. Factors that have squeezed the industry in the last ten years are also giving its creative people more chances.

Knight, Arthur. "Cinema on a Shoestring." *Playboy* 9 (No. 4, Apr 62) 64–66. From Stanley Kubrick's *Killer's Kiss* to *Black Orpheus*: new film makers.

Walsh, Moira. "Films: A Retraction." *America*

109 (26 Oct 63) 494–496. Discussion of the tribulations of independently produced feature films.

Bean, Robin. "Muscle Mayhem." *F&F* 10 (No. 9, June 64) 14–18. Hammer Production Company and American International Pictures and their films.

Levy, Alan. "Peekaboo Sex, or How to Fill a Drive-In." *Life* 59 (16 July 65) 81–82+. Detailed report on American International Pictures.

Johnson, Albert. "The Dynamic Gesture: New American Independents." *FQ* 19 (No. 4, Summer 66) 6–11. Focus on Vic Morrow and *Deathwatch,* Mary Ellen Bute's *Passages from Finnegan's Wake,* and other independent features brought to the San Francisco festival by Johnson.

Borgzinner, Jon. "Made a Good Movie Lately?"

Life 65 (11 Oct 68) 92–99+. The young generation of film makers.

Bean, Robin, and David Austen. "U.S.A.: Confidential." *F&F* 15 (No. 2, Nov 68) 16–28. On the films made by American International Pictures.

"The Old Hollywood: They Lost It at the Movies." *Newswk* 75 (2 Feb 70) 66–67. Old traditions make way for the new wave.

Welles, Orson. "But Where Are We Going?" *Look* 34 (3 Nov 70) 34–36. New age of artistic control by the young director will perhaps create a new golden age in film.

"The New Movies." *Newswk* 76 (7 Dec 70) 62–74. New directors Dennis Hopper, Robert Rafelson, John Korty; actors Robert Redford, Donald Sutherland; actresses Carrie Snodgress, Sally Kellerman; new heroes epitomized by Jack Nicholson in *Five Easy Pieces.*

4e. Europe Since 1930

"How They Control Movies Abroad." *Lit Dig* 114 (6 Aug 32) 22. European countries organizing film institutes to study effects of film.

Birrell, Francis. "Film-Going in London and Paris." *New S&N* 5 (21 Jan 33) 73–74. Comparison of exhibition practices in two cities.

Buchanan, Donald W. "The Art of the European Film." *Queens Q* 40 (Nov 33) 568–576. Surveys industry in Russia, Germany, and France.

"Films Abroad." *Living Age* 350 (July 36) 441–443. Brief survey, including British.

"Films in Birth." *Living Age* 351 (Nov 36) 251–253. Prospects in Russia and France.

Sadoul, Georges. "A Letter from Paris." *Films* 1 (No. 1, Nov 39) 91–96. Report on French and German production.

Smith, Brian. "Movies in Malta." *S&S* 11 (No. 44, Spring 43) 86–87. A personal account of film exhibition there.

Weinberg, H. G. "European Film in America." *Th Arts* 32 (Oct 48) 48–49. Current import status and a selection of titles discussed.

Jarrico, Paul. "They Are Not So Innocent Abroad." *New Rep* 120 (31 Jan 49) 17–19. European attempts to develop their own studios and film productions after the war in a love/hate relationship with U.S. movies.

Foose, Thomas T. "1950's Foreign Imports." *FIR* 2 (Jan 51) 13+. The British were the best.

Griffith, Richard. "European Films and American Audiences." *SRL* 34 (13 Jan 51) 52–54+. Analysis of European film trends and their acceptance in the U.S.

Houston, Penelope. "In Perspective." *S&S* 19 (Mar 51) 431–432. Unlike literature, "in the

cinema, all's change"; a brief history of European film, suggesting that a little more stability might be a good thing.

Koeves, Tibor. "Celluloid Crusaders." *UN World* 5 (Mar 51) 35–37+. An analysis of Italian, French, and English movie makers.

Knight, Arthur. "Mediterranean Movie Making." *Sat Rev* 36 (24 Oct 53) 49–50. The notable increase in joint production of films on the Continent.

"Glamour-Imported." *NYTM* (15 Nov 53). See 2b(2).

"Beauty Abroad." *Coronet* 36 (Aug 54). See 2b(2).

"Foreign Film Fare." *NYTM* (6 Mar 55) 26–27. A survey of contemporary films from abroad.

Nichols, M. "Foreign Accent in Starlets." *Coronet* 40 (Aug 56). See 2b(4).

"Queens of the Foreign Hollywoods." *NYTM* (10 Nov 57). See 2b(2).

Dyer, Peter John. "The Realists—a Return to Life." *F&F* 6 (No. 2, Nov 59) 12–14+. Post-World War II European film making.

Alpert, Hollis. "Show of Strength Abroad." *Sat Rev* 48 (24 Dec 60) 43–45. French, Swedish, and English movie industry: are foreign films better?

Gerasimov, Sergei. "The Class of Conscience." *F&F* 7 (No. 6, Mar 61) 7+. Films reflect the social conditions of Western world; emphasis on films of Fellini and New Wave.

"Angry Cry Against a Sinful City." *Life* 50 (12 May 61) 54–55. *La Dolce Vita* and some other current imports.

Harris, Jack. "A Sudden Surge of Magnetic Males." *Life* 51 (15 Sep 61). See 2b(2).

Peck, Seymour. "Europe's New Symbols of

169

Femininity." *NYTM* (24 Sep 61) 54–55. Photos of current European actresses.

Duprey, Richard A. "Bergman and Fellini, Explorers of the Modern Spirit." *Cath World* 194 (Oct 61) 13–19+. Lengthy study on *La Dolce Vita* and *The Virgin Spring*, and comparison of the two directors.

Young, Vernon. "European Film Notebook." *Hudson Rev* 14 (Winter 61–62) 580–585. Discussion of the "hate England" trend in British cinema from 1958 on; why Swedish films cannot provide escapism for audiences; landmarks of the New Wave.

Bauer, Jerry. "Newer Wave." *Th Arts* 46 (July 62) 22–24. On the second "new wave" in France and Italy.

Peck, Seymour. "Leading Men, European Style." *NYTM* (18 Nov 62) 106–107. Photos of leading European stars.

Gilliatt, Penelope. "Bad Good Films." *Vogue* 141 (1 Jan 63) 124+. Some recent trends in European film.

"Pictorial: Europe's New Sex Sirens." *Playboy* 10 (Sep 63). See *2b(6)*.

Greene, M. "Some Very Winning Europeans." *Life* 55 (20 Dec 63). See *2b(2)*.

"Les Girls; New Faces." *Time* 84 (21 Aug 64). See *2b(4)*.

Kauffmann, S. "Film Thoughts from Abroad." *New Rep* 151 (24 Oct 64) 22–25. Notes from a three-month tour in eight countries.

"Where the Action Is; Symposium." *Sat Rev* 48 (25 Dec 65) 10–22+. The movie scene is European in 1965.

"Common Market's Glamour Stock." *Life* 60 (28 Jan 66). See *2b(4)*.

Knight, Arthur. "New Life for the New Wave." *Sat Rev* 49 (20 Aug 66) 38. Music Corporation of America backs Truffaut, Chabrol, Losey, and other European directors.

Holleaux, André. "Subsidy Under the Common Market . . ." *JSPG* (June 67). See *6a(3)*.

Vietheer, George. "The Journal Looks at Foreign Film Subsidies." *JSPG* (June 67). See *6a(3)*.

"Hi-Ho, Denario!" *Time* 90 (4 Aug 67) 56–57. On the making of Italian Westerns in Spain.

Madsen, Axel. "A Cinematic Love Affair: European Style." *Cinema* (Calif) 3 (No. 6, Winter 67). See *2c*.

Strick, Philip. "Brussels Conference." *S&S* 37 (Summer 68) 127. Common Market countries fear withdrawal of U.S. production money but can't decide what to do.

4e(1). GREAT BRITAIN AND IRELAND

[See also *8c(2a)*.

[See 5, Biography: *Lindsay Anderson, Michael Anderson, Ken Annakin, Anthony Asquith, Roy Baker, Michael Balcon, Sidney Bernstein, John Boorman, Peter Brook, Henry Cornelius, John Davis, Basil Dearden, Anatole De Grunwald,*

Clive Donner, Terence Fisher, Bryan Forbes, Cyril Frankel, Sidney Furie, Sidney Gilliat, Jack Gold, Graham Greene, Val Guest, Peter Hall, Robert Hamer, Alfred Hitchcock, Seth Holt, Ken Hughes, Alexander Korda, David Lean, J. Lee-Thompson, Richard Lester, Don Levy, Joseph Losey, Alexander Mackendrick, Wolf Mankowitz, Maxwell Munden, Silvio Narizzano, George Pearson, Harold Pinter, Michael Powell, J. Arthur Rank, Carol Reed, Michael Reeves, Karel Reisz, Michael Relph, Tony Richardson, Ken Russell, G. B. Shaw, Ralph Thomas, Peter Ustinov, Peter Watkins, Michael Winner, Peter Yates.]

Marshall, Norman. "Reflections on the English Film." *Bookman* 81 (Oct 31) 71–72. Why film is an art form unsuited to the English character and temperament.

Lejeune, C. A. "The British Film and Others." *Fortnightly Rev* 143 (Mar 35) 285–294. Reviews British film industry; the studios at Elstree, Ealing, and Shepherd's Bush; British Film Institute; the GPO film unit.

Holmes, Winifred. "British Films and the Empire." *S&S* 5 (No. 19, Autumn 36) 72–74. Historical and critical comments on film making and film viewing in New Zealand, Canada, India, South Africa, and Australia.

"Unpopularity Contest." *Current Hist* (Sep 37). See *2b(2)*.

Hitchcock, Alfred. "Directors' Problems." *Living Age* 354 (Apr 38). See *2c*.

McCullie, Hector. "Oh! London." *S&S* 7 (No. 26, Summer 38) 73–74. London and provincial cinema viewers compared.

Wilson, Norman. "The Voice of Scotland." *S&S* 15 (No. 57, Spring 46) 20–21. Film production there.

Harman, A. Jympson. "Truth and British Films." *S&S* 15 (No. 57, Spring 46). See *7a(1)*.

Wollenberg, H. H. "British Films Overseas." *S&S* 15 (No. 60, Winter 46–47). See *7e*.

Goldsmith, I. G. "Made in England." *Screen Writer* 2 (Jan 47). See *2d*.

Huff, Theodore. "Sadoul and Film Research." *Hwd Q* 2 (No. 2, Jan 47). See *4a(1)*.

Manvell, Roger. "Clearing the Air." *Hwd Q* 2 (No. 2, Jan 47) 174–178. There is a growing minority audience in England and room in the industry for individual artists; much of the British public likes the realistic element in U.S. films.

Clarke, T. E. B. "Screenwriter and Director in a British Studio." *Screen Writer* 3 (June 47) 14–16. Describes how he worked successfully with director Charles Crichton on three films, and gives advice to other writers on writer-director relationships and the step-by-step development of a shooting script.

Paxton, John. "Coffee in a Teacup: Notes on an English Adventure." *Hwd Q* 3 (No. 1, Fall 47) 34–40. Reminiscences by the screenwriter for James Hilton's novel *So Well Remembered;* the British say American pictures are unrealistic; is the British character, as J. B. Priestley suggests, "antithetical to drama"?

Noble, Peter. "A Survey of Film Periodicals, II: Great Britain." *Hwd Q* 3 (No. 2, Winter 47–48). *See 1b(2).*

Vargas, A. L. "The Future of the British Film Writer." *S&S* 16 (No. 64, Winter 47–48) 161–162. He is generally held in low esteem.

Clarke, T. E. B. "British Writers Speak Out." *Screen Writer* 3 (No. 8, Jan 48). *See 2d(1).*

Lee, Norman. "Hollywood! You've Been Warned." *Screen Writer* 3 (Feb 48) 28–31. British pictures are getting better, partly because writers are being left free to direct and produce their own works.

Whitebait, William. "New Precision in Film Reviewing." *New S&N* 39 (21 Jan 50). *See 3b.*

Patmore, Derek. "British Producers Adopt Continental Methods." *FIR* 1 (Mar 50) 17+. Newly formed independent producing companies; current films shown in London.

Wright, Basil, Henry Cornelius, Thorold Dickinson, Anthony Havelock-Allan, Rosamund John, Frank Launder, Rachael Low, James Minter, Guy Morgan. "Round Table on British Films." *S&S* 19 (May 50) 114–122. Economics, subjects, style, and other topics.

Patmore, Derek. "Word from Britain." *FIR* 1 (May–June 50) 12+. Currently successful films showing in England.

Queval, Jean. "France Looks at British Films." *S&S* 19 (July 50) 198–200. Since *Brief Encounter,* the French have, generally, liked British films; admiration for the "documentary school"; Queval feels there is "an utter lack of pulchritude" in British life and films, and that this, together with violence, is what French audiences want.

Patmore, Derek. "A London Newsletter." *FIR* 1 (Sep 50) 15–16. The future for British production looks brighter: *Trio* and others.

Wagner, Geoffrey. "The Lost Audience." *QFRTV* 6 (No. 4, Summer 52) 338–350. Columbia University author looks at British industry (especially producer Filippo del Giudice) and prescribes more intelligence and independence, not the kind of opposition from Rank and others that faced *Henry V.*

Gray, Hugh. "The Eternal Problem." *QFRTV* 6 (No. 4, Summer 52) 354–360. Loss of audience and predictions of doom for the drama have been going on "from Aeschylus to Zanuck"; answering article, "The Lost Audience," by Geoffrey Wagner, pp. 338–350 in same issue, reminds us that Korda and Balcon also had successes.

Young, Colin. "Continental and Otherwise: The Specialized Cinema in Britain." *QFRTV* 9 (No. 1, Fall 54) 33–45. UCLA graduate

student reports on art theatres, film societies, and censorship in England and his native Scotland.

Oughton, Frederick. "Man with a Roving Eye." *F&F* 1 (No. 5, Feb 55). *See 2c.*

Marks, Louis. "All About Kids." *F&F* 1 (No. 6, Mar 55). *See 2b(10).*

Powell, Dilys. "The Everyman." *S&S* 25 (Summer 55) 43. Brief profile of a Hampstead specialized cinema house on its twenty-fifth anniversary.

Watts, Stephen. "The Future of Film and TV in Britain." *QFRTV* 10 (No. 4, Summer 56) 364–373.

"Discovery: British Women Are Beautiful." *Look* 20 (21 Aug 56). *See 2b.*

Mulock, Al. "School for Actors." *F&F* 3 (No. 1, Oct 56). *See 2b(1).*

Watts, Stephen. "The Public Goes for Quality." *JSPG* 4 (No. 2, Nov 56). *See 7b(1a).*

Gunston, David. "Eyes and Ears of the World." *F&F* 3 (No. 5, Feb 57). *See 2d(5).*

Hitchcock, Alfred. "Murder, With English on It." *NYTM* (3 Mar 57). *See 5, Alfred Hitchcock.*

Lennard, Robert. "How We Find the Stars of Tomorrow." *F&F* 3 (No. 7, Apr 57) 8–9. Casting director explains how various British stars were discovered.

Quayle, Anthony. "Society and the Actor." *F&F* 3 (No. 10, July 57). *See 2b(1).*

Hume, Rod. "Gentlemen in England." *F&F* 3 (No. 12, Sep 57). *See 2b.*

Field, Mary. "Children in Cinema." *F&F* 4 (No. 7, Apr 58). *See 7b(3a).*

"British Feature Directors." *S&S* 27 (Autumn 58) 289–304. An alphabetical listing of eighty British directors, with titles of their films and critical paragraphs about their work; also a list of seventeen film studios.

Rotha, Paul, *et al.* "The Critical Issue." *S&S* 27 (Autumn 58). *See 3b.*

Conrad, Derek. "What Makes the British Laugh?" *F&F* 5 (No. 5, Feb 59) 7+. John and Roy Boulting discuss the British sense of humor.

"A Free Hand." *S&S* 28 (No. 2, Spring 59). *See 2c.*

Hill, Derek. "A Writers' Wave?" *S&S* 29 (Spring 60). *See 2d.*

Lassally, Walter. "The Dead Hand." *S&S* 29 (Summer 60). *See 2a(5).*

"Idleness Enriched." *Economist* 199 (24 June 61) 1384+. Design, programs, and clientele of London's "cartoon news cinema."

Stonier, G. W. "Life with Whitebait." *New S&N* 62 (6 Oct 61). *See 3b(1).*

Mortimer, John. "Life in Celluloid." *Spectator* 207 (24 Nov 61). *See 2d(1).*

"The Front Page." *S&S* 31 (Spring 62) 55. Editorial on the still-lagging British "breakthrough" in film: "is it our literary tradition which damps down British cinema?"

Hill, Derek. "The Short Film Situation." *S&S* 31 (Summer 62). *See 4a(5)*.

"British-American." *Movie* (No. 1, June 62) 8–9. A graph attempts to compare the directorial talent in British and American film industries.

Cowie, Peter. "The Face of '63: No. 1—Britain." *F&F* 9 (No. 5, Feb 63) 19–27. British actors, producers, and directors who will make an impact on films in 1963.

Johnson, Ian. "Have the British a Sense of Humor?" *F&F* 9 (No. 6, Mar 63) 48–53. British humor 1939–1963.

"How to Get into Films." *F&F* 9 (No. 10, July 63) 11–14. A number of young people in the British film industry answer questions about getting into the industry.

Meehan, Thomas. "Friday Night and Saturday Night." *New Yorker* 39 (19 Oct 63). *See 3b(4)*.

Alpert, Hollis. "Happiness Is a Film-Maker in London." *Sat Rev* 48 (25 Dec 65) 10–13+.

"Moviemaking: Slow, Damp, and Better Now Than Hollywood." *Esq* 66 (July 66) 60–61. Short list of movie people working in London.

McGillivray, David. "The Crowded Shelf." *F&F* 15 (No. 12, Sep 69) 14–22. Films that have never been released in Britain.

Robinson, David. *"Around Angel Lane."* *S&S* 39 (Summer 70) 132–133. Some biographical notes about young English director Barney Platts-Mills and comments about this feature film, also entitled *Bronco Bullfrog*.

"The Crisis We Deserve." *S&S* 39 (Autumn 70) 172–178. Questionnaire basically asks what film makers feel about the context—not only economic—in which pictures are now being made in England; young British film makers Kevin Billington, John Boorman, Kevin Brownlow, James Clark, Dick Clement, and Peter Hall give their views.

4e(1a). Historical Surveys

Ervine, John. "Actor and the Cinema." *London Mercury* 33 (Mar 36) 482–492. The development of "mechanized" entertainment (i.e., cinema and television) was fatal to the concert hall, the opera, and theatre. Discussion (Apr 36) 619–623 and (May 36) 51–52.

Seton, Marie. "The British Cinema." *S&S* 6 (No. 21, Spring 37) 5–8. From 1896 to 1907.

Seton, Marie. "The British Cinema: 1907–1914." *S&S* 6 (No. 22, Summer 37) 64–67.

Sharar, Dewan. "Twenty-two Soho Square: British Movietone News." *Great Britain and the East* 49 (29 July 37) 162–163. Brief historical survey.

Seton, Marie. "The British Cinema: 1914." *S&S* 6 (No. 23, Autumn 37) 126–128. An overview of the films and the film scene August–December 1914.

Seton, Marie. "War." *S&S* 6 (No. 24, Winter 37–38) 182–185. The British film in wartime, 1915–1920.

Seton, Marie. "Silent Shadows." *S&S* 7 (No. 25, Spring 38) 31–33. British cinema, 1920–1927.

Young, Howard Irving. "British Studios in Wartime." *Screen Writer* 1 (Feb 46) 11–17. After a shutdown at first, they kept right on making and showing pictures.

Sadoul, Georges. "Early Film Production in England." *Hwd Q* 1 (No. 3, Apr 46) 249–259. French critic and historian credits the "Brighton School" with perhaps the earliest use of close-ups (G. A. Smith, 1901?) and montage chase sequences. See objecting letter by Theodore Huff *Hwd Q* 2 (No. 2, Jan 47) 203–206.

Balcon, Michael. "The British Film During the War." *Penguin F Rev* 1 (Aug 46) 66–73. A renaissance: causes and effects.

Hepworth, Cecil. "Those Were the Days." *Penguin F Rev* 6 (Apr 48) 33–39. Reminiscences by a pioneer of the earliest days of cinematography.

Price, Peter. "The Impresario Urge." *S&S* 19 (Nov 50) 290–293. An article dealing with the British producers who dared to attempt their dreams: Alexander Korda and Filippo del Giudice.

Pratley, Gerald. "Who Invented the Movies?" *FIR* 2 (Aug–Sep 51) 13–15. An analysis of the historical importance of William Friese-Greene with some reference to the biographical film *The Magic Box*.

Ramsaye, Terry. "Friese-Greene Is a Legend." *FIR* 2 (Aug–Sep 51) 15–18. Informed Britons do not believe in him as a movie inventor.

Crow, Duncan. "The First Golden Age." *S&S* 23 (Jan–Mar 54) 148–151+. How sound was introduced; early history of British cinema, including the effects of the Cinematograph Act of 1928, which placed a quota on film imports and stimulated domestic British production.

Crow, Duncan. "The Advent of Leviathan." *S&S* 23 (Apr–June 54) 191–193+. Second article in a history of British cinema; events between 1927 and 1936; the formation of Gaumont-British Picture Corporation (1927) and Associated British Cinemas, Ltd. (1928).

Spottiswoode, Raymond. "The Friese-Greene Controversy: The Evidence Reconsidered." *QFRTV* 9 (No. 3, Spring 55) 217–230. No adequate evidence exists to establish the true contribution of this British inventor to the development of the motion picture.

Manvell, Roger. "The Oldest Man in Films." *F&F* 1 (No. 11, Aug 55) 8+. The contributions of George Albert Smith, recently honored by the British Film Academy.

Allen, K. S. "Golden Anniversary." *F&F* 1 (No. 12, Sep 55) 10. John P. Harris' nickelodeon first showed films in June of 1905.

Lassally, Walter. "The Cynical Audience." *S&S* 26 (Summer 56). *See 7b(1a).*

Lambert, Gavin. "Notes on the British Cinema." *QFRTV* 11 (No. 1, Fall 56) 1–13. Realism came before the documentary movement, from Hitchcock and Balcon; Korda brought elegance, Pascal, an obsession to do Shaw's plays; not much social commitment among feature makers.

Gray, Martin. "The Shape of Things Past." *F&F* 5 (No. 5, Feb 59). *See 2k.*

Acres, Sidney Birt. "The First Command Film Performance." *Cinema Studies* 1 (No. 2, Dec 60) 49–57. Author's father took news film of prince and princesses, and they wanted to see it.

Coe, Brian. "Wordsworth Donisthorpe." *Cinema Studies* 1 (No. 3, Aug 61) 51–54. Pioneer in British cinematography filed first patent in 1876.

Williams, David. "Early Film Criticism in Leicester." *Cinema Studies* 1 (No. 4, Dec 61) 68–71. There were nine picture theatres there in 1911, and as early as 1896–1898 there were two newspaper reviewers.

Johnson, Ian. "We're All Right, Jack." *F&F* 8 (No. 12, Sep 62) 44–48. Review of the past ten years of British film making.

Balcon, Michael. "Sir Michael Balcon Writes as One Professional Survivor to Another." *Silent Picture* (No. 2, Spring 69) 8–9. The usefulness of George Pearson's autobiography *Flashback* (London: Allen & Unwin, 1957) as a story of the British film industry.

Durgnat, Raymond. "TV's Young Turks." *F&F* 15 (No. 6, Mar 69) 4–10; (No. 7, Apr 69) 26–30. Two-part study of the work of British film directors who began with television work.

Eves, Vicki. "Britain's Social Cinema." *Screen* 10 (No. 6, Nov–Dec 69) 51–66. Such films are comparatively rare.

Honri, Baynham. "The Samuelson Saga." *Silent Picture* (No. 5, Winter 69–70) 2–7. History of the Samuelson Film Manufacturing Company, Ltd. (started in 1906) and the films they made.

Johnston, Claire, and Jan Dawson. "Declarations of Independence." *S&S* 39 (Winter 69–70). *See 8d.*

Gifford, Denis. "Pimple." *Silent Picture* (No. 6, Spring 70) 2–7. An interview with Joe Evans, the brother of "Pimple" (Fred Evans), a British slapstick comedy star of 1912–1916; Joe discusses his work as scriptwriter.

4e(1b). Critical Studies of British Cinema

Herring, Robert. "The Funny Side of the Screen." *Close Up* 7 (No. 6, Dec 30) 397–403. The cinema scene in London.

Birt, Dan. "Be British." *Close Up* 8 (No. 4, Dec 31) 284–286. Great Britain has failed to produce a British film.

Grierson, John. "Future for British Films." *Spectator* 148 (14 May 32) 691–692. British films should concentrate more on scope and action than provincial charades of London's West End.

Myres, J. L. "Film in National Life." *Spectator* 148 (11 June 32) 825–826. Discussion of report of the Committee on Education and Cultural Films considering problems of mass taste, propriety, and reflection of national self-consciousness.

Dukes, Ashley. "The English Scene." *Th Arts* 17 (Mar 33) 188–192. Survey of current British entertainment.

Baldwin, Oliver. "Fatuity of British Films." *Bookman* 84 (July 33) 192. British films should rely more on literary sources and less on West End theatre.

Lindsay, Philip. "Filming England's History." *Bookman* 84 (July 33) 193. Why costume films always will be a popular genre.

Dukes, Ashley. "The English Scene." *Th Arts* 18 (Nov 34) 822–829. Survey of British screenwriting.

Greene, Graham. "The Middle-Brow Film." *Fortnightly Rev* 145 (No. 139, Mar 36) 302–307. English versus American films; objections to Hitchcock; why no good British comedies?

Brogan, D. W. "Screen World: Symposium." *Spectator* 160 (14 Jan–4 Feb 38) 80–81. The American picture is better than the British: more intelligent, more entertaining, more varied, and more courageous.

Asquith, Anthony. "Wanted: A Genius." *S&S* 7 (No. 25, Spring 38) 5–6. More brilliant film directors are now wanted.

Mason, A. E. W. "The Artistic Future of the Films." *Royal Soc of Arts J* 86 (22 July 38) 890–900. A plea for artistic originality in the film industry (responsive producers, original scripts, etc.).

Wright, Basil. "Cinema." *Spectator* 161 (30 Sep 38) 515. Brief comments on failures and accomplishments of the British cinema.

De Rochemont, Richard. "As America Sees It." *S&S* 10 (No. 37, Spring 41) 6–7. American reactions to British war films and a plea for films which show Great Britain on the offensive.

Hardy, H. Forsyth. "Vital Background for Drama." *S&S* 12 (No. 47, Oct 43) 68–69. The need for more realistic use of British background for dramatic films.

Robertson, E. Arnot. "Women and the Film." *Penguin F Rev* 3 (Aug 47) 31–35. A woman complains of the treatment of love, mothers, and old age; British pictures are good, just the same.

Lean, David. *"Brief Encounter." Penguin F Rev* 4 (Oct 47) 27–35. Gratified by the modest success of his film in the U.S., the director suggests British films now have "a style and nationality of their own."

Mathieson, Muir. "Developments in Film Music." *Penguin F Rev* 4 (Oct 47) 41–46. The work of leading British composers in film.

Lambert, Gavin. "British Films." *Sequence* (No. 2, Winter 47) 9–14. Survey of recent titles; prospects for the future.

Vargas, A. L. "British Films and Their Audiences." *Penguin F Rev* 8 (Jan 49) 71–76. Simple, everyday themes will put the cinema back in touch with the public.

Anderson, Lindsay. "British Cinema: The Descending Spiral." *Sequence* (No. 7, Spring 49) 6–11. A series of disappointments.

"Nyoka's Perils." *Newswk* 33 (27 June 49) 87. Two new British adventure serials.

Panter-Downes, Mollie. "Letter from London." *New Yorker* 25 (10 Dec 49) 126. What Great Britain needs for better box office—more films like *The Third Man*.

Ellis, Olivia. "Entertainment for Young Audiences." *CSMM* (24 Dec 49) 11. Cites achievements of Children's Entertainment Films.

Rayner, Henry. "Nothing to Laugh At." *S&S* 19 (Apr 50). *See 4k(1)*.

Balcon, Michael. "The Feature Carries on the Documentary Tradition." *QFRTV* 6 (No. 4, Summer 52) 351–353. Pictures such as *Seven Days to Noon* draw on the approach of British documentary. Reprinted from *UNESCO Courier*.

"Why War?" *S&S* 24 (Jan–Mar 55) 117. Brief note: too many British war pictures?

Houston, Penelope. "The Undiscovered Country." *S&S* 25 (Summer 55) 10–14. The British cinema: Will it snap back from its postwar trend to mediocre escapism? The fluid American society (with a tradition of individual rebellion and nonconformity against authority) compared to British stability; some British releases of 1955.

Knight, Arthur, *et al.* "Hard Lines for the British Films." *Film* (No. 5, Sep–Oct 55) 10–14. Knight's negative view of the British film scene is countered by several British figures.

Kurnitz, H. "Britannia Rules the Chuckle." *Holiday* 19 (Apr 56) 80+. *See 4k(1)*.

Regent, Roger. "Britain Without a Passport." *F&F* 3 (No. 4, Jan 57) 10–11. French critic bemoans the decline of British comedies such as *Passport to Pimlico*.

"Replies to a Questionnaire." *S&S* 26 (Spring 57) 180–185. Various contributors from fields other than cinema reply to questions about the social relevance of cinema as an art, and about the critical attitude in Great Britain at that time; responding to the theme in Lindsay Anderson's article "Stand Up! Stand Up!" are Kingsley Amis, John Osborne, Kenneth Tynan, and others. *See 3a(6)*.

Everson, William K. "British Humor on the Screen." *FIR* 8 (Nov 57) 433–442. An analysis of the 1932–1938 "golden age" of British comedy film; Alec Guinness' appeal was international and "essentially un-British."

Marcorelles, Louis. "Indictment." *Film* (No. 14, Nov–Dec 57) 4. British cinema: the reasons for its ineptitude.

Wright, Basil, *et al.* "What's Wrong with British Films?" *Film* (No. 14, Nov–Dec 57) 5–15.

Carstairs, John Paddy. "British Laugh-Makers." *F&F* 4 (No. 4, Jan 58) 9–10. Style of British film humor.

Hamilton, Guy, *et al.* "The British Cinema." *Film* (No. 15, Jan–Feb 58) 6–12.

"Jolly Old England." *Américas* 11 (Jan 59) 38. Reprint of an article from Mexican film magazine *Séptimo Arte* about British humor in films.

Stonier, G. W. "What Hopes for British Films?" *Sat Rev* 42 (19 Dec 59) 14–15. *New Statesman and Nation* film critic sees future in Lindsay Anderson, Karel Reisz, Tony Richardson, Jack Clayton.

Saltzman, Harry. "New Wave Hits British Films." *F&F* 6 (No. 7, Apr 60) 11+. On producing realistic films in Great Britain.

Robinson, David. "As Others See Us." *S&S* 29 (Summer 60) 116. Note on Soviet writers' "perceptive article" on recent British films seen in Moscow.

"Screen Holds the Eye: Images of the New Society." *Times Lit Supplement* 3056 (No. 208, 9 Sep 60) xxviii. How the British cinema can break away from its traditionally class-bound, conformist reputation.

Dyer, Peter John. "Young and Innocent." *S&S* 30 (Spring 61). *See 4k(10)*.

Riley, Philip. "Restricting Realism." *London Mag* new series 1 (No. 2, May 61) 70–76. Against the current trends in realistic British films.

Riley, Philip. "Second Thoughts on British Films." *London Mag* new series 1 (No. 4, July 61) 91–96. The individual film artist against the industry.

Kael, Pauline. "Commitment and the Strait-Jacket." *FQ* 15 (No. 1, Fall 61) 4–13. "The semi-documentary surface" of recent British films satisfies *Sight and Sound* critics as "commitment," but *Saturday Night and Sunday Morning* cheats by ending with the hero's resignation; *Look Back in Anger* and *The Entertainer* are better because more despairing and tragic.

Hammond, Brian. "The Shape of Things to Come?" *Motion* (No. 3, Spring 62) 42–43. The new realism of Resnais and Cassavetes offers a challenge to the British cinema.

Johnson, Ian. "The Reluctant Stars." *F&F* 8 (No. 8, May 62). *See 2b(2)*.

Perkins, V. F. "The British Cinema." *Movie* (No. 1, June 62) 2–7. Criticism of the

British cinema and its lack of importance. "British Cinema." *Film* (No. 36, Summer 63) 16–24. With comments on *This Sporting Life*.

Durgnat, Raymond. "Old Wine in New Bottles." *Film* (No. 39, Spring 64) 32–33. Weaknesses in the new British films.

French, Philip. "Marriage in the British Cinema." *20th Century* 172 (Spring 64) 107–116. Analysis of the presentation of marriage in British films, with reference to the similarities between *Brief Encounter* and *Room at the Top*.

Durgnat, Raymond. "Vote for Britain!" *F&F* (No. 7, Apr 64) 9–14; (No. 8, May 64) 10–15; (No. 9, June 64) 38–43. British films reflect British ideological controversies, including British elections; three articles.

Relph, Michael. "Does Wardour Want New Ideas? Or the Same Old . . . ?" *F&F* 10 (No. 9, June 64) 12–13. A plan for the future of British production.

French, Philip. "Right Kind of Englishman?" *20th Century* 173 (Autumn 64) 44–45. The British cinema is likely to lag behind the theatre, novel, and television in its response to changing ideas about society.

French, Philip. "The Alphaville of Admass." *S&S* 35 (Summer 66) 106–111. "Or how we learned to stop worrying and love the boom"; survey of London's fame as "the swinging city" and its impact on the British cinema; the films of Richard Lester; *Darling, Alfie* and *Morgan;* whereas "the conformity of the British cinema from 1958 to 1963 was a conformity of subject matter, now it is one of treatment."

Anderson, Lindsay. "Class Theatre, Class Film." *TDR* 11 (Fall 66) 122–129. British film industry aims movies toward the middle-class audience; interview by Paul Gray.

Eimerl, Sarel. "Bundles from Britain." *Reporter* 36 (6 Apr 67) 40–44. Current trends in British film.

Casty, Alan. "The New Style in British Rebels and Their Films." *Midwest Q* 9 (No. 2, Jan 68) 139–153.

Young, Vernon. "London Film Chronicle: Variation on a Personal Theme." *Hudson Rev* 21 (Spring 68) 159–165. Reflections on *The War Game, Privilege, A Man for All Seasons, Accident, Far from the Madding Crowd,* and *The Whisperers* as related to the British national character and class system.

Woodman, Ross. "Artists as Filmmakers." *Arts Canada* 25 (June 68). See 6c(3).

Robinson, David. "Case Histories of the Next Renascence." *S&S* 38 (Winter 68–69) 36–40. The author briefly summarizes the past British "swinging cinema" and introduces nine new film makers who in general indicate strong preference for the "well-made film"; Anthony Harvey's *The Lion in Winter* and

the unashamed romanticism of Kevin Billington's *Interlude* might indicate a cycle of historical romances.

Jarvie, Ian. "Media and Manners—Film and Society in Some Current British Films." *FQ* 22 (No. 3, Spring 69) 11–17. Looking backward at "realistic movements" usually reveals them as romantic; this is true of much of the "north country" film making in England; the newest "TV wave" seems to reflect a group of directors more than society; *Poor Cow* and others.

Durgnat, Raymond. "Brain Drains: Drifters, Avant-Gardes and Kitchen Sinks." *Cinema* (Cambridge) (No. 3, June 69) 12–15. A criticism of the narrowness of most British films.

Chanan, Michael. "Commitment and Disillusion: British Cinema 1956–1969." *Art International* 13 (Oct 69) 61–64. The early and late films of Tony Richardson, Karel Reisz, Lindsay Anderson contrasted; the British "Free Cinema" movement, in which these directors played a significant part.

"Some Funny Talk." *F&F* 6 (No. 6, Mar 70). See 4k(1).

Dawson, Jan, and Claire Johnston. "More British Sounds." *S&S* 39 (Summer 70). See 8d.

4e(1c). Economic Status of the Industry

Bord, R. "First Steps Toward a Workers' Film Movement." *Close Up* 6 (No. 1, 1930) 66–69.

Dukes, Ashley. "London Scene: Theatre and the Talkies." *Th Arts* 14 (June 30) 466–475. Surveys condition of British entertainment industry.

Duckworth, Leslie. "Blockheads." *Close Up* 7 (No. 4, Oct 30) 167–169. British exhibitors ignore provincial audiences during the summer.

Oakley, Herbert S. "Luck of the British Film." *Fortnightly Rev* 135 (Jan 31) 72–79. Surveys the progress of British film industry.

"Warners in England." *Time* 18 (21 Sep 31) 41. Jack Warner announces new studio in Middlesex to evade British quota restrictions.

Griffith, Hubert. "Films and the British Public." *19th Century* 112 (Aug 32) 190–200. English film industry's emulation of Hollywood.

Dent, Arthur. "From Producer to Picture Theatre." *S&S* 2 (No. 5, Spring 33) 11–12. A discussion of the machinery of film distribution.

Brandt, George. "Why British Films Fail." *Rev of Reviews* (London) 82 (No. 518, 10 Mar 33) 59–62. Why Hollywood films are more commercially successful than British films.

Biery, Ruth, and Eleanor Packer. "England Challenges Hollywood." *SEP* 206 (29 July 33) 12–13+. Survey of British film industry.

Rowson, S. "Value of Remittances Abroad for Cinematograph Films." *Royal Statist Soc J* 97 (No. 4, 1934) 633–640.

Rowson, Simon. "Economics of the Film Trade." *S&S* 3 (No. 11, Autumn 34) 105–106. Excerpts from address to British Association on the Relation of Film to National Life.

"Britain Invades U.S. Market with Improved Shows." *Newswk* 4 (18 Aug 34) 23. Gaumont-British program for production.

Phillips, H. "London's New Movie Metropolis." *Travel* 65 (Sep 35) 20–21.

Rowson, S. "Statistical Survey of the Cinema Industry in Great Britain in 1934; With Discussion." *Royal Statist Soc J* 99 (No. 1, 1936) 67–129.

Pringle, Henry F. " 'Ollywood on the Thames." *SEP* 209 (26 Sep 36) 10–11. Status of British industry, including "quota quickies," low-cost production, and the need for stars.

Vallance, Aylmer. "Future of British Films." *New S&N* 13 (1 May 37) 708–709. Economic factors necessary for survival of industry.

Grierson, John. "Film Situation." *London Mercury* 36 (Sep 37) 459–463. Examination of British film production shows American affiliations and interests exist because of need for distribution outside of Great Britain.

Vallance, Aylmer. "Patriotism on the Screen." *New S&N* 14 (13 Nov 37) 785–786. Battle with Hollywood for dominance of British audiences and exhibitors.

Dalrymple, Ian. "Screen World: The British Films." *Spectator* 160 (28 Jan 38) 125–126. The failures of the British film industry at the end of the first quota period.

Smith, Brian. "Nationalise!" *S&S* 9 (No. 36, Winter 40–41) 60–61. A call for the nationalization of the British film industry.

Balcon, Michael. "Rationalise!" *S&S* 9 (No. 36, Winter 40–41) 62–63. An argument against the nationalization of the British film industry.

Elvin, George H. "British Labour Problems." *S&S* 10 (No. 40, Spring 42) 79–81. Effects of the war on the film industry.

Thomas, F. L. "Whither Our Business?" *S&S* 10 (No. 40, Spring 42) 64–67. The effect of wartime on film production, exhibition, and distribution.

"Future of British Films." *New S&N* 28 (12 Aug 44) 103. Discussion of the recommendations made by the Cinematograph Films Council on growth of monopolies in British film industry; reply (19 Aug 44) 120.

Bower, Dallas. "No Celluloid Utopia." *New S&N* 28 (2 Sep 44) 151. Condition of British film industry in 1939–1940; discussion (9 Sep 44) 168.

Grierson, John. "Hollywood International." *Nation* 160 (6 Jan 45). *See 7e(1).*

"Government Films and Second-Features." *New S&N* 32 (10 Aug 46) 95–96. New film-making policy may curtail or eliminate the necessity of producing second features.

Elvin, George H. "Trade Unionism in the British Film Industry." *Penguin F Rev* 3 (Aug 47) 42–48.

"Films Take the Cut: The Decision to Impose a Duty of 300 Per Cent Ad Valorem on the Earnings of Imported Films." *Spectator* 179 (15 Aug 47) 195.

"A Look at the Books." *Time* 50 (22 Dec 47) 67–68. J. Arthur Rank opens the books of his General Cinema Finance Corporation to the public; his producing companies are all in financial difficulty.

Abrams, Mark. "The British Cinema Audience." *Hwd Q* 3 (No. 2, Winter 47–48). *See 7b(1b).*

Wyatt, W. "Parliament and Film Monopolists." *New S&N* 35 (10 Jan 48) 24–25. British film audiences spend £15 million on American imports per year and far less on home productions; reply (24 Jan 48) 73.

Anderson, Lindsay. "A Possible Solution." *Sequence* (No. 3, Spring 48) 7–10. British factory atmosphere has driven away artists; independent small-scale production is the only hope.

Dawson, Anthony H. "British and American Motion Picture Wage Rates Compared." *Hwd Q* 3 (No. 3, Spring 48). *See 6c(2).*

Harrison, Stella. "Letter from London." *Canad Forum* 28 (Apr 48) 6–7. British film-production emergency and the American impasse.

"Target for British Films." *New S&N* 35 (19 June 48) 490. Exhibitors should support home film industry.

Baxter, R. K. Neilson. "The Structure of the British Film Industry." *Penguin F Rev* 7 (Sep 48) 83–90. A survey of present production facilities.

Low, Rachael. "The Implications Behind the Social Survey." *Penguin F Rev* 7 (Sep 48) 107–112. An examination of the statistics recently gathered in Britain on cinema attendance.

Rotha, Paul. "Film Crisis." *Spectator* 182 (11 Feb 49) 177–178. Statistics on British feature film production and comments on the problems of rising costs and lack of proper financing.

Betts, E. "Independent Film Producer." *New S&N* 37 (12 Feb 49) 148. Independent producers' role not clearly defined in the Film Act (1948). Discussion (19 Feb 49) 181; (26 Feb 49) 205; (5 Mar 49) 228; (12 Mar 49) 251–252; (26 Mar 49) 301; (23 Apr 49) 405; (7 May 49) 472.

"On the Rocks." *New S&N* 37 (19 Mar 49) 267–368. British film-industry slump.

"Failure in Films." *New S&N* 38 (12 Nov 49)

539–540. Impending disaster in British film industry.

Griffith, Richard. "Where Are the Dollars?" *S&S* 19 (Dec 49) 33–34; (Jan 50) 39–40; (Mar 50) 44–45. American markets for British films; distribution by Rank Organization through Universal may work for a time; United Artists spent money in the wrong places; how *Henry V* and others fared in smaller theatres; the author's advice about subjects and budgets; three articles.

Woodhouse, C. M. "The Latest Film Crisis." *Spectator* 183 (16 Dec 49) 848–849. Major problems in the British film industry stem from the fear of risking economic consequences of free competition.

Crow, Duncan. "Days of Reckoning: Home Truths." *S&S* 19 (Jan 50) 9–12. The financial crisis is caused by high entertainment tax, uneconomical distribution, and undue perfectionism in production.

Davenport, Nicholas. "Common Sense on the Film Crisis." *S&S* 19 (Jan 50) 12. Not volume but quality can save the industry: survival of the fittest.

Abrams, Mark. "The British Cinema Audience, 1949." *Hwd Q* 4 (No. 3, Spring 50). *See 7b(1b).*

"More Grief for Movie Exports." *Bus Wk* (15 July 50) 108–110. The sick film industry in Great Britain and how it affects the Hollywood industry.

"Up for Air." *Newswk* 36 (31 July 50) 78–79. Great Britain's depressed film industry; the hope for aid from government and Hollywood.

Hurst, Brian Desmond. "The Lady Vanishes." *S&S* 19 (Aug 50) 253–255. The parlous state of the British film industry.

Davenport, N. "Hollywood and Mr. Wilson." *New S&N* 40 (19 Aug 50) 197. Great Britain cannot increase production volume without sacrificing quality.

Griffith, Richard. "The Audience Over 35." *FIR* 1 (Sep 50) 19–23. The British have learned the hard way to appeal to U.S. minority audiences through art theatres.

Gray, J. C. "Outlook for British Films." *Political Q* 21 (Oct 50) 384–394. Economic problems.

Crow, Duncan. "The Protected Industry: The Need for Protection." *S&S* 19 (Dec 50) 317–318. The economic crisis in the British film industry; the history of legislation, beginning with the Cinematograph Act of 1927.

Crow, Duncan. "The Protected Industry: Closing the Gap." *S&S* 19 (Feb 51) 391–392. The problem of restoring confidence in the industry so that more private investors will help; the so-called Gater Report found the most serious deficiency to be a lack of proper preproduction planning.

Crow, Duncan. "The Protected Industry: Pro-

tecting the Producer." *S&S* 19 (Mar 51) 429–430. Government regulations, exhibitor profits, appeals for the government to lessen the entertainment tax, and the operation of the National Film Finance Association.

Crow, Duncan. "The Protected Industry: Summing Up." *S&S* 19 (Apr 51) 460+. The selection committee of the Board of Trade, which allocates films' major circuits, turned down the Anglo-American agreement.

Koval, Francis. "British Films in Europe." *S&S* 20 (May 51) 10–11. Koval feels that the European market is being neglected; he recommends partnership with a foreign country as a distribution method.

Davenport, N. "No Festival for Films." *New S&N* 41 (9 June 51) 643. Discussion of British film crisis; discussion (16 June 51) 683.

Fay, Gerald. "Films and Finance." *Spectator* 188 (23 May 52) 668. Comments on *The British Film Industry,* a report by Political and Economic Planning detailing the history of British film finance.

Davenport, N. "Ailing Child." *New S&N* 43 (14 June 52) 696. How to make British productions pay and stop American films from cornering the market; reply (21 June 52) 731.

Rotha, Paul. "Films and Dollars." *New S&N* 44 (30 Aug 52) 230–231. American remittances for the year estimated at $125 million, part of which may be invested in American-controlled British location productions; reply (6 Sep 52) 266.

"The Front Page." *S&S* 23 (July–Sep 53) 7. Editorial assessment of British film costs, income, and Eady fund.

"The Front Page: How Goes the Enemy?" *S&S* 23 (Apr–June 54) 175. Editorial comment on the progress of TV in England.

"Telemeter." *S&S* 23 (Apr–June 54) 170. Note on British reactions to pay-TV.

"The Front Page: Britain and the Film Festivals." *S&S* 24 (July–Sep 54) 3. Editorial suggests more participation.

"The Front Page." *S&S* 24 (Spring 55) 169. Status of British industry: only TV takes newcomers.

French, Sir Henry. "How Films Work." *F&F* 1 (No. 7, Apr 55) 6–7. The problems facing the British film industry: the internal operation of the system of production and distribution in England.

French, Henry. "Money for Films." *F&F* 1 (No. 8, May 55) 8. Problems of financing.

"The Front Page." *S&S* 25 (Summer 55) 3. Editorial on English unions' resistance to newcomers.

French, Sir Henry. "No White Sheets." *F&F* 1 (No. 9, June 55) 12. The economic recovery of the British film industry from the crisis of 1947–1950.

Kingsley, David. "Out of the Crisis." *F&F* 1 (No. 11, Aug 55) 6–7. The purpose of the National Film Finance Corporation.

Elvin, George. "How Cinema Might Die." *F&F* 1 (No. 11, Aug 55) 8. The attitude of the members of the unions toward the threat of commercial television.

"When Screens Overlap (Cinema Trade and Television)." *Economist* 176 (17 Sep 55) 963–964. Analysis of television's effect on cinema box office.

Forlong, Michael. "Truth Is Better Than Fiction." *F&F* 2 (No. 11, Aug 56) 4+. The director of *Shetland Bus,* made on small budget in Norway, discusses the need for screen projects to be smaller and less expensive.

"Empty Cinemas." *Fortune* 54 (Nov 56) 83. While American films do well in Great Britain, British films rarely leave U.S. art houses.

Roud, Richard. "Britain in America." *S&S* 26 (Winter 56–57) 119–123. What kind of British film appeals to American audiences; films shown in the U.S.—their success or failure, by company.

"Big Screen Shrinks." *Economist* 182 (16 Feb 57) 573–575. Television is seen as having cornered the entertainment market and cinema is on the decline.

"No Leaks from Sir David (About the Cinema Tax)." *Economist* 182 (9 Mar 57) 793. Remarks on the increase of levy paid to producers by exhibitors.

"Accounting for Rationalisation." *Economist* 183 (18 May 57) 621. Suggestions for voluntary reorganization of cinema exhibitors' association.

"Television Makes Its Mark." *Economist* 184 (20 July 57) 244+. Impact of television on cinema compounded by the fact that television now produces its own movies.

Crow, Duncan. "From Screen to Screen." *S&S* 27 (Autumn 57) 61–63. Theatre films sold to British TV; a few statistics and titles.

Baker, Peter. "Talent Is So Expensive." *F&F* 3 (No. 12, Sep 57) 16. Film-production economics in Great Britain.

Houston, Penelope. "Time of Crisis." *S&S* 27 (Spring 58) 167–175. A sharp decline in paid admissions, studio layoffs and shutdowns, an increase in the television industry, and taxes levied by the government have wrought a crisis in Great Britain; audiences, production policies, cost of production, government aid, exhibition; cinema and television.

Whitebait, William. "Closing Down." *New S&N* 55 (15 Mar 58) 331. Report on recent closing of many movie theatres in Great Britain.

"Cinemas and Television: Fido, the Watch Dog; What Is the Right Size?" *Economist* 188 (30 Aug 58) 695. Suggestions for cutting losses in British film industry, including the closing of half the theatres.

Road, Sinclair. "Consequences of the Crisis." *Film* (No. 17, Sep–Oct 58) 4–5. When cinema ceases to be the main form of mass entertainment, drastic changes begin to take place in film making itself.

Orrom, Michael. "The Cinema in Transition." *Film* (No. 19, Jan–Feb 59) 10–12. Television's effect.

del Giudice, Filippo. "They Forgot the Public *Also* Had Intelligence." *F&F* 5 (No. 5, Feb 59) 12+. Producer looks at film-industry economics.

"The Front Page." *S&S* 28 (Nos. 3–4, Summer–Autumn 59) 109–110. The National Film Finance Corporation has lost only £127,000 annually and ought to be continued.

Hill, Derek. "Defence Through FIDO." *S&S* 28 (Nos. 3–4, Summer–Autumn 59) 183–184. Theatre owners in England try to keep feature films from being sold to TV.

Woods, Fredrick. "Take *That,* You Swine." *F&F* 5 (No. 11, Aug 59) 6. Problems with the British support films.

"Is the Stitch in Time? British Newsreels Eligible for Subsidy." *Economist* 193 (7 Nov 59) 564+. New Cinematograph Act includes newsreels in quota of British films that theatres are compelled to show.

Archibald, Lord. "Independents Plus U.S. Participation Key to Britain's Production Level." *JSPG* (Dec 59) 7–9. Chairman of British Federation of Film Makers comments on system in the two countries.

"Films: A Shortage of Product." *Economist* 195 (7 May 60) 556+. Fall in audience attendance causes a steady reduction in number of feature films produced.

"Levy—At Home and Abroad." *Economist* 195 (25 June 60) 1368. Suggestions for raising the film levy.

"The Cost of Independence: An Enquiry." *S&S* 30 (Summer 61) 107–113. Among the respondents: producer Anthony Perry, writer Kenneth Cavander, directors Tony Richardson and Carl Foreman, and John Terry, managing director of the National Film Finance Corporation.

Relph, Michael. "My Idea of Freedom." *F&F* 7 (No. 12, Sep 61) 22. Producer writes of the changes in production and the advantages of independents.

"In the Common Market: A Wider Screen for Britain." *S&S* 31 (Winter 61–62) 32–34. Independent organization (Economist Intelligence Unit) reports on the likely effects of Britain's proposed entry: subsidies, coproduction, and other problems.

Hill, Derek. "International Film Season." *S&S* 32 (Spring 63) 66. Foreign films on BBC get huge audiences; theatre people plan reprisals against distributors.

Mortimer, John. "Second Opinion." *F&F* 9 (No. 8, May 63) 11. Producer writes on the comparative economics of *Dock Brief* and *Lunch Hour.*

Balcon, Michael. "The Money in Films." *F&F* 9 (No. 10, July 63) 9–10. Independent producers, especially his Bryanston Organisation.

Houston, Penelope. "The Power of the Circuits." *S&S* 32 (Autumn 63) 174. Cinematograph Films Council examines restrictive effect of Rank and ABC dominating best theatres.

Davenport, Nicholas. "Film Crisis." *Spectator* 212 (20 Dec 63) 830–831. British independent producers are facing extinction; controversy over trading practices and suggestions for adopting the French system, whereby government loans are granted on artistic merit.

Houston, Penelope. "Whose Crisis?" *S&S* 33 (Winter 63–64) 26–28. A summary of the crisis situation the British film industry is sharing with most European film industries —declining audience, overproduction, projects without backers, cinema shutdowns, and completed films which cannot find theatres.

Cameron, Ian. "Saving the Cinema." *Spectator* 212 (7 Feb 64) 178+. Comments on the poor quality of cinema theatres and the policies of the distributors and exhibitors.

Gillett, John. "State of the Studios." *S&S* 33 (Spring 64) 55–61. The plight of the British film industry: only four features in British studios, three of them being made by American directors; visits with Roger Corman and Blake Edwards, filming *Masque of the Red Death* and *A Shot in the Dark.*

Houston, Penelope. "The British Lion Stakes." *S&S* 33 (Spring 64) 73–74. Brief chronicle of acrimony and bidding for assets of British Lion; government's role debated.

Forbes, Bryan. "England: Dispatch from the Combat Zone." *Show* 4 (Apr 64) 82–83. England's movie crisis based on overproduction, narrowing of distribution facilities, a backlog of unreleased films, lack of good new films.

Hsura, Bernard. "The Patterns of Power." *F&F* 10 (No. 7, Apr 64) 49–56. Recent history of British production and distribution as influenced by the major theatre chains.

Cameron, Ian. "Hard Night Out." *Spectator* 213 (10 July 64) 45–46. Report on the Federation of British Film Makers market-research project.

"Who Shows What to Whom?" *Economist* 212 (8 Aug 64) 571. Speculations on the outcome of the investigation of cinema chains by the Monopolies Commission.

"Parcelling Out." *Economist* 213 (12 Dec 64) 1268+. Cinema Exhibitors Association's decision to sell the television rights to films more than five years old is fatal to the Film Industry Defence Organisation.

Houston, Penelope. "Occupied Industry." *S&S* 34 (Spring 65) 59–60. In the face of American financial domination of perhaps seventy percent of first features, the National Film Finance Corporation has a new agreement to select projects and get release through the Rank Organization.

Gillett, John. "Happening Here." *S&S* 34 (Summer 65). *See 6c(3).*

Silvey, Robert, and Judy Kenyon. "Why You Go to the Pictures." *F&F* 11 (No. 9, June 65) 5. Statistical analysis of British movie attendance.

Houston, Penelope. "England, Their England." *S&S* 35 (Spring 66) 54–56. American film companies' invasion of London; some speculations on pros and cons; biggest problem of the British film industry is to get finance from British sources.

Hutchinson, Tom. "By Their Films Shall Ye Know Them." *20th Century* 175 (Summer 66) 18–19. Why Britain should join the Common Market and seek European concepts about film making for use by British technicians.

Rotha, Paul. "Britain's Dollar-Dominated Films." *New S&N* 71 (24 June 66) 925–926.

"Film Monopolists." *Economist* 221 (5 Nov 66) 586–587. Institute of Economic Affairs study.

Coleman, John. "British Films." *New S&N* 72 (18 Nov 66) 754. The current British film situation.

Houston, Penelope. "Monopoly." *S&S* 36 (Winter 66–67) 15–16. Note on Monopolies Commission Report, especially the Rank and ABC theatre chains.

Kelly, Terence. "Chicken-Hearted Champions of Competition." *F&F* 13 (No. 4, Jan 67) 34–35. Digest of the Monopolies Commission Report on the British film industry's structure and trading practices.

Guback, Thomas. "American Interests in the British Film Industry." *Q Rev Econ and Bus* 7 (Summer 67) 7–21.

Perkins, V. F. "Forced to Be Free or Doing Business in a Graveyard." *Movie* (No. 15, Spring 68) 17–19. Recommendations for changes in the legislation affecting the British film industry.

"Representative Minority." *Economist* 227 (6 Apr 68) 48–49. Comments on the Cinematograph Film Council's report "Review of Films Legislation."

Taylor, John Russell. "Backing Britain." *S&S* 38 (Summer 69) 112–115. What American film companies have been doing recently in Great Britain; interviews with Jay Kanter, in charge of European feature production for Universal, and Michael Flint, in charge for Paramount.

Eves, Vicki. "The Structure of the British Film Industry." *Screen* 11 (No. 1, Feb 70) 41–54. Relations with U.S., exhibitors, independents.

Houston, Penelope. "Films Bill." *S&S* 39 (Spring 70) 72. Films Bill renews quotas, Eady Fund, and National Film Finance Corporation.

Austen, David. "Profits of Gloom." *F&F* 16 (No. 7, Apr 70) 4–8. Financial state of British industry in the 1940s.

Wakely, Michael. "Situation Hopeless But Not Serious." *F&F* 16 (No. 8, May 70) 6–9. Financial state of British film industry in the 1950s and 1960s.

Sinclair, Andrew. "Who Killed the Film?" *New S&N* 80 (23 Oct 70) 512–513. Author who adopted and directed his novel *The Breaking of Bumbo* for Bryan Forbes' production group distributes the blame for the decline of British production.

Terry, John. "The Future of the British Film Industry." *Screen* 11 (Nos. 4–5, 1970) 115–128.

4e(1d). Individual Companies

"Will Elstree Eclipse Hollywood?" *Lit Dig* 116 (16 Sep 33) 14. Douglas Fairbanks and son join British film studio.

"Britain's Best." *Time* 26 (9 Sep 35) 44+. Development of talkies; remarks on Alexander Korda.

Desmond, R. W. "Hollywood's Challenge from Britain." *CSMM* (5 Aug 36) 8–9. New films and performers for Alexander Korda.

"In Golden Square." *Time* 28 (2 Nov 36) 60–61+. John Maxwell, chairman of Associated British Picture Corporation, plans take-over of Gaumont-British.

Hobson, Harold. "Glamour Out of Drudgery." *CSMM* (16 Dec 36) 9. A visit to Denham Studios in Buckinghamshire, where *Fire Over England* is being shot and *I, Claudius* prepared by Alexander Korda.

"Hollywood Still Waves; Gaumont-British Troubles." *Bus Wk* (13 Mar 37) 35–36. Gaumont-British tries to crash the American market; difficulties encountered.

Hobson, H. "Town of Make-Believe." *CSMM* (1 Dec 37) 9. Denham Studios in Buckinghamshire.

"Films Across the Sea." *New S&N* 27 (11 Mar 44) 167–168. Mr. Rank's attempt to wrest worldwide domination of the film industry away from Hollywood; details on economic and power structures in Hollywood. Discussion (18 Mar) 189; (26 Mar) 206; (2 Apr) 224; (8 Apr) 241.

"Big Business in Films." *New S&N* 30 (11 Aug 45) 87. "J. Arthur Rank has become a junior partner in American film capitalism."

Bennett, Charles. "Rank Enthusiasm." *Screen Writer* 1 (Nov 45) 24–29. An appreciation of British postwar films, the J. Arthur Rank Studio, and the producers and directors there; some assumptions about why British films are more appealing to Britishers than Hollywood films.

Clarke, M. "Mr. Rank's Gesture." *New S&N* 32 (19 Oct 46) 280. Board established to supervise exhibition of independently produced films in Great Britain.

Pope-Hennessy, James. "Film Studio." *Spectator* 178 (6 June 47) 649–650. Report on tour of Sir Alexander Korda's studios at Shepperton, Middlesex, and the production of *Ideal Husbands* and *Anna Karenina*.

"Shot in the Arm." *Time* 52 (6 Dec 48). See *8e*.

Lancaster, Osbert. "Posters for British Films." *Arch Rev* 105 (Feb 49). See *6d(3)*.

"Rank's Retreat." *Time* 54 (24 Oct 49) 96–97. The drop in J. Arthur Rank's movie production.

"Mr. Rank's Crisis." *Spectator* 183 (11 Nov 49) 624. British film industry can now be regarded as a major national asset, but it is hampered by unsound financial structures.

"Rocking Empire." *Time* 54 (21 Nov 49) 92. J. Arthur Rank and his Odeon Theatres in serious money trouble.

"Twilight of Rank." *Newswk* 34 (21 Nov 49) 91. The financial plight of film magnate J. Arthur Rank and its possible effects on the British film industry.

"Rank's Movie Magic Fails." *Bus Wk* (3 Dec 49) 105. Reasons behind his near collapse; impact on U.S. movie industry.

Read, Jan. "'Pregnant with Jeopardy.'" *Hwd Q* 4 (No. 4, 1950). See *2d(1)*.

Knight, Arthur. "A Visit to Ealing." *Sat Rev* 34 (13 Oct 57) 44–45. Brief profile of England's Ealing Studios.

"Tight Little Ealing." *Time* 59 (14 Apr 52) 106. Ealing Studios' non-formula films.

"End of the Keel." *Time* 63 (14 June 54) 97. The death of British Lion Films, founded by Sir Alexander Korda.

"New Venture." *S&S* 24 (Oct–Dec 54) 60. Independent Harlequin Company makes *Stolen Journey*.

"Rank's Secret." *Bus Wk* (2 July 55) 68. J. Arthur Rank puts his empire in trust.

Tynan, Kenneth. "Tight Little Studio: Home of the Good British Movies?" *Harper's* 211 (Aug 55) 52–55. Sir Michael Balcon and Ealing Studios.

"Ealing Studios." *S&S* 25 (Winter 55–56) 117. Note on Sir Michael Balcon's films now that studio has been sold to BBC-TV.

"British Films." *S&S* 25 (Spring 56) 169. Balcon and Rank: future plans.

"The Front Page." *S&S* 27 (Summer 57) 3. Changes in distribution: Korda films sold to TV in England.

"Attendances and the Levy." *Economist* 186 (4 Jan 58) 58. Rank's film production plans trimmed because of decline in cinema attendance and recent entertainments taxation.

"Production Alliance." *S&S* 28 (Nos. 3–4, Summer–Autumn 59) 133. Note on new Bryanston Films, similar to American United Artists.

"More Power to the Independent Elbow." *Economist* 198 (11 Feb 61) 591. As an economy move, British Lion and Columbia Pictures to merge.

"Rank Organisation: Sting in the Tail." *Economist* 199 (15 Apr 61) 258. Stock and dividend payments.

Attenborough, Richard. "Two in Harmony." *F&F* 7 (No. 12, Sep 61) 9. Advantages of independent production companies like his Allied Film Makers.

Morgan, John. "Wounded Lion." *New S&N* 67 (3 Jan 64) 5–6. The British Lion affair; why producers need to be more independent of the monopolies.

Boulting, John, and Roy Boulting. "Years of the Lion." *Spectator* 212 (3–10 Jan 64) 5. Two-part article on the plight of the independent British film producer; brief historical survey of treatment of the independent and also British Lion Films.

"Lion Tamer Wanted?" *Economist* 211 (25 Apr 64) 406. Problems of production control at British Lion, now under Sir Michael Balcon's direction.

Bean, Robin. "Muscle Mayhem." *F&F* 10 (No. 9, June 64). See 4d(2).

Shivas, Mark. "British Lion." *Movie* (No. 14, Autumn 65) 1–4. British Lion and its relation to British film making and the government.

Heard, Colin. "Hammering the Box Office." *F&F* 15 (No. 9, June 69) 17–18. On the films of Hammer Films, Ltd.

Houston, Penelope. "Forbes' First Fifteen." *S&S* 38 (Autumn 69) 182–183. Note on plans of Bryan Forbes' regime as chief of production at Associated British.

4e(1e). Censorship and Morality

Richardson, Dorothy M. "The Censorship Petition." *Close Up* 6 (No. 1, 1930) 7–11. The account of a petition for the revision of film censorship.

Herring, Robert. "The English Censorship." *Close Up* 6 (No. 4, 1930) 269–272.

Duckworth, Leslie B. "It Rests with Local Authorities." *Close Up* 6 (No. 4, 1930) 272–277; (No. 5, 1930) 392–394. One person's experience with censorship regulations.

Bond, R. "Acts Under the Acts." *Close Up* 6 (No. 4, 1930) 278–283. British censorship problems.

Bond, R. "Dirty Work." *Close Up* 7 (No. 2, 1930) 98–100. A reaction against the British government's response to Russian films.

Mendus, I. M. Banner. "Films and the Law I Sing." *Close Up* 7 (No. 3, 1930) 163–168. A note on the law governing the showing of films in England, Wales, Scotland, and Northern Ireland.

Herring, Robert. "Three Funny Stories." *Close Up* 7 (No. 5, Nov 30) 304–309. Recent censorship events in Great Britain and the state of British film production.

Robson, William A. "British Films Are Pure." *Nation* 13 (19 Nov 30) 547–548. Censorship not the answer.

Young, G. Gordon. "On Film Patrol." *Close Up* 8 (No. 2, June 31) 108–110. Comments on the London Public Morality Council's attitude toward film.

"Filthy Films in England." *Lit Dig* 111 (17 Oct 31) 19. Court and Church react against movie morals.

Griffith, H. "Films and the British Public." *19th Century* 112 (1932) 190–200. Morality is regulated by suburban audiences.

"Sex Films in England." *Living Age* 342 (Apr 32) 182–183. Australians attack "low moral tone" of English talkies.

Ashley, Walter. "Standards of Film Censorship." *S&S* 1 (No. 3, Autumn 32) 68–69. Recent criteria used; some of the better films were prohibited for children.

"A Halt to Sunday Movies in England." *Lit Dig* 115 (18 Mar 33) 17. Church rejects appeal for movies on Sunday.

Macaulay, R. "Marginal Comments." *Spectator* 154 (25 Jan 35) 117; (29 May) 976. Recent call for stricter film censorship and control raises age-old questions.

Dalrymple, Ian. "Film Censorship." *Spectator* 155 (29 Nov 35) 895–896. Appeal for lighter censorship and more tolerance toward the motion pictures from official censorship bodies.

Gardner, Frank M. "Letters from an English Cousin." *Wilson Lib Bul* 10 (Dec 35) 264+. Surveys English method of film censorship.

"No Particular Taste." *Time* 26 (9 Dec 35) 25–26. On Great Britain's Board of Film Censors.

"Politics on the Screen." *S&S* 5 (No. 18, Summer 36) 20–21. Politics and censorship related to recent films.

Herring, Robert. "Religion and the Screen." *S&S* 5 (No. 19, Autumn 36) 75–77. The influence of religious groups on censorship.

Wright, Basil. "Censor's Certificate." *Spectator* 161 (21 Oct 38) 651. Aims, powers, and discretion of the British Board of Censors, with predictions on general rise in censorship.

Moore, Beatrix. "Censor the Censor!" *S&S* 7 (No. 28, Winter 38–39) 149. An interview with G. W. Pabst, in which he decries the censor's attitudes toward public taste.

Martin, K. "Public Opinion: Censorship During the Crisis." *Political Q* 10 (Jan 39) 134–138.

Curtailment of freedom of press and cinema by British government during the Munich crisis.

Farndale, W. E. "Sunday Cinemas; a New Power." *London Q Rev* 166 (Jan 41) 106–108. A new order from the Defense Regulations allowing cinemas to open on Sundays.

Hitchner, Dell G. "English Film Censorship During the Munich Crisis." *SW Soc Sci Q* 23 (Sep 42) 133–139.

"Films and the State." *New S&N* 32 (14 Dec 46) 436–437. Call for censorship reform.

Watkins, A. T. L. "Film Censorship in Britain." *Penguin F Rev* 9 (May 49) 61–66. Secretary of British Board of Film Censors explains their concern about films that may lower moral standards, give offense to reasonable people, or injure children.

Watkins, A. T. L. "Censorship in Britain." *FIR* 2 (Mar 51) 17–23. Secretary of British Board of Film Censors writes on their method of classifying films.

"The Front Page." *S&S* 21 (Oct–Dec 51) 51. Editorial comments on the "X," special adults-only, category of films.

"Film Censorship." *New S&N* 43 (8 Mar 52) 262. Nonflammable 16mm films are exempt from censorship and control.

"Report on the 'X.'" *S&S* 23 (Jan–Mar 54) 123–124+. A definition of the "X" certificate; a list of films given the certificate; some comments on its successes and weak points.

Everson, William K. "Cut Copies." *S&S* 24 (Oct–Dec 54) 92–94. A brief history of censored films; some whose endings were considered too "downbeat" for American audiences, while Europe got to see the original version; in general, British censors seem more concerned with undue violence than with sex, while American censors ignore most violence and concentrate on sex.

"X in a Spot." *Economist* 174 (1 Jan 55) 20. Questions bases of British Board of Film Censors' rating system with emphasis on recent "X" rating of *Spare the Rod*.

Watkins, A. T. L. "Nobody Loves the Censor!" *Film* (No. 3, Feb 55) 20–22. Secretary of of the British Board of Film Censors discusses the grounds and means of censorship.

De La Roche, Catherine. "Don't Shoot the Censor." *F&F* 1 (No. 7, Apr 55) 12. Suggestions for revisions in the British Board of Film Censors; arguments for and against censorship as a policy.

Wilcox, John. "The Small Knife: Britain." *S&S* 25 (Spring 56) 206–210. History and procedures of British Board of Film Censors.

Dyer, Peter John. "Censored!" *F&F* 3 (No. 5, Feb 57) 11–13; No. 6 (Mar 57) 9–11+; No. 7 (Apr 57) 11–14. A history of official and unofficial film censorship in Great Britain from 1910; a three-part article.

Quigly, Isabel. "Kindest Cuts." *Spectator* 198

(8 Feb 57) 177. Techniques of classification (X, A, or U), employed by the British Board of Film Censors.

Watkins, Arthur. "The Censor Answers His Critics." *F&F* 3 (No. 8, May 57) 8. Secretary of the British Board of Film Censors replies to the earlier articles of Peter John Dyer.

Gunston, David. "Film Censor in Britain." *Contemp Rev* 191 (June 57) 342–346. The nature of censorship and the rating system used by the British Board of Film Censors.

Hunnings, Neville M. "The Origins of Censorship in England." *S&S* 27 (Winter 57–58) 151–154. A study of censorship before the Cinematograph Act of 1909, the act itself, and the progressive legal restraints which formed the history of film censorship in England.

Duperley, Denis, and Geoff Donaldson. "Will Britain See These Films?" *F&F* 4 (No. 8, May 58) 31. Will censors pass two German films on homosexuality?

"Censors' Stag Party?" *Economist* 187 (24 May 58) 690. Censors of the Brighton Watch Committee exclude female members from watching film review screenings.

Thompson, J. Lee. "The Censor Needs a Change." *F&F* 4 (No. 9, June 58) 8. Inconsistency in awarding the "X."

Trevelyan, John. "Censored!—How and Why We Do It." *F&F* 4 (No. 9, June 58) 8+. By newly appointed secretary to British Board of Film Censors.

"Censored." *S&S* 28 (No. 2, Spring 59) 65. John Trevelyan, British film censor, lectures at National Film Theatre.

"Questions of Censorship." *S&S* 29 (Summer 60) 116. Note on opening of Gala Film Theatre Clubs for adult audiences, including films banned or cut.

Whitebait, William. "This Nanny!" *New S&N* 60 (9 July 60) 48. Description of the members of the British Board of Film Censors, with reasons they censored various films.

Whitebait, William. "This Censorship." *New S&N* 60 (30 July 60) 153–154. Pressures from the British Board of Film Censors often cause companies to abandon motion-picture projects.

Trevelyan, John. "The 'X' in Britain." *JSPG* (Sep 61) 9–11. Secretary of the British Board of Film Censors discusses classification as it operates in Britain, with the predominant concern of protection of children.

McDougall, Gordon. "To Deprave and Corrupt?" *Motion* (No. 2, Winter 61–62) 5–8. An examination of the method and aims of film censorship in Great Britain.

Perkins, V. F., *et al.* "Censorship." *Movie* (No. 6, Jan 63) 16–21. Censorship in Britain is explored through interviews with John Trevelyan, secretary of the British Board of

Film Censors, and with Robert Aldrich and Joseph Losey.

Hunnings, Neville. "Censorship in London." *S&S* 35 (Winter 65–66) 20–21. New working of license law omits "morality" and adds race hatred.

Trevelyan, John. "New Film Categories." *Film* (No. 58, Spring 70) 16. Secretary of the British Board of Film Censors discusses new systems of classification.

Trevelyan, John. "Film Censorship in Great Britain." *Screen* 11 (No. 3, Summer 70) 19–30. Secretary of British Board of Film Censors on the board's history, finances, composition, methods of operation, policies, recent changes.

4e(1f). Subsidies and Quotas

Blakeston, Oswell. "Facts for Finance." *Close Up* 9 (No. 1, Mar 32) 29–30. Discussion of the Quota Act in Great Britain.

Montagu, Ivor. "The Moyne Report." *S&S* 5 (No. 20, Winter 36–37) 120–122. A discussion of the report of the committee which investigated the working of the 1927 Cinematograph Act, or the Quota Act.

Board of Trade, *et al.* "Quota—Cost and Quality." *S&S* 6 (No. 22, Summer 37) 75–76. Board of Trade proposals for a new cinematograph act; reactions.

Wright, Basil. "British Films and Quota." *Spectator* 159 (9 July 37) 54–55. Advantages and disadvantages of the quota system; proposals of the Moyne Commission to remedy major problems.

Hardy, H. Forsyth. "A Measure for Optimists." *S&S* 7 (No. 25, Spring 38) 18–19. Analysis of the New Cinematograph Film Act of 1938.

"Films Council." *Spectator* 163 (28 July 39) 133. How the New Film Act is working and how the Cinematograph Films Council is fulfilling its functions.

Manvell, Roger. "The Cinema and the State: England." *Hwd Q* 2 (No. 3, Apr 47) 289–293. Recent books propose further involvement of government in film financing.

MacKenzie, N. "Films and Quotas: How Far Should the New Bill Differ from the Old Act?" *New S&N* 33 (21 June 47) 451–452. Suggestions for revisions of 1938 New Film Act, about to expire. Discussion 33 (28 June) 475; 34 (2 Aug) 92.

Wright, Basil. "Law and the Screen." *Spectator* 180 (9 Jan 48) 40–41. Explanation of the new Cinematograph Act pending before Parliament.

Wyatt, W. "Champagne for Hollywood." *New S&N* 35 (20 Mar 48) 231. The changes produced by the Film Act of 1948.

"Crisis in Britain." *Time* 53 (14 Feb 49) 92. British film industry failing; government creates Film Finance Corporation.

Webb, J. E. "British Attitude Toward Film Quotas; Letter to Motion Picture Association." *US Dept of State Bul* 20 (26 June 49) 825.

"Film Finance and Policy." *New S&N* 39 (22 Apr 50) 446. Work of Film Finance Corporation.

"Support for the Film Industry." *New S&N* 39 (29 Apr 50) 473. Film Finance Corporation backed more than half of the features most recently produced.

"The Front Page: National Film Finance Corporation." *S&S* 19 (June 50) 147–148. Editorial based on first annual report of government subsidy agency.

Crow, Duncan. "The Protected Industry: The Quota and the Fund." *S&S* 19 (Jan 51) 357–358. Quota schemes have not solved the production problems; the subsidy system requires payments by exhibitors into the British Film Production Fund.

"Keeping Films Going." *Spectator* 188 (2 May 52) 567. Brief remarks on the importance of the quota system. Discussion (9 May) 616; (16 May) 644.

"Films in Trouble." *New S&N* 45 (14 Feb 53) 166. The Eady scheme (for subsidizing film production) may not be extended because exhibitors are losing money on the entertainment tax.

Crow, Duncan. "The Monsoon Case." *S&S* 22 (Apr–June 53) 150. Court rejects plea that a British company actually "made" a film financed by Americans.

"The Twin Pillars." *S&S* 23 (Jan–Mar 54) 114. British Film Production Fund is voluntarily continued for three years.

"Films and Finance." *Spectator* 192 (12 Mar 54) 279. Brief comments on proposed National Film Finance Corporation Loan. Reply (19 Mar) 323.

Davenport, Nicholas. "Film Fracas." *Spectator* 192 (30 Apr 54) 510. Complaints from the film industry on recent small budget of £3½ million. Discussion (7 May) 543; (14 May) 582; (17 Sep) 335; additional Davenport comment (3 Sep) 296.

"British Lion Collapses." *New S&N* 47 (5 June 54) 718. Government receiver will close British Lion's production program and new company will concentrate only on distribution.

Knight, Arthur. "Hard Lines for the British Film." *Sat Rev* 38 (7 May 55) 31. Disaster hits British film making when the National Film Finance Corporation forecloses on Korda's British Lion.

Crow, Duncan. "Economic Front." *S&S* 26 (Winter 56–57) 116. Proposals for continuing British subsidy.

"Specialized Bank (the National Film Finance Corporation)." *Economist* 183 (1 June 57) 818.

"The Front Page." *S&S* 27 (Summer 58) 217. Editorial on films and activities of British Film Institute Experimental Production Committee.

"Business or Show Business?" *Economist* 196 (23 July 60) 390. Why the National Film Finance Corporation is losing money.

"In the Black: British Lion." *Economist* 196 (13 Aug 60) 672. Film company's net profits for 1959.

Davenport, Nicholas. "Subsidising Films." *Spectator* 205 (2 Sep 60) 349. Certain types of films financed by the National Film Finance Corporation tend to drive audiences away rather than attract them.

"Film Financing: Judgment and Luck." *Economist* 199 (21 June 61) 1406. Profits of the National Film Finance Corporation for 1960.

"Lion Not So Mangy." *Economist* 200 (12 Aug 61) 655. Success of the second reconstruction of British Lion Films.

"Christmas Circus: What Sort of Lion?" *Economist* 210 (4 Jan 64) 46–47. British Lion wants the government to retain 50% interest in the company.

Davenport, Nicholas. "British Lion—A Solution." *Spectator* 212 (17 Jan 64) 85. Suggestions for abolishing the National Film Finance Corporation and turning British Lion into a British United Artists.

"What Am I Bid?" *Economist* 210 (18 Jan 64) 230. British Lion lost a large amount of money and the government wants to sell the company.

"Cinelion Embalmed." *Economist* 210 (8 Feb 64) 532. Controversy over the sale of British Lion.

"Lion: Kind Owner Wanted." *Economist* 210 (14 Mar 64) 1020+. Bids received for British Lion.

"Owner Found." *Economist* 210 (21 Mar 64) 1128. Sir Michael Balcon's group is chosen for new ownership of British Lion.

"British Film Production Fund." *JSPG* (June 64) 29–30. How the Eady subsidy plan operates.

"State Film Loans: Subsidise Nice People." *Economist* 212 (19 Sep 64) 1160. National Film Finance Corporation does not attract producers whose films are likely to succeed commercially.

"Back in Business." *S&S* 35 (Autumn 66) 170. British Film Institute Production Board (formerly Experimental Film Fund, 1952–1962) has a little money to lend.

Gilbert, Robert W. "Foreign Film Subsidies as an Aspect of Financing." *JSPG* 10 (No. 3, Sep 68). *See 6a(3).*

Perkins, V. F. "Supporting the British Cinema." *Movie* (No. 16, Winter 68–69) 13–15. Toward a more positive relationship between the government and the cinema industry.

"Bank of Soho Square." *Economist* 232 (2

Aug 69) 56–57. Problems with pending film legislation and the financial losses of the government film bank.

"Eady Money, Not Easy Money." *JSPG* (Sep 69) 8+. Up-to-date explanation of British film subsidy.

Terry, John. "Film Financing in the United Kingdom." *JSPG* (Sep 70) 32–34. By the managing director of the National Film Finance Corporation; its overall record.

4e(1g). Ireland

Hutchins, Patricia. "The Mountain and the Swan." *S&S* 8 (No. 31, Autumn 39) 107–108. Notes on the Irish cinema.

O'Laoghaire, Liam. "Dublin to Killarney." *S&S* 9 (No. 35, Autumn 40) 52. A brief history of the Irish cinema and its film-society movement.

O'Laoghaire, Liam. "Developments in Eire." *S&S* 12 (No. 45, Summer 43) 12–14. The film scene in Ireland, particularly the role of film education.

O'Dwyer, Kelvin. "The Child and the Cinema in Eire." *S&S* 15 (Summer 46). *See 1a(4).*

Hutchins, Patricia. "News from Ireland." *S&S* 16 (No. 62, Summer 47) 50–51.

Gerrard, John. "The Irish Screen." *S&S* 16 (No. 64, Winter 47–48) 159–160.

Gerrard, John. "A History of Irish Production." *S&S* 17 (No. 65, Spring 48) 20–23.

Gerrard, John. "Irish Censorship—or Fighting for Cleaner Cinema." *S&S* 18 (Summer 49) 81–82.

Conluain, Proinsias O. "Ireland's First Films." *S&S* 23 (Oct–Dec 53) 96–98. An account of film making in Ireland 1910–1915, mainly concerned with the work of an American, Sidney Olcott, who shot a number of films there.

4e(2). FRANCE AND BELGIUM

[See 5, Biography: *Yves Allegret, René Allio, Claude Autant-Lara, Georges de Beauregard, Jacques Becker, Mag Bodard, Robert Bresson, Marcel Carné, André Cayatte, Claude Chabrol, René Clair, René Clement, Henri-Georges Clouzot, Jean Cocteau, Philippe De Broca, Jacques Demy, Michel Deville, Jean Epstein, Louis Feuillade, Georges Franju, Abel Gance, Philippe Garrel, Jean-Luc Godard, Jean Gremillon, Sacha Guitry, Christian Jacque, Alain Jessua, Marin Karmitz, Albert Lamorisse, Roger Leenhardt, Louis Lumière, Louis Malle, Chris Marker, Georges Méliès, Jean-Pierre Melville, Max Ophuls, Marcel Pagnol, Jean Painlevé, Charles Pathé, Jacques Prévert, Raimu, Jean Renoir, Alain Resnais, Jacques Rivette, Alain Robbe-Grillet, Eric Rohmer, Jean Rouch, Charles Spaak, Jacques Tati, Maurice Tourneur, François Truffaut, Agnès Varda, Jean Vigo.*]

Stenhouse, Charles E. "A British Eye on Paris." *Close Up* 6 (No. 6, 1930) 508–520; 7 (No. 1, 1930) 21–37. Recent film events in Paris.

Blakeston, Oswell. "It Happened in Bruxelles." *Close Up* 7 (No. 6, 1930) 404–417. A personal account of film viewing.

Lenauer, Jean. "Talkie Diseases of the French Cinema." *Close Up* 10 (No. 3, Sep 33) 235–243. Aesthetic and financial problems.

Clarrière, Georges. "Specialised Cinema in France." *S&S* 3 (No. 10, Summer 34) 61–62. Peculiarities of French film audience reactions.

Rose, Felix. "*Ciné Actualité*." *S&S* 7 (No. 26, Summer 38). *See 8b.*

Holmes, Winifred. "Evil Eye in Belgium." *S&S* 7 (No. 27, Autumn 38) 113–115. The film industry.

"News from Belgium." *S&S* 11 (No. 44, Spring 43) 90. Film making in an occupied country.

Boyer, Charles. "Advanced Training for Film Workers: France." *Hwd Q* 1 (No. 3, Apr 46). *See 1a(3).*

Vedrès, Nicole. "French Cinema." *Penguin F Rev* 2 (Jan 47) 70–73. Current productions.

Vedrès, Nicole. "French Cinema Takes Stock." *Penguin F Rev* 3 (Aug 47) 81–83. After the Cannes film festival.

Vedrès, Nicole. "Criticism and French Cinema." *Penguin F Rev* 4 (Oct 47) 105–108. The excesses of the French press in writing about its native film industry.

L'Institut des Hautes Etudes Cinématographiques. "A Survey of Film Periodicals, III: France (as of Nov 1, 1947)." *Hwd Q* 3 (No. 2, Winter 47–48). *See 1b(2).*

Pirosh, Robert. "Outside U.S.A." *Screen Writer* 3 (Jan 48) 27–29. Writer worked with René Clair on new form of narration instead of dubbing; he reports on the much different role of producer and others in France.

Vedrès, Nicole. " 'It's Typically French.' " *Penguin F Rev* 5 (Jan 48) 73–76. This kind of audience judgment does not see the true humanistic style of French cinema.

Sauvage, Leo. "Open Letter to New York Film Critics." *Nation* 167 (10 July 48). *See 3b.*

Vorontzoff, Alexis N. "French Film Publications (August 1944–December 1948): A Preliminary List to a Basic Bibliography—Part I." *Hwd Q* 5 (No. 2, Winter 50). *See 1b(2).*

Vorontzoff, Alexis N. "French Film Publications (August 1944–December 1948): A Preliminary List to a Basic Bibliography—Part III." *QFRTV* 6 (No. 1, Fall 51). *See 1b(2).*

Seton, Marie. "Taking Eisenstein to France." *Film* (No. 2, Dec 54) 19–21. An account of talks on Eisenstein given by the author to cinema clubs in France.

"French Stars and Their Performances." *F&F* 2 (No. 1, Oct 55) 8–9. Photos with brief biographies.

Tessoneau, Rémy. "The French Institute of Cinema (IDHEC)." *JUFPA* 10 (No. 1, Fall 57). *See 1a(3c).*

Collin, Philippe. "The French Laughter Makers." *F&F* 4 (No. 2, Nov 57) 15–16+. French film comedians.

"Four Authors in Search of a Film." *F&F* 5 (No. 8, May 59) 10–11+. Four French writers discuss film making.

Whitcomb, J. "New French Movie Stars." *Cosmopolitan* 149 (Aug 60). *See 2b(4).*

Roud, Richard. "The French Line." *S&S* 29 (Autumn 60) 166–171. Among French critics the *politique des auteurs* is carried to extremes; the main difference is the supremacy of form over content.

"Mecca for Film Trade." *Bus Wk* (17 Apr 65). *See 7e.*

Genêt. "Letter from Paris." *New Yorker* 41 (15 May 65). *See 4k(3).*

Houston, Penelope. "Perspectives 1970." *S&S* 34 (Summer 65) 121. Summary of French survey of audience tastes.

de Pomerai, Odile. "Novelist Turns to Films: Jean Giono and the Cinema." *20th Cent Lit* 12 (July 66) 59–65. French writer, now seventy, adapts for screen his novel *Un Roi sans divertissement*.

Moats, A.-L. "Film That Shook France; *L'Aveu,* or, *The Confession*." *Nat Rev* 22 (29 Dec 70) 1406. Reports reactions of French political groups to view of Communism reflected in *The Confession* (Costa-Gavras).

4e(2a). Historical and Critical Surveys

Cavalcanti, Alberto. "Evolution of Cinematography in France." *Experimental Cinema* 1 (No. 2, June 30) 5–6.

Werth, Alexander. "Walls! Walls!" *CQ* 1 (No. 2, Winter 32) 93–95. French talkies are all confined to small sets.

Taylor, D. F. "French Movie Today." *CQ* 2 (No. 1, Autumn 33) 26–28. Experimental period seems to be past.

Rose, Felix. "Cinema in France: 1936." *S&S* 6 (No. 22, Summer 37) 71–74. A survey of French cinema during 1936.

Hamilton, James Shelly. "Artistic Motion Pictures." *Design* 41 (Dec 39) 22–25. Discussion of French renaissance of film art, with special emphasis on Pagnol's *Harvest*, Duvivier's *The End of Day*, and Renoir's *La Marsellaise* and *Grand Illusion*.

"News from Occupied France." *S&S* 13 (No. 49, May 44) 11–12. Films seen in that country.

Kirstein, Lincoln. "French Films During the Occupation." *Bul Museum of Mod Art* 12 (No. 3, Jan 45) 16–20.

Hackett, Hazel. "The French Cinema During the Occupation." *S&S* 15 (No. 57, Spring 46) 1–3.

Hackett, Hazel. "The French Cinema Since the Liberation." *S&S* 15 (No. 58, Summer 46) 48–52.

Vedrès, Nicole. "The French Cinema Since 1944." *Penguin F Rev* 1 (Aug 46) 74–79.

Anderson, Lindsay. "Some French Films—and a Forecast." *Sequence* (No. 1, Dec 46) 4–11. An overview of films made in the last ten years and a note on the threat to the industry imposed by the quota law (Blum-Byrnes Agreement).

Novik, William. "Four Years in a Bottle." *Penguin F Rev* 2 (Jan 47) 45–53. A critical study of French film production under the occupation.

Brunius, Jacques B. "Rise and Decline of an 'Avant-Garde.' " *Penguin F Rev* 5 (Jan 48) 53–63. French film 1919–1932.

Grunberg, I. "Film Directors in France." *Life & Letters Today* 56 (Feb 48) 153–157. A brief review of the merits of Jacques Becker, René Clair, and Pierre Prévert, with critical comments on the state of the French film industry.

Lambert, Gavin. "French Cinema: The New Pessimism." *Sequence* (No. 4, Summer 48) 8–12. Recent postwar films.

Morrison, George. "The French Avant-Garde." *Sequence* (No. 4, Summer 48) 30–34; (No. 5, Autumn 48) 29–34; (No. 6, Winter 48–49) 32–37. In three parts: the earliest works, the years 1924–1929, and "the last stage," 1930–1934; lists of important films.

Auriol, Jean-George. "Contemporary French Cinema." *Penguin F Rev* 8 (Jan 49) 51–70. Directors and writers, old and new.

Sadoul, Georges. "The French Cinema 1948–1949." *S&S* 18 (Spring 49) 58–59.

Lambert, Gavin. "French Cinema—Writers and Directors." *Sequence* (No. 9, Autumn 49) 98–104. The sound period, with its emphasis on writing.

Debrix, Jean. "The Cinema's Place in Present-Day France." *FIR* 1 (Feb 50) 20–22. Intellectual curiosity about cinema since the war; IDHEC and the remarkable spread of French film societies.

Sadoul, Georges. "The Postwar French Cinema." *Hwd Q* 4 (No. 3, Spring 50) 233–244. Directors; economic problems; some documentaries.

Bourgeois, Jacques. "Varying Techniques of French Directors." *FIR* 1 (May–June 50) 13+. Newsletter from Paris; new films by Clair, Allegret, Melville.

Debrix, Jean R. "1950 in France." (Tr. Dorothy Milburn.) *FIR* 2 (Jan 51) 14–18. Quality succumbed to quantity.

Knight, Arthur. "What's Happened to French Films?" *Sat Rev* 35 (24 May 52) 33. Changing conditions in France result in fewer films on American screens: work by Duvivier, Becker, Pagnol.

Queval, Jean. "French Films Since the War." *S&S* 22 (Jan–Mar 53) 102–108. Also some of the directors who have contributed most.

Grayson, Helen. "French Scene." *Sat Rev* 37 (13 Mar 54) 48+. Maintaining an audience in France for French short subjects; how they can be seen in America.

Hine, A. "What Has Happened to French Movies?" *Holiday* 16 (Oct 54) 28+. The decline of the French film.

Wolfenstein, Martha, and Nathan Leites. "Trends in French Films." *J Soc Issues* 11 (No. 2, 1955) 42–51. Analysis of recurring themes in 1947–1955 French cinema and predictions on new trends.

Billard, Ginette, and Pierre Billard. "Sixty Glorious Years of French Cinema." *F&F* 2 (No. 1, Oct 55) 4–6.

Grossvogel, David I. "Play of Light and Shadow: A Directional Error." *Yale French Studies* (No. 17, 1956) 75–85. A brief history of French film in terms of its poetic illusion.

Billard, Ginette. "Les Boys of French Cinema." *F&F* 2 (No. 12, Sep 56) 10–11. Survey of great French actors.

Goretta, Claude. "Aspects of French Documentary." *S&S* 26 (Winter 56–57). *See* 8c(2).

Baker, Peter. "France Makes Them So Xy." *F&F* 3 (No. 4, Jan 57) 11. British critic bemoans the decline of French sensitivity and the increase of French sensationalism and sex.

Butcher, M. "Films from France: A Survey of the Post-War French Cinema." *Dublin Rev* 231 (No. 473, Summer 57) 74–83. Directors, such as Cocteau, Bresson, and Clement.

Marcorelles, Louis. "French Cinema: The Old and the New." *S&S* 27 (Spring 58) 190–195. Cinema seems to be a consuming intellectual passion of the new generation in France, but there is "a tendency toward critical pedantry, dryness, the systematization of judgments"; comments on Astruc, Vadim, Malle, Chabrol.

Dyer, Peter John. "Some Personal Visions." *F&F* 5 (No. 2, Nov 58) 13–15+. Causes and effects of French avant-garde 1924–1934.

Dyer, Peter John. "Journey into the Night." *F&F* 5 (No. 10, July 59) 12–14+. French film makers' interest in romantic pessimism and fate.

Durgnat, Raymond. "A Look at the Old and New Waves." *F&F* 6 (No. 10, July 60) 28+. Old and new French films at the National Film Theatre.

Weightman, J. G. "Watching Old Films." *20th Century* 168 (Aug 60) 168–172. Generally harsh comments about the National Theatre's retrospective of French films (1933–1955).

Durgnat, Raymond. "On the Crest of the 'Wave.'" *F&F* 7 (No. 1, Oct 60) 9+. A review of French cinema history.

Brunius, Jacques, *et al.* "The French Film." *Film* (No. 26, Nov–Dec 60) 10–19. Several authors discuss the work of Carné, Vigo, Renoir, Truffaut, Bresson, Tati, and Chabrol.

Durgnat, Raymond. "The Mirror for Marianne." *F&F* 9 (No. 2, Nov 62) 48–55. The last ten years in French film making.

Milne, Tom. "The Real Avant-Garde." *S&S* 32 (Summer 63) 148–152. Historical survey of the French silent cinema: Louis Delluc, Abel Gance, Raymond Bernard, and Louis Feuillade were (in terms of innovations) the real avant-garde.

Truffaut, François. "A Certain Tendency of the French Cinema." *CdC in Eng* (No. 1, Jan 66). See *3b*(2).

Rosenblatt, Daniel. "Behind the Lines: France." *F Soc Rev* 4 (No. 3, 1968). See *4k*(12).

Blumer, Ronald. "The Camera as Snowball: France 1918–1927." *CJ* 9 (No. 2, Spring 70) 31–39. "Impressionist" film makers, encouraged by the critic Louis Delluc, who also made films, wanted to increase the virtuosity of the cinema; Epstein and L'Herbier tried superimposition and out-of-focus shots to suggest states of mind; Gance threw the camera around in a snowball fight.

4e(2b). "New Wave" (1959) and After

Grenier, C. "New Wave at Cannes." *Reporter* 20 (23 July 59) 39–41. Some background information about French New Wave directors, such as Truffaut, Chabrol, Marcel Camus.

Sadoul, Georges. "Notes on a New Generation." *S&S* 28 (Nos. 3–4, Summer–Autumn 59) 111–117. New film makers in France include Marcel Camus, Jacques Baratier, Jean Rouch, Claude Bernard-Aubert, Georges Franju, Alain Resnais, Claude Chabrol, François Truffaut.

Billard, Ginette. "The Men and Their Work." *F&F* 6 (No. 1, Oct 59) 7–8. Brief descriptions of the major directors of the New Wave.

"Meeting '*La Nouvelle Vague*' . . ." *F&F* 6 (No. 1, Oct 59). See *3d*.

Chapsal, Madeleine. "Sins Out of Context." *Reporter* 20 (12 Nov 59) 31–32. Controversy over Vadim's *Les Liaisons Dangereuses* in France.

"New Wave." *Time* 74 (16 Nov 59) 114+. Brief report on the young film makers of France.

Burch, Noel. "*Qu'est-ce que la Nouvelle Vague?*" *FQ* 13 (No. 2, Winter 59) 16–30. The beginnings of the New Wave and a dis-

paraging comment on its proponents; an exception is Hanoun's *Une Simple Histoire,* which is praised at considerable length.

Weber, Eugen. "An Escapist Realism." *FQ* 13 (No. 2, Winter 59) 9–16. Early work by Camus, Malle, Chabrol, Resnais examined in terms of both content and treatment.

Rouch, Jane. "The Young Lions of the French Film Industry." *JSPG* (Dec 59) 16–18. Wife of Jean Rouch reports on latest works.

"Refined Depravity." *America* 102 (12 Dec 59). See *7b*(6).

Alpert, Hollis. "New Wave: Orpheus in Rio." *Sat Rev* (19 Dec 59) 12–13. *Black Orpheus* in the context of the revitalization of French cinema; part of *Saturday Review* report "The New Frankness in Films."

Butcher, Maryvonne. "France's Film Renascence." *Commonweal* 71 (8 Jan 60) 414–416.

Grenier, C. "Renaissance of French Movies." *NYTM* (20 Mar 60) 44–45.

Holland, Norman N. "How New? How Vague?" *Hudson Rev* 13 (Summer 60) 270–277. The New Wave directors favor a point-of-view approach closer to a novelist's vision than that of a cinéaste.

Genêt. "Letter from Paris." *New Yorker* 36 (13 Aug 60) 88+. Moral concern over New Wave French films.

Weightman, J. G. "New Wave in French Culture." *Commentary* 30 (Sep 60) 230–240. The New Wave seen as part of a broader phase of sophisticated anarchism within a framework of authority and prosperity occurring in French culture.

Todd, Oliver. "Letter from Paris." *New S&N* 60 (5 Nov 60) 691–692. Pros and cons of the New Wave.

Siclier, Jacques. "New Wave and French Cinema." *S&S* 30 (Summer 61) 116–120. A survey of the state of the New Wave, including a long list of the working directors and their projects in 1959 and 1960, which shows that "everyone now wants to make a film"; criticism of Resnais and Godard for turning their backs on authentic social reality and into formal abstraction that does not interest the mass public.

Marcorelles, Louis. "Interview with Truffaut." *S&S* 31 (Winter 61–62). See *5, François Truffaut.*

Tyler, Parker. "The Lady Called 'A'; Or, If Jules and Jim Had Only Lived at Marienbad." *F Cult* (No. 25, 1962) 21–24. Recent French pictures: *Last Year at Marienbad,* Truffaut's *Jules and Jim,* and *Paris Is Ours.*

Strick, Philip. "*Lola* Shrugs Off That Shadow." *Motion* (No. 3, Spring 62) 26–29. Relationships between Demy's *Lola,* the French New Wave, and the American film.

Roud, Richard. "The Left Bank." *S&S* 32 (Winter 62–63) 24–27. Besides the *Cahiers du Cinéma* group, there are other new French film makers who share enough similarities to be called a group; Agnès Varda, Chris Marker, and Alain Resnais all feel, unlike Truffaut and Godard, that "personal problems and emotions should be seen in a social context."

Graham, Peter. "The Face of '63: No. 4—France." *F&F* 9 (No. 8, May 63) 13–21. French actors, directors, and producers who will make an impact on film making in 1963.

Young, Colin. "Conventional—Unconventional." *FQ* 17 (No. 1, Fall 63) 14–30. Recent developments in European cinema, particularly the alteration of traditional concepts of narrative and motivation; emphasis on Bresson and Godard; exposition "belongs to a day and age when we believed that people did things 'for reasons.'"

Gary, Romain. "The Foamy Edge of the Wave." *Show* 4 (Apr 64) 75–76. Survey of the accomplishments of the New Wave in France and why its directors appear more interesting and imaginative in print than on film.

Graham, Peter. *"Cinéma-Vérité* in France." *FQ* 17 (No. 4, Summer 64). *See 8c(3).*

Jacob, Gilles. *"Nouvelle Vague* or *Jeune Cinéma?" S&S* 34 (Winter 64–65) 4–8. Notes on the apparent collapse of the New Wave in France; there is hostility too; a dialogue with Alain Jessua, director of *La Vie à l'envers,* confirms these feelings.

Taylor, Stephen. "After the *Nouvelle Vague." FQ* 18 (No. 3, Spring 65) 5–11. In particular, Truffaut's *Soft Skin* and Godard's *Contempt;* "the crisis of regroupment" after the initial success of the New Wave.

Jacob, Gilles, and Claire Clouzot. "Letter from Paris." *S&S* 34 (Autumn 65) 160–163. Alain Resnais talks about his three new projects, among them *La Guerre est finie;* a visit to the set of Jacques Tati's new film, *Playtime;* a report on the critics' response to Godard's *Alphaville.*

Kotlowitz, R. "What's Going on in Paris?" *Harper's* 234 (Jan 67) 101–103. A "newsletter" on current films.

Ross, T. J. "A First Generation: On the New Wave and Claude Chabrol." *December* 9 (Nos. 2–3, Summer–Fall 67) 163–175.

Gollub, Judith. "French Writers Turned Film Makers." *F Her* 4 (No. 2, Winter 68–69). *See 3f(2).*

4e(2c). Economic Status of the Industry

Peet, Creighton. "French Film Studios." *Outlook* 159 (25 Nov 31) 403+. Traces development of French cinema industry.

Chavance, Louis. "American Movies in France." *Canad Forum* 12 (Mar 32) 220–222. While American films shaped French cinema audience, lack of talkies imported is hurting French film industry.

Petsche, Maurice. "French Cinema." *Living Age* 349 (Nov 35) 243–247. Reviews the decline in French film industry and suggests government subsidy.

"French Earn More from U.S. Movies, So They Turn Their Studios into Factories." *US News & World Report* 24 (2 Apr 48) 65.

Sadoul, Georges. "Crisis Over France." *S&S* 17 (No. 66, Summer 48) 94–95. Cinema's financial problems.

"Foreign Showcase: Paris Theatre." *Newswk* 32 (20 Sep 48) 98. French effort to meet increasing American taste for foreign films.

"New Feathers for Pathé: Paris Theatre." *Time* 52 (20 Sep 48) 91–92. The opening of Pathé's Paris Theatre in Manhattan occasions a look backward at Pathé's importance in world cinema.

MacDougall, Allan Ross. "Paris Cinemas of Yesteryear and Today." *FIR* 1 (Apr 50) 14–16+. Onetime secretary and biographer of Isadora Duncan recalls an afternoon spent with her in Paris in 1919 before attending a French motion-picture theatre where he first encountered the French custom of tipping the usher.

Debrix, Jean. "40 Million Frenchmen Aren't Enough." *FIR* 1 (Oct 50) 11–14. From 1946 to 1949, the average cost per feature film made in France rose from $45,000 to $110,000; the Byrnes-Blum Agreement of 1946, later revised, set quotas, but while production costs soared, the quality of French films sagged.

Steinhouse, H. "Films in France." *New S&N* 42 (8 Sep 51) 247. Revision of Paris film accord (1948) seen as an anti-American measure.

"Glamorous Gauls: French Movie Actresses." *Life* 33 (1 Dec 52) 115–118.

"Film Facts and Figures." *Yale French Studies* (No. 17, 1956) 107–108. Statistics and data on France's Centre National de la Cinématographie.

"A Boost for French Films." *Bus Wk* (30 June 56) 103–104. French movie men promote its stars and movies, including Martine Carol.

Lisbona, Joseph. "Panorama: The French Cinema in 1956." *Film* (No. 11, Jan–Feb 57) 20–21. A brief account of the French film-making industry during the year.

Marcorelles, Louis. "Paris Notes!" *S&S* 26 (Spring 57) 172. Coproduction and the dangers of Americanization in France.

Thuillier, Jean. "On Being an Iron Hand." *F&F* 7 (No. 1, Oct 60) 16. Why production in France can be truly independent; by a French producer.

Billard, Ginette. "No Free French." *F&F* 7 (No. 5, Feb 61) 39. Review of current production situation in France.

Houston, Penelope. "The Rewards of Quality." *S&S* 31 (Spring 62). *See 6a(3)*.

"BB or Bust." *Newswk* 61 (25 Feb 63) 76. Financial troubles of the French movie industry.

Salomon, Barbara. "The Franglais Film." *Nation* 199 (10 Aug 64) 57–59. American influence on French movie industry after World War II.

"Great Come-&-See-It Day." *Time* 85 (9 Apr 65) 62+. French film exhibitors fight for financial life.

Fixx, J. F. "The Great Gallic Welcome." *Sat Rev* 48 (25 Dec 65) 14–17. American films and film makers take over Italy.

Degrand, Claude. "Film Subsidy in France." *JSPG* (June 67) 37–40.

Jacob, Gilles. "Hollywood *sur* Seine." *S&S* 36 (Autumn 67) 162–166. French film companies have tried to solve some of their alarming financial problems by becoming dependent on U.S. investment; François Truffaut and his "Americanized" *The Bride Wore Black; Far from Vietnam,* which denounces American policies in Southeast Asia, is financed by film makers.

Sainsbury, Peter. "New French Cinema." *Afterimage* (No. 2, Autumn 70) 56–58. Three new French independent companies working outside the established film industry.

4e(2d). Censorship

"Intelligent Censorship." *Commonweal* 20 (15 June 34) 186. On French Catholic rating system.

Salemson, Harold. "A Film at War." *Hwd Q* 1 (No. 4, July 46) 416–419. Jean Renoir's *La Marseillaise* was shown in Tunis just after its liberation from the Germans in 1943, but withdrawn after a week of enthusiastic audience response.

De La Roche, Catherine. "The Censors Have No Code." *F&F* 1 (No. 9, June 55) 13. Censorship in France: recent decisions.

Waters, Roy. "The Small Knife: France." *S&S* 25 (Spring 56) 210–211+. Censorship there serves politics.

Marcorelles, Louis. "*L'Affaire* Vadim." *S&S* 29 (Winter 59–60) 20–21. *Les Liaisons Dangereuses* was not banned but was denied export.

Stein, Elliott. "Suzanne Simonin, Diderot's Nun." *S&S* 35 (Summer 66) 130–133. Case history of censorship problems with the Jacques Rivette film *La Religieuse* in France.

Godard, Jean-Luc. "My Anger Has to Strike." *Atlas* 11 (June 66) 375. Letter to André Malraux about his censoring of the film *La Religieuse.*

De Cleen, Edmond. "Cinema Without Censor." *Film* (No. 55, Summer 69) 11–12. In Belgium.

4e(3). ITALY

[*See 5, Biography: Michelangelo Antonioni, Marco Bellocchio, Bernardo Bertolucci, Dino De Laurentiis, Francesco De Robertis, Giuseppe De Santis, Vittorio De Sica, Gianni Di Venanzo, Luciano Emmer, Federico Fellini, Pietro Germi, Ermanno Olmi, Pier Paolo Pasolini, Carlo Ponti, Francesco Rosi, Roberto Rossellini, Franco Rossi, Mario Soldati, Alberto Sordi, Luchino Visconti, Luigi Zampa, Cesare Zavattini, Franco Zeffirelli.*]

Franzero, C. M. "The Educational Cinema in Italy." *S&S* 2 (No. 5, Spring 33) 6–8. The Luce Institute and its positive influence upon cinema in Italy.

Noxon, G. F. "Italy's 'International' Institute." *CQ* 3 (No. 1, Autumn 34). *See 1a(2)*.

Margolis, Herbert F. "Luciano Emmer and the Art Film." *S&S* 16 (No. 61, Spring 47) 1–3. The recent work of some experimental Italian film makers, led by the anti-Fascist Emmer.

"Hollywood in Italy." *NYTM* (25 Sep 49). *See 7d(1)*.

"Sexy Signore." *Life* 31 (3 Sep 51) 62–64. Strongly influenced by Anna Magnani, young Italian starlets emerge from the neorealist movement.

"Rich Crop of Beauties." *Life* 33 (20 Oct 52) 112–113. Young Italian actresses, including Gina Lollobrigida.

"Which Is Glamor?" *Collier's* 131 (3 Jan 53). *See 2b(2)*.

"Youth and Beauty, Native and Imported, Bolster New Italian Movie Industry." *Newswk* 42 (31 Aug 53) 66–68.

D'Alessandro, A. "Italian Movie Stars." *Cosmopolitan* 136 (Feb 54) 44–49. Italy's burgeoning star system: Magnani, Mangano, Lollobrigida, others discussed.

"Hollywood on the Tiber." *Time* 64 (16 Aug 54) 54–56. Gina Lollobrigida's biography; other Italian stars; booming movie production.

Seton, Marie. "Italian Cine-Clubs." *Film* (No. 5, Sep–Oct 55) 18–20. Aspects of film viewing, film study, and film censorship in Italy, as revealed through the author's presentations of Eisenstein material to the cine clubs.

"Idols of Italy." *Look* 19 (15 Nov 55) 100+. Movie stars.

Rauch, Robert J. "An American in a European Film School." *JUFPA* 10 (No. 1, Fall 57). *See 1a(3c)*.

Lane, John Francis. "Italy's New Curves." *F&F* 4 (No. 6, Mar 58) 12. Italian actors now wear jeans.

Weaver, William. "Letter from Italy." *Nation* 190 (19 Mar 60) 260–261. Italy's reaction to Fellini's *La Dolce Vita;* Ernesto Rossi's book *The State as Filmmaker.*

Lerman, Leo. "Basics on Italian Cinema." *Mlle*

54 (Dec 61) 68–71. A sampling of directors, actors, writers, ideas.

Renton, Bruce. "Letter from Italy." *Nation* 196 (2 Mar 63) 187–188. Report on the threat to Italo-German relations because of Nanni Loy's film *The Four Days of Naples.*

Zavattini, Cesare. "The New *Free* Newsreels." *Cinéaste* 3 (No. 2, Fall 69). *See 8b.*

Prottri, Danielle. "Letter from Italy." *Cinéaste* 3 (No. 3, Winter 69–70). *See 8b.*

4e(3a). Historical and Critical Surveys

Cavalcanti, Alberto. "Notes on the Cinema in Italy." *S&S* 6 (No. 22, Summer 37) 68. Italian films shown at Venice.

Scherk, Alfred. "The Italian Film Industry in Transition." *Penguin F Rev* 1 (Aug 46) 80–83.

Makins, William Cooper. "The Film in Italy." *S&S* 15 (No. 60, Winter 46–47) 126–129.

Vesselo, Arthur. "The Italian Cinema Before the Liberation." *S&S* 16 (No. 61, Spring 47) 6–7.

Reid, Adrian. "The Short Film in Italy." *S&S* 17 (No. 68, Winter 48–49) 166+. Rise of the short film after the war.

MacClintock, Lander. "Road from Rome." *Th Arts* 33 (Dec 49) 37–41. Italy's film output 1920–1945.

Venturi, Lauro. "Prevailing Trends in Italy's Film Industry." *FIR* 1 (Apr 50) 7–8. Italian neorealism reduced acting jobs; comic Totò and the one-to-one shooting ratio of his films.

Luce, Candida. "Incoherence in Italian Films." *FIR* 1 (Oct 50) 15–18. Anonymous actress says American films are preferred by Italians, along with Italian slapstick comedies; peculiarities of Italian production.

Verdone, Mario. "The Italian Cinema from Its Beginnings to Today." *Hwd Q* 5 (No. 3, Spring 51) 270–281. Editor of *Bianco e Nero* discusses trends, directors, stars; foreign producers in Italy.

Lane, John Francis. "Italy in London." *F&F* 1 (No. 1, Oct 54) 6–7. Second Italian Film Festival: *La Strada, I Vitelloni*, others; background to the festival.

Brunel, Christopher. "London's Italian Festival." *FIR* 6 (Apr 55) 181–182. Brief description of the 1955 London Festival of Italian Films.

Hartung, Philip T. "Screen." *Commonweal* 62 (15 Apr 55) 48. The Museum of Modern Art's retrospective—50 Years of Italian Cinema.

Kass, Robert. "50 Years of Italian Cinema." *FIR* 6 (Aug–Sep 55) 313–317. Thumbnail reviews of films presented at the Museum of Modern Art in a retrospective showing of representative Italian films of the last fifty years.

Lane, John Francis. "The Italian Laugh-Makers." *F&F* 4 (No. 8, May 58) 9–10+. History of Italian film comedy.

Bryan, J. "Cinema City." *Holiday* 27 (Apr 60) 127+. Italian film past and present.

Lane, John Francis. "The Money in Muscles." *F&F* 6 (No. 10, July 60). *See 4k(4).*

Marinucci, Vinicio. "Fact, Fiction and History Were in at the Beginning." *F&F* 7 (No. 4, Jan 61) 15–16+. History of the Italian cinema, part 1.

Marinucci, Vinicio. "History—Before and After Mussolini." *F&F* 7 (No. 5, Feb 61) 37–38+. History of Italian cinema, part 2.

Marinucci, Vinicio. "The Theatre Supplies the Funny Men." *F&F* 7 (No. 7, Apr 61) 33–35. History of Italian cinema, part 3.

Marinucci, Vinicio. "Eroticism and the Good Earth." *F&F* 7 (No. 8, May 61) 33–34. Italian film history, part 4.

Marinucci, Vinicio. "Development of Realism with a Sense of Humor." *F&F* 7 (No. 9, June 61) 31–32.

Marinucci, Vinicio. "Search for New Styles in Musicals." *F&F* 7 (No. 10, July 61) 33–34. History of Italian musicals.

Marinucci, Vinicio. "The Crisis That Led to Better Things." *F&F* 7 (No. 11, Aug 61) 41. Decline of comedy, musical, and documentary films in Italy led to development of sophisticated comedy and dramatic film.

Eames, David. "Cinecittà." *Show* 2 (Feb 62) 64–71. Notes on this Italian movie studio; remarks on the German occupation and postwar Italian film making.

Whitehall, Richard. "Days of Strife and Nights of Orgy." *F&F* 9 (No. 6, Mar 63). *See 4k(4).*

Lane, John Francis. "The Face of '63: No. 3—Italy." *F&F* 9 (No. 7, Apr 63) 11–21. Italian directors, actors, and producers likely to make an impact on films of 1963.

"New Times, New Writers." *Economist* 210 (28 Mar 64) 1264+. Relationship between postwar Italian fiction and film.

Connolly, Robert. "Moravia on Italian Film." *F Com* 2 (No. 3, Summer 64) 33. The novelist spoke at the Metropolitan Museum.

Fenin, George N. "Behind the Lines: Italy." *F Soc Rev* 4 (No. 3, 1968). *See 4k(12).*

4e(3b). Neorealism and After

King, Hugh Barty. "Seven Americans." *S&S* 15 (No. 59, Autumn 46) 83–84. How *Open City* came to be shown in America and how *Paisan* was made.

Emmer, Luciano, and Enrico Gras. "The Film Renaissance in Italy." *Hwd Q* 2 (No. 4, July 47) 353–358. The production situation just after the war; brief chronology of leading films written by film makers.

Genêt. "Letter from Rome." *New Yorker* 24 (5 Feb 49) 89. Brief discussion of Italian neorealism.

Eisner, Lotte. "Notes on Some Recent Italian Films." *Sequence* (No. 8, Summer 49) 52–58. Critique of recent work by Vergano, De Santis, Lattuada, Zampa, De Sica.

Jacobson, Herbert L. "De Sica's *Bicycle Thieves* and Italian Humanism." *Hwd Q* 4 (No. 1, Fall 49) 28–33. Discussion of some leading film makers, with emphasis on De Sica, who seems to be saying that "in a crisis a man must help himself," a philosophy of individualism.

"Movie Bad Girls: Rags and Riots Lead to Italian Film Success." *Life* 27 (7 Nov 49) 108–110. Actresses "let their hair and morals down" in neorealist roles.

Lambert, Gavin. "Notes on a Renaissance." *S&S* 19 (Feb 51) 399–409. A long article on the Italian cinema, with the stress on individual directors rather than collective trends: early history, the 1930s and the rise of De Sica to prominence in 1943; Luchino Visconti, Renato Castellani, Roberto Rossellini, and lesser-known but promising directors, Antonioni, Lattuada, Emmer, De Santis; the myth of neorealism.

Hawkins, Robert F. "In Rome, the People Are Movie Stars." *NYTM* (21 Sep 52) 22–23+. Neorealism in Italy.

"Italian Film Invasion." *Life* 33 (20 Oct 52) 107–113. Includes sketches of directors Visconti and Rossellini.

Lambert, Gavin. "Further Notes on a Renaissance." *S&S* 22 (Oct–Dec 52) 61–65. Neorealism has expanded to a point at which it can no longer be classified; De Sica, Zavattini, Castellani, Visconti, Germi, Malaparte; expanding commercialism is a danger.

Kumlien, G. D. "Artless Art of Italian Films." *Commonweal* 58 (22 May 53) 177+. Roots and uniqueness of neorealism.

Kass, Robert. "The Italian Film Renaissance." *FIR* 4 (Aug–Sep 53) 326–348. Critical review of films since 1944, including lesser works and directors, exploitation themes, and influence of U.S. market.

Zavattini, Cesare. "Some Ideas on the Cinema." *S&S* 23 (Oct–Dec 53) 64–69. One of the leading writers of the Italian postwar renaissance says: "Life is not what is related in stories; life is another matter. To understand it involves a minute, unrelenting, and patient search . . . being able to observe reality, not to extract fictions from it."

Hine, A. "Italian Movies." *Holiday* 15 (Feb 54) 11+. Films, directors, and performers that have brought into vogue the postwar Italian films.

Lambert, Gavin. "The Signs of Predicament." *S&S* 24 (Jan–Mar 55) 147–151+. The promising crop of neorealist directors (De Sica, Visconti, Castellani, Rossellini, De Santis, etc.) face the prospect of becoming a commercially uninviting risk in an increasingly

commercial Rome; these directors must also face political "chamber of commerce" opposition to their themes; comments on *Umberto D, Senso, I Vitelloni,* and *La Strada.*

Griffith, Richard. "Moment in Which We Live." *Th Arts* 39 (May 55) 24–25+. Italian neorealism and why it seems to be surviving its success.

Wilson, John S. "Italian Film Story: Renaissance Revisited." *Th Arts* 39 (May 55) 68–69+. The Italian film is not just a postwar phenomenon.

"New Names." *S&S* 25 (Winter 55–56) 119–121. Photographs and thumbnail biographies of new Italian directors: Antonioni, De Seta, Emmer, Fellini, Lizzani, De Santis, Maselli, Rossi.

Pacifici, Sergei J. "Notes Toward a Definition of Neorealism." *Yale French Studies* (No. 17, 1956) 44–52.

Hawkins, Robert. "Italian Notes." *S&S* 26 (Summer 56) 6.

Evans, Jon. "We Want to See." *Film* (No. 11, Jan–Feb 57) 5–7. An account of Italian neorealism, its theoretical problems, and some recent films which seem to promise new directions.

Hawkins, Robert. "Italian Notes." *S&S* 27 (Summer 57) 4. An American "invasion" of sorts; Fellini's plans.

Barzini, Luigi, Jr. "The Motion Picture Industry." *Atlantic* 202 (Dec 58) 178–181. Neorealist art and box-office pressures of Italian movie industry.

Almendros, Nestor. "Neorealist Cinematography." *F Cult* (No. 20, 1959) 39–43.

Lane, John Francis. "A Style Is Born." *F&F* 5 (No. 7, Apr 59) 13–15+. The Italian influence on films.

Lane, John Francis. "The Italian Look." *F&F* 6 (No. 3, Dec 59) 31. Recent films of Alberto Sordi, Vittorio De Sica, and Maurizio Arena.

Lane, John Francis. "Yes! Fellini Has Started Something." *F&F* 6 (No. 8, May 60) 31. Other current Italian directors.

Morandini, Morando. "The Year of *La Dolce Vita.*" *S&S* 29 (Summer 60) 123–127. Editor of Italian film magazine *Schermi* comments on various directors.

Dworkin, Martin S. "Dissenting Screen: Films of Social Protest." *Cath World* 191 (Sep 60). See 3a(6).

Grenier, Cynthia. "Three Adventurous Italians." *Sat Rev* (24 Dec 60) 46–47. Current works of Antonioni, Fellini, and Visconti are the most exciting films coming out of Europe; part of *Saturday Review* report "Are Foreign Films Better?"

Rhode, Eric. "Why Neo-Realism Failed." *S&S* 30 (Winter 60–61) 26–32. The film makers did not understand realism (as George Lukacs understands it) or the complexity of society;

De Sica and Rossellini were naïve; only Visconti's *La Terra Trema* was a truly realist film.

Lovell, Alan. "Italian Cinema Today." *New S&N* 61 (3 Feb 61) 189. Italian cinema enjoys its first resurgence since neorealism with the films of Antonioni, Fellini, De Sica and Visconti.

Alpert, Hollis. "Film: The Italians Again." *Sat Rev* 44 (11 Feb 61) 41–42. Recent developments since neorealism.

Pepper, Curtis G. "Rebirth in Italy: Three Great Movie Directors." *Newswk* 58 (10 July 61) 66–68. Report on Fellini, Antonioni, and Visconti: their work, their thoughts about society and each other.

Young, Vernon. "The Moral Cinema: Notes on Some Recent Films." *FQ* 15 (No. 1, Fall 61) 14–21. Rebelling against their own late-blooming "social progress and its urbanizing of the soul," Italian film makers continue to be concerned with moral conflicts: De Sica in *Two Women,* Visconti less interestingly in *Rocco and His Brothers;* other works by Zurlini, Bolognini, Damiani.

"Italy After the Liberation: Reality and Neo-realism." *Times Lit Supplement* 3111 (13 Oct 61) 710–711. Traces Italy's return to realism after the war as a freeing of cultural life from the excesses and limitations of the Fascist world.

Lane, John Francis. "The Triumph of Italy's Realism." *F&F* 8 (No. 3, Dec 61) 38–39. Italian realism in Pasolini, De Seta, and Olmi.

Harcourt, Peter. "Toward a New Neo-Realism." *London Mag* new series 2 (No. 3, June 62) 70–74; (No. 4, July 62) 45–48. Films of De Sica and of the new Italian film makers; in two parts.

Lane, John Francis. "Oh! Oh! Antonioni." *F&F* 9 (No. 3, Dec 62) 58–66. Survey of the past ten years of film making in Italy.

Connelly, Robert. "Three Italian Films." *F Com* 1 (No. 6, Fall 63) 34–38. Production notes and critiques of *The Leopard, La Terra Trema,* and *Il Posto* (*The Sound of Trumpets*).

LaBadie, Donald W. "From Neo-Real to Sur-Real." *Show* 4 (Apr 64) 84. Discussion of the new directions in Italian cinema as dominated by Fellini; brief comments on the films of Gregoretti, Ferreri and Germi.

Gough-Yates, Kevin. "The Destruction of Neo-Realism." *F&F* 16 (No. 12, Sep 70) 14–22. Study of the neorealist "movement," which has never been defined.

4e(3c). Films in the 1960s

Lane, John Francis. "The New Realists of Italy: Five Directors." *F&F* 7 (No. 4, Jan 61) 20–21+. Mauro Bolognini, Gillo Pontecorvo, Florestano Vancini, Francesco Rosi, Franco Rossi: each director speaks about his work.

Pasolini, Pier Paolo. "Intellectualism . . . and the Teds." *F&F* 7 (No. 4, Jan 61) 17+. The cinema in Italy.

Nichols, Mike. "Save My Seat." *New Yorker* 37 (18 Nov 61). See 3b(4).

Castello, Giulio Cesare. "*Cinema Italiano* 1962." *S&S* 32 (Winter 62–63) 28–33. The social and psychological preoccupations are still based on realism; Antonioni's *Eclipse* and Francesco Rosi's *Salvatore Giuliano* and other films reviewed.

Di Giammatteo, Fernaldo. "Marienbadism and the New Italian Directors." *FQ* 16 (No. 2, Winter 62–63) 20–25. Brusati and Petri may have been infected, but De Seta, Olmi, Rosi, and Pasolini seem to be resisting.

"*La Dolce Far Niente.*" *Time* 81 (1 Mar 63) 46. First public reactions to *8½.*

Lane, John Francis. "A Case of Artistic Inflation." *S&S* 32 (Summer 63) 130–135. Rome, as "New Hollywood," went off the tracks with such pretentious films as *The Condemned of Altona, The Leopard,* and Fellini's *8½.*

Bennett, Joseph. "Italian Film: Failure and Emergence." *Kenyon Rev* 26 (Autumn 64) 738–747. The recent films of Fellini, Antonioni, and Visconti are disappointing, the vitality of Italian film is transferred to the works of Bolognini, Germi, Ferreri, Rosi, Damiani, and Loy.

Young, Vernon. "Italian Film: Left Hand, Right Hand." *Hudson Rev* 17 (Autumn 64) 431–439. Rosi's *The Easy Life* (*Il sorpasso*) exemplifies what's happening in Italian cinema today; additional comments on Damiani's *La Noia,* Bolognini's *Il Bell'Antonio* and *La Corruzione.*

"Horse, Italian Style." *Newswk* 65 (28 June 65) 88. Italy produces Westerns.

"The Double-Neos." *Newswk* 67 (21 Feb 66) 98+. Italy's "new wave"; De Seta, Bertolucci, Bellochio, and Pasolini rebelling against Italy's film establishment.

"The Forty-Cent Stars." *Newswk* 67 (21 Mar 66) 105+. Italian comics Franchi and Ingrassia produce over twenty-three spoofs in two years.

Paolucci, A. "Italian Film: Antonioni, Fellini, Bolognini." *Mass Rev* 7 (Summer 66) 556–567. Italian directors have put their films to the test of public approval, avoiding the extremes of Hollywood films and the personalized films of the avant-garde in the U.S.

Fox, William Price. "Wild Westerns, Italian Style." *SEP* 241 (6 Apr 68) 50–52+. Making of low-budget cowboy movies in Rome.

Lane, John Francis. "Italy's Angry Young Directors." *F&F* 15 (No. 1, Oct 68) 74–80.

Lane, John Francis. "Love and Anger." *F&F* 15 (No. 12, Sep 69) 32–34. On current Italian films.

Prottri, Danielle, and Alberto Cattini. "Political Engagement in the Italian Cinema." *Cinéaste* 3 (No. 4, Spring 70) 28+. Discussion of Italian films which represent a Marxist approach.

Wallington, Mike, and Chris Frayling. "The Italian Western." *Cinema* (Cambridge) (Nos. 6–7, Aug 70). See *4k(2)*.

Georgakas, Don. "Revolutionary Cinema—Italian Style." *Cinéaste* 4 (No. 3, Winter 70–71) 33–34. The films; the distribution problems.

4e(3d). Economic Status of the Industry

Slater, L. "Road to Rome." *Newswk* 33 (7 Feb 49). See *7d(1)*.

"Hollywood on the Tiber." *Time* 55 (26 June 50) 92+. Filming of *Quo Vadis?*

"Rome's New Empire." *Time* 60 (14 July 52) 86–87.

"Memo from Rome." *US News & World Report* 36 (23 Apr 54) 69–70. American invasion of studios in Italy.

Kumlien, G. D. "Defeat at the Box Office." *Commonweal* 64 (4 May 56) 120–121. The reasons for the crisis of the Italian film industry.

"Italian Movies, the Last Act?" *US News & World Report* 41 (17 Aug 56) 82–84.

Weaver, William. "Letter from Rome." *Nation* 184 (12 Jan 57) 47–48. Financial and censorship problems of Italian movie industry.

"Drive-In Cine; Photographs." *NYTM* (29 Sep 57). See *6e(2a)*.

"Fine Italian Hand." *Newswk* 61 (28 Jan 63). See *7c(5)*.

Castello, Giulio Cesare. "Crisis in Rome." *S&S* 33 (Autumn 64) 171–172. A gloomy report on the state of the Italian cinema; mostly American films are being produced.

Plateroti, Arnaldo. "Italian Government Subsidy and Union Labor." *JSPG* (June 67) 25–28+.

Nowell-Smith, Geoffrey. "Italy *Sotto Voce*." *S&S* 37 (Summer 68) 145–147. Dubbing, opposed in a manifesto by such Italian film makers as Antonioni, Lattuada, Bellocchio, and Pontecorvo, is a symptom of the economic crisis of the Italian cinema and of American influence on Italian film production.

Lane, John Francis. "Long Live Crisis." *F&F* 16 (No. 7, Apr 70) 63–67. Current crisis in the Italian film industry.

4e(3e). Censorship

"Italian Movie Code." *Commonweal* 62 (20 May 55) 173. Italian restrictions on their films do not mean more universal acceptance of them. Discussion 62 (17 June 55) 279–280.

Kumlien, G. D. "Sex in Italian Films." *Commonweal* 62 (15 July 55) 370–371. Barriers to creativity and glamor ahead under Italy's new censorship code.

"Goodbye to the Lollos?" *New S&N* 52 (7 July

56) 3. Italy is trying to pass an amended law in support of the film industry.

Borghese, Elizabeth Mann. "Letter from Florence." *Nation* 194 (17 Feb 62) 154–156. Confusion of the laws on motion-picture and theatre censorship in Italy.

Bachmann, Gideon. "Censorship—Italy." *Film* (No. 38, Winter 63) 11–13. Leftist trends in the Italian cinema, with particular reference to the work of Pasolini.

"Seduced and Amended." *Time* 85 (11 June 65) 39. The Italian government's debate over film censorship.

"This Is Doris Day?" *Newswk* 65 (21 June 65) 48+. Lollobrigida and Virna Lisi in *The Dolls* threaten to bring down the Italian government.

4e(4). GERMANY, AUSTRIA, HOLLAND, SWITZERLAND

[See 5, Biography: *Hans Albers, Karl Freund, Emil Jannings, Fritz Lang, Carl Mayer, Friedrich Murnau, Richard Oswald, G. W. Pabst, Erich Pommer, Leni Riefenstahl, Volker Schloendorff, Sybilla Schmitz, Bernhard Wicki.*]

Bryher. "Berlin: April 1931." *Close Up* 8 (No. 2, June 31) 126–133. A discussion of recent films shown in Berlin.

Kraszna-Krausz, A., and G. W. Pabst. "Before the Microphone of German Broadcasting." *Close Up* 8 (No. 2, June 31) 122–126. The film industry in Germany and other topics.

Herring, Robert. "New German Cinema." *London Mercury* 24 (Oct 31). See *4d*.

Hulsker, T. "News Out of Holland." *CJ* 1 (No. 1, Autumn 32) 26–27.

"Austrian Films Meet Their Censor." *Living Age* 349 (Sep 35) 84–86. Austrian films must be cut to please German censor.

Holmes, Winifred. "Forty Years." *S&S* 7 (No. 26, Summer 38) 57–59. Films and filming in the Netherlands.

Winge, John H. "The Laughter of the Gods." *S&S* 7 (No. 28, Winter 38–39) 146–148. A brief description of the death of Austrian cinema.

de Jaeger, C. T. "Austria's Film Future." *S&S* 12 (No. 48, Jan 44) 100–102. Effects of the war.

Podselver, Judith. "Motion Pictures in Central Europe." *Screen Writer* 2 (May 47). See *4e(9b)*.

Smith, G. Buckland. "The German Film Institute." *S&S* 16 (No. 62, Summer 47). See *1a(2)*.

Wollenberg, H. H. "The Scene in Switzerland." *S&S* 16 (No. 64, Winter 47–48) 144–147.

Wollenberg, H. H. "The Return of the Austrian Film." *S&S* 17 (No. 67, Autumn 48) 111–112.

Schulberg, Stuart. "For the Record: 'Of All

People.'" *Hwd Q* 4 (No. 2, Winter 49).
See *7f.*

"Black Angel." *Life* 28 (20 Mar 50). *See 2b(10).*

Gesek, Ludwig. "Our Newsletter from Vienna." *FIR* 1 (Sep 50) 17–18+. The post-World War II history of the Austrian film, by the editor of a cinema periodical there.

Ford, Charles. "Grandeur and Decadence of UFA." *FIR* 4 (June–July 53) 266–268. Brief history of the Universum Film Aktiengesellschaft, and its twenty-five-year domination of the German film industry, now ended.

"Acting Beauties." *Life* 36 (10 May 54) 127–128. Four German stage and screen stars.

Genschow, Gustov. "They Put Talent Before Publicity." *F&F* 3 (No. 3, Dec 56) 10–11. German actors.

Donaldson, Geoffrey. "Dutch Courage." *F&F* 3 (No. 4, Jan 57) 12+. History of the Dutch film industry.

Hauff, Eberhard. "The German Institute for Film and Television." *JUFPA* 10 (No. 1, Fall 57). *See 1a(3c).*

Bohm, Karlheinz. "The World Before Us." *F&F* 6 (No. 5, Feb 60). *See 2b.*

De Vaal, Jan. "Film Research in the Netherlands." *Cinema Studies* 1 (No. 1, Mar 60) 9–12. Plans and priorities; discovery of an English-Dutch coproduction of 1922.

Heaword, Rosemary. "An Early Anglo-Dutch Co-Production." *Cinema Studies* 1 (No. 3, Aug 61) 57–58. Little is known about *The Black Tulip.*

"Very Educational." *Nation* 196 (20 Apr 63). *See 7f.*

"Rock 'Em, Sock 'Em." *Newswk* 61 (17 June 63). *See 7c(5).*

"'The Future Is Entirely Ours'—The Sound-and-Picture Outline for Leni Riefenstahl's *Triumph of the Will.*" *F Com* 3 (No. 1, Winter 65). *See 2d(4).*

Cowie, Peter. "Dutch Films." *FQ* 19 (No. 2, Winter 65–66) 41–46. The directors are independent, they work mostly with short films, and they have a love-hate relationship with the sea; since Joris Ivens there have been John Ferno, Bert Haanstra, Fons Rademakers, and others.

Stephenson, Ralph. "Films from Holland." *Film* (No. 44, Winter 65–66) 34–36.

Schenk, Rolf. "Is There a Swiss Film Industry?" *F Soc Rev* (Oct 67) 36–37. A brief description, postwar.

Bragin, John. "Behind the Lines: Germany." *F Soc Rev* 4 (No. 3, 1968). *See 4k(12).*

Cowie, Peter. "Where Are We Going Now?" *Film* (No. 59, Summer 70) 4–8. The past and future of Dutch film.

4e(4a). German Silent Films

Kraszna-Krausz, A. "Proletarian of the Film." *Close Up* 6 (No. 6, 1930) 485–492. The

decline of production opportunities in Germany.

"Talkies in Germany." *Living Age* 338 (1 May 30) 291. German language affected by American talkies.

Sadleir, Michael. "Cinema in Germany." *New S&N* 35 (9 Aug 30) 568. Comparison of German and British audiences.

Haensel, Curt. "German Stage and Talkie." *Th Arts* 15 (June 31) 462–474.

Peet, Creighton. "German Studios." *Outlook* 159 (21 Oct 31) 249. Relates visit to Germany, with comments on movie industry, stars, and current production.

Melnitz, William W. "Aspects of War and Revolution in the Theater and Film of the Weimar Republic." *Hwd Q* 3 (No. 4, Summer 1948–Summer 1949) 372–378. As director of several theatres during the period, the author is concerned mostly with plays; his conclusion is that there was, especially from 1919 to 1925, a "strong devotion to the republican" idea of government.

Eisner, Lotte H. "Ach, the Kammerspiel." (Tr. by David A. Mage.) *FIR* 3 (May 52) 229–232. The psychological film in Germany, including *The Last Laugh* and *New Year's Eve,* discussed in an excerpt from *The Demonic Screen,* published in France, also in *The Haunted Screen* (University of California Press, 1969).

Whitford, Frank. "Expressionism in the Cinema." *Studio Inter* 179 (Jan 70) 24–27. An examination of the relationship between the German cinema and the visual arts between 1919 and 1925.

Eisner, Lotte. "Some Notes on Lost German Films." *Silent Picture* (No. 8, Autumn 70) 20–21. A plea for more archival work to preserve nitrate films, particularly for the period 1913–1919, when the war closed off distribution and no archival work was going on.

4e(4b). Nazi Period

Villard, Oswald Garrison. "On the German Front." *Nation* 132 (14 Jan 31) 37–39. German government and National Socialists ban *All Quiet on the Western Front.*

Chéronnet, Louis. "German Cinema." *Living Age* 343 (Jan 33) 441–444. French critic lauds German film industry and sees connections to German national character.

"Mechanical Mouse." *SRL* 10 (11 Nov 33). *See 2h(3).*

"Bergner Banned." *Time* 23 (19 Mar 34). *See 7e(3).*

"Nazi Movies Through Russian Eyes." *Living Age* 347 (Nov 34) 270–271. Dmitri Bukhartsev describes German films.

"Film Ideals of Present-Day Germany." *S&S* 4 (No. 14, Summer 35) 58–59. Excerpts from an address by Joseph Goebbels in which he attempts to enumerate laws and purposes of the film.

Holmes, Winifred. "Hamburg Cinema." *S&S* 8 (No. 29, Spring 39) 18–20. A typical film program.

Lieu, Alfree. "Nazi Film Did Not Impress Shanghai Audience." *China Weekly Rev* 94 (9 Nov 40). See *4f(3)*.

Reichenheim, J. O. "The German Film." *S&S* 10 (No. 38, Summer 41) 19–20. The German film before the war and the subsequent effect of the Nazi party.

"Nazi Plans." *S&S* 10 (No. 38, Summer 41) 30–31. German plans for the use of the cinema.

"Scenes from the Nazi Horror News-Film." *Illus London News* 99 (13 Sep 41) 334–335.

Kracauer, Siegfried. "Conquest of Europe on the Screen: The Nazi Newsreel, 1939–1940." *Social Research* 10 (Sep 43) 337–357. Analysis of the Nazi newsreel (1939–1940) as a part of the German system of war propaganda; cinematic devices overcome critical resistance.

"Axis Newsreels." *Life* 15 (13 Dec 43). See *8b*.

"The Reich Institute for Film and Slides in Science and Education." *S&S* 14 (No. 55, Oct 45) 88–90. How the institute functioned.

Schulberg, Budd. "The Celluloid Noose." *Screen Writer* 2 (Aug 46) 1–15. The writer worked for the U.S. government at the close of World War II collecting Nazi films and newsreels about Germany to use in the Nuremberg trials to help convict the Nazi leaders; he describes this film footage.

Altmann, John. "Movies' Role in Hitler's Conquest of German Youth." *Hwd Q* 3 (No. 4, Summer 1948–Summer 1949) 379–386. Excerpts from author's forthcoming book *Nazi Film Propaganda* include the organization of the propaganda machine; techniques used to enslave children; Goebbels' role; Karl Ritter's philosophy: "My movies deal with the unimportance of the individual."

Altmann, John. "The Technique and Content of Hitler's War Propaganda Films, Part I: Karl Ritter and His Early Films." *Hwd Q* 4 (No. 4, Summer 50) 385–391. *Traitors* (1935) and *Patriots* (1936).

Altmann, John. "The Technique and Content of Hitler's War Propaganda Films, Part II: Karl Ritter's 'Soldier' Films." *Hwd Q* 5 (No. 1, Fall 50) 61–72. The "heroic" films of the 1930s that impressed young men with the idea that "senseless, sacrificial death has its value"; *Cadets* (1939) deals with the possibility of defeat and ways of harassing a conqueror.

"Dr. Goebbels at the Cinema." *S&S* 29 (Aug 50) 235–238. Taken from Goebbels' diary during the war; reactions to the propaganda films of his enemies; feelings about the Nazi film movement, Leni Riefenstahl, and UFA.

Marcorelles, Louis. "The Nazi Cinema: 1933–1945." *S&S* 25 (Autumn 55) 65–69. Nazi cinema was controlled by a few companies; its role was chiefly to provide escape; but in the documentary, Nazi cinema was at its best.

Fielding, Raymond. "The Nazi German Newsreel." *JUFPA* 12 (No. 3, Spring 60) 3–5. Gift to UCLA of twenty-eight newsreels (1939–1942) reveals differences from American newsreels: they were longer, always narrated, and dramatically structured.

Luft, Herbert G. "Shadow of the Swastika." *F&F* 7 (No. 2, Nov 60) 10–11. Kurt Gerron (Gerson), German actor, forced to direct propaganda film for the Nazis during World War II from a concentration camp, *Hitler Presents a Town to the Jews*.

Hull, David Stewart. "Forbidden Fruit: The Harvest of the German Cinema, 1939–1945." *FQ* 14 (No. 4, Summer 61) 16–30. The politically oriented films and directors of the period; one of the few entertainment films mentioned, *Baron Munchausen*, is given some artistic consideration.

Blobner, Helmut, and Herbert Holba. "Jackboot Cinema." *F&F* 9 (No. 3, Dec 62) 11–20. Study of political propaganda films of the Third Reich; a list of key films.

Hoffmann, Hilmar. "Manipulation of the Masses Through the Nazi Film." *F Com* 3 (No. 4, Fall 65) 34–39. Artistic director of Oberhausen short-film festival reports on a closed showing of Nazi feature films and comments on their propaganda goals.

Leiser, Erwin. "Germany, Awake!" *F Com* 3 (No. 4, Fall 65) 40. Comments on his own film which uses clips from thirty Nazi films.

"The Nazis Return." *F&F* 12 (No. 7, Apr 66) 36–39. Films popular in Germany during the Third Reich.

Luft, Herbert G. "The Screen as a Propaganda Weapon: Germany." *Cinema* (Calif) 5 (No. 2, 1969) 24–26. Films made during the Third Reich.

4e(4c). West Germany Since World War II

Joseph, Robert. "Cinema: Comment and Criticism." *Arts & Arch* 62 (July 45) 16+. Programs of films in the Allied-occupied areas of Germany.

Joseph, Robert. "American Films in Germany —A Report." *Screen Writer* 1 (May 46) 10–14. Efforts toward "re-education of the German people"; films chosen for this task; reactions in Germany.

Joseph, Robert. "Cinema: The Germans See Their Concentration Camps." *Arts & Arch* 63 (Sep 46) 14+. Effects of a documentary in postwar Germany.

Joseph, Robert. "German Film Production Today." *Screen Writer* 2 (Dec 46) 22–33. Under American Zone Information Control Division, progress has been slow.

Joseph, Robert, and Gladwin Hill. "Our Film Program in Germany." *Hwd Q* 2 (No. 2, Jan 47) 122–130. Film officer for Berlin under occupation program defends list of films allowed into Germany; *New York Times* reporter Hill suggests U.S. feature films won't do what is needed.

Wollenberg, H. H. "The Revival of the German Film." *S&S* 16 (No. 61, Spring 47) 9–11.

Ickes, Paul. "The New German Film and Its International Prospects." *Penguin F Rev* 4 (Oct 47) 95–99. German film still reflects the philosophy that cinema should direct the mind rather than reflect the present.

Luft, Herbert G. "A Study of the German Screen." *Screen Writer* 3 (Nov 47) 11–12. *Murderers Among Us* is a relatively honest film, but there is still no admission of collective guilt.

"German Movies Turn to Stark Realism in Bid for Recognition in World Market." *US News & World Report* 24 (30 Jan 48) 63. *And Over Us the Sky* and *Shadowed Marriage* discussed.

Larsen, Egon. "Germany." *S&S* 17 (No. 66, Summer 48) 75–79. A new film industry?

Larsen, Egon. "The Emergence of a New Film Industry." *Hwd Q* 3 (No. 4, Summer 48–Summer 49) 387–394. Expanded reprint from *Sight and Sound* of German journalist's report on slow revival of German film industry; message films; treatment of Jews; see also objection to optimistic tone by Herbert Luft and letter from Stuart Schulberg offering list of documentaries made by occupation government 4 (No. 2, Winter 49) 206–208.

Wollenberg, H. H. "From Adolf Hitler to Stewart Granger." *S&S* 18 (Summer 49) 63–65. Postwar German film preferences: films with Granger in British zone; two German productions.

Silverman, Dore. "The Film in Germany." *S&S* 18 (Summer 49) 66–68.

Mayer, Arthur L. "Disquiet on the Western Front." *Th Arts* 34 (May 50) 47–50. Mayer as head of the motion-picture branch of military government in Germany.

Walter, H. "German Students Seek Peace with the Jews; Behind the Fight Against Nazi Movie-Makers." *Commentary* 14 (Aug 52) 124–130. Students protest showing of Veit Harlan's *Hanna Ammon* because of film maker's former role as star director for Goebbels and maker of *Jew Suess*.

"Movies Find Cheap New Location." *Life* 36 (10 May 54) 86+. Germany's low production costs encourage foreign producers.

Schulberg, Stuart. "The German Film: Comeback or Setback?" *QFRTV* 8 (No. 4, Summer 54) 400–404. Producer of feature films for American-owned film company in Wiesbaden briefly describes West German industry since 1947 and lack of originality in films.

Patalas, Enno. "The Contemporary West German Film as a Social Symptom." *F Cult* 1 (No. 4, 1955) 9–12. An artistic crisis.

"Kuba, the Great." *Newswk* 45 (21 Mar 55) 104+. Biography of German woman film magnate Ilse Kubaschewski.

Patalas, Enno. "Terminal 'Zero'—Germany's Latest Experimental Film." *F Cult* 2 (No. 9, 1956) 10–13. Analysis of Herbert Vesely's *Nicht Mehr Fliehen* (*Flee No More*), with discussion of his earlier film *An Diesen Abenden* (*On These Evenings*).

Zurbuch, Werner. "German Notes." *S&S* 26 (Summer 56) 6.

Patalas, Enno. "The German Waste Land." *S&S* 26 (Summer 56) 24–27. The failure of the postwar West German film industry to produce worthwhile films; some suggested reasons and a few exceptions (Vesely and others).

de Laurot, Edouard. "Germany 1957—Tradition and Experiment." *F Cult* 3 (No. 12, 1957) 7–9. The beginning of a German avant-garde which the author views as a reaction against the commercial industry; it does not avoid the contemporary realities of postwar German society.

Luft, Friedrich. "Postwar Film." *Atlantic* 199 (Mar 57) 186. Short account of German cinema.

Eisner, Lotte. "The German Cinema Loses Its Way." *Film* (No. 12, Mar–Apr 57) 9–12.

Fenin, George N., and William K. Everson. "The European Western." *F Cult* (No. 20, 1959). *See 4k(2).*

"Tycoon Named Ilse." *Time* 74 (12 Oct 59) 84. Woman is boss of a German studio.

Luft, Herbert G. "Germany Today." *JSPG* (Dec 59) 10–13. Recent film making.

Zurbuch, Werner. "Young German Directors." *FQ* 14 (No. 3, Spring 61) 65.

Donaldson, Geoffrey. "The Shadow Still Remains." *F&F* 7 (No. 9, June 61) 33–34. Post-World War II production in Germany.

Vas, Robert. "Fifteen Years After: Notes from West Germany." *S&S* 30 (Autumn 61) 201–203. Films include Bernard Wicki's *The Bridge* and Helmut Kautner's *Black Gravel*.

Bean, Robin. "Nein Neue Welle." *F&F* 8 (No. 7, Apr 62) 12+. Decline of German films.

Vas, Robert. "'Papa' and His Children." *S&S* 31 (Summer 62) 121. Note on manifesto by twenty-six young directors in Germany and a grant to them by the older producers.

Bean, Robin. "The Face of '63: No. 5—Germany." *F&F* 9 (No. 9, June 63) 41–48. German actors, directors, and producers who are likely to make an impact on the films of 1963; East and West Germany.

Bean, Robin. "Hand Up, Hans!" *F&F* 11 (No. 1, Oct 64) 53. Current German films.

Gregor, Ulrich. "The German Film in 1964: Stuck at Zero." *FQ* 18 (No. 2, Winter 64–65) 7–21. Neither established German directors (Kautner, Staudte, Wicki) nor the French New Wave–influenced "Oberhausen group" (the Viennese Herbert Vesely, Hans Jurgen Pohland from Berlin, Ferdinand Khittl from Munich) seem to have found public or critical acceptance; perhaps television, film schools, and film magazines will help. See also letter from D. S. Hull and Gregor's reply 19 (No. 1, Fall 65) 63–64.

Schoenbaum, David. "Letter from Germany." *S&S* 34 (Winter 64–65) 32–33. There is support for opera and theatre, but subsidies and prizes for films are erratic; one young distributor, Hanns Eckelkamp in Duisburg, shows and publicizes imported films and plans to produce.

Cohen, Jules. "The Chronic Crisis in West German Film." *F Com* 3 (No. 1, Winter 65) 32–35. A critical report on the films of Lang, Dieterle, Siodmak, Kautner, Thiele, Wicki, Staudte, Zbonek, and Vesely.

Patalas, Enno. "The *Kolberg* Case." *S&S* 35 (Winter 65–66) 22–23. Veit Harlan's last film for Goebbels has now been shown uncut in Germany, with introduction and epilogue.

Bucher, Felix. "Twenty Years of German Post-War Films." *Camera* 45 (No. 11, Nov 66) 56.

"Fade—And Come-Back?" *Economist* 223 (22 Apr 67) 342. Controversy over certain scenes in the film version of Gunter Grass' *Cat and Mouse*.

Falkenberg, B. "New Wave German Style." *Partisan Rev* 35 (Fall 68) 599–604. Theoretical bases of recent German films.

Baxter, Brian. "Werner Herzog and Jean-Marie Straub." *Film* (No. 54, Spring 69) 35–36. Critical and historical remarks on the work of two German directors.

"Young German Film." *F Com* 6 (No. 1, Spring 70) 32–45. Reprint from *Der Spiegel*, Hamburg weekly (No. 53, 1967), traces work of various young directors from shorts seen at Oberhausen in 1961 through films subsidized by government beginning in 1965.

von Praunheim, Rosa. "Stories of Revolution." *F&F* 16 (No. 8, May 70) 88–89. On West German underground film making.

Thoms, Albie. "German Underground." *Afterimage* (No. 2, Autumn 70) 44–55. The current scene.

4e(5). SCANDINAVIA

Hardy, H. Forsyth. "The Cinema in Scandinavia." *S&S* 6 (No. 23, Autumn 37) 129–132.

Hardy, H. Forsyth. "Lighthearted Vikings." *S&S* 6 (No. 24, Winter 37–38) 174–175.

Denmark and Norway are emphasized in this study of Scandinavian films.

Ege, Friedrich. "The Land Closed with Seven Seals." *S&S* 7 (No. 25, Spring 38) 20–21. An overview of the film industry in Finland.

Ege, Friedrich. "Orko." *S&S* 9 (No. 35, Autumn 40) 46. A sketch of Orko, who helped to build the Finnish cinema.

Jackson, Ragna. "The Scandinavian Film." *Penguin F Rev* 2 (Jan 47) 74–79; 3 (Aug 47) 62–67. Early Scandinavian films as part of world film industry; contemporary work; two articles.

Geis, Gilbert. "Municipal Motion-Picture Theatre Ownership in Norway." *QFRTV* 9 (No. 1, Fall 54). *See 6e.*

Card, James. "Influences of the Danish Film." *Image* 5 (No. 3, Mar 56) 51–57. In particular, compares August Blom's *Atlantis* with the films of D. W. Griffith.

Milne, Tom. "Cold Tracks." *S&S* 32 (Winter 62–63) 13–14. Norwegian films are few, but *Kalde Spor* deserves to be seen.

Schickel, Richard. "Scandinavian Screen." *Holiday* 40 (Nov 66) 156–157+. Current trends.

Wynne-Ellis, Michael. "Finland." *S&S* 38 (Autumn 69) 182. New films "youngish, critical and teeming with social comment."

4e(5a). Denmark

[See 5, Biography: Carl Dreyer, Asta Nielsen.]

Holmes, Winifred. "Your Freedom Is at Stake!" *S&S* 15 (No. 60, Winter 46–47). *See 8c(4).*

Podselver, Judith. "Motion Pictures in Denmark." *Hwd Q* 3 (No. 2, Winter 47–48). Correspondent from Paris describes work by Dreyer.

Cockshott, Gerald. "Films in Denmark." *S&S* 17 (No. 67, Autumn 48) 114–116.

Neergaard, Ebbe. "The Rise, the Fall, and the Rise of Danish Film." *Hwd Q* 4 (No. 3, Spring 50) 217–232. Director of Danish government film office traces history from 1906 through the "great period" (1911–1914) to Dreyer (from 1920), wartime documentaries, and after.

Neergaard, Ebbe. "Feature Films Preferred by Danish Youth." *QFRTV* 7 (No. 3, Spring 53) 279–290. Ten films most often named by fifteen-to-twenty-four age group in four different kinds of districts.

Ford, Charles. "Danish Films." *FIR* (Feb 54) 72–74. Brief history of the Danish film industry of the silent film era; Carl Dreyer's *The Passion of Joan of Arc* was a French product made in Paris.

Neergaard, Ebbe. "*The Word.*" *S&S* 24 (Spring 55) 172+. Carl Dreyer's new film a popular success in Denmark.

Marcussen, E. B. "Danish Film Production." *Am Scandinavian Rev* 43 (Dec 55) 328–346. The influence of documentary film seen as key to understanding the core of postwar Danish cinema.

Duperley, Denis. "Age Comes First." *F&F* 3 (No. 9, June 57) 11. Danish actors.

Monty, Ib. "Report from Denmark." *S&S* 35 (Spring 66) 70. How the cinema tax is distributed: prizes, film education, production guarantees, etc.

4e(5b). Sweden

[*See 5, Biography: Ingmar Bergman, Jorn Donner, Vilgot Sjöman, Victor Sjöstrom (also spelled Seastrom), Mauritz Stiller, Arne Sucksdorff, Mai Zetterling.*]

Yunkers, Adja. "Swedish Cinema." *Life & Letters Today* 15 (No. 5, Autumn 36) 171–174. The work of Sjöstrom and Stiller: unlike that of contemporary Swedish cinema.

Idestam-Almquist, Bengi. "Motion Picture in Sweden." *Am Scandinavian Rev* 29 (June 41) 120–136. Garbo, Bergman, and other actresses seen as evidence of Swedish cinema's importance and the effectiveness of the training at the national dramatic theatre.

Linder, T. "The Film in Sweden." *S&S* 12 (No. 45, Summer 43) 2–5.

Wallace, Irving. "Smorgasbord Circuit." *Collier's* 118 (21 Dec 46). See 2b(5).

Hardy, H. Forsyth. "The Swedish Film Today." *S&S* 16 (No. 64, Winter 47–48) 131–133.

Lawrence, Eric. "The Motion Picture Industry in Sweden." *Hwd Q* 5 (No. 2, Winter 50) 182–188. Early directors; economic problems; censorship.

Kolaja, Jiri. "Swedish Feature Films and Swedish Society." *Hwd Q* 5 (No. 2, Winter 50) 189–194. Summary of a 1948 Stockholm study of 543 features, 1929–1947, their subjects (social stratification, sex, success, etc.), their happy or unhappy endings.

"Success from Sweden: Foreign Intrigue." *Newswk* 38 (5 Nov 51) 58.

De La Roche, Catherine. "Swedish Films." *FIR* 4 (Nov 53) 461–464. "Outspoken, often poetically sensual"; appraisal of leading directors, including Ingmar Bergman, Alf Sjöberg, and Gustave Molander.

de Laurot, Edouard. "Swedish Cinema—Classic Background and Militant Avantgarde." *F Cult* 2 (No. 10, 1956) 18–20. The experimental film in relation to Sweden's cinematic tradition.

Ulrichsen, Erik. "Scandinavian Notes." *S&S* 26 (Spring 57) 173. A new film, *The Seventh Seal,* by "the most daring and talented of younger Scandinavian film makers," Ingmar Bergman, is awaited with interest.

Burke, P. E. "Young Talent Is Soon Discovered." *F&F* 3 (No. 6, Mar 57) 16–17. Young Swedish actors.

"Around the World." *F&F* 5 (No. 1, Oct 58) 14. On Arne Sucksdorff and Rolf Blomberg.

Borgh-Lindahl, Gunnel. "Swedish Love Life and . . . Laughter." *F&F* 5 (No. 1, Oct 58) 7. On three Swedish directors: Kjellgren, Ekman, Kjellin.

Waldenkranz, Rune. "How Great Our Adventure." *F&F* 5 (No. 1, Oct 58) 9–11+. Swedish film from 1940–1958.

Burke, P. E. "Giving Silent Classics Sound Reincarnation." *F&F* 5 (No. 1, Oct 58) 12–13. New Swedish films are remakes of older ones.

Svanstrom, Ragnhild. "Those Comedians Can Crash the Frontier." *F&F* 5 (No. 1, Oct 58) 15+. History of Swedish comedians.

Dymling, Carl Anders. "Swedish Film Industry Beset by Tax, TV and Other Problems." *JSPG* (Dec 59) 26–27.

Morrisett, Ann. "The Swedish Paradox." *S&S* 30 (Autumn 61) 192–194. The Swedish film industry's worst slump in years; work by Alf Sjöberg, Arne Sucksdorff, and Ingmar Bergman.

Morrisett, Ann. "Sweden: Paradise and Paradox." *FQ* (No. 1, Fall 61) 22–29. The rise of TV and a slump in filming, the deaths of Victor Sjöstrom and Carl Anders Dymling (head of Svensk Filmindustri since 1942)—will the "family feeling" of Swedish film making survive?

Young, Vernon. "After Bergman . . ." *S&S* 32 (Spring 63) 96–99. New Swedish films are generally bad and lifeless: Vilgot Sjöman's *Mistress* and Gunnar Hellström's *Chance.*

"How Sweden's Film God Brings in the Kronor." *Bus Wk* (29 Feb 64) 128–130. The box-office success of Ingmar Bergman in Sweden and abroad.

Coleman, John. "Not to Speak About Bergman." *New S&N* 68 (21 Aug 64) 255–256. Swedish cinema for the past decade centers around Bergman; comments on the emerging style of Jörn Donner.

Fleisher, Frederic. "The Harry Schein Plan." *S&S* 34 (Winter 64–65) 17. For Swedish tax assistance to quality productions, for a film institute and a film school.

Dewey, Lang. "Parthenogenesis Swedish Style." *Film* (No. 45, Spring 66). See 7e(5).

Sjöman, Vilgot. "Catching the Rare Moment." *TDR* 11 (Fall 66) 102–105. Interview by Paul Gray covering influence of Bergman and other aspects of Swedish film making.

Schein, Harry. "Swedish Subsidies Are No Subsidies." *JSPG* (June 67) 29–32.

Cowie, Peter. "Swedish Films at Sorrento." *F Com* 6 (No. 2, Summer 70) 22–25. Editor of *International Film Guide* critically summarizes films seen at festival.

Fleisher, Frederic. "Export or Die." *F Com* 6 (No. 2, Summer 70) 36–37. Everyone denies that Swedish films are tailored for foreign audiences, but the Sandrews company gets about half its income from abroad.

Waldekranz, Rune. "Young Swedish Cinema— In Relation to Swedish Film Tradition." *F Com* 6 (No. 2, Summer 70) 38–43. Echoes of Sjöstrom and Stiller.

4e(5c). Censorship

Lawrence, Eric. "Film Censorship in Sweden." *Hwd Q* 5 (No. 3, Spring 51) 264–269. A continuation of Lawrence's article on Swedish motion-picture industry (Winter 50).

Geis, Gilbert. "Film Censorship in Norway." *QFRTV* 8 (No. 3, Spring 54). See *7e(3)*.

Marcussen, Elsa B. "Films for Children in Scandinavia." *Am Scandinavian Rev* 45 (Mar 57) 22–34. Censorship standards and the founding of organizations to promote children's films.

Hunnings, Neville. "Tribulations of a Censor." *S&S* 33 (Spring 64) 74. Censor board in Sweden wants to abolish itself but bans *491*.

Walsh, Francis P. "Film Censorship in Sweden." *Contemp Rev* 205 (Apr 64) 212–214.

Gross, L. "After Nudity, What, Indeed?" *Look* 33 (29 Apr 69) 80. Censorship battles in Sweden over Vilgot Sjöman's film *I Am Curious (Yellow)*.

Hunnings, Neville. "Censorship: On the Way Out?" *S&S* 38 (Autumn 69) 201–202. The impact of Danish and Swedish liberalized censorship laws.

4e(6). SPAIN AND PORTUGAL

[See 5, Biography: Juan Bardem, L. G. Berlanga, Luis Buñuel, José Luis Font.]

Costa, Alves. "The Cinema in Portugal." *Close Up* 7 (No. 6, Dec 30) 379–386.

Costa, Alves. "Notes on the Portuguese Cinema." *Close Up* 8 (No. 1, Mar 31) 17–18.

Costa, Alves. "News from Portugal." *Close Up* 8 (No. 2, June 31) 141–142.

Costa, Alves. "The Censorship in Portugal." *Close Up* 10 (No. 2, June 33) 203.

Costa, Alves. "Portugal." *Close Up* 10 (No. 4, Dec 33) 336–341.

Joseph, Robert. "A Festival for Fascism." *Arts & Arch* 61 (Aug 44) 20+. U.S. governmental and motion-picture-industry involvement in support of fascist Spain.

Aragao, Armando. "The Film in Portugal." *S&S* 17 (No. 65, Spring 48) 36–38.

Patmore, Derek. "A Newsletter from Madrid." *FIR* 1 (July–Aug 50) 5–6+. Spain's newest actors and directors; American film production in Spain; Spanish film production potential.

"Boom in Spain." *Time* 65 (6 June 55) 106. U.S. producers plan ten major pictures in Spain because of cheap labor.

Aranda, Francisco. "Giving Them Blood." *F&F* 6 (No. 9, June 60) 28+. Films of Manuel de Oliveira and Portuguese films generally.

Cobos, Juan. "Spanish Heroism." *F&F* 7 (No. 2, Nov 60) 9+. The difficulties of production in Spain: censorship and distribution; Mario Ferreri's *The Wheelchair*.

Aranda, Francisco. "Celluloid Armada." *F&F* 7 (No. 11, Aug 61) 37–38. Recent Spanish production.

Cobos, Juan. "Franco's Three Wise Monkeys . . ." *F&F* 9 (No. 4, Jan 63) 67–71. Survey of the last ten years of film making in Spain.

Cobos, Juan. "The Face of '63: The Spanish Influence." *F&F* 10 (No. 1, Oct 63) 39–43. Spanish actors, directors, and producers likely to make an impact on the films of 1963.

Laurie, Edith. "New Changes on the Spanish Film Scene." *F Com* 2 (No. 4, Fall 64) 37–40. San Sebastian film festival and comments on Spanish films.

"The Reign of Spain." *Time* 85 (26 Feb 65) 60+. Film companies at work in Spain.

Ross, Walter S. "Something for Everyone." *Sat Rev* 48 (25 Dec 65) 18–20. Film production in Spain—Jules Dassin, David Lean, and Richard Lester; part of *Saturday Review* report "Where the Action Is."

Clouzot, Claire. "The Young Turks of Spain." *S&S* 35 (Spring 66) 68–69. New Spanish film activity by a group of fifteen young film makers, twelve of them graduates of official school of cinematography.

DeGorter, Fred. "Spain—a Second Hollywood?" *Cinema* (Calif) 3 (No. 2, Mar 66) 34–35. American films made in Spain.

Schickel, Richard. "Spanish Films: Paradoxes and Hopes." *Harper's* 235 (Sep 67) 127–129. Concentrates on Carlos Saura, director of *The Hunt*.

4e(7). GREECE

[See 5, Biography: Michael Cacoyannis, Costa-Gavras.]

Carter, Sydney. "Greek Films: 1946." *S&S* 15 (No. 60, Winter 46–47) 133–134.

McDonald, Donna. "Dimitrios, the Greek." *Take One* 1 (No. 7, 1967) 7–9. A humorous account of film exhibition in Greece.

Safilios-Rothschild, C. " 'Good' and 'Bad' Girls in Modern Greek Movies." *J Marriage & Family* 30 (Aug 68) 527–531. In Greek films the identification of the "good" girl as poor and, conversely, the "bad" as rich is reflective of traditional class values and serves the purpose of perpetuating those values.

4e(8). RUSSIA

[See 5, Biography: Grigori Alexandrov, Boris Barnet, Sergei Bondarchuk, Nikolai Cherkas-

sov, Grigori Chukrai, Mark Donskoi, Alexander Dovzhenko, Sergei Eisenstein, Friedrich Ermler, Sergei Gerasimov, Grigori Kozintsev, Lev Kuleshov, Ivan Mosjoukine, V. I. Pudovkin, Ivan Pyriev, Samson Samsonov, Dziga Vertov, Eugene Zamiatin.]

Attasheva, Pearl. "News of the Soviet Cinema." *Close Up* 7 (No. 3, 1930) 177–183.

Marshall, H. P. J. "The Kino Olympiad: Moscow." *Close Up* 7 (No. 3, 1930) 168–176. Notes on recent Russian films.

Potamkin, Harry A. "The New Kino." *Close Up* 8 (No. 1, 1931) 64–70. Recent Soviet films.

Godwin, Murray. "Sociology, Fate, Form and Films." *New Rep* 67 (3 June 31). See *3b(2)*.

"Film in Moscow." *Spectator* 147 (31 Oct 31) 565–566. Reactions of a Moscow audience to propaganda in Russian film *The Pathway to Life.*

Popkin, Zelda F. "Camera Explorers of the New Russia." *Travel* 58 (Dec 31) 37–40+. Surveys Soviet ethnographic and geographic films.

Potamkin, Harry A. "Tendencies in the Soviet Film." *New Masses* 7 (No. 12, June 32) 18. "Instead of the 'grand' films of Eisenstein and Pudovkin, there is now intimacy of contact."

Schoeni, Helen. "Production Methods in Soviet Russia." *CQ* 2 (No. 4, Summer 34) 210–214.

Ford, Richard. "Moscow Goes to the Movies." *S&S* 6 (No. 21, Spring 37) 9–11. Industry and theatres in Soviet Russia.

Sharar, Dewan. "Film in Soviet Russia." *Great Britain and the East* 49 (16 Sep 37) 395. Report on T. Dickinson and A. Lawson's paper "The Cine-Technician," detailing the scope and progress of the film industry in Soviet Russia.

Montagu, Ivor. "The Soviet Film Industry." *S&S* 10 (No. 39, Autumn 41) 48–50. During the sound period.

Swingler, R. "Sense of History in Soviet Films." *Labour Monthly* 24 (Feb 42) 62–63.

Farber, M. "Russian Victory." *New Rep* 109 (11 Oct 43). See *8b.*

Joseph, Robert. "Russia Fights with Films." *Arts & Arch* 62 (Apr 45) 22–23+. Russian film industry, including exhibition.

Simonov, Konstantin. "The Soviet Film Industry." *Screen Writer* 2 (June 46). See *2d.*

De La Roche, Catherine. "Escapism and Soviet Culture." *S&S* 15 (No. 60, Winter 46–47) 141–142. The Stalinist demand for a more direct relation between art and society.

De La Roche, Catherine. "Scenic Design in the Soviet Cinema." *Penguin F Rev* 3 (Aug 47) 76–80. Past and current designers: Egorov, Kozlovsky, and Eisenstein.

Macleod, Joseph. "Stereoscopic Film." *S&S* 16 (No. 63, Autumn 47). See *2m(2).*

Burov, Semyon. "Realism the Basis of Soviet Film Art." *Penguin F Rev* 4 (Oct 47). See *3a(2).*

De La Roche, Catherine. "The Soviet Cinema and Youth." *Penguin F Rev* 4 (Oct 47) 109–113. Opportunities for young people in production.

De La Roche, Catherine. "The Soviet Cinema and Science." *Penguin F Rev* 5 (Jan 48) 77–81. Cinema in the USSR is used more and more to popularize science.

De La Roche, Catherine. "Actors of the Soviet Cinema." *Penguin F Rev* 6 (Apr 48) 104–110. The Moscow Art Theatre and a review of some actors now in Soviet films.

De La Roche, Catherine. "The State Institute of Cinema and the Film Actors' Theatre in Moscow." *S&S* 17 (No. 66, Summer 48) 101–102.

"Night at the Movies in Moscow." *Time* 55 (20 Feb 50) 30. Description of Moscow's theatres.

Hunkin, Elizabeth. "Moscow Entertainment." *Spectator* 185 (27 Oct 50) 414. Soviet audiences, their tastes and reactions to opera, ballet, drama, and cinema.

Rimberg, John. "The Soviet Film Industry Today." *QFRTV* 11 (No. 2, Winter 56) 149–153. Co-author of *The Soviet Film Industry* (Praeger, 1955) gives statistics and recent personnel changes.

Medvedev, A. "Birth of a Film-Maker." *F&F* 5 (No. 4, Jan 59) 12. Training at the Soviet Institute of Cinematography.

Frankel, Tobia. "Sovietski Ekran." *NYTM* (15 Mar 59) 52+. Russia's version of a movie magazine.

Weeks, Edward. "The Peripatetic Reviewer." *Atlantic* 205 (Mar 60) 108+. Visit to film studios at Leningrad; present situation in Russian movie industry.

Hill, Steven P. "Soviet Film Criticism." *FQ* 14 (No. 1, Fall 60) 31–40. Film books and magazines; from *Iskusstvo Kino*, the critical journal, is drawn an extensive report on films and film reviewing in the USSR.

Davidov, Alexander. "Exchange Is Not Robbery." *F&F* 7 (No. 6, Mar 61) 33. On foreign distribution of Soviet films.

Feyder, Mikhail. "The Cinemas." *F&F* 7 (No. 6, Mar 61) 10+. Soviet film exhibition.

Semenov, Rostislav. "The Studios." *F&F* 7 (No. 6, Mar 61) 11. Soviet film production.

Vengherov, Vladimir. "Give Me Actors—Not Stars." *F&F* 7 (No. 6, Mar 61) 12+. Soviet director writes about directing in USSR.

Kapler, Alexei. "Fury Behind a Pen." *F&F* 7 (No. 6, Mar 61) 13. Writing for Soviet films.

Guroshev, Alexander. "Giving Youth Its Chance." *F&F* 7 (No. 6, Mar 61) 14. Training in the Soviet State Institute of Cinematography.

Ivanov, Boris. "Our 'Method.' " *F&F* 7 (No. 6, Mar 61) 14+. Acting technique at Soviet State Institute of Cinematography.

Nicolaiev, George. "A Place for Experiment." *F&F* 7 (No. 6, Mar 61) 33. Development of Lenfilm Studios.

Vysotzky, Michael. "Giving Them Real Stereo." *F&F* 7 (No. 6, Mar 61) 33. Mosfilm chief engineer on dimensional sound.

Chukhrai, Grigori. "Keeping the Old on Their Toes." *F&F* 9 (No. 1, Oct 62) 26. Russian director on Russian film making generally.

"More About Novosti." *F Com* 1 (No. 4, 1963) 20–22. Boris Burkov, board chairman of Novosti Press Agency in Moscow, answers questions by Soviet-born student at Columbia, Tanya Osadca, about distribution of news material abroad, including films.

Hill, Steven P. "Film Archive Work in the USSR." *F Soc Rev* (Jan 66) 16–21. A description of the resources and activities of the Soviet All-Union Federal Archive.

Kapler, Alexei. "Mosfilms." *Atlas* 12 (Nov 66) 45–47. Vulgar scripts lead to vulgar films.

Chukhrai, Grigori. "Incentive to Talent." *F&F* 13 (No. 3, Dec 66) 58. Moscow Experimental Film Studio.

"Giant Soviet Film Factory Succeeds with a New Soft Sell." *Life* 62 (7 Apr 67) 65–81+. Behind the scenes at Mosfilm; includes a report, "A Moscow Moviegoer Hunts for a Thriller," by Peter Young.

Roud, Richard. "Through an Ideology Darkly." *Sat Rev* (23 Dec 67) 13–14+. Distortion in in the interpretation and evaluation by U.S. critics (such as MacDonald and Warshow) of Soviet cinema because of political ramifications; part of *Saturday Review* report, "Filmmaking Behind the Iron Curtain."

Hibbin, Nina. "Social Passions." *F&F* 14 (No. 10, July 68) 48–50. Soviet film week at the National Film Theatre.

Hill, Steven P. "A Mosaic of Recent Soviet Writings on Cinema." *F Com* 5 (No. 1, Fall 68) 21–48. Specialist in Soviet film and theatre, professor in department of Slavic languages and literatures at University of Illinois, has selected and translated published Soviet articles about film.

Zusman, E. "Soviet Theaters: To Build or Not to Build." *F Com* 5 (No. 1, Fall 68) 36–37. Head of Film Exhibition-Distribution Board for Far East Coast Territory writes from Vladivostok of the problems of getting a loan from the national bank for theatres in rural areas because it takes so much longer (ten years) to pay it back. Translated by Steven Hill from *Sovetskoe Kino* (6 Jan 68).

Hill, Steven P. "Art vs. Box Office in the USSR." *F Soc Rev* 4 (No. 8, 1969) 30–36. Translation of an account, published in *Iskusstvo Kino,* of a round-table discussion dealing with Russian attendance problems.

Hibbin, Nina. "Living On with Lenin." *F&F* 16 (No. 10, July 70) 25–26. Films shown during the Lenin centenary.

4e(8a). Historical and Critical Surveys

Potamkin, Harry Alan. "Film Problems of Soviet Russia." *Experimental Cinema* 1 (No. 1, Feb 30) 3–4.

Popkin, Zelda F. "Russia Goes to the Movies." *Outlook* 155 (28 May 30) 129–131+. Survey of Soviet cinema and film personalities.

Braver-Mann, Barnet G. "The Cinema of Experience." *Left* 1 (No. 1, Spring 31) 80–83. Soviet films as visualization of experience rather than of sentimentality.

Kaufmann, N. "The Evolution of the Soviet Cinema." *Left* 1 (No. 1, Spring 31) 73–78. A short history. Translation from the German of "Film and Foto, 1929."

Stern, Seymour. "Two Films Against Imperialism." *Left* 1 (No. 1, Spring 31) 83–91. On *China Express* and *Storm Over Asia.*

Mirsky, D. S. "Background of the Russian Films." *London Mercury* 24 (May 31) 53–64. Russia has exercised a major influence on the arts for the last fifty years, particularly film technique.

Mirsky, D. S. "Soviet Films." *Virginia Q Rev* 7 (Oct 31) 522–532. Relationship between science and art of the cinema as seen in rise of Soviet School of film directors, particularly Eisenstein.

Kraszna-Krausz, A. "The First Russian Sound Films." *Close Up* 8 (No. 4, Dec 31) 300–303.

Seton, Marie. "New Trends in Soviet Cinema." *CQ* 3 (No. 3, Spring 35) 149–152; continued (No. 4, Summer 35) 210–214. *Chapayev* and the recent Moscow Cinema Conference; speeches by Eisenstein and others.

Eastman, F. "Motion Pictures in Russia." *Chris Cent* 53 (9 Sep 36) 1185–1187.

MacDonald, Dwight. "Soviet Cinema 1930–1940, A History." *Partisan Rev* (July; Aug–Sep 38; Winter 39). The influence of political committees on the art of the film.

Marshall, Herbert. "Cinema in Russia." *London Mercury* 38 (Oct 38) 545–552. Graduate of the Higher Academy of Cinema in Moscow discusses Russian film history and production.

Beiswanger, George. "Soviet Russia at War: Theatre and Film in Action." *Th Arts* 26 (Nov 42) 682–689.

Eisenstein, Sergei. "Soviet Cinema." *Art and Industry* 34 (May 43) 153–157. Excerpts from an article written on the occasion of the twentieth anniversary of the Soviet cinema.

De La Roche, Catherine. "Development of Soviet Cinema." *S&S* 14 (No. 56, Winter 45–46) 111–113. Brief historical account.

Leyda, Jay. "Prologue to the Russian Film." *Hwd Q* 2 (No. 1, Oct 46) 35–41. Preprint of first half of chapter one of author's book *Kino*: early history (reprint Macmillan, 1972).

De La Roche, Catherine. "The Moscow Script Studio and Soviet Screenwriting." *Penguin F Rev* 2 (Jan 47) 64–69. The history of script-writing in Soviet Russia.

Leyda, Jay. "Prologue to the Russian Film (Part Two)." *Hwd Q* 2 (No. 2, Jan 47) 164–173. The second half of the first chapter of author's *Kino: 1903–1908.*

Feldman, Harry, and Joseph Feldman. "The Claims for Soviet Movies." *FIR* 2 (June–July 51) 24–29. Denial of originality in the films and of clarity in Soviet theory.

Ford, Charles. "Russian Films Before the Soviets." *FIR* 4 (Nov 53) 472–474. A short history of Big Five studios, run by Ermolieff, Khanjonkoff, Kharitonoff, Drankoff, and Trofimoff.

Minchinton, John. *"The Gorky Trilogy."* F&F 1 (No. 4, Jan 55) 14. Comparison of Maxim Gorky's stories and the films by Mark Donskoi.

Warshow, R. "Re-Viewing the Russian Movies." *Commentary* 20 (Oct 55) 321–327. Aesthetically the great silent films are as successful as ever, but this is "a triumph of art over humanity"; *Tsar to Lenin* is at least a record of actual events; Eisenstein was a "skilled hack and a philistine."

Stern, Seymour. "The Soviet Directors' Debt to Griffith." *FIR* 7 (May 56). *See 5, D. W. Griffith.*

Leyda, Jay. "Two-Thirds of a Trilogy." *FQ* 12 (No. 3, Spring 59) 16–22. The political climate surrounding the filming and subsequent failure to complete *Ivan the Terrible;* the actors' indignation at Eisenstein's usage of *mise-en-scène.*

Dyer, Peter John. "Russian Youth in Uproar." *F&F* 5 (No. 11, Aug 59) 12–14+. History of Soviet film making.

Yourenev, R. "A Short History of Soviet Cinema." *F&F* 7 (No. 6, Mar 61) 15–16+. Russian writes of Soviet film history.

Vas, Robert. "Sunflowers and Commissars." *S&S* 31 (Summer 62) 148–151. Aspects of the Soviet period in the 1930s when montage was set aside and the new weapon was sound: everything had to be constructive, impersonal, didactic.

Hill, Steven P. "A Classic Must Be Treated with Care." *F Soc Rev* (Nov 66) 24–25. The possibility of some Soviet films' having been reedited.

Knight, Arthur. "The Bright Spring, the Bleak Winter." *Sat Rev* (23 Dec 67) 12–13. Survey of film making in the Soviet Union from origins to postwar period; part of *Saturday Review* report "Filmmaking Behind the Iron Curtain."

Hill, Steven P. "Behind the Lines: Russia." *F Soc Rev* 4 (No. 3, 1968). *See 4k(12).*

Luft, Herbert G. "The Screen as a Propaganda Weapon: Russia." *Cinema* (Calif) 5 (No. 4, 1969) 18–21. Primarily the silent period.

Baskakov, Vladimir. "After the Revolution." *F&F* 16 (No. 1, Oct 69) 62–68. Origins and general history of Soviet cinema.

Leyda, Jay. "Between Explosions." *FQ* 23 (No. 4, Summer 70) 33–38. Privately produced films after the October revolution in Russia.

4e(8b). Trends Since World War II

Anstey, Edgar. "Cinema: Current Trends in Soviet Production." *Spectator* 174 (16 Mar 45) 243. Russian film criticism as key to trends in Soviet film production.

De La Roche, Catherine. "Soviet Cinema." *Spectator* 175 (6 July 45) 7. Developments in postwar Soviet cinema as planned and directed by the All-Union Cinema Committee in Moscow.

De La Roche, Catherine. "Recent Developments in Soviet Russia." *Penguin F Rev* 1 (Aug 46) 84–89.

"Moscow Movies Edit History, Too, For Effect." *US News & World Report* 25 (19 Nov 48) 76. The background of *The Young Guard.*

"Red Virtue Routs Western Villainy." *Life* 26 (6 June 49) 63–65. Report on anti-U.S. content of *Meeting on the Elbe.*

"The Hair of the Dog." *Time* 54 (17 Oct 49) 29. Foreign films turned to propaganda in Russia, including *The Last Round* and *The School of Hate.*

Wollenberg, H. H. "Soviet Cinema's Change of Heart." *S&S* 20 (June 51) 56–59. Present-day Soviet cinema is only a means of propaganda; Pudovkin himself stated publicly in recent years that the development of montage destroyed the pictorial value of the films and lessened the impact of acting.

Anderson, Joseph L. "Soviet Films Since 1945: 1." *FIR* 4 (Jan 53) 7–14. Stalin and other cultural, scientific, and military heroes contrast with American and British villains.

Anderson, Joseph L. "Soviet Films Since 1945: 2." *FIR* 4 (Feb 53) 64–73. Documentaries, newsreels and cartoons; the shortage of scripts, especially comedies; the rise and fall of the "no-conflict theory"; the inability of film-school graduates to get directing jobs; war films. See letter (Apr 53) 204 for sources used by author.

Blake, Patricia. "Marxist Musicale: The Calf-Length Tutu." *Reporter* 8 (12 May 53) 35–37. A look at Russian movies, based on *Concert of Stars.*

"Love in Russian Movies." *Scholastic* 64 (7 Apr 54) 19. Love, as a legitimate movie subject, approved by the Russian rulers.

"Reds'-Eye View of U.S." *Life* 37 (11 Oct 54) 36+. The Russians make a crude, effective hate-America film, *Silvery Dust,* to be shown in the USSR and satellite countries.

"Moscow's Uncle Tom." *Newswk* 45 (2 May 55) 40. Two Russian propaganda films depicting America's persecution of its black people.

"Corn from Moscow." *Newswk* 45 (27 June 55) 88. A look at the Soviet film industry.

Hazell, Frank. "Soviet Film Makers Have New Freedom." *F&F* 2 (No. 3, Dec 55) 9. Manager of British National Film Theatre reports on a visit to Moscow.

"Love on the Two-Year Plan." *Time* 66 (19 Dec 55) 94. Soviet film week in Paris.

Gillett, John. "Between the Acts." *S&S* 25 (Spring 56) 201–204. After the great formative period, Soviet films have been little more than party-line biographies and dehumanized war chronicles; some newer films which indicate a promising trend.

Vasiliev, V. "Soviet Film-Makers Need *Less* Freedom." *F&F* 2 (No. 9, June 56) 14+. Abbreviation of article in *Iskusstvo Kino* (No. 8). Organization and economic faults of current Russian production.

Hardcastle, Leslie. "Soviet Notes." *S&S* 26 (Autumn 56) 60.

Alexandrov, Grigory V. "*Potemkin*—and After." *F&F* 3 (No. 7, Apr 57) 10+. Current film making in Moscow.

"Soviet Movie Shows Reach for the Moon." *Time* 70 (28 Oct 57) 24–25. A cinema prediction from the USSR.

Frankel, Max. "Soviet Boy Now Gets Tractor and Girl." *NYTM* (23 Mar 58) 50+. Post-Stalin film renews its acquaintance with the facts of life.

Grenier, Cynthia. "Soviet Cinema: The New Way." *S&S* 27 (Summer 58) 236–237. Promising trends: more humanly frail and complex characters, a new maturity in the stories, and an added emphasis on love.

Yurenev, R. "Young Talent Has Changed Soviet Cinema." *F&F* 4 (No. 9, June 58) 11. New directors and actors appraised.

Gerasimov, Sergei. "Social Realism and Soviet Cinema." *F&F* 5 (No. 3, Dec 58) 11–13+. Freedom of the artist in Russia.

Robinson, David. "Russia Revisited." *S&S* 29 (Spring 60) 70–75. Travel diary of visit by Robinson and Lindsay Anderson to the Soviet film centers; the quality lacking in films and in contemporary life is excitement; many so-called contemporary films still deal with the last war.

Khanyutin, Yuri. "Youth Has Its Fling." *F&F* 6 (No. 7, Apr 60) 12+. Soviet film of the 1950s.

Baker, Peter. "The Other Side of the Curtain." *F&F* 7 (No. 6, Mar 61) 9+. Report on a tour through USSR.

Vas, Robert. "Humanist Sputniks." *S&S* 30 (Summer 61) 151–152. New modernism in the Soviet cinema seen in a determined pursuit of contemporary subjects; Kalatozov's *The Letter That Was Not Sent* and Chukrai's *Ballad of a Soldier.*

Bergman, Ingmar. "Away with Improvisation— This Is Creation." *F&F* 7 (No. 12, Sep 61) 13. On some current Soviet films, especially *Lady with the Little Dog.*

Karaganov, Alexander. "Once More on the New Generation." *F Cult* (No. 24, 1962). *See 3a(6).*

Miller, Warren. "From Red Banners to Ballads." *Horizon* 4 (Mar 62) 110–112. Current Russian films.

Hibbin, Nina. "Ivan the Magnificent." *F&F* 9 (No. 5, Feb 63) 56–61. Survey of the past ten years of film making in the USSR.

Gillett, John. "Moscow Roundabout." *S&S* 32 (Autumn 63) 187–189. Some impressions from the Moscow Film Festival, in which Gillett gives clues to current thinking among Soviet film makers and critics.

"The Critic Speaks." *Newswk* 63 (24 Feb 64) 39–40. Soviet Defense Minister gives advice on handling Russian military theme in films.

Shabad, Theodore. "Thaw in Soviet Movies?" *NYTM* (22 Mar 64) 26–27. Stills from recent Soviet films.

Kuliojanov, Lev. "USSR: The Newly Proper Study of Mankind." *Show* 4 (Apr 64) 81. Remarks from the head of the Department of Film Production of the USSR Film Committee on modern Soviet cinema as based on interest in the moral value and purity of the new man (i.e., Schweitzer's *A Strange Family* and Mironer's *Spring on Zarechnaya Street*); relationship between contemporary and classic Soviet cinema.

"Passé Parable." *Newswk* 65 (1 Feb 65) 30–31. Soviet film *The Chairman* is parable of Nikita Khrushchev.

"Russian Studios Steal a Scene from Hollywood." *Bus Wk* (3 July 65) 22–23. Changes in Russian film toward easing of propaganda, profit seeking, and demand for the star system.

"Saturday Night at the Movies." *Time* 86 (12 Nov 65) 44. Stalin and Trotsky portrayed in new Russian film.

Hibbin, Nina. "See No Evil?" *F&F* 12 (No. 5, Feb 66) 43–46. Recent trends in Soviet films.

Hill, Steven P. "The Soviet Film Today." *FQ* 20 (No. 4, Summer 67) 33–52. Since Stalin's death, the industry, the directors, the politics, the films; based on a fifty-day visit and eighty-four feature films seen; new attention to technique and to individual artistic expression.

Hibbin, Nina. "Looking East." *F&F* 13 (No. 9, June 67) 16–18. On recent Soviet films.

Fondiller, H. V. "From Russia, with Love." *Pop Photog* 61 (July 67) 70–71. Prize-winning film by Soviet amateur shows universality of Mother's Day.

Varshavsky, Y. "From Generation to Generation." *F&F* 13 (No. 11, Aug 67) 42–46. Current Soviet thinking about film, including those made in the West.

"The Russian Six." *F&F* 13 (No. 12, Sep 67) 27–29. On six new Russian directors.

Kozintsev, Gregory. "The New Film-Makers." *Sat Rev* (23 Dec 67) 15+. Russian director writes on the current Soviet cinema; part of *Saturday Review* report "Film-Making Behind the Iron Curtain."

Hill, Steven P. "Inquisition in the Other Eden." *F Com* 5 (No. 1, Fall 68) 22–23. Introduction (by editor of series of articles in this issue of *Film Comment*) to article by Eugene Gabrilovich; background and brief details of persons blacklisted under Stalin and during the postwar period.

Gabrilovich, Eugene. "Stories of What Has Passed." *F Com* 5 (No. 1, Fall 68) 23–27. Soviet screenwriter tells personal story of his blacklisting in 1949 (for a year or more) and remembers an earlier encounter with Stalin at Gorky's house; translated by Steven Hill from *Iskusstvo Kino* (No. 2, 1966) 41–45; annotated filmography.

Leiser, Erwin. *"Ordinary Fascism."* *F Com* 5 (No. 1, Fall 68) 50–51. Co-director of West Berlin Film and TV School describes a new Soviet film by Mikhail Romm which attempts through hitherto unknown archive material to show the dangers and attractions of fascism for the average man.

Hudson, Roger. "Letter from Moscow." *Film* (No. 53, Winter 68–69) 10–15. Contemporary Russian film-making activities.

Hill, Steven P. "Recent Russian Films." *F Soc Rev* 4 (No. 8, 1969) 22–29.

4e(9). EASTERN EUROPE

[See 5, Biography: Paul Fejos, Miklós Jancsó, George Pal, Istvan Szabo.]

Wollenberg, H. H. "Behind 'The Iron Curtain.'" *S&S* 14 (No. 56, Winter 45–46) 116–117. A brief account of film in Hungary, Bulgaria, and Poland.

Seton, Marie. "Yugoslav Films: The First Two Years." *S&S* 16 (No. 62, Summer 47) 47–49.

Sinetar, George. "The Hungarian Film." *S&S* 16 (No. 62, Summer 47) 52.

Sheridan, Paul. "Hungary Starts Again." *S&S* 16 (No. 64, Winter 47–48) 151–153.

Rosio, Bengt. "The Cinema in Eastern Europe." *S&S* 18 (Spring 49) 1–4.

Driscoll, John P. "Tito and Celluloid." *QFRTV* 7 (No. 2, Winter 52) 129–134. Describes several government propaganda films and contrasts a cinematic Yugoslav film with a rhetorical one from Russia on a similar subject.

Benton, W. "Satellite Culture and Mr. Marx." *Th Arts* 40 (Nov 56) 70–71+. Czechoslovakia's Minister of Culture on "socialist realism"; the chief of the film division on recent Czech films; the chief of the Hungarian film industry on recent Hungarian pictures.

Marcorelles, Louis. "Hungarian Cinema." *S&S* 26 (Winter 56–57) 124–130. The state of the art in Hungary a few weeks before the revolt in October 1956.

Vucicevic, Branko. "The Yugoslav Film Comes to Maturity." *F Cult* 3 (No. 14, 1957) 5–6+. The development of the post-World War II Yugoslav film industry—feature and experimental film production.

Brunel, Christopher. "Hungary's Films." *Film* (No. 11, Jan–Feb 57) 22–23.

Donaldson, Geoffrey. "East German Courage." *F&F* 3 (No. 6, Mar 57) 8+. East German film makers' current productions attempt to revive traditions of UFA.

Marcorelles, Louis. "Report on Hungary." *S&S* 27 (Winter 57–58) 112. Note on political effects of October rising.

Butcher, Maryvonne. "Films and Freedom." *Commonweal* 69 (17 Oct 58). See 7c.

"Propaganda." *S&S* 28 (Winter 58–59) 4. From East German studios, banned by British censors.

Grenier, Cynthia. "The Celluloid Thaw." *Reporter* 20 (5 Feb 59) 35–37. New trend of Polish, Hungarian, Czech, and Russian films.

Vas, Robert. "Yesterday and Tomorrow: New Hungarian Films." *S&S* 29 (Winter 59–60) 31–34. The years 1954–1956 proved how rich the Hungarian cinema is in talent, but there is a revival of autocracy in the film industry; except for a few recent productions, such as Károly Makk's *House Under the Rocks*, most films are straightforward propaganda pieces.

Neal, Fred Warner. "The Yugoslav New Course." *FQ* 14 (No. 2, Winter 60) 62–63. Decentralization of production and censorship.

Hibbin, Nina. "Peasant Cinema." *F&F* 8 (No. 4, Jan 62) 19–21+. Film critic of *The London Daily Worker* on the growth of socialist realism in Hungary.

Hitchens, Gordon. "Recurrent Themes in East German Film." *F Com* 1 (No. 2, Summer 62) 70–73. Quotations from catalogs.

Laurie, Edith. "Film Making in Bulgaria." *F Com* 2 (No. 2, 1964) 40–42.

Vas, Robert. "Out of the Plain." *S&S* 35 (Summer 66) 151–152. Brief report on the state of Hungarian cinema, including Miklós Jancsó's *The Round-Up*.

Magyar, Balint. "The Early Hungarian Cinema." *Cinema Studies* 2 (No. 3, Mar 67) 54–57. Report on a compilation film of early reels, including Lumière footage from 1896.

Hemming, Roy, and William Johnson. "The Lively Arts." *Senior Scholastic* 91 (12 Oct 67) 26. On Eastern European film.

Gheorghiu, Mihnea. "Young Faces, Young Hearts." *Sat Rev* 50 (23 Dec 67) 16–17. Rumanian cinema; part of *Saturday Review* report "Film-Making Behind the Iron Curtain."

Toeplitz, Jerzy. "Cinema in Eastern Europe." *CJ* 8 (No. 1, Fall 68) 2–11. Twice head of the Polish film school at Lodz, Dr. Toeplitz describes differences in historical development in several countries and the subtle changes in "socialist realism" since the time of Stalin; based on lecture at University of Kansas.

Nogueira, Rui, and Nicoletta Zalaffi. "All Men Are Film-Makers." *Film* (No. 53, Winter 68–69) 32–33. An interview with the Yugoslav film maker Vatroslav Mimica, who discusses his own work.

Forman, Rose. "Television for Children, Socialist Style." *F Com* 5 (No. 2, Fall 69) 66–69. Reports on children's films made in Poland, Czechoslovakia, Hungary, Yugoslavia, Bulgaria.

Harnack, Curtis. "Film Scene at Pula." *Nation* 209 (15 Dec 69) 676+. Report on the Yugoslav Film Festival.

Budgen, Suzanne. "The Festival of the Hungarian Feature Film—Pecs, 1969." *Screen* 11 (No. 2, 1970) 58–63.

Crick, Philip. "Three East European Directors—Makavejev, Menzel, Jancsó." *Screen* 11 (No. 2, 1970) 64–71.

"New Wave in Hungary." *Newswk* 75 (12 Jan 70) 75. The more liberal atmosphere fostered by Communist party chief Janos Kadar.

Oppenheim, Norbert. "Makavejev in Montreal." *S&S* 39 (Spring 70) 73. A few questions about the Yugoslav director's preferences.

Robinson, David. "Quite Apart from Miklós Jancsó . . ." *S&S* 39 (Spring 70) 84–89. Brief history of the Hungarian cinema; the work of three directors in their forties, Andras Kovács, János Herskó and Péter Bacsó, plus younger new talents.

Young, V. "Films from Hungary and Brazil." *Hudson Rev* 23 (Spring 70) 116–121.

4e(9a). Poland

[*See* 5, *Biography: Walerian Borowczyk, Wojciech Has, Roman Polanski, Jerzy Skolimowski, Andrzej Wajda.*]

Cenkalski, Christina, and Eugene Cenkalski. "Polish Film Builds for the Future." *Hwd Q* 2 (No. 3, Apr 47) 294–296. Recent history of state agency Film Polski.

Brinson, Peter. "How to Build a Film Industry." *F&F* 1 (No. 12, Sep 55) 8. In Poland.

Rohonyi, C. "Polish Film and Theatre Posters; With German and French Texts." *Graphis* 12 (Jan 56) 68–77+.

Moskowitz, Gene. "The Uneasy East." *S&S* 27 (Winter 57–58) 136–140. The state of the art in Poland; the author interviews Aleksander Ford; the philosophy of Polish cinema since the bloodless revolution which gave the country more freedom from Russia; the work of directors Andrzej Munk, Jerzy Kawalerowicz, and others.

Bukowiecki, Leon. "Polish Cinema After World War II." *F Cult* 4 (No. 16, 1958) 7–10.

Bukowiecki, Leon. "Early Polish Films." *F&F* 4 (No. 12, Sep 58) 12.

Bukowiecki, Leon. "Modern Polish Cinema." *F&F* 5 (No. 3, Dec 58) 28+. Rise of Polish films after World War II.

Michalek, Boleslaw. "Warsaw: The Rate for the Job." *S&S* 29 (Spring 60) 68. Note on new method of paying film salaries in accordance with box office.

Michalek, Boleslaw. "The Polish Drama." *S&S* 29 (Autumn 60) 198–200. A report on the developments of Polish cinema since *A Generation* and *Kanal*: a new note of mockery; Aleksander Ford's spectacle *The Teutonic Knights;* attempts by several young film makers to come to grips with contemporary questions.

Lovell, Alan. "Polish Cinema Today." *New S&N* 60 (17 Dec 60) 970. Comments on the National Film Theatre's season of new Polish films, with emphasis on Andrzej Munk's *Eroica* and Andrzej Wajda's *Lotna*.

Hull, David Stewart. "New Films from Poland." *FQ* 14 (No. 3, Spring 61) 24–29. Has the impetus disappeared from the revolution in Polish cinema? Some recent films by Wajda, Morgenstern, Kaniewska, Rozewicz.

Baker, Peter. "Another Word for It." *F&F* 8 (No. 2, Nov 61) 11–12+. Polish political conditions and recent films.

Williamson, D. C. "Dealing with the Establishment." *F&F* 8 (No. 2, Nov 61) 13–14+. The Polish film industry and the establishment.

Munk, Andrzej. "National Character and the Individual." *F&F* 8 (No. 2, Nov 61) 15+. How national character influences the film artist.

"Polish Cinema." *Film* (No. 31, Spring 62) 22–27. A survey of recent films, actors, directors.

Michalek, Boleslaw. "Warsaw Notes." *S&S* 34 (Summer 65) 122. Novelists become film makers; Tadeusz Konwicki has just finished *Salto*.

Kaluzynski, Zygmunt. "Film Polski." *Atlas* 12 (Nov 66) 47–48. Lack of creativity in two Polish films, *The Ashes* and *Pharaoh*.

Hill, Steven P. "Some Recent Polish Films."

F Soc Rev (Feb 68) 18–22. Brief remarks on recent films by Wajda and Konwicki.

"Poland." *S&S* 37 (Summer 68) 129. Purges following student demonstrations take anti-Jewish turn as Jerzy Toeplitz is removed as film-school rector and Aleksander Ford deposed as artistic director of studio film unit.

Hedges, Charles. "Poland." *Film* (No. 56, Autumn 69) 10–14. Recent Polish cinema.

4e(9b). Czechoslovakia

[See 5, Biography: *Milos Forman, Pavel Hobl, Jan Kadar, Jiri Menzel, Karel Zeman*.]

Santar, Karel. "The Brief History of the Czech Motion Pictures." *Close Up* 8 (No. 1, Mar 31) 34–37.

Plicka, Karel. *"On the Mountains and in the Valleys." Close Up* 8 (No. 2, June 31) 96–99. The Czech director discusses his film of the same title.

Santar, Karel. "The Film in Czechoslovakia." *CQ* 1 (No. 2, Winter 32) 96–99.

Jezek, Svatopluk. "The Events of Czech Film." *Close Up* 9 (No. 4, Dec 32) 237–241. An account of Czech film during recent years.

Santar, Karel. "*Prague Castle* and Other Czech Shorts." *Close Up* 10 (No. 2, June 33) 125–127.

Weiss, Jiri. "Film in Czechoslovakia." *S&S* 11 (No. 44, Spring 43) 92–94.

Hofman, J. "Czech Cartoons." *S&S* 15 (No. 60, Winter 46–47) 125.

Tempest, Peter. "The Czechoslovak Film Industry." *Sequence* (No. 1, Dec 46) 13–14. Recent organization and development.

Manvell, Roger. "The Film in Czechoslovakia." *S&S* 15 (No. 60, Winter 46–47) 130–132.

Podselver, Judith. "Motion Pictures in Central Europe." *Screen Writer* 2 (May 47) 30–34. On Czech and Austrian film making.

Dent, Alan. "Czechoslovakiana." *Illus London News* 210 (17 May 47) 530. Czech film festival in Glasgow, with emphasis on *Men Without Wings*.

Brichta, Jindrich. "The Three Periods of the Czechoslovak Cinema." *Penguin F Rev* 3 (Aug 47) 53–58.

Karpf, R. "Cinema Block-Head." *NYTM* (14 Dec 47) 32. Note on Czech puppet characters.

Weiss, Jiri. "Czech Cinema Has Arrived." *F&F* 5 (No. 6, Mar 59) 8+. Weiss answers questions about film.

Bocek, J. "Czechoslovak Puppet Films; with German and French Texts." *Graphis* 16 (Sep 60). See *2h(6)*.

Broz, Jaroslav. "Grass Roots." *F&F* 11 (No. 9, June 65) 39–42. History of Czechoslovakian cinema.

Bachmann, Gideon. "Is There Really a New Wave in Czech Films—and Will It Last?"

Film (No. 43, Autumn 65) 10–14. A visit to Czechoslovakia.

Hooper, Mary. "Forman." *Film* (No. 45, Spring 66) 34–35. A digest of Milos Forman's remarks about the Czech film industry, the position of the directors, and the new vitality.

"Spotlight on Prague." *Newswk* 68 (18 July 66) 93–94. New films, directors, and writers of the Czech movie industry.

"Sweet Light from a Dark Casino." *Time* 88 (29 July 66) 44. A report on the Czech film renaissance.

Svoboda, Josef. "Laterna Magika." *TDR* 11 (Fall 66). See *3f(1)*.

"Will They Listen to the Tales of Hoffmann?" *Economist* 222 (4 Feb 67) 407. Appointment of Karel Hoffmann as Czech Minister of Culture and Information seen as sign of less restraint on future Czech cinema.

"Czech New Wave." *Time* 89 (23 June 67) 97. Report on films shown recently at the Museum of Modern Art in New York.

Bachmann, G. "Miracle in Prague." *Atlas* 14 (July 67) 54–58. Analysis of the development of Czechoslovakian film since 1962.

Gilliatt, Penelope. "Current Cinema." *New Yorker* 43 (1 July 67) 54+. Current trends in Czech film.

Madsen, Axel. "This Year at Marienbad." *S&S* 36 (Autumn 67) 176–177. Note on political problems of Czech directors.

Cohen, Jules. "Elmar Klos and Jan Kadar." *F Com* 4 (Nos. 1–2, Fall–Winter 67) 68–72. Czech directors of *The Shop on Main Street* discuss their film.

Forman, Milos. "Chill Wind on the New Wave." *Sat Rev* 50 (23 Dec 67) 10–11+. Surveys history of film making in Czechoslovakia; part of *Saturday Review* report "Film-Making Behind the Iron Curtain."

Zalman, Jan. "Question Marks on the New Czechoslovak Cinema." *FQ* 21 (No. 2, Winter 67–68) 18–27. Dangers of official censure of some films and of officially requiring that films make money; older directors seem to be able to challenge accepted myths, but younger ones are criticized for unintelligible symbolism; critical descriptions of a number of films.

Liehm, Antonin J. "A Reckoning of the Miracle." *F Com* 5 (No. 1, Fall 68) 64–69. The twenty-five or more directors of Czechoslovakia, more than a new wave, represent a film culture, but not a mass culture; both historical tales and crazy comedy reflect a series of catastrophes in their country's history and the lack of illusion of the younger generation.

Bond, Kirk. "The New Czech Film." *F Com* 5 (No. 1, Fall 68) 70–79. Critical analysis of six features, including *Diamonds of the Night* and *Daisies*.

Dewey, Lang. "The Czechoslovak Cinema: Go! Stop! Go!" *Film* (No. 52, Autumn 68) 20–32. Its history; the work of the Prague Film School; recent films and directors.

Morgenstern, J. "Fragile Freedom." *Newswk* 72 (2 Sep 68) 66–67. The Czech new wave in political danger.

Skvorecky, Josef. "The Birth and Death of the Czech New Wave." *Take One* 2 (No. 8, 1969) 9–12. Historical background; critique of the work of Forman, Chytilova, Nemec, and Schorm; work in progress.

Deitch, Gene. "An American in Prague." *F Lib Q* 2 (No. 4, Fall 69). *See 4k(9).*

Forman, Rose. "Czech Film Festival." *F Lib Q* 2 (No. 4, Fall 69). *See 4k(9).*

"The Czechs in Exile." *Newswk* 76 (27 July 70) 70–71. A portrait of Czech film directors in the U.S.: Kadar, Forman, and Passer.

Dewey, Langdon. "Czechoslovakia: Silents into Sound." *Film* (No. 60, Autumn 70) 4–7. An overview of transition from silent film to sound, and the work of certain directors during this period.

4f. Asia

"Mood-Sharpening in Manila." *Time* 17 (26 Jan 31) 28. President of municipal board declares U.S. movies cause crime, vice, and imitative Philippine films.

Seton, Marie. "Turkish Prelude." *Close Up* 10 (No. 4, Dec 33) 309–315. Film making and viewing in Turkey.

Marshall, J. "Flicker Jitters." *Collier's* 98 (12 Sep 36) 66–68. Chinese and Japanese films.

Sharar, Dewan. "Film Prospects in Palestine." *Great Britain and the East* 49 (28 Oct 37) 601. American films predominate in spite of strict censorship problems.

Wright, R. H. "Chop Ruma Besar." *S&S* 7 (No. 27, Autumn 38) 111–112. Film publicity and film viewing in the Far East.

Wright, R. H. "Our Picture Show." *S&S* 7 (No. 28, Winter 38–39) 152–154. Film responses in upper Malaya, especially to Mickey Mouse.

Sazonov, Alexei. "Activity in Middle Asia." *S&S* 13 (No. 50, July 44) 35–36.

Young, R. B. "A Note on Singapore and Malaya." *S&S* 17 (No. 65, Spring 48) 9.

Freeden, Herbert. "Film Production in Palestine." *S&S* 17 (No. 67, Autumn 48) 117–119.

Harris, E. "Film Production Problems and Activities in Palestine." *Penguin F Rev* 5 (Jan 48) 36–41.

Chase, L. "Hollywood, P. I." *SEP* 221 (4 Dec 48) 12. Sampaguita Pictures, Inc., in the Philippines.

"Film Queens of Asia." *Life* 31 (31 Dec 51) 50–51.

Durgnat, R. E. "Oriental Notebook." *S&S* 24 (Oct–Dec 54) 79–84. Film making in Japan and Hong Kong, past, present, and future; anti-Americanism and the influence of the West and Western stories.

Castle, Eugene W. "Tearful Movies, Turkish Delight." *Am Mercury* 81 (Dec 55) 127–129. A survey of recent Turkish film making.

Ismail, U. "Film Industry." *Atlantic* 197 (June 56) 141. Brief history of the Indonesian film industry.

Peterson, A. D. C. "Kris into Ploughshare."

Spectator 206 (10 Mar 61) 323–325. Comments on government film unit in Malaya and how documentaries translate the issues of this emerging nation for the villager.

"Asia and Movies." *America* 108 (19 Jan 63) 64. Discussion of amount of film production in the Orient.

Blake, B. "Prodigious Outputs of the East." *Life* 55 (20 Dec 63) 166–179+. The film industry in Asia.

MacCann, Richard Dyer. "Films and Film Training in the Republic of Korea." *JUFPA* 16 (No. 1, 1964) 4–6+. The industry makes more than a hundred features a year, the government, forty or more informational and documentary subjects; report on a State Department advisory mission by the author.

Gessner, Peter. "Films from the Vietcong." *Nation* 202 (24 Jan 66). *See 7f.*

Prachasai, Kiat. "Bangkok's Burgeoning Film Industry." *Cinema* (Calif) 3 (No. 4, Dec 66) 38–39. On Thailand's cinema.

Laporte, R. "Director Charming (Prince Sihanouk)." *Atlas* 14 (Dec 67) 53–54. The making of *Shadows Over Angkor*, directed by Cambodia's Prince Sihanouk for Khemara Pictures.

"Lights, Camera, Sihanouk." *Time* 92 (6 Dec 68) 47+. Description of Prince Sihanouk's two feature-length films at Cambodia's first international film festival.

Hitchens, Gordon. "The Short, Fruitful Film Career of Norodom Sihanouk (A Prince)." *Take One* 2 (No. 7, 1969) 19. In Cambodia.

Kayumov, Malik. "Documentary in Uzbekistan." *F Com* 5 (No. 2, Spring 69) 22–23. Interview by E. Semenov in *Sovetskoe Kino* (16 Nov 68), translated by Steven Hill; director stresses importance of emotion and dramatic structure as opposed to news reporting.

"Films from North Vietnam and the N.L.F." *F Com* 5 (No. 2, Spring 69) 85. Annotated list of fourteen available from group in New York.

Hitchens, Gordon. "Filmmaking Under the

Bomb." *F Com* 5 (No. 2, Spring 69) 86–87. Conversation with North Vietnamese film and information personnel at the Leipzig festival.

Cuong, Ma Van. "Newsreel and Documentary Photography in North Vietnam." *F Com* 5 (No. 2, Spring 69) 88.

Issari, Ali. "Development of Film Production in Iran." *JUFA* 22 (No. 4, 1970) 117–118. Describes program begun under Point 4 to make films in order to allow an illiterate population to learn new farming, health, and sanitation techniques, aided by production crews from U.S. universities.

Williams, Don G. "Universities in Overseas Production." *JUFA* 22 (No. 4, 1970) 119–121. The Syracuse University overseas film contracts, especially the Iran project, which was the initial venture in film making and film training for overseas governments.

Constantino, R. "Hollywood's Subversion of the Philippines." *Atlas* 19 (May 70) 55–56. Americanized, the Filipino films show a loss of indigenous national values.

4f(1). JAPAN

[*See* 5, Biography: *Heinosuke Gosho, Sussumu Hani, Kon Ichikawa, Masaki Kobayashi, Akira Kurosawa, Toshiro Mifune, Kenji Mizoguchi, Nagisa Oshima, Yasujiro Ozu, Hiroshi Teshigahara.*]

Koch, Carl. "Japanese Cinema." *Close Up* 8 (No. 4, Dec 31) 296–299. Japanese use of a speaker to comment on the films.

Ogino, Y. "Japanese Film Problems: 1932." *Close Up* 10 (No. 1, Mar 33) 61–66.

"Film Censor Held Liberal in Japan." *Trans-Pacific* 21 (4 May 33) 16. But kissing and politics are watched carefully.

Venables, E. K. "The Cinema in Japan." *S&S* 2 (No. 7, Autumn 33) 87–88. A personal account of an afternoon spent at the Japanese talkies.

Ogino, Y. "Japan as Seen in Films." *Close Up* 10 (No. 4, Dec 33) 353–360.

Iwasaki, Akira. "Honourable Movie-Makers." *S&S* 6 (No. 24, Winter 37–38) 194–197. Development of film making in Japan.

Cunninghame, R. R. "The Japanese Cinema Today." *S&S* 17 (No. 65, Spring 48) 16–18.

Anderson, Joseph L. "The Other Cinema." *S&S* 19 (Mar 51) 452. The postwar development of the Japanese film industry.

Deverall, R. L. G. "Red Propaganda in Japan's Movies." *America* 90 (14 Nov 53) 172–174.

Conant, Theodore R. "Anti-American Films in Japan." *FIR* 5 (Jan 54) 8–11. Since the occupation's end the leftist unions have participated in making films which show American soldiers as degraded oppressors; two were made by Kurosawa before he escaped the "progressive movement."

Anderson, Joseph L. "Japanese Film Periodicals." *QFRTV* 9 (No. 4, Summer 55). *See* 1b(2).

Card, James. "Japanese Film Masterpieces." *Image* 5 (No. 4, Apr 56) 84–87. Six films added to the George Eastman collection.

Schorer, Mark. "Japan's Delinquents: Children of the Sun and Moon." *Reporter* 15 (18 Oct 56) 35–37. The action films of youthful Shintaro Ishihara; an interview.

Schecter, Leona Protas. "War II on Japanese Screens." *FIR* 8 (Mar 57) 108–110. An analysis of the Japanese documentary *Thus Fought Japan,* created from official U.S. and Japanese newsreels, as both pacifistic and anti-American.

Anderson, Joseph L. "The Department of Cinema at Nihon University." *JUFPA* 10 (No. 4, Summer 58). *See* 1a(3c).

"Friend of Motion Pictures." *New Yorker* 34 (17 Jan 59) 20–21. Interview of Mrs. Kazuko Komori, writer on Japanese and foreign actors and actresses.

Ikeda, Gishin. "The Japanese Film Industry in 1959." *JSPG* (Dec 59) 19–21. Number of films, by company and by subject; imports.

Richie, Donald. "Japan: The Younger Talents." *S&S* 29 (Spring 60) 78–81. Three directors: Kon Ichikawa, Nasaki Kobayashi, and Yasushi Nakahira; some new documentary and experimental films.

"Pearl Harbor, Japanese View." *NYTM* (13 Nov 60). *See* 9, Storm Over the Pacific.

"Zen Commandments." *Time* 78 (11 Aug 61) 37. A Japanese company makes *The Life of Buddha.*

Sklarewitz, Norman. "White Villains Wanted: $8.33 a Day." *Show* 2 (July 62) 63+. Why foreigners are in great demand to act as spies, brothelkeepers, and felons in Japan's movie industry.

"Yank Movie Man of Japan." *Ebony* 18 (July 63) 45–46+. Story of Arthur "Chico" Lourant, black American star of Japanese film, radio, and television.

Yoshiyama, Tats. "The Benshi." *F Com* 2 (No. 2, 1964) 34–35. Brief description and history of the function of the man who customarily narrated and acted out dialogue for silent films in Japan.

Ray, Satyajit. "Calm Without, Fire Within." *Show* 4 (Apr 64). *See* 4f(2).

Clayburn, Peter. "Chanbara." *S&S* 33 (Summer 64) 123. Near-supernatural exploits of *ninja* (spies in the feudal era) are still popular film stories for Japanese.

"Outdoing Olympia?" *Newswk* 64 (21 Sep 64). *See* 8c(2).

"Monster-*San.*" *Newswk* 64 (19 Oct 64) 110+. Japanese monster movies.

"A Conversation with Two Japanese Film Stars." *F Com* 3 (No. 1, Winter 65) 61–63. Noboru Nayaka and his wife, Kyoko Kishida, star of *Woman in the Dunes,* talk at Brooklyn College about the film and about theatrical training in Japan.

"Rising Sun Is Blue." *Time* 86 (5 Nov 65) 93. Japanese industry turns to erotic films to fight television.

Steele, Robert. "Japanese Underground Film." *F Com* 4 (Nos. 1–2, Fall–Winter 67) 74–79. Descriptions of a number of works, including the erotic ones by Takahiko Iimura which caused a riot at Yale.

Gillett, John. "Coca-Cola and the Golden Pavilion." *S&S* 39 (Summer 70) 153–156. A diary of Gillett's trip to Japan to attend Expo 70 and its film festival and to do research; meetings with Kon Ichikawa and Akira Kurosawa.

4f(1a). Historical and Critical Studies

Ogino, Y. "Film Criticism in Japan." *Close Up* 9 (No. 2, June 32) 107–114. The state of film criticism in certain film magazines.

Anderson, Joseph L. "The History of Japanese Movies." *FIR* 4 (June–July 53) 277–290. Kurosawa, Shimizu, and others; the industry and actors; recent contemporary (*Kindaigeki*) dramas.

Richie, Donald. "Where the Silver Screen Has Turned to Gold." *Th Arts* 38 (Mar 54) 80–83+. Japanese film—"an overlay of Western manners on an idea which is basically Japanese."

Burr, H. A. "Two-Sword Hombres." *Atlantic* 194 (Oct 54) 104–105. A brief look at the Japanese Western: the samurai movie.

"Exquisite New Films from Japan." *Life* 37 (15 Nov 54) 89–92+. *Gate of Hell, Golden Demon, Ugetsu.*

Shio, Sakanishi. "Dilemma of Japanese Film World." *Japan Q* 2 (April–June 55) 219–223. Caught between East and West in terms of audience expectations.

Strauss, Harold. "My Affair with Japanese Movies." *Harper's* 211 (July 55) 54–59. The Japanese "aesthetic" of film with roots in traditional theatre and painting; parallels with Kabuki and Noh.

Young, Vernon. "Reflections on the Japanese Film." *Art Dig* 29 (Aug 55) 20–21. Basic passions and crises in *Rashomon, Ugetsu, Gate of Hell.*

Young, Vernon. "Japanese Film: Inquiries and Inferences." *Hudson Rev* 8 (Fall 55) 436–442. Attempt to clarify Western misconceptions.

Miner, Earl Roy. "Japanese Film Art in Modern Dress." *QFRTV* 10 (No. 4, Summer 56) 354–363. Former military government official in Japan contrasts historical genres with stories of modern problems only recently seen in this country.

Iwasaki, Akira. "The Japanese Cinema." *Film* (No. 10, Nov–Dec 56) 6–10. A brief discussion of the most important Japanese films which have not been exported.

Anderson, J. L. "Seven from the Past." *S&S* 27 (Autumn 57) 82–87. A short history of the Japanese cinema before World War II; Kinugasa, Ozu, Mizoguchi, Yamanaka, a war film by Tasaka.

Anderson, Lindsay. "Two Inches Off the Ground." *S&S* 27 (Winter 57–58) 131–132+. A study praising the work of Kurosawa, Mizoguchi, and Ozu; reports on *Ikiru* and *Tokyo Story,* Japanese films which offer the sense of inspiration suggested by the title (a reference to Zen).

Gillett, John. "Discovering the Japanese Cinema." *Film* (No. 16, Mar–Apr 58) 9–12. Based upon the recent showing of Japanese films at the National Film Theatre.

Richie, Donald, and Joseph Anderson. "Traditional Theater and the Film in Japan." *FQ* 12 (No. 1, Fall 58) 2–9. Arguing that there is little influence on Japanese film by traditional theatre, the authors then discuss the better-known forms of theatre such as Noh and Kabuki, contrasting these forms with cinema; exceptions, such as the Kabuki-like *Song of Narayama,* are discussed.

Stanbrook, Alan. "The Break with the Past." *F&F* 6 (No. 6, Mar 60) 9–11+. History of Japanese film.

Stanbrook, Alan. "Oriental Talent." *F&F* 6 (No. 7, Apr 60) 13–14+. Concluding analysis of Japanese film.

Richie, Donald. "A Personal Record." *FQ* 14 (No. 1, Fall 60) 20–30. Interviews with and discussions of Kurosawa, Kinoshita, Toyoda, Yoshimura, Mifune, Hani; the "Japaneseness" of their films; the role of critics in Japan; Richie's memories of personal encounters while writing, with Joseph Anderson, the history of Japanese films.

Richie, Donald. "Learn About *Shibui* from Japanese Films." *House Beautiful* 102 (Sep 60) 107–109. Mood and atmosphere: the austerity that becomes elegance.

"East Goes West." *Esq* 56 (Aug 61) 91–97. Picture story on the changing traditions of Japanese movie industry.

Foster, Hugh G. "Japan; the Peculiar Films." *Holiday* 30 (Oct 61) 112–113+. Descriptions of a dozen Japanese films, including *Ikiru,* which show prevailing sadness.

Iwabutchi, M. "Japanese Cinema 1961." *F Cult* (No. 24, 1962) 85–88. Survey of "best films" and directors.

Richie, Donald. "The Face of '63: No. 6—Japan." *F&F* 9 (No. 10, July 63) 15–18+. Japanese actors, directors, and producers likely to make an impact on films in 1963.

Cohen, Jules. "A Season of Japanese Films." *F Soc Rev* (Jan 68) 12–16. Brief comments on New York's Museum of Modern Art program.

Oberbeck, S. K. "Samurai to *Shomin-geki.*" *Newswk* 75 (11 May 70) 96–98. Review of New York's Museum of Modern Art Japanese film series.

4f(1b). Economic Status of the Industry

Lindstrom, Siegfried F. "The Cinema in Cinema-Minded Japan." *Asia* 31 (Dec 31) 768–775+. Profile of moviegoing in Japan and film-production methods.

Butcher, Harold. "Japan Goes to the Movies." *Travel* 64 (Apr 35) 51–53+. Survey of Japanese film industry.

"Sex Is Taboo in Dai Nippon, But Not in Manchukuo Films." *China Weekly Rev* 93 (31 Aug 40) 492–493. Japanese takeover of Manchurian motion-picture company and subsequent banning of American films.

Wollenberg, H. H. "The Situation in Japan." *S&S* 15 (No. 58, Summer 46) 65.

Granada, Yole. "Glamour Replaces Banzai." *UN World* 2 (Feb 48) 28–31. Japanese movie production after the war; samurai films explained.

"The Sword Swingers." *Time* 64 (8 Nov 54) 104+. Japanese movie makers' comeback.

Ozaki, Koji. "Popular Entertainments of Japan." *Atlantic* 195 (Jan 55) 148–151. The rise in Japanese box office receipts since *Rashomon; Ugetsu, Gate of Hell, Tale of Genji* discussed.

Iwabutchi, Masayoshi. "1954 in Japan." *S&S* 24 (Spring 55) 202–205. There were 373 feature films produced and over a hundred documentaries during that year, including *Always in My Heart* (Oba), *They Were Twelve* (Kinoshita). and *Gate of Hell* (Kinugasa).

Richie, Donald. "The Unexceptional Japanese Films." *FIR* 6 (June–July 55) 273–277. Rarely can a Japanese producer please both foreign and domestic audiences; *Always in My Heart* and other emotional stories are more popular in Japan than *Rashomon.*

"For Japan's Films, a Hard Choice." *Bus Wk* (11 Feb 56) 114. Two kinds of products, modern and classic.

Hart, Henry. "New York's Japanese Film Festival." *FIR* 8 (Mar 57) 97–101. Descriptions of several films provided by Japanese producers with government assistance.

Harrington, Clifford V. "Japanese Filmmaking Today." *FIR* 8 (Mar 57) 102–107. An appraisal of today's Japanese film industry, with a report on the production of *Export of Women,* directed by Yutaka ("Jack") Abe during a visit to the Nikkatsu studio outside of Tokyo.

Hart, Henry. "The 2nd Japanese Film Festival." *FIR* 9 (Mar 58) 125–128. New York showings sponsored by the leading studios of Japan.

Prouse, Derek. "Report from Japan." *S&S* 27 (Summer 58) 218. Brief note: studios, production costs, Imai's new film.

Gibney, Frank. "The Teeming World of Japanese Films." *Show* 2 (July 62) 56–57+. Days in the lives of Japanese film makers; lesser-known movies.

4f(2). INDIA AND CEYLON

"Lord Irwin and the Movies." *Chris Cent* 48 (29 July 31). See 7e.

Kelen, Margit. "Hollywood in India." *Travel* 62 (Feb 34) 36–38+. On Indian film industry.

Cressey, Paul Frederick. "The Influence of Moving Pictures on Students in India." *Am J of Sociology* 41 (Nov 35) 341–350. Questionnaire shows foreign films are small influence on audience impressions of Europe and America.

Singh, G. P. "Cinema in India." *Great Britain and the East* 45 (26 Dec 35) 822. Rapid growth and popularity of cinema in India, based on appeal of Western culture, makes film especially beneficial for stimulating social reform.

Singh, G. P. "Hollywood and India." *Spectator* 155 (27 Dec 35) 1063–1064. Enormous growth of cinema theatres and popularity of Hollywood films in India, as fulfillment of need for spectacular entertainment, may arouse population to revolt against current living conditions. Reply 156 (14 Feb 36) 257.

Cressey, P. "The Influence of Moving Pictures on Students in India." *Am J of Sociology* 41 (1935–1936) 341–350.

Sharar, Dewan. "Cinema in India; Its Scope and Possibilities." *Great Britain and the East* 48 (15 Apr 37) 542–543. Reactions of Indian audiences to foreign sound films; illiterates prefer bad Indian films to good foreign imports because of language barriers.

Brock, R. W. "British Film Producers and India." *Great Britain and the East* 48 (22 Apr 37) 597. India possesses all the essentials for a great film industry except the technical knowledge which British film producers stand ready to supply.

Bhattacharya, Bhabani. "India at the Pictures." *Spectator* 158 (23 Apr 37) 756–757. Indian audiences have extreme difficulty understanding English as spoken in the cinema.

Sharar, Dewan. "Cinema in India: Its Scope and Possibilities; with Discussion." *Asiatic Rev* 33 (July 37) 459–481. Historical survey.

"Work of the Motion Picture Society of India." *Great Britain and the East* 49 (15 July 37) 84–85.

Sharar, Dewan. "British Films in India." *Great Britain and the East* 49 (26 Aug 37) 305.

Five times as many American as British films shown in India.

Murthy, Krishna. "Screen World: Foreign Films in India." *Spectator* 160 (4 Feb 38) 174. Future of foreign films in India uncertain; rising preference for Indian films seen in rising popularity of Indian stars.

Abbas, Ahmad. "Silver Jubilee." *S&S* 7 (No. 26, Summer 38) 64–66. A brief history of film in India.

Vijaya-Tunga, J. "The Supremely Beautiful Isle." *S&S* 7 (No. 26, Summer 38) 67–68. Cinema in Ceylon.

"Development of the Film Industry." *Great Britain and the East* 52 (30 Mar 39) 357–358. Financial backing of Indian film industry by the Cine Finance and Banking Corporation.

Lindsay, Harry. "India's Place in Empire Films; with Discussion." *Asiatic Rev* 35 (Apr 39) 207–217. The film holdings of the Empire Film Library of the Imperial Institute.

Abbas, K. Ahmad. "Film in India." *Life & Letters Today* 25 (May 40) 184–194. Scope and growth; social and cultural conditions.

Murthy, K. K. "Conditions in India." *S&S* 9 (No. 34, Summer 40) 33–34. Indian cinema and the effect of war.

Abbas, K. Ahmad. "The Wind in India." *S&S* 9 (No. 35, Autumn 40) 47. Cinema in India; reactions to *Gone with the Wind*.

"Films of India and Burma from the Lawrence Thaw Cinematograph Expedition." *Asiatic Rev* 37 (July 41) 522–524.

Shaw, Alexander. "India and the Film." *Asiatic Rev* (No. 38, July 42) 271–279. Film production, distribution, and exhibition in India.

Moorhouse, Sydney. "Bengal Studio." *S&S* 13 (No. 52, Jan 45) 91–93. Brief account of Indian film making.

Berko, F. "The Film in India: A Review of the War Years." *S&S* 14 (No. 55, Oct 45) 84–86.

Holmes, Winifred. "Postscript to India." *S&S* 15 (No. 58, Summer 46) 43–45. Information films of India.

Vittachi, Tarzie. "Ceylon and the Cinema." *S&S* 16 (No. 61, Spring 47) 12–13.

Keene, Ralph. "Cast and Caste." *Penguin F Rev* 4 (Oct 47) 47–51. Social problems of making a documentary in India.

Rahim, N. K. "The Film in India." *Penguin F Rev* 4 (Oct 47) 69–75.

Abbas, Khwaja Ahmad. "The Mirror of India." *Th Arts* 32 (Feb 48) 51–53. Films mirroring India's customs, social and religious makeup; some comparison with U.S. films.

Dickinson, Thorold. "Indian Spring." *Penguin F Rev* 6 (Apr 48) 62–72. A survey of India for the Rank Organization; location work there not recommended for the time being.

Allen, William D. "World's Second Biggest Film Maker." *FIR* 1 (Feb 50) 6–10. Produc-

tion, distribution, and exhibition of motion pictures in India.

Motwane, Harnam. "Production in India." *FIR* 1 (Oct 50) 19–21. A survey of the state of the Indian film industry by one of its film producers; factors requiring attention.

Patel, Baburao. "Stardom in India." *FIR* 2 (Jan 51) 32–36. Perils include abuse for giving charity to Hindu relief, in the case of a young girl, Madhubala.

Howard, Jack. "The Film in India." *QFRTV* 6 (No. 3, Spring 52) 217–227. UCLA journalism student interviews UCLA theatre-arts student, Ahmed Lateef, about economics, stars, and studios in his country.

Rama-Rau, S. "Letter from Bombay." *New Yorker* 28 (3 May 52) 89–90. Brief look at censorship in Indian films.

Cort, D. "Biggest Star in the World." *Th Arts* 36 (Aug 52) 24–26+. Film acting in India.

Trumbull, Robert. "Focus on the Future." *NYTM* (12 Oct 52) 51–52. In India, U.S. money and know-how help Indians make twelve short documentary films designed to raise standards of living.

Trumbull, Robert. "Movies Are Booming—in Bombay." *NYTM* (5 July 53) 14–15+.

Thomas, Donald, and Harish Kumar Mehra. "The Indian Film." *Atlantic* 192 (Oct 53) 131–133. Comparisons with Hollywood; discussion of the Bengal, Maharashtra, Bombay, and Punjab studios.

Garga, B. D. "Background to the Indian Film." *S&S* 23 (Jan–Mar 54) 158–169. Indian film maker and critic gives a brief history of Indian cinema, primarily the earlier period.

Seton, Marie. "The Indian Film." *Film* (No. 4, Mar 55) 23–26. Since India's independence there has appeared a trend toward the dramatic film, the core of which springs from a realistic social issue.

Gargi, Balwant. " 'Now Trot!' Said the Man." *F&F* 1 (No. 9, June 55) 10–11. Indian scriptwriter discusses realism in Indian films.

Carstairs, G. M. "Indian Films." *Spectator* 195 (1 July 55) 16+. Festival of Indian films at the Scala Theatre is first major presentation in Europe of the world's second largest film industry.

Silverman, Dore. "No Rest for the Actor." *F&F* 2 (No. 2, Nov 55) 25. Industry and censorship in India.

Jones, Dorothy B. "Foreign Sensibilities." *FIR* 6 (Nov 55). See *7a(1)*.

Seton, Marie. "Journey Through India." *S&S* 26 (Spring 57) 198–202. The experiences of a film critic as she toured India, showing films, seeing films, and talking about them.

"Hollywood in the East." *Newswk* 50 (5 Aug 57) 44+. Report on growing Indian movie industry.

Peries, Lester. "A Film-Maker in Ceylon." *S&S* 27 (Autumn 57) 99–100. All of the Sinhalese films made before Peries' *Rekava* (*The Line of Destiny*) were, in fact, South Indian productions, made in studios; the frustrations and joys of making the film with ordinary people as actors.

"New Maharajahs." *Time* 73 (5 Jan 59) 58. Report on the film industry in India.

"Indispensable Queen." *Time* 74 (31 Aug 59) 52–53. The young woman who provides the singing voice for India's screen actresses.

Andrews, Robert Hardy. "Wanted: More Hollywood Films for Far (and Near) East Fans." *JSPG* (Dec 59) 22–25. Especially India and Pakistan.

Sarha, Kolita. "Indian Family." *F&F* 6 (No. 9, June 60) 29. Current Indian film making.

Ray, S. K. "New Indian Directors." *FQ* 14 (No. 1, Fall 60) 63–64.

Hunnings, Neville. "The Origins of Film Censorship in India." *Cinema Studies* 1 (No. 2, Dec 60) 25–32.

Sarha, Kolita. "Discovering India." *F&F* 7 (No. 3, Dec 60) 13+. Film production in India is world's third largest.

Ray, Satyajit. "Calm Without, Fire Within." *Show* 4 (Apr 64) 86–87. Discussion of national traits in Indian and Japanese films, the absence of a naturalistic tradition in the visual arts, quality of disciplined acting and pacing.

Laurie, Edith. "To Have or Not to Have a Film Festival." *F Com* 3 (No. 3, Summer 65) 18–23. India invites competition of foreign films for first festival; government policy and even censorship might change under new minister of information and broadcasting, Indira Gandhi.

Ray, Satyajit. "Healthy Flicker." *Atlas* 12 (Oct 66) 54–55. Film making in India.

Levine, Faye. "Life, Love and the Movies in India." *Atlantic* 218 (Nov 66) 90–93. Reflections by a Fulbright scholar.

Garga, Bhagwan D. "India's Ancient Heroes on Celluloid." *UNESCO Courier* 20 (Dec 67) 43+. On the use of Indian myth in its cinema.

Beveridge, James. "India's Mass Medium." *F Lib Q* 2 (No. 1, Winter 68–69) 25–30+. Features, documentaries, and TV: a general report.

Das Gupta, Chidananda. "Indian Cinema Today." *FQ* 22 (No. 4, Summer 69) 27–35. Hindi film formulas try to reach a mass audience but middle-class pressure (as in Indian life generally) tends to censor the themes and also to suppress individual artists in regional production centers.

4f(3). CHINA, TAIWAN, HONG KONG

"Motion Pictures in the Far East." *Far Eastern Rev* 28 (Nov 32) 532+. Review of production, distribution, and exhibition in northern China.

Burdon, Wilbur. "Chinese Reactions to the Cinema." *Asia* 34 (Oct 34) 594–600. Discussion of Chinese filmgoing and social changes brought about by movies.

"Chinese Sensitive to Western Movie Presentation." *China Weekly Rev* 71 (23 Feb 35) 416–417. The filming of *The Good Earth* and the success of actress Anna May Wong are seen as indicators of change in Hollywood's attitude toward China.

Kong, Alexed Y. L. "Chinese Film Industry." *China Weekly Rev* 72 (16 Mar 35) 101.

Moorad, George L. "Chinese Talkies." *Asia* 35 (Oct 35) 614–619. Realism and stark tragedy seen as dominating notes in Chinese movies.

Treat, Ida. "China Makes Its Own Movies." *Travel* 67 (June 36) 32–35. Since 1931, floods, usurers, foreign domination, and other home-grown subjects; most are still imitative of Western models.

Chien, P. Y. "China's Film Magnate, T. J. Holt, To Seek Ideas Abroad for Development of Moving Picture Industry." *China Weekly Rev* 79 (27 Feb 37) 437–438. Report on Holt's tour of European and American film industries.

Sharar, Dewan. "Film Industry in China." *Great Britain and the East* 49 (21 Oct 37) 568. The closing of China's film industry since the outbreak of war.

Löwenthal, R. "Public Communications in China Before July, 1937." *Chinese Soc & Polit Sci Rev* 22 (Apr 38) 47–50. Chinese film production, distribution, and exhibition; charts of film supply and films censored.

"China's Propaganda Cartoons." *China Weekly Rev* 85 (25 June 38). See 7b(5).

Lieu, Alfree. "Nazi Film Did Not Impress Shanghai Audience." *China Weekly Rev* 94 (9 Nov 40) 323.

Shaw, Lau. "Hollywood Films in China." *Screen Writer* 2 (Nov 46) 1–6. Author of *Rickshaw Boy* surveys the history of film viewing in China and recommends for this audience stories that are easy to understand, entertaining, and instructive.

Blakeston, Oswell. "Chinese Interview." *S&S* 18 (Spring 49) 12–13. Brief encounter in England with Chinese film executive.

"Ex-Smasheroo." *Time* 57 (11 June 51) 32. Shanghai movie *The Life of Wu Hsun* under Chinese government attack.

Barisse, Rita. "New Life—New Films." *F&F* 1 (No. 5, Feb 55) 89. New films being made in China under the revolutionary impulse.

Barisse, Rita. "The Chinese Way." *F&F* 1 (No. 6, Mar 55) 5. Critique of *The White-Haired Girl* as an example of Chinese film making.

Houn, Z. "Motion Pictures and Propaganda in

Communist China." *Journalism Q* 34 (1957) 481–492.

Elegant, Robert S. "Red China's Big Push." *Newswk* 50 (30 Sep 57) 124+. Chinese Communist drive to win the movie markets of Southeast Asia.

"What Makes Run Run Run?" *Time* 75 (30 May 60) 54–55. The Shaw Brothers, Asian film magnates in Hong Kong.

Leyda, Jay. "The Chinese Adventure." *F&F* 6 (No. 12, Sep 60) 11+. Chinese films currently available to the West.

"Twelve Golden Gongs." *Newswk* 57 (20 Mar 61) 100–101. Chinese films, mostly made in Hong Kong, as seen in New York and San Francisco.

Jarvie, Ian. "Hong Kong Notes." *S&S* 33 (Winter 63–64) 22. Mandarin films lean on theatrical traditions.

"Film in the Chinese People's Republic." *F Com* 2 (No. 2, 1964) 27–29. Two articles: one from a U.S. Information Agency research report, the other a review of a "Chinese countryside" film in a Peking literary magazine.

Topping, Seymour. "By Mao: Librettos and Scenarios." *NYTM* (25 Oct 64) 40–41. Stills from Red Chinese films.

Liu, A. "Movies and Modernization in Communist China." *Journalism Q* 43 (1966) 319–324.

Weakland, J. H. "Themes in Chinese Communist Films." *Am Anthropologist* 68 (Apr 66) 477–484. Analysis of 1962–1964 Red Chinese fictional films for signs of sociocultural changes.

"Imperial Dynasty." *Newswk* 67 (11 Apr 66) 109–109A. Chinese films made by the Shaw Brothers of Hong Kong.

"Asian Westerns Take a Bow in the Occident." *Bus Wk* 6 (10 Aug 68) 48–49. Report on Hong Kong movie mogul Run Run Shaw.

Zhelahovtsev, Z. "A Soviet Reporter's View of Cinema in the Chinese People's Republic." *F Com* 5 (No. 1, Fall 68) 29–32. As witness of the Red Guards' "cultural revolution" in 1966, the author describes critical assaults on Russian films and "all the production of entire studios" in China; *Red Pack,* about a peddler, described, and some documentaries; translated by Steven Hill from *Sovietsky Ekran* (1967, No. 8).

Scher, Mark F. "Film in China." *F Com* 5 (No. 2, Spring 69) 8–21. National secretary of the China-America People's Friendship Association reports on history of Chinese films; themes of recent films, mostly about the hard life before Communism or about the battles of the revolution; *The East Is Red,* a stage pageant on film; animation, documentaries, and distribution problems.

4g. Africa

van der Poel, H. R. "The Film in South Africa." *CQ* 2 (No. 2, Winter 33–34) 104–105.

Davis, J. M. "Cinema and Missions in Africa." *Inter Rev of Missions* 25 (July 36) 378–383. Experiment in the use of educational films by Protestant missionaries among the Bantu tribes.

"South African Developments." *S&S* 6 (No. 21, Spring 37) 15–16. Report by South Africa Department of Education used as basis for discussions of film and education in that country.

Chirgwin, A. M. "Films and the African." *Spectator* 159 (3 Dec 37) 986. Remarks on report of the International Missionary Council ("The African and the Cinema"); how film was used in Africa for educational purposes.

Woolliams, Gordon F. "Nigerian Nights." *S&S* 7 (No. 25, Spring 38) 13. The opening of the first cinema in Lagos, Nigeria. Response and argument (No. 26, Summer 38) 83.

Parker, A. P. *"Lasheen." S&S* 7 (No. 28, Winter 38–39) 142–145. A discussion of the Egyptian historical film and the Egyptian film industry.

Schauder, Leon. "South Africa, I Presume!"

S&S 8 (No. 30, Summer 39) 55–57. An account of the film industry in South Africa and a plea for more documentaries about South Africa.

Gale, W. D. "Southern Rhodesian Plans." *S&S* 11 (No. 43, Winter 42–43) 58–60. For a film institute.

Gutsche, T. "South African Cinema." *S&S* 12 (No. 46, Autumn 43) 31–33.

Hawton, Michael S. "North African News." *S&S* 12 (No. 48, Jan 44) 86–87.

Coley, Capt. "The First Feature in Afrikaans." *S&S* 15 (No. 57, Spring 46) 19–20. Film production in South Africa.

Reid, Colin. "Celluloid in Arabia." *S&S* 15 (No. 58, Summer 46) 66. Brief notes on the Arabian and Egyptian film industries.

Dickinson, Thorold. "Search for Music." *Penguin F Rev* 2 (Jan 47) 9–15. Looking for African music to film the story of Kisenga, the composer from Tanganyika, *Men of Two Worlds.*

Berry, Donald. "South Africa and the Cinema." *S&S* 16 (No. 63, Autumn 47) 93–95. History of films produced, film studios, exhibition.

Connolly, Brian M. "Southern Rhodesia—Is This Your Country?" *S&S* 17 (No. 65,

Spring 48) 7–9. Various aspects of films made for and about Rhodesia.

Toledano, Edward. "Supercolossal, Arab Style." *NYTM* (27 Mar 49) 50–51. Cairo's films all follow a familiar pattern: slick fantasy, glamorous stars, and lots of singing.

El-Mazzaoui, Farid. "Film in Egypt." *Hwd Q* 4 (No. 3, Spring 50) 245–250. Pioneers, directors, distributors, studios, theatres, films (fifty a year).

Spurr, Norman F. "Report on *Zonk*." *S&S* 20 (June 51) 61–62. The reaction of various African audiences to a musical film done there with an all-African cast.

Spurr, Norman F. "Movies in Africa." *FIR* 2 (Dec 51) 43–46. A report on two audience-reaction tests on an all-African audience seeing an all-African cast in a film called *Zonk* made by African Film Productions, Ltd., in South Africa and two Colonial Film Unit productions, *Pamba*, made in Uganda, and *Watoto Wa Leo*, made in Tanganyika. Reprinted from *Sight and Sound* (June 1951).

"Yankee Doodle on the Rand." *Time* 62 (27 July 53). *See 6e(1)*.

Tanner, Alain. "Recording Africa." *S&S* 26 (Summer 56). *See 8c(2)*.

Vaughn, Jimmy. "The Dark Continent in the Wrong Light." *F&F* 5 (No. 4, Jan 59) 10+. British and American films' treatment of Africa.

"Kinematografeion." *Economist* 196 (20 Aug 60) 708–709. Going to the cinema in Tripoli.

Wilson, John. "Film Illiteracy in Africa." *Canad Communications* 1 (No. 4, Summer 61) 7–14. The difference in film conventions between the sophisticated West and a preliterate society.

Rouch, Jean. "The Awakening African Cinema." *UNESCO Courier* 15 (Mar 62) 10–15. Recent films and topics.

Padgaonkar, Dilip. "Ivory Coast." *S&S* 36 (Spring 67) 70–71. Note on showing films in a northern town: *Pather Panchali* not accepted in face of familiar Indian musical films; *Breathless* a hit.

Morgenthau, Henry. "Guide to African Films." *Africa Report* 13 (May 68) 52–54. Several brief reference works on African films exist; review of UNESCO catalogue.

Elnaccash, A. "Egyptian Cinema: A Historical Outline." *African Arts* 2 (No. 1, Autumn 68) 52–55+.

Morgenthau, H. "On Films and Filmmakers." *Africa Report* 14 (May–June 69) 71–75. TV documentary maker and organizer of Brandeis University African Film Festival reports on films by or about Africans, including three by Ousmane Sembene.

Le Roy, Marie Claire. "Africa's Film Festival." *Africa Report* 15 (Apr 70) 27–28. Screenings in Upper Volta's newly nationalized cinemas, including *Mandabi;* short interview with its director, Ousmane Sembene.

Peters, Alaba. "Film and TV in Africa." *Africa Report* 15 (Nov 70) 21. Brief general statement; technical and standardization problems.

Mortimer, Robert A. "Engaged Film-Making for a New Society." *Africa Report* 15 (Nov 70) 28–30. New directors in Senegal; Ousmane Sembene, Mahama Johnson Traore, and others; distribution problems.

4h. Latin America

[*See 5, Biography: Jorge Sanjines (Bolivia)*.]

Pound, Louise. "Hollywood Slang in Spanish Translations." *Am Speech* 14 (Feb 39) 67–70. Difficulties with translating American slang into Spanish.

Wanger, Walter. "Film Phenomena: Film World Looks to Latin America." *Sat Rev* 26 (17 Apr 43) 42–43. Nelson Rockefeller enlists the film to acquaint the United States with life and activities in Latin-American countries.

del Castillo, Ramón. "The Cinema in Latin America." *S&S* 12 (No. 47, Oct 43) 58–60.

del Castillo, Ramón. "The Cinema in Chile." *S&S* 15 (No. 60, Winter 46–47) 121–124. Including comments on foreign intervention.

Attwood, A. W. "The Cinema in Guayaquil." *S&S* 16 (No. 61, Spring 47) 14. Ecuador's largest city.

Plaskitt, Peter. "Report from Latin America." *S&S* 16 (No. 62, Summer 47) 49.

Lowry, Walker. "Movies with a Latin Accent." *NYTM* (14 Nov 48) 19+. A report on the film industry in Latin America, with emphasis on Mexico.

Tavares de Sá, H. "Hollywood Needs Latin America." *Américas* 1 (Oct 49) 2–7. How Latin America relates to the problems of the movie industry as a whole.

Allen, William D. "Spanish-Language Films in the U.S." *FIR* 1 (July–Aug 50) 1–4+. Spain, Mexico, Argentina, and Cuba send films to 400 theatres located primarily either in New York City or the southeast area of the country; the stars, the quality, quantity, and content of these films and the leading critic, "Babby" Quintero.

"Coke Tells How to Make a Movie." *Américas* 4 (Nov 52) 8+. Biography of Jorge Délano Frederick, "Coco," a Chilean journalist, cartoonist, movie director, and producer, plus his own humorous recollections.

Wagner, Robert W. "Report from Latin America." *JUFPA* 10 (No. 1, Fall 57) 3+. Films, film clubs, and production among the universities.

Wagner, Robert W., and O. S. Knudsen. "UFPA Visits Latin America." *JUFPA* 12 (No. 1, Fall 59) 6–9. The authors toured eight countries (omitting Argentina and Mexico); they report on production facilities, distribution, theatres, cine clubs, and university training in film.

Gillett, John. "South of the Border." *S&S* 29 (Autumn 60) 188–191. An account of the state of the Latin-American film: excessive plots and excessive music, except for Luis Buñuel and Torre-Nilsson.

"Facts and Figures of the Americas." *Américas* 16 (Oct 64) 47. Tables giving film attendance rates and production rates in Latin America, compared with the U.S.

Dew, Edward. "A Letter from Peru." *F Com* 3 (No. 3, Summer 65) 40. Report on unfavorable audience response to *La Intimidad de los Parques,* based on two stories by Julio Cortazar.

"Walter Achugar on Latin American Cinema." *Cinéaste* 4 (No. 3, Winter 70–71) 35+. The head of the Third World Cinemathèque in Montevideo, Uruguay, discusses goals and problems.

4h(1). MEXICO

[See 5, Biography: Alphonso Bedoya, Gabriel Figueroa.]

Carter, Adam. "Motion Pictures in Mexico." *Pan Am Union Bul* 67 (Mar 33) 218–219. Reviews 1932 period in Mexican film industry as "brilliant era."

Chavez, Carlos. "Films by American Governments: Mexico." *Films* 1 (No. 3, Summer 40) 20–21. Brief statement, with reference to *The Wave* (by Paul Strand) and *Humanidad* (by Adolfo Best-Maugard).

del Castillo, Ramón. "Mexican Cinema." *S&S* 13 (No. 51, Oct 44) 55–57.

Nugent, Frank. "Hollywood Invades Mexico." *NYTM* (23 Mar 47). *See 9, The Fugitive.*

Kahn, Gordon. "Letter from Mexico." *Screen Writer* 3 (June 47) ii+. Working conditions of screenwriters there.

del Castillo, Ramón. "Religious Films of Mexico." *S&S* 16 (No. 64, Winter 47–48) 155–157.

Oliver, Maria Rosa. "The Native Films of Mexico." *Penguin F Rev* 6 (Apr 48) 73–79. Including a report on Cantinflas, Mexico's comic genius.

"Hollywood Discovers New Fields in Mexico." *US News & World Report* 24 (11 June 48) 65.

Wollenberg, H. H. "Mexican Screen-Art." *S&S* 18 (Spring 49) 27–28. Especially the work of Emilio Fernández.

Silberstein, B. G. "Assignment in Mexico." *Am Photog* 43 (Oct 49) 610–611. A travelogue, including a visit to a movie set and a description of the acting style of Mexican actor Cantinflas.

Askenazy, Natalia. "Movieland Stretches Southward." *FIR* 1 (May–June 50) 14–15+. A newsletter from Mexico City: production plans (Mexican and American), theatres, censorship, an interview with cameraman Gabriel Figueroa.

Askenazy, Natalia. "The Two Kinds of Mexican Movies." *FIR* 2 (May 51) 35–39. Analysis of the leading director of each faction: Julio Bracho, a Rightist, and Emilio Fernández, a Leftist; the Rightists dominate the industry.

Waynes, L. "Mexican Movies Grow Up." *Th Arts* 35 (Nov 51) 46–47+. Recent success for Mexican movies—views of Emilio Fernández, director, and stars such as Cantinflas; amusing parallels with Hollywood.

Fournier Villada, R. "He Makes Mexico Laugh." *Américas* 5 (No. 3, Mar 53) 6–8+. A biography of Cantinflas, including a short description of other Mexican comics.

Nicholson, Irene. "Memoirs of a Mexican." *S&S* 23 (July–Sep 53). *See 8c(4).*

Seton, Marie. "Eisenstein's Images and Mexican Art." *S&S* 23 (July–Sep 53). *See 5.*

Ross, Betty. "Back to the Golden Era." *F&F* 1 (No. 11, Aug 55) 7. The ideas behind current Mexican film productions.

Nicholson, Irene. "Mexican Films: Their Past and Their Future." *QFRTV* 10 (No. 3, Spring 56) 248–252. Co-editor of London magazine *Film Art* discusses Toscano, Eisenstein, Buñuel, Cantinflas, *Raíces,* musicals, young writers. See letter from Paul Rotha 11 (No. 3, Spring 56) 248–252.

Aranda, Francisco. "The Rise of Mexican Film." *F&F* 6 (No. 3, Dec 59) 8+. History of Mexican films.

Young, Colin. "Letter from Mexico." *FQ* 14 (No. 1, Fall 60) 62–63. Financing and production; news of commercial production and of Buñuel.

Fernández, Emilio. "After the Revolution." *F&F* 9 (No. 9, June 63) 20. Films in Mexico.

Michel, Manuel. "Mexican Cinema: A Panoramic View." *FQ* 18 (No. 4, Summer 65) 46–55. Mexican critic writes comprehensive history of the industry, which is dominated by a government-supported monopoly and makes over and over the same popular genres with the same stars; "a director's cinema has never existed in Mexico."

Lash, Vivian. "Experimenting with Freedom in Mexico." *FQ* 19 (No. 4, Summer 66) 19–24. The first experimental cinema contest for full-length films in Mexico sponsored by cinema workers; description of four prize-winners.

4h(2). CUBA

del Castillo, Ramón. "Cuban Cinema." *S&S* 16 (No. 61, Spring 47) 8. Past and present.

Meisler, Stanley. "Cuba's Frenzied Culture." *Nation* 191 (24 Dec 60) 504–505. Movie industry discussed briefly.

Brook, Peter. "The Cuban Enterprise." *S&S* 30 (Spring 61) 78–79. Despite the fact that there is no audience for Spanish-speaking art films in Latin America, Brook saw during his visit to Cuba promising signs in the activities of the new Cuban state film institute.

Sutherland, Elizabeth. "Cinema of Revolution —90 Miles from Home." *FQ* 15 (No. 2, Winter 61–62) 42–49. Post-Castro cinema, produced and distributed by the Cuban Institute of Cinematographic Art and Industry; descriptions of films.

Johnson, William. "Report from Cuba." *FQ* 19 (No. 4, Summer 66) 31–36. Touring the ICAIC—the government agency for controlling Cuba's film activity; films, imported films, theatres, and equipment; the Cinemateca.

Douglas, Maria Eulalia. "The Cuban Cinema." *Take One* 1 (No. 12, 1968) 6–9. An historical account of post-revolution Cuban cinema.

Engel, Andi. "Solidarity and Violence." *S&S* 38 (Autumn 69) 196–200. The Cuban Institute of Cinematographic Art and Film Industry; three of its most important directors, Tomás Gutiérrez Alea, Humberta Solás, and Santiago Alvarez.

4h(3). BRAZIL

[*See 5, Biography: Alberto Cavalcanti, Glauber Rocha.*]

Peixoto, Mario. *"Limits."* *Close Up* 9 (No. 1, Mar 32) 47–49. The director discusses his film *Limits,* the first Brazilian avant-garde film.

de Araujo, Roberto. "Films by American Governments: Brazil." *Films* 1 (No. 3, Summer 40) 22–25. Government decrees about film; some educational production since 1937.

Viany, Alex. "Production in Brazil." *FIR* 2 (Feb 51) 28–32.

Barbosa e Silva, Florentino. "On the Brazilian Screen." *Américas* 5 (June 53) 13–16. A detailed study of the Brazilian movie industry and its history, including audience attendance.

de Almeida Prado, D. "Dramatic Renaissance." *Atlantic* 197 (Feb 56) 157–160. The resurgence of theatre and cinema in Brazil.

Fenin, George N. "Film Progress in Brazil." *QFRTV* 10 (No. 3, Spring 56) 253–256. From four films in 1950 to twenty-three in 1954; influence of Cavalcanti; relationship with government.

Neusbaum, Frank. "Breakthrough in Brazil." *JUFPA* 14 (No. 3, 1962) 4–7. A staff member describes a Point 4 program for audiovisual training, motion-picture translation, and 16mm educational film production in Brazil.

Playfair, Guy. "Festivals and a Revolution." *S&S* 33 (Autumn 64) 169–170. Brazilian films.

"Hollywood Producers Go Rolling Down to Rio." *Bus Wk* (25 Sep 65) 32–33. U.S. and foreign film companies discover advantages of production in Brazil.

Tuten, Frederic. "Brazil's Cinema." *Vogue* 152 (1 Oct 68) 152.

Nogueira, Rui, and Nicoletta Zalaffi. "Brasil Año 1970." *Cinema* (Cambridge) (No. 5, Feb 70) 14–20. Round-table discussion on the Cinema Novo with four of its prominent directors and one producer.

Young, V. "Films from Hungary and Brazil." *Hudson Rev* 23 (Spring 70). *See 4e(9).*

Viany, A. "Old and New in Brazilian Cinema." *TDR* 14 (Winter 70) 141–144. Cinema Novo in the context of Brazil's film-making history.

Rocha, Glauber. "Beginning at Zero: Notes on Cinema and Society." *TDR* 14 (Winter 70) 144–149. Brazilian Cinema Novo as an alternative, creative response to the films being made in Brazil that were influenced by Hollywood and were not truly representative of Brazilian culture and society.

4h(4). ARGENTINA

[*See 5, Biography: Fernándo Solanos, Leopoldo Torre-Nilsson.*]

Tew, H. P. "Cinema in the Argentine." *Close Up* 6 (No. 2, 1930) 140–145. Argentine responses to world cinema.

Hurrie, William G. "The Argentine Republic and Its Film Industry." *S&S* 8 (No. 31, Autumn 39) 93–96.

del Castillo, Ramón. "The Cinema in Argentina." *S&S* 14 (No. 55, Oct 45) 80–82.

del Castillo, Raymond. "The Cinema in Argentina." *Penguin F Rev* 4 (Oct 47) 100–104. A brief survey of the present status of production.

"Movies in Argentina Hit by Import Bans." *US News & World Report* 24 (5 Mar 48) 67.

Norgate, Matthew. "The Argentine Cinema." *S&S* 17 (No. 66, Summer 48) 65–67.

del Castillo, Ramón. "Humanity in the Argentine Cinema." *S&S* 18 (Spring 49) 25–27.

Clark, Jacqueline. "Report from the Argentine." *FIR* 1 (Mar 50) 16+. Conditions affecting motion-picture production and exhibition in Buenos Aires.

Potenze, Jaime. "Argentine Movies." *Américas* 6 (Aug 54) 20–23+. Extended study of the history and present situation including foreign movies, new stars, and internationally famous movies.

di Nubila, Domingo. "Argentina Way." *F&F* 7 (No. 3, Dec 60) 16+; (No. 4, Jan 61) 41–42. Two articles by a critic from Buenos Aires on Argentine cinema.

Vinacua, Rodolfo. "Speaking of Argentina: A Survey of Recent Cultural Trends." *Américas* 13 (Dec 61) 24–27. Includes a review of current film trends.

Torre-Nilsson, Leopoldo. "How to Make a New Wave." *F&F* 9 (No. 2, Nov 62) 19–20. New rise of film in Argentina.

Playfair, Guy. "Argentina." *S&S* 34 (Autumn 65) 175–176. Note on government aid for "A" pictures; new young directors.

Solanos, Fernándo, and Octavio Getino. "Toward a Third Cinema." *Cinéaste* 4 (No. 3, Winter 70–71). See *3a(6)*.

4i. Canada

[See also *2h(5)*.

[See 5, *Biography: Larry Kent, Allan King, Don Owen, Donald Shebib*.]

Cowan, James A. "Problems in Celluloid." *Canad Mag* 73 (Feb–Mar 30) 4–5+. Discussion of Canadian film industry, with call for more than mere sentimentality.

Nelson, J. C. "Movie Finds Its Voice." *Canad Mag* 73 (May 30) 10+. On dubbing Canadian films for English-speaking audiences.

Elston, Laura. "What and Why of Movie Censorship." *Canad Mag* 79 (May 33) 6+. Attacks central censorship for entire nation of Canada as exorbitant and morally unjust.

Trent, John. "In Defense of the Undefended." *Canad Mag* 80 (Sep 33) 10+. Profile on activities and workings of Ontario Censor Board.

Buchanan, Donald. "For the Intelligent Filmgoer." *Canad Forum* 15 (Feb 36). See *1a(1)*.

Harrold, E. W. "The Cinema in Canada." *S&S* 6 (No. 24, Winter 37–38) 208–209.

"Films by American Governments: The Dominion of Canada." *Films* 1 (No. 3, Summer 40) 25–33. Early activities of Motion Picture Bureau; first wartime work of National Film Board under John Grierson.

Buchanan, D. "Canada on the World's Screen." *Canad Geographical J* 22 (Feb 41) 70–81. The history and function (in both peace and war) of the Canadian Film Board.

Lambert, R. S. "The Canadian Scene." *S&S* 10 (No. 38, Summer 41) 23–24.

Buchanan, Donald. "Promoting Democracy with the 16mm Film." *Canad Forum* 22 (Mar 43) 351–352. The work of the Canadian National Film Board.

Mackay, James. "Animation in the Canadian Film." *Studio* 129 (Apr 45). See *2h(5)*.

"Film Board." *Canad Forum* 27 (Sep 47) 123–124. Plea for attention to National Film Board in its difficulties with government support and organization. Reply: R. McLean 27 (Nov 47) 187.

"Fight Over Films." *Newswk* 35 (2 Jan 50) 28. The future of the Canadian National Film Board; Parliamentary disputes over finances and political allegiances.

Wright, Basil. "Documentary: Flesh, Fowl, or . . . ?" *S&S* 19 (Mar 50) 43+. "An attempt to sort out" what happened at the National Film Board of Canada when Commissioner Ross McLean was not reappointed.

Parker, Gudrun. "A Comment on Canadian Films." *Canad Art* 8 (No. 1, Autumn 50) 24–28. Development and trends.

Dawson, Anthony. "Motion Picture Production in Canada." *Hwd Q* 5 (No. 1, Fall 50) 83–99. Production, theatres, and U.S. distribution.

Starr, Cecile. "New Ideas on Film in Canada." *Sat Rev* 35 (7 June 52) 36–37. The Canadian Film Board makes all Canada a studio and treats nearly every possible topic.

Pratley, Gerald. "Canada's Film Awards." *FIR* 3 (June–July 52) 277–280. The winning films; *Newfoundland Scene*, "Film of the Year," reviewed.

McLaren, Norman. "Notes on Animated Sound." *QFRTV* 7 (No. 3, Spring 53). See *2g(2c)*.

Starr, Cecile. "Ideas on Film." *Sat Rev* 36 (8 Aug 53) 36–38. About Crawley Films, Canada's leading commercial producer of sponsored and educational movies.

Pratley, Gerald. "Canada's National Film Board." *QFRTV* 8 (No. 1, Fall 53) 15–27. History and challenges faced by government agency; relationship with CBC.

"The Amazing Crawleys." *Scholastic* 65 (22 Sep 54) 13+. Canadian educational-film company.

Durst, John. "Canada Calling." *F&F* 1 (No. 11, Aug 55) 10. Production in Canada: the National Film Board and Crawley Films.

Starr, Cecile. "For Canada and the World." *Sat Rev* 39 (10 Nov 56) 26–27. A survey of the work of the National Film Board of Canada on the occasion of the opening of its first permanent headquarters; recent films.

Bossin, Hye. "Production in Canada." *JSPG* (Dec 59) 28–29.

Crick, Philip. "The National Film Board of Canada." *Film* (No. 34, Winter 62) 42–44. Brief historical statement and account of the NFBC's work.

Junker, Howard. "The National Film Board of Canada: After a Quarter Century." *FQ* 18 (No. 2, Winter 64–65) 22–29. A sketch of the early history; some recent films; last year's statistics; television and *cinéma vérité* phases; the frustrations of the French; the first feature films.

Harcourt, Peter. "The Innocent Eye." *S&S* 34 (Winter 64–65) 19–23. The National Film Board of Canada, especially the old Unit B, which has produced *City of Gold, Universe, The Living Machine* and *Lonely Boy;* comments by executive producer Tom Daly; a brief summary of the activities of the French-language units.

"A Cinema of Dispossession." *CdC in Eng* (No. 4, 1966) 40–53. The film making of French Canadians; Michel Brault, Gilles Groulx, Claude Jutra, Arthur Lamothe, Jean-Pierre Lefebvre answer questions about the artistic and economic development of Canadian cinema; other statements on cinema in Quebec.

McLean, Grant. "The National Film Board of Canada—Present Status and Future Plans." *JUFPA* 18 (No. 1, 1966) 16–20. Its expanded program, now including fictional and feature-length films; its philosophy; its experimental program; a report by a board executive.

LaMarsh, Judy. "Close-Up on Bill C-204." *Take One* 1 (No. 1, 1966) 4–5. Why the Canadian government believes in helping the Canadian film industry.

Morris, Peter. "Canada's First Movie Mogul." *Take One* 1 (No. 1, 1966) 6–7. A brief description of the work of the Canadian film pioneer Ernest Shipman.

"Two Canadian Film-Makers." *Take One* 1 (No. 2, 1966) 13–16. An interview with two Canadian film makers, Arthur Lamothe and Jean-Claude Labrecque.

Madsen, Axel. "Effervescence in Canada: The Birth of a New Film Industry." *Cinema* (Calif) 3 (No. 4, Dec 66) 30–32.

Pratley, Gerald. "A Lusty, Loveable Brawl . . . Etc." *Take One* 1 (No. 3, 1967). *See 3b.*

Slade, Mark. "The God with the Luminous Navel." *Take One* 1 (No. 3, 1967) 11–13. A report of the National Film Board's Summer Institute.

Madsen, Axel. "*Pour la Suite du* Canada." *S&S* 36 (Spring 67) 68–69. Note on general developments in Quebec cinema.

Taylor, N. A. "Canada Views Subsidy." *JSPG* (June 67) 33–36.

Kardish, Larry. "Canadian Cinema: A Brief Perspective." *Medium* 1 (No. 1, Summer 67)

38–47. The industry in Canada; types of films from different film organizations.

Durniak, J. "National Film Board of Canada." *Pop Photog* 60 (June 67) 77–81.

Bryant, Peter. "Making a Film in Bella Coola." *Take One* 2 (No. 7, 1969). *See 9, Noohalk.*

Blumer, Ronald. "NFB: Is This the End?" *Take One* 2 (No. 3, 1969) 12–13. Problems related to the board's survival.

Vineberg, Dusty. "New Man at the Film Board." *Take One* 2 (No. 8, 1969) 13–14. The NFB and its new head, Sydney Newman.

Farber, Manny. "Films at Canadian Artist '68: Art Gallery of Ontario." *Arts Canada* 26 (Feb 69) 28–29. Impressions of films shown in the Canadian Artists 1968 competition.

Hénaut, Dorothy Todd. "Film as an Instrument for Social Change." *Arts Canada* 26 (Feb 69) 34–35. A report on the National Film Board's Challenge for Change program.

Hénaut, Dorothy Todd. "Implicating People in the Process of Change." *F Lib Q* 2 (No. 4, Fall 69) 44–47. The National Film Board of Canada's Challenge for Change program.

Prichard, P. S. "Photographer to a Nation." *Américas* 21 (Sep 69) 36–41. National Film Board of Canada.

Summers, Bob. "Challenge for Change." *Cinéaste* 3 (No. 4, Spring 70) 16–18. A review of the program sponsored by the National Film Board of Canada.

Summers, Bob, and Gary Crowdus. "A Discussion with Tony Kent." *Cinéaste* 3 (No. 4, Spring 70) 18–20. The distribution coordinator discusses the work of Canada's Challenge for Change project.

Cronenberg, David. "Film-Making in Canada." *Film* (No. 58, Spring 70) 27–28. An overview of the film-making situation in Canada.

Aellen, Werner. "The Independent Filmmaker: A West Coast View." *Arts Canada* 27 (April 70). *See 6c(3).*

McPherson, Hugo. "The Future of the Moving Image." *Arts Canada* 27 (Apr 70). *See 3a(6).*

Youngblood, Gene. "New Canadian Cinema: Images from the Age of Paradox." *Arts Canada* 27 (Apr 70) 7–14.

Watson, Patrick. "Challenge for Change." *Arts Canada* 27 (Apr 70) 14–20. A review of the National Film Board Challenge for Change program (community use of videotape and film).

Charlesworth, Roberta. "The Quiet Revolution —Film in Education." *Arts Canada* 27 (Apr 70) 21–23. The present-day and potential use of film in all levels of education in Canada.

Ryan, Terry. "Six Filmmakers in Search of an Alternative." *Arts Canada* 27 (Apr 70) 25–27. Today's concern for the rights of man manipulated by technology; the film makers are Arthur Lipsett, Derek May, Robin Spry,

Pierre Hébert, Ryan Larkin, Norman Mc-Laren.

Coté, Guy L. "Anybody Making Shorts These Days?" *Arts Canada* 27 (Apr 70) 35–38. On the Quebec film makers' shift in emphasis from short- to feature-film making: its results and future.

Yates, Norman. "Filmmakers in Edmonton: An Interim Report." *Arts Canada* 27 (Apr 70)

46–48. A report on film making in Edmonton (Alberta), Canada.

Pringle, D. "New Film in Toronto." *Arts Canada* 27 (Apr 70) 50–54.

Mackay, David. "The 60-Second Capital." *Arts Canada* 27 (Apr 70) 55–56. A brief discussion of the Canadian film industry as related to TV commercials, technological advances, and the future of educational film making.

4j. Australia and New Zealand

Harris, James. "New Zealand Newsreels." *S&S* 13 (No. 50, July 44) 38–39.

Goldschmidt, Eric. "The Development of Australian Films." *Hwd Q* 3 (No. 3, Spring 48) 311–315. From 1909 to the Film Board in 1945.

Duncan, Catherine. "As Others See Us." *S&S* 17 (No. 65, Spring 48) 12–14. Films for the Department of Immigration by the Australian Film Board.

Goldschmidt, Eric. "Australian Production." *S&S* 17 (No. 66, Summer 48) 64. A reply to an earlier article by Catherine Duncan.

Watt, Harry. "You Start from Scratch in Australia." *Penguin F Rev* 9 (May 49) 10–16. Director describes difficulties of making the features, *The Overlanders* and *Eureka*.

Batlett, Norman. "Film Library Idea Catches on in Australia." *Lib J* 75 (15 Jan 50)

125–127. The Commonwealth National Library at Canberra, Australia, has film collection and is distributing agency for the Australian National Film Board.

Mirams, Gordon. "Drop That Gun!" *QFRTV* 6 (No. 1, Fall 51). *See 7e(3)*.

Reid, Russell. "New Zealand's Film Production." *FIR* 2 (Oct 51) 36–37. National film unit set up on John Grierson's recommendation.

Merralls, James. "Australian Notes." *S&S* 27 (Autumn 58) 276. Overseas companies come, but there is no indigenous feature production.

Pattison, Barrie. "The Australian Cinema: An Outline History." *Cinema Studies* 1 (No. 8, Dec 63) 185–194.

Higham, Charles. "Australian Blues." *S&S* 39 (Winter 69–70) 15–16. Note on recent films by Australians and by visitors.

4k. Types of Fiction Films

Wright, Basil. "Let's Be Perverts." *CQ* 1 (No. 1, Autumn 32) 23–25. Pathological cases on film—films by Lang, Pabst, LeRoy, Stroheim, and others.

Roseheimer, Arthur, Jr. "You Make Your Movies." *S&S* 16 (No. 62, Summer 47) 58–59. Films are often made in thematic cycles.

Skeffington-Lodge, T. C. "Projection of Decadence." *Spectator* 180 (2 Apr 48) 403. "Psychological" films reflect current decadence as they neither amuse, instruct, uplift, nor provide escape from monotony.

Sward, Keith. "Boy and Girl Meet Neurosis." *Screen Writer* 4 (Sep 48) 8–10+. "Psychiatric" films settle for "the obvious, the superficial, or the bizarre."

Smith, A. Morton. "The Circus in the Movies." *Hobbies* 53 (Nov 48) 35. Preview of films to feature circus setting.

Peer, Robert. "Hollywood—A Psychological Trend." *S&S* 18 (Spring 49) 54. Pictures that deal with psychoanalysis.

Edwards, Catherine C. "Family Films Are Box Office." *Parents Mag* 24 (May 49) 34–35. A summary of family films by various studios.

"New Fad in Movies: Disease." *Life* 28 (15 May 50) 85–90. Cancer, polio, smallpox, the plague.

"The Favorite Film Stories." *Image* 1 (No. 1, Jan 52) 2–3. Group of basic narratives used repeatedly; tragedies: Jesus and Dr. Jekyll; gypsies: Carmen.

Everson, William K. "The Decline of Charm." *S&S* 23 (Apr–June 54). *See 3b(2)*.

Kurnitz, H. "Antic Arts: Monarchy Makes a Comeback." *Holiday* 20 (Aug 56) 71+. The current crop of films about royalty.

Gow, Gordon. "Success . . . Without the Excess." *F&F* 4 (No. 11, Aug 58) 7+. Standards for suspense films.

Tyler, Parker. "Film Letter: On the Cult of Displaced Laughter." *Kenyon Rev* 20 (Fall 58) 628–633. Recent themes in cinema based on disillusionment with institutions; Par Lo Duca's *L'Erotisme au Cinéma* and Michel Laclos' *Le Fantastique au Cinéma*.

Young, Vernon. "Condemned Man Escapes: Five Films on the Subject." *Hudson Rev* 12 (Winter 59–60) 561–569. Discussion of struggles for survival in *Nine Lives, Scott of the Antarctic, Un Homme Condamné à Mort*

S'Est Echappé, Duped Till Doomsday, The Real End of the Great War, and *An Eye for an Eye.*

Dyer, Peter John. "Youth and the Cinema (2): Candid Camera." *S&S* 29 (Spring 60) 61–65. The cinema's approach to today's younger generation: the European scene and Hollywood's influence upon it, in particular in postwar France.

Hill, Derek. "Women in Love." *London Mag* new series 1 (No. 3, June 61) 65–71. On films that show how women feel when they fall in love.

Alloway, Lawrence. "On the Iconography of the Movies." *Movie* (No. 7, Feb 63). *See 3b.*

Osborn, Elodie. "New York on Screen." *Art in America* 52 (Oct 64) 80–89. Survey of short documentaries and art films about New York City.

Coffey, Warren. "Types and Anti-Types." *Commentary* 42 (Aug 66) 54–59. The "parodic anti-type" as the reversal, mockery, or ironic treatment of conventions, styles, or audience expectations, as evidenced in some of the best contemporary films.

Jahiel, Edwin. "The Ring and the Lens: Films on Boxing." *F Soc Rev* (Sep 66) 26–28. A brief account of American boxing films.

Spears, Jack. "Baseball on the Screen." *FIR* 19 (No. 4, Apr 68) 198–217.

Hewetson, Alan. "Comics in Cinema." *Cinema* (Calif) 5 (No. 4, 1969) 2–7. On comic books that have been made into movies or serials.

Stein, Ruthe. "The Youth Phenomenon in Films." *Cinéaste* 3 (No. 2, Fall 69) 13. The emphasis on youth in recent films such as *Alice's Restaurant, The Graduate, Easy Rider, Joanna, Goodbye, Columbus.*

Ryall, Tom. "The Notion of Genre." *Screen* 11 (No. 2, 1970) 22–32. Westerns and gangster pictures "certainly constitute genres," but the idea of using classical models is unsatisfactory; using a complex of subjects, themes, and iconography might help in teaching.

Buscombe, Edward. "The Idea of Genre in the American Cinema." *Screen* 11 (No. 2, 1970) 33–45. The setting, the clothes, certain physical objects and attitudes toward them—the outer visual conventions—are perhaps more important in a popular genre such as the Western than are history, archetypes, or auteurs.

Carson, L. M. Kit. "The Loser Hero." *Show* (Jan 70) 38–43. Short history of the motorcycle movie from *The Wild One* to *Little Fauss and Big Halsy;* American motorcycle filmography included (1953–1970).

Hyatt, Hannah. "The River, a Creative Symbol." *F Lib Q* 3 (No. 2, Spring 70) 26–29. A review of river films: *The River* (1939), *Forgotten River* (1965), *Mekong—River of Asia* (1966); includes a list of such films.

Didion, Joan. "Nine Bike Movies in Seven Vroom! Days." *Life* 68 (8 May 70) 4. A short critique of the motorcycle film as a reflection of its audience.

Collins, Richard. "Genre: A Reply to Ed Buscombe." *Screen* 11 (Nos. 4–5, 1970) 66–75.

Tudor, Andrew. "Genre: Theory and Mispractice in Film Criticism." *Screen* 11 (No. 6, 1970) 33–43.

Levitt, Rosalind. "Happy or Not, Those Days Are Here Again." *Show* (23 July 70) 12–19. Discussion of the lure of 1930s themes in films and plays as based on across-the-decades sympathy of the rootlessness of the Depression era (*The Damned, Bonnie and Clyde, They Shoot Horses, Don't They?, Myra Breckinridge*).

Bromwich, David. "Hollywood Discovers 'The Revolution.'" *Dissent* 17 (No. 6, Nov–Dec 70) 569–574. On recent Hollywood films that deal with the "revolution," especially on college campuses.

4k(1). COMEDIES

Saalschutz, L. "Mechanisms of Cinema." *Close Up* 6 (No. 4, 1930). *See 8c(1).*

Corrigan, Beatrice. "Harlequin in America." *Canad Forum* 14 (Nov 33) 62–65. Traces *commedia dell'arte* in work of U.S. film comedians.

"The Pie in Art." *Nation* 139 (7 Nov 34) 524. Lauds Mack Sennett.

Roach, Hal. "The Gag's the Thing." *Pop Mech* 63 (May 35) 712–715. Comedy director discusses methods for slapstick laughter.

Eustis, M. "Custard Pie to Cartoon." *Th Arts* 22 (Sep 38) 675–681. How films enhanced the already traditional theatrical pantomime; from Sennett to Disney.

Nugent, F. S. "Movie Humor, No Laughing Matter." *NY Times* (3 Mar 40) 6. What will make an audience laugh and why? Lubitsch and others comment.

"Comedy Has Its Limits." *Chris Cent* (26 June 40) 816–817. Objections to *The Great Dictator.*

Crowther, B. "Cavalcade of Movie Comics." *NYTM* (20 Oct 40) 6–7.

"Movies Discover a Gold Mine in Screwball Army and Navy Comedies." *Life* 10 (23 June 41) 37–40.

Ferguson, O. "Flag for a Gag." *New Rep* 106 (5 Jan 42) 22. Objections to wartime army comedies: "the pattern openly shuns all subtlety and sense."

Reese, H. A. "Older the Gag, the Louder the Laugh." *SEP* 214 (25 Apr 42) 19+. Subtitled "How Abbott and Costello Have Proved It."

Isaacs, H. R. "Laugh, and You Laugh Alone." *Th Arts* 29 (Apr 45). *See 3a(4).*

"Movie 'Roads' Lead to Box-Office Gold." *Look* 11 (No. 26, 23 Dec 47) 90. Comedy series with Bing Crosby, Bob Hope, and Dorothy Lamour has grossed $17 million and there are more productions planned.

"That Slapstick Is Good for What Ails You." *Collier's* 121 (17 Apr 48) 98. Editorial lamenting absence of screen comedy.

Winge, John H. "Decline and Fall of Comedy." *S&S* 17 (No. 66, Summer 48) 96–97.

Knight, Arthur. "The Two-Reel Comedy: Its Rise and Fall." *Penguin F Rev* 9 (May 49) 39–46. From 1916 to 1928 the great comedians could take time to make short films funny; now they are so poor it is a good thing the double feature is squeezing them out.

Agee, J. "Comedy's Greatest Era." *Life* 27 (5 Sep 49) 70–82. A nostalgic look at the great silent comedians: Keaton, Chaplin, Lloyd, and Langdon.

Hine, A. "Movies." *Holiday* 7 (Feb 50) 15–16+. Nostalgia for the old style of screen comedy and disdain for modern actionless, intellectual comedy.

Raynor, Henry. "Nothing to Laugh At." *S&S* 19 (Apr 50) 68–73. Four new English comedies suggest a look back at earlier efforts.

"Do You Remember . . . Our Gang?" *Negro Dig* 9 (Dec 50) 69–70. Traces the show-business career of Eugene Jackson, a member of the gang in Hal Roach's "Our Gang" comedies.

Kracauer, Siegfried. "Silent Film Comedy." *S&S* 21 (Aug–Sep 51) 31–32. Accidents and the often malevolent nature of human life were the soul of slapstick comedy, from the storyless farces of France in the early 1900s to America in the 1920s. Speech seemed to put an end to all of this and who alone has survived? Harpo Marx.

Knight, Arthur. "The 2-Reel Comedy—Its Rise and Fall." *FIR* 2 (Oct 51) 29–35. Survey of silent and early sound era; revised version of an article written for *Penguin Film Review* (May 49).

Wilson, Liza, and David McClure. "Ma and Pa Kettle: Hollywood Gold Mine." *Collier's* 128 (8 Dec 51) 22–23+. The story of Percy Kilbride and Marjorie Main, stars of the Kettle series.

Callenbach, Ernest. "The Comic Ecstasy." *FIR* 5 (Jan 54). *See 3a(4).*

Wilson, N. Hope. "The Kettles." *FIR* 5 (Dec 54) 524–526. The "Ma and Pa Kettle" series: the reasons for their popularity in certain areas, how the movie conception of the characters differs from Betty McDonald's original, *The Egg and I.*

Sufrin, Mark. "The Silent World of Slapstick (1912–1916)." *F Cult* 2 (No. 10, 1956) 21–22. The freaks, the tricks, the quality of fable.

Thomas, Ralph. "My Way with Screen Humour." *F&F* 2 (No. 5, Feb 56). *See 5, Ralph Thomas.*

Kurnitz, H. "Britannia Rules the Chuckle." *Holiday* 19 (Apr 56) 80+. Comparison of American and British comedies.

Schein, Harry. "What Is Film Humor?" *QFRTV* 11 (No. 1, Fall 56) 24–32. Swedish film critic proposes three main types of screen humor—reformer, humorist, court jester—and gives special attention to *Mr. Hulot's Holiday,* Danny Kaye, and the Swedish Pavel Romel.

Badger, Clarence G. "Early Days of Movie Comedies." *Image* 6 (No. 5, May 57) 104–113. Reminiscences by a director of the early silent-comedy days.

Tati, Jacques. "Make Them Laugh." *F&F* 3 (No. 11, Aug 57) 15. Comparison between Tati's Hulot and Chaplin's Charlie.

Collin, Philippe. "The French Laughter Makers." *F&F* 4 (No. 2, Nov 57). *See 4e(2).*

Everson, William K. "British Humor on the Screen." *FIR* 8 (Nov 57). *See 4e(1b).*

Carstairs, John P. "British Laugh-Makers." *F&F* 4 (No. 4, Jan 58). *See 4e(1b).*

"Sight Gag Revival." *Life* 44 (3 Feb 58) 8–9. Stills from Robert Youngson's *The Golden Age of Comedy.*

Weales, G. "Movies: Where Are the Clowns of Yesteryear?" *Reporter* 18 (6 Mar 58) 39–41. An appeal for the return of early motion-picture humor, the humor of comedians from the time of Sennett through W. C. Fields and the Marx Brothers.

Lane, John F. "The Italian Laugh-Makers." *F&F* 4 (No. 8, May 58). *See 4e(3a).*

Thomaier, William. "Early Sound Comedy." *FIR* 9 (May 58) 254–262. A review of the 1934–1941 so-called screwball American screen comedy, which includes such films as *It Happened One Night* and *A Night at the Opera.* See also letter to editor (June–July 58) 350.

Dyer, Peter John. "Cops, Custard—and Keaton." *F&F* 4 (No. 11, Aug 58) 13–15+. First of two articles on American silent comedy and its European parallels; part of series on world history.

Svanstrom, Ragnhild. "Those Comedians Can Crash the Frontier." *F&F* 5 (No. 1, Oct 58). *See 4e(5b).*

"Saved at the Altar." *Life* 45 (22 Dec 58) 148–153. Modern-day stars reenact a Mack Sennett chase.

Conrad, Derek. "What Makes the British Laugh?" *F&F* 5 (No. 5, Feb 59). *See 4e(1).*

De Sica, Vittorio. "British Humor?" *F&F* 5 (No. 7, Apr 59) 10. Reflections on the similarity between British and Italian humor; filmography.

Houston, Penelope. "Conscience and Comedy." *S&S* 28 (Nos. 3–4, Summer–Autumn 59)

161–163. Jacques Tati is in the great tradition, but *I'm All Right, Jack* seems the "work of soured liberals"; more audacity is needed.

Dyer, Peter John. "They Liked to Break the Rules." *F&F* 6 (No. 1, Oct 59) 12–14+. American sound comedy (except Chaplin and the musical).

Sellers, Peter. "A Serious Look at Laughter." *F&F* 6 (No. 6, Mar 60) 7+. Comedy actor writes on comedy.

Disney, Walt. "Humour: My Sixth Sense." *F&F* 7 (No. 5, Feb 61). *See 5, Walt Disney.*

"Two-Reeler's Return." *New Yorker* 37 (23 Sep 61) 34–36. Films by Hal Roach and Mack Sennett to be shown on television.

Panama, Norman. "Comedy at the Crossroad." *F&F* 8 (No. 8, May 62) 25+. Director talks about comedy films.

Perkins, V. F. "Comedies." *Movie* (No. 5, Dec 62) 21–22. An analysis of Howard Hawks' comic tendencies and techniques.

Johnson, Ian. "Have the British a Sense of Humor?" *F&F* 9 (No. 6, Mar 63). *See 4e(1).*

Eyles, Allen. "Uncle Sam's Funny Bone." *F&F* 9 (No. 7, Apr 63) 45–49. The need for a new spirit in American comedies.

Sheed, Wilfred. "Pitfalls of Pratfalls." *Commonweal* 78 (5 July 63) 402–404. The Boulting Brothers' comedies.

Hrusa, Bernard. "The Lost Art of Comedy." *Film* (No. 37, Autumn 63) 25–29; No. 38 (Winter 63) 31–34.

McCaffrey, Donald W. "The Evolution of the Chase in Silent Screen Comedy." *J Soc Cin* 4 (1964) 1–8. Includes description of climactic sequence in *Girl Shy,* when Harold Llyod employs eight different vehicles to get to the scene of a wedding.

Peck, Seymour. "Hollywood Laughs It Up." *NYTM* (23 Feb 64) 16–17. Stills from recent comedies.

Jarvie, Ian. "In Praise of Romantic Comedy." *Film* (No. 42, Winter 64) 39–41.

Walsh, Moira. "Vacuous Comedies." *America* 112 (27 Mar 65) 437–438. Their characteristics.

MacDonald, Dwight. "Films: Present-Day versus Old-Time Comedies." *Esq* 63 (June 65) 14+. In an extensive analysis of film comedy (and five recent bad examples) MacDonald insists upon three rules: (1) It must be quick; (2) the comic hero must be attractive; (3) comedy can be sadistic in a fanciful world where nobody really gets hurt.

Durgnat, Raymond. "World of Comedy." *F&F* 11 (No. 10, July 65) 8–13; (No. 11, Aug 65) 10–15. Toward a definition of comedy and of the "gag."

Durgnat, Raymond. "The World Turned Upside Down." *F&F* 11 (No. 12, Sep 65) 8–12. On comedy: how it works by creating a world of reversals.

Duprey, R. A. "Laughter Needs a Renaissance." *Cath World* 202 (Oct 65) 63–64.

Durgnat, Raymond. "Breaking the Laugh Barrier." *F&F* 12 (No. 1, Oct 65) 16–20. Absurdity and satire in comedy.

Ronan, H. "Rise and Fall and Rise of Slapstick." *Senior Scholastic* 87 (7 Oct 65) 21.

Durgnat, Raymond. "Hoop-De-Doo for Mr. L and Mr. H." *F&F* 12 (No. 2, Nov 65) 14–19. On film comedy: Keaton, Langdon, Lloyd, Marx Brothers, and Laurel and Hardy.

Durgnat, Raymond. "Subversion in the Fields." *F&F* 12 (No. 3, Dec 65) 42–48. About satires on the American way of life.

Durgnat, Raymond. "Life's a Drag, Isn't It?" *F&F* 12, No. 4 (Jan 66) 40–46. Comedy After World War II.

Trevelyan, C. F. "Slapstick to Satire." *US Camera* 29 (Sep 66) 70–73. Exaggeration is the basis of all comedy, and it uses the natural activities of our life, no matter how simple these acts may seem.

Ford, Corey. "When They Really Knew How to Laugh." *McCall's* 95 (Nov 67) 82–83+. On the film comedians of the 1920s.

Leventhal, Howard, and William Mace. "The Effect of Laughter on Evaluation of a Slapstick Movie." *J of Personality* 38 (1970) 16–30.

McCaffrey, Donald. "The Golden Age of Sound Comedy." *Screen* 11 (No. 1, Feb 70) 27–40. Brief outline includes Keaton, Fields, Laurel and Hardy, Andy Hardy series.

Mast, Gerald. *"The Gold Rush* and *The General." CJ* 9 (No. 2, Spring 70). *See 3c.*

"Some Funny Talk." *F&F* 6 (No. 6, Mar 70) 8+. Discussion by Peter Barnes with Spike Mulligan, Bernard Braden, and Ted Ray on British film comedy.

Rogers, Peter. "Carrying on Instinctively." *F&F* 16 (No. 9, June 70) 70–73. Interview with the producer of the "Carry On . . ." films.

4k(2). WESTERNS

[See also 7b(4).]

McNichols, C. L. "Picture Horse, Styles in Movie Mounts." *Rev of Reviews* 95 (Feb 37) 71. The world has become horse-conscious because of the "oaters."

Carroll, Sidney. "Lo, the Poor Cowboy." *Esq* 18 (Nov 42) 47+. Casual history of Western films, based on interview with director George Marshall.

Stoddard, Frank. "Top Ten Western Stars." *Good Housekeeping* 116 (Mar 43) 49+. Stars, plots, and "strict code of ethics" discussed.

Kahn, Gordon. "Lay That Pistol Down." *Atlantic* 173 (Apr 44) 105–108. Fear of the world audience has reduced the tough Western hero to a singing cowboy.

Daugherty, Frank. "Singing Western." *CSMM* (29 Apr 44) 89.

"Hollywood Rides Again." *NYTM* (19 Aug 45) 16–17. Brief pictorial look at forthcoming Westerns.

Marshall, J. "Westerns Are Back in the West." *Collier's* 116 (8 Dec 45) 22–23+. Westerns stage a revival after war handicaps are removed.

Natteford, Jack, and Luci Ward. "Trite, Stale—and Profitable?" *Screen Writer* 1 (May 46) 15–20. A survey of film Westerns and criteria for judging innovations in them.

Natteford, Jack, and Luci Ward. "Problems of the Outdoor Action Writer." *Screen Writer* 2 (Oct 46) 15–19. The Western as melodrama "partially divorced from reality"; the special problems involved in creating "believable fantasy."

"Horse Opera: Western Movies." *Life* 21 (7 Oct 46) 93–99. A brief history; how one is made.

Zimet, Julian. "Regarding the Horse Opera." *Screen Writer* 2 (Nov 46) 15–19. Discusses the appeal of Westerns to children, the positive values they express, and the quiet they induce when similar successes are not achieved by the viewer.

Natteford, Jack, and Luci Ward. "The Economics of the Horse Opera." *Screen Writer* 3 (No. 8, Jan 48) 21–24. Most Westerns are sold at a flat rate to theatres and any unexpected increase in box office does not go to the production company; if the writer wants to make a reputation for money-making scripts, he'd better work for the big-time specials.

"Hoss Opera Rides Again." *NYTM* (19 Sep 48) 24–25. The Western, Hollywood's contribution to film art, changes only in terms of bigger budgets, as it continues to allow the viewer the comforts of a mythical past.

"The Great American Horse Opera." *Life* 26 (10 Jan 49) 42–46. Photographer sets up typical scenes from new film *Yellow Sky* with props only, in order to show stylized tradition of the Western.

Rogers, Roy. "Don't Shoot, Ma! Cowboy Fever." *American* 148 (Aug 49) 28–29. Roy Rogers tells how he broke into pictures; the dangers and assets of Westerns.

Brady, Thomas F. "Hollywood Goes More Thataway." *NYTM* (20 Aug 50) 24–25. One-fourth of current pictures are Westerns.

Elkin, Frederick. "The Psychological Appeal of the Hollywood Western." *J Educ Soc* 24 (No. 1, Sep 50) 72–86. Action and simplicity appeal to certain psychological needs.

Knight, Arthur. "Westerns Ho." *Sat Rev* 35 (1 Mar 52) 23+. The Western film is "sure-fire" box office, but a warning is sounded against endless repetition.

Rowland, Roy. "The Western as History." *FIR* 3 (May 52) 220–223. Distortions and misrepresentations of American history happen in many films, but history isn't too clear in some cases, says this director.

Markfield, Wallace. "The Inauthentic Western." *Am Mercury* 75 (Sep 52) 82–86. A comparison of the old-style Western with the new.

Franklin, Eliza. "Westerns, First and Lasting." *QFRTV* 7 (No. 2, Winter 52) 109–115. Brief history of Western film.

Rieupeyrout, Jean-Louis. "The Western: A Historical Genre." *QFRTV* 7 (No. 2, Winter 52) 116–128. Article reprinted from *Cahiers du Cinéma* examines the Western film and suggests it is often pretty close to history, despite accusations of violence, superficiality, and stereotypes; John Ford's *My Darling Clementine* and *Fort Apache* analyzed with approval.

Everson, William K. "Europe Produces Westerns, Too." *FIR* 4 (Feb 53) 74–79. Hans Albers makes them in Germany, and one imitation at least has occurred in England (set in Africa) and Russia.

"Fifty Years Going That-a-Way." *NYTM* (5 Apr 53) 20–21. Quick history of the Western film, with stills from *The Great Train Robbery* to *Shane*.

Jacobson, Herbert L. "Cowboy, Pioneer, and American Soldier." *S&S* 22 (Apr–June 53) 189–190. The Western kept the traditions of persistence, individualism, and inventiveness alive in an essentially peaceful nation, until they were needed in the two world wars.

Harbert, Ruth. "Fifty Years of Westerns." *Good Housekeeping* 137 (July 53) 17. The Hollywood Western celebrates its golden anniversary: from *The Great Train Robbery* to *Shane*.

"The Crowded Prairie." *Time* 62 (23 Nov 53) 114. Hollywood busy with twenty-two variations on the same Western theme.

Warshow, Robert. "The Westerner." *Partisan Rev* 21 (Mar 54) 190–203. He is "the last gentleman," who does what he "has to do," and is therefore a killer of men and naturally alone; variations in the conventions in *High Noon*, *My Darling Clementine*, *Shane*, and other films.

Pratt, John. "In Defence of the Western." *F&F* 1 (No. 2, Nov 54) 8. The American film industry and the Western; it's an entertainment formula, a tradition, a cliché.

Schein, Harry. "The Olympian Cowboy." *Am Scholar* 24 (No. 3, Summer 55) 309–320. Analysis of plot types in Westerns; hatred of women; moral conflicts; different versions of Jesse James; godlike heroes.

"Le Western." *Time* 66 (4 July 55) 70. European critics' examination of the Western film.

Fenin, George. "The Western—Old and New." *F Cult* 2 (No. 8, 1956) 7–10. Since World War II, as André Bazin suggests, there is an advance in interpretation; examples of films, sequences, and characters.

Sufrin, Mark. "Where the Handclasp's a Little Stronger." *Sat Rev* 39 (25 Aug 56) 26. Brief analysis of the Western genre—its appeal, its evolution in Hollywood.

Walker, Stanley. "The Western Still Rides High." *NYTM* (28 Apr 57) 26–27+. History of the Western.

Terraine, John. "The End of the Trail." *F&F* 3 (No. 10, July 57) 9+. Recent changes in the genre of the Western.

Miller, Alexander. "The Western—A Theological Note." *Chris Cent* 74 (27 Nov 57) 1409+.

Pratt, George. "The Posse Is Riding Like Mad." *Image* 7 (No. 4, Apr 58) 76–85; 7 (No. 7, Sep 58) 152–161. Two articles on Westerns and their stars 1907–1914.

Fenin, George N., and William K. Everson. "The European Western." *F Cult* (No. 20, 1959) 59–71. Especially in Germany.

Emery, F. E. "Psychological Effects of the Western Film: A Study in Television Viewing." *Human Relations* 12 (No. 3, 1959) 195–229.

Holland, Norman N. "Psychiatry in Pselluloid." *Atlantic* 203 (Feb 59). See 7a(4).

Woods, Frederick. "Hot Guns and Cold Women." *F&F* 5 (No. 6, Mar 59) 11+. Conventions in the Western.

Bradshaw, B. "They Still Go Thisaway and Thataway in the Red Rock Country." *Ariz Highways* 35 (May 59) 6–9.

Dyer, Peter John. "A Man's World." *F&F* 5 (No. 8, May 59) 13–15+. Influences on American Westerns to 1940 and their influence on other genres.

"First Scenes in Movies' Westerns." *Life* 46 (18 May 59) 101–102. Stills from *The Great Train Robbery* (section of article on the American West).

Bluestone, George. "The Changing Cowboy: From Dime Novel to Dollar Film." *Western Humanities Rev* 14 (1960) 331–337. Adult Westerns.

Nussbaum, Martin. "Sociological Symbolism of the Adult Western." *Social Forces* 39 (Oct 60) 25–28. The "first folk-type art form to have features of universality"; the Western's special recurring aspects: exciting places, unique heroes, individualism, contact with nature, grappling with good and evil, and the gun.

Homans, Peter. "Puritanism Revisited: An Analysis of the Contemporary Screen-Image Western." *Studies in Pub Com* 3 (Summer 61) 73–84. The hero's inner control when faced with evil temptation goes through a change when there is a villain who must be destroyed; the responsibility for that falls upon the adversary, who always shoots first.

Saisselin, Remy G. "Poetics of the Western."

Brit J Aesthetics 2 (No. 2, Apr 62) 159–169. "A vehicle of escape into a world of heroism and adventure," the Western is to American culture what the medieval knight and his horse were to Europe, part of a myth in which character need not be credible.

Cawelti, John. "Prolegomena to the Western." *Studies in Pub Com* (No. 4, Autumn 62) 57–70. A reaction against an earlier article (issue No. 3) by Peter Homans; an attempt to outline the problems involved in exploring the cultural meaning of such popular art forms as the Western.

LaBadie, Donald W. "The Last Roundup." *Show* 2 (Sep 62). See 2b(2).

Everson, William K. "Sixty-Year Saga of the Horse Opera." *NYTM* (14 Apr 63) 74–75. Stills showing the history of the Western.

Weaver, John D. "Destry Rides Again, and Again, and Again." *Holiday* 34 (Aug 63) 77–80+. The omnipresence of the Western and the cowboy.

Moser, D. "Western Hero." *Life* 55 (20 Dec 63) 104–109. The widespread, long-lasting popularity of the Western.

"Horse, Italian Style." *Newswk* 65 (28 June 65). See 4e(3c).

Whitehall, Richard. "The Heroes Are Tired." *FQ* 20 (No. 2, Winter 66–67) 12–24. History of the American Western seen by an English critic; Peckinpah's realism seems the way of the future.

Godfrey, Lionel. "A Heretic's View of the Western." *F&F* 13 (No. 8, May 67) 14–20. A film critic who does not like the Western.

Sarris, Andrew. "Films: From *The Great Train Robbery* to the Great Society." *Arts Mag* 41 (Summer 67) 20–21. The enduring qualities of the American Western film.

Barsness, John. "A Question of Standard." *FQ* 21 (No. 1, Fall 67) 32–37. The gap between myth and reality of the West in motion pictures is seen in two prototypes: myth in *High Noon*, reality in *The Misfits*.

Hughes, Albert. "Jesse James: Outlaw with a Halo." *Montana* 17 (No. 4, Oct 67) 60–75. Subtitled "The Magazine of Western History," this issue presents an extensive study of the movies which have misrepresented the James family as heroes.

Cawelti, John G. "The Gunfighter and Society." *Am West* 5 (No. 2, Mar 68) 30–35+. "Group involvement" Westerns such as *Bonanza* (on TV) echo the middle-class dream of escape to suburbia, but movies such as *The Gunfighter* represent "society's ambiguous dependence on, and abhorrence of, violence."

Fox, William Price. "Wild Westerns, Italian Style." *SEP* 241 (6 Apr 68). See 4e(3c).

Sutton, M. L. "Non-Hero Western." *Writers Dig* 48 (June 68) 45. A lament for the nonheroic Western.

Brode, Douglas. "Reflections on the Tradition of the Movie Western." *Cinéaste* 2 (No. 2, Fall 68). *See 3c, Bonnie and Clyde.*

Schickel, Richard. "Decline and Fall of the Western." *Life* 65 (20 Sep 68) 16.

Gordon, Alex. "Trivia." *Cinema* (Calif) 5 (No. 1, 1969) 34–37. A history of "B" Westerns and stars.

Joseph, Robert. "The New American Mythology." *Cinema* (Calif) 5 (No. 2, 1969) 32–35. Motorcycles instead of horses.

"Ford and Kennedy on the Western." *FIR* 20 (No. 1, Jan 69) 29–33. Dialogue between John Ford and Burt Kennedy.

Boatright, Mody C. "The Formula in Cowboy Fiction and Drama." *Western Folklore* 28 (Apr 69) 136–145. Basic cowboy types and plots.

McArthur, Colin. "The Roots of the Western." *Cinema* (Cambridge) (No. 4, Oct 69) 11–13. The relationship of the Western film to America.

Ross, T. J. "Fantasy and Form in the Western." *December* 12 (Nos. 1–2, 1970) 158–169. Qualities of this genre; juxtaposing the 1920s Westerns with those of the 1960s; speculation that we may be moving past the heyday of this genre.

Crist, Judith, Bruce Kane, Philip K. Scheuer, Joel Reisner. "Special Report: The Western." *Action* 5 (No. 3, May–June 70) 11–29. The "top dozen" Westerns; articles dealing with Sam Peckinpah and Henry Hathaway.

Brackman, J. "Films." *Esq* 73 (June 70) 68. The Westerns of Sam Peckinpah, particularly *The Wild Bunch:* a portrait of his Old West.

Wallington, Mike, and Chris Frayling. "The Italian Western." *Cinema* (Cambridge) (Nos. 6–7, Aug 70) 31–38. The inflections of form and content, and a detailed treatment of Sergio Leone.

Willett, Ralph. "The American Western: Myth and Anti-Myth." *J Pop Cult* 4 (No. 2, Fall 70) 455–462.

4k(3). SCIENCE FICTION, SUPERNATURALISM, HORROR

Jaffray, Norman R. "The Spine Chillers." *SEP* 205 (29 Apr 33) 61. Poem about horror films.

Hubler, R. G. "Scare 'Em to Death and Cash In." *SEP* 214 (23 May 42) 20–21+. What makes the movie horror thriller scary and why; *Frankenstein* analyzed; makeup techniques.

Tyler, Parker. "Supernaturalism in the Movies." *Th Arts* 29 (June 45) 362–366+. Witty exploration of many recent film ghosts.

Myers, Henry. "Weird and Wonderful." *Screen Writer* 1 (July 45) 19–23. Val Lewton's "horror films" at RKO are suggestive and modern, not old-fashioned Gothic.

Meeker, O. "Screamy-Weamies." *Collier's* 117 (12 Jan 46). *See 6d(1).*

Siodmak, Curt. "In Defense of the Ghouls." *Screen Writer* 1 (Feb 46) 1–6. Horror films and their relationship to subconscious drives and emotions; like the myth and fairy tale, they "are based on complex and fundamental wishes and desires."

Kracauer, S. "Hollywood's Terror Films: Do They Reflect an American State of Mind?" *Commentary* 2 (Aug 46) 132–136. Certain terror films, while sometimes rooted in wartime propaganda, nevertheless reflect uncertainties, inner disintegration, and mental disturbances.

Crowther, B. "Outer Space Comes of Age." *Atlantic* 189 (Mar 52) 91–92. How space operas might supplant the Western.

Harrington, Curtis. "Ghoulies and Ghosties." *S&S* 21 (Apr–June 52) 157–161. The technical tricks of film to create mystical effects; the Germans have always seemed to love mysticism and demonstrated it well with films such as *The Golem, Siegfried,* and *Nosferatu;* Dreyer's *Vampyr.*

Harrington, Curtis. "Ghoulies and Ghosties." *QFRTV* 7 (No. 2, Winter 52) 191–202. Reprint from *Sight and Sound* offers history of fantasy and horror films.

Houston, Penelope. "Glimpses of the Moon." *S&S* 22 (Apr–June 53) 185–188. Some of Hollywood's ventures into space and science fiction.

Addams, Charles. "Movie Monster Rally." *NYTM* (9 Aug 53) 16–17. King Kong, Frankenstein, and Dracula, among others, form a gallery of "memorable meanies."

"Bloodstream Green." *Time* 62 (19 Oct 53) 112–113. The biggest assortment of horror movies since the Frankenstein days of the 1930s; list of new productions.

"Og, Gog, and Magog." *Time* 62 (16 Nov 53). *See 7c(5).*

Everson, William K. "Horror Films." *FIR* 5 (Jan 54) 12–23. Eight categories; many plot synopses.

Fisher, David. "The Angel, the Devil, and the Space Traveler." *S&S* 23 (Jan–Mar 54) 155–157. Some of the devices, dramatic and technical, used to portray supernatural events and beings: he cites *All That Money Can Buy, La Beauté Diable, It's a Wonderful Life,* and *Orphée.*

Everson, William K. "A Family Tree of Monsters." *F Cult* 1 (No. 1, 1955) 24–30. Discussion of Universal's original movie monsters: *Dracula, Frankenstein, The Mummy, The Wolf Man,* and their eventual followups.

"Shock Around the Clock." *Time* 70 (9 Sep

57) 110. Horror and rock-and-roll films: new movies combine the genres.

Karloff, Boris. "My Life as a Monster." *F&F* 4 (No. 2, Nov 57) 11+. Karloff comments on horror movies.

"Ghastly Look of a Film Fad." *Life* 43 (11 Nov 57) 16–17. A gallery of stills from current horror films.

Farber, Marjorie. "Bride of Sputnik." *F Cult* 4 (No. 17, 1958) 12–14. Some extended remarks on science-fiction films and the tendency toward adoration of scientific progress.

Brustein, Robert. "Film Chronicle: Reflections on Horror Movies." *Partisan Rev* 25 (Spring 58) 288–296. Horror films covertly embody certain underground assumptions about science which reflect popular opinion.

Dyer, Peter John. "All Manner of Fantasies." *F&F* 4 (No. 9, June 58) 13–15+. European school of fantasy and horror—magicians, waxworks, Gothic castles; seventh article in world history of cinema.

Dyer, Peter John. "Some Nights of Horror." *F&F* 4 (No. 9, June 58) 13–15+. Eighth in series on world cinema; second on horror films.

"Monstrous for Money." *Newswk* 52 (14 July 58) 84. Latest science-horror film, *The Fly,* and teenage audience's responses.

"Stiff Competitors." *Time* 72 (4 Aug 58) 66. The promotion of horror films.

"All Horrid . . ." *S&S* 27 (Autumn 58) 278. Horror films planned as *Teenage Werewolf* and *The Fly* garner much cash; British Hammer Films may make *Frankenstein Created Woman,* starring Brigitte Bardot.

Knight, Arthur. "Tired Blood." *Sat Rev* 41 (18 Oct 58) 57–58. On the comeback of the horror film.

Gehman, Richard. "The Hollywood Horrors." *Cosmopolitan* 145 (Nov 58) 38–42. State of the monster business; possible psychological effects.

Grotjahn, Martin. "Horror—Yes, It Can Do You Good." *F&F* 5 (No. 2, Nov 58) 9. Psychiatrist writes on psychological advantages of horror films for viewers.

"Lovers of Frankenstein; Are Horror Films Such Good Business?" *Economist* 189 (6 Dec 58) 868–870.

Hill, Derek. "The Face of Horror." *S&S* 28 (Winter 58–59) 6–11. Recent deplorable elaborations—from "sci-fi" monsters to the ugliness of the "clinical cult" and close views of operations.

Hodgens, Richard. "A Brief, Tragical History of the Science Fiction Film." *FQ* 13 (No. 2, Winter 59) 30–39. Critical appraisal of the cycle begun by *Destination Moon* and *The Thing;* the sense of actual possibility, of puzzle, and of surprise are essentials of good "sci-fi," but most movies settle for horror.

Holland, Norman. "Good Bad Movie." *Atlantic* 203 (Jan 59). *See 3b(4).*

"Gold from Ghouls." *Time* 73 (6 Apr 59) 46–47.

"Queer for Fear." *Time* 74 (3 Aug 59) 58. William Castle releases *The Tingler.*

Lourie, Gene. "A Background to Horror." *F&F* 6 (No. 5, Feb 60) 14. About directing horror films.

Kobler, John. "Master of Movie Horror." *SEP* 232 (19 Mar 60). *See 5, William Castle.*

Cohen, Herman. "On Being a Teenage Werewolf." *F&F* 6 (No. 12, Sep 60) 15+. Director talks about his horror films.

Morsberger, R. E. "Shakespeare and Science Fiction." *Shakespeare Q* 12 (Spring 61) 161. Note on similarity of *Forbidden Planet* (MGM, 1956) and *The Tempest.*

"Blood Pudding." *Time* 78 (1 Sep 61) 50. A survey of current horror films.

"Back from the Dead." *Newswk* 59 (22 Jan 62) 80. Human monster comes back in the person of Vincent Price in a series of Edgar Allan Poe stories.

Price, James. "Hail Horrors, Hail Infernal World." *London Mag* new series 2 (No. 11, Feb 63) 67–72. On the horror genre.

Shayon, Robert Lewis. "Screens and Screams." *Sat Rev* 46 (20 Apr 63) 44. Hitchcock's "shudder-frontier" in *Psycho, The Birds,* and others.

Arnold, Francis. "Out of This World." *F&F* 9 (No. 9, June 63) 14–18. On science-fiction films.

Price, James. "The Dark House." *London Mag* new series 3 (No. 5, Aug 63) 67–71. On the "dark house" genre of thriller as a parallel to the film theatre.

Hamblin, Dora Jane. "Go On, Frighten Us to Death, We Love It!" *Life* 55 (30 Aug 63) 40. The attraction of horror films.

Connor, Edward. "The Return of the Dead." *FIR* 15 (No. 3, Mar 64) 146–160. Study of this theme in cinema.

Brower, B. "Vulgarization of American Demonology." *Esq* 61 (June 64) 94–99+. Demise of the serious horror movie in American culture.

Fischer, Terence. "Horror Is My Business." *F&F* 10 (No. 10, July 64). *See 5, Terence Fischer.*

"Old-Master Monsters and the New Breed." *Look* 28 (8 Sep 64) 48–49. Famous monsters of filmland, their creators, and their psychological effect on children.

Dyer, Peter John. "Z Films." *S&S* 33 (Autumn 64) 179–181. Some notes on horror films, and in particular the work of Roger Corman; *The Masque of the Red Death* and *The Stranger* are discussed at considerable length.

"Monster-*San*." *Newswk* 64 (19 Oct 64). *See 4f(1).*

Genêt. "Letter From Paris." *New Yorker* 41 (15 May 65) 171–172. Horror-movie center in the theatre Le Dragon.

"The Horror Film: An Exhibition and Film Series at the Museum of Modern Art, New York." *Camera* 44 (No. 7, July 65) 30–33.

Sontag, Susan. "Imagination of Disaster." *Commentary* 40 (Oct 65) 42–48. The science-fiction film and the "aesthetics of destruction"; excerpt from her book *Against Interpretation* (Farrar, Straus and Giroux, 1966).

"Return of Batman." *Time* 86 (26 Nov 65) 60+. Re-release of the old serials.

Ellison, Harlan. "Three Faces of Fear." *Cinema* (Calif) 3 (No. 2, Mar 66) 4–8+. A theory of film horror from the works of Val Lewton; see also letter by DeWitt Bodeen 3 (No. 4, Dec 66), 23.

"Rape of the Future." *Esq* 65 (May 66) 112–116. Pictures from science-fiction films with short comments, and a short interview with Arthur C. Clarke, writer of *2001*.

Glazebrook, Philip. "The Anti-Heroes of Horror." *F&F* 13 (No. 1, Oct 66) 36–37.

Spinrad, Norman. "Stanley Kubrick in the 21st Century." *Cinema* (Calif) 3 (No. 4, Dec 66). *See 9, 2001: A Space Odyssey.*

Denne, John D. "Society and the Monster." *December* 9 (Nos. 2–3, Summer–Fall 67) 180–183. Three kinds of monster stories: good versus evil; a struggle between strong opponents; vindication of the status quo.

Stanbury, C. M. "Monsters in the Movies." *December* 10 (No. 1, 1968) 174–177. Stanbury traces the mythological symbolism in the monster and science-fiction film.

Siodmak, Curt. "Sci-Fi or Sci-Fact?" *F&F* 15 (No. 2, Nov 68) 63–64.

Kane, Joe. "Nuclear Films." *Take One* 2 (No. 6, 1969) 9–11. A sometimes humorous, sometimes serious attempt to create and classify a genre from films dealing with the end of the world.

Gross, E. "Witchcraft and the Movies." *Commentary* 47 (Jan 69) 68–71. "Psychic sciences" are popular now because "the unexplained and the terrifying were never so great as they are right now"; hence *Rosemary's Baby* reaches an enormous audience.

Halliwell, Leslie. "The Baron, the Count, and Their Ghoul Friends." *F&F* 15 (No. 9, June 69) 12–16; (No. 10, July 69) 12–16. Horror films from the classic period of the mid-1930s to the early 1940s; two articles.

Hitchens, Gordon. " 'A Breathless Eagerness in the Audience' . . . Historical Notes on Dr. Frankenstein and His Monster." *F Com* 6 (No. 1, Spring 70) 49–51. Stage presentations of Mary Wollstonecraft Shelley's book.

"Movies: Ghouls, Ghosts, and Banshees." *McCall's* 97 (Mar 70) 12+. Brief history of the horror film in general: American International Pictures as a producer.

Ellison, Harlan. "Them or Us." *Show* (Apr 70) 44–47+. Survey of science-fiction movies.

Tarratt, Margaret. "Monsters from the Id." *F&F* 17 (No. 3, Dec 70) 38–42. Study of science-fiction films.

4k(4). HISTORICAL, SPECTACLE, ADVENTURE FILMS

Lindsay, Philip. "Filming England's History." *Bookman* 84 (July 33). *See 4e(1b).*

Lindsay, Philip. "The Camera Turns on History." *CQ* 2 (No. 1, Autumn 33) 10–11. Consultant for *Henry VIII* praises the inspiring qualities of costume pictures. See reply (No. 2, Winter 33–34) 111.

Schulberg, B. P. "Motion Picture as an Educator." *Overland Monthly and Outwest Mag* new series 91 (Sep 33) 121. Many entertainment films teach history, says Paramount executive.

Beard, Charles R. "Why Get It Wrong?" *S&S* 2 (No. 8, Winter 33–34) 124–125. Recent British films reveal historical inaccuracies.

Walsh, James J. "The Movies and History." *Commonweal* 20 (20 July 34) 299–300. Movies create false backgrounds in minds of young generation regarding people and places of history.

Petrie, Sir Charles. "Historical Film." *19th Century* 117 (May 35) 613–623. Surveys handicaps of historical films.

Courtney, W. B. "Stupendous, Colossal, Gorgeous." *Collier's* 96 (28 Sep 35) 15–16+. Prospects for spectacles, color talkies.

Field, Mary. "Making the Past Live." *S&S* 4 (No. 15, Autumn 35) 132–134. Films with historical inaccuracies.

Liotta, J. V. "Motion Pictures and the Library." *Lib J* 61 (1 Feb 36) 102–103. Cleveland Public Library links new movies such as *The Crusades* with lists of history books (on free bookmarks).

Hearnshaw, F. J. C. "History on the Film." *Fortnightly Rev* 145 (new series 139, June 36) 665–671. Truth in history is difficult, and Shakespeare made changes for dramatic reasons, but certain feature-film makers could do better, *Disraeli*, for example.

Sharar, Dewan. "Should Historical Films Be Accurate?" *Great Britain and the East* 49 (20 Sep 37) 479. *The Crusades* and *The Charge of the Light Brigade* typical of American cinema's inaccuracy.

Renoir, Jean. "Farthingales and Facts." *S&S* 7 (No. 26, Summer 38). *See 5, Jean Renoir.*

Laver, James. "Dates and Dresses." *S&S* 8 (No. 30, Summer 39) 50–51. Women are to blame for many of the inaccuracies in historical films.

Dugan, James. "Facts on the Wind." *New Masses* 34 (23 Jan 40) 28–30. The first of

227

two articles exposing the historical inaccuracies of *Gone with the Wind.*

Dugan, James. "Reconstruction and *GWTW.*" *New Masses* 34 (30 Jan 40) 28–30. Second of two articles exposing the historical inaccuracies of *Gone with the Wind.*

Churchill, D. W. "Hollywood Goes Historical." *NYTM* (4 Aug 40) 6–7. Detailing the rise of the historical film, this article also lists types, techniques, and researches involved.

Munsan, F. "Movies and History." *SRL* 24 (3 May 41) 9. The movie version of John Brown in *Santa Fe Trail* is the springboard for this discussion of what comprises a relevant historical film.

Packard, F. "Gay Nineties." *New Yorker* 17 (31 May 41) 60–61. This lively account deals with the movies' concept of the "gay nineties."

Koch, Howard. "The Historical Film—Fact and Fantasy." *Screen Writer* 1 (Jan 46) 1–10. Including defense of author's script for *Mission to Moscow.*

Hine, A. "The Nondocumentary Jungle Movie." *Holiday* 6 (Nov 49) 22+. Its evolution from thrills to documentary to tongue in cheek.

Morgan, James. "Coronatiana, USA." *S&S* 23 (July–Sep 53) 43–46. Deviations from English history in *Young Bess, The Sword and the Rose,* and *Elizabeth and Essex.*

Everson, William K. "Film Spectacles." *FIR* 5 (Nov 54) 459–471. The author classifies authentic spectacle films as historical epics, "disaster" films, Westerns on an epic scale, musicals and comedies which contain genuine spectacle, and "stunt" films (*King Kong*), fantasies (*The Thief of Bagdad*), and futuristic dramas (*Metropolis*).

"Reviving Hollywood Spirits." *Bus Wk* (13 Nov 54) 116–119. With the exception of RKO, every production company is making money with spectacles.

Robinson, David. "Spectacle." *S&S* 25 (Summer 55) 22–26+. Cinema was born into a world of theatrical spectacles, which were the fashion on stage at that time; Robinson cites early French, English, American, and Italian spectacles and discusses Griffith's *Intolerance;* the spectacle has been dying since its zenith, forty years ago; only wide screen and De Mille kept it alive.

Scharper, Phillip J. "Hollywood and History." *America* 93 (25 June 55) 332–334. Historical movies are both artistically debased and historically distorted due to Hollywood's refusal to "stand before history humbly and gaze at it honestly."

De Mille, Cecil B. "Forget Spectacle—It's the Story That Counts." *F&F* 3 (No. 1, Oct 56). *See 5, C. B. De Mille.*

Connor, Edward. "The Genealogy of Zorro." *FIR* 8 (Aug–Sep 57) 330–333+. A survey of the Zorro films and the actors who played the title role.

Dyer, Peter J. "Some Mighty Spectacles." *F&F* 4 (No. 5, Feb 58) 13–15+. Film spectacles, especially those of the silent period; part of a series on film history.

Dyer, Peter John. "From Boadicea to Bette Davis." *F&F* 5 (No. 4, Jan 59) 13–15+. Period and historical films in Britain and America.

Dyer, Peter John. "The Rebels in Jackboots." *F&F* 5 (No. 6, Mar 59) 13–15+. Historical films; nationalist propaganda of European costume films related to *Birth of a Nation.*

Coughlan, Robert. "Generals' Mighty Chariots: *Ben-Hur.*" *Life* 47 (16 Nov 59) 118–120+. History of the various stage and screen productions of *Ben-Hur,* with a biographical sketch of Lew Wallace.

Tate, Thad W., Jr. "The American Past and Film: An Historian's View." *JUFPA* 12 (No. 4, Summer 60) 10–13+. Researcher at Colonial Williamsburg warns against the "pageant approach" and suggests specific themes for the historical film maker.

Lane, John Francis. "The Money in Muscles." *F&F* 6 (No. 10, July 60) 9+. Italian spectaculars after *Ben-Hur,* especially those of the late 1950s.

Connor, Edward. "The 12 Tarzans." *FIR* 11 (No. 8, Oct 60) 452–463.

Green, Peter. "Movies Make Hay with the Classical World." *Horizon* 3 (May 61) 52–57. Hollywood epics viewed by the former director of classical studies at Selwyn College, Cambridge.

Wright, Peter. "Nazi Crimes and Punishment—The Films." *Motion* (No. 2, Winter 61–62) 17–19. A consideration of the films dealing with the Nazi period.

Heston, Charlton. "Mammoth Movies I Have Known." *F&F* 8 (No. 7, Apr 62) 16–17. On epic films.

Fadiman, William. "Blockbusters or Bust?" *F&F* 9 (No. 5, Feb 63) 64–65. Hollywood decides to get back its audience by producing expensive spectaculars.

Whitehall, Richard. "Days of Strife and Nights of Orgy." *F&F* 9 (No. 6, Mar 63) 8–14. The Italian spectacle.

Houston, Penelope, and John Gillett. "The Theory and Practice of Blockbusting." *S&S* 32 (Spring 63) 68–74. Multimillion-dollar epics seem to draw big audiences; high costs tend to rule out subtle stories; comments on *El Cid, The Longest Day,* and *Lawrence of Arabia.*

Silke, James R. "And Then Came the Dancing Girls." *Cinema* (Calif) 1 (No. 5, Aug–Sep 63) 15–18. Spectacle films.

Durgnat, Raymond. "Epic." *F&F* 10 (No. 3, Dec 63) 9–12. A study of the "epic" film.

"Hollywood's Fabulous History of the Film." *Life* 55 (20 Dec 63) 146–155. World history in stills from Hollywood films.

Behlmer, Rudy. "Robin Hood on the Screen." *FIR* 16 (No. 2, Feb 65) 91–109. Discusses the different actors who have played Robin Hood over the years.

Price, James. "Three Views of History." *London Mag* new series 4 (12 Mar 65) 80–83. On the ways to make films about historical events.

Behlmer, Rudy. "Swordplay on the Screen." *FIR* 16 (No. 6, June–July 65) 362–382. Review of the art as practiced by Valentino, Flynn, Fairbanks, *et al*.

Gow, Gordon. "Thrill a Minute." *F&F* 13 (No. 4, Jan 67) 4–11. Adventure films of the 1960s.

Crist, Judith. "Down with Bigness!" *Ladies' Home J* 84 (Jan 67) 55. Against current spectaculars.

Farber, Stephen. "The Spectacle Film: 1967." *FQ* 20 (No. 4, Summer 67) 12–22. *The Bible, Hawaii, Khartoum, Grand Prix, The Sand Pebbles*.

French, Philip. "Qualified Epics." *London Mag* new series 8 (No. 3, June 68) 95–98.

McNeill, W. H. "Historian and Historical Films." *Editors Dig* 34 (Jan 69) 38–40.

Sragow, Michael. "*Becket* and *The Lion in Winter*." *F Soc Rev* 5 (No. 4, Dec 69) 36–43. Glenville's *Becket* and Harvey's *The Lion in Winter* analyzed as Hollywood historical epic, and against actual historical and theatrical counterparts.

Jowett, Garth S. "The Concept of History in American Produced Films: An Analysis of the Films Made in the Period 1950–61." *J Pop Cult* 3 (No. 4, Spring 70) 799–813.

Rubenstein, Leonard. "Fascism Revisited." *F Soc Rev* 6 (No. 3, Nov 70) 43–46; (No. 4, Dec 70) 43–47. Articles dealing with films about Nazi Germany.

4k(5). RELIGIOUS FILMS

[See also 8e.]

Bregy, K. "What of Catholic Movies?" *Commonweal* 28 (12 Aug 38) 406–408. A Catholic looks at the ways movies have dealt with his faith.

Buchanan, Andrew. "These Religious Pictures." *S&S* 7 (No. 28, Winter 38–39) 155–156. There is not only a place for the religious film to be shown in churches but also for the religious factor in commercial films.

Burton, T. "Books into Pictures." *SRL* 21 (13 Apr 40) 21. A critical look at Hollywood's attempts to make books into movies, this article focuses on the religious film.

"Celluloid Revival." *Time* 43 (24 Apr 44) 48–49. Hollywood once again to make religious films.

Burke, J. A. V. "Signs of a Renaissance." *Commonweal* 50 (13 May 49) 113–115. Religion in films can avoid sentimentalism and has a right to make use of the screen (examples: *Monsieur Vincent, Dr. Laennac,* and *The Divine Tragedy*).

Elkin, Frederick. "God, Radio, and the Movies." *Hwd Q* 5 (No. 2, Winter 50) 105–114. *The Next Voice You Hear,* produced by Dore Schary, offers an opportunity to discuss the positive aspects of religion in films.

"First Christian Western." *Time* 58 (8 Oct 51) 107. Billy Graham starring in *Mr. Texas*.

Lavery, Emmet. "Some Live by Faith." *Cath World* 174 (Feb 52) 339–345. The author of *The First Legion* and *The Magnificent Yankee* studies the spiritual values of Hollywood and the films about religion or religious characters.

"*Quo Vadis?*" *Chris Cent* 69 (26 Mar 52) 359–361. An attack on Hollywood and *Quo Vadis?* for believing that with a religious subject its spectacle-sex-violence will be forgiven.

Miller, W. "Hollywood and Religion." *Religion in Life* 22 (No. 2, 1953) 273–279.

"Trend." *Time* 61 (29 June 53) 92. Biblical films pay off.

Miller, William Lee. "It May Be Box Office, But Is It the Bible?" *Reporter* 9 (29 Sep 53) 42–44. A critical study of Hollywood "religious" pictures, including *Salome*.

"Movie Scenario: The Bible." *NYTM* (11 Oct 53) 32–33. Stills from films with Biblical themes, including *The Ten Commandments* (1923) and *Ben-Hur* (1926).

Klausler, Alfred P. "*Martin Luther,* the Story of a Film." *Chris Cent* 70 (21 Oct 53) 1195–1198. Hollywood blamed for not backing this Protestant effort.

Fisher, David. "The Saint in the Cinema." *S&S* 23 (Oct–Dec 53) 93–95. The stereotype of religious persons: *I Confess, Monsieur Vincent, Journal d'un Curé de Campagne,* and *Passion de Jeanne d'Arc*.

"Scripture on Wide Screen." *Time* 63 (14 June 54) 72–74. Hollywood making Biblical movies, including *The Robe, Ten Commandments*.

Healy, Roger. "The Noble Experiment." *America* 91 (7 Aug 54) 460–461. Catholic group tries to equal the box office of *Martin Luther* with story of Pope Pius X called *The Secret Conclave,* but theatre loses money.

Hine, A. "Biblical Films." *Holiday* 16 (Nov 54) 28–31. The popularity of Biblical "epics."

Boyd, Malcolm. "All Films Are Theological!" *Chris Cent* 71 (1 Dec 54) 1456–1457. What is a religious film? Concern for the way Hollywood describes almost all films as "religious."

De La Roche, Catherine. "Fingers in the Pie." *F&F* 1 (No. 12, Sep 55) 13. The author examines a religious revival in films.

"Preacher Is Not Exhibit A." *Chris Cent* 73 (4 Apr 56). *See 7a(4)*.

Bort, David. "Religion on the Screen." *FIR* 7 (Nov 56) 439–442. American-produced religious feature films have for the most part failed to inform the masses about the nature and purposes of religion.

"Hollywood Knows, Mr. A." *Time* 70 (5 Aug 57) 61. A Catholic critic accuses Hollywood of exploiting the church in its films.

Burke, John A. V. "Religion in the Cinema." *F&F* 4 (No. 1, Oct 57) 13–15+. History of films with religious themes and/or characters.

Boyd, Malcolm. "How Does the Secular Press Interpret Religious Movies?" *Religion in Life* 27 (Spring 58) 276–285.

Connor, Edward. "Angels on the Screen." *FIR* 9 (Aug–Sep 58) 375–379. Characterizations of angels in films such as *The Man Who Could Work Miracles* (1937) and *Cabin in the Sky* (1943).

Connor, Edward. "Demons on the Screen." *FIR* 10 (Feb 59) 68–77. A review of the films known to the author in which the portrayal of one or more demons or of devil worship in any form is included, as well as those in which human beings are "possessed."

Boyd, M. "God and De Mille in Hollywood." *Chris Cent* 76 (25 Feb 59) 230–231. Written at the time of the death of C. B. De Mille: an attack on Hollywood "religious" movies.

"Bible Against Itself." *Chris Cent* 76 (28 Oct 59) 1235–1236. Reply *America* 102 (14 Nov 59) 175. Attack on Hollywood's Biblical spectacles.

Harrell, John G. "Religious Films: Fact and Forecast." *Chris Cent* 77 (6 Apr 60) 413–414. Appeal for a new tradition of religious-film making to go beyond Hollywood's theatricality.

"Rhapsody on a Theme by Spyros P. Skouras." *Chris Cent* 77 (7 Sep 60) 1015. Comment on choice of a Russian for role of Christ.

"Hollywood Presents Too Many Kings." *Chris Cent* 77 (28 Sep 60) 110. Attack on Hollywood Biblical extravaganzas.

Harrell, John G. "A Theology for Film Making." *Chris Cent* 78 (2 Aug 61) 930–931. Characteristics of good religious films.

"Wide-Screen Gospel." *Newswk* 58 (7 Aug 61) 69. Clergymen disturbed by too many Bible films.

Crowther, Bosley. "Good Book Is a Great Script." *NYTM* (31 Dec 61) 10–11. Films based on the Bible.

Walsh, Moira. "Otto Preminger Looks at the Catholic Church." *Cath World* 198 (Mar 64) 365–371. How does one go about making a movie (*The Cardinal*) about a religious institution one distrusts and does not understand?

"Jesus as a Clown." *Newswk* 63 (27 Apr 64) 96. Robert Moses, president of the New York World's Fair, offended by religious film, *Parable*.

Archer, Eugene. "Hollywood and the Bible." *Show* 4 (Dec 64) 30–36+. Historical survey of the Biblical screen epic, with comments from sociologists and religious leaders on their lasting appeal; emphasis on Huston's *The Bible* and George Stevens' *The Greatest Story Ever Told*.

Boyd, Malcolm. "Who Speaks for the Church?" *Chris Cent* 82 (21 Apr 65) 493–495. Criticizes the stance adopted by leading churchmen that any movie with a religious topic is good regardless of how banal and cliché-ridden it may be; prefers *Nothing But a Man* to *The Greatest Story Ever Told*. Discussion 82 (23 June 65) 815.

Clinton, F. "What Is a Catholic Film?" *Nat Rev* 21 (4 Nov 69) 1125–1126. Historical sketch of titles.

4k(6). MUSICALS, OPERA, DANCE

[See also 2b(8), 2g(2), 8a(4).]

Arvey, V. "Present-Day Musical Films and How They Are Made Possible." *Etude* 49 (Jan 31) 16–17.

Weiss, Trude. "The First Opera-Film." *Close Up* 9 (No. 4, Dec 32) 242–245. Comments on *The Bartered Bride,* a German film directed by Max Ophuls, from Smetana's comic opera.

Tibbett, L. "Opera Can Be Saved by the Movies." (Ed. by H. H. Taubman.) *Pictorial Rev* 34 (Feb 33) 8–9+.

"Opera Via Talkies." *Musician* 40 (June 35) 4. Editorial surveys recent interest in movie operas.

Skinner, Richard Dana. "A Letter to Walter Damrosch." *North Amer Rev* 240 (Sep 35) 278–283. Asks conductor to bring Wagner music-dramas to screen.

Danilova, Alexandra. "Classical Ballet and the Cinema." *S&S* 4 (No. 15, Autumn 35) 107–108. Russian ballerina argues for the use of film to preserve ballet and for higher standards of ballet in current films.

Lawler, H. "Opera on the Screen." *Etude* 54 (May 36) 283–284.

Davenport, M. "Machine-Made Prima Donnas." *Rdrs Dig* 28 (May 36) 91. No mistakes in movie operas, because only the best is recorded; excerpt from *Stage.*

Martini, Nino. "And Now the Movies." *Etude* 54 (June 36) 349–350. Opera films.

Laine, Juliette. "Operetta and the Sound Film." *Etude* 56 (June 38) 359–360. Advice to aspiring movie singer-actresses by Jeannette MacDonald.

Tindall, Glenn M. "Music and the Movies." *School and Society* 48 (3 Dec 38) 721–724. Tribute to the musical film; its educational use.

Rosenheimer, A. "Towards the Dance Film." *Th Arts* 26 (Jan 42) 56–58+. The contributions of Astaire, Berkeley, and Clair in integrating film and dance.

Paul, E. "Musical and Low." *Atlantic* 176 (July 45) 109+. The trends and styles of Hollywood musicals: a humorous attack.

Morton, Lawrence. "Chopin's New Audience." *Hwd Q* 1 (No. 1, Oct 45) 31–33. *A Song to Remember* sent thousands of people to the record shops for Chopin music; see also brief note 1 (No. 4, July 46) 440.

Crichton, Kyle (ed.). "Gamble with Music." *Collier's* 117 (23 Mar 46) 22–23. Problems in filming a musical versus stage musical productions.

Keller, Hans. "Revolution or Retrogression?" *S&S* 16 (No. 62, Summer 47) 63–64. Critical reactions to the film version of the opera *The Barber of Seville*.

"Behind the Golden Curtain." *Harper's* 196 (Jan 48) 96. The Metropolitan Opera goes to the multitudes via cinema.

Vaughan, David. "Dance in the Cinema." *Sequence* (No. 6, Winter 48–49) 6–13.

Eames, Marian. "Gray Thoughts on *Red Shoes*." *FIR* 1 (Dec 50) 20–24. Devotee of ballet finds little to praise in the "extravaganza."

Graham, Ronnie. "Stale, Flat and Profitable." *FIR* 2 (Feb 51) 25–27+. Informal survey of Hollywood musicals.

Bauer, Leda. "Twice-Told Tales." *Th Arts* 35 (June 51) 39–41+. Opera into film—limitations and failures; emphasis on *Tales of Hoffmann*.

Todd, A. "From Chaplin to Kelly." *Th Arts* 35 (Aug 51) 50–51. A history of the dance in film from silents to Astaire, Berkeley, and finally Gene Kelly.

"MGM Musicals." *Life* 32 (14 Apr 52) 116–118. Such stars as Fred Astaire, the Champions, and Gene Kelly promise box-office success.

Newton, Douglas. "Poetry in Fast and Musical Motion." *S&S* 22 (July–Sep 52) 35–37. The musical film is the least pretentious and most genuine poetic film which has yet been produced.

"Trio of Films." *Dance Mag* 27 (Apr 53) 34–35. Choreography in *The Story of Three Loves, Lili,* and *The 5,000 Fingers of Dr. T.*

Dietz, Howard. "The Musical Band Wagon Keeps on Rollin' Along." *Look* 17 (No. 16, 11 Aug 53) 93–95. History of the Hollywood musical comedy, particularly *The Band Wagon*.

Nagrin, D. "American in the Fiji Islands." *Dance Mag* 28 (Feb 54) 35–37. Choreographing native dances in *His Majesty O'Keefe*.

De La Roche, Catherine. "Song and Dance." *F&F* 1 (No. 1, Oct 54) 12–13. Preview of season of pioneers of the modern musical at the National Film Theatre.

"Song and Dance." *S&S* 24 (Oct–Dec 54) 95–100. Photographic section on American and British musicals; National Film Theatre has program of these films.

"Dance in the Movies." *Dance Mag* 28 (Nov 54) 20–27. A surge of movie musicals keeps choreographers on their toes.

Kracauer, Siegfried. "Opera on the Screen." *F Cult* 1 (No. 2, 1955) 19–21. Some analysis of Abel Gance's *Louise* (1939), Menotti's *The Medium* (1951), and Powell and Pressburger's *Tales of Hoffmann* (1951).

Lerman, Leo. "Dance in the Movies." *Dance Mag* (Jan 55) 9. Two new musicals: *Deep in My Heart* and *There's No Business Like Show Business*.

"Opera Season, To Taste." *Harper's* 210 (Jan 55) 87. Differences in American and Italian treatments of opera on film.

Jablonski, Edward. "Filmusicals." *FIR* 6 (Feb 55) 56–69. A historical survey that begins with MGM's *Broadway Melody* (1929).

"Elephant's Eye." *New Yorker* 31 (10 Sep 55) 33–35. Interchange of discussion about set designing for *Oklahoma!* and publicity for *Guys and Dolls*.

Levy, Louis. "Britain *Can* Make Good Musicals." *F&F* 2 (No. 4, Jan 56) 13. Musical director of Associated British Studios says Americans learned from Jessie Mathews.

Baker, Peter. "Tough Guys Set a New Pattern." *F&F* 2 (No. 4, Jan 56) 15. Serious dramatic material has changed the movie musical.

Knight, Arthur. "Opera Night at the Movies." *Sat Rev* 39 (24 Mar 56) 31–32. Qualities of operas that hamper their translation into films.

Connor, Edward. "The Composer on the Screen." *FIR* 7 (Apr 56). See 7a(4).

Terry, Walter. "The Dance." *Etude* 74 (May 56) 17+. *The Ballet of Romeo and Juliet,* a Soviet dance movie, starring Galina Ulanova, compared to American modern dance; camera work and acting recognized.

Vaughan, David. "After the Ball." *S&S* 26 (Autumn 56) 89–91+. *Singin' in the Rain, An American in Paris, Guys and Dolls,* and others seem to represent a decline from *On the Town*.

Hrusa, Bernard. "On the Musical." *Film* (No. 14, Nov–Dec 57) 16–19; No. 15 (Jan–Feb 58) 17–18. Brief account of its development; two articles.

Knight, Arthur. "Dance and Film: An Appraisal." *Dance Mag* 34 (Feb 60) 30–31+.

The creative and reproductive tendencies of film.

Peck, Seymour. "Again the Movies Sing and Dance." *NYTM* (2 July 61) 16–17. Production stills from recent musicals.

Fry, Annette. "Opera on Main Street." *Opera News* 26 (31 Mar 62) 8–13. A "Grand Opera Film Festival" series for local theatres.

"Big Season for Musicals: *Jumbo, Gypsy,* and *Bye Bye Birdie.*" *Look* 26 (14 Aug 62) 38–39+.

"September Calendar." *Dance Mag* 36 (Sep 62) 36–37+. Report on a Gene Kelly dance-film festival at the Museum of Modern Art in New York.

Knight, Arthur. "The Year They Almost Stopped Dancing." *Dance Mag* 36 (Dec 62) 16–17. Review of musicals in 1962.

Cutts, John. "Bye Bye Musicals." *F&F* 10 (No. 2, Nov 63) 42–45. Adaptation of stage musicals versus original screen musicals.

Palatsky, Eugene. "Pavlova Rediscovered!" *Dance Mag* 38 (Dec 64) 34–36. The rediscovery of a thirty-year-old movie, *The Immortal Swan,* restores the ballerina's art to full view.

Thompson, Thomas. "Tuning U.S. Musicals to Overseas Box Office." *Life* 58 (12 Mar 65). *See 7e(1).*

Anderson, Jack. "Towards a Dance Film Library." *Dance Mag* 39 (Sep 65) 40–42. Efforts of Genevieve Oswald, curator of the New York Public Library Dance Collection.

Spaeth, Sigmund. "Winning Friends for Opera." *Opera News* 30 (11 Dec 65) 8–11. Includes an appraisal of operatic movies.

Comolli, Jean-Louis. "Dancing Images." *CdC in Eng* (No. 2, 1966). *See 5, Busby Berkeley.*

Godfrey, Lionel. "A Heretic Looks at Musicals." *F&F* 13 (No. 6, Mar 67) 4–8. Film critic writes against Hollywood musicals.

Vallance, Tom. "Soundtrack." *Film* (No. 49, Autumn 67) 35–37. Return of the film musical.

Hudson, Peggy, and Roy Hemming. "The Lively Arts." *Senior Scholastic* 91 (28 Sep 67) 42–43. On the Kraft Music Hall TV special *The Hollywood Musical.*

Bach, Steven. "The Hollywood Idiom: Give Me That Old Soft Shoe." *Arts Mag* 42 (Dec 67–Jan 68) 15–16. The American musical film: its development and future.

Compton, Gardner. "Film Dance and Things to Come." *Dance Mag* 42 (Jan 68). *See 2a.*

Rizzo, Francis. "Shadow Opera: Hollywood Musical Fakes." *Opera News* 32 (3 Feb 68) 8–12. A history of Hollywood operas.

Sidney, George. "Three Ages of the Musical." *F&F* 14 (No. 9, June 68) 4–7. Interview on the musical.

Ronan, Margaret. "The Lively Arts." *Senior Scholastic* 94 (7 Feb 69) 16+. A quick history of film musicals as they change from escapism to serious themes.

Terry, Walter. "Fabulous Find in the Files." *Sat Rev* 52 (8 Mar 69) 113–115. Isadora Duncan and other dancers in movies.

Pleasants, H. "Screen and the Voice." *Opera News* 34 (17 Jan 70) 8–13. Transferring opera to the screen.

Jones, Robert T. "Movie Time at the Opera." *Time* 96 (27 July 70) 56. Report on festival of operatic films.

Jacobson, Robert, and Irving Kolodin. "Weber and Wagner at the Lincoln Center Opera Fest." *Sat Rev* 53 (1 Aug 70) 35. Report on the "Opera on Film" festival in New York's Philharmonic Hall; the Hamburg State Opera's contribution to cinematic opera.

"Rolf Lieberman." *New Yorker* 46 (29 Aug 70) 21–22. Interview: his work as the director of the Hamburg State Opera as well as his operatic films.

"Opera on Film." *Opera News* 35 (5 Sep 70) 21. Weber's *Der Freischütz;* others.

4k(7). BIOGRAPHIES

[See also 7a(4).]

Freeman, Joseph. "Biographical Films." *Th Arts* 25 (Dec 41) 900–906. Biographical forms in literature, theatre, and film.

Hartung, P. T. "Man or the Star." *Commonweal* 39 (31 Dec 43) 281. Brief consideration of the difficulties inherent in biographical films (i.e., Paul Muni's *Pasteur*), and concise reviews of Hollywood wartime attempts.

Kaufman, George S. "Notes for a Film Biography." *New Yorker* 21 (11 Aug 45) 26–27. An acid comment on the movie biography, stimulated by a viewing of *Rhapsody in Blue.*

Knox, Alexander. "On Playing Wilson." *Hwd Q* 1 (Oct 45). *See 2b(1).*

Crowther, Bosley. "Living Biographies, Hollywood Style." *NYTM* (20 Jan 46) 24–25+. Newest trend: romantic biography and the problem of glamorous stereotypes.

"Presidential Stars." *NYTM* (20 Oct 46). *See 2b(6).*

"Hollywood and Science." *Sci Illus* 3 (May 48) 8–10. On movies of famous scientists.

Knight, Arthur. "Take Any Life, Take Mine." *Sat Rev* (3 May 52) 31+. Why biographies are rarely suited to the movies; some recent efforts are above average.

Pichel, Irving. "*Martin Luther:* The Problem of Documentation." *QFRTV* 8 (No. 2, Winter 53) 172–185. Director describes his efforts to achieve a sense of filmed reality in this biography.

Hill, Derek. "Napoleon '55." *F&F* 1 (No. 6, Mar 55) 10. Comparison of Marlon Brando in *Desirée* with earlier Napoleons on the screen.

Gilbert, Lewis. "Drama from the Lives of Men Around Us." *F&F* 2 (No. 12, Sep 56) 9. The British director of *Reach for the Sky*, a feature-length biography of Douglas Bader, discusses the problem of dealing with factual events on film.

Roman, Robert C. "Lincoln on the Screen." *FIR* 12 (No. 2, Feb 61) 87–112.

Peck, Seymour. "Bringing Life to the Movies." *NYTM* (15 July 62) 16–17. Production stills of recent filmed biographies.

Steele, Robert. "A New Film on the Genius of Eugene O'Neill." *F Com* 4 (No. 4, Summer 68) 18–21. Analysis of background and content of biography presented by a Boston TV station.

Madsen, Axel. "The Great Race." *S&S* 37 (Autumn 68) 182. Producers vie with each other to film life of Che Guevara.

Boyajian, Cecile Starr. "Film Portraits." *F Lib Q* 3 (No. 3, Summer 70) 11–15. Biographies of famous artists and performers: traditional approaches versus *cinéma vérité*.

4k(8). EROTIC FILMS

[See also 7b(6), 7c.]

"Speaking of Pictures . . . These Movie Kisses Are Now Museum Pieces." *Life* 4 (7 Feb 38) 4–5. From library of Museum of Modern Art, some poses no longer allowed by code.

Crowther, Bosley. "Evolution of the Movie Kiss." *NYTM* (22 Dec 46) 21+. Varying techniques and positions.

"Movie Kisses . . . Now and Then." *Look* 11 (No. 12, 10 June 47) 62–67. Pictorial essay of film kisses through the years.

"Solid B.O." *Life* 25 (27 Sep 48) 89–92. Profits are down, so "girl movies" are more important than ever.

Hine, Al. "Siren Song." *Holiday* (Mar 51). See 2b(6).

Wald, Jerry, and Norman Krasna. "The Hollywood Kiss." *Look* 15 (No. 21, 9 Oct 51) 36–42. Illustrated history of the kiss in Hollywood films written by producers.

Harrington, Curtis. "The Erotic Cinema." *S&S* 22 (Oct–Dec 52) 67–74+. Harlow, Garbo, Dietrich, Crawford, and some of the films which demonstrate trends in erotic themes: *Greed, Extase, The Blue Angel,* and *The Joyless Street.*

Peck, Seymour. "It Must Be More Than Sex." *NYTM* (14 Sep 58). See 2b(6).

"Sexports." *Time* 76 (19 Sep 60). See 7e(1).

Phelps, Donald. "A Second Look at Pornography." *Kulchur* 1 (No. 3, 1961) 57–73. On the rising acceptance of pornography.

Rhode, Eric. "Sensuality in the Cinema." *S&S* 30 (Spring 61) 93–95. Film makers are obsessed with the erotic; what constitutes a sensual film? The only four the author regards

as truly sensual are Visconti's *Ossessione,* Becker's *Casque d'Or,* Eisenstein's *Que Viva Mexico* and Renoir's *Déjeuner sur l'Herbe.*

"Nudeniks." *Time* 77 (23 June 61) 51. Small Hollywood producers fill the market with cheaply made sex films.

Durgnat, Raymond. "The Dark Gods." *F&F* 8 (No. 1, Oct 61) 14–16+. Eroticism in cinema: definitions and points of departure.

Durgnat, Raymond. "Saturnalia in Cans." *F&F* 8 (No. 2, Nov 61) 33–34+. Eroticism in cinema: deviationists.

Durgnat, Raymond. "From Pleasure Castle to Libido Motel." *F&F* 8 (No. 4, Jan 62) 13–15+. Eroticism in cinema: the subconscious.

Durgnat, Raymond. "Flames of Passion—*All Next Week.*" *F&F* 8 (No. 5, Feb 62) 16–18+. Eroticism in cinema: the sacred and the profane.

Durgnat, Raymond. "Some Mad Love and the Sweet Life." *F&F* 8 (No. 6, Mar 62) 16–18+. Eroticism in cinema: analysis of French and Italian styles.

"A Primer of Passion." *Show* 2 (Mar 62) 65–66. Satiric photographic survey of how Hollywood has filmed various love situations over the years as interpreted by Sid Caesar and Celeste Holm.

Durgnat, Raymond. "Another Word for It." *F&F* 8 (No. 7, Apr 62) 13–15+. Eroticism in cinema: symbolism.

Durgnat, Raymond. "Midnight Sun." *F&F* 8 (No. 8, May 62) 21–23. Eroticism and the cosmos.

Moller, David. "Nuderama." *F Com* 1 (No. 2, Summer 62) 18–20. Report on nudist films and film houses.

Ferrer, Frank. "Exploitation Films." *F Com* 1 (No. 6, Fall 63). See 6c(3).

Mahon, Barry. "The Truth, the Whole Truth, and Nothing But the Truth About Exploitation Films." *F Com* 2 (No. 2, 1964) 1–13. Producer of *Nutty Nudes* and other films, who worked with Errol Flynn for two years, is interviewed by Gordon Hitchens on costs, grosses, censorship, and audience reactions.

Hoffman, F. A. "Prolegomena to a Study of Traditional Elements in the Erotic Film." *J Am Folklore* 78 (Apr 65) 143–148. After viewing 280 of them, Hoffman looks on erotic films as part of the tradition of folklore or myth that is as common in traditional motifs as, for example, the tradition of deception in comedy.

Knight, Arthur, and Hollis Alpert. "The History of Sex in the Cinema—Part 1, The Original Sin." *Playboy* 12 (No. 4, Apr 65) 127. Earliest attempts to show sex in film and peep shows discussed, together with the rise of zealous censorship.

Knight, Arthur, and Hollis Alpert. "The History of Sex in the Cinema—Part 2: Compounding the Sin." *Playboy* 12 (No. 5, May 65) 134–138. Sex graduates from peep show to movie house in decade 1910–1920—and the concurrent censorship reaction.

Knight, Arthur, and Hollis Alpert. "The History of Sex in the Cinema—Part 3: The 20's." *Playboy* 12 (No. 6, June 65) 155–160.

Knight, Arthur, and Hollis Alpert. "The History of Sex in the Cinema—Part 4: European Sex Stars of '20's." *Playboy* 12 (No. 7, Aug 65) 114–120.

Knight, Arthur, and Hollis Alpert. "The History of Sex in the Cinema—Part 5: Sex Stars of the '20's." *Playboy* 12 (No. 9, Sep 65) 170–177.

Knight, Arthur, and Hollis Alpert. "The History of Sex in the Cinema—Part 6: The 30's in America." *Playboy* 12 (No. 11, Nov 65) 150–157.

Krassner, Paul. "How Soft Was My Pornography." *Take One* 1 (No. 2, 1966) 11–12. A humorous discussion: "soft-core" pornography in advertising and commercials.

McGillivray, David. "A Maiden Voyage into Moving Pornography." *Film* (No. 47, Winter 66) 36–37. One person's account of seeing a pornographic film and finding it invigorating.

Knight, Arthur, and Hollis Alpert. "The History of Sex in the Cinema—Part 7: Europe in the 30's." *Playboy* 13 (No. 2, Feb 66) 134–141. Films exploiting sexual themes were made in Europe because of restrictions of Production Code in U.S.

Knight, Arthur, and Hollis Alpert. "The History of Sex in the Cinema—Part 8: Sex Stars of the 30's." *Playboy* 13 (No. 4, Apr 66) 142–149. Gable, West, Garbo, Lombard, Turner, Lamour, Grable.

Whitehall, Richard. "The Face of the Vampire." *Cinema* (Calif) 3 (No. 3, July 66) 11–15. "Vamps" of the cinema, particularly Theda Bara; the era of the *femme fatale* and through the present time.

Knight, Arthur, and Hollis Alpert. "The History of Sex in the Cinema—Part 9: The Forties, War and Peace in Hollywood." *Playboy* 13 (No. 8, Aug 66) 120–128.

Knight, Arthur, and Hollis Alpert. "The History of Sex in the Cinema—Part 10: The 1940's, Europe." *Playboy* 13 (No. 9, Sep 66) 172–178+.

Knight, Arthur, and Hollis Alpert. "The History of Sex in the Cinema—Part 11: Sex Stars of the Forties (U.S.A.)." *Playboy* 13 (No. 10, Oct 66) 150–164. Private lives and public images of "love goddesses" (Betty Grable, Veronica Lake, Esther Williams) and "matinee idols" (Peck, Bogart, Gable).

Knight, Arthur, and Hollis Alpert. "The History of Sex in the Cinema—Part 12: The Fifties—Hollywood Grows Up." *Playboy* 13 (No. 11, Nov 66) 162+. Hollywood's attack on

social problems with new maturity; also problems of censorship.

Knight, Arthur, and Hollis Alpert. "The History of Sex in the Cinema—Part 13: Sex Stars of the Fifties." *Playboy* 13 (No. 12, Dec 66) 232+.

Knight, Arthur, and Hollis Alpert. "The History of Sex in the Cinema—Part 14: Sex Stars of the Fifties." *Playboy* 14 (No. 1, Jan 67) 95–108. Sex images—on screen and off—of such stars as Monroe, Loren, Lollobrigida, Taylor, Novak; the increasingly permissive audience; also Brando, Dean, Hudson.

Knight, Arthur, and Hollis Alpert. "The History of Sex in the Cinema—Part 15: The Experimental Films." *Playboy* 14 (No. 4, Apr 67) 136–143. Emshwiller (*Relativity*), Buñuel, Cocteau, Dulac; from 1920s to present.

Knight, Arthur, and Hollis Alpert. "The History of Sex in the Cinema—Part 16: The Nudies." *Playboy* 14 (No. 6, June 67) 124–135. History from 1930s (so-called Main Street films), 1940s ("jungle adventures"), 1950s–1960s ("educational" tours of nudist camps), to known stars of late 1960s.

Knight, Arthur, and Hollis Alpert. "The History of Sex in the Cinema—Part 17: The Stag Film." *Playboy* 14 (No. 11, Nov 67) 154–158. The enduring stereotypes.

Knight, Arthur, and Hollis Alpert. "The History of Sex in the Cinema—Part 18: The 1960's, Hollywood Unbuttons." *Playboy* 15 (No. 4, Apr 68) 138–149. Unprecedented nudity produced by increasingly permissive moral attitudes.

Knight, Arthur, and Hollis Alpert. "The History of Sex in the Cinema—Part 19: The 1960's, Eros Unbound in Foreign Films." *Playboy* 15 (No. 7, July 68) 130–145. Increasing explicitness of films from early part of decade (*La Dolce Vita, Never on Sunday*) to *I Am Curious* (*Yellow*)—"as explicit as you can get in or out of a stag film."

Phillips, Gene D. "The Boys on the Bandwagon." *Take One* 2 (No. 8, 1969) 6–8. Homosexual themes in American and British films.

Knight, Arthur, and Hollis Alpert. "The History of Sex in the Cinema—Part 20: Sex Stars of the 60's." *Playboy* 16 (No. 1, Jan 69) 157–172. Taylor, Loren, Bardot, Mastroianni, Connery.

Lithgow, James, and Colin Heard. "*Underground U.S.A.* and the Sexploitation Market." *F&F* 15 (No. 11, Aug 69) 18–29.

Knight, Arthur, and Hollis Alpert. "Sex in the Cinema—1969." *Playboy* 16 (No. 11, Nov 69) 168–181. Increasing freedom on screen in words and pictures.

Fadiman, William. "Speaking Out." *F&F* 16 (No. 8, May 70) 27–28. On the current trend toward sexploitation films in the Hollywood major studios.

Schickel, Richard. "Porn and Man at Yale." *Harper's* 241 (July 70) 34–38. Russ Meyer film festival at Yale; some discussion of Meyer's films.

Keneas, A. "True Blue." *Newswk* 76 (13 July 70) 91–92. Getting sex on the screen by labeling it documentary: Danish imports.

Knight, Arthur, and Hollis Alpert. "Sex in the Cinema: 1970." *Playboy* 17 (No. 11, Nov 70) 152–164. Anything can be seen on screen: interracial sex, homosexuality, underground (Warhol), documentary sex films; forces of reaction are readying a counter-attack.

4k(9). STORIES FOR CHILDREN AND YOUTH

[See also 7b(3).]

Jones, I. W. "Children and the Movies." *Ladies' Home J* 48 (Sep 31) 21+. "Film Topics: The Children's Cinema." *Rev of Reviews* (London) 84 (No. 527, 10 Dec 33) 64. Films made for children.

Eastman, Fred. "How to Select Movies for Children." *Parents Mag* 9 (Mar 34) 18–19+.

Hecht, G. J. "How to Get Better Movies for Your Children." *Parents Mag* 9 (Sep 34) 15+.

Farr, William. "Films for Children." *S&S* 3 (No. 12, Winter 34–35) 162–164. Making and exhibiting them.

"Films for Children." *S&S* 5 (No. 20, Winter 36–37) 128–129. A report on the Conference on Films for Children, organized by the British Film Institute.

Bernstein, Sidney. "What the Film Trade Has Done." *S&S* 5 (No. 20, Winter 36–37) 133–135. An outline of the film industry's attempt to provide films for children.

Lasch, F. C. "Movie Values for Boys and Girls." *Parents Mag* 12 (Dec 37) 26–27. A plea for better selectivity regarding movies for children.

"Children's Matinees." *S&S* 11 (No. 41, Summer 42) 18–20. The Odeon Theatrs in Great Britain attempt to create special programs for children.

Llewellyn, Michael Gareth. "The Kind of Film for Children." *S&S* 14 (No. 55, Oct 45) 77–79. Films should not talk down or preach to them.

Field, Mary. "Children and the Entertainment Film." *S&S* 15 (No. 58, Summer 46) 46–47. Planning more suitable stories.

Gorney, Sondra. "The Puppet and the Moppet." *Hwd Q* 1 (No. 4, July 46). See *2h(6).*

Meadow, Noel, and Harry L. Ober. "Adults Not Admitted . . ." *Screen Writer* 2 (Nov 46) 19–23. New York's Children's Saturday Matinee Club caters to the ten- to twelve-year-old audience; the need for good chil-

dren's films rather than films for an adult with a ten- to twelve-year-old mentality.

Gorney, Sondra. "On Children's Cinema: America and Britain." *Hwd Q* 3 (Fall 47) 56–62. U.S. so-called children's films are not produced with the young audience in mind; Mary Field's children's film project for J. Arthur Rank.

Edwards, C. "Films That Live Again for Children." *Parents Mag* 22 (Oct 47) 36–37.

Nathan, P. S. "Books into Films: Saturday Matinee Plan." *Publishers Weekly* 152 (25 Oct 47) 2100. Children's film library set up by the Motion Picture Association.

Schooling, Patricia. "Children's Entertainment Films." *S&S* 16 (No. 64, Winter 47–48) 172–175. Children's Entertainment Films produces films exclusively for children.

"Films for Children: Flow Has Been Reduced to a Trickle." *Good Housekeeping* 129 (Sep 49) 11+.

Hillard, J. "Children's Classics." *Wilson Lib Bul* 24 (Nov 49) 248.

Daly, Rosemary. "Films for Fledglings." *SRL* 32 (19 Nov 49) 58. Report on the film program of the Brooklyn Children's Museum.

Ellis, Olivia. "Entertainment for Young Audiences." *CSMM* (24 Dec 49). See *4e(1b).*

"The Front Page: Children and the Cinema." *S&S* 19 (July 50) 189–190. Summary of an official report; Rank will no longer make children's films.

"Children's Film Library Grows." *CSMM* (4 Nov 50) 20. Motion Picture Association offers list of past and present features they say children like.

Starr, Cecile. "Ideas on Film: Kid Stuff." *SRL* 33 (18 Nov 50) 44–45. Report on 16mm children's film programs as good replacement for TV.

Raynor, Henry. "Heaven Lies About Us." *S&S* 19 (Dec 50) 319–322. Films about children are not always films children like to see; they tend to like the comic-book villain without redeeming features.

Pfeiffer, K. "3,000,000 Children Have a Saturday Date." *Parents Mag* 26 (Feb 51) 44–45+. Plans for a children's film library to keep matinee films available for children.

Stevenson, Grace, and Ruth Hewett. "Films for Children." *Lib J* 76 (15 Apr 51) 721. Selection standards and a variety of films.

"Republic of Childhood Documentary Based on Children's Books." *Publishers Weekly* 160 (27 Oct 51). See *8c(4).*

Bunting, Caroline K. "Filming Young Readers for Globe-Circling Picture." *Lib J* 76 (15 Dec 51). See *8c(4).*

Hills, Janet. "Children's Films." *S&S* 21 (Apr–June 52) 179–181+. Some of the Rank Organisation's Children's Entertainment Films and some of the formulas by which they work; new UNESCO publication discusses children's films.

Edwards, Roy. "The Fifth Columnists." *S&S* 23 (July–Sep 53). *See 7a(2)*.

"The Children's Film Foundation." *Nature* 172 (No. 4390, 19 Dec 53) 1134. Foundation which distributes, produces, and exhibits special entertainment films for children.

Butcher, Maryvonne. "British Foundation for Children's Films." *America* 91 (17 July 54) 399–401. Objectives: production, promotion, and exhibition of suitable films.

Starr, Cecile. "Your Children's Movies." *Sat Rev* 37 (13 Nov 54) 28+. Hollywood has established a Children's Film Library with low exhibition rentals; some children's films discussed.

Field, Mary. "Children's Taste in Films." *QFRTV* 11 (No. 1, Fall 56) 14–23. British pioneer in educational films and founder of Children's Entertainment Films for J. Arthur Rank tells what kind of films children really want; history of CEF.

Baum, Frank. "The Oz Film Co." *FIR* 7 (Aug–Sep 56) 329–333. Story of the failure of the Oz Film Manufacturing Company, which built one of the largest pre-World War I film studios in Hollywood for the sole purpose of making children's fantasy films based on the famous Oz fairy tales; the studio was headed by the author of the stories, L. Frank Baum.

Starr, Cecile. "Fiction, Fantasy and Fairy Tales on Film." *House Beautiful* 98 (Oct 56) 212–213+.

"Films for Children Dodos?" *America* 96 (10 Nov 56) 142. Call for the revival of films for children.

Starr, Cecile. "Something for the Children." *Sat Rev* 38 (12 Nov 56) 28. Outstanding children's films at the Edinburgh Film Festival.

Finley, James F. "TV for Me, If Teens Rule Screens." *Cath World* 184 (Feb 57) 380. Attack on Elvis Presley and other teenage movies.

Marcussen, Elsa. "Films for Children in Scandinavia." *Am Scandinavian Rev* 45 (Mar 57). *See 4e(5c)*.

"Sideburns and Sympathy." *Time* 71 (3 Mar 58) 82. Kansas City theatre owner turns to production for teen market.

"Tall Tales Told About Tiny Folk." *Life* 45 (15 Dec 58) 45–46. *The Seventh Voyage of Sinbad* and *Tom Thumb* are both about miniature people.

Schindel, Morton. "Picture Books into Films." *Lib J* 84 (15 Jan 59) 224–226. As told by this producer of films for children.

Dyer, Peter John. "Youth and the Cinema (1): The Teenage Rave." *S&S* 29 (Winter 59–60). *See 7a(2)*.

"Lamorisse's New Balloon." *Time* 76 (24 Oct 60). *See 5, Albert Lamorisse*.

Neiss, Laura. "Teen-Agers of America, Arise!" *Seventeen* 22 (Jan 63) 10. On the teenage image in films.

Peterson, Sidney. "You Can't Pet a Chicken." *Atlantic* 211 (Mar 63). *See 7a(2)*.

Hartung, P. T. "Children's Hour." *Commonweal* 78 (6 Sep 63) 539. Reviews of children's films.

Bean, Robin. "Keeping Up with the Beatles." *F&F* 10 (No. 5, Feb. 64) 9–12. Study of films for teenage audiences.

Limbacher, James L. "Movies Are Better Than Ever." *Lib J* 89 (15 May 64) 2152–2155. Children's Film Foundation features listed.

Radnitz, Robert B. "On Creating Films for Children." *Horn Bk* 40 (Aug 64) 415–417.

Ehrlich, H. "Hollywood's Teen-Age Gold Mine." *Look* 28 (3 Nov 64) 60–64+. Teen-age beach-party pictures.

Ransom, J. "Beach-Blanket Babies." *Esq* 64 (July 65) 90–95. Teenage beach movies.

Lewis, Richard Warren. "Those Swinging Beach Movies." *SEP* 238 (31 July 65) 83–87.

Lapinski, Susan. "In My Opinion." *Seventeen* 25 (Mar 66) 26. A sixteen-year-old girl is against the beach-ski-surf-rock soap operas.

Kael, Pauline. "Movies for Young Children." *McCall's* 93 (June 66) 36+. "Cheating" movies versus good animal and undersea adventures: *Born Free* and *Around the World Under the Sea*.

"Fallen Angels." *Newswk* 68 (15 Aug 66) 84. American International Pictures revises formula of juvenile beach-party pictures.

Rubbo, Michael. "Love and Life in Children's Films." *Take One* 1 (No. 7, 1967) 20–22. A discussion of the values in children's films, especially those made in Czechoslovakia and England.

Schindel, M. "Confessions of a Book Fiend." *Lib J* 92 (15 Feb 67) 858–859. Morton Schindel, president of Weston Woods Studios, produces films and filmstrips based on children's books.

"Z as in Zzzz or Zowie." *Time* 89 (5 May 67) 61. James Nicholson and Samuel Arkoff of American International Pictures make films for teenagers.

Morgenstern, Joseph. "What the Kids Should See." *Newswk* 70 (18 Sep 67) 92+. On children's films and television programs.

Parks, Lanetta W. "Small Triumphs." *F Lib Q* 1 (No. 4, Fall 68) 45–46. Suggestions for films for teenagers at public libraries.

Reed, Rex. "Films for the Popcorn Brigade." *Holiday* 45 (June 69) 20+. Reviews of movies for children.

Walsh, Moira. "Films for Children." *America* 121 (19 July 69) 48. Review of three current "good" children's films.

Forman, Rose. "Television for Children, Socialist Style." *F Com* 5 (No. 2, Fall 69). *See 4e(9).*

Pellowski, Anne. "Children's Cinema: International Dilemma or Delight?" *F Lib Q* 2 (No. 4, Fall 69) 5–11. A survey of the international situation in films especially for children; includes bibliography of materials on children's films.

Mannon-Tissot, Thalia. "Innovation Through Trial and Error." *F Lib Q* 2 (No. 4, Fall 69) 13–15. The film program for children at the Brooklyn Public Library.

Marcussen, Elsa B. "Cine-Chain Links Nations." *F Lib Q* 2 (No. 4, Fall 69) 17–20. Activities of the International Centre of Films for Children and Young People worldwide.

Deitch, Gene. "An American in Prague." *F Lib Q* 2 (No. 4, Fall 69) 20–23. An animated-film maker writes of the films he has made for children in the last ten years in Czechoslovakia.

Forman, Rose. "Czech Film Festival." *F Lib Q* 2 (No. 4, Fall 69) 23–24+. Report on the children's film studio in Gottwaldov, Czechoslovakia.

Weightman, John. "Outsider Rides Again." *Encounter* 33 (Nov 69). *See 7a.*

4k(10). CRIME AND SPY THRILLERS

[See also 7b(4).]

Williamson, A. Edmund. "Ridding Local Movies of Gangster Films." *Am City* 45 (Sep 31). *See 7c(2a).*

Thomson, H. Douglas. "Detective Films." *S&S* 4 (No. 13, Spring 35) 10–11. Brief attempt to define them.

Sayers, Dorothy L. "Detective Stories for the Screen." *S&S* 7 (No. 26, Summer 38) 49–50. Writer gives advice to producers.

Shearer, Lawrence. "Crime Certainly Pays on the Screen." *NYTM* (5 Aug 45) 17+. Extensive look at the rash of "hard-boiled" crime movies and their possible psychological implications; reference to writer Raymond Chandler.

Houseman, John. "Today's Hero: A Review." *Hwd Q* 2 (No. 2, Jan 47). *See 7a(5).*

Warshow, Robert. "The Gangster as Tragic Hero." *Partisan Rev* 15 (Feb 48) 240–244. He is a man of the city, with a drive for success; at the same time he represents a rejection of the demands of modern life.

Hitchcock, Alfred. "Enjoyment of Fear." *Good Housekeeping* 128 (Feb 49) 39, 241–243. The plot must be valid, while the character identified with remains safe.

Wolfenstein, Martha, and Nathan Leites. "Crime Patterns in Today's Movies." *FIR* 1 (Mar 50) 11–15. The different treatment given in American, British, and French films.

Henry, Clayton R., Jr. "Crime Films and Social Criticism." *FIR* 2 (May 51) 31–34. Critical

analyses of the American mystery films, *The Maltese Falcon, Murder My Sweet, Asphalt Jungle,* and *The Third Man;* they indicate that "crime flourishes because the common man avoids his responsibilities to the society in which he lives."

Tynan, Kenneth. "Cagney and the Mob." *S&S* 20 (May 51). *See 7a(5).*

Durgnat, R. E. "Ways of Melodrama." *S&S* 21 (Aug–Sep 51) 34–40. Its mixture in various films, good and bad.

"Public Enemy No. 1." *NYTM* (21 June 53) 23. The French shoot a satire on gangster films on location in New York.

Rogers, W. P. "Nothing Comic About Crime." *Vital Speeches* 20 (1 Feb 54) 244–245.

Connor, Edward. "The Mystery Film." *FIR* 5 (Mar 54) 120–123. How audiences are kept in the dark; actors who have played sleuths.

Connor, Edward. "The 6 Charlie Chans." *FIR* 6 (Jan 55). *See 2b(6).*

Grace, Harry. "A Taxonomy of American Crime Film Themes." *J Soc Psych* 42 (Aug 55) 129–136. A brief attempt to classify crime themes of American feature films according to their developmental periods and to gain insight into the social dynamics of a mass communication culture.

Houston, Penelope. "The Private Eye." *S&S* 26 (Summer 56) 22–23+. Films made from the novels of Raymond Chandler, the detective-story writer: "The more vicious forms of corruption are presented so objectively that the oblique social comment may easily be interpreted merely as a cynical gesture of despair." Comments by Chandler on *Farewell, My Lovely, The Big Sleep, The Maltese Falcon, The Lady in the Lake,* and his scripts for *Double Indemnity* and *Strangers on a Train.*

Connor, Edward. "The 12 Bulldog Drummonds." *FIR* 7 (Oct 56) 394–397. A survey of the portrayal of the role of international adventurer Bulldog Drummond by different actors in films 1922–1951.

Schorer, Mark. "Japan's Delinquents." *Reporter* 15 (18 Oct 56). *See 4f(1).*

De La Roche, Catherine. "The Cinema—Mirror of Our Times?" *Film* (No. 11, Jan–Feb 57). *See 7a(1).*

Farber, Manny. "Underground Films." *Commentary* 24 (Nov 57). *See 3b.*

Connor, Edward. "The 9 Philo Vances." *FIR* 9 (Mar 58) 133–137, 154. The characterization of the role of the detective by Williaim Powell, Basil Rathbone, Warren William, Paul Lukas, Edmund Lowe, and others.

"Will Hollywood Never Learn?" *America* 99 (12 Apr 58) 40. Indictment of Hollywood's bent for crime and corruption films.

Dyer, Peter John. "The Murderers Among Us." *F&F* 5 (No. 3, Dec 58). *See 4d.*

Wilson, Richard. "Hoodlums: The Myth or

Reality." *F&F* 5 (No. 9, June 59) 10. Director prefers to make gangster films about real gangsters.

Siodmak, Robert. "Hoodlums: The Myth." *F&F* 5 (No. 9, June 59) 10, 35. Director of gangster films likes to make films about fictional gangsters rather than real ones.

Connor, Edward. "The 4 Ellery Queens." *FIR* 6 (No. 6, June–July 60) 338–342. Brief discussion of the detective films and the actors who played the title role.

Dyer, Peter John. "Young and Innocent." *S&S* 30 (Spring 61) 80–83. A historical survey of prewar British thrillers, with Hitchcock leading the way; two "discoveries" unseen since the 1930s are Hitchcock's *Secret Agent* and Arthur Woods' *They Drive by Night*.

Hull, David Stewart. "International Delinquency." *Film* (No. 28, Mar–Apr 61) 28–30. Brief account of recent European and Japanese films dealing with juvenile delinquency.

Eyles, Allen. "A Killing or Two." *Motion* (No. 3, Spring 62) 17–22. The gangster film.

Whitehall, Richard. "Crime, Inc." *F&F* 10 (No. 4, Jan 64) 7–12; (No. 5, Feb 64) 17–22; (No. 6, Mar 64) 39–44. Three-part study of crime films: rackets, gangsters, G-men, public enemies.

"The Bond Wagon." *Newswk* 63 (11 May 64) 96+. Bizarre props and gold-painted girl help account for success of the James Bond movies.

"James Bond's Girls." *Vogue* 144 (July 64) 74–77. Pictures.

Houston, Penelope. "007." *S&S* 34 (Winter 64–65) 14–16. The James Bond films and the Ian Fleming stories.

"Bondomania." *Time* 85 (11 June 65) 59. The popularity of James Bond films.

"007 Girls." *Time* 86 (10 Sep 65) 53. New movies about female spies.

Johnson, Ian. "007 Plus Four." *F&F* 12 (No. 1, Oct 65) 5–8. On the James Bond movies.

Stewart-Gordon, James. "007—The Spy with the Golden Touch." *Rdrs Dig* 87 (Oct 65) 113–117. On the creation of the James Bond character.

Lawrenson, Helen. "Fu Manchu Strikes Again." *Holiday* 39 (Feb 66) 128+. New cycle of films.

"Spies Who Came into the Fold." *Time* 87 (4 Mar 66) 105–106. Analysis of the espionage craze in current films.

Carpenter, Richard G. "007 and the Myth of the Hero." *J Pop Cult* 1 (No. 2, 1967) 79–89. James Bond is in the tradition of the questing mythic heroes of the past—Achilles, Jason, Hercules.

Roseman, Eugene. "In My Opinion." *Seventeen* 26 (Feb 67) 268. An eighteen-year-old is against Bogart and his "hippie" fans.

"The Many Lives of James Bond." *Esq* 67 (Mar 67) 73–85. Centers on *You Only Live Twice*.

Kahan, Saul. "The Absurd Horrors of Spying." *F&F* 13 (No. 8, May 67) 46–47. On the film *The Defector*.

Palance, Leo. "When the Private Eye Was King: Nuanced Hero in a Dark Scene." *Arts Mag* 42 (Sep–Oct 67) 16–17. Brief examination of the private-detective genre of the 1940s in film and literature (Howard Hawks, Raymond Chandler, Dashiell Hammett, Ross MacDonald, etc.).

French, Philip. "Incitement Against Violence." *S&S* 37 (Winter 67–68) 2–8. Cycles in American gangster films from the early 1930s up to Arthur Penn's *Bonnie and Clyde* and Roger Corman's *The St. Valentine's Day Massacre;* how films influenced the real gangsters' life-style; what they seem to say in different eras.

Geduld, Carolyn and Harry. "From Kops to Robbers: Transformation of Archetypal Figures in the American Cinema of the Twenties and Thirties." *J Pop Cult* 1 (No. 4, Spring 68). *See 4d.*

Godfrey, Lionel. "Martinis Without Olives." *F&F* 14 (No. 7, Apr 68) 10–14. On new and old private-detective films.

Schrader, Paul. "They're Young . . . They're in Love . . . They Kill People." *Cinema* (Calif) 5 (No. 2, 1969) 28–29. On *Bonnie and Clyde, The Big Bounce,* and *Pretty Poison.*

Durgnat, Raymond. "Spies and Ideologies." *Cinema* (Cambridge) (No. 2, Mar 69) 5–13. The ideological basis of several spy films.

Durgnat, Raymond. "The Family Tree of the Film *Noir.*" *Cinema* (Cambridge) (Nos. 6–7, Aug 70) 49–56. Historical sketch; cycles, concerns, variation.

4k(11). RACE RELATIONS FILMS

[See also 7a(2), 7a(3), 7b(2).]

Kronenberger, L., and J. T. McManus. "Motion Pictures, the Theater, and Race Relations." *Annals of Am Acad Polit and Soc Sci* 244 (Mar 46) 152–158. How films have dealt with social problems: a title-by-title rundown.

Nathan, P. S. "Books into Films." *Publishers Weekly* 150 (21 Dec 46) 3302. Is the screen learning to speak out against racial and religious bigotry?

Margolis, Herbert F. "The Hollywood Scene: The American Minority Problem." *Penguin F Rev* 5 (Jan 48) 82–85. Success of *Crossfire,* plans for *Gentleman's Agreement.*

Mayer, Robert. "Hollywood Report." *S&S* 17 (No. 65, Spring 48) 32–34. Controversial new films such as *Gentleman's Agreement.*

Wollenberg, H. H. "The Jewish Theme in Contemporary Cinema." *Penguin F Rev* 8 (Jan 49) 46–50. The revelation of anti-Semitism in the U.S. through the cinema.

"Sweepstakes: Movies with Social Consciousness." *Time* 53 (21 Mar 49) 98. Films on "the Negro problem," such as *Pinky, Intruder in the Dust.*

Tyler, Parker. "Hollywood as a Universal Church." *Am Q* 2 (1950) 165–176. Emphasis on racial assimilation as ideology of some films.

Nathan, Paul S. "Books into Films." *Publishers Weekly* 157 (21 Jan 50) 260. Movies dealing with anti-Negro prejudice.

Winnington, Richard. "Negro Films." *S&S* 19 (Jan 50) 27–30. A discussion of some of the "color-bar" films made in Hollywood, such as *Home of the Brave, Pinky,* and *Lost Boundaries;* all three seem to be couched in a compromise and leave the basic problems untouched with happy Hollywood endings.

Knight, Arthur. "The Negro in Films Today." *FIR* 1 (Feb 50) 14–19. New, questioning treatment of the American Negro in four films: *Home of the Brave, Pinky, Intruder in the Dust,* and *Lost Boundaries.*

Ellis, Robert. "Hollywood Director Speaks Out." *Negro Dig* 9 (Jan 51) 42–44. Mark Robson discusses his new race relations film *Lights Out* and his pride in having directed the first anti-Jim Crow film, *Home of the Brave.*

Weales, Gerald. "Pro-Negro Films in Atlanta." *FIR* 3 (Nov 52). *See 7b(1b).*

Johnson, Albert. "Beige, Brown or Black." *FQ* 13 (No. 1, Fall 59) 38–44. *Island in the Sun* is at least a turning point in the history of race relations pictures because it deals with miscegenation.

Axthelm, Kenneth W. "Minority Groups: Our Majority Audience." *F Lib Q* 1 (No. 3, Summer 68) 25–29. Films to use to interest minority groups.

4k(12). FILMS ABOUT WAR AND PEACE

Santelli, Cesar. "Children and War Films." *Living Age* 338 (1 Aug 30). *See 7b(3).*

"War Films: For and Against." *Lit Dig* 110 (29 Aug 31) 14–15. French critics offer opinions on propaganda in film.

"Truth About War." *Commonweal* 15 (13 Jan 32) 285. Praises *The Big Parade, What Price Glory?, All Quiet on the Western Front,* among others, for stressing brutality of war.

Sydney, John. "Films and Peace." *S&S* 3 (No. 11, Autumn 34) 110–112. A survey of the films which deal with war and peace.

Evans, Frederick. "War and Child Opinion." *S&S* 4 (No. 15, Autumn 35). *See 7b(3a).*

Cummings, M. "War on the Screen: Can It Foster Peace?" *Delineator* 129 (July 36) 10–11.

Levin, Meyer. "Glory Poison for the Screen." *Rdrs Dig* 29 (Dec 36) 101–102. Pictures changed or dropped because they were too "antimilitaristic" for foreign nations; condensed from *Esquire.*

Fischer, John. "It's Zero Hour, Hollywood." *New Masses* 44 (8 Sep 42) 16–17. In order to be fully useful in the war effort, Hollywood must stop presenting war situations in terms of the prewar plot formulas and devices.

Isaacs, H. R. "Shadows of War." *Th Arts* 26 (Nov 42) 689–696. Hollywood's version.

Reavis, W. C. "War Films Available to School and Adult Audiences." *School Rev* 51 (Apr 43) 205. List of titles.

Williams, J. R. "Britain Makes the Movie a Weapon of War." *Am Federationist* 50 (May 43). *See 8c(2a).*

Farber, Manny. "Movies in Wartime." *New Rep* 110 (3 Jan 44) 16–20. Stereotyped plots and "enemies."

Mayer, Arthur L. "Post-War Preambles: IV. Films for Peace." *Th Arts* 28 (Nov 44) 642–649.

Jones, Dorothy B. "The Hollywood War Film: 1942–1944." *Hwd Q* 1 (No. 1, Oct 45). *See 4d.*

Nichols, Dudley. "Men in Battle: A Review of Three Current Pictures." *Hwd Q* 1 (No. 1, Oct 45) 34–39. Screenwriter looks at *The Story of G. I. Joe, Counterattack,* and *A Bell for Adano.*

Fearing, Franklin. "Warriors Return: Normal or Neurotic?" *Hwd Q* 1 (No. 1, Oct 45) 97–109. Films concerned with civilian-soldier relationships after the war; UCLA professor of psychology objects to *I'll Be Seeing You* as reflecting a psychiatric view that all soldiers "are more or less permanently damaged by war service." See dissenting letter (with reply) (No. 3, Apr 46) 321–328, listed in *7a(4).*

Hine, A. "Movies." *Holiday* 6 (Sep 49) 19–20+. List and description of World War II films; some novels and plays about the war that might make excellent films.

"World War II on the Screen." *NYTM* (11 Sep 49) 24–25. Stills from a group of current films.

Slater, L. "War Over Hollywood." *Newswk* 36 (28 Aug 50) 76–78. Hollywood's hesitancy to plan Korean War films.

Reisz, Karel. "Milestone and War." *Sequence* (No. 14, 1952) 12–16. A critique of Lewis Milestone's war films.

"Why War?" *S&S* 24 (Jan–Mar 55). *See 4e(1b).*

"War in Hollywood." *Newswk* 50 (16 Sep 57) 118+. William Wellman's *Darby's Rangers* and his other combat movies.

Gillett, John. "Westfront, 1957." *S&S* 27 (Winter 57–58) 122–127. Films about World War II: *The Bridge on the River Kwai, Attack, Men in War, Bitter Victory, The Way Ahead,* and others; the social and political attitudes that generated them.

Zavattini, Cesare. "First Outline for a Film on Peace." *F Cult* (No. 20, 1959) 3–7.

de Laurot, Edward. *"Vive la Guerre!"* F Cult (No. 20, 1959) 7–11. An antiwar script outline.

Butcher, Maryvonne. "Enemy on Film." *Commonweal* 69 (20 Mar 59) 642–644. Discussion of war films.

Robinson, David. "The Old Lie." *S&S* 31 (Autumn 62) 201–203. Milestone's *All Quiet on the Western Front* and Chaplin's *Shoulder Arms* were perhaps the greatest statements on World War I by the generation which fought it; comments on selected films about World War I.

"Coming: The End of the World." *Newswk* 61 (4 Mar 63) 84+. Movie flirtations with nuclear war; comments by directors and producers (*On the Beach, Fail-Safe*).

Jones, James. "Phoney War Films." *SEP* 236 (30 Mar 63) 64–67. In a movie, the heroes cannot lose.

Bachmann, Gideon. "What Price Glory?" *Film* (No. 36, Summer 63) 26–32. The use of sex and/or propaganda, the incitement to hatred, and the use of violence, make war films truly obscene.

Whitehall, Richard. "1 . . . 2 . . . 3?" *F&F* 10 (No. 11, Aug 64) 7–12. A study of the war film.

Prideaux, T. "Take Aim: Fire at the Agonies of War." *Life* 55 (20 Dec 63) 115–118+. Two new antiwar films: *The Victors* and *Dr. Strangelove.*

Knight, A. "Films for Peace." *Sat Rev* 47 (19 Dec 64) 23. International Peace Film Festival at Los Alamos.

Kniper, John. "Civil War Films: A Quantitative Description of a Genre." *J Soc Cin* 5 (1965) 81–89. There were 359 of them in the decade 1910–1919, the peak year being 1913; of 457 films studied, 42% were on the side of the South and only 29% for the North.

Dworkin, Martin S. "Clean Germans and Dirty Politics." *F Com* 3 (No. 1, Winter 65) 36–41. German generals seem to have been nonpolitical according to some British and American films about World War II; comments on *The Desert Fox, The Young Lions, The Enemy Below,* and *I Aim at the Stars.*

Guy, Rory. "Hollywood Goes to War." *Cinema* (Calif) 3 (No. 2, Mar 66) 22–29. Movies of World War II.

Spears, Jack. "World War I on the Screen." *FIR* 17 (No. 5, May 66) 274–292; 17 (No. 6, June–July 66) 247–265. Contemporary films.

Soderbergh, P. A. *"Aux Armes!* The Rise of the Hollywood War Film, 1916–1930." *South Atlantic Q* 65 (Autumn 66) 509–522. The development of various plot patterns of standard "blood-and-thunder" war films (1916–1930), with special reference to D. W. Griffith and King Vidor.

Soderbergh, Peter A. "On War and the Movies: A Reappraisal." *Centennial Rev* 11 (1967) 405–418.

Arlen, Michael J. "The Air." *New Yorker* 42 (21 Jan 67) 75–76+. Treatment of World War II in films and on TV.

"Kill Cong: No Films on Vietnamese War from Hollywood." *Nation* 204 (10 Apr 67) 453. An editorial.

"Cinematic Escalation." *Atlas* 13 (May 67) 20. Analysis of the appeal of American war films.

Behlmer, Rudy. "World War I Aviation Films." *FIR* 18 (No. 7, Aug–Sep 67) 413–444. During 1925–1966.

"John Wayne's Green Beret." *Nation* 205 (11 Dec 67) 614. An editorial opposing his film *The Green Berets.*

Madsen, Axel. "The Big Silence." *S&S* 37 (Winter 67–68) 18–19. *The Green Berets* has finished shooting in Georgia but little else, pro or con, has been done in Hollywood on the Vietnam war.

Rosenblatt, Daniel. "Behind the Lines: France." *F Soc Rev* 4 (No. 3, 1968) 17–23. World War I in the French film.

Bragin, John. "Behind the Lines: Germany." *F Soc Rev* 4 (No. 3, 1968) 24–29. World War I in the German film.

Fenin, George N. "Behind the Lines: Italy." *F Soc Rev* 4 (No. 3, 1968) 30–33. World War I in Italian films, with special emphasis on Monicelli's *La Grande Guerra.*

Hill, Steven P. "Behind the Lines: Russia." *F Soc Rev* 4 (No. 3, 1968) 34–41. World War I in the Russian film.

Thompson, Richard. "Behind the Lines: America." *F Soc Rev* 4 (No. 3, 1968) 42–45. World War I in American films.

Soderbergh, Peter A. "The Grand Illusion: Hollywood and World War II, 1930–1945." *U of Dayton Rev* 5 (1968) 13–22.

Madsen, Axel. "Vietnam and the Movies." *Cinema* (Calif) 4 (No. 1, Spring 68) 10–13. Movies set in Vietnam war.

Ball, Robert O. "A Study of War." *F Soc Rev* (Apr 68) 42–46. Outline of a film course section dealing with war.

Halliwell, Leslie. "Over the Brink." *F&F* 14 (No. 12, Sep 68) 55–60; 15 (No. 1, Oct 68) 59–64. Films made during World War II; two articles.

Soderbergh, Peter A. "The War Films." *Discourse* (Winter 68) 87–91.

Bielecki, Stanley. "Zanuck Goes to War." *F&F* 15 (No. 11, Aug 69) 56–60. About *Tora! Tora! Tora!* and *Patton.*

Grossman, E. "Bloody Popcorn." *Harper's* 241 (Dec 70) 32–40. A comparison of *M*A*S*H, Patton,* and *Catch-22* as new movie approaches to war.

5. Biography

[See also 3b(1), 8c, 10.]

A

Uselton, Roi A. "**Renée Adorée.**" *FIR* 19 (No. 6, June–July 68) 345–357. Career of French-born actress of the 1920s and 1930s; film chronology.

Lundquist, Gunnar. "**Hans Albers.**" *FIR* 16 (No. 3, Mar 65) 150–177. Career of little-known German actor who enjoyed great popularity in his native country.

Silke, James R. "**Lola Albright** . . . First a Woman.**" *Cinema* (Calif) 1 (No. 3, 1962–1963) 16–19.

Fenin, George. "An Interview with **Robert Aldrich.**" *F Cult* 2 (No. 10, 1956) 8–9. The American director talks of his films.

Aldrich, Robert. "The High Price of Independence." *F&F* 4 (No. 9, June 58) 7+. Comments on characters in his own films, his reputation abroad, changes in Hollywood; a bit of autobiography.

Aldrich, Robert. "Learning from My Mistakes." *F&F* 6 (No. 9, June 60) 9+. Why his last two films, *The Angry Hills* and *The Phoenix,* failed.

Jarvie, Ian. "Hysteria and Authoritarianism in the Films of **Robert Aldrich.**" *F Cult* (Nos. 22–23, 1961) 95–111. A detailed analysis of Aldrich's style, from *Apache* through *The Angry Hills.*

Aldrich, Robert. "Hollywood . . . Still an Empty Tomb." *Cinema* (Calif) 1 (No. 3, 1962–1963) 4–6+. Interview with director.

Mayersberg, Paul. "**Robert Aldrich.**" *Movie* (No. 8, Apr 63) 4–5. A brief overview of Aldrich's work.

Cameron, Ian, and Mark Shivas. "Interview with **Robert Aldrich.**" *Movie* (No. 8, Apr 63) 8–11. A biography and filmography are appended to this interview in which the director discusses his work.

Eyles, Allen. "The Private War of **Robert Aldrich.**" *F&F* 13 (No. 12, Sep 67) 4–9. On his career, especially *The Dirty Dozen.*

Greenberg, Joel. "**Robert Aldrich.**" *S&S* 38 (Winter 68–69) 8–13. An interview with a "veteran of countless Hollywood in-battles, and creator of a body of films which . . . reflect . . . his preoccupation with the morality and ethics of violence in an amoral, violent world."

Aldrich, Robert. "Why I Bought My Own Studio." *Action* 4 (No. 1, Jan–Feb 69) 7–10.

"Alexandrov in London." *S&S* 23 (Jan–Mar 54) 116. Note on visit by Russian director **Grigori Alexandrov.**

Knight, Derrick. "**Alexandre Alexeieff.**" *Film* (No. 22, Nov–Dec 59) 9–11. Brief remarks on the animated-film maker living and working in Paris.

Allégret, Yves. "Why I Choose the Unusual." *F&F* 2 (No. 1, Oct 55) 12. French director prepares *La Meilleure Part.*

Blasi, Ralph. "**Dede Allen**—The Force on the Cutting Room Floor." *Show* (Jan 70). See 2f.

"Interview: **Woody Allen.**" *Playboy* 14 (No. 5, May 67) 63–72. Comedian talks about *Casino Royale, What's New, Pussycat?*

Godard, Jean-Luc, and Michel Delahaye. "Two Arts in One: **René Allio** and Antoine Bourseiller." *CdC in Eng* (No. 6, Dec 66). See 3f(1).

Zavriew, André. "**René Allio.**" *Film* (No. 54, Spring 69) 36–37. Interview with French director.

Young, Christopher. "**June Allyson.**" *FIR* 19 (No. 9, Nov 68) 537–547. Career and film listing.

Young, Christopher. "**Judith Anderson.**" *FIR* 21 (No. 4, Apr 70) 193–196. Film index, with a few brief comments.

Anderson, Lindsay. "Sport, Life, and Art."

Readers are advised to acquaint themselves with the range of categories throughout the bibliography in the search for specific subjects. In some cases, cross-categorical comparisons are directly suggested. In general, however, each article is placed under one category only. Cross-references on individual articles have been kept to a minimum.

Entries are in chronological order of publication under each category. Exceptions are: Part 5, Biography, in which the order is alphabetical by name; Part 9, Case Histories of Film Making, which is alphabetical by film title; and 3c and 8c(4), also alphabetical by title.

Directors of French "new wave" films at a meeting organized by Unifrance Film at the Cannes Film Festival (1959). From left to right (front row), François Truffaut, Raymond Vogel, Louis Felix, Edmond Séchan; (second row), Edouard Molinaro, Jacques Baratier, Jean Valère; (third row), François Reichenbach, Robert Hossein, Jean-Daniel Pollet, Roger Vadim, Marcel Camus; (back row), Claude Chabrol, Jacques Doniol-Valcroze, Jean-Luc Godard, Jacques Rozier.

F&F 9 (No. 5, Feb 63) 15–18. Interview on *This Sporting Life* and on Anderson's film criticism.

Cowie, Peter. "An Interview with **Lindsay Anderson**." *FQ* 17 (No. 4, Summer 64) 12–14. Concerning his film *This Sporting Life*, its reception, and the middle-class critical response to the new working-class stories on film.

Anderson, Lindsay. "Class Theatre, Class Film." *TDR* 11 (Fall 66). *See 4e(1b)*.

Oughton, Frederick. "Bantam-Heavyweight Director." *F&F* 1 (No. 7, Apr 55) 13. The career of **Michael Anderson**, new British director.

"Michael Anderson." *F&F* 2 (No. 5, Feb 56) 3. Sketch of director's career at thirty-five.

"Ursula Andress: She Said Yes to Dr. No." *Cinema* (Calif) 1 (No. 4, June–July 63) 21–25. Profile of actress.

Shipman, David. "The All-Conquering Governess." *F&F* 12 (No. 11, Aug 66) 16–20. On the acting career of **Julie Andrews.**

"Filmography of **Kenneth Anger**." *F Cult* (No. 31, 1963–1964) 8–9. From *Who Has Been Rocking My Dream Boat?* (1941) to *Scorpio Rising* (1962–1963).

"*Spider* Interviews **Kenneth Anger**." *Spider* 1 (No. 3, 15 Apr 65) 5–7+. About this early underground film maker's *Scorpio Rising* and his projected *Kustom Kar Kommandos.*

"An Interview with **Kenneth Anger**." *F Cult* (No. 40, Spring 66) 68–71. Reprint from *Spider* magazine.

Martin, Bruce, and Joe Medjuck. "**Kenneth Anger**." *Take One* 1 (No. 6, 1967) 12–15. Interview and comments about Anger and his work.

Cornwall, Regina. "On **Kenneth Anger**." *December* 10 (No. 1, 1968) 156–158. *Scorpio Rising;* his fascination with magic and cult activity.

Rayns, Tony. "Lucifer: A **Kenneth Anger** Kompendium." *Cinema* (Cambridge) (No. 4, Oct 69) 23–31. Analysis of the films, influences upon him, comments by Anger.

"Life of a Wordsmith." *Time* 85 (16 Apr 65) 76+. A portrait of screenwriter **Edward Anhalt.**

Annakin, Ken. "In the Vast Outdoors." *F&F* 6 (No. 10, July 60) 15+. He discusses his films, especially *Swiss Family Robinson.*

Antonioni, Michelangelo. "There Must Be a Reason for Every Film." *F&F* 5 (No. 7, Apr 59) 11. Reflections on his approach to film making.

Manceaux, Michèle, Richard Roud, and Penelope Houston. "Michelangelo Antonioni." *S&S* 30 (Winter 60–61) 4–13. An interview by a correspondent of *L'Express;* Roud's critical analysis covers his first five films; Houston offers a study of *L'Avventura.*

Antonioni, Michelangelo. "Reflections on the

Film Actor." *F Cult* (Nos. 22–23, 1961). *See 2c.*

Labarthe, André S. "Interview with **Michelangelo Antonioni**." *NY F Bul* 2 (No. 8, 1961) 6–9. His philosophy of film making.

Labarthe, André S. "**Michelangelo Antonioni's** Complete Filmography." *NY F Bul* 2 (No. 9, 1961) 5–8.

Antonioni, Michelangelo. "Eroticism—The Disease of Our Age." *F&F* 7 (No. 4, Jan 61) 7. The Italian director discusses his attitude toward film making.

Lane, John Francis. "Exploring the World Inside." *F&F* 7 (No. 4, Jan 61) 9+. Analysis of **Michelangelo Antonioni's** work for the cinema.

Antonioni, Michelangelo. "Making a Film Is My Way of Life." *F Cult* (No. 24, 1962) 43–45. Neorealism was all right in its day; now we must try to examine inner thoughts.

Antonioni, Michelangelo. "A Talk with **Michelangelo Antonioni** on His Work." *F Cult* (No. 24, 1962) 45–62. The Italian director visits the students at the Centro Sperimentale di Cinematografía in Rome; transcript of his talk, questions and answers; from *Bianco e nero.*

Clay, Jean. "**Michelangelo Antonioni**: a Great Master of the Italian Renaissance." *Réalités* (English ed.) (No. 139, June 62) 39–43. An overview of the director's work and life, with quotes and observations made on the set of *Eclipse.*

Cameron, Ian. "**Michelangelo Antonioni**." *FQ* 16 (No. 1, Fall 62) 1–58. Descriptions of the films from *Cronace di un amore* (1950) to *L'Eclisse* (1962), plus the shorts; some brief extracts from screenplays.

Alpert, Hollis. "A Talk with **Antonioni**." *Sat Rev* 45 (27 Oct 62) 27+.

Strick, Philip. "**Antonioni**." *Motion* (No. 5, 1963) 3–59. Entire issue devoted to an analysis of his work, with a foreword by the film maker.

Barthelme, Donald. "L'lapse." *New Yorker* 39 (2 Mar 63). *See 3b(4)*, **Michelangelo Antonioni.**

Antonioni, Michelangelo. "The Hollywood Myth Has Fallen!" *Pop Photog* 53 (July 63). *See 3a(2).*

Antonioni, Michelangelo. "The Event and the Image." *S&S* 33 (Winter 63–64). *See 3a(2).*

Nowell-Smith, Geoffrey. "Shape Around a Black Point." *S&S* 33 (Winter 63–64) 15–20. An analysis of **Antonioni's** *The Eclipse;* his other films and his general attitude to life and the cinema are also discussed.

Houston, Penelope. "Keeping Up with the **Antonionis**." *S&S* 33 (Autumn 64). *See 3b(2).*

Davis, Melton S. "Most Controversial Director." *NYTM* (15 Nov 64) 34–35+. On the career of Italian director **Michelangelo Antonioni.**

Godard, Jean-Luc. "Interview with **Michelangelo Antonioni.**" *Movie* (No. 12, Spring 65) 31–34. The Italian director discusses his work, particularly *Red Desert.*

Godard, Jean-Luc. "Night, Eclipse, Dawn . . . an Interview with **Michelangelo Antonioni.**" *CdC in Eng* (No. 1, Jan 66) 19–29. Style, meaning, and character in *Red Desert.*

"**Antonioni's** Hypnotic Eye on a Frantic World." *Life* 62 (27 Jan 67) 62B–65.

"**Antonioni** Talks About His Work." *Life* 62 (27 Jan 67) 66–67.

Garis, R. "Watching **Antonioni.**" *Commentary* 43 (Apr 67) 86–89. Reply with rejoinder 44 (Aug 67) 14–17.

Barzini, L. "Adventurous **Antonioni.**" *Holiday* 41 (Apr 67) 99–100+.

"On the Scene: **Michelangelo Antonioni.**" *Playboy* 14 (No. 7, June 67) 125. Brief sketch after success of *Blow-Up.*

Kinder, Marsha. "**Antonioni** in Transit." *S&S* 36 (Summer 67) 132–137. *Blow-Up* seems to focus on new, ambiguous forms of art, yet moves at a vigorous pace; this is not a complete break with earlier films.

"Interview: **Michelangelo Antonioni.**" *Playboy* 14 (No. 11, Nov 67) 77–88. *Blow-Up,* nudity on screen, interpretation of characters in his films, his early career.

Andrew, J. Dudley. "The Stature of Objects in **Antonioni's** Films." *TriQuarterly* 11 (Winter 68) 40–59. Objects, shapes, and colors are used by the Italian director to reveal character.

Bosworth, P. "**Antonioni** Discovers America." *Holiday* 45 (Mar 69) 64–65+.

Hamilton, J. "**Antonioni's** America." *Look* 33 (18 Nov 69) 36–40.

Samuels, C. T. "**Antonioni.**" *Vogue* 155 (15 Mar 70) 96–97. Interview.

Gow, Gordon. "**Antonioni** Men." *F&F* 16 (No. 9, June 70) 40–46. Study of the male characters in his films.

Samuels, Charles Thomas. "An Interview with **Antonioni.**" *F Her* 5 (No. 3, Spring 70) 1–12. "The film I would like to make is a film with characters in a vacuum, with absolutely nothing behind them."

Hernacki, Thomas. "**Michelangelo Antonioni** and the Imagery of Disintegration." *F Her* 5 (No. 3, Spring 70) 13–21. A critique of his films which are "built on the solitude, the emotional waste, and the spiritual desert of modern man."

Samuels, Charles T. (ed.). "**Antonioni.**" *Vogue* 155 (15 Mar 70) 96–97+. An interview with the director on his theories of art and film.

Tudor, Andrew. "**Antonioni:** The Road to Death Valley." *Cinema* (Cambridge) (Nos. 6–7, Aug 70) 22–30. Major themes in **Antonioni's** films.

Gindoff, B. "Thalberg Didn't Look Happy: Or, with **Antonioni** at Zabriskie Point." *FQ* 24 (Fall 70) 3–6.

Arkin, Alan. "After Alan Arkin." *F&F* 14 (No. 2, Nov 67) 4–7. Interview about his career.

Jablonski, Edward, and William R. Sweigart. "**Harold Arlen.**" *FIR* 13 (No. 10, Dec 62) 605–614. Career of composer Arlen with chronology of his film music.

Tozzi, Romano. "**George K. Arthur.**" *FIR* 13 (No. 3, Mar 62) 151–171. Biography of actor who became a successful producer of shorts; film chronology.

Vermilye, Jerry. "**Jean Arthur.**" *FIR* 17 (No. 6, June–July 66) 329–346. Career of actress Jean Arthur from silents to *Gunsmoke.*

Arletty. "Strictly *Entre Nous.*" *Penguin F Rev* 7 (Sep 48) 17–24. Reminiscences of her beginnings as an actress.

Virmaux, Alain. "Artaud and Film." *TDR* 11 (Fall 66) 154–155. Antonin Artaud's contribution to cinema and influence on various film makers.

Asquith, Anthony. "The Play's the Thing." *F&F* 5 (No. 5, Feb 59) 13. His approach to filming; filmography.

Cowie, Peter. "This England." *F&F* 10 (No. 1, Oct 63) 13–17. On the films of **Anthony Asquith.**

Balcon, Michael. "Anthony Asquith: 1902–1968." *S&S* 37 (Spring 68) 77. Tribute to British director.

Eustis, M. "Actor-Dancer Attacks His Part: **Fred Astaire.**" *Th Arts* 21 (May 37) 371–386. Astaire's techniques in suiting the dance to the film medium; biography included.

Pratley, Gerald. "**Fred Astaire's** Film Career." *FIR* 8 (Jan 57) 12–19. Life and career of the dancer-singer-actor; index to his films.

Conrad, Derek. "Two Feet in the Air." *F&F* 6 (No. 3, Dec 59) 11–13+. **Fred Astaire,** the man and his movies.

O'Hara, John. "There's No One Quite Like **Astaire.**" *Show* 2 (Oct 62) 76–77+. His film career.

Higham, Charles. "Meeting **Mary Astor.**" *S&S* 33 (Spring 64) 74. A few of her reminiscences.

Ratcliffe, Michael. "**Richard Attenborough.**" *F&F* 9 (No. 11, Aug 63) 15–17. On his acting career in films.

Hanson, Curtis Lee. "An Actor's Actor." *Cinema* (Calif) 3 (No. 2, Mar 66) 9–12. Interview with actor **Richard Attenborough.**

Attenborough, Richard. "Elements of Truth." *F&F* 15 (No. 9, June 69) 4–8. Interview about his career.

De La Roche, Catherine. "The Fighter." *F&F* 1 (No. 4, Jan 55) 12. The work and latest film (*The Red and the Black*) of the French director **Claude Autant-Lara.**

Durgnat, Raymond. "The Rebel with Kid

Gloves." *F&F* 7 (No. 1, Oct 60) 11+. Analysis of **Claude Autant-Lara's** work for the cinema, part 1.

Durgnat, Raymond. "Colette—and a Modern Devil." *F&F* 7 (No. 2, Nov 60) 17+. Analysis of **Claude Autant-Lara's** work for the cinema, part 2.

"On the scene: **Aram Avakian.**" *Playboy* 17 (No. 8, Aug 70) 149. Sketch of producer-director of *End of the Road* and film editor of *The Miracle Worker*.

Adamson, Joe. "You Couldn't Get Chaplin in a Milk Bottle." *Take One* 2 (No. 9, 1970) 10–14. An interview with American animation director **Tex Avery**, who worked at Warner Brothers.

Milne, Tom. "The Difference of **George Axelrod.**" *S&S* 37 (Autumn 68) 164–169. Former radio and TV writer talks about Hollywood and his films, including *Seven-Year Itch* and *Lord Love a Duck*.

Hanhardt, John. "**George Axelrod** and *The Manchurian Candidate*." *F Com* 6 (No. 4, Winter 70–71) 9–13. The screenwriter's contribution compared with that of director John Frankenheimer; filmography.

Aznavour, Charles. "Acting on My Emotions." *F&F* 7 (No. 1, Oct 60) 17. The French actor discusses his work.

B

Hagen, Ray. "**Lauren Bacall.**" *FIR* 15 (No. 4, Apr 64) 217–236. Biography and film listing of American actress.

Polt, Harriet. "The Films of **Bruce Baillie.**" *F Com* 2 (No. 4, Fall 64) 50–53. Film maker from South Dakota who started Canyon Cinema group in San Francisco has "acutely sensitive eyes and ears" but remains somewhat incoherent and vague; descriptions of *On Sundays, Mr. Hayashi, To Parsifal*, and *Mass*.

Baillie, Bruce. "Symposium." *Arts in Soc* 4 (No. 1, Winter 67) 88–89. Director's responses to questionnaire.

Stein, Jerome. "**Fay Bainter.**" *FIR* 16 (No. 1, Jan 65) 27–46. Career and film listing.

LaBadie, Donald W. "**Carroll Baker:** Free Agent." *Show* 1 (Dec 61) 60–61. Comments on the film-acting career of Carroll Baker from *Giant* to *Something Wild*.

Baker, Roy. "Discovering Where the Truth Lies." *F&F* 7 (No. 8, May 61) 17+. The producer-director discusses his attitude toward film making.

Baker, Stanley. "Playing the Game." *F&F* 16 (No. 11, Aug 70) 30–34. On his acting; filmography.

Houston, Penelope. "Survivor." *S&S* 32 (Winter 62–63) 15. A chat with **Sir Michael Balcon,** whose involvement with British film production has lasted for over forty years; he

comments on its present situation and prospects of pay-TV.

Tynan, Kenneth. "Ealing: The Studio in Suburbia." *F&F* 2 (No. 2, Nov 55) 4. **Michael Balcon's** early career.

Tynan, Kenneth. "Ealing's Way of Life." *F&F* 2 (No. 3, Dec 55) 10. **Michael Balcon's** middle-class comedies avoid sex and never criticize England.

Slide, Anthony. "Britain's Queen of Happiness." *Silent Picture* (No. 2, Spring 69) 10–14. A biographical sketch of **Betty Balfour** and her work with George Pearson.

"**Lucien Ballard:** Cinematographer." *Cinema* (Calif) 5 (No. 4, 1969) 47. A note on a few of his films.

Bodeen, DeWitt. "**Theda Bara.**" *FIR* 19 (No. 5, May 68) 266–287. Career and film listing.

"The Arrest." *S&S* 25 (Spring 56) 170. **Juan Bardem** arrested and released in Spain while making *Calle Major*.

"New Names: Spain." *S&S* 25 (Spring 56) 212–213. Photos and thumbnail profiles of directors **Juan Bardem** and L. G. Berlanga.

Bardem, Juan A. "Spanish Highway." *F&F* 3 (No. 9, June 57) 6. Influence of neorealism on Bardem's work.

Silke, James R. "The Tragic Mask of Bardolatry." *Cinema* (Calif) 2 (No. 2, 1962) 27–29. Profile of **Brigitte Bardot.**

Durgnat, Raymond. "B.B." *F&F* 9 (No. 4, Jan 63) 16–18. On **Brigitte Bardot's** image as sex symbol.

Maurois, André. "B.B.: The Sex Kitten Grows Up." *Playboy* 11 (No. 7, July 64) 84–92. In words and pictures, a famous writer traces **Brigitte Bardot's** growing professional maturity from *And God Created Woman* to *Contempt*.

Hill, Steven P. "In Memoriam: Russian Film-Makers." *F Cult* (No. 38, 1965) 63–65. Eulogy for the Russian film maker and actor **Boris Barnet**; filmography.

Kusmina, Ellen. "A Tribute to **Boris Barnet.**" *F Com* 5 (No. 1, Fall 68) 33. Actress writes about working habits of comedy director. Translated by Steven Hill from *Sputnik Kinofestivalia* (No. 4, 8 July 67) 6.

Rosenberg, Bernard, and F. William Howton. "The Self-Discovery of a Documentary Film-maker." *F Com* 6 (No. 1, Spring 70) 6–15. **Arthur Barron** talks with sociologists about his early life, education through the Ph.D. in sociology, finding the documentary medium, making of each of his films.

Barron, Arthur. "Network Television and the Personal Documentary." *F Com* 6 (No. 1, Spring 70) 16–19. Film maker objects to news orientation, prefers to "groove with the film" and to dramatize life as Flaherty did.

Barron, Arthur. "The Intensification of Reality." *F Com* 6 (No. 1, Spring 70) 20–25. Documentary director tells Ohio University group his experiences in shooting three CBS-TV programs seeking modern parallels to *The Grapes of Wrath, Babbitt,* and *Moby Dick;* Barron expresses his view that the film maker may be a catalyst in the situation and use "everything in the bag of tricks" to show what is really true; filmography.

Berger, Spencer M. "The Royal Family in Films." *Image* 6 (No. 10, Dec 57) 232–239. A biographer of the **Barrymores** reviews the film careers of Ethel and Lionel.

Brady, Tom. "Miss [Ethel] **Barrymore** at 70." *NYTM* (14 Aug 49) 22–23.

Downing, Robert. "**Ethel Barrymore**." *FIR* 10 (Aug–Sep 59) 385–389. Brief review of the life and career of actress Ethel Barrymore (1879–1959).

Gray, Bert. "An **Ethel Barrymore** Index." *FIR* 14 (June–July 63) 357–360. Filmography.

Berger, Spencer M. "The Film Career of **John Barrymore**." *FIR* 3 (Dec 52) 481–499. Filmography.

Berger, Spencer M. "The Film Career of **John Barrymore**." *Image* 6 (No. 1, Jan 57) 4–11. A friend of the Barrymores reviews the actor's film work.

Barrymore, Lionel. "We Barrymores!" (Ed. by L. Shipp.) *SEP* 223 (19 Aug 50) 17–19; (26 Aug 50) 32–33; (2 Sep 50) 36–37; (9 Sep 50) 34; (16 Sep 50) 34; (23 Sep 50) 34.

"**Lionel Barrymore**." *Image* 3 (No. 9, Dec 54) 63. Brief biography.

Downing, Robert. "**Lionel Barrymore** 1878–1954." *FIR* 6 (Jan 55) 8–12. Brief survey of the theatrical and film career of the late actor.

Gray, Bert. "A **Lionel Barrymore** Index." *FIR* 13 (No. 4, Apr 62) 220–235. His films.

Jacobs, Jack. "**Richard Barthelmess**." *FIR* 9 (Jan 58) 12–21. Career of the actor with a descriptive index to his seventy-five films of both the silent and sound eras.

Knight, Arthur. "Film Producer." *Scholastic* 66 (6 Apr 55) 6. An interview with **Hall Bartlett**, a young producer, writer, and director of *Unchained.*

Bartlett, Hall. "Kicking the Cliché Down the Stairs." *F&F* 7 (No. 2, Nov 60) 8+. The American director talks about his films; among them *Navajo, All the Young Men.*

Stang, Joanne. "Movie (Title) Mogul." *NYTM* (1 Dec 57) 86+. On **Saul Bass**, designer of animated sequences and titles.

"Motion Picture Titles by S. Bass." *Print* 11 (May–June 58) 17–38. Illustration of the work of Saul Bass in a variety of media (film titles, ads, posters, record album covers, etc.); an appraisal of his accomplishments.

Kane, Bruce, and Joel Reisner. "A Conversation with **Saul Bass**." *Cinema* (Calif) 4 (No. 3, Fall 68). *See 2h(7).*

Aison, Everett. "**Saul Bass**: The Designer as Filmmaker." *Print* 23 (Jan–Feb 69) 90–94+. A review of his work in motion pictures; includes an interview.

Bodeen, DeWitt. "**Florence Bates**." *FIR* 17 (No. 10, Dec 66) 641–666. Career of this veteran character actress.

Beatty, Warren. "The First Ten Seconds—They Shape the Way Ahead." *F&F* 7 (No. 7, Apr 61) 7–8+. Interview with the American actor.

Hanson, Curtis Lee. "An Interview with **Warren Beatty**." *Cinema* (Calif) 3 (No. 5, Summer 67) 7–10. Star-producer focuses on *Bonnie and Clyde.*

"Oldtimer." *Time* 62 (13 July 53) 90+. **William Beaudine, Sr.,** now director of TV films.

Scheuer, Philip K. "Sixty Years in Films." *Action* 4 (No. 4, July–Aug 69) 17–18. American director **William Beaudine, Sr.**

Billard, Ginette. "Interview with **Georges de Beauregard**." *FQ* 20 (No. 3, Spring 67) 20–23. French producer of films by Godard, Demy, and Varda describes his role.

De La Roche, Catherine. "The Stylist." *F&F* 1 (No. 6, Mar 55) 6. The career of **Jacques Becker,** French film maker.

Lisbona, Joseph. "Microscope Director." *F&F* 3 (No. 3, Dec 56) 6. On the work of **Jacques Becker;** filmography.

Baxter, Brian. "**Jacques Becker** and *Montparnasse 19.*" *Film* (No. 17, Sep–Oct 58) 13–14.

"**Becker—Sjöström**." *S&S* 29 (Spring 60) 96–98. Short tributes to **Jacques Becker,** who died in Paris in February, and to Victor Sjöström, who died in January at the age of eighty; there is also a slightly abridged translation of Ingmar Bergman's address at the Swedish Film Academy, in which he pays homage to Sjöström.

Guillermo, Gilberto Pérez. "**Jacques Becker:** Two Films." *S&S* 38 (Summer 69) 142–147. An extensive study of *Casque d'or* and *Le Trou,* which the author sees as falling into the French tradition of poetry.

"**Beckett**." *New Yorker* 40 (8 Aug 64) 22–23. Production of **Samuel Beckett's** first screenplay for Evergreen Theatre with Buster Keaton playing the major role.

Norman, Marc. "**Alphonso Bedoya** in America." *Cinema* (Calif) 5 (No. 4, 1969) 17. Notes on this actor's fourteen American films (after 170 made in Mexico).

Johnston, Alva. "**Wallace Beery**." *New Yorker* (9 Nov 35) 22–27. Profile of the actor.

Bellocchio, Marco. "The Sterility of Provocation." *CdC in Eng* (No. 7, Jan 67) 58. Statement by the Italian director.

Thomsen, Christian Braad. "**Bellocchio**." *S&S* 37 (Winter 67–68) 14–16. Marco Bellocchio's ideas about politics; his film *China Is Near* is presently banned in Italy because of its provocative criticism of the Italian petit-bourgeois family and of liberal political action.

Tuten, Frederic. "*China Is Near:* An Interview with **Marco Bellocchio**." *Cinéaste* 4 (No. 1, Summer 70) 24–25. The Italian director discusses his work.

"Jean-Paul Belmondo." *F&F* 7 (No. 1, Oct 60) 5. Sketch of the French actor's career.

"Two Actors." *F&F* 7 (No. 1, Oct 60). *See 5, Jean-Louis Trintignant*. About **Jean-Paul Belmondo.**

Shipman, David. "Belmondo." *F&F* 10 (No. 12, Sep 64) 7–11. On the acting career of Jean-Paul Belmondo.

Towne, Robert. "Bogart and **Belmondo**." *Cinema* (Calif) 3 (No. 1, Dec 65). *See 5, Humphrey Bogart.*

Grenier, Richard. "Son of Bogie." *Esq* 65 (Jan 66) 66–69+. Portrait of **Jean-Paul Belmondo.**

Eliscu, Lita. "**Jordan Belson** Makes Movies." *Show* (Jan 70) 57–59. Comments on Belson's experimental films: *L.S.D., Momentum, Phenomena,* and others; production details and his influence on commercial films such as *2001;* illustrated with color frames from *Momentum.*

Benedek, Laslo. "People in My Hands." *F&F* 4 (No. 9, June 58) 9+. About directing.

Ringgold, Gene. "**Constance Bennett**." *FIR* 16 (No. 8, Oct 65) 472–495. Career and film listings.

Farber, Stephen. "The Writer in American Films." *FQ* 21 (No. 4, Summer 68). *See 2d(1)*. About **Robert Benton.**

Bergman, Ingmar. "I Am a Conjurer." *F&F* 2 (No. 12, Sep 56) 14–15. Personal reflections on film making; part one of two-part article.

Bergman, Ingmar. "Dreams and Shadows." *F&F* 3 (No. 1, Oct 56) 15–16.

Ulrichsen, Erik. "**Ingmar Bergman** and the Devil." *S&S* 27 (Summer 58) 225–230. Influenced by the plays of Strindberg and by his puritanical upbringing, demoniacal elements seem to have a fascination for him; some of Bergman's early films discussed.

Weightman, J. G. "**Bergman**, an Uncertain Talent." *20th Century* 164 (Dec 58) 566–572. Ingmar Bergman's films seen as genuinely folk and poetic works.

Stanbrook, Alan. "An Aspect of **Bergman**." *Film* (No. 20, Mar–Apr 59) 10–13. Brief analysis of Ingmar Bergman's work through *Wild Strawberries.*

Bergman, Ingmar. "Conversation Piece." *F&F* 5 (No. 8, May 59) 31. Imaginary conversation between a fictional writer and Bergman.

Archer, Eugene. "The Rack of Life." *FQ* 12 (No. 4, Summer 59) 3–16. Analysis of the films of Ingmar Bergman from *Torment* to *The Magician* on the theme of man's search for meaning in a hostile universe; Bergman's technique; his company of players.

Bergman, Ingmar. "Each Film Is My Last." *F&F* 5 (No. 10, July 59) 8+. Reflections on film making; filmography.

Oldin, Gunnar. "Ingmar Bergman." *Amer-Scand Rev* 47 (No. 3, Sep 59) 250–257. A few early insights: he directed a play "holding a hammer in his hand," and to some he seemed "a genuine buffoon."

Moonman, Eric. "Summer with **Bergman**." *Film* (No. 21, Sep–Oct 59) 18–22. The relationship of Bergman to the Swedish film industry and other contemporary directors.

Wiskari, Werner. "Another **Bergman** Gains Renown." *NYTM* (20 Dec 59) 20–21+. On the career of Ingmar Bergman.

Pechter, William S. "**Ingmar Bergman**: A Study." *TDR* 5 (No. 2, 1960) 94–101. He is more interested in film as a conceptual medium than a visually poetic one.

"A Baffling Movie Master." *Life* 48 (22 Feb 60) 59–60+. Brief view of **Ingmar Bergman.**

Croce, Arlene. "The **Bergman** Legend." *Commonweal* 71 (11 Mar 60) 647–649. Bergman is within the tradition of Swedish film.

"I Am a Conjurer." *Time* 75 (14 Mar 60) 60–62+. Long feature article on **Ingmar Bergman.**

Ross, Walter. "Strange Vision of **Ingmar Bergman**." *Coronet* 48 (Oct 60) 57–71.

Bond, Kirk. "The World of **Ingmar Bergman**." *NY F Bul* 2 (No. 6, 1961) 6–10. Generous evaluation of Bergman's work, particularly *The Seventh Seal* and *The Magician.*

Dymling, Carl Anders. "Rebel with a Cause." *F&F* 7 (No. 5, Feb 61) 35. **Ingmar Bergman**: a personal viewpoint by a producer who sponsored him.

Cowie, Peter. "Resolving the Conflict." *Motion* (No. 1, Summer 61) 18–20. Analysis of **Ingmar Bergman's** films, with particular attention to *Virgin Spring, Seventh Seal,* and *So Close to Life.*

Duprey, Richard A. "**Bergman** and Fellini, Explorers of the Modern Spirit." *Cath World* 194 (Oct 61). *See 4e.*

Dienstfrey, Harris. "Success of **Ingmar Bergman**." *Commentary* 32 (Nov 61) 391–398. Also discussion 33 (Apr 62) 348.

Alpert, Hollis. "Style Is the Director." *Sat Rev* 44 (23 Dec 61) 39–41. On **Ingmar Bergman**; part of *Saturday Review* report "Film Directors at Work."

Blackwood, Caroline. "The Mystique of Ingmar Bergman." *Encounter* (London) 16 (No. 4, Apr 61) 54–57. A director of "rabid anti-intellectualism," his formula is "the Supernatural and Sex, decked out with Symbols"; he makes "children's films for adults."

Degnan, James P. "Through a Dark, Glassily." *Atlantic* 212 (Sep 63). *See 3b(4)*. About **Ingmar Bergman.**

Hedlund, Oscar. "**Ingmar Bergman**, the Listener." *Sat Rev* 47 (29 Feb 64) 47–49.

Bergman as man, husband, and Swede; how he views the relationship of film and music.

"Interview: **Ingmar Bergman.**" *Playboy* 11 (No. 6, June 64) 61–68. Bergman talks on his personality, critics; American "New Wave" film makers, *The Silence* and some of his other films.

Steene, B. "Archetypal Patterns in Four **Ingmar Bergman** Plays." *Scandinavian Studies* 37 (Feb 65) 58–76. Relationship of themes and protagonists with the myth of the Fall and the legend of Faust.

Steene, Birgitta. "The Isolated Hero of **Ingmar Bergman.**" *F Com* 3 (No. 2, Spring 65). *See 7a(5).*

Fleisher, Frederic. "Ants in a Snakeskin." *S&S* 34 (Autumn 65) 176. Note on **Ingmar Bergman**'s speech accepting Erasmus prize in Amsterdam: "Religion and the arts are kept alive for sentimental reasons. . . . I push with the other ants" because of curiosity and hunger for expression.

Scott, James F. "The Achievement of **Ingmar Bergman.**" *J Aesthetics and Art Criticism* 24 (No. 2, Winter 65) 263–272.

Godard, Jean-Luc. "Bergmanorama." *CdC in Eng* (No. 1, Jan 66) 56–62. **Ingmar Bergman** the ultimate auteur versus the *mise-en-scène* of Visconti or the imitativeness of Vadim.

Comstock, W. Richard. "**Ingmar Bergman:** Assessment at Midpoint." *F Soc Rev* (Apr 66) 12–18. A brief critique of the director's work.

Bergman, Ingmar. "Each Film Is My Last." *TDR* 11 (Fall 66) 94–101. Bergman discusses the creative process and film making.

Loney, G. "German in the Theatre." *Mod Drama* 9 (Sep 66) 70–77. **Ingmar Bergman**, general manager of Sweden's Royal Dramatic Theater, returns to film making with *Persona*.

Hamilton, William. "**Ingmar Bergman** on the Silence of God." *Motive* 27 (No. 2, Nov 66) 36–41. Theology professor discusses the trilogy *Through a Glass Darkly, Winter Light,* and *The Silence.*

Bergman, Ingmar. "The Serpent's Skin." *CdC in Eng* (No. 11, Sep 67) 24–29. The Swedish film maker speaks of his need for artistic expression.

Newman, Edwin. " 'My Need to Express Myself in a Film.' " *F Com* 4 (Nos. 1–2, Fall–Winter 67) 58–62. Transcript of interview with **Ingmar Bergman** in Stockholm for WNBC-TV.

Lothwall, Lars-Olof. "**Ingmar Bergman**?" *Take One* 2 (No. 1, 1968) 16–18. An interview with the Swedish director in which he discusses his films, particularly *Shame.*

Silverstein, Norman. "**Ingmar Bergman** and the Religious Film." *Salmagundi* 2 (No. 3, Spring–Summer 68) 53–66. On Bergman's "religious" films as a substitute for religion among intellectuals.

Björkman, Stig, *et al.* "Interview with **Ingmar Bergman.**" *Movie* (No. 16, Winter 68–69) 2–8. Bergman discusses various aspects of his work.

Riffe, Ernest. "**Bergman:** Through a Filmmaker Darkly." *Take One* 2 (No. 3, 1969) 11. A brief, unpleasant critic's encounter with Ingmar Bergman, which may have been written by the director himself.

Cantor, J. "**Ingmar Bergman** at Fifty." *Atlantic* 223 (Mar 69) 150+.

Young, V. "Cinema Borealis." *Hudson Rev* 23 (Summer 70) 252–274. Background to **Ingmar Bergman**'s films; including 1940s' Swedish filmic climate, Strindbergian influence, and the evolution of a God-Demon metaphysical image.

Bergman, Ingmar. "My Three Powerfully Effective Commandments." *F Com* 6 (No. 2, Summer 70) 9–12. The Swedish writer-director's way of working with script and studio; he says he tries (1) to be entertaining at all times, (2) to obey his artistic conscience at all times, and (3) to make each film as if it were his last.

Bergman, Ingmar. "The Snakeskin." *F Com* 6 (No. 2, Summer 70) 14–15. Art, the Swedish director says, no longer can influence our lives, but curiosity still drives him to do it; art is like a snakeskin filled with ants that make it move.

"Biography, **Ingmar Bergman.**" *F Com* 6 (No. 2, Summer 70) 16–18. Comments, including sentences from reviews, on his films; bibliography of works by and about Bergman, pp. 20–21.

Steene, Birgitta. "Images and Words in **Ingmar Bergman**'s Films." *CJ* 10 (No. 1, Fall 70) 23–33. The shift from "gothic" to "ascetic" since *The Seventh Seal;* the trilogy offers greater emphasis on the human face and suggests that language is increasingly untrustworthy as a means of conveying love.

Tynan, Kenneth. "The Abundant Miss Bergman." *F&F* 5 (No. 3, Dec 58) 9–10+. Article on **Ingrid Bergman**, based on interview; biography and films.

Vermilye, Jerry. "An **Ingrid Bergman** Index." *FIR* 12 (No. 5, May 61) 280–294. Film listings, with comments on each film.

Ross, Lillian. "**Ingrid Bergman.**" *New Yorker* (21 Oct 61) 100–103. Profile of the actress.

Bowers, Ronald L. "**Ingrid Bergman.**" *FIR* 19 (No. 2, Feb 68) 71–88. Career and film listing.

"100 Lighted Violins." *Newswk* 66 (13 Dec 65) 104+. Tribute to **Busby Berkeley** at New York's Gallery of Modern Art.

Comolli, Jean-Louis. "Dancing Images." *CdC in Eng* (No. 2, 1966) 22–25. The spectacle of **Busby Berkeley**'s images reveals directly the dream nature of the cinematographic spectacle.

Brion, Patrick, and René Gilson. "Interview with **Busby Berkeley**." *CdC in Eng* (No. 2, 1966) 26–41. American director discusses his films, career, and techniques; filmography by Ralph Crandall.

Jenkinson, Philip. "The Great Busby." *Film* (No. 45, Spring 66) 30–33. **Busby Berkeley**, as represented in the retrospective at the National Film Theatre.

Thomas, John. "The Machineries of Joy." *F Soc Rev* (Feb 67) 28–30. Brief comments on a collection of clips from **Busby Berkeley** films.

Roman, Robert C. "**Busby Berkeley**: Retrospect on a Hollywood Dance Film-Maker of the Thirties." *Dance Mag* 42 (Feb 68) 34–39+.

Murray, William. "Return of **Busby Berkeley**." *NYTM* (2 Mar 69) 26–27+. On the career of the director of spectacular musical sequences in Hollywood.

"New Names: Spain." *S&S* 25 (Spring 56). *See 5, Juan Bardem.* About **L. G. Berlanga**.

Cobos, Juan. "Spanish Fighter." *F&F* 4 (No. 5, Feb 58) 12. On **Luis Berlanga**'s films.

Berlanga, Luis. "The Day I Refused to Work." *F&F* 8 (No. 3, Dec 61) 9+. On *Placido* and Berlanga's decision to film only when he is free.

Scher, Saul N. "**Irving Berlin**'s Filmusic." *FIR* 9 (May 58) 225–234. All but one of his stage musicals have been filmed, and he has worked on many other movies.

Ford, Charles. "**Sarah Bernhardt**." (Tr. by Anne and Thornton K. Brown.) *FIR* 5 (Dec 54) 515–518. A short survey of the intermittent film career of Sarah Bernhardt, which ran from 1908 (*Elizabeth, Queen of England*) to 1923 (*La Voyante*).

Hilliard-Hughes, Albert. "**Sarah Bernhardt** on the Screen." *Silent Picture* (No. 7, Summer 70) 9–10. An annotated index of seven films in which she appeared.

Godfrey, Lionel. "The Music Makers." *F&F* 12 (No. 12, Sep 66) 36–40. On the film music of **Elmer Bernstein** and Jerry Goldsmith.

"**Sidney Bernstein**." *F&F* 1 (No. 4, Jan 55) 3. A sketch of British film exhibitor turned television producer.

Bragin, John. "A Conversation with **Bernardo Bertolucci**." *FQ* 20 (No. 1, Fall 66) 39–44. He was a poet, but stopped writing "reconstruction of past moments" and turned to film, which "made me discover that there is a future."

Johnston, Alva. "**Russell Birdwell**." *New Yorker* (19 Aug 44) 22–28; (26 Aug 44) 26–34; (2 Sep 44) 24–28; (9 Sep 44) 30–38. Profile of the publicist.

"**D. W. Griffith** and **Billy Bitzer** Pose for Still." *Image* 7 (No. 3, Mar 58). *See 5, D. W. Griffith.*

Burke, P. E. "Fame Came Too Soon to Miss Julie." *F&F* 3 (No. 10, July 57) 10. **Anita** **Björk** returns to Sweden after unsuccessful stay in Hollywood.

Burke, P. E. "The Man Who Would Make His Mistakes Again." *F&F* 5 (No. 1, Oct 58) 8. On **Gunnar Björnstrand**.

Diehl, Digby. "A Talk with **Noel Black**." *Action* 4 (No. 5, Sep–Oct 69) 14–17. Young American director.

Baker, Peter. "A Star Without the Limelight." *F&F* 2 (No. 6, Mar 56) 5. Interview with **Claire Bloom**.

Batten, Mary. "Interview with **James Blue**." *F Com* 1 (No. 5, Summer 63) 2–14. The director of *The Olive Trees of Justice* talks about the making of that film with non-professional actors in Algeria and his hopes for new kinds of American films; brief biography.

Johnston, Alva. "**A. C. Blumenthal**." *New Yorker* (4 Feb 33) 19–23. Profile of theatre owner.

"Producer." *New Yorker* 44 (4 Jan 69) 25–27. How **Mag Bodard** became producer of *The Umbrellas of Cherbourg, The Young Girls of Rochemont, Le Bonheur,* and *La Chinoise.*

Russell, Lee. "**Budd Boetticher**." *New Left Rev* (No. 32, July–Aug 65) 78–83. Study of his films.

Russell, Lee. "The Films of **Budd Boetticher**." *December* 9 (Nos. 2–3, Summer–Fall 67) 135–139. A study of his films.

Wicking, Christopher. "**Budd Boetticher**." *Screen* 10 (Nos. 4–5, July–Oct 69) 9–31. Screenwriter on American director's films.

Schrader, Paul. "**Budd Boetticher**: A Case Study in Criticism." *Cinema* (Calif) 6 (No. 2, 1970) 23–29. For Boetticher's films the auteur theory seems inadequate; selected bibliography.

Jenson, Lee. "The Return of **Budd Boetticher**." *Adam Film World* 2 (No. 6, Aug 70) 21–25+. An extensive interview with the American director in which he discusses his own work and the problems of working in the industry.

"**Dirk Bogarde**." *F&F* 1 (No. 11, Aug 55) 3. Career sketch of the British actor.

Whitehall, Richard. "**Dirk Bogarde**." *F&F* 10 (No. 2, Nov 63) 13–16. On the acting career of Dirk Bogarde.

Barnes, Peter. "Gunman No. 1." *F&F* 1 (No. 12, Sep 55) 12. The career of **Humphrey Bogart**.

Cooke, Alastair. "Epitaph for a Tough Guy." *Atlantic* 199 (May 57) 31–35. The career of **Humphrey Bogart**.

McCarty, Clifford. "**Humphrey Bogart** 1899–1957." *FIR* 8 (May 57) 193–204. The life and career of the late actor, with a descriptive index to his seventy-five films.

Towne, Robert. "**Bogart** and Belmondo." *Cinema* (Calif) 3 (No. 1, Dec 65) 4–7.

Brooks, Louise. "**Humphrey** and Bogey." *S&S*

36 (Winter 66–67) 18–23. Hollywood star of the 1920s recalls the career of **Humphrey Bogart,** and the man she knew on and off the screen; the changes in his screen personality; how he met Mayo Methot.

Houston, Penelope. "Hitchcockery." *S&S* 37 (Autumn 68). *See 7b(4).* About **Peter Bogdanovich.**

Marshall, J. "Nothing to It; Making Movies Is as Easy as Building a Skyscraper." *Collier's* 117 (18 May 46) 65+. Unorthodox history of **Benedict Bogeaus,** independent producer.

Gillett, John. "Thinking Big." *S&S* 39 (Summer 70) 135–136. Note on **Sergei Bondarchuk,** Russian actor-director, in London for English dubbing of *Waterloo.*

Springer, John. "Beulah Bondi." *FIR* 14 (May 63) 282–291. Career study of this character actress. Filmography.

Farber, Stephen. "The Writer in American Films." *FQ* 21 (No. 4, Summer 68). *See 2d(1).* About **John Boorman.**

Brown, John Lindsay. "Islands of the Mind." *S&S* 39 (Winter 69–70) 20–23. **John Boorman,** the author feels, is the most important of the younger generation of English directors; even in large-scale Hollywood productions, such as *Point Blank* and *Hell in the Pacific,* an island image recurs.

Stuart, Michael. "Star." *Close Up* 7 (No. 1, 1930) 41–46. Comments on the film star **Irving Booth.**

Strick, Philip. "The Theatre of **Walerian Borowczyk.**" *S&S* 38 (Autumn 69) 166–171. Polish-born short-film maker and animator, onetime partner of Jan Lenica, has made films in France for ten years; recently he has moved to "conventional" features.

Agel, Henri. "**Frank Borzage.**" *NY F Bul* 2 (Nos. 12, 13, 14, 1961) 4. The lyricism of this director.

Thurston, Wallace. "The Films of **Charles Boultenhouse.**" *Kulchur* 4 (No. 16, Winter 64–65) 75–78. A study of his experimental films.

Bouvril. "Trying to Find My Style." *F&F* 7 (No. 1, Oct 60) 14. The French actor discusses his work.

Behlmer, Rudy. "Clara Bow." *FIR* 14 (Oct 63) 451–465. Career study of this actress. Filmography.

Robinson, David, Tom Milne, and John Russell Taylor. "Twenties Show People." *S&S* 37 (Autumn 68). *See 4b.* About **Clara Bow.**

Barnett, L. "Happiest Couple in Hollywood; **Brackett** and Wilder Are Movies' No. 1 Writing Team." *Life* 17 (11 Dec 44). *See 5, Billy Wilder.*

Springer, John. "Charles Brackett." *FIR* 11 (No. 3, Mar 60) 129–140. Career of Charles Brackett, writer turned producer; with film index.

Bodeen, DeWitt. "Alice Brady." *FIR* 17 (No.

9, Nov 66) 555–587. Career of early actress in film; also film chronology.

Tyler, Parker. "Stan Brakhage." *F Cult* 4 (No. 18, 1958) 23–25. Brief analysis of Brakhage's early films, from *Interim* to *Loving.*

Sutherland, Donald. "A Note on **Stan Brakhage.**" *F Cult* (No. 24, 1962) 84–85. The focus is mainly on Brakhage's *Prelude: Dog Star Man.*

Sitney, P. Adams. *"Anticipation of the Night* and *Prelude.*" *F Cult* (No. 26, 1962) 54–57. Analysis of two **Stan Brakhage** films.

Brakhage, Stan. "Metaphors on Vision." *F Cult* (No. 30, 1963). A thirty-page collection of writings on film as Brakhage sees it; preceding is a ten-page interview by P. Adams Sitney.

Hill, Jerome. "Brakhage and Rilke." *F Cult* (No. 37, 1965) 13–14. Hill compares the first ten *Songs* of Stan Brakhage to the *Duino Elegies* of Rilke.

Hill, Jerome, and Guy Davenport. "Two Essays on **Brakhage** and His Songs." *F Cult* (No. 40, Spring 66) 8–12.

Brakhage, Stan. "Symposium." *Arts in Soc* 4 (No. 1, Winter 67) 79–82. Director's responses to questionnaire.

Brinson, Peter. "The Brooder." *F&F* 1 (No. 1, Oct 54) 9. Life and career of **Marlon Brando.**

Capote, Truman. "Marlon Brando." *New Yorker* (9 Nov 57) 53–100. Profile of actor.

Rush, Barbara. "Brando—The Young Lion." *F&F* 4 (No. 6, Mar 58) 10. Actress in *The Young Lions* writes about Marlon Brando.

Malden, Karl. "The Two Faces of Brando." *F&F* 5 (No. 11, Aug 59) 7. Actor writes about Brando as director and actor.

McVay, Douglas. "The Brando Mutiny." *F&F* 9 (No. 3, Dec 62) 24–30. On his work as an actor and director.

Steele, Robert. "Meet **Marlon Brando.**" *F Her* 2 (No. 1, Fall 66). *See 8c(4).*

Winge, John Hans. "Brecht and the Cinema." *S&S* 26 (Winter 56–57) 144–147. Playwright **Bertolt Brecht** moved to Los Angeles after Hitler came to power; he collaborated with Fritz Lang on *Hangmen Also Die* and returned to Germany in 1949.

Coté, Guy L. "Interview with **Robert Breer.**" *F Cult* (No. 27, 1962–1963) 17–20. The painter and film maker Robert Breer is interviewed about his work, especially *A Man and His Dog Out for Air;* filmography.

Geltzer, George. "**Herbert Brenon.**" *FIR* 6 (Mar 55) 116–125. Writer, editor, producer, and, since 1912, director, including *Peter Pan, Dancing Mothers,* and *Beau Geste;* his comments on individual actors.

Douchet, Jean. "Bresson on Location." *Sequence* (No. 13, 1951) 6–8. A brief interview with **Robert Bresson** during the shooting of *Diary of a Country Priest.*

Lambert, Gavin. "Notes on **Robert Bresson.**" *S&S* 23 (July–Sep 53) 35–39. " 'Difficult,' probably, is the word for Bresson's films; difficult because the experience they communicate is not only a personal, but a fairly private one"; Lambert discusses three: *Les Anges du péché, Les Dames du Bois de Boulogne,* and *Journal d'un curé de campagne.*

Monod, Roland. "Working with **Bresson.**" *S&S* 27 (Summer 57) 30–32. Written by a man Bresson chose to play an imprisoned pastor in *Un Condamné à mort s'est échappé;* how this director-writer works and how he thinks; reprint from *Cahiers du Cinéma* (Nov 56).

Baxter, Brian. "**Robert Bresson.**" *Film* (No. 17, Sep–Oct 58) 9–10.

Roud, Richard. "The Early Work of **Robert Bresson.**" *F Cult* (No. 20, 1959) 44–52.

Ford, Charles. "**Robert Bresson.**" (Tr. by Anne and Thornton K. Brown.) *FIR* 10 (Feb 59) 65–67+. An appraisal of three of his four films: *Angels of Sin* (1943), *Diary of a Country Priest* (1951), and *A Condemned Man Escaped* (1956).

Greene, Marjorie. "**Robert Bresson.**" *FQ* 13 (No. 3, Spring 60) 4–10. A study of the man himself, his technique with actors, his sense of art and mysticism in the cinema, and his control over his work, based on conversations with him in Paris.

Roud, Richard. "French Outsider with the Inside Look." *F&F* 6 (No. 7, Apr 60) 9–10+. On **Robert Bresson's** early film work.

Cameron, Ian. "An Interview with **Robert Bresson.**" *Movie* (No. 7, Feb 63) 28–29. The French director discusses various aspects of his work, with particular emphasis on *Joan of Arc.*

Merleau-Ponty, M., and Jean-Luc Godard. "The Testament of Balthazar." *CdC in Eng* (No. 6, Dec 66) 44–45. Brief paragraphs which appear to be the words of **Robert Bresson** chosen by the authors.

Godard, Jean-Luc, and Michel Delahaye. "The Question: Interview with **Robert Bresson.**" *CdC in Eng* (No. 8, Feb 67) 5–27. The French film maker discusses his latest film, *Au Hasard Balthazar,* and the manner in which it puts a question; the importance of chance in life; the impossibility of working with professional actors.

Skoller, Donald S. "Praxis as a Cinematic Principle in the Films of **Robert Bresson.**" *CJ* 9 (No. 1, Fall 69) 13–22. "Some revelation of process, the process of the spirit or will making its way or asserting itself within a set of circumstances"—this is what Bresson seems to try to do in *A Condemned Man Escaped* and in *The Diary of a Country Priest.*

Armes, Roy. "The Art of **Robert Bresson.**" *London Mag* new series 10 (No. 7, Oct 70) 77–80.

"Undergraduate Enterprise." *S&S* 12 (No. 46, Autumn 43) 49. Plans for **Peter Brook's** undergraduate production of a film based on Sterne's *A Sentimental Journey.*

Brook, Peter. "The French Gave Me My Freedom." *F&F* 7 (No. 1, Oct 60) 7–8+. Interview with the British director.

Bachmann, Gideon. "**Peter Brook** Putting into Question." *Film* (No. 29, Summer 61) 17–19. The director comments upon recent developments in film making.

Houston, Penelope, and Tom Milne. "Interview with **Peter Brook.**" *S&S* 32 (Summer 63) 108–113. On the basis of his three films, *The Beggar's Opera, Moderato Cantabile,* and *Lord of the Flies,* he comments on the relationship between theatre and cinema in Great Britain.

Taylor, John Russell. "**Peter Brook,** or the Limitations of Intelligence." *S&S* 36 (Spring 67) 80–84. Brook's fourth film, *Marat/Sade,* again suggests his theatre work doesn't easily translate into film; he lacks the instinct for the unifying idea of the whole.

Card, James. "The 'Intense Isolation' of **Louise Brooks.**" *S&S* 27 (Summer 58) 240–244. Her career as an actress began and ended in the 1920s; she seemed to cast a spell over her audiences and those who worked with her; she played in *Canary Murder Case, Diary of a Lost Girl,* and *Love 'Em and Leave 'Em.*

Brooks, Louise. "Pabst and Lulu." *S&S* 34 (Summer 65) 123–127. Louise Brooks, Hollywood star of the 1920s, recalls G. W. Pabst, the German director, and her experiences as Lulu under his direction in *Pandora's Box.*

Robbins, Fred. "What Makes **Mel Brooks** Run?" *Show* (17 Sep 70) 12–15. On location in Yugoslavia for the filming of Mel Brooks' second film, *The Twelve Chairs.*

Joyce, Paul. "**Richard Brooks** and *Lord Jim.*" *Film* (No. 42, Winter 64) 27+. An interview.

Cameron, Ian, *et al.* "**Richard Brooks.**" *Movie* (No. 12, Spring 65) 2–9. An interview with the director during the making of *Lord Jim.* He discusses all of his work.

Mayersberg, Paul. "Conservative Idealist." *Movie* (No. 12, Spring 65) 10–12. **Richard Brooks'** work is seen as reflecting a conservative, idealist philosophy.

Brooks, Richard. "Foreword to *Lord Jim.*" *Movie* (No. 12, Spring 65) 15–16. The film maker writes about the film he made of Conrad's novel.

Vallance, Tom. "Filmography of **Richard Brooks.**" *Movie* (No. 12, Spring 65) 16–17.

Hanson, Curtis Lee. "A Conversation with **Charles Bronson.**" *Cinema* (Calif) 3 (No. 1, Dec 65) 8–10.

"Samuel Bronston." *F&F* 7 (No. 2, Nov 60) 5. Career sketch of the independent producer of *King of Kings*.

"Brain in Spain." *Time* 82 (12 July 63) 57. A portrait of **Samuel Bronston**.

"Interview: **James Brown**." *Playboy* 15 (No. 2, Feb 68) 51–66. Football, acting (*Dirty Dozen*), Black Power, and civil rights.

Sanders, Charles L. "Film Star **Jim Brown**." *Ebony* 24 (Dec 68) 192–194+.

Johnston, Alva. "**Joe E(van) Brown**." *New Yorker* (7 July 45) 26–33. Profile of the comedian.

Geltzer, George. "**Tod Browning**." *FIR* 4 (Oct 53) 410–416. His career and films, which include *The Unholy Three, Dracula,* and *Freaks*.

Guy, Rory. "Horror: The **Browning** Version." *Cinema* (Calif) 1 (No. 4, June–July 63) 26–28. Tribute to Tod Browning.

Lambert, Gavin. "Personal Pleasures: Some Films by **James Broughton**." *S&S* 21 (Oct—Dec 51) 88+. Lambert describes these films as having a genuine poetic freshness which is analogous to Vigo; comments on *Mother's Day, Adventures of Jimmy, Looney Tom,* and *Four in the Afternoon*.

Broughton, James. "Film as a Way of Seeing." *F Cult* (No. 29, 1963). *See 3a.*

Robinson, David. "Jacques Brunius." *S&S* 36 (Summer 67) 118–119. Tribute to actor-director-writer-critic.

Bryan, Julien. "Adventures of a Roving Cameraman." *Pop Mech* 71 (June 39); 72 (July 39). *See 8c(2b)*.

Marill, Alvin H. "**Yul Brynner**." *FIR* 21 (No. 8, Oct 70) 457–472. Career and film listing.

Buchholz, Horst. "The Ego and I." *F&F* 8 (No. 7, Apr 62) 9–10. Interview about his acting.

Dunham, Harold. "**John Bunny**." *Silent Picture* (No. 1, Winter 68–69) 11–14. "The screen's first comic fat man" (first film in 1910; died 1915); his life and films.

Barcia, J. Rubia. "**Luis Buñuel**'s *Los Olvidados*." *QFRTV* 7 (No. 4, Summer 53) 392–401. Personal friend of Buñuel (Spanish teacher at UCLA) also analyzes director's films and career.

Richardson, Tony. "The Films of **Luis Buñuel**." *S&S* 23 (Jan–Mar 54) 125–130. Biography and interview: *L'Age d'or, Subida al cielo, El, Robinson Crusoe,* and *Los Olvidados* described.

Doniol-Valcroze, Jacques, and André Bazin. "Conversation with **Buñuel**." *S&S* 24 (Spring 55) 181–185. Excerpts from a taped interview.

"**Buñuel** in London." *S&S* 25 (Autumn 55) 61. Brief note on director's films at National Film Theatre.

Barnes, Peter. "The Rebel Who Grew Up." *F&F* 1 (No. 12, Sep 55) 9. Brief encounter with **Luis Buñuel**.

Buñuel, Luis. "**Buñuel** on **Buñuel**." *FIR* 6 (Oct 55) 425–426. Letter to editor in which the Spanish director responds to comments on his work, especially *El* (*This Strange Passion*), and his "love for the instinctive and the irrational."

Aubry, Daniel, and J. M. Lacor. "**Luis Buñuel**." *FQ* 12 (No. 2, Winter 58) 7–9. In interview, the Spanish director claims he often inserts a scene making fun of opera, uses mostly dolly shots in *Nazarin,* and cuts every film in his mind before shooting; he approves of Bresson and Kubrick.

Riera, Emilio Garcia. "The Eternal Rebellion of **Luis Buñuel**." *F Cult* (No. 21, 1960) 42–60. Analysis of the films of the Spanish director; filmography included.

Prouse, Derek. "Interviewing **Buñuel**." *S&S* 29 (Summer 60) 118–119. In Mexico while making *The Young One*.

Buñuel, Luis. "The Cinema, an Instrument of Poetry." *NY F Bul* 2 (No. 2, 1961). *See 3a.*

Aranda, J. F. "Surrealist and Spanish Giant." *F&F* 8 (No. 1, Oct 61) 17–18+. Analysis of the work of **Buñuel**.

Aranda, J. F. "Back from the Wilderness." *F&F* 8 (No. 2, Nov 61) 29–30+. Conclusion of analysis of films of **Buñuel**.

Kanesaka, Kenji. "Interview with **Luis Buñuel**." *F Cult* (No. 24, 1962) 75–76. Buñuel interviewed about his work, the *Nouvelle Vague,* and Japanese cinema.

Robinson, David. "The Old Surrealist." *London Mag* new series 2 (No. 8, Nov 62) 66–72. On **Luis Buñuel**.

Hammond, R. M. "The Literary Style of **Luis Buñuel**." *Hispania* 46 (No. 3, 1963) 506–513. His scripts can be studied with a view to serious literary criticism.

Fuentes, Carlos. "**Luis Buñuel**: The Macabre Master of Movie Making." *Show* 3 (Nov 63) 81+. Why Buñuel (at sixty-three) is more avant-garde than any of the young film makers; his directorial career; censorship problems.

Carson, Robert. "**Luis Buñuel**: An Eye in the Wilderness." *Holiday* 37 (Apr 65) 123–124+.

Buñuel, Luis. "Interview at Cannes." *Cinema* (Calif) 2 (No. 6, July–Aug 65) 38.

Hammond, Robert M. "Louis Alcoriza and the Films of **Luis Buñuel**." *F Her* 1 (No. 1, Fall 65) 25–34. Films written by Alcoriza, including six in collaboration with Buñuel; commentary and chronology.

Milne, Tom. "The Mexican **Buñuel**." *S&S* 35 (Winter 65–66) 36–39. Despite the limitations—tight budgets, rapid shooting schedules, etc.—Milne also finds the true Buñuel signature in his early Mexican films.

Fieschi, Jean-André. "The Angel and the Beast: **Luis Buñuel**'s Mexican Sketches." *CdC in Eng* (No. 4, 1966) 18–25. A reassessment of the five films, seldom seen or praised, which Buñuel made in Mexico.

Price, James. "The Andalusian Smile: Reflections on **Luis Buñuel**." *Evergreen Rev* 10 (No. 40, Apr 66) 24–29. Sadist and fetishistic elements, yes, but acceptance of human nature is the central theme.

Buñuel, Juan. "A Letter by Juan Buñuel on *Exterminating Angel*." *F Cult* (No. 41, Summer 66) 66–67. Some interpretation of his father's film in a letter to Herman Weinberg about **Luis Buñuel**.

Kanesaka, Kenji. "A Visit to **Luis Buñuel**." *F Cult* (No. 41, Summer 66) 60–65. At the time he was making *Simon of the Desert*.

Harcourt, Peter. "Luis Buñuel: Spaniard and Surrealist." *FQ* 20 (No. 3, Spring 67) 2–19. Analysis especially of *Los Olvidados, Nazarin, Viridiana*, and *Diary of a Chambermaid;* perhaps Buñuel's pessimism comes in part from the bitter defeat of the republicans in the Spanish war; in his films goodness is almost always defeated by the forces of darkness.

Carrière, Jean-Claude. "The Buñuel Mystery." *Show* (Apr 70) 58–62. Comments by Buñuel's collaborator-scriptwriter (*The Diary of a Chambermaid, The Monk, Belle de Jour,* and *The Milky Way*), about his temperament, directing style, handling of actors, script construction, and the religious influence in his films.

Brinson, Peter. "Prince from Wales." *F&F* 1 (No. 8, May 55) 13. The career of actor **Richard Burton**, now in *Prince of Players*.

"Interview: **Richard Burton**." *Playboy* 10 (No. 9, Sep 63) 51–63. Burton talks on early life, acting, his roles, plays and playwrights, *Cleopatra*, Liz Taylor, and Dylan Thomas.

Meehan, Thomas. "Success, Et Cetera." *Show* 4 (Oct 64) 32–33+. Conversation with **Richard Burton** and Elizabeth Taylor about their childhood goals and present successes.

Weinberg, Gretchen. "An Interview with **Mary Ellen Bute**." *F Cult* (No. 35, 1964–1965) 25–28. On the filming of *Finnegan's Wake*.

Johnston, Alva. "**Charles Butterworth**." *New Yorker* (27 July 35) 20–26. Profile of the actor.

C

Cacoyannis, Michael. "A Matter of Size." *F&F* 6 (No. 4, Jan 60) 13+. Greek director answers questions on film making generally.

Stanbrook, Alan. "Rebel with a Cause." *Film* (No. 24, Mar–Apr 60) 16–19. A brief outline of the work of the Greek director **Michael Cacoyannis**.

Cacoyannis, Michael. "Greek to Me." *F&F* 9 (No. 9, June 63) 19. His preferences in making films.

Dallas, Athena. "**Michael Cacoyannis**." *F Com* 1 (No. 6, Fall 63) 44–45. Brief profile.

Cacoyannis, Michael. "Symposium." *Arts in Soc* 4 (Winter 67) 62–64. Director's response to a questionnaire.

Kirstein, Lincoln. "Cagney and the American Hero." *Hound & Horn* 5 (Apr 32) 465–467. About **James Cagney**.

Miller, Don. "James Cagney." *FIR* 9 (Aug–Sep 58) 361–374. The actor's career and films, which are descriptively indexed in chronological order.

Oakes, Philip. "Interview with **James Cagney**." *S&S* 28 (Winter 58–59) 24–25.

Cagney, James. "James Cagney Talking . . ." *F&F* 5 (No. 6, Mar 59) 12+. Cagney answers questions about himself and his films.

Steinem, Gloria. "Maurice Joseph Micklewhite, What's 'E Got?" *NYTM* (4 Dec 66) 66–67+. On the career of British actor **Michael Caine**.

"Interview: **Michael Caine**." *Playboy* 14 (No. 7, July 67) 47–58. Early life, entrance into films, his film and private image.

Caine, Michael. "Playing Dirty." *F&F* 15 (No. 7, Apr 69) 4–10; (No. 8, May 69) 15–18. Interview on actor's career and general outlook; two articles.

Cambridge, Godfrey. "Godfrey Cambridge's Open-Door Policy." *Look* 33 (7 Jan 69) 76–77. Brief career study of Godfrey Cambridge; followed by Cambridge's remarks on responsibility of black performers to ease racial tensions.

"Orpheus Distending." *Time* 76 (19 Sep 60) 62+. A portrait of **Marcel Camus**, French director.

Oliver, Marie Rose. "Cantinflas." *Hwd Q* 2 (No. 3, Apr 47) 253–256. Admiring description by Argentine writer of personality and methods of the Mexican comedian.

Ross, Betty. "Mexico's Chaplin." *S&S* 17 (No. 66, Summer 48) 87–89. About **Cantinflas**.

Gerald, Yvonne. "The Comedy of Cantinflas." *FIR* 9 (Jan 58) 6–11. Analysis of the Mexican film comedian, Mario Moreno Cantinflas, comparing him with Danny Kaye, Charlie Chaplin, Alec Guinness, and Jacques Tati.

"Interview: **Truman Capote**." *Playboy* 15 (No. 3, Mar 68) 51–62. Writer talks about *In Cold Blood*, violence in U.S., *Breakfast at Tiffany's*.

Johnston, A. "Capra Shoots as He Pleases." *SEP* 210 (14 May 38) 8–9. Methods and biography of **Frank Capra**, from Sennett gagman to director.

"How **Frank Capra** Makes a Hit Picture." *Life* 5 (19 Sep 38) 46–47. Twelve posed pictures of the director with Harry Cohn, moviola, etc., while working on *You Can't Take It with You.*

Daugherty, F. "He Has the Common Touch." *CSMM* (9 Nov 38) 5. **Frank Capra** explains how he alters the tone of satirical plays.

Hellman, G. T. "Thinker in Hollywood: **Frank Capra.**" *New Yorker* 16 (24 Feb 40) 23–28. Capra's rise to the top as a director; some of his views on the motion picture.

Hamman, M. "Meet **Frank Capra** Making a Picture." *Good Housekeeping* (Mar 41) 11+.

Harriman, M. C. "Mr. & Mrs. **Frank Capra.**" *Ladies' Home J* 58 (Apr 41) 35+.

Biberman, Herbert. "**Frank Capra**'s Characters." *New Masses* 40 (8 July 41) 26–27. Capra has allowed a theory—that politics is of no use—to overwhelm the dynamic characterization and democratic social philosophy of his earlier films; hence an apparently antifascist film with a fascist message, *Meet John Doe.*

Wechsberg, J. "Meet **Frank Capra.**" *Rdrs Dig* 51 (Oct 47) 80–83. His biography and methods.

Salemson, Harold J. "Mr. **Capra**'s Short Cuts to Utopia." *Penguin F Rev* 7 (Sep 48) 25–34. Praise for the American director's film career.

Stanbrook, Alan. "Ya Gotta Have Heart." *F&F* 6 (No. 12, Sep 60) 6+. Comparison of **Frank Capra** and Richard Quine films.

Capra, Frank. "Do I Make You Laugh?" *F&F* 8 (No. 12, Sep 62) 14–15. Reflections on the general state of film and something about his early days in Hollywood.

Pechter, William S. "American Madness." *Kulchur* 3 (No. 12, Winter 63) 64–72. Like Mark Twain, **Frank Capra** is a folk artist; he deals with the mythology of innocence and corruption; but he has comic genius, with the realism this requires.

Price, James. "**Capra** and the American Dream." *London Mag* new series 3 (No. 10, Jan 64) 85–93. Capra's films of the 1930s.

Richards, Jeffrey. "**Frank Capra** and the Cinema of Populism." *Cinema* (Cambridge) (No. 5, Feb 70) 22–28. Filmography on pp. 31–33.

Lane, John Francis. "C. C." *F&F* 9 (No. 4, Jan 63) 19–21. On **Claudia Cardinale** as sex symbol.

Manvell, Roger. "**Marcel Carné.**" *S&S* 15 (No. 57, Spring 46) 4–6. *Les Enfants du Paradis* and other works by this French director.

Lodge, J. F. "The Cinema of **Marcel Carné.**" *Sequence* (No. 1, Dec 46) n.p. (11–13).

Lambert, Gavin. "**Marcel Carné.**" *Sequence* (No. 3, Spring 48) 16–25. Detailed analysis of the French director's work; filmography.

Stanbrook, Alan. "The **Carné** Bubble." *Film* (No. 22, Nov–Dec 59) 12–15. An evalua-

tion, often negative, of the French director's work.

Springer, John. "**Nancy Carroll.**" *FIR* 7 (Apr 56) 157–163. The motion-picture career of this former star.

Springer, John. "A **Nancy Carroll** Index." *FIR* 15 (No. 5, May 64) 287–291. Original article on Miss Carroll appeared in 1956 without a film index.

Carson, L. M. Kit. "A Voice-Over." *F Lib Q* 2 (No. 3, Summer 69) 20–22. The film maker talks about his films and *cinéma vérité* in general.

"People of Talent (1): **Maria Casarès.**" *S&S* 24 (Spring 55) 201. "The cinema has offered little . . . apart from *Orphée.*"

Casarès, Maria. "Actress Faces the Camera." *World Theatre* 8 (No. 1, 1959) 43–52. Recollections of the author's encounters with the cinema, particularly in Carné's *Les Enfants du Paradis* and Bresson's *Les Dames du Bois de Boulogne.*

Taylor, John Russell. "Cassavetes in London." *S&S* 29 (Autumn 60) 177–178. Note on actor **John Cassavetes** and his film *Shadows.*

Cassavetes, John. ". . . And the Pursuit of Happiness." *F&F* 7 (No. 5, Feb 61) 7–8+. Interview with the American actor-director.

Cassavetes, John. "*Faces.*" *Cinema* (Calif) 4 (No. 1, Spring 68) 24–28. Interview with director.

Austen, David. "Masks and Faces." *F&F* 14 (No. 12, Sep 68) 4–8. Interview with **John Cassavetes** on his film career.

"The Faces of the Husbands." *New Yorker* 45 (15 Mar 69) 32–33. A talk with **John Cassavetes** about *Faces* and the making of *Husbands.*

"On the Scene: **John Cassavetes.**" *Playboy* 17 (No. 4, Apr 70) 183. Biographical sketch of actor-director.

Kobler, John. "Master of Movie Horror." *SEP* 232 (19 Mar 60) 30–31+. On the career of American director **William Castle.**

Stainton, Walter H. "**Irene Castle.**" *FIR* 13 (No. 6, June–July 62) 347–358. Career and biography of dancer who was in twenty silent pictures.

Cavalcanti. "Cavalcanti in Brazil." *S&S* 22 (Apr–June 53) 152. Note on the director's current work and plans.

De La Roche, Catherine. "Cavalcanti in Brazil." *S&S* 24 (Jan–Mar 55) 119. He has produced four films and directed three; *O Canto do mar* was criticized as "remote from Brazilian actuality."

Monegal, Emir Rodriguez. "**Alberto Cavalcanti.**" *QFRTV* 9 (No. 4, Summer 55) 341–358. Reprint, as translated by UCLA film student Thomas Caulfield, of article in Spanish in magazine *Film* (Sep 53); the career and films of the Brazilian director at home and abroad; his advice to young documentary producers; filmography.

Minish, Geoffrey. "Cavalcanti in Paris." *S&S* 39 (Summer 70) 135. Brazilian living again in Paris recalls happier days directing in England and opposition of U.S. companies to his 1950 return to Brazil.

"A French Winner at Venice." *FIR* 1 (Oct 50) 8–10. Analysis of the French film about euthanasia, *Justice est faite* (*Justice Is Done*), and its director **André Cayatte**, who got into films through a law suit as an attorney.

Millar, Gavin. "The Necessity for Love." *Motion* (No. 3, Spring 62) 11–16. Structure and themes in five films of **Claude Chabrol**.

Cameron, Ian. "The Darwinian World of **Claude Chabrol**." *Movie* (No. 10, June 63) 4–9.

Fieschi, Jean-André. "Wait and See." *Movie* (No. 10, June 63) 10–13. Brief comments on some of the **Chabrol** films which have not been shown in Britain.

Fieschi, Jean-André, and Mark Shivas. "Interview with **Claude Chabrol**." *Movie* (No. 10, June 63) 16–20. The French director discusses his films.

Gow, Gordon. "When the New Wave Became Old Hat." *F&F* 13 (No. 6, Mar 67) 20–24; (No. 7, Apr 67) 26–31. Study of the films of **Claude Chabrol**; two articles.

Baxter, Brian. "**Claude Chabrol**." *Film* (No. 54, Spring 69) 31–32. Brief quotes from Chabrol on his own work.

Dewey, Langdon. "Chabrol Rides the Waves." *Film* (No. 55, Summer 69) 32–33. A brief overview of Chabrol's work, including a filmography.

Wood, Robin. "**Chabrol** and Truffaut." *Movie* (No. 16, Winter 69–70) 16–24.

Allen, Don. "**Claude Chabrol**." *Screen* 11 (No. 1, Feb 70) 55–65. His career; response to Roy Armes' analysis of *Les Biches* in March–April (1969) issue; rejoinder by Armes, pp. 66–67.

Milne, Tom. "**Chabrol**'s Schizophrenic Spider." *S&S* 39 (Spring 70) 58–62. Claude Chabrol's work and themes; Milne considers him the best technician in France and lists three dominant images in Chabrol's seventeen films: the castle, the family, and the intruder.

Ciment, Michel, *et al.* "**Claude Chabrol** Interviewed." *Movie* (No. 18, Winter 70–71) 2–9.

Wilson, Harry. "The Dark Mirror." *Sequence* (No. 7, Spring 49) 19–22. An appreciation of **Raymond Chandler** as a writer of thrillers and his effect on the Hollywood film, including those based on his works.

Mitchell, George. "**Lon Chaney**." *FIR* 4 (Dec 53) 497–510. Biography and filmography of the actor noted for grotesque characters.

Braff, Richard E. "A New **Lon Chaney** Index." *FIR* 21 (No. 4, Apr 70) 217–242.

Weinberg, Herman G. "Prelude to a Criticism of the Movies." *Close Up* 8 (No. 1, Mar 31) 62–64. Critical comments on **Charlie Chaplin**.

Bartlett, Arthur C. "**Charlie Chaplin**'s No-Man." *American* 112 (Oct 31). See 6d(1).

"**Charles Spencer Chaplin**." *New Yorker* (23 May 35) 9–10. Profile of actor-director.

Churchill, Winston S. "Everybody's Language." *Collier's* 96 (26 Oct 35) 24+. **Chaplin**, the master of pantomime, should stay with his art and not necessarily try to make talking pictures; a partial biography and appreciation of Chaplin by the future British political leader.

Waley, H. D. "Is This Charlie?" *S&S* 7 (No. 25, Spring 38) 10–12. An attempt to clarify which films **Chaplin** actually made for Keystone in 1914.

Cooke, A. "**Charlie Chaplin** at 50." *Atlantic* 164 (Aug 39) 176–185. This look at both "Charlie" and "Charles" Chaplin also comments on film's permanence as an art.

Frye, Northrop. "The Great Charlie." *Canad Forum* 21 (Aug 41) 148–150. The importance of **Chaplin** in American culture.

Eisenstein, S. M. "Charlie the Kid." *S&S* 15 (No. 57, Spring 46) 12–14. The childlike nature of **Chaplin**'s perception.

Eisenstein, S. M. "Charlie the Grown Up." *S&S* 15 (No. 58, Summer 46) 53–55. Eisenstein further discusses the work and appeal of **Chaplin**.

Renoir, Jean. "**Chaplin** Among the Immortals." *Screen Writer* 3 (July 47) 1–4. French film director describes the parallels in the careers of Chaplin and Molière, and defends Chaplin's film *Monsieur Verdoux* as an expression of a true and great artisan.

Frye, Northrop. "The Eternal Tramp." *Here and Now* 1 (No. 1, Dec 47). **Chaplin**'s various portrayals of the "tramp" in his movies, emphasizing *Monsieur Verdoux*.

Raynor, Henry. "**Chaplin** as Pierrot." *Sequence* (No. 7, Spring 49) 30–33. An analysis of his humor.

Capp, Al. "The Comedy of **Charlie Chaplin**." *Atlantic* (Feb 50) 25–29. Theoretical approach by comic-strip artist.

Huff, Theodore. "**Chaplin** as Composer." *FIR* 11 (Sep 50) 1–5. Violinist, cellist, composer, and conductor, as well as supervisor of musical cue sheet for his own silent features; an analysis of *City Lights*.

Grace, Harry A. "**Charlie Chaplin**'s Films and American Culture Patterns." *J Aesthetics and Art Criticism* 10 (No. 4, June 52) 353–363. An analysis of the themes of Chaplin's films.

"**Charlie Chaplin**." *Nation* 175 (4 Oct 52) 287. McCarran immigration law threatens to prevent Chaplin from returning to the U.S.

Greene, Graham. "Dear Mr. **Chaplin**." *New*

Rep 127 (13 Oct 52) 5. An open letter on the occasion of the denial of Charlie Chaplin's reentry into the U.S.

"One Chaplin, Many Moods." *NYTM* (19 Oct 52) 56–57. Photographs.

Kerr, W. "Lineage of *Limelight.*" *Th Arts* 36 (Nov 52) 72–75. What happens when Chaplin starts to speak; includes comments on *Great Dictator* as well.

Huie, William. "Mr. Chaplin and the Fifth Freedom: The Sovereign Right to Be a Fool." *Am Mercury* 75 (Nov 52) 123–128. An attack on a letter to Chaplin from Graham Greene printed in *New Republic.*

Genêt. "Letter from Paris." *New Yorker* 28 (15 Nov 52) 175–176. Charlie Chaplin's visit to Paris.

"The Laugh's on Us." *Nation* 175 (15 Nov 52) 440. Chaplin's tour of Europe turned into an expression of anti-American crowd sentiment after immigration authorities threatened not to let him come back.

Lambert, Gavin. "The Elegant Melancholy of Twilight." *S&S* 22 (Jan–Mar 53) 123–127. An extensive review of Chaplin's film *Limelight;* a discussion of some of the other films he has made; "at 63, Chaplin has executed an imaginative portrait of the artist as an old man and shown his creative powers to be at their height."

Neiman, Gilbert. "Charlie Chaplin." *New Mexico Q* 23 (Spring 53) 77–90. "Or, the Absurdity of Scenery"—an essay on the occasion of the publication of books by Theodore Huff and Robert Payne.

Stonier, G. W. "After *Limelight?*" *New S&N* 55 (9 May 53) 542. Remarks addressed to Chaplin on his move to England; brief résumé of his career. Reply by John Grierson (16 May) 581.

Tyler, Parker. "Chaplin: The Myth of the Immigrant." *Western Rev* 18 (Autumn 53) 74–80. Woman as a romantic ideal was the basic attitude Chaplin brought with him from England; *Limelight* is a final symbolic statement of this.

Micha, René. "Chaplin as Don Juan." *S&S* 23 (Jan–Mar 54) 132–137. Micha cites instances in his many films in which Chaplin, as actor or director, seems almost unconsciously to come to the Don Juan legend.

Queval, Jean. "In Search of Charlie." *S&S* 24 (July–Sep 54) 4. Note on author's visit to 3 Pownall Terrace, Chaplin's boyhood home.

Warshow, Robert. "Film Chronicle: A Feeling of Sad Dignity." *Partisan Rev* 21 (No. 6, Nov–Dec 54) 664–675. "How cold a heart" —Chaplin wants to be loved, not to love us; *Limelight* is his "story of a clown who lost his funny-bone."

Gibbons, Tom. "Chaplin as Chaplin." *Film* (No. 3, Feb 55) 16–18. Neither satirist nor social philosopher, merely a good film maker.

Baker, Peter. "Clown with a Frown." *F&F* 3 (No. 11, Aug 57) 7–9+. History of Charlie Chaplin and his films.

Hinxman, Margaret. "Interview with Chaplin." *S&S* 27 (Autumn 57) 76–79. The differences between comedy and tragedy; favorite gags; an antipolitical statement.

Dyer, Peter John. "The True Face of Man." *F&F* 4 (No. 12, Sep 58) 13–15+. Survey of Chaplin's films; tenth article in series on world film history.

Beaumont, Charles. "Chaplin." *Playboy* (Mar 60) 81–89. His personal problems.

Spears, Jack. "Chaplin's Collaborators." *FIR* 13 (No. 1, Jan 62) 18–38. Stories of men and women such as Henry Lehrman and Mabel Normand whose assistance in direction and camera work Chaplin never acknowledged.

Brownlow, Kevin. "The Early Days of Charlie Chaplin." *Film* (No. 40, Summer 64) 12–15. Comments on Chaplin's silent-film career in America.

McVay, Douglas. "A Proper Charlie." *F&F* 11 (No. 2, Nov 64) 10–15. On twelve of Charlie Chaplin's two-reelers.

Cates, Peter. "The Little Fellow's Portrait." *F&F* 11 (No. 3, Dec 64) 11–13. Discussion of Chaplin's autobiography.

Robinson, David. "Chaplin Meets the Press." *S&S* 35 (Winter 65–66) 20. He announces in London his new film, *A Countess from Hong Kong.*

Brooks, Louise. "Charlie Chaplin Remembered." *F Cult* (No. 40, Spring 66) 5–6. Double dates with Follies girls.

Hamblin, D. J. "Passionate Clown Comes Back." *Life* 60 (1 Apr 66) 80–86. Charlie Chaplin.

Bentley, Eric. "Charlie Chaplin and Peggy Hopkins Joyce." *Moviegoer* (No. 3, Summer 66) 10–16. *A Woman of Paris* indicates that Chaplin was as capable of melodrama as of farce.

Mellor, J. G. "The Making of Charlie Chaplin." *Cinema Studies* 2 (No. 2, June 66) 19–25. His earliest roles in English music halls.

"The Custard Pie of Creation." *Newswk* 67 (6 June 66) 90–94. At seventy-seven, Charlie Chaplin directs *A Countess from Hong Kong* and talks about his life and art.

Meyerhold, Vsevelod. "Two Lectures." *TDR* 11 (Fall 66). See *3f(1).* About Chaplin.

Merryman, R. "Ageless Master's Anatomy of Comedy." *Life* 62 (10 Mar 67) 80–84+. Interview with Chaplin.

Kenner, H. "Anatomy of Tepidity." *Nat Rev* 19 (30 May 67) 599–600. About Chaplin.

Madden, David. "Harlequin's Stick, Charlie's Cane." *FQ* 22 (No. 1, Fall 68). See *3f(1).* About Chaplin.

Rosen, Philip G. "The Chaplin World-View."

CJ 9 (No. 1, Fall 69) 2–12. His sociopolitical views as revealed in public statements and writings.

"Charlie Chaplin's *Monsieur Verdoux* Press Conference." *F Com* 5 (No. 4, Winter 69) 34–42. Recorded in 1947 by George Wallach, then a director for radio station WNEW, Chaplin responds to questions about his politics, his patriotism, and his message pictures.

Hickey, Terry. "Accusations Against Charles Chaplin for Political and Moral Offenses." *F Com* 5 (No. 4, Winter 69) 44–57. Based on M.A. thesis at Boston University, expanded in collaboration with Jonathan Hoops; includes extracts from trial records and newspaper reports.

Kitses, Jim. "The Rise and Fall of the American West: Borden Chase Interviewed." *F Com* 6 (No. 4, Winter 70–71) 14–21. What Howard Hawks did to the *Red River* ending; how little Anthony Mann adds to a script; comments on King Vidor, Bill Seiter, and the blacklist; filmography of Chase screenplays.

Carr, Chauncey L. "Ruth Chatterton." *FIR* 13 (No. 1, Jan 62) 7–17. On the occasion of her death, career and films of this American actress.

Buck, Tony. "Cherkassov's *Don Quixote.*" *S&S* 27 (Autumn 58) 320–322. Notes from the diary of Nikolai Cherkassov, the Russian actor who played Don Quixote in the Kozintsev version of the film; compares it to the novel and to the stage and opera versions, both of which he has done; condensed from *Iskusstvo Kino.*

Herlinghaus, Hermann. "A Talk with Grigori Chukhrai." *F Cult* (No. 26, 1962) 34–39. The Russian director is interviewed about his work, with special attention to *The Forty First* and *Ballad of a Soldier.*

Ogden, Ronald. "Art of René Clair." *Bookman* 82 (Apr 32) 64–66. He has utilized sound to make the talkies a completely new and distinctive art form.

"The Art of René Clair." *Living Age* 342 (Apr 32) 181–182. Profile of French director.

"René Clair Indicts the Film 'Industry.'" *Lit Dig* 114 (20 Aug 32). See 2c.

Potamkin, Harry A. "René Clair and Film Humor." *Hound & Horn* 6 (No. 1, Oct–Dec 32) 114–123. An appraisal of the French director's style and films.

Causton, Bernard. "Conversations with René Clair." *S&S* 1 (No. 4, Winter 32–33) 111–112. French film director discusses his own work.

Institut des Hautes Études Cinématographiques. "*Le Silence est d'or:* A Student Film Analysis." *Hwd Q* 3 (No. 3, Spring 48). See 3c. About René Clair.

Lambert, Gavin. "René Clair." *Sequence* (No.

6, Winter 48–49) 21–29. Analysis of his films; chronological index.

Koval, Francis. "Interview with Clair." *S&S* 19 (Mar 50) 9–11. Summary of earlier work; directing *La Beauté du diable;* his quoted interpretation of the Faust story.

Koval, Francis. "To the Legend of Faust." *FIR* 2 (Jan 57) 19–20. "René Clair adds the Gallic touch," since the Germanic legend lacks logic; changes in the story, as reported in *Sight and Sound.*

Manvell, Roger. "Debate with a Past Self." *S&S* 21 (Jan–Mar 52). See 3a. About René Clair.

"René Clair in Moscow." *S&S* 25 (Winter 55–56) 130–132. Interview by four members of a French newspaper, after his return from a week of French films in Russia; his reactions to Russian films.

Claire, René. "Nothing Is More Artificial than Neo-Realism." *F&F* 3 (No. 9, June 57) 7+. Making of *Porte des Lilas.*

Ford, Charles. "Cinema's First Immortal." *FIR* 11 (No. 9, Nov 60) 513–518. Biography of René Clair, upon his election to the Académie Française.

Hudson, Roger. "Putting the Magic in It." *S&S* 35 (Spring 66). See 2f. About James Clark, editor.

Bodeen, DeWitt. "Marguerite Clark." *FIR* 15 (No. 10, Dec 64) 611–636. Career and film listing for silent-film star.

Archer, Eugene. "Woman Director Makes the Scene." *NYTM* (26 Aug 62) 46+. On the career of Shirley Clarke.

Clarke, Shirley. "The Cool World." *F&F* 10 (No. 3, Dec 63) 7–8. Interview on Harlem and the New York film makers.

Polt, Harriet. "Shirley Clarke at Venice." *F Com* 2 (No. 2, 1964) 31–32. Brief interview, originally in a Czech magazine, mostly about *The Cool World.*

Berg, Gretchen. "Interview with Shirley Clarke." *F Cult* (No. 44, Spring 67) 53–55. As published in *Dance Perspectives.*

Soltero, Jose. "Shirley Clarke on *Jason.*" *Medium* 1 (No. 2, Winter 67–68) 62–64. Recorded interview with director: problems of distribution and of making a personal film that is "objective."

Cowie, Peter. "Clayton's Progress." *Motion* (No. 3, Spring 62) 34–36+. Analysis of British director Jack Clayton.

McVay, Douglas. "The House That Jack Built." *F&F* 14 (No. 1, Oct 67) 4–11. On the directing career of Jack Clayton, especially *The Pumpkin Eater.*

Koval, Francis. "Interview with Clément." *S&S* 19 (June 50) 149–151. René Clément frequently chooses to use nonactors, as he did in *Les Maudits;* "this doesn't mean I'm a neo-realist."

Eisner, Lotte H. "Style of René Clément." *F*

Cult 3 (No. 12, 1957) 21; (No. 13) 11. Draws heavily on the director's lecture on his own films at the Sorbonne to comment on specific films and extracts; two parts in successive issues.

Clément, René. "On Being a Creator." *F&F* 7 (No. 1, Oct 60) 39. The French director's view of coproductions.

McVay, Douglas. "The Darker Side of Life." *F&F* 13 (No. 3, Dec 66) 19–26. Study of the films of René Clément.

Hamilton, Jack. "Montgomery Clift." *Look* 13 (No. 15, 19 July 49) 56–61. The life and career of the American actor; photographs by Stanley Kubrick.

Cole, Clayton. "Eyes That Say More Than Words." *F&F* 2 (No. 12, Sep 56) 13+. Montgomery Clift.

Roman, Robert C. "Montgomery Clift." *FIR* 17 (No. 9, Nov 66) 541–554. At the time of his death, a biography and film chronology.

Hunter, Tim. "A Man's Cameraman." *On Film* (1970) 72–76. Interview with William Clothier, who has photographed Westerns for Ford, Hawks, Wellman, and Wayne.

Tennant, Sylvia. "Henri-Georges Clouzot." *Film* (No. 8, Mar–Apr 56) 20–24. The French director is capable of provoking and controlling audience reactions.

Sety, Gerard. "Clouzot: He Plans Everything from Script to Screen." *F&F* 5 (No. 3, Dec 58) 7. Working with Henri-Georges Clouzot on *Spies*.

Schrader, Paul. "An Interview with Henri-Georges Clouzot." *Cinema* (Calif) 5 (No. 4, 1969) 14–15.

Hanson, Curtis Lee. "James Coburn on Acting, Directors, Hollywood, and Movies." *Cinema* (Calif) 3 (No. 1, Dec 65) 11–13. Interview.

Wallis, C. G. "The Blood of a Poet." *Kenyon Rev* 6 (No. 1, Winter 44) 24–42. On Jean Cocteau.

Koval, Francis. "Interview with Cocteau." *S&S* 19 (Aug 50) 229–231+. "This is, to my mind, the real task of the film: to express ideas which cannot be adequately expressed by any other means."

Lambert, Gavin. "Cocteau and Orpheus." *Sequence* (No. 12, Autumn 50) 20–32. A detailed analysis of Jean Cocteau's films, with references to his other works.

Cocteau, Jean. "Conversation." *S&S* 22 (July–Sep 52). *See 3a.*

Cocteau, Jean. "Cocteau." *Film* (No. 4, Mar 55) 8–11. Extracts from Cocteau's letters to Mary Hoeck regarding *Orphée* and *Les Enfants terribles.*

Jean, Raymond. "Dialogue Between the Movie-Going Public and a Witness for Jean Cocteau." *QFRTV* 10 (No. 2, Winter 55) 160–166. University of Pennsylvania professor of French literature creates an imaginary dialogue based on an actual interview with Cocteau.

Casares, Maria. "On Cocteau as a Film Director." *World Theatre* 8 (No. 1, Spring 59) 51.

Bukowiecki, Leon. "Testament." *F&F* 8 (No. 2, Nov 61) 28+. Analysis of Jean Cocteau's film *Testament of Orpheus.*

"Death and the Poet." *Show* 4 (Jan 64) 74–75. Brief comments on *The Testament of Orpheus* as Cocteau's epitaph.

Oxenhandler, Neal. "On Cocteau." *FQ* 18 (No. 1, Fall 64) 12–14. *Testament of Orpheus* recapitulates Cocteau's films, plays, and life; he always insisted that "films are not public but private . . . not entertainment but art."

Steegmuller, F. "Onward and Upward with the Arts." *New Yorker* 45 (27 Sep 69) 130–134+. Jean Cocteau.

Brown, F. "Image of Cocteau." *Nation* 211 (19 Oct 70) 379.

Pacheco, Joseph B., Jr. "Claudette Colbert." *FIR* 21 (No. 5, May 70) 268–282. Career and film listing.

Knight, Arthur. "Interview with Jack Cole in New York." *Dance Mag* 30 (May 56). *See 2b(8).*

Jacobs, Jack. "Ronald Colman." *FIR* 9 (Apr 58) 175–189. Life and career of the actor with a descriptive index of his films made in England (incomplete) and U.S.

Bodeen, DeWitt. "Betty Compson." *FIR* 17 (No. 7, Aug–Sep 66) 396–418. Career and film listings.

Brown, Robert K. "Interview with Bruce Conner—Part 1." *F Cult* (No. 33, 1964) 15–16. Conner doesn't discuss his film *A Movie.*

Conner, Bruce. "Conner: 'I Was Obsessed . . .'" *F Lib Q* 2 (No. 3, Summer 69) 23–27. The film maker on his film *Report,* on the assassination of President John Kennedy.

"Bruce Conner." *F Com* 5 (No. 4, Winter 69) 16–25. Conversation with the San Francisco experimental-film maker recorded at 1968 Flaherty Seminar.

"Interview: Sean Connery." *Playboy* 12 (No. 11, Nov 65) 75–84.

"The Star Who Didn't Come Home." *Show* 2 (May 62) 100–101. About the popularity of Eddie Constantine in the French cinema.

Lindsay, Michael. "Interview with Eddie Constantine." *Cinema* (Calif) 4 (No. 4, 1968) 16–18. "I want to look like Humphrey Bogart."

Nolan, Jack Edmund. "Eddie Constantine." *FIR* 19 (No. 7, Aug–Sep 68) 431–454. Career and films.

Clarens, Carlos. "Gary Cooper." *FIR* 10 (Dec 59) 557–595. Life and career of the American actor, whose eighty-seven films are descriptively indexed and surveyed.

Guy, Rory. "Gary Cooper was a Great Actor,

No, He Was Not! He Was . . ." *Cinema* (Calif) 2 (No. 3, Oct–Nov 64) 15–19. Article, pictures, filmography.

Behlmer, Rudy. "**Merian C. Cooper.**" *FIR* 17 (No. 1, Jan 66) 17–49. Career of this producer.

O'Dell, Paul. "**Miriam Cooper:** Forgotten Star." *Silent Picture* (No. 4, Autumn 69) 5–9. With filmography.

Sternfeld, Frederick W. "Copland as a Film Composer." *Musical Q* 37 (Apr 51) 161–175. **Aaron Copland's** style and career; an intensive study of his Academy Award-winning score of *The Heiress,* explaining the relationship between the mood and the music.

Taylor, John Russell. "**Francis Ford Coppola.**" *S&S* 38 (Winter 68–69) 21. Brief quotes on his directing approach and *Finian's Rainbow.*

Scheuer, Philip K. "On the Road with *The Rain People.*" *Action* 4 (No. 1, Jan–Feb 69) 4–6. Interview with **Francis Ford Coppola.**

Coppola, Francis Ford. "The Dangerous Age." *F&F* 15 (No. 8, May 69) 4–10. Interview about his film career.

Dyer, Peter John. "Z Films." *S&S* 33 (Autumn 64). *See 4k(3).* About **Roger Corman.**

Joyce, Paul. "**Roger Corman** Starts the Long Ride Home." *Film* (No. 43, Autumn 65) 28–32. An interview in which the director discusses his work.

Alloway, Lawrence. "Son of Public Enemy." *Arts Mag* 41 (Nov 66) 25–26. The iconography and genre of **Roger Corman's** cinema; the emerging slang: swastika as the "S" on Superman's chest.

"Senjamyson." *Take One* 1 (No. 9, 1968) 8–11. An interview with Jay Sayer about the making of *The Viking Women* and *The Sea Serpent,* on which he worked as writer, actor, and casting director for **Roger Corman,** who directed the films.

Collins, Alan. "A Letter from **Roger Corman.**" *Take One* 1 (No. 12, 1968) 13–14. Corman discusses his work and answers some questions put by Collins.

Diehl, Digby. "**Roger Corman:** A Double Life." *Action* 4 (No. 4, July–Aug 69) 10–14. Interview.

Diehl, Digby. "**Roger Corman:** The Simenon of the Cinema." *Show* (May 70) 26–30+. Comments on the film-making career of Roger Corman (110 films in fifteen years) with budget figures, production and direction techniques included for some films.

Strick, Philip. "Ma Barker to Von Richthofen." *S&S* 39 (Autumn 70) 179–183. An interview with director **Roger Corman.**

Medjuck, Joe, and Alan Collins. "An Interview with **Roger Corman.**" *Take One* 2 (No. 12, 1970) 6–9. While shooting *Von Richthofen and Brown.*

De La Roche, Catherine. "The Independent." *F&F* 1 (No. 5, Feb 55) 11+. Review of the career of British film director **Henry Cornelius.**

Johnson, Albert. "Interviews with **Hubert Cornfield** and Paul Wendkos." *FQ* 15 (No. 3, Spring 62) 39–46. Two graduates of University of Pennsylvania discuss their films and careers (Cornfield—*The Third Voice;* Wendkos—*Angel Baby*).

"**Hubert Cornfield.**" *F&F* 8 (No. 10, July 62) 5. Brief biography of new director.

Higham, Charles. "Report from the Slide Area." *S&S* 31 (Autumn 62) 177. **Hubert Cornfield's** films and plans.

Georgakas, Dan, and Gary Crowdus. "**Costa-Gavras** Talks About Z." *Cinéaste* 3 (No. 3, Winter 69–70) 12–16. The Greek director discusses his work and politics.

Costa-Gavras. "Pointing Out the Problems." *F&F* 16 (No. 9, June 70) 32–36. Interview about his film career.

"On the Scene: **Costa-Gavras.**" *Playboy* 17 (No. 11, Nov 70) 205. Director talks briefly on Z and political situation in Greece.

Courtenay, Tom. "*The Loneliness of the Long Distance Runner.*" *F&F* 8 (No. 12, Sep 62) 10–11. On his acting in his first three films.

Coutard, Raoul. "Light of Day." *S&S* 35 (Winter 65–66) 9–11. An article reprinted from *Le Nouvel Observateur* by the cameraman for Godard, Demy, and others; some of the special innovations and frustrations of working with Godard.

Lennon, Peter. "Cameraman-Director **Raoul Coutard:** Sergeant of the Cinema." *Show* (17 Sep 70) 16–19. Coutard's career as a cameraman; interview mainly about his own first film, *Hoa Binh,* in Vietnam.

McClelland, Douglas. "**Jeanne Crain.**" *FIR* 20 (No. 6, June–July 69) 357–367. Career and film listing of actress.

"**Joan Crawford.**" *S&S* 21 (Apr–June 52) 162–164. Title of series: "They Made Me a Myth."

Card, James. "The Film Career of **Joan Crawford.**" *Image* 5 (No. 1, Jan 56) 14–17. Filmography by George Pratt.

Quirk, Lawrence J. "**Joan Crawford.**" *FIR* 7 (Dec 56) 481–501. A study of the film career of Joan Crawford that divides it into five periods: (1) (1925–1929), a "jazz honey" and "Charleston queen"; (2) (1930–1933), a modern girl with an egocentric *Weltschmerz;* (3) (1934–1940), a glamour clothes horse; (4) (1941–1952), a dramatic actress; and (5) (1953 to date), a star emeritus; included is an index to her seventy-three films.

Braun, Eric. "Forty Years a Queen." *F&F* 11 (No. 8, May 65) 7–14. On the career of **Joan Crawford.**

Bowers, Ronald L. "**Joan Crawford:** Latest Decade." *FIR* 17 (No. 6, June–July 66) 366–369. Six recent pictures.

Crisp, Donald. "We Lost So Much Dignity as We Came of Age." *F&F* 7 (No. 3, Dec 60) 7+. Interview with American actor and film maker whose career in Hollywood spans two generations.

Ross, Lillian. "Hume Cronyn." *New Yorker* (21 Oct 61) 103–111. Profile of the actor.

Marill, Alvin H. "Bing Crosby." *FIR* 19 (No. 6, June–July 68) 321–344. Career and film listing.

Condon, Frank. "Cruze, Director." *Collier's* 97 (28 Mar 36) 17+. **James Cruze** is making pictures again; his career in silent films.

Geltzer, George. "James Cruze." *FIR* 5 (June–July 54) 283–291. Historical survey of the 1911–1938 film career of the director of *The Covered Wagon* and *Washington Merry-Go-Round*.

Houston, Penelope. "Cukor and the Kanins." *S&S* (Spring 55). *See 2d(4).* About **George Cukor**.

Tozzi, Romano V. "George Cukor." *FIR* 9 (Feb 58) 53–64. Life and career of the director, with an index of the forty-four films with which he was associated as dialogue director, co-director, or director.

Cukor, George. "On a Note of Courage." *JUFPA* 11 (No. 2, Winter 59) 21. The director who was fired by the producer of *Gone with the Wind* reminds USC film students not to be frightened by failures.

Reid, John Howard. "So He Became a Lady's Man." *F&F* 6 (No. 11, Aug 60) 9–10+. Analysis of **Cukor's** work for the cinema—part 1.

Reid, John Howard. "Women and Still More Women." *F&F* 6 (No. 12, Sep 60) 10+. Conclusion of an analysis of films of **George Cukor**.

Overstreet, Richard. "Interview with George Cukor." *F Cult* (No. 34, 1964) 1–16. How the producers recut *A Star Is Born* and *The Chapman Report;* comments on directing, on actors, and directors.

Gillett, John, and David Robinson. "Conversation with George Cukor." *S&S* 33 (Autumn 64) 188–193. "Now I, having started in the theatre, am for better or worse an interpretative director, and the text always determines the way I shoot a picture." Cukor recalls his early days, M-G-M, and Irving Thalberg, his actresses, failures, and successes.

Seidenbaum, A. "Why They Let George Do It." *McCall's* 92 (Oct 64) 189–190. **George Cukor's** way of directing *My Fair Lady*.

Higham, Charles. "George Cukor." *London Mag* new series 5 (No. 2, May 65) 61–69. Study of the man and his films.

Martin, Pete. "Hollywood's Champion Language Assassin." *SEP* 220 (2 Aug 47) 22–23+. The personal style of director **Michael Curtiz**.

Nolan, Jack Edmund. "Michael Curtiz." *FIR* 21 (No. 9, Nov 70) 525–548. Career of one of Hollywood's most prolific directors; film listing.

Minchinton, John. "Zbigniew Cybulski." *Film* (No. 48, Spring 67) 26. An appreciation in memory of the Polish actor.

D

Bodeen, DeWitt. "Bebe Daniels." *FIR* 15 (No. 7, Aug–Sep 64) 413–443. Career and film listings of silent-movie actress.

Higham, Charles, and Joel Greenberg. "North Light and Cigarette Bulb." *S&S* 36 (Autumn 67). *See 2e.* About **William Daniels**, cameraman.

Cook, Page. "Ken Darby." *FIR* 20 (No. 6, June–July 69) 335–356. Career of one of Hollywood's leading voice orchestrators; film listing.

Roman, Robert C. "Linda Darnell." *FIR* 17 (No. 8, Oct 66) 473–486. On the occasion of her death, a biography and film chronology.

Weinberg, Herman G. "In Memoriam, H. D'Abbadie D'Arrast, 1897–1968." *F Com* 5 (No. 3, Fall 69) 36–45. About the Chaplin protégé who made eight films in the Lubitsch fashion; chronology of his films; excerpts from reviews.

Billard, Ginette. "But Darrieux Seeks New Horizons." *F&F* 2 (No. 1, Oct 55) 10. Brief biography of French star **Danielle Darrieux**.

Whitehall, Richard. "Danielle Darrieux." *F&F* 8 (No. 3, Dec 61) 12–13+. Analysis of her films; filmography.

Grenier, Cynthia. "Jules Dassin." *S&S* 27 (Winter 57–58) 141+. Interview with the exiled American director.

Bluestone, George. "An Interview with Jules Dassin." *F Cult* 4 (No. 17, 1958) 3–4. How this American director found himself on a blacklist; how he was offered *Rififi*.

Lane, John Francis. "I See Dassin Make *The Law*." *F&F* 4 (No. 12, Sep 58) 28–29. Comments by Jules Dassin on his *Naked City* and others while directing a new film in Italy.

Dassin, Jules. "Style and Instinct." *F&F* 16 (No. 5, Feb 70) 22–26; (No. 6, Mar 70) 66–70. Two-part interview about his Hollywood period and later career.

Whitehall, Richard. "On the 3:10 to Yuma." *F&F* 9 (No. 7, Apr 63) 51–54. Analysis of **Delmer Daves'** films.

Whitehall, Richard. "A Summer Place." *F&F* 9 (No. 8, May 63) 48–51. Conclusion of analysis of films of **Delmer Daves**.

Wicking, Christopher. "Interview with **Delmer Daves**." *Screen* 10 (Nos. 4–5, July–Oct 69) 55–66.

Wallington, Mike. "Auteur and Genre: The Westerns of **Delmer Daves**." *Cinema* (Cambridge) (No. 4, Oct 69) 6–9. Themes, iconography, and technique in Daves' work.

Robinson, David, Tom Milne, and John Russell Taylor. "Twenties Show People." *S&S* 37 (Autumn 68). *See 4b.* About **Marion Davies**.

Kendall, Philip. "**Marion Davies**." *Silent Picture* (No. 7, Summer 70) 2–8.

D'Avino, Carmen. "Symposium." *Arts in Soc* 4 (No. 1, Winter 67) 90–93. Director's responses to questionnaire.

Stack, Dennis. "Animation, Pixilation, and Mr. **D'Avino**." *Cinema* (Calif) 4 (No. 4, 1968) 24. On animator Carmen D'Avino.

Flanner, Janet. "**Bette Davis**." *New Yorker* (20 Feb 43) 19–29. Profile of the actress.

"**Bette Davis**." *Look* 10 (No. 16, 6 Aug 46) 19–23. Life and career of the American actress.

Lambert, Gavin. "Portrait of an Actress: **Bette Davis**." *S&S* 21 (Aug–Sep 51) 12–19. A description of the shooting of a complicated scene for *Another Man's Poison*, with Bette Davis at work; comments on her career, from her arrival in Hollywood in 1930.

Raper, Michell. "Mannerisms—in the Grand Manner." *F&F* 1 (No. 12, Sep 55) 7. The career of **Bette Davis**.

Quirk, Lawrence J. "**Bette Davis**." *FIR* 6 (Dec 55) 481–499. A survey of the career, the sixty-five films, and the four marriages of the film actress; an index of her films, with an appraisal by the author.

Cole, Clayton. "I Was Not Found on a Soda Fountain Stool." *F&F* 2 (No. 8, May 56) 6. Interview with **Bette Davis**.

Baker, Peter. "All About Bette." *F&F* 2 (No. 8, May 56) 7–9. General article on **Bette Davis**' life and films; on pp. 11–13, "Her Films and the Men Who Made Them."

Davis, Bette. "I Think . . ." *F&F* 5 (No. 8, May 59) 27+. Her opinions on almost everything.

Shipman, David. "What Ever Happened to **Bette Davis**?" *F&F* 9 (No. 7, Apr 63) 8–9. A study of her career.

Dyer, Peter John. "Meeting Baby Jane." *S&S* 32 (Summer 63) 118–120. An interview with **Bette Davis** while she was promoting *What Ever Happened to Baby Jane?* in England; comments on the director, Bob Aldrich, and on the careers of the two leading actresses, Bette Davis and Joan Crawford.

Davis, Bette. "What Is a Star?" *F&F* 11 (No. 12, Sep 65) 5–7. Interview about her career and being a star.

Carey, Gary. "The Lady and the Director: **Bette Davis** and William Wyler." *F Com* 6 (No. 2, Fall 70) 18–24. Wyler's attempts "to liberate certain sides" of Davis' personality in *Jezebel, The Letter,* and *The Little Foxes.*

"**John Davis**: Producers' President." *F&F* 2 (No. 2, Nov 55) 3. Biography of the British executive.

Curtis, Richard. "Ossie Davis: Cinema Comes to Harlem." *Action* 4 (No. 6, Nov–Dec 69) 12–14. The black American actor, playwright, and director discusses his work, particularly *Cotton Comes to Harlem*.

"Interview: **Sammy Davis, Jr.**" *Playboy* 13 (No. 12, Dec 66) 99–124. Actor's early life, present feelings on comedy, and views on national issues.

Shipman, David. "**Doris Day**." *F&F* 8 (No. 11, Aug 62) 14–16+. Study of her acting career.

Capp, Al. "The Day Dream." *Show* 2 (Dec 62) 72–73+. Why **Doris Day** is the most valuable star property in Hollywood today; biographical comments; brief remarks from Day about interviews.

Cole, Clayton. "The Dean Myth." *F&F* 3 (No. 4, Jan 57) 17. Examination of the cult of **James Dean**.

Bean, Robin. "Dean—Ten Years After." *F&F* 12 (No. 1, Oct 65) 12–15. Ten years after the death of James Dean; the Dean myth and the actors who would replace him.

Westerbeck, Colin J., Jr. "Some Out-Takes from Radical Film-Making: **Emile De Antonio**." *S&S* 39 (Summer 70) 140–143. How this documentary-compilation film maker gets his backing; his rejection of narration; his pursuit of out-takes for his film on the Kennedy assassination; other films.

"Dearden and Relph: Two on a Tandem." *F&F* 12 (No. 10, July 66) 26–33. On the films of director **Basil Dearden** and producer Michael Relph.

Miller, Warren. "Jester of the New Wave." *Horizon* 4 (Jan 62) 109–110. The career of **Philippe De Broca**.

De Grunwald, Anatole. "The Champagne Set." *F&F* 11 (No. 5, Feb 65) 7–8. Interview on his film-producing career, especially *The Yellow Rolls Royce.*

Doyle, Neil. "**Olivia De Havilland**." *FIR* 13 (No. 2, Feb 62) 71–85. Career and film list for the American actress.

De Hirsch, Storm. "Astral Daguerreotype." *F Cult* (No. 33, 1964) 9–13. Experimental-film maker responds to questions under hypnosis; special language and visions developed in trance state over ten years.

"No, But I Saw the Picture." *Time* 79 (26 Jan 62) 80–81. A portrait of **Dino De Laurentiis**, Italian producer.

Bean, Robin. "Reaching for the World." *F&F* 11 (No. 5, Feb 65) 9–15. On the acting career of **Alain Delon**.

Delon, Alain. "Creating with a Passion." *F&F* 16 (No. 9, June 70) 6–12. Interview on his acting and producing; filmography.

Bodeen, DeWitt. "**Dolores Del Rio**." *FIR* 18

(No. 5, May 67) 266–283. Career and film listing of the actress.

Nugent, Frank S. "Sixty Reels of De Mille." *NYTM* (10 Aug 41) 10+. Legends of **Cecil B. De Mille** on his sixty-first birthday.

Van Ryn, F. "When You See Paramount, Remember **De Mille**." *Rdrs Dig* 41 (Sep 42) 35–38. Brief biography.

Lardner, Ring, Jr. "The Sign of the Boss." *Screen Writer* 1 (Nov 45) 1–12. An uncomplimentary sketch of **Cecil B. De Mille**, centering around his conflict with the American Federation of Radio Artists.

"De Mille's Newest Bathtub Scene." *Look* 10 (No. 25, 10 Dec 46) 56–59. Famous bathtub scenes from the films of Cecil B. De Mille.

Feldman, Joseph, and Harry Feldman. "**Cecil B. De Mille's** Virtues." *FIR* 1 (Dec 50) 1–6. Simplification, symbolic situations, and technical craftsmanship.

Harcourt-Smith, Simon. "The Siegfried of Sex." *S&S* 19 (Feb 51) 410–412+. **De Mille's** early career, his exploitation of sex appeal, and some of his later films, including *Samson and Delilah*.

Johnson, Albert. "The Tenth Muse in San Francisco." *S&S* 24 (Jan–Mar 55). *See 2c.* About **Cecil B. De Mille**.

"Going Like 70." *Time* 65 (9 May 55). *See 5, Samuel Goldwyn.* About **Cecil B. De Mille**.

"The Milestone." *JSPG* (Feb 56) 8–19+. Tributes to **Cecil B. De Mille** offered by Jesse L. Lasky, Samuel Goldwyn, Barney Balaban, Y. Frank Freeman.

De Mille, Cecil B. "After 70 Pictures." *FIR* 7 (Mar 56) 97–102. Address given by De Mille on receiving the Milestone Award of the Screen Producers Guild on 22 January 1956, in which he states many of his beliefs regarding motion pictures, including a rejection of the idea that stories should leave out "the fact that life has a seamy side."

Hill, Gladwin. "Most Colossal of All." *NYTM* (12 Aug 56) 16+. A profile of director **Cecil B. De Mille** as he completes his greatest effort: *The Ten Commandments*.

De Mille, Cecil B. "Forget Spectacle—It's the Story That Counts." *F&F* 3 (No. 1, Oct 56) 7. An interview by Clayton Cole.

Baker, Peter. "Showman for the Millions." *F&F* 3 (No. 1, Oct 56) 9–14. On **Cecil B. De Mille's** life and work; filmography.

Card, James. "The Greatest Showman on Earth." *Image* 5 (No. 9, Nov 56) 196–201. Notes on the career of **Cecil B. De Mille**.

"De Mille's Legacy of Epics: His Work and His Life." *Life* 46 (2 Feb 59) 26–30. A pictorial review of the showman's career.

Boyd, M. "God and **De Mille** in Hollywood." *Chris Cent* 76 (25 Feb 59) 230–231. *See 4k(5).* About **Cecil B. De Mille**.

De Mille, Cecil B. "De Mille's Epic Story of Films' First Epic." *Life* 47 (19 Oct 59) 154–

156+. De Mille describes the beginnings of his career: the making of *The Squaw Man;* from the autobiography written with Donald Hayne.

De Mille, Agnes. "Goodnight, C. B." *Esq* 61 (Jan 64) 119–131. A celebrated niece writes about her uncle, **Cecil B. De Mille**, the effect of his death, his accomplishments during his lifetime, and then goes back through scattered parts of his life in great detail.

Geltzer, George. "**William C. De Mille**." *FIR* 7 (June–July 56) 264–271. In 1914 he entered the film industry as an extra in his brother Cecil's sixth film; after that he wrote and directed films for over fifteen years; in 1941 he became head of the University of Southern California's drama department, and his second wife, Clara Beranger, taught screenwriting in the cinema department.

Roud, Richard. "Rondo Galant." *S&S* 33 (Summer 64) 136–139. The world of French writer-director **Jacques Demy** on the basis of his three films, *Les Parapluies de Cherbourg, Lola,* and *La Baie des Anges.*

Billard, Ginette. "**Jacques Demy** and His Other World." *FQ* 18 (No. 1, Fall 64) 23–27. This French director is a pure *metteur en scène,* "no more 'committed' than a ballet choreographer"; his films are fantasies and all take place in provincial towns.

Kinder, Marsha. "Interview with **Jacques Demy**." *F Her* 2 (No. 3, Spring 67) 17–24.

Scheuer, Philip K. "Frenchman in Hollywood." *Action* 3 (No. 6, Nov–Dec 68) 10–13. Interview with **Jacques Demy**.

Demy, Jacques. "Lola in Los Angeles." *F&F* 16 (No. 7, Apr 70) 12–16. Interview on his films.

Most, Mary. *"Une Créature du Cinéma."* *Cinema* (Calif) 5 (No. 1, 1969) 10–12. Interview with actress **Catherine Deneuve**.

Hanson, Curtis Lee. "Cock a Doodle Doo." *Cinema* (Calif) 3 (No. 3, July 66) 17–19. Article on **John Derek's** direction of his second feature.

Arnheim, Rudolf. "To **Maya Deren**." *F Cult* (No. 24, 1962) 1–2. Eulogy for the avant-garde film maker.

Deren, Maya. "Notes, Essays, Letters." *F Cult* (No. 39, Winter 65) 1–86. Comments on her own films; a bibliography; articles from *The Village Voice,* with additions; reprint of "An Anagram of Ideas on Art, Form and and Film," published as a chapbook by Alicat Book Shop, 1946.

Jarratt, Vernon. "**Francesco De Robertis**." *S&S* 17 (No. 65, Spring 48) 27–28. A brief description of the Italian director's work.

Lyons, E. "**Louis De Rochemont**: Maverick of the Movies." *Rdrs Dig* 55 (July 49) 23–27. Ex-newsreel cameraman who re-created actual events.

Gehman, Richard B. "**De Rochemont**, Pictorial Journalist." *Th Arts* 35 (Oct 51) 58–59. Low-cost, nonstar, factual films.

Zolotow, Maurice. "Want to Be a Movie Star?" *SEP* 224 (29 Mar 52) 24–25+. Shooting outside the studios using nonprofessionals— the story of **Louis De Rochemont**.

Hart, Henry. "De Rochemont's *Windjammer*." *FIR* 9 (May 58). See *2m(3)*.

Lane, John Francis. "De Santis and Italian Neo-Realism." *S&S* 19 (Aug 50) 245–247. **Giuseppe De Santis** has made a box-office success (*Bitter Rice*); biography.

Koval, Francis. "Interview with De Sica." *S&S* 19 (Apr 50) 61–63. Comments on **Vittorio De Sica**'s *Bicycle Thief* and the necessity "to transpose reality into the poetical plane."

"Vittorio De Sica." *F&F* 1 (No. 2, Nov 54) 3. A brief profile of the Italian director and actor.

Lane, John Francis. "Edinburgh President." *F&F* 1 (No. 12, Sep 55) 4–5. Interview with **Vittorio De Sica**: a discussion of his latest film, *Gold of Naples*.

De Sica, Vittorio. "The Most Wonderful Years of My Life." *F&F* 2 (No. 3, Dec 55) 5–6. Translation by John Francis Lane. How the Italian director got into films; the making of *The Gates of Heaven* (never released) and *Shoeshine*.

De Sica, Vittorio. "Money, the Public, and *Umberto D*." *F&F* 2 (No. 4, Jan 56) 28–29. Also about the making of *Bicycle Thief*.

De Sica, Vittorio. "Hollywood Shocked Me." *F&F* 2 (No. 5, Feb 56) 12–13. The director's visit there; his work for Selznick on *Terminal Station;* third of a series.

De Sica, Vittorio. "I Must Act to Pay My Debts." *F&F* 2 (No. 6, Mar 56) 7. Last of four articles; note by translator, John Francis Lane.

Sargeant, Winthrop. "Profiles: Bread, Love, and Neo-Realismo." *New Yorker* 33 (29 June 57) 35–36+; (6 July 57) 35–36+. A lengthy study of **Vittorio De Sica** in two parts.

McVay, Douglas. "Poet of Poverty." *F&F* 11 (No. 1, Oct 64) 12–16; (No. 2, Nov 64) 51–54. Two articles on the directing career of **Vittorio De Sica**.

Price, James. "The Case of **De Sica**." *London Mag* new series 4 (No. 9, Dec 64) 76–79. On the director-actor.

Nogueira, Rui, and Nicoletta Zalaffi. "**Michel Deville**." *Film* (No. 55, Summer 69) 28–29. Interview with the French director.

Machlin, Milt. "I. A. L. Diamond—The Wit of Billy Wilder." *Show* (Jan 70) 8+. Diamond's script collaboration with Billy Wilder since 1956 as an attempt to maintain the standards of the sophisticated comedies of the 1930s; brief remarks from Diamond.

Koval, Francis. "Interview with Dieterle." *S&S* 19 (May 50) 107–109. **William Dieterle:** brief biography and comments on *Vulcano,* just finished.

Luft, Herbert G. "William Dieterle." *FIR* 8 (Apr 57) 148–156+. The director began his work in films as an actor in Germany in 1909; as a writer and director in 1923; in 1930, directing in Hollywood. See also his letter in *FIR* 8 (May 57) 234, and Luft's response in *FIR* 8 (June–July 57) 301.

Pinto, Alfonso, and Francisco Rialp. "The Films of **William Dieterle**." *FIR* 19 (No. 8, Oct 68) 499–514. Companion index to (Apr 57) article on career of the actor-director.

George, Manfred. "Marlene Dietrich's Beginning." *FIR* 3 (Feb 52) 77–80. Her association with the German film industry until 1930 and the events that led to her role of Lola in *The Blue Angel,* directed by von Sternberg.

Hemingway, Ernest. "Tribute to Mamma from Papa Hemingway." *Life* 33 (18 Aug 52) 92. Comments on **Marlene Dietrich**.

Sargeant, Winthrop. "Dietrich and her Magic Myth." *Life* 33 (18 Aug 52) 86–90+. Lengthy story of actress Marlene Dietrich: her public and private life.

Knight, Arthur. "Marlene Dietrich." *FIR* 5 (Dec 54) 497–514. "Notes on a living legend," with an annotated list of her films.

Lane, John Francis. "Give Her Dirt—and Hard Work." *F&F* 3 (No. 3, Dec 56) 13–14. **Marlene Dietrich** working on *Monte Carlo Story*.

Whitehall, Richard. "*The Blue Angel*." *F&F* 9 (No. 1, Oct 62) 19–23. On the acting career of **Marlene Dietrich**.

Higham, Charles. "Dietrich in Sydney." *S&S* 35 (Winter 65–66) 23. Note on her views of von Sternberg (who never informed the cast of the stories of his pictures); other recollections.

Carr, Harry. "The Only Unpaid Movie Star." *American* (Mar 31) 55–57+. Profile of **Walt Disney**, with brief biographical background and details on animation of Mickey Mouse.

Seldes, Gilbert. "Walt Disney." *New Yorker* (19 Dec 31) 23–27. Profile of artist-producer.

Mann, Arthur. "Mickey Mouse's Financial Career." *Harper's* 168 (May 34) 714–721. Profile of **Walt Disney**.

Mullen, S. "**Walt Disney**, Master of Cartoons." *Scholastic* 26 (18 May 35) 10–11.

Hollister, P. "**Walt Disney**: Genius at Work." *Atlantic* 166 (Dec 40) 689–701. This saga about "the Pied Piper of our time" shows the history, output, technique, and philosophy of Disney and his production company.

"Mr. and Mrs. Disney." *Ladies' Home J* 58 (Mar 41) 20+. Walt Disney's life story told on the occasion of the production of *Fantasia*.

Low, David. "Leonardo da **Disney**." *New Rep* 106 (5 Jan 42) 16–18. A comparison between Leonardo da Vinci and Walt Disney as artists.

"But Is It Art?": **Walt Disney** Doesn't Care." *Bus Wk* (10 Feb 45). *See 6b(2).*

Reid, Ashton. "**Mr. Disney**'s Dream World." *Collier's* 115 (24 Feb 45) 33. A short history of Disney's career in animation.

Ericsson, Peter. "**Walt Disney**." *Sequence* (No. 10, New Year 50) 159–170. Overview of Disney's work, including chronological index to his work.

Alexander, J. "Amazing Story of **Walt Disney**." *SEP* 226 (31 Oct 53) 24–25; (7 Nov 53) 26–27.

"A Silver Anniversary for Walt and Mickey." *Life* 35 (2 Nov 53) 82–90. A chronicle of Disney's career: from Mickey Mouse to current "true-life adventures."

Lubin, Edward R. "**Disney** Is Still Creative." *FIR* 5 (Mar 54) 115–118.

Low, David. "Leonardo da **Disney**." *New Rep* 131 (22 Nov 54) 40–43. Reprinted from 106 (5 Jan 42) 16–18. Disney as an artist who uses his brains.

"Father Goose." *Time* 64 (27 Dec 54) 42–46. **Walt Disney**'s biography, work, and social impact; the story of Mickey Mouse.

Miller, Diane Disney. "My Dad, **Walt Disney**." (Ed. by Pete Martin.) *SEP* 229 (24 Nov 56) 78+; (1 Dec 56) 28–29+; (8 Dec 56) 38–39+; (15 Dec 56) 36–37+; (22 Dec 56) 24+; (29 Dec 56) 24+; (5 Jan 57) 24+.

Disney, Walt. "Humour: My Sixth Sense." *F&F* 7 (No. 5, Feb 61) 6. An attempt to analyze the business of making people laugh.

Wolters, L. "Wonderful World of **Walt Disney**." *Today's Health* 40 (Apr 62) 26–31.

"Wide World of **Walt Disney**." *Newswk* 60 (31 Dec 62) 48–51.

De Roos, Robert. 'Magic Worlds of **Walt Disney**.' *National Geographic* 124 (Aug 63) 157D, 158–207. With editorial comment by M. B. Grosvenor; the life and art of Walt Disney and a tour of Disneyland.

Davidson, B. "Fantastic **Walt Disney**." *SEP* 237 (7 Nov 64) 66–68.

Sayers, Frances. "Too Long at the Sugar Bowls." *Lib J* 90 (15 Oct 65) 4538. Frances Sayers, children's librarian, takes issue with claim by California educator that **Walt Disney** is "the greatest educator of this century."

"AFA Honors **Walt Disney**." *Am Forestry* 72 (Dec 66) 10. American Forestry Association says Disney has instilled love of wild things in hearts of children and adults.

Deneroff, Harvey. "**Walt Disney** (1901–1966)." *F Soc Rev* (Dec 66) 10–11. A brief account of his work.

Morgenstern, J. "**Walt Disney** (1901–1966) Imagineer of Film." *Newswk* 68 (26 Dec 66) 68–69.

Rider, David. "**Walt Disney**." *Film* (No. 48, Spring 67) 21–25. An appreciation of Disney's work, particularly his appeal to children.

"**Disney**'s Legacy." *Newswk* 69 (2 Jan 67) 58–59.

Brewer, R. "**Walt Disney**, RIP." *Nat Rev* 19 (10 Jan 67) 17.

Reddy, J. "Living Legacy of **Walt Disney**." *Rdrs Dig* 90 (June 67) 165–170.

Maltin, Leonard. "**Walt Disney**'s Films." *FIR* 18 (No. 7, Oct 67) 457–469. Film index only.

Disney, R. "Unforgettable **Walt Disney**." *Rdrs Dig* 94 (Feb 69) 212–218.

Marx, W. "**Disney** Imperative." *Nation* 209 (28 July 69) 76–78.

Gillett, John. "**Gianni di Venanzo**." *S&S* 35 (Summer 66) 150. Brief tribute to cameraman who worked with Antonioni, Fellini, and others.

Bodeen, DeWitt. "**Richard Dix**." *FIR* 17 (No. 8, Oct 66) 487–519. Career and film chronology.

"**Edward Dmytryk**: Double Bill." *F&F* 4 (No. 9, June 58) 5. Brief biography of the American director.

Tozzi, Romano. "**Edward Dmytryk**." *FIR* 13 (No. 2, Feb 62) 86–101. Career of editor turned "serious-minded" director; film listings.

Doermer, Christian. "The Image Shapers." *F&F* 9 (No. 3, Dec 62) 76–77. Interview with the actor about his films.

Johnson, Albert. "The Tenth Muse in San Francisco." *S&S* 26 (Summer 56). *See 5, Gene Kelly.* About **Stanley Donen**.

Donen, Stanley. "Giving Life an Up-Beat." *F&F* 4 (No. 9, June 58) 7+. Director looks back.

McVay, Douglas. "Moanin' for **Donen**." *Film* (No. 27, Jan–Feb 61) 20–25. Brief comments on the work of Stanley Donen, including a filmography.

McVay, Douglas. "The Art of **Stanley Donen**." *NY F Bul* 2 (No. 9, 1961) 10–12. An analysis of his later films, particularly *Pajama Game* and *Funny Face;* filmography.

Cameron, Ian, and Mark Shivas. *"What's New, Pussycat?" Movie* (No. 14, Autumn 65) 12–16. An interview with the film's director, **Clive Donner**, who discusses this film and his work.

Joyce, Paul. "Nothing But the Best?" *Film* (No. 45, Spring 66) 16–21. Interview with **Clive Donner**.

Donner, Clive. "The Urge of Some People." *F&F* 15 (No. 10, July 69) 4–8. Interview about his career.

Donner, Jörn. "After Three Films." *S&S* 35 (Autumn 66) 190–195. A highly personal account of Donner's transition from film critic to film maker; his problems as a Finn making films in neighboring Sweden; some comments on Ingmar Bergman.

"**Jörn Donner**: An Outsider at Home." *F&F* 15

(No. 3, Dec 68) 70–72. On his film career.

Reyner, Leslie. "Jörn Donner." *Film* (No. 54, Spring 69) 33–35. Brief comments on the director's work.

Donner, Jörn. "After Six Films." *S&S* 39 (Spring 70) 75–79. Since his *Sight and Sound* article "After Three Films" (Autumn 66), Donner has made three more films, returned to Finland, and found himself involved in production as well as direction; a personal record.

De La Roche, Catherine. "**Mark Donskoi.**" *Sequence* (No. 5, Autumn 48) 20–27. An analysis of the Russian scriptwriter and director, including a filmography.

Fox, Charles. "The Gorki Trilogy—The Poetry of Cinema." *Film* (No. 3, Feb 55) 8–12. A discussion of the Russian films directed by **Mark Donskoi.**

Whitehall, Richard. "D.D." *F&F* 9 (No. 4, Jan 63) 21–23. On **Diana Dors** as sex symbol.

Maltin, Leonard. "**Gordon Douglas:** Making of a Pro." *Action* 5 (No. 6, Nov–Dec 70) 19–21. Interview with the director.

Bond, R. "**Dovjenko** on the Sound Film." *Close Up* 7 (No. 4, Oct 30). *See 3a(1).*

Jacobs, Lewis. "**Dovzhenko.**" *Left* 1 (No. 1, Spring 31) 78–79. A brief history of the Russian director's work.

Moore, John C. "Pabst, **Dovjenko:** A Comparison." *Close Up* 9 (No. 3, Sep 32). *See 5, G. W. Pabst.*

"**Dovzhenko** at 60." *S&S* 25 (Autumn 55) 62. Note on his future projects.

Montagu, Ivor. "**Dovzhenko:** Poet of Life Eternal." *S&S* 27 (Summer 57) 44–48. The life, theories, and work of the Soviet director of *Earth* and *Arsenal*, who died last year.

Shibuk, Charles. "The Films of Alexander **Dovzhenko.**" *NY F Bul* 2 (No. 11, 1961) 7–9; 2 (Nos. 12, 13, 14, 1961) 11–13. Examination of all films of "the cinema's greatest lyric poet"; in two parts.

Robinson, David. "**Dovzhenko.**" *Silent Picture* (No. 7, Summer 70) 11–14. His early, "juvenile" work.

Mahoney, S. "**Robert Downey** Makes Vile Movies." *Life* 67 (28 Nov 69) 63–66+.

Siegel, Joel. "The Greta Garbo of Filmmakers: **Robert Downey** Just Wants To Be Left Alone." *December* 12 (Nos. 1–2, 1970) 127–134. Interview; his career.

"**Downey's** *Pound.*" *New Yorker* 46 (28 Feb 70) 30–32. A visit to the set of *Pound* and an interview with director Robert Downey.

"Tugboat Annie." *Time* 22 (7 Aug 33) 23–24. Cover story on career of **Marie Dressler.**

Bond, Kirk. "Léger, Dreyer, and Montage." *Creative Art* 11 (No. 2, Oct 32). *See 5, Ferdinand Léger.* About **Carl Dreyer.**

Winge, John H. "Interview with **Dreyer.**" *S&S* 19 (Jan 50) 16–18. His proposed project, a

film on the life of Christ, to be shot in Israel.

Rowland, Richard. "**Carl Dreyer's** World." *Hwd Q* 5 (No. 1, Fall 50) 53–60. Columbia University English professor compares *The Passion of Joan of Arc* and *Day of Wrath*, suggesting that Dreyer does not change his individualistic style.

Moor, P. "Tyrannical Dane: **C. Dreyer.**" *Th Arts* 35 (Apr 51) 34–38. Onstage, a "master, crackpot and lunatic," offstage, gracious; speculations on his Christus scenario (never filmed).

Dreyer, Carl Theodore. "Film Style." *FIR* 3 (Jan 52) 15–21. Director recounts the elements that determined the style of his approach when he directed *Day of Wrath*; a defense of "slowness."

Card, James. "Visit with **Carl Th. Dreyer.**" *Image* 2 (No. 9, Dec 53) 61. A brief account.

Trolle, Borge. "The World of **Carl Dreyer.**" *S&S* 25 (Winter 55–56) 122–127. His actors and themes.

Schein, Harry. "Mankind on the Border." *QFRTV* 10 (No. 3, Spring 56) 257–261. Translation of Swedish magazine article on the work of **Carl Dreyer**, especially his latest film, *Ordet*.

Luft, Herbert G. "**Carl Dreyer**—A Master of His Craft." *QFRTV* 11 (No. 2, Winter 56) 181–196. Life, works, philosophy, plans; latest film, *Ordet*.

Luft, Herbert. "**Dreyer.**" *F&F* 7 (No. 9, June 61) 11. An interview with **Carl Dreyer.**

Cowie, Peter. "**Dreyer** at 75." *F&F* 10 (No. 6, Mar 64) 45–46. On his films.

Wright, Elsa Gress. "Danish Film: The Living **Dreyer.**" *Kenyon Rev* 26 (Autumn 64) 747–751. Comments on the career of Carl Dreyer and analysis of *The Passion of Joan of Arc*.

Kelman, Ken. "**Dreyer.**" *F Cult* (No. 35, 1964–1965) 1–9. Analysis of the films of Carl Dreyer; filmography.

Bond, Kirk. "The World of **Carl Dreyer.**" *FQ* 19 (No. 1, Fall 65) 26–38. "Dreyer is the most modern of all silent directors"; *The President* is an extraordinary first film; later his theme becomes a symbolic one, the Death of the Master and the coming of a new life.

Milne, Tom. "Darkness and Light: **Carl Theodor Dreyer.**" *S&S* 34 (Autumn 65) 167–172. A study of Dreyer's style and themes; emphasis on early silent films.

Delahaye, Michel. "Between Heaven and Hell: Interview with **Carl Dreyer.**" *CdC in Eng* (No. 4, 1966) 7–17. The Danish film maker in a lengthy commentary on his own work, including *Gertrud*.

Trolle, Borge. "An Interview with **Carl Th. Dreyer.**" *F Cult* (No. 41, Summer 66) 58–60. Mostly about *Gertrud*.

Lerner, Carl. "'My Way of Working Is in Relation to the Future.'" *F Com* 4 (No. 1, Fall 66) 62–67. A conversation with Danish director **Carl Dreyer.**

Duperley, Denis. "**Carl Dreyer:** Utter Bore? or Total Genius?" *F&F* 14 (No. 5, Feb 68) 45–46. Interview about his career.

Hart, Henry. "**Carl Theodore Dreyer:** 1889–1968." *FIR* 19 (No. 4, Apr 68) 193. One-page obituary.

Drum, Dale D. "**Carl Dreyer's** Shorts." *FIR* 20 (No. 1, Jan 69) 34–54.

Dreyer, Carl. "Dreyer in Double Reflection." *Cinema* (Calif) 6 (No. 2, 1970) 8–15. An annotated translation of Dreyer's 1946 essay "A Little on Film Style," by Gwen Morgan and Donald Skoller, with annotations by Donald Skoller.

Brakhage, Stan. "**Carl Theodore Dreyer.**" *Caterpillar* (No. 14, Jan 71) 58–72. A study of his films.

Dullea, Keir. "Portrait of a Young Actor on His Way to the Top." *F&F* 12 (No. 3, Dec 65) 5–9. Interview on his acting career.

Madden, James C. "**Irene Dunne.**" *FIR* 20 (No. 10, Dec 69) 621–635. Career and film listing of the actress.

E

Weinberg, Gretchen. "**Arnold Eagle.**" *F Cult* (No. 41, Summer 66) 87–90. Interview with cameraman who worked with Hans Richter and knew Flaherty.

Schrader, Paul. "Poetry of Ideas: The Films of **Charles Eames.**" *FQ* 23 (No. 3, Spring 70) 2–19. His multiscreen work for world fairs, his optimism about problem solving through the sciences and communication, his work for IBM; filmography.

Solbert, O. N. "**George Eastman,** Amateur." *Image* 2 (No. 8, Nov 53) 49–56. His contributions to photography and film.

Johnson, Albert. "Conversation with **Roger Edens.**" *S&S* 27 (Spring 58) 179–182. Roger Edens worked in, produced, or wrote many of the great Hollywood musicals since 1936.

Blackton, J. S. "Interview with **Thomas Alva Edison.**" *School Arts* 31 (Dec 31) supp 9–12.

Franklyn, Irwin. "**Blake Edwards.**" *FIR* 10 (Apr 59) 249–250. Brief letter on American director's career.

Hauduroy, Jean-François. "Sophisticated Naturalism: Interview with **Blake Edwards.**" *CdC in Eng* (No. 3, 1966) 21–26. The American film maker discusses his career, his beginnings as an actor, work in radio as a scriptwriter, early films.

Haller, Robert. "*Peter Gunn:* The Private Eye of **Blake Edwards.**" *F Her* 3 (No. 4, Summer 68) 21–27. In the tradition of the best mystery writers.

Hanson, Curtis Lee. "Samantha and the Look." *Cinema* (Calif) 3 (No. 2, Mar 66) 15–18. On actress **Samantha Eggar.**

O'Konor, Louise. "The Film Experiments of **Viking Eggeling.**" *Cinema Studies* 2 (No. 2, June 66) 26–31. Especially *Diagonal Symphony;* bibliography.

Gohrn-Ohm, M. "**Hasse Ekman.**" *Am Scandinavian Rev* 36 (Mar 48) 47–53. Biographical comments on the actor-director's career.

Koval, Francis. "Interview with Emmer." *S&S* 19 (Jan 51) 354–356. **Luciano Emmer,** Italian director of films about art, has made his first feature film, the story of a particular day when the lives of five people become entangled by fate; profile of his life, works, and possible future as a director.

Emshwiller, Ed. "Symposium." *Arts in Soc* 4 (No. 1, Winter 67) 83–85. Director's responses to questionnaire.

"Long Way from Hollywood." *Woman's Home Companion* 83 (Nov 56) 22. A short introduction of **Morris Engel** and Ruth Orkin, husband-wife team who made *The Little Fugitive* and *Lovers and Lollipops.*

Howard, Clifford. "Eisenstein in Hollywood." *Close Up* 7 (No. 2, 1930) 139–142. On **Sergei Eisenstein.**

Brody, Samuel. "Paris Hears **Eisenstein.**" *Close Up* 6 (No. 4, 1930) 283–289. An account of a lecture given at the Sorbonne by Eisenstein.

Blakeston, Oswell. "Two Little Stories." *Close Up* 8 (No. 3, Sep 31) 211–214. One deals with Eisenstein's visit to Hollywood, the other, with his visit to England.

Wilson, Edmund. "Eisenstein in Hollywood." *New Rep* 68 (4 Nov 31) 320–322. Description of Russian director's stay in Hollywood and current work in Mexico.

Eisenstein, Sergei M. "Mexican Film and Marxian Theory." *New Rep* 69 (9 Dec 31) 99–100. Soviet director replies to Edmund Wilson, saying, "We are no longer little boys who run away from home to see Indians stick feathers in their hair or cannibals pass rings through their noses."

"**Eisenstein's** Monster." *Time* 19 (2 May 32) 24. What the Russian director told the press about his sojourn in Hollywood.

"**Eisenstein's** Plans." *Living Age* 342 (July 32) 462–463. Returning from U.S., Soviet director tells about *American Tragedy* and *Que Viva Mexico!*

Potamkin, Harry A. "**Eisenstein** and the Theory of Cinema." *Hound & Horn* 6 (No. 4, July–Sep 33) 678–689. An analysis and critique of the Russian film maker's theory of montage, including some developmental history of his ideas.

Eisenstein, Sergei M. "Through Theatre to Cinema." *Th Arts* 20 (Sep 36). See *3f(1).*

Wollenberg, H. H. "Two Masters." *S&S* 17 (No. 65, Spring 48). See 5, *Ernst Lubitsch.* About **Sergei M. Eisenstein.**

Montagu, Ivor. "Sergei Eisenstein." *Penguin F Rev* 7 (Sep 48) 10–16. A personal reminiscence and review of the Russian director's work on the occasion of his death.

Barbarow, George. "Eisenstein and Some Artistic Dilemmas." *Hudson Rev* 2 (No. 3, 1949) 467–472. A discussion of Eisenstein's personality and some of the cinematic problems that involved him as they emerge from his writing in *Film Sense* and *Film Form* and the context of his times.

Solski, W. "End of Sergei Eisenstein: Case History of an Artist Under Dictatorship." *Commentary* 7 (Mar 49) 252–260.

Seton, Marie. "Vignettes of Eisenstein." *FIR* 2 (Apr 51) 29–31. Anecdotes about him contained in a letter from his biographer, Marie Seton, to Herman G. Weinberg.

Seton, Marie, Karel Reisz, and Lewis McLeod. "Editing: Unfair to Eisenstein." *S&S* 20 (June 51). See 2f.

Ingster, Boris. "Sergei Eisenstein." *Hwd Q* 5 (No. 4, Summer 51) 380–388. Author met Eisenstein in 1922, worked with him, came to Hollywood with him; how the director first became interested in film and was influenced by American films.

Seton, Marie. "Eisenstein's Images and Mexican Art." *S&S* 23 (July–Sep 53) 8–13. How Mexican art and culture influenced Eisenstein in his unfinished film *Que Viva Mexico!*

Eisenstein, Sergei M. "Sketches for Life." *F&F* 4 (No. 7, Apr 58) 12+. The importance of graphic art in Eisenstein's film making.

Eisenstein, Sergei M. "One Path to Colour." *S&S* 30 (Spring 61). See 2e(2).

Kuiper, John B. "Stage Antecedents of the Film Theory of S. M. Eisenstein." *Educ Th J* 13 (Dec 61) 259–263. His theatrical background.

Leyda, Jay. "The Care of the Past." *S&S* 31 (Winter 61–62) 47. An account of Leyda's findings in the Eisenstein collection at the Central Government Archives in Moscow; these included Eisenstein projects hitherto unknown.

Kuiper, John B. "Cinematic Expression: A Look at Eisenstein's Silent Montage." *Art J* 22 (Fall 62). See 3a(5).

Berson, Arnold, and Joseph Keller. "Shame and Glory in the Movies." *Nat Rev* 16 (14 Jan 64). See 7b(5). About Sergei M. Eisenstein.

Gottesman, Ronald. "Sergei Eisenstein and Upton Sinclair." *S&S* 34 (Summer 65) 142–143. Two letters by Sinclair to Stalin reprinted from Gottesman's forthcoming book on the correspondence between Eisenstein and Sinclair; cablegram from Stalin about Danashevsky and Eisenstein reproduced.

Brakhage, Stan. "Sergei Eisenstein." *Caterpillar* (Nos. 15–16, Apr–July 71) 107–135. On his films.

Wunscher, Catherine. "Jean Epstein, 1897– 1953." *S&S* 23 (Oct–Dec 53) 106. Tribute to the French director who made *La Chute de la maison Usher* (1928), *Finis Terrae* (1929), and *Le Tempestaire* (1947); his films were slow and rhythmic, full of poetic images of men and nature.

Bachmann, Gideon (ed.). "Jean Epstein." *Cinemages* 2 (1955) 1–54. An entire issue devoted to the French director; a comprehensive presentation of his work in the U.S., articles by and about Epstein, a filmography and bibliography.

Trauberg, Leonid. "A Fragment of Ermler." *F&F* 14 (No. 6, Mar 68) 51. On Friedrich Ermler's work.

Mills, J. "Why Should He Have It?" *Life* 66 (7 Mar 69) 62–78. Biography of Robert Evans, boss of Paramount Studios.

F

Herring, Robert. "Interview with Douglas Fairbanks." *Close Up* 6 (No. 6, 1930) 504–508. Fairbanks discusses plans for working with Eisenstein.

Lambert, Gavin. "Fairbanks and Valentino: The Last Heroes." *Sequence* (No. 8, Summer 49) 77–80. Films of the two American actors briefly described.

Fairbanks, Douglas, Jr. "Producing vs. Acting." *FIR* 8 (Oct 57) 383–386. The author reviews his acting and producing careers in film and TV and appraises the advantages he has found, especially in producing.

Barrett, Marvin. "Alice Faye, I Love You." *Show* 2 (July 62) 8–9. Recollection of her films.

Wunscher, Catherine. "Paul Fejos." *FIR* 5 (Mar 54) 124–127. The international career of the Hungarian director whose first American film was *The Last Moment*, with a $5,000 budget.

Wiener, Willard L. "Charmer for a Nice Fee." *Collier's* 124 (6 Aug 49) 27+. On agent Charles Feldman.

Havemann, Ernest. "Packages of Stars." *Life* 28 (17 Apr 50) 107–108+. Agent Charles Feldman, originator of the "package" deal.

Bluestone, George. "An Interview with Federico Fellini." *F Cult* 3 (No. 13, 1957) 3–4+. Fellini talks mainly about neorealism and *La Strada*.

Fellini, Federico. "Fellini: A Personal Statement." *Film* (No. 11, Jan–Feb 57) 8–9. Fellini discusses the nature of his work, particularly in *La Strada* and *I Vitelloni*, and how he relates to neorealism.

Stanbrook, Alan. "The Hope of Fellini." *Film* (No. 19, Jan–Feb 59) 17–20. An analysis of his work.

Fellini, Federico. "My Sweet Life." *F&F* 5 (No. 7, Apr 59) 7. Reflections on past films and the future *La Dolce Vita*.

Lane, John Francis. "**Fellini** Tells *Why*." *F&F* 6 (No. 9, June 60) 30. Fellini answers questions about the controversy over *La Dolce Vita*.

Fellini, Federico. "The Bitter Life—of Money." *F&F* 7 (No. 4, Jan 61) 13+. The Italian director discusses his most recent film, *La Dolce Vita*.

Neville, R. "Poet Director of the Sweet Life." *NYTM* (14 May 61) 17+. **Federico Fellini**.

Johnson, Ian. "Dreams, Fantasy, and Reality." *Motion* (No. 1, Summer 61) 10–13. Fellini's films seen as an articulation of dreams and reality, fantasy and simplicity.

Peri, Enzo. "**Federico Fellini**: An Interview." *FQ* 15 (No. 1, Fall 61) 30–33. Fellini talks of neorealism, *La Dolce Vita*, an upcoming film he plans (but didn't make), his offers from America.

Duprey, Richard A. "Bergman and **Fellini**, Explorers of the Modern Spirit." *Cath World* 194 (Oct 61). *See 4e.*

Fellini, Federico. "End of the Sweet Parade: *Via Veneto*." *Esq* 59 (Jan 63) 98–108+. A film maker takes a last look at his own creation: *Via Veneto*.

Navone, John J. "**Fellini's** *La Dolce Italia*." *Commonweal* 77 (15 Mar 63) 639–641. Communication with others is Fellini's truest joy.

Lewalski, B. "Federico **Fellini's** *Purgatorio*." *Mass Rev* 5 (No. 3, 1964) 567–573. A comparison of *8½* to Dante's *Purgatorio:* the world of Fellini's films.

Bachmann, Gideon. "Interview with **Federico Fellini**." *S&S* 33 (Spring 64) 82–87. While making *8½*, the Italian director makes special point of his opposition to intellectual labeling, to the people who ask, "What does it mean?"

Bachmann, Gideon. "Disturber of the Peace: **Federico Fellini**." *Mlle* 60 (Nov 64) 152–153+. An elaborate interview of Fellini by a writer of his biography at the time of filming *Juliet of the Spirits*.

Ross, Lillian. "Profiles: *10½*." *New Yorker* 41 (30 Oct 65) 63–66+. Article in the form of a script of a movie showing **Federico Fellini** at work.

Kast, Pierre. "Giulietta and Federico: Visit with **Fellini**." *CdC in Eng* (No. 5, 1966) 24–33. The director discusses his current production, *Juliet of the Spirits*.

Davis, Melton S. "First the Pasta, Then the Play." *NYTM* (2 Jan 66) 10–11+. The careers of Italian director **Federico Fellini** and his actress wife, Giulietta Masina.

"Interview: **Federico Fellini**." *Playboy* 13 (No. 2, Feb 66) 55–66. Fellini discusses his conception of himself as a "storyteller," his past, and the relation of his films to human experience.

Ross, T. J. "The Dance of the Homeless: On the World of **Fellini's** Films." *December* 8 (No. 1, Spring 66) 103–116. On the persistent image of dance in Fellini's films and its significance.

Harcourt, Peter. "The Secret Life of **Federico Fellini**." *FQ* 19 (No. 3, Spring 66) 4–19. Except for *I Vitelloni* and the sketch for *Boccaccio 70*, Fellini's films appear to be imprisoned in a private world; underneath is a subliminal and mystical response to life expressed through forms of cinematic movement countering the dark shadows of the city squares at night.

Walter, Eugene. "The Wizardry of **Fellini**." *F&F* 12 (No. 9, June 66) 19–26. Interview and study of Fellini.

Fellini, Federico. "I Was Born for the Cinema." *F Com* 4 (No. 1, Fall 66) 77–84. Interview conducted by Irving R. Levine for WNBC-TV *Open Mind* series.

Aliaga, Joseph. "**Fellini's** Mystery." *Medium* 1 (No. 1, Summer 67) 27–37. *La Strada* as the preeminent Fellini film compared with others.

Wood, Robin. "The Question of **Fellini** Continued." *December* 9 (Nos. 2–3, Summer–Fall 67) 140. Fellini's intrusion into his films.

Fellini, Federico. "Fellini on Fellini on *Satyricon*." *Cinema* (Calif) 5 (No. 3, 1969) 2–13. Seven pages of direct quotations followed by a two-page interview.

Eason, Patrick. "Notes on Double Structure and the Films of **Fellini**." *Cinema* (Cambridge) (No. 2, Mar 69) 22–26.

Alpert, Hollis. "**Fellini** at Work." *Sat Rev* 52 (12 July 69) 14–17.

Herman, David. "**Federico Fellini**." *Am Imago* 26 (No. 3, Fall 69) 251–268. A thematic investigation into the world of Fellini's films.

Rhode, Eric. "Gherardi in London." *S&S* 39 (Winter 69–70). *See 5, Piero Gherardi.* About **Federico Fellini**.

Myhers, John. "**Fellini's** Continuing Autobiography." *Cinema* (Calif) 6 (No. 2, 1970) 40–41. An attempt to relate aspects of Fellini's *Satyricon* to his personal life and development as an artist.

Langman, B. "Working with **Fellini**." *Mlle* 70 (Jan 70) 74–75.

Moravia, Alberto. (Tr. by S. Morini.) "**Federico Fellini** on *Satyricon*." *Vogue* 155 (1 Mar 70) 168–171+. Film maker talks with novelist.

Rollin, B. "**Fellini**: He Shoots Dreams on Film." *Look* 34 (10 Mar 70) 48–53.

Fellini, Federico. "**Fellini's** Formula." *Esq* 74 (Aug 70) 18–24+. Thoughts on working for TV in Italy; directing by Fellini.

Bodeen, DeWitt. "**Elsie Ferguson**." *FIR* 15 (No. 9, Nov 64) 551–574. Career and film listing for silent-film actress.

"**Fernandel**." *F&F* 1 (No. 8, May 55) 3. Career sketch of the French actor.

Gerald, Yvonne. "**Fernandel's** Comic Style."

FIR 11 (No. 3, Mar 60) 141–144. Brief piece on the French comedian.

Fernandel. "I'm an Actor, Not a Comedian." *F&F* 7 (No. 1, Oct 60) 15. The French actor discusses his career.

London, Julie. "The Two Faces of Ferrer." *F&F* 4 (No. 9, June 58) 12. Singer chosen to act in *The Great Man* reports on José **Ferrer** as director.

Ferrer, José. "Cyrano and Others." *F&F* 8 (No. 10, July 62) 13–14+. Actor-director answers questions.

Hill, Gladwin. "Jet Propulsion, Hollywood Type." *Collier's* 126 (29 July 50) 28–29+. Story of **Mel Ferrer**, star and director.

Lacassin, Francis. "**Louis Feuillade**." *S&S* 34 (Winter 64–65) 42–47. Life and career of the man who made hundreds of films and wrote all but half a dozen of his own scripts for series called *Les Vampires, Judex, Tih Minh,* and *Fantômas.*

McVay, Douglas. "**Edwige Feuillère**." *F&F* 7 (No. 3, Dec 60) 14–15+. The film work of the French actress.

"**Mary Field**." *F&F* 1 (No. 12, Sep 55) 3. Sketch of a film maker who began the production of films for children.

Johnston, Alva. "**W. C. Fields**." *New Yorker* (2 Feb 35) 23–26; (9 Feb 35) 25–28; (16 Feb 35) 22–26. Profile of the comedian.

Tynan, Kenneth. "Toby Jug and Bottle." *S&S* 19 (Feb 51) 395–398. A humorous account of some of the antics of **W. C. Fields**, his jokes and his life, in an extended review of of the book *W. C. Fields: His Follies and Fortunes,* by Robert Lewis Taylor (Doubleday, 1949).

Markfield, W. "Dark Geography of **W. C. Fields**." *NYTM* (24 Apr 66) 32–33+.

Robinson, David. "Dukinfield Meets McGargle." *S&S* 36 (Summer 67) 125–129. **W. C. Fields**, *né* Dukinfield; the relationships between art and life in his work, between Fields and his creations, notably Eustace P. McGargle of *Poppy.*

McVay, Douglas. "Elysian Fields." *Film* (No. 50, Winter 67) 22–23. Praise for the work of **W. C. Fields**.

Sicre, J. Gomez. "Depth of Focus." *Américas* 2 (May 50) 24–28. A brief biography of Mexican **Gabriel Figueroa**, photographer of *The Fugitive, The Pearl,* and *Pueblerina.*

Finch, Peter. "How I Learnt to Laugh at Myself." *F&F* 4 (No. 12, Sep 58) 7. British actor on acting.

Finch, Peter. "Peter, Peter, Pumpkin Eater." *F&F* 10 (No. 9, June 64) 7–8. Interview about his acting.

Finch, Peter. "The Mind's Eye." *F&F* 16 (No. 11, Aug 70) 4–10. Interview about his acting career; filmography.

Marcorelles, Louis. "Talking About Acting: Albert **Finney** and Mary Ure." *S&S* 30 (Spring 61). *See 2b(1).*

Fischer, Terence. "Horror Is My Business." *F&F* 10 (No. 10, July 64) 7–8. Interview with the director about his horror films.

Houston, Penelope. "Visits to Babylon: **F. Scott Fitzgerald** and Hollywood." *S&S* 21 (Apr–June 52) 153–156. Fitzgerald's reactions to Hollywood taken from his works.

Grierson, John. "Flaherty." *CQ* 1 (No. 1, Autumn 32) 12–17. Talking with **Robert Flaherty** while he was making *Man of Aran,* Grierson reports, "He was more full of detailed anecdote than of the theory of cinema."

Schrire, David, and John Grierson. "Evasive Documentary." *CQ* 3 (No. 1, Autumn 34). *See 8c(1).* About **Robert Flaherty.**

Hobson, Harold. "Man of Films." *CSMM* (6 Nov 35) 8. Reviews **Flaherty**'s *Man of Aran* with comments on plans for *Elephant Boy.*

"Documentary Daddy: **Robert Joseph Flaherty**." *Time* 37 (3 Feb 41) 69.

Foster, Inez Whitely. "Partners and Pioneers." *CSMM* (15 Jan 49) 5. Portrait of **Robert Flaherty** and his wife.

Taylor, Robert Lewis. "Moviemaker." *New Yorker* 25 (11 June 49) 30–34+; (18 June 49) 28–32+; (25 June 49) 28–32+. Extensive biography with much early personal background of **Robert Flaherty.**

Houston, Penelope. "Interview with **Flaherty**." *S&S* 19 (Dec 49) 16–18. Documentary director was in London to arrange distribution for *Louisiana Story;* how much he enjoyed making this film; he is still an explorer; brief summary of career.

Gray, Hugh. "**Robert Flaherty** and the Naturalistic Documentary." *Hwd Q* 5 (No. 1, Fall 50) 41–48. UCLA professor tells of his own encounter with Flaherty on an interview, then takes on the problem of staged scenes in documentary as an aspect of reconstruction in art; Flaherty did "naturalistic," not "sociological" films, and he saw "through to the essentials."

Knight, Arthur. "Flaherty Festival." *SRL* 34 (6 June 51) 27–28. Review of the career of Robert Flaherty.

Flaherty, Robert. "Film: Language of the Eye." *Th Arts* 35 (May 51) 30–36. Documentary director recounts making of *Nanook, Moana,* and *Louisiana Story:* "Film is the great pencil of the modern world"; based on article in magazine of Screen Directors Guild.

Grierson, John. "**Flaherty** as Innovator." *S&S* 21 (Oct–Dec 51) 64+. *Nanook,* truly a revolution in cinema, violated all the traditions of the 1920s, not just in style and subject matter, but in technical things, such as choice of lenses, angles, available light; it was this film and *Moana* which encouraged Grierson to enter government film making.

Weinberg, Herman G. "A Farewell to Flaherty." *FIR* 2 (Oct 51) 14–16. Author recounts his last meeting with Robert Flaherty.

Huston, John. "Regarding **Flaherty**." *Sequence* (No. 14, 1952) 17–18. A personal reminiscence of Robert Flaherty.

Flaherty, Frances. "The **Flaherty** Way." *Sat Rev* 35 (13 Sep 52) 50+. How the eye and experience of the explorer enhance the work of Flaherty.

Bachmann, Gideon. "Bob." *Film* (No. 21, Sep–Oct 59) 23–27. Several film figures discuss **Robert Flaherty** and his work.

van Dongen, Helen. "**Robert J. Flaherty** 1884–1951." *FQ* 18 (No. 4, Summer 65) 3–14. His mysterious monologues about modern civilization that never became instructions on how to cut *The Land;* his reluctance "to shoot something I thought was needed" for *Louisiana Story;* the documentary director who was really a storyteller, as seen by the editor who actually created the structure of the oil-drilling sequence.

Cameron, Ian, *et al.* "*Barabbas:* A Discussion." *Movie* (No. 1, June 62). *See 3c.* About **Richard Fleischer**.

Fleischer, Richard. "Don't Throw Them Away." *F&F* 17 (No. 3, Dec 70) 20–25. Interview on his career; filmography.

Fleischner, Bob. "Symposium." *Arts in Soc* 4 (No. 1, Winter 67) 85–87. Director's responses to questionnaire.

Reid, John Howard. "The Man Who Made *G.W.T.W.*" *F&F* 14 (No. 3, Dec 67) 12–17. On the career of **Victor Fleming**.

Reid, John Howard. "**Fleming**: The Apprentice Years." *F&F* 14 (No. 4, Jan 68) 39–46. Continuation of career of Victor Fleming.

Spears, Jack. "**Robert Florey**." *FIR* 11 (No. 4, Apr 60) 210–231. Varied career of Hollywood director; film listing.

Higham, Charles. "Visitors to Sydney." *S&S* 31 (Summer 62) 120. Note on **Robert Florey**, who has been technical adviser, writer, and director in Hollywood for forty years.

Thomas, Anthony. "**Errol Flynn**." *FIR* 11 (No. 1, Jan 60) 7–17. On occasion of Flynn's death, summary of what the man was "really like"; film list by Robert Roman.

Cutts, John. "Requiem for a Swashbuckler." *Cinema* (Calif) 3 (No. 5, Summer 67) 17–19. On **Errol Flynn**.

Cutts, John. "Requiem for a Swashbuckler." *F&F* 17 (No. 1, Oct 70) 14–18. On the heroic image of **Errol Flynn**.

Hill, Derek. "Press Conference." *S&S* 27 (Summer 57) 4. Note on visit by **Henry Fonda**, who says he will make no more films with John Ford; Sidney Lumet's organizational talent astonishing (*Twelve Angry Men*).

Morton, Frederick. "The Unspectacular Hero."

Holiday 24 (Nov 58) 117–120+. About **Henry Fonda**.

Springer, John. "**Henry Fonda**." *FIR* 11 (No. 9, Nov 60) 519–538. Career and film listings.

Ross, Lillian. "**Henry Fonda**." *New Yorker* (28 Oct 61) 61–72. Profile of the actor.

Cowie, Peter. "**Fonda**." *F&F* 8 (No. 7, Apr 62) 23+. On the acting career of Henry Fonda.

Fonda, Henry. "Fonda on Fonda." *F&F* 9 (No. 5, Feb 63) 7–8. On his acting on stage and in films.

Hagen, Ray. "**Fonda**: Without a Method." *F&F* 12 (No. 9, June 66) 40–46. On Henry Fonda's acting style and career.

Hanson, Curtis Lee. "Reflections on 40 Years of Make-Believe." *Cinema* (Calif) 3 (No. 4, Dec 66) 11–17. Interview with **Henry Fonda**.

Logan, Joshua. "Fonda Memories." *Show* (Apr 70) 6+. Excerpt from *The Fondas,* by John Springer (Citadel, 1970); recollections on the acting career of Henry Fonda.

Reif, Tony, and Iain Ewing. "Fonda." *Take One* 2 (No. 3, 1969) 6–10. An interview with **Peter Fonda**.

"Interview: Peter Fonda." *Playboy* 17 (No. 9, Sep 70) 85. On being "cult-hero"; his political views.

Katz, Jon. "An Interview with **José Luis Font**." *F Com* 1 (No. 2, Summer 62) 25–45. Film writer, critic, and documentary director talks about American films, Bardem, Berlanga, Buñuel, Bergman, Spanish censorship and subsidy, the Spanish audience.

Carlyle, John. "**Joan Fontaine**." *FIR* 14 (Mar 63) 146–159. Career study of the actress; filmography.

Adler, Richard. "*King Rat*." *Cinema* (Calif) 3 (No. 1, Dec 65) 32–35. Interview with actor-writer-director **Bryan Forbes**.

Forbes, Bryan. "Breaking the Silence." *F&F* 6 (No. 10, July 60) 7–8+. His experiences as writer, especially for *The Angry Silence.*

"John Ford's Big Brother." *Image* 1 (No. 2, Feb 52) 3. The career (in brief) of **Francis Ford**, American film actor.

Daugherty, Frank. "**John Ford** Wants It Real." *CSMM* (21 June 41) 5. Interview with John Ford, who discusses "social significance" and drama in film.

Ericsson, Peter. "**John Ford**." *Sequence* (No. 2, Winter 47) 18–25. Analysis of recent Ford films, including a filmography.

Nugent, F. S. "Hollywood's Favorite Rebel." *SEP* 222 (23 July 49) 25+. **John Ford**'s life and accomplishments in the movie industry. Also *Rdrs Dig* 55 (Oct 49) 53–57.

Anderson, Lindsay. "*They Were Expendable* and **John Ford**." *Sequence* (No. 11, Summer 50) 18–31. Using *They Were Expendable* as a lesser-known example of Ford's greatness, a positive, analytical argument is made for most of his work.

Anderson, Lindsay. "**John Ford**." *FIR* 2 (Feb

51) 5–16. His work is a portrayal of the righteous man and is unconcerned with contemporary issues; condensed from British film magazine *Sequence.*

Anderson, Lindsay. *"The Quiet Man." Sequence* (No. 14, 1952) 73–77. An encounter with **John Ford,** in Ireland for *The Quiet Man.*

Johnson, G. "**John Ford:** Maker of Hollywood Stars." *Coronet* 35 (Dec 53) 133–140.

Cockshott, Gerald. "The Curious Cult of **John Ford.**" *Film* (No. 2, Dec 54) 8–10+. A negative analysis of Ford's work. Two replies "in praise of John Ford" in (No. 3, Feb 55) 25–26.

Johnson, Albert. "The Tenth Muse in San Francisco." *S&S* 24 (Spring 55) 206–208. Notes taken from a lecture given by Kenneth Macgowan at the San Francisco Museum of Art on the work of **John Ford,** especially *Young Mr. Lincoln,* which Macgowan produced.

Mitry, Jean. "**John Ford.**" (Tr. by Anne and Thornton K. Brown from *Cahiers du Cinéma.*) *FIR* 6 (Aug–Sep 55) 305–309. He chooses *Stagecoach, The Long Voyage Home, The Informer, Prisoner of Shark Island,* and *The Sun Shines Bright* as the favorites of all the films he has made; his working relationships with the studios regarding scripts, production, and editing; his liking for situations in which characters come face to face with a powerful force in a tragic moment and reveal themselves as they are.

"The Front Page." *S&S* 25 (Autumn 55) 59. Editorial on **John Ford**'s films showing at National Film Theatre: a poet's world not unlike that of Jean Renoir.

Baker, Peter G. "**John Ford.**" *F&F* 2 (No. 2, Nov 55) 19. Response to Ford's films at National Film Theatre series.

Cutts, John. "Press Conference." *S&S* 25 (Spring 56) 170. John Wayne talks about **John Ford.**

Reed, A. C. "**John Ford.**" *Ariz Highways* 32 (Apr 56) 4–11.

Killanin, Michael. "Poet in an Iron Mask." *F&F* 4 (No. 5, Feb 58) 9+. Interview with **John Ford.**

Gillett, John. "Working with Ford." *S&S* 29 (Winter 59–60) 21–22. Note on Martin Rackin's experiences with John Ford's self-assurance.

Barkun, Michael. "Notes on the Art of **John Ford.**" *F Cult* (No. 25, 1962) 9–13. Analysis of the style of John Ford, with special emphasis on *The Informer* and *Fort Apache.*

McVay, Douglas. "The Five Worlds of **John Ford.**" *F&F* 8 (No. 9, June 62) 14–17+. Analysis of his films, their music, themes, and actors.

Mitchell, George J. "The Films of **John Ford.**" *FIR* 14 (Mar 63) 129–145. Filmography only, with comments on stories.

Bogdanovich, Peter. "Autumn of **John Ford.**" *Esq* 61 (Apr 64) 102–104+. Ford's character in life and at work gradually emerges through replays back to specific incidents in his life—on the set, during different scenes, at home.

Mitchell, George J. "Ford on Ford." *FIR* 15 (No. 6, June–July 64) 321–332. Thoughts on film and life by John Ford.

"**Ford** on Ford." *Cinema* (Calif) 2 (No. 2, July 64) 42. Discussion at UCLA by John Ford.

Cherniak, Samuel. "Toward *Liberty Valance.*" *Moviegoer* (No. 2, Summer–Autumn 64) 34–37. **John Ford**'s *The Horse Soldiers* seen as a turning point in the attitude toward the West which will be realized in the questioning of *The Man Who Shot Liberty Valance.*

Russell, Lee. "**John Ford.**" *New Left Rev* (No. 29, Jan–Feb 65) 69–73. Study of his films.

Kennedy, Burt. "A Talk with **John Ford.**" *Action* 3 (No. 5, Sep–Oct 68). *See 5, Burt Kennedy.*

Beresford, Bruce. "Decline of a Master: **John Ford.**" *Film* (No. 56, Autumn 69) 4–7.

Kennedy, Burt. "Our Way West." *F&F* 16 (No. 1, Oct 69) 30–32. An interview with **John Ford** on his Westerns.

Houston, Penelope, and Kenneth Cavander. "Interview with **Carl Foreman.**" *S&S* 27 (Summer 58) 220–223+. The screenwriter-producer left America after the McCarthy hearings; he feels *The Key* is, in a way, a sequel to *High Noon,* portraying an individual alone against a society.

Alpert, Hollis. "Something Worth Fighting For." *Sat Rev* 46 (28 Dec 63). *See 6c(3).* About **Carl Foreman.**

Foreman, Carl. "A Sense of Adventure." *F&F* 16 (No. 2, Nov 69) 14–16. Interview on filming generally.

Foreman, Carl. "Confessions of a Frustrated Screenwriter." *F Com* 6 (No. 4, 1970–1971). *See 2d(1).*

Dyer, Peter John. "Star-Crossed in Prague." *S&S* 35 (Winter 65–66) 34–35. **Milos Forman,** the Czech director, likes to poke gentle fun at characters; his films *Peter and Pavla* and *A Blonde in Love* examined.

Gow, Gordon. "Red Youth." *F&F* 12 (No. 5, Feb 66) 32–33. Study of young characters in some of the films of **Milos Forman.**

Levy, Alan. "Watch Out for the Hook, My Friend." *Life* 62 (20 Jan 67) 77–80+. **Milos Forman** in America.

Forman, Milos. "Closer to Things." *CdC in Eng* (No. 7, Jan 67) 57–58. Statement at Pesaro in 1965.

Blue, James, and Gianfranco de Bosio. "Interview with **Milos Forman.**" *CdC in Eng* (No. 8, Feb 67) 53–54. The Czechoslovakian film maker discusses his film *Loves of a Blonde.*

Polt, Harriet. "Getting the Great Ten Percent: An Interview with **Milos Forman.**" *F Com* 6

(No. 2, Fall 70) 58–63. Director of *Loves of a Blonde* talks about his films and others, nonprofessional actors, and the film he was then planning to make in America.

"William Fox Presents." *Newswk* 2 (2 Dec 33) 22–23. Fox testifies before Senate Banking and Currency Subcommittee.

"On the Road to Hilaria." *American* 147 (Feb 49) 105. Brief profile of Barney Fradkin, gag man for Hope and Crosby.

Roberts, Katharine. "Acting in a Business Way." *Collier's* 95 (16 Mar 35) 14+. Interview with Kay Francis.

Parish, James, Jr., and Gene Ringgold. "Kay Francis." *FIR* 15 (No. 2, Feb 64) 65–83. Biography and film listing for the American actress.

Grenier, Cynthia. "Franju." *S&S* 26 (Spring 57) 186–190. The life and work of Georges Franju, France's documentary-film maker, who directed *Hôtel des Invalides, En Passant par la Lorraine,* and *Sang des bêtes.*

Price, James. "Undertones." *London Mag* new series 5 (No. 1, Apr 65) 72–75. On the films of Franju, especially *Thérèse Desqueyroux.*

Frankel, Cyril. "What Establishes a Style?" *F&F* 7 (No. 12, Sep 61) 10. British director writes of style in his films.

Mayersberg, Paul. "John Frankenheimer." *Movie* (No. 5, Dec 62) 35. Elements of a personal style in the director's work.

Fenwick, J. H. "Black King Takes Two." *S&S* 33 (Summer 64) 114–117. An article comparing John Frankenheimer's four early pictures with the achievements of his latest successful political thrillers, *Manchurian Candidate* and *Seven Days in May.*

Thomas, John. "John Frankenheimer, the Smile on the Face of the Tiger." *FQ* 19 (No. 2, Winter 65–66) 2–13. Extended opinions about the films, beginning with the assumption that this director has dealt with the ambiguities of American life in a descent from liberal optimism to nihilism.

Casty, Alan. "Realism and Beyond: The Films of John Frankenheimer." *F Her* 2 (No. 2, Winter 66–67) 21–33. The conflict between the demands of plot and realistic form.

Higham, Charles. "Frankenheimer." *S&S* 37 (Spring 68) 91–93. John Frankenheimer's schooling, television work, and most important films.

Filmer, Paul. "Three Frankenheimer Films: A Sociological Approach." *Screen* 10 (Nos. 4–5, July–Oct 69) 160–173.

Au Werter, Russell. "John Frankenheimer." *Action* 5 (No. 3, May–June 70) 6–9. Interview.

Bodeen, DeWitt. "Pauline Frederick." *FIR* 16 (No. 2, Feb 65) 69–90. Career and film listing.

Freed, Arthur. "Making Musicals." *F&F* 2

(No. 4, Jan 56) 9–12+. MGM producer writes of twenty-five-year history.

Luft, Herbert G. "Karl Freund." *FIR* 14 (Feb 63) 93–108. Career study of this cinematographer.

Deschner, Donald. "Karl Freund." *Cinema* (Calif) 5 (No. 4, 1969) 24–27. The contributions of this cinematographer to early German films.

Thomas, Anthony. "Hugo Friedhoffer." *FIR* 16 (No. 8, Oct 65) 496–510. Career of one of Hollywood's leading composers.

Russell, Lee. "Samuel Fuller." *New Left Rev* (No. 23, Jan–Feb 64) 86–89. Study of his films.

Fuller, Samuel. "What Is Film?" *Cinema* (Calif) 2 (No. 2, July 64) 21–24.

Goodman, Ezra. "Low-Budget Movies with Pow." *NYTM* (28 Feb 65) 42–43+. On the career of director Samuel Fuller.

Hanson, Curtis Lee. "*Caine*—A New Film by Samuel Fuller." *Cinema* (Calif) 3 (No. 6, Winter 67) 30–31. Filmography (titles only).

Wollen, Peter. "Notes Toward a Structural Analysis of the Films of Samuel Fuller." *Cinema* (Cambridge) (No. 1, Dec 68) 26–29.

Canham, Kingsley. "The World of Samuel Fuller." *Film* (No. 55, Summer 69) 4–10. A critical analysis including a filmography.

Canham, Kingsley. "Samuel Fuller's Action Films." *Screen* 10 (No. 6, Nov–Dec 69) 80–92.

McArthur, Colin. "Samuel Fuller's Gangster Films." *Screen* 10 (No. 6, Nov–Dec 69) 93–101.

Björkman, Stig, and Mark Shivas. "Samuel Fuller: Two Interviews." *Movie* (No. 17, Winter 69–70) 25–31. In two separate interviews, the director discusses various aspects of his work.

Farber, Manny. "The Films of Sam Fuller and Don Siegel." *December* 12 (Nos. 1–2, 1970) 170–174. Visuals, morals, and moods.

Christie, Ian Leslie, *et al.* "Samuel Fuller." *Cinema* (Cambridge) (No. 5, Feb 70) 6–8. Interview.

Koszarski, Richard. "Jules Furthman." *F Com* 6 (No. 4, Winter 70–71) 26–31. How much did the work of this prolific screenwriter contribute to the careers of Sternberg, Hawks, and others? Filmography.

G

Duvillars, Pierre. "Jean Gabin's Instinctual Man." (Tr. by Dorothy Milburn.) *FIR* 2 (Mar 51) 28–31. Key roles played by Jean Gabin all have the common denominator of being characters trapped by civilized life and doomed to destruction.

Nolan, Jack E. "Jean Gabin." *FIR* 14 (Apr 63) 193–209. Career study and filmography.

Cowie, Peter. "Jean Gabin." *F&F* 10 (No. 5, Feb 64) 13–16. Study of his acting career.

Fowler, Dan C. "Clark Gable." *Look* 11 (No. 14, 8 July 47) 64–71.

Clarens, Carlos. "Clark Gable." *FIR* 11 (No. 10, Dec 60) 577–597. Biography written on Gable's death; also film listing.

Koval, Francis. "France's Greatest Director." *FIR* 3 (Nov 52) 436–442+. Interview with **Abel Gance**; his plans to use the triptych screen again for the life of Christ.

Brownlow, Kevin. *"The Charm of Dynamite." Film* (No. 54, Spring 69) 8–12. An interview with **Abel Gance**, including remarks about the film *The Charm of Dynamite*, which treats the making of *Napoleon* and includes scenes heretofore thought lost.

Brownlow, Kevin. "Abel Gance: Spark of Genius." *F&F* 16 (No. 2, Nov 69) 32–37+. On the years that led up to Gance's *Napoleon*, a section from Kevin Brownlow's book *The Parade's Gone By* (Ballantine, 1969).

Virgilia, Sapieha. "Greta Garbo." *New Yorker* (7 Mar 31) 28–31. Profile of actress.

Young, Stark. "Film Note: Greta Garbo." *New Rep* 72 (28 Sep 32) 176–178. Her remoteness puzzles the public but it has something to do with her talent.

Canfield, Mary Cass. "Letter to Garbo." *Th Arts* 21 (Dec 37) 951–960.

Huff, Theodore. "The Career of Greta Garbo." *FIR* 2 (Dec 51) 1–17. A brief summary with a list of her films, a production still from each.

Tynan, Kenneth. "Garbo." *S&S* 23 (Apr–June 54) 187–190+. Impressions of Garbo during an interview; Tynan's ideas on how she appeals, to whom she appeals, and with whom she compares.

"Greta Garbo." *F&F* 1 (No. 10, July 55) 3. Career sketch of the film actress.

Fleet, Simon. "Garbo: The Lost Star." *F&F* 3 (No. 3, Dec 56) 14. Greta Garbo's flight from publicity.

Levy, Alan. "Garbo Walks." *Show* 3 (June 63) 60–61+. Remarks on the Greta Garbo cult as it exists today and how fans still wait outside her New York apartment for a glimpse of her.

Whitehall, Richard. "Garbo—How Good Was She?" *F&F* 9 (No. 12, Sep 63) 42–48. Analysis and history of her acting career.

Gronowicz, Antoni. "Garbo: The Falling Leaves." *December* 6 (No. 1, Spring 65) 100–103. A brief interview with some biographical comments.

Barthes, Roland. "Garbo's Face." *Moviegoer* (No. 3, Summer 66) 8–9.

Gronowicz, Antoni. "Garbo." *J Pop Cult* 2 (No. 1, Summer 68) 91–98. A brief interview, with biographical comments.

Gronowicz, Antoni. "Garbo." *Arts in Soc* 5 (No. 3, Fall–Winter 68) 466–468. Interview with some biographical comments.

Nordberg, Carl Eric. "Greta Garbo's Secret." *F Com* 6 (No. 2, Summer 70) 26–35. According to a Stockholm critic, she usually played a virtuous *femme fatale*, a passionate puritan who has only a moment of love and then gives up life—or the rest of her life—in payment.

Vincent, Mal. "Ava Gardner." *FIR* 16 (No. 6, June–July 65) 343–357. Career and film listing.

Bachmann, Gideon. "Interview with **Jack Garfein**." *Film* (No. 27, Jan–Feb 61) 26–31. The American writer-director discusses his work.

Johnson, Albert. "Jack Garfein: An Interview." *FQ* 17 (No. 1, Fall 63) 36–43. His film *Something Wild* is the springboard for a discussion of creative American film making and the problems of the independent.

Roman, Robert C. "John Garfield." *FIR* 11 (No. 6, June–July 60) 325–338. Career and film list for the American actor.

"Star Turn: **Judy Garland**." *S&S* 20 (June 51) 53. Judy Garland's appearance at the London Palladium, her first on the stage in sixteen years, brought some comments about her past career and successes; how the star image changes as the stars mature.

Rosterman, Robert. "Judy Garland." *FIR* 13 (No. 4, Apr 52) 206–219. Biography and career; film chronology.

Brinson, Peter. "The Great Come-Back." *F&F* 1 (No. 3, Dec 54) 4–5. A review of the career of **Judy Garland** on the release of *A Star Is Born*.

McVay, Douglas. "Judy Garland." *F&F* 8 (No. 1, Oct 61) 10–11+. Analysis of her film work; filmography.

Higham, Charles, and Joel Greenberg. "North Light and Cigarette Bulb." *S&S* 36 (Autumn 67). *See 2e*. About **Lee Garmes**, cameraman.

Garnett, Tony. "An Interview." *Afterimage* (No. 1, Apr 70), 12 pages. The author is interviewed, discussing his role and theories as a producer of political films.

Hartog, Simon. "An Interview with **Philippe Garrel**." *Afterimage* (No. 2, Autumn 70) 59–63. The French film maker discusses his work and film making in France.

Luft, Henry G. "Greer Garson." *FIR* 12 (No. 3, Mar 61) 152–176. Biography and film list.

Lane, John Francis. "Italy's Man of a Thousand Faces." *F&F* 5 (No. 7, Apr 59) 29. On **Vittorio Gassman**.

Carr, Chauncey L. "Janet Gaynor." *FIR* 10 (Oct 59) 470–478+. Life and motion-picture career of the American actress, with a descriptive index to her thirty-five films since 1926.

Hudson, Roger. "Sergei Gerasimov." *Film* (No. 54, Spring 69) 12–17. An interview with the

Russian director-producer-teacher about his own work and film making in Russia.

Germi, Pietro. "Man Is Not Large Enough for Man." *F&F* 12 (No. 12, Sep 66) 25–29. Interview about Italian director's outlook on life.

Jablonski, Edward C., and Milton A. Caine. "Gershwin's Movie Music." *FIR* 2 (Oct 51) 23–28. George Gershwin's career in Hollywood and an appraisal of the use of his music in films.

Rhode, Eric. "Gherardi in London." *S&S* 39 (Winter 69–70) 16–17. Designer Piero Gherardi talks about his work for Fellini.

Erengis, George P. "Cedric Gibbons." *FIR* 16 (No. 4, Apr 65) 217–232. Career of art director of MGM for three decades.

Quirk, Lawrence J. "John Gilbert." *FIR* 7 (Mar 56) 103–110. A biography of the American silent-screen star, through a survey of his films until his death in 1936.

Davis, Henry R., Jr. "A John Gilbert Index." *FIR* 13 (No. 8, Oct 62) 477–483.

De La Roche, Catherine. "Launder and Gilliat." *S&S* 15 (No. 59, Autumn 46). *See 5, Frank Launder.* About Sidney Gilliat.

Enley, Frank. "Film in the Making: *State Secret.*" *S&S* 19 (Dec 49) 10–12. Location in the Dolomites for entertainment film; biography of director Sidney Gilliat and brief note on cinematographer Robert Krasker.

Bodeen, DeWitt. "Dorothy Gish." *FIR* 19 (No. 7, Aug–Sep 68) 393–414. Biography and films of silent-film actress.

Gish, Lillian. "Silence Was Our Virtue." *F&F* 4 (No. 3, Dec 57) 9. Reflections on her early career.

"Conversation with Lillian Gish." *S&S* 27 (Winter 57–58) 128–130. She discusses D. W. Griffith, with whom she worked for nine years, gives her views on her profession, and talks of some of her films.

Tozzi, Romano. "Lillian Gish." *FIR* 13 (No. 10, Dec 62) 577–602. Career and film list.

Gish, Lillian. "Life and Living." *F&F* 16 (No. 4, Jan 70) 12–15. Television interview on her film career.

Gish, Lillian. "Lillian Gish . . . Director." *Silent Picture* (No. 6, Spring 70) 12–13. Her trying experience of making *Remodelling Her Husband;* from a recorded interview.

Godard, Jean-Luc. "But 'Wave' Adds Brightness." *F&F* 7 (No. 12, Sep 61) 7+. Interview about his beginning in film making.

Godard, Jean-Luc. "An Interview." *NY F Bul* 3 (No. 5, 1962) 3–12. His critical work and his films up to *My Life to Live;* more by Warren Sonbert on p. 13.

Godard, Jean-Luc. "Taking Pot Shots at *The Riflemen.*" *NY F Bul* 3 (No. 5, 1962) 14–15. The director responds to French critics on his film *Les Carabiniers.*

Sarris, Andrew. "A Movie Is a Movie Is a Movie Is a." *NY F Bul* 3 (No. 5, 1962) 17–19. An assessment of Jean-Luc Godard's career, noting his dialectical approach to film making and reality; on pp. 20–24, an annotated chronology of his life and works.

Milne, Tom. "Jean-Luc Godard and *Vivre sa vie.*" *S&S* 32 (Winter 62–63) 9–12. In an interview recorded at the London Film Festival, Godard answers questions about directing, editing, improvisation, and his future projects; following is Milne's review of *Vivre sa vie.*

Fieschi, Jean-André. "Godard." *Movie* (No. 6, Jan 63) 21–25. An analysis of Godard's work, with particular emphasis on *Vivre sa vie.*

Sarris, Andrew. "Waiting for Godard." *F Cult* (No. 33, 1964) 2–8. The work of Jean-Luc Godard has been delayed in reaching the U.S., except for *Breathless;* he represents a disintegration of categories in modern cinema.

Clay, Jean. "Jean-Luc Godard: The French Cinema's Most Negative Asset." *Réalités* (English-language edition) Jan 64.

Marcorelles, Louis. "Jean-Luc Godard's Half-Truths." *FQ* 17 (No. 3, Spring 64) 4–7. Brief examination of a man "erratic, tormented, uncertain"; his films show his tendency for reality on the wing and "verbal delirium"; Godard "is bold, but he remains a man of letters."

Feinstein, Herbert. "An Interview with Jean-Luc Godard." *FQ* 17 (No. 3, Spring 64) 8–10. Problems encountered in making *Contempt:* artistic freedom and Joe Levine.

Price, James. "Behind Dark Glasses." *London Mag* new series 4 (No. 11, Feb 65) 78–82. On Jean-Luc Godard.

Godard, Jean-Luc. "Godard on Pure Film." *Cinema* (Calif) 2 (No. 5, Mar–Apr 65) 38. Comment on *The Married Woman.*

Price, James. "A Film Is a Film: Some Notes on Jean-Luc Godard." *Evergreen Rev* 9 (No. 38, Nov 65) 46–53.

Sharits, Paul J. "Red, Blue, Godard." *FQ* 19 (No. 4, Summer 66) 24–29. The use of color in Godard's *A Woman Is a Woman* and *Contempt;* thematic, narrative, and symbolic functions.

Goldman, Judith. "Godard: Cult or Culture?" *F&F* 12 (No. 9, June 66) 36–37. Will his early style continue?

Wittig, Monique. "Lacunary Films." *New S&N* 72 (15 July 66) 102. Godard and the process of discontinuity.

Wood, Robin. "Jean-Luc Godard." *New Left Rev* (No. 39, Sep–Oct 66) 77–83. Study of his work. Reply by Lee Russell, pp. 83–87.

Godard, Jean-Luc. "One or Two Things." *S&S* 36 (Winter 66–67) 2–6. Why he is making two films at the same time; his attitudes toward film making and the world. Reprinted from *Le Nouvel Observateur.*

Godard, Jean-Luc. "Modern Life." *Take One* 1

(No. 3, 1967) 7–10. The French film director discusses modern life, his films (particularly *Two or Three Things That I Know About Her* and *Made in U.S.A.*), and the influences upon him.

Godard, Jean-Luc. "Three Thousand Hours of Cinema." *CdC in Eng* (No. 10, May 67) 10–15. Journal on his activities in film.

Bertolucci, Bernardo. "Versus Godard." *CdC in Eng* (No. 10, May 67) 16–17. A comparison of *Two or Three Things That I Know About Her* and *Made in U.S.A.*

Delahaye, Michel. "Jean-Luc Godard and the Childhood of Art." *CdC in Eng* (No. 10, May 67) 18–29. A critique of *Masculin-Féminin* seen in the context of Godard's other films.

Delahaye, Michel. "Jean-Luc Godard or the Urgency of Art." *CdC in Eng* (No. 10, May 67) 32–37. The cinematic world of Godard.

Thompson, Richard. "Jean-Luc—Cinema—Godard." *December* 9 (Nos. 2–3, Summer–Fall 67) 143–158.

Moullet, Luc. "Jean-Luc Godard." *CdC in Eng* (No. 12, Dec 67) 22–23. Godard's beginnings as a film maker: *Breathless*.

Fieschi, Jean-André. "The Difficulty of Being Jean-Luc Godard." *CdC in Eng* (No. 12, Dec 67) 38–43. *Une Femme est une femme* as a clarification of Godard as auteur: a critique of the film.

Mussman, Toby. "Godard as Godard." *Medium* 1 (No. 2, Winter 67–68) 20–32. Godard's theory of film making: involving the audience intellectually rather than emotionally.

"Godard in Hollywood." *Take One* 1 (No. 10, 1968) 13–17. Excerpts from a panel in Hollywood moderated by Kevin Thomas and consisting of Godard, Samuel Fuller, King Vidor, Roger Corman, Peter Bogdanovich.

Sokolov, Raymond A. "The Truth 24 Times a Second." *Newswk* 71 (12 Feb 68) 90–91. A short biography and filmography of Jean-Luc Godard and his impact on movies.

Federman, Raymond. "Jean-Luc Godard and Americanism." *F Her* 3 (No. 3, Spring 68) 1–10+. Godard in his films portrays the illusion of Americanism and attempts to destroy the illusions of the cinema.

Siegel, Joel E. "Between Art and Life: The Films of Jean-Luc Godard." *F Her* 3 (No. 3, Spring 68) 11–22+. Godard has brought film into line with the concerns of contemporary artists in other fields; film is a fiction and a documentary record of the creation of that fiction.

Sarris, Andrew. "Jean-Luc Versus Saint Jean." *F Her* 3 (No. 3, Spring 68) 27–30. Fragmentation, depletion of emotional energy, exploitation of mannerisms, superficial political rhetoric—Godard is no longer interesting.

Sontag, Susan. "Godard." *Partisan Rev* 35

(Spring 68) 290–313. Thorough analysis, critique, and defense of French director Jean-Luc Godard.

Macbean, James Roy. "Politics and Poetry in Two Recent Films by Godard." *FQ* 21 (No. 4, Summer 68) 14–20. *La Chinoise* and *Two or Three Things That I Know About Her* examined in terms of revolution in art and society.

Clouzot, Claire. "Godard and the U.S." *S&S* 37 (Summer 68) 110–114. An article concerning Jean-Luc Godard's tour of American colleges with *La Chinoise;* the apparent difficulties he ran into with students and critics, his evolution from aestheticism to sociopolitical consciousness.

Farber, Manny. "The Films of Jean-Luc Godard." *Artforum* (Oct 68) 58–61.

Blum, Peter, and David Ehrenstein. "Two or Three Things We Know About Godard." *December* 10 (No. 1, 1968) 164–173. Four films.

Godard, Jean-Luc. "Struggle on Two Fronts." *FQ* 22 (No. 2, Winter 68–69) 20–35. Taped interview reprinted from *Cahiers du Cinéma* (No. 194, Oct 67).

Silverstein, Norman. "Godard and Revolution." *Salmagundi* (No. 9, Spring 69) 44–60. Godard is not so interested in social change as in the relation between art and life.

Crofts, Stephen. "The Films of Jean-Luc Godard." *Cinema* (Cambridge) (No. 3, June 69) 27–32. Traits and concerns of the characters in his films.

Ross, W. S. "Splicing Together Jean-Luc Godard." *Esq* 72 (June 69) 72–75. With interview.

Weightman, John. "Whatever Happened to Godard?" *Encounter* 33 (Sep 69) 56–59. *Le Gai Savoir* and other recent films seen as signs of Godard's increasing cinematic incoherence.

Goodwin, Michael, Tom Luddy, and Naomi Wise. "The Dziga Vertov Film Group in America." *Take One* 2 (No. 10, 1970) 9–27. An extended interview with Jean-Luc Godard and Jean-Pierre Gorin, including a recent filmography and separate critical comments by various authors on *Le Gai Savoir, Wind from the East, A Film Like Any Other,* and *One P.M.;* film as an instrument of political action.

Godard, Jean-Luc. "Dziga Vertov Notebook." *Take One* 2 (No. 11, 1970) 7–9. Sketches and comments in Godard's production notebook.

Allard, Pierre. "Godard: A Select Bibliography." *Take One* 2 (No. 11, 1970) 11.

Dawson, Jan. "Raising the Red Flag." *S&S* 39 (Spring 70) 90–91. An article concerning Jean-Luc Godard's "declaration of war on the bourgeoisie" in his films *Weekend, British Sounds,* and *Le Gai Savoir.*

Godard, Jean-Luc. *"British Sounds, Pravda."* *Afterimage* (No. 1, Apr 70) 14 pages. Descriptions and critique commenting on his two films and political cinema; a brief, two-page introduction by Peter Sainsbury.

Silverstein, Norman. "**Godard** and Revolution." *F&F* 16 (No. 9, June 70) 96–106. His films about revolution.

Hamulian, Leo. "Waiting for **Godard**." *J Pop Cult* 4 (No. 1, Summer 70) 308–312. On his films.

McBride, Joseph. *"See You at Mao."* *S&S* 39 (Summer 70) 136. **Godard** shows this film at University of Wisconsin; a brief critical study of his answers to questions.

Spiers, David. "Interview with **Jack Gold**." *Screen* (Nos. 4–5, July–Oct 69) 115–128. Former BBC documentary director talks about his first feature, *The Bofors Gun*.

Godfrey, Lionel. "The Music Makers." *F&F* 12 (No. 12, Sep 66). *See 5, Elmer Bernstein*. About **Jerry Goldsmith**.

Johnston, A. "The Great Goldwyn." *SEP* 209 (8 May 37) 5–7+; (22 May 37) 24–25+; (5 June 37) 20–21+; (19 June 37) 23+. Series of articles on **Samuel Goldwyn**, his "touch," personality, films, and company.

Busch, Noel. "Maker of Stars: A Close-Up of **Samuel Goldwyn**." *Cinema Arts* 1 (No. 1, June 37) 69. The way he was influenced, and what he influenced.

Woolf, S. J. "Story Makes the Movie—Interview with **Samuel Goldwyn**." *NYTM* (14 Nov 43) 18–20.

Butterfield, R. "Sam Goldwyn." *Life* 23 (27 Oct 47) 126–128+. Lengthy study beginning with *The Squaw Man*.

Anderson, Lindsay. "**Goldwyn** at Claridges." *Sequence* (No. 13, 1951) 9+. A brief interview with Samuel Goldwyn and discussion of his film *Edge of Doom*.

Goldwyn, Frances. "I Love Making Movies with Sam." *Woman's Home Companion* 80 (Apr 53) 34–35+. Big stars, studio gossip, trials and triumphs, told by **Samuel Goldwyn's** wife.

"Another American Visitor." *S&S* 23 (July–Sep 53) 3–4. **Samuel Goldwyn** speaks at a Critics' Circle luncheon.

Pryor, Thomas. "The **Goldwyns**—and *Guys and Dolls*." *Collier's* 135 (29 Apr 55) 62–65. A portrait of Sam and Frances Goldwyn, business as well as marital partners, while filming Goldwyn's sixty-eighth picture.

"Going Like 70." *Time* 65 (9 May 55) 106. Producer **Samuel Goldwyn** and Cecil B. De Mille, both seventy-three still going strong.

Wainwright, Loudon. "One-Man Gang Is in Action Again." *Life* 46 (16 Feb 59) 102–104+. The story of **Samuel Goldwyn** and *Porgy and Bess*. Same article in *Rdrs Dig* 74 (May 59) 275–276+ with the title "Last of the Hollywood Moguls."

"**Samuel Goldwyn** Said." *JSPG* (Mar 59) 4–5+. His remarks on the occasion of the Milestone dinner; responsibilities to the stockholders.

Peck, Seymour. "Best of **Goldwyn**." *NYTM* (26 Aug 62) 34–35. Photos from Samuel Goldwyn's "great" pictures.

"Creating with Enthusiasm." *Nation's Business* 54 (Nov 66) 46–48+. An interview with **Samuel Goldwyn.**

Luft, Herbert G. "**Samuel Goldwyn**." *FIR* 20 (No. 10, Dec 69) 585–604. Career of the producer; film chronology.

Houston, Penelope. "Cukor and the Kanins." *S&S* 24 (Spring 55). *See 2d(4)*. About **Ruth Gordon.**

Anderson, J. L., and Donald Richie. "The Films of **Heinosuke Gosho**." *S&S* 26 (Autumn 56) 76–81. Though he is known in Japan for his films on contemporary life, only two have been shown in the West: *Where Chimneys Are Seen* and *An Inn at Osaka*.

Mayer, M. "**Elliot Gould** as the Entrepreneur." *Fortune* 82 (Oct 70). *See 6c(3)*.

"Interview: **Elliot Gould**." *Playboy* 17 (No. 11, Nov 70) 77–94.

Daugherty, Frank. "**Paul Green** in Hollywood." *Close Up* 9 (No. 2, June 32) 81–86. The American writer discusses movies, Hollywood, and the theatre.

Nolan, Jack Edmund. "**Graham Greene's** Movies." *FIR* 15 (No. 1, Jan 64) 23–43. How the author's works have fared on the screen.

French, Philip. "Screen **Greene**." *London Mag* new series 8 (No. 1, Apr 68) 54–57. On the films from Graham Greene novels or screenplays.

Phillips, G. D. "**Graham Greene**: On the Screen." *Cath World* 209 (Aug 69). *See 3f(2)*.

"People of Talent (5): **Joan Greenwood**." *S&S* 25 (Spring 56) 191. Her performances and manner of speaking.

Hackett, Hazel. "**Jean Grémillon**." *S&S* 16 (No. 62, Summer 47) 60–62. The French director's work.

Chowl, Hay. "Mickey's Rival." *Close Up* 6 (No. 6, 1930) 493–495. An account of **John Grierson** working on a puppet film.

Ellis, Jack C. "The Young **Grierson** in America, 1924–1927." *CJ* 8 (No. 1, Fall 68) 12–21. The man who was to become the founder of the documentary-film movement in England studied at the University of Chicago on a Rockefeller grant, visited Hollywood, wrote for *The New York Sun*, and met Walter Lippmann, William Allen White, Robert Flaherty.

Ellis, Jack C. "**John Grierson's** First Years at the National Film Board." *CJ* 10 (No. 1, Fall 70) 2–14. How the first director of the NFB chose his staff and apprentices; his conflict with the old Motion Picture Bureau; a chapter from a forthcoming biography of John Grierson by a professor of film at Northwestern University.

Blumer, Ronald. "**John Grierson: I Derive My Authority from Moses.**" *Take One* 2 (No. 9, 1970) 17–19. An interview with the British documentary-film pioneer.

Watkins, Fred. "**Corinne Griffith** Today." *FIR* 10 (Nov 59) 566–568. Letter to editor based on interview with actress now campaigning against income tax.

MacKaye, M. *"Birth of a Nation."* *Scribner's* 102 (Nov 37) 40–46+. Detailed history and significance of both **D. W. Griffith** and this film; pictures included.

Stern, S. "Pioneer of the Film Art: **D. W. Griffith.**" *NYTM* (10 Nov 40) 16–17+.

Ackland, Rodney. "The Bubble—Reputation." *S&S* 12 (No. 45, Summer 43) 8–11. **D. W. Griffith**'s reputation seems to be pushed farther and farther back with each new wave of good films.

Braverman, B. "**David Wark Griffith**, Creator of Film Form." *Th Arts* 29 (Apr 45) 240–250. Biography inspired by the then-current showings of his work at the Museum of Modern Art in New York.

Noble, Peter. "A Note on an Idol." *S&S* 15 (No. 59, Autumn 46) 81–82. **Griffith**'s racist tendencies.

Griffith, D. W., and Seymour Stern. *"The Birth of a Nation."* *S&S* 16 (No. 61, Spring 47) 32–35. Griffith and Stern reply to Peter Noble's earlier charge of Griffith's racism. Further letters and responses in 16 (No. 63, Autumn 47) 119 and 17 (No. 65, Spring 48) 49–50.

Stern, Seymour. "The **Griffith** Controversy." *S&S* 17 (No. 65, Spring 48) 49–50. Answering further attacks on Griffith.

"Movies Lose Their Great Pioneer." *Life* 25 (2 Aug 48) 31–33+. A brief obituary for **D. W. Griffith.**

"Last Dissolve." *Time* 52 (2 Aug 48) 72. Epitaph for **D. W. Griffith**, with a brief biography.

Barrymore, Lionel, Cecil B. De Mille, Tony Gaudio, Lillian Gish, F. Hugh Herbert, Julian Johnson, Mack Sennett, Mae Marsh, Scena Owen, and Mary Pickford. "**David Wark Griffith**: 1875–1948." *Screen Writer* 4 (Aug 48) 2–4+.

Agee, James. "**David Wark Griffith.**" *Nation* 167 (4 Sep 48) 264–266. Eulogy of Griffith's gift for the unforgettable image, the sense of life in even his poorest work.

Stern, Seymour. "**D. W. Griffith**: An Appreciation." *S&S* 17 (No. 67, Autumn 48) 109–110. On the occasion of his death, July 23.

Stern, Seymour. "**D. W. Griffith** and the Movies." *Am Mercury* 68 (Mar 49) 308–319.

An assessment of Griffith's stature in American film history.

Feldman, Joseph, and Harry Feldman. "The **D. W. Griffith** Influence." *FIR* 1 (July–Aug 50) 11–14+. Specific scenes in Italian and American films may reflect his work.

Dickinson, Thorold. "**Griffith** and the Development of the Silent Film." *S&S* 21 (Oct–Dec 51) 84–86+. Griffith's entire career, from the Louisville stage to New York and Hollywood.

Stern, Seymour. "**Griffith** and Poe." *FIR* 2 (Nov 51). See 3f(2).

Stern, Seymour. "11 East 14th Street." *FIR* 3 (Oct 52) 399–406. The New York address of the American Mutoscope and Biograph Company, where **D. W. Griffith** worked until 1913; this article surveys this early portion of Griffith's career and contains a letter to the author from Griffith's cameraman, Bitzer, with a firsthand account of his association with Griffith.

Johnson, Albert. "The Tenth Muse in San Francisco." *S&S* 24 (Jan–Mar 55). See 2c. About **D. W. Griffith.**

Stern, Seymour. "The Cold War Against **David Wark Griffith.**" *FIR* 7 (Feb 56) 49–59. The Soviet cultural "conspiracy" to rewrite cinema history and destroy the eminence of Griffith; the author's categorical defense.

Card, James. "Influences of the Danish Film." *Image* 5 (No. 3, Mar 56). See 4e(5). About **D. W. Griffith.**

Stern, Seymour. "The Soviet Directors' Debt to **Griffith.**" *FIR* 7 (May 56) 202–209. Filmic techniques the great Russian silent-film directors borrowed from Griffith; comparative examples.

Pratt, George. "In the Nick of Time." *Image* 6 (No. 3, Mar 57) 52–59. New findings about the early career of **D. W. Griffith.**

Salerno, Anthony. "**Griffith** in Louisville." *FIR* 8 (Apr 57) 187–189. Letter to editor quotes *Louisville Courier-Journal* (17 Feb) article by Edmund Rucker, who knew **D. W. Griffith** as a boy and later interviewed him.

Vaughan, D. "Victor Sjöström and **D. W. Griffith.**" *Film* (No. 15, Jan–Feb 58). See 5, *Sjöström.*

"**D. W. Griffith** and Billy Bitzer Pose for Still." *Image* 7 (No. 3, Mar 58) 66–67. Their work together.

Dyer, Peter John. "Rediscovery: The Decline of a Mandarin." *S&S* 28 (Winter 58–59) 44–47. **D. W. Griffith**'s work did not decline so much as some critics say; his later films, including *Isn't Life Wonderful?, Abraham Lincoln,* and *The Struggle.*

Carr, Chauncey. "**D. W. Griffith.**" *FIR* 10 (Mar 59) 188–190. Notes on reminiscences by art librarian at University of Louisville published in *Courier-Journal* (18 Jan 59).

Stern, Seymour. "Biographical Hogwash: I

and II." *FIR* 10 (May 59) 284–296; (June–July 59) 336–343. *Star Maker,* the story of D. W. Griffith by Homer Croy (Duell, 1959), Stern considers "a fraud and a hoax from beginning to end"; detailed contradictions of Croy's book.

Goodman, Paul. "**Griffith** and the Technical Innovations." *Moviegoer* (No. 2, Summer–Autumn 64). *See 3a(1).*

Batman, Richard. "**D. W. Griffith**: The Lean Years." *Calif Hist Soc Q* 44 (1965) 195–204. The last years of his life.

Niemeyer, G. Charles. "David Wark Griffith: In Retrospect, 1965." *F Her* 1 (No. 1, Fall 65) 13–23. Biography and preference list of his films by author on occasion of series at Museum of Modern Art.

Bucher, Felix. "**David Wark Griffith**—A Pioneer of the Cinema: Reconsidered Today." *Camera* 44 (No. 12, Dec 65) 6–11.

Silverstein, Norman. "**D. W. Griffith** and Anarchy in American Films." *Salmagundi* 1 (No. 2, Winter 66) 47–58. Griffith has fathered a cinema that is rich in its language but lacking in depth of thought and fullness of aesthetic achievement.

Meyer, Richard J. "The Films of **David Wark Griffith**." *F Com* 4 (Nos. 1–2, Fall–Winter 67) 92–105. Executive of educational TV station in New York reports on content of forty-two films screened at Museum of Modern Art.

Kuiper, John B. "The Growth of a Film Director." *J Lib Congress* 25 (Jan 68) 25–30. Notes on **D. W. Griffith**'s Biograph years, with particular reference to the films now available from the paper-print collection.

O'Dell, Paul. "Biograph, **Griffith**, and Fate." *Silent Picture* (No. 1, Winter 68–69) 2–6. Fate as a theme in Griffith's early Biograph films, with a list of nineteen films in which fate is an important aspect.

Sklar, R. "**Griffith**'s Russian Fans." *Nation* 211 (21 Sep 70) 249–250.

Brakhage, Stan. "**David Wark Griffith**." *Caterpillar* 4 (No. 1, Oct 70) 103–121. On the man and his work.

O'Dell, Paul. "The Rise and Fall of Free Speech in America." *Silent Picture* (No. 9, Winter 70–71). *See 7c(1a).* About **D. W. Griffith**.

Guest, Val. "British Films Were Never Bad." *F&F* 7 (No. 1, Oct 60) 34. Review of the British director's career.

Hill, Derek. "Man of Many Faces." *F&F* 1 (No. 5, Feb 55) 12. Interview with British actor, **Alec Guinness**, on the set of *The Prisoner.*

McVay, Douglas. "**Alec Guinness**." *F&F* 7 (No. 8, May 61) 12–13+. Analysis of the career of the British actor.

Meehan, Thomas. "Between Actors—a Conversation." *Show* 4 (Dec 64). *See 3f(1).* About **Alec Guinness**.

Guinness, Alec. "Life with a Pinch of Salt." *F&F* 12 (No. 2, Nov 65) 5–6+. Interview about his acting.

Marcorelles, Louis. "**Sacha Guitry**." *S&S* 27 (Autumn 57) 101. Tribute to the French stage and screen director, perhaps best known for his historical films; cinema, he said, "does not have to pose social problems. It is a magic lantern."

H

Hall, Peter. "In Search of a Revolution." *F&F* 15 (No. 12, Sep 69) 40–44. On his work in films and theatre.

Lockart, Freda Bruce. "Interview with Hamer." *S&S* 21 (Oct–Dec 51) 74–75. The preposterous or absurd story treated as realistically as possible—this is the only consistent tendency of **Robert Hamer**, the director of *Dead of Night* and *Kind Hearts and Coronets.*

Jennings, C. Robert. "It's All George." *Show* 4 (May 64) 74–76+. Career and life-style of actor **George Hamilton**.

Green, Stanley. "Hammerstein's Film Career." *FIR* 8 (Feb 57) 68–77. A review of the Broadway and Hollywood career of **Oscar Hammerstein II**.

Downing, Robert. "**Walter Hampden**." *FIR* 6 (Aug–Sep 55) 310–312. Career of the actor, including reference to his many silent and sound films.

Blue, James. "**Susumu Hani**." *F Com* 5 (No. 2, Spring 69) 24–25. As one of series of interviews with directors about their handling of untrained actors, Blue talks with Japanese director about his short film *Children Who Draw* and his first feature, *Bad Boys;* filmography.

Roman, Robert C. "**Cedric Hardwicke**." *FIR* 16 (No. 1, Jan 65) 8–26. Films and career.

Markopoulos, Gregory. "The Erasing Influence." *Vision [Film Comment]* 1 (No. 1, Spring 62) 24–25. Early work of experimental-film maker **Curtis Harrington**.

Palmer, John. "Interview with **Curtis Harrington**." *F Cult* (No. 34, 1964) 38–48. Harrington discusses his early experimental work, as well as the work of other avant-garde film makers.

Harris, Richard. "My Two Faces." *F&F* 11 (No. 7, Apr 65) 5–6. Interview on his acting career.

Behlmer, Rudy. "**Rex Harrison**." *FIR* 16 (No. 10, Dec 65) 593–610. Career and film credits.

Dunham, Harold. "**Bobby Harron**." *FIR* 14 (Dec 63) 607–618. Career study of this silent-film actor. Filmography.

Dunham, Harold. "Mae Marsh, **Robert Har-**

ron and D. W. Griffith." *Silent Picture* (No. 4, Autumn 69). *See 5, Mae Marsh.*

Hudson, Roger. "Putting the Magic in It." *S&S* 35 (Spring 66). *See 2f.* About **Anthony Harvey** as film editor.

Scheuer, Philip K. "**Anthony Harvey:** Director's Guild Award Winner." *Action* 4 (No. 3, May–June 69) 11–13. An interview with the director of *The Lion in Winter,* who discusses his own work and directing in general.

Harvey, Laurence. "Following My Actor's Instinct." *F&F* 8 (No. 1, Oct 61) 22. Working in Hollywood.

Stanbrook, Alan. "**Laurence Harvey.**" *F&F* 10 (No. 8, May 64) 42–46. Study of his acting career.

Pinto, Alfonso. "**Lillian Harvey.**" *FIR* 21 (No. 8, Oct 70) 478–509. Career of German actress of the 1920s and 1930s.

Gelder, R. Van. "Two-Gun Man at 70." *NYTM* (8 Dec 40) 13. **W. S. Hart** talks about the good old days.

Mitchell, George. "**William S. Hart.**" *FIR* 6 (Apr 55) 145–154. His boyhood near the Sioux reservation in Dakota territory, his acting career in New York, his film work for Thomas Ince in Santa Monica and for Paramount; "his not always reliable autobiography, *My Life East and West,* was published in 1929." See also letter by Mitchell, *FIR* 6 (May 55) 251.

Card, James. "The Films of **William S. Hart.**" *Image* 5 (No. 3, Mar 56) 60–63. Filmography by George Pratt.

Toeplitz, Krzystov-Teodor. "The Films of **Wojciech Has.**" *FQ* 18 (No. 2, Winter 64–65) 2–6. This "literary" director doesn't fit in any Polish school; his studies of decadence are nostalgic and sympathetic, but "the search for constructive values is going on continually" and sometimes the bohemian rebel offers the answers; "to make some positive contribution to life," Has says, "is difficult."

Reid, John Howard. "The Best Second Fiddle." *F&F* 9 (No. 2, Nov 62) 14–18. On the films of **Henry Hathaway.**

"Jack Hawkins." *F&F* 1 (No. 6, Mar 55) 3. Sketch of the British film actor.

Hall, Dennis John. "Gentleman Jack." *F&F* 16 (No. 12, Sep 70) 74–81. Study of the acting career of **Jack Hawkins.**

Rivette, Jacques, and François Truffaut. "**Howard Hawks.**" (Tr. by Anne and Thornton Brown from *Cahiers du Cinéma.*) *FIR* 7 (Nov 56) 443–452. The American director interviewed after he finished *Land of the Pharaohs;* the best drama involves danger, a comedy, embarrassment; his work with Faulkner and friendship with Hemingway; his films listed.

Agel, Henri. "**Howard Hawks.**" *NY F Bul* 3 (No. 4, 1962) 7–9. His mastery of both comedy and drama; his utilization of the basic genres of American film: Westerns, gangster films, war films.

Dyer, Peter John. "Sling the Lamps Low." *S&S* 31 (Summer 62) 134–139. A skeptical treatment of **Howard Hawks'** career: "He can in no way be described as an innovator . . . his best films have often been his most unoriginal"; analysis of major films.

Sarris, Andrew. "The World of **Howard Hawks** —Part I." *F&F* 8 (No. 10, July 62) 20–23+. From *Scarface* to *Air Force,* the director's films assessed; his comedy is "the defeat of intelligence and dignity by the gratuitous elements of modern life."

Sarris, Andrew. "Masculine Codes and Useless Creatures." *F&F* 8 (No. 11, Aug 62) 44–48. Conclusion of analysis of films of **Howard Hawks.**

Bogdanovich, Peter, Jacques Rivette, Mark Shivas, V. F. Perkins, and Robin Wood. "**Howard Hawks.**" *Movie* (No. 5, Dec 62) 7–34. His films and personal style, including a long interview with the director; filmography.

Hawks, Howard. "Man's Favorite Director." *Cinema* (Calif) 1 (No. 6, Nov–Dec 63) 10. Focus on his actresses in interview.

Russell, Lee. "**Howard Hawks.**" *New Left Rev* (No. 24, Mar–Apr 64) 82–85. Study of his films.

Thompson, Richard. "Hawks at 70." *December* 8 (No. 1, Spring 66) 126–136. On Hawks, especially *Red Line 7000.*

Hawks, Howard. "Gunplay and Horses." *F&F* 15 (No. 1, Oct 68) 25–27. Interview about his films.

Wellman, William, Jr. "**Howard Hawks:** The Distance Runner." *Action* 5 (No. 6, Nov–Dec 70) 8–11.

Smith, Colin. "**Will Hay.**" *Film* (No. 16, Mar–Apr 58) 13–15. A brief account of the film work of the comic actor.

Downing, Robert. "**Helen Hayes'** Golden Jubilee." *FIR* 7 (Feb 56) 62–66. A review of benefit performance for American Theater Wing at the Waldorf-Astoria saluting the actress' fifty years in theatre and films; a list of her films.

McClelland, Douglas. "The Brooklyn Bernhardt." *F&F* 11 (No. 6, Mar 65) 11–15. On the acting career of **Susan Hayward.**

McClelland, Douglas. "**Susan Hayward.**" *FIR* 13 (No. 5, May 62) 266–276. Career and film listing.

Monroe, Keith. "**Leland Hayward.**" *Life* 25 (20 Sep 48) 128–145+. A lengthy profile of the agent-producer.

Hart, Henry. "**Leland Hayward.**" *FIR* 6 (June–July 55) 257–260. Brief biography and report on his activities as a producer of plays and films, with a remark on the peculiar choice of Billy Wilder to direct *The Spirit of St. Louis.*

Laitin, J. "Up in Edie's Room." *Collier's* 136 (2 Sep 55). See *2i.* About **Edith Head,** costume designer.

Werner, M. R. "Yellow Movies." *New Yorker* 16 (14 Sep 40) 77–84. **William Randolph Hearst's** motion-picture company, Cosmopolitan Productions.

Houston, Penelope. "Scripting: The Return of Hecht." *S&S* 21 (Aug–Sep 51) 30. The lifting of the ban on films by **Ben Hecht** leads the author to discuss Hecht's career, his comedies and thrillers.

Fuller, Stephen. "**Ben Hecht: A Sampler.**" *F Com* 6 (No. 4, Winter 70–71) 33–39. Author of forthcoming book on Hecht shares some quotations from his writings about writing in Hollywood: "I spent more time arguing than writing"; filmography.

Morgan, James. "Hecht-Lancaster Productions." *S&S* 25 (Summer 55). See *6c(3).* About **Harold Hecht.**

Brooks, Richard. "Swell Guy." *Screen Writer* 3 (Mar 48) 13–17. Memories of **Mark Hellinger,** columnist and producer.

Johnston, Claire. "**Monte Hellman.**" *Cinema* (Cambridge) (Nos. 6–7, Aug 70) 39–41. An analysis of his films; filmography.

Herring, Robert. "But Something Quite Different Is Needed." *Close Up* 7 (No. 2, 1930) 90–97. Comments on film acting, with particular emphasis on the German actress **Brigitte Helm.**

Seligson, M. "Hollywood's Hottest Writer—**Buck Henry.**" *NYTM* (19 July 70) 10–11+. His method of working and his past experience in screenwriting.

Viotti, Sergio. "Britain's Hepburn." *F&F* 1 (No. 2, Nov 54) 7. The career of British film actress **Audrey Hepburn.**

Brett, Simon. "**Audrey Hepburn.**" *F&F* 10 (No. 6, Mar 64) 9–12. On her acting career.

Thorpe, Edward. "Katie Could Do It." *F&F* 1 (No. 9, June 55) 5. The career of actress **Katharine Hepburn.**

Mason, George. "Katharine the Great." *F&F* 2 (No. 11, Aug 56) 7. Working with **Katharine Hepburn** in *Iron Petticoat.*

Tozzi, Romano V. "**Katharine Hepburn.**" *FIR* 8 (Dec 57) 481–502. Her career in films and plays; a descriptive index to her thirty-two films.

Bowers, Ronald L. "Hepburn Since '57." *FIR* 21 (No. 7, Aug–Sep 70) 423–425. The five films Katharine Hepburn has done since 1957.

Cowie, Peter. "**Katharine Hepburn.**" *F&F* 9 (No. 9, June 63) 21–23. Study of her acting career, especially her films.

McCarty, Clifford. "**Victor Herbert's** Filmusic." *FIR* 8 (Apr 57) 183–185. Original mu-

sical scores written for silent films by Victor Herbert 1916–1924.

Cook, Page. "**Bernard Herrmann.**" *FIR* 18 (No. 7, Aug–Sep 67) 398–412. Career of film-music composer.

Higham, Charles. "**Charlton Heston.**" *S&S* 35 (Autumn 66) 169–170. Note on his recent physical chores in pictures.

Austen, David. "It's All a Matter of Size." *F&F* 14 (No. 7, Apr 68) 4–6. Interview with **Charlton Heston** about his career.

Watts, Stephen. "**Alfred Hitchcock** on Music in Films." *CQ* 2 (No. 2, Winter 33–34). See *2g(2a).*

Hitchcock, Alfred. "My Own Methods." *S&S* 6 (No. 22, Summer 37) 61–63.

Hitchcock, Alfred. "Directors' Problems." *Living Age* 354 (Apr 38). See *2c.*

Maloney, Russell. "**Alfred Joseph Hitchcock.**" *New Yorker* (10 Sep 38) 28–32. Profile of the director.

Wagner, W. "Hitchcock, Hollywood Genius." *Current Hist* 52 (24 Dec 40) 13–14. Profile of Hitchcock also deals with his films.

Jacobs, Lewis. "Film Directors at Work: I. **Alfred Hitchcock;** II. Frank Capra." *Th Arts* 25 (Mar 41) 225–232.

Johnston, Alva. "300-Pound Prophet Comes to Hollywood: **Alfred Hitchcock.**" *SEP* 215 (22 May 43) 12–13+. "Hitchcock has transformed thrillers into high screen art."

Nugent, Frank S. "Mister **Hitchcock** Discovers Love." *NYTM* (3 Nov 46) 12–13+. The master of thrills turns to romance in *Notorious* and *Spellbound.*

Kane, L. "Shadow World of **Alfred Hitchcock.**" *Th Arts* 33 (May 49) 32–40. Emphasis on the post-1939 films.

Anderson, Lindsay. "**Alfred Hitchcock.**" *Sequence* (No. 9, Autumn 49) 113–124. Analysis, with film index.

Turner, John B. "On Suspense and Other Film Matters." *FIR* 1 (Apr 50) 21–22+. Among **Hitchcock's** answers to questions: "Although all of us in the movies have been somewhat influenced by D. W. Griffith, I suppose, I can't say that any producers of movies have influenced me greatly."

Harcourt-Smith, Simon. "*Stage Fright* and **Hitchcock.**" *S&S* 19 (July 50) 207–208. *Stage Fright* is judged one of his frequent failures; he proved by *39 Steps, The Lady Vanishes,* and *Shadow of a Doubt* that he has genius; has it run down with sheer boredom?

Pratley, Gerald. "**Alfred Hitchcock's** Working Credo." *FIR* 3 (Dec 52) 500–503. Interview for the Canadian Broadcasting Company while shooting *I Confess* in Quebec.

"**Alfred Hitchcock:** Master of Thrills." *F&F* 2 (No. 3, Dec 55) 3. Biographical note with one quotation.

De La Roche, Catherine. "Conversation with

Hitchcock." *S&S* 25 (Winter 55–56) 157–158. Hitchcock gives his opinions on good thrillers, some comments on *To Catch a Thief,* and some thoughts on directing.

"Alfred Hitchcock, Director." *Newswk* 47 (11 June 56) 105–108. His box-office eminence.

Havemann, E. "We Present **Alfred Hitchcock**." *Th Arts* 40 (Sep 56) 27–28. Influences on Hitchcock as a director; elements of a suspense story.

Havemann, E. "His Pleasure Is Scaring People." *Rdrs Dig* 69 (Sep 56) 165–168. Brief portrait of **Alfred Hitchcock**.

Hitchcock, Alfred. "Hitchcock Speaking." *Cosmopolitan* 141 (Oct 56) 66–67. Interview in which he discusses television, scripts, Hollywood.

Hitchcock, Alfred. "Murder, With English on It." *NYTM* (3 Mar 57) 17+. Hitchcock on "high crime" in English life.

Martin, Pete. "I Call on **Alfred Hitchcock**." *SEP* 230 (27 July 57) 36–37+. An interview about TV, movies, and crime.

Hitchcock, Alfred. "Alfred Hitchcock Talking . . ." *F&F* 5 (No. 10, July 59) 7+. General comments on film making.

Brean, Herbert. "Master of Suspense Explains His Art." *Life* 47 (13 July 59) 72+. An interview with **Alfred Hitchcock**, with attention paid to *North by Northwest.*

Whitcomb, Jon. "Master of Mayhem." *Cosmopolitan* 147 (Oct 59) 22–25. **Alfred Hitchcock** interview.

Pett, John. "A Master of Suspense." *F&F* 6 (No. 2, Nov 59) 9–10+. Analysis of the work of **Alfred Hitchcock**.

Pett, John. "Improving on the Formula." *F&F* 6 (No. 3, Dec 59) 9–10+. Conclusion of article on films of **Alfred Hitchcock**.

Douchet, Jean. "Hitch and His Public." *NY F Bul* 2 (No. 7, 1961) 1+. An examination of catharsis in **Hitchcock**'s films through the voyeur theme in *Rear Window* and *Psycho.*

Agel, Henri. "**Alfred Hitchcock**." *NY F Bul* 2 (No. 15, 1961) 9–11. An attempt to define the themes of Hitchcock's work as evil, sin, despair, and grace.

Cameron, Ian. "**Hitchcock** and the Mechanisms of Suspense." *Movie* (No. 3, Oct 62) 4–7. The devices Hitchcock uses to create suspense, with particular reference to *The Man Who Knew Too Much.*

Higham, Charles. "**Hitchcock**'s World." *FQ* 16 (No. 2, Winter 62–63) 3–16. "The mechanics of creating terror and amusement" are all he understands; he is at his best in films dominated by "morbidity, physical disgust, . . . libidinous sadism"; opinions on all his films.

Cameron, Ian, and V. F. Perkins. "**Hitchcock**." *Movie* (No. 6, Jan 63) 4–6. An interview with the director in which he discusses various aspects of his films, including *The Birds.*

Cameron, Ian. "**Hitchcock**: Suspense and Meaning." *Movie* (No. 6, Jan 63) 8–12. Aspects of the director's personal style.

Perkins, V. F. "*Rope.*" *Movie* (No. 7, Feb 63) 11–13. A discussion of **Hitchcock**'s body of films, its emphasis on the power of evil, and particular remarks on *Rope.*

Wertham, Fredric. "*Redbook* Dialogue." *Redbook* 120 (Apr 63). See 7b(4). About **Alfred Hitchcock**.

"**Hitchcock** on Style." *Cinema* (Calif) 1 (No. 5, Aug–Sep 63) 4. Interview; focus on *The Birds.*

Houston, Penelope. "The Figure in the Carpet." *S&S* 32 (Autumn 63) 159–165. The *politique des auteurs* and the case of **Alfred Hitchcock**: Is there a continuing thread during the last twelve years? Irrationality becomes more important in the stories, but he is still more interested in method than in morality.

Truffaut, François. "Skeleton Keys." *F Cult* (No. 32, 1964) 63–67. The work of **Alfred Hitchcock**. Reprinted from *Cahiers du Cinéma.*

Pechter, William S. "The Director Vanishes." *Moviegoer* (No. 2, Summer–Autumn 64) 37–50. An analysis of **Hitchcock**'s work; two crucial turning points are *North by Northwest* and *The Birds.*

"Truffaut." *New Yorker* 40 (31 Oct 64). See 5, *François Truffaut.* About **Alfred Hitchcock**.

Cameron, Ian, and Richard Jeffery. "The Universal **Hitchcock**." *Movie* (No. 12, Spring 65) 21–24. A discussion of the universal aspects of Hitchcock's work, with particular emphasis on *The Birds* and *Marnie.*

Bazin, André. "**Hitchcock** vs. Hitchcock." *CdC in Eng* (No. 2, 1966) 51–59. Two conversations with the director; Bazin surprises him with a proposed common theme of "transfer of personality."

Truffaut, François. "Skeleton Keys." *CdC in Eng* (No. 2, 1966) 61–66. With a comment on Bazin's interview with the director (on previous pages), Truffaut tries to show that in *Shadow of a Doubt* and other films, **Hitchcock** focuses on questions of identity.

Chabrol, Claude. "**Hitchcock** Confronts Evil." *CdC in Eng* (No. 2, 1966) 67–71. **Hitchcock**'s world view revealed in his films as a Catholic conception of the universe: life as the battle for man's salvation.

Crawley, Budge, *et al.* "**Hitchcock**." *Take One* 1 (No. 1, 1966) 14–17. An interview in which the director discusses his work, such as *Psycho,* and particularly *Torn Curtain,* his most recent work.

Russell, Lee. "**Alfred Hitchcock**." *New Left Rev* (No. 35, Jan–Feb 66) 89–93. Study of his films.

Vermilye, Jerry. "An **Alfred Hitchcock** Index." *FIR* 17 (No. 4, Apr 66) 231–248.

Bond, Kirk. "The Other **Alfred Hitchcock**." *F Cult* (No. 41, Summer 66) 30–35. In some of his earliest films, subtlety and tender moments.

Sonbert, Warren. "**Alfred Hitchcock**: Master of Morality." *F Cult* (No. 41, Summer 66) 35–38. Comparison of *Marnie* with earlier films.

Hitchcock, Alfred. "Hitchcock and the Dying Art." *Film* (No. 46, Summer 66) 9–15. The director discusses his work, his methods, stars, audiences, television, and some of his own films.

Hitchcock, Alfred. "Symposium." *Arts in Soc* 4 (Winter 67) 66–68. Director's responses to a questionnaire.

Madsen, Axel. "Who's Afraid of **Alfred Hitchcock?**" *S&S* 37 (Winter 67–68) 26–27. Writer-producer Ernest Lehman talks about his scripts for *The Sound of Music, Who's Afraid of Virginia Woolf?,* and *North by Northwest.*

"A Talk with **Alfred Hitchcock**." *Action* 3 (No. 3, May–June 68) 8–10.

Braudy, Leo. "Hitchcock, Truffaut, and the Irresponsible Audience." *FQ* 21 (No. 4, Summer 68) 21–27. Objections to Truffaut's book-length interview with Hitchcock [*Hitchcock* (Simon and Schuster, 1969)] for its failure to show his manipulation of the audience and his latent voyeurism; long analysis of *Psycho.*

Houston, Penelope. "Hitchcockery." *S&S* 37 (Autumn 68). *See 7b(4).* About **Alfred Hitchcock**.

Millar, Gavin. "Hitchcock Versus Truffaut." *S&S* 38 (Spring 69) 82–88. A response to Truffaut's book, *Hitchcock* (Simon and Schuster, 1969); Miller cannot find any general philosophy of life in the conversations recorded; Hitchcock's stories have ideas in them, but "they are for the most part simple, unitary ideas." On pp. 87–88 is a review of Truffaut's *The Bride Wore Black.*

Wollen, Peter. "Hitchcock's Vision." *Cinema* (Cambridge) (No. 3, June 69) 2–4. Recurrent concerns in his films.

Durgnat, Raymond. "The Strange Case of **Alfred Hitchcock**." *F&F* 16 (No. 5, Feb 70) 58–62. Chronological study of his films, in ten successive issues, concluding in *F&F* 17 (No. 2. Nov 70) 35–37.

Samuels, Charles T. "Hitchcock." *Am Scholar* 39 (Spring 70) 295–304. A survey of his films: Hitchcock as an excellent craftsman, but "primitive" major director, an exploiter of the "immediate experience."

Mundy, Robert. "Another Look at **Hitchcock**." *Cinema* (Cambridge) (Nos. 6–7, Aug 70) 10–12. His use of color, imagery, and ideology.

Belton, John. "Reply to Samuels' Article on 'Hitchcock.'" *Am Scholar* 39 (Autumn 70) 728–731. Belton objects to Samuels' use of the term "primitive" and of Hitchcock's own comments on his films as supportive evidence.

Walker, Michael. "The Old Age of **Alfred Hitchcock**." *Movie* (No. 18, Winter 70–71) 10–13. An attempt to place the American director's *Topaz* within the body of Hitchcock's work.

Hobl, Pavel. "One Kind of Film-Making." *TDR* 11 (Fall 66) 150–153. Discussion of career and films of this Czechoslovakian film maker; interview by Paul Gray.

Holden, William. "I'm Old-Fashioned—and This Is Why." *F&F* 7 (No. 4, Jan 61) 37+. The American actor discusses his career.

Gough-Yates, Kevin. "Seth Holt." *Screen* 10 (No. 6, Nov–Dec 69) 4–23. Interview with the British director who began as a documentary editor.

Houston, Penelope. "Interview with **John Houseman**." *S&S* 31 (Autumn 62) 160–165. In London to produce *In the Cool of the Day,* he talks about a producer's responsibilities, his earlier films, his television programs, directors he has worked with, including Vincente Minnelli, Orson Welles, Joseph Mankiewicz.

Dickens, Homer. "Leslie Howard." *FIR* 10 (Apr 59) 198–207. Life and career of the late actor; a descriptive index to his twenty-five films which includes their British titles.

Conrad, Derek. "Living Down a Classic." *F&F* 4 (No. 8, May 58) 12. On **Trevor Howard**.

Whitehall, Richard. "**Trevor Howard**." *F&F* 7 (No. 5, Feb 61) 12–13+. Analysis of the work of the British film actor.

Everson, William K. "**William K. Howard**." *FIR* 5 (May 54) 224–229. A summary of the 1921–1946 film career of the late director who made *White Gold, The Power and the Glory,* and *Fire Over England;* a list of his pictures.

Crichton, K. "Camera! Personal History of **James Wong Howe**." *Collier's* 99 (12 June 37) 19+.

Davis, Sylvester. "The Photography of **James Wong Howe**." *Calif Arts and Arch* 56 (No. 4, Oct 39) 9.

Knight, Arthur. "Camera Eye." *Scholastic* 64 (28 Apr 54) 6. Interview with **James Wong Howe**.

Jacobs, Jack. "**James Wong Howe**." *FIR* 12 (No. 4, Apr 61) 215–241. Biography of cameraman; film listing.

Higham, Charles, and Joel Greenberg. "North Light and Cigarette Bulb." *S&S* 36 (Autumn 67) *See 2e.* About **James Wong Howe**.

Robinson, David. "Evolution of a Cartoonist." *S&S* 31 (Winter 61–62) 17. Note on career of **John Hubley** at Disney, UPA, and after.

Archibald, Lewis. "**John Hubley**." *FLQ* 3 (No. 2, Spring 70) 5–10. The animated films and career of film maker John Hubley.

Hubler, Richard G. "The Hughes Method." *Screen Writer* 2 (June 46) 12–16. Condemns **Howard Hughes'** method of film making—as in *The Outlaw*—as pure opportunism, in which Southwest history is mechanically perverted for the sake of profit.

Hughes, Ken. "Those Nutty Intellectuals." *F&F* 9 (No. 4, Jan 63) 9–10. Interview with the British director.

Nin, Anaïs. "'Poetics of the Film." *F Cult* (No. 31, 1963–1964) 12–14. A lecture given at the University of Chicago on the films of **Ian Hugo**: *Ai-Ye, Jazz of Lights,* and *Venice Etude One* (incorporated in *The Gondola Eye);* filmography.

Hunter, Jeffrey. "Actor's Choice." *F&F* 8 (No. 7, Apr 62) 14+. Interview on his life and acting.

Davidson, Bill. "**Ross Hunter:** The Last Dream Merchant." *Show* 2 (Aug 62) 74–75+. How this Hollywood producer has lured millions of women back to the movies with films with gorgeous sets, gowns, jewels, tears.

Fowler, Dan. "Walter Huston's Bad Boy John." *Look* 13 (No. 10, 10 May 49) 40–47. The life and career of American director **John Huston**.

Farber, Manny. "Hollywood's Fair-Haired Boy; **John Huston**." *Nation* 168 (4 June 49) 642. Objections to Huston as "arty," "Eisensteinian," message mad, and static.

Griffith, Richard. "Wyler, Wellman, and **Huston**." *FIR* 1 (Feb 50). *See 5, William Wyler.*

Agee, James. "Undirectable Director—**John Huston**." *Life* 29 (18 Sep 50) 128–130+.

Reisz, Karel. "Interview with **Huston**." *S&S* 21 (Jan–Mar 52) 130–132. He has worked on the script for each of his films, especially for details of description and characteristic behavior, to give the actors better insight into the character; on location for *African Queen.*

"**John Huston.**" *F&F* 1 (No. 1, Oct 54) 3. A sketch: his best films are clearly conceived, efficiently executed, and typically American.

Godley, John. "In the Wake of the Whale: **John Huston**." *Vogue* 126 (15 Nov 55) 118–119+. Taking a screen test for John Huston.

de Laurot, Edouard. "An Encounter with **John Huston**." *F Cult* 2 (No. 8, 1956) 1–4. Excerpts from a conversation with the American director, with emphasis on *Moby Dick.*

"Director **John Huston**; a Remarkable Man and the Movies in '56." *Newswk* 47 (9 Jan 56) 67–70. John Huston's life, his ability to entertain.

Barnes, Peter. "The Director on Horseback." *QFRTV* 10 (No. 3, Spring 56) 281–287. British film writer suggests decline of John Huston's directing quality because he has made too many films away from the U.S.

"**John Huston** Hits a Double." *Look* 22 (25 Nov 58) 106+. Short production report on *The Roots of Heaven* and *The Barbarian and the Geisha.*

Archer, Eugene. "**John Huston**—The Hemingway Tradition in American Film." *F Cult* (No. 19, 1959) 66–101. Study of the career of the American film director, his fifteen feature films and three documentaries.

Bester, Alfred. "**John Huston's** Unsentimental Journey." *Holiday* 25 (May 59) 111+. His career and directorial approach.

Archer, Eugene. "Taking Life Seriously." *F&F* 5 (No. 12, Sep 59) 13–14+. Films of **John Huston**.

Archer, Eugene. "Small People in a Big World." *F&F* 6 (No. 1, Oct 59) 9–10+. On **John Huston**; conclusion of two-part article.

Agee, James. "Agee on **Huston**." *F&F* 9 (No. 11, Aug 63) 35–38. Short selection reprinted from *Life* (1950), on Huston's films.

Bachmann, Gideon. "How I Make Films: An Interview with **John Huston**." *FQ* 19 (No. 1, Fall 65) 3–13. Everything depends on the idea of the specific film itself; sometimes the words are as important as the actions; actors do not need much help; economy in everything.

Mayersberg, Paul. "**Huston's** Reflections." *Movie* (No. 15, Spring 68) 25–26. A discussion of John Huston's work, with particular reference to *Reflections in a Golden Eye.*

Taylor, John Russell. "**John Huston** and the Figure in the Carpet." *S&S* 38 (Spring 69) 70–73. A study of John Huston's search for style and self-definition after *The Maltese Falcon;* "cool, noncommittal distance" may be the key to his "aesthetic abstraction" not only visually, but in his scripts.

Sarris, Andrew. "**John Huston:** Young at Heart." *Show* (Jan 70) 28–29. Remarks on the directing career of John Huston; brief biographical comments; incomplete filmography; based on material in his book *The American Cinema* (Dutton, 1969), pp. 56–58.

Vermilye, Jerry. "**Walter Huston.**" *FIR* 11 (No. 2, Feb 60) 70–83. His films and biography, with list of his films.

Kerner, Bruce. "An Interview with **Kenneth Hyman**." *Cinema* (Calif) 4 (No. 2, Summer 68) 5–9. New executive in charge of production at Warner Brothers–Seven Arts talks about his program and his earlier work with Sidney Lumet as producer on *The Hill.*

I

Richie, Donald. "The Several Sides of **Kon Ichikawa**." *S&S* 35 (Spring 66) 84–86. Ichikawa's first picture was an animated film, and was followed by a series of satirical comedies, then the tragedy of *The Burmese Harp, Punishment Room, Enjo,* and *Kagi.*

Milne, Tom. "The Skull Beneath the Skin." *S&S* 35 (Autumn 66) 185–189. **Kon Ichikawa's** work, including his early minor films.

Ichikawa, Kon, *et al.* "The Uniqueness of Kon Ichikawa." *Cinema* (Calif) 6 (No. 2, 1970) 30–31. A translated symposium in which the director and others discuss his work.

Pratt, George. "See Mr. Ince." *Image* 5 (No. 5, May 56) 100–111. Silent producer and director **Thomas Ince** seen in the light of new research.

Mitchell, George. "Thomas H. Ince." *FIR* 11 (No. 8, Oct 60) 464–484. Career, biography, and personal recollections of the American director.

Ince, Elinor. "Thomas Ince." *Silent Picture* (No. 6, Spring 70) 14–15. A letter from Elinor Ince to George Pratt of Eastman House, explaining that her husband's death was not murder and giving the details of how he died.

Godfrey, Lionel. "The Private World of **William Inge.**" *F&F* 13 (No. 1, Oct 66) 19–24. The writer's career.

Geltzer, George. "Hollywood's Handsomest Director." *FIR* 3 (May 52) 213–219. The career of **Rex Ingram,** with a record of his ideas on film making as contained in an article from *Motion Picture Classic* (July 1921); a list of his films 1916–1933.

O'Laoghaire, Liam. "**Rex Ingram** and the Nice Studios." *Cinema Studies* 1 (No. 4, Dec 61). *See 6c(4).*

Higham, Charles. "Isherwood on Hollywood." *London Mag* new series 8 (No. 1, Apr 68) 31–38. An interview with **Christopher Isherwood** on his writing for films.

Hulsker, J. "Joris Ivens." *CQ* 1 (No. 3, Spring 33) 148–151. Interview, especially about the documentary director's trip to Russia.

MacLeish, Archibald. "The Cinema of **Joris Ivens.**" *New Masses* 24 (24 Aug 37) 18. Documentary should be conceived as analogous to the realistic novel; if so, Ivens might be recognized by both critics and public as a great film maker.

Stebbins, Robert, and Jay Leyda. "Joris Ivens: Artist in Documentary." *Mag of Art* 31 (July 38) 392–399+. A study of Ivens' films with emphasis on *Spanish Earth.*

Ivens, Joris. "Apprentice to Films." *Th Arts* 30 (Mar–Apr 46) 179–184+. Personal account of a lifelong contact with the film medium; a philosophic and technical chronicle.

Grenier, Cynthia. "Joris Ivens: Social Realist Versus Lyric Poet." *S&S* 27 (Spring 58) 204–207. A new film by the veteran documentary film maker, *The Seine Meets Paris;* Ivens has for years been making communist propaganda films; Grenier speaks of his political and social ideals and of some of the other films he has made.

J

Farber, Stephen. "The Writer II: An Interview with **Alexander Jacobs.**" *FQ* 22 (No 2, Winter 68–69) 2–14. After analysis of parts of script compared with film of *Point Blank,* author questions screenwriter about other details and his relationship with John Boorman, the director.

"How a New Film Maker Made It in Hollywood." *Bus Wk* (16 Sep 67) 188–190+. Story of independent producer **Arthur P. Jacobs.**

Houston, Penelope. "The Horizontal Man." *S&S* 38 (Summer 69) 116–120. A study of Hungarian **Miklós Jancsó's** films and his style; he is "a master of the artistic atrocity" and his "films are dream documents of civil war, in which all the guilts are shared."

Price, James. "Polarities: The Films of **Miklós Jancsó.**" *London Mag* new series 9 (No. 5, Aug–Sep 69) 189–194.

Truscott, Harold. "**Emil Jannings**—A Personal View." *Silent Picture* (No. 8, Autumn 70) 5–16. His roles in his films; people and studios he worked with; the quality of Jannings' acting in specific roles.

Jaque, Christian. "Making It International." *F&F* 7 (No. 1, Oct 60) 10. French director aims to give his films international appeal.

Wright, Basil. "**Humphrey Jennings.**" *S&S* 19 (Dec 50) 311. His early career and *Spare Time,* one of his first films; a tribute just after he died.

Vedrès, Nicole, and Gavin Lambert. "**Humphrey Jennings.**" *S&S* 20 (May 51) 24–26. Admiration for the man and his work; Lambert describes *Listen to Britain* in some detail, and other films.

Anderson, Lindsay. "Only Connect." *S&S* 23 (Apr–June 54) 181–186. Some personal reactions to the work of British documentary director **Humphrey Jennings;** his method of "connection by contrast and juxtaposition"; a sequence from *A Diary for Timothy.*

Dand, Charles H. "Britain's Screen Poet." *FIR* 6 (Feb 55) 73–78. A personal estimate of the films of **Humphrey Jennings;** without the demands of wartime he might never have made films.

Callenbach, Ernest. "The Importance of **Humphrey Jennings.**" *FQ* 15 (No. 2, Winter 61–62) 2–3. Editorial introduction to articles on the British documentary director says his patriotism and national pride may not "teach us what is to be said," but we can learn from his lyricism and sense of grace.

Anderson, Lindsay. "Only Connect: Some Aspects of the Work of **Humphrey Jennings.**" *FQ* 15 (No. 2, Winter 61–62) 5–12. Affectionate descriptions of Jennings' wartime documentaries; pictorial sequence from *A Diary for Timothy.* Reprinted from *S&S* (Apr–May 54).

Jennings, Humphrey. "Working Sketches of an Orchestra." *FQ* 15 (No. 2, Winter 61–62) 12–18. Excerpts from notes for a film that was never made—visual impressions of London Symphony rehearsals and a performance, with proposed informal dialogue.

Noxon, Gerald. "How **Humphrey Jennings** Came to Film." *FQ* 15 (No. 2, Winter 61–62) 19–26. Personal account of Jennings' early days at Cambridge and initial exposure to film with Grierson's GPO film unit.

Sansom, William. "The Making of *Fires Were Started*." *FQ* 15 (No. 2, Winter 61–62) 27–29. Fireman employed as an actor in this film recalls reenactment methods and personality of documentary director **Humphrey Jennings**.

Merralls, James. "**Humphrey Jennings**: A Biographical Sketch." *FQ* 15 (No. 2, Winter 61–62) 29–34.

Delahaye, Michel. "Meeting with **Alain Jessua**." *CdC in Eng* (No. 11, Sep 67) 36–43. The French film maker speaks of his films and his career.

Silverman, Dore. "Hollywood's Peripatetic Trailer." *S&S* 18 (Spring 49) 22–24. Brief profile and question-and-answer session with **Eric Johnston**, president of MPA.

Hume, Rod. "She Saw the Vision and Became the Star." *F&F* 2 (No. 9, June 56) 15. **Jennifer Jones** biography; filmography.

Doyle, Neil. "**Jennifer Jones**." *FIR* 13 (No. 7, Aug–Sep 62) 390–400. Career and film listing.

Conrad, Derek. "Success Was Not Enough for Sunset Boulevard." *F&F* 4 (No. 9, June 58) 9. Career of German actor **Curt Jurgens**.

K

"Director." *New Yorker* 41 (12 Feb 66) 23–25. Talk with Czech director **Jan Kadar** during the New York premiere of *The Shop on Main Street*.

Taylor, F. J. "King and Queen of Color: Dr. and Mrs. **H. T. Kalmus**." *Rdrs Dig* (Aug 44). *See 2e(2).*

Taylor, F. J. "Mr. Technicolor." *SEP* 222 (22 Oct 49) 26–27. A close-up of Dr. **Herbert T. Kalmus**.

Houston, Penelope. "Cukor and the Kanins." *S&S* 24 (Spring 55). *See 2d(4).* About **Garson Kanin**.

Gordon, Alex. "**Boris Karloff**." *Cinema* (Calif) 5 (No. 1, 1969) 6–7. A list of his films (titles and dates only).

Roman, Robert C. "**Boris Karloff**." *FIR* 15 (No. 7, Aug–Sep 69) 389–412. Career and film listing.

Gerard, Lillian. "**Boris Karloff**, the Man Behind the Myth." *F Com* 6 (No. 1, Spring 70) 46–49. "Urbane, dignified, affable, kind": a personal reminiscence.

Crowdus, Gary, and Irwin Silber. "Towards a Proletarian Cinema." *Cinéaste* 4 (No. 4, Fall 70) 21–27. An interview with the French director **Marin Karmitz**, with notes about his film *Comrades*.

Wiener, Willard L. "The Happiest Man in Hollywood." *Collier's* 126 (30 Dec 50) 32–33+. On American International's **Sam Katzman**.

"Jungle Sam." *Time* 60 (1 Dec 52) 62. Producer **Sam Katzman**'s movies.

"Meet Jungle Sam." *Life* 34 (23 Mar 53) 79–82. Independent producer **Sam Katzman** makes "awful" movies, which always make money.

de Laurot, Edouard L., and Jonas Mekas. "An Interview with **Boris Kaufman**." *F Cult* 1 (No. 4, 1955) 4–6. The Hollywood cameraman's work with Kazan and Vigo.

Baker, Peter. "Kaye Dreams Are Hard to Capture on Film." *F&F* 2 (No. 3, Dec 55) 8. Assessment and biography of **Danny Kaye**.

Archer, Eugene. "**Elia Kazan**—The Genesis of a Style." *F Cult* 2 (No. 8, 1956) 5–7+. Kazan's style is analyzed from *A Tree Grows in Brooklyn* through *East of Eden*.

"A Quiz for **Kazan**." *Th Arts* 40 (Nov 56) 30–31+. Elia Kazan's stage and screen direction; the work of Tennessee Williams; *Baby Doll*.

Archer, Eugene. "Genesis of a Genius." *F&F* 3 (No. 3, Dec 56) 7–9. **Elia Kazan**'s work; filmography.

Archer, Eugene. "The Theatre Goes to Hollywood." *F&F* 3 (No. 4, Jan 57) 13–14. Second of a two-part article on **Elia Kazan**.

"**Elia Kazan**." *F&F* 7 (No. 7, Apr 61) 5. Career sketch of the American director.

Kazan, Elia. "The Young Agony." *F&F* 8 (No. 6, Mar 62) 26–27+. Interview about his filming and general philosophy.

Fixx, James F. "Who Cares What the Boss Thinks?" *Sat Rev* 46 (28 Dec 63) 14–15. The past, present, and future of director **Elia Kazan**, with comments about *America, America*. Part of *Saturday Review* report "The Anti-Formula Film."

Miller, Arthur. "Arthur Miller Ad-Libs on **Elia Kazan**." *Show* 4 (Jan 64) 54–56+. As part of article on his stage directing, brief comments on the scripting of the film *America, America;* and elements of Kazan's directing technique.

Delahaye, Michel. "A Natural Phenomenon: Interview with **Elia Kazan**." *CdC in Eng* (No. 9, Mar 67) 12–39. The American director discusses his career and his films, especially *America, America* and *Splendor in the Grass;* on pp. 8–11 is a selection of Kazan's statements; filmography and biography by Patrick Brion, pp. 36–39.

Bishop, Christopher. "The Great Stone Face."

FQ 12 (No. 1, Fall 58) 10–14. An examination of **Buster Keaton,** his films, their aesthetics, the "metaphysics" of the Keaton character; comparisons with Chaplin and Lloyd; also an interview with him, about techniques, sound comedy, and the new comedians.

Baxter, Brian. "**Buster Keaton.**" *Film* (No. 18, Nov–Dec 58) 8–11. Career and films.

Robinson, David. "Rediscovery: Buster." *S&S* 29 (Winter 59–60) 41–43. **Buster Keaton** is a poet, and he acts with his whole being; a tribute to Keaton, whose long-unseen features *Our Hospitality* and *The Cameraman* have appeared again in England.

Brownlow, Kevin. "**Buster Keaton.**" *Film* (No. 42, Winter 64) 6–10. Interview.

Gillett, John, and James Blue. "Keaton at Venice." *S&S* 35 (Winter 65–66) 26–30. Buster Keaton talks about the way he worked out some of his elaborate effects in *Our Hospitality, Seven Chances, Steamboat Bill, Jr., The General,* and *Sherlock Junior.*

Friedman, Arthur B. "**Buster Keaton:** An Interview." *FQ* 19 (No. 4, Summer 66) 2–5. Originating gags and plot lines for *The Navigator* and *Seven Chances.*

McCaffrey, Donald W. "The Mutual Approval of **Keaton** and Lloyd." *CJ* 6 (1966–1967) 9–15. A report of interviews with Buster Keaton and Harold Lloyd, comparing gags, preview systems, and their opinions of each other.

Houston, Penelope. "The Great Blank Page." *S&S* 37 (Spring 68) 63–67. A long article inspired by the National Film Theatre's **Buster Keaton** season in London; no theorist of comedy, he nevertheless knew what he wanted and stressed "real hazards"; his personality, unlike Chaplin's, is "American and free."

Kauffmann, Stanley. "**Buster Keaton** Festival." *New Rep* 163 (24 Oct 70) 24+. Reviews and story about Raymond Rohauer, who put the festival together.

Druxman, Michael B. "**Howard Keel.**" *FIR* 21 (No. 9, Nov 70) 549–570. Career and film listing.

Isaacs, Hermine R. "**Gene Kelly.**" *Th Arts* 30 (Mar 46) 149–156. How the dancer adjusts himself to the camera; comments by Kelly.

"**Gene Kelly:** Dancing Dynamo." *F&F* 2 (No. 4, Jan 56) 3. Brief biography.

Johnson, Albert. "The Tenth Muse in San Francisco." *S&S* 26 (Summer 56) 46–50. A report of a lecture given by **Gene Kelly** at the San Francisco Museum of Art; his work as a dancer in films, the dance as an art form, and the advantages and disadvantages of film over theatre; as a postscript, Johnson discusses the career of one of Kelly's collaborators, Stanley Donen, on *Cover Girl, On the Town, Singin' in the Rain,* and others.

Behlmer, Rudy. "**Gene Kelly.**" *FIR* 15 (No. 1, Jan 64) 6–22. Biography; film listing.

Cutts, John. "Kelly, Dancer, Actor, Director." *F&F* 10 (No. 11, Aug 64) 38–42; (No. 12, Sep 64) 35–37. On the career of Gene Kelly; two parts.

Hanson, Curtis Lee. "Interview with **Gene Kelly.**" *Cinema* (Calif) 3 (No. 4, Dec 66) 24–28.

Hanson, Curtis Lee. "Interview with **Burt Kennedy.**" *Cinema* (Calif) 4 (No. 1, Spring 68) 14–18.

Kennedy, Burt. "A Talk with John Ford." *Action* 3 (No. 5, Sep–Oct 68) 6–9. An interview and comments; both directors speak.

"Ford and **Kennedy** on the Western." *FIR* 20 (No. 1, Jan 69). *See 4k(2).*

Notkin, Richard. "The Times and Trials of **Larry Kent.**" *Take One* 1 (No. 4, 1967) 4–6. An interview with the Canadian film maker.

Tozzi, R. V. "**Jerome Kern.**" *FIR* 6 (Nov 55) 452–459. A historical survey of the life and career of the late composer.

Braun, Eric. "From Here to Esteem." *F&F* 16 (No. 8, May 70) 22–26. On the work of **Deborah Kerr;** see also April and June issues.

Kelly, Quentin. "Actor . . . Without Dungarees." *F&F* 3 (No. 9, June 57) 9. On **John Kerr.**

Jamison, Barbara B. "Kidd from Brooklyn." *NYTM* (13 June 54) 42+. Profile of choreographer **Michael Kidd.**

Kidd, Michael. "The Camera and the Dance." *F&F* 2 (No. 4, Jan 56) 7. Dancer and choreographer on his work for *Seven Brides for Seven Brothers* and *Guys and Dolls.*

Rosenthal, Alan. "The Fiction Documentary." *FQ* 23 (No. 4, Summer 70). *See 8c(4).* About **Allan King.**

Shibuk, Charles, and Christopher North. "The Life and Films of **Henry King.**" *FIR* 9 (Oct 58) 427–433. A study of the career of the director of *Tol'able David* who made more than forty pictures at 20th Century-Fox, including *Lloyd's of London, The Story of Bernadette, Twelve O'Clock High* and *The Gunfighter.*

Cherry, Richard. "**Henry King:** The Flying Director." *Action* 4 (No. 4, July–Aug 69) 6–8. Interview and comments.

Lewin, Robert. "**King Brothers:** Makers of Cheapies." *Life* 25 (22 Nov 48) 118–122. Three ex-pinball kings who became producers, Morry, Frank, and Hymie Kozinsky, who took the name of King.

Michel, Walter S. "In Memoriam of **Dimitri Kirsanov,** a Neglected Master." *F Cult* 3 (No. 15, 1957) 3–5. Introduction to Kirsanov's work; some analysis of *Ménilmontant,* including stills and a breakdown of two of the film's sequences into shots.

"The King of Intermissions." *Time* 86 (9 July 65). *See 6e(1).* About **Eugene V. Kline,** exhibitor.

Weinberg, Gretchen. "**Arthur Kleiner.**" *F Cult* (No. 41, Summer 66) 83–86. Interview with head of music department of Museum of Modern Art in New York.

Kline, Herbert. "Films Without Make-Believe." *Mag of Art* 35 (Feb 42). *See 8c(2).*

Silke, James R. "*Harakiri*, Kobayashi, Humanism." *Cinema* (Calif) 1 (No. 4, June–July 63) 32. Interview and article on **Masaki Kobayashi,** director of *Harakiri.*

Watts, Stephen. "**Alexander Korda** and the International Film." *CQ* 2 (No. 1, Autumn 33) 12–15. Interview the day after the first showing of *Henry VIII* suggests that a film's international popularity may stem from its national characteristics.

Courtney, W. B. "New Worlds for Alexander." *Collier's* 97 (15 Feb 36) 25+. Career of **Alexander Korda.**

"Underdog Now Lion: **Korda** Becomes Leading English Producer." *Lit Dig* 122 (18 July 36) 19–21.

Gilliat, Sidney, Graham Greene, and Ralph Richardson. "Sir **Alexander Korda.**" *S&S* 25 (Spring 56) 214–215. Brief tributes to the British producer, who died 23 January 1956.

Dalrymple, Ian. "**Alexander Korda.**" *QFRTV* 11 (Spring 57) 294–309. Writer-director-producer writes tribute to late British film producer; his career and philosophy.

Lejeune, C. A. "**Alexander Korda**: A Sketch." *S&S* 4 (No. 13, Spring 65) 5–6.

Thomas, Anthony. "**Erich Wolfgang Korngold.**" *FIR* 7 (Feb 56) 89–90. A short review of the life and career of Korngold, who has written operas and the original scores for such films as *King's Row, Captain Blood,* and *Anthony Adverse.*

Callenbach, Ernest, and Albert Johnson. "Feature Production in San Francisco: An Interview with **John Korty.**" *FQ* 19 (No. 3 Spring 66) 20–25. The making of a first feature, *Crazy Quilt;* the transition from documentaries to actors and scripts.

"Korty." *New Yorker* 46 (6 June 70) 27–28. Interview with John Korty: how he got into films and the making of *Riverrun.*

Goodwin, Michael. "Camera: **Laszlo Kovacs.**" *Take One* 2 (No. 12, 1970) 12–16. An interview and comments on the American cinematographer who shot *Targets, Easy Rider, Five Easy Pieces,* and other recent "new wave" films.

Kozintsev, Grigori. "The Hamlet Within Me." *F&F* 8 (No. 12, Sep 62) 20. Soviet director of *Hamlet* on his film and Shakespeare in general.

Kozintsev, Grigori. "Over the Parisiana." *S&S* 32 (Winter 62–63) 46–47. This fragment from the author's memoirs, entitled *The Deep Screen,* reprinted from the Soviet journal *Novy Mir,* recalls the early 1920s when he came to the cinema with Trauberg and made such prewar Soviet classics as *The New Babylon* and *The Maxim Trilogy.*

"Gregory Kozintsev." *Film* (No. 49, Autumn 67) 27–29. Interview with the Russian director.

Small, Collie. "Genius on a Low Budget." *Collier's* 126 (16 Sep 50) 26–27+. On **Stanley Kramer.**

Crowther, Bosley. " 'A' Movies on 'B' Budgets." *NYTM* (12 Nov 50) 24–25+. **Stanley Kramer.**

"Mr. **Kramer** Has Come Up Fast." *Life* 29 (20 Nov 50) 76.

Kramer, Stanley. "The Independent Producer." *FIR* 2 (Mar 51) 1–4+.

Houston, Penelope. "**Kramer** and Company." *S&S* 22 (July–Sep 52) 20–23+. A new kind of producer, who has made a number of successful films about social problems.

"Half a Step Behind." *Time* 62 (14 Dec 53) 108. **Stanley Kramer**'s partnership with Columbia Pictures ends and he organizes an independent company.

Durnick, J. "Talk with **Stanley Kramer**—Creative Side of Motion Picture Making." *Pop Photog* 37 (Sep 55) 106–107+.

Bogdanovich, Peter. "Dore Schary–**Stanley Kramer** Syndrome." *NY F Bul* 1 (Nos. 12, 13, 14, 1960). *See 5.* **Dore Schary.**

Kramer, Stanley. "Politics, Social Comment and My Emotions." *F&F* 6 (No. 9, June 60) 7–8+. Interview.

"Talk with the Director." *Newswk* 56 (17 Oct 60) 114+. **Stanley Kramer** at the time of *Judgment at Nuremberg.*

Crowther, Bosley. "Hollywood's Producer of Controversy." *NYTM* (10 Dec 61) 76–79. On the career of **Stanley Kramer.**

Tracy, Spencer, and Montgomery Clift. "An Actor's Director." *F&F* 8 (No. 4, Jan 62) 10. Two stars of *Judgment at Nuremberg* write about **Stanley Kramer.**

Cowie, Peter. "The Different One." *F&F* 9 (No. 6, Mar 63) 15–19. On **Stanley Kramer**'s films and his decline in critical popularity in recent years.

Kramer, Stanley. "Send Myself the Message." *F&F* 10 (No. 5, Feb 64) 7–8. Interview.

Omatsu, Mary. "Guess Who Came to Lunch?" *Take One* 1 (No. 9, 1968) 20–21. Interview with **Stanley Kramer;** his address to University of Toronto students.

Kramer, Stanley. "Nine Times Across the Generation Gap." *Action* 3 (No. 2, Mar–Apr 68). *See 7b(1a).*

Sitney, P. Adams. "Kubelka Concrete (Our Trip to Vienna)." *F Cult* (No. 34, 1964) 48–51. The work of the Austrian experimental-film maker **Peter Kubelka.**

Mekas, Jonas. "Interview with **Peter Kubelka.**"

F Cult (No. 44, Spring 67) 42–47. His "underground" films.

Stang, Joanne. "Film Fan to Film Maker." *NYTM* (12 Oct 58) 34+. Career of American director **Stanley Kubrick**.

Noble, Robin. "Killers, Kisses . . . Lolita." *F&F* 7 (No. 3, Dec 60) 11–12+. **Stanley Kubrick**'s work for the cinema.

Reynolds, Charles. "Interview with **Kubrick**." *Pop Photog* 47 (Dec 60) 144–145+. "A good film is, in the end, a film for which you have great affection."

Kubrick, Stanley. "Words and Movies." *S&S* 30 (Winter 60–61) 14. The director of *Lolita* comments on the adaptations of novels to the screen, and on the writer-director relationship; "directing should be nothing more or less than a continuation of the writing."

Kubrick, Stanley. "How I Stopped Worrying and Love the Cinema." *F&F* 9 (No. 9, June 63) 12–13. Comments on his own films.

Tornabene, Lyn. "Contradicting the Hollywood Image." *Sat Rev* 46 (28 Dec 63) 19–21. Career study on **Stanley Kubrick**; part of *Saturday Review* report "The Anti-Formula Film."

Milne, Tom. "How I Learned to Stop Worrying and Love **Stanley Kubrick**." *S&S* 33 (Spring 64) 68–72. Survey of Kubrick's films; each charts an obsession which brings disaster.

Price, James. "**Stanley Kubrick**'s Divided World." *London Mag* new series 4 (No. 2, May 64) 67–70.

Russell, Lee. "**Stanley Kubrick**." *New Left Rev* (No. 26, Summer 64) 71–74. Study of his films.

Burgess, Jackson. "The 'Anti-Militarism' of **Stanley Kubrick**." *FQ* 18 (No. 1, Fall 64) 4–11. What this American director is really concerned with is public morality, "the dubiety and ambiguity of human moral choices," and in *Dr. Strangelove* the stupidity of depending on "infallible" machines; novelist Burgess analyzes *Fear and Desire*, *Paths of Glory* as well.

Alpert, Hollis. "Offbeat Director in Outer Space." *NYTM* (16 Jan 66) 14–15+. Career of **Stanley Kubrick**.

Bernstein, Jeremy. "Profiles: How About a Little Game?" *New Yorker* 42 (12 Nov 66) 70–72+. Study of **Stanley Kubrick** and his career at the time he was making *2001*.

French, Philip. "**Stanley Kubrick**." *London Mag* new series 8 (No. 4, July 68) 68–71.

"Interview: **Stanley Kubrick**." *Playboy* 15 (No. 9, Sep 68) 85+. Director of *2001* discusses metaphysics.

Kubrick, Stanley. "Critics and Film." *Action* 4 (No. 1, Jan–Feb 69). See 3b.

Kuchar, George. "George Kuchar Speaks on Films and Truth." *F Cult* (No. 33, 1964) 14–15. Underground-film maker says, "Nature is my inspiration."

Kuchar Brothers. "Filmography of the Kuchar Brothers." *December* 7 (No. 1, Spring 65) 152–154. A filmography with annotations.

Kuchar, Mike. "Symposium." *Arts in Soc* 4 (No. 1, Winter 67) 94–97. Director's responses to questionnaire.

Hill, Steven P. "Kuleshov—Prophet Without Honor?" *F Cult* (No. 44, Spring 67) 1–38. A three-day taped "bio-interview" with the Russian pioneer and further answers to questions by mail; annotated filmography; introduction.

Taylor, Richard. "Lev Kuleshov, 1899–1970." *Silent Picture* (No. 8, Autumn 70) 28. The Russian director's theories and films.

Leyda, Jay. "The Films of Kurosawa." *S&S* 24 (Oct–Dec 54) 74–78+. A vigorous, competitive film industry since the war has encouraged artists in Japan; *Drunken Angels*, *Rashomon*, and *Living* are discussed; **Akira Kurosawa**'s films express pity and humanity.

McVay, Douglas. "The Rebel in a Kimono." *F&F* 7 (No. 10, July 61) 9–10+. Analysis of the films of **Kurosawa**.

Richie, Donald. "Dostoevsky with a Japanese Camera." *Horizon* 4 (July 62) 42–47. **Kurosawa** and his films.

West, Anthony. "The Art of Akira Kurosawa." *Show* 2 (July 62) 58–62. Themes of Kurosawa's films: death, destiny, and society's effect on the individual.

Iida, Shinbi. "**Kurosawa**." *Cinema* (Calif) 1 (No. 5, Aug–Sep 63) 28. Article followed by interview.

Richie, Donald. "Kurosawa on Kurosawa." *S&S* 33 (Summer 64) 108–113; (Autumn 64) 200–203. Notes of Kurosawa's comments looking back over the body of his work, from his first picture in 1943, *Judo Saga*, to *Sanjuro* (1962); two articles.

Ortolani, Benito. "Films and Faces of **Akira Kurosawa**." *America* 113 (2 Oct 65) 368–371. Discussion of influences on Kurosawa, his themes, and critical response to his films.

Bucher, Felix. "Akira Kurosawa—Hiroshi Teshigahara." *Camera* 45 (No. 9, Sep 66) 50–55. A study of the two Japanese film directors.

L

Roman, Robert C. "Alan Ladd." *FIR* 15 (No. 4, Apr 64) 199–216. On the occasion of his death, a biography and film listing.

"Universal to Cowdin." *Time* 27 (23 Mar 36). See 6b(2). About **Carl Laemmle**.

Uselton, Roi A. "Barbara LaMarr." *FIR* 15 (No. 6, June–July 64) 352–369. Career and film listing of silent-film actress.

"Lamorisse's New Balloon." *Time* 76 (24 Oct 60) 65–66. A report on *Voyage in a Balloon* and a brief look at its director, **Albert Lamorisse**.

Morgan, James. "Hecht-Lancaster Productions." *S&S* 25 (Summer 55). *See 6c(3).* About **Burt Lancaster.**

Lancaster, Burt. "Hollywood Drove Me to a Double Life." *F&F* 8 (No. 4, Jan 62) 10+. Lancaster explains how and why he is a producer.

Schuster, Mel. "**Burt Lancaster.**" *FIR* 20 (No. 7, Aug–Sep 69) 393–408. Career and film listing.

Ferguson, Otis. "Behind the Camera: Lang." *New Rep* 104 (23 June 41) 858; (30 June 41) 887; 105 (7 July 41) 21. Personal background on **Fritz Lang**, based on interviews.

Lang, Fritz. "Happily Ever After." *Penguin F Rev* 5 (Jan 48) 22–29. Classic tragedy is too negative for modern man's faith in himself; "the highest responsibility of the film creator is to reflect his times" and what is wanted now is the "affirmative ending" in which virtue triumphs through struggle.

Eisner, Lotte H. "The German Films of Fritz Lang." *Penguin F Rev* 6 (Apr 48) 53–61. The expressionistic style of Lang's films is consistent despite new national influences or the changing of the times.

Lambert, Gavin. "Fritz Lang's America." *S&S* 25 (Summer 55) 15–21; (Autumn 55) 92–97. The status of the German film industry when Fritz Lang left in 1934; a few films from Lang's German period and those he has made in America; two articles.

Hart, Henry. "Fritz Lang Today." *FIR* 7 (June–July 56) 261–263. A brief interview with the Austrian-born director, including a comment on brutality as a substitute for the belief in hell.

Taylor, John Russell. "The Nine Lives of Dr. Mabuse." *S&S* 31 (Winter 61–62) 43–46. Certain themes run inescapably through **Fritz Lang's** career.

Lang, Fritz. "Fritz Lang Talks About Dr. Mabuse." *Movie* (No. 4, Nov 62) 4–5. The various Mabuse films he has made.

Bartlett, Nicholas. "The Dark Struggle." *Film* (No. 32, Summer 62) 11–13. The films of Fritz Lang; comments taken from an interview with the director.

Lang, Fritz. "Talks About the Problems of Life Today." *F&F* 8 (No. 9, June 62) 20–21.

Madsen, Axel. "**Lang.**" *S&S* 36 (Summer 67) 108–112. Fritz Lang's films and his attitude toward the film medium; a present-tense interview-essay.

Berg, Gretchen. "**Fritz Lang.**" *Take One* 2 (No. 2, 1968) 12–13. Interview; his own work and Godard's *Contempt.*

Chamberlin, Philip. "The Films of **Fritz Lang** at the L. A. County Museum." *Cinema* (Calif) 5 (No. 3, 1969) 38–39. Brief notes on each showing.

Joannides, Paul. "Aspects of **Fritz Lang.**" *Cinema* (Cambridge) (Nos. 6–7, Aug 70)

6–9. His moral sensitivity, unity of theme, metaphysical precariousness, imagery, use of movement.

Schonert, Vernon L. "**Harry Langdon.**" *FIR* 18 (No. 7, Oct 67) 470–485. Career and film chronology.

Lardner, Ring, Jr. "My Life on the Blacklist." *SEP* 234 (14 Oct 61) 38–40+.

Geist, Kenneth. "The Films of **Ring Lardner, Jr.**" *F Com* 6 (No. 4, Winter 70–71) 45–49. The screenwriter's films and experiences under conditions of the blacklist; filmography.

Johnston, Alva. "**Jesse L. Lasky.**" *New Yorker* (10 July 37) 18–24. Profile of producer.

Lasky, Jesse L., and Don Weldon. "I Was a Star Maker." *McCall's* 84 (July 57) 34+. Excerpt from autobiography, *I Blow My Own Horn* (Doubleday, 1957); beginnings of the movie industry in America.

"Amateur Activities: *Saturday Night.*" *S&S* 19 (Dec 49) 32. Derek York and **Walter Lassally** make a thirty-minute story film; Bryan Forbes in the cast.

Hudson, Roger. "The Secret Profession." *S&S* 34 (Summer 65). *See 2e.* About **Walter Lassally,** cameraman.

"New-Wave Producer Hits Jackpot." *Bus Wk* (3 Jan 70). *See 6c(3).* About **Michael S. Laughlin.**

McVay, Douglas. "The Intolerant Giant." *F&F* 9 (No. 6, Mar 63) 20–24. On the acting career of **Charles Laughton.**

Vermilye, Jerry. "**Charles Laughton.**" *FIR* 14 (May 63) 257–275. Career study, filmography.

De La Roche, Catherine. "Launder and Gilliat." *S&S* 15 (No. 59, Autumn 46) 94–95. An analysis of the work of Sidney Gilliat and **Frank Launder,** writer-producer-directors.

Robinson, David. "The Lighter People." *S&S* 24 (July–Sep 54) 39–42+. **Stan Laurel** and Oliver Hardy knew how to play on the audience's ability to recognize old gags and they seemed to have an infinite capacity for variations on a single theme.

Verb, Boyd. "Laurel Without Hardy." *FIR* 10 (Mar 59) 153–158. Interview with Stan Laurel.

Barnes, Peter. "Cuckoo." *F&F* 6 (No. 11, Aug 60) 15+. Review of the career of **Laurel** and Hardy.

"L. & H. Cult." *Time* 90 (14 July 67) 74. On the recent popularity of **Laurel** and Hardy.

Pope, Dennis. "**Stanley Laurel** and Oliver Norvell Hardy." *Film* (No. 49, Autumn 67) 32–34. A brief historical and critical overview of the comedians' work.

Everson, William K. "The Crazy World of **Laurel** and Hardy." *Take One* 1 (No. 9, 1968) 16–19.

Amory, Cleveland. "Trade Winds." *Sat Rev* 52 (12 July 69). *See 7b(1c).* About **Laurel** and **Hardy.**

Cain, James M. "**Vincent Sargent Lawrence.**" *Screen Writer* 2 (Jan 47) 11–15. Memorial essay on this screenwriter.

"Swifty the Great." *Time* 79 (2 Feb 62) 54–55. Agent **Irving Lazar.**

Heller, Joseph. "Irving Is Everywhere." *Show* 3 (Apr 63) 104–105+. Comments on the career and life-style of Hollywood agent **Irving Lazar.**

Heller, Joseph. "Irving Is Everywhere." *F&F* 9 (No. 12, Sep 63) 9–10+. On **Irving Lazar,** Hollywood writer's agent.

Bachmann, Gideon. "The Frontiers of Realist Cinema: The Work of **Ricky Leacock.**" *F Cult* (Nos. 22–23, 1961). *See 8c(3).*

Marcorelles, Louis. "The Deep Well." *Contrast* 3 (No. 5, Autumn 64) 246–249. An interview with **Richard Leacock.**

Blue, James. "One Man's Truth—An Interview with **Richard Leacock.**" *F Com* 3 (No. 2, Spring 65) 15–23. The *cinéma vérité* director talks about his film *Happy Mother's Day,* his objections to "fake real films when the camera jumps around," and the future of theatrical versus realistic films.

Pichel, Irving. "*This Happy Breed* and *Great Expectations.*" *Hwd Q* 2 (No. 4, July 47) 408–411. Two **David Lean** films, of which the latter surprisingly gives us a "greater sense of reality." See also letter *Hwd Q* 3 (No. 1, Fall 47) 87–89 on characterization in Dickens' novel.

Lean, David. "What You Can Learn from Movies." *Pop Photog* 42 (Mar 58). *See 1a.*

Watts, Stephen. "David Lean." *FIR* 10 (Apr 59) 245–246. Brief letter on British director's career.

McVay, Douglas. "Lean—Lover of Life." *F&F* 5 (No. 11, Aug 59) 9–10+. **David Lean's** films.

Lean, David. "Out of the Wilderness." *F&F* 9 (No. 4, Jan 63) 11–15. Interview with the director, especially on *Lawrence of Arabia.*

Higham, Charles. "**David Lean.**" *London Mag* new series 4 (No. 10, Jan 65) 74–83. On Lean's career.

Alpert, Hollis. "**David Lean** Recipe: A Whack in the Guts." *NYTM* (23 May 65) 32–33+.

Westerbeck, C. L., Jr. "Lean Years." *Commonweal* 93 (18 Dec 70) 302–303. A review of **David Lean's** career, culminating in a short critique of *Ryan's Daughter.*

Lee-Thompson, J. "The Still Small Voice of Truth." *F&F* 9 (No. 7, Apr 63) 5–6. Director offers comments on his films, especially *Taras Bulba.*

Marcorelles, Louis. "Interview with **Roger Leenhardt** and **Jacques Rivette.**" *S&S* 32 (Autumn 63) 168–173. According to *Cahiers,* Leenhardt, sixty, is the spiritual father

of the French New Wave; he has made about thirty short films and two features; Rivette, thirty-five, is also a critic and a director of short films and *Paris nous appartient;* they talk about cinema, critics, the role of the writer.

Fraser, Graham. "A Gentle Revolutionary." *Take One* 1 (No. 7, 1967) 10–13. A discussion of the work of **Jean-Pierre LeFebvre,** the Canadian film maker.

Bond, Kirk. "Léger, Dreyer, and Montage." *Creative Art* 11 (No. 2, Oct 32) 134–139. **Fernand Léger** compared with the Danish director.

"On the Scene: **Ernest Lehman.**" *Playboy* 14 (No. 2, Feb 67) 142. Screenwriter who did movie version of *Who's Afraid of Virginia Woolf?*

Nogueira, Rui. "*Psycho,* Rosie and a Touch of Orson." *S&S* 39 (Spring 70) 66–70. How **Janet Leigh** began her acting career; the director-actor relationship with Josef von Sternberg, Orson Welles, Alfred Hitchcock, Bob Fosse, and John Frankenheimer.

Raper, Michell. "They Called Her a Dresden Shepherdess." *F&F* 1 (No. 11, Aug 55) 5. The career of actress **Vivien Leigh.**

Bowers, Ronald L. "**Vivien Leigh.**" *FIR* 16 (No. 7, Aug–Sep 65) 403–418. Biography and film listings.

Maltin, Leonard. "A Visit with **Mitchell Leisen.**" *Action* 4 (No. 6, Nov–Dec 69) 7–8. Hollywood director discusses his work at Paramount from the 1920s through the 1940s.

Lemmon, Jack. "Such Fun to Be Funny." *F&F* 7 (No. 2, Nov 60) 7. Interview with the American actor.

"Interview: **Jack Lemmon.**" *Playboy* 11 (No. 5, May 64) 57–64. Lemmon discusses actors, his films, theories of acting, and films in general.

Baltake, Joe. "**Jack Lemmon.**" *FIR* 21 (No. 1, Jan 70) 1–13. Biography and film list.

Lerner, Carl. "Odyssey from Hollywood to New York." *F Com* 2 (No. 4, Fall 64) 2–11. Film editor who began as assistant at Columbia Pictures and for Wyler, Hawks, and Rogosin, tells interviewer Judy Lotz about the editor's relationship to different kinds of directors and his experiences as writer-director of *Black Like Me.*

"Straight-Shooter: From Uniform Folder to Director-Producer." *Lit Dig* (13 Feb 37) 20+. Director-producer **Mervyn LeRoy.**

Beatty, J. "Mervyn of the Movies." *American* 126 (July 38) 32–33+. **Mervyn LeRoy** and the life of film directors and producers in general.

LeRoy, Mervyn. "The Making of Mervyn Le-Roy." *FIR* 4 (May 53) 220–225. An excerpt from LeRoy's book *It Takes More Than Talent* (Knopf, 1953); how he began as an actor, comic, wardrobe assistant, and second cameraman.

French, Philip. "**Richard Lester.**" *Movie* (No. 14, Autumn 65) 5–11. An analysis of the director's work.

Bluestone, George. "Lunch with **Lester.**" *FQ* 19 (No. 4, Summer 66) 12–16. His early work on *The Goon Show;* techniques on the Beatles' films.

Richardson, Boyce. "**Dick Lester** and His War." *Take One* 1 (No. 8, 1967) 4–6. A discussion of Lester's work, with particular reference to *How I Won the War.*

Lester, Richard. "The Art of Comedy." *Film* (No. 48, Spring 67) 16–21. The director discusses his work.

"**Richard Lester.**" *New Yorker* 43 (28 Oct 67) 50–51. Interview with the American director who works in England.

Cameron, Ian, and Mark Shivas. "An Interview with **Richard Lester.**" *Movie* (No. 16, Winter 68–69) 16–28. Also filmography.

Prelutsky, B. "What's **Richard Lester** Trying To Do?" *Holiday* 45 (Apr 69) 82–83+. Survey of Lester's career as a feature-film maker, accusing the director of superficiality and modishness.

"A Simple Guy." *Newswk* 55 (22 Feb 60) 100+. Producer **Joseph E. Levine.**

"Joe Unchained." *Time* 77 (24 Feb 61) 64–65. A portrait of **Joseph E. Levine.**

O'Neil, P. "Super Salesman of Super Colossals." *Life* 53 (27 July 62) 76–78B+. **Joseph E. Levine.**

Hamill, Katherine. "Supercolossal, Well, Pretty Good: World of **Joe Levine.**" *Fortune* 69 (Mar 64) 130–132+.

Tomkins, Calvin. "Profiles." *New Yorker* 43 (16 Sep 67) 55–56+. On **Joe Levine,** producer and executive of Embassy Pictures.

Beresford, Bruce. "**Don Levy.**" *Cinema* (Cambridge) (No. 2, Mar 69) 14–17. An interview with the British film maker.

Kass, Robert. "**Jerry Lewis** Analyzed." *FIR* 4 (Mar 53) 119–123. The neighborhood freak, a child only a mother could love—this is his role, and it is very far from true comedy.

Hume, Rod. "Martin and **Lewis**—Are Their Critics Wrong?" *F&F* 2 (No. 6, Mar 56) 10. Brief assessment of the history and work together of Dean Martin and Jerry Lewis.

Taylor, John Russell. "**Jerry Lewis.**" *S&S* 34 (Spring 65) 82–85. *Cahiers du Cinéma* discovered him after fifteen years in the critical wilderness; his special talents, early films with Frank Tashlin, and the films he wrote and directed himself.

Madsen, Axel. "America's Uncle: Interview with **Jerry Lewis.**" *CdC in Eng* (No. 4, 1966) 26–31. The film maker discusses his acceptance by the French critics and his early directing experiences; *The Bellboy;* four different reviews of *The Family Jewels* on pp. 31–39.

Sarris, Andrew. "Editor's Eyrie." *CdC in Eng* (No. 4, 1966) 64–66. Editor's generally negative judgment of **Jerry Lewis.**

Alpert, Hollis. "*LeRoi du* Crazy." *NYTM* (27 Feb 66) 28–29+. The French reaction to **Jerry Lewis,** and the story of his career.

Hanson, Curtis Lee. "Point of View." *Cinema* (Calif) 3 (No. 4, Dec 66) 50. Comment on director **Jerry Lewis.**

Farber, Manny. "Films." *Nation* 172 (14 Apr 51) 353–354. On the death of a very unorthodox artist, **Val Lewton;** how he was misplaced in Hollywood, what made his films unique.

Bodeen, DeWitt. "**Val Lewton.**" *FIR* 14 (Mar 63) 210–225. Personal recollections by author; biography and career study of this producer who made a number of horror films; filmography.

Ellison, Harlan. "Three Faces of Fear." *Cinema* (Calif) 3 (No. 2, Mar 66). *See 4k(3).* About **Val Lewton.**

"**Rolf Lieberman.**" *New Yorker* 46 (29 Aug 70). *See 4k(6).*

Linder, Carl. "Notes and Writings." *F Cult* (No. 35, 1964–1965) 29–32. Linder's film writings and notes, the latter mostly relating to his film *The Devil Is Dead.* See also his letter about San Francisco film makers pp. 65–67.

Linder, Carl. "An Interview with Carl Linder." *December* 7 (No. 1, Spring 65) 155–159.

Barrios, Gregg. "Naming Names: The Films of **Carl Linder.**" *FQ* 22 (No. 1, Fall 68) 41–46. The sometimes Boschean vision of this experimental-film maker: *The Devil Is Dead, Overflow,* and *Closed Mondays.*

Spears, Jack. "**Max Linder.**" *FIR* 16 (No. 5, May 65) 272–291. Career of the motion picture's "first truly international star."

Litvak, Anatole. "A Cutter at Heart." *F&F* 13 (No. 5, Feb 67) 16–17. Interview on his career and films.

Nolan, Jack Edmund. "**Anatole Litvak.**" *FIR* 18 (No. 9, Nov 67) 548–573. Career and films of director.

Marshall, Jim. "Back to the Mines." *Collier's* 117 (1 June 46) 58+. **Harold Lloyd** back at work for Preston Sturges.

Calman, Mel. "Meeting with **Harold Lloyd.**" *S&S* 28 (Winter 58–59) 4. Conversation at a restaurant.

Freidman, Arthur B. "Interview with **Harold Lloyd.**" *FQ* 15 (No. 4, Summer 62) 7–13. How he worked backward from a climactic gag to the establishing story; surmounting obstacles "gives you the opportunity to create comedy."

Garringer, Nelson E. "**Harold Lloyd.**" *FIR* 13 (No. 7, Aug–Sep 62) 407–422. Career and film listing.

Lloyd, Harold. "The Funny Side of Life." *F&F* 10 (No. 4, Jan 64) 19–21. Interview about comedy and his films.

McCaffrey, Donald W. "The Mutual Approval of Keaton and Lloyd." *CJ* 6 (1966–1967). *See 5, Buster Keaton.*

Lloyd, Harold. "The Serious Business of Being Funny." *F Com* 5 (No. 3, Fall 69) 46–57. Visiting the University of Michigan Cinema Guild (managed by Hubert Cohen) in November 1966, Lloyd comments on the surprise gag (it has "a sharper laugh to it"), the hard work of planning and previewing, the amount of directing he did ("always in on it"), and his films generally.

Schoenfeld, Bernard C. "The Mistakes of David Loew." *Screen Writer* 1 (Oct 45) 1–7. An appreciative account of David Loew and the courageous stand he made against political censors, and against those in the Hollywood establishment who advised against his making *The Southerner* with Jean Renoir as director.

Kahn, Ely Jacques, Jr. "Joshua Logan." *New Yorker* (4 Apr 53) 38–65; (11 Apr 53) 37–67. Profile of director.

Davidson, Bill, and Joshua Logan. "My Greatest Crisis." *Look* 22 (5 Aug 58) 54+. Logan tells how he made it as a director on Broadway and in Hollywood; see also 22 July 58.

Gow, Gordon. "Gold Diggers of 1969." *F&F* 16 (No. 3, Dec 69) 12–16. Interview with Joshua Logan on his film directing.

Milson, Sylvia. "He Chose Slow Walk to Success." *F&F* 2 (No. 10, July 56) 10. On career of Herbert Lom.

Busch, Noel F. "A Loud Cheer for the Screwball Girl." *Life* 5 (17 Oct 38) 48–51+. Profile of comedienne Carole Lombard.

Dickens, Homer. "Carole Lombard." *FIR* 12 (No. 2, Feb 61) 70–86. Biography and films.

"Goffredo Lombardo." *F&F* 7 (No. 4, Jan 61) 5. Career sketch of the Italian producer.

Carey, Gary. "Written on the Screen: Anita Loos." *F Com* 6 (No. 4, Winter 70–71) 51–55. Her scripts for Douglas Fairbanks, Constance Talmadge, and Jean Harlow; filmography.

Lane, John Francis. "Neapolitan Gold." *F&F* 3 (No. 7, Apr 57) 9+. Sophia Loren.

Moravia, Alberto. "This Is Your Life: Sophia Loren." *Show* 2 (Sep 62) 54–57. Interview; how she began her acting career; some comments on Carlo Ponti; preceded by pictorial feature, pp. 49–53.

Silke, James R. "Sophia Loren: Earth Mother." *Cinema* (Calif) 2 (No. 1, Feb–Mar 64) 20.

White, W. L. "Pare Lorentz." *Scribner's* 105 (Jan 39) 7–11+. The head man of U.S. government motion pictures, his films, his ingenuity, personal dramatics, and jousts with Hollywood.

McEvoy, J. P. "Young Man with a Camera: Pare Lorentz." *Rdrs Dig* 37 (Aug 40) 73–76. Biography, from film critic to film maker.

Black, C. M. "He Serves Up America: Pare Lorentz." *Collier's* 106 (3 Aug 40) 22+. The documentary-film maker's struggles in Hollywood and work with the government.

"Rare Treat." *Newswk* 58 (25 Sep 61) 100. TV series, Pare Lorentz *on Film;* short biography of the director.

"Conscience of the Thirties." *Newswk* 72 (5 Aug 68) 6. Pare Lorentz, who made *The River,* has a "consulting firm" today and doesn't like TV documentaries.

Luft, Herbert G. "Peter Lorre." *FIR* 11 (No. 5, May 60) 278–284. Brief piece on the actor; film list.

Dyer, Peter John. "Fugitive from Murder." *S&S* 33 (Summer 64) 125–127+. The life and acting career of Peter Lorre; his struggle against being stereotyped as Mr. Murder.

Houston, Penelope, and John Gillett. "Conversations with Nicholas Ray and Joseph Losey." *S&S* 30 (Autumn 61). *See 5, Nicholas Ray.*

Mayersberg, Paul. "Contamination." *Movie* (No. 9, May 63) 31–34. Joseph Losey's work; emphasis on *The Damned.*

Losey, Joseph. "The Monkey on My Back." *F&F* 10 (No. 1, Oct 63) 11+. On his style of film making and some of his films.

Brunius, Jacques. "Joseph Losey and *The Servant.*" *Film* (No. 38, Winter 63) 27–30. Interview.

Jacob, Gilles. "Joseph Losey, or the Camera Calls." *S&S* 35 (Spring 66) 62–67. In his study of the director's films, the author makes clear his reservations about Losey and his "journeying in search of a style."

Durgnat, Raymond. "Losey: Modesty and Eve." *F&F* 12 (No. 7, Apr 66) 26–33; (No. 8, May 66) 28–33. On the filming career of Joseph Losey; second article entitled "Losey: Pattern Maids."

Price, James. "Themes of Dispassion." *London Mag* new series 6 (No. 4, July 66) 93–97. On the films of Joseph Losey.

Durgnat, Raymond. "The Cubist Puritanism of Joseph Losey." *Film* (No. 50, Winter 67) 10–12.

Phillips, Gene D. "The Critical Camera of Joseph Losey." *Cinema* (Calif) 4 (No. 1, Spring 68) 22–34+.

Strick, Philip. "Mice in the Milk." *S&S* 38 (Spring 69) 77–79. An account of Joseph Losey's *Boom* and *Secret Ceremony,* which together with *Accident* form "an immaculate trilogy of introspection" and resist, "almost tangibly, the invasion of the critic, interpreter, or commentator, turning him away with a reflective, flawless surface."

Eason, Patrick, and Tony Rayns. "Joseph Losey." *Cinema* (Cambridge) (No. 3, June 69) 17–21. An interview.

Dunham, Harold. "**Bessie Love.**" *FIR* 10 (Feb 59) 86–99. Her career began with *Intolerance;* her roles surveyed in silent pictures and early musical comedies; a descriptive index of her ninety-two films.

Love, Bessie. "On Working Behind the Camera." *F&F* 8 (No. 10, July 62) 16+. Silent-era actress works as script clerk on wartime film in England.

Ringgold, Gene. "**Myrna Loy.**" *FIR* 14 (Feb 63) 69–92. Career study; filmography.

Braun, Eric. "**Myrna Loy on Comedy.**" *F&F* 14 (No. 6, Mar 68) 9–11. Interview on her life and films.

"**Ernst Lubitsch.**" *Time* 19 (No. 5, 1 Feb 32) 48. Lubitsch's way of directing (following a review of *The Man I Killed*).

"Versatility of Mr. Lubitsch." *Living Age* 350 (June 36) 325–327. *London Observer* interview: "In America, you can put over the most serious drama if it is salted with humor. You must learn to laugh at things."

Wollenberg, H. H. "Two Masters." *S&S* 17 (No. 65, Spring 48) 46–48. A discussion of Lubitsch and Eisenstein—their differences and similarities.

Wollenberg, H. H. "Ernst Lubitsch." *Penguin F Rev* 7 (Sep 48) 61–67. The part Lubitsch played in the emergence of cinema art.

Weinberg, Herman G. "A Tribute to Lubitsch." *FIR* 2 (Aug–Sep 51) 3–12. A survey of his career with a letter in which Lubitsch appraises his own films.

Lubitsch, Ernst. "Letter to Herman Weinberg." *F Cult* (No. 25, 1962) 38–45. Reproduction of personal letter in which Lubitsch attempts to point out the important phases of his career.

Auriol, Jean-Georges. "*Chez Ernst.*" *CdC in Eng* (No. 9, Mar 67) 54–55. The world of the films of Ernst Lubitsch; first published in *La Revue du Cinéma* (Sep 48).

Reisch, Walter, *et al.* "A Tribute to Lubitsch, 1892–1947." *Action* 2 (No. 6, Nov–Dec 67) 14–15. By several friends.

Green, Calvin. "Lubitsch: The Trouble with Paradise." *F Soc Rev* 4 (No. 4, 1968) 18–33; 4 (No. 5, 1969) 19–34. Brief notes in two parts on some Lubitsch films presented at the Museum of Modern Art in New York.

"**Sidney Lumet.**" *F&F* 6 (No. 11, Aug 60) 5. Sketch of the director's career.

Bogdanovich, Peter. "An Interview with Sidney Lumet." *FQ* 14 (No. 2, Winter 60) 18–23. Comments on television, his own films, and the differences between the theatre and cinema, Hollywood and the independent producer.

Bean, Robin. "The Insider." *F&F* 11 (No. 9, June 65) 8–13. Sidney Lumet interviewed on his film making.

Petrie, Graham. "The Films of Sidney Lumet: Adaptation as Art." *FQ* 21 (No. 2, Winter

67–68) 9–18. Emphasis on *A Long Day's Journey into Night* and *The Pawnbroker.*

Farber, Stephen. "Lumet in '69." *S&S* 38 (Autumn 69) 190–195. Reevaluation of Sidney Lumet, director of *The Pawnbroker* and *The Hill,* who does not write and usually uses established material; a character's past and present seem to interest him; *Bye Bye Braverman* has "pathos and freshness of observation."

Browne, Mallory. "Artisan in Light." *CSMM* (7 Aug 35) 3. Profile of Louis Lumière.

"Lumière Jubilee." *Time* 26 (18 Nov 35) 19–20.

Sadoul, Georges. "Lumière—The Last Interview." *S&S* 17 (No. 66, Summer 48) 68–70. Film pioneer discusses the early years and his role.

Vermilye, Jerry. "Ida Lupino." *FIR* 10 (May 59) 266–283. Writer, director, producer, and actress; an index to her fifty-nine films since 1933.

Lupino, Ida. "Me, Mother Directress." *Action* 2 (No. 3, May–June 67) 14–15. The American actress discusses her career and her movement into directing.

Weinberg, Gretchen. "Interview with Len Lye." *F Cult* (No. 29, 1963) 40–45. Speculations by the animator from New Zealand who won the prize at Brussels and was an inspiration to Norman McLaren.

Lye, Len. "Is Film Art?" *F Cult* (No. 29, 1963). *See 3a.*

Cavalcanti, Alberto. "Presenting Len Lye." *S&S* 16 (No. 64, Winter 47–48) 134–136. His experimental work in animation.

"Len Lye Speaks at the Film Makers Cinematheque." *F Cult* (No. 44, Spring 67) 49–51. His own career in animated film.

M

Tyler, Parker. "Willard Maas." *F Cult* (No. 20, 1959) 53–58. The career of the experimental-film maker; analysis of *Geography of the Body, Image in the Snow,* and *Narcissus.*

MacArthur, James. "Creating an Illusion." *F&F* 7 (No. 3, Dec 60) 9+. The young American actor talks about his work.

Bodeen, DeWitt. "Jeanette MacDonald." *FIR* 16 (No. 3, Mar 65) 129–144. Career and film listing.

Dunne, Philip. "Kenneth Macgowan—A Man to Remember." *JSPG* (June 63) 23–24+. Tribute to editor-producer-professor who started film teaching at UCLA.

Dickson, Robert G. "Kenneth Macgowan." *FIR* 14 (Oct 63) 475–487. Career study of the producer; filmography.

Cutts. John. "Mackendrick Finds the Sweet Smell of Success." *F&F* 3 (No. 9, June 57) 8–9+. Alexander Mackendrick's five British films before going to Hollywood.

Wald, Malvin. "Profile of a Filmmaker." *JUFPA* 16 (No. 2, 1964). *See 8c(4)*. About **Kent Mackenzie**.

Bean, Robin. "The Two Faces of Shirley." *F&F* 8 (No. 5, Feb 62) 11–12+. Interview with **Shirley MacLaine** about her work.

Stein, Jeanne. "Aline MacMahon." *FIR* 16 (No. 10, Dec 65) 616–632. Biography and film listing of the American actress.

MacMurray, Fred. "I've Been Lucky." *SEP* 235 (24 Feb 62) 36–37+. Autobiography—as told to Pete Martin.

Kobler, John. "Tempest on the Tiber." *Life* 28 (13 Feb 50) 115–118+. A "close-up" of Italian actress **Anna Magnani**.

Whitehall, Richard. "Anna Magnani." *F&F* 7 (No. 10, July 61) 15–16+. Analysis of the acting of Anna Magnani.

Toback, James. "At Play in the Fields of the Bored." *Esq* 70 (Dec 68) 150–155+. On the personality and literary career of **Norman Mailer**; also a description of Mailer and his friends making a movie.

Roddy, Joseph. "Latest Model **Mailer**." *Look* 33 (27 May 69) 22–28. Norman Mailer's writing, acting, directing careers.

Moshier, W. Franklyn. "Marjorie Main." *FIR* 17 (No. 2, Feb 66) 96–114. Career and film listing for actress who played Ma Kettle.

Malden, Karl. "What the Hell, I'm a Frank Guy." *Cinema* (Calif) 2 (No. 1, Feb–Mar 64) 26. Interview with actor.

"Louis Malle." *Film* (No. 39, Spring 64) 14–16. Interview.

Gow, Gordon. "Louis Malle's France." *F&F* 10 (No. 11, Aug 64) 14–18. A study of his films.

Price, James. "Night and Solitude: The Cinema of **Louis Malle**." *London Mag* new series 4 (No. 6, Sep 64) 73–75.

Russell, Lee. "Louis Malle." *New Left Rev* (No. 30, Mar–Apr 65) 73–76. A study of his films.

Birrell, Francis. "Art of Mamoulian." *New S&N* 4 (26 Nov 32) 657. American director **Rouben Mamoulian** should be regarded as one of the few film artists.

Robinson, David. "Rouben Mamoulian: Painting the Leaves Black." *S&S* 30 (Summer 61) 123–127. An interview with the twenty-six-year-old director; his innovations with sound and color; his stars; comments on his work film by film.

Nugent, Frank S. "All About Joe." *Collier's* 127 (24 Mar 51) 24–25+. On writer-director **Joseph Mankiewicz**.

Mankiewicz, Joseph. "Putting on the Style." *F&F* 6 (No. 4, Jan 60) 9+. Interview with Mankiewicz about his life and films.

Reid, John Howard. "Cleo's Joe." *F&F* 9 (No. 11, Aug 63) 44–48; (No. 12, Sep 63) 13–16. On the film career of **Joseph L. Mankiewicz**; in two parts.

Bontemps, Jacques, and Richard Overstreet. "Measure for Measure: Interview with **Joseph L. Mankiewicz**." *CdC in Eng* (No. 8, Feb 67) 28–52. The American director discusses his ideas, his career, and his films; filmography and biography by Patrick Brion.

Sarris, Andrew. "Mankiewicz of the Movies." *Show* (Mar 70) 26–30+. Report on the directing career of Joseph L. Mankiewicz as a microcosm of film history (1929–1970); includes remarks on *Citizen Kane*, brief biographical sketch, working with Paramount, MGM, and Fox, association with F. Scott Fitzgerald, and the demise of the Hollywood system.

"Wolf Mankowitz." *F&F* 1 (No. 3, Dec 54) 3. A sketch of the British screenwriter, film maker, novelist, and authority on chinaware.

"The Crusader." *Time* 81 (22 Mar 63) 56. A portrait of **Abby Mann**, screenwriter.

Reid, John Howard. "Mann and His Environment." *F&F* 8 (No. 4, Jan 62) 11–12+; (Feb 62) 19–20+. Life and films of **Anthony Mann**; second article titled "Tension at Twilight."

Fenwick, J. H., and Jonathan Green-Armytage. "Now You See It: Landscape and **Anthony Mann**." *S&S* 34 (Autumn 65) 186–189. An interview with Mann and a study of hallmarks of his work; an apparent conscious reliance on location.

Missiaen, Jean-Claude. "'A Lesson in Cinema': Interview with **Anthony Mann**." *CdC in Eng* (No. 12, Dec 67) 44–59. The film maker discusses his films and his career; brief biography and detailed filmography by Patrick Brion and Olivier Eyquem.

Wicking, Christopher, and Barrie Pattison. "Interviews with **Anthony Mann**." *Screen* 10 (Nos. 4–5, July–Oct 69) 32–54.

Reid, John Howard. "Portraying Life with Dignity." *F&F* 8 (No. 6, Mar 62) 19–20+. Analysis of the work of director **Daniel Mann**.

Reid, John Howard. "Marty and Other Squares." *F&F* 8 (No. 7, Apr 62) 20+. Analysis of the films of **Delbert Mann**.

Mann, Ann. "What Is a Mann?" *Action* 2 (No. 4, July–Aug 67) 9+. A description of the new president of the Directors Guild, Delbert Mann, by his wife.

Mann, Delbert. "Symposium." *Arts in Soc* 4 (No. 1, Winter 67) 69–70. Director's responses to questionnaire.

McClure, Michael. "Defense of **Jayne Mansfield**." *F Cult* (No. 32, 1964) 24–27.

Thruelsen, R. "Hollywood's Plane Crasher." *SEP* 50 (14 Apr 56). *See 2j(3)*. About **Paul Mantz**.

Tozzi, Romano. "Fredric March." *FIR* 9 (Dec 58) 545–571. Life and career of the stage and film star, with a descriptive index to his sixty-two films.

Barber, Rowland. "**Ann-Margret**: New Star in the West." *Show* 2 (Sep 62) 68–69+. Her rise to Hollywood stardom.

Bodeen, DeWitt. "**Frances Marion**." *FIR* 20 (No. 2, Feb 68) 71–91; (No. 3, Mar 69) 129–152. Career and film index of the early screenwriter.

Jacob, Gilles. "**Chris Marker** and the Mutants." *S&S* 35 (Autumn 66) 164–168. A study of this French director's films, which have taken him from Russia and China to Cuba; stress on the short film *La Jetée*.

Brown, Robert. "Interview with **Gregory Markopoulos**." *F Cult* (No. 32, 1964) 6–8. His life and films—*Psyche, Swain, Twice a Man*, etc.

Markopoulos, Gregory. "Symposium." *Arts in Soc* 4 (No. 1, Winter 67) 77–78. Director's responses to questionnaire.

Markopoulos, Gregory. "The Driving Rhythm." *F Cult* (No. 40, Spring 66) 31–34. Lecture on his films, especially *Twice a Man;* continued (Summer 66) 17–21.

Slide, Anthony. "**Percy Marmont**'s Hollywood." *Silent Picture* (No. 7, Summer 70) 15–17. An interview in which the actor tells about how he got started in films, his films, and life in Hollywood in the 1920s.

Dunham, Harold. "**Mae Marsh**." *FIR* 9 (June–July 58) 306–321. Life and career of silent-film actress Mae Marsh, who jumped up and down so frequently for D. W. Griffith; a descriptive index of fifty-four of her films.

Dunham, Harold. "**Mae Marsh**, Robert Harron and D. W. Griffith." *Silent Picture* (No. 4, Autumn 69) 10–17.

Marshall, George. "55 Years in the Movies." *Action* 5 (No. 6, Nov–Dec 70) 2–6.

Diehl, Digby. "What We Have Here Is a Failure to Communicate." *Show* (9 July 70) 20–23+. The acting career of **Strother Martin** from bit parts to "starring" bad guys, with comments from Martin on playing stereotypes.

"Interview: **Lee Marvin**." *Playboy* 16 (No. 1, Jan 69) 59–78. Star talks about violence on the screen.

"*Horse Feathers*." *Time* 20 (15 Aug 32) 24–45. History of **Marx Brothers** and their performances.

Rowland, Richard. "American Classic." *Hwd Q* 2 (No. 3, Apr 47) 264–269. An appreciation of the **Marx Brothers**' films.

Rowland, Richard. "American Classic." *Penguin F Rev* 7 (Sep 48) 68–76. A study of the **Marx Brothers**. Reprinted from *Hollywood Quarterly*.

Kurnitz, Harry. "Return of the **Marx Brothers**." *Holiday* 21 (Jan 57) 95+. Review of their film career.

Perelman, S. J. "The Winsome Foursome." *Show* 1 (Nov 61) 34–38. **Marx Brothers** and Perelman's relationship with them while scripting *Monkey Business*.

Marx, Groucho. "Groucho Writes." *Take One* 1 (No. 11, 1968) 14–15. A few letters which Groucho Marx wrote to Warner Brothers when they objected to the Marx Brothers making a film called *A Night in Casablanca*.

Davis, Metton S. "First the Pasta, Then the Play." *NYTM* (2 Jan 66). *See 5, Federico Fellini*. About **Giulietta Masina**.

Peavy, Charles. "The Films of **Richard Mason**." *Cinéaste* 2 (No. 4, Spring 69) 4–5+. Thematic discussion of this black director's films; ghetto film-making programs; film as a socializing tool.

Stein, Jeanne. "**Raymond Massey**." *FIR* 14 (Aug–Sep 63) 389–402. Career study; filmography.

"**Richard Massingham**." *S&S* 23 (July–Sep 53) 53. Brief obituary for British actor-director-humorist.

Mackie, Philip. "The Troubled Man." *S&S* 24 (Spring 55) 213+. A tribute to **Richard Massingham**: actor, director, producer, medical doctor, and comedian.

"Interview: **Marcello Mastroianni**." *Playboy* 12 (No. 7, July 65) 49–56.

Shenker, I. "Man Who Made Apathy Irresistible: Italy's **M. Mastroianni**." *NYTM* (12 Dec 65) 54–55+.

Chamberlin, Anne. "The Great Undashing Lover of Our Time." *SEP* 239 (13 Aug 66) 81–85. The career of **Marcello Mastroianni**.

Everson, William. "**Rudy Maté**: His Work with Carl Dreyer." *F&F* 2 (No. 2, Nov 55) 7. Interviewed in New York while directing *Miracle in the Rain*.

Luft, Herbert G. "**Rudolf Maté**." *FIR* 15 (No. 8, Oct 64) 480–499. Career of cameraman turned director.

Mayer, Carl. "I Remember . . ." *S&S* 7 (No. 28, Winter 38–39) 157. The German scriptwriter discusses his work in the cinema and includes an excerpt from the directions for *Sylvester*.

Wilhelm, Wolfgang. "**Carl Mayer**." *S&S* 13 (No. 50, July 44) 32. Tribute to the German screenwriter.

Daugherty, Frank. "The Screen's Greatest Poet." *FIR* 4 (Mar 53) 129–132. A tribute to the late German film writer **Carl Mayer**.

Luft, Herbert G. "Notes on the World and Work of **Carl Mayer**." *QFRTV* 8 (No. 4, Summer 54) 375–392. Life and work of German screenwriter; production circumstances of *The Last Laugh, Sunrise*, and other films.

Luft, Herbert G. "**Carl Mayer**, Screen Author." *CJ* 8 (No. 1, Fall 68) 29–38. This screenwriter made an important contribution to the direction of his films because of his specific shot descriptions; opening scenes of *Sunrise* from the script; Mayer's later life.

Pringle, Henry F. "**Louis Burt Mayer.**" *New Yorker* (28 Mar 36) 26–31; (4 Apr 36) 26–30. Profile of the producer.

"Metro-Goldwyn-Mayer: **Louis B. Mayer** Bosses the Biggest Movie-Making Machine." *Life* 15 (27 Sep 43). *See 6b(2).*

"Birthday: Metro-Goldwyn-Mayer." *Time* 54 (11 July 49) 91. **L. B. Mayer** of MGM, a brief biography.

Shearer, Lloyd. "Metro-Goldwyn Without **Mayer.**" *Th Arts* 35 (Sep 51) 56–57+. Thoughts on the retirement of Louis B. Mayer.

Saroyan, William. "Best Angel God Ever Saw." *SEP* 236 (16 Nov 63) 94–95. On the career of **L. B. Mayer**, head of MGM studios.

Cohen, Art, and Terry Hickey. "**Al Maysles** and The Showman." *JUFPA* 16 (No. 2, 1964). *See 8c(3).*

Reynolds, C. "Focus on **Al Maysles.**" *Pop Photog* 54 (May 64) 128–131. His career so far; diagrammed photograph of his equipment.

Haleff, Maxine. "The Maysles Brothers and 'Direct Cinema.'" *F Com* 2 (No. 2, 1964) 19–23. **Albert** and **David Maysles** talk about their films on Joe Levine and the Beatles and the work they did for Godard; comments by interviewer on their careers.

Blue, James. "Thoughts on *Cinéma Vérité* and a Discussion With the **Maysles Brothers.**" *F Com* 2 (No. 4, 1964) 22–30. Ford Foundation grantee comments on latter-day "mystique" of nonpreconception, then interviews film makers who believe research puts them "at a disadvantage" in showing what really happens.

Sitton, Bob. "'An Interview: **Albert** and **David** Maysles.**" *F Lib Q* 2 (No. 3, Summer 69) 13–18. The film makers discuss their films.

Greenfeld, J. "**Paul Mazursky** in Wonderland." *Life* 69 (4 Sep 70) 51–54+. New director shoots his second film, *Alex in Wonderland.*

Bodeen, DeWitt. "**May McAvoy.**" *FIR* 19 (No. 8, Oct 68) 482–498. Career and film listing of "child-woman" actress of 1920s and 1930s.

Hagen, Ray. "**Mercedes McCambridge.**" *FIR* 16 (No. 5, May 65) 292–312. Career and films of the actress.

McCamy, Colin. "Symposium." *Arts in Soc* 4 (No. 1, Winter 67) 98–103. Director's responses to questionnaire.

Martin, Pete. "Going His Way." *SEP* 219 (30 Nov 46) 14–15+. Life with Academy Award-winning director **Leo McCarey.**

Daney, Serge, and Jean-Louis Noames. "Taking Chances: Interview with **Leo McCarey.**" *CdC in Eng* (No. 7, Jan 67) 42–54. American director of comedies discusses his films.

Crosby, Bing, and David Butler. "Remembering **Leo McCarey.**" *Action* 4 (No. 5, Sep–Oct

69) 11–13. Two friends remember the work of the American director.

O'Brien, Geoffrey. "**Leo McCarey.**" *On Film* (1970) 29.

Thomas, Anthony. "**Tim McCoy.**" *FIR* 19 (No. 4, Apr 68) 218–244. Career and film listing of the Western star.

McEnery, Peter. "The Harmful Formula." *F&F* 10 (No. 10, July 64) 15. Interview with the actor about his career.

Parish, James R., and Gene Ringgold. "**Dorothy McGuire.**" *FIR* 15 (No. 8, Oct 64) 466–479. Career and film listing.

Johnston, Alva. "**Victor McLaglen**, Master of the Light Horse." *Woman's Home Companion* 63 (Nov 36) 20–21+. His physical prowess, his careers in boxing and policing, his fear of a Red revolution.

"Movies Without a Camera, Music Without Instruments." *Th Arts* 36 (Oct 52) 16–17. Brief note on **Norman McLaren.**

Jordan, William E. "**Norman McLaren:** His Career and Techniques." *QFRTV* 8 (No. 1, Fall 53) 1–14. Canadian animator's work on film with and without a camera; illustrations from films and comments on McLaren's theories; filmography.

Borshell, Allan. "Blinkity, Blank." *Film* (No. 7, Jan–Feb 56) 22. An analysis of **Norman McLaren's** work.

Weinberg, Gretchen. "Mc *et Moi.*" *F Cult* (No. 25, 1962) 46–47. "A spiritual portrait" of the Canadian film maker **Norman McLaren.**

Callenbach, Ernest. "The Craft of **Norman McLaren.**" *FQ* 16 (No. 2, Winter 62–63) 17–19. Subheading: "Notes on a lecture given at the 1961 Vancouver film festival."

MacDermot, Anne. "Etchcraft on Celluloid." *UNESCO Courier* 17 (Jan 64) 20–23. About the Canadian short-film maker **Norman McLaren.**

Cutler, May Ebbitt. "The Unique Genius of **Norman McLaren.**" *Canad Art* 22 (May–June 65) 8–17.

Rosenthal, Alan. "**Norman McLaren** on *Pas de Deux.*" *JUFA* 22 (No. 1, 1970) 8–15. Interview with the Canadian animation director published in author's *Documentary in Action* (University of California, 1971).

Anderson, Bert, and William Sloan. "An Interview with **Norman McLaren.**" *F Lib Q* 3 (No. 2, Spring 70) 13–17. The Canadian animator discusses his films.

Armbrister, Trevor. "A Loser Makes It Big: **Steve McQueen.**" *SEP* 240 (14 Jan 67) 26–29.

Levy, Alan. "Voice of the Underground Cinema." *NYTM* (19 Sep 65) 70+. About **Jonas Mekas**, editor of *Film Culture* magazine.

Méliès, Georges. "The Silver Lining." *S&S* 7 (No. 25, Spring 38) 7–9. French film maker reminisces about the laughter and pleasure that went on behind the camera during production.

Brakhage, Stan. "Georges Méliès." *Caterpillar* (No. 11, Spring 70) 2–14. A study of the man and his films.

O'Leary, Liam. "Raquel Meller." *Cinema Studies* 2 (No. 4, June 67) 61–64. Biography of the silent star in Spain and France.

Breitbart, Eric. "An Interview with Jean-Pierre Melville." *F Cult* (No. 35, 1964–1965) 15–19.

Milne, Tom. "*Le Deuxième Souffle.*" *S&S* 36 (Spring 67) 85–87. Jean-Pierre Melville's new film is different from his previous thrillers.

Nogueira, Rui, and François Truchaud. "A Samurai in Paris." *S&S* 37 (Summer 68) 118–123. An interview with Jean-Pierre Melville, who began his career in the 1940s, on his latest production, *Le Samourai,* and other films.

Menjou, Adolphe. "Man of Two Worlds—and 250 Movies." *F&F* 7 (No. 11, Aug 61) 8–9. Reflections on his stay in Hollywood from 1920, and on his career.

Kolodny, Irving. "The Man Who Made *Closely Watched Trains.*" *Action* 3 (No. 3, May–June 68) 13–14. An account of a meeting with Jiri Menzel, including quotations.

Levy, Alan. "A Promised Land . . ." *NYTM* (9 Feb 69) 28–29+. On the career of Czech director Jiri Menzel.

Losano, Wayne A. "Romance and Irony in the Films of Russ Meyer." *J Pop Cult* 4 (No. 1, Summer 70) 286–291. Application of the traditional literary terms to his films.

Schickel, Richard. "Porn and Man at Yale." *Harper's* 241 (July 70). *See 4k(8).* About Russ Meyer.

LaBadie, Donald W. "Toshiro Mifune: Japan's Top Sword." *Show* 3 (May 63) 79–80+. His acting career; films made with Kurosawa; Hollywood's false picture of Japan.

Milius, John. "Toshiro Mifune: An Appreciation." *Cinema* (Calif) 3 (No. 6, Winter 67) 26–28. On the Japanese actor.

Gambol, Juliette. "An Interview." *Cinema* (Calif) 3 (No. 6, Winter 67) 27+. With Toshiro Mifune, Japanese actor.

Guy, Rory. "An Interview with Toshiro Mifune." *Cinema* (Calif) 5 (No. 1, 1969) 28–31.

Goodman, Ezra. "Directed by Lewis Milestone." *Th Arts* 27 (Feb 43) 111–119. Life and techniques of this freelance director.

Reisz, Karel. "Milestone and War." *Sequence* (No. 14, 1952). *See 4k(12).*

Feinstein, Herbert. "Interview with Lewis Milestone." *F Cult* (No. 34, 1964) 25–27. At San Francisco film festival.

"Stuart Millar." *Film* (No. 33, Autumn 62). *See 6c(1).*

Gray, Martin. "Without a Formula." *F&F* 3 (No. 5, Feb 57) 6. Director David Miller and his *The Opposite Sex* and *The Story of Esther Costello.*

Johnson, Ian. "Mills." *F&F* 8 (No. 9, June 62) 22–23+. On the acting career of John Mills.

Harcourt-Smith, Simon. "Vincente Minnelli." *S&S* 21 (Jan–Mar 52) 115–119. His career, his talents, some of his films.

Johnson, Albert. "The Films of Vincente Minnelli: Part I." *FQ* 12 (No. 2, Winter 58) 21–35. "The director-as-artist, working freely in a milieu that is too often accused of insensitivity"; analysis of his films from *Cabin in the Sky* (1942) to *The Bad and the Beautiful* (1952); detailed scene descriptions.

Johnson, Albert. "The Films of Vincente Minnelli: Part II." *FQ* 12 (No. 3, Spring 59) 32–42. From *The Band Wagon* (1952) to *Some Came Running* (1958) as Minnelli turns to other genres than the musical with increasing frequency; Johnson finds a consistent tendency toward stylization whatever the subject matter.

McVay, Douglas. "The Magic of Minnelli." *F&F* 5 (No. 9, June 59) 11+.

Minnelli, Vincente. "The Rise and Fall of the Musical." *F&F* 8 (No. 4, Jan 62) 9. Interview; his general reflections on filming and his own films.

Shivas, Mark. "Minnelli's Method." *Movie* (No. 1, June 62) 17–18. His attention to detail; his refusal to write his own scripts; particular aspects of *Four Horsemen of the Apocalypse.*

"No Method: Vincente Minnelli." *Movie* (No. 1, June 62) 20–24. Parts of the script for *Four Horsemen of the Apocalypse* are interfaced with an interview with the American director, in which he discusses the film.

Reynolds, C. "Interview with Vincente Minnelli." *Pop Photog* 51 (July 62) 106–107+.

Serebrinsky, Ernesto, and Oscar Garaycochea. "Vincente Minnelli: Interviewed in Argentina." *Movie* (No. 10, June 63) 23–28. The director discusses his films and his work; filmography on pp. 33–35.

Galling, Dennis Lee. "Vincente Minnelli." *FIR* 15 (No. 3, Mar 64) 129–140. Career and films of American director.

Ames, Aydelott. "Mary Miles Minter." *FIR* 20 (No. 8, Oct 69) 473–489. Career of silent-screen actress; film list by DeWitt Bodeen pp. 490–495.

"The Big M's." *Time* 77 (23 June 61) 51. A look at the Harold and Walter Mirisch Hollywood production company.

Ringgold, Gene. "Robert Mitchum." *FIR* 15 (No. 5, May 64) 257–279. Biography and film listing of the American actor.

Mitchell, George, and William K. Everson. "Tom Mix." *FIR* 8 (Oct 57) 387–397. Life and film career of the actor-writer-director who brought showmanship to the Western.

Richie, Donald, and J. L. Anderson. "**Kenji Mizoguchi.**" *S&S* 25 (Autumn 55) 76–81. A thorough discussion of his work since 1922, when he directed his first picture; his life almost traces the different phases of Japanese cinema.

Mocky, **Jean-Pierre.** "Penetrating the Commercial Barrier." *F&F* 8 (No. 1, Oct 61) 9+. Interview with the actor-writer.

Allan, Rupert. "**Marilyn Monroe** . . . A Serious Blonde Who Can Act." *Look* 15 (No. 22, 23 Oct 51) 40–47. Her life and career.

Baker, Peter. "The **Monroe** Doctrine." *F&F* 2 (No. 12, Sep 56) 12. Marilyn Monroe interviewed.

Odets, Clifford. "To Whom It May Concern: **Marilyn Monroe.**" *Show* 2 (Oct 62) 67+. Her acting career and Hollywood's treatment of her.

Roman, Robert C. "**Marilyn Monroe.**" *FIR* 13 (No. 8, Oct 62) 449–468. On the occasion of her death, a biography and film chronology.

Fenin, George. "M. M." *F&F* 9 (No. 4, Jan 63) 23–24. On **Marilyn Monroe** as sex symbol.

Billard, Ginette. "Rough Stuff from the Song Man." *F&F* 2 (No. 11, Aug 56) 13. On **Yves Montand.**

Smith, Jack. "The Perfect Filmic Appositeness of **Maria Montez.**" *F Cult* (No. 27, 1962–1963) 28–32. A tribute to the film actress.

Reynolds, Quentin. "Man with a Union Card." *Collier's* 103 (1 Apr 39) 22+. As member of Screen Actors Guild, **Robert Montgomery** works for better conditions for actors.

Spears, Jack. "**Colleen Moore.**" *FIR* 14 (Aug–Sep 63) 403–424. Career study of the actress; filmography.

"People of Talent (3): **Agnes Moorehead.**" *S&S* 25 (Autumn 55) 84. Her films and style.

Bowers, Ronald L. "**Agnes Moorehead.**" *FIR* 17 (No. 5, May 66) 293–314. Career and film chronology.

"**Kenneth More.**" *F&F* 1 (No. 7, Apr 55) 3. Career sketch of the British actor.

Stanbrook, Alan. "The Star They Couldn't Photograph." *F&F* 9 (No. 5, Feb 63) 10–14. On **Jeanne Moreau,** her life and acting on stage and film.

Duras, Marguerite. "The Affairs of **Jeanne Moreau.**" *Show* 3 (Mar 63) 174–175+. Her acting career; comments from Moreau on why she chose particular roles.

Collins, Larry, and Dominique Lapierre. "The Name Is **Moreau** (Not Bardot)." *NYTM* (21 Mar 65) 46–47+. On the career of actress Jeanne Moreau.

Jennings, C. Robert. "**Jeanne Moreau.**" *SEP* 238 (10 Apr 65) 86–88. The French actress' roles.

Lindsay, Michael. "An Interview with **Jeanne Moreau.**" *Cinema* (Calif) 5 (No. 3, 1969) 15–17. Her comments on directors: Antonioni, Malle, Welles, and Truffaut.

Bodeen, DeWitt. "**Antonio Moreno.**" *FIR* 18 (No. 6, June–July 67) 325–344. Biography and film chronology of actor of the 1920s.

Morley, **Robert.** "I Hate Acting." *F&F* 11 (No. 10, July 65) 5–7. Interview about the actor and his career.

O'Leary, Liam. "**Ivan Mosjoukine.**" *Silent Picture* (No. 3, Summer 69) 11–15; (No. 5, Winter 69–70) 13–16. Actor who exiled himself from Russia to Paris; second article includes French films he acted in and directed.

Godfrey, Lionel. "Flawed Genius." *F&F* 13 (No. 4, Jan 67) 47–52. On the films of **Robert Mulligan.**

Blakeston, Oswell. "**Maxwell Munden**—A New Signature." *S&S* 17 (No. 68, Winter 48–49) 194. British scenarist-director-producer.

Astruc, Alexandre. "Fire and Ice." *CdC in Eng* (No. 1, Jan 66) 69–73. **F. W. Murnau** is the greatest poet cinema has ever known because he conveys themes through his employment of all the elements of the *mise-en-scène.*

Schonert, Vernon L. "**James Murray.**" *FIR* 19 (No. 10, Dec 68) 618–623. Brief career of one of the stars of King Vidor's *The Crowd.*

Anderson, Thom. "**Eadweard Muybridge.**" *F Cult* (No. 41, Summer 66) 22–24. Brief survey of the photographs of human and animal movement by this pioneer.

N

Phillips, Gene. "**Silvio Narizzano:** Portrait of a Film-Maker." *Take One* 1 (No. 9, 1968) 6–7. An interview with the British-Canadian director and an analysis of his films.

Austen, David. "*Blue.*" *F&F* 14 (No. 11, Aug 68) 5–9. Interview with director **Silvio Narizzano** about *Blue* and other films.

Nash, Johnny. "My Way to Escape." *F&F* 5 (No. 12, Sep 59). *See 2b(7).*

Coulson, Alan A. "**Anna Neagle.**" *FIR* 18 (No. 3, Mar 67) 149–178. Biography and film listing for the British actress.

George, Manfred. "**Hildegarde Neff.**" *FIR* 6 (Nov 55) 445–448. Life and career of the German actress.

"Director-Artist." *Life* 16 (19 June 44) 65–66+. Pictorial sketch of director **Jean Negulesco** at work with his canvas between takes of *The Conspirators.*

Spears, Jack. "**Marshall Neilan.**" *FIR* 13 (No. 9, Nov 62) 517–540. Career and film chronology of the director.

Nelson, **Gene.** "Working in Hollywood." *Dance Mag* 30 (May 56). *See 2b(8).*

Casty, Alan. "A Story About People, That's My Clay—An Interview with **Ralph Nelson.**"

F Com 3 (No. 3, Summer 65) 2–10. Biography and filmography; director who began in TV says, "Every project takes on its own style"; discusses *Lilies of the Field, Once a Thief,* and other films.

Jacobs, Jack. "**Alfred Newman.**" *FIR* 10 (Aug–Sep 59) 403–414. His life and musical career; an index to the films he has provided the music for, in the role of either conductor-composer or music director-adaptor.

Farber, Stephen. "The Writer in American Films." *FQ* 21 (No. 4, Summer 68) *See 2d(1).* About **David Newman.**

Eyles, Allen. "The Other Brando." *F&F* 11 (No. 4, Jan 65) 7–11. Study of the career of **Paul Newman.**

Newman, Paul. "Success Begins at 40." *F&F* 12 (No. 4, Jan 66) 5–8. Interview about his career as an actor.

Wilson, Jane. "**Paul Newman:** What If My Eyes Turn Brown?" *SEP* 241 (24 Feb 68) 26–30+. His career and directing of *Rachel, Rachel.*

"Interview: **Paul Newman.**" *Playboy* 15 (No. 7, July 68) 59–74. His movies, his campaigning for Eugene McCarthy, his theories of acting.

Diehl, Digby. "The Anti-Hero as Director." *Action* 4 (No. 3, May–June 69) 15–18. An interview with **Paul Newman** in which he discusses directing and *Rachel, Rachel.*

Pattinson, Ivan. "The Villain of the Piece." *F&F* 1 (No. 4, Jan 55) 7. A review of the career and analysis of the stage personality of British actor **Robert Newton.**

Jensen, Paul. "The Career of **Dudley Nichols.**" *F Com* 6 (No. 4, Winter 70–71) 56–63. The screenwriter, best known for his work with John Ford, wrote articles about the need for the word to bow to the image, but his own desire to express important ideas and to be respectful of important plays resulted in rather traditional scripts; filmography.

"Interview: **Mike Nichols.**" *Playboy* 13 (No. 6, June 66) 63–74. Views of the director of *Who's Afraid of Virginia Woolf?*

Nichols, Mike. "It Depends on How You Look at It." *F&F* 15 (No. 2, Nov 68) 4–8. Interview about this director's films.

"Some Are More Yossarian Than Others." *Time* 95 (15 June 70) 66–68+. Production and critique of *Catch-22;* profile of director **Mike Nichols.**

Gelmis, Joseph. "**Mike Nichols** Talks About His Films." *Atlantic* 225 (Feb 70) 71–77. Interview about *Catch-22* and previous films.

Winge, John H. "**Asta Nielsen.**" *S&S* 19 (Apr 50) 58–59. Brief tribute to and description of the Danish actress, who has not been able to work in recent years.

"The Screen's First Tragedienne: **Asta Nielsen.**" *Image* 4 (No. 3, Mar 55) 24. Brief biography of the Danish actress.

Luft, Herbert G. "**Asta Nielsen.**" *FIR* 7 (Jan 56) 19–26. The Danish actress' career in silent films, including *Hamlet* (1922), in which she portrayed the title role, and one talkie.

Thomas, Anthony. "**David Niven.**" *FIR* 20 (No. 2, Feb 62) 92–100. Career biography; index by Clifford McCarty pp. 101–117.

Spolar, B., and M. Hammond. "How to Work in Hollywood and Still Be Happy." *Th Arts* 37 (Aug 53) 80+. Composer **Alex North**'s formula.

Reisner, Joel, and Bruce Kane. "An Interview with **Alex North.**" *Cinema* (Calif) 5 (No. 4, 1969) 42–45. This composer came to Hollywood to work for Elia Kazan, after doing several documentaries.

Bodeen, DeWitt. "**Ramon Novarro.**" *FIR* 18 (No. 9, Nov 67) 528–547. Career and film chronology.

Bodeen, DeWitt. "**Ramon Novarro.**" *Silent Picture* (No. 3, Summer 69) 3–10. A biographical sketch, by a friend, of Ramon Novarro—his breaks, setbacks, and changing character.

O

Martin, David. "**George O'Brien.**" *FIR* 13 (No. 9, Nov 62) 541–561. Career and film listing of the Western actor.

Alpert Hollis. "View from the 28th Floor." *Sat Rev* (24 Dec 66). *See 6b(2).* About **Robert H. O'Brien,** MGM executive.

Mitchell, George. "**Sidney Olcott.**" *FIR* 5 (Apr 54) 175–181. The late director's silent-film career, which began in 1907 and ended in 1927, after precedent-making location trips to Florida, Ireland, and to Palestine for *From the Manger to the Cross.*

Hicks, Schuyler. "A Lady to Remember." *Cinema* (Calif) 1 (No. 5, Aug–Sep 63) 1–5. Portrait of **Edna May Oliver** on her death.

Brinson, Peter. "The Real Interpreter." *F&F* 1 (No. 7, Apr 55) 4–5. Sir **Laurence Olivier** as the interpreter of Shakespeare; comments on three films.

McVay, Douglas. "Hamlet to Clown." *F&F* 8 (No. 12, Sep 62) 16–19. On **Laurence Olivier**'s acting career.

Hart, Henry. "**Laurence Olivier.**" *FIR* 18 (No. 10, Dec 67) 593–612. Career and film listing.

Coleman, Terry. "**Olivier** Now." *Show* (June 70) 42–47. Comments on the acting career of Sir Laurence Olivier (on both stage and screen), with emphasis on the filming of *Three Sisters* at Shepperton Studios (also directed by Olivier).

Solomos, George Paul. "**Ermanno Olmi.**" *F Cult* (No. 24, 1962) 35–36. Brief note on the Italian director of *Il Posto.*

Houston, Penelope. "The Organisation Man." *S&S* 33 (Spring 64) 78–81. An appraisal of *Il Posto* and its little-known director **Ermanno**

Olmi; "work has been one of the great neglected subjects of the contemporary cinema."

Bachmann, Gideon. "Ermanno Olmi: The New Italian Films." *Nation* 198 (25 May 64) 540–543. Renaissance in Italian films by Olmi and others in northern Italy, especially in Milan.

Lane, John Francis. "Ermanno Olmi: 'The Cinema Is Life, Life Is the Cinema.' " *S&S* 39 (Summer 70) 148–152. Director of *Il Posto* says he still is very much outside present Italian cinema and its themes: "The cinema is a vehicle for ideas; it is not an object." . . . One searches for "reasons behind the individual tragedies."

Koval, Francis. "Interview with Ophuls." *S&S* 19 (July 50) 192–194+. Former actor **Max Ophuls** traces his career, assesses his own films.

Archer, Eugene. "**Ophuls** and the Romantic Tradition." *Yale French Studies* (No. 17, 1956) 3–5. Appraisal of director Max Ophuls' aesthetic as entirely divorced from issues of contemporary civilization.

Mason, James, Peter Ustinov, *et al.* "**Max Ophuls.**" *S&S* 27 (Summer 57) 49–50. Tributes to the director, who died on 26 March 1957.

Sarris, Andrew. "Memory and **Max Ophuls.**" *Moviegoer* (No. 3, Summer 66) 2–7. Tribute and analysis; his use of the movie camera.

Williams, Forrest. "The Mastery of Movement: An Appreciation of **Max Ophuls.**" *F Com* 5 (No. 4, Winter 69) 70–74. Mostly about *Letter from an Unknown Woman;* brief biography.

Koch, Howard. "Script to Screen with **Max Ophuls.**" *F Com* 6 (No. 4, Winter 70–71) 41–43. Reminiscence of working with the French director, especially on *Letter from an Unknown Woman.*

"Long Way from Hollywood." *Woman's Home Companion* 83 (Nov 56). *See 5, Morris Engel.* About **Ruth Orkin.**

Cameron, Ian. "**Nagisa Oshima.**" *Movie* (No. 17, Winter 69–70) 7–15. Comments on Oshima's work, with an interview and a filmography.

"Oshima." *Film* (No. 58, Spring 70) 4–6. A brief overview of the work of the Japanese director **Nagisa Oshima.**

Luft, Herbert G. "**Richard Oswald.**" *FIR* 9 (Oct 58) 443–449. Career of the international writer and film director who has made more than 200 German, Austrian, French, and American films.

"Interview: **Peter O'Toole.**" *Playboy* 12 (No. 9, Sep 65) 91–100. Rising British actor.

Owen, Don. "Adrift in a Sea of Mud." *Take One* 1 (No. 6, 1967) 4–6. The Canadian film maker discusses his work and his future plans.

Richie, Donald. "The Later Films of **Yasujiro Ozu.**" *FQ* 13 (No. 1, Fall 59) 18–25. His spare techniques and his almost exclusive use of the family drama.

Milne, Tom. "Flavour of Green Tea Over Rice." *S&S* 32 (Autumn 63) 182–186. The development, subject matter, and style of **Yasujiro Ozu,** frequently described as the most Japanese of directors.

Richie, Donald. "**Yasujiro Ozu:** The Syntax of His Films." *FQ* 17 (No. 2, Winter 63–64) 11–16. Grammar (episodes, simple shots, cuts), structure (circular sequence), tempo (psychological) are all part of Ozu's "oblique" method of film making, which has only one object, the revelation of character.

Ryu, Chishu. "**Yasujiro Ozu.**" *S&S* 33 (Spring 64) 92. A leading actor in almost all his films since the war provides these reminiscences about the Japanese director, who died in December.

Hatch, Robert. "The Family of **Ozu.**" *Nation* 198 (22 June 64) 638–639. New York festival shows films by Japanese director Yasujiro Ozu.

Nakamura, Haruji, and Leonard Schrader. "**Ozu** Spectrum." *Cinema* (Calif) 6 (No. 1, 1970) 2–8. Introduction; two interviews about his films from *Kinema Jumpo;* brief article by actor Chishu Ryu; and a short article by Yasujiro Ozu himself from *Kinema Jumpo.*

P

Moore, John C. "Pabst, Dovjenko: A Comparison." *Close Up* 9 (No. 3, Sep 32) 176–182. About **G. W. Pabst.**

Potamkin, Harry Alan. "**Pabst** and the Social Film." *Hound & Horn* 6 (No. 2, Jan–Mar 33) 293–305. History of the German film maker's beginnings in cinema, analysis of his style and films.

Patris, Ludo. "**G. W. Pabst** and *Don Quixote.*" *CQ* 1 (No. 4, Summer 33). An interview about his intentions on this film.

Daugherty, Frank. "The **Pabst** Arrival." *Close Up* 10 (No. 4, Dec 33) 332–335. Brief comments on Pabst and his work, including quotes from the German director.

Kracauer, Siegfried. "Analysis of **Pabst.**" *S&S* 16 (No. 61, Spring 47) 21–25. An extract from Kracauer's book *From Caligari to Hitler* (Princeton University Press).

Bachmann, Gideon (ed.) "**G. W. Pabst.**" *Cinemages* 3 (May 55) 1–94. An entire issue devoted to Pabst, including an index to his work, biographical notes, and six articles on Pabst by various authors.

Card, James. "Out of Pandora's Box." *Image* 5 (No. 7, Sep 56) 148–155. New light on **G. W. Pabst** from his lost star, Louise Brooks.

Luft, Herbert G. "G. W. Pabst." *FIR* 15 (No. 2, Feb 64) 93–116. Life and films.

Brooks, Louise. "Pabst and Lulu." *S&S* 34 (Summer 65). *See 5, Louise Brooks.*

Luft, Herbert G. "G. W. Pabst." *F&F* 13 (No. 7, Apr 67) 18–24. On the man and his career.

Luft, Herbert G. "G. W. Pabst." *Cinema* (Calif) 3 (No. 6, Winter 67) 15–17+.

Eisner, Lotte. "Meeting with Pabst." *S&S* 36 (Autumn 67) 209. Personal recollections, on the death of German director G. W. Pabst in May 1967.

Stuart, John. "Working with Pabst." *Silent Picture* (No. 8, Autumn 70) 25–26. Actor reminisces about being directed by G. W. Pabst in *L'Atlantide*.

Ford, Charles. "Marcel Pagnol." *FIR* 21 (No. 4, Apr 70) 197–203. Biography and film chronology of the French producer-director-writer.

Maddison, John. "The World of Jean Painlevé." *S&S* 19 (Aug 50) 249–252. This maker of scientific films is also an explorer of the beauties of the universe.

Seton, Marie. "George Pal." *S&S* 5 (No. 18, Summer 36) 13. Critical comments on cartoon and puppet films by a young Hungarian who makes them.

Knight, Arthur. "Hermes Pan, Who Is He?" *Dance Mag* 34 (Jan 60) 40–43. Dance director.

Lindsay, Michael. "Gordon Parks Talks About *Learning Tree*." *Cinema* (Calif) 5 (No. 1, 1969) 14–19. Interview with the black American director on his first feature film.

Cherry, Richard. "The Many Worlds of Gordon Parks." *Action* 4 (No. 2, Mar–Apr 69) 12–15. Interview with the American director.

Parsons, Harriet. "What Producers Do." *FIR* 5 (Oct 54). *See 2a(3).*

McClelland, Douglas. "Eleanor Parker." *FIR* 13 (No. 3, Mar 62) 135–148. Career and films of the American actress.

Murray, William. "Letter from Rome." *New Yorker* 38 (21 Apr 62) 167–169. Pier Paolo Pasolini, his subject matter and *Accattone*.

"Pier Paolo Pasolini: An Epical-Religious View of the World." (Tr. by Michael Graham and Latizia Ciotti Miller.) *FQ* 18 (No. 4, Summer 65) 31–45. Influenced, he says, by Dreyer, Chaplin, and Mizoguchi, and by the painting of Masaccio, the novelist-director is doubtful if he can define realism and points out that in Italy there is no "average language," hence any actor's lines are "fictitious"; transcript of an appearance before the film school in Rome, before he had begun *The Gospel According to St. Matthew.*

Hitchens, Gordon. "Pier Paolo Pasolini and the Art of Directing." *F Com* 3 (No. 4, Fall 65) 20–24. Production notes and responses to *The Gospel According to St. Matthew;* biographical sketch of director; poem by Pasolini blaming Pope Pius XII for not doing more for the poor.

Blue, James. "Pier Paolo Pasolini." *F Com* 3 (No. 4, Fall 65) 25–32. Interview emphasizes director's way of handling actors, trained and untrained, in *The Gospel According to St. Matthew.*

Pasolini, Pier Paolo. "Symposium." *Arts in Soc* 4 (No. 1, Winter 67) 72–76. Director's responses to questionnaire.

Gervais, Marc. "Pier Paolo Pasolini: Contestators." *S&S* 38 (Winter 68–69) 2–7. A short history of the difficulties encountered by *Edipo Re* and *Teorema;* an extensive analysis of both films.

Bragin, John. "Pier Paolo Pasolini: Poetry as a Compensation." *F Soc Rev* 4 (No. 5, 1969) 12–18; (No. 6, 1969) 18–28; (No. 7, 1969) 35–40. Critique in three parts of the Italian director's work.

Gough-Yates, Kevin. "Pier Paolo Pasolini and the "Rule of Analogy." *Studio Inter* 177 (Mar 69) 117–119. The influence of painting on his work.

Macdonald, Susan. "Pasolini: Rebellion, Art, and a New Society." *Screen* 10 (No. 3, May–June 69) 19–34. The connections between his personal life and his films.

Purdon, Noel. "Pasolini: The Film of Alienation." *Cinema* (Cambridge) (Nos. 6–7, Aug 70) 14–21. Structural and formal methods Pasolini uses to create the sense of alienation.

Chandler, David. "Keep the People Nice." *Collier's* 127 (5 May 51) 26–27+. On producer Joe Pasternak.

Shipp, Cameron. "Never Make an Audience Think!" *SEP* 226 (6 Feb 54) 32–33+. Profile of Joe Pasternak, producer of musicals for MGM.

"Charles Pathé Honored." *Image* 3 (No. 7, Oct 54) 47. At congress (1954) of European film technicians.

Sadoul, Georges. "Napoleon of the Cinema." *S&S* 27 (Spring 58) 183. Charles Pathé began with phonographs and a peep show; later he had studios, laboratories, and theatres all over the world; he sold virtually his entire empire, and lived on, a wealthy man, until December 1957.

Pearson, George. "Lambeth Wall to Leicester Square." *S&S* 7 (No. 28, Winter 38–39) 150–151. An early British film figure reminisces.

O'Dell, Paul. "Pearson on Film." *Silent Picture* (No. 2, Spring 69) 2. Impressions of George Pearson, British movie pioneer, on a TV show about him.

Honri, Baynham. "George Pearson Remembered." *Silent Picture* (No. 2, Spring 69) 3–4.

Dickinson, Thorold. "Working with Pearson." *Silent Picture* (No. 2, Spring 69) 5–7. Anecdotal account of George Pearson in the 1920s.

Pearson, George. "George Pearson, The Man and His Art." *Silent Picture* (Spring 69) 15–18. Quotes primarily on his films.

Stein, Jeanne. "Gregory Peck." *FIR* 18 (No. 3, Mar 67) 129–145. Career and film listing.

"Wanted: Sam Peckinpah." *Cinema* (Calif) 1 (No. 4, June–July 63) 4–6+. Interview with the film maker.

Callenbach, Ernest. "A Conversation with Sam Peckinpah." *FQ* 17 (No. 2, Winter 63–64) 3–10. Descriptions of his first two films and two of his TV scripts, followed by a lively discussion.

McArthur, Colin. "Sam Peckinpah's West." *S&S* 36 (Autumn 67) 180–183. "Paradox is central to his vision."

McCarty, John Alan. "Sam Peckinpah and *The Wild Bunch*." *F Her* 5 (No. 2, Winter 69–70) 1–10+. Review of films and writing career.

Medjuck, Joe. "Sam Peckinpah Lets It All Hang Out." *Take One* 2 (No. 3, 1969) 18–20. Interview with the American director, including discussion of *The Wild Bunch*.

Schrader, Paul. "Sam Peckinpah Going to Mexico." *Cinema* (Calif) 5 (No. 3, 1969) 19–25. His troubles, his film *The Wild Bunch*, and his "fascist edge."

Farber, Stephen. "Peckinpah's Return." *FQ* 23 (No. 1, Fall 69) 2–11. Close analysis of *The Wild Bunch*, followed by an interview with Sam Peckinpah, the director, who says he identifies with outlaws.

Whitehall, Richard. "Talking with Peckinpah." *S&S* 38 (Autumn 69) 172–175. Sam Peckinpah reminisces about his pioneer ancestors and his own youth in central California; he also comments on *Major Dundee*, badly cut by the studio, his new film *The Wild Bunch*, and his TV writing.

Cutts, John. "Shoot!" *F&F* 16 (No. 1, Oct 69) 4–8. Interview with Sam Peckinpah about his career.

Armes, Roy. "Sam Peckinpah." *London Mag* new series 9 (No. 12, Mar 70) 101–106.

Brower, Brock. "An Untheatrical Director Takes the Stage." *NYTM* (20 May 62) 32–33+. On the career of Arthur Penn.

Mayersberg, Paul. *"The Miracle Worker* and *The Left-Handed Gun*." *Movie* (No. 3, Oct 62) 26–28. A comparison of the two films made by Arthur Penn, noting the common elements such as the problems of communication between people and the virtual uselessness of the spoken word.

Penn, Arthur. "*Bonnie and Clyde*: Private Morality and Public Violence." *Take One* 1 (No. 6, 1967). *See 9, Bonnie and Clyde.*

Hanson, Curtis Lee. "An Interview with Arthur Penn." *Cinema* (Calif) 3 (No. 5, Summer 67) 11–16.

Lindsay, Michael. "An Interview with Arthur Penn." *Cinema* (Calif) 5 (No. 3, 1969) 32–36.

Hillier, Jim. "Arthur Penn." *Screen* 10 (No. 1, Jan–Feb 69) 5–12. Brief survey and analysis of Penn's published views about American myths.

Wood, Robin. "Arthur Penn in Canada." *Movie* (No. 18, Winter 70–71) 26–36. An extensive interview with the American director; special mention of *Little Big Man*, which he was then shooting.

Gray, Martin. "Seeing Himself as Others See Him." *F&F* 3 (No. 3, Dec 56) 15. François Perier, the French actor, on acting and his career.

"Anthony Perkins." *Cinema* (Calif) 2 (No. 5, Mar–Apr 65) 17–19. Actor discusses acting and directors in interview.

Bean, Robin. "Pinning Down the Quicksilver." *F&F* 11 (No. 10, July 65) 44–49. Anthony Perkins talks about his acting career.

Bayer, William. "Interview with Frank Perry." *F Com* 1 (No. 5, Summer 63) 15–22. The director of *David and Lisa* talks about his intentions in that film, the work of other directors, and the difficulty of getting three minutes of film completed each day; brief biography.

Boeth, Richard. "New Face, Old Pro." *Sat Rev* 46 (28 Dec 63) 21–23. How Frank Perry, independent film maker, got backing for *David and Lisa* and became an independent director; part of *Saturday Review* report "The Anti-Formula Film."

Tyler, Parker. "Sidney Peterson." *F Cult* (No. 19, 1959) 38–43. The career of this experimental film maker.

Philipe, Gérard. "In the Margin." *Sequence* (No. 7, Spring 49) 23. The young French actor comments from his own experience on the nature of film making.

Billard, Ginette. "Philipe, the Actor, May End His Career." *F&F* 2 (No. 1, Oct 55) 10. Biography of Gérard Philipe, French star.

Phillips, Leslie. "Criticism Follows Success." *F&F* 7 (No. 8, May 61) 20. A British free-lance actor discusses his career.

Pleasence, Donald. "Taking the Pick." *F&F* 8 (No. 11, Aug 62) 11–12. Reflections on his acting career.

"Irving Pichel (1891–1954)—'Wonderful to Have Had You with Us.'" *QFRTV* 9 (No. 2, Winter 54) 109–123. Memorial article about Irving Pichel, teacher, writer, actor, and director, with letters from friends.

"Shrewd." *Time* 17 (11 May 31) 46. Mary Pickford is buying up her old pictures to destroy them so that she will not look "ridiculous in 20 years."

Harriman, Margaret Case. "Mary Pickford." *New Yorker* (7 Apr 34) 29–33. Profile of the actress.

Card, James. "The Films of **Mary Pickford**." *Image* 8 (No. 4, Dec 59) 172–191. Article includes a selective list of her early short films and complete list of her features.

Spears, Jack. "**Mary Pickford's** Directors." *FIR* 17 (No. 2, Feb 66) 71–95. Reviews Pickford's relations with directors such as Ince, Griffith, Kirkwood, and Olcott.

Marill, Alvin H. "**Walter Pidgeon**." *FIR* 20 (No. 9, Nov 69) 528–548. Career and film chronology.

English, Richard. "Gaudiest Producers in Hollywood, Pine and Thomas." *SEP* 225 (3 Jan 53). See 6d. About **Bill Pine** and partner.

Nelson, G. "Harold Pinter Goes to the Movies." *Chicago Rev* 19 (No. 1, 1966) 33–43. Influences of film on **Pinter's** work.

Weinberg, Gretchen. "Interview with **Ernest Pintoff**." *F Cult* (No. 31, 1963–1964) 54–58. About his short films *The Critic, The Interview*.

MacDonald, Dwight. "Complete Works of **Ernest Pintoff**." *Esq* 61 (Apr 64). See 2h(4).

Selby, Stuart. "**Ernest Pintoff**, Fireman." *F Com* 2 (No. 3, Summer 64) 4–9. Maker of six shorts, five of them animated, including *The Critic*, makes a feature, *Harvey Middleman, Fireman;* notes on location work and on Pintoff's themes.

Poitier, Sidney. "They Call Me a Do-It-Yourself Man." *F&F* 5 (No. 12, Sep 59) 7+. Black actor writes of working his way into the profession.

Poitier, Sidney. "Talking of Corruption." *F&F* 7 (No. 11, Aug 61) 7. The actor would like to direct a picture about corruption in society.

Weinberg, Gretchen. "Interview with **Roman Polanski**." *S&S* 33 (Winter 63–64) 32–33. Taped during Polanski's visit to New York for the festival showing of his *Knife in the Water;* opinions about film making in Poland, his short films, and some films he had seen.

Delahaye, Michel, and Jean-André Fieschi. "Landscape of a Mind: Interview with **Roman Polanski**." *CdC in Eng* (No. 3, 1966) 28–35. His beginnings in Polish cinema; *Repulsion, Knife in the Water, Cul-de-Sac*.

Bucher, Felix. "To Mark Time: Questions to **Roman Polanski**." *Camera* 45 (No. 3, Mar 66) 50–53.

"On the Scene: **Roman Polanski**, Pole Vaulting." *Playboy* 13 (No. 10, Oct 66) 162. Films he has made, plus brief biography.

Kahan, Saul. "Transylvania, **Polanski** Style." *Cinema* (Calif) 3 (No. 3, Dec 66) 7–9. On Roman Polanski—primarily about his work on *The Vampire Killers*, a spoof of the horror film.

Engle, Harrison. "**Polanski** in New York." *F Com* 5 (No. 1, Fall 68) 4–11. Expatriate Polish director interviewed by American short-film maker; emphasis on *Rosemary's Baby;* extracts from reviews; biography; filmography.

Ross, T. J. "**Roman Polanski**, *Repulsion*, and the New Mythology." *F Her* 4 (No. 2, Winter 68–69) 1–10+. The intrusion of the world on the hero or heroine; "the cry of the maddened spirit" against "the harsh compromises of the mundane world."

McArthur, Colin. "**Polanski**." *S&S* 38 (Winter 68–69) 14–16. "Within the carpet-bag term avant-garde, there are two major influences on Polanski: the theatre of the absurd and surrealism"; the career and trademarks of Roman Polanski, who is of all Polish film makers the least Polish. Analysis of *Rosemary's Baby* on following pages by Beverle Houston and Marsha Kinder.

Reisner, Joel, and Bruce Kane. "An Interview with **Roman Polanski**." *Cinema* (Calif) 5 (No. 2, 1969) 10–15.

McCarty, John Alan. "The **Polanski** Puzzle." *Take One* 2 (No. 5, 1969) 18–21. A study of the director's thematic intentions.

Polanski, Roman. "Satisfaction—A Most Pleasant Feeling." *F&F* 15 (No. 7, Apr 69) 15–18. On his films and the macabre.

Nairn, Tom. "**Roman Polanski**." *Cinema* (Cambridge) (No. 3, June 69) 22–26. Analysis of his themes and structures; with a filmography.

Pollard, Michael J. "The Sexy Flying Machine That Burst from a Cloud." *F&F* 15 (No. 2, Nov 68) 10–12. Interview about his acting career.

Pechter, William. "**Abraham Polonsky** and *Force of Evil*." *FQ* 15 (No. 3, Spring 62) 47–54. An analysis of *Body and Soul* and *Force of Evil;* appended is an interview in which Polonsky discusses the Hollywood blacklist, his early life, and his films.

Pechter, William. "Parts of Some Time Spent with **Abraham Polonsky**." *FQ* 22 (No. 2, Winter 68–69) 14–19. While directing *Tell Them Willie Boy Is Here;* some comments on the blacklist.

Canham, Kingsley. "**Polonsky**." *Film* (No. 58, Spring 70) 12–15. An overview of the work of the American writer-director Abraham Polonsky.

Cook, Jim, and Kingsley Canham. "**Abraham Polonsky** Interviewed." *Screen* 11 (No. 3, Summer 70) 57–73.

Luft, Herbert G. "**Erich Pommer**." *FIR* 10 (Oct 59) 457–469; (Nov 59) 518–533. Two-part study of the German film producer who rose to become the production head of the giant UFA Studios in Germany in 1923 and was responsible for many of the best-known films of the period; his later work in England and the U.S.

"**Ponti**." *New Yorker* 45 (5 Apr 69) 31–32. An interview with Italian producer **Carlo Ponti**; his comments on director-producers, and on some American films; his list of the greatest directors.

Arnold, H. J. P. "Herbert Ponting as a Cinematographer." *Cinema Studies* 2 (No. 3, Mar 67) 47–53. His perfectionism and willingness to take risks in the Antarctic and elsewhere.

Spears, Jack. "Edwin S. Porter." *FIR* 22 (No. 6, June–July 70) 327–354. Career and film listing of first outstanding figure in U.S. picture production.

Thomas, Anthony. "Dick Powell." *FIR* 12 (No. 5, May 61) 267–273. Biography; index by Robert Roman pp. 274–279.

Green, O. O. "Michael Powell." *Movie* (No. 14, Autumn 65) 17–20. A discussion of this British director's work.

Jacobs, Jack. "William Powell." *FIR* 9 (Nov 58) 497–509. Life and career of the actor, with a descriptive index to his ninety-five films.

Roman, Robert C. "Tyrone Power." *FIR* 10 (Jan 59) 5–17+. Biography of the late star, including the films in which he appeared, with the author's appraisal of his roles; index to his films. See also letters (Mar 59) 188.

Preminger, Otto. "Your Taste, My Taste . . . and the Censor's." *F&F* 6 (No. 2, Nov 59) 7+. Interview with Preminger, especially about *Anatomy of a Murder*.

Reid, John Howard. "Both Sides of the Camera." *F&F* 7 (No. 5, Feb 61) 15–16. Analysis of Otto Preminger's work for the cinema, part I.

Reid, John Howard. "Fabulous Saints and Sinners." *F&F* 7 (No. 6, Mar 61) 31–32+. Conclusion of study of films of Otto Preminger.

Archer, Eugene. "Why Preminger?" *Movie* (No. 2, Sep 62) 11–30. Evaluations of Preminger's films; interview with him about *Advise and Consent*.

"Interview with Otto Preminger." *Movie* (No. 4, Nov 62) 18–20. The director discusses his work, especially *Advise and Consent*.

Mayersberg, Paul. "Carmen and Bess." *Movie* (No. 4, Nov 62) 21–25. Analysis of two of Otto Preminger's films, *Carmen Jones* and *Porgy and Bess;* filmography.

Knight, Arthur. "How to Rate a Critic." *Sat Rev* (26 Dec 64). *See 3b*. About Otto Preminger.

Sarris, Andrew. "Preminger's Two Periods—Studio and Solo." *F Com* 3 (No. 3, Summer 65) 12–16. Critical analysis of Otto Preminger, a "director with the personality of a producer" who achieves a "sombre quality" by keeping "his characters in the same frame"; biography follows article.

Cameron, Ian, *et al.* "An Interview with Otto Preminger." *Movie* (No. 13, Summer 65) 14–16. While preparing to work on *Bunny Lake Is Missing*.

Ross, Lillian. "Profiles: Anatomy of a Commercial Interruption." *New Yorker* 41 (19 Feb 66) 42–46+. Article in form of script showing Otto Preminger at work.

Meehan, Thomas. "Otto the Terrible." *SEP* 240 (8 Apr 67) 26–31. On the career of Otto Preminger.

McGuinness, Richard. "Otto Preminger." *On Film* (1970) 36. Comment on the director's life and films.

Bogdanovich, Peter. "Otto Preminger." *On Film* (1970) 37–52. Interview, including report on the making of *Laura*.

Schickel, Richard. "1962: The Year of Paula Prentiss." *Show* 2 (Jan 62) 51–52. The old Hollywood myth of chance discovery is not totally dead after all.

Preston, Catherine Craig. "The Movies and I." *FIR* 8 (Aug–Sep 57) 334–337. As told to John Springer; a short biography of the actress and wife of actor Robert Preston which also surveys his film career.

Peper, William. "Robert Preston." *FIR* 19 (No. 3, Mar 68) 129–141. Career and film listings.

Hackett, Hazel. "Jacques Prévert—Script-Writer and Poet." *S&S* 15 (No. 60, Winter 46–47) 137–139. A critical appreciation.

Anderson, Lindsay. "Encounter with Prévert." *S&S* 23 (July–Sep 53) 4. Note on a visit with the French screenwriter.

Price, Vincent. "Mean, Moody, and Magnificent." *F&F* 11 (No. 6, Mar 65) 5–8. Interview about his acting career.

Marill, Alvin H. "Vincent Price." *FIR* 20 (No. 5, May 69) 276–292. Career and film chronology.

Price, Vincent. "Black Cats and Cobwebs." *F&F* 15 (No. 11, Aug 69) 52–54. On his work in horror films.

Seton, Marie. "A Conversation with V. I. Pudovkin." *S&S* 2 (No. 5, Spring 33) 13–14. His own work and that of his contemporaries in the Soviet Union.

Potamkin, Harry A. "Pudovkin and the Revolutionary Film." *Hound & Horn* 6 (No. 3, Apr–June 33) 480–493. The Russian film maker's beginnings in film; discussion of his films and theoretical writings.

Waddington, C. H. "Two Conversations with Pudovkin." *S&S* 17 (No. 68, Winter 48–49) 159–161.

Weinberg, Herman G. "Vsevelod Pudovkin." *FIR* 3 (Aug–Sep 53) 325–327. A tribute to the late Russian director, with a short survey of his career.

Wright, Basil. "V. I. Pudovkin: 1893–1953." *S&S* 23 (Oct–Dec 53) 105. A tribute, with comments on his works.

Donskoy, Mark. "While His Heart Beat: A tribute to Ivan Pyriev." (Tr. by Steven Hill; no source given.) *F Com* 5 (No. 1, Fall 68) 34–35. Veteran director who once was head of Mosfilm and gave first job to Gregory

Chukhrai is here praised by the director of the Gorky trilogy.

Q

Stanbrook, Alan. "Ya Gotta Have Heart." *F&F* 6 (No. 12, Sep 60). *See 5, Frank Capra.* About director **Richard Quine.**

Johnson, Ian. "**Anthony Quinn.**" *F&F* 8 (No. 5, Feb 62) 13–15+. Analysis of the actor's films; filmography.

Marill, Alvin H. "**Anthony Quinn.**" *FIR* 19 (No. 8, Oct 68) 465–481. Biography and film listing.

Simons, Mary. "The Loving World of **Anthony Quinn.**" *Look* 33 (1 Apr 69) 48–50. An interview.

Quinn, Anthony. "Competing with Myself." *F&F* 16 (No. 5, Feb 70) 6–10. Interview about his acting.

R

"**Bob Rafelson.**" *New Yorker* 46 (24 Oct 70) 41–42. Interview with the director on his films.

Raft, George. "You've Got to Be Tough with Hollywood." *F&F* 8 (No. 10, July 62) 15+. But actor says, "I have always felt I should do what the public wants."

Jacobson, Herbert L. "Homage to **Raimu.**" *Hwd Q* 3 (No. 2, Winter 47–48) 169–171. Brief summary of life and work of late French actor who played men of middle age who seek "peace and limited contentment . . . by the powers of love and reason."

Bronner, Edwin. "**Luise Rainer.**" *FIR* 6 (Oct 55) 390–393. Her film career consisted of more than two Academy Awards, for *The Great Ziegfeld* (1936) and *The Good Earth* (1937).

Stein, Jeanne. "**Claude Rains.**" *FIR* 14 (Nov 63) 513–528. Career study of the actor; filmography.

Thomas, Anthony. "**David Raksin.**" *FIR* 14 (Jan 63) 38–41. Career study of this film-music composer; lists his "film compositions."

Hart, Henry. "**Terry Ramsaye** (1885–1954)." *FIR* 5 (Oct 54). *See 4a(1).*

Aitken, John. "Question of Rank." *Screen Writer* 1 (Aug 45) 1–8. On **J. Arthur Rank,** his studios, theatres, and world market hopes.

Wickmore, Francis Sill. "**J. Arthur Rank.**" *Life* (Oct 45) 107–121.

McEvoy, J. P. "Philosophy of **J. Arthur Rank.**" *Rdrs Dig* 52 (May 48) 40–43. Subheading: "Revealing glimpses of a British tycoon."

Lindsey, Cynthia. "The New Hollywood Tycoon." *Show* 4 (Oct 64) 44–46+. Rise of **Martin Ransohoff;** how he upsets stereotyped notions about the Hollywood producer.

Hanson, Curtis Lee. "**Martin Ransohoff.**" *Cin-*

ema (Calif) 2 (No. 6, July–Aug 65) 19–24. Interview with producer.

Dunne, John G. "Hollywood's Heedless Horseman." *Holiday* 38 (Dec 65) 111–112+. The career of **Martin Ransohoff.**

Cutts, John. "Superswine!" *F&F* 15 (No. 6, Mar 69) 65–67. On **Basil Rathbone's** career.

"People of Talent (4): **Aldo Ray.**" *S&S* 25 (Winter 55–56) 141. Biography and "natural" personality.

Bodeen, DeWitt. "**Charles Ray.**" *FIR* 19 (No. 9, Nov 68) 548–580. Career and film listing of "Ince's Wonder Boy" actor.

Belz, C. I. "Film Poetry of **Man Ray.**" *Criticism* 7 (Spring 65) 117–130. His works are prophetically relevant to contemporary film makers such as Antonioni, Resnais, Truffaut.

Agel, Henri. "**Nicholas Ray.**" *NY F Bul* 2 (No. 11, 1961) 10–11. An analysis of Ray's lyricism as opposed to his social content; includes filmography.

Houston, Penelope, and John Gillett. "Conversations with **Nicholas Ray** and **Joseph Losey.**" *S&S* 30 (Autumn 61) 182–187. Biography of both directors, who, besides being born in the same town in Wisconsin, also arrived at the cinema via theatre and radio, and made their first films for RKO; Ray talks about critics, his favorite directors, and the filming of *Savage Innocents* and *Rebel Without a Cause;* Losey looks back to his Hollywood years, and names *The Prowler* as his favorite film of this period.

Barr, Charles. "**Nicholas Ray:** Adding Up the Details." *Motion* (No. 3, Spring 62) 23–26. Special attention to *King of Kings* and *The James Brothers.*

Perkins, V. F. "The Cinema of **Nicholas Ray.**" *Movie* (No. 9, May 63) 4–10. Emphasis in his films; filmography by David Thomson and Kieran Hickey on pp. 11–13.

Aprà, Adriano, *et al.* "Interview with **Nicholas Ray.**" *Movie* (No. 9, May 63) 14–24.

Ray, Satyajit. "A Long Time on the Little Road." *S&S* 26 (Spring 57) 203–205. Director gives some of his philosophy of film and describes the feelings he had while making **Pather Panchali.**

Gray, Hugh. "**Satyajit Ray.**" *FQ* 12 (No. 2, Winter 58) 4–7. The Indian artist and director talks about his start in the cinema and his film **Pather Panchali.**

Croce, Arlene. "*Pather Panchali* and *Aparajito.*" *F Cult* (No. 19, 1959) 44–50. Long discussion of two **Satyajit Ray** films.

McVay, Douglas. "The Ray Trilogy." *Film* (No. 24, Mar–Apr 60) 21–24. Brief analysis of Satyajit Ray's *Pather Panchali* and the two sequels.

Grimes, Paul. "Indian Moviemaker Who Flees Escape." *NYTM* (26 June 60) 42–43. On **Satyajit Ray.**

Rhode, Eric. "**Satyajit Ray:** A Study." *S&S* 30

(Summer 61) 133–136. "In what way," asks Ray, "can man control the world, and what is the price he must pay for trying to do so?" Rhode considers this as the Promethean theme behind all Ray's films; discussion of the Apu trilogy.

Stanbrook, Alan. "The World of Ray." *F&F* 12 (No. 2, Nov 65) 55–58. On the films of Satyajit Ray.

Melik, Amita. "Reluctant God." *S&S* 35 (Winter 65–66) 21–22. Note on recent critical responses to Satyajit Ray films in India.

Ray, Satyajit. "From Film to Film." *CdC in Eng* (No. 3, 1966) 12–19+. Introduction by Georges Sadoul; the Indian film maker talks about his life, how he began to make films with *Pather Panchali* and his later films; filmography.

Das Gupta, Chidananda. "Ray and Tagore." *S&S* 36 (Winter 66–67) 30–34. Analysis by editor of *Indian Film Culture* of Satyajit Ray's themes and characters that project the Tagore era, the nineteenth-century Bengal renaissance, rather than a modern India with its social and economic problems: "There is no anger, no sense of urgency, and no obvious partisanship for the forces of change. In this sense of resignation and fatality, Ray is Indian to the core."

Glushanok, Paul. "On Ray." *Cinéaste* 1 (No. 1, Summer 67) 3–6. Satyajit Ray's films have such impact because everything is so subtly implied—and then the threads are drawn together.

"Maestro." *New Yorker* 43 (22 July 67) 25–27. Current projects and future plans of Satyajit Ray.

Blue, James. "Satyajit Ray." *F Com* 4 (No. 4, Summer 68) 4–17. Bengali film director interviewed in Calcutta; filmography and biography; emphasis on securing believable performances from untrained actors in the Apu trilogy.

Taper, Bernard. "At Home in Calcutta." *Harper's* 239 (Dec 69) 40–42+. About Satyajit Ray, Indian director.

Ray, Satyajit. "The Oriental Master." *Film* (No. 57, Winter 69–70) 7–8. The Indian director discusses his own work.

Isaksson, Folke. "Conversation with Satyajit Ray." *S&S* 39 (Summer 70) 114–120.

Pechter, William S. "India's Chekhov." *Commonweal* 93 (16 Oct 70) 71–72. Brief survey and judgment of films by Satayajit Ray.

Hunter, Jack F. "Ronald Reagan." *FIR* 18 (No. 4, Apr 67) 207–220. Career and film listing.

Meehan, Thomas. "Between Actors—A Conversation." *Show* 4 (Dec 64). See *3f(1)*. About Robert Redford.

Redgrave, Michael. "I Am Not a Camera." *S&S* 24 (Jan–Mar 55). See *2b(1)*.

De La Roche, Catherine. "Master of His Des-

tiny." *F&F* 2 (No. 3, Dec 55) 11. Career of Michael Redgrave, British actor.

Goodman, E. "Carol Reed." *Th Arts* 31 (May 47) 57–59. He discusses his own films and American and British films in general.

Breit, Harvey. "I Give the Public What I Like." *NYTM* (15 Jan 50) 18–19. A profile of British director Carol Reed, previewing his film The Third Man.

De La Roche, Catherine. "A Man with No Message." *F&F* 1 (No. 3, Dec 54) 15. A study of British director Carol Reed.

Sarris, Andrew. "Carol Reed in the Context of His Time." *F Cult* 2 (No. 10, 1956) 14–17; 3 (No. 11, 1957) 11–14+. In two parts, the career of the British director from its beginning to *Trapeze;* his patriotic contributions, his handling of actors.

Sarris, Andrew. "First of the Realists." *F&F* 3 (No. 12, Sep 57) 9–10+. Analysis of the work of Carol Reed.

Sarris, Andrew. "The Stylist Goes to Hollywood." *F&F* 4 (No. 1, Oct 57) 11–12+. Conclusion of article on Carol Reed's films.

Fawcett, Marion. "Sir Carol Reed." *FIR* 10 (Mar 59) 134–141. The films he has directed since 1934 discussed critically, in chronological order; no separate index.

Reed, Oliver. "All Wound Up and Ready to Go." *F&F* 13 (No. 9, June 67) 4–8. Interview on his career and acting.

Wood, Robin. "In Memoriam: Michael Reeves." *Movie* (No. 17, Winter 69–70) 2–6. A tribute to the British director and a description of his films.

Bodeen, DeWitt. "Wallace Reid." *FIR* 17 (No. 4, Apr 66) 205–230. Career of movie idol of 1910s and 1920s.

Weaver, Randolph T. "*Prince Achmed* and Other Animated Silhouettes." *Th Arts* 15 (June 31). See *2h(5)*. About Lotte Reiniger.

White, E. W. "Lotte Reiniger and Her Art." *Horn Bk* 15 (Jan 39). See *2h(5)*.

Coté, Guy. "Flatland Fairy Tales." *Film* (No. 1, Oct 54) 16–18. A personal account of a visit to a British studio of Lotte Reiniger, maker of silhouette films.

"She Made First Cartoon Feature." *F&F* 2 (No. 3, Dec 55) 24. Lotte Reiniger now makes silhouette films in London.

"The Films of Lotte Reiniger." *F Cult* 2 (No. 9, 1956) 20. Short piece on her "silhouette" films.

"Karel Reisz." *F&F* 7 (No. 5, Feb 61) 5. Career sketch of the British director.

Phillips, Gene. "An Interview with Karel Reisz." *Cinema* (Calif) 4 (No. 2, Summer 68) 53–54. Director of *Morgan* talks briefly of that film and of *Isadora*, now ready for shooting; the "moment" of social realism in Great Britain, he says, has passed.

"Dearden and Relph: "Two on a Tandem.""

F&F 12 (No. 10, July 66). *See 5, Basil Dearden.* About **Michael Relph.**

LaBadie, Donald W. "What Makes Remick Walk?" *Show* 3 (Feb 63) 80–81+. Acting career of **Lee Remick**; comparison with Bette Davis as a symbol of the "lost generation" of the 1920s and 1930s; Remick as prototype of the "found generation" of the 1950s and 1960s.

Renoir, Jean. "Farthingales and Facts." *S&S* 7 (No. 26, Summer 38) 51–52. French director on history in his films.

Renoir, Jean. "Starting Point." (Tr. by D. S. Moore.) *Life & Letters Today* 23 (Dec 39) 353–363. Personal recollections of early childhood and major influences in his career as a film director.

Ray, Satyajit. "Renoir in Calcutta." *Sequence* (No. 10, New Year 1950) 146–150. Notes on Jean Renoir's visit to India and his plans to make a film there.

Allison, Gordon. "Jean Renoir." *Th Arts* 35 (Aug 51) 18+. Brief history and news of his new film, *The River.*

Renoir, Jean. "Personal Notes." *S&S* 21 (Apr–June 52) 152–153. The French director's feelings about working conditions.

Renoir, Jean. "I Know Where I'm Going." (Tr. by David A. Mage.) *FIR* 3 (Mar 52) 97–101. Cinema, a "collective" art, can help depict the collective evolution of mankind; now is a time of increasing goodwill.

Rivette, Jacques, and François Truffaut. "Renoir in America." *S&S* 24 (July–Sep 54) 12–17. Renoir gives his impressions of Hollywood, where he made five films, and describes the pleasures and problems involved in shooting them; he discusses *Swamp Water, This Land Is Mine, The Southerner, Diary of a Chambermaid,* and *Woman on the Beach.*

Rivette, Jacques, and François Truffaut. "Renoir in America." *FIR* 5 (Nov 54) 449–456. A self-appraisal of his own career in Hollywood by the French director. Reprinted from *Sight and Sound.*

Billard, Ginette. *"French Can-Can." F&F* 1 (No. 4, Jan 55) 15. An interview on the set with **Jean Renoir.**

"Jean Renoir: Painter's Son." *F&F* 2 (No. 1, Oct 55) 3. Brief biography with one quotation.

Bazin, André. "Cinema and Television." *S&S* 28 (Winter 58–59) 26–30. Interview with **Jean Renoir** and Roberto Rossellini, just before Bazin's death, as reprinted from *France Observateur;* includes remarks on co-production and films for TV.

Dyer, Peter John. "Renoir and Realism." *S&S* 29 (Summer 60) 130–135+. A study of Renoir's silent films and his development as a "naturalistic" film maker; not until *Rules of the Game* did Renoir turn his back on Zolaism.

Bachmann, Gideon. "A Conversation with **Jean Renoir.**" *Contact* 2 (No. 5, June 60) 9–24. An interview with the director on his films and views on film making; originally recorded 23 June 1956.

Whitehall, Richard. "Painting Life with Movement." *F&F* 6 (No. 9, June 60) 13–14. **Renoir's** films.

Whitehall, Richard. "The Screen Is His Canvas." *F&F* 6 (No. 10, July 60) 29–30+. Conclusion of analysis of **Jean Renoir's** films.

Callenbach, Ernest, and Roberta Schuldenfrei. "The Presence of Jean Renoir." *FQ* 14 (No. 2, Winter 60) 8–10. Brief portrait as he directs his new play, *Carola,* at University of California, Berkeley.

Bazin, André. "New Meaning of Montage." *F Cult* (Nos. 22–23, 1961). *See 3a(5).* About **Jean Renoir.**

Maynard, Virginia. "A Rehearsal with **Jean Renoir.**" *Educ Th J* 13 (No. 2, May 61) 92–98. For a production of his play *Carola* at University of California at Berkeley.

Marcorelles, Louis. "Conversation with **Jean Renoir.**" *S&S* 31 (Spring 62) 78–83. His new film, *Le Caporal épinglé;* "I don't really bother much about linking shots, physical devices to link action"—the thing that counts for Renoir is the emotional link; his opinions on the English and American cinema, freedom, and criticism.

Harcourt, Peter. "Jean Renoir." *London Mag* new series 2 (No. 9, Dec 62) 56–60. On the man and his work.

"Jean Renoir." *Cinema* (Calif) 2 (No. 1, Feb–Mar 64) 12–14+. Interview.

Russell, Lee. "Jean Renoir." *New Left Rev* (No. 25, May–June 64) 57–60. A study of his films.

Svatek, Peter, *et al.* "Questions and Answers with **Jean Renoir.**" *Take One* 1 (No. 7, 1967) 4–6. French film director on his own work and that of other film makers.

Delahaye, Michel, and Jean-André Fieschi. "My Next Films: Interview with **Jean Renoir.**" *CdC in Eng* (No. 9, Mar 67) 40–52.

Madsen, Axel. "Renoir at 72." *Cinema* (Calif) 4 (No. 1, Spring 68) 36–37.

Nogueira, Rui, and François Truchaud. "Interview with **Jean Renoir.**" *S&S* 37 (Spring 68) 56–59. Questions about his films; on pp. 60–62 are extracts from his speech at the Academy Cinema in London, where *La Marseillaise* opened: "Slowly I discovered that to make films was . . . perhaps a way to discover reality."

Millar, Daniel. "The Autumn of Jean Renoir." *S&S* 37 (Summer 68) 136–141. Renoir's post-American films.

Gilliatt, Penelope. "Profiles: *Le Meneur de Jeu.*" *New Yorker* 45 (23 Aug 69) 34–36+. A long interview with **Jean Renoir.**

Sesonske, Alexander. "Renoir: A Progress

Report." *Cinema* (Calif) 6 (No. 1, 1970) 17–20. Interview; his plans in 1968 for his latest film; author is working on a book about the French director.

Burch, Noel. "A Conversation with **Alain Resnais.**" *FQ* 13 (No. 3, Spring 70) 27–29. Discussion of *Hiroshima, Mon Amour,* the short films, other directors.

Grenier, Cynthia. "Explorations in the Unconscious." *Sat Rev* 44 (23 Dec 61) 37–38. Study of **Alain Resnais.**

Resnais, Alain. "Alain Resnais Speaks at Random." *NY F Bul* 3 (No. 2, 1962) 16–17. A selection of quotes from the director, followed by a filmography.

Archer, Eugene. "Director of Enigmas." *NYTM* (18 Mar 62) 54–55. On the career of French director **Alain Resnais.**

Stanbrook, Alan. "The Time and Space of **Alain Resnais.**" *F&F* 10 (No. 4, Jan 64) 35–38.

Nowell-Smith, Geoffrey. "**Alain Resnais.**" *New Left Rev* (No. 27, Sep–Oct 64) 84–88. Study of his films.

Pechter, William S. "On **Alain Resnais.**" *Moviegoer* (No. 1, Winter 64) 26–33. Resnais' *Marienbad* and *Hiroshima* seen as films about persuasion.

Resnais, Alain. "The War Is Over." *F&F* 13 (No. 1, Oct 66) 40–42. Interview.

Lacassin, Francis. "Dick Tracy Meets Muriel." *S&S* 36 (Spring 67) 101–102. **Alain Resnais,** besides being a director, is also a comic-strip enthusiast.

Roud, Richard. "Memories of **Resnais.**" *S&S* 38 (Summer 69) 124–129. Alain Resnais' beginnings as director and some of the people who have influenced him.

Markopoulos, Gregory. "The Golden Poet." *F Cult* (No. 27, 1962–1963) 20–21. **Ron Rice** and his film *Senseless.*

Rice, Ron. "Diaries, Notebooks, Documents." *F Cult* (No. 39, Winter 65) 87–126. Includes scripts and diagrams by the experimental-film maker.

"**Ralph Richardson.**" *F&F* 7 (No. 8, May 61) 5. Career sketch of the British actor.

Coulson, Alan A. "**Ralph Richardson.**" *FIR* 20 (No. 8, Oct 69) 457–472. Career and film listings.

Houston, Penelope, and Louis Marcorelles. "Two New Directors." *S&S* 28 (Winter 58–59) 31–34. **Tony Richardson** on location for *Look Back in Anger;* Jacques Rivette as he films *Paris nous appartient,* also a film about young people and their reaction to the world.

Richardson, Tony. "The Man Behind an Angry-Young-Man." *F&F* 5 (No. 5, Feb 59) 9+. Interview on directing as Richardson was making *Look Back in Anger.*

Young, Colin. "**Tony Richardson:** An Interview in Los Angeles." *FQ* 13 (No. 4, Summer 60) 10–15. He talks about various Woodfall films in work and completed and says he never wants to do another play he has staged himself.

Alpert, Hollis. "Britain's Angry Young Director." *Sat Rev* 43 (24 Dec 60) 48–49. Interview with **Tony Richardson;** part of *Saturday Revue* report "Are Foreign Films Better?"

Richardson, Tony. "The Two Worlds of Cinema." *F&F* 7 (No. 9, June 61) 7+. Interview with Richardson on Hollywood versus independent work.

Moller, David. "Britain's Busiest Angry Young Man." *F Com* 2 (No. 1, Winter 64) 3–8. Critical survey of films directed and produced by **Tony Richardson.**

Durgnat, Raymond. "*The Loved One.*" *F&F* 12 (No. 5, Feb 66) 19–23; (No. 6, Mar 66) 37–40. On **Tony Richardson's** films; two articles.

Lellis, George. "Recent **Richardson:** Cashing the Blank Check." *Take One* 2 (No. 1, 1968) 10–13. Critical examination of Tony Richardson's films.

Lellis, George. "Recent **Richardson**—Cashing the Blank Cheque." *S&S* 38 (Summer 69) 130–133. A critical study of *The Charge of the Light Brigade* and other Tony Richardson films; the author sees his work as mediocre, but interesting; he has ability to handle dialogue.

Lawrenson, Helen. "The Richman Era." *Show* 2 (June 62) 74–77+. The singing career of **Harry Richman,** his film performances, relationship to Hollywood and Clara Bow.

Mekas, Jonas. "**Hans Richter** on the Nature of Film Poetry." *F Cult* 3 (No. 11, 1957) 5–8. Richter interviewed about his films *Ghosts Before Breakfast, Dreams That Money Can Buy, Rhythm 21, 8 by 8.*

Young, Vernon. "Painter and Cinematographer **Hans Richter:** A Retrospective of Four Decades." *Arts Mag* 33 (Sep 59) 48–55. His contribution to space art and time art (1921–1957).

Richter, Hans. "From Interviews with Hans Richter During the Last Ten Years." *F Cult* (No. 31, 1963–1964). *See 3a.*

"The Case of **Leni Riefenstahl.**" *S&S* 29 (Spring 60) 68. Note on withdrawal of British Film Institute invitation for a talk on her works.

Gunston, David. "**Leni Riefenstahl.**" *FQ* 14 (No. 1, Fall 60) 4–19. Some description of her films under the Nazis; more on her early history as an actress in Dr. Arnold Fanck's Alpine films; "*Triumph of the Will* could not have been made by anyone not fanatically at one with the events depicted."

Muller, Robert. "Romantic Miss **Riefenstahl.**" *Spectator* 206 (10 Feb 61) 179–180. Why Leni Riefenstahl made *Triumph of the Will;* her war activities related to propaganda films.

Berson, Arnold. "The Truth About Leni." *F&F* 11 (No. 7, Apr 65) 15–19. On the films and life of **Leni Riefenstahl.**

Hitchens, Gordon. "An Interview with a Legend." *F Com* 3 (No. 1, Winter 65) 5–11. **Leni Riefenstahl** talks of *Triumph of the Will, Olympia,* and films she now wants to make.

"Biographical Sketch of **Leni Riefenstahl.**" *F Com* 3 (No. 1, Winter 65) 12–15.

Gregor, Ulrich. "A Comeback for **Leni Riefenstahl?**" *F Com* 3 (No. 1, Winter 65) 24–25. West Berlin film critic says even *Olympia* is fascist in spirit, that Riefenstahl contradicts herself about Goebbels' support of *Triumph,* that her films not be suppressed but should be placed in the political context of the times.

Gardner, Robert. "Can the Will Triumph?" *F Com* 3 (No. 1, Winter 65) 28–31. Harvard lecturer and director of anthropology films speaks of **Leni Riefenstahl** as candid, naïve, and careless about ideas; he interviewed her and describes her cutting room and incidents connected with *Triumph of the Will.*

"Letters from Readers." *F Com* 3 (No. 3, Summer 65) 81–87. Mostly favorable judgments on the issue (Winter 65) devoted to **Leni Riefenstahl;** one negative letter prompts a long reply from editor Gordon Hitchens explaining the magazine's purpose.

Delahaye, Michel. "Leni and the Wolf: Interview with **Leni Riefenstahl.**" *CdC in Eng* (No. 5, June 66) 48–55. Her career as dancer, actress, and film director in Germany; extensive technical comments on *The Blue Light, Triumph of the Will, Olympia, Tiefland;* present plans for African films.

Brownlow, Kevin. "**Leni Riefenstahl.**" *Film* (No. 47, Winter 66) 14–19. An interview with the German director.

Rotha, Paul, Kevin Brownlow, and **Leni Riefenstahl.** "**Leni Riefenstahl.**" *Film* (No. 48, Spring 67) 12–15. Rotha objects to the attempt by Brownlow and Riefenstahl to whitewash the latter's past and they reply to his objections.

Corliss, Richard. "**Leni Riefenstahl:** A Bibliography." *F Her* 5 (No. 1, Fall 69) 27–36.

Richards, Jeffrey. "**Leni Riefenstahl:** Style and Structure." *Silent Picture* (No. 8, Autumn 70) 17–19. *Triumph of the Will* as visual propaganda.

McVay, Douglas. "The Best and the Worst of **Martin Ritt.**" *F&F* 11 (No. 3, Dec 64) 43–48. A study of his films.

Godfrey, Lionel. "Tall When They're Small." *F&F* 14 (No. 11, Aug 68) 42–48. The films of **Martin Ritt.**

Cooper, Texas Jim. "**Tex Ritter.**" *FIR* 21 (No. 4, Apr 70) 204–216. Career and film listing.

Roman, Robert C. "**Thelma Ritter.**" *FIR* 20 (No. 9, Nov 69) 549–568. At the time of her death, career and filmography of this actress.

Houston, Penelope, and Louis Marcorelles. "Two New Directors." *S&S* 28 (Winter 58–59). *See 5, Tony Richardson.* About **Jacques Rivette.**

Marcorelles, Louis. "Interview with Roger Leenhardt and **Jacques Rivette.**" *S&S* 32 (Autumn 63) *See 5, Roger Leenhardt.*

Roach, Hal. "Living with Laughter." *F&F* 11 (No. 1, Oct 64) 23–25. Reflections on his career, especially on comedians he knew.

Slide, Anthony. "Hal Roach on Film Comedy." *Silent Picture* (No. 6, Spring 70) 2–7. Recorded interview; anecdotal account of teams he worked with (Our Gang, Laurel and Hardy) and his preference for collective comedy versus a one-man show; the basis of slapstick.

McCann, Barry. "**Alain Robbe-Grillet.**" *Film* (No. 51, Spring 68) 22–27. The French writer-director's work; critical comments on his major concerns.

Ward, John. "**Alain Robbe-Grillet.**" *S&S* 37 (Spring 68) 86–90. Novelist and scriptwriter for Alain Resnais has turned to film making himself; author feels his literary style is not immediately translatable into film terms in his own works *L'Immortelle* and *Trans-Europ-Express.*

Hart, Henry. "**Cliff Robertson.**" *FIR* 20 (No. 3, Mar 69) 153–163. Career and film index for the actor.

McKelway, St. Clair. "**Bill Robinson.**" *New Yorker* (6 Oct 34) 26–28; (13 Oct 34) 30–34. Profile of the actor.

Eyles, Allen. "**Edward G. Robinson.**" *F&F* 10 (No. 4, Jan 64) 13–17. A study of his film career.

Roman, Robert C. "**Edward G. Robinson.**" *FIR* 17 (No. 7, Aug–Sep 66) 419–446. Career and film listing.

Ellis, Robert. "Hollywood Director Speaks Out." *Negro Dig* 9 (Jan 51). *See 4k(11).* About **Mark Robson.**

Luft, Herbert G. "**Mark Robson.**" *FIR* 19 (No. 5, May 68) 288–309. Career of the director.

Delahaye, Michel, Pierre Kast, and Jean Narboni. "An Interview with **Glauber Rocha.**" *Afterimage* (No. 1, Apr 70) 20 pages. His work, theories, and politics.

Crowdus, Gary, and William Starr. "*Cinema Novo* vs. Cultural Colonialism: An Interview with **Glauber Rocha.**" *Cinéaste* 4 (No. 1, Summer 70) 2–9+. The Brazilian director discusses the *Cinema Novo* movement, his own films and political base.

Hitchens, Gordon. "The Way to Make a Future: A Conversation with **Glauber Rocha.**" *FQ* 24 (No. 1, Fall 70) 27–30. The Brazilian director objects to Ernest Callenbach's analysis of his film *Antonio das Mortes (FQ*

[Winter 69–70]) and insists on divorcing it from Marxism and Freudianism.

Green, Stanley. "**Richard Rodgers'** Filmusic." *FIR* 7 (Oct 56) 398–405. His career in films and associations with Lorenz Hart and Oscar Hammerstein.

Cohen, Saul B. "**Michael Roemer** and Robert Young, Film Makers of *Nothing But a Man*." *F Com* 3 (No. 2, Spring 65) 8–13. Background, content, and methods of shooting this film; filmography of both men; two brief extracts from reviews.

Widmark, Anne. "Conversation with **Michael Roemer**." *F Her* 3 (No. 2, Winter 67–68) 29–33. Drama and nonfiction in *Nothing But a Man* by Roemer and Robert Young.

Dickens, Homer. "**Ginger Rogers**." *FIR* 17 (No. 3, Mar 66) 129–155. Career and film listing.

Davis, Peter. "**Rogosin** and Documentary." *F Cult* (No. 24, 1962) 25–28. Criticism of **Lionel Rogosin**, who seems to reject optimism but does not show enough of the truth.

Zalaffi, Nicoletta, and Rui Nogueira. "**Eric Rohmer**." *Film* (No. 51, Spring 68) 27–30. An interview with the director and comments on his work.

Clarens, Carlos. "**Eric Rohmer**: *L'Amour Sage*." *S&S* 39 (Winter 69–70) 6–9. Rohmer's four filmed *contes moraux* all have the same theme, including *La Collectionneuse* and *Ma Nuit chez Maud*; Rohmer was chief editor of *Cahiers du Cinéma* until 1963; his work with TV documentaries has encouraged him to work with "feelings buried deep in our consciousness."

Geltzer, George. "**Ruth Roland**." *FIR* 11 (No. 9, Nov 60) 539–548. American actress who was in serials.

Clark, Roy. "**Alex Romero** Compares Hollywood and Broadway." *Dance Mag* 36 (Jan 62) 42–45. Interview with Romero, film choreographer.

Rose, William. "*It's a Mad, Mad, Mad, Mad, World*." *Film* (No. 37, Autumn 63) 30–33. The writer of the original idea for the film talks about his own career and Kramer's film.

Lane, John Francis. "A Neapolitan Eisenstein." *F&F* 9 (No. 11, Aug 63) 51–53. On the films of **Francesco Rosi**.

"**Francesco Rosi**." *Film* (No. 39, Spring 64) 12–14. An interview with the Italian director.

Lane, John Francis. "*The Moment of Truth*." *S&S* 33 (Autumn 64) 169. **Francesco Rosi** on location in Spain.

Bachmann, Gideon. "**Francesco Rosi**: An interview." *FQ* 18 (No. 3, Spring 65) 50–56. A Neapolitan who studied law, the director of *Hands Over the City* feels that his own research into corruption can be a participation (for himself and for his viewers) in the continuing mastery of democratic proc-

esses; he tries to find stories in the life around him.

Rosi, Francesco. "Moments of Truth." *F&F* 16 (No. 12, Sep 70) 6–10. Interview.

Ordway, Peter. "Prophet with Honor: **Roberto Rossellini**." *Th Arts* 33 (Jan 49) 49–51. On his way of working, from *Open City* to *Amore*.

Venturi, Lauro. "**Roberto Rossellini**." *Hwd Q* 4 (No. 1, Fall 49) 1–13. His documentaries and early films; the making of *Open City* and others; filmography.

Harcourt-Smith, Simon. "The Stature of **Rossellini**." *S&S* 29 (Apr 50) 86–88.

Koval, Francis. "Interview with **Rossellini**." *S&S* 19 (Feb 51) 393–394. "The struggle between faith and mere opportunism" he feels is one of his characteristic concerns; "I am not a pessimist at all. I am only a realist."

Murray, W. "The Man Who Knows No Rules." *UN World* 7 (May 53) 44–47. **Roberto Rossellini**'s career; filming of *Europe 51*.

Scherer, Maurice, and François Truffaut. "Interview with **Roberto Rossellini**." *F Cult* 1 (No. 2, 1955) 12–14. Interview with Roberto Rossellini reprinted from *Cahiers du Cinéma*.

Bazin, André. "Cinema and Television." *S&S* 28 (Winter 58–59). See 5, Jean Renoir. Interview with **Roberto Rossellini** and Jean Renoir.

Bazin, André. "New Meaning of Montage." *F Cult* (Nos. 22–23, 1961). See 3a(5). About **Roberto Rossellini**.

Sarris, Andrew. "**Rossellini** Rediscovered." *F Cult* (No. 32, 1964) 60–63. He is far more revolutionary than Antonioni; the zoom lens is now appropriate for him because it "follows man without ever crowding in close enough to lose man's context."

Casty, Alan. "The Achievement of **Roberto Rossellini**." *F Com* 2 (No. 4, Fall 64) 17–21. Critical review of career and films of the Italian director, described as exhibiting "excesses of an intense sincerity" and moving in style from the "jagged" images of wartime through "grandiose symbolism" to "loosely episodic lyricism."

Phelps, Donald. "**Rossellini** and *The Flowers of Saint Francis*." *Moviegoer* (No. 1, Winter 64) 19–25. In Roberto Rossellini's work there is a symmetry of weaknesses and strengths; special attention to *The Flowers of St. Francis*.

Russell, Lee. "**Roberto Rossellini**." *New Left Rev* (No. 42, Mar–Apr 67) 69–71. Study of his films.

Soltero, José, and Toby Mussman. "Interview with **Roberto Rossellini**." *Medium* 1 (No. 2, Winter 67–68) 56–61. His themes; film versus TV, color versus black and white, etc.

Hart, Henry. "Notes on **Robert Rossen**." *FIR* 13 (No. 6, June–July 62) 333–334. Brief career description of the director, with film list annotated by Henry Burton pp. 335–340 and by John Springer pp. 341–342.

Rossen, Robert. "The Face of Independence." *F&F* 8 (No. 11, Aug 62) 7. General reflections on his films.

Casty, Alan. "The Films of Robert Rossen." *FQ* 20 (No. 2, Winter 66–67) 3–12. A study of his characters, who have "a certain inner natural force" which they cannot "fully identify or control."

Noamès, Jean-Louis. "Lessons Learned in Combat: Interview with Robert Rossen." *CdC in Eng* (No. 7, Jan 67) 20–29. The American film maker speaks of his career and his films: *All the King's Men, Lilith* (review on p. 32), *The Hustler* (review on p. 31); filmography by Patrick Brion on pp. 38–41.

Stein, Daniel. "An Interview with Robert Rossen." *Arts in Soc* 4 (No. 1, Winter 67) 46–58.

Casty, Alan. "Robert Rossen." *Cinema* (Calif) 4 (No. 3, Fall 68) 18–22. Retrospective study of his films.

Dark, Chris. "Reflections on Robert Rossen." *Cinema* (Cambridge) (Nos. 6–7, Aug 70) 57–61. Thematic aspects of Rossen's films, particularly *The Hustler*.

Rossi, Franco. "Oh, the Smog Bites." *Cinema* (Calif) 1 (No. 4, June–July 63) 16–18. Interview with Rossi, director of *Smog*.

Luft, Herbert G. "Rotha and the World." *QFRTV* 10 (No. 1, Fall 55) 89–98. Life and works of British documentary film maker and film historian Paul Rotha.

Blue, James. "The Films of Jean Rouch." *F Com* 4 (Nos. 1–2, Fall–Winter 67) 80–91. Filmography of *cinéma vérité;* comment on the new phrase "direct cinema"; biography of French ethnographer-cameraman Rouch; conversation with him; additional conversation of Rouch with Jacqueline Veuve, who has worked with him.

Soltero, José. "On Jean Rouch." *Medium* 1 (No. 2, Winter 67–68) 52–55. His films as an effort to understand the individual's experience, using *The Lion Hunters* for a detailed example.

Spigelgass, Leonard. "Damon Runyon." *Screen Writer* 2 (Mar 47) 23–27. An appreciative essay by a screenwriter who worked with him on adapting his stories.

Goodwin, Michael, and Naomi Wise. "Getting Richard Rush Straight." *Take One* 2 (No. 8, 1969) 17–19. Interview with the American director.

Hagen, Ray. "Jane Russell." *FIR* 14 (Mar 63) 226–235. Career study; filmography.

Russell, Ken. "Ideas for Films." *Film* (No. 19, Jan–Feb 59) 13–15. How an idea arises and takes form in film.

Russell, Ken. "Shock Treatment." *F&F* 16 (No. 10, July 70) 8–12. Interview about his career, especially his next film, on Tchaikovsky; filmography.

Phillips, Gene D. "An Interview with Ken Russell." *F Com* 6 (No. 2, Fall 70) 10–17. Professor talks with British director about his films, especially *Women in Love* and his BBC series of biographies.

Ringgold, Gene. "Rosalind Russell." *FIR* 21 (No. 10, Dec 70) 585–610. Career and film chronology.

Falkenberg, Paul. "Sound Montage: A Propos de Ruttmann." *F Cult* (Nos. 22–23, 1961) 59–62. An article on the pioneer German documentary-film maker Walter Ruttmann, with an emphasis on his film *Weekend*.

"People of Talent (2): Robert Ryan." *S&S* 25 (Summer 55) 37. Brief biography and analysis.

Stein, Jeanne. "Robert Ryan." *FIR* 19 (No. 1, Jan 68) 9–27. Career and film chronology.

S

"Not So Sad Sack." *Time* 80 (27 July 62). *See 6e(1).* About Ben Sack, exhibitor.

Hardy, Forsyth. "Leontine Sagan." *CQ* 1 (No. 2, Winter 32) 85–88. Woman director of *Maedchen in Uniform* interviewed.

Saks, Gene. "Well, How Do You Like Directing Movies?" *Action* 2 (No. 2, Mar–Apr 67) 10–11. A former stage director and actor describes his reactions to directing his first film, *Barefoot in the Park*.

Saltzman, Harry. "Blazing the Trail." *F&F* 15 (No. 12, Sep 69) 4–7. Interview about his changing role as producer.

Hill, Steven P. "Interview with Samson Samsonov." *F Cult* (No. 42, Fall 66) 118–133. A traditional director-producer in the Russian "new wave" tells his life story; brief reviews of his pictures by Hill.

"A Talk with Jorge Sanjines." *Cinéaste* 4 (No. 3, Winter 70–71) 12. The Bolivian director discusses his film *Blood of the Condor.*

Schaffner, Franklin. "The Best and Worst of It." *F&F* 11 (No. 1, Oct 64) 9–11. Interview about his films, especially *The Best Man.*

Wilson, David. "Franklin Schaffner." *S&S* 35 (Spring 66) 73–75. A study of the career of the director who came into films through stage and television, and has directed only three features: *The Stripper, The Best Man,* and the eleventh-century Normandy epic *The War Lord.*

"An Interview with Franklin Schaffner." *Cinéaste* 3 (No. 1, Summer 69) 11–16+. American director discusses his films.

Kaufman, Stanley Lloyd, Jr. "The Early Franklin J. Schaffner." *FIR* 20 (No. 7, Aug–Sep 69) 409–418. Interview by a Yale undergraduate.

Munroe, Dale. "Director **Franklin Schaffner:** From *Planet of the Apes* to *Patton.*" *Show* (6 Aug 70) 16–17. Problems with location logistics in *Patton,* production details, etc.

Boal, Sam. "Plan for Hollywood—by Schary." *NYTM* (6 Feb 49) 16+. Profile of **Dore Schary,** production head of MGM.

Whitney, Dwight. "The Schary Script." *Collier's* 124 (19 Nov 49) 22–23+. On Dore Schary's *Battleground* and Schary as studio boss at MGM.

"Schary, the Messenger." *Newswk* 35 (29 May 50) 82. Biography of Dore Schary; his role in the American film industry.

Lambert, Gavin. "A Line of Experiment." *S&S* 19 (Mar 51). See 4d. About **Dore Schary.**

"Making the Decision on 3-D Movies." *Bus Wk* (15 Aug 53) 78–84+. Daily routine of **Dore Schary,** vice-president in charge of production for Loew's Inc.; including a short biography.

Bogdanovich, Peter. "Dore Schary–Stanley Kramer Syndrome." *NY F Bul* 1 (Nos. 12–14, 1960) 12–14. "Middle artists" caught between the desires to make both art and money.

Spelman, Franz. "The Explosive Schell Family." *Show* 3 (Jan 63) 62–65+. European and Hollywood acting careers of **Maximilian, Maria, Carl,** and **Immy Schell.**

Pringle, Henry F. "**Nicholas M. Schenck.**" *New Yorker* (30 Apr 32) 22–25. Profile of MGM executive.

Cooke, Alan. "Amateur Activities: Mount Pleasant Productions." *S&S* 19 (Jan 50) 41–42. **John Schlesinger** and Cooke make two short films.

Schlesinger, John. "Blessed Isle or Fool's Paradise." *F&F* 9 (No. 8, May 63) 8–10. Interview about the future of young British film makers and his *Billy Liar.*

Weinberg, Gretchen. "**John Schlesinger** at the Sixth Montreal International Film Festival." *F Her* 1 (No. 1, Fall 65) 42–44. Comments on *Darling* and on other directors.

Schlesinger, John. "A Buck for Joe." *F&F* 16 (No. 2, Nov 69) 4–8. Interview about his film career.

Phillips, Gene. "**John Schlesinger,** Social Realist." *F Com* 5 (No. 4, Winter 69) 58–63. Associate of National Center for Film Study talks with the British director in New York and comments on several of his films; biography and filmography.

Spiers, David. "**John Schlesinger** Interviewed." *Screen* 11 (No. 3, Summer 70) 3–18.

Hall, William. "**John Schlesinger,** Award Winner." *Action* 5 (No. 4, July–Aug 70) 4–10. Interview.

Nogueira, Rui, and Nicoletta Zalaffi. "**Volker Schloendorff:** The Rebel." *Film* (No. 55,

Summer 69) 26–27. Interview with the German director.

"**Sybille Schmitz:** 1909–1955." *Image* 4 (No. 4, Apr 55) 31–32. Brief biography of the German actress.

Brownlow, Kevin, "**B. P. Schulberg.**" *Film* (No. 51, Spring 68) 8–13. Career of the Paramount producer and executive.

Turner, Charles L. "**Victor Seastrom.**" *FIR* 11 (No. 5, May 60) 266–277; (No. 6, June–July 60) 343–355. In two parts; career of the Swedish actor and director, with separate lists of his films. *See also 5, Victor Sjöström* (Swedish spelling).

Seaton, George. "Getting Out on a Limb." *F&F* 7 (No. 7, Apr 61) 9+. The American director discusses his attitude toward film making.

Brown, Vanessa. "**George Seaton.**" *Action* 5 (No. 4, July–Aug 70) 21–23. Report on the American director by an actress.

LaBadie, Donald W. "Everybody's Galatea." *Show* 3 (Aug 63) 76–77+. Acting career of **Jean Seberg** from Preminger's discovery to Godard's *Breathless.*

McVay, Douglas. "The Man Behind." *F&F* 9 (No. 8, May 63) 44–47. **Peter Sellers'** zany style of comedy films.

Seltzer, Walter. "In the Middle of It All." *F&F* 10 (No. 10, July 64) 42–43. On his productions, especially *Man in the Middle.*

"Selznick and Milestone." *Time* 18 (3 Aug 31) 26. Producer and director form company to make only six pictures a year; the **David Selznick** legend.

"Selznick Out." *Time* 20 (26 Dec 32) 36. RKO production chief David Selznick resigns.

"Thalberg's Shoes." *Time* 21 (3 Apr 33) 34. While Irving Thalberg recuperates on a trip to Europe, **D. O. Selznick** is announced as a new vice-president of MGM and announces cast for *Dinner at Eight.*

Lane, John Francis. "They Call It the **Selznick** Touch." *F&F* 4 (No. 4, Jan 58) 8+. Interview with David O. Selznick during the filming of *A Farewell to Arms.*

Behlmer, Rudy, and Henry Hart. "**David O. Selznick.**" *FIR* 14 (June–July 63) 321–339. Career study.

Brownlow, Kevin. "**David O. Selznick.**" *Film* (No. 43, Autumn 65) 6–9. An interview with the producer.

"Amazing Selznicks." *Collier's* 101 (4 June 38) 19+. The careers of David and **Myron Selznick.**

Beatty, Jerome. "A Star-Maker Whose Recipe Is Anything for a Laugh." *American* (Jan 31) 40–42+. Brief biographical sketch of **Mack Sennett,** with comments on nature of comedy.

"Custard Pie Classics." *NYTM* (8 June 47) 28–29. A pictorial look at the art and stars of **Mack Sennett.**

Pryor, Thomas. "Then and Now." *NYTM* (22 Feb 53) 27. **Mack Sennett**, at sixty-eight, looks back to his role in the silent era of screen comedy.

Giroux, Robert. "**Mack Sennett**." *FIR* 19 (No. 10, Dec 68) 593–612; 20 (No. 1, Jan 69) 1–28. Biography.

Nogueria, Rui. "The Lily in the Valley." *S&S* 38 (Autumn 69) 184–187. Interview with **Delphine Seyrig**, star of *L'Année dernière à Marienbad* and *Muriel*, who talks about Alain Resnais and other directors.

Knight, Arthur. "Fun Man." *Sat Rev* 44 (26 Aug 61) 24. **Stanley Shapiro**, young comedy writer.

Crowther, Bosley. "Maestro of Sophisticated Comedy." *NYTM* (18 Nov 62) 36+. On the career of Hollywood writer **Stanley Shapiro**.

Mycroft, Walter. "Shaw—and the Devil to Pay." *F&F* 5 (No. 5, Feb 59) 14–15+. **G. B. Shaw**'s active part in the filming of his plays.

Roman, Robert C. "G. B. S. on the Screen." *FIR* 11 (No. 7, Aug–Sep 60). See *3f(2)*. About **George Bernard Shaw**.

Alpert, Hollis. "The Joys of Uncertainty." *Sat Rev* (29 Dec 62) 16–17. **Irwin Shaw**, former screenwriter, turns director; part of *Saturday Review* report "The Lonely Art of Film-Making."

Guerin, Ann, and Henry Grossman. "Running Figure in a Landscape." *Show* (Jan 70) 61+. Interview with **Robert Shaw** on film acting.

Jacobs, Jack. "**Norma Shearer**." *FIR* 11 (No. 7, Aug–Sep 60) 290–405. Career, biography, and film listing for actress.

Shebib, **Donald**. "McLuhan's Child." *New Yorker* 46 (21 Nov 70) 47–49. Interview with the Canadian director about his life, past films, and the making of his recent film *Goin' Down the Road*.

Springer, John. "**Sylvia Sidney**." *FIR* 17 (No. 1, Jan 66) 6–16. Career and film listing for the actress.

Hanson, Curtis Lee. "Interview with **Don Siegel**." *Cinema* (Calif) 4 (No. 1, Spring 68) 4–9. Filmography.

Bogdanovich, Peter. "Working Within the System." *Movie* (No. 15, Spring 68) 1–16. An extensive filmography and interview with Hollywood director **Donald Siegel**, who discusses his own work and the problems of working within the industry.

Austen, David. "Out for the Kill." *F&F* 14 (No. 8, May 68) 4–9; (No. 9, June 68) 10–15. Study of the films of **Don Siegel**, in two parts.

Siegel, Don. "The Anti-Heroes." *F&F* 15 (No. 4, Jan 69) 22. Interview about his career generally and reflections on film making.

Mundy, Robert. "**Don Siegel**: Time and Motion,

Attitudes and Genre." *Cinema* (Cambridge) (No. 5, Feb 70) 10–13.

Farber, Manny. "The Films of Sam Fuller and **Don Siegel**." *December* 12 (Nos. 1–2, 1970). See *5, Sam Fuller*.

"**Sol Siegel**: Sign of Leo." *F&F* 4 (No. 11, Aug 58) 5. Sketch of the producer.

Signoret, Simone. "On Being Under the Director's Spell." *F&F* 8 (No. 9, June 62). See *2c*.

Vallance, Tom, and Allen Eyles. "**Alexander Singer**." *Film* (No. 38, Winter 63) 4–6. A brief description of the work and career of this new American director.

Marshman, D. "Mister Siodmak." *Life* 23 (25 Aug 47) 100–102. The work and struggles of director **Robert Siodmak**.

Taylor, [J.] Russell. "Encounter with Siodmak." *S&S* 28 (Nos. 3–4, Summer–Autumn 59) 180–182. **Robert Siodmak** comments on each of his films.

Nolan, Jack Edmund. "**Robert Siodmak**." *FIR* 20 (No. 4, Apr 69) 218–252. Career of the director of suspense films; chronology.

Joannides, Paul. "Two Films by **Douglas Sirk**." *Cinema* (Cambridge) (Nos. 6–7, Aug 70) 62–64. Analysis of *A Time to Love and a Time to Die* and *All That Heaven Allows*, indicating that they are the work of a single intelligence.

Krohn, Sven. "Convention Be Damned." *Atlas* 12 (Aug 66) 55–56. **Vilgot Sjöman** seen as successor to Bergman and ignored thus far only because of his interest in socially unacceptable behavior.

Vaughan, D. "**Victor Sjöström** and D. W. Griffith." *Film* (No. 15, Jan–Feb 58) 13–15+. Comparison of the two directors' work, indicating greater depth in the films of Sjöström. *See also 5, Victor Seastrom* (American spelling).

"Becker-Sjöström." *S&S* 29 (Spring 70). *See 5, Jacques Becker*.

Fleisher, Frederic. "**Victor Sjöström**: Pioneer of the Swedish Film." *Am Scandinavian Rev* 48 (Sep 60) 250–258. The director and his work.

Skolimowski, Jerzy. "The Twenty-first." *CdC in Eng* (No. 7, Jan 67) 55–57. Interview with the Polish film maker.

Toeplitz, Krzysztof-Teodor. "**Jerzy Skolimowski**: Portrait of a Debutant Director." *FQ* 21 (No. 1, Fall 67) 25–31. Sudden appearances nowadays of new names in film, especially rebels: Skolimowski is one of those who have lost faith in the kind of film that confronts important social problems.

Delahaye, Michel. "Passages and Levels: Interview with **Jerzy Skolimowski**." *CdC in Eng* (No. 12, Dec 67) 5–21. The Polish film maker discusses his theoretical concerns.

Thomsen, Christian Braad. "**Skolimowski**." *S&S* 37 (Summer 68) 142–144. Jerzy Skolimowski, young Polish director, in Denmark, where he wanted to shoot his next film; he discusses two of his six films, *Le Départ,* which he made in France, and *Hands Up,* which he made in Poland in 1967 and which is now banned there.

Blum, Peter. " 'An Accusation That I Throw in the Face of My Generation'—A Conversation with the Young Polish Director, **Jerzy Skolimowski.**" *F Com* 5 (No. 1, Fall 68) 12–20. Group interview; biography and annotated filmography.

Coughlan, Robert. "**Spyros Skouras** and His Wonderful CinemaScope." *Life* 35 (20 July 53) 81–84+.

"**Spyros P. Skouras.**" *F&F* 1 (No. 5, Feb 55) 3. Sketch of the 20th Century-Fox executive.

"Tally Ho." *Time* 80 (6 July 62) 38. 20th Century-Fox board of directors retires president **Spyros Skouras:** salary cut and total loss of power.

Coulson, Alan. "**Everett Sloan.**" *Film* (No. 37, Autumn 63) 13–15. Biographical sketch of the American actor.

Hudson, Roger. "The Secret Profession." *S&S* 34 (Summer 65). *See 2e.* About **Douglas Slocombe.**

De Carl, Lennard. "**Alexis Smith.**" *FIR* 21 (No. 6, June–July 70) 355–377. Career and film listings.

Sitney, P. Adams. "**Harry Smith** Interview." *F Cult* (No. 37, 1965) 4–13. Biographical information on this avant-garde film maker.

"**Fernando Solanas:** An Interview." *FQ* 24 (No. 1, Fall 70) 37–43. Reprinted from *Cinéthique* (Paris) No. 3, 1969.

Volpi, Gianni, *et al.* "Cinema as a Gun: An Interview with **Fernando Solanos.**" *Cinéaste* 3 (No. 2, Fall 69) 18–24+. Argentine director discusses his background and purposes, Latin-American cinema, and his own film, *La Hora de los Hornos.*

Jarratt, Vernon. "**Mario Soldati.**" *S&S* 17 (No. 66, Summer 48) 71–74. Italian novelist and director critically presented.

James, Howard. "**Elke Sommer:** A Celluloid Pagan." *Cinema* (Calif) 1 (No. 3, 1962–1963) 24–25.

Mazzetti, Lorenza. "People of Talent: **Alberto Sordi.**" *S&S* 26 (Summer 56) 51. He exposes the Italian character, but the audience loves him; his first important role in cinema, *The White Sheik.*

"On the Scene: **Terry Southern.**" *Playboy* 11 (No. 8, Aug 64) 116. Brief description of his career and works (*Candy, Dr. Strangelove*) and his philosophy as reflected in his writings.

Hammond, Robert M. "Writer vs. Director." *F Cult* 3 (No. 15, 1957) 5–7. An interview with the French film writer **Charles Spaak,** concerning the importance of scenarios; the

films he has written; the directors he has worked with.

"Talk with a Moviemaker." *Newswk* 54 (28 Dec 59) 64–65. Producer **Sam Spiegel.**

Fixx, James F. "The **Spiegel** Touch: Filming *Lawrence of Arabia.*" *Sat Rev* 45 (29 Dec 62) 13–15. How Sam Spiegel operates as a producer.

"Emperor." *Time* 81 (19 Apr 63) 67–68. Producer **Sam Spiegel:** career and life.

Stamp, Terence. "Frames and Feelings." *F&F* 15 (No. 3, Dec 68) 4–10. Interview about his acting and directors he has worked for.

Stamp, Terence. "Acting on Instinct." *F&F* 15 (No. 4, Jan 69) 4–10. Interview about his acting career.

"Biographical Note: **Barbara Stanwyck.**" *Th Arts* 35 (Aug 51) 36–37.

Ringgold, Gene. "**Barbara Stanwyck.**" *FIR* 14 (Dec 63) 577–602. Career study of the actress; filmography.

Ford, Charles. "**Ladislas Starevitch.**" *FIR* 9 (Apr 58). *See 2h(6).*

Richter, Hans. "**Frank Stauffacher.**" *F Cult* 1 (Nos. 5–6, 1955) 4–5. Eulogy for the San Francisco artist and film maker.

Geltzer, George. "**Mal St. Clair.**" *FIR* 5 (Feb 54) 56–61. Too sophisticated for Sennett, he became a success with critics as a comedy director (often using a minimum of titles), but was uncomfortable with sound.

"The Year of the Steigers." *Cinema* (Calif) 3 (No. 2, Mar 66) 18–21+. Interview with actor **Rod Steiger** and his wife, actress Claire Bloom.

"*Cinema* Interviews **Steiger.**" *Cinema* (Cambridge) (No. 1, Dec 68) 12–17. Is Rod Steiger an auteur of his films? Filmography.

"Interview: **Rod Steiger.**" *Playboy* 16 (No. 7, July 69) 61–74. Discusses health and food, his films, censorship, drugs, Hollywood and his relation to it, family life, acting, politics.

Hall, Dennis John. "Method Master." *F&F* 17 (No. 3, Dec 70) 28–32. On the career of actor **Rod Steiger.**

Martin, Pete. "The Man Who Made the Hit Called *Shane.*" *SEP* 226 (8 Aug 53) 32–33+. The life, work, and "touch" of **George Stevens.**

Houston, Penelope. "*Shane* and **George Stevens.**" *S&S* 23 (Oct–Dec 53) 71–76. *Shane* a hopeful trend in Westerns; biography of the director; a sequence in still pictures from and a short comment on the film *A Place in the Sun* also included.

Archer, Eugene. "**George Stevens** and the American Dream." *F Cult* 3 (No. 11, 1957) 3–4+. A detailed analysis of *A Place in the Sun, Shane,* and *Giant,* plus a survey of Stevens' stylistic origins, from *Alice Adams* to *I Remember Mama;* filmography.

Luft, Herbert G. "**George Stevens.**" *FIR* 9 (Nov 58) 486–496. Career of director

George Stevens, including an index to his twenty-three films, from *The Cohens and Kelleys in Trouble* (1933) to *The Diary of Anne Frank* (1958).

Knight, Arthur. "The Lost Art of Editing." *Sat Rev* (20 Dec 58). *See 2f.* About **George Stevens.**

Stasey, Joanne. "Hollywood Romantic." *F&F* 5 (No. 10, July 59) 9–10+. Films of **George Stevens.**

Bartlett, Nicholas. "Sentiment and Humanism." *Film* (No. 39, Spring 64) 26–29. A note on the films of **George Stevens.**

Heston, Charlton. "*Greatest Story* Diaries." *Cinema* (Calif) 2 (No. 4, Dec–Jan 64–65) 4–7. Star's close-up of director **George Stevens** at work.

Silke, James R. "A Monograph of **George Stevens'** Films." *Cinema* (Calif) 2 (No. 4, Dec–Jan 64–65) 8–16.

Stevens, George. "Stevens Talks About Movies." *Cinema* (Calif) 2 (No. 4, Dec–Jan 64–65) 17–25. His life in films.

Silke, James R. "The Picture." *Cinema* (Calif) 2 (No. 4, Dec–Jan 64–65) 26–35. How **George Stevens** uses land, actors, light, color, movement, and action.

McVay, Douglas. "Greatest—Stevens." *F&F* 11 (No. 7, Apr 65) 10–14; (No. 8, May 65) 16–19. Two-part study of the film career of George Stevens.

Beresford, Bruce. "**George Stevens.**" *Film* (No. 59, Summer 70) 12–14. An attempt to describe and assess the American director's work.

Maltin, Leonard, "**George Stevens:** Shorts to Features." *Action* 5 (No. 6, Nov–Dec 70) 12–14. Interview.

Bodeen, DeWitt. "**Anita Stewart.**" *FIR* 19 (No. 3, Mar 68) 145–181. Career and film chronology of silent-film actress.

Carey, Gary. "The Many Voices of **Donald Ogden Stewart.**" *F Com* 6 (No. 4, Winter 70–71) 74–79. A few satiric novels, a great deal of "play doctoring" for movies, only two originals, political leftism (from his wife, Ella Winter?); filmography.

Hume, Rod. "Small Talk Star." *F&F* 2 (No. 10, July 56) 4. The work of **James Stewart.**

Sweigart, William R. "**James Stewart.**" *FIR* 15 (No. 10, Dec 64) 585–605. Career to date and film chronology.

Stewart, James. "That's Enough for Me." *F&F* 12 (No. 7, Apr 66) 19–22. Interview about the advantages of acting and about his acting.

Idestam-Almquist, Bengi. "The Man Who Found Garbo." *F&F* 2 (No. 11, Aug 56) 10–11+. On the work of **Mauritz Stiller.**

Sjöström, Victor. "As I Remember Him." *F Com* 6 (No. 2, Summer 70) 48–50. Swedish director-actor recalls his friendship with the Finnish-born director **Mauritz Stiller.**

Stockwell, Dean. "Believe in the Part . . .

and See It Grow." *F&F* 6 (No. 7, Apr 60) 8+. Interview with Stockwell about his acting.

"**Dean Stockwell** on a Long Day." *Cinema* (Calif) 1 (No. 3, 1962–1963) 10–12. Interview with the actor.

Stokowski, Leopold. "My Symphonic Debut in the Films." *Etude* 54 (Nov 36) 685.

Ardmore, Jane K. "Home Is a Movie Set." *Parents Mag* 33 (Apr 58). *See 2a.* About **Andrew** and **Virginia Stone.**

Mason, James. "Filmaking." *FIR* 9 (May 59) 282–824. In letter to editor, actor praises location shooting by producer-director **Andrew Stone** and his wife Virginia.

Blakeston, Oswell. "The Romantic Cinema of **Henri Storck.**" *Arch Rev* 69 (No. 414, May 31) 173. Belgian director of documentary art films.

Stothart, Herbert, Jr. "**Herbert Stothart.**" *FIR* 21 (No. 10, Dec 70) 622–642. Career of a pioneer in film music composing, of the 1920s and 1930s.

Lawrenson, Helen. "The Route from Anne Frank to Camille is Straight Down the Appian Way." *Show* 2 (July 62) 69. **Susan Strasberg's** acting career.

Straub, Jean-Marie. "Frustration of Violence." *CdC in Eng* (No. 7, Jan 67) 58–59. Brief statement by the director, followed by review of *Unreconciled.*

Armes, Roy. "**Jean-Marie Straub.**" *London Mag* new series 10 (No. 6, Sep 70) 65–70.

Wyler, William, and **Barbra Streisand.** "Symbiosis Continued." *Action* 3 (No. 2, Mar–Apr 68). *See 5, William Wyler.* About Barbra Streisand.

"On the Scene: **Joseph Strick.**" *Playboy* 15 (No. 9, Sep 68) 177. Brief report on the producer-director of *Ulysses* and *The Savage Eye.*

Sturges, John. "How the West Was Lost!" *F&F* 9 (No. 3, Dec 62) 9–10. On his work in general; on the Hollywood Western.

Cherry, Richard. "Capsule of **John Sturges.**" *Action* 4 (No. 6, Nov–Dec 69) 9–11. The American producer-director discusses his own work.

Crowther, Bosley. "When Satire and Slapstick Meet." *NYTM* (27 Aug 44) 14–15. **Preston Sturges,** the man and his films.

Ericsson, Peter. "**Preston Sturges.**" *Sequence* (No. 4, Summer 48) 22–29. A critique of the American director's films.

Kracauer, Siegfried. "**Preston Sturges** or Laughter Betrayed." *FIR* 1 (Feb 50) 11–13+. Critical analyses of seven films.

Gow, Gordon. "Conversation with **Preston Sturges.**" *S&S* 25 (Spring 56) 182–183. On a BBC radio program *Talking of Films,* he discusses writer-directors, the film he was making at the time of the interview, *The*

Notebook of Major Thompson, and working conditions of the French industry.

King, Nel, and G. W. Stonier. "**Preston Sturges.**" *S&S* 28 (Nos. 3–4, Summer–Autumn 59) 185–186. Two tributes to the American director after his death.

Farber, Manny, and W. S. Poster. "**Preston Sturges: Success in the Movies.**" *F Cult* (No. 26, 1962) 9–16. His witty economy and non-sequiturs; "the most original movie talent produced in recent years; the most complex and puzzling" yet relevant to the "contemporary American psyche."

Jonsson, Eric. "**Preston Sturges** and the Theory of Decline." *F Cult* (No. 26, 1962) 17–21.

Houston, Penelope. "**Preston Sturges.**" *S&S* 34 (Summer 65) 130–134. The American comedy writer-director in whose films the victory is likely to go to "plain human silliness and gullibility."

Budd, Michael. "Notes on **Preston Sturges** and America." *F Soc Rev* (Jan 68) 22–26.

Sarris, Andrew. "**Preston Sturges** in the Thirties." *F Com* 6 (No. 4, Winter 70–71) 81–85. Early screenplays of the writer, who became a director in 1940; special analysis of *The Power and the Glory;* complete filmography.

Hardy, Forsyth. "The Films of **Arne Sucksdorff.**" *S&S* 17 (No. 66, Summer 48) 60–63+. An analysis of the Swedish director's work.

Ericsson, Peter. "**Arne Sucksdorff.**" *Sequence* (No. 7, Spring 49) 24–29. His work, including filmography.

De La Roche, Catherine. "**Arne Sucksdorff's** Adventure." *S&S* 23 (Oct–Dec 53) 83–86+. Just finishing his first feature film, *The Great Adventure,* which deals mainly with the animals he sees and knows in his native Sweden, Sucksdorff gives some of his ideas about film making.

De La Roche, Catherine. "Film-Maker on His Own." *F&F* 1 (No. 2, Nov 54) 11. Survey of **Arne Sucksdorff's** short subjects.

"**Arne Sucksdorff.**" *Image* 4 (No. 5, May 55) 40. Brief filmography of the Swedish film maker.

"**Arne Sucksdorff.**" *Cinema* (Calif) 2 (No. 6, July–Aug 65) 39. Short interview and comment on *Children of Copacabana.*

Jacobs, Jack. "**Margaret Sullavan.**" *FIR* 11 (No. 4, Apr 60) 193–207. Life and films of the American actress.

"**David Susskind.**" *Film* (No. 33, Autumn 62). See 6c(1).

Harriman, Helena Case. "**Gloria Swanson.**" *New Yorker* (18 Jan 30) 24–27. Profile of the actress.

Brownlow, Kevin. "**Gloria Swanson.**" *Film* (No. 41, Autumn 64) 7–10. The American actress discusses her early career.

Bodeen, DeWitt. "**Gloria Swanson.**" *FIR* 16 (No. 4, Apr 65) 193–216. Career to date, and film chronology.

Robinson, David, Tom Milne, and John Russell Taylor. "Twenties Show People." *S&S* 37 (Autumn 68). *See 4b.* About **Gloria Swanson.**

Nogueira, Rui. "I Am Not Going to Write My Memoirs." *S&S* 38 (Spring 69) 58–62. Gloria Swanson recalls her long career, including *Madame Sans-Gêne, Nero's Weekend, Queen Kelly,* and *Sunset Boulevard;* she also talks about Sam Wood, with whom she made ten pictures, Cecil De Mille, Allan Dwan, and D. W. Griffith.

Bodeen, DeWitt. "**Blanche Sweet.**" *FIR* 16 (No. 9, Nov 65) 549–579. Career and film listing of the silent-film actress.

Sitton, Robert. "Hungarian Director Szabo Discusses His Film *Father.*" *F Com* 5 (No. 1, Fall 68) 58–63. *New York Times* writer interviews **Istvan Szabo** on WBAI, Pacifica Radio.

T

Bodeen, DeWitt. "**Constance Talmadge.**" *FIR* 18 (No. 10, Dec 67) 613–630. Career and film listing of the silent-film actress.

Spears, Jack. "**Norma Talmadge.**" *FIR* 18 (No. 1, Jan 67) 16–54. Career and film chronology.

Bogdanovich, Peter. "**Frank Tashlin**—An Interview and an Appreciation." *F Cult* (No. 26, 1962) 21–33. Filmography included.

Bogdanovich, Peter. "**Tashlin!**" *Movie* (No. 7, Feb 63) 14–15. An interview with the American director.

Cameron, Ian. "**Frank Tashlin** and the New World." *Movie* (No. 7, Feb 63) 16–23. An analysis of Tashlin's work, especially in thematic terms; filmography and biography.

Bogdanovich, Peter. "**Tashlin's** Cartoons." *Movie* (No. 16, Winter 68–69) 38–39. A listing of some of the cartoons which Frank Tashlin directed.

Queval, Jean. "*Jour de Fête.*" *S&S* 19 (June 50) 165–166. **Jacques Tati,** his career as a comedian and film maker.

Mayer, Andrew C. "The Art of **Jacques Tati.**" *QFRTV* 10 (No. 1, Fall 55) 19–23. Government attorney and film fan regrets episodic nature of French comedian's films.

Simon, John K. "Hulot; or The Common Man as Observer and Critic." *Yale French Studies* (No. 23, 1959) 18–25. **Jacques Tati's** comic essence as deliberately allied with social context.

Woodside, Harold. "**Tati** Speaks." *Take One* 2 (No. 6, 1969) 6–8. Notes on, and an interview with, the French director-actor.

Armes, Roy. "The Comic Art of **Jacques Tati.**" *Screen* 11 (No. 1, Feb 70) 68–80.

Meehan, Thomas. "Success, Et Cetera." *Show* 4 (Oct 64). *See 5, Richard Burton.* About **Elizabeth Taylor.**

Israel, Lee. "Rise and Fall of **Elizabeth Taylor.**" *Esq* 67 (Mar 67) 96–99+.

Essoe, Gabe. "**Elizabeth Taylor.**" *FIR* 21 (No. 7, Aug–Sep 70) 393–410. Career and film chronology.

Bowers, Ronald L. "**Robert Taylor.**" *FIR* 18 (No. 1, Jan 63) 1–15. Career and film chronology.

Austin, John. "The **William Desmond Taylor** Mystery." *Show* (3 Sep 70) 18–19. Circumstances surrounding the unsolved death of this silent-film director.

Temple, Gertrude. "Bringing Up Shirley." *American* 119 (Feb 35) 26–27+ The mother of **Shirley Temple** tells how her daughter got into the movies.

Black, **Shirley Temple**. "Tomorrow I'll Be Thirty." *Good Housekeeping* 145 (Nov 57) 114–115+. Reflections on her life.

Terry-Thomas. "Playing Myself and Others." *F&F* 8 (No. 3, Dec 61) 11. Reflections on the British comedian's current films.

Bucher, Felix. "Akira Kurosawa—**Hiroshi Teshigahara.**" *Camera* 45 (No. 9, Sep 66). *See 5, Akira Kurosawa.*

"Metro-Goldwyn-Mayer." *Fortune* 6 (Dec 32). *See 6b(2).* About **Irving Thalberg.**

Fiskin, Jeffrey Alan. "An Interview with **Marlo Thomas.**" *Cinema* (Calif) 5 (No. 4, 1969) 8–10. Actress from TV has made her first feature, *Jenny.*

Thomas, Ralph. "My Way with Screen Humour." *F&F* 2 (No. 5, Feb 56) 5. By the director of *Doctor in the House.*

Sternfeld, Frederick W. "Current Chronicle." *Musical Q* 35 (Jan 49). *See 2g(2d).* About **Virgil Thomson.**

"Theme Song." *Time* 62 (14 Sep 53) 108. Composer **Dimitri Tiomkin** and popular theme songs.

"Philosopher." *New Yorker* 30 (15 Jan 55) 20. **Mike Todd** discusses his projected filming of *War and Peace.*

Sayre, Joel. "**Mike Todd** and His Big Bug-Eye." *Life* 38 (7 Mar 55) 140–142+. A lengthy profile containing a detailed account of the Todd-AO process.

Hornblow, Arthur, Jr. "The Great **Todd** Revolution." *JSPG* (June 63) 15–20. Mike Todd, his wide-screen projects, and the skeptics he proved wrong.

Toland, Gregg. "Motion Picture Cameraman." *Th Arts* 25 (Sep 41) 646–654. The cameraman for *Citizen Kane* discusses his work in that film and in general.

Koenig, Lester. "**Gregg Toland**, Film-Maker." *Screen Writer* 3 (Dec 47) 27–33. Director of cinematography comments on *The Best Years of Our Lives,* other cameramen, directors, writers, and the star system.

Slocombe, Douglas. "The Work of **Gregg Toland.**" *Sequence* (No. 8, Summer 49) 67–76. The Hollywood cameraman's films. See also letter in (No. 9, Autumn 49) 112.

Mitchell, George. "A Great Cameraman." *FIR* 7 (Dec 56) 504–512. A study of the late cinematographer **Gregg Toland** and his career, which included *Wuthering Heights, The Grapes of Wrath,* and *Citizen Kane.*

Roman, Robert C. "**Marta Toren.**" *FIR* 10 (Aug–Sep 59) 445–446. Letter to editor gives life story and career of then Swedish actress, who died at thirty.

Trajtenberg, Mario. "Torre-Nilsson and His Double." *FQ* 15 (No. 1, Fall 61) 34–41. Discovered by a small Cannes audience for *End of Innocence* in 1957, **Leopoldo Torre-Nilsson** gets little support in his own Buenos Aires; using mostly novels written by his wife, Beatriz Guido, he often deals with adolescents faced by corruption.

Di Nubila, Domingo. "An Argentine Partnership." *F&F* 7 (No. 12, Sep 61) 17–18+. On **Leopoldo Torre-Nilsson.**

Botsford, Keith. "**Leopoldo Torre-Nilsson:** The Underside of the Coin." *Show* 2 (Nov 62) 84–85+. Elements of Argentine society depicted in his films.

Soltero, José. "Interview with **Leopoldo Torre-Nilsson.**" *Medium* 1 (No. 1, Summer 67) 20–26. At the time of filming *Monday's Child* in Puerto Rico.

Tourneur, Jacques. "Taste Without Clichés." *F&F* 12 (No. 2, Nov 56) 9–11. Interview about American film-making career of the son of Maurice Tourneur.

Geltzer, George. "**Maurice Tourneur.**" *FIR* 12 (No. 4, Apr 61) 193–214. Biography and film list of the French director.

Hill, Derek. "Sixty Round the Bend." *F&F* 1 (No. 8, May 55) 5. The career of **Spencer Tracy.**

Cowie, Peter. "**Spencer Tracy.**" *F&F* 7 (No. 9, June 61) 8–9+. Study of the films of Spencer Tracy.

Tozzi, Romano. "**Spencer Tracy.**" *FIR* 17 (No. 10, Dec 66) 601–634. Career and film chronology.

Hagen, Ray. "**Claire Trevor.**" *FIR* 14 (Nov 63) 541–552. Career study of the actress; filmography.

"Two Actors." *F&F* 7 (No. 1, Oct 60) 13+. Interview with **Jean-Louis Trintignant** and Jean-Paul Belmondo.

Haskell, Molly. "**Jean-Louis Trintignant.**" *Show* (20 Aug 70) 34–38. Remarks on his acting career; comments on what it was like to work with directors such as Rohmer, Robbe-Grillet, Bertolucci.

Brož, J. "The Puppet Film as an Art." *F Cult* 1 (Nos. 5–6, 1955) 19–20. An interview with the Czech film-maker **Jiří Trnka:** *Prince*

Bayaya, The Good Soldier Shweik, Old Czech Legend.

Brož, Jaroslav. "An Interview with the Puppet-Film Director, **Jirí Trnka**." *Film* (No. 7, Jan–Feb 56) 16–19.

"Trnkaland." *Newswk* 67 (28 Mar 66) 99. **Jirí Trnka**, celebrated Czech animator, displays his craft at the World's Fair in Montreal.

Smith, Maynard T. "**Lamar Trotti**." *FIR* 9 (Aug–Sep 58) 380–384. A prolific screenwriter and producer who worked at 20th Century-Fox; an index to his fifty-four films, which included *Young Mr. Lincoln* and *The Ox-Bow Incident*. See also letter to editor by Dudley Nichols in 9 (Oct 58) 473.

"On Film: Visit with **F. Truffaut**." *New Yorker* 36 (20 Feb 60) 36–37. Chatty account of Truffaut's visit in New York after *The 400 Blows* was made.

Franci, R. M., and Marshall Lewis. "A Conversation with **François Truffaut**." *NY F Bul* 2 (Nos. 12, 13, 14, 1961) 5–10. Auteur theory, Renoir, and the New Wave.

Marcorelles, Louis. "Interview with **Truffaut**." *S&S* 31 (Winter 61–62) 35–37. Having just completed *Jules and Jim*, François Truffaut discusses his own situation and that of the young French cinema; reprinted from *France Observateur*.

Franci, R. M., and Marshall Lewis. "Conversations with **François Truffaut**." *NY F Bul* 3 (No. 3, 1962) 16–25. His early films and the auteur theory; *Jules and Jim* and cinema as a popular medium; filmography.

Truffaut, François. "*Jules and Jim*, Sex and Life." *F&F* 8 (No. 10, July 62) 19. Comments on New Wave and his own films.

Shatnoff, Judith. "**François Truffaut**—The Anarchist Imagination." *FQ* 16 (No. 3, Spring 63) 3–11. Detailed look at three films: *The 400 Blows, Jules and Jim,* and *Shoot the Piano Player;* "Truffaut does as he pleases. . . . As soon as we settle down with one metaphor, he jars us out and into another, perhaps one which is contradictory.

"**François Truffaut**—an Interview." *FQ* 17 (No. 1, Fall 63) 3–13. The French director comments on his sojourn as movie critic, other New Wave directors, the American cinema, and his films; he is especially critical of the way *Shoot the Piano Player* turned out; reprinted from *Cahiers du Cinéma* (Dec 62).

Oxenhandler, Neal. "**Truffaut**, Heir to Apollinaire." *Shenandoah* 15 (No. 2, Winter 64) 8–13. Each has a moral universe.

"**Truffaut**." *New Yorker* 40 (31 Oct 64) 45–46. Talk with Truffaut about his book *Hitchcock* (Simon and Schuster, 1967).

Nowell-Smith, Geoffrey. "**François Truffaut**." *New Left Rev* (No. 31, May–June 65) 86–90. A study of his films.

Klein, Michael. "The Literary Sophistication of **François Truffaut**." *F Com* 3 (No. 3, Summer 65) 24–29. Graduate student in English analyzes *Shoot the Piano Player* and *Jules and Jim* in terms of dislocation and irony, concluding that a haunting work of art is a result of manipulation.

Jacob, Gilles. "The 400 Blows of **François Truffaut**." *S&S* 37 (Autumn 68) 190–191. Truffaut defends the stand he took in favor of the Cinémathèque and his role in helping to bring the Cannes Film Festival to an abrupt halt.

Houston, Penelope. "Hitchcockery." *S&S* 37 (Autumn 68). See 7b(4). About **François Truffaut**.

De Gramont, Sanche. "Life-Style of *Homo Cinematicus*." *NYTM* (15 June 69) 12–13+. On **Truffaut**: a kind of interview, in which Truffaut talks about how he works.

Wood, Robin. "Chabrol and **Truffaut**." *Movie* (No. 16, Winter 69–70). See 5, *Claude Chabrol.*

Truffaut, François. "Is Truffaut the Happiest Man on Earth?" *Esq* 74 (Aug 70) 67+. Truffaut's thoughts on his film making and on other directors.

"**Truffaut**." *New Yorker* 46 (17 Dec 70) 35–37. Interview with director on his last ten years in film and his thoughts on America.

Scully, Frank. "Scully on Tully." *Screen Writer* 3 (Aug 47) 8–10. A memorial essay on screenwriter **Jim Tully**.

Hanson, Curtis Lee. "Two for the Show." *Cinema* (Calif) 3 (No. 6, Winter 67) 4–8+. Interview with **Lawrence Turman**, producer of *The Graduate*.

Valentino, Lon. "For Love of Lana." *Show* (Jan 70). See 7b(1c). About **Lana Turner**.

U

Marcorelles, Louis. "Talking about Acting: Albert Finney and **Mary Ure**." *S&S* 30 (Spring 61). See 2b(1).

Ustinov, Peter. "Doing It All at Once." *F&F* 6 (No. 8, May 60) 5+. Ustinov answers questions on his work as writer and actor.

Bachmann, Gideon. "**Ustinov**." *Film* (No. 30, Winter 61) 18–21. An interview with Peter Ustinov; his own work and his theories about film.

V

Canby, Vincent. "Czar of the Movie Business." *NYTM* (23 Apr 67) 38–39+. Biography of MPA President **Jack Valenti** and his first year's work at the job.

Lambert, Gavin. "Fairbanks and **Valentino**: The Last Heroes." *Sequence* (No. 8, Summer 49). See 5, *Douglas Fairbanks.*

Huff, Theodore. "The Career of **Rudolph Valentino**." *FIR* 3 (Apr 52) 145–163. Brief

estimate of the silent-film star, with a list
of his films.

Card, James. "**Rudolph Valentino.**" *Image* 7
(No. 5, May 58) 106–112. The legend and
the life of the American film star.

Marberry, M. M. "The Overloved One." *Am
Heritage* 16 (No. 5, Aug 65) 84–86+. The
funeral of **Rudolph Valentino** and the publicity seekers who sought to gain from it.

Mencken, H. L. "On Hollywood—and **Valentino.**" *CJ* 9 (No. 2, Spring 70). *See 7d.*

Christgau, R. "**Vanderbeek:** Master of Animation." *Pop Photog* 57 (Sep 65) 106–111. His
equipment, career, and methods.

Christgau, Robert. "**Vanderbeek.**" *Cavalier* 17
(No. 9, July 67) 61–65. Career of this early
underground-film maker.

Mekas, Jonas, and Edouard de Laurot. "The
American Documentary—Limitations and
Possibilities." *F Cult* 2 (No. 9, 1956) 6–9.
Interview with **Willard Van Dyke** about such
problems as a definition of documentary,
government sponsorship, and the moral responsibilities of the film maker.

Engle, Harrison. "Thirty Years of Social Inquiry
—an Interview with **Willard Van Dyke.**" *F
Com* 3 (No. 2, Spring 65) 24–37. Documentary-film maker comments on his own
films, the underground, collaboration in documentary, Lorentz and Flaherty; annotated
filmography of his forty-three productions.

Zuckerman, Art. "Focus on **Willard Van Dyke.**"
Pop Photog 56 (Apr 65) 118–119+. His
career as documentary director.

Beatty, Jerome. "He Brings 'Em Back in Cans."
American 118 (Aug 34) 76–77+. Profile of
director W. S. Van Dyke.

Johnston, Alva. "**W. S. Van Dyke.**" *New
Yorker* (28 Sep 35) 20–24. Profile of the
director.

Peavy, Charles D. "An Afro-American in Paris:
The Films of **Melvin Van Peebles.**" *Cinéaste*
3 (No. 1, Summer 69) 2–3. A brief description of this black American's directing work.

"On the Scene: **Melvin Van Peebles.**" *Playboy*
17 (No. 9, Sep 70) 195. Biographical sketch.

Varda, Agnès. "The Underground River." *F&F*
16 (No. 6, Mar 70) 6–10. Interview on her
filming career.

Herring, Robert. "**Conrad Veidt.**" *Close Up* 7
(No. 4, Oct 30) 270–272. An interview and
comments on the work of the German actor.

Vertov, Dziga. "The Writings of Dziga Vertov."
F Cult (No. 25, 1962) 50–65. Selected
writings and manifestos (*Kinoks-Revolution,
Notebooks, Kine Eye Lectures*) of the Russian documentary-film maker.

Giercke, Christoph. "**Dziga Vertov.**" *Afterimage* (No. 1, Apr 70) 6 pages. Comments
on some Vertov texts.

Gray, Michael. "No Swan Song for Director
Charles Vidor." *F&F* 2 (No. 9, June 56) 12.
Biographical piece, with filmography.

Dunham, Harold. "**Florence Vidor.**" *FIR* 21
(No. 1, Jan 70) 21–49. Biography of the
silent-film actress.

Harrington, Curtis. "The Later Years: **King
Vidor's** Hollywood Progress." *S&S* 22 (Apr–
June 53) 179–182+. Three years of unemployment after the failure of *An American
Romance* may have led this American
director to increasing slickness and exaggeration, beginning with *Duel in the Sun.*

Perkins, V. F., and Mark Shivas. "An Interview
with **King Vidor.**" *Movie* (No. 11, July–Aug
63) 7–10.

Higham, Charles. "**King Vidor.**" *F Her* 1
(No. 4, Summer 66) 15–25. His most characteristic films assert the values of the America
of the backwoods.

"**King Vidor** at NYU." *Cinéaste* 1 (No. 4,
Spring 68) 2–8+. A transcribed interview
with the director; lengthy discussion of *The
Crowd, Hallelujah,* and *The Big Parade;*
comments on Eisenstein and Warhol.

Greenberg, Joel. "War, Wheat and Steel." *S&S*
37 (Autumn 68) 192–197. Extensive interview with **King Vidor**, who directed his first
feature in 1918, and his most recent, *Solomon
and Sheba,* in 1959; the title refers to three
themes he managed to put on film.

Greenberg, Joel. "**Salka Viertel.**" *S&S* 35
(Spring 66) 70–71. Note on expatriate writer
who was a friend of Greta Garbo and wrote
several of her films; her memoirs are in
preparation.

Cavalcanti, Alberto. "**Jean Vigo.**" *Cinema Q*
(Edinburgh) 3 (No. 2, Winter 35) 86–88.

Kracauer, Siegfried. "**Jean Vigo.**" (Tr. by William Melnitz.) *Hwd Q* 2 (No. 3, Apr 47)
261–263. Descriptions of two films by the
young French director, *Zéro de conduite* and
L'Atalante.

Zilzer, Gyula. "Remembrance of **Jean Vigo.**"
Hwd Q 3 (No. 2, Winter 47–48) 125–128.
Short, vivid biography of the noted French
film maker by a man who worked with him.

Barbarow, George. "The Work of **Jean Vigo.**"
Politics 5 (No. 1, Winter 48) 37–38. Analysis
of Vigo's films, especially *Zéro de conduite.*

Ashton, Dudley Shaw. "Portrait of Vigo." *Film*
(No. 6, Dec 55) 20–23. Jean Vigo, his life
and his films.

Rhode, Eric. "**Jean Vigo.**" *Encounter* 26 (Feb
66) 37–42. The French director's anarchistic
style and his influence on Truffaut's *400
Blows.*

Lane, John Francis. "The Hurricane Visconti."
F&F 1 (No. 3, Dec 54) 8–9. Background of
the director **Luchino Visconti** and of his new
film, *Senso.*

Castello, Giulio Cesare. "**Luchino Visconti.**"
S&S 25 (Spring 56) 184–190+. Biography
of the Italian director responsible for *Ossessione, Bellissima, La Terra trema,* and *Senso;*
close analysis of these films.

Lane, John Francis. "Visconti—The Last Decadent." *F&F* 2 (No. 10, July 56) 11–12.

Dyer, Peter John. "The Vision of Visconti." *Film* (No. 12, Mar–Apr 57) 22–24.

Doniol-Valcroze, Jacques, and Jean Domarchi. "Visconti Interviewed." *S&S* 28 (Nos. 3–4, Summer–Autumn 59) 144–147+. His work with Renoir and his films through *Senso*.

Poggi, Gianfranco. "Luchino Visconti and the Italian Cinema." *FQ* 13 (No. 3, Spring 60) 11–22. Critical study of the films from *Ossessione* to *White Nights*, the historical and realistic perspectives in each, and the contrast with the neorealism of Rossellini and De Sica.

Visconti, Luchino. "The Miracle That Gave Man Crumbs." *F&F* 7 (No. 4, Jan 61) 11. The Italian director discusses his attitude toward film making.

Aristarco, Guido. "The Earth Still Trembles." *F&F* 7 (No. 4, Jan 61) 12+. Italian critic examines current trends in the films of Visconti.

Minoff, Leon. "Luchino Visconti—New Old Master." *Sat Rev* 45 (29 Dec 62) 18–19+. Career study; part of report *Saturday Review* "The Lonely Art of Film-Making."

Johnson, Ian. "Visconti's *Rocco*." *Motion* (No. 3, Spring 62) 5–10+. An analysis of Luchino Visconti's work, with emphasis upon *Rocco and His Brothers* and the film maker's realistic tendencies.

Lucas, Christopher. "Monica Vitti." *Show* 1 (Oct 61) 102–103. Her acting career.

O'Leary, Liam. "Arthur von Gerlach—The Unknown Director. *Silent Picture* (No. 8, Autumn 70) 23–24. Only two films survive from his short career.

Pringle, Henry F. "Josef von Sternberg." *New Yorker* (28 Mar 31) 26–29. Profile of the director.

Harrington, Curtis. "The Dangerous Compromise." *Hwd Q* 3 (No. 4, Summer 48–Summer 49) 405–415. Experimental-film maker declares Josef von Sternberg declined as director because of submission to commercial pressures.

Harrington, Curtis. "Arrogant Gesture." *Th Arts* 34 (Nov 50) 42–45+. Josef von Sternberg and his productions.

von Sternberg, Josef. "More Light." *S&S* 25 (Fall 55). See 2e.

von Sternberg, Josef. "A Taste for Celluloid." *F&F* 9 (No. 10, July 63) 40–42. Interview about the director's life and films.

Smith, Jack. "Belated Appreciation of V. S." *F Cult* (No. 31, 1963–1964) 4–5. Brief tribute to the work of Josef von Sternberg.

Nugent, John. "The Puppeteer." *Newswk* (29 Mar 65) 88–89. Josef von Sternberg discusses his autobiography with a journalist.

Bogdanovich, Peter. "Josef von Sternberg." *Movie* (No. 13, Summer 65) 17–25. A biography, filmography, and interview.

Green, O. O. "Six Films of Josef von Sternberg." *Movie* (No. 13, Summer 65) 26–31. Analysis of *The Blue Angel, Dishonored, Morocco, Scarlet Empress, The Devil Is a Woman,* and *Shanghai Gesture*.

Stein, Elliott. *"Fun in a Chinese Laundry."* *S&S* 34 (Autumn 65) 202–204. A lengthy review of Josef von Sternberg's autobiography, *Fun in a Chinese Laundry* (Macmillan, 1965), evaluated as containing a great deal of self-puffery and a fine chapter on lighting.

Weinberg, Herman G. "Josef von Sternberg." *F Her* 1 (No. 2, Winter 65–66) 13–17. Excerpt from *Josef von Sternberg* (Paris: Editions Seghers, 1966): symbolism, eroticism, and mannerisms in his films.

Macklin, F. A. "Interview with Josef von Sternberg." *F Her* 1 (No. 2, Winter 65–66) 2–11. Questioned about his films, von Sternberg steadfastly refuses to answer; filmography included.

Brownlow, Kevin. "Sternberg." *Film* (No. 45, Spring 66) 4–10. Comments and quotes from an interview with Josef von Sternberg.

Russell, Lee. "Josef von Sternberg." *New Left Rev* (No. 36, Mar–Apr 66) 78–81. Study of his films.

Mayer, H. A. *"Queen Kelly* and Queen Victoria." *Close Up* 8 (No. 2, June 31) 136–138. Comments on the work of Erich von Stroheim.

Noble, Peter. "Stroheim—His Work and Influence." *S&S* 16 (No. 64, Winter 47–48) 163–166. Erich von Stroheim.

Noble, Peter. "The Man You Love to Hate." *Th Arts* 34 (Jan 50) 22–27+. Erich von Stroheim, now an "exile" in a Seine château, is "a solid boxoffice star in France"; his biography, his films, and the characters he has played.

Schwerin, Jules V. "The Resurgence of von Stroheim." *FIR* 1 (Apr 50) 3–6+. Von Stroheim undertook the responsibilities of the combined roles behind the camera for the sake of artistic unity, whereas this practice today by studio executives is done in the name of economy.

Lambert, Gavin. "Stroheim Revisited: The Missing Third in the American Cinema." *S&S* 22 (Apr–June 53) 165–171+. His association with D. W. Griffith and some of the films he later directed, including a review of *Greed*, which Erich von Stroheim considered his only "real picture."

Reisz, Karel. "Stroheim in London." *S&S* 23 (Apr–June 54) 172. Visiting for fourteen-week season of his films at National Film Theatre.

Everson, William K. "Erich von Stroheim: 1885–1957." *FIR* 8 (Aug–Sep 57) 305–314. An appraisal of his career and films which does not take too seriously the charges that *Greed* was ruined and his talent completely misunderstood in Hollywood. See also letters in 8 (Oct 57) 423–428 and 8 (Nov 57) 476.

Curtiss, T. Quinn. "The Last Years of von Stroheim." *F Cult* 4 (No. 18, 1958) 3–5. By "an old friend . . . who saw him constantly" during his last ten years.

Watts, Richard. "A Few Reminiscences." *F Cult* 4 (No. 18, 1958) 5–7. About Erich von Stroheim.

Eisner, Lotte H. "Homage to an Artist." *F Cult* 4 (No. 18, 1958) 7–8. To Erich von Stroheim.

von Stroheim, Erich. "Erich von Stroheim Introduces *The Merry Widow*." *F Cult* 4 (No. 18, 1958) 9–11. A transcription of introductory remarks to a screening at the Palais des Beaux-Arts, Brussels, 28 November 1955.

Arnheim, Rudolf. "Portrait of an Artist." *F Cult* 4 (No. 18, 1958) 11–13. Discussion of Erich von Stroheim and his films *Foolish Wives, Wedding March,* and *Greed.*

Eisner, Lotte H. "Notes on the Style of Stroheim." *F Cult* 4 (No. 18, 1958) 13–19. Griffith's influence and differences from Lubitsch.

Marion, Denis. "Erich von Stroheim: The Legend and the Fact." *S&S* 31 (Winter 61–62) 22–23+. Film critic of *Le Soir* of Brussels wrote a book on von Stroheim and then further researched the birth and background of the director; his father was a hatmaker; Erich volunteered for the Austrian army but deserted and emigrated within a year.

von Sydow, Max. "Working with Bergman." *F&F* 6 (No. 11, Aug 60) 7. Interview with the Swedish film actor.

W

Hanson, Curtis Lee. "Two for the Show." *Cinema* (Calif) 3 (No. 6, Winter 67) 4–8+. Interview with Ray Wagner, producer of *Petulia.*

Wajda, Andrzej. "Destroying the Commonplace." *F&F* 8 (No. 2, Nov 61) 9+. Interview about his own film making and films in general.

Austen, David. "The Wajda Generation." *F&F* 14 (No. 10, July 68) 14–17. On the Polish director Andrzej Wajda's trilogy.

Toeplitz, Krzysztof-Teodor. "Wajda *Redivivus*." *FQ* 23 (No. 2, Winter 69–70) 37–41. Andrzej Wajda's new films, *Everything for Sale* and *A Fly Hunt,* demonstrate that he has taken leave of military stories and is confronting formal problems of reality and individual needs—a "new and vigorous period of creativity."

Goodman, Ezra. "How to Be a Hollywood Producer." *Harper's* 196 (May 48) 413–423.

A typical day with Warners producer Jerry Wald; his personal history.

"Book Buyer." *Time* 72 (6 Oct 58). See *3f(2)*. About Jerry Wald.

Gehman, Richard. "What Makes Jerry Run?" *Cosmopolitan* 147 (July 59) 76–81. Producer Jerry Wald and his movies.

"Run, Run, Run." *Newswk* 54 (20 July 59) 94. Movie producer Jerry Wald.

Barber, Rowland. "The Mighty Soundtrack in Bungalow Ten." *Show* 2 (Mar 62) 86–91. Why Jerry Wald is one of Hollywood's most successful producers; his career as a scriptwriter, his box-office successes.

Arlen, Michael J. "At Last! The Mighty Marvelous Waldmachine." *Esq* 57 (May 62) 128–129+. Jerry Wald, a "dependent" independent producer and his contribution to the film industry; his interest in making classics into screenplays.

Zucker, Phyllis. "Robert Walker." *FIR* 21 (No. 3, Mar 70) 136–145. Career and film chronology of this actor.

Nolan, Jack Edmund. "Edgar Wallace." *FIR* 18 (No. 2, Feb 67) 71–85. Biography and comments on author whose works were made into films; film chronology.

Wallach, Eli. "My Strange Dilemma." *F&F* 7 (No. 11, Aug 61) 19. General reflections on his career and writing.

Wallach, Eli. "In All Directions." *F&F* 10 (No. 8, May 64) 7–8. Interview on his acting career and acting in general.

"Face to Face with a Boy Whose Life Was Changed by a Movie." *Seventeen* 25 (Oct 66) 143. On Lew Wallach, actor in *Up the Down Staircase.*

Austen, David. "Following No Formula." *F&F* 16 (No. 3, Dec 69) 4–8. Interview with producer Hal Wallis on the industry and his career.

Conley, Walter. "Raoul Walsh—His Silent Films." *Silent Picture* (No. 9, Winter 70–71) 2–18. Quotations from secondary sources; his work with Griffith and his films; his style as a director and his character as an actor.

Walters, Charles. "On the Bright Side." *F&F* 16 (No. 11, Aug 70) 12–18. On his directing career.

Griggs, John. "Here Was an Actor!" *FIR* 3 (Mar 52) 118–124+. Enthusiastic appreciation for the abilities of Henry B. Walthall; survey of his films, which the actor-author collects.

"Walter Wanger." *F&F* 7 (No. 3, Dec 60) 5. Career sketch of the American producer.

Brownlow, Kevin. "The Early Days of Walter Wanger." *Film* (No. 39, Spring 64) 10–11. Biographical note on the American producer.

Malanga, Gerard. "Andy Warhol." *Kulchur* 4 (No. 16, Winter 64–65) 37–39. An interview.

Junker, Howard. "Andy Warhol, Movie Maker."

Nation 200 (22 Feb 65) 206–208. Filmography, on-set account of filming, and informal interview.

Ehrenstein, David. "An Interview with **Andy Warhol**." *F Cult* (No. 40, Spring 66) 41.

Stoller, James. "Beyond Cinema: Notes on Some Films by **Andy Warhol**." *FQ* 20 (No. 1, Fall 66) 35–38. There's a sadness about the whole ambience, but his "art" is worth listening to when it openly mingles film and gossip.

Tyler, Parker. "Dragtime and Drugtime; or Film à la **Warhol**." *Evergreen Rev* 11 (No. 46, Apr 67) 28–31. Tyler considers the nature of time in Warhol's films, in the light of the drug experience.

Berg, Gretchen. "Nothing to Lose: Interview with **Andy Warhol**." *CdC in Eng* (No. 10, May 67) 38–43. Andy Warhol speaks about himself and his films.

Whitehall, Richard. "Whitehall with **Warhol**." *Cinema* (Calif) 3 (No. 6, Winter 67) 20–24. A personal impression and appraisal.

Lugg, Andrew M. "On **Andy Warhol**." *Cinéaste* 1 (No. 3, Winter 67–68) 9–13; (No. 4, Spring 68) 12–15+. His development from painter to film maker; stylistic discussion of *Empire*.

Berg, Gretchen. "Andy." *Take One* 1 (No. 10, 1968) 10–11. A personal account of **Andy Warhol**, his personality and his work in 1965.

Brill, Judith. "**Andy Warhol** Superartist." *F Lib Q* 1 (No. 4, Fall 68) 15–18. A film made about the film maker in his own style which tells about his career as an artist.

Carroll, Paul. "What's a **Warhol**?" *Playboy* 16 (No. 9, Sep 69) 132. Examination of content of Warhol's films.

Perreault, John. "**Andy Warhol**." *Vogue* 155 (1 Mar 70) 165–166+. A talk with the film director; an interpretation of his work.

Kent, Leticia (ed.). "It's Hard to Be Your Own Script." *Vogue* 155 (1 Mar 70) 167+. **Andy Warhol** talks about his films.

Rayns, Tony. "**Andy Warhol** Films Inc: Communication in Action." *Cinema* (Cambridge) (Nos. 6–7, Aug 70) 42–47. Interviews with Paul Morrissey and Joe D'Allesandro, with supplementary text on Warhol's work.

Heflin, Lee. "Notes on Seeing the Films of **Andy Warhol**." *Afterimage* (No. 2, Autumn 70) 30–33. A personal observation of the works.

Pomeroy, Ralph. "An Interview with **Andy Warhol**." *Afterimage* (No. 2, Autumn 70) 34–39. The director discusses his work and his life, informally.

"**Warner Brothers**." *Fortune* 16 (Dec 37). See *6b(2)*.

Connolly, Vera L. "Backstage in the Talkies." *Delineator* 116 (Mar 30) 14+. Interview with producer **Jack Warner**.

Warner, Jack L., with Dean Jennings. *"My First Hundred Years in Hollywood."* Mc-*call's* 91 (Sep 64) 72–73+; 92 (Oct 64) 128–129+; (Nov 64) 100–101+. Excerpts from producer's book (Random House, 1965).

"On the Scene: **Peter Watkins**." *Playboy* 15 (No. 6, June 68) 157. About the youngest producer ever to get Academy Award (for documentary *The War Game*).

Watkins, Peter. "Left, Right, Wrong." *F&F* 16 (No. 6, Mar 70) 28–29. Interview on his career.

Morton, Lawrence. "Music from the Films: A CBC Broadcast." *Hwd Q* 5 (No. 2, Winter 50) 132–137. Interview with **Franz Waxman**, composer for films (a radio script).

Cook, Page. "**Franz Waxman**." *FIR* 19 (No. 7, Aug–Sep 68) 415–430. Survey of his scores for films, with comments on some of them; list of films for which he composed music 1930–1960.

Gray, Martin. "No-Contract Star." *F&F* 3 (No. 6, Mar 57) 15. **John Wayne** explains why he works for John Ford without a contract.

Wayne, John. "Why I Turned Producer and Director." *JSPG* (Sep 60) 23–24. Because he wanted to make *The Alamo*.

Didion, Joan. "**John Wayne**." *SEP* 238 (14 Aug 65) 76–79. The actor's career.

Hall, Dennis John. "Tall in the Saddle." *F&F* 16 (No. 1, Oct 69) 12–19. Study of **John Wayne**'s acting career.

Jennings, Dean. "He Breaks Hollywood's Rules." *SEP* 228 (26 May 56) 48–49+. Swiss producer **Lazar Wechsler** makes low-budget films of high quality.

"Anatomy of an Amateur." *Newswk* 53 (20 Apr 59). See *2b(6)*. About **Joseph Welch**.

"Interview: **Raquel Welch**." *Playboy* 17 (No. 1, Jan 70) 75–90. On being a sex symbol, sex trends in movies, her sex life, sex trends in society, male domination.

Downer, A. S. "Orson and the Carpenters." *Sewanee Rev* 52 (Jan 44) 127–136. **Orson Welles**, whatever he does, is essentially a producer of startling effects.

Drake, Herbert. "Orson Welles: He's Still a Four-Ply Genius." *Look* 11 (No. 17, 19 Aug 47) 50–55. His former press agent writes about Hollywood's only actor-writer-producer-director; Welles adds his comments.

Koval, Francis. "Interview with **Welles**." *S&S* 19 (Dec 50) 314–316. "In my opinion, the writer should have the first and last word in film-making"; critics overstress the importance of images; "I definitely prefer to act on the stage."

Kerr, W. "Wonder Boy **Welles**." *Th Arts* 35 (Sep 51) 50–51+. He seems to have "let himself turn into a buffoon" but we should remember he is not only a ham actor but a first-rate producer and director.

MacLiammoir, Michael. "**Orson Welles**." *S&S*

24 (July–Sep 54) 36–38+. Some personal impressions of Welles, with a catalog of his talents and eccentricities.

"Winged Gorilla." *New S&N* 51 (No. 1298, 21 Jan 56) 65–66. On **Orson Welles** and his work.

Grigs, Derick. "**Orson Welles**: Conversation at Oxford." *S&S* 29 (Spring 60) 82–83. Remarks on the theatre, the press, Hollywood, morality, and some directors he likes or dislikes.

Stanbrook, Alan. "The Heroes of **Welles**." *Film* (No. 28, Mar–Apr 61) 12–16. A description of the heroes in Orson Welles' films.

Cowie, Peter. "**Orson Welles**." *F&F* 7 (No. 7, Apr 61) 10–11+. The relationship of Welles the actor to Welles the director.

Tynan, Kenneth. "**Orson Welles**: My Signature Against the World" (Part I). *Show* 1 (Oct 61) 64–69; "**Orson Welles**: Genius Without Portfolio" (Part II). (Nov 61) 60–65.

Fleischer, Richard. "Case for the Defense." *F&F* 9 (No. 1, Oct 62) 14. Director writes about **Orson Welles** as actor in two of his films.

Tyler, Parker. "**Orson Welles** and the Big Experimental Film Cult." *F Cult* (No. 29, 1963) 30–35. He constantly fails brilliantly; his stories reflect himself; he is the scorpion (in the Arkadin story) who stings the frog (producer); esteem for him is based on his intentions.

Lane, John Francis. "The Trial of **Orson Welles**." *F&F* 9 (No. 6, Mar 63) 70. General discussion by Welles of films, his own and others.

Pechter, William S. "Trials." *S&S* 33 (Winter 63–64) 5–9. Critical essay on **Orson Welles'** adaptation of Franz Kafka's *The Trial*, plus generally negative reevaluation of Welles' work.

Cobos, Juan, Miguel Rubio, and J. A. Pruneda. "A Trip to Don Quixoteland: Conversations with **Orson Welles**." *CdC in Eng* (No. 5, June 66) 34–47. The director discusses his films *The Trial, Lady from Shanghai, Falstaff;* ideas for projects; his method of working; comments on Hemingway, on other film directors.

Tynan, Kenneth. "Interview: **Orson Welles**." *Playboy* 14 (No. 3, Mar 67) 53–64. His early life, *Falstaff*, Antonioni, Fellini, Kubrick, trends in film making.

Johnson, William. "**Orson Welles**: Of Time and Loss." *FQ* 21 (No. 1, Fall 67) 13–24. Telescoping and other such manipulations of time in Welles films; themes of loss of innocence; contradictions within characters.

Daney, Serge. "**Welles** in Power." *CdC in Eng* (No. 11, Sep 67) 16–19. The concept of power in the films of Orson Welles.

"Special Report: **Orson Welles**." *Action* 4 (No. 3, May–June 69) 23–35. Comments by peo-

ple who worked on *Citizen Kane,* other people who knew Welles, and Arthur Knight, who reappraises the film; Welles writes a note on the *War of the Worlds* broadcast.

McBride, Joseph. "**Welles** Before Kane." *FQ* 23 (No. 3, Spring 70) 19–22. Description of an experimental film, *The Hearts of Age,* made by Orson Welles and William Vance for a Todd School drama festival when Welles was nineteen.

Higham, Charles. "*It's All True*." *S&S* 39 (Spring 70) 92–98. A reprinted chapter of Higham's book on **Orson Welles** (University of California, 1970), concerning the history of one of the most famous of Welles' uncompleted projects: the Latin-American material shot under the general title of *It's All True*.

Wilson, Richard. "It's Not Quite All True." *S&S* 39 (Autumn 70) 188–193. A response to Higham's article; **Welles'** longtime associate gives his own account of this ill-fated film.

Griffith, Richard. "Wyler, **Wellman** and Huston." *Fir* 1 (Feb 50). *See 5, William Wyler.*

Brownlow, Kevin. "**William Wellman**." *Film* (No. 44, Winter 65–66) 7–11. An interview with the American director.

Hanson, Curtis Lee. "A Memorable Visit with an Elder Statesman." *Cinema* (Calif) 3 (No. 3, July 66) 20–32. An interview, with photographs, in which **William Wellman** talks about his career and advises young directors on how to crack Hollywood.

Wellman, William, Jr. "**William Wellman**: Director Rebel." *Action* 5 (No. 2, Mar–Apr 70) 13–15. A biographical survey of Wellman's work, with critical notes.

Johnson, Albert. "Interviews with Hubert Cornfield and **Paul Wendkos**." *FQ* 15 (No. 3, Spring 62). *See 5, Hubert Cornfield.*

Austen, David. "Improvizations on an Original Theme." *F&F* 14 (No. 4, Jan 68) 4–7. Interview with **Paul Wendkos** on his film-directing career.

Werner, Oskar. "Mistress Cinema." *F&F* 13 (No. 2, Nov 66) 19–22. Interview about his acting career.

Troy, William. "**Mae West** and the Classic Tradition." *Nation* 137 (8 Nov 33) 547–548. The actress reflects tradition of burlesque.

Arbus, Diane. "**Mae West**: Emotion in Motion." *Show* 5 (Jan 65) 42–45. Description of Mae West's home in Santa Monica and comments on the lasting quality of her legend on the occasion of her seventy-first birthday.

Braun, Eric. "Doing What Comes Naturally." *F&F* 17 (No. 1, Oct 70) 27–32. On **Mae West**.

Braun, Eric. "One for the Boys." *F&F* 7 (No. 2, Nov 70) 38–42. Conclusion of a study of **Mae West**; filmography.

Sanford, John. "Nathanael West." *Screen Writer* 2 (Dec 46) 10–13. A memorial essay by a personal friend on the novelist and film writer.

Callenbach, Ernest, and Albert Johnson. "The Danger Is Seduction: An Interview with Haskell Wexler." *FQ* 21 (No. 3, Spring 68) 3–14. His work as director of photography on *Virginia Woolf* and *In the Heat of the Night;* early work for Irvin Kershner; comments on *cinéma vérité,* the role of the cameraman, his own film *The Bus.*

Jones, R. B. "Haskell Wexler and the Cool Medium." *Take One* 2 (No. 4, 1969) 5. Notes and a statement by the American cameraman-director.

Edwards, Roy. "Movie Gothick." *S&S* 27 (Autumn 57) 95–98. James Whale, an Englishman who came to America and found success directing *Frankenstein* (1931), *The Bride of Frankenstein, The Invisible Man, The Old Dark House,* was known for his inventive treatments of horror stories and for an off-beat vein of humor.

Thomaier, William, and Robert F. Fink. "James Whale." *FIR* 13 (No. 5, May 62) 277–296. Career of horror-film director.

Davies, Wallace E. "Truth about Pearl White." *FIR* 10 (Nov 59) 537–548. The facts and the fiction of her background prior to her success in serials such as *The Perils of Pauline.* See also letter by Frank Leon Smith in 10 (Dec 59) 634–637.

Whitney, John H. "A.S.I.D. Talk-Design Conference, Catalina, 1962." *F Cult* (No. 37, 1965) 21–24. His process of "motion graphics."

Lamont, Austin. "An Interview with John Whitney." *F Com* 6 (No. 2, Fall 70) 28–33. Maker of abstract films tells his autobiography, his work with optical printers and computers, the work of his brother, James; filmography.

"John Whitney 2." *F Com* 6 (No. 2, Fall 70) 34–38. Discussion at Flaherty Seminar about the dot-and-line system the film maker has been working on at IBM, which he calls a "fluid musical experience for the eye to perceive"; he predicts the possibility of real-time feedback similar to spontaneous improvisation, but suggests the best-quality work will not come that way.

Wicki, Bernard. "Lesson of the Hate Makers." *F&F* 8 (No. 7, Apr 62) 11–12. Interview on his first two films.

Widmark, Richard. "Creating Without Compromise." *F&F* 8 (No. 1, Oct 61) 7–8. His reflections on his work as actor and producer.

Coen, John. "Producer-Director Cornel Wilde." *F Com* 6 (No. 1, Spring 70) 52–61. Interview, biography, filmography of the film star.

Wilde, Cornel. "Survival!" *F&F* 17 (No. 1, Oct 70) 4–10. Interview on his films and general view of life; filmography.

Barnett, L. "Happiest Couple in Hollywood: Brackett and Wilder Are Movies' No. 1 Writing Team." *Life* 17 (11 Dec 44) 100–104+. Lengthy study of the respective careers of Billy Wilder and Charles Brackett.

Luft, Herbert G., and Charles Brackett. "Two Views of a Director—Billy Wilder." *QFRTV* 7 (No. 1, Fall 52) 58–69. Critic suggests Wilder's increasing cynicism; Brackett, producer-writer who has collaborated with Wilder, denies this, citing his rich humor.

Schulberg, Stuart. "A Communication: A Letter About Billy Wilder." *QFRTV* 7 (No. 4, Summer 53) 434–436. Response to articles by Luft and Brackett.

Wilder, Billy. "One Head Is Better Than Two." *F&F* 3 (No. 5, Feb 57) 7. Reflections on his directing career.

Hume, Rod. "A Sting in the Tale." *F&F* 3 (No. 5, Feb 57) 8. Billy Wilder's humor.

McVay, Douglas. "The Eye of a Cynic." *F&F* 6 (No. 4, Jan 60) 11–12+. On the films of Billy Wilder.

Schumach, M. "Wilder and Funnier Touch." *NYTM* (24 Jan 60) 30+. Study of Billy Wilder's personality and working methods.

"Policeman, Midwife, Bastard." *Time* 75 (27 June 60) 75–76. A portrait of director Billy Wilder.

Simon, John. "Belt and Suspenders." *Th Arts* 46 (July 62) 20–21+. On the films of Billy Wilder.

Higham, Charles. "Cast a Cold Eye: The Films of Billy Wilder." *S&S* 32 (Spring 63) 83–87. "Together with Alfred Hitchcock, Billy Wilder remains the English-speaking cinema's most persistently cynical director"; even *Ace in the Hole* exploits the sensationalism it purports to attack; a consistently negative view, film by film.

"Interview: Billy Wilder." *Playboy* 10 (No. 6, June 63) 57–66. Early career, views on Hollywood, his image as a comedy director.

Lemon, Richard. "Well, Nobody's Perfect." *SEP* 239 (17 Dec 66) 30–34+. On the career of Billy Wilder.

Higham, Charles. "Meet Whiplash Wilder." *S&S* 37 (Winter 67–68) 21–23. Billy Wilder's methods of writing and directing; his early career; the original opening for *Sunset Boulevard;* the origin of *Ace in the Hole.* (*The Fortune Cookie* was called *Meet Whiplash Willie* in England.)

Spiller, David. "The World of Wilder." *London Mag* new series 8 (No. 3, June 68) 76–82.

Mundy, Robert. "Wilder Reappraised." *Cinema* (Cambridge) (No. 4, Oct 69) 14–22. His main spheres of concern and devices; interview with the director and I. A. L. Diamond, who has co-scripted many of his films.

McBride, Joseph, and Michael Wilmington.

"The Private Life of **Billy Wilder.**" *FQ* 23 (No. 4, Summer 70) 2–9. With serious material and a farcical and ironic style, Wilder is usually concerned with some sort of swindle; special analysis of *Some Like It Hot* and *Ace in the Hole.*

Brown, Vanessa. "**Billy Wilder.**" *Action* 5 (No. 6, Nov–Dec 70) 16–18. Excerpts from her Voice of America broadcast interview.

Wilson, John. *"The Revolutionary."* *S&S* 39 (Winter 69–70) 18–19. Note on Harvard graduate **Paul Williams** making this film.

Roberts, Meade. "Williams and Me." *F&F* 6 (No. 11, Aug 60) 7+. A description of how **Tennessee Williams** works on the film scripts of his own plays.

Whitehall, Richard. "Poet . . . But Do We Know It?" *F&F* 6 (No. 11, Aug 60) 8+. A study of **Tennessee Williams'** work in film.

Bean, Robin. "The Importance of Being . . . What's 'Is-name." *F&F* 14 (No. 5, Feb 68) 4–10. Interview with **Michael Winner** about his career.

Spiers, David. "An Interview with **Michael Winner.**" *Screen* 10 (No. 3, May–June 69) 5–18. Rise of the British director.

Buckley, Michael. "**Shelley Winters.**" *FIR* 21 (No. 3, Mar 70) 146–160. Career and film listing.

Robinson, David. "A New Clown." *S&S* 23 (Apr–June 54) 213. **Norman Wisdom's** first film, *Trouble in Store,* was not very good, but the TV star made it a box-office hit.

Marks, Louis. "Top Billing." *F&F* 1 (No. 3, Dec 54) 10–11. An assessment of the work of British comic actor **Norman Wisdom;** his latest film, *Trouble in Store.*

Stark, Samuel. "**Robert Wise.**" *FIR* 14 (Jan 63) 5–22. Career study of the American director; filmography.

"New Producer." *New Yorker* 39 (14 Sep 63) 33–35. *The Cool World* at Venice Film Festival; a talk with its producer, **Frederick Wiseman.**

Mamber, Stephan. "The New Documentaries of **Frederick Wiseman.**" *Cinema* (Calif) 6 (No. 1, 1970) 33–40. Analysis of his four films as investigations of institutions—"government at its point of direct impact"; interview on pp. 38–40.

Handelman, Janet. "An Interview with **Frederick Wiseman.**" *F Lib Q* 3 (No. 3, Summer 70) 5–9. The documentary-film maker speaks about his films.

McWilliams, Donald E. "**Frederick Wiseman.**" *FQ* 24 (No. 1, Fall 70) 17–26. About this documentary director's way of working; lengthy quotations.

"Mr. Documentary." *Time* 80 (7 Dec 62) 65–66. **David Wolper** produces documentary films for TV.

"Young King David." *Newswk* 64 (23 Nov 64). *See 8c(2b).* **David Wolper.**

Kempton, Murray. "**Natalie Wood:** Mother, Men and the Muse." *Show* 2 (Mar 62) 50–53. Her acting career.

Isaacs, Hermine R. "**William Wyler,** Director with a Passion and a Craft." *Th Arts* 31 (Feb 47) 20–24. Life, techniques, and philosophy, with numerous films cited.

Griffith, Richard. "**Wyler,** Wellman and Huston." *FIR* 1 (Feb 50) 1–4+. An adaptation from his contribution to Paul Rotha's *The Film Till Now* (Funk & Wagnalls, 1949).

Chandler, David. "Willy Makes the Stars Tremble." *Collier's* 125 (4 Feb 50) 26–27+. On director **William Wyler.**

Reisz, Karel. "The Later Films of **William Wyler.**" *Sequence* (No. 13, 1951) 19–30. A discussion of the films made after *Dead End* by the American director.

Heston, Charlton. "The Questions No One Asks About Willy." *F&F* 4 (No. 11, Aug 58) 9+. About **William Wyler's** directing methods; preparations for *Ben-Hur.*

Reid, John Howard. "A Little Larger Than Life." *F&F* 6 (No. 5, Feb 60) 9–10+. Analysis of the work of **William Wyler.**

Reid, John Howard. "A Comparison of Size." *F&F* 6 (No. 6, Mar 60) 12+. Conclusion of analysis of work of **William Wyler.**

Brownlow, Kevin. "The Early Days of **William Wyler.**" *Film* (No. 37, Autumn 63) 11–13.

"**William Wyler.**" *Cinema* (Calif) 2 (No. 6, July–Aug 65) 39. Short interview at Cannes.

Heston, Charlton. "What I Want, and Don't Want, from My Director." *Action* 2 (No. 1, Jan–Feb 67). *See 2c.* On **William Wyler.**

Hanson, Curtis Lee. "**William Wyler.**" *Cinema* (Calif) 3 (No. 5, Summer 67) 22–28. Interview with the director; filmography with commentary on pp. 29–35.

Wyler, **William,** and Barbra Streisand. "Symbiosis Continued." *Action* 3 (No. 2, Mar–Apr 68) 17–18. The two personalities discuss their relationship in the making of *Funny Girl.*

Carey, Gary. "The Lady and the Director: Bette Davis and **William Wyler.**" *F Com* 6 (No. 2, Fall 70). *See 5, Bette Davis.*

Y

Yates, Peter. "The Suggestive Experience." *F&F* 15 (No. 11, Aug 69) 4–7. Interview about his career.

Lawrenson, Helen. "**Susannah York.**" *Show* 2 (Jan 62) 68–69. Her acting career, including the film *Freud.*

Bowers, Ronald L. "**Loretta Young.**" *FIR* 20 (No. 4, Apr 69) 193–217. Career and film listing.

Cohen, Saul B. "Michael Roemer and **Robert Young,** Film Makers of *Nothing But a Man.*" *F Com* 3 (No. 2, Spring 65). *See 5, Michael Roemer.*

Young, Robert. "How I Won the War of the Sexes by Losing Every Battle." *Good Housekeeping* 154 (Jan 62) 44+. Personal recollections by the movie star.

Lane, John Francis. "Young Romantic." *F&F* 13 (No. 5, Feb 67) 58–60. On the films of **Terence Young**.

Z

Werth, Alexander. "A Soviet Writer Takes to Cinema." *CQ* 2 (No. 2, Winter 33–34) 101–103. **Eugene Zamiatin**, novelist and playwright; his projects in Russia and in Paris.

Bluestone, George. "Luigi Zampa." *FQ* 12 (No. 2, Winter 58) 10–12. In a brief interview the Italian director condemns the current state of film censorship, both civil and ecclesiastic, in Italy and its effect on his own films.

Pringle, Henry F. "Brains in the Front Office." *Collier's* 93 (6 Jan 34) 20+. On **Darryl Zanuck** and 20th Century-Fox.

Johnston, Alva. "Darryl Francis Zanuck." *New Yorker* (10 Nov 34) 24–28; (17 Nov 34) 24–29. Profile of the producer.

"New Deal in Hollywood." *Time* 21 (1 May 33) 35. Restoration of industry salary cuts came a week late at Warners and **Darryl Zanuck** resigned to form his own company with Joseph Schenck; his biography.

McEvoy, J. P. "He's Got Something; D. F. Zanuck." *SEP* 212 (1 July 39) 16–17+. Biography of Darryl Zanuck; comments from other film makers; *The Public Enemy* discussed.

Busch, N. "Darryl Zanuck: Last of the Wonder Boys." *Life* 10 (14 Apr 41) 96–100. How to run a one-man studio.

"One-Man Studio." *Time* 55 (12 June 50) 64–66. **Darryl F. Zanuck** biography.

Whitney, Dwight. "Hollywood Story of Darryl Zanuck." *Coronet* 28 (Sep 50) 58–63. His movie career.

"Zanuck Rides Again." *Time* 80 (3 Aug 62) 51.

Havemann, E. "Darryl Zanuck: Last of the Movie Moguls." *McCall's* 91 (Oct 63) 134–135. Brief biography and assessment of producer as he takes on job as president of 20th Century-Fox.

Canby, Vincent. "D. Z.: The Last Tycoon." *NYTM* (17 Mar 68) 32–33+. On the career of 20th Century-Fox executive **Darryl F. Zanuck**.

Ehrlich, H. "Zanuck: Last of the Red-Hot Star-Makers." *Look* 34 (3 Nov 70) 69–71. Interview with **Darryl Zanuck** about his creation of movie stars.

Medjuck, Joe. "Frank Zappa." *Take One* 2 (No. 2, 1968) 8–9. An interview in which the musician discusses his career as film maker, with particular reference to *Uncle Meat*, which is both album and film.

Lane, John Francis. "Za and Co." *F&F* 1 (No. 2, Nov 54) 9. **Cesare Zavattini**, the Italian scenarist and theorist: his work and recent productions.

Zavattini, Cesare. "Pages from My Diary." *F&F* 4 (No. 8, May 58) 11+. Unconnected reflections from his journal about how the Italian screenwriter views life and filming.

Devlin, P. "I Know My Romeo and Juliet." *Vogue* 151 (1 Apr 68) 34+. About director **Franco Zeffirelli**.

Libuse, Konradova. "Putting on a Style." *F&F* 7 (No. 9, June 61) 35+. Work of Czech director **Karel Zeman**.

Knight, Arthur. "Fred Zinnemann." *FIR* 2 (Jan 51) 21–24+. His career and approach to film making, especially for *Teresa*.

Hart, Henry. "Zinnemann on the Verge." *FIR* 4 (Feb 53) 80–81. Remarks by Fred Zinnemann on various aspects of production and the requisites of a good director; he plans to add the role of producer.

"Fred Zinnemann, Oscar Winner." *Vogue* 123 (1 May 54) 110. Brief note.

Johnson, Albert. "The Tenth Muse in San Francisco (3)." *S&S* 25 (Autumn 55) 102–104+. An account of one of a series of showings and lectures given by the San Francisco Museum of Art; some questions and answers by **Fred Zinnemann**, who directed *The Search*.

Crist, Judith. "Movie Maker." *Scholastic* 67 (17 Nov 55) 6. Short interview with director **Fred Zinnemann**.

Zinnemann, Fred. "A Conflict of Conscience." *F&F* 6 (No. 3, Dec 59) 7+. Zinnemann answers a number of questions about his films.

Schickel, Richard. "Fred Zinnemann: Quiet Man on the Set." *Show* 4 (Aug 64) 80–81+. Rise of the American film director as controlling force behind the cinema within the studio system; remarks from Zinnemann on the process of refining a film.

Zinnemann, Fred. "Zinnemann Talks Back." *Cinema* (Calif) 2 (No. 3, Oct–Nov 64) 20–22+. Interview with the director.

Reid, John Howard. "A Man for All Movies." *F&F* 13 (No. 8, May 67) 4–11; (No. 9, June 67) 11–15. Two articles on the films of **Fred Zinnemann**.

Zinnemann, Fred. "Some Questions Answered." *Action* 2 (No. 3, May–June 67) 22–23. In an interview the American director discusses his own career and work.

Farr, William. "Adolph Zukor: 1912–37." *S&S* 5 (No. 20, Winter 36–37) 126–127. Brief survey of Paramount executive's career up to this time.

"Paramount." *Fortune* 15 (Mar 37). See 6b(2). About **Adolph Zukor**.

"An American Visitor." *S&S* 23 (Jan–Mar 54) 115. Brief report of **Adolph Zukor**'s talk to London critics' luncheon.

6. Motion Picture Industry

6a. Analyses of Business Conditions

[*See also 3b(2), 4d, 7b(1).*]

Torbert, Hugh. "Our Nickelodeon Athens." *North Am Rev* 229 (June 30) 683–689. Reasons for mediocrity in American films; organization of the industry.

Hays, Will H. "The Cinema of Tomorrow." *Ladies' Home J* 47 (July 30) 6+. Review of progress made in movie industry.

"Lost Illusion." *Lit Dig* 109 (6 June 31) 18. Frenchman ranks U.S. industries by value of product; movies rank seventy-fifth, behind perfume and ice cream.

Lilly, Joseph. "Hope for Hollywood." *Outlook* 158 (17 June 31) 206–207+. Sees artistic values of movies rising as industry grows.

Peet, Creighton. "Happy New Year, Etc. Etc." *Outlook* 159 (30 Dec 31) 567. Surveys present situation in Hollywood.

Ahern, Maurice L. "Midas and the Microphones." *Commonweal* 15 (6 Apr 32) 628–629. Suggests movie men—not bankers—should run industry.

"State of the Industry." *Time* 18 (27 June 32) 24. After worst year in history, film companies cut production costs, reshuffle executives.

Trumbo, Dalton. "Hollywood Pays." *Forum* 89 (Feb 33) 113–119. Sees industry as producer-oriented with no need for bankers.

Trumbo, Dalton. "The Fall of Hollywood." *North Am Rev* 236 (Aug 33) 140–147. Bankers, nepotism, contracts, and talkies destroy vigor of movies.

Hughes, Rupert. "Calamity, with Sound Effects." *New Outlook* 162 (Sep 33) 21–26. Novelist surveys difficulties which have befallen movie industry.

"Fever Chart for Hollywood." *American* 128 (Oct 39) 67–74. A study by the Carnegie Corporation, directed by L. C. Rosten.

Russel, Bob. "A Letter from Hollywood." *Films* (U.S.) 1 (No. 1, Nov 39) 97–103. Economic situation; production plans.

Goldwyn, Samuel. "Hollywood Is Sick." *SEP* 213 (13 July 40) 18–19+. The double feature is hurting the industry.

McEvoy, J. P. "Fear over Hollywood." *Rdrs Dig* 38 (Jan 41) 62–65. A look at Hollywood in a slump; a discussion of block booking, "B" pictures, and the double feature (with solutions).

"Slump." *Time* 37 (30 June 41) 65. "Most likely cause: the paucity of good pictures."

Isaacs, Hermine Rich. "Profits and Prestige." *Th Arts* 25 (Sep 41) 666–672. The two are no longer mutually exclusive.

"Trouble in Paradise." *New Rep* 116 (24 Feb 47) 41. Because of antitrust laws and the decentralization of Hollywood, movie profits were up, but production employment was down.

Crichton, Kyle. "Hollywood Headache." *Collier's* 120 (20 Sep 47) 18–19. Production is down, Hollywood unemployment up; Great Britain enacts currency blockage legislation.

Ornstein, William. "You Can't Scare the Movies." *Screen Writer* 3 (Nov 47) 17–18. Magazine editor guesses movie theatres are here to stay.

Moley, Raymond. "Movie Troubles, Past and Present." *Newswk* 30 (8 Dec 47) 92. Cyclical theory of Hollywood's slumps and their results.

"Trouble in Hollywood." *Life* 24 (23 Feb 48) 55–56+. Soaring costs, loss of foreign revenue, and bad films cause a crisis in the postwar industry. The solution: belt tightening and better films.

"An Industry Gets over the Jitters." *Newswk* 31 (10 May 48) 58.

Readers are advised to acquaint themselves with the range of categories throughout the bibliography in the search for specific subjects. In some cases, cross-categorical comparisons are directly suggested. In general, however, each article is placed under one category only. Cross-references on individual articles have been kept to a minimum.

Entries are in chronological order of publication under each category. Exceptions are: Part 5, Biography, in which the order is alphabetical by name; Part 9, Case Histories of Film Making, which is alphabetical by film title; and 3c and 8c(4), also alphabetical by title.

Warner Brothers studio in Burbank, about 1955.

Mayer, Arthur L. "An Exhibitor Looks at Hollywood." *Screen Writer* 4 (June–July 48) 6–7+. Independent production doesn't seem to cause "any substantial advance" in artistic standards; getting rid of block booking and "B" pictures will not be a good thing; other trends.

Brennan, Frederick H. "Memo to the Moguls of Hollywood." *NYTM* (25 July 48) 14+. A screenwriter says that mass production, mismanagement, and other evils of big business are to blame for the industry's troubles.

"Worries of Movie-Makers." *US News & World Report* 24 (25 June 48) 31. The end of an era in Hollywood blamed on TV, higher costs, fading foreign market.

Milestone, Lewis. "First Aid for a Sick Giant." *New Rep* 120 (31 Jan 49) 15–17. Director says Hollywood needs to combat its own manufactured hysteria with forceful, positive public relations.

"Movies: End of an Era?" *Fortune* 39 (Apr 49) 98–102+. "There is no crisis," says Eric Johnston; analysis of the total situation suggests he is mistaken.

Schulberg, Budd. "The Frightened City." *Nation's Business* 37 (Aug 49) 36–38+. Are better movies the cure for the ills of Hollywood or is the industry too sick to live?

Hart, Henry. "The Industry in 1950." *FIR* 1 (Apr 50) 9–11+. Treasurer of the National Board of Review reports on the 1950 annual conference and addresses by such men as George Sidney, Bertram Bloch, and George J. Schaefer on the downward trend in motion-picture theatre attendance.

Houseman, John. "Hollywood Faces the Fifties." *Harper's* 200 (Apr 50) 50–59; (May 50) 51–59. The conditions—psychological and economic—that are plunging Hollywood into fading box-office and artistic doldrums.

Cerf, Bennett. "Trade Winds." *Sat Rev* 33 (15 July 50) 4. Report on the industry's slow recovery from recent ill-fortune.

Alpert, H. "Critics' Choice." *Th Arts* 35 (Aug 51) 42–43+. Box-office slumps are causing a reevaluation of Hollywood methods.

"Alphabet Soup." *Newswk* 38 (6 Aug 51) 83. Producers and exhibitors get together in an attempt to find solution to diminishing profits; Council of Motion Picture Organizations, new public-relations group.

Coughlan, Robert. "Now It Is Trouble That Is Supercolossal in Hollywood." *Life* 31 (13 Aug 51) 102–108+. An examination of Hollywood's financial crisis; the most promising solution: pay-TV.

Bauer, Leda. "In the Cool, Cool, Cool of the Evening." *Th Arts* 35 (Sep 51) 32–33+. What entertainment will revive Hollywood box office—more musicals?

"Movie Men's Discovery: Better Pictures Pay Off." *US News and World Report* 31 (19

Oct 51) 42–43. General industry situation.

Sayers, Jack. "Who Says Hollywood Is Dying?" *Look* 15 (No. 22, 23 Oct 51) 143–151.

Hine, A. "Hollywood and Hine." *Holiday* 10 (Dec 51) 31+. The state of the industry at year's end; what it's doing, what it's planning.

"Hollywood Hope: Extravaganzas and TV Quickies." *Newswk* 39 (16 June 52) 72+. How and why movie business is picking up.

"Critical Times." *Time* 62 (21 Sep 53) 106. Movie production slowed down; changes in the self-censorship system because of TV's competition.

"The Year in Films." *Time* 62 (28 Dec 53) 55–56. Summary of the year 1953.

Jamison, Barbara. "And Now Super-Colossal Headaches." *NYTM* (10 Jan 54) 20–21+. Innovations to bring the audience back.

"Memo from Hollywood: Fewer, Better Films." *US News & World Report* 36 (22 Jan 54) 48–49.

"Comeback—And Why." *Newswk* 44 (13 Sep 54) 104+. Reasons for a student boom in filmgoing.

Goldwyn, Samuel. "As I See It." *JSPG* (Nov 54) 6–7+. A realistic analysis of the industry's present prosperity, accompanied by a note of warning not to make too many pictures.

Emler, Dr. William. "Hollywood Economics." *F Cult* 1 (No. 3, 1955) 28. Decline of the "B" picture.

Lincoln, F. "Comeback of the Movies." *Fortune* 51 (Feb 55) 127–131. The advent of 3-D, Cinerama, drive-ins, the double feature, CinemaScope; United Artists and Universal.

"Movies: Boomlet to Boon?" *Newswk* 45 (7 Mar 55) 73–76. Reasons for the film industry's gradual recovery.

"Getting Them Back to the Movies." *Bus Wk* (22 Oct 55) 58+. With *Alexander the Great* Hollywood lures the audience away from TV: "Make them big, show them big, sell them big."

Mayer, Arthur. "Myths, Movies, and Maturity." *Sat Rev* 39 (7 Apr 56) 7–8. Studios are selling movies to television, leasing part of their facilities to independent producers, and selling to the foreign market, which supplies 50% of the income.

"New Blood, New Bounce Make Hollywood Studios Hum." *Bus Wk* (22 Sep 56) 106–108+. New crop of owners and managers; the tie-in with TV; where profits come from.

James, T. F. "Movie Business." *Cosmopolitan* 141 (Oct 56) 20–22+. Hollywood's box-office slump: ills and assets.

Ardrey, Robert. "What Happened to Hollywood?" *Reporter* 16 (24 Jan 57) 19–22. A screenwriter's examination of the reasons Hollywood is going broke; see reply by Dore Schary (18 Apr 57).

"Out of Focus." *Newswk* 49 (25 Feb 57)

85–86. Some of Hollywood's changes: shrinking studios, shrinking production schedules, producing units leaving town.

Schary, Dore. "Hollywood: Fade Out, Fade In." *Reporter* 16 (18 Apr 57) 20–25. Answer to Robert Ardrey (24 Jan 57), concerning the current crisis in Hollywood and some future speculations.

Hodgins, Eric. "Amid Ruins of an Empire a New Hollywood Arises." *Life* 42 (10 June 57) 146–150+. Analysis of changing Hollywood: glamor superseded by big business.

Alpert, Hollis. "Ten Years of Trouble." *Sat Rev* (21 Dec 57) 9–11. Describes readjustments the big studios are being forced to make as consumer demand has lessened; part of *Saturday Review* report "The Big Change in Hollywood."

"Wolf." *Time* 70 (23 Dec 57) 70. A theatre owner predicts the collapse of the big studios.

Mayer, Arthur. "Hollywood: Save the Flowers." *Sat Rev* 41 (29 Mar 58) 11–13+. Some of the forces that are determining Hollywood's future.

"What's Ahead in the Movies." *Changing Times* 12 (Aug 58) 6.

Fadiman, William. "In This Corner, Hollywood." *Sat Rev* 42 (19 Dec 59) 9–11+. Columbia's story editor assesses "art-industry" problems.

Schallert, Edwin. "Evolution or Devolution?" *JSPG* (Mar 60) 15–18. Surveys of industry situation suggests producers should continue to make the pictures.

"Movies Move Out." *Economist* 195 (30 Apr 60) 422. Century City real-estate development on 20th Century-Fox back lot.

Scheuer, Philip K. "Hollywood—Fabulous Invalid?" *JSPG* (Sep 60) 1–5+. Los Angeles film critic discusses TV, rising cost of production, increasing foreign production, drop in American film output, etc.

Wald, Jerry. "Bury Us Not on the Lone Prairie." *JSPG* (Sep 60) 5–8. Hollywood "is still very much alive and kicking"; gross receipts and corporate profits have risen, new talent is coming in.

Scheuer, Philip K. "Hollywood—An Invalid?" *FIR* 11 (No. 8, Oct 60) 449–451. Movie Critic of *Los Angeles Times* analyzes Hollywood's present crisis (editor bills him as "Kenneth").

Mayer, Arthur. "Growing Pains of a Shrinking Industry." *Sat Rev* 44 (25 Feb 61) 21–23+. The traumatic effect TV had on moviemaking; how the industry is fighting back.

Alpert, Hollis. "Cinema's Ins and Outs." *Sat Rev* 47 (29 Aug 64) 166–169. The industry and its financing since TV.

Alpert, H., A. Knight, J. G. Fuller. "Do the Movies Have a Future?" *Sat Rev* 47 (29 Aug 64) 166–172. Status differences between old-line producers and the new independent

breed, in arranging financing, production, and distribution.

Champlin, Charles. "The American Motion Picture: 1966." *Sat Rev* 49 (24 Dec 66) 11–25. Film making for TV has given Hollywood more security but the theatre business is in good shape, too.

"Hollywood's New Leader." *Bus Wk* (7 Jan 67) 80–84. 20th Century-Fox under Darryl Zanuck sees new revenue from "blockbuster films" and renting of TV films.

Howe, A. N. "A Trio in Need of Harmony." *JSPG* (Sep 69) 21–23. If only producers, distributors, and exhibitors could agree on long-term goals!

"Last Days of Babylon?" *Forbes* 104 (1 Nov 69) 65–66+. Survey of studio assets, income, audience expectations.

"Hollywood: Will There Ever Be a 21st Century-Fox?" *Time* 95 (9 Feb 70) 57–58. The problems of the studios in a time when people aren't going to the movies and TV is providing overwhelming competition.

Greenspan, Lou, Don Carle Gillette, A. W. Howe, Arthur Mayer, Jack Valenti, Philip Dunne, Thomas Pryor, William Fadiman. "The Journal Looks at Hollywood and the State of the Industry." *JSPG* (Mar 70) 1–32.

Fadiman, W. "Hollywood: Shivering in the Sun." *New Rep* 162 (27 June 70) 17–19. The death of Hollywood as film capital of the world: rising costs, loss of customers, TV, competition from foreign films, take-over by the conglomerates.

6a(1). FINANCE AND BOX-OFFICE INCOME

"Sound, Shekels, and Shylocks." *World's Work* 60 (Nov 31) 51–53+. Surveys connections between Wall Street and Hollywood.

Howard, Sidney. "Hollywood on the Slide." *New Rep* 72 (9 Nov 32) 350–353. Playwright sees Hollywood's financial difficulty as example of foolish capitalism; reply by A. B. Kuttner 73 (14 Dec 32) 129–130.

"Then Came the Dawn." *Bus Wk* (8 Feb 33) 12. Receivership for RKO and Paramount Publix.

"Mickey Mouse, Financier." *Lit Dig* 116 (21 Oct 33). See *2h(3)*.

Weir, Hugh (ed.). "Wild Money." *SEP* 206 (2 Dec 33) 8–9+; (16 Dec 33) 18–19+; (6 Jan 34) 32+; (3 Feb 34) 26+; (10 Feb 34) 26–27+. Fictionalized account of banker's adventure in movies.

"Movie Business Picking Up." *Lit Dig* 117 (31 Mar 34) 41.

"Came the (Movie) Dawn." *Bus Wk* (9 Nov 35) 18. Wall Street moves into industry to reorganize movie producers.

"There's Always a Catch; Once It Was Sound, Now Color." *Newswk* 6 (7 Dec 35) 36.

Reviews financial records of major companies.

"Bulging Box Office Tills." *Lit Dig* 121 (15 Feb 36) 40. C. F. Morgan article in *The Magazine of Wall Street* says decency is making money.

"Film Industry Dreams of Greater Profits in Celluloid as Sales Soar." *Lit Dig* 122 (19 Sep 36) 46.

"Movies Hit Prosperity Trail." *Bus Wk* (21 Nov 36) 22. Net earnings and deficits 1929–1936; RKO trying to get out of bankruptcy.

"Box Office Speaks." *Chris Cent* 53 (25 Nov 36) 1552–1553.

"Prospectus." *Time* 31 (6 June 38) 38–40. A look at the coming year in cinema, with a breakdown of all the major production companies, including their budgets.

Goodman, Ezra. "Hollywood Is Worried." *S&S* 8 (No. 31, Autumn 39) 106. Financial and other recent problems in the film-industry capital.

"Movie Trade Bemoans Unhappy Lot." *Bus Wk* (29 June 40) 22–23.

Nugent, F. S. "Hollywood Counts the Pennies." *NYTM* (30 Aug 42) 14–15+. Subtitled: "How Pictures May Be Affected by War Economics."

"Prosperity Row." *Time* 40 (16 Nov 42) 92+. Wartime government restrictions on film makers may limit production after the biggest box-office year in history.

"Big Movie Year." *Bus Wk* (13 Feb 43) 37–38. Attendance and receipts push to new records despite wartime troubles.

"Movie March." *Newswk* 22 (26 July 43) 54+. Economic considerations of rising movie attendance.

"Hollywood Wows Wall Street." *Bus Wk* (11 May 46) 58+. Why Hollywood is reaping a wartime harvest, both at the box office and in Wall Street.

Warner, Harry P. "Television and the Motion Picture Industry." *Hwd Q* 2 (No. 1, Oct 46) 11–18. Lawyer compares cost figures on production, talent, advertising, etc.

Borneman, Ernest. "Rebellion in Hollywood. A Study in Motion Picture Finance." *Harper's* 193 (Oct 46) 337–343. High taxes encourage one-picture deals and complicated financing.

Brown, J. M. "The Midas Touch." *Sat Rev* 29 (12 Oct 46) 36–38. The contrasts between the expenses of foreign films as opposed to the expenses of American films.

"Hollywood a Postwar Record Breaker." *Bus Wk* (7 Dec 46) 96. A chart listing comparative earnings of the Big Five proves postwar Hollywood booming.

"Movie Industry's Headaches." *US News & World Report* 22 (13 June 47) 22. Unexpected postwar earnings, costs, closing foreign markets—all are part of the headache.

"Boffo Sensational." *Time* 49 (23 June 47)

82+. Hollywood's reply to a recent box-office slump.

"Super Colossal Economies." *Newswk* 30 (1 Sep 47) 77. Because of the foreign market slump, Hollywood begins to "economize."

Odlum, F. B. "Financial Organization of the Motion Picture Industry." *Annals of Amer Acad of Polit and Soc Sci* 254 (Nov 47) 18–25. A cent-by-cent account of the expenses, investments, profits, taxes, etc., of the entire industry, with a breakdown of the five major companies.

"Problems Face Movie Makers." *Bus Wk* (6 Dec 47) 94+. Problems include rising costs, declining attendance, and a 75% British tax on film rentals.

Dawson, Anthony H. "Motion Picture Economics." *Hwd Q* 3 (No. 3, Spring 48) 217–240. Financial history of the large companies; taxes, profits, salaries, theatre chains, other topics in comprehensive survey; charts and graphs.

"The Take in 1947." *Time* 51 (5 Apr 48) 94. Studio earnings.

"Hollywood Earnings Continue to Slide." *Bus Wk* (7 Aug 48) 86. A tabulation shows how much profits have dropped.

McWilliams, Carey. "Oilmen Invade Hollywood." *Nation* 167 (16 Oct 48) 429. "Brash young men from Texas" are pouring money into movies.

"All Is Bright." *Time* 52 (27 Dec 48) 58. Soaring costs, failing receipts, TV all contribute to gloom of moviedom.

Brady, Thomas F. "This Is Where the Money Went." *New Rep* 120 (31 Jan 49) 12–15. Charts and graphs of exhibition profits, production-distribution profits, expenditures in salaries and production since 1940.

"Spotlight on the Woe." *Newswk* 33 (18 Apr 49) 71. Sales, costs, and receipts of U.S. films in 1948.

"Hollywood Is a Little Better Off." *Bus Wk* (23 July 49) 61–62. A tabulation of earnings of studios; serious long-range problems.

"Movie Makers Meet Postwar Problems." *Bus Wk* (1 Oct 49) 26. Producers cut costs; a look at foreign revenue and domestic revenue.

"Hollywood Shakes Its Slump." *Bus Wk* (11 Feb 50) 82–84. Earnings, TV, production.

Robbins, Harold. "The Dollars and Cents in Tomorrow's Movies." *FIR* 1 (Mar 50) 18–20+. Author of *The Dream Merchants* (Knopf, 1949) and budget and planning analyst for Universal-International Pictures discusses the financial setbacks of American film companies since 1947 and the subsequent introduction of successful low-budget European films; predicts that Hollywood will make better films from smaller budgets.

Nathan, Paul S. "Books into Films." *Publishers Weekly* 157 (1 Apr 50) 1592. Current box-office troubles.

"Movies: New Sick Industry." *Bus Wk* (25 Nov 50) 26. Reasons for the box-office slump.

"New Millionaires at M.G.M." *Time* 57 (19 Feb 51) 98.

"Comeback in Hollywood." *Time* 58 (1 Oct 51) 98. Box office better than in 1950.

"Movies Come out of the Dog House." *Bus Wk* (10 Nov 51) 140–142. Moviemakers' earnings 1939–1951.

"Gloomy Movies." *Bus Wk* (7 June 52) 126+. Loew's, Inc., and United Paramount slash quarterly dividends.

"Fat '52." *Newswk* 41 (30 Mar 53) 90. Financial figures for the industry.

"Tax Stays on Movies." *Time* 62 (17 Aug 53) 90.

"Sick Report." *Time* 61 (4 May 53) 102. Losses of movie industry blamed on federal admission tax and TV.

"Reviving Hollywood Spirits." *Bus Wk* (13 Nov 54). *See 4k(4).*

Schary, Dore. "Movie Grosses." *FIR* 6 (Apr 55) 155–157. A satirical short story by MGM's vice-president in charge of production: progressive exaggeration of box-office returns.

"Box Office Recovery." *Economist* 175 (18 June 55) 1049–1050. Analysis of 1953–1954 fall in box-office receipts and subsequent innovations being used to recapture audience.

Sanders, Terry B. "The Financing of Independent Feature Films." *QFRTV* 9 (No. 4, Summer 55) 380–389. UCLA graduate student tells how companies are set up and the meaning of such terms as "risk-capital group," "completion-money group"; the role of the distribution company and the bank; the redistribution of monies earned.

"Movie Industry Is Split Over Why Business Is Better." *Bus Wk* (10 Sep 55) 54. How much of a comeback is the movie business really making?

Knight, Arthur. "Rehearsals at the Box Office." *Sat Rev* 38 (31 Dec 55) 26. Movies (particularly independently produced) need more attendance to support more artistic efforts.

"Entertainment's Stepchild." *Economist* 181 (29 Dec 56) 1130–1131. Report from Los Angeles on increasing costs of film production and drop in annual movie attendance.

"Vanishing Moviegoer." *Time* 71 (10 Feb 58) 100. A report on dwindling movie attendance.

"Malaise of the Movies." *America* 99 (19 Apr 58) 99. Statistics concerning the box-office slump and speculations on the future.

Havemann, Ernest. "Business of Show Business: Riches or Ruin." *Life* 45 (22 Dec 58) 180–183+. Financial aspects, both movie and theatre.

"Mad Money." *Time* 73 (19 Jan 59) 66+. Some examples of financing in Hollywood.

"Movies' Profit Lights Brighten." *Bus Wk* (7 May 60) 156–158+. Large audiences, big profits from big pictures, and businesslike management revive film companies.

"It's Side Assets That Count." *Bus Wk* (17 Sep 60) 175+. Market standings of major film companies; trend toward diversification.

"*Cleopatra*'s Prospects." *Fortune* 67 (May 63) 234. Financial assets and profits—how they are normally divided.

"Speculating in Spectaculars." *Fortune* 67 (May 63) 232+. How to rate motion-picture stocks.

"Can Cleo Pay It Back?" *Bus Wk* (8 June 63) 48–50. Fox's strategy to recoup *Cleopatra* costs.

"*Cleopatra* Touch." *Economist* 207 (15 June 63) 1138. Survey of finances for *Cleopatra*.

"Movie Screens Get Back Some Silver." *Bus Wk* (31 Aug 63) 41–42+. Recent attendance trends and theatre-building boom.

"Reel Money." *Newswk* 64 (7 Dec 64) 79. Earning reports of movie companies rising.

Howe, A. H. "How Movies Are Financed." *FIR* 7 (No. 1, Jan 66) 1–5.

"Upsurge for the Movies." *Time* 90 (28 July 67) 51. The current economic state of Hollywood.

"Communications; A 'Bum' Year for a 'Glamorous' Industry." *Forbes* 101 (1 Jan 68) 162–163. Short financial report on broadcasters, publishers, and motion pictures for the year of 1967.

"Why Don't They Get a New Script?" *Forbes* 103 (15 June 69) 30–31. Leadership and money problems of 20th Century-Fox and MGM.

"Hollywood and Bust." *Economist* 233 (29 Nov 69) 69–70. Financial losses in Britain and America follow decline in cinema attendance.

Knebel, F. "Hollywood: Broke and Getting Rich." *Look* 34 (3 Nov 70) 50–52.

6a(2). RELATIONS WITH TELEVISION

[See also 2m(4).]

Hughes, Pennethorne. "Her Public We!" *Close Up* 7 (No. 5, Nov 30) 325–328. The tele-cinema may solve some of the problems of film exhibition and censorship.

Daugherty, Frank. "Movies Woo Television." *CSMM* (22 Dec 37) 3.

Hurd, V. D. "Hollywood Opportunity." *CSMM* (1 July 39) 8. What will TV do to the movies? Some pitfalls and opportunities for film are discussed in this context.

DeForest, L. "Movies to Rescue Television." *Sci Dig* 11 (May 42) 34–38. Financial investment in the development of workable television by the motion-picture industry.

De Jaeger, C. T. "Television and the Films." *S&S* 12 (No. 47, Oct 43) 63–65. How they might combine for entertainment and information.

"Hollywood Digs In." *Bus Wk* (24 Mar 45) 92+. Leaders in cinema are anxious to become involved in television.

Daugherty, Frank. "Will Hollywood Televise?" *CSMM* (3 July 48) 5.

Cross, Peter D. "Television—End of Films?" *S&S* 17 (No. 67, Autumn 48) 131–132.

"Television: Movies' Friend or Foe?" *US News & World Report* 26 (7 Jan 49) 24–25.

"The Hollywood TV Invasion." *Consumer Reports* 14 (Feb 49) 86–87. The plans and deals of Big Five motion-picture producers.

Goldwyn, Samuel. "Hollywood in the Television Age." *NYTM* (13 Feb 49) 15. Goldwyn argues that movies cannot defeat television, so the two mediums must join forces, perhaps in some type of pay-TV.

Brecher, Edward. "Movies and Television." *Consumer Reports* 14 (Apr 49) 187. British films will be seen on television because Hollywood's Big Five keeps them out of the theaters.

"TV Produces—On Film." *Bus Wk* (15 Oct 49) 70–73. Use of film in television has become big business: a review and report.

"Television and Movies." *Good Housekeeping* 129 (Nov 49) 219. Reviews impact of TV on movies.

Goldwyn, Samuel. "Hollywood in the Television Age." *Hwd Q* 4 (No. 2, Winter 49) 145–151. Hollywood producer thinks TV will improve entertainment standards of theatrical films, predicts pay-TV.

Goldwyn, Samuel. "Television's Challenge to the Movies." *NYTM* (26 Mar 50) 17. The two industries should pool their talents.

"Foot in the Door?" *Time* 55 (1 May 50) 82–84. Film companies move into production for television.

"Pandora's Box." *Time* 55 (29 May 50) 86+. TV's effect on movie industry.

Mayer, Arthur. "Are Movies Better Than Ever?" *SRL* 33 (17 June 50) 9–10+. Analysis of the way the motion-picture industry is reacting to the threat of television.

"TV—Movie Policy." *Bus Wk* (1 July 50) 21. Speculation on FCC's decision: Can movie makers go into television?

Luther, Rodney. "Television and the Future of Motion Picture Exhibition." *Hwd Q* 5 (No. 2, Winter 50) 164–177. Various ways some theatre people are attempting to come to terms with TV; "modified theatre exhibition will continue."

"Anguish's Success." *Newswk* 37 (26 Feb 51) 45. Toby Anguish leases films to TV stations.

Hughes, Rupert. "TV Won't Ruin Everything." *FIR* 2 (Mar 51) 24–27+.

"End of an Era." *Time* 57 (28 May 51) 100. The end of Hollywood's Golden Era blamed on TV.

"Hollywood Romance." *Time* 57 (18 June 51) 100. American Federation of Musicians agrees to the sale of films to TV on conditions favorable to the union.

Crichton, Kyle. "View from the East." *Th Arts* 35 (Aug 51) 44+. Is television a rival of Hollywood, or is it merely the enemy of motion-picture theatres?

Shearer, Lloyd. "Hollywood Dilemma." *Th Arts* 35 (Aug 51) 10–11+. Television—and what the studios are doing about it.

Goldwyn, Samuel. "Is Hollywood Through?" *Collier's* 128 (29 Sep 51) 18–19+. Producer rejects danger from television.

MacKaye, Milton. "Big Brawl; Hollywood vs. Television." *SEP* 224 (19 Jan 52) 17–19+; (26 Jan 52) 30+; (2 Feb 52) 30+.

"Hollywood and TV." *Life* 32 (25 Feb 52) 20+. Editorial argues that the two industries are beneficial to each other.

"Hollywood Learns How to Live with TV." *Bus Wk* (9 Aug 52) 46–48.

"Really Happy Marriages Don't Start This Way." *Collier's* 130 (20 Sep 52) 78. The competition between TV and the movie industry.

Walters, F. "Government Sides with TV." *Th Arts* 36 (Oct 52) 79–81. Feud with the movie industry.

"Competition Is Coming." *Newswk* 40 (24 Nov 52) 82–83. Proposed merger between American Broadcasting Company and United Paramount Theaters.

"Something Worth Seeing." *Collier's* 130 (20 Dec 52) 78. An editorial that sees TV as a good competitor to the movie industry, not as a threat.

Hawley, L. "Look What TV's Doing to Hollywood!" *SEP* 225 (7 Feb 53) 34–35.

Howard, Jack. "Hollywood and Television—Year of Decision." *QFRTV* 7 (No. 4, Summer 53) 359–369.

"TV and Film: Marriage of Necessity." *Bus Wk* (15 Aug 53) 108–110. Theatrical films sold; commercials; kinescoped shows; films made for television.

Rule, John T. "Movies and TV: Murder or Merger?" *Atlantic* 192 (Oct 53) 55–58. Explanation of new processes; also an argument that TV can be the "savior" of cinema.

"Recruits from Hollywood." *Time* 62 (5 Oct 53) 80+. Has Hollywood finally given in to TV?

Goldwyn, Samuel. "Movies' Best Years Ahead: Television Is No Threat." *US News & World Report* 36 (5 Mar 54) 38–43.

Manvell, Roger. "Peep Show Bogey." *F&F* 1 (No. 2, Nov 54) 10. How film producers are trying to meet the threat of television.

Manvell, Roger. "Can Cinema Survive?" *F&F* 1 (No. 3, Dec 54) 13. A discussion of the coexistence of television and film: Will film last?

"Movie Makers Look for Gold on the TV Screen." *Bus Wk* (23 Apr 55) 154–156.

Schwartz, Delmore. "Films—TV." *New Rep* 133 (18 July 55) 21–22. The threat of TV to Hollywood.

"Thirty-five British Films Bought by ABC for Video Showing." *Bus Wk* (30 July 55) 54.

"Free Movies Every Night." *Time* 66 (1 Aug 55) 54–55. General Teleradio sells first backlog of old films for re-release on TV.

"TV's Effect on Movies, Sports." *US News & World Report* 39 (2 Sep 55) 43.

"TV Pays $2-Million for RKO Film Library." *Bus Wk* (31 Dec 55) 46.

"Hollywood Finally Sells to TV." *Bus Wk* (28 Jan 56) 54. The beginning of television purchase of Hollywood films: RKO film library.

"Films for TV." *Bus Wk* (3 Mar 56) 115. As predicted, more film companies are ready to follow RKO in selling their films to television.

"More Than Half of Movie Houses Reported Doing Poorly." *Bus Wk* (24 Mar 56) 52–53. A brief assessment of the movie industry's declining economic condition, much of it due to television.

Springer, John. "Farewell, Frankie . . . Bye, Bye, Blanche!" *FIR* 7 (May 56), 198–201. Feature motion pictures purchased for television; a list of films having been telecast as of May 1956; title's reference is to Frankie Darro and Blanche Mehafey, of the older, cheaper "B" productions.

Knight, Arthur. "Film and TV—A Shotgun Marriage?" *QFRTV* 10 (No. 4, Summer 56) 374–390. When is film better for TV than "live" TV?

"Stock of Aged MGM Movies Released to TV for $20-Million." *Bus Wk* (1 Sep 56) 63.

"Return of the Oldtimers." *Time* 68 (10 Sep 56) 95. Films sold to television.

"Nation's Fourth TV Net Sets Up with Films." *Bus Wk* (22 Sep 56) 52. National Telefilm Associates.

"More Films for TV." *Bus Wk* (10 Nov 56) 59. Deal between 20th Century-Fox and National Telefilm Associates, Inc., gives 390 pre-1948 films to television.

"Here Comes Hollywood." *Time* 68 (12 Nov 56) 106–108. Hollywood will have difficulty competing with films on television.

"Nothing But Movies." *Newswk* 48 (12 Nov 56) 106. National Telefilm Associates distributing films to television.

"Will Feature Films Reshape TV?" *Bus Wk* (24 Nov 56) 131–132+. Networks are basically opposed to including films in primetime slots.

Bachmann, Gideon. "The Impact of Television on Motion Pictures." *F Cult* 3 (No. 12, 1957) 3–6+. Gilbert Seldes, Fred Zinnemann, John Houseman, Boris Kaufman, Fritz Lang, Stanley Kramer, and Otto Preminger discuss TV's artistic and economic challenge; extracts from a series of radio interviews.

Houston, Penelope. "Hollywood in the Age of Television." *S&S* 26 (Spring 57) 175–179. It has ceased to be an expanding industry.

Sharnick, John. "Old, Old Movies in the New, New Medium." *House and Garden* 3 (Mar 57) 22–23. Films on television.

Canby, Vincent. "Telemovies." *FIR* 8 (Apr 57) 145–147. Condensed from *Motion Picture Herald;* eventually theatre chains will also provide movies on TV receivers for the second or third run for a fee.

Lavery, Emmett. "Hollywood's Future." *Commonweal* 66 (19 Apr 57) 57–59. Hollywood and television.

Alpert, Hollis. "Ten Years of Trouble." *Sat Rev* 40 (21 Dec 57) 9–11. Hollywood and television.

"What TV Is Doing to the Movie Industry." *US News & World Report* 44 (7 Feb 58) 88–90. Reports from Hollywood and New York.

"TV Gets Paramount's Pre-1948 Films." *Bus Wk* (15 Feb 58) 44. Last big package of pre-1948 films has been sold for television distribution by Paramount Picture Corporation.

Foster, H. "Celluloid Jungle." *Holiday* 29 (Jan 61) 115–116. Surveys old movies on TV.

Warner, Jack, Jr. "Teamwork, the Key to Creativity." *JSPG* (Mar 63) 19–22. Second-generation producer's view of relationship between industry and TV.

Alpert, Hollis. "Now the Earlier, Earlier Show." *NYTM* (11 Aug 63) 22–23. Old movies now seen on TV in prime time.

"Reel Attraction." *Newswk* 66 (15 Nov 65) 116–118. The problems of films on television.

"Colonel Bogey's March." *Time* 88 (7 Oct 66) 80. Films on TV outrate all other programs.

"At the Movies!" *Newswk* 68 (10 Oct 66) 99. Blockbuster films on television: *The Bridge on the River Kwai, North by Northwest,* and others.

Brown, Stanley. "Hollywood Rides Again." *Fortune* 74 (Nov 66) 181–182+. Effect of televised movies on the motion-picture industry.

"New Gold in the Hollywood Hills." *Time* 88 (25 Nov 66) 108+. Selling old movies to TV.

"Bombs Away?" *Newswk* 68 (5 Dec 66) 68. The supply of films for television is diminishing.

Champlin, Charles. "Can TV Save the Films?" *Sat Rev* (24 Dec 66) 11–13. Broadcast of *The Bridge on the River Kwai* suggests big benefits for both. Part of *Saturday Review* report "The American Motion Picture: 1966."

"Flick Boom." *Newswk* 70 (6 Nov 67) 104. Films for television are almost depleted, causing prices to skyrocket on those which remain.

6a(3). ASSISTANCE BY GOVERNMENT

[See also 7f.]

McCarthy, Frank. "I Borrowed the British Navy." *Look* 17 (No. 17, 25 Aug 53). *See 9, Sailor of the King.*

Johnston, Eric. "Our Biggest Bargain in Foreign Policy." *JSPG* (Dec 59) 4–6. Discusses the U.S. government's Informational Media Guaranty program, which has provided U.S. dollars for foreign countries to buy American films, books, and magazines valued at $150-million in the past ten years.

Javits, Jacob K. "The Federal Government and the Living Arts." *JSPG* (Mar 60) 7–10. Senator from New York argues for federal support of a U.S. Arts Foundation that would make the arts available to the whole country rather than just a few rich cities; visual arts would come later, after more experience.

Mirisch, Walter M. "Make Way for Tomorrow?" *JSPG* (Dec 60) 21–24. Advocates an American version of the British Eady Plan, a box-office tax benefiting motion-picture producers, which saved the British film industry.

Wolffers, Jules. "To Hold a Mirror . . ." *JSPG* 6 (No. 8, Mar 61) *See 7e(2).*

Houston, Penelope. "The Rewards of Quality." *S&S* 31 (Spring 62) 71–72. The French state cinema-aid law emphasizes quality (advancement of cinema art, cultural significance, or support for propaganda goals); short films are especially assisted; examples given of amounts collected by specific films.

"The Hexagon." *Time* 80 (13 July 62) 54. The Pentagon helps Hollywood in production of military films.

Stevens, George, Jr. "The Motion Picture—A National Cultural Poverty Area?" *JUFPA* 16 (No. 4, 1964) 3+. There is little public respect for film as an art form in this country, little financial support for it, and little recognition of it by the government and the "intellectual élite"; the opening of the Kennedy Center for the Performing Arts presents a chance to change these attitudes;

a speech to the Washington, D.C., Film Council.

"States and Cinemas." *S&S* 36 (Winter 66–67) 26–29. The pattern of subsidy and state aid in the seven film-making countries of Western Europe. Some of the questions asked: Is entertainment tax payable on cinema tickets? Is national production aided by a subsidy system? Is there a system of reward for "quality"? Is there some special form of aid to short films?

Allen, Irving. "Subsidy Creates Mediocrity." *JSPG* (June 67) 19–20.

Degrand, Claude. "Film Subsidy in France." *JSPG* (June 67). *See 4e(2c).*

Holleaux, André. "Subsidy Under the Common Market." *JSPG* (June 67) 13–16. Proposals for European community subsidy of films to replace coproduction schemes.

Howe, A. H. "Hollywood or Europe." *JSPG* (June 67). *See 6c(4).*

Kuchel, Thomas. "Protecting the American Film Industry." *JSPG* (June 67) 17–18+. California senator opposes subsidy, suggests tax advantages.

Plateroti, Arnaldo. "Italian Government Subsidy and Union Labor." *JSPG* (June 67). *See 4e(3d).*

Schein, Harry. "Swedish Subsidies Are No Subsidies." *JSPG* (June 67). *See 4e(5b).*

Taylor, N. A. "Canada Views Subsidy." *JSPG* (June 67). *See 4(i).*

Vietheer, George. "The *Journal* Looks at Foreign Film Subsidies." *JSPG* (June 67) 1+. Report by vice-president of U.S. Motion Picture Export Association, covering practices of twenty countries, mostly European.

Fadiman, William. "Should American Films Be Subsidized?" *Sat Rev* 50 (5 Aug 67) 14–17+.

Fadiman, William. "Public Money for Private Gain." *F&F* 14 (No. 8, May 68) 47–49. Subsidizing American films.

Deedy, J. "News and Views." *Commonweal* 88 (28 June 68) 426. Government aids in production of *The Green Berets.*

Gilbert, Robert W. "Foreign Film Subsidies as an Aspect of Financing." *JSPG* 10 (No. 3, Sep 68) 3–8.

"Darryl's Antic." *New Rep* 160 (28 June 69) 11. Bill to prohibit military aid to commercial movies because of Darryl Zanuck's *Tora! Tora! Tora!*

6b. Distribution

[See also 7e(1).]

"Ownership and Control of Moving Picture Companies." *Fortune* 13 (Feb 36) 144. "Appendix B" for a longer article on "Jews in America."

"Film Arbitration." *Bus Wk* (25 Jan 41) 18. The motion-picture industry sets up machinery to settle its old trade disputes.

"Films Across the Sea." *New S&N* 27 (11 Mar 44). *See 4e(1d).*

Swenson, S. "The Entrepreneur's Role in Introducing the Sound Motion Picture." *Polit Sci Q* 63 (Sep 48) 404–423. Businessmen: their actual behavior compared with entrepreneurial behavior as described in economic theory.

"The Expensive Art." *FQ* 13 (No. 4, Summer 60) 19–34. Discussion by John Adams, Shirley Clarke, Edward Harrison, Bill Kenly, Elodie Osborn, and Amos Vogel about the problems of distributing foreign and independent films; Harrison starts off with the information that it costs $20,000 just to prepare and promote a finished picture.

Mayer, Arthur, Max Youngstein, Robert Lippert, Walter Reade, Jr., Glenn Norris, Norton Ritchey, Alfred Daff, James Burkett. "The *Journal* Looks at Motion Picture Distribution." *JSPG* (Dec 61) 3–22. Producers, theatre men, and distribution executives criticize the system, especially the inequities of profit splits and the duplications in booking offices around the world; independents are developing new, streamlined methods.

"Distribution of Independent Films." *F Cult* (No. 42, Fall 66) 46–75. Symposia, various meetings on this subject, at fourth New York Film Festival.

Levine, Joe. "Joe Levine on Joe Levine." *JSPG* (Sep 68) 29–30. Why he merged with Avco —for money to use and more freedom.

Solomon, Benjamin W. "Accounting Aspects of Producer-Distributor Relations." *JSPG* 10 (No. 3, Sep 68) 17–20.

Arkoff, Samuel Z. "Famous Myths of the Film Industry." *JSPG* (Sep 69) 3–7. An independent distributor says exhibitors will always be at odds with distributors.

Youngstein, Max E. "How Much Muscle Do You Have?" *JSPG* (Sep 69) 13–15. An independent producer talks about relations with distributors.

Silver, Charles. "For a Fair Distribution of Film Wealth." *F Com* 6 (No. 2, Fall 70) 2–4. Former Brandon Films executive complains about the fate of unusual films; it seems to be the fault of distributors, exhibitors, and the audience.

6b(1). MONOPOLIES AND MERGERS

Bennett, Ralph Culver. "Merger Movement in the Motion Picture Industry." *Annals of Am Acad of Polit and Soc Sci* 147 (Jan 30) 89–94. Analysis of legal aspects in Fox's proposed absorption of Loew's, Inc., and Warners' control of Stanley Company and First National.

Eastman, Fred. "Who Controls the Movies?" *Chris Cent* 47 (5 Feb 30) 173–175.

"Vast Interests Now Have a Voice in the Talkies." *Bus Wk* (17 Sep 30) 22–23. Paris Sound Picture Conference resolves patent infringement.

Wellesby, Norah. "The Story of Gideon Nathan." *North Am Rev* 230 (Dec 30) 687–692. Fictitious account of small distributor and his adventures with block booking.

"Good Motive, Good Result No Defense Against Sherman Act." *Bus Wk* (3 Dec 30) 12. U.S. Supreme Court acts against uniform contracts and credit agreements between producers and distributors.

"Busting the Movie Trust." *Lit Dig* 107 (13 Dec 30) 11. Paramount and First National hit with antitrust decisions.

"Movies and Rotten Eggs." *Chris Cent* 48 (28 Jan 31) 127–128. Condemns Sidney Kent, vice-president of Paramount, for upholding validity of block booking.

"Movie Exhibitors Ask for a Sponge." *Chris Cent* 48 (4 Feb 31) 156. Allied Theatre Owners of Texas ask for legal power to break block booking.

"The Motion Picture Combine." *Canad Forum* 11 (Aug 31) 405–406. On Famous Players in Canada and Paramount's monopoly.

"Movie Block-Booking to Be Tested." *Chris Cent* 49 (23 Mar 32) 373. Cleveland exhibitors sue MPPDA.

"Block-Booking Outlawed in Chicago." *Chris Cent* 49 (20 Apr 32) 501–502.

"Movie Exhibitors Ask Church Cooperation." *Chris Cent* 50 (1 Feb 33) 140+. Harrison's Reports editor and exhibitors are against block booking.

Donavon, William, and Breck P. McAllister. "Consent Decrees in the Enforcement of Federal Anti-Trust Laws: The Moving Picture Industry." *Harvard Law Rev* 46 (No. 6, Apr 33) 929–931. Exhibitor contracts, block booking, zoning.

"New Mexico Outlaws Block-Booking." *Chris Cent* 50 (17 May 33) 644–645.

"Wisconsin Delivers Body Blow to Block-Booking." *Chris Cent* 50 (12 July 33) 900. State Supreme Court rules against United Artists in theatre suit.

"Shamed Citizen." *Time* 22 (4 Dec 33) 34–36. William Fox tells U.S. Senate Committee on Banking and Currency his attempts to get two attorneys general to approve his purchase of MGM.

"Block-Booking Must Go!" *Chris Cent* 50 (20 Dec 33) 1600–1601. But new NRA code does not deal with it.

"Harrison Says Hays Must Go." *Chris Cent* 51 (21 Mar 34) 381. Another attack on block booking.

Short, W. H. "Block-Booking Must Go!" *Parents Mag* 9 (Apr 34) 13.

"New Attack on Block-Booking: Bill Number H. R. 8686." *Chris Cent* 51 (30 May 34) 715.

LeSourd, Howard M. "Block-Booking—Cause or Camouflage?" *Lit Dig* 117 (9 June 34) 28.

"Fox Film Feature." *Bus Wk* (23 June 34) 16–18. Federal courts support Fox's Tri-Ergon patents.

"Movie Climax." *Bus Wk* (20 Oct 34) 18. Supreme Court refuses to review challenges to Fox's Tri-Ergon patents on projector fly-wheel and double-film process.

"Fox After Hounds." *Time* 24 (22 Oct 34) 42. Does William Fox still have a claim on certain sound patents?

"Fox Loses." *Bus Wk* (9 Mar 35) 10–11. U.S. Supreme Court holds two Fox Tri-Ergon patents invalid.

Harrison, P. S. "Give the Movie Exhibitor a Chance!" *Chris Cent* 52 (19 June 35) 819–821. Analysis of block booking and Hays office propaganda for it.

"Lawsuit in St. Louis." *Time* 26 (14 Oct 35) 58–59. Antitrust charge against Warner Brothers, RKO, and Paramount.

"Sound Settlement: ERPI Waives Provisions in Movie Contracts." *Bus Wk* (18 Jan 36) 16. Result of suit by RCA against Bell Telephone.

"Uncle Sam Sits in on Producers' Game of Freeze-Out." *Newswk* 7 (7 Mar 36) 30. The Skourases in St. Louis and other independent theatre owners couldn't get Fox, Paramount, or RKO pictures; Justice Department asks injunction against companies.

"Free the Movies Now!" *Chris Cent* 53 (25 Nov 36) 454. Bills to prohibit block booking.

"Fateful Hour for the Movies." *Chris Cent* (27 May 36) 757. Proposed legislation to abolish block booking and blind selling.

"Hollywood and Radio." *Bus Wk* (6 Nov 37) 27. Hollywood studios and stars move into the radio business.

"Ask Film Booking Law." *Bus Wk* (19 Feb 38) 22–23. The reasons small theatres strove to stop block booking.

"Blocked: Prohibitory Bill Goes Over." *Bus Wk* (25 June 38) 20. Neely Bill passes Senate but lags in House.

"Movie Anti-Trust Suit, Who Cares?" *Bus Wk* (30 July 38) 17–18. Thurman Arnold tries to determine public interest in the movie antitrust suit.

"Constructive Effort: Trust Busting Procedure." *Time* 32 (1 Aug 38) 37.

Dugan, James. "The Film Trust on Trial." *New Masses* 28 (16 Aug 38) 5–6.

McConnell, B. M. "Is the Motion-Picture Industry a Monopoly?" *CSMM* (14 Sep 38) 14.

Sherburne, E. C. "Letter to a Movie Goer." *CSMM* (30 Nov 38) 5. A defense of the U.S. government's suit against eight major film companies to end the practice of block booking.

Isaacs, Hermine R. "Film in the Court." *Th Arts* 22 (Dec 38) 907–909. The government's bill of complaint for violation of the Sherman Anti-Trust Law.

"Movies Are Anti-Trust Test." *Bus Wk* (17 June 39) 14–15. Efforts to prevent the Department of Justice from imposing an anti-trust suit on Hollywood production.

"Arnold Scorns Movie Code." *Bus Wk* (26 Aug 39) 43. Thurman Arnold refuses to drop antitrust suit.

Depinet, N. E., and J. Roosevelt. "Abolish Movie Block-Booking?" *Rotarian* 56 (Jan 40) 24–25. Two detailed arguments—pro and con.

"Pass the Neely Bill!" *Chris Cent* 57 (21 Feb 40) 240–241. Advocates the outlawing of block booking and blind selling.

"Legion of Decency and the Big Eight: Motion Picture Block-Booking." *Chris Cent* 57 (20 Mar 40) 373.

Ferguson, Otis. "Weep No More, My Ladies." *New Rep* 102 (3 June 40) 760–761. Block booking and double bills are not the source of bad picture making; we should become aware of excellent directors instead.

"Film Trust Truce Near." *Bus Wk* (31 Aug 40) 39. The signing of the consent decree by five companies and the events leading up to it.

"Movies Arbitrate." *Bus Wk* (2 Nov 40) 15. The specification of the consent decree that disputes will be handled by the American Arbitration Association.

"Is This the End of Block-Booking?" *Chris Cent* 57 (6 Nov 40) 1364. Written after five companies signed the consent decree.

"Consent Decree." *Time* 36 (11 Nov 40) 70–71. A short history of block booking and blind selling and a look at the government consent decree designed to stop such action.

"Movie Agreement: Consent Decree Signed by Five Companies." *Scholastic* 37 (11 Nov 40) 4.

"Arbitration for the Movies Is the Fruit of Consent Decree." *Newswk* 16 (2 Dec 40) 45–46.

"Movie Dynamite? Bill Now Being Pushed in Minnesota." *Bus Wk* (5 Apr 41) 30. Allied Theatre Owners of the Northwest try to overhaul the movie industry's consent decree.

Davidman, Joy. "Monopoly Takes a Screen Test." *New Masses* 39 (24 June 41) 28–30. About monograph by the Temporary National Economic Committee, *The Movie Industry—Patterns of Control.*

"Antitrust Scenario." *Bus Wk* (6 Sep 41) 32+. Independent exhibitors still not satisfied with consent decree offered by major film producers and Department of Justice.

"Movie Relief." *Bus Wk* (29 Nov 41) 44. Federal court lifts consent-decree provisions so that producers can sell in Minnesota and comply with state law there.

"Movie Pact Flops." *Bus Wk* (20 June 42) 33–34. Vital portions of famous consent decree now inoperative—block booking is on the way back.

"Movie Tribunals." *Bus Wk* (20 Feb 43) 38+. Future of antitrust arbitration system rests with successor to Thurman Arnold, Assistant Attorney General, now elevated to federal judiciary.

"Movie Divorce: U.S. Reopens Suit to Force Big Five to Give Up Exhibiting Pictures." *Bus Wk* (12 Aug 44) 84–86.

"Movie Surrender? Industry's Limited Front in Anti-Trust Case Is Reported Cracking." *Bus Wk* (17 Nov 45) 16.

"Scophony Suit." *Bus Wk* (22 Dec 45) 90+. Justice Department charges that American and British companies monopolized television patents for Movie reproduction.

"Smashing Blow at Movie Monopoly." *Chris Cent* 63 (20 Mar 46) 356. Subsequent runs in same area barred until three weeks have elapsed; possible effects on the movie distributor of the Supreme Court's decision.

"New Film Decree." *Bus Wk* (22 June 46) 19–20. Recent decision on block booking and blind selling occasions this résumé of empire building in Hollywood.

"Divorce Denied: Moviemakers Shoved Through Antitrust Grinder." *Time* 47 (24 June 46) 82+. Manhattan federal court rules out block booking, but major companies allowed to keep theatres.

Nathan, F. S. "Books into Films." *Publishers Weekly* 150 (24 Aug 46) 808. What will be the results of the abolition of block booking and collapsible corporations?

"U.S. Court Decision Ends Block-Booking." *Chris Cent* 63 (28 Aug 46) 1027.

"No Film Peace: Antitrust Against Eight Motion Picture Producers." *Bus Wk* (26 Oct 46) 41–42.

"Nobody's Pleased with New Movie Decree Regulating Trade Practices." *Bus Wk* (11 Jan 47) 16.

Brady, R. A. "Problem of Monopoly: Status of Anti-Trust Action." *Annals of Am Acad of Polit and Soc Sci* 254 (Nov 47) 125–136.

Mayer, Arthur L. "An Exhibitor Begs for 'B's.'" *Hwd Q* 3 (No. 2, Winter 47–48) 172–177. Abolition of block booking has taken away the opportunity for innovation and the development of new talents that used to occur along with the formula "B"-budget films.

"Independents' Day; Final Decisions of Supreme Court." *Time* 51 (17 May 48) 91–92. Separation of producer and exhibitor.

"Bid to Buy ABC." *Bus Wk* (4 Dec 48) 96. 20th Century-Fox wants to take over broadcasting company and all its works; may get at least controlling interest.

"Paramount Gives In." *Time* 53 (7 Mar 49) 95–96. Paramount Pictures, Inc., to split into two separate companies, one to make and distribute movies, the other to operate theatres, as result of U.S. consent decree in antitrust case.

"Consent Decree Ends Color-Film Anti-Trust Suit." *Bus Wk* (11 Mar 50) 25. Technicolor must open up its color-film process to any would-be licensee.

"New Picture." *Time* 55 (13 Mar 50) 88. Technicolor, Inc., has agreed in a consent decree to make its process, skilled know-how, and 152 patents available to others.

"Grim Choice for Hollywood." *Bus Wk* (24 June 50) 26. Supreme Court orders five companies to get out of theatres or production.

"Triple Damage Hits Movies." *Bus Wk* (14 Oct 50) 54+. A wave of civil antitrust suits.

"Warners Split." *Bus Wk* (6 Jan 51) 92. Movie company agrees to form separate production and exhibition concerns.

Borneman, Ernest. "United States vs. Hollywood: The Case History of an Anti-Trust Suit." *S&S* 19 (Feb 51) 418–420+. Brief history of the production, distribution, and exhibition setup in the United States, beginning with the early days; control of all of the first-run theatres meant the virtual annihilation of competition and led to many abuses; this eventually brought on the antitrust suit.

Borneman, Ernest. "United States vs. Hollywood: The Case History of an Anti-Trust Suit." *S&S* 19 (Mar 51) 448–450. The court order, and the problems it failed to solve.

"Linking Movies with Television." *Commonweal* 54 (8 June 51) 203–204. Merger of ABC with United Paramount chain: a dangerous "standardization" of the arts?

Levin, Harvey. "How Much Merger in Television?" *Nation* 173 (13 Oct 51) 299–300. The projected merger of ABC-TV with United Paramount Theaters raises doubts for the artistic future of either medium.

"When Greek Meets Greek." *Time* 59 (16 June 52) 88+. Movie companies sued by lawyer Nick Spanos for activities against independent theatre owners.

"Movies, TV Join Hands." *Bus Wk* (22 Nov 52) 34. FCC is set to approve merger of Paramount Theaters with ABC; result will be the entrance of movies into television.

Begeman, Jean. "One-Party Television, Too?" *New Rep* 128 (23 Feb 53) 12–14. Doubts about ABC-TV merger with United Paramount Theaters.

Starr, Cecile. "Case of the Feature Film." *Sat Rev* (9 May 53) 36. The government's antitrust suit condemning practices restricting 16mm film rentals.

"Sherman Act Redefinition." *Time* 63 (18 Jan

54) 86+. The Crest Theater sues film distributors for conspiracy.

"Color Clash." *Newswk* 44 (12 July 54) 60. Pathé Laboratories, Inc., has charged Technicolor, Inc., with monopolizing the film-laboratory business.

Whitney, S. N. "Vertical Disintegration in the Motion Picture Industry." *Am Econ Rev* 45 (May 55) 491–498. The impact of federal government antitrust laws; history.

Cassidy, Ralph. "Monopoly in Motion Picture Production and Distribution: 1908–15." *S Calif Law Rev* 32 (No. 4, 1959).

"U.S. to Appeal TV Film Ruling." *Bus Wk* (13 Aug 60) 53–54. Justice Department plans to appeal federal court ruling absolving film companies of antitrust charges in distribution of pre-1940 movies for TV.

"Movie Block-Booking Hit Again." *Bus Wk* (10 Dec 60) 38. Ruling against package sale of films to TV stations parallels 1948 Supreme Court ruling against block booking.

"How Goldberg Views the Late Show." *Bus Wk* (10 Nov 62) 142. Supreme Court says block booking is illegal for TV too.

"Good-by, Nancy Drew." *Newswk* 60 (19 Nov 62) 106. Supreme Court rules that it is illegal for movie distributors to subject television stations to block booking.

"Theatre Chain to Make Films." *Bus Wk* (6 July 63) 22. Reversal of ruling separating production and exhibition to allow National General Corporation to produce and distribute films.

"Hollywood's Big Brothers." *Economist* 220 (30 July 66) 445–446. Consolidated Foods takeover of United Artists is typical of holding companies' rising control of motion-picture industry.

"Movies Get New Moguls." *Bus Wk* (8 Feb 69) 29–30. Report on conglomerate mergers with Hollywood studios.

6b(2). INDIVIDUAL COMPANIES

[*See also 4d(1).*]

"Utility Magnate Buys Out Fox." *Bus Wk* (16 Apr 30) 30.

Condon, Frank. "Over the Bridge to the Movies." *SEP* 204 (16 Jan 32) 31+. Paramount Studio at Astoria, New York.

"Lasky Out." *Time* 20 (26 Sep 32) 26. Sam Katz is behind changes at Paramount.

"Metro-Goldwyn-Mayer." *Fortune* 6 (Dec 32) 50–64+. Economic profile of company; biography and personal estimate of Irving Thalberg.

"Mr. Rockefeller Inherits the Movies." *Chris Cent* 50 (8 Feb 33) 183–184. Has he acquired RKO because of its bankruptcy?

"John D. Rockefeller, Jr., Inherits the American Movies." *China Weekly Rev* 64 (18 Mar 33) 83–84. Rockefeller's financial backing of Radio City has inadvertently made him almost sole owner of RKO.

"Big Bankrupt." *Time* 21 (27 Mar 33) 23. Paramount Publix Corporation takes voluntary bankruptcy.

"Talkie Money." *Bus Wk* (23 Sep 33) 22. Paramount bankrupt.

"Fox Film: Odlum and British Firm Now Big Stockholders." *Newswk* 3 (5 May 34) 25.

"Fox Film Recovery." *Bus Wk* (8 June 35) 21–22. Fox merges with 20th Century Pictures.

"Movie Epic." *Bus Wk* (24 Aug 35) 18–19. Fox Film merger with 20th Century.

"The Men Who Revived Paramount Go to Work on RKO." *Newswk* 6 (16 Nov 35) 30+. Investment company buys RCA's interest in RKO.

"Universal to Cowdin." *Time* 27 (23 Mar 36) 47. Carl Laemmle sells 80% interest for $5,500,000 to J. Cheever Cowdin, backed by Eastman money; biography of Laemmle.

"Film Shake-Up: Paramount Stockholders Refuse to Reelect Otterson as Director." *Lit Dig* 121 (27 June 36) 38.

"Again, Paramount." *Time* 27 (29 June 36) 54. Joseph P. Kennedy advises on production and management.

"Paramount Pictures Inc." *Fortune* 15 (Mar 37) 86–96+. Economic profile of company; biography and personal estimate of Adolph Zukor.

"Warner Brothers Pictures, Inc." *Fortune* 16 (Dec 37) 110–113+. Economic profile of company; comments on the brothers' personalities.

"Loew's Inc., the World's Most Profitable Trust." *Fortune* 20 (Aug 39) 24–31. Loew's, Inc., the men who run it, the pictures it makes (through MGM), and the antitrust suit leveled against it.

Potamkin, Harry A. "The Cinematized Child." *Films* 1 (No. 1, Nov 39) *See 1a(4)*.

"Hollywood Lawsuit." *Bus Wk* (12 Oct 40) 57–59. The plan to merge Universal with a holding company brings action.

Delehantz, Theodore. "The Disney Studio at War." *Th Arts* 27 (Jan 43) 31–39.

"Metro-Goldwyn-Mayer: Louis B. Mayer Bosses the Biggest Movie Making Machine." *Life* 15 (27 Sep 43) 60–75.

Isaacs, Hermine Rich. "Presenting the Warner Brothers." *Th Arts* 28 (Feb 44) 99–108.

"But Is It Art?: Walt Disney Doesn't Care." *Bus Wk* (10 Feb 45) 72+. Walt Disney Productions discussed as a $7-million business enterprise with a great postwar future in fields other than strictly screen entertainment.

"Schoolmaster M-G-M." *Newswk* 27 (20 May 46). *See 8a*.

"Super-Super: New Corporation, Universal-International." *Time* 48 (12 Aug 46) 88. Merger to make "A" pictures exclusively.

"Hollywood in New York." *NYTM* (22 Dec 46) 44. RKO-Pathé's new studios in New York make New York a film center once again.

"Big Frog." *Time* 49 (13 Jan 47) 83. Universal-International Pictures moves into 16mm with a subsidiary called United World Films.

"M-G-M Records." *Bus Wk* (15 Feb 47) 79+. MGM launches a long-expected tie-up with a record company, initiating a trend.

"Paramount: Oscar for Profits." *Fortune* 35 (June 47) 88–95+. Up from bankruptcy.

"Blue Skies: M-G-M." *Time* 53 (21 Feb 49) 102. With Dore Schary in charge of production, MGM production is picking up.

"Paramount Chooses Films." *Bus Wk* (19 Mar 49) 98+. Two major movie companies get rid of their theatres.

"Comeback?" *Time* 56 (24 July 50) 74. United Artists sold to Paul V. McNutt and syndicate of Eastern investors.

"U.A. Mystery Sale." *Newswk* 36 (24 July 50) 54. Paul V. McNutt purchases control of United Artists.

"Who Bought United Artists?" *Bus Wk* (12 Aug 50) 78–79. "Nobody knows who backed McNutt syndicate or exactly how much U.A. cost, but it's clear that Pickford and Chaplin sold out because U.A. needed capital to finance films and the banks balked."

"Trio Unites to Save United Artists." *Bus Wk* (28 Apr 51) 102–105. Young businessmen have formula to bring film distributor out of red: buy up competitor (Eagle Lion Classics), switch to mass distribution.

"The Brother Act Retires." *Time* 57 (14 May 51) 101–103. The Warner brothers announce they are arranging to sell control.

"Warners' for Sale." *Newswk* 37 (14 May 51) 80.

"Movie Pay Cut." *Bus Wk* (26 May 51) 134+. Executives of 20th Century-Fox Film Corporation asked to take "voluntary" pay cuts.

"Warner Bros. to Buy Million of Own Shares." *Bus Wk* (14 July 51) 114. Move to reduce capitalization of the company.

"MGM Musicals." *Life* 32 (14 Apr 52). *See 4k(6).*

"M-G-M's Economy." *Newswk* 40 (21 July 52) 74. Plans for 1952–1953, centered around a tighter budget.

"Re-United Artists." *Time* 61 (23 Feb 53) 94.

"Happy Ending." *Bus Wk* (28 Feb 53) 121–122. United Artists has once more become a major factor in movie distribution: Krim and associates have been successful.

"Battle of the 20th Century." *Time* 61 (13 Apr 53) 98. Charles Green, spokesman for Fox stockholders, charges Skouras and Zanuck with mismanagement.

"RKO: It's Only Money." *Fortune* 47 (May 53) 122–127.

"Twentieth Century-Fox Becomes Battleground." *Bus Wk* (9 May 53) 29. Stockholders vote on whether to keep or change the system of "cumulative" voting used in electing the board of directors.

"Hughes Sells Control of RKO Theatres Corp." *Bus Wk* (14 Nov 53) 76. Howard Hughes sells stock he had held in trusteeship.

"Hughes Coup." *Bus Wk* (13 Feb 54) 33. Speculation about Hughes' motives in offering to buy RKO assets.

"Hughes Upsets the Market." *Time* 63 (15 Feb 54) 91.

"RKO Approves a Deal." *Time* 63 (22 Feb 54) 96.

"Bargain Day at RKO." *Time* 63 (24 Mar 54) 86.

"$23.5 Million Check." *Time* 63 (12 Apr 54) 102. Howard Hughes buys all RKO assets and becomes the nation's only sole owner of a major motion-picture studio.

"Two to the Rescue." *Newswk* 44 (20 Sep 54) 75+. Since 1951, Robert S. Benjamin and Arthur B. Krim doing well as executives of United Artists.

"Mavericks on the Range." *Newswk* 45 (18 Apr 55) 79–80. Problems at the annual meeting of Republic Pictures Corporation.

"General Tire Goes Hollywood." *Bus Wk* (23 July 55) 32. General Tire and Rubber Company buys the assets of RKO Radio Pictures from Howard Hughes.

"Howard Hughes Exit." *Newswk* 46 (25 July 55) 70.

"RKO." *S&S* 25 (Autumn 55) 64. Note on Howard Hughes and his studio, now sold to subsidiary of General Tire and Rubber Company.

"Hughes and Odlum Move Closer." *Bus Wk* (8 Oct 55) 59–60. Merger approaches between Hughes' RKO's corporate shell and Floyd Odlum's Atlas Corporation.

Coughlan, Robert. "O'Neills' Money Machine." *Life* 39 (5 Dec 55) 186–190+. Story of the O'Neill family, owners of General Tire and Rubber Company, which bought the RKO studios: their decision to go into the movie business.

"Odlum-RKO Deal." *Bus Wk* (24 Dec 55) 28. Directors of RKO and four smaller companies agree to merge their firms with Atlas Corporation.

"That Big RKO Deal." *Newswk* 47 (9 Jan 56) 55.

"Quick Turn-Around on RKO Fills Everybody's Pockets." *Bus Wk* (14 Jan 56) 52. Profits made by Thomas F. O'Neill of General Teleradio, Inc. since purchase of RKO Radio Pictures from Howard Hughes.

"Boston to Hollywood." *Time* 67 (21 May 56) 96–97. Serge Semenenko's investment in Warner Brothers.

Brown, Sandford. "Lights, Camera, Profits." *Newswk* 48 (16 July 56) 73–76. Diversification of RKO Teleradio Pictures.

"Banker's the Star." *Newswk* 48 (23 July 56) 63–64. Serge Semenenko purchases control of Warner Brothers.

"Loew Blow." *Time* 68 (12 Nov 56) 97–98. A management fight in Loew's, Inc.

"Peace Dove That Roosted at Loew's Succumbs as Proxy Battle Looms." *Bus Wk* (27 July 57) 46.

Hughes, Emmet J. "M.G.M.: War Among the Lion Tamers." *Fortune* 56 (Aug 57) 98–103. The fight for control of Loew's, Inc.

"Loew's Insurgents Pick Up New 'Directors' to Make a Quorum as Foes Stay Away." *Bus Wk* (3 Aug 57) 36.

"Gun Fight at the MGM Corral." *Time* 70 (5 Aug 57) 69. Battle over control of MGM's corporate assets.

"Roars at M-G-M." *Newswk* 50 (5 Aug 57) 73.

"More on a Muddle." *Newswk* 50 (12 Aug 57) 72. Battle over who has control over MGM.

"Explosion on the Movie Lot." *Bus Wk* (17 Aug 57) 43–47+. Loew's, Inc., board of directors splits down the middle.

Sheehan, Robert. "Cliff-Hanger at MGM." *Fortune* 56 (Oct 57) 134–135+.

"M-G-M's Sick Lion (Loew's, Inc., The World's Biggest Motion Picture and Theater Enterprise)." *Economist* 185 (26 Oct 57) 310.

"Caging the Lion." *Newswk* 50 (28 Oct 57) 82–84. Showdown between Loew's president Joseph R. Vogel and an opposition group headed by Joseph Tomlinson.

"Loew's Woes." *Time* 70 (28 Oct 57) 91. Loew's, Inc., gives President Joseph R. Vogel solid control.

"Film Company Branches into TV." *Bus Wk* (9 Nov 57) 133–136. United Artists and television.

Knight, Arthur. "The United Artists Story." *Sat Rev* 40 (21 Dec 57) 12–13. Financial situation after change of administration in 1951. Part of *Saturday Review* report "The Big Change in Hollywood."

"Twentieth Century City." *Time* 71 (13 Jan 58) 81. 20th Century-Fox in the building business.

Bloom, Murray T. "What Two Lawyers Are Doing in Hollywood." *Harper's* 216 (Feb 58) 42–49. Robert Benjamin and Arthur Krim rejuvenate United Artists.

North, Christopher. "MGM Is Here to Stay." *FIR* 9 (Apr 58) 166–170. A report of the MGM stockholders after the recent proxy fight.

"Hollywood Happy Ending." *Time* 71 (28 Apr 58) 90–92. Robert Benjamin and Arthur Krim report profits at United Artists.

"Derring-Doers of Movie Business." *Fortune* 57 (May 58) 137–141+. Arthur Krim and Robert Benjamin put United Artists on its feet again.

"Truce at Loew's." *Bus Wk* (10 Jan 59) 100. Nathan Cummings buys block of stock from dissidents and pledges support to President Joseph R. Vogel.

"The Slow Buck." *Newswk* 53 (19 Jan 59) 70. Loew's, Inc., earnings; resignation of dissident Joseph Tomlinson.

"Story Behind Paramount Pictures." *Changing Times* 15 (July 61) 34.

"Perils of Spyros." *Newswk* 58 (21 Aug 61) 70. Spyros P. Skouras returned as president of 20th Century-Fox.

"Skouras Wins Chance to Write New Script." *Bus Wk* (28 Oct 61) 104.

"Period of Adjustment." *Time* 79 (25 May 62) 73. MCA, Inc., plans to "revitalize the film industry."

"Dragon Slayer." *Newswk* 60 (6 Aug 62) 62–63. Darryl Zanuck and associated interests regain control of board of directors and bring back Spyros P. Skouras as the chairman at 20th Century-Fox. See also (9 July 62) 62–64 and (16 July 62) 64–66.

"Casualties at Fox." *Time* 50 (7 Sep 62) 63.

Levine, Joseph E. "Dead the Movie Industry Is Not!" *Cinema* (Calif) 1 (No. 3, 1963) 23. Article on films Embassy Pictures is distributing.

"Can Fox Keep *Cleopatra* Afloat?" *Bus Wk* (16 May 64) 25–26.

McDonald, J. "Now the Bankers Come to Disney." *Fortune* 73 (May 66) 138–141.

Alpert, Hollis. "View from the 28th Floor." *Sat Rev* (24 Dec 66) 17–19+. President Robert O'Brien's decision making at MGM. Part of *Saturday Review* report "The American Motion Picture: 1966."

"Walt Disney's Legacy." *Economist* 221 (24 Dec 66) 1327. Film holdings and the plans for Disney World and Mineral King.

"Fight in the Lion's Den." *Time* 89 (3 Mar 67) 87. President Robert H. O'Brien and chief stockholder Philip J. Levin struggle for control of MGM.

"MGM's Own Drama." *Bus Wk* (4 Mar 67) 126–128.

"Fight Over MGM." *Newswk* 69 (6 Mar 67) 68–70.

"Back to Work?" *Time* 89 (17 Mar 67) 94. Proxy fight for control of MGM leaves President Robert O'Brien in control.

"Cecil B. De Bluhdorn?" *Newswk* 69 (29 May 67) 82. Changes in Paramount ownership.

"Newest Life of Leo the Lion." *Time* 90 (1 Sep 67) 59–60. Philip J. Levin sells his shares in MGM and ends his fight to win control.

"End of a Lion Hunt: P. J. Levin Sells Shares."
Newswk 70 (4 Sep 67) 59. At MGM.

Dunne, John Gregory. "20th Century-Fox."
Take One 2 (No. 2, 1968) 6–7. A personal
account of experiences with the studio and
with Richard and Darryl Zanuck.

"Son of Zanuck Stars at Twentieth Century."
Bus Wk (14 Sep 68) 76–78.

"New Scene at MGM." *Newswk* 72 (28 Oct
68) 102.

"MGM Gets New Leading Man." *Bus Wk* (14
Dec 68) 48.

"New Showdown Looms." *Bus Wk* (2 Aug 69)
66. MGM stockholder Kirk Kerkorian threatens to offer $35 per share for one million
shares of MGM common stock.

"MGM Cliff-Hanger." *Newswk* 74 (4 Aug 69)
70–71.

"Eurodollars Finance the New MGM Drama."
Bus Wk (16 Aug 69) 41–42.

"Coup That Won MGM." *Time* 94 (3 Oct 69)
94.

"New Lion Roars." *Bus Wk* (11 Oct 69) 47.
MGM report.

"Disney Without Walt." *Newswk* 74 (20 Oct
69) 90.

"James Aubrey Makes Comeback." *Bus Wk*
(25 Oct 69) 40. MGM report.

"Return of Smiling Jim." *Time* 94 (3 Oct 69)
80. Aubrey president of MGM.

"Again the Smiling Cobra." *Newswk* 74 (3
Nov 69) 84–85. New president at MGM,
James Aubrey.

"Dash of Bitters for a Bronfman." *Bus Wk* (8
Nov 69) 60. At MGM.

"Paramount's Lot." *Newswk* 74 (10 Nov 69)
84. Speculation on proposed sale of studios.

Murray, T. "Men Who Followed Mickey
Mouse." *Dun's Rev* 94 (Dec 69) 34–38. At
Disney Studio.

"Teaching MGM's Lion New Tricks." *Bus Wk*
(3 Jan 70) 44. The salvage techniques of
President James T. Aubrey, Jr.

Canham, Kingsley. "The Studio." *Screen* 11
(No. 1, Feb 70) 81–86. Brief history of 20th
Century-Fox.

"The Day the Dream Factory Woke Up." *Life*
68 (27 Feb 70) 38–43. Paramount's house-
cleaning sale: selling its studio and revising
its accounting.

"Movies: Ghouls, Ghosts, and Banshees." *Mc-
Call's* 97 (Mar 70) *See 4k(3)*.

Fleming, K. "Dreams for Sale." *Newswk* 75
(4 May 70) 36–37. The MGM auction of
props.

"MGM Is Cutting More Than Film." *Bus Wk*
(9 May 70) 23. The streamlining of MGM's
equipment and staff by new president James
T. Aubrey.

"Memories on the Block." *Life* 68 (22 May 70)
42–50. Pictorial essay on MGM's properties

auction, with a brief story on the legends of
Hollywood.

Higham, Charles. "Gather Ye Rosebud . . ."
S&S 39 (Summer 70) 134. Brief report on
MGM props auction.

6b(3). MOTION PICTURE ASSOCIATION

[See also 7c(2), 7c(4), 7c(6).]

"Federal Council v. Hays." *Time* 18 (6 July
31) 20–21. *Churchman* and *Christian Century* cause Federal Council of Churches to
"investigate" MPPDA and Hays office; some
council members had been on Hays' payroll.

"Hays Poll." *Time* 19 (21 Mar 32) 36. Decline
of film attendance of about 30% in two
years stirs Will Hays to send out 150,000
questionnaires.

"Helper for Hays?" Filmdom's Effort to Sign
Up Eric A. Johnston." *Bus Wk* (24 Mar 45)
32+.

"Movie Czar Cast in Larger Role." *Bus Wk*
(22 Sep 45) 7. Some forecasting concerning
moviedom's new "czar"—Eric Johnston.

"Exit King Log." *Time* 46 (1 Oct 45) 86–87.
Will Hays' abdication from the throne of
filmdom—enter Eric Johnston.

"Johnston's Premiere." *Bus Wk* (27 Oct 45)
33–34+. Eric Johnston, president of U.S.
Chamber of Commerce, applies his well-
known reasonableness to Hollywood's labor
squabbles.

"New Movie Czar Picks Krug of WPB as His
Grand Duke." *Bus Wk* (27 Oct 45) 34–37.

Isaacs, Hermine R. "Fine Spirits: Eric Johnston
and the Hays Office." *Th Arts* 29 (Nov 45)
637. What will happen when the new
"movie czar" takes office? Some surmises
and a look at recent significant films.

Burnup, Peter. "Reflections on the Johnston
Visit." *S&S* 15 (No. 60, Winter 46–47)
143–144. MPAA President Eric Johnston's
visit to England.

"First 100 Days." *Time* 88 (2 Sep 66) 38.
Jack Valenti and the MPAA.

Canby, Vincent. "Czar of the Movie Business."
NYTM (23 Apr 67). *See 5, Jack Valenti*.

Valenti, Jack. "The 'Foreign Service' of the
Motion Picture Association of America."
JSPG (Mar 68) 21–25. The Motion Picture
Export Association knows foreign markets.

6b(4). NEW METHODS: 16mm, PAY-TV, CARTRIDGES

[See also 2n.]

"New Film Library Rents 16mm Talkies at
$2 a Reel." *Newswk* 4 (14 July 34) 22.

Krows, Arthur Edwin. "The Exhibitor Says
'No.'" *New Outlook* 165 (May 35) 31–36.
Study of nontheatrical distribution.

Eastman, F. "Chances the Movies Are Missing." *Chris Cent* 54 (12 May 37) 617–618. Importance of the nontheatrical film.

Fawcett, John. "Join the Navy and See the Movies." *Cinema Arts* 1 (No. 3, Sep 37) 21–22. U.S. Navy as the biggest single film distributor in the world; how it chooses its films on the basis of raising sailors' "morale."

McCullie, Hector. "The Cinema Goes to the Patron." *S&S* 11 (No. 42, Autumn 42) 51–52. Cinema vans carry films to scattered groups of people during wartime in England.

Grierson, John. "Pictures Without Theaters." *Nation* 160 (13 Jan 45) 37–39. Advocates international exchange of documentary films on 16mm.

Heather, J. F. C. "Our Show." *S&S* 14 (No. 55, Oct 45) 82–83. Village mobile shows and a comment about children's reactions.

"New Age A-Coming?" *Life* 28 (20 Feb 50) 36. Commander MacDonald, president of Zenith Radio, has begun televising first-run movies in Chicago on a "pay as you see" television basis.

Harrison, P. S. "Telemeter." *FIR* 5 (Feb 54) 68–71. Pay-TV system inaugurated in an experimental trial in Palm Springs with the premiere of *Forever Female.*

Starr, Cecile. "Ideas on Film." *Sat Rev* 37 (14 Aug 54) 26–27. Survey of 16mm exhibition activity across America, from private organizations to museums and archives.

"Movie Exhibitors Fear Forced Sale of 16mm Film." *Bus Wk* (8 Oct 55) 54. The Justice Department's so-called 16mm antitrust case.

Spears, Jack. "Telemovies Begin." *FIR* 8 (Oct 57) 369–374. A report of the pay-TV experiment among 300 subscribers in Bartlesville, Oklahoma, by Video Independent Theatres, Inc.

LeRoy, Mervyn. "Motion Pictures and Pay-TV." *Atlantic* 200 (Dec 57) 84–86.

Perlberg, William. "We're Still Losing Ground." *JSPG* (Mar 59) 8–9+. Film producer argues the merits of pay-TV for saving the film industry.

Fabian, S. H., Paul MacNamara, Robert J. O'Donnell, Mervyn LeRoy, Emanuel Celler, Edmund Hartmann, Oren Harris, Jack Gould, Ralph Bellamy, Frank Stanton, Harold Fellows. "The Journal Looks at Pay-TV." *JSPG* (June 59) 3–24.

Chamberlin, Philip. "Allies, Not Enemies." *FQ* 14 (No. 2, Winter 60) 36–39. The battle between theatrical and nontheatrical film exhibitors and the problem of wider exposure for the "art" film; some case histories and solutions for bridging these gaps.

Jones, Dorothy B. "16mm—Box Office Threat or Promise?" *JSPG* (Dec 61) 23–27. This kind of distribution can increase motion-picture audiences by making available fine films of the past, and thereby increasing respect for film; contract stipulations are that 16mm films do not compete with commercial theatres.

"Pay-TV Revisited . . .The Journal Takes Another Look." *JSPG* (Sep 64) 3–41. Various authors, including the head of FCC (E. William Henry). Congressman Emanuel Celler, Sylvester Weaver, Ralph Bellamy, and others, debate the issue.

"This Film for Hire." *Holiday* 36 (Dec 64) 145–148. Home viewing of feature and documentary films?

Junker, Howard. "New Perils Awaiting the Serious Drinker." *F Com* 3 (No. 3, Summer 65) 34–37. French company tries to popularize Scopitone, a jukebox with pictures; some are directed by Claude Lelouch.

Forsdale, Louis. "8—The Paperback of Films." *F Lib Q* 2 (No. 1, Winter 68–69) 8–11. Rosy future for 8mm films in libraries; brief articles by librarians follow.

Macdonald, Susan. "16mm Film Availability." *Screen* 10 (No. 6, Nov–Dec 69) 45–50.

Guber, Peter. "The New Ballgame: The Cartridge Revolution." *Cinema* (Calif) 6 (No. 1, 1970) 21–31.

Kahlenberg, Richard, and Chloe Aaron. "The Cartridges Are Coming." *CJ* 9 (No. 2, Spring 70) 2–12. Digest of special report prepared for American Film Institute board of trustees by its assistant director: differing systems, moves toward standardization, plans for marketing and programming, lists of equipment and distribution companies.

Hart, Henry. "Cassettes." *FIR* 21 (No. 9, Nov 70) 521–524.

6c. Production and Production Costs

[*See also* 9.]

Thalberg, Irving, and Hugh Weir. "Why Motion Pictures Cost So Much." *SEP* 206 (4 Nov 33) 10–11+. MGM producer surveys Hollywood industry.

Goldwyn, Samuel. "Do We Pay Our Picture Stars Too Much?" *SEP* 206 (17 Feb 34) 8–9+. Producer surveys incomes in Hollywood.

"Salaries." *Newswk* 4 (28 July 34) 24. NRA survey reports 110 film people get more than President Roosevelt.

Zeisler, K. F. "Costs—A Barrier to Culture." *Antioch Rev* 7 (Mar 47) 45–54. Cultural contributions made impossible by costs of film technology.

Betts, Ernest. "The Price of Film-Making." *S&S* 18 (Spring 49) 44–45. Not economy but creative excitement makes profitable pictures.

"Cutting Costs of Make-Believe." *Bus Wk* (27 May 50) 54+. The Motion Picture Research Council develops cheaper materials and equipment.

Dawson, Anthony. "Patterns of Production and Employment in Hollywood." *Hwd Q* 4 (No. 4, Summer 50) 338–353. Former research assistant at UCLA Industrial Relations Institute uses figures from the *Hollywood Reporter* for 1937–1940 and 1945–1948.

Parsons, L. O. "How Much Is Talent Worth?" *Cosmopolitan* 137 (Oct 54) 16. Some stars, directors, and producers are now working on a strict percentage basis.

"Script for Success." *Time* 73 (27 Apr 59) 86+. How Hollywood handles production costs.

Bevis, Donald L. "Moments of Truth." *FIR* 10 (Aug–Sep 59) 400–402+. A review of the economics of a film production, including the budget, which is broken down by the production estimator, or budget director, from the script; included are various wages and salary scales.

Noble, John Wesley. "Big Gamble on the Stars." *SEP* 232 (18 June 60) 26–27+. Accidents and stars and the company that insures them, Fireman's Fund Insurance Company.

"Shoot Only When Covered." *Time* 76 (12 Dec 60) 60–62. The business of film insurance.

"Fade Out for Blockbuster Films?" *Bus Wk* (20 Oct 62) 172–174+. Should Hollywood move from blockbusters to less expensive films to fit in with the movement of theatres to the suburbs?

Brandt, Harry, Aubrey Schenck, Meade Roberts, Ivan Tors, Robert W. Selig. "The Journal Looks at Today's Market for Budget Pictures." *JSPG* 11 (No. 4, June 63) 3–14. Producers, writers, and theatre men write about low-cost productions.

Bart, Peter. "$upercollossaliti$." *Sat Rev* 49 (24 Dec 66) 14–16. Rising production costs because of demands of a clique of stars; part of *Saturday Review* report "The American Motion Picture: 1966."

Alpert, H. "Where Does the Money Go?" *Sat Rev* 49 (24 Dec 66) 16. Excessive costs of film making.

Stulberg, Gordon. "Hollywood Transition." *Sat Rev* (28 Dec 68) 20. Hollywood shifts its initiative from the big studio film and mass production to the "individual picture" and production on a qualitative rather than quantitative basis; part of *Saturday Review* report "The Now Movie."

6c(1). STUDIO SYSTEM

[See also 2a(1), 4d(1), 6b(2).]

"Celluloid Aesthetics." *Nation* 130 (26 Mar 30) 352. Film director says the more a film costs, the more the rental.

"Winnie Sheehan Stars in Movieland Guessing Game." *Newswk* 6 (27 July 35) 27. Profiles of film magnates Winfield Sheehan, Joseph Schenck, Darryl Zanuck, and others.

Delehanty, Thorton. "Czars Fall on Hollywood." *North American Rev* 242 (Dec 36) 258–268. Film critic for *New York Post* says "lust for power" and fear of losing power explains much of the Hollywood product as well as the response to foreign and censorship pressures.

Graves, Janet. "Hollywood Trademarks." *Cinema Arts* 1 (No. 3, Sep 37) 39. A breakdown of the studios, their differences, their fortes and weak points, and the people who work in them.

Seldes, Gilbert. "Are the Foreign Films Better?" *Atlantic* 184 (Sep 49) 49–52. Hollywood needs a more flexible system of production.

Schary, Dore. "How I Cut Costs." *FIR* 1 (Nov 50) 1–3+. Chapter 10 in Schary's book *Case History of a Movie* (Random House, 1950) discusses the preproduction planning phase of *The Next Voice You Hear*.

Spinrad, Leonard. "End of an Era." *FIR* 7 (Apr 56) 145–146. The economic reasons for the decline of the production head of the major studio.

Hart, Henry. "The Vanishing Executive Producer." *FIR* 7 (Aug–Sep 56) 326–328+. Extended review of the television play *The Film Maker*, by Malvin Wald and Jack Jacobs.

"Stuart Millar." *Film* (No. 33, Autumn 62) 33–36. American producer discusses his experience with the major studios.

"David Susskind." *Film* (No. 33, Autumn 62) 26–32. TV producer on his experience with major film studios.

"Three to Get Ready." *Time* 91 (12 Apr 68) 101+. Young masters of production at biggest studios—Fox's Richard Zanuck, Warner's Kenneth Hyman, and Paramount's Robert Evans.

Aldrich, Robert. "Why I Bought My Own Studio." *Action* 4 (No. 1, Jan–Feb 69) See 5, *Robert Aldrich*.

Mills, J. "Why Should He Have It?" *Life* 66 (7 Mar 69). See 5, *Robert Evans*.

David, S. "Secrets of the Hollywood Establishment." *Esq* 74 (Aug 70) 64–65+. Thoughts on the Hollywood scene by a Hollywood producer: a defense of traditional methods.

Preminger, Ingo. "M*A*S*H Notes." *Esq* 74 (Aug 70) 60–61+. The new system of production in the studios as exemplified by the film *M*A*S*H;* the economics of the new film.

6c(2). LABOR RELATIONS

[See also 2b(3), 2d(3).]

Ziesse, Francis E. "America's Highest Paid Labor Body." *Am Federationist* 37 (May 30) 570–576. Formation, rules, and standards of the International Alliance of Theatrical and Stage Employees.

Kohler, A. "Some Aspects of Conditions of Employment in the Film Industry." *International Labour Rev* 23 (June 31) 773–804. United States compared with other countries.

"Effects of Technological Changes upon Employment in the Amusement Industry." *Monthly Labor Rev* 32 (Aug 31) 261–267. Suggests amount of theatrical stage labor seriously affected by rapid development of motion picture.

Crone, Berta. "Occupations, Today and Tomorrow." *New Outlook* 161 (June 33) 2+. Surveys movies' jobs in perspective of all industrial employment.

"Movies and Radio Join Varied Brood of Blue Eagle." *Newswk* 2 (9 Dec 33) 34. NRA salary code in effect for movies and broadcasting.

Chaplin, John R. "Hollywood Goes Closed Shop." *Nation* 142 (19 Feb 36) 225–226. IATSE has shut out IBEW as labor union, but this encourages writers, actors, and even directors to consolidate their guilds. Will the Academy as company union disappear?

Broun, Heywood. "Boys in the Higher Brackets." *Nation* 144 (15 May 37) 565. Why the Screen Actors Guild should support striking technicians in Hollywood; importance of unions to their members discussed.

Dugan, James. "Goldwyn's Hairshirt." *New Masses* 27 (17 May 38) 27–28. Samuel Goldwyn's complaints about business falling off will be used as justifications for layoffs in Hollywood and to attack the Hollywood unions.

Ross, M. "C.I.O. Loses Hollywood." *Nation* 149 (7 Oct 39) 374–377. A comprehensive look at the loss of Hollywood labor by the CIO to the AFL; history of the International Alliance of Theatrical and Stage Employees.

Muir, F. "All Right Gentlemen, Do We Get the Money?" *SEP* 212 (27 Jan 40) 9–11+. The story of Willy Bioff and the IATSE; history of Hollywood's union conflicts.

"War Hits Hollywood." *Bus Wk* (3 Feb 40) 49–50. Hollywood's 15,000 craftsmen face 10% wage reduction because of foreign business losses caused by the war.

Joseph, Robert. "Re: Unions in Hollywood." *Films (US)* 1 (No. 3, Summer 40) 34–50. Early days of the Academy (when it was a bargaining agent), the Writers Guild and the Actors Guild.

Bower, A. "White-Collar Workers in the Motion Picture Industry." *Nation* 152 (1 Mar 41) 249. The plight of office workers in Hollywood and the subsequent formation of the Screen Office Employees Guild.

McWilliams, Carey. "Racketeers and Movie Makers." *New Rep* 105 (27 Oct 41) 533–535. Background on International Alliance of Theatrical and Stage Employees and its president, Willie Bioff.

"Bioff Show." *Newswk* 18 (10 Nov 41) 52+. Federal charges of extortion against Bioff and Brown, officials of the IATSE.

"Movie Tempest: Screen Extras Drive for Own Union." *Bus Wk* (29 July 44). *See 2b(9).*

"Screen Extras Win." *Bus Wk* (23 Dec 44). *See 2b(9).*

"Movie-Struck: Hollywood Walkout over Union Jurisdiction Ties Up Studios." *Bus Wk* (17 Mar 45) 106+.

"Record at Stake." *Bus Wk* (8 Sep 45) 106+. "Movie studio strikers are up against the 25-year tradition that producers have never lost a strike; National Labor Relations Board decision is due."

Ward, George. "Rhapsody in Black and Blue." *Nation* 161 (20 Oct 45) 395–396. Dispute over the right of employees to belong to unions of their own choice.

"Peace in Studios." *Bus Wk* (3 Nov 45) 107–108. All Hollywood strikers are reinstated under settlement while jurisdictional issues are discussed or arbitrated.

Seiler, C. "Hollywood Rebellion." *New Rep* 113 (5 Nov 45) 597–599. The Conference of Studio Unions breaks the grip of the IATSE, which sought to control all unions in the movie industry.

"Collective Bargainer's Guide to Hollywood." *Bus Wk* (13 July 46) 80. The employer groups and unions.

"Stuffed Duck?" *Time* 48 (12 Aug 46) 86–88. Increased pay demands from the Screen Cartoonists Guild led to layoffs at the Disney studio.

"It's Second-Run." *Bus Wk* (5 Oct 46) 100. Carpenters and sympathizers have walked off Hollywood sets in a "retake" of jurisdictional squabbles.

"Hold Your Hats, Boys." *Time* 48 (7 Oct 46) 22–23. Competition between IATSE and Conference of Studio Unions over jurisdiction of carpenters and painters.

"Hollywood Puts On a Strike Thriller." *Life* 21 (14 Oct 46) 29–35.

Montgomery, Robert. "President of Film Actors' Union Condemns the Strike." *Life* 21 (14 Oct 46) 32. Explanation of the stand taken by the Screen Actors Guild in the strike by Hollywood Conference of Studio Unions.

"More Trouble in Paradise." *Fortune* (Nov 46) 154+. Labor troubles in Hollywood.

"Melodrama in Movie Strike." *Bus Wk* (9 Nov 46) 85–86. Current strike of carpenters and other tradesmen in Hollywood; a permanent arbitrator has been hired, Joseph Keenan.

Graham, Garrett. "Peace in Our Time." *Screen Writer* 2 (Feb 47) 25–29. Argues against the violence of strikers and nonstrikers in the CSU-IATSE jurisdictional dispute and urges plebiscite.

"Justice, Hollywood Style." *Life* 22 (17 Mar 47) 40–41. Mass picketing of Hollywood studios led to numerous arrests and a problem for the courts in Los Angeles.

"Makeup Men Sue." *Bus Wk* (7 June 47) 108. Makeup Artists and Hair Stylists Local 706 of the IATSE is sued for a supposedly restrictive and arbitrary closed shop.

Dunne, George. "Peace in Jail." *Commonweal* 46 (20 June 47) 230–233. Herb Sorrell (CSU) and the Hollywood–Los Angeles labor picture. Reply with rejoinder by O. Carlson, 47 (17 Oct 47) 11–14.

"Noisy Drone Among the B's." *New Rep* 117 (1 Sep 47) 12. The congressional investigation of Hollywood labor troubles: jurisdictional fight between CSU and IATSE.

Ross, Murray. "Labor Relations in Hollywood." *Annals of Am Acad of Polit and Soc Sci* 254 (Nov 47) 58–64. A comprehensive history, from the days of the open shop, of the various unions and guilds.

Dawson, Anthony H. "British and American Motion Picture Wage Rates Compared." *Hwd Q* 3 (No. 3, Spring 48) 241–247. Parallel columns by function; see also objection to use of certain figures by union official in Great Britain, 3 (No. 4, no date) 446–448, and reply by Dawson.

Brewer, Roy M. "Movies for Labor: Hollywood Film Council of A.F. of L. Leads the Way." *Am Federationist* 55 (July 48) 10–11. Established in 1947 to unite the efforts of many organizations within the industry.

Dawson, Anthony A. P. "Hollywood's Labor Troubles." *Industrial and Labor Relations Rev* 1 (July 48) 638–647. Economic background of jurisdictional disputes, strikes, featherbedding, and less publicized Hollywood disputes.

"Gone Are the Winds: Hollywood Labor Finds Peace." *Fortune* 40 (Nov 49) 206+.

"And Now Pay Cuts." *Newswk* 37 (28 May 51) 66–67.

"Hollywood Evolves $20-a-Month Pensions." *Bus Wk* (16 Oct 54) 176. An agreement with seventy unions and guilds.

"Strange Strike in Hollywood." *US News & World Report* 48 (8 Feb 60) 78–79.

Perlberg, William. "The Dollar and the Strike." *JSPG* (Mar 60) 1–2+. The actors' and writers' guilds would be better advised to seek a pension fund than to strike for percentages of films sold to TV.

"Peace in Hollywood?" *Newswk* 55 (7 Mar 60) 75–76. Screen Actors Guild on the brink of a strike over sale of post-1948 films to TV.

"Strike Halts Movie-Making." *Bus Wk* (12 Mar 60) 34.

"Hollywood Strike Is a Gloomy Omen." *Life* 48 (21 Mar 60) 20–25.

"Strike in a Ghost Town." *Time* 75 (21 Mar 60) 57–59. Screen Actors Guild follows screenwriters on strike: independent producers agree to sign.

Houston, Penelope. "After the Strike." *S&S* 28 (Summer 60). See 4d.

Knight, Arthur. "Meanwhile, Back in Hollywood." *Sat Rev* (25 Dec 65) 21. Hollywood no longer desirable as "the" place to make films because of pressure by unions and guilds for excessive pay; part of *Saturday Review* report "Where the Action Is."

"An Historic Occasion." *Action* 2 (No. 4, July–Aug 67) 10–11. Meeting of representatives of the Directors Guild of America with representatives of Great Britain's Association of Cinematograph, Television and Allied Technicians.

Murphy, A. D. "Students: Stay Out of Hollywood." *Cinéaste* 2 (No. 2, Fall 68) 7–8. An attack on unionism in the Hollywood system, which is keeping young people out.

"Movie Unions Waive Rights." *US News & World Report* 68 (6 Apr 70) 72. An interpretation of new requirements by film unions designed to encourage a return to Hollywood production.

Freeland, Nat. "Yonkers in Los Angeles, Portobello Road in Burbank." *Show* (20 Aug 70) 26–31. Comments on the building of supersets by the IATSE, with breakdown of craft locals typically involved in set building.

6c(3). INDEPENDENT PRODUCTION

[See also 4d(2), 8d.]

Condon, Frank. "Poverty Row." *SEP* 207 (25 Aug 34) 30+. On inexpensive Hollywood films.

"New Firm Backs Faith in Movies' Colorful Future." *Newswk* 6 (19 Oct 35) 31. Formation of Selznick International Pictures, Inc.

Farber, Manny. "Independents' Day." *New Rep* (28 Aug 44) 248. Cheaper movies on independent basis give more room for experimentation.

"Battle of Reno: Fight of Independent Producers Against Movie Monopoly." *Bus Wk* (7 Oct 44) 90–94.

"Nelson in Movies." *Bus Wk* (30 June 45)

22. Subtitled: "Major Battle Between Eight Producers and Independents."

"Show Business: Pine-Thomas Pictures." *Time* 46 (6 Aug 45) 82+. Independent production for average audiences.

"Independent Income; Independent Producers." *Time* 46 (5 Nov 45) 84. The "corporation fade-out": independents can make more money.

Barbarow, George. "Do We Need Hollywood?" *Politics* (May 46) 167–168. Inexpensive features are possible.

Capra, Frank. "Breaking Hollywood's Pattern of Sameness." *NYTM* (5 May 46) 18+. The independent producer's influence on Hollywood is for a return to individuality plus craftsmanship.

Marshall, J. "Nothing to It; Making Movies Is as Easy as Building a Skyscraper." *Collier's* 117 (18 May 46). *See 5, Benedict Bogeaus.*

"Sanctuary Closed; Single-Picture Corporations Attacked by United States." *Bus Wk* (3 Aug 46) 26+.

"End of the Honeymoon." *Time* 48 (5 Aug 46) 80. The "collapsible corporation" is out, says Internal Revenue; end of the "quickie" independent companies.

Borneman, E. "Rebellion in Hollywood: Study in Motion Picture Finance." *Harper's Bazaar* (Oct 46) 337–343. The movement within Hollywood toward more independent production.

Armstrong, Arthur A. "What's Happening to the Single-Picture Corporation?" *Screen Writer* 2 (Nov 46) 24–27. Its tax benefits and how they are being wrongfully threatened by the Commissioner of Internal Revenue.

Nelson, Donald M. "The Independent Producer." *Annals of Amer Acad of Polit and Soc Sci* (1947) 49–57.

"Price of Liberty." *Time* 49 (26 May 47) 88. Independents Wyler, Capra, Stevens sell their Liberty Films Company to Paramount.

Marlowe, Frederic. "The Rise of the Independents in Hollywood." *Penguin F Rev* 3 (Aug 47). Brief list of directors.

"Hollywood's Newest Studio." *Look* 2 (No. 20, 30 Sep 47) 90–91. The Enterprise Company uses profit-sharing plan to attract stars and directors.

Blakeston, Oswell. "The Aesthetic and Economic Revolution of Independent Frame." *S&S* 17 (No. 65, Spring 48) 34–35. The term "independent frame" is used by the author to describe both production and artistic aspects of decision making that can achieve economy and freedom.

"Small Wonder, Eagle Lion." *Time* 53 (28 Feb 49) 88. Eagle Lion, the first addition to big-time U.S. film studios in fourteen years, is making profits.

"$10 Million Newcomer: National Exhibitors Film Company." *Time* 54 (11 July 49) 92. For financing independent producers.

"Hollywood's Angels Stage a Revival." *Bus Wk* (6 May 50) 98–101. Investors back independent productions; still headaches.

"Taking a Flier in Movies." *Commonweal* 52 (19 May 50) 142. Hollywood's enthusiasm over independent film's success bodes only danger to the creative film maker in the future.

"Big Deal." *Time* 56 (28 Aug 50) 72–73. Independent production plans of Jerry Wald and Norman Krasna at RKO.

Lupino, Ida. "New Faces in New Places." *FIR* 1 (Dec 50). *See 2b(4).*

Kramer, Stanley. "The Independent Producer." *FIR* 2 (Mar 51). *See 5, Stanley Kramer.*

"Mayer of Cinerama." *Newswk* 40 (3 Nov 52) 83. Louis B. Mayer is chosen as chairman of the board of Cinerama Productions.

"Cinerama: A Wall Street Hit?" *Bus Wk* (8 Nov 52) 171–172. Uncertainty regarding financial success and security of the new Cinerama, Inc.

Bartlett, Hall. "The Fighting Independent." *JSPG* (Nov 54) 8–9. The struggling independent producer's troubles with financing and distribution.

Bartlett, Hall. "The Fighting Independent." *FIR* 6 (Feb 55) 49–55. The author's experiences as the producer of *Navajo, Crazylegs,* and *Unchained.*

Morgan, James. "Hecht-Lancaster Productions." *S&S* 25 (Summer 55) 38–42+. The background of the two partners, Harold Hecht, a student of the theatre, dancer and dance director, and literary agent, and Burt Lancaster, an acrobat with the circus, stage actor, and bit player in films; descriptions of some of the films: *Apache, Vera Cruz, Marty.*

Sanders, Terry B. "The Financing of Independent Feature Films." *QFRTV* 9 (No. 4, Summer 55). *See 6a(1).*

Bradley, David, Norman McLaren, Adrian Brunel. "Making Films on Small Budgets." *Film* (No. 6, Dec 55) 12–19.

"Hollywood Revolution." *Time* 67 (5 Mar 56) 106. Big studio production giving way to independent production spearheaded by United Artists.

"Whitney's Adventure." *Newswk* 47 (21 May 56) 116. Multimillionaire C. V. Whitney returns to film production.

"Top Branch." *Time* 68 (3 Sep 56) 74. Independent production team: Harold Hecht and Burt Lancaster.

Chayefsky, Paddy. "Art Films—Dedicated Insanity." *Sat Rev* 40 (21 Dec 47) 16+. Author describes from firsthand experience problems involved in making an art film— and profitably; part of *Saturday Review* report "The Big Change in Hollywood."

"Shift to Independents." *Newswk* 51 (20 Jan 58) 76.

Chayefsky, Paddy. "Art Films—They're Dedicated Insanity." *F&F* 4 (No. 8, May 58). *See 2d.*

"Hecht-Hill-Lancaster." *F&F* 4 (No. 12, Sep 58) 5. Brief history of partners in independent production, including Harold Hecht and Burt Lancaster.

"Cash for the Film Independents." *Bus Wk* (8 Nov 58) 68+. New financing system assures flow of bank funds to independent producers.

Youngstein, Max E. "The Independent's Progress." *Sat Rev* 41 (20 Dec 58) 13. In 1951 one percent, today 50% of important films are "independent"; part of *Saturday Review* report "The Film: Survey of the Craft and Its Problems."

Mekas, Jonas. "A Call for a New Generation of Film Makers." *F Cult* (No. 19, 1959) 1–3. The editor of *Film Culture* calls for a "free" (independent and low-budget) American cinema.

Knight, Arthur. "Creative Films in America?" *Sat Rev* (24 Dec 60) 50–51. Independent film making discussed at Antioch College conference on film; part of *Saturday Review* report "Are Foreign Films Better?"

"Film Unions and the Low-Budget Independent Film Production—An Exploratory Discussion." *F Cult* (Nos. 22–23, 1961) 134–150. A discussion by former union official James Degangi, Louis Stoumen, Willard Van Dyke, Shirley Clarke, and Jonas Mekas; appended is a group of memoranda on "The Methods and Problems of Film Financing."

The New American Cinema Group. "The First Statement of the Group." *F Cult* (Nos. 22–23, 1961) 131–133. A statement of principles by twenty-three independent film makers, including *Film Culture* editor Jonas Mekas, 30 September 1960: low budgets, personal expression, and no censorship.

Sutherland, Elizabeth. "New York's New Wave of Movie Makers." *Horizon* 3 (Mar 61) 12–19. Introduction to eight film makers: Francis Thompson, Sidney Meyers, Robert Frank, Lionel Rogosin, John Cassavetes, Shirley Clarke, Richard Leacock, and Bert Stern.

Fenin, George N. "The Skyscraper Experiment." *F&F* 7 (No. 7, Apr 61) 12+. Independent film makers in America.

Douglas, Kirk. "Using My Two Heads." *F&F* 7 (No. 9, June 61) 10+. Cooperation is the key to independent productions.

Richardson, Tony. "The Two Worlds of Cinema." *F&F* 7 (No. 9, June 61). *See 5, Tony Richardson.*

"The Cost of Independence: An Enquiry." *S&S* 30 (Summer 61). *See 4e(1c).*

Moskowitz, Gene. "Can the Outsiders Connect?" *F&F* 7 (No. 10, Jul 61), 14+. History of New York City independents and their chances of succeeding.

"Personal Creation in Hollywood: Can It Be Done?" *FQ* 15 (No. 3, Spring 62) 16–34. Fred Zinnemann, John Houseman, Irvin Kershner, Terry Sanders, and Kent Mackenzie in symposium with critics Colin Young, Gavin Lambert, Pauline Kael on their experiences with various types of "independent" production.

MacCann, Richard Dyer. "Independence, with a Vengeance." *FQ* 15 (No. 4, Summer 62) 14–21. As the studios reduced production in the face of TV competition, they released actors and others from contracts; independent companies began to spring up, headed by actors and agents; these new companies, even more afraid of the box office than the studios, tend to protect their single shots with the same old sex and violence.

"Cinerama's Star is Rising." *Bus Wk* (28 Jul 62) 126–128.

Knight, Arthur. "Studios Without Walls." *Sat Rev* 45 (29 Dec 62) 11+. New directions in film production; the Mirisch Company works independently through United Artists; part of *Saturday Review* report "The Lonely Art of Film-Making."

"You Got to Have Mom." *Newswk* 61 (21 Jan 63) 91. Independent producers: the King Brothers.

Schiffer, George. "The Business of Making Art Films." *F Com* 1 (No. 5, Summer 63) 23–27. Lawyer traces the heartbreaking process of financing and producing independent films.

Ferrer, Frank. "Exploitation Films." *F Com* 1 (No. 6, Fall 63) 31–33. Production budgets, relationship with theatres, distributors.

Alpert, Hollis. "Something Worth Fighting For." *Sat Rev* 46 (28 Dec 63) 16–18. Carl Foreman's views on the struggle for survival of the independent film maker; part of *Saturday Review* report "The Anti-Formula Film."

Knight, Arthur. "The Flip Side." *Sat Rev* 46 (28 Dec 63) 20. Independent film making; part of *Saturday Review* report "The Anti-Formula Film."

Boeth, Richard. "The Flaw in the Ointment." *Sat Rev* 46 (28 Dec 63) 23–24. Independents are seeking stars and anticipating the objections of studio heads in their desire to make money; hence the pathetic film year of 1963; part of *Saturday Review* report "The Anti-Formula Film."

Aldrich, Robert. "What Ever Happened to American Movies?" *S&S* 33 (Winter 63–64) 21. Artistic projects such as *Marty* can't be financed except by cross-collateralizing with big-budget star vehicles; Aldrich hopes to do this.

Gessner, Robert. "A Reexamination of the Art Versus Industry Question." *J Soc Cin* 4 (1964) 27–30. Artistic independence is the new possibility, but it is still true that it takes more than one person to make a film.

Fadiman, William. "Cowboys and Indies." *F&F* 10 (No. 6, Mar 64) 51–52. On the rise of independent producers and their more serious films.

Knight, A. "Declarations of Independents." *Sat Rev* 47 (23 May 64) 33–34. Except for Warner and Disney, the traditional relationship between the studio and its productions has all but disappeared.

Bermel, Albert. "Four New Ways to Make a Movie." *Harper's* 229 (Oct 64) 76–81. Some American films produced by freelancers.

Gillett, John. "Happening Here." *S&S* 34 (Summer 65) 138–141. Three British features, *It Happened Here, Four in the Morning,* and *Herostratus;* the problems connected with such independent film making.

Rubin, Joan Alleman. "Staking Out a New World of Film." *Mlle* 62 (Mar 66) 170–171+. New movie makers Susan Berns, Gene and Carole Marner, and Barbara Rubin.

Cobbing, Bob. "London Co-op." *Film* (No. 47, Winter 66) 32–35. An account of the creation of the London Filmmakers Cooperative, based on the similar organization in New York.

Sarris, Andrew. "Illusions and Independents." *Sat Rev* 49 (24 Dec 66) 23–25. Is the "independent cinema" really an alternative to Hollywood; part of *Saturday Review* report "The American Motion Picture: 1966."

Hartman, Charles. "The New and Independent Film-Maker." *F Soc Rev* (Nov 67) 27–31. Brief comments on Shirley Clarke, D. A. Pennebaker, and others.

Woodman, Ross. "Artists as Filmmakers." *Arts Canada* 25 (June 68) 35. Report on the London Filmmakers Cooperative.

Murphy, A. D. "New Room at the Top." *Sat Rev* 51 (28 Dec 68) 21–22+. Opportunities for young film makers.

Stulberg, Gordon. "Hollywood Transition." *Sat Rev* 51 (28 Dec 68) 20. The methods of the old Hollywood contrasted with the new "individual pictures."

"New Kind of Movie Shakes Hollywood." *Bus Wk* (3 Jan 70) 40–41. How budget films made on location aim at younger audiences: without stars, big studios, etc.

"New-Wave Producer Hits Jackpot." *Bus Wk* (3 Jan 70) 41. The production style and history of Michael S. Laughlin, a young Hollywood producer.

Aellen, Werner. "The Independent Filmmaker: A West Coast View." *Arts Canada* 27 (Apr 70) 49.

Sweeney, Louise. "The Movie Business Is Alive and Well and Living in San Francisco." *Show* (Apr 70) 34–37+. The workings of new American independent company, Zoetrope, with comments on Francis Ford Coppola, John Korty, George Lucas, Robert Dalva, *et al.*

Winner, Michael. "The Work of an Independent Producer-Director." *Screen* 11 (No. 3, Summer 70) 78–87. It is "immensely hard and arduous physical work."

"The Kids at Cannon." *Time* 96 (31 Aug 70) 60. Christopher Dewey and Dennis Friedland talk about their new production company, the Cannon Group, which has sponsored such films as *Joe* and *Jump.*

Mayer, M. "Elliott Gould as the Entrepreneur." *Fortune* 82 (Oct 70) 108–111+. The association of Gould and Jack Brodsky: their production company in operation.

"New Hollywood Is the Old Hollywood." *Time* 96 (7 Dec 70) 72–73. Distribution problems of John Cassavetes and his film *Husbands:* Hollywood hasn't really given more control to the director.

6c(4). PRODUCTION OUTSIDE OF HOLLYWOOD

[See also 2k(4), 7e.]

Patterson, Frances Taylor. "Will Hollywood Move to Broadway?" *New Rep* 61 (5 Feb 30) 297–299. Weighs question of filming in California or New York.

Whang, Paul K. "Will *The Good Earth* Be Filmed in China?" *China Weekly Rev* 67 (17 Feb 34) 450. Pros and cons.

"Hollywood Misses Cue." *Bus Wk* (16 Dec 39) 24. La Guardia's efforts to lure the movie industry back to New York.

Kline, H. "Film Making in Mexico City." *Th Arts* 27 (Nov 43) 679–688. Early coproduction problems.

Crowther, Bosley. "Hollywood Versus New York." *NYTM* (3 Aug 47) 10–11+. The arguments for each as a movie capital.

"Through the Loophole." *Time* 62 (6 July 53) 81–82. Hollywood production moves abroad.

McDonald, Gerald D. "U.S. Filmaking Abroad." *FIR* 5 (June–July 54). *See 4b.*

"Hollywood—In Paris and Rome." *NYTM* (11 Sep 55) 54–55. American films such as *Trapeze* and *War and Peace* are shot on foreign locations.

"Hollywood Unions Say Too Many Films Are Shot Abroad." *Bus Wk* (16 Feb 57) 169.

Mankiewicz, Joseph L. "Shoot It in Tanganyika." *Sat Rev* (21 Dec 57) 14. Brief note on using natural locations; part of *Saturday Review* report "The Big Change in Hollywood."

Richmond, Ted. "Why Go to Spain?" *JSPG* (Dec 59) 30–33. By producer who made *Solomon and Sheba* there.

Schnee, Charles H. "A Confidential Memo." *JSPG* (Dec 59) 14–15+. "To: An American producer who wants to film abroad—and return to Hollywood safe and sane"—some practical suggestions.

Barnwell, John, and Nick Archer. "The Orient Is the Place." *JSPG* (Mar 60) 21–24. Advice on how to produce pictures there.

Knight, Arthur. "Hollywood Moves East." *JSPG* (Sep 60) 15–17. Critic arrives in California to discover films are being largely shot elsewhere.

Zanuck, Darryl F. "Shoot It Where You Find It!" *JSPG* (Dec 60) 3–4+. "You should only produce abroad when you have to—and certainly not for economic reasons, because they are nonexistent"; producer comments on pictures he made at home and overseas.

Douglas, Kirk. "All Roads Lead to . . . Hollywood." *JSPG* (Dec 60) 5–6. Actor-producer tells why he chose to shoot *Spartacus* in Hollywood rather than abroad.

Perlberg, William. "What Do You Mean, Run-Away Production!" *JSPG* (Dec 60) 7–8+. Veteran producer discusses shooting *The Counterfeit Traitor* overseas.

Wald, Jerry. "Oh, To Be in Hollywood . . ." *JSPG* (Dec 60) 9–10+. More Hollywood production? Make it more economical, reduce overhead, alter the tax structure, put more variety into the product.

Foreman, Carl. "To Film or Not Abroad—That Is Not the Question." *JSPG* (Dec 60) 11–12+. *Guns of Navarone* was shot in Greece not only because it was suitable to the story but because of the encouragement and help offered by the Greek government.

Mirisch, Harold J. "Why Runaway?" *JSPG* (Dec 60) 13–14+. Filming abroad should be a "last alternative."

Schneer, Charles H. "All the World's a Stage." *JSPG* (Dec 60) 15–16. Advantages of filming abroad: foreign locales, subsidies, lower costs in some places.

Aller, Herbert. "Should Foreign Filming Be Stopped?" *JSPG* (Dec 60) 17–18+. Business representative of cameramen's union warns that the jobs of Hollywood technicians, the Hollywood community, and the American way of life are endangered.

Corman, Roger. "Foreign Production for the Medium-Budget Producer." *JSPG* (Dec 60) 19–20+. Moderate saving in cost is balanced by greater difficulty in shooting.

Foreman, Carl. "Of Peregrinating Producers." *Sat Rev* (24 Dec 60) 52–53. When it's worthwhile to shoot a film on location; part of *Saturday Review* report "Are Foreign Films Better?"

North, Christopher. "The Abandonment of Hollywood." *FIR* 12 (No. 1, Jan 61) 14–19. Why more films are being produced abroad.

O'Laoghaire, Liam. "Rex Ingram and the Nice Studios." *Cinema Studies* 1 (No. 4, Dec 61) 71–77. The American director took the studios over for his own and made *Mare Nostrum* there in 1924.

"Moviemaker, Stay Home." *Bus Wk* (26 Jan 63) 68. Union requests for more "made in America" films.

Huston, John, Mark Robson, Jud Kinberg, Charles Schneer, Mitchell Kowal, Robert Siodmak. "The Journal Looks at Hollywoodians Away from Home." *JSPG* (Mar 63) 3–14. Directors, producers, and an actor examine reasons for and against making pictures away from Hollywood.

Spiegel, Sam. "Hollywood—One World Concept." *JSPG* (June 63) 21–22. Producers must be free to go abroad just as distributors are free to seek audiences overseas.

Vietheer, George. "Blocked Motion Picture Funds." *JSPG* (June 64) 35–36. Motion Picture Export Association report on countries where these funds still exist.

Alpert, Hollis. "Happiness Is a Film-Maker in London." *Sat Rev* 48 (25 Dec 65) 10–13+. They leave Hollywood partly because producers and directors feel they have more "freedom." Part of *Saturday Review* report "Where the Action Is."

Ross, Walter S. "Something for Everyone." *Sat Rev* 48 (25 Dec 65). See 4e(6).

Sughrue, John J. "What's a Documentary?" *Action* 1 (No. 1, Sep–Oct 66). See 8c(1).

"For Movies: A Boom, But New Worries in Hollywood." *US News & World Report* 61 (17 Oct 66) 120–122+. Film making moves abroad; can subsidy keep it at home?

Siodmak, Curt. "Filming Behind the Iron Curtain." *Action* 1 (No. 2, Nov–Dec 66) 16–17. In Czechoslovakia.

"Movie Making: Another U.S. Invasion of Europe." *US News & World Report* 62 (20 Mar 67) 113–114+.

Howe, A. H. "Hollywood or Europe." *JSPG* (June 67) 21–24. Reasons film producers go to Europe analyzed; U.S. subsidy proposed to balance such temptations abroad.

Slide, Anthony. "The O'Kalems." *Cinema Studies* 2 (No. 5, Sep 67) 77–79. Kalem Company let Sidney Olcott go to Ireland to make films in 1910.

Alpert, Hollis. "Hollywood in Budapest." *Sat Rev* 50 (23 Dec 67) 20+. Notes on the American-Hungarian production of *The Fixer;* part of *Saturday Review* report "Film-Making Behind the Iron Curtain."

Greenspan, Lou, George Ornstein, Samuel Marx, Melville Shavelson, John Dales, Sheldon Leonard, Charles Schneer, Robert Andrews. "The Journal Looks at Filming Abroad." *JSPG* (Mar 68) 1–20+.

Zook, Douglas-Paul. "Film in Boston—HELP!" *Cinéaste* 2 (No. 4, Spring 69) 9. Critique of

Boston as a film city and a call for interested students and film makers to organize against dismal situation.

Ronan, Margaret. "Hollywood East." *Senior Scholastic* 95 (1 Dec 69) 18. Using foreign locations adds atmosphere, cuts costs, and increases monetary returns for current films.

Norman, Phillip. "Believe It or Not, They're Still Making Movies in Europe." *Show* (June 70) 37–39. Comments on the Hollywood recession and American-financed films made in Europe (especially Great Britain), with statements from Michael Winner, Leslie Lindley, Mark Rosen, and Joseph Shaftel.

6d. Sales

"Movies Begin Million-Dollar Drive." *Bus Wk* (3 Sep 38) 22–23. The story of "Motion Pictures' Greatest Year"—a concentrated effort by the entire industry to bolster lagging attendance.

Home, H. "Cooperation That Counts: Promotion of Books Made into Movies." *Publishers Weekly* 144 (4 Sep 43) 808–810.

"Old Films Pay Off." *Bus Wk* (19 Oct 46) 40. Wartime habit of re-releasing old films initiates a profitable excuse to do same in peacetime.

Nathan, P. S. "Books into Films: Revivals." *Publishers Weekly* 152 (16 Aug 47) 650. Hollywood is reissuing features.

"Twice-Told Tales." *Good Housekeeping* 131 (Nov 50). See 2d.

Pichel, Irving. "Crisis and Incantation." *Hwd Q* 5 (No. 3, Spring 51) 213–223. "Incantations" of advertising and exploitation can't equal the appeal of good screen stories; three qualities to be sought in stories, with examples from existing films.

English, Richard. "Gaudiest Producers in Hollywood, Pine and Thomas." *SEP* 225 (3 Jan 53) 22+. Press agents turned producers —Bill Pine and Bill Thomas—and how they send stars out on the road to drum up business.

Knight, Arthur. "The Reluctant Audience." *S&S* 22 (Apr–June 53) 191–192. A detailed report on how *Henry V* was successfully sold out in cities and small towns by direct appeal to opinion makers, literary clubs, schools, and others.

Hurd, Reggie, Jr. "Re-issues." *FIR* 4 (Dec 53). *See 1a.*

Perlberg, William. "New Birds in the Old Forest." *JSPG* (Apr 55) 4+. An independent producer's answer to this issue's central question, "How do they sell our pictures?"

Rhoden, E. C. "Should We Pick Up the TV Tab?" *JSPG* (Apr 55) 5+. President of National Theatres gives the theatre operator's views on marketing problems, especially "preselling."

Schary, Dore. "Hollywood's Public Relations." *FIR* 6 (Dec 55) 500–502. Bitter journalists, tawdry studio publicity, dishonest advertising, and prejudiced attacks on controversial films make it hard for the motion-picture

industry to keep its record straight; MGM production chief defends *Blackboard Jungle*.

Lederer, Richard. "I Don't Know Anything About Advertising, But . . ." *JSPG* (Sep 69) 25–27. Warners advertising executive advises producer how to respond ("reluctantly") to every step in the promotion process.

6d(1). PUBLICITY

[See also 9.]

Bartlett, Arthur C. "Charlie Chaplin's No-Man." *American* 112 (Oct 31) 78+. Profile of Carlyle T. Robinson, press agent for Chaplin during 1931 European tour.

Hughes, Rupert. "A Brief for Hollywood." *SEP* 206 (3 Mar 34) 23+. Subtitled "A Worm's Eye View of Hollywood Publicists."

Peace, M. "Ballyhoodlums." *SEP* 209 (15 Aug 36) 16–17+. How the Hollywood publicity man gives a girl glamor.

Meynell, Francis. "This Publicity Business." *S&S* 5 (No. 19, Autumn 36) 66–68. A plea for more sophisticated film advertising.

Taylor, F. J. "Publicity Build-Up for a Class A Film." *Scribner's* 105 (Mar 39) 16–19+. Publicity for *Union Pacific* is the springboard for this examination of picture promotion in general.

Farnol, L. "Hollywood Build-Up." *Th Arts* 25 (Apr 41) 297–306. Proceeds on the thesis that public interest governs publicity, not vice versa; details Hollywood's methods of publicity.

"Hollywood's Clamor-Boys." *Am Mercury* 54 (Jan 42) 85–92. Movie publicity business is as bizarre as the town's reputation.

"Filmese." *Am Speech* 17 (Apr 42) 131. Hollywood publicity releases seen as source of new jargon.

"Hollywood Unit Man." *SEP* 215 (21 Nov 42) 114–117. Role of the studio publicity man in exploiting new films and stars.

Johnston, Alva. "Russell Birdwell." *New Yorker* (19 and 26 Aug; 2 and 9 Sep 44). *See 5, Russell Birdwell.*

Pryor, Thomas. "Stars in New York." *NYTM* (Apr 45) 46. The publicity arrangements for stars.

Meeker, O. "Screamy-Weamies." *Collier's* 117 (12 Jan 46) 42+. Publicity and promotion campaigns for Universal's horror films.

Jones, P. "Scarred Veteran of the Screen: Interview with B. Hill." *Forum* 105 (Feb 46). *See 4b.*

Kaufman, Wolfe. "What Is the Answer?" *Screen Writer* 1 (May 46) *See 3b.*

Wechsberg, J. "They Make the Stars Glitter." *Rdrs Dgt* 50 (Feb 47) 99–101. Some publicity stunts.

Marshman, D. "Love That Movie!" *Life* 22 (10 Feb 47) 73–74+. The publicity for *Duel in the Sun.*

"Film Version of *The Egg and I* Gets $850,000 Promotion." *Publishers Weekly* 151 (15 Mar 47) 1629–1630.

Hubler, Richard G. "As I Remember Birdie." *Screen Writer* 3 (Sep 47) 13–15. Memories of Russell Birdwell and his publicity campaign for the film *The Outlaw,* starring Jane Russell.

Adlem, Eric Lorraine. "Film Stamps." *S&S* 17 (No. 67, Autumn 48) 125. Stamps issued to commemorate films and film personalities.

"Outside Work: Colossal Spectacular." *New Yorker* 24 (11 Sep 48) 26–27. Example of Hollywood publicity—promotion of Ingrid Bergman's *Joan of Arc.*

"Step a Little Closer, Folks." *Time* 52 (29 Nov 48) 96. Some publicity stunts by exhibitors.

Frank, S. "Hollywood's Ballyhoo Boys." *SEP* 221 (11 Dec 48) 34–35.

"Deluge, Film Promotion for *Samson and Delilah.*" *Time* 54 (29 Aug 49) 74. Paramount's publicity stunts for the film.

"In the Flesh." *Time* 54 (21 Nov 49) 101. Personal-appearance tours.

Sharp, Dolph. "Hollywood's Headline Hunter." *Coronet* 27 (Mar 50) 44–46. On newsman Earl Hays.

Hine, A. "Man Who Made the World *Samson-and-Delilah* Conscious." Holiday 7 (Apr 50) 8+. Hollywood publicity man Richard Condon discusses his work for *Samson and Delilah.*

Gordon, Jay E. "There's Really No Business Like Show Business." *QFRTV* 6 (No. 2, Winter 51) 173–185. Some suggestions for overcoming industry stagnation in publicity ideas.

"Colossal." *Time* 59 (7 Apr 52) 102. Exploitation of *Quo Vadis?*

"There's Still No Business Like It." *QFRTV* 7 (No. 1, Fall 52) 70–76. Letters in response to Jay Gordon's article on publicity for movies: William Perlberg, Nunnally Johnson, Jerry Wald, Gilbert Seldes included; see 6 (No. 2, Winter 51) 173–185.

"Hoopla Over Hans." *Look* 17 (24 Feb 53) 76+. Picture essay of Sam Goldwyn giving *Hans Christian Andersen* two premieres on TV with stars.

"Hollywood's Press: Why Stars Are in Your Eyes." *Newswk* 43 (22 Feb 54) 62–64.

"Hucksters Hawking American Womanhood." *America* 92 (9 Oct 54) 30. Ads for *The Barefoot Contessa.*

Thurber, James. "Hark, the *Herald Tribune, Times,* W.O.R. and All the Other Angels Sing!" *New Yorker* 32 (14 Apr 56) 40–41. The sound and fury of publicity for *The Conqueror.*

McPherson, Mervyn. "A Sucker Every Second, But . . ." *F&F* 2 (No. 10, July 56) 9. Early Hollywood publicity representative to Great Britain talks about publicity.

Golding, David. "Keep the Drums Rolling." *JSPG* (Nov 56) 10+. Selling movies—new publicity trends.

"Stiff Competitors." *Time* 72 (4 Aug 58). *See 4k(3).*

"Please Release Us!" *Chris Cent* 78 (13 Dec 61) 1511. Some quotes of publicity releases for *King of Kings.*

Knight, Arthur. "The Care and Feeding of Critics—a Public Relations Function?" *JSPG* (Mar 62) 15–16+. Pet peeves about Hollywood publicity men—they don't provide enough accurate information about film, misrepresent critic's reviews, prejudge his estimate.

Brodsky, Jack, and Nathan Weiss. "The *Cleopatra* Papers." *Esq* 60 (Aug 63) 33–41. Exchange of letters, cables, and notes of two publicity managers of 20th Century-Fox in Rome and New York.

Oulahan, R. "Well-Planned Crawford." *Life* 56 (21 Feb 64) 11–12. Star Joan Crawford on tour plugging *Straitjacket.*

Hamilton, J. "Virna Lisi: Experiment in Star-Making." *Look* 29 (18 May 65) 60–66. Elaborate explanation of mass publicity campaign by George Axelrod; the "star-maker's role."

"Hollywood Changes Script on Sightseers." *Bus Wk* (10 July 65). *See 1a.*

Barry, L. "Super 8 on the Back Lot." *Pop Photog* 59 (Aug 66). *See 1a.*

Dermer, Irwin. "The Photographer and the Cinema." *Camera* 6 (No. 2, Feb 67) 20–29+. Author describes his experiences as publicity photographer for various films.

"Rubberneck Rush." *Newswk* (21 Aug 67). *See 1a.*

Kane, Bruce, and Joel Reisner. "Angles." *Cinema* (Calif) 4 (No. 2, Summer 68) 12–15. Russell Birdwell recalls some of his publicity campaigns for movies, including *Gone with the Wind, Beau Geste,* and *The Outlaw.*

"If You Want to Visit a Hollywood Studio." *Good Housekeeping* 167 (July 68). *See 1a.*

"Building a Dowry for *Funny Girl.*" *Bus Wk* (28 Sep 68) 82–84. Report on Columbia Pictures pre-release promotion campaign.

6d(2). PREMIERES AND PREVIEWS

Johnston, William A. "Air Follies." *SEP* 202 (31 May 30) 13+. On typical Hollywood premiere and movie production details.

Pringle, Henry F. "Star Torture." *Collier's* 96 (14 Dec 35) 25+. On previews.

McEvoy, J. P. "Hollywood Premeer." *SEP* 210 (12 Feb 38) 10.

Costello, M. "They Pronounce It Pre-meer." *Commonweal* 33 (10 Jan 41) 294–296. This glimpse at a "gala" opening provides behind-the-scenes commentary about film premieres in general.

"Haiti Goes to the Movies." *Our World* 7 (Aug 52) 46–53. 20th Century-Fox stages junket to show off *Lydia Bailey.*

"The Customer Is the Boss." *Life* 34 (2 Feb 53) 45–48. Sneak preview cards for *The Bad and the Beautiful* said it was "too long"; pictures of several scenes that were cut out afterward.

Hurd, Reggie, Jr. "Preview Nights in Westwood Village." *FIR* 5 (Feb 54) 52–55. Value of the sneak preview; descriptions of audience response.

"Movies Are Wetter Than Ever." *Life* 38 (10 Jan 55) 67–68. Howard Hughes' *Underwater!* (RKO) is previewed underwater in Silver Springs, Florida, to an audience equipped with air tanks and face masks.

"Way Down Under: Preview of *Underwater!* at Silver Springs, Florida." *New Yorker* 30 (22 Jan 55) 24–25.

Knight, Arthur. "Damp Art of Movieselling: Staging a Junket." *Sat Rev* 38 (29 Jan 55) 25–26. The promotional trip to Florida to premiere *Underwater!;* advertising campaigns of the early 1950s.

Levin, Bernard. "Night Out with Mr. Todd." *Spectator* 198 (10 May 57) 609–611. Press attendance of *Around the World in 80 Days* screening at the tenth Cannes Film Festival.

Knight, Arthur. "Showmanship." *Sat Rev* 48 (5 June 65) 37. Warner Brothers Studio Tours and the premiere of *The Great Race.*

6d(3). ADVERTISING

[See also 7c(1a).]

"Movie Promises and Performance." *Chris Cent* 48 (25 Feb 31) 260. Notes Paramount advertising as violation of Hays Code.

"Picture of the Ape and the African Maiden." *China Weekly Rev* 56 (14 Mar 31) 38. Call for censorship of exaggerated Hollywood advertisements.

"Cinemadvertising." *Time* 17 (25 May 31) 58. Protests against plugs for various products by Warners and Paramount short subjects.

Teilhet, Darwin. "Propaganda Stealing the Movies." *Outlook* 158 (27 May 31) 112–113+. Complains about obvious advertising within feature films.

"Macy's vs. Movies." *Time* 19 (18 Jan 32) 22. Advertising director calls movie ads exaggerated; gets replies.

"Celluloid Sin." *Nation* 134 (29 June 32) 714. Sees movie advertising as diffusion of normal audience interests.

"Film Trailers." *Lit Dig* 122 (1 Aug 36) 20. They have some censorship problems in certain states.

"Hollywood Jargon." *Am Speech* 12 (Apr 37). *See 7b(1c).*

"Firms Get Free Ads in Movies." *Bus Wk* (2 Sep 39) 26. Products receive plugs because film directors want realism; a look at manufacturers' relations with Hollywood.

"Movie Promotion Up." *Bus Wk* (8 June 40) 47. Because of the pinch of war losses, producers counter with more advertising and publicity for films.

Morgan, H. "Industry Watches the Movies for Public Trends." *Nation's Business* 28 (July 40) 20–22+. How Hollywood influences product selling; detailed listing of "Mickey Mouse" items sold everywhere.

Farber, M. "Signs of the Double-Cross: Movie Theatre Advertising." *New Rep* 112 (4 June 45) 791. The false, garish advertising of many movies.

Williams, John Elliot. "They Stopped at Nothing." *Hwd Q* 1 (No. 3, Apr 46) 270–278. Examples of exaggerated newspaper advertising for movies; some of the better pioneer publicity men of the 1920s.

Minton, Arthur. "Marlovian 42 Street: Folkways of the Megalopolis." *Social Forces* 24 (May 46) 393–397. Comparisons of various reviewers' comments with the extreme statements of "placards employing a heroic idiom" in front of Times Square theatres.

Whiteside, T. "Zooming Up from a Pinpoint." *New Rep* 117 (22 Sep 47) 25–27. Hilarious look at movie trailers and how they are made.

"Desperate." *New Yorker* 23 (11 Oct 47) 26. The "adjective-mongers" in advertising and publicity.

Blakeston, Oswell. "The Tie-Up Comes of Age." *S&S* 17 (No. 67, Autumn 48) 122–123. Manufacturers selling products that relate to specific films.

Sutherland, Donald. "Bogus Ballyhoo." *S&S* 17 (No. 67, Autumn 48) 121. American film advertising slogans in England.

Lancaster, Osbert. "Posters for British Films." *Arch Rev* 105 (Feb 49) 88–89. A brief outline of the rise and fall of quality poster-advertising art: Ealing Studio poster work.

Bass, S. "Film Advertising; with German and French Texts." *Graphis* 9 (No. 48, 1953) 276–289+.

"Movie Commercials." *Fortune* 49 (Mar 54) 204. Alexander Film Company of Colorado

Springs is one of the nation's oldest; makes film ads for theatres and TV.

"*New York Times'* Movie Ads." *America* 90 (6 Mar 54) 585. An alarm seen in the lowered moral tone.

"Lewd and Vulgar Movie Ads." *America* 91 (29 May 54) 240. *The French Line,* starring Jane Russell, seen as a disgrace to American journalism.

"Ad Nauseam." *Time* 64 (19 July 54) 76. Examples of Hollywood advertising in bad taste.

Doff, John. "Making Film Ads." *F&F* 1 (No. 5, Feb 55) 10. From the viewpoint of an advertising film producer.

"Trouble Over Torsos." *Life* 38 (7 Mar 55) 38–39. In ads for RKO's *Underwater!* showing Jane Russell skin-diving, was the body stolen from a drawing of someone else?

Stebbins, Hal. "Motion Picture Advertising . . . Is It?" *JSPG* (Apr 55) 13–26. President of his own advertising agency discusses how successful film advertising is.

"U.S. Movie Ads in the Orient." *America* 93 (7 May 55) 143. Concern over their eroticism and morbid sensationalism.

Gregory, James. "A Documentary Gets the Hard Sell." *FIR* 7 (Nov 56) 453–456. Columbia's advertising campaign for the undersea documentary *The Silent World.*

"Movie Ads and Decency." *America* 96 (8 Dec 56) 292. Advertising industry itself calls for self-control.

Finley, James F. "Film and TV." *Cath World* 185 (June 57) 221. Short comment on Arlene Dahl's suing Universal Pictures for "heating up the movie ads."

"Double-Talk in the Times." *America* 97 (29 June 57) 360. Plea for the abolition of salacious ads.

"Ad Men Urge Cleanup." *America* 97 (31 Aug 57) 535. Some publishers blast recent advertising.

"Bardot and the Ad-Men." *America* 99 (10 May 58) 188–189. Must journalism continue to sensationalize advertisements of the films of Brigitte Bardot?

"Oscars for Commercials." *Time* 72 (6 Oct 58) 51–52. The Fifth Annual Festival of Screen Advertising Services.

"Goya's Girl Goes Aloft." *Life* 46 (27 Apr 59) 116. Advertising for *The Naked Maja.*

Wills, F. H. "Hans Hillmann's Film Posters; with German and French Texts." *Graphis* 15 (July 59) 344–349.

"Tulsa Vetoes Immoral Movie Ads." *Am Mercury* 90 (Feb 60) 47–48. Reprint: Tulsa's newspaper adopts a code.

Youngstein, Max E. "The Press and Motion Pictures." *JSPG* (Sep 60) 9–10+. Movie distributors get "shabby treatment": news-paper rules as to kinds of advertising accepted, increased advertising rates for films, etc.

Bresler, Jerry, Albert M. Pickus, Paul N. Lazarus, Jr., Roger Lewis, Ernest Emerling, Clark Ramsay, Harry Goldberg, Gordon S. White, Frank Whitbeck, James Meade, Robert T. Gillham. "The Journal Looks at Motion Picture Advertising." *JSPG* (June 61) 3–31. Producers, theatre men, and the head of the MPA advertising code discuss quality, costs, and controls of film advertising.

Rotzler, W. "Advertising for Film and Theatre; with German and French Texts." *Graphis* 18 (Mar 61) 100–117.

"Watch My Line." *Time* 79 (5 Jan 62) 40–41. Stars battle over billing.

Grande, L. M. "Advertising: For Mature Adults." *America* 106 (27 Jan 62) 558–559.

McKnight, Felix R. "How Hollywood Looks to the American Press." *JSPG* (Mar 62) 5–6. Dallas newspaper editor notes criticism of the new freedom in film subject matter and urges better controls on "obscene advertising copy." See reply by MGM advertising manager (June 62).

Cameron, Ian. "Future for the Cinema." *Spectator* 212 (6 Mar 64) 313–314. The evolution of advertising in the cinema with emphasis on Joe E. Levine's publicity.

"Censoring Sex." *Time* 85 (12 Feb 65) 71. *Los Angeles Times* screen board censors movie ads.

"The Journal Looks at Movie Advertising Censorship." *JSPG* (June 65) 3–32. Newspapermen, film salesmen, a critic, and retired director of advertising code offer opinions; policies of three newspapers included.

Fischer-Nosbisch, Fritz. "Film Poster Today: *Camera* Questions." *Camera* 45 (No. 5, May 66) 40–47. An interview about the role of a designer today working with photography and the film poster.

"Laundering the Sheets." *Time* 93 (30 May 69) 54. Analysis of movie-ad censorship in various newspapers.

Lazarus, Paul. "The Wet Finger Method for Evaluating Film Success." *JSPG* (Sep 69) 31–33. Grosses for trailers give an idea of the success of most pictures; examples of bookings.

Austen, David. "All Next Week . . ." *F&F* 16 (No. 1, Oct 69) 79. On the trailers used to advertise next week's attractions in the theatres.

"You've Seen the Movie, Now Read the Ad." *Time* 96 (12 Oct 70) 80. Studios offer to use or mention products in their films if the manufacturers will, in return, promote the film in their own advertising.

6e. Theatres

"Movie Profits and Poisoned Pictures." *Chris Cent* 47 (7 May 30) 580. Deplores stress on profit in movie industry and calls for moral responsibility from exhibitors.

Blakeston, Oswell. "Enough—No More." *Close Up* 7 (No. 5, Nov 30) 310–313. The use of excessive architectural features in recent cinema theatres.

"Easy Money for the Movies." *Chris Cent* 48 (8 Apr 31) 468. Deplores use of advertising films in theatres.

Dutton, William. "Getting on in the World." *SEP* 203 (23 May 31) 49+. New jobs in motion-picture theatres.

"Newspapers Put an End to Advertising Movies." *Bus Wk* (8 July 31) 22. Advertising shorts withdrawn from theatres by newspaper pressure.

"Effects of Technological Changes Upon Employment in the Motion-Picture Theaters of Washington, D.C." *Monthly Labor Rev* 33 (Nov 31) 1005–1018. Surveys labor conditions, noting change from silent to sound movies affecting projectionists and musicians.

"Gladys Glycerine, Theatre Owner, Banker, Cry Real Tears Together." *Bus Wk* (10 Aug 32) 14–15. Readjustment to capital basis allowing profits from smaller income.

Shand, P. Morton. "Building the Shell of the Screen." *S&S* 1 (No. 4, Winter 32–33) 104–105. The need for building spaces designed exclusively for cinema viewing.

"Movie Home Rule." *Bus Wk* (18 Jan 33) 16. Big theatre chains moving to decentralize.

Johnston, Alva. "A. C. Blumenthal." *New Yorker* (4, 11 Feb 33). *See 5, A. C. Blumenthal.*

"Wages and Hours of Stage Employees and Motion-Picture Machine Operators." *Monthly Labor Rev* 36 (May 33) 1111–1115. Compares salaries reported by local unions.

Nyman, Kenneth. "Profit or Prestige?" *S&S* 3 (No. 10, Summer 34) 51–55. Problems of film exhibition.

"Premium Thriller." *Bus Wk* (8 Dec 34) 24. Free premiums at theatres mean boom for manufacturer but headache for exhibitor.

Leathart, J. R. "Cinema Façade." *S&S* 4 (No. 13, Spring 35) 12–13. Brief comments on cinema architecture.

Kresensky, R. "Bank Night." *Chris Cent* 52 (14 Aug 35) 1034–1035. Colorful article on drawings for money put up by theatres.

Rowson, Simon, *et al.* "Two-Feature Programme." *S&S* 4 (No. 16, Winter 35–36), 166–169. A number of authors discuss the relative value and popularity of the double feature.

"Bank Night." *Time* 27 (3 Feb 36) 57–58. How theatres handle money give-aways on Mondays to increase business.

"Bank Night." *New Rep* 86 (6 May 36) 363–365. Detailed description of this lottery method of enticing the public to go to the movies.

"Bank Night." *Lit Dig* 123 (6 Mar 37) 36.

Shaw, H. F. "Do You Hold Hands at the Movies?" *American* 124 (Aug 37) 38–39. A theatre manager's bank night and other headaches.

Lorentz, P. "Movie Platform." *Lit Dig* 123 (7 Aug 37) 23. A protest against double bills, and a plea for more short subjects.

Sprague, J. R. "Small-Town Movie Theatre." *SEP* 210 (14 Aug 37) 23+. A detailed look at all types of movie houses, how they operate, at what expense, and how affected by block booking.

"Screen Fans Organize to Bite Hand That Feeds Them Double Features." *Newswk* 10 (4 Oct 37). *See 7b(1c).*

Fink, F. "Down with Doubles." *Lit Dig* 124 (27 Nov 37). *See 7c(2).*

Parkhill, F. "Bank Night Tonight." *SEP* 210 (4 Dec 37) 20–21. The efforts of movie exhibitors to bolster faltering attendance.

"Doublefeaturitis." *Sci Am* 158 (Feb 38) 73. An attack on the "double-feature" policy.

"Double Trouble." *Time* 31 (21 Feb 38) 55. The popularity of theatres showing double features.

"Double Movie Scrap." *Bus Wk* (5 Mar 38). *See 7c(2).*

"Glamour Under Fire." *Bus Wk* (14 May 38) 18+. Independent exhibitors cause sensation by advertisement denying the box-office value of the big stars.

Ferguson, O. "Doldrum Weather." *New Rep* 96 (31 Aug 38) 104–105. Crowded conditions in movie theatres.

Crowther, B. "Double-Feature Trouble." *NYTM* (14 July 40) 8. Written at the time of Samuel Goldwyn's poll to determine the fate of the double feature, this article explores the why's, pros and cons.

Fuller, W. R. "The Exhibitor's Part." *S&S* 10 (No. 37, Spring 41). In wartime England.

Cross, Elizabeth. "Plain Words to the Exhibitor." *S&S* 10 (No. 39, Autumn 41) 44–45.

Edwards, C. C. "One for the Money." *Parents Mag* 16 (Oct 41) 26–27+. Industry is making a belated effort to discourage double bills.

Wilson, E. "Big Pie Plate." *SEP* 214 (20 June 42) 19+. Dish salesman Jack Price provides free crockery to attract movie audiences.

Nugent, F. S. "Double, Double, Toil and Trouble: Do Hollywood and the Exhibitors

Really Want to Get Rid of the Double Feature?" *NYTM* (17 Jan 43) 11+.

"How to Run a Theatre: Movie Exhibitor Attempts to Cope with Aggressive Adolescence." *Time* (22 Nov 43) 94–96.

Cross, Elizabeth. "More Carping." *S&S* 13 (No. 51, Oct 44) 70–71. Arguments against certain film programs, specifically those which use too many shorts before the feature.

"Theater Fight in Open." *Bus Wk* (21 Oct 44) 39. The struggle by independents to open more theatres in wartime.

"1,212% Profit." *Time* 48 (19 Aug 46) 81–82. Business dealings of Charles P. Skouras of National Theaters Corporation.

"Tax on Movies." *Bus Wk* (7 Dec 46) 95–96. Cities are turning to taxes on theatre admissions to increase their revenues.

Skouras, Charles P. "The Exhibitor." *Annals of Am Acad of Polit and Soc Sci* (1947) 26–30.

"Boxoffice Pinch." *Bus Wk* (4 Oct 47) 62+. Theatre owners face the prospect of having to pay higher film rentals.

"What's Playing at the Grove? Independent Movie Operator." *Fortune* 38 (Aug 48) 94–99. Fighting for better clearance rulings and the right to bid for first-run pictures.

Spottiswoode, Raymond. "Children in Wonderland?" *SRL* 31 (13 Nov 48) 60. The lack of interest by local theatres in presenting films made for children.

Hine, A. "Film Palaces." *Holiday* 5 (May 49) 23–26. A history of the movie house: emphasis on splash gives way to comfort.

"Prelude to Divorce?" *Time* 53 (16 May 49) 91–92. Joe Schenck's resignation at 20th Century-Fox to devote all his time to theatres.

"Room for 48, 150, 147." *Time* 53 (13 June 49) 98. Statistics on mushrooming movie theatres throughout the world.

"Popcorn Bonanza." *Life* 27 (25 July 49) 41–44. "Fans are eating movie exhibitors out of the red."

Hine, A. "Man Who Bucked the Movie Producer-Distributor Monopoly." *Holiday* 7 (Mar 50) 22+. Independent theatre-chain owner William Goldman discusses movies, distribution, theatres, movie companies, and trends.

Clarke, Michael. "Censorship by Violence?" *S&S* 19 (Apr 50) 60. Anti-British U.S. film about Palestine taken off the screen by authorities because of audience disturbances.

Allen, William D. "Spanish-Language Films in the U.S." *FIR* 1 (July–Aug 50). See *4h*.

Cerf, Bennett. "Tradewinds." *SRL* 34 (31 Mar 51) 4+. Reprinted letter by Irving Hoffman on woes of motion-picture theatre owners.

Edmonds, Lawrence. "Fleapit Nights." *S&S* 21 (Oct–Dec 51) 87. A humorous visit to the typical lower-class theatres that play cheap or sensational films.

"Honor Night." *Time* 60 (24 Nov 52) 108. A theatre owner's protest against tax on movie tickets.

Bunn, M. "Back to the Picture Show!" *American* 154 (Dec 52). See *7b(1b)*.

"Warming Up for a New Take-Off." *Bus Wk* (21 Nov 53) 108+. Stanley Warner Corporation teaming up old Warner theatre circuit and new Cinerama.

Geis, Gilbert. "Municipal Motion Picture Theatre Ownership in Norway." *QFRTV* 9 (No. 1, Fall 54) 79–91. History, organization, financial problems.

"Cinema Count." *Newswk* 44 (18 Oct 54) 100. The number of theatres in U.S.

Tennant, Sylvia. "Why Do We Sit Through the Second Feature?" *Film* (No. 2, Dec 54) 26–28. Second features are categorized and their virtues and liabilities noted.

"Bid for Teens." *Bus Wk* (14 May 55). See *7b(3)*.

Dyer, Peter John. "Those First-Rate Second Features." *F&F* 2 (No. 12, Sep 56) 17. Report on good but ordinary films that fill lower half of double bill.

Cole, H. A. "Need for Facts." *JSPG* (Nov 56) 7+. A pioneer Texas exhibitor tells how research won the battle for tax cuts for the motion-picture exhibitor.

Moscow, Robert. "Showmanship." *JSPG* (Nov 56) 8+. Exhibitor in Atlanta discusses how to sell motion pictures.

Reade, Walter, Jr. "Stop the Fighting." *JSPG* (Nov 56) 8+. Exhibitor says exhibitors, producers, and distributors should get together to make money.

Mayer, Arthur. "Hollywood's Favorite Fable." *FQ* 12 (No. 2, Winter 58) 13–20. The myth of the virtuous producer-distributor and the wicked exhibitor; block booking with cancellation privileges and film production by exhibitors should be resumed in place of competitive bidding.

Pickus, Albert M. "An Exhibitor Speaks." *JSPG* (June 60) 3+.

Hall, B. M. "Best Remaining Seats." *Am Heritage* 12 (Oct 61). See *4b*.

Raven, Simon. "Home from Home." *Spectator* 207 (24 Nov 61) 736–738. Some theatres in Great Britain are social gathering places where audiences have little regard for what is taking place on the screen.

Eyles, Allen, and Marcus Eavis. "Focus on Exhibition." *Motion* (No. 2, Winter 61–62) 13–16+. Exhibition and distribution practices must be changed.

Martin, Pete. "20-Cartoons-20." *Kulchur* 2 (No. 5, Spring 62). See *2h(1)*.

Leglise, Paul. "Hidden Face of the Cinema: An Audience of 12,000,000,000." *UNESCO Courier* 16 (Feb 63). See *7e(1)*.

Slide, Anthony. "William Morton and His Cinemas." *Cinema Studies* 1 (No. 8, Dec 63) 197–199. Exhibitor in Hull (England).

Williams, David. "Notes About Film Projection." *Cinema Studies* 1 (No. 8, Dec 63) 195–197. Interview with L. A. Taylor, chief projectionist of Regal Cinema, Newbury, with fifty years' experience.

DeRome, Peter. "Off-Broadway Cinema." *S&S* 33 (Winter 63–64). *See 4a.*

Tiffen, C. E. "British Cities Try Municipal Movie Houses." *Am City* 79 (Apr 64) 154.

"The Early Cinema in Eastbourne." *Cinema Studies* 1 (No. 9, June 64) 226–228. Report by a group of students at BFI Summer School held there.

Nowell-Smith, Geoffrey. "Chasing the Gorgon." *S&S* 34 (Spring 65) 60–61. Catching "art" movies and others at out-of-the-way theatres in Manchester; sociology of audiences.

Callenbach, Ernest. "Temples of the Seventh Art." *S&S* 35 (Winter 65–66) 12–17. We are neglecting to use imagination in movie-theatre architecture: the stripped-down style is not exciting.

O'Connor, Charles. "Earnings in Motion Picture Theater Industry, April 1966." *Monthly Labor Rev* 90 (Apr 67) 48–51. U.S. Bureau of Labor Statistics tables covering all theatre personnel.

McDonald, Donna. "Dimitrios, The Greek." *Take One* 1 (No. 7, 1967). *See 4e(7).*

Comolli, Jean-Louis. "Notes on the New Spectator." *CdC in Eng* (No. 7, Jan 67) 60–61. The new cinema should be shown in theatres of light rather than darkness so that the spectator may confront life and the world on the screen instead of dreams and escape.

Huntley, John. "The Cinema Comes to Birmingham." *Cinema Studies* 2 (No. 5, Sep 67) 79–82. Press clippings, 1896.

Corwin, Sherrill. "Prophets and Profits." *JSPG* (Sep 69) 9–12. Exhibitor talks about relations with distributors.

Mayer, Michael F. "A Scrap of Paper." *JSPG* (Sep 69) 17–19. The film rental contract with the exhibitor.

Lamson, R. D. "Measured Productivity and Price Change: Some Empirical Evidence on Service Industry Bias, Motion Picture Theaters." *J Polit Econ* 78 (Mar–Apr 70) 291–305. An economic analysis of productivity in relation to motion-picture theatres.

North, Christopher. "Film History for Exhibitors." *FIR* 21 (No. 8, Oct 70). *See 4d.*

6e(1). CASE STUDIES

Blake, Frances. "Something New in the Motion Picture Theatre." *Close Up* 10 (No. 2, June 33) 154–157. The film activities of the Fine Arts Theatre in Boston.

Coxhead, Elizabeth. "Towards a Co-operative Cinema." *Close Up* 10 (No. 2, June 33)

133–137. Notes on the work of the Academy Cinema, on Oxford Street, which shows specialist films.

"All-Cartoon Theater." *Newswk* 4 (20 Oct 34). *See 2h.*

Lindgren, E. H. "Preserving Entertainment Films." *S&S* 4 (No. 14, Summer 35) 69. An interview with the manager of the Forum Cinema, noted for its repertory policy and for reviving the best films of the past.

Blank, A. H. "Whozinnit?" *American* 121 (Jan 36) 28–29+. Head of corporation operating seventy-five theatres in Iowa, Nebraska, and Illinois reports on favorite stars of the year according to his receipts.

"Income, Costs, Admissions All Going Up." *Newswk* 10 (13 Sep 37) 30. The Roxy Theatre—how its fortunes rose and fell with the Depression years, and how it is typical of the movie industry in general.

Roney, C. B. "Show Lady: Managing a Moving Picture Theater in Milford, Michigan." *SEP* 211 (18 Feb 39) 23+.

McCullie, Hector. "An Exhibitor Hits Back." *S&S* 10 (No. 40, Spring 42) 76–78. The problems faced by one of them.

Huntley, John. "The First Picture House in the World." *S&S* 16 (No. 63, Autumn 47) 102. The Blackburn Cinema, one of the oldest.

"New Feathers for Pathé: Paris Theatre." *Time* 52 (20 Sep 48). *See 4e(2c).*

"Victim." *New Yorker* 25 (26 Nov 49). *See 8b.*

Andrus, Edythe F. "Ladies, Please Remove Your Hats." *CSMM* (31 Dec 49) 15. Opening of new film theatre in Augusta, Michigan.

Drum, Dale D. "Silent Movies in Los Angeles." *FIR* 3 (Nov 52) 450–454. Mr. and Mrs. John Hampton's North Fairfax Avenue theatre and how it came to be.

"Yankee Doodle on the Rand." *Time* 62 (27 July 53) 84+. Biography of African Theatres' chairman John Schlesinger.

Smythe, Dallas, Parker B. Lusk, and Charles A. Lewis. "Portrait of an Art Theater Audience." *QFRTV* 8 (No. 1, Fall 53). *See 7b(1b).*

Bond, Edwin. "How to Be a Film Exhibitor." *S&S* 23 (Jan–Mar 54) 154. A humorous article dealing with some of the many hazards one might face if one took seriously the glowing ads for the sale of motion-picture theatres.

"Movie House with a Past." *NYTM* (28 Mar 54) 39. The Fifth Avenue Playhouse in New York has been a mecca for serious film enthusiasts since 1926, when it opened with *The Cabinet of Dr. Caligari.*

Halliwell, Leslie. "Strictly for Eggheads." *S&S* 23 (Apr–June 54) 201–202. The case history of a small cinema, out of business because of the slump, that came back as an art house; failures are noted; some of the older, better films.

Zolotow, M. "Most Fabulous Movie Theater

in the World." *Rdr Dig* 66 (June 55) 131–134. New York's Radio City Music Hall.

Griggs, John. "A 1914 Victory." *FIR* 6 (Aug–Sep 55) 318–324. A true suspense story: a theatre owner, about to be forced out of business, found his young assistant had a kind of projector an indifferent distributor needed almost as badly as he needed a print of *The Spoilers*.

Powell, Dilys. "The Everyman." *S&S* 25 (Summer 55). See *4e(1)*.

Fleming, T. J. "Portrait of a Happy Theatre Owner." *Cosmopolitan* 141 (Oct 56) 58–59. Don Rugoff discusses "the way to a viewer's heart."

"Old Days, Sixty Cents." *Newswk* 53 (27 Apr 59) 114. California movie theatre showing silent films exclusively.

"The King of Intermissions." *Time* 86 (9 July 65) 93–94. Portrait of Eugene V. Klein of National General Corporation.

"Not So Sad Sack." *Time* 80 (27 July 62) 65. Portrait of Ben Sack, independent theatre owner.

"Music Hall: Still the No. 1 Hit." *Bus Wk* (25 Dec 65) 46–49.

Paletz, David, and Michael Noonan. "The Exhibitors." *FQ* 19 (No. 2, Winter 65–66) 14–40. Interviews with three exhibitors: an executive of Pacific Drive-Ins, the owner of a Los Angeles independent art house, and the manager of a "nudie cutie" house; booking procedures, audiences, business procedures, and scheduling.

Weinberg, Gretchen. "David Fine." *F Cult* (No. 41, Summer 66) 87. Interview with owner of Cameo Theater in New York, a "Russian-Greek-nudie house."

6e(2). NEW FORMS

[See also 2m, 6b(4).]

Pawley, Frederick Arden. "Design of Small Motion Picture Theatres." *Arch Rec* 71 (June 32) 429–438+. Studies building type and construction methods.

Schlanger, Ben. "The Small Motion Picture Theatre." *Arch Rec* 75 (June 34) 534–535. Architect sees "need for, and desirability of, new and smaller movie theaters."

"Storm King Theatre and Shops, Cornwall-on-Hudson, N.Y." *Arch Rec* 78 (Oct 35) 278–282.

"Big Export Trade Seen in Prefab Theaters." *Sci Dig* 19 (Jan 46) 15–16. The National Theatres Amusement Company announces plans for American-style prefab movie houses as part of export trade.

Dreyfuss, Henry. "Four-Square Theater." *Hwd Q* 2 (No. 4, July 47) 367–370. Industrial designer proposes rear-projection four-sided screen (by mirrors) for audience seated on four sides of room looking toward the center,

in order to get away from a screen enlarged merely for the benefit of the back rows.

"Modern Theatre." *Life* 27 (10 Oct 49) 67–68. An architect designs and builds a movie theatre made solely from laminated wood.

Robinson, David. "Building a Cinema." *S&S* (Winter 56–57) 137–139+. A history of cinema architecture through a number of different eras; new national film theatre was to be built and the article ends with a description of the proposed structure.

Bogard, Will. "The Film Chamber at New Cinema Workshop." *Cinéaste* 2 (No. 3 Winter 68–69) 16. A report on a twenty-two-foot half-cylindrical chamber with a half-spherical screen area built at the Workshop in Pittsburgh in order to study the effects of film viewing.

Cargin, Peter. "Alternative Cinema." *Film* (No. 58, Spring 70) 7–9. Specialist cinemas, film societies, television.

6e(2a). Drive-Ins

"Drive-In Theatre." *Bus Wk* (5 Aug 33) 19. See also *Lit Dig* 116 (22 July 33) 19. Camden, N.J., has first drive-in theatre.

"Movie Theatre Lets Cars Drive Right In." *Pop Sci* 123 (Aug 33) 19. Camden, N.J.

"Drive-In Movie Holds Four Hundred Cars." *Pop Mech* 60 (Sep 33) 326. Camden, N.J.

"Ozoners." *Time* 51 (26 Apr 48) 96. How outdoor theatres are improving.

Best, K., and K. Hillyer. "Movies Under the Stars." *Rdrs Dig* 53 (Sep 48) 117–119. A short look at the history of drive-ins.

"Fly-In Theatre Near Asbury Park, N.J." *Sci Dig* 24 (Sep 48) 94.

"Twice as Many Drive-In Theaters?" *Bus Wk* (1 Jan 49) 44–45. Costs and competition discussed.

"Moon-Washed." *New Yorker* 25 (1 Oct 49) 20. The phenomenon of the drive-in.

Cullman, Marguerite W. "Double-Feature—Movies and Moonlight." *NYTM* (1 Oct 50) 22. A report on the successful drive-in movie business.

Durant, John. "Movies Take to the Pastures." *SEP* 223 (14 Oct 50) 24–25. Top box office at the drive-in.

"Drive-In with a Balcony." *Bus Wk* (30 June 51) 70. Theatre in San Francisco on terraced slope.

Luther, Rodney. "Drive-In Theaters: Rags to Riches in Five Years." *Hwd Q* 5 (No. 4, Summer 51) 401–411. From 1946 to 1951, about 2,000 of them.

"Drive-In Film Business Burns Up the Prairies." *Life* 31 (24 Sep 51) 104–106+. In a time of financial crisis drive-in theatres bring back some of the "lost audience" over age thirty-five.

Hine, A. "The Drive-Ins." *Holiday* 12 (July 52) 6. The past, present, and future of drive-in theatres.

"Drive-In Theatres: Happy But Griping." *Bus Wk* (9 May 53) 129. The drive-in magnates' complaints about TV, 3-D, admissions tax, and cars.

"Drive-Ins Steal the Show." *Bus Wk* (15 Aug 53) 114. Comparison with indoor movie theatres and survey of youngsters' entertainment preferences.

"The Family 'Drives In.'" *NYTM* (26 June 55) 16. Drive-in theatres have become both respectable and successful.

Taylor, Frank J. "Big Boom in Outdoor Movies." *SEP* 229 (15 Sep 56) 31+.

"Growth in Drive-Ins." *Commonweal* 65 (16 Nov 56) 166.

"Colossal Drive-In." *Newswk* 50 (22 July 57) 85–87. "All-Weather Drive-In," on the Sunrise Highway in N.J.

"Million-Dollar Drive-In Offers Films, Fun and Food." *Pop Sci* 171 (Sep 57) 118–121. Pictures of luxury drive-ins.

"Drive-In Cine; Photographs." *NYTM* (29 Sep 57) 32. Pictures of Italy's (Europe's?) first drive-in.

"Drive-In Lie-In." *Newswk* 62 (8 July 63) 78. Short history of drive-in theatres.

6e(2b). Art Houses and Multiplexes

Hakim, Eric. "Specialised Cinema or Film Society." *S&S* 3 (No. 9, Spring 34) 10–12. Suggestions for setting up specialized theatres, apart from film societies, which will show noncommercial or unusual films.

Oakley, C. A. "Mr. Cosmo Takes a Bow." *S&S* 9 (No. 33, Spring 40) 9. The Cosmo, first cinema outside of London expressly built for the exhibition of Continental and repertory feature films.

Cohn, Herbert. "Running a Specialist Theatre." *S&S* 11 (No. 41, Summer 42) 9–11. During wartime.

Harris, Elizabeth M. "The Function of the Specialized Cinema." *Penguin F Rev* 6 (Apr 48) 80–86. To show foreign films or British films of high quality; to improve the standards of commercial British films.

Dellow, Richard. "Provincial Specialist Theatres." *S&S* 17 (No. 67, Autumn 48) 129–130. Theatre in Bedford, England, illustrates the problems such theatres face.

"Afterhours: Opening of Paris Theatre, New York." *Harper's* 197 (Dec 48) 95. French vulgarity and pretentious films. Response 198 (Feb 49) 14.

"Sureseaters." *Time* 54 (17 Oct 49) 100. Small art-theatre boom.

Griffith, Richard. "The Audience over 35." *FIR* 1 (Sep 50). See *4e(1c)*.

Alpert, Hollis. "Strictly for the Art Houses." *SRL* 34 (28 Apr 51) 27. A criticism of "art houses" and their audiences. Reply by Ernest Callenbach (26 May 51) 24.

"Quality and Service: An Answer to the Movie Slump?" *Bus Wk* (15 Sep 51) 116–118+.

Movie houses like country clubs—a cure for the box office?

Frank, Stanley. "Sure-Seaters Discover an Audience." *Nation's Business* 40 (Jan 52) 34–36+. Art houses compared with regular movie theatres.

"The Good Old Silents." *Time* 60 (20 Oct 52). See *4b*.

Twomey, John E. "Some Considerations on the Rise of the Art-Film Theater." *QFRTV* 10 (No. 3, Spring 56) 239–247.

Marcorelles, Louis. "*Cinémas d'Essai.*" *S&S* 27 (Autumn 57) 58. Note on formation of international art-theatre federation at Cannes.

"Film Chain Finds Cures for Box Office Blues." *Bus Wk* (22 Mar 58) 72–73+. Louis Sher operates thirteen "art" theatres for adults only across the country; his methods are drawing in large audiences.

"A Managerial Revolution." *Sat Rev* 43 (18 June 60) 26. Art theatre managed by Daniel Talbot.

"Making a Loud Dollar." *Newswk* 56 (15 Aug 60) 80. Daniel Talbot and the New Yorker Art Theater.

Kael, Pauline. "Fantasies of the Art House Audience." *S&S* 31 (Winter 61–62). See *3b(2)*.

"Art House Boom." *Newswk* 59 (28 May 62) 102.

Alpert, Hollis. "Something New in Movie Communication: A Double-Decker Theatre." *Sat Rev* 45 (9 June 62) 54–55.

"Twin Cinemas: Flexible Showcase for Films." *Arch Forum* 117 (Sep 62) 120–123. Report on a new twin cinema in New York City.

Schoenstein, Ralph. "What Time Does the Coffee Go On?" *Sat Rev* 46 (28 Dec 63) 17. About art theatres.

Cowie, Peter. "Art Cinemas in Alliance." *S&S* 35 (Summer 66) 117. Note on International Confederation of Art Cinemas; no British or American members.

Houston, Penelope. "Cinecenta." *S&S* 38 (Winter 68–69) 21–22. Note on opening of four small (150-seat) cinemas.

"Four-in-One Cinema." *Cinema* (Calif) 5 (No. 3, 1969) 27–30. Cinecenta in London has four 150-seat theatres; diagram included.

"The Boutique Cinemas." *F&F* 15 (No. 4, Jan 69) 31–33. On the opening of a theatre in London that includes four individual film theatres in one building.

"Quads, Sixplexes and Up." *Newswk* 74 (8 Sep 69) 71. The rise of multiple theatres.

"The Movie Theater Gets Cut to Size." *Bus Wk* (14 Mar 70) 29. Trans-Lux Corporation and others open 1970s' version of the nickelodeon: minitheatres.

"Snorkel Theater." *Arch Forum* 133 (Oct 70) 54–55. New "non-building" in New York houses cinema literally undergound with ticket booth topside.

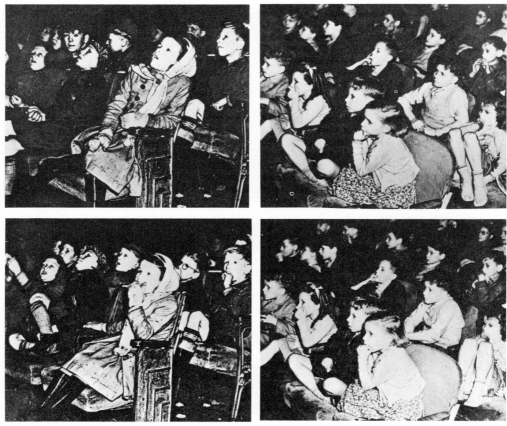

Children in Hull and in London (at right) watching violent scenes in *Comanche Territory*. (Reproduced from Mary Field, *Children and Film*.)

7. Film and Society

7a. Film Content as a Reflection of Society

[See also 3a(2), 3a(6).]

Klingender, F. D. "The New Deal and the American Film." *CQ* 3 (No. 4, Summer 35) 197–201. *Massacre, Dangerous Age,* and even Mae West represent social criticism; but this trend is already over and fantasy has returned.

Calverton, V. F. "Cultural Barometer." *Current Hist* 48 (Feb 38) 54–56.

Riegel, O. W. "Nationalism in Press, Radio and Cinema." *Am Sociological Rev* 3 (Aug 38) 510–515. The major media are best equipped to neutralize the trend toward emotional nationalism, yet have not done so; minimal attention to cinema.

Hauser, Arnold. "The Film as a Product of Society." *S&S* 8 (No. 32, Winter 39–40) 129–132. The various ways in which films represent the society that produces them.

Mok, M. "Slumming with Zanuck." *Nation* 150 (3 Feb 40) 127–128. Relates the power of big business to social conditions and the film industry, occasioned by the people who came to the preview of Darryl Zanuck's *The Grapes of Wrath.*

Cross, Elizabeth. "Rural Plea." *S&S* 9 (No. 36, Winter 40–41) 65. A plea for more films which will reveal the life of people in the country.

Pinthus, Kurt. "History Directs the Movies." *Am Scholar* 10 (Oct 41) 483–497. Social and historical forces—and demands for entertainment—reflected in film.

Jones, Dorothy B. "Quantitative Analysis of Motion Picture Content. *Pub Opin Q* 6 (Sep 42), 411–428. The socially significant aspects of film content, among these being the identity, wants, and values of the major characters.

Grant, Elspeth. "From Pearl White to Pearl Harbour." *S&S* 11 (No. 43, Winter 42–43) 61–62. Movies which falsify the facts of human life.

Fox, Milton. "Art of the Movies in American Life." *J Aesthetics and Art Criticism* 3 (No. 9, 1944) 39–52. Mass-entertainment characteristics; distribution and exhibition; Hollywood tradition.

De Voto, Bernard. "Easy Chair." *Harper's* 194 (Feb 47). See 3a(2).

Mercey, Arch A. "Social Uses of the Motion Picture." *Annals of Am Acad of Polit and Soc Sci* 250 (Mar 47) 98–104. How the postwar film has developed in news value, government use, etc.

Tyler, Parker. "The Horse." *S&S* 16 (No. 63, Autumn 47). See 3a(5).

Zinnemann, Fred. "Different Perspective." *S&S* 17 (No. 67, Autumn 48) 113. Argument for a certain kind of dramatic documentary material for contemporary films.

Jones, Dorothy B. "Quantitative Analysis of Motion Picture Content." *Pub Opin Q* 14 (No. 3, 1950) 554–558. Hollywood picture types and content analysis of 1,200 films (1917–1947).

Elkin, Fred. "The Value Implications of Popular Films." *Sociology and Social Research* 38 (1954) 320–322.

Houseman, John. "How—and What—Does a Movie Communicate?" *QFRTV* 10 (No. 3, Spring 56). See 3a.

Rosenberg, Milton J. "Mr. Magoo as Public Dream." *QFRTV* 11 (No. 4, Summer 57). See 2h(1).

Martin, Dick. "Cards on the Screen." *Hobbies* 63 (Dec 58) 122–123. Playing cards used in movies.

Readers are advised to acquaint themselves with the range of categories throughout the bibliography in the search for specific subjects. In some cases, cross-categorical comparisons are directly suggested. In general, however, each article is placed under one category only. Cross-references on individual articles have been kept to a minimum.

Entries are in chronological order of publication under each category. Exceptions are: Part 5, Biography, in which the order is alphabetical by name; Part 9, Case Histories of Film Making, which is alphabetical by film title; and 3c and 8c(4), also alphabetical by title.

Losey, Joseph. "Mirror to Life." *F&F* 5 (No. 9, June 59) 7+. Social content in films.

MacFadden, Patrick. "Letting Go." *F Soc Rev* 4 (No. 1, 1968). *See 2h(3)*.

Yoshimaya, Tats. "Film News from the Fiftieth State." *F Com* 1 (No. 4, 1963). *See 4d*.

Farber, Manny. "Hard Sell Cinema." *December* 10 (No. 1, 68) 141–146. Farber cites the "middle-class blitz" of jazz, painting, and the novel, and traces its manifestations in the cinema.

Taylor, John Russell. "Larking Back." *S&S* 37 (Spring 68). *See 2k*.

Durgnat, Raymond. "Spies and Ideologies." *Cinema* (Cambridge) (No. 2, Mar 69). *See 4k(10)*.

Weightman, John. "Outsider Rides Again." *Encounter* 33 (Nov 69) 46–50. Lance Robson's *Varieties of the Picaresque* used as model for an analysis of society as it relates to *Easy Rider, Goodbye, Columbus* and *Midnight Cowboy*.

Steiner, Shari. "Europe and America: A Question of Self-Image." *Sat Rev* (27 Dec 69). *See 3a(6)*.

Jowett, Garth S. "The Concept of History in American Produced Films: An Analysis of Films Made in the Period 1950–1961." *J Pop Cult* 3 (No. 4, Spring 70). *See 4d*.

Weimer, H. R. "The Cinema and the City." *J Pop Cult* 3 (No. 4, Spring 1970) 825–831. A study of the treatment of the city in films 1908–1970.

7a(1). NATIONAL TYPES

[See also 7e.]

Carter, H. "Spirit of the Nations Revealed in Their Films." *World Today* 55 (May 30) 526–535.

Whang, Paul K. "Boycotting American Movies." *World Tomorrow* 13 (Aug 30) 339–340. Complains about unfair Chinese stereotype (from *China Weekly Review*).

Modern, Klara. "The Vienna of the Films." *Close Up* 9 (No. 2, June 32) 129–131. A plea for a more honest film treatment of the capital of Austria.

Ogino, Y. "Japan as Seen in Films." *Close Up* 10 (No. 4, Dec 33). *See 4f(1)*.

Knight, Eric M. "Synthetic America." *CQ* 2 (No. 2, Winter 33–34) 87–90. Philadelphia film critic suggests that U.S. films show only cardboard conventions, not the varieties of American life; Westerns, *I Am a Fugitive, State Fair,* Mae West, and the newsreels show some of the truth.

Patterson, F. T. "Bread and Cinemas: In Defense of that Battered Stepchild, the Movies." *North Am Rev* 246 (Dec 38) 259–266. The movie as a reflection of American culture.

Sancton, Thomas. "The New York Myth." *New Rep* 107 (27 July 42) 112–114. Polemic against wartime image of America in film, radio, and magazines which stresses urban, acquisitive values.

Joseph, Robert. "From Hun to Nazi by Way of the Motion Picture." *Calif Arts and Arch* 60 (No. 5, June 43) 18+. The treatment of the Germans in Hollywood films during the two world wars.

Lambert, R. S. "The Screen Englishman." *S&S* 13 (No. 51, Oct 44) 60. A Canadian view.

Harman, A. Jympson. "Truth and British Films." *S&S* 15 (No. 57, Spring 46) 15–16. Images of national life.

Jacobs, Arthur. "Foreign Policy and Cinema." *S&S* 15 (No. 59, Autumn 46) 102–105. A comparison of Nazism as it was and as it was portrayed on the screen.

Pozner, Vladimir. "Adult or Adulterated?" *Screen Writer* 2 (Apr 47) 14–17. Condemns Hollywood's treatment of foreign locales in films because the characterization of foreigners is demeaning.

Powdermaker, Hortense. "An Anthropologist Looks at the Movies." *Annals of Am Acad of Polit and Soc Sci* 254 (Nov 47) 80–87. How they reflect the face of America.

Sutherland, Donald. "Scotland . . . and the Screen." *S&S* 17 (No. 68, Winter 48–49) 162–163. A criticism of the image of Scotland on the screen.

Kracauer, Siegfried. "National Types as Hollywood Presents Them." *Pub Opin Q* 13 (No. 1, 1949) 53–72. Foreign characters as reflection of popular attitudes; analysis of treatment of British and Russian characters in Hollywood films 1933–1949.

"Portrayal of Foreigners by Hollywood." *Sci Newsletter* 55 (4 June 49) 356. Dr. Siegfried Kracauer's concern about American films making little attempt to capture reality of Russian characters (for example).

Kracauer, Siegfried. "How American Films Portray Foreign Types." *FIR* 1 (Mar 50) 21–22+. American screen images of British types are more or less true likenesses while the popular portrayals of cliché Russian stereotypes are not.

Houston, Penelope. "Mr. Deeds and Willie Stark." *S&S* 19 (Nov 50). *See 4d*.

Kolaja, Jiri. "Swedish Feature Films and Swedish Society." *Hwd Q* 5 (No. 2, Winter 50). *See 4e(5b)*.

Grace, Harry A. "Charlie Chaplin's Films and American Culture Patterns." *J Aesthetics and Art Criticism* 10 (No. 4, June 52). *See 5, Charlie Chaplin*.

Jones, Dorothy B. "Foreign Sensibilities." *FIR* 6 (Nov 55) 449–451. Although the 1952 production *Bengal Brigade* was carefully prepared at Universal to meet the expectations of India, it has not been granted a license there.

De La Roche, Catherine. "The Cinema—Mirror of Our Times?" *Film* (No. 11, Jan–Feb 57) 10–14. The various ways in which thriller films, their themes and motifs, might be a reflection of national attitudes.

Atkinson, Alex. "The Dusenberg Place." *Atlantic* 199 (Mar 57). See *3b(4)*.

Dooley, Roger B. "The Irish on the Screen." *FIR* 8 (May 57) 211–217; 8 (June–July 57) 259–270.

Butcher, Maryvonne. "National Traits in Movies." *Commonweal* 68 (22 Aug 58) 513–516.

Schary, Dore. "Our Movie Mythology." *Reporter* 22 (3 Mar 60) 39–42.

Shatnoff, Judith. "The Warmer Comrade." *FQ* 20 (No. 1, Fall 66) 28–34. "Images of political necessity" change over the years: "Soviet success has been simultaneously acknowledged and disparaged" in *Dr. Zhivago* and *The Russians Are Coming.*

Safilios-Rothschild, C. " 'Good' and 'Bad' Girls in Modern Greek Movies." *J Marriage & Family* 30 (Aug 68). See *4e(7)*.

Durgnat, Raymond. "The 'Yellow Peril' Rides Again." *F Soc Rev* 5 (No. 2, 1969) 36–40. Brief notes on the Oriental image in several films.

Young, Vernon. "Movies and National Character." *F&F* 15 (No. 5, Feb 69) 15–20. Films that reflect the country of their origin.

Friedman, Norman L. "American Movies and American Culture, 1946–1970." *J Pop Cult* 3 (No. 4, Spring 70). See *4d*.

Holtan, Orley. "The Agrarian Myth in *Midnight Cowboy, Alice's Restaurant, Easy Rider,* and *Medium Cool.*" *J Pop Cult* 4 (No. 1, Summer 70) 273–285.

Cohen, Larry. "America as Film, Film as America." *Art in America* 58 (Sep 70) 68–73. Current films use the national landscape (*Midnight Cowboy, Petulia, Easy Rider, Medium Cool*).

7a(2). STEREOTYPES: MINORITIES, WOMEN, CHILDREN

[See also 2b(7), 4k(11).]

Davidman, Joy. "Women: Hollywood Version." *New Masses* 44 (14 July 42) 28–31. Hollywood films are full of "male chauvinism" despite the fact that sexual equality is one of the democratic aims of the war.

Humboldt, Charles. "Caricature by Hollywood." *New Masses* 44 (28 July 42) 29–30. Movies distort the position of women in America and ignore their fight for social equality, thus helping to maintain their inferior status.

Goodman, Ezra. "Hollywood and Minorities." *Asia* 43 (Jan 43) 34–35.

Trumbo, D. "Minorities and the Screen." *Arts & Arch* 61 (No. 2, Feb 44) 16–17+.

"Attack Movie Stereotypes of Minorities." *Chris Cent* 63 (18 Dec 46) 1525. Several films draw criticism for contributing to racial caricature.

Ager, Cecilia. "Women Only." *Mlle* (Apr 47) 234+. The woman's picture.

Robertson, E. Arnot. "Women and the Film." *Penguin F Rev* 3 (Aug 47). See *4e(1b)*.

Chandler, David. "The Corporate Author: An Essay in Literary Criticism." *Screen Writer* 3 (Dec 47) 45–47. A satirical essay on the recurring clichés in Hollywood films resulting from different studio attitudes toward mothers, women, heroes, etc.

De La Roche, Catherine. "That 'Feminine Angle.'" *Penguin F Rev* 8 (Jan 49) 25–34. The difference of potential appeal to men and women in film audiences; the star system.

Whitman, Howard. "What Hollywood Doesn't Know About Women." *Collier's* 123 (5 Mar 49) 18–19+. On Hollywood's "ideal woman."

Tyler, Parker. "The Film: Revival of the Matriarchic Spirit." *Accent* 11 (No. 2, 1952) 104–112. A discussion of some films emphasizing female wisdom and initiative.

Edward, Roy. "The Fifth Columnists." *S&S* 23 (July–Sep 53) 21–23+. "It is a mistake to believe, as most people do, that children are innocent, lovable, and amusing. It would be more true to say that they are dangerous fifth columnists, they love only themselves or others of their own breed." The portrayal of children in three films: *Zéro de Conduite* (Vigo), *Jeux Interdits* (Clement), and *Los Olvidados* (Buñuel).

Spears, Jack. "The Indian on the Screen." *FIR* 10 (Jan 59) 18–35. Either a stereotyped villain or a stereotyped noble savage: a lengthy survey of Hollywood's portrayal of the American Indian from approximately 1908 through 1958; some of the better-known American Indian actors.

Dyer, Peter John. "The Face of the Goddess." *F&F* 5 (No. 9, June 59). See *4d*.

Dyer, Peter John. "Youth and the Cinema (1): The Teenage Rave." *S&S* 29 (Winter 59–60) 26–30. How Hollywood sets about reaching the teenager and the image it presents of him; the James Dean cult of the 1950s: *Gidget, High School Confidential, Blue Denim,* and *The Young Stranger.*

Neiss, Laura. "Teen-agers of America, Arise!" *Seventeen* 22 (Jan 63). See *4k(9)*.

Peterson, Sidney. "You Can't Pet a Chicken." *Atlantic* 211 (Mar 63) 126–129. Study of child cult, corresponding to primitivism; early and late Disney; the animated cartoon and the audience.

Lapinski, Susan. "In My Opinion." *Seventeen* 25 (Mar 66). *See 4k(9).*

Gough-Yates, Kevin. "The Heroine." *F&F* 12 (Nos. 8–11, May–Aug 66). *See 7a(5).*

Friar, Ralph. "White Man Speaks with Split Tongue, Forked Tongue, Tongue of Snake." *F Lib* Q 3 (No. 1, Winter 69–70) 16–23+. A history of Hollywood's presentation of the American Indian in film, followed by annotated filmography of recent pro-Indian pictures (by William Vickrey).

7a(3). BLACK EXPERIENCE

[See also 1a(5), 2b(7), 4k(11).]

Delehanty, Thornton. "Reform in Movieland." *Negro Dig* 1 (Jan 43) 63–65. Brief description of a projected all-black cast film, *Thanks, Pal,* to be directed by William Le Baron; news of other forthcoming films about Negroes.

Foster, Joseph. "Hollywood and the Negro." *New Masses* 53 (28 Oct 44) 28–29. Hollywood has always falsified its portrait of the Negro, but change is beginning because of the appearance of screenwriters who care and because of the impetus of the war.

Hardwick, Leon H. "Negro Stereotypes on the Screen." *Hwd Q* 1 (No. 2, Jan 46) 234–236. Brief historical note, with list of eleven recent films.

Weisman, A. "He Passed as a Negro." *Negro Dig* 9 (Oct 51). *See 9, Lost Boundaries.*

Cameron, Earl. "Negro in Cinema." *F&F* 3 (No. 8, May 57) 9–11. Historical study.

Vaughn, Jimmy. "The Dark Continent in the Wrong Light." *F&F* 5 (No. 4, Jan 59). *See 4g.*

Dworkin, Martin S. "The New Negro on the Screen." *Progressive* 24 (Oct 60) 39–41, (Nov 60) 33–36, (Dec 60) 34–36 and 25 (Jan 61) 36–38. A more idealized picture emerges in the 1950s.

"Hollywood and the Negro." *New Rep* 145 (11 Dec 61) 5. NAACP pressure on industry for more Negro roles.

Sidney, P. Jay. "Anti-Negro Propaganda in Films." *Vision [Film Comment]* 1 (No. 1, Spring 62) 22–23. As servants, as "problems," or even if excluded, the Negro role in America is distorted.

Williams, Robert. "Stereotypes of Negroes in Film." *F Com* 1 (No. 2, Summer 62) 67–69. Based on notes for Chicago University Documentary Film Group series.

Cripps, Thomas R. "The Reaction of the Negro to the Motion Picture *Birth of a Nation.*" *Historian* 25 (May 63) 244–262. Protests and riots led to cuts in the film in some cities.

Sloan, William J. "The Documentary Film and the Negro: The Evolution of the Integration Film." *J Soc Cin* 5 (1965). *See 8c(2b).*

Johnson, Albert. "The Negro in American Films: Some Recent Works." *FQ* 18 (No. 4, Summer 65) 14–30. Close analysis of several films, including *Lilies of the Field, The Cool World,* and *Nothing But a Man;* many others mentioned.

Sugy, Catherine. "Black Men or Good Niggers?" *Take One* 1 (No. 8, 1967) 18–21. A discussion of race and racism in recent films.

Cripps, Thomas R. "Death of Rastus: Negroes in American Films Since 1945." *Phylon* 28 (Fall 67) 267–275. Censorship is one of the most persistent influences on the maintenance of cinema stereotypes.

Boyd, Malcolm. "The Hollywood Negro: Changing Image." *Chris Cent* 84 (6 Dec 67) 1560–1561. Sidney Poitier; earlier films about Negroes.

Madsen, Axel. "The Race Race!! or Too Late Blues." *Take One* 1 (No. 11, 1968) 16–17. Some films dealing with Negro themes or directed by Negroes; *Uptight* and *The Learning Tree.*

Bigby, John. "Fade to Black." *Take One* 1 (No. 12, 1968). *See 1a(4).*

Neal, Larry. "Film and the Black Cultural Revolution." *Arts in Soc* 5 (No. 2, Summer–Fall 68) 348–350. A call for black film makers to record the black experience.

Madsen, Axel. "Too Late Blues." *S&S* 37 (Autumn 68) 184. Controversies over black violence (*Uptight,* in production) and black history (*Confessions of Nat Turner,* purchased by David Wolper).

Cripps, T. R. "Movies in the Ghetto." *Negro Dig* 18 (Feb 69) 21–27+.

Stein, Ruthe. *"Uptight." Cinéaste* 2 (No. 4, Spring 69) 4–5+. Notes on blacks in contemporary film; special emphasis on Dassin's *Uptight*—part of an issue largely devoted to both blacks in film and the black film maker.

"NCOMP Charges Hollywood Lacks Black Sensitivity." *Chris Cent* 86 (10 Sep 69). *See 7c(2b).*

Cripps, Thomas R. "Paul Robeson and the Black Identity in Movies." *Mass Rev* 11 (1970) 468–485.

Nelsen, Anne K., and M. Hart. "The Prejudicial Film: Progress and Stalemate, 1915–1967." *Phylon* 31 (1970) 142–147. Comparison of *The Birth of a Nation* and *Hurry Sundown.*

Chelminski, R. " 'Cotton' Cashes In." *Life* 69 (28 Aug 70). *See 9, Cotton Comes to Harlem.*

7a(4). PROFESSIONAL IMAGES

[See also 4k(7).]

Kirstein, Lincoln. "Cagney and the American Hero." *Hound & Horn* 5 (Apr 32). See 5, *James Cagney.*

Cooper, E. Newbold. "College in the Movies." *School and Society* 40 (17 Nov 34) 664–665. Claims college life in movies ludicrous.

"Hollywood in the Bronx." *Time* 35 (29 Jan 40). *See 4d(2).*

Lafferty, H. M. "Hollywood Versus the School Teacher." *School and Society* 62 (11 Aug 45) 92–94. It seems that all vocations are treated glamorously on the screen, except for school teachers; a plea for a change.

Fearing, Franklin. "The Screen Discovers Psychiatry." *Hwd Q* 1 (No. 2, Jan 46) 154–158. In *Spellbound* and *Love Letters,* for example.

Phinney, Milt. "Please Quit Libeling Us." *Screen Writer* 1 (Mar 46) 32–37. A complaint about the false and degraded image of newspapermen in feature films.

Grinker, Roy E., and John P. Spiegel. "The Returning Soldier: A Dissent." *Hwd Q* 1 (No. 3, Apr 46) 321–328. Authors attacked by Franklin Fearing (No. 1, Oct 45) 97–109—listed in *4k(12)*—defend their book *Men Under Stress* and suggest he is too devoted to theory to know how the men really feel; in reply Fearing says they are only concerned with a minority of clinical cases.

Tyler, Parker. "Schizophrenic Motifs in the Movies: The Comedic Use of the Retarded Mental Reflex." *Sewanee Rev* 54 (July 46) 489–503.

Smith, Theodore. "A Factual Study of Judges, Lawyers, etc. in Motion Pictures of 1946." *Am Bar Assoc J* 33 (No. 7, 1947) 649.

Fearing, Franklin. "Psychology and the Films." *Hwd Q* 2 (No. 2, Jan 47) 118–121. Doubts about a recent cycle of films in which psychiatrists are all-wise or insane.

Kubie, Lawrence S. "Psychiatry and the Films." *Hwd Q* 2 (No. 2, Jan 47) 113–117. Dangers of portraying dreams on the screen.

Bruce, Margaret B. "Librarians à la Hollywood." *Wilson Lib Bul* 22 (May 48) 692–693. She is tired of Hollywood's view of librarians and others.

"Doctors as Hollywood Sees Them." *Sci Dig* 34 (Oct 53) 60. British medical journal's comments on the unorthodoxy of their diagnoses.

Tyler, Parker. "Hollywood: The Artist Portrayed and Betrayed." *Art News* 52 (Feb 54) 30–33. How popular myths and stereotypes control the treatment of Toulouse-Lautrec and his art in John Huston's *Moulin Rouge;* other examples cited, Gauguin in *The Moon and Sixpence,* Michelangelo in *The Titan, et al.*

Dworkin, M. S. "Movie Psychiatrics." *Antioch Rev* 14 (Dec 54) 484–491. Films misinform by oversimplifying and incorrectly using psychological terminology.

Spears, Jack. "The Doctor on the Screen." *FIR*

6 (Nov 55) 436–444. Medical stories (about a hundred) have usually been successful; historical survey. See also letter 6 (Dec 55) 542.

"Preacher Is Not Exhibit A." *Chris Cent* 73 (4 Apr 56) 413. Hollywood accused of bias against Protestantism.

Connor, Edward. "The Composer on the Screen." *FIR* 7 (Apr 56) 164–170. A survey of films, domestic and foreign, depicting the lives of famous composers, appraising their authenticity.

Feinstein, Herbert. "Lana, Marlene, Greta, et al.: The Defense Rests." *FQ* 12 (No. 1, Fall 58) 30–34. How Hollywood mangles courtroom procedure.

"These Films Delve into the Shadows." *F&F* 5 (No. 2, Nov 58) 8+. View by a psychiatrist of film's treatment of psychiatry.

Hirsch, Walter. "The Image of the Scientist in Science Fiction: A Content Analysis." *Am J of Sociology* 63 (59) 506–512.

Holland, Norman N. "Psychiatry in Pselluloid." *Atlantic* 203 (Feb 59) 105–107. Critical view of psychoanalysis in the movies and a satire suggesting what the Western is likely to become if the trend goes on.

Schwartz, J. "The Portrayal of Educators in Motion Pictures 1950–1958." *J Educ Soc* 34 (1960) 82–90.

Fine, Benjamin. "Does Hollywood Hate Teachers?" *JSPG* (Mar 62) 7–10. Stereotyped images of teachers could be changed by the power of Hollywood.

7a(5). HEROES, HEROINES, VILLAINS

[See also 2b(6).]

Vesselo, Arthur. "Villains, Heroes, and Hobgoblins." *S&S* 7 (No. 25, Spring 38) 14–16. The function of villainy and heroism in the viewer's response to a film.

Farber, M. "Hero in American Movies." *New Rep* 109 (18 Oct 43) 521–523.

Houseman, John. "Today's Hero: A Review." *Hwd Q* 2 (No. 2, Jan 47) 161–163. The "tough" movie has no "moral energy" and may represent the "neurotic personality" of the USA in 1947; *The Big Sleep* a current example; see also response by Lester Asheim 2 (No. 4, July 47) 414–416.

Nugent, Frank S. "Calvalcade of Hollywood Heroes." *NYTM* (4 May 47) 12–13+. A survey of the male hero type from Charles Ray to Bogart's Philip Marlowe.

Asheim, Lester. "The Film and the Zeitgeist." *Hwd Q* 2 (No. 4, July 47) 414–416. Social scientist objects to article by John Houseman in 2 (No. 2, Jan 47) 161–163 criticizing "tough" movies as representing the "neurotic personality" of the USA and calls attention to "the whole universe of the popular film" as a better guide; see also Houseman rejoinder in 3 (No. 1, Fall 47) 89–90.

Deming, Barbara. "The Villain-Hero: I." *FIR* 2 (Mar 51) 32–36. An analysis of the role of the protagonist in *Dragonwyck* (1946), *Undercurrent* (1946), and *The Strange Love of Martha Ivers* (1946).

Deming, Barbara. "Non-Heroic Heroes: II." *FIR* 2 (Apr 51) 32–38. Condensed from *Running Away from Myself* (Grossman, 1969) in which the author analyzes *None But the Lonely Heart* (1944) and *It's a Wonderful Life* (1946).

Tynan, Kenneth. "Cagney and the Mob." *S&S* 20 (May 51) 12–16. It was an artistic triumph to reject the humorless black villain and the pure hero; yet Cagney, with his charm which allows us to believe it was really not his fault, has accidentally become a corrupting influence.

Houston, Penelope. "The Heroic Fashion." *S&S* 21 (Oct–Dec 51) 61–63. Some comments on the pure heroes of old, who fought real enemies for simple causes, and did so without words; the Hemingway influence has been strongly felt; British heroes, heroes during the war, the postwar hero, and the ever-sacrosanct Western hero.

Halsey, E. "Defective as Movie Hero." *Commonweal* 55 (8 Feb 52) 444–445. Movies such as *A Place in the Sun* and *A Streetcar Named Desire* are decadent: such films no longer portray "representative man" but the neurotic fool in a villainous society. Discussion 55 (29 Feb 52) 518–520, (14 Mar 52) 568–569.

Fishwick, M. "Aesop in Hollywood: The Man and the Mouse." *Sat Rev* 37 (10 July 54) 7–9. Fairbanks and Mickey Mouse—two American heroes manufactured in Hollywood.

Elkin, Fred. "Popular Hero Symbols and Audience Gratifications." *J Educ Psych* 29 (1955) 97–107.

Weales, Gerald. "The Crazy, Mixed-Up Kids Take Over." *Reporter* 15 (13 Dec 56) 40–41. New movie heroes Dean, Brando, Presley.

Brustein, Robert. "America's New Culture Hero." *Commentary* 25 (No. 2, 1958) 123–129. Marlon Brando's roles and other rebels in film; they are more conformist than they seem.

Cole, Clayton. "The Breeding Boys." *F&F* 5 (No. 9, June 59) 26–27+. Film heroes since World War II.

Alexander, A. J. "A Modern Hero: The Non-genue." *F Cult* (Nos. 22–23, 1961) 81–91. The emergence of a bonafide modern film hero—the female—which has "reached its fullest expression in *Room at the Top, The Fugitive Kind,* and *Hiroshima Mon Amour.*

Stanbrook, Alan. "The Heroes of Welles." *Film* (No. 28, Mar–Apr 61). See 5, *Orson Welles.*

Lewis, Richard Warren. "Hollywood's New Breed of Soft Young Men." *SEP* 235 (1 Dec 62). See 2b(2).

Trachtenberg, S. "The Hustler as Hero." *Antioch Rev* 22 (Winter 62–63) 427–434. Robert Rossen's *The Hustler* and other American films.

"An International Survey on the Film Hero." *International Soc Sci J* 15 (1963) 113–119. Changes in French, Yugoslav, and Polish hero images.

Gilliatt, Penelope. "The Hollywood Nursery." *Harper's* 226 (June 63) 87–90. The infantilism of Hollywood heroines.

Steene, Birgitta. "The Isolated Hero of Ingmar Bergman." *F Com* 3 (No. 2, Spring 65) 68–78. Exegesis of *Seventh Seal, Wild Strawberries, Through a Glass Darkly,* and *Winter Light.*

Stewart-Gordon, James. "007—The Spy with the Golden Touch." *Rdrs Dig* 87 (Oct 65). See 4k(10).

Gough-Yates, Kevin. "The Hero." *F&F* 12 (No. 3, Dec 65) 11–16; (No. 4, Jan 66) 11–16. Study of the hero in films, epic, romantic, and Byronic.

Gough-Yates, Kevin. "The Hero." *F&F* 12 (No. 5, Feb 66) 23–30; (No. 6, Mar 66) 25–30. In film: the unwilling hero, the antihero, the tragic hero; two articles.

Gough-Yates, Kevin. "The Heroine." *F&F* 12 (No. 8, May 66) 23–27; (No. 9, June 66) 27–32; (No. 10, July 66) 38–43; (No. 11, Aug 66) 45–50. The heroine as possessor of masculine traits in times of crisis; yet happiness never comes for the woman when she takes over male role; the antiheroine; the "good-bad" girl and the fallen angel; four articles.

Whitehall, Richard. "The Heroes Are Tired." *FQ* 20 (No. 2, Winter 66–67). See 4k(2).

Carpenter, Richard G. "007 and the Myth of the Hero." *J Pop Cult* 1 (No. 2, 1967). See 4k(10).

King, Larry. "Battle of Popcorn Bay." *Harper's* 234 (May 67) 50–54. Heroes in World War II films.

Farber, Stephen. "The Outlaws." *S&S* 37 (Autumn 68) 170–176. A long study of the criminal heroes of John Boorman's *Point Blank,* Penn's *Bonnie and Clyde,* and Richard Brooks' *In Cold Blood;* not social message but social despair is in these films.

Saud, Mark. "The Hero in Contemporary Cinema." *Medium* 1 (No. 2, Winter 67–68) 2–14. The film hero as the contemporary folk hero.

Carson, L. M. Kit. "The Loser Hero." *Show* (Jan 70). See 4k.

7b. Audiences and Effects

7b(1). WHAT THE AUDIENCE WANTS

[See also 1a, 3a(4), 6a.]

"Movies and the Eyesight." *Lit Dig* 108 (21 Mar 31) 24. Conditions of viewing may cause eye irritation.

Ferguson, Otis. "Doldrum Weather." *New Rep* 96 (31 Aug 38) 104–105. What the movie audience is like—free, happy, likely to be raucous sometimes, not bound by tradition.

Hauser, Arnold. "Notes on the Sociology of the Film." *Life & Letters Today* (Dec 38) 80–87. The cinema audience expects a romantic and reassuring view of society.

Bell, Oliver. "Sociological Aspects of the Cinema." *Nature* 144 (1939) 520. Need for more research on audiences.

Crowther, Bosley. "Reality or Escape." *NYTM* (14 June 42) 16–17. Some guides to public taste for films during wartime.

Crowther, Bosley. "Movies Follow the Flag." *NYTM* (13 Aug 44) 18–19. The efforts to show films to soldiers overseas.

Finch, P. "No Show Tonight." *SEP* (18 Nov 44) 6. Vignette of films shown to sailors in wartime.

Montani, A., and G. Pietranera. "First Contribution to the Psycho-analysis and Aesthetics of Motion-Pictures." *Psychoanalytic Rev* 33 (No. 2, 1946) 177–196. Possible psychoanalytic basis of the motion picture and its appeal to individuals and groups.

Gordon, Jay E. "Operation Celluloid." *Hwd Q* 2 (No. 4, July 47) 416–419. German prisoners of war in the U.S. were shown feature films; the top ten favorites included two dog stories.

"Convicts See a Movie of Their Own Escape." *Life* 25 (2 Aug 48). *See 9, Canon City.*

Hodgins, Eric. "What's with the Movies?" *Life* 26 (16 May 49) 97–106. Panel discussions by critics, scholars, exhibitors, and consumers on the relationship of film to its audience.

Elkin, Frederick. "The Psychological Appeal of the Hollywood Western." *J Educ Soc* 24 (No. 1, Sep 50). *See 4k(2).*

Prindeville, Trego. "Movies and the G.I." *FIR* 4 (Oct 53) 405–409. Viewing films in Korea, especially films about that war (*Retreat, Hell*).

Everson, William K. "Audience Reactions." *FIR* 7 (Dec 56) 513–517+. The varying responses to different genres of films by ethnic and cultural groups (Germany, England, New York).

Geltzer, George. "The Deaf and the Talkies." *FIR* 8 (Aug–Sep 57) 315–319. As told to Frank Leon Smith. A firsthand appraisal of the 120,000 deaf members of the American theatregoing and TV audience.

Kraft, Richard. "Others Seats Than Mine." *NY F Bul* 1 (No. 8, 1960) 4–7. A humorous article on the types of audiences which attend old movies in New York.

"First Movies: A Poll." *Show* 3 (Apr 63) 79–80. Prominent Americans describe their first movie experiences; remarks from Dean Rusk, Pierre Salinger, Walker Percy, *et al.*

Gans, H. J. "The Rise of the Problem-Film: An Analysis of Changes in Hollywood Films and the American Audience." *Social Problems* 11 (No. 4, 1964) 327–335. A wide-ranging discussion guessing at how production decisions are made based on responses to "subcultures" in the audience: this explains the "increase" in problem pictures.

"Movies: The Big Flick Kick." *Look* 29 (9 Mar 65). *See 4a(2).*

Hosie, S. W. "Have You Seen *Shoes?*" *America* 120 (31 May 69) 651–652. The Catholic audience response to *The Shoes of the Fisherman.*

Durgnat, Raymond. "Art and Audience." *Brit J Aesthetics* 10 (1970) 11–24.

7b(1a). History and Opinions

Jones, Harold Ellis, and Herbert S. Conrad. "Rural Preferences in Motion Pictures." *J Soc Psych* 1 (Aug 30) 419–423. Sees strong Puritanical tradition as reason for adverse criticism of *The Last Laugh* and Charlie Chaplin.

Orton, William. "But Is It Art?" *Atlantic* 149 (May 32) 586–597. Appeal to producers to recognize artistic taste of audiences.

"Give the Public a Chance." *SRL* 10 (14 July 34) 804. Public really wants value in films, not shocking sensation.

"Battle at the Box Office." *Collier's* 94 (11 Aug 34) 54. Better films will be given to audiences demanding them.

"Screen Morals." *New S&N* 8 (17 Nov 34) 712–713. Enjoyment of Harold Lloyd's *The Catspaw* seen as a farcical fulfillment of audience's common wish to be powerful.

Depinet, Ned E. "Movies and the Public: The Position of the Film Producer." *Rotarian* 48 (Feb 36) 37–44. It's a complex business, at the mercy of the whims of the audience.

Vijaya-Tunga, J. "The Pavilion of Purple Light." *S&S* 7 (No. 27, Autumn 38) 109–110. The author's personal experiences in film viewing lead him to believe that the cinema appeals to the inherent laziness in man.

Cookman, M. "What Do Women of America

Think About Entertainment?" *Ladies' Home J* 56 (Feb 39) 63–64.

Lewin, W. "Movie Audience Behavior." *Scholastic Life* 25 (Mar 40) 162. A decalogue based on student discussions and suggestions.

Mayer, A. L. "Who Wants Good Movies?" *Nation* 150 (20 Apr 40) 511–512. The view that the releasing of good movies (e.g., socially oriented as opposed to escapist) depends upon the general moviegoing public; written at the time such social commentaries as *The Grapes of Wrath* and *Of Mice and Men* were released.

Dieterle, William. "What the Public Thinks It Wants." *Calif Arts and Arch* 57 (No. 6, June–July 40) 21+. Censorship, the economics of the motion-picture industry, and the future of quality films.

Glenn, Charles. "Box Office Revolt." *New Masses* 36 (16 July 40) 30–31. The people are rejecting war films, but this does not mean they want escape films.

Bergman, L. "Added Feature: The Movie Audience." *NYTM* (1 Dec 40) 9. A humorous psychological study of the movie audience.

Foster, Joseph. "Whose Bad Taste?" *New Masses* 57 (6 Nov 45) 30–31. Bosley Crowther's argument that the movie audience does not want honest, realistic films is nonsense and betrays his class bias.

Powdermaker, Hortense. "An Anthropologist Looks at the Movies." *Annals of Am Acad of Polit and Soc Sci* (1947) 80–87. Films substitute for real relationships in a lonely society.

Borneman, E. W. G. "Public Opinion Myth." *Harper's* 195 (July 47) 30–40. Alexander Korda and the author both object to Hollywood's total servitude to audience research.

Gassner, John. "Theatre Arts." *Forum* 108 (Nov 47) 315–319. The English tax on U.S. film prompts this examination of Hollywood and its failure to relate properly to the public.

Taylor, G. R. "What the Film Public Wants." *New S&N* 35 (28 Feb 48) 171–172. Questions mentality of general cinema audience.

Seldes, G. "How Dense Is the Mass?" *Atlantic* 182 (Nov 48) 23–27. A call to make movies once more for the "grown-up" audience, thereby restoring good box office.

Reisman, Leon. "Cinema Technique and Mass Culture." *Am Q* 1 (No. 4, 1949) 314–325. Needs and desires the movies fulfill for their audiences, not so much through story as by methods of execution.

Mauerhofer, Hugo. "Psychology of Film Experience." *Penguin F Rev* 8 (Jan 49) 103–109. There is therapy in escape from everyday reality.

"What's Wrong with the Movies?" *Time* 53 (28 Feb 49) 88. An exhibitor's poll shows that people think movies are too highbrow,

not "wholesome" enough, not Protestant-oriented.

"The Power of a Woman." *Time* 54 (14 Nov 49) 101. Hollywood's box-office slips blamed on underestimating the power of a woman.

Tyler, P. "Lament for the Audience—and a Mild Bravo." *Kenyon Rev* 12 (No. 4, 1950) 689–696. Elements which make up an enlightened film audience confined to limited minority in New York City.

"Women and the Box Office." *Good Housekeeping* 130 (May 50) 16–17+. Some new films predicted to be hits because of women.

"What the Public Wants." *Time* 58 (23 July 51) 82. Exhibitors as guides to public taste.

Sisk, J. P. "Passion in a New Dimension!" *Commonweal* 59 (23 Oct 53). *See 2m(1)*.

Palmer, C. A. "Commercial Practices in Audience Analysis." *JUFPA* 6 (No. 3, Spring 54) 9–10. Producer of factual film criticizes various methods of predicting responses to fiction and nonfiction films, urging early concern about the objective, the right audience, the "residual impression," whenever a film is intended as a tool.

Fenin, George N. "Motion Pictures and the Public." *F Cult* 1 (No. 1, 1955) 15–18. The author argues for a revision of the mercantile mentality of the American motion-picture industry and a greater respect for public taste.

Skinner, John. "Censorship in Films and Dreams." *Am Imago* 12 (1955) 223–240. Repetition of myth-making activity provides temporary release for audience.

"Movies, Literally for the Millions." *America* 92 (12 Mar 55) 606. Statistics on moviegoers, in U.S. and abroad; concern over censorship and protection from crime in the movies.

Schary, Dore. "Why We Don't Always Make 'Family' Movies." *Good Housekeeping* 141 (Sep 55) 44+. Schary's contention that "a family picture is any good picture, regardless of its subject."

Lassally, Walter. "The Cynical Audience." *S&S* 26 (Summer 56) 12–15. Film societies and special cinemas, art houses and the like, have made part of today's audience more appreciative of good films; the author compares the films of the optimistic 1930s with those of the cynical 1950s.

Wald, Jerry. "The Long Sellers." *Lib J* 81 (1 Oct 56) 2131–2134. A study of people's reading habits tells this film producer what direction film entertainment should take.

Watts, Stephen. "The Public Goes for Quality." *JSPG* (Nov 56) 9+. English critic on English tastes in film.

"Wanted, Better Motion Pictures for the Family Trade." *Consumer Bul* 41 (Sep 58) 38+. An editorial.

Wanamaker, Sam. "Facing Facts." *Film* (No.

18, Nov–Dec 58) 6–7. There is a more discriminating audience.

Harmon, Sidney. "Some Ideas on Producing Motion Pictures in 1959." *JSPG* (Sep 59) 7–10. Needed: seminars on subject matter and on the public mind.

Robson, Mark. "Talking to Myself." *JSPG* (Sep 59) 13–14. The public really wants to "go deeper."

Olsen, M. "Motion Picture Attendance and Social Isolation." *Sociological Q* 1 (1960) 107–116. They are closely correlated.

"Will Sex and Violence in Motion Pictures Really Pay Off?" *Consumer Bul* 43 (Feb 60) 32–33. An editorial noting mounting audience discontent over movie sex and violence.

Gibson, John E. "Your Taste in Movies Gives You Away." *Sci Dig* 417 (Mar 60) 63–65. On the relationship of movie preferences and personality.

Kael, Pauline. "Fantasies of the Art House Audience." *S&S* 31 (Winter 61–62). *See 3b(2)*.

Walsh, Moira. "Making Mature Movie Viewers." *America* (3 Nov 62) 978–982. Discussion of proper audience responses to film, and of film artists' obligations to truths which have human value.

Holland, Norman. "The Puzzling Movies: Their Appeal." *J Soc Cin* 3 (1963). *See 3a*.

Nowell-Smith, Geoffrey. "Movie and Myth." *S&S* 32 (Spring 63). *See 3b*.

Kael, Pauline. "The Freedom to Make Product." *New Yorker* 44 (16 Mar 68) 152+. An analysis of the appeal of the movies to an audience.

Kramer, Stanley. "Nine Times Across the Generation Gap." *Action* 3 (No. 2, Mar–Apr 68) 11–13. The American director discusses his visits to nine university campuses and the students' reactions to his latest film, *Guess Who's Coming to Dinner?*

Alpert, Hollis. "*The Graduate* Makes Out." *Sat Rev* 51 (6 July 68) 14–15+. A lengthy study of the phenomenal success of *The Graduate*.

"More Fun Films Wanted, Less Sex and Violence." *Consumer Bul* 51 (Sep 68) 13–14. An editorial.

Schillaci, Anthony. "Film as Environment." *Sat Rev* 15 (28 Dec 68) 8–14+. Youthful American audiences influence the films of the 1960s; dialogue and other literary values rapidly outmoded; youthful film makers also influence evolution of the cinema. Part of *Saturday Review* report "The Now Movie."

Cohen, Larry. "The New Audience: From Andy Hardy to Arlo Guthrie." *Sat Rev* (27 Dec 69) 8–11+. Youth audience for motion pictures has grown and changed. Part of *Saturday Review* report "The Art That Matters."

7b(1b). Surveys

Abbott, Mary Allen. "Motion Picture Preferences of Adults and Children." *School Rev* 41 (Apr 33) 278–283. Experiment shows "definite similarities . . . common sources of enjoyment."

"*Fortune* Survey: Moving Pictures." *Fortune* 13 (Apr 36) 222. About one-fourth of respondents claimed they went to the movies once a week and 13% went more often.

Ford, Richard. "What One Public Says It Likes." *S&S* 6 (No. 22, Summer 37) 70. Questionnaire given to some film audiences in England.

"*Fortune* Survey: Movies and Movie Stars." *Fortune* 16 (July 37) 103–104. Many statistics concerning polls covering cross-sections of the U.S.

Dyer, Ernest. "What Do They Like?" *S&S* 7 (No. 26, Summer 38) 78–79. A questionnaire administered to the Tyneside Film Society.

Hoellering, F. "Films: Reactions of Some Regular Movie-Goers." *Nation* 147 (10 Dec 38) 638–639.

"Boy Meets Facts." *Time* 38 (21 July 41) 73. Findings of the Audience Research Institute (Gallup) contradict Hollywood's claims of audience size and interests.

Lassner, R. "Sex and Age Determinants of Theatre and Movie Interests." *J Gen Psych* 31 (Oct 44) 241–271.

Zanker, R. R. "Children's Likes and Dislikes." *S&S* 13 (No. 51, Oct 44) 73–75. A questionnaire.

"Gallup Gadget: Device for Determining Audience Reaction to Movies." *Bus Wk* (3 Feb 45) 80.

Crowther, Bosley. "It's the Fans Who Make the Films." *NYTM* (24 June 45) 14. Gallup's systematic opinion samplings determine what kinds of films people like best.

Fiske, M., and L. Handel. "Motion Picture Research: Content and Audience Analysis." *J of Marketing* 11 (1946) 129–134.

"Audience Penetration and Want-to-See." *Time* 48 (22 July 46) 94.

Cirlin, B. D., and J. N. Peterman. "Pre-Testing a Motion Picture: A Case History." *J Soc Issues* 3 (1947) 39+. Like/dislike button-pushing and charting.

Doscher, Luelyne. "The Significance of Audience Measurements in Motion Pictures." *J Soc Issues* 3 (1947) 51–57. Criticism of dependence on pretesting likes and dislikes.

Wolff, H. "Pretesting Movies." *Sci Illus* 2 (Feb 47) 44–45.

Shaw, Robert. "Package Deal in Film Opinions." *Screen Writer* 2 (Mar 47) 28–37. On Dr. George Gallup's motion-picture research system, including mechanized audience-reaction testing, and pre-release story, idea, and title testing.

MacDougall, Ronald. "Reactions to Audience Reaction." *Screen Writer* 2 (Apr 47) 29–31. Criticizes the validity of Dr. Gallup's audience research as a basis for decisions on film making (reported in March issue).

"Electric Movie Reviewers Record Reaction to Film." *Pop Mech* 87 (May 47) 149. How audience reactions are wired by rheostats.

Lazarsfeld, Paul F. "Audience Research in the Movie Field." *Annals of Am Acad of Polit and Soc Sci* 254 (Nov 47) 160–168. Structure and characteristics of audiences; how they are surveyed; effects on subsequent films.

Abrams, Mark. "The British Cinema Audience." *Hwd Q* 3 (No. 2, Winter 47–48) 155–158. The young male lower-income film fan is also likely to be a gambler, according to this economist's survey; comparisons with reading habits, class, etc.

Heisler, F. "A Comparison of the Movie and Non-Movie Goers of the Elementary School." *J Educ Research* 41 (1948) 541–546.

"How to Sell a Movie." *Look* 12 (No. 22, 26 Oct 48) 52–55. Audience Research, Inc., run by Dr. George Gallup, pretests the market for the film industry.

"Quarter's Polls on Moving Pictures." *Pub Opin Q* 13 (No. 2, 1949) 359–360. On quality of current motion pictures, attendance patterns, likes/dislikes; response descriptions.

"Public Taste in Entertainment; *Fortune* Survey." *Fortune* 39 (Mar 49) 39–40. General opinion: fewer good movies are being made now than two or three years ago.

Abrams, Mark. "The British Cinema Audience, 1949." *Hwd Q* 4 (No. 3, Spring 50) 251–255. The box-office decline since his earlier article; audience structure not altered.

"Film and Public: *Chance of a Lifetime*." *S&S* 19 (Jan 51) 349–350. A survey taken of one hundred London cinemagoers and what they said about a film, *Chance of a Lifetime*, dealing with factory workers who take over management for a time, but are happy to see the bosses return; the film was denied release by the circuits on the grounds that it was not "box office," but, for the first time, the government stepped in and forced release.

England, Leonard. "The Critics and the Box-office." *S&S* 20 (June 51). See *3b*.

Haley, Jay. "The Appeal of the Moving Picture." *QFRTV* 6 (No. 4, Summer 52) 361–374. Various studies indicate basic desire for escape.

Weales, Gerald. "Pro-Negro Films in Atlanta." *FIR* 3 (Nov 52) 455–462. A New York college graduate from Indiana attempts an objective survey of individual reactions of Southern Negroes and whites to such pictures as *Pinky, Home of the Brave, Intruder in the Dust; Lost Boundaries, Imitation of Life*, and *The Birth of a Nation* were banned by the censor. Reprinted in *Phylon* 13 (Dec 52) 298–304.

Bunn, M. "Back to the Picture Show!" *American* 154 (Dec 52) 34–35+. Exhibitors' survey shows that Bowery Boys and Ma and Pa Kettle are tops with the public.

Handel, Leo A. "Hollywood Market Research." *QFRTV* 7 (No. 3, Spring 53) 304–310. Author of *Hollywood Looks at Its Audience* (University of Illinois, 1950) summarizes measurement methods used, past and present.

Neergaard, Ebbe. "Feature Films Preferred by Danish Youth." *QFRTV* 7 (No. 3, Spring 53). See *4e(5)*.

"Drive-Ins Steal the Show." *Bus Wk* (15 Aug 53). See *6e(2a)*.

Smythe, Dallas W., Parker B. Lusk, and Charles A. Lewis. "Portrait of an Art Theatre Audience." *QFRTV* 8 (No. 1, Fall 53) 28–50. Professor of communications at University of Illinois (and associates) interviewed 728 patrons of the Illini theatre in Champaign-Urbana.

Smythe, Dallas W., John R. Gregory, Alvin Ostrin, Oliver P. Colvin, and William Moroney. "Portrait of a First-Run Audience." *QFRTV* 9 (No. 4, Summer 55) 390–409. Professor of communication research at University of Illinois (and associates) sample a downtown audience and ask how often they attend, which films they like, etc.

"*Pacific Destiny*." *Film* (No. 9, Sep–Oct 56). See *9, Pacific Destiny*.

Sindlinger, Albert E. "The Role for Research." *JSPG* (Nov 56) 6+. Opinion researcher describes his method of gauging "know-about" and intensity of desire to see specific movies; "the public only knows what it wants right after it has been stimulated to want it."

"Why Guess?" *JSPG* (Nov 56) 7+. Universal International's report on the value of opinion research.

Scott, E. M. "Personality and Movie Preference." *Psych Reports* 3 (1957) 17–18. Choice of movies attended is related in many instances to central aspects of personality, as shown in an experiment conducted with university students.

Few, Roger. "What Sends Them?" *S&S* 27 (Winter 57–58) 114. Brief report on 1,000 people who waited in line to see a film in England.

"They Like, and Dislike." *Newswk* 52 (4 Aug 58) 69. Albert E. Sindlinger is public-opinion pollster and business analyst for Hollywood's audiences.

Dumazedier, Joffre. "The Cinema and Popular Culture." *Diogenes* (No. 31, Fall 60) 103–113. Implications of UNESCO survey of audience expectations in Annecy, France; active and passive attitudes to be gauged in other countries.

Rose, Ernest D. "Motion Picture Research and the Art of the Film Maker." *JUFPA* 15 (No. 2, 1963) 8–11+. The role of film theory for the film maker: to explain why certain techniques are more effective than others, to predict audience reactions, and thus to control them; specific studies in audience reactions.

Dronberger, Ilse. "Student Attitudes Toward the Foreign Film." *JUFPA* 17 (No. 1, 1965) 6–9+. Reactions at Indiana University to a series.

Silvey, Robert, and Judy Kenyon. "Why You Go to the Pictures." *F&F* 11 (No. 9, June 65). *See 4e(1c)*.

Anast, Philip. "Differential Movie Appeals as Correlates of Attendance." *Journalism Q* 44 (1967) 86–90. Frequent filmgoers tend to be more interested in sex and violence and also tend to believe in the "reality" of movies.

Hershey, Lenore. "What Women Think of the Movies." *McCall's* 94 (May 67) 28+. Responses to a recent questionnaire.

Wanderer, J. J. "In Defense of Popular Taste: Film Ratings Among Professionals and Lay Audiences." *Am J of Sociology* 76 (Sep 70) 262–272. Presents statistical evidence for a correlation of upper-middle-class taste and critics' taste in evaluating movies.

7b(1c). Fans, Fan Magazines, Columnists

[See also 2b(2).]

Whipple, Leon (ed.). "Toys for Demos." *Survey* 63 (1 Jan 30) 434+. Surveys movie magazines.

"Screen Language." *Am Speech* 11 (Feb 36) 77. Fan magazines seen as source of word coining.

"Hollywood Jargon." *Am Speech* 12 (Apr 37) 161. Movie ads and fan magazines analyzed for new jargon.

Baskette, K. "Angle Worms." *SEP* 210 (11 Sep 37) 22–23. Activities and problems of the Hollywood fan-magazine writers.

"Screen Fans Organize to Bite Hand That Feeds Them Double Features." *Newswk* 10 (4 Oct 37) 25.

Trewin, J. C. "Came the Night!" *S&S* 7 (No. 27, Autumn 38) 105–106. The author's personal account of seeing films for the first time, as a child, in a Cornish village.

Dudley, F. "Usually They Want Something." *Ladies' Home J* 58 (Jan 41) 25+. What happens when movie fans write to their favorites.

Crowther, Bosley. "Those Amazing Movie Fans." *NYTM* (26 Apr 42) 15+. The 500,000 members of fan clubs and their implications for the film industry.

"Vultures of Hollywood: Life Through the Fan Magazine." *Am Mercury* 56 (Mar 43) 345–350. An anonymous "fan-magazine writer"

tells how to "dish out gossip just short of slander."

"Day with Sidney Skolsky: Hollywood Columnist Sees Stars from Dawn to Dark." *Life* 14 (3 May 43) 102–105. Photos of Skolsky with stars.

Crowther, Bosley. "It's the Fans Who Make the Films." *NYTM* (24 June 45).

Benson, B. "Read Your Character by the Stars." *Ladies' Home J* 64 (Mar 47) 76–77+. In listing your favorite movie stars, you reveal your own personality and socio-economic position.

Kahn, G. "The Gospel According to Hollywood." *Atlantic* 179 (May 47) 98–102. Extensive history and analysis of the phenomenon of the movie fan magazine.

"Opinion Leaders." *Time* 51 (12 Apr 48) 100. Trouble for film magazines when the studios cancelled 60% of their advertising in them; fan publications as myth makers.

"Who Is Your Favorite Star? *Companion* Poll." *Woman's Home Companion* 75 (June 48) 7–8. This poll continued with annual reports in June through 1955.

Knepper, Max. "Hollywood's Barkers." *S&S* 19 (Jan 51) 359–362. Report on typical stories and styles in fan magazines and their relationship to the studios.

Hopper, Hedda. *"From Under My Hat." Woman's Home Companion* 79 (Aug 52) 42–43+. Hedda tells about herself and reveals stories she has known about Hollywood stars; excerpt from her book, *From Under My Hat* (Doubleday, 1952).

Sisk, J. P. "Life in the Movie Magazines." *Commonweal* 61 (1955) 634–635.

"Fans Choose." *Newswk* 45 (14 Feb 55) 90. *Photoplay Magazine* announces the results of its popularity poll.

Quirk, Lawrence J. "Quirk of *Photoplay*." *FIR* 6 (Mar 55) 97–107. The life and career of James R. Quirk, first managing editor of *Photoplay,* with cited testimony of their association with Quirk by such notables as Louella Parsons, Robert E. Sherwood, and Terry Ramsaye.

Sisk, J. P. "Life in the Movie Magazines." *Commonweal* 61 (18 Mar 55) 634–635. Regardless of their worthlessness, these publications provide for our psychological needs.

Baker, Peter. "When Private Lives Are Public Property." *F&F* 3 (No. 6, Mar 57) 12. MGM makes *Slander,* about magazines that prey on movie stars' activities.

"The Polite Inquisitor." *Newswk* 49 (17 June 57) 75. Joe Hyams of *The New York Herald Tribune,* one of the 350 Hollywood correspondents.

Tupper, Lucy. "The Gentle Influence." *FIR* 9 (Oct 58) 434–442. How the author was encouraged by her moviegoing to read books films were based on, admire the stars, and become aware of social problems.

Dickens, Homer, *et al.* "Unforgotten Movie Scenes." *FIR* 10 (Feb 59) 100–106. Fans send in a symposium of favorite scenes from past films.

Farber, Manny. "The Fading Movie Star." *Commentary* 36 (July 63) 55–60. The evolution of movies in the last ten years has brought about the disappearance of the mysterious interactions between actors and fans.

Roseman, Eugene. "In My Opinion." *Seventeen* 26 (Feb 67). *See 4k(10).*

Reisner, Joel. "The Cinematic Acolyte." *Cinema* (Calif) 5 (No. 4, 1969) 13. The new movie "fan."

Fane, Marlene. "Writing for the Fan Magazine Field." *Writer's Dig* 49 (May 69) 36–40. Tips by the editor of *Movie Life.*

Amory, Cleveland. "Trade Winds." *Sat Rev* 52 (12 July 69) 8–9. The Sons of the Desert, a Laurel and Hardy fan club, honoring the comedy team.

Valentino, Lon. "For Love of Lana." *Show* (Jan 70) 72–74. Comments on Lana Turner from film buff with a collection of 20,000 photographs of her.

7b(2). INFLUENCE AND EFFECTS OF FILMS

[*See also 3a(6), 4k(11).*]

"That Slim Movie Figure." *Lit Dig* 115 (27 May 33) 23. Scientists suggest boyish female figure popular because of projection distortion.

"The Influence of Motion Pictures on Interiors." *Calif Arts and Arch* 50 (Nov 36). *See 2k(1).*

Hampton, E. L. "1,200-Mile Style Parade; World's Style Capital Moved to Hollywood." *Nation's Business* 25 (Apr 37) 78+. How the movies have initiated apparel and furniture and fixture trends.

Cressey, P. "The Motion Picture Experience as Modified by Social Background and Personality." *Am Sociological Rev* 3 (1938) 516–525. What the audience brings to the movies.

"Film and Radio Gleanings." *Am Speech* 13 (Oct 38) 139–140. Comments on film and radio as source of slang.

Thorpe, M. "Hollywood Sets the Style." *Current Hist* 51 (Nov 39) 35–37. The influences of Hollywood on national customs—from dress to toys.

Sondern, F., and C. N. Schrader. "Hollywood Handles Dynamite." *Commonweal* 35 (12 Dec 41) 195–197. The influence of Hollywood on fashions, manners, speech, and general behavior—and potentially on politics, morals, and important social questions.

"Why the Movies Are Influencing American

Taste." *House Beautiful* 84 (July 42). *See 2k(2).*

Stuhl, D. M. "Movies for Shut-Ins." *Recreation* (Dec 43) 19–20. The effect, particularly recuperative, of films on audiences; Volunteer Film Organization discussed.

"New March of Time Program Features Books." *Publishers Weekly* 146 (28 Oct 44). *See 8b(2).*

Morton, Lawrence. "Chopin's New Audience." *Hwd Q* 1 (No. 1, Oct 45). *See 4k(6).*

Crocker, H. "Assignment in Hollywood." *Good Housekeeping* 122 (Mar 46). *See 2k(2).*

Schlichter, Karl. "The Irresponsibles." *Screen Writer* 1 (Mar 46) 21–26. Describes the portrayal of diseases in films such as *A Song to Remember* and *The Bells of St. Mary's;* people are misguided in the handling of their own ailments.

Shearer, L. "The Three Most Popular Movie Sets of the Last Twenty Years and What They Mean." *House Beautiful* 88 (Dec 46). *See 2k(2).*

Wall, W. D. "Notes in Passing." *Arts & Arch* 72 (May 55) 11+. How little we know about the effect the cinema exerts on the daily lives of people.

Gehman, Richard. "The Hollywood Horrors." *Cosmopolitan* 145 (Nov 58). *See 4k(3).*

"Happy Inventions." *House and Garden* 121 (Jan 62). *See 2k(2).*

7b(2a). Opinions

"The Moral Movies." *Commonweal* 11 (8 Jan 30) 270. Questions whether movies are positive deterrent to crime and wrongdoing.

Hays, Will H. "The Movies Are Helping America." (Ed. by Campbell MacCulloch.) *Good Housekeeping* 96 (Jan 33) 44–45+. Movies spread knowledge and are improving morally.

Schire, David. "The Psychology of Film Audiences." *S&S* 2 (No. 8, Winter 33–34). *See 8c(1).*

Blumer, H. "The Molding of Mass Behavior Through the Motion Picture." *Pub of Am Soc Society* 29 (1936) 115–127. The tendency is to separate the individual from group mores (unlike folk tales).

Quigley, M. "Public Opinion and the Motion Picture." *Pub Opin Q* 1 (1937) 129+. They influence each other.

Phillips, H. A. "Movies Move the World." *Rotarian* 52 (June 38) 23–26. The influence of movies on habits and fashions.

Loveman, Amy. "Knowledge and the Image." *SRL* 28 (8 Feb 41) 8. A defense of the educational potential of the film medium as an aid to reading.

Frakes, Margaret. "Drinking in the Movies." *Chris Cent* 60 (17 Mar 43) 325–327. Drinking in films wrongly influences young viewers and foreign audiences.

Mealand, Richard. "Books into Films: Increasing Influence of the Picture." *Publishers Weekly* 148 (6 Oct 45) 1674. In praise of the salutary influence of movies on the reading and thinking habits of the public.

Perry, E. L. "Hollywood: Postwar Challenge." *CSMM* (8 Dec 45) 6. Films can help the world, but will this influence be viewed as propaganda?

Road, Sinclair. "The Influence of the Film." *Penguin F Rev* 1 (6 Aug 46) 57–65. Film has an educational job to do, in and out of theatres throughout the world; new developments at UNESCO and elsewhere.

Cohen, Elliott. "Letter from a Movie Maker." *Commentary* 4 (1947) 344–349. Does *Crossfire* backfire by presenting anti-Semitism?

Miller, Carl G. "Our Hollywood Competitors." *Education* 67 (Feb 47) 396. A deploring look at Hollywood's sometimes unfortunate influence on youth and adults.

Fearing, Franklin. "The Influence of the Movies on Attitudes and Behavior." *Annals of Am Acad of Polit and Soc Sci* (Nov 47) 70–79. Psychological and social implications of the link between movies and audiences; symbolism and social strata.

Johnston, Eric. "Motion Picture as a Stimulus to Culture." *Annals of Am Acad of Polit and Soc Sci* 254 (Nov 47) 98–102.

Quigley, Martin. "The Importance of the Entertainment Film." *Annals of Am Acad of Polit and Soc Sci* 254 (Nov 47) 65–69. Its impact on society; the need for self-restraint.

Kracauer, Siegfried. "Pictorial Deluge." *Transformation: Arts, Communication, Environment* 1 (No. 1, 1950) 52–53. In American mass culture we are submerged by pictures and at the same time prevented from really perceiving them.

De Mille, Cecil B. "A Man Is No Better Than What He Leaves Behind Him." *JSPG* (Feb 56) 5–7+. SPG Milestone Award speech about the influence of motion pictures, especially overseas.

Jenkins, Ivor. "Caligari to Clinic: Psychiatry in the Film." *Film* (No. 11, Jan–Feb 57) 15–18. The possible relationship between film and psychiatry, especially as reflected in the appeal of the film to the unconscious.

Grotjahn, Martin. "Horror—Yes, It Can Do You Good." *F&F* 5 (No. 2, Nov 58). *See 4k(3)*.

Crist, Judith. "Sex and Violence in Movies and TV: How Harmful Are They?" *Good Housekeeping* 169 (Aug 69) 59–61+. Includes quotes on the subject from celebrities.

7b(2b). Research

"Psychological Tests to Determine the Effectiveness of the Talking Picture." *School and Society* 35 (5 Mar 32) 312. Public school experiments in New York; Camden and Elizabeth, New Jersey; other towns.

Rosenthal, S. P. "Changes of Socio-Economic Attitudes Under Radical Motion Picture Propaganda." *Archives of Psych* (No. 166, 1934) 5–46.

Cressey, Paul G. "Motion Picture Experience as Modified by Social Background and Personality." *Am Sociological Rev* 3 (Aug 38) 516–525. Effect of movies on social attitudes.

Bell, Oliver. "Sociological Aspects of the Cinema." *Nature* 144 (No. 3646, 16 Sep 39) 520. Proposals for research in the areas of the sociological and psychological effects of film.

Paterson, Andrew W. "An Experiment in Pupil Appraisal." *S&S* 12 (No. 47, Oct 43) 70–72. An attempt to use film as a way of heightening powers of observation and attention.

French, A. Seymour. "A Youth Club Leads." *S&S* 12 (No. 48, Jan 44) 83–86. One youth club uses films to heighten analytical skills.

Low, Rachael. "Audience Research." *S&S* 15 (No. 60, Winter 46–47) 150–151. Most of it has been more misleading than helpful.

Raths, L. E., and F. N. Trager. "Public Opinion and *Crossfire*." *J Educ Soc* 21 (1948) 345–368. School children in Ohio become slightly less prejudiced after seeing this film.

Rosen, Irwin C. "The Effects of the Motion Picture *Gentleman's Agreement* on Attitudes Towards Jews." *J of Psychology* 26 (1948) 525–536.

Hulett, J. E., Jr. "Estimating the Net Effect of a Commercial Motion Picture on the Trend of Local Opinion." *Am Sociological Rev* 14 (1949) 263–275. Study of *Sister Kenny* and attitudes toward polio treatment in Champaign-Urbana (Illinois). Critique on pp. 550–552.

Gray, B. "Social Effects of the Film." *Sociological Rev* 42 (1950) 135–144. Although film may have some antisocial results, many negative criticisms of film are exaggerated and misrepresented.

Cooper, Eunice, and Helen Dinerman. "Analysis of the Film *Don't Be a Sucker*: A Study in Communication." *Pub Opin Q* 15 (No. 2, 1951) 243–264. Reactions of adult and high-school groups to a film on the futility of intergroup prejudice.

Goldberg, H. D. "The Role of 'Cutting' in the Perception of the Motion Picture." *J Applied Psych* 35 (1951) 70–71. A brief report of an experiment indicating that perceptual responses are geared to the edited film as a whole rather than individual scenes.

Fearing, Franklin. "A Word of Caution for the Intelligent Consumer of Motion Pictures." *QFRTV* 6 (No. 2, Winter 51) 129–142. UCLA psychology professor finds little research to support effects of films on violent behavior or racial attitudes, but proposes better education of the "consumer."

Carpenter, C. R. "Recent Progress at the Instructional Film Research Program." *JUFPA* 6 (No. 3, Spring 54) 13–15. Head of department of psychology at Pennsylvania State University summarizes findings on effectiveness of instructional films; one suggestion is that responses vary more with viewer background than by film stimuli.

Rose, Nicholas. "Some Comments on Motion Picture Research." *JUFPA* 6 (No. 3, Spring 54) 3–8. Report on infrared study of audience reactions to feature film *The Life of Riley,* plus a diagram of varying responses to any joke.

Goldberg, A. "The Effects of Two Types of Sound Motion Pictures on the Attitudes of Adults Towards Minorities." *J Educ Soc* 29 (1956) 386–391. Dramatic film had effect; documentary did not.

Maccoby, Eleanor, and W. Wilson. "Identification and Observational Learning from Films." *J of Abnormal & Social Psych* 55 (1957) 76–87.

Maccoby, Eleanor, and R. Burton. "Differential Movie-Viewing Behaviour of Male and Female Viewers." *J of Personality* 26 (1958) 259–267.

Spiegelman, Marvin. "Effect of Personality on the Perception of a Motion Picture." *J of Projective Techniques* 19 (No. 4, 1958) 461–464.

Emery, F. E. "Psychological Effects of the Western Film: A Study in Television Viewing." *Human Relations* 12 (No. 3, 1959). *See 4k(2).*

Kantor, Bernard R. "Cinema Research." *JUFPA* 11 (No. 2, Winter 59) 17–18. Reference to audience research work by Dr. Nicholas Rose at USC Cinema Department.

Catton, W. R. "Changing Cognitive Structure as a Basis for the Sleeper Effect." *Social Forces* 38 (1960) 348–354. An experiment using the film *Neighbors.*

Middleton, Russell. "Ethnic Prejudice and Susceptibility to Persuasion." *Am Sociological Rev* 25 (Oct 60) 679–686. Effect of the film *Gentleman's Agreement* on racial prejudices.

McCoy, E. P. "Influence of Color on Audiences' Rated Perception of Reality in the Film." *AV Com Rev* 10 (Jan 62). *See 2e(2).*

Fleming, Malcolm. "What Is a Good Film?" *JUFPA* 15 (No. 4, 1963) 8–9+. A film is good if it elicits the desired response; more scientific testing needed to establish why some techniques work and others do not, to provide guidelines for future film makers.

Rose, Ernest D. "Image, Sound, and Meaning." *JUFPA* 18 (No. 2, 1966) 21–23. Experiments aimed at finding how much weight the audience attaches to the visual images and to the sound track of a film, and how meaning

is resolved out of conflicting images and track.

Salomon, G., and R. E. Snow. "Specification of Film Attributes for Psychological and Educational Research Purposes." *AV Com Rev* 16 (1968) 225–244.

Williams, Robert C. "Film Shots and Expressed Interest Levels." *Speech Monographs* 35 (No. 2, June 68) 166–169. An attempt to prove that interest is increased by the use of close-ups.

Tudor, Andrew. "Film and the Measurement of Its Effects." *Screen* 10 (Nos. 4–5, July–Oct 69) 148–159. Emotional impact seems to be there, but better theory and method are needed to measure it.

7b(3). EFFECTS ON CHILDREN AND YOUTH

[See also 4k(9), 7c(6).]

Santelli, César. "Children and War Films." *Living Age* 338 (1 Aug 30) 664–670. Recommendations for showing war films to school children.

"Appraising Films for Young People." *School Rev* 39 (May 31) 329–330. Reviews evaluation method of *Educational Screen.*

"A New Plan to Bring Children into Movie Theatres." *Chris Cent* 48 (12 Aug 31) 1013. Hays Office attacked for violating rules of SPCC regarding children and movies.

Duckworth, Leslie B. "Certain General Conclusions." *Close Up* 8 (No. 3, Sep 31) 207–211. Analysis of the report of the Birmingham Cinema Inquiry Committee's report of the effect of the cinema upon children.

"Children to Aid Elevation of Film Standards." *Lit Dig* 116 (30 Dec 33) 20. Nationwide tests show rising generation will raise level of taste.

Cressey, P. "The Motion Picture as Informal Education." *J Educ Soc* 7 (1934) 504–515. Children are influenced by leisure choices.

"The Establishment of a Children's Film Board." *School and Society* 39 (24 Feb 34) 240–241. Dr. W. W. Charters urges motion-picture producers to establish children's departments.

Dale, Edgar. "Helping Youth to Choose Better Movies." *Parents Mag* 9 (Apr 34) 26–27+.

"English Children and the Movies." *Social Service Rev* 26 (Mar 52) 87. A brief report on the increase in the number of English children attending the cinema between 1931 and 1948.

"Bid for Teens." *Bus Wk* (14 May 55) 114+. Texas movie chain gives special prices to bring teenagers back to movies.

"America in the Eyes of Foreign Teen-Agers." *Senior Scholastic* 70 (15 Feb 57). *See 7e(2).*

"Teen-Agers and the Movies." *Sci Dig* 41 (Apr 57) 47.

"Monstrous for Money." *Newswk* 52 (14 July 58). *See 4k(3).*

Mirams, Gordon. "How the Cinema Affects Children." *UNESCO Courier* 14 (Mar 61) 24–28. Annotated bibliography.

"Old-Master Monsters and the New Breed." *Look* 28 (8 Sep 64). *See 4k(3).*

Richard, J. "Foggy Mountain." *Antioch Rev* 28 (Fall 68). *See 3b.*

7b(3a). Opinions

Eastman, Fred. "Our Children and the Movies." *Chris Cent* 47 (15 Jan 30) 110–112. Part of series "The Menace of the Movies."

"Should Children Go to the Movies?" *Parents Mag* 5 (Feb 30) 14–16+. Also *Lit Dig* 104 (1 Mar 30) 23. Opinion of National Film Estimate Service is that "the average child under ten should not be allowed to attend the usual commercial motion picture show."

Seitz, Don C. "Wanted: A Children's Hour at the Movies." *Parents Mag* (Mar 30) 16+. Outlines plan to "boycott bad movies for your children and organize to obtain good ones."

Rinehart, M. R. "Your Child and the Movies." *Ladies' Home J* 48 (Apr 31) 8–9+.

Eastman, Fred. "Are Movies Fit for Children?" *Parents Mag* 6 (Oct 31) 20–21+.

Cockerell, T. D. A. "The New Education." *School and Society* 38 (21 Oct 33) 536–538. Response to Forman's *Our Movie-Made Children* (Macmillan, 1933).

"Seeking to Improve Motion-Picture Standards." *Lit Dig* 117 (24 Mar 34) 22. Discussion of the effect of films on children centered on the activities of the Motion-Picture Research Council and the National Board of Review.

Dearborn, George Van Ness. "Children at the Movies." *School and Society* 40 (28 July 34) 127–128. Physician claims talkies are unsound for children.

Dyer, Ernest. "Training Film Taste." *S&S* 3 (No. 11, Autumn 34) 134–136. Children's tastes especially.

"Freedom of the Films." *Spectator* 154 (25 Jan 35) 109–110. Archbishop of Canterbury questions effect of films on children and illiterates and general influence on national character. Reply (8 Feb) 209.

"Children at the Movies." *School and Society* 41 (15 June 35) 810–811. British Home Office recommendations for movie improvement.

Evans, Frederick. "War and Child Opinion." *S&S* 4 (No. 15, Autumn 35) 111–113. War films are seen as generally producing a positive attitude among children toward peace.

De Mille, William. "Mickey vs. Popeye." *Forum* 94 (Nov 35). *See 2h(1).*

Read, C. Stanford. "Children at the Cinema." *19th Century* 118 (Dec 35) 750–762. Psy-

chologist's view of moviegoing experience and effects on children.

Miller, Emanuel. "What Children Like." *S&S* 5 (No. 20, Winter 36–37) 131–132. Also a theoretical statement of the effects of certain films upon children.

Rowson, Simon. "The Dimensions of the Problem." *S&S* 5 (No. 20, Winter 36–37) 129–130. Relationship between children and the cinema; from a paper delivered to the Conference on Films for Children.

Broun, Heywood. "Written from a Ridge." *Commonweal* 31 (17 Nov 39) 97–98. The impact of censorship and the trivialities of fan magazines on children.

Mackenzie, C. "Movies and the Child: The Debate Rages On." *NYTM* (23 June 40) 9+. A sampling of opinions and surveys revealing what kinds of movies children like; opinions on censorship.

Gruenberg, S. M. "New Voices Speak to Our Children." *Parents Mag* 16 (June 41) 23+. The influence of questionable movies, radio, and magazines on children.

Mackenzie, Catherine. "Movies and Superman." *NYTM* (12 Oct 41) 22. Children's reactions to movie horrors, radio crime, and comics; response to an article in the *Journal of Pediatrics;* horror movies (like comics) may provide a necessary catharsis for dull, frustrated young lives.

Gittins, John. "The Child's Approach." *S&S* 11 (No. 41, Summer 42) 4–6. The relation between children's actions, attitudes, and films they see and analyze.

Bean, Keith F. "A Letter to Oliver Bell." *S&S* 12 (No. 46, Autumn 43) 35–39. The influence of films upon children requires more substantial film fare for them.

"Film and the Child Mind." *New S&N* 32 (31 Aug 46) 150. Effects of films seen by children. Discussion (7 Sep) 172, (14 Sep) 189, (21 Sep) 208.

Henry, G. H. "Shakespeare's Heavy Rivals: Radio. Movies. Tabloids; Can We Rescue Our Schools?" *Survey Graphic* 36 (Mar 47) 187–189.

"Making Amusements Safe for Youth." *Etude* 66 (Oct 48) 579+. Influence of printing press, radio, and motion picture; replies to this editorial from people responsible for mass media.

Wall, W. D., and E. M. Smith. "The Film Choices of Adolescents." *Brit J Educ Psych* 19 (1949) 121–136.

Riesman, David. "Movies and Audiences." *Am Q* 4 (1952) 195–202. They help young people to be "other-directed."

Friedson, Elliot. "Adult Discount: An Aspect of Children's Changing Taste." *Child Development* 24 (1953) 39–49.

Feller, Dan. "Films and Delinquency." *FIR* 6 (Nov 55) 433–435. They can make delinquents worse, but the average child will not be harmed.

"Maturity and Movies." *America* 94 (31 Dec 55) 366+. When do children become adults?

"Old Films on TV." *America* 98 (22 Feb 58) 583. With more films on television than in the theatres, parents must be watchful about what their children see.

Field, Mary. "Children in Cinema." *F&F* 4 (No. 7, Apr 58) 9–10. How children view films; the Children's Film Foundation.

Spock, Benjamin. "Television, Radio, Comics, and Movies." *Ladies' Home J* 77 (Apr 60) 61+.

Whitehorn, Katherine. "Swinging the Censor." *Spectator* 205 (26 Aug 60) 320. Questions recent rating of *Ben-Hur* as suitable fare for children.

Wolf, Anna W. M. "TV, Movies, Comics: Boon or Bane to Children?" *Parents Mag* 36 (Apr 61) 46–48+.

Crist, Judith. "How Old Is Mature?" *Ladies' Home J* 84 (May 67) 89. The effect of films on children.

Stang, J. "Should Children See Violent Movies?" *Current* 92 (Feb 68) 40–41.

Ebert, Roger. "Just Another Horror Movie, Or Is It?" *Rdrs Dig* 94 (June 69) 127–128 (condensed from *Chicago Sun-Times*). *The Night of the Living Dead,* which includes cannibalism, was not classified by Walter Reade for mature audiences.

7b(3b). Research

Sullenger, T. Earl. "Modern Youth and the Movies." *School and Society* 32 (4 Oct 30) 459–461. Sociological study of movie preferences.

"Films and the Child." *Spectator* 146 (13 June 31) 927–928. Cinema Enquiry Committee criticized because of overriding disapproval of cinema and lack of concrete conclusions.

"Gangster Movies and Children." *Chris Cent* 48 (12 Aug 31) 1015–1016. Cites specific incidents of adverse moral effects movies have on children.

"Studying the Problem of Motion Pictures in England and America." *School Rev* 39 (Sep 31) 491–495. Quotes *London Times Educational Supplement* article reviewing current efforts to study effects of movies on English children.

"British Youth Dislikes Love in the Movies." *Lit Dig* 111 (17 Oct 31) 22. Comedy and adventure most successful British movies.

Ervine, St. John. "Cinema and the Child." *Fortnightly Rev* 137 (Apr 32) 426–443. From questionnaire on moviegoing habits of British children, raises questions about moral impact.

Eastman, Fred. "Your Child and the Movies." *Chris Cent* 50 (3 May 33) 591–593; (10 May 33) 620–622; (17 May 33) 653–655;

(24 May 33) 688–690; (31 May 33) 718–720; (7 June 33) 750–752; (14 June 33) 779–781. Preliminary reports on the Payne fund studies about to be published in book form.

" 'A Lotta T'ings' Learned in the Movies." *Lit Dig* 115 (13 May 33 16–17. Review of psychological studies of movie effects on children.

Rorty, James. "New Facts About Movies and Children." *Parents Mag* 8 (July 33) 18–19+. Reports results from tests on children, their pulse rates, and movies' effects.

Rorty, James. "How the Movies Harm Children." *Parents Mag* 8 (Aug 33) 18–19+. Summarizes evidence presented by the Payne Fund Studies concerning movies as factor in teaching delinquency and crime.

Williams, J. Harold. "Attitudes of College Students Towards Motion Pictures." *School and Society* 38 (12 Aug 33) 222–224. Study based on reactions to Thurstone attitude scale.

"The Effect of Motion Pictures on Children." *Elementary School J* 34 (Oct 33) 85–88. Announces books published through Motion Picture Research Council, with summary of H. J. Forman's *Our Movie-Made Children* (Macmillan, 1933).

"The Moving Picture Habits of High School Students." *School and Society* 39 (17 Mar 34) 338–339. National Council of Teachers of English experiment offers recommendations.

Louttit, C. M. "Motion Pictures and Youth: A Review." *J Applied Psych* 18 (Apr 34) 307–316. A review of a series of studies published by the Indiana University Psychological Clinics.

Knight, Eric. "Rampant Reformers." *CQ* 2 (No. 4, Summer 34) 227–230. Brief critique of Payne fund studies for U.S. Motion Picture Research Council; money could better have been spent on children's films than on attacking Hollywood's influence on children.

De Feo, Luciano. "Movies and the Public: Effects on the World's Children." *Rotarian* 48 (Feb 36) 37–39. Director of International Educational Cinematographic Institute, formed by the League of Nations at Mussolini's suggestion, compares studies in different countries.

Shultz, G. D. "Movies and Radio, Blessing or Bane?" *Better Homes and Gardens* 15 (Mar 37) 78+. Scientific research into the emotional reactions of children to scenes of love and violence.

"Just Like the Movies." *Lit Dig* 124 (11 Dec 37) 4. The effect of films on children; emphasis on *Dead End*.

"Cultural Influence of the Cinema." *School and Society* 50 (9 Sep 39) 340. A look at the report of The League of Nations Advisory

Committee on Social Questions (with a juvenile emphasis).

Keliher, Alice V. "Children and Movies: A Critical Summary of the Scientific Literature." *Films* 1 (No. 4, Summer 40) 40–48. Payne fund studies and others.

Preston, M. I. "Children's Reactions to Movie Horrors and Radio Crime." *J of Pediatrics* 19 (1941) 147–168.

Valentine, E. R. "Are Movies Good or Bad for Them?" *NYTM* (30 Mar 41) 8–9+. Through a visit to a typical children's matinee, parents, educators, psychologists study children's reactions to the film medium.

Wiese, M., and S. Cole. "A Study of Children's Attitudes and the Influence of a Commercial Motion Picture." *J of Psychology* 21 (1946) 151–171. *Tomorrow the World* shown to children.

"Speaking of Pictures—The Wiggle Test." *Life* 25 (23 Aug 48) 16–18. A test devised by the Children's Film Library to measure children's attention to films: pictures are of a showing of *The Sea Hawk*.

Wall, W. D., *et al.* "The Adolescent and the Cinema." *Educational Rev* 1 (Oct 48) 34–46; (Feb 49) 119–130. Studies of retention of images by boys and girls in British Midlands.

"Lassie on Trial." *New Yorker* 24 (30 Oct 48) 16–17. Amusing afternoon with the Johnston office's children's preview to study youthful reactions to movies.

Wall, W. D., and W. A. Simson. "The Effects of Cinema Attendance on the Behaviour of Adolescents as Seen by Their Contemporaries." *Brit J Educ Psych* 19 (1949) 53–61.

"Picking 'Em Out of the Hat." *Scholastic* 53 (5 Jan 49) 3. National poll of high-school student moviegoing.

Field, Mary. "Unfinished Project." *S&S* 18 (Spring 49) 8–11. An experiment in recording with sound and film the reactions of children to films; stills.

"Cinema as a Substitute." *Spectator* 185 (10 Nov 50) 451. The report *Children and the Cinema,* made by the Social Survey Division of the Central Office of Information, concludes cinema is a harmless pastime for most children.

Wall, W. D. "The Emotional Responses of Adolescent Groups to Certain Films." *Brit J Educ Psych* 20 (1951) 153; 21 (1951) 81–88.

Freidson, Eliot. "Consumption of Mass Media by Polish-American Children." *QFRTV* 9 (No. 1, Fall 54) 92–101. The habits of seventy-nine schoolboys with respect to movies, TV, and comic books.

"Juvenile Delinquency (Motion Pictures)." *F Cult* 1 (Nos. 5–6, 1955) 14–16. Excerpts from hearings before the Subcommittee to Investigate Juvenile Delinquency of the Committee of the Judiciary, United States

Senate, Eighty-fourth Congress, first session. "Movies' Effect Depends on Mood of Audiences." *Sci Newsletter* 68 (17 Sep 55) 191. Study of ten- and eleven-year-olds.

Albert, R. S. "The Role of Mass Media and the Effect of Aggressive Film Content upon Children's Aggressive Responses and Identification Choices." *Genetic Psychology Monographs* 55 (1957) 211–285.

Depaul, Brother. "Youth Looks at Movies." *America* (19 Jan 63) 76–78. Discussion of a questionnaire about tastes in films sent by the author to Catholic high-school and college students.

Carlson, Harry. "Movies and the Teenager." *JSPG* (Mar 63) 23–26+. Lutheran minister surveyed 3,000 high-school students in La Habra, California, on movies they liked, movies that affected their lives, etc.

7b(4). VIOLENCE IN FILMS

[See also 3b(2), 4k(2), 4k(10).]

"Gang Films." *Commonweal* 14 (10 June 31) 143–144. Knights of Columbus condemn gangster films.

"Effects of Gang Movies." *Outlook* 158 (8 July 31) 296–297. Finds argument against gang movies unconvincing.

"A Shot Heard Round the Country." *Lit Dig* 110 (25 July 31) 20–21. Effects of gang films on children in Montclair, New Jersey.

Pitkin, Walter B. "Screen Crime vs. Press Crime." *Outlook* 158 (29 July 31) 398–399+. Suggests movies and tabloids must be discussed together in exploitation of crime.

Cochran, Mary Lue. "Movies and Young Criminals." *Nat Educ Assoc J* 21 (May 32) 169. Questions effects of gangster films on children.

"Are Gang Films Wholesome?" *Lit Dig* 115 (4 Mar 33) 23. Child Study Association and National Board of Review asserts that gang films *are* wholesome.

Vesselo, Arthur. "Crime Over the World." *S&S* 6 (No. 23, Autumn 37) 135–137. The treatment of violence and bloodshed in the major film-producing countries.

Thompson, B. J. "Clinics in Crime." *Commonweal* 29 (14 Apr 39) 686–687. Under guise of entertainment, TV and radio have given complete clinical instruction in crime to countless children.

Durant, J. "Touch On and Off." *Collier's* 106 (31 Aug 40). *See 2b(6).*

Houseman, John. "Violence, 1947: Three Specimens." *Hwd Q* 3 (No. 1, Fall 47) 63–65. The public seems to want violent entertainment, but rarely is it used to produce an absorbing and valid film; *Brute Force,* because of its complete unreality, is an immoral film; *Body and Soul, Crossfire* also examined.

Muhlen, N. "Comic Books and Other Horrors: Prep School for Totalitarian Society?" *Commentary* 7 (Jan 49) 80–87. Effects of violent movies and comic books.

Freund, Arthur J. "The Mass Media Before the Bar." *Hwd Q* 4 (No. 1, Fall 49) 90–97. Chairman of an American Bar Association committee objects to violence and unrealistic presentation of crime and justice in the media; *Brute Force,* one example; he believes harm can be proved and laws should be passed.

Mirams, Gordon. "Drop That Gun!" *QFRTV* 6 (No. 1, Fall 51). See *7e(3)*.

Culshaw, John. "Violence and the Cartoon." *Fortnightly Rev* 170 (Dec 51). See *2h(1)*.

Beaumont, Charles. "The Heavies." *Playboy* 12 (No. 2, Feb 52). See *2b(6)*.

"Violence and Brutality in the Movies." *Sci Dig* 35 (Mar 54) 31. *Providence Journal*'s short comment on violence.

"New High in Movie Heels." *NYTM* (18 Apr 54). See *2b(6)*.

Knight, Arthur. "Cheez It, the Cops!" *Sat Rev* 37 (2 Oct 54) 43–44. *Rogue Cop, Dragnet, Shield for Murder, Pushover,* and *Private Hell 36:* each of these movies depicts a policeman who uses his office as a license to commit brutality or make illegal financial gain.

Maccoby, Eleanor, H. Levin, and B. M. Selya. "The Effect of Emotional Arousal on the Retention of Aggressive and Non-Aggressive Movie Content." *Am Psychologist* 10 (1955) 359+. Angered viewer remembers violence more.

Anderson, Lindsay. "The Last Sequence of *On the Waterfront.*" *S&S* 24 (Jan–Mar 55). See *3c*.

Hughes, Robert. "*On the Waterfront,* a Defense and Some Letters." *S&S* 24 (Spring 55). *See 3c.*

"Sex and Violence Justified." *America* 92 (5 Mar 55) 583–584. An editorial attacking a feature article by director Robert Aldrich.

Maccoby, Eleanor, H. Levin, and B. M. Selya. "The Effects of Emotional Arousal on the Retention of Film Content: 'A Failure to Replicate.'" *J of Abnormal and Social Psych* 50 (1956) 3–11. Frustrated subjects didn't remember even the violence very well; compare 1955 study.

Siegel, A. "Film-Mediated Fantasy Aggression and Strength of Aggressive Drive." *Child Development* 27 (1956) 365–378.

"How Others See Us on Films." *America* 95 (8 Sep 56). See *7e(2)*.

"Movies, TV Rapped." *Senior Scholastic* 75 (21 Oct 59) 27. Teachers criticize violence in movies and TV.

Dworkin, Martin. "*The Desperate Hours* and the Violent Screen." *Shenandoah* 11 (No. 2, 1960). *See 3c, The Desperate Hours.*

Wertham, Fredric. "How Movie and TV Violence Affects Children." *Ladies' Home J* 77 (Feb 60) 58–59+.

Lovaas, O. I. "Effect of Exposure to Symbolic Aggression on Aggressive Behavior." *Child Development* 32 (1961) 37–44. Cartoon's aggression seems to encourage children to do more hitting.

Mussen, Paul, and Eldred Rutherford. "Effects of Aggressive Cartoons on Children's Aggressive Play." *J of Abnormal and Social Psych* 62 (1961) 461–464.

Feschbach, S. "The Stimulating Versus Cathartic Effects of a Vicarious Aggressive Activity." *J of Abnormal and Social Psych* 63 (1961) 381–385.

Lord, Robert. "Not for Children!" *JSPG* (Sep 61) 25–27. Writer defends sex and violence as necessary ingredients in a dramatic medium.

Walters, R., E. Thomas, and C. Acker. "Enhancement of Punitive Behavior by Audiovisual Displays." *Science* 136 (1962) 872–873. Toronto University experiments with adults suggest that the knife-fight scene in *Rebel Without a Cause* increases aggressive behavior even in adults.

Lineberry, W. P., and E. R. Floyd. "Violence Bores Me." *Senior Scholastic* 81 (14 Nov 62) 23.

Bandura, Albert, Dorothea Ross, and Sheila Ross. "Imitation of Film-Mediated Aggressive Models." *J of Abnormal and Social Psych* 66 (1963) 3–11.

Berkowitz, Leonard, and Edna Rawlings. "Effect of Film Violence on Inhibition Against Subsequent Aggression." *J of Abnormal and Social Psych* 66 (1963) 405–412. It is found to heighten hostility in this experiment.

Berkowitz, Leonard, R. Corwin, and M. Heironimus. "Film Violence and Subsequent Aggressive Tendencies." *Pub Opin Q* 27 (1963) 217–229. If "fantasy aggression appears socially justified" in a film story, the effect may be to release restraints in real life.

Walter, R., and E. Thomas. "Enhancement of Punitiveness by Visual and Audio-Visual Displays." *Canad J of Psych* 17 (1963) 244–255.

Durgnat, Raymond, and Ian Johnson (eds.). "Companion to Violence and Sadism in the Cinema." *Motion* (No. 4, Feb 63) 3–50. A compendium of thoughts on cinema violence and sadism—nature of aggression, genres, films, actions, directors, trends, articles, and notes signed and unsigned by the editors, Peter Cowie, Philip Strick, *et al.*

Wertham, Fredric. "*Redbook* Dialogue." *Redbook* 120 (Apr 63) 70–71+. Conversation with Alfred Hitchcock on violence in films.

Berkowitz, Leonard. "Film Violence and Subsequent Aggressive Tendencies." *Pub Opin Q* 27 (June 63) 217–229.

Bandura, Albert. "What TV Violence Can Do

to Your Child." *Look* (22 Oct 63) 46–52. Films shown to four-year-olds in Palo Alto, California, resulted in imitation of aggressive actions, a contradiction of the so-called catharsis theory of violence in drama; summary of Stanford University studies and also of Walters experiments with adults at University of Toronto.

Berkowitz, Leonard. "The Effects of Observing Violence." *Sci Am* 210 (Feb 64) 35–41. Reply with rejoinder, Paul Goodman 210 (June 64) 8. Report of recent findings that films "induce hostile behavior."

"Picture of Violence." *Newswk* 63 (24 Feb 64) 91. Effect of filmed violence.

French, P. "Violence in the Cinema." *20th Century Studies* 173 (Winter 64–65) 115–130. Some movies explore violence, others exploit it, but this is natural for cinema and not persuasive for the audience.

Hicks, David J. "Imitation and Retention of Film-Mediated Aggressive Peer and Adult Models." *J of Personality and Soc Psych* 2 (1965) 97–100.

Berkowitz, Leonard, and R. G. Geen. "Film Violence and the Cue Properties of Available Targets." *J of Personality and Soc Psych* 3 (1966) 525–530. The effect is not necessarily to increase hostility toward everyone.

Lovibond, S. H. "The Effect of Media Stressing Crime and Violence Upon Children's Attitudes." *Social Problems* 15 (1967) 91.

"Don't Watch This Part, Honey, I'll Tell You When It's Over." *Esq* 68 (July 67) 60–63. Violence in movies.

Morgenstern, Joseph. "The Thin Red Line." *Newswk* 70 (28 Aug 67) 82–83. Films can be a laboratory for the study of violence, the consequence of violent life; a second look at *Bonnie and Clyde.*

Wertham, Fredric, John Trevelyan, Sherrill Corwin, Judith Crist, Arthur Penn, David Levy, Malvin Wald, Saul David, G. William Jones, Charles Champlin, James Wall, Jay Emanuel. "The Journal Looks at Violence in Films." *JSPG* (Dec 67) 3–38.

Hofsess, John. "Death Valley, U.S.A." *Take One* 1 (No. 11, 1968) 6–9. The relationship between the media and society, with particular reference to violence.

Krassner, Paul. "Ten Advantages of Violence." *Take One* 1 (No. 11, 1968) 12–13. The ironic advantages of media violence.

Schickel, Richard. "Violence in the Movies." *Rev of Existential Psych and Psych* 8 (1968) 169–178.

Wertham, Fredric. "Film Violence—Is It Necessary?" *Take One* 1 (No. 11, 1968) 9–12. The screen should help society struggle against violence and hate, rather than creating an atmosphere in which these are looked upon as normal.

Kozloff, Max. "*In Cold Blood.*" *S&S* 37 (Sum-

mer 68) 148–150. A critical analysis of Richard Brooks' *In Cold Blood,* from Truman Capote's script and novel, and Luchino Visconti's *The Outsider,* based on Albert Camus' novel *L'Etranger;* the moral standpoints from which they view similarly destructive acts of murder.

Wertham, Fredric. "Is So Much Violence in Film Necessary?" *Cinéaste* 2 (No. 1, Summer 68) 4–6+. It exploits and contorts values for the young.

Knight, Arthur. "Anything for a Laugh." *Sat Rev* 51 (20 July 68) 38. A study of audiences and violence on the screen.

Houston, Penelope. "Hitchcockery." *S&S* 37 (Autumn 68) 188–189. Reviews of two films, *The Bride Wore Black* and *Targets,* both dealing with multiple killings and both influenced by Hitchcock; the directors, François Truffaut and Peter Bogdanovich, are both former critics who interviewed the master lovingly and lengthily.

Beck, Calvin T. "Knocking the Establishment's View of Violence, Or: Cubing the Squares." *Cinéaste* 2 (No. 3, Winter 68–69) 10. Rebuttal to Wertham article attacking unnecessary film violence, with author stressing its less conventional meanings.

Hartmann, Donald P. "Influence of Symbolically Modeled Instrumental Aggression and Pain Cues on Aggressive Behaviour." *J of Personality and Soc Psych* 11 (1969) 280–288. Film violence influenced delinquents to take aggressive action.

Armstrong, Michael. "On Violence . . ." *F&F* 15 (No. 6, Mar 69) 20–31. History of violence in the film.

Kniveton, B. H., and G. M. Stephenson. "The Effect of Pre-Experience on Imitations of an Aggressive Film Model." *Brit J of Soc and Clinical Psych* 9 (1970) 31–36. Children who played before seeing filmed violence were less affected by it.

Noble, G. "Film Mediated Aggressive and Creative Play." *British J of Soc and Clinical Psych* 9 (1970) 1–7. Six-year-olds played with war toys more after seeing a war film.

Rocha, Glauber. "The Aesthetics of Violence." *Afterimage* (No. 1, Apr 70). See 3a(6).

Brown, Roger. "Social Concern, the Mass Media, and Violence." *Screen* 11 (Nos. 4–5, 1970) 3–15.

Eves, Vicki. "The Effects of Violence in the Mass Media." *Screen* 11 (No. 3, Summer 70) 31–42. Sociology graduate concludes there is no evidence of any link with violent behavior in life as opposed to an experimental situation.

7b(5). PROPAGANDA IN FILMS

[See also 3a(6).]

"The Prophets of the New Age." *Cath World* 136 (Mar 33) 732–733. Reprint from *The*

Dublin Review suggests movies give out the gospel of socialism.

Grierson, John. "Propaganda." *S&S* 2 (No. 8, Winter 33–34) 119–121. The uses of propaganda, its relation to education theory and the needs of human beings.

Cousins, E. G. "Cinema and Propaganda." *Bookman* 85 (Mar 34) 480–481. The film industry should not shun the propaganda film.

Onderdonk, Francis S. "The Peace Films Caravan." *World Tomorrow* 17 (28 June 34) 334–335. Requests donations to group which shows films, presents speakers on the League of Nations, and distributes pacifist literature.

Hale, Oron James. "Nationalism in Press, Films, and Radio." *Annals of the Am Acad of Polit and Soc Sci* 175 (Sep 34) 110–116. Expression of alarm over "warlike preservation of peace" by media, news bias, government control, and propaganda.

Villard, Oswald Garrison. "Propaganda in the Movies." *Nation* 139 (12 Dec 34) 665. Condemns militarism in movies, Hearst, censorship.

Ames, Richard Sheridan. "The Screen Enters Politics." *Harper's* 170 (Mar 35) 473–482. Asks whether Hollywood will produce more propaganda after the newsreel campaign against Upton Sinclair in California.

Riegel, O. W. "Nationalism in Press, Radio, and Cinema." *Am Sociological Rev* 3 (1938) 510–515.

Seldes, G. "Motion Pictures." *Scribner's* 103 (Apr 38) 65–66. Increasing use of movies for social propaganda; for example, business films in reply to government films.

"China's Propaganda Cartoons." *China Weekly Rev* 85 (25 June 38) 114. Film used to combat Japan's undeclared war on China.

Pearson, R. M. "Artist's Point of View: Films for Democracy." *Forum* 101 (Mar 39) 175.

Nugent, F. S. "Hollywood Waves the Flag." *Nation* 148 (8 Apr 39) 398–400. A discussion of recent cycles in film, with emphasis on the latest, nationalism.

Quigley, Martin. "This Propaganda Question." *S&S* 8 (No. 30, Summer 39) 47–49. Arguments against film propaganda.

Barry, I. "Film as a Recording Machine." *SRL* 20 (12 Aug 39) 12. The propaganda potential of film and how it may merely express the moods of the time.

Miller, C. R., and L. Minsky. "Movies and Propagandizing." *Survey Graphic* 28 (Nov 39) 713–716. A discussion at the Williamstown Institute of Human Problems.

Buchanan, Andrew. "Prince Propaganda." *S&S* 8 (No. 32, Winter 39–40) 128. The pros and cons of propaganda, especially in relation to depicting Great Britain.

"Movie Warning to Neutrals: Film *Feuertaufe* (*Blood Baptism*)." *Living Age* 358 (June 40) 360–361. A look at this German propaganda film and its effects on English films of the time.

Glenn, Charles. "The Cameras Shoot for War." *New Masses* 35 (11 June 40) 31. The antiwar movement is strong in Hollywood, but not among the producers, who are in the process of turning out war propaganda.

Wright, Basil. "Propaganda by Films." *Spectator* 164 (21 June 40) 837.

McDonald, John. "Films and War Propaganda." *Pub Opin Q* 4 (Sep 40) 519–522; continued in 5 (Mar 41) 127–129. Hollywood and Washington use of film for public-opinion formation.

"Film at War." *New S&N* 20 (7 Sep 40) 230–231. The British government has failed to make full use of film for propaganda purposes.

Frakes, Margaret. "Time Marches Back: Propaganda for Defense." *Chris Cent* 57 (16 Oct 40). See 8b(2).

"Documentary Film, an Instrument of Propaganda and Morale." *Th Arts* 24 (Nov 40). See 8c(1).

Bower, A. "Films: Latin American and Other Problems." *Nation* 152 (15 Feb 41) 192–193. Hollywood and politics—a look at possible film ventures on controversial and propagandist themes.

"Films Conquer Nations." *S&S* 10 (No. 37, Spring 41) 4–5. The role of propaganda in British and German films.

Bryan, A. J. "Library Film Forums on National Defense." *Lib J* 66 (15 Mar 41) 241–243. Deals with film programs designed to strengthen civilian morale in wartime.

Nye, Gerald P. "Our Madness Increases as Our Emergency Shrinks." *Vital Speeches* 7 (15 Sep 41) 720–723. Senator Nye says: "Movies . . . have become the most gigantic engines of propaganda in existence to rouse the war fever in America and plunge this nation to her destruction."

Bruner, J. S., and G. Fowler. "Strategy of Terror: Audience Response to *Blitzkrieg im Westen.*" *J of Abnormal Psych* 36 (Oct 41) 561–574. The varied response to this German war-propaganda film shows that counter-propaganda can be used effectively.

Cousins, Norman. "Our Heroes." *Sat Rev* 24 (25 Oct 41). See 7c(3).

Davidman, Joy. "Cameras as Weapons." *New Masses* 45 (8 Dec 42) 28–29. There is more to praise in government documentary efforts than in entertainment films.

Zanuck, Darryl F. "Free Speech on the Silver Screen: An Antidote to Nazi Poison on Celluloid." *Free World* 9 (Mar 45) 58–61.

Paul, E. "Of Film Propaganda." *Atlantic* 176 (Sep 45) 123+. A sharp objection to propaganda films which seek to win friends for the Allies.

Bean, Keith. "On Immorality." *S&S* 14 (No. 55,

Oct 45) 72–74. Certain narrow nationalistic themes in films are seen as irresponsible and immoral.

Siggins, A. J. "What Is the Film Doing for Mankind?" *New Vistas* 1 (No. 9, Apr 46) 27–33. British and American films produce confusion when they undertake propaganda; films should have objectives beyond national considerations.

Rosten, Leo C. "Movies and Propaganda." *Annals of Am Acad of Polit and Soc Sci* 254 (Nov 47) 116–124. Even mildly controversial films, films which break away from the "libidinous contortions" of the boy-girl formula, are often labeled "propagandist."

Altmann, John. "Movies' Role in Hitler's Conquest of German Youth." *Hwd Q* 3 (No. 4, Summer 48–Summer 49). *See 4e(4b).*

"The Hair of the Dog." *Time* 54 (17 Oct 49). *See 4e(8b).*

Altmann, John. "The Technique and Content of Hitler's War Propaganda Films, Part I: Karl Ritter and His Early Films." *Hwd Q* 4 (No. 4, Summer 50). *See 4e(4b).*

Wollenberg, H. H. "The Strange Story of *Titanic.*" *S&S* 19 (Aug 50) 239–240. German film version of the *Titanic* disaster (made under Goebbels in 1943) said to be anti-British, portraying selfish capitalism, etc.

Altmann, John. "The Technique and Content of Hitler's War Propaganda Films, Part II: Karl Ritter's 'Soldier' Films." *Hwd Q* 5 (No. 1, Fall 50). *See 4e(4b).*

Brown, John Mason. "Ugh!" *SRL* 33 (7 Oct 50) 46–48. How the filming of *Hiawatha* could be regarded as communist propaganda.

Deverall, R. L. G. "Red Propaganda in Japan's Movies." *America* 90 (14 Nov 53). *See 4f(1).*

"Reds'-Eye View of U.S." *Life* 37 (11 Oct 54). *See 4e(8b).*

"Moscow's Uncle Tom." *Newswk* 45 (2 May 55). *See 4e(8b).*

De La Roche, Catherine. "Truth and Propaganda in the Cinema." *Film* (No. 12, Mar–Apr 57) 25–29.

"Cinema Cold War in Asia." *America* 99 (12 July 58) 406. How a Red Chinese cartoon character ("Little White") exemplifies efforts at cinema propaganda.

Vas, Robert. "Sorcerers or Apprentices." *S&S* 32 (Autumn 63) 199–203. The propaganda film, having become an everyday occurrence (i.e., commercials), may have lost its drive, and with it the stimulating role it has played so often in the history of cinema; its development during the 1930s in England, Russia, in Nazi films, and in the works of Humphrey Jennings.

Greenberg, Stanley S. "Operation Persuasion." *JUFPA* 16 (No. 2, 1964) 4–6+. The film *Operation Abolition,* about the House Un-American Activities Committee, was used in a communication research study against the same film footage with a different narration (*Operation Correction*).

Berson, Arnold E., and Joseph Keller. "Shame and Glory in the Movies." *Nat Rev* 16 (14 Jan 64) 17–21. A discussion of Leni Riefenstahl and Sergei Eisenstein.

Hoffmann, Hilmar. "Manipulation of the Masses Through the Nazi Film." *F Com* 3 (No. 4, Fall 65). *See 4e(4b).*

MacFadden, Patrick. "The Jaundiced Screen." *Take One* 1 (No. 1, 1966) 8–10. Comments on the propaganda films made by North Vietnam and the United States.

"Propaganda Films About the War in Vietnam." *F Com* 4 (No. 1, Fall 66) 4–39. Descriptions of visuals and tape-recorded narration for two Vietcong films, the U.S. Army film *Why Vietnam?,* and *While Brave Men Die* (produced by Donald C. Bruce, Fulton Lewis III, and Roy Burlew, Jr.); brief descriptions of a North Vietnam feature, *Days of Protest* (made by Jerry Stoll in San Francisco), and *Time of the Locust* (directed by Peter Gessner).

Commager, Henry Steele. "On the Way to 1984: Analysis of Film *Why Vietnam?,* and Arguments Against Carrying War Propaganda into the Classroom." *Sat Rev* 50 (15 Apr 67). *See 7f(1a).*

Gowland, P. "Our Movies Fought City Hall, and Won!" *Pop Photog* 65 (Nov 69) 124–125+. Hollywood people help make film *Save Our Stream* and another that prevented freeway from replacing a beach.

Tracy, P. "The New Newsreel." *Commonweal* 91 (13 Feb 70) 532–533. A group of people who make radical films reflecting their individual viewpoints.

"How to Keep the Unions Out of the Plant." *Bus Wk* (18 Apr 70) 78. *Labor Unions in America* is used by companies to prevent unionization; description of contents.

7b(6). MORALITY IN FILMS

[See also 3b(2), 4k(8).]

Eastman, Fred. "The Menace of the Movies." *Chris Cent* 47 (15 Jan 30) 75–78. Re-examination of morality in movies eight years after Hays began clean-up; articles continue under various titles through Feb 12.

"Good Citizenship and the Movies." *Chris Cent* 47 (26 Feb 30) 262–264. Restatement of Dr. Eastman's proposals to clean up film in "The Menace of the Movies."

Eastman, Fred. "What's To Be Done with the Movies?" *China Weekly Rev* 52 (10 May 30) 427. Suggestions for cleaning up the movies. Reprinted from *Christian Century.*

"The Movie Barons Take Notice." *Chris Cent* 47 (18 June 30) 774–776. Answers Carl

Milliken's charge that coverage of movie morals is biased.

"A Year of the Movies." *Chris Cent* 47 (31 Dec 30) 1616–1618. Summarizes year's campaign against movie immorality.

"After Hours: A Very Moving Picture." *World's Work* 60 (Sep 31) 50. Assails movie producers as money-hungry and laments weakness of morality crusade.

Eastman, Fred. "What Can We Do About the Movies?" *Parents Mag* 6 (Nov 31) 19+. Attacks motion-picture trust as responsible for movies' harmful morals.

"Another Year of the 'Hays-Cleaned' Movies." *Chris Cent* 49 (27 Jan 32) 108. Attacks movies' concentration on adultery and sex.

Twombly, Clifford G. "Have the Movies Cleaned Up?" *Chris Cent* 49 (13 Apr 32) 480–482. See also *Lit Dig* 113 (30 Apr 32) 16.

"Are the Movies Any Cleaner?" *Lit Dig* 113 (30 Apr 32) 16. Commentary on Clifford Twombly's article in *Christian Century*.

"The Child—Movies—Missions." *Missionary Rev* 56 (July 33) 348–349. Calls for religious awakening to moral duty in films.

Peters, Charles C. "The Relation of Motion Pictures to Standards of Morality." *School and Society* 39 (31 Mar 34) 414–415. Suggests producers lose rather than gain by antagonizing current morality.

Oglesby, Catherine. "The Movie Problem." *Ladies' Home J* 51 (May 34) 142. Summary of opinions of film morality by women's groups.

"Let Us Center Our Fire." *Commonweal* 20 (29 June 34) 225–226. Calls for unity in attack on movie morals.

Rorty, James. "It Ain't No Sin!" *Nation* 139 (1 Aug 34) 124–127. Finds uproar over movie morals a colossal misunderstanding.

Bigelow, William Frederick. "Movie Tangle." *Good Housekeeping* 99 (Sep 34) 4. Cautions against overreaction to "indecent" movies.

Israel, Edward L. "Morals and the Movies." *Forum* 92 (Oct 34) 200–203. Survey of religious groups and attacks on movie morals.

Wray, R. P. "Do Motion Pictures Conflict with Standards of Morality?" *Education* 55 (Oct 34) 108–114.

Shipler, G. E. "Church and the Movies." *Nation* 139 (10 Oct 34) 409–410. Reply to John Rorty's article 139 (1 Aug 34).

Peterson, F. "Germs That Attack the Mind." *Education* 55 (Nov 34) 187–188.

"Bulging Box Office Tills." *Lit Dig* 121 (15 Feb 36). *See 6a(1).*

"Hollywood Produces a New Alibi." *Chris Cent* 64 (5 Feb 47) 165. Attack on Hollywood's handling of drinking scenes in films.

"Canned Burlesque." *Time* 57 (16 Apr 51) 104+. Recording the "strip" shows: one

version for strict cities, another for wide-open ones.

Shaw, George Bernard. "The Cinema as a Moral Leveler." *S&S* 22 (Oct–Dec 52) 66+. A reprint from *New S&N* (27 June 1914): "The nameless exponents of a world-wide vulgarity (vulgarity is another name for morality) have complete possession of the cinema."

Hine, A. "The Kiss." *Holiday* 15 (May 54) 23–24. History of the movie kiss.

Weinberg, Herman G. "Hollywood, O Hollywood!" *F Cult* 1 (No. 3, 1955) 7–11. An excerpt of a chapter from Weinberg's *Saint Cinema* (Drama Book Shop, 1972). A study of the morals of the screen.

"European Bishops on Movies." *America* 93 (9 Apr 55) 30–31. Moral dangers of modern movies to be read in all the churches of France.

Alpert, Hollis. "Sexual Behavior in the American Movie." *Sat Rev* 39 (23 June 56) 9–10. Hollywood's concept of treating the subject and its sinners has changed from one of complete public scorn to one of personal remorse, but often keeps the happy ending. Discussion 39 (14 July 56) 21; (18 Aug 56) 21.

Wald, Jerry. "Sex in Movies." *FIR* 7 (Aug–Sep 56) 309–313. A well-known producer says the movies merely mirror sexual mores; like the stage's classical tradition of handling violence offstage, a more adult theatrical film should handle indecency offscreen.

"Reflections on a Condemned Film: *Baby Doll*." *America* 96 (5 Jan 57) 386. Comments on "art" and "bad taste": they cannot coexist.

"Trouble with *Baby Doll*." *Time* 69 (14 Jan 57) 100.

Scott, N. A., Jr. "*Baby Doll* Furor." *Chris Cent* 74 (23 Jan 57) 110–112. Review and discussion on reactions and morality.

Dyer, Peter John. "Some Silent 'Sinners.'" *F&F* 4 (No. 6, Mar 58) 13–15+. Silent films' view of sin and sinners; part of a history of films.

"Candor Can Become Cancer." *America* 101 (16 May 59) 324–325. Candor and frankness in films should not override "delicacy."

"Clean Up Hollywood?" *Newswk* 54 (7 Sep 59) 54–55. Protestant National Council charges growing use of sex and violence.

"Refined Depravity." *America* 102 (12 Dec 59) 340. The New Wave demonstrates depravity clothed in the garb of superior technique.

Knight, Arthur. "The New Frankness in Films." *Sat Rev* (19 Dec 59) 18+.

Zinsser, William K. "Bold and Risky World of 'Adult' Movies." *Life* 48 (29 Feb 60) 78–86+. A survey of the new sexual frankness and freedom in Hollywood films. Same *Rdrs*

Dig 76 (June 60) 65–69 with title "Mature Movies or Merely Salacious?"

"How Sick Is Our Entertainment?" *Senior Scholastic* 77 (7 Dec 60) 22–23. Analysis of current movies featuring violence, sex, etc.

"Do You Like the New Movies?" *Consumer Bul* 44 (Jan 61) 33. An editorial against unwholesome films.

Wharton, Don. "How to Stop the Movies' Sickening Exploitation of Sex." *Rdrs Dig* 78 (Mar 61) 37–40. Plea to stay away from "sick" films.

Crowther, Bosley. "Sex in the Movies." *Coronet* 50 (June 61) 44–48. Recent films are plainly meant to shock.

"Big Leer." *Time* 77 (9 June 61) 55–56. New Hollywood films explore previously censorable themes.

Bunzel, Peter. "Outbreak of New Films for Adults Only." *Life* 52 (23 Feb 62) 88–96+. More sexual frankness in Hollywood films and the chance of tighter censorship.

"Undress Films Coming." *America* 107 (7 Apr 62) 6. Discussion of British nudist films for U.S. distribution.

Shurlock, Geoffrey. "The More Things Change . . . Or, Onward and Upward with the Arts." *JSPG* (June 62) 21–26. Hollywood Production Code administrator gives extracts from various attacks on stage and screen morality including 1583, 1896, and recent years.

Crowther, Bosley. "Which Movies Should You See?" *Seventeen* 21 (Oct 62) 120–121+. On the recent candid treatment of "bold" themes.

Koningsberger, Hans. "Love in Another Country (Where They Order It Better)." *Horizon* 5 (May 63) 110–112. The film portrayal of love's consummation.

Davidson, Muriel. "Are Movies Fit for Our Families?" *Good Housekeeping* 157 (July 63) 94–97+. Quotes from prominent actors, directors, and religious leaders concerning the state and direction of movies.

Johnson, Ian, and Raymond Durgnat. "Puritans Anonymous." *Motion* 6 (Autumn 63). *See 4a(3).*

Sontag, Susan. "Feast for Open Eyes." *Nation* 198 (13 Apr 64). *See 3c.*

Wagner, Geoffrey. "Muckmanship." *Nat Rep* 16 (16 June 64) 502–503. On sexual freedom in the "new American cinema" (underground).

Thompson, Thomas. "Wilder's Dirty-Joke Film Stirs a Furor." *Life* 58 (15 Jan 65) 52+. *Kiss Me, Stupid* arouses a moral controversy.

Roddy, Joseph. "After Nudity What?" *Look* 29 (9 Mar 65) 36–38. A list of films the author found repugnant; quality is going down because of lack of censorship and taste.

Wall, James M. "Toward Christian Film Criteria." *Chris Cent* 82 (16 June 65) 775–778. Discussion 82 (11 Aug 65) 994+. Problem of obtaining freedom of artistic expression in view of the temptation to exploit salaciousness for its own sake.

"Nudity in Films." *America* 112 (26 June 65) 895. Discussion of the stand on film nudity by the bishops of the Catholic Church in the United States.

Armstrong, O. K. "Must Our Movies Be Obscene?" *Rdrs Dig* 87 (Nov 65) 154–156.

Comden, Betty. "To Those of You Who Remember Eric Linden in *Are These Our Children?*, I Say: 'Are These Our Parents?' " *Esq* 65 (Jan 66) 12–20. Spoof on "the decaying morals of our parents," who should be sheltered from sex films.

Thompson, Thomas. "Surprising Liz in a Film Shocker." *Life* 60 (10 June 66) 87–92. *Who's Afraid of Virginia Woolf?* sparks controversy.

"Is Nothing Obscene?" *Time* 88 (4 Nov 66) 70+. Swedish film *491.*

Black, Shirley Temple. "Sex at the Box Office." *McCall's* 94 (Jan 67) 45+. Shirley Temple on "adult" films.

Eller, Vernard. "Nude Morality." *Chris Cent* 84 (24 May 67) 689–691. Reply with rejoinder, 84 (12 July 67) 919. Man stripping before man; man stripping before God—the differences.

Aliaga, Joseph. "Pornography and the Film." *Medium* 1 (No. 1, Summer 67) 48–54. Economics; descriptions; the basic "line of action"; the sad state of society that makes pornography what it is.

Mannes, Marya. "Adult Movies." *McCall's* 95 (May 68) 16+. Current trends in "adult" films.

"Where the Boys Are." *Time* 91 (28 June 68) 80+. Discussion of Hollywood's sudden interest in homosexuality in films.

Walsh, M. "Nudity in Films." *America* 118 (29 June 68) 818–819.

"For $250,000 It's Worth It." *Life* 66 (31 Jan 69) 76–77. New wave of sex epics makes actress Anne Heywood a star.

"Goodness, Truth and Popcorn." *Chris Today* 13 (25 Apr 69) 22. The Christian will have to battle for truth and goodness at the movies.

Farber, Leslie H. "My Wife, the Naked Movie Star." *Harper's* 238 (June 69) 49–55. Sexual illusion and twisted morality in film as seen by a psychiatrist.

Sarris, Andrew. "Censorship: A View from New York." *S&S* 38 (Autumn 69). *See 7c(1a).*

Reck, T. S. "Come Out of the Shower, and Come Out Clean." *Commonweal* 90 (26 Sep 69). *See 4d.*

Skrade, Carl. "Theology and Films." *JUFA* 22

(No. 1, 1970) 16–27. Analyzes *The Dirty Dozen, How I Won the War, The Red Desert,* some Westerns for their treatment of such religious concerns as man's significance and man's sense of horror.

Blake, R. "Secular Prophecy in an Age of Film." *J of Relig Thought* 27 (Spring–Summer 70) 63–75.

Schickel, Richard. "Obscenity in Films." *Life* 68 (10 Apr 70) 12. Language in films seen as an expression of our culture and a reflection of a time of great national stress.

Alpert, Hollis. "Mine Eyes Have Seen the Glory." *Sat Rev* 53 (16 May 70) 56. The current state of film obscenity trials: are the new sexual-information films harmful to the community?

Detweiler, Robert. "The Moral Failure of *Bob and Carol and Ted and Alice.*" *J Pop Cult* 4 (No. 1, Summer 70). See 3c.

Brudnoy, D. "Losing It at the Movies." *Nat Rev* 22 (1 Dec 70) 1309–1311. Discussion of movies as a mirror of, not a cause of, society's increasing moral permissiveness.

7c. Social, Political, and Legal Restraints

[See also 4k(8), 7b(4), 7b(6).]

Eastman, Fred. "What's to Be Done with the Movies?" *Chris Cent* 47 (12 Feb 30) 202–204. Part of series "The Menace of the Movies."

Eastman, Fred. "Next Move for Better Movies." *Chris Cent* 48 (29 Apr 31) 570–573. With Senate movie-control bills defeated, Eastman outlines program for film clean-up.

Orton, William. "Hollywood Has Nothing to Learn." *Atlantic* 147 (June 31) 681–689. Review of Hollywood's censorship struggle, suggesting need for more artistic freedom.

Hullinger, Edwin Ware. "Fumigating the Movies." *North Am Rev* 233 (May 32) 445–449. Wall Street turns its attention to Hollywood.

Furnas, J. C. "False Fronts in Hollywood." *Virginia Q Rev* 8 (July 32) 337–349. Discussion of moral and aesthetic attacks on Hollywood movies and the industry's attempts to reconcile the two.

Howard, Clifford. "Film Morals." *Close Up* 10 (No. 3, Sep 33) 271–273. A plea for more humane understanding of film censorship.

"Save the Grown-ups!" *Nation* 138 (28 Mar 34) 348. Tongue-in-cheek recommendations for adult censorship.

Oglesby, Kate. "Toward Federal Censorship of Movies?" *Th Arts* 18 (Apr 34) 314. Letter to editor attacks Henry Forman's *Our Movie-Made Children* (Macmillan, 1933).

Berchtold, William E. "The Hollywood Purge." *North Am Rev* 238 (Dec 34) 503–512. Reviews history of movie censorship.

"A Plea to Our Censors." *SRL* 11 (22 Dec 34) 384. Points out dangers inherent in censorship.

"Decency and Censorship." *Chris Cent* 53 (29 July 36) 1030–1032.

Shaw, Bernard. "Saint Joan Banned; Film Censorship in the United States." *London Mercury* 34 (Oct 36) 490–496. The Hays Office and Catholic Action Group are assuming control of the public's artistic recreations.

"How Shall the Films Be Safeguarded?" *Scho-lastic* 29 (21 Nov 36) 6–7+. A symposium.

McEvoy, J. P. "Back of Me Hand to You." *SEP* 24 (24 Dec 38) 8–9+. Joseph Breen of the Hays office and his relationship with the Catholic Legion of Decency—history and influence of both.

Ferguson, Otis. "Legion Rides Again." *New Rep* 105 (22 Dec 41) 861. The code and the pressure groups versus quality films.

Joseph, Robert. "In Defense of the Films as Public Art and Industry." *Arts & Arch* 61 (May 44) 32+. Against the investigations and suspicions of governmental agencies and individuals.

Ernst, Morris. "Freedom to Read, See, and Hear." *Harper's* 191 (July 45) 51–53. A plan for release of restrictions on the chief communications media, including films.

Eastman, F. "Motion Pictures and American Culture." *Recreation* 40 (July 46) 228. Censorship and decency codes not enough to get better pictures; some solutions offered.

Nathan, George Jean. "If Hollywood Came to Dunsinane." *Am Mercury* 63 (Nov 46) 598–604. How the theatre would fare under U.S. and Hollywood restraints.

"The Freedom of the Screen." *Screen Writer* 3 (No. 2, July 47) 8–21. Issues of censorship, the code, and congressional investigation reviewed in several pieces by Martin Field, Vladimir Pozner, Morris Cohn, Bernard Schoenfeld; report on Eric Johnston's visits to all studios.

Koenig, Lester. "Conference on Thought Control." *Screen Writer* III (Aug 47) 11–15. A report of nine panel discussions on the various arts and how they are being affected adversely by direct and indirect political pressure, accusations, censorship; sponsor was Progressive Citizens of America and its Hollywood Council of the Arts, Sciences and Professions.

Pichel, Irving. "Areas of Silence." *Hwd Q* 3 (No. 1, Fall 47) 51–55. Theatrical imitation and big business fears keep film from doing controversial subjects.

Pichel, Irving. "On Freedom of the Screen." *Screen Writer* III (Nov 47) 1–4. Dramas present misbehavior but don't necessarily support it; both dramatists and censors should recognize this.

Luraschi, Luigi. "Censorship at Home and Abroad." *Annals of Am Acad of Polit and Soc Sci* 254 (Nov 47) 147–152. The kinds of censorship in movies, why they are necessary, and how they benefit the public and the movie industry as well.

"Censors Raise a Howl." *Life* 25 (25 Oct 48) 57–60. A brief survey of contemporary censorship: the banning of *Oliver Twist* in the U.S.; the closing of Disney's *Bambi* in the USSR.

"Fadeout for Censors?" *Time* 54 (28 Nov 49) 82. The case of *Lost Boundaries*.

Nathan, Paul. "Books into Films." *Publishers Weekly* 159 (20 Jan 51) 254–255. The Code and Bureau of Customs.

Spaeth, Otto L. "Fogged Screen." *Mag of Art* 44 (Feb 51) 44. Director of American Federation of Arts speaks out against banning of Rossellini's *The Miracle* and a program of Charlie Chaplin films. See also letter 44 (May 51) 194.

Barr, Alfred H., Jr. "Fogged Screen—Reply." *Mag of Art* 44 (May 51) 194. A long letter to the editor condemning the censoring of *The Miracle* and *The Bicycle Thief*.

Seldes, G. "Short Angry View of Film Censorship." *Th Arts* 35 (Aug 51) 56–57. The dwindling privilege of free expression in film corresponds to dwindling free expression in schools, politics, etc.

Rice, Elmer. "Entertainment in the Age of McCarthy." *New Rep* 128 (13 Apr 53) 14–17. The devious ways pressure is brought to bear on U.S. films.

"Hullabaloo over *The Moon Is Blue*." *Life* 35 (13 Jul 53) 71–72+. Trouble with the Breen office and the Catholic Legion of Decency.

"Editorial: A Free Screen?" *Life* 36 (8 Feb 54) 28. The Supreme Court decision declaring the censoring of *La Ronde* and *M* unconstitutional does not alter the need for up-to-date self-censorship by the industry.

"Trend Toward Laxity?" *Time* 65 (30 May 55) 84. A widening breach between the Production Code and the Roman Catholic Legion of Decency.

"How Do You See the Movies? As Entertainment and Offensive at Times or as a Candid Art." *Newswk* 56 (8 Aug 55) 50–51. America's movie censorship.

"Volunteer Censors." *New Rep* 134 (23 Jan 56) 4–5. Both the Legion of Decency and the MPAA Code seem to be losing influence and power.

Cogley, John. "*Baby Doll* Controversy." *Commonweal* 65 (11 Jan 57) 381. Author says no civil-rights issue is at stake.

Ardrey, Robert. "Hollywood: The Toll of the Frenzied Forties." *Reporter* 16 (21 Mar 57) 29–33. Screenwriter's recollections about moral and political pressures.

Butcher, Maryvonne. "Films and Freedom." *Commonweal* 69 (17 Oct 58) 65–67+. Strict political and cultural control in Eastern Europe produces creative films.

Wirt, Frederick M. "To See or Not to See: The Case Against Censorship." *FQ* 13 (No. 1, Fall 59) 26–31. Censorship offends democracy because it promotes irresponsible exercise of power through vague standards, it brings the state too deeply into things which should be personally decided, and it blocks the free play of ideas central to democracy.

Knight, Arthur. "The New Frankness in Films." *Sat Rev* 42 (19 Dec 59) 18+. Reviews movie battles with censorship and current situation.

"A New Look at Movie Censorship." *Senior Scholastic* 77 (11 Jan 61) 8–9+. A forum on the pros and cons.

Schumach, Murray. "The Censor as Movie Director." *NYTM* (12 Feb 61) 15+. The influence of censorship and the code in current film making.

"New Look at Movie Censorship?" *Senior Scholastic* 78 (1 Mar 61) 4. Discussion.

Holmes, M. "Mother Speaks Up for Censorship." *Today's Health* 40 (Jan 62) 50–51+.

Crosby, John. "Speaking Out: Movies Are Too Dirty." *SEP* 235 (10 Nov 62) 8+.

"Censorship Now." *Film* (No. 43, Autumn 65) 4–5+. A realistic view of censorship and a plea for methods to improve the censor's task.

Elkin, Fred. "Censorship and Pressure Groups." *Phylon* (Spring 66) 71–80.

Valenti, Jack. "A Message to Film-Makers." *Action* 3 (No. 2, Mar–Apr 68) 19–21. The problems of censorship and freedom of the screen.

Clayton. George. "Classification—and the Right to be 'Obscene' But Not Absurd." *Cinema* (Calif) 5 (No. 2, 1969) 22–23. Opinion piece on the Hollywood code, censorship, and rating systems.

Huffman, James. "Movies and the Moral Flux." *Chris Today* 13 (4 July 69) 32–33. MPAA and the National Catholic Office for Motion Pictures.

7c(1). CENSORSHIP IN THE U.S.

7c(1a). History and Opinions

[See also 6d(3).]

Weinberg, Herman G. "The Cinema and the Censors." *Close Up* 7 (No. 4, Oct 30) 252–259. Censorship in America.

"Censor and the Screen." *State Government* 7 (Sep 34) 183–186. A brief discussion of the censorship movement and an examination of state censorship boards.

Ernst, Morris L. "Sense and Censorship." *Cinema Arts* 1 (No. 2, July 37) 18–21. Brief history; differences in state laws; the decision-making process.

Calverton, V. F. "Cinema Censorship." *Current Hist* 50 (Mar 39) 47.

Hamman, M. "Do You Want Your Movies Censored?" *Good Housekeeping* 110 (Apr 40) 13+. Many movies cited to show that, despite censorship, American films are the least restricted in the world.

"Administrative Censorship Limits Several Films." *Publishers Weekly* 149 (16 Feb 46) 1136.

"Movie Censorship." *Life* 21 (28 Oct 46) 79–82+. How films are altered to fit U.S. censorship laws; both foreign and domestic films discussed.

Frank, S. "Headaches of a Movie Censor." *SEP* 220 (27 Sep 47) 20–27. A visit with a state movie censor and a history of censorship in Hollywood.

Knepper, M. "Don't Chain the Movies!" *Forum* 108 (Nov 47) 265–269. A call for change in censorship policies.

Lang, Fritz. "Freedom of the Screen." *Th Arts* 31 (Dec 47) 52–55. A plea for a reexamination of the goals of censorship.

Tyler, Parker. "Wanted: The Whole Film Package." *Nation* 168 (25 June 49) 711. Questions the fixed length of films and the butchery of censorship.

Levy, Herbert M. "The Case Against Film Censorship." *FIR* 1 (Apr 50) 1–2+. Staff counsel for the American Civil Liberties Union discusses expanding trends of censorship in the U.S. since 1915.

"Sniffing Out the Sin in the Cinema." *Collier's* 125 (13 May 50) 78. Against film censorship proposal.

"The Censor." *Time* 56 (25 Dec 50) 56. The trouble: too many of them.

"Censor in the Barnyard." *Time* 58 (29 Oct 51). *See 2h.*

Knight, Arthur. "Those Censors Again." *Sat Rev* 36 (21 Nov 53) 51. Is a documentary record film such as *Latuko* subject to the same censorship as the entertainment film?

London, Ephraim S. "The Freedom to See." *Nation* 177 (19 Dec 53) 544–545. The state of movie censorship and a personal opinion about "licensing."

"Movies an Ever Growing Moral Problem." *American* 90 (30 Jan 54) 432. Supreme Court against film censorship.

Mayer, Arthur. "A Movie Exhibitor Looks at Censorship." *Reporter* 10 (2 Mar 54) 35–40.

Lehman, Milton. "Who Censors Our Movies?" *Look* 18 (6 Apr 54) 86–92. An exploration of the "jungle of censorship" state by state

and in Hollywood. Discussion (4 May) 18; (18 May) 16.

Fearon, John. "Movies and Morals." *America* 91 (5 June 54) 277–279. Author's advice on censorship: movies should not lower the average moral standard.

Buckley, Michael J. "State Censorship of Movies." *Cath World* 180 (Oct 54) 24–27. Voluntary codes having failed, the state has the duty to step in and guard the common good.

Everson, William K. "Cut Copies." *S&S* 24 (Oct–Dec 54). *See 4e(1e).*

Flick, Hugo M. "A Wide-Angle Look at Censorship." *F Cult* 1 (No. 3, 1955) 1–3. Head of New York State Motion Picture Division defends law requiring licensing of motion pictures prior to public exhibition.

"The Censors." *Time* 66 (25 July 55) 86. Films in trouble with censors.

"Movies and Censorship: *The Man with the Golden Arm* and *The Prisoner*." *Commonweal* 63 (6 Jan 56) 345. Subject alone as a basis for restraint is not enough; treatment too should be considered.

LaBarre, H. "Why Movies Are Censored." *Cosmopolitan* 141 (Oct 56) 72–75. Are we moving toward relaxation of restrictions as cultural standards change and foreign films arrive?

Knight, Arthur. "Lady Chatterley's Lawyer." *Sat Rev* 42 (25 July 59) 25+. Defends freedom of films from censorship.

"State and the Films." *America* 103 (13 Aug 60) 526. How to safeguard a nation's morals when film censors are losing their power.

"Bluer Movies, Not-So-Blue Noses." *Life* 49 (5 Dec 60) 46. Is more censorship needed?

Wald, J. "Movie Censorship: The First Wedge." *Sat Rev* 44 (8 Apr 61) 53–54. Discussion 44 (13 May 61) 67–68.

Mayer, Arthur. "How Much Can the Movies Say?" *Sat Rev* 45 (3 Nov 62) 18–20+. Proposal to give theatre owners the responsibility of censorship; views of parents, theatre owners, and the Motion Picture Association.

Batten, Mary. "An Interview with Ephraim London." *F Com* 1 (No. 4, 1963) 2–19. Comments on various local and state censorship boards and the status of the legal concept of obscenity by the man who argued the *Miracle* case before the Supreme Court.

Scott, Barbara. "Motion Picture Censorship and the Exhibitor." *F Com* 2 (No. 4, Fall 64) 56–60. Attorney for Motion Picture Association reviews current cases and attacks the idea of statutory classification of audiences.

Pilpel, Harriet F. "How Can You Do That?" *Publishers Weekly* 190 (26 Dec 66) 55–56. In favor of community standards for censorship in general (film and nonfilm); case of Genet's *Un Chant d'Amour.*

"What Is the State of the Law?" *Current* 92 (Feb 68) 42–49.

Sarris, Andrew. "Censorship: A View from New York." *S&S* 38 (Autumn 69) 202–203. The situation there is now one of the most liberated; Sarris gives his views on the whole sexual revolution in the cinema.

O'Dell, Paul. *"The Rise and Fall of Free Speech in America."* *Silent Picture* (No. 9, Winter 70–71) 19–20. A review of Griffith's pamphlet, published after *The Birth of a Nation,* in which the director makes a strong statement on censorship as a threat not only to artistic freedom but to knowledge.

7c(1b). Local Practices

"Grand Rapids Demands Better Movies." *Chris Cent* 50 (12 Apr 33) 483. A movement to give local directors of public welfare the power to regulate the pictures shown.

"Keeping the Movies Pure." *Nation* 137 (8 Nov 33) 528. Doubts effectiveness of the New York Board of Censors.

"Licensing Motion Pictures in New York State." *School and Society* 40 (17 Nov 34) 654–655. Review of year's work by censor board.

"Sound and Fury over Free Speech." *Lit Dig* 123 (May 37) 3–4. Decision against Kansas newsreel censorship.

"Boner in Memphis." *Collier's* 115 (2 June 45) 78. Local censorship of a film because of a Negro cast member ("Rochester").

"Higher Criticism in Memphis." *Time* 46 (13 Aug 45) 20.

"Moral Breach." *Time* 54 (31 Oct 49). *See 8c(4).*

Velie, Lester. "You Can't See That Movie." *Collier's* 125 (6 May 50) 11–14+. Reviews local censorship actions.

Alpert, Hollis. "Talk with a Movie Censor." *SRL* 35 (22 Nov 52) 21+. Discussion (13 Dec 52) 22 and (27 Dec 52) 23. Dr. Hugh Flick, New York state censor, discusses procedures, policies, effects of court decisions, especially *The Miracle, La Ronde.*

Cummings, Ridgely. "Film Censorship in Los Angeles?" *New Rep* 139 (2 Sep 58) 3+. Controversy over a list of films, including *Un Chien Andalou.*

Levy, Herman M. "Industry Case Digest." *JSPG* (Dec 60) 27–29. A lower court decision against the Pennsylvania censorship law.

"Who Bans What." *Newswk* 57 (13 Feb 61) 89–90+. Censors in Atlanta and elsewhere.

"Freedom and Film." *F Com* 1 (No. 3, 1962) 21–22. Notes on local censorship in U.S.

"Defense Against Dirt." *Time* 95 (9 Mar 70) 20. A day with the Board of Motion Picture Censors of Maryland.

Kunkin, Art. "Pornography Wins in Los Angeles." *F&F* 16 (No. 10, Jul 70) 60–61.

Editor of *The Los Angeles Free Press* writes on recent court case.

7c(1c). Supreme Court Decisions

"Limit on Movie Censorship." *Bus Wk* (31 May 52) 33. Supreme Court's decision on *The Miracle* extends the free-speech guarantee to the movies.

"Free Cinema." *Time* 59 (2 June 52) 22. The case of *The Miracle.*

"Another Miracle Needed." *Nation* 174 (7 June 52) 537. The Supreme Court's decision to reverse the ban on Rossellini's *The Miracle.*

"Freedom of Film." *Newswk* 39 (9 June 52) 91. The Supreme Court's ruling that movies have the same Constitutional freedom as speech and the press.

"Court Finds Sacrilege No Legal Concept." *Chris Cent* 69 (11 June 52) 693. Roberto Rossellini's *The Miracle* and the Supreme Court decision.

"*Miracle* Decision." *Commonweal* 56 (13 June 52) 235–236. The Supreme Court decision on *The Miracle* case is assessed and endorsed.

"*Miracle* Decision." *New Rep* 126 (23 June 52) 8.

Walters, F. "Supreme Court Ruling on *The Miracle* and *Pinky.*" *Th Arts* 36 (Aug 52) 74–77.

"Movie Censorship Gets Shakier." *Bus Wk* (9 Jan 54) 33. The industry's own code criticized; Supreme Court cases.

"Freedom to Film." *Time* 63 (25 Jan 54) 23. The cases of *La Ronde* and *M.*

"Supreme Court: No State Film Bans." *Newswk* 43 (25 Jan 54) 27.

"Censoring the Censors." *New Rep* 130 (1 Feb 54) 5. The Supreme Court's reversal of bans on *The Miracle* and *La Ronde* does *not* mean censorship is dead.

"Court Strikes Down Censorship Acts." *Chris Cent* 71 (3 Feb 54) 132. Concern for the moral standards of the nation and the Supreme Court in cases of *La Ronde* and *M.*

Clancy, W. P. "Freedom of the Screen." *Commonweal* 59 (19 Feb 54) 500–502. Applauding Supreme Court's decision overruling bans on *La Ronde, The Miracle.* Reply with rejoinder 59 (12 Mar 54) 578–579.

"One Man's Obscenity." *Time* 70 (25 Nov 57) 33. Supreme Court ruling on *The Game of Love.*

"Adultery Is an Idea." *Time* 74 (13 July 59) 44. U.S. Supreme Court decision on *Lady Chatterley's Lover.*

"High Court's Ruling on Sex in Movies: *Lady Chatterley's Lover.*" *US News & World Report* 47 (13 July 59) 50.

"Public Morals and the Constitution: Film Version of *Lady Chatterley's Lover.*" *America* 101 (18 July 59) 526–527. A case history and criticism of the Supreme Court decision which declared the New York film-licensing law unconstitutional.

"Movie Censorship Upheld." *America* 104 (4 Feb 61) 582.

Smith, R. H. "Supreme Court's Affirmation of Official Censorship." *Publishers Weekly* 179 (6 Feb 61) 68. On the Times Film Corporation case.

"Retreat From Freedom." *Chris Cent* 78 (8 Feb 61) 163–164. Reply (14 June 61) 749. Editorial on the U.S. Supreme Court case of *Don Juan* and the freedom of expression.

"Free Speech and Movies." *Commonweal* 73 (10 Feb 61) 495–496. Supreme Court on *Times Film Corporation* v. *Chicago.*

"Censoring Movies." *Commonweal* 74 (31 Mar 61) 17. *Times Film Corporation* v. *Chicago.*

"Censoring the Censors." *Time* 85 (12 Mar 65) 72. U.S. Supreme Court decision on Maryland censorship law.

Fleishman, Stanley. "Movies, Politics, and the Supreme Court." *JSPG* (Sep 68) 35–38. Quotations from recent cases on obscenity.

7c(1d). Films Censored

"U.S. Jury Tries and Condemns Czech Moving Picture." *Newswk* 6 (6 July 35) 18. Banning of *Ecstasy.*

"Pretty, Witty Nelly." *Wilson Lib Bul* 10 (Oct 35) 136+. *Nell Gwyn,* banned in U.S., said to be a superior picture; cites defect of inflexibility in film censorship.

Earle, G. H. "*Spain in Flames;* Reply with Rejoinder." *Nation* 144 (10 Apr 37) 396. Why censorship of this film was inexcusable; effects of war propaganda films discussed.

"*Spain in Flames:* Film Censorship." *Nation* 144 (27 Mar 37) 340–341. Comment on Pennsylvania's ban on Spanish Civil War documentary.

Munro, W. C. "Cameras Don't Lie." *Current Hist* 46 (Aug 37) 37–42. Suppressed newsreels of the South Chicago strike massacre pose a censorship question.

"Freedom of Film and Press." *Chris Cent* 55 (2 Feb 38) 136–137. An attack on movie censorship spurred by the banning by Chicago police of a *March of Time* film concerning Nazi Germany.

"Classic into Movie." *Publishers Weekly* 133 (5 Feb 38) 727. Problems, particularly censorship, involved in D. O. Selznick's *Tom Sawyer.*

"New York Censors Release *Harvest.*" *Publishers Weekly* 136 (23 Sep 39) 1263. Previously censored French film released.

"Censorship: *Oliver Twist.*" *Nation* 167 (30 Oct 48) 479. Criticism of the British film for representing a Jew in the worst tradition of cruel caricature.

"Is Movie Censorship Legal?" *Bus Wk* (3 Dec 59) 23. The movie *Lost Boundaries,* produced by Louis De Rochement, discussed as a test case on whether precensorship is constitutional.

"The Censor." *Time* 57 (8 Jan 51) 72. Roberto Rossellini's *The Miracle.*

" 'Ways of Love' Controversy." *Life* 30 (15 Jan 51) 59–60+. New York license commissioner tries unsuccessfully to stop the showing of Rossellini's *The Miracle.*

Wohlforth, Robert. "People and Pickets in Front of Paris Theater Where *Miracle* Is Being Shown." *New Rep* 124 (5 Feb 51) 13.

"*The Miracle.*" *Time* 57 (19 Feb 51) 60–61.

"By Order of the Board." *Time* 57 (26 Feb 51) 98+. Case of *The Miracle.*

"*Miracle* Film Banned by New York State Regents." *Publishers Weekly* 159 (3 Mar 51) 1131.

Hart, Henry. "*The Miracle* and *Oliver Twist.*" *FIR* 2 (May 51) 1–6. Two cases of censorship examined.

Marshall, Margaret. "Notes by the Way, the *Miracle* Case." *Nation* 173 (24 Nov 51) 451. The decision on *The Miracle* will affect the whole future of cinema as a form of communication.

"*La Ronde* Has Censor Trouble." *Life* 32 (21 Jan 52) 56.

"Chicago Police Ban *The Miracle.*" *Publishers Weekly* 162 (30 Aug 52) 820.

"*Limelight* Out." *Time* 61 (9 Feb 53) 96. *Limelight* banned because investigation of Chaplin's political activities not completed.

"Cutting a Queen's Choice." *Life* 36 (29 Mar 54) 97–98. A nude bathing scene with Gina Lollobrigida in René Clair's *Beauties of the Night* is fit for a queen (of England) but not for U.S. censors.

"Russell Rumpus, Little Rock." *Bus Wk* (10 Apr 54) 172. *The French Line,* starring Jane Russell, banned in Little Rock.

de Laurot, Edward L. "The Price of Fear." *F Cult* 1 (No. 3, 1955) 3–6+. Detailed analysis of the significance of the deletions made for U.S. premiere of Clouzot's *Wages of Fear,* a practice which the author concludes is prejudicial to the general public interest.

Irvine, Keith. "Film You Won't See: Mutilated Version of *Wages of Fear.*" *Nation* 181 (6 Aug 55) 109–110. The distributor's cutting of Clouzot's film is symptomatic of America's fear of reality on the screen.

"Brigitte at the Bar." *Time* 71 (24 Feb 58) 98. Controversy in Philadelphia over *And God Created Woman.*

"Lady Chatterley's Licence." *Economist* 192 (25 July 59) 218. U.S. Supreme Court refuses to grant a license to French film version of *Lady Chatterley's Lover.*

"Censorship of Movies." *New Rep* 144 (27 Feb 61) 8. Problems of *Don Juan* in Chicago.

Haines, F. "Art in Court: City of Angels Vs. *Scorpio Rising.*" *Nation* 199 (14 Sep 64)

123–125. Analysis of theory of redeeming social value in art accused of obscenity.

"Goldfarb Case Fought by Anti-Censorship Forces." *Publishers Weekly* 187 (18 Jan 65) 105–106.

"Popular Mechanics of Sex." *Time* 96 (28 Sep 70) 58–63. The decision of the U.S. Court of Appeals to release the Swedish film *Language of Love.*

"Burden on the Censor." *Newswk* 65 (29 Mar 65) 88. Danish *A Stranger Knocks* in court: more freedom for producers.

"Guilt Despite Association." *Time* 88 (16 Dec 66) 82. California court decision on Genet's *Un Chant d'Amour.*

"*Ars Longa* . . . Censoring of *Ulysses.*" *Time* 89 (12 May 67) 49.

"Grove to Fight U.S. Film Seizure." *Publishers Weekly* 193 (5 Feb 68) 46. Case of Swedish film *I Am Curious (Yellow).*

"Curiouser and Curiouser." *Newswk* 72 (9 Dec 68) 111. United States Court of Appeals decision on *I Am Curious (Yellow).*

Carter, J. M. "Witness for Obscenity." *Lib J* 95 (July 70) 2431. A theatre manager and projectionist on trial in Jackson, Mississippi, for showing *The Fox:* report by a witness for the defense.

7c(2). PRIVATE PRESSURE GROUPS

Richardson, Anna Steese. "Talking Pictures and Community Taste." *Woman's Home Companion* 57 (Jan 30) 32. Director of Good Citizen Bureau reviews guidelines for tasteful films.

Gilman, Catheryne Cooke. "Better Movies— But How?" *Woman's J* 15 (Feb 30) 10–12. President of Federal Motion Picture Council of America says "no" to women's organizations cooperating with film industry for better movies.

"Good Citizenship and the Movies." *Chris Cent* 47 (26 Feb 30). *See 7b(6).*

Winter, Alice Ames. "And So to Hollywood." *Woman's J* 15 (Mar 30) 7–9. Recommends women's organizations cooperate with film industry for better movies.

"Exposing Another Attempt at Camouflage." *Chris Cent* 47 (5 Mar 30) 293. Committee on the Use of the Motion Picture in Religious Education proves not to be independent of the industry. Discussion (19 Mar 30) 371.

Eastman, Elaine Goodale. "Handmaidens of Hollywood?" *Chris Cent* 48 (25 Feb 31) 268–270. Outlines failures of women's club in cleaning up movies.

"Fixing the Blame for Bad Pictures." *Lit Dig* 110 (18 July 31) 18. Summary of religious attacks and industry's defense.

"Demand Growing for Social Control of Movies." *Chris Cent* 48 (21 Oct 31) 1301.

Reviews religious and educational groups' calls for legislation.

Richardson, Anna Steese. "It's Up to the Box Office." *Woman's Home Companion* 58 (Nov 31) 54. Suggests boycott unless films are bettered.

"Women Demand Movie Investigation." *Chris Cent* 48 (9 Dec 31) 1549. Recommendations from International Council of Women.

Marriot, V. E. "P.T.A. and the Movies." *Chris Cent* 50 (25 Jan 33) 124. New program is against any "cooperation" with movie industry's hypocrisy.

White, Lillian McKim. "Better Week-End Movies." *Parents Mag* 8 (Mar 33) 28. Suggests that paid advertisements of motion pictures suitable for children be put in the newspaper each weekend.

"Who Supports the National Board of Review?" *Chris Cent* 51 (28 Feb 34) 276–277. "Passed" implies approval; producers thus gain support for their films.

"Churches War Against Obscenity." *Lit Dig* 117 (3 Mar 34) 21.

"This Way to Better Movies." *Chris Cent* 51 (7 Mar 34) 312–313. The objectives of the Motion Picture Research Council to oppose block booking, publicize the Payne Fund reports, and encourage community control of theatres.

"Youth and Morals." *Time* 23 (2 Apr 34) 30. Motion Picture Research Council has Mrs. August Belmont as new president; funds sought now that Payne Fund studies are completed.

Belmont, E. "Bettering Motion Pictures." *New Rep* 78 (18 Apr 34) 273–274. Letter to the editor: the Motion Picture Research Council has moved from investigation to action (from its president, Eleanor R. Belmont).

Gilman, Catheryne Cooke. "The Movie Problem." *Ladies' Home J* 51 (July 34) 104–105. Summary of program of National Congress of PTA.

"Movie Consumers." *Survey* 70 (July 34) 221. Cites success of religious groups in boycott threats.

"A Successful Crusade." *Nat Rep* 22 (July 34) 10. Cites religious movement against movies as success.

"Farewell Broadway!" *Chris Cent* 51 (25 Jul 34) 966–968. Heywood Broun and ACLU question censorship threat concealed in boycott of movies.

"Film Boycott." *Newswk* 3 (30 June 34) 20; 4 (7 July 34) 5; (14 July 34) 33; (21 July 34) 22; (28 July 34) 21. Churchmen of all sects protest.

"Better Movies." *Sci Am* 151 (Sep 34) 121. Commends religious attacks on movies.

Pringle, Henry F. "Panic over Hollywood." *American* 118 (Oct 34) 24–25+. Hollywood producers face boycott of "salacious, indecent, vulgar" pictures.

Walters, Raymond. "A Conference of National Organizations Interested in Motion Pictures." *School and Society* 40 (6 Oct 34) 451–453.

"Is the Movie Victory Won?" *Chris Cent* 51 (14 Nov 34) 1446–1448. Only temporarily, but better pictures are coming.

"New Move for Screen Reform." *Lit Dig* 119 (19 Jan 35) 18. Motion Picture Foundation acts as advisors to Catholics, Protestants, Jews.

"Marching Against Hollywood." *Wil Lib Bul* 9 (Sep 34) 28; (Nov 34) 138+; (Feb 35) 316–317. Traces religious movement against film immorality.

"Movie Moguls Cleaning Up the Screen." *Lit Dig* 119 (27 Apr 35) 18. Religious movements appear successful.

Fink, F. "Down with Doubles." *Lit Dig* 124 (27 Nov 37) 13–15. The forming of the Anti-Movie Double Feature League of America.

"Double Movie Scrap." *Bus Wk* (5 Mar 38) 45. Proposed Chicago ordinance limiting double features is held up as PTA backtracks.

Taylor, W. "Secret Movie Censors: Behind the Attack on *Blockade.*" *Nation* 147 (9 Jul 38) 38–40. Claims theatre chains privately agree not to show certain films; projectionist unions also have influence.

Sage, M. "Hearst over Hollywood: Matter of Orson Welles' Film, *Citizen Kane.*" *New Rep* 104 (24 Feb 41). *See 9, Citizen Kane.*

Peattie, Donald. "Nature of Things." *Audubon Mag* 44 (Sep 42) 266–269. Organized sportsmen protest Walt Disney's *Bambi* while others applaud its message on hunters.

Metzger, C. R. "Pressure Groups and the Motion Picture Industry: Influence Upon Producers in Selection of Screen Material." *Annals of Am Acad of Polit and Soc Sci* 254 (Nov 47) 110–115.

"National Board Reviewing Committees in 1949." *FIR* 1 (Feb 50) 38. The Review Committee, the Schools Motion Picture Committee, the Exceptional Film Committee, the Committee on Nontheatrical Films, and the National Motion Picture Council.

Ramsaye, Terry. "Forty Years of the National Board." *FIR* 1 (Feb 50) 23–24. Some of the background that led to the foundation of the National Board of Review of Motion Pictures.

"Futility of Censorship." *Nation* 172 (17 Feb 51) 147. Attempts by religious groups to censor public entertainments suggest return to separation of church and state.

"Your Town and the Movies." *FIR* 2 (Apr 51) 1–5. Staff of the National Board of Review of Motion Pictures urges the establishment of more motion-picture councils and lists their activities and benefits.

"Censorship, Private Brand." *Bus Wk* (24 Nov 51) 130–131. New TV code and movie incidents spotlight rise in censorship by private groups.

Edwards, Clara. "Women and Better Films." *FIR* 7 (Mar 56) 111–113. National Chairman of Motion Pictures of the National Council of Women lists her duties and ten of the fifty-two films her organization supports for 1956.

Engel, Samuel G. "Motion Pictures, Fine Wares for the Wary." *PTA Mag* 53 (Sep 58) 29. Parents share the responsibility with film producers for what films children see.

Limbacher, James L. "Movies Are Better Than Ever." *Lib J* 89 (15 May 64) 2152–2155. Surveys consumer groups in U.S. and Great Britain which attempt to improve children's film fare: Children's Film Library, Teaching Films Custodians, Schools Motion Picture Committee, Children's Film Foundation.

Boyd, M. "Church's Word to the Film Industry." *Chris Cent* 83 (9 Mar 66) 305–306. 1965 motion-picture awards of National Catholic Office for Motion Pictures and the broadcasting and film commission of the National Council of Churches.

7c(2a). Local Action

Williamson, A. Edmund. "Ridding Local Movies of Gangster Films." *Am City* 45 (Sep 31) 112–113. Chamber of Commerce Better Films Committee in New Jersey curtail showing of gangster films by mayor's power over theatre license renewal.

Browne, Alice B. "How Our Town Got Better Movies." *Parents Mag* 7 (Jan 32) 28+. Hillsdale (Illinois) PTA movie chairman describes plan.

Wright, C. M. "Community Stands on Its Rights." *Chris Cent* 49 (3 Aug 32) 961. Local committee prevents showing of *Scarface* in East Orange, New Jersey.

Campbell, Harold G. "Moving Pictures and School Children." *School and Society* 39 (30 June 34) 837. Study to determine how schools can pressure for more wholesome films.

Walker, Hannah R. "How We Got Better Movies in Glen Ellyn." *Rotarian* 73 (Nov 48) 14–16. The whole town helps pick them through a Children's Film Council.

Lucht, Mrs. W. A. "Time for a Movie Movement?" *Rotarian* 74 (Mar 49) 3. An answer to letters asking how Children's Film Council works in Glen Ellyn, Illinois.

"Baltimore Does It Quietly." *America* 98 (8 Feb 58) 526. How quietly persuasive people can effectively work for censorship.

Haymaker, Frank. "Better Movies for Your Children." *PTA Mag* 52 (Apr 58) 16–18. How one community brings good films to its children.

Eastman, Fred. "Ungrading Hometown Movies." *Chris Cent* 76 (14 Jan 59) 47–48. Report on Claremont, California, citizens trying to get better movies by pressuring exhibitors.

Moffett, Hugh. "Sexy Movies? Chadron, Nebraska, Tries Gentle Persuasion." *Life* 66 (30 May 69) 52B–52D+. Women against "adult" films.

7c(2b). Catholic

"A Priest Reviews the Pictures." *Chris Cent* 48 (7 Jan 31) 5. Pressure to cancel his radio movie reviews.

"Catholic Church and the Movies." *Chris Cent* 51 (18 Apr 34) 515–516. Firmer tone in Catholic attacks.

"Catholics Attack Obscenity on the Screen." *Lit Dig* 117 (5 May 34) 22. Nationwide movement to refuse patronage.

"Catholic Crusade for Better Movies." *Chris Cent* 51 (16 May 34) 652. National Catholic welfare conference wants pledges not to see objectionable pictures.

"Decency Plus!" *Chris Cent* 51 (13 June 34) 790–791. A million Catholics have signed new pledge of Legion of Decency; the Reverend Daniel Lord is disillusioned with code he helped write.

"Movies' Last Chance." *Chris Cent* 51 (20 June 34) 822–824. Praise for Catholic boycott.

"Legion of Decency Presses Film Boycott." *Lit Dig* 117 (23 June 34) 19.

"Legion of Decency (Cont'd)" *Time* 24 (2 July 34) 18. Archbishop of Cincinnati, leader in setting up Legion of Decency, announces producers' jury for Production Code is abolished and Joseph Breen's power increased; other results of Legion pressure across the country.

Angly, Edward. "Boycott Threat Is Forcing Movie Clean-Up." *Lit Dig* 118 (7 July 34) 7+. MGM cancels *The Postman Always Rings Twice,* Goldwyn scratches *Barbary Coast,* and Paramount cleans up *It Ain't No Sin.*

Angly, Edward. "Film Boycott Moves Hollywood to Action." *Lit Dig* 118 (14 July 34) 7+. Pope gives crusade his blessing; producers publicly announce "era of sophistication."

"Cardinal's Campaign." *Time* 24 (16 July 34) 28. First Legion of Decency classification of pictures; other developments.

Jones, Llewellyn. "Cardinal Mundelein Attacks." *Chris Cent* 51 (18 July 34) 945–946. How the Catholics are developing their boycott.

Skinner, Richard Dana. "Movies and Morals." *Commonweal* 20 (27 July 34) 329. Summary of Legion of Decency precepts.

"Campaign Against Objectionable Motion Pictures." *Cath World* 139 (Aug 34) 617–618.

Reviews Legion of Decency and other steps to raise moral tone of motion pictures.

"Catholic Drive for Decency." *Chris Cent* 51 (15 Aug 34) 1037–1039. It doesn't reach the corporate structure of the industry (block booking) or the general distortions of life shown on screens.

"Progress of the Legion of Decency." *Commonweal* 20 (17 Aug 34) 375–376. It is having a real impact.

Collins, Michael. "What Next in Hollywood?" *Commonweal* 20 (31 Aug 34) 421–423. Cites defect in Legion of Decency in absence of agreement upon "indecent" and "immoral."

McMahon, Joseph H. "The Battle for Decency." *Commonweal* 20 (7 Sep 34) 441–443. Restatement of principles behind Legion of Decency.

Flaherty, Miriam R. "Sentimentality and the Screen." *Commonweal* 20 (5 Oct 34) 522–523. Questions role of Legion of Decency and calls for Church to recognize documentary film.

Schwegler, Edward S. "What Next, Legion of Decency?" *Commonweal* 21 (16 Nov 34) 84–86. Calls for national list of movie ratings.

" 'I Condemn.' " *Time* 24 (17 Dec 34) 32. First Legion of Decency pledge read at Mass in thousands of Catholic churches.

Boyle, T. O'R. "We Are All Censors." *Commonweal* 21 (21 Dec 34) 226–228. Defense of Legion of Decency.

"Legion of Decency Campaign Intensified." *Lit Dig* 118 (22 Dec 34) 20. Protestants join Catholic crusade.

"Black Side of a White List." *Nation* 140 (9 Jan 35) 34. Suggests Legion of Decency is dealing in religious censorship.

"Legion of Decency's First Year." *Chris Cent* 52 (27 Mar 35) 392–394. Decency is not enough; artists should be freed to make great pictures.

"Vatican over Hollywood." *Nation* 143 (11 July 36) 33. Influence of Legion of Decency on the making of films is unjustified.

"Hollywood Encyclical." *Time* 28 (13 July 36) 50. Extracts from Pope Pius XI statement praising Legion of Decency and deploring "loss of innocence so often suffered in motion picture theaters."

"Encyclical on Motion Pictures." *Cath World* 143 (Aug 36) 618–619. Synopsis of Pius XI July statement in favor of "combating whatever contributes to lessening the people's sense of decency and honor."

Wyatt, E. V. "Wolves in Celluloid." *Cath World* 143 (Aug 36) 599–602. Various urgings of Pope Pius XI that cinema be reviewed by Catholic agencies; "good" ones approved.

"Shaw Alarmed at Censorship." *Newswk* 8 (19 Sep 36) 44. Report on lengthy George Bernard Shaw letter to *New York Times* on

Catholic attempt to precensor United Artists production of *Saint Joan.*

"GBS and the Catholic Censorship." *New Rep* 88 (23 Sep 36) 173. Comment on Shaw's letter to *New York Times,* revealing list of changes demanded by Catholic Action organization before *Saint Joan* could be made into a movie by Hollywood.

"Shaw on Catholic censorship." *Chris Cent* 53 (23 Sep 36) 1244. Reply with rejoinder (7 Oct 36) 1332.

Farrell, James T. "GBS Interviews the Pope." *Nation* 143 (3 Oct 36) 387–388. An imaginary conversation in which Shaw protests attempts to stop plans for *Saint Joan* in Hollywood.

Yeaman, E. "Catholic Movie Censorship." *New Rep* 96 (5 Oct 38) 233–235. A critical look at rulings by the Legion of Decency.

"How Are the Movies?" *Commonweal* 30 (4 Aug 39) 358–359. Cinema from a Catholic point of view.

"Legion of Decency's Attack Shelves Garbo Film." *Chris Cent* 58 (17 Dec 41) 1564. *Two-Faced Woman* suggests that Hollywood cannot be trusted; some outside, powerful agency must check on it.

Ferguson, O. "Legion Rides Again." *New Rep* 105 (22 Dec 41) 861. "I don't think the Legion wants a few objectionable things taken out so much as it wants an issue."

Whelan, Robert. "The Legion of Decency." *Am Mercury* 60 (June 45) 655–663. The history, philosophy, and influence of this minority pressure group.

"Moviegoing Morals." *Time* 47 (27 May 46) 60. Policies of the Catholic Legion of Decency.

"Censorship Shortened These *Duel* Scenes." *Look* 11 (No. 12, 10 June 47). *See 9, Duel in the Sun.*

Blanshard, Paul. "Roman Catholic Censorship." *Nation* 166 (8 May 48) 499–502. The movies are "selling a phony morality" because of the closed-mindedness of censorship organizations such as the Legion of Decency.

Burke, John A. V. "The Church, the Cinema and Censorship." *S&S* 17 (No. 66, Summer 48) 85–86. The Roman Catholic Church position on film censorship.

"Taking Films Seriously." *Commonweal* 53 (10 Nov 50) 123. Films such as *Dieu A Besoin des Hommes* present a problem for Catholic critics: do adult treatments of religious topics need to be kept from viewer when, as here, the theme can be construed as anticlerical?

"Catholic Censorship of *The Miracle.*" *New Rep* 124 (29 Jan 51) 7. Shall the authority of the Catholic Church extend beyond its communicants in banning *The Miracle?*

Seldes, Gilbert. "Pressures and Pictures." *Nation* 172 (3 Feb 51) 104–106; (10 Feb 51) 132–134. Threatened censorship of Rossellini's *The Miracle* prompts examination of Catholic pressures.

"*The Miracle* and Related Matters." *Commonweal* 53 (2 Mar 51) 507. Some second thoughts on how well Catholicism was served by the Church's blast against this film.

Clancy, W. P. "Catholic as Philistine." *Commonweal* 53 (16 Mar 51) 567–569. Appraisal of Church action on *The Miracle.*

Crowther, Bosley. "Strange Case of *The Miracle.*" *Atlantic* 187 (Apr 51) 35–39. The "calculated showdown test of strength" between the Legion of Decency and the distributors of *The Miracle.*

"Miracle on 58th Street." *Harper's* 202 (Apr 51) 106–108. The steps Catholic groups took to ban Rossellini's *The Miracle* in New York.

"The Critics and the Guardians." *Commonweal* 57 (19 Dec 52) 271. It is time for Catholic concern with film criticism to move beyond the Legion of Decency approach.

Kerr, Walter. "Catholics and Hollywood." *Commonweal* 57 (19 Dec 52) 275–277. Catholic criticism is driving itself into "an unattractive, and philosophically untenable corner" if it continues to judge the value of a film by its "proselytizing content."

Lavery, Emmet. "Is Decency Enough?" *Commonweal* 57 (19 Dec 52) 278–279. Critique of Legion's effectiveness; why not support good films and let the rest go?

"The Cardinal and Caroline." *Time* 61 (22 June 53) 33. Martine Carol in *Un Caprice de Caroline Chérie* displeases the Church in France.

"Catholics and the Movies." *Commonweal* 62 (3 June 55) 219–220. Deplores the Catholic as philistine; asks for more careful policies by the Legion.

"Major Papal Statement on Movies." *America* 93 (9 July 55) 361. Film censorship by authoritative public bodies is still justified.

"Bishops on the Movies." *America* 94 (10 Dec 55) 293. The Catholic Bishops of the U.S. feel that too many movie producers are becoming lax in the application of the production code.

"Film and Its Audiences: *Letters from My Windmill* and National Legion of Decency." *Commonweal* 63 (3 Feb 56) 449–450. Catholic audiences in Europe and America disagree as to whether this film is objectionable.

"Movie Morality." *Time* 67 (11 June 56) 76. A Jesuit urges National Legion of Decency to be stricter.

"Legion's Political Judgment." *Commonweal* 64 (3 Aug 56) 431. The Legion of Decency is attempting the impossible task of making a moral judgment of a film entirely apart from artistic considerations: *Storm Center* got a separate classification as a particularly objectionable movie.

"Should It Be Suppressed? *Baby Doll*." *Newswk* 48 (31 Dec 56) 59. The Catholic Legion of Decency condemns it.

"*Baby Doll*." *Commonweal* 65 (11 Jan 57) 371–372. Discussion of what should constitute the Catholic Church's response to *Baby Doll* and films like it.

Lee, Robert E. A. "Censorship: A Case History." *Chris Cent* 74 (Feb 57) 163–165. Roman Catholic Church and film biography *Martin Luther*.

Cogley, John. "More on *Baby Doll*." *Commonweal* 65 (1 Feb 57) 465. Economic boycotts by Catholics are disfunctional, and these raise civil-rights issues.

"Lonely George and *Martin Luther*." *America* 96 (16 Mar 57) 668. Catholics who do not demonstrate against objectionable films show "cowardly betrayal of principle."

Welch, R. J. "*Martin Luther* Film." *America* 96 (23 Mar 57) 698–700. The Catholic objections.

"Oscars and Good Taste." *America* 97 (13 Apr 57). *See 3d.*

"Public Opinion on Censorship." *America* 97 (8 June 57) 295. How the "common man's" opinions coincide with the Legion of Decency's.

"Highlights of the New Encyclical." *America* 97 (28 Sep 57) 669. Analyzing Pope Pius' "Remarkable Inventions" document: movies, radio, and TV should serve man's moral development.

"Legion's Second Spring." *America* 98 (9 Nov 57) 152. The National Legion of Decency is adopting a more positive approach in its evaluation of films.

"Legion Still Needed." *America* 98 (18 Jan 58) 442. Editorial.

"Movies Improve a Bit." *America* 100 (20 Dec 58) 360. Statistics on ratings with the new "A" category—A-I, A-II, A-III.

"Positive Look at Films." *America* 100 (3 Jan 59) 387. The National Legion of Decency will hereafter recommend films as well as rate them objectionable.

"*Nun's Story*—Filmed." *America* 101 (23 May 59) 356. Statement by the National Legion of Decency on the film of *The Nun's Story*.

"Rating the Legion." *America* 102 (12 Dec 59) 344–345.

Little, Thomas F. "Why Film Control?" *JSPG* (Sep 61) 15–16. Executive secretary of National Legion of Decency describes its system of classifying films and recommends a self-imposed system for the film industry.

Durgnat, Raymond. "Cupid vs. the Legion of Decency." *F&F* 8 (No. 3. Dec 61) 16–18+. Eroticism in cinema: the mass media and their public.

"Sex and Celluloid." *Newswk* 58 (11 Dec 61)

57. U.S. Roman Catholic hierarchy calls on the film industry to mend its morals.

"Legion of Decency." *America* 110 (9 May 64) 624–625.

Walsh, M. "Right Conscience About Films." *America* 110 (9–16 May 64) 657–658+. Defense of Legion of Decency film-rating policy.

"Moral or Immoral?" *Newswk* 64 (28 Dec 64) 53–54. Billy Wilder's *Kiss Me, Stupid* and problems with the National Legion of Decency.

"Catholic Film Newsletter." *America* 112 (16 Jan 65) 68.

Walsh, Moira. "Lost Ladies and Bad Logic." *America* 112 (6 Mar 65) 334. The greatest obstacle to freedom in the film is not the Legion of Decency but rather the "ignorance and misinformation" of filmgoers, encouraged by film makers.

Walsh, M. "Films: Condemnation of *The Pawnbroker*." *America* 112 (5 June 65) 838–839.

"*Sexy Nights* Didn't Last." *America* 113 (14 Aug 65) 149. *Sexy Girls* and *Sexy Nights* picketed by a Catholic youth club in New Guiana (South America).

"Changing Legion of Decency." *Time* 86 (3 Dec 65) 77–78.

Little, T. "Modern Legion and Its Modern Outlook." *America* 113 (11 Dec 65) 744–746.

"Catholic Film Awards." *America* 114 (19 Feb 66) 247.

Macklin, F. Anthony. "Editorial: Who Is Immoral?" *F Her* 1 (No. 3, Spring 66) 1+. Against the condemned rating given by the National Catholic Office for Motion Pictures.

Holloway, Ronald. "The Changing Legion." *F Soc Rev* (Sep 66) 25.

"The Double Standard." *Time* 89 (28 Apr 67) 104. The National Catholic Office for Motion Pictures.

Phillips, G. "No More Ratings?" *America* 117 (11 Nov 67) 560–561.

"1968 NCOMP Film Awards." *America* 118 (23 Mar 68) 365. Also (6 Apr 68) 450–451; (27 Apr 68) 553–554.

"Film Nudity and NCOMP." *America* 118 (15 June 68) 764.

Corliss, Richard. "The Legion of Decency." *F Com* 4 (No. 4, Summer 68) 24–61. M.F.A. thesis in film-radio-television at Columbia University by graduate of "nineteen years of education in Catholic schools"; history and policies, with special attention given to *The Outlaw, The Miracle, A Streetcar Named Desire, Baby Doll*.

"NCOMP Developments." *America* 120 (19 Apr 69) 468. Reply G. Phillips 120 (24 May 69) 601.

Walsh, Moira. "*Teorema*." *America* 120 (10 May 69) 569–570. Pasolini's *Teorema* and the International Catholic Film Office.

Berry, L. "No Vatican Oscar for *Teorema*." *Commonweal* 90 (23 May 69) 292–293. International Catholic Film Office disavows best-film award given at Venice Film Festival; Pasolini's reactions.

Corliss, R. "Still Legion, Still Decent?" *Commonweal* 90 (23 May 69) 288–293. Reply (27 June 69) 423. Critique and recent history of NCOMP judgments.

"NCOMP charges Hollywood Lacks Black Sensitivity." *Chris Cent* 86 (10 Sep 69) 1157.

7c(2c). Protestant

"The Federal Council Weighs the Movies." *Chris Cent* 48 (15 July 31) 918–920. Summary of Federal Council of Churches' findings on movies.

"The Presbyterians Seem Fed Up with Elder Hays." *Chris Cent* 49 (8 June 32) 725–726. Presbyterians' resolution cites producers as untrustworthy.

Tullis, D. D. "Presbyterians Endorse Catholic Campaign for Movie Decency." *Chris Cent* 51 (27 June 34) 870. Cleveland churches pass resolution.

"Protestantism and Jewry Join Catholics in Movie Ban." *Chris Cent* 51 (4 July 34) 884–885.

"The Movie Boycott." *Nation* 139 (11 July 34) 34. Protestants join Catholics.

Bailey, A. W. "Movies and the Public: A Candid Assay from an American." *Rotarian* 48 (Feb 36) 39–42. "Entertainments should be regulated by the public interest," says Connecticut clergyman.

"Spanking the Movies." *Lit Dig* 122 (11 July 36) 20. Federal Council of Churches report finds Will Hays and Joseph Breen still allow drinking and gambling to look attractive.

"Echo of Bernadette." *Newswk* 24 (14 Aug 44) 83. Committee seeks to promote production of religious films reflecting Protestant ideals.

"Sermons in Films." *Newswk* 30 (10 Nov 47) 68. The Protestant Film Commission's purpose and films.

"Better Than Censorship, Protestant Motion Picture Council." *National Council* 3 (May 53) 6–7.

"Protestant Sensibilities Interest Hollywood." *National Council* 6 (Apr 56) 23.

"Films Irk the Council." *America* 101 (Sep 59) 683. Protest against sex and violence in motion pictures, made by the National Council of Churches of Christ; suggests Council ally with the Catholic Legion of Decency.

"Fire and Fall Back." *Time* 74 (7 Sep 59) 50. Hollywood battles the National Council of Churches.

"Religion and the Media." *America* 103 (18 June 60) 366. The National Council of Churches echoes the Catholic Legion's pleas for more discrimination in viewing tastes.

Spencer, Harry C. "Christianity and the Censor-ship of Television, Radio and Film." *Religion in Life* 30 (Winter 60–61) 17–31.

Trotter, F. T. "Church Moves Toward Film Discrimination." *Religion in Life* 38 (Summer 69) 264–276. The film-awards nominations of the National Council of Churches are chosen from outstanding American films of artistic merit.

7c(2d). Political Pressure and Blacklisting

[See also 7d(2).]

Howe, B. A. "Reds Take to Stage and Screen." *Nat Rep* 23 (Jan 36) 22–23+; (Feb 36) 22–23. Propaganda in the U.S. through organizations, plays, and films, according to the associate editor of this "magazine of fundamental Americanism"; list of Soviet film showings by theatre in second article.

Platt, David. "The Screen: Paramount and Pinkerton." *New Masses* 20 (14 July 36) 29. Calls for a protest to prevent Paramount from filming the life of Allan Pinkerton, the "Red-baiter, strike-breaker, and reactionary."

Ellis, Peter. "The Screen." *New Masses* 23 (13 Apr 37) 27–28. Reports the formation of Associated Film Audiences to organize the audience to press for "pro-labor, anti-war, and generally progressive films."

"Politics in Hollywood." *New Rep* 110 (26 June 44) 847–848. The red scare in Hollywood results in the formation of the Motion Picture Alliance.

Koch, Howard. "I'm Standing on My Head." *Screen Writer* 2 (Feb 47) 19–24. Events in his life—such as writing the *Mission to Moscow* screenplay—which look subversive to the Daughters of the American Revolution; other writers under attack.

"Hollywood Handles the Theme of Loyalty." *New Yorker* 23 (6 Dec 47) 33. Hollywood's blacklisting of political leftists increases the favorable atmosphere for Communism.

Carlson, Oliver. "Communist Record in Hollywood." *Am Mercury* 66 (Feb 48) 135–143. An exposé of Communist infiltration in the film industry giving names, numbers, and front organizations.

"SWG Takes Court Action Charging Blacklist Conspiracy." *Screen Writer* 4 (June–July 48) 1–2+. Digest of formal complaint under Clayton Act, filed by Screen Writers Guild and thirty American writers against trade groups and producers who followed suggestion of House Un-American Activities Committee.

"Hollywood Film Writers." *Nation* 168 (15 Jan 49) 59. Ten Hollywood writers discharged and blacklisted because of Communist activities.

"Film Rights to Albert Maltz's New Novel." *Nation* 168 (14 May 49) 543. "Anti-Communist hiring policy" is criticized because it applies to the entire work of certain writers, regardless of content or subject matter.

McWilliams, C. "Hollywood Gray List." *Nation* 169 (19 Nov 49) 491–492. Studio tendency to drop certain Hollywood personalities as "political offenders."

Clarke, Michael. "Censorship by Violence?" *S&S* 19 (Apr 50). *See 6e.*

"Dangerous Thoughts, This Property Is Condemned." *Nation* 171 (25 Nov 50) 485. The "morals clause" in actor contracts and how it has been misused politically.

"Trouble at RKO." *Time* 59 (21 Apr 52) 104+. Howard Hughes gets rid of Communist suspects.

Kerby, P. "Legion Blacklist." *New Rep* 126 (16 June 52) 14–15. The "loyalty" check by which the studios are trying to win the confidence of the American Legion.

Endore, Guy. "Life on the Blacklist." *Nation* 175 (20 Dec 52) inside cover.

"Mr. Ferrer and Mr. Chaplin: Threat by American Legion." *Nation* 176 (31 Jan 53) 90.

"The Process of Dissolution." *Commonweal* 57 (6 Feb 53) 441. The censorship of Chaplin's *Limelight.*

Murray, William. "*Limelight,* Chaplin and His Censors." *Nation* 176 (21 Mar 53) 247–248. The American Legion calls Chaplin a Communist.

"Seeing Red in Hollywood." *Newswk* 48 (9 July 56) 94+. Hollywood's blacklisting of over 200 suspected Communists.

"Eric Johnston Tells How Hollywood Licked the Reds." *US News & World Report* 41 (23 Nov 56) 161.

Poe, Elisabeth. "Credits and Oscars." *Nation* 184 (30 Mar 57). *See 2d(3).*

"The Unremarkable Mr. Rich." *Nation* 184 (13 Apr 57) 306. Speculation on the probably blacklisted writer using the pseudonym of "Robert Rich," Oscar winner for writing *The Brave One.*

"Hollywood Whodunit: An Oscar, Who Won It?" *Life* 42 (15 Apr 57) 161–162. Mysterious screenwriter—blacklisted?

Trumbo, Dalton. "Blacklist—Blackmarket." *Nation* 184 (4 May 57) 383–387. Consequences of blacklisting of Hollywood Ten on the tenth anniversary of the case. Reply 185 (17 Aug 57) inside cover.

Cogley, John. "Matter of Ritual." *Commonweal* 66 (10 May 57) 149. Dalton Trumbo, Carl Foreman, and the blacklist.

Cutts, John, and Penelope Houston. "Blacklisted." *S&S* (Summer 57) 15–19+. Based on John Cogley's book *Report on Blacklisting* (Meridian, 1956); events before, during, and after the 1947 hearing by the House Un-American Activities Committee.

Jacobs, Paul. "Good Guys, Bad Guys, and Congressman Walter." *Reporter* 18 (15 May 58) 29–31. How Columbia Pictures finally dared to hire a blacklisted writer, Carl Foreman, to produce four pictures; his behind-scenes meeting with Congressman Walter, who accepted his confession without naming others.

"Blacklist Fadeout." *Time* 73 (26 Jan 59) 77.

"That's Me." *Newswk* 53 (26 Jan 59). *See 3d.*

Cogley, John. "Not So Defiant Ones." *Commonweal* 69 (20 Feb 59) 541. Hollywood's cynical application of the blacklist.

Lardner, Ring, Jr. "My Life on the Blacklist." *SEP* 234 (14 Oct 61). *See 5, Ring Lardner, Jr.*

Benedict, J. "Movies Are Redder Than Ever." *Am Mercury* 91 (Aug 60) 3–23. A detailed account of how Communist and Communist-leaning writers, performers, directors, and producers have all but taken over the industry.

Bessie, Alvah. "The Non-Existent Man." *Contact* 2 (No. 6, Oct 60) 83–96. One of the Hollywood Ten writes about the Congressional investigation and what he has done since.

Levin, Bernard. "Seven Years' Hard." *Spectator* 206 (30 June 61) 943–945. The screenwriting career of Louis Pollack and his difficulties with the Un-American Activities Committee.

"Anti-Red Rally." *Newswk* 58 (30 Oct 61) 20–21. *Hollywood's Answer to Communism* shown on TV; criticism of Hollywood for doing it.

Bessie, Alvah. "Dissolve To." *Contact* 4 (No. 5, July–Aug 64) 19–24. A fictional movie script on his experiences as one of the Hollywood Ten.

"California Group Attacks Film Makers and Broadcasters." *F Com* 3 (No. 3, Summer 65) 53–54. Extensive quotations from a pamphlet called *Red Stars* urging people to fight against Communists in the movie business.

Bessie, Alvah. "Jail, Freedom and the Screenwriting Profession." *F Com* 3 (No. 4, Fall 65) 56–67. One of the Hollywood Ten talks about people on and off the blacklist after the Congressional investigations of Communist party membership in Hollywood; extracts from reviews of Bessie's book *Inquisition in Eden* (Macmillan, 1965).

Biberman, Herbert. "American People and Freedom of the Screen." *F Com* 3 (No. 4, Fall 65) 67–69. Polemical statement by one of Hollywood Ten (cited in 1947 for contempt by Committee on Un-American Activities) declaring that the First Amendment is now inoperative.

MacFadden, Patrick, *et al.* "Blacklisted!" *Take One* 1 (No. 5, 1967) 10–15. Brief note on the background of blacklisting in America, with personal accounts by Millard Lampell and Herbert Biberman.

7c(3). FEDERAL INVESTIGATIONS

[See also 3a(6), 7f.]

"May Investigate Movie Industry." *Chris Cent* 48 (25 Mar 31) 418–419. Reports on Senate resolution.

"Movie Makers Bank on Willkie to Foil the Propaganda Inquiry." *Newswk* 18 (15 Sep 41) 51+.

Nye, Gerald P. "Our Madness Increases as Our Emergency Shrinks." *Vital Speeches* 7 (15 Sep 41). *See 7b(5).*

"Propaganda or History?" *Nation* 153 (20 Sep 41) 241–242. Senate investigation of "provocative" anti-Nazi films.

"Hollywood in Washington." *Time* 38 (22 Sep 41) 13. Senate investigation of prowar films as seen by *The Hollywood Reporter*'s Jack Moffitt.

"Senate Isolationists Run Afoul of Willkie in Movie Warmonger Hearings." *Life* 11 (22 Sep 41) 21–25. Wendell Willkie is defense counsel for Hollywood as Senate subcommittee investigates films "calculated to drag the U.S. into a European conflict."

Straight, Michael. "The Anti-Semitic Conspiracy." *New Rep* 105 (22 Sep 41) 362–363. Nye Committee investigating industry (and anti-Nazi movies) reflects anti-Semitism as well as isolationism.

"Warmongering Movies?" *Scholastic* 39 (22 Sep 41) 6. The Senate investigation.

Frakes, Margaret. "Why the Movie Investigation?" *Chris Cent* 58 (24 Sep 41) 1172–1174. Article supporting the Senate investigation of anti-Nazi propaganda.

Cousins, Norman. "Our Heroes." *Sat Rev* 24 (25 Oct 41) 10. Investigation by Senate committee into charges of war propaganda.

Willkie, Wendell. "Senate's Threat to Free Speech: Movie Investigation Highlights Dangers." *Life* 11 (3 Nov 41) 42+.

Isaacs, H. R. "Fact Is Stranger Than Fiction." *Th Arts* 25 (Dec 41) 881–883. Subtitle: "Trial of Willie Bioff and George E. Browne and the Investigation of War Propaganda in Motion Pictures."

"Kefauver Versus Hollywood." *Time* 65 (27 June 55) 88. Juvenile delinquency investigation.

7c(3a). Proposals for Regulation

"The Movies Before Congress." *Chris Cent* 47 (21 May 30) 646–647. Supports Brookhart and Hudson bills to outlaw block booking and to license films.

Howard, Clifford. "Shadow over Hollywood." *Close Up* 7 (No. 1, 1930) 47–51. Outline of the national censorship bill pending before Congress.

Gilman, Catheryne Cooke. "Government Regulations for the Movies." *Chris Cent* 48 (26 Aug 31) 1066–1068.

"Senator Brookhart's New Movie Bills." *Chris Cent* 49 (16 Mar 32) 341. Proposals for investigation of Hays office and for outlawing block booking.

"Dreadful Results of a Movie Nightmare." *Chris Cent* 49 (4 May 32) 564. Declares Senate bill for movie investigation has nothing to do with censorship.

Eastman, Fred. "Movies in Politics." *Chris Cent* 49 (15 June 32) 763–765. Calls for passage of movie-control legislation.

Howard, Clifford. "Storm over Hollywood." *Close Up* 10 (No. 2, June 33) 192–193. The possibility of government intervention in the Hollywood industry.

"New Movie Bill Takes Hays' Code in Earnest." *Chris Cent* 50 (9 Aug 33) 1005. Representative Wright Patman of Texas proposes federal motion-picture commission (four members of which shall be women) to forbid a film to enter interstate commerce if it tends to corrupt morals, to incite to crime, or promote international war.

Eastman, Fred. "Social Issues in the Movie Code." *Chris Cent* 50 (20 Sep 33) 1170–1171. Proposed NRA code forbids nontheatrical showings of features, allows block booking.

"Catholic Women Protest Movie Code." *Chris Cent* 50 (11 Oct 33) 1259–1260. Spokesmen call draft of NRA code ineffective.

"President and the Movie Code." *Chris Cent* 50 (25 Oct 33) 1326–1328. Telegram to President protests Hays office domination of proposed NRA code.

Hecht, George J. "A Model Movie Law." *Parents Mag* 8 (Nov 33) 23+. Publisher outlines plan for regulating children's attendance at movies.

"Movie Code and the Independents." *Chris Cent* 50 (1 Nov 33) 1358. Independent producers and exhibitors against proposed NRA code.

"Will Dr. Lowell Accept?" *Chris Cent* 50 (13 Dec 33) 1565. President of Harvard asked to be member of NRA movie-code authority.

"The Motion Picture Code Authority and Dr. A. Lawrence Lowell." *School and Society* 38 (30 Dec 33) 863. President of Harvard declines post on NRA code board.

Wilson, P. W. "Motion Pictures Move into the New Deal." *Lit Dig* 117 (6 Jan 34) 9+. Roosevelt refuses to establish federal censorship.

"President Lowell Declines Code Appointment." *Chris Cent* 51 (10 Jan 34) 44–45. Harvard president attacks block booking in letter to NRA administrator.

"Mrs. Bagley and the N.R.A." *Chris Cent* 51 (17 Jan 34) 77–78. New England civic leader also refuses to join NRA code board.

"A National Program for Motion Pictures."

Nat Educ Assoc J 23 (Dec 34) 251. Details legislative bill proposed by Motion Picture Research Council.

Price, Thompson. "The Government Goes to Hollywood." *New Outlook* 165 (Feb 35) 11–16+. Film industry faced with threats of censorship and indictments for alleged monopoly.

Ryskind, Morrie. "Hollywood Tea Party." *Nation* 142 (6 May 36) 581. Members of the film industry show their opposition to sedition bill.

"Tempest in a Hollywood Teapot: OWI Order." *Th Arts* 27 (Feb 43) 71–72. Office of War Information to preview Hollywood films; controversy over war films designed as entertainment.

McDonald, John. "Will Hays's New Rival: Government Review." *Nation* 156 (3 Apr 43) 484–486. Office of War Information proposes prerelease review of films to standardize "voluntary propaganda requirements."

"The Purity Test." *Time* 55 (27 Mar 50) 99. The federal government to police the morals of movie performances; a bill introduced by Senator Edwin C. Johnson including a disapproval of Rossellini-Bergman case.

"Movie Morals: Whose Business." *US News & World Report* 28 (21 Apr 50) 21–22. Senator Edwin C. Johnson's demand for public regulation of Hollywood's private morals; Hollywood's defense by Eric Johnston.

"Man with a Mission." *Time* 55 (1 May 50) 86. Reaction to Senator Edwin C. Johnson's attempt to improve Hollywood's morals by federal licensing of players and producers.

Mayer, Michael F. "Film Censorship in the Nation's Capital." *F Com* 2 (No. 2, 1964) 47–48. Statement before Senate committee on the District of Columbia, protesting bill for injunctive relief against obscene films.

7c(3b). Un-American Activities Committee

Koch, Howard. "Mr. Rankin Has Made Me Self-Conscious." *Screen Writer* 1 (Sep 45) 8–11. Congressman's accusation of Communist associations makes writer wonder if his behavior could be examined in practically every aspect.

Corwin, E. "Report from Hollywood." *New Rep* 116 (26 May 47) 9. Negative view of investigations of Communism; excerpts from hearings.

"Reds Gone Hollywood." *Newswk* 29 (26 May 47) 27–28.

Graham, Garrett. "Witch-Hunting in Hollywood." *Screen Writer* 3 (June 47) 17–21. Details some of the political accusations leveled against Hollywood and the Writers Guild; attacks the attackers in Washington and Sacramento.

Nathan, P. "Just How Subversive Are the Movies?" *Publishers Weekly* 151 (7 June 47) 2843. A questioning look at the ideas and effects of the hearings.

Shaffer, S. "Red Scenario: House Un-American Activities Committee Investigation in Hollywood." *Newswk* 30 (25 Aug 47) 22. Witnesses scheduled.

Trivers, Paul. "Town Meeting Tonight!" *Screen Writer* 3 (Oct 47) 31–33. Describes a *Town Meeting of the Air* program on the question "Is There *Really* a Communist Threat in Hollywood?" Emmet Lavery, Screen Writers Guild president, and Lela Rogers, mother of actress Ginger Rogers, took part.

"From Wonderland: Un-American Activities Committee Investigation into Communism in Hollywood." *Time* 50 (27 Oct 47) 25. Testimony of Sam Wood.

"Hollywood on the Hill." *Time* 50 (3 Nov 47) 22–23. Excerpts from testimony.

Walton, W. "Kangaroo Court Under Klieg Light." *New Rep* 117 (3 Nov 47) 8–9. Attack on J. Parnell Thomas and the Un-American Activities Committee.

Burnham, P. "Hollywood Affliction." *Commonweal* 47 (7 Nov 47) 84–85. The Communist problem in Hollywood: industry employees contributing to party causes, Burnham says, are generally creative people unhappy with their work but who stay because it pays well. This moral laziness spawns guilt feelings and a desire to contribute to an organization whose aim is the overthrow of the system.

Habe, H. "War Against the Writers." *New S&N* 34 (8 Nov 47) 367. Hollywood investigation of "potential" Communist influence in films by Thomas Committee.

Olson, S. "Movie Hearings." *Life* 23 (24 Nov 47) 137–138. Comprehensive report on the Un-American Activities Committee.

Kahn, Gordon, Norman Corwin, Lillian Hellman, Salka Viertel, Roland Kibbee, William Wyler, Emmet Lavery, Howard Koch. "Freedom vs. Fear: The Fight for the American Mind." *Screen Writer* 3 (No. 7, Dec 47) 1–26. Responses to the Un-American Activities Committee investigation by magazine's editor, Screen Writers Guild members, and others.

"Hollywood Super-Purge." *Newswk* 30 (8 Dec 47) 24–25. Hollywood, on the heels of the hearings, officially resolves to clean house of subversives.

"Paradise Lost?" *Time* 51 (19 Jan 48) 87–88. The "red scare" is slowing down the pulse of Hollywood and threatening future production.

Ross, Lillian. "Onward and Upward with the Arts." *New Yorker* 23 (21 Feb 48) 32–48. Effects of the Thomas Committee subversive-activities investigations on the film capital; interview with Humphrey Bogart, E. G. Robinson, and Lauren Bacall; Hollywood will make the same uncontroversial, bland movies as before.

" 'Days of Wrath.' " *Sequence* (No. 3, Spring 48) 11–12. A brief statement on the Congressional committee hearings and their effect on Hollywood.

Arnold, Thurman, Abe Fortas, Paul Porter. "A Letter from Thurman Arnold." *Screen Writer* 3 (Mar 48) 6–8. Statement of principles written by legal counsel for Screen Writers Guild; opposition to producers' blacklist of employees named by Un-American Activities Committee.

Cerf, Bennett. "Trade Winds." *Sat Rev* 31 (17 Apr 48) 5–6. Report on recent developments in Hollywood, with emphasis on Communist investigations.

"Court and the Ten." *New Rep* 120 (3 Jan 49) 8. The dismissal of the Hollywood Ten is denounced by a federal judge.

"Un-American Activities." *S&S* 19 (June 50) 168. A half-page article discussing the hearing and outcome of the 1947 Congressional Committee on Un-American Activities.

"Hollywood Eight." *New Rep* 123 (10 July 50) 8. The rest of the Hollywood Ten accused of Communist activities are indicted.

"Command Performance." *Time* 57 (2 Apr 51) 94. Ten members of the movie industry accused of Communist activities.

"Larry Parks in Red Face." *Newswk* 37 (2 Apr 51) 21. The appearance of Larry Parks, Howard da Silva, and Gale Sondergaard.

"The Adventurer." *Time* 57 (23 Apr 51) 104. Actor Sterling Hayden.

"More Hollywood Reds." *Newswk* 37 (23 Apr 51) 36+. Some of the screenwriters, directors, and actors whose names came up before the House Un-American Activities Committee.

"Hollywood Serial Story." *Newswk* 37 (7 May 51) 26.

"Operation Hollywood." *Time* 57 (7 May 51) 98+.

English, Richard. "What Makes a Hollywood Communist?" *SEP* 223 (19 May 51) 30–31+. Edward Dmytryk, one of "The Ten" in Hollywood charged for Communism, tells of his experiences.

"Hollywood Show." *Newswk* 37 (4 June 51) 19. Testimony by actor José Ferrer, writer Budd Schulberg, and director Frank Tuttle.

"More Red Than Herring." *Time* 57 (4 June 51) 100. More people accused of Communist activities.

Shannon, W. V. "Hollywood Returns to the Stand." *New Rep* 124 (25 June 51) 21–22. House Un-American Activities Committee meets Budd Schulberg, José Ferrer, E. G. Robinson.

Bloom, Hannah. "Hollywood Hearings." *Nation* 173 (13 Oct 51) 304. Four years of investigations by the House Committee on Un-American Activities.

"Hollywood Meets Frankenstein." *Nation* 174 (28 June 52) 628–631. The House Un-American Activities Committee and the American Legion send the film industry into panicky retreat.

"The Name Droppers." *Time* 61 (23 Mar 53) 108. Hollywood names accused of Communist activities file suit for blackmail.

Fenton, Frank. "Hollywood's Message." *Nation* 79 (13 Nov 54) 424.

"Artists Are Also Citizens." *America* 93 (17 Sep 55) 583. Answer to two critics of *New York Times* on the House Un-American Activities Committee's investigation and on the case of *Blackboard Jungle*.

Tailleur, Roger. "Elia Kazan and the House Un-American Activities Committee." (Tr. from the French by Alvah Bessie.) *F Com* 4 (No. 1, Fall 66) 43–58. Survey of general period of investigations by an editor of *Positif;* many footnoted corrections by editor.

"HUAC-adoo: Part One." *Take One* 2 (No. 4, 1969) 7–13. Excerpts from testimony given to the Committee on Un-American Activities, Washington, October 1947, by Jack Warner, Louis B. Mayer, Ayn Rand, Robert Taylor, Lela B. Rogers.

"HUAC-adoo: Part Two." *Take One* 2 (No. 5, 1969) 6–14. Continuation of excerpts from testimony given in Washington, October 1947, by John Howard Lawson, Dalton Trumbo, Alvah Bessie, Herbert Biberman, Dore Schary, Ring Lardner, Jr., and Bertolt Brecht.

Cook, Jim. "Un-American Activities." *Screen* 11 (No. 3, Summer 70) 74–77. Brief summary of U.S. Congress political investigations of Hollywood.

7c(4). HOLLYWOOD PRODUCTION CODE

[*See also 6a(3), 7c(6).*]

Eastman, Fred. "The Menace of the Movies." *Chris Cent* 47 (15 Jan 30). *See 7b(6).*

"Will Hays and the Presbyterians." *Chris Cent* 47 (12 Mar 30) 325. Suggests Hays misused his religious connections.

"Doctor Macfarland and the Motion Picture Producers." *Chris Cent* 47 (9 Apr 30) 452. General Secretary of Federal Council of Churches of Christ resigns because of payments from Hays office.

"The Movies Are 'Converted' Again!" *Chris Cent* 47 (9 Apr 30) 454–455. Announcement of new Hays Code.

"The New Moral Code for the Talkies." *Lit Dig* 105 (12 Apr 30) 9–10.

"Hollywood Promises." *Commonweal* 11 (16 Apr 30) 667–668. Attacks Hays Code as weak and unviable.

"Morals for Movies." *Outlook* 154 (16 Apr 30) 612.

"Virtue in Cans." *Nation* 130 (16 Apr 30) 441. Summary of the Hays Code.

Winter, Alice Ames. "Motion Picture's Self-Correction." *Woman's J* 15 (June 30) 49+. Associate director of Public Relations for MPPA announces new code.

"Movies, Ethics and Children." *J of Home Econ* 22 (July 30) 578–580. The Hays Code in detail.

Brown, Arthur J. "New Code of Motion Pictures." *Missionary Rev* 53 (Sep 30) 680–681.

"Ethics of Motion Picture Advertisers." *J of Home Econ* 22 (Oct 30) 855–856. Reviews Hays Code's advertising directives.

Barrows, Edward M. "Motion-Pictures: Success Through Self-Regulation." *Rev of Reviews* 85 (Mar 32) 32–35. Reviews social and industrial achievement of movies since 1895.

Shaw, Albert. "Will Hays: A Ten-Year Record." *Rev of Reviews* 85 (Mar 32) 30–31. Congratulates Hays on successful handling of movie morality.

"Movie Censors That Hear Their Master's Voice." *Chris Cent* 49 (13 July 32) 877. According to Harrison's Reports, Colonel Jason Joy visited various censor boards and "coincidentally" got *Scarface* approved by most of them.

"Little Gems from Jason Joy." *Chris Cent* 49 (10 Aug 32) 973. Excerpts from report of MPA executive's trip to enlighten local censor boards on forthcoming product.

"Milliken Lining Up Protestants to Aid Films." *Chris Cent* 49 (26 Oct 32) 1292. Editorial pointing to ex-Governor Carl Milliken's mission for the Motion Picture Association.

Hapgood, Norman. "Will Hays and What the Pictures Do to Us." *Atlantic* 151 (Jan 33) 75–84. When decentralization of Hays' power comes, improvement of movies is likely to follow.

"Celluloid Czar." *Nation* 137 (19 July 33) 62. Indicts Hays as irresponsible.

"Deluded Women: Hays Office and Women's Clubs." *Chris Cent* 50 (6 Dec 33) 1527–1529. Facts are juggled in motion-picture reports provided for women's clubs.

Benson, M. "Will the Code Bring Better Movies?" *Parents Mag* 9 (June 34) 26+.

"Hollywood Wins a Truce." *Commonweal* 20 (20 July 34) 295–296. Joe Breen joins Hays office for stricter enforcement of code.

Angly, Edward. "Producers Cleansing Films, But Will Reform Last?" *Lit Dig* 118 (21 July 34) 7+.

"A Vigorous Broom." *Publishers Weekly* 126 (21 July 34) 196–197. Hopes code will not eliminate literary masterpieces.

Eastman, Fred. "Now Watch Mr. Hays!" *Chris Cent* 51 (19 Sep 34) 1172–1173. Will he

apply the $25,000 fine if disapproved picture is released?

Davenport, Walter. "Pure as the Driven Snow." *Collier's* 94 (24 Nov 34) 10–11+. On Joseph I. Breen, Hays office censor.

Furnas, J. C. "Moral War in Hollywood." *Fortnightly Rev* 143 (Jan 35) 73–84. Surveys 1934 as year of reformation in U.S. movies.

"Reformers Look Back on First Year and Find It Good." *Newswk* 6 (17 Aug 35) 16–17. Reform movement sees year as one of "unprecedented cleanliness."

Berman, Sam. "Hays Office." *Fortune* 18 (Dec 38) 68–72+. Extensive history of the office and the man himself; structure of the office and ties with production companies detailed.

Redman, B. R. "Pictures and Censorship." *SRL* 19 (31 Dec 38) 3–4+. A criticism and survey of the Motion Picture Producers and Distributors of America (the Hays office); a sharp attack on the producers involved.

"Rash of Censorship." *Newswk* 13 (13 Mar 39) 34. Conflicts between the Hays office and Warner Brothers in 1939.

Salemson, Harold J. "A Question of Morals." *Screen Writer* 1 (Apr 46) 1–7. This writer argues that the Production Code has not accomplished its purpose of preserving good taste in films; on the contrary, the sexual understatement required by the code has "called forth the most libidinous fantasia" in the audience.

Rivkin, Allen. "Hollywood Letter." *Free World* 11 (June 46) 50–51. Self-censorship of Johnston office; objections explained in detail.

"Cleavage and the Code." *Time* 48 (5 Aug 46) 98. Joseph Breen tries to describe to the puzzled British Hollywood's censorship code.

Nathan, P. S. "Books into Films." *Publishers Weekly* 150 (31 Aug 46) 1041. The Production Code not only limits American film but may standardize foreign output as well.

"Play Safe But Be Suggestive." *New Rep* 115 (30 Dec 46) 907–909. A criticism of J. I. Breen and the Production Code; a call for modification.

"Laura Clocks the Kisses." *American* 144 (Oct 47) 118. A visit with a censor for Motion Picture Producers Association.

Collins, Richard. "The Screen Writer and Censorship." *Screen Writer* 3 (Oct 47) 15–17. Official thought control of the code and self-censorship exercised by film makers stifle creativity.

Inglis, Ruth. "Need for Voluntary Self-Regulation." *Annals of Am Acad of Polit and Soc Sci* 254 (Nov 47) 153–159. Plea for a more cooperative kind of self-regulation; history of Hollywood code.

Quigley, Martin. "The Importance of the Entertainment Film." *Annals of Am Acad of Polit and Soc Sci* 254 (Nov 47). See 7b(2a).

Shurlock, Geoffrey. "Motion Picture Production Code." *Annals of Am Acad of Polit and Soc Sci* 254 (Nov 47) 140–146. What it is; how it is administered; how it is enforced; its accomplishments.

Schary, Dore. "Censorship and Stereotypes." *SRL* 32 (30 Apr 49) 9–10. A defense of the film industry's code.

"Banned *Bicycle*." *Newswk* 35 (13 Mar 50) 78. Motion Picture Association seal of approval denied to *The Bicycle Thief;* De Sica's refusal to delete the "offending portions."

"*Bicycle Thief* Banned by Motion Picture Association of America." *New Rep* 122 (13 Mar 50) 9.

"Censor's Censor." *Time* 55 (13 Mar 50) 94. *The Bicycle Thief* censored.

"Evil-Minded Censors." *Life* 28 (13 Mar 50) 40. Editorial criticizes censoring of *The Bicycle Thief* by the Motion Picture Association of America.

"Twist Twists." *Newswk* 36 (18 Dec 50) 93. The Production Code withholds approval of *Oliver Twist* on the grounds that Alec Guinness's performance as Fagin humiliates the Jewish race.

Vizzard, John A. "Is the Code Democratic?" *FIR* 2 Nov 51) 1–3. Member of code administration says its purpose is not to suppress films, but to see that they neither repel the intelligent, nor offend the innocent; the "arty" set thinks adult films have to be about adultery.

Knight, Arthur. "Ring Around *The Moon Is Blue*." *Sat Rev* 36 (27 June 53) 33–36. Challenges to the Production Code: *The Bicycle Thief, La Ronde*.

Sheerin, John B. "*Moon Is Blue*." *Cath World* 177 (Aug 53) 325. The distribution of this film is a campaign to break down the self-regulation of the movie industry.

"Censored." *Look* 17 (25 Aug 53) 41–43. *From Here to Eternity:* stills shown from a censored sequence.

"Movie Producers Stand by the Code." *America* 89 (19 Sep 53) 587. The case of *The Moon Is Blue* causes alarm.

"The Censors." *Time* 63 (11 Jan 54) 80, (1 Feb 54) 72. Has the time come to change the Production Code?

"Shall Movies Exploit Filth for Profit?" *Chris Cent* 71 (13 Jan 54) 37. An attack on Samuel Goldwyn for trying to ease the film code on morals.

"Revising the Code." *Commonweal* 59 (22 Jan 54) 392. Is the Production Code inflexible—written for children? Reply—M. Quigley 59 (26 Feb 54) 527–529. Quigley denies it.

"Modernize the Movie Production Code?" *America* 90 (23 Jan 54) 409. The impact of TV seen in the efforts to change the code.

"Movie Issue." *Commonweal* 59 (5 Feb 54)

442. Should the Production Code be revised?

Goodman, Walter. "Who Censors Your Movies?" *New Rep* 130 (22 Feb 54) 12–14. Discussion (22 Mar 54) 22. A history of the code from 1922, as Goldwyn calls for renovation.

"Producers Defend the Code." *America* 90 (27 Feb 54) 551. Eight major movie producers see no need for code changes.

Parsons, L. O. "Hollywood and Censorship." *Cosmopolitan* 136 (Apr 54) 8. Censorship is necessary for good business; Mae West was never so popular as Mary Pickford.

Herbert, F. Hugh. "A Person Can Develop a Code." *JSPG* (Aug 54) 7+. President of Screen Writers Guild suggests that the production code (and its administration) may be unduly hard on the producers of motion pictures and unduly lenient toward movie advertising.

Wald, Jerry. "Dollars and Sense and Censorship." *JSPG* (Aug 54) 6+. Producer argues for the value of the production code in protecting the industry and that "the Code has never stood in the way of good picture making."

Vizzard, John A. "Changing Times." *JSPG* (Aug 54) 12–13. A member of the Production Code administration argues that for the code to change with the times may be "a long step backwards"; what is accepted in a given society may not be "acceptable to people of reason and decency."

"*French Line*." *Commonweal* 60 (6 Aug 54) 428. Showing of Hughes' film in defiance of code in drive-ins is irresponsible.

"Is the Movie Code Being Junked?" *America* 93 (28 May 55) 227.

"Strange Reports About the Code." *America* 93 (25 June 55) 326. The Screen Directors Guild of America in defense of the industry's code, criticized.

Hart, Henry. "Economic Censorship." *FIR* 6 (Dec 55) 507–510. A report on a meeting at which Morris Ernst told plans for legal action against the MPAA's refusal to grant a code seal to *I Am a Camera*, claiming that small companies were being discriminated against.

Knight, A. "Hollywood Takes on Narcotics." *Sat Rev* 38 (17 Dec 55) 27–29. Production Code is slowly being modified and is dwindling in overall effect.

Quigley, Martin J. "The Motion-Picture Production Code." *America* 94 (10 Mar 56) 630–632. Firsthand report on the formation of the code. Discussion (31 Mar 56) 705; 95 (14 Apr 56) 45; (26 May 56) 213.

"Code Changes." *Newswk* 48 (24 Dec 56) 70.

"New Code." *Time* 68 (24 Dec 56) 61. The self-censorship code's first major overhaul in a quarter century.

"Production Code and *Baby Doll*." *America* 96

(29 Dec 56) 367. Doubts about its effectiveness.

North, Christopher. "The New Production Code." *FIR* 8 (Jan 57) 20–25. Motion Picture Association Code as revised and approved December 11, 1956; comments on specific changes.

Driver, Tom F. "The New Movie Code." *Chris Cent* 74 (2 Jan 57) 6.

"New Code Appraised." *America* 96 (5 Jan 57) 384. Martin Quigley comments on recent revisions of the Motion Picture Association's Code.

Morley, R. "Code and the Church." *Newswk* 49 (7 Jan 57) 72. Editorial column: Revision has strengthened the code, but "there is need to watch the watchers."

Wald, Jerry, and Mark Robson. "The Code Doesn't Stultify." *FIR* 8 (Dec 57) 503–506. Well-known producer and director believe it's necessary and nonrestrictive.

"Decoded." *Time* 72 (3 Nov 58) 78. The obsolescence of the old Production Code.

Shurlock, Geoffrey. "Caution, Soft Shoulders." *JSPG* (Mar 59) 10+. Director of Production Code administration discusses public repercussions of the liberalized code.

Wald, Jerry. "The Code and Common Sense." *JSPG* (Mar 59) 11+. The Production Code does not stand in the way of good art, and it protects the film industry from outside censorship.

Hamilton, Jack. "Hollywood Bypasses the Production Code." *Look* 28 (29 Sep 59) 80+. Examples of breaking the code, interviews and opinions of many Hollywood figures.

Mirisch, Walter, Gerald Kennedy, John Houseman, Richard Coe, Michael Blankfort, Geoffrey Shurlock, Max Youngstein, William Mooring, Sumner Redstone, Charles Alicoate, George Cukor. "The Journal Looks at the Production Code: Should It Be Abolished?" *JSPG* (Mar 65) 3–38. Administrator of the code (Shurlock) and various producers, critics, etc., debate the issue in separate articles.

"Morality Crisis." *Newswk* 65 (19 Apr 65) 98+. List of films which have broken the code.

"When Bare Breasts Are Decent." *Time* 88 (30 Sep 66) 56+. The new Production Code.

"Three-and-a-Half Square." *Newswk* 68 (3 Oct 66) 22. Hollywood's new code.

"New Movie Code: Motion Picture Association of America." *Senior Scholar* 89 (7 Oct 66) 17.

Valenti, Jack. "Motion Picture Code and the New American Culture." *PTA Mag* 61 (Dec 66) 16–19. Optimistic forecast for American film under the new production code.

Dart, Peter. "Breaking the Code: A Historical Footnote." *CJ* 8 (No. 1, Fall 68) 39–41. The case of Howard Hughes' *The Outlaw.*

"New Movie Code: Clean Up or Cover Up?" *Senior Scholastic* 93 (25 Oct 68) 5–8+.

Walsh, Moira. "Of Ratings, Psychos, Etc." *America* 120 (22 Mar 69) 343–345. Discussion of the Production Code's rulings on several recent films.

7c(5). COPYRIGHT, TITLES, LIBEL

[See also 2d(2).]

Liddy, Sylvester J. "Copyright Infringement by Film Exhibitor." *Sci Am* 147 (July 32) 61. Announces court ruling giving protection to films like that of plays or other dramatic compositions.

"Russian Princess Asks Court to Halt Rasputin Film." *Newswk* 2 (4 Nov 33) 14. Princess Youssoupoff sues MGM, claiming libel in *Rasputin and the Empress.*

"Princess Wins *Rasputin* Suit." *Newswk* 3 (10 Mar 34) 13. Jury awards $126,875 against MGM film in libel suit.

"Dinner in London." *Time* 24 (20 Aug 34) 37. The woman lawyer who defeated MGM in the *Rasputin* libel case.

Zissu, Leonard. "The Copyright Dilemma of the Screen Composer." *Hwd Q* 1 (No. 3, Apr 46) 317–320. Commercial practices versus property rights.

"Lady of Many Titles." *American* 145 (Apr 48) 119. Brief profile of Margaret Ann Young, director of the title-registration bureau of the Motion Picture Association.

Menagh, F. "Monitor of Movie Titles." *SEP* 221 (7 Aug 48) 52.

Weinberg, Herman G. "A Problem in Film Ethics." *FIR* 1 (July–Aug 50) 7–10+. Two pictures with a single theme: Joseph von Sternberg's 1931 *Morocco* and the Mexican *Enamorado,* made more recently.

Lindey, Alexander. "Plagiarism in the Movies." *FIR* 3 (Aug–Sep 52) 323–334. A chapter from *Plagiarism and Originality* (Harper, 1952) surveys many specific films named in lawsuits based on claims of plagiarism.

"Og, Gog, and Magog." *Time* 62 (16 Nov 53) 106. *The Great Green Og* and *Gog;* two horror pictures have title trouble.

"The Front Page." *S&S* 26 (Spring 57) 171. An editorial against recutting of films for another market, which changes the director's intention.

Walbridge, Earle F. "Films A Clef." *FIR* 9 (Mar 58) 113–124. Films that closely follow the lives of real people; lawsuits that have resulted; plagiarism cases.

"Fine Italian Hand." *Newswk* 61 (28 Jan 63) 89. Reuse of successful titles as a way to profits in Italy's movie industry.

"Rock 'Em, Sock 'Em!" *Newswk* 61 (17 June 63) 90. West German film industry renames American films.

Schiffer, George. "The Law and the Use of Music in Film." *F Com* 1 (No. 6, Fall 63) 39–43.

Schiffer, George. "Privacy, Publicity, and Unfair Competition." *F Com* 2 (No. 1, Winter 64) 20–28. Detailed advice on specific cases governing rights of persons "in their names, portraits, pictures, reputations, performances," and other copyright and equity situations.

"Right of Privacy and Property." *Time* 84 (25 Dec 64) 54.

"Appellate Court Reverses John Goldfarb Decision." *Publishers Weekly* 187 (22 Feb 65) 133–134. Continuation 187 (22 Mar 65) 51; 187 (29 Mar 65) 25. University of Notre Dame suit against movie *John Goldfarb, Please Come Home.*

Hunnings, Neville. "Copyright." *S&S* 36 (Summer 67) 138–140. The problems of archives and the rights to show old films.

Katz, Arthur S. "The Creative Process and the Law." *JSPG* 10 (No. 3, Sep 68) 9–12+.

Lloyd, Boardman. " 'Disk Television': Recurring Problems in the Performance of Motion Pictures." *JSPG* 10 (No. 3, Sep 68) 13–16.

Tannenbaum, Samuel W. "Copyright Law: Titles in the Entertainment Field." *JSPG* 10 (No. 3, Sep 68) 21–23.

"Title Registration in Motion Pictures." *JSPG* (Sep 68) 24–27. Official statement on this bureau of Motion Picture Association which offers voluntary protection in the absence of copyrights.

Calmann, Rudolf. "Unfair Competition in Ideas." *JSPG* (Sep 68) 29–33. The courts in some states protect such ownership.

Pilpel, H. F., and K. P. Norwick. "But Can You Do That?" *Publishers Weekly* 196 (29 Dec 69) 37–38. Privacy cases, including *The Titicut Follies.*

7c(6). AUDIENCE CLASSIFICATION

[See also 6b(3), 7a(3), 7c(4).]

"Fighting for Freedom from Hollywood." *Chris Cent* 51 (31 Jan 34) 141. *Parents Magazine* proposes local licensing law limiting children's attendance to approved shows for family audience on weekends.

"Children at the Movies." *Commonweal* 23 (17 Jan 36) 312. New York City ordinance bars unaccompanied children under sixteen.

"Minor Matters." *Time* 28 (20 July 36) 36. Children under sixteen now not allowed to go alone to New York City theatres and sit in special section up front under a matron's supervision.

"Movies for Minors." *Lit Dig* 122 (24 Oct 36) 24–25. Magazines and committees guide parents.

"The Front Page." *S&S* 28 (No. 2, Spring 59) 55. Editorial: Not only films but cinemas might be classified.

"Classify the Films?" *America* 102 (10 Oct 59) 31.

Hift, Fred. " 'Classification'—Boon or Doom for Hollywood?" *Sat Rev* 42 (19 Dec 59) 16+. Motion-picture ratings, pro and con; part of *Saturday Review* report "The New Frankness in Films."

"Classify or Collapse." *America* 102 (16 Jan 60) 440. Directive to Hollywood to consider the youthful viewers.

Johnston, Eric. "Classification: A Noise or an Echo?" *JSPG* (Sep 61) 3–6. President of Motion Picture Association argues that classification of entertainment is censorship, intruding on parental authority, and that it solves none of the problems people want it to solve.

Gardiner, Harold C., S.J. "Film Classification? Yes!" *JSPG* (Sep 61) 7–8. It is an informative device and a reminder to parents of their responsibility to supervise their children.

Pickus, Albert M. "Information, the Key to Classification." *JSPG* (Sep 61) 13–14. Theatre Owners of America have a Film Content Informational Service, which analyzes film content, including scenes of sex and violence, enabling theatre owners to assess for themselves the type of audience the film should play to; TOA president is personally in favor of MPA classification.

Coe, Richard L. "Why Doesn't Someone Do Something?" *JSPG* (Sep 61) 17–19. Classification should be an individual responsibility.

Schnee, Charles. "White Star, Asterisk, Black Star." *JSPG* (Sep 61) 21–22. President of Writers Guild of America argues for self-classification by movie industry; each film should be classified before shooting starts.

Mack, S. Franklin. "What About Classification?" *JSPG* (Sep 61) 23–24. Representative of National Council of Churches rejects censorship but advocates classification.

"Parents, Children, and Films." *America* (15 Dec 62) 1235. A call for an advisory classification system to protect children.

Nathan, P. "Rights and Permissions: Motion Picture Classification." *Publishers Weekly* 182 (17 Dec 62) 29.

"Confusing the Issue." *America* 108 (5 Jan 63) 3. Criticism of Bosley Crowther's argument against a system of advisory film classification.

"Film Classification Defied." *America* 3 (5 Dec 64) 730. Attempt by distributors of *Malamondo* to ignore review boards that rate films.

Knight, A. "Who's to Classify?" *Sat Rev* 49 (26 Feb 66) 42+. Report on church groups' choices.

Fitzgerald, John E. "Film Classification: A Viewpoint." *Cath World* 204 (Oct 66) 32–36. Censorship or a responsible act? *Who's Afraid of Virginia Woolf?* and other examples.

Smith, Margaret Chase. "Sick Movies, a Menace to Children." *Rdrs Dig* 91 (Dec 67) 139–142. Senator from Maine approves audience classification.

Valenti, Jack, Richard Randall, Bosley Crowther, James Webb, Patrick Sullivan, Anne Childress, Gerald Kennedy, Saul David, G. William Jones, John Trevelyan, George Slaff, R. W. McDonald, Philip Harling. "The Journal Looks Again at Classification—What Now?" *JSPG* (June 68) 4–44. The MPA is still using the label "Suggested for Mature Audiences," but the Supreme Court in the Dallas case indicated that classification by law was acceptable; critics, ministers, and other observers, together with a few industry people, argue the question.

"Film Classification." *America* 119 (12 Oct 68) 310–311. Discussion of new MPAA system.

"New Ratings for Movies." *Senior Scholastic* 93 (18 Oct 68) supp 6–7. Questions and answers.

"Adults Only for Some Films Now." *US News & World Report* 65 (21 Oct 68) 22. Explanation of new classification code.

"Movies: G, M, R, X." *Newswk* 72 (21 Oct 68) 98+.

"New X Film Rating: Protective or Permissive?" *Senior Scholastic* 93 (25 Oct 68) 9–10.

"Step Toward Maturity." *Commonweal* 89 (25 Oct 68) 101–102. An editorial.

Nathan, Paul. "Not for Children." *Publishers Weekly* 194 (28 Oct 68) 50.

"Film-Makers Opt for Self-Policing." *Chris Cent* 85 (30 Oct 68) 1361.

Kauffmann, Stanley. "Sex Symbols." *New Rep* 159 (2 Nov 68) 30+. An analysis of ratings by the MPA.

"X Marks the Spot." *Newswk* 72 (2 Dec 68) 96+. The head of a major American theatre chain, Walter Reade, Jr., refuses to follow the movie industry's rating plan.

Michener, James A. "GMRX: An Alternative to Movie Censorship." *Rdrs Dig* 94 (Jan 69) 87–93. Explains recent sex and violence in U.S. films and describes new rating system.

Robinson, Sally. "What Should Parents See?" *Seventeen* 28 (Jan 69) 42+. A seventeen-year-old selects films for adults.

Whitehorn, Ethel. "Motion Picture Industry Has Devised an Audience-Suitability Rating System." *PTA Mag* 63 (Jan 69) 39.

Zinsser, William. "The New Movie Ratings." *Life* 66 (7 Feb 69) 11.

"X Marks the Spot." *Newswk* 73 (24 Feb 69) 101. The effects of the film industry's movie-classification program.

Sloan, William. "Code Control." *F Lib Q* 2 (No. 2, Spring 69) 33–36. The Film Library Information Council states its opposition to the classification scheme of the Motion Picture Association of America as censorship.

Robinson, Sally. "In My Opinion." *Seventeen* 28 (Mar 69) 22. A seventeen-year-old is against new rating system.

Knight, Arthur. "G as in Good Entertainment." *Sat Rev* 52 (1 Mar 69) 40. Discussion of problems inherent in Motion Picture Association's self-classification process.

"Can the New Movie Classification Code Bring Back the Customers?" *Consumer Bul* 52 (May 69) 15–16. An editorial.

"Keys to the New Movie Codes." *Good Housekeeping* 168 (June 69) 162.

Miller, E. (ed). "G, M, R and X: Opinions on Sex, Violence, Nudity in Films and the New Rating Code." *Seventeen* 28 (July 69) 82–83+. A symposium by young people.

Greenspan, Lou, Robert Steele, Anne Childress, Fredric Wertham, James Wall, Martin Dworkin, Art Buchwald, Gerald Kennedy, Frank Kelly, Richard Coe, Bernard Kantor. "The Journal Looks at the Film Rating Race." *JSPG* (Dec 69) 1–36. Editor asked various people outside the industry: What is your opinion of the rating system which was put into effect on November 1, 1968?

"The M-Rating Dies to Help Films Live." *Bus Wk* (7 Feb 70) 104–106. The switch from M to GP rating by the MPAA after complaints from distributors that M was hurting business.

Hunnings, Neville. "AA and X." *S&S* 39 (Spring 70) 71–72. Note on change in British classification: X is for over eighteen, AA for over fourteen, and adults don't have to come to A's with children.

Schickel, R. "Whatever Became of the Family Movie?" *Life* 69 (11 Sep 70) 10. There is no way to tell what is in a GP movie; only one-sixth of pictures in five months got G ratings; are movies ceasing to be mass art?

Boyd, G. N. "Movies and the Sexual Revolution: Should the Ratings Be Revised?" *Chris Cent* 87 (23 Sep 70) 1124–1125.

Shalit, G. "Rating Game." *Look* 34 (3 Nov 70) 82–89. What self-classification means and implies.

7d. Hollywood's Way of Life

[See also 2b(2), 3b(3), 7b(1c).]

Sheean, Vincent. "Hollywood." *Commonweal* 12 (11 June 30) 151–152. The unreality of the place which has captured the imagination of America. Responses (9 July 30) 284 and (30 July 30) 344.

Weber, Joe, and Lew Fields. "There's No Place

Like Hollywood." *Collier's* 86 (19 July 30) 10+. A look at Hollywood by two men from the theatre.

McNutt, Patterson. "Why I Hate Hollywood." *Outlook* 157 (28 Jan 31) 140–141+. Rejection of movie-making activities from personal experience.

Condon, Frank. "Harnessing the Humming Bird." *SEP* 203 (13 June 31) 33+. Reports on life in Hollywood.

"Is Hollywood So Bad?" *Lit Dig* 110 (11 July 31) 18. Actor George Arliss defends Hollywood.

Benchley, Robert. "A Possible Revolution in Hollywood." *Yale Rev* 21 (Sep 31) 100–110. Calls Hollywood "one of the dullest centres in the country" and calls for "a little well-staged, imaginative debauchery."

Condon, Frank. "If They Needed Passports." *SEP* 204 (12 Sep 31) 37+. On Hollywood stars' real names.

Dreiser, Theodore. "The Real Sins of Hollywood." *Liberty* 9 (11 June 32) 6–11.

Oursler, Fulton. "Is Hollywood More Sinned Against Than Sinning?" *Liberty* 9 (18 June 32) 22–25.

Cantor, Eddie, and David Freedman. "Who's Hooey in Hollywood." *SEP* 204 (16 Apr 32) 6–7+; (21 May 32) 28+; 205 (2 July 32) 9+. Star describes life in movie town.

Wylie, I. A. R. "Gone Hollywood." *Harper's* 165 (June 32) 11–20. On affectations of movie people.

Shawell, J. "Hollywood's Untold Tales." *Picture Rev* 33 (Aug 32) 12–13+.

Speare, Dorothy. "Hollywood Madness." *SEP* 206 (7 Oct 33) 26–27+. Focuses on Hollywood as dreamland.

Rorty, James. "Dream Factory." *Forum* 94 (Sep 35) 162–165. Suggests movie material infects those who produce it.

"Hollywood Is a Wonderful Place." *Life* 2 (No. 18, 3 May 37) 28–37. "The army of extras"; candid photos of the town; pictures and careers of Gary Cooper, Sylvia Sidney, Carole Lombard, Claudette Colbert.

Sayre, Joel and Gertrude. "What We Liked About Hollywood." *Scribner's* 103 (Mar 38) 24–25. A list of happy memories by two screenwriters.

Jones, G. "Knights of the Keyhole." *Collier's* 101 (16 Apr 38) 25–26+. The Hollywood gossip mill.

White, E. B. "One Man's Meat." *Harper's* 179 (July 39) 217–219. A famed journalist looks at Hollywood's standard of living.

Schulberg, Budd. "The Hollywood Novel." *Films* 1 (No. 2, Spring 40) 68–78. History of types and reviews of eight recent ones.

Arliss, George. "Londoner Looks at Hollywood." *Current Hist* 51 (Mar 40) 39–41+.

Ferguson, Otis. "To the Promised Land." *New Rep* 105 (14 July 41) 49–52; (4 Aug 41) 150–153; (18 Aug 41) 219–221; (8 Sep 41) 304–306; (22 Sep 41) 369–371; (13 Oct 41) 473–475; (24 Nov 41) 697–699. Humorous series on film production—and living—in Hollywood.

Brush, Katharine. "It's Not My Hollywood." *Good Housekeeping* 113 (Nov 41) 43+. Impressions of Hollywood by an outsider.

Crichton, Kyle. "Hollywood Holocaust: No Gas, No Hired Help, No Money!" *Collier's* 111 (13 Feb 43) 16+. Difficulties caused by government wartime restrictions.

Green, Abel. "Report from Hollywood." *SRL* 28 (14 Apr 45) 31. Life is different out there, but hardworking.

Leonard, Harold. "Hollywood." *S&S* 14 (No. 54, July 45) 39–42. Hollywood's interest in cultural activities is bound by its authoritarian and business structures.

Leonard, Harold. "Present and Accounted For." *S&S* 15 (No. 59, Autumn 46) 86–88. The story of twenty Hollywood personalities, what they did while serving in the armed forces, and their future plans on returning to Hollywood.

Cahn, Robert. "Heart of Hollywood." *CSMM* (15 Mar 47) 6. Voluntary contributions have built and maintain a home for veteran workers in the industry.

Crowther, Bosley. "Hollywood Starts Over." *Nation's Business* 36 (Oct 48) 47–49+. The problem of actors' morals; industry programs to give movies a better moral tone.

Shaw, Irwin. "Hollywood People." *Holiday* 5 (1949) 53–61.

Schulberg, Budd. "Hollywood: Its Life and Industry Ranging from 'Amazingly Colossal' to 'Ztinks.'" *Holiday* 5 (Jan 49). See 4a(2).

"Hollywood Wildcats." *Time* 54 (10 Oct 49) 93. Hollywood stars as oilmen.

Schary, Dore. "Exploring the Hollywood Myth." *NYTM* (9 Apr 50) 14+. The popular stereotype hurts the industry.

"Selling the Sizzle." *Commonweal* 52 (21 Apr 50) 38. A rebuttal to the contention that Hollywood is immoral; such publicity is its worst enemy.

Trumbo, Dalton. "The Graven Image." *Th Arts* 34 (July 50) 32–35. The Oscar season; the Hollywood way of life as an agreeable, humdrum community where there are no more thieves, rapists, murderers than in any other community.

"The World Inside." *S&S* 19 (Dec 50) 323–327. A number of extracts, mainly from novels, about the world of cinema.

Hine, A. "The Movie Mind." *Holiday* 9 (Apr 51) 6+. A review of some books that try to psychoanalyze Hollywood.

Russell, Rosalind. "They Still Lie About Hollywood." *Look* 15 (No. 14, 3 July 51) 36–43.

Meyerhoff, H. "*The New Yorker* in Hollywood." *Partisan Rev* 18 (Sep 51) 569–574.

Satirical piece on writer (presumably Lillian Ross) wrestling with her conscience to write about John Huston and the Hollywood movie colony.

Huff, Theodore. "Hollywood on Hollywood." *FIR* 4 (Apr 53) 171–183. Movies about movies traced from Sennett through *A Star Is Born, Sunset Boulevard,* and *The Bad and the Beautiful.*

Schulberg, Budd. "It Was Great to Be a Boy in Hollywood." *Holiday* 17 (Jan 55). *See 4a(2).*

Uselton, Roi A. "Death by Automobile." *FIR* 6 (Dec 55) 511–516. Survey of the notable Hollywood film personalities who have died from one cause or another while in an automobile, from Florence LaBadie to James Dean. See also brief letter 7 (Jan 56) 43.

Rosten, Leo. "Hollywood Revisited." *Look* 20 (10 Jan 56) 17–28. The author of *Hollywood: The Movie Colony, The Movie Makers* (reprinted Arno Press, 1971) gives a psychological X-ray of the movie colony—its manners, conflicts, morals.

Uselton, Roi A. "Death by Airplane." *FIR* 7 (May 56) 210–214. Airplane disasters that took the lives of eight film stars.

Gehman, R. "Hollywood and Its People." *Cosmopolitan* 141 (Oct 56) 46–51. Examination of the effects of Hollywood on its people: sex, religion, real estate, psychiatrists discussed.

Home, William Douglas. "Looking-Glass Men." *Spectator* 198 (4 Jan 57) 8–10. Impressions of life in Hollywood.

Ardrey, Robert. "Hollywood's Fall into Virtue." *Reporter* 16 (21 Feb 57) 13–17. A screenwriter examines what has killed the Hollywood legend. Discussion 16 (4 Apr 57) 4.

Uselton, Roi A. "Death by Suicide." *FIR* 8 (Apr 57) 156–166. Brief life stories of players who committed suicide, including Max Linder, Lupe Velez, Herman Bing, and Carole Landis.

Dooley, Roger B., and Robert Kass. "Fade-Out." *FIR* 8 (Aug–Sep 57) 327–329. A treatment for a proposed film about Hollywood.

"From a Hollywood Window You Can See Almost Anything." *Look* 23 (17 Mar 59) 47–50+.

Lom, Herbert. "Hollywood as I Saw It." *F&F* 5 (No. 11, Aug 59) 8+. Personal impressions, by an actor.

Douglas, Kirk. "Is the Industry Meeting Its Responsibilities?" *JSPG* (Sep 59) 11–12. Facetious article about change of style in Hollywood life—no more diamond tie clasps.

Serling, Rod. "Somebody Asked Me, Therefore . . ." *JSPG* (Sep 59) 3–6. TV scriptwriter turned screenwriter discusses hypersensitivity of Hollywood and other things that occur to him.

Elliott, Summer Locke. "The Cracked Lens: Notes on Hedda, Hollywood, TV, and Me." *Harper's* 221 (Dec 60) 78+. What happens when a writer of TV plays produces a documentary called *Hedda Hopper's Hollywood.*

Davidson, Bill. "Place in the Sun." *Show* 1 (Oct 61) 80–83. Excerpts from author's book *The Real and the Unreal* (Harper, 1961); the "image" of Hollywood versus the actualities of the film industry.

Parsons, Louella. "First to Know." *McCall's* 89 (Nov 61) 76–79+. Condensation of *Tell It to Louella* (Putnam's, 1961).

Lokke, V. L. "A Side Glance at Medusa: Hollywood, the Literature Boys, and Nathanael West." *Southwest Rev* 46 (Winter 61) 35–45. Hollywood's Sickness is representative of what is happening in society.

Hopper, Hedda. *"The Whole Truth and Nothing But."* *McCall's* 90 (Oct 62) 110–113+; (Nov 62) 104–105+. Excerpts from her book; Hollywood's most famous feuds (Doubleday, 1962).

Ross, Michael. "Stars in Your Eyes." *Travel* 119 (Feb 63) 38–40. There is a Tanner Grey Lines tour of Hollywood homes that drives through one studio (Universal) but it takes "pull" to get inside and watch.

Fadiman, William. "Lingua California Spoken Here." *F&F* 9 (No. 7, Apr 63) 60–61. On the argot of Hollywood.

Zimmer, Jill Schary. "With a Cast of Thousands." *McCall's* 91 (Nov 63) 130–133+. Excerpts from book recalling Hollywood childhood by daughter of onetime production head of MGM, Dore Schary.

Fadiman, William. "The Talkies." *F&F* 10 (No. 10, July 64) 48–49. Conversation in Hollywood is limited—to film topics.

Jennings, C. Robert. "Hollywood: The Rat Race in Neo-Babylon." *Show* 5 (Apr 65) 11+. What it's like to live in Hollywood and be an interviewer of the movie stars.

Kael, Pauline. "Incredible Shrinking Hollywood." *Holiday* 39 (Mar 66) 86–93+. Today's Hollywood, its themes and preoccupations.

"Moviemaking: Slow, Damp, and Better Now Than Hollywood." *Esq* 66 (July 66). *See 4e(1).*

Swanson, Gloria. "Hollywood Sunset." *Esq* 66 (Aug 66) 76–81. Nostalgic look at the old dream factory compared to Hollywood today; author comments on stills.

Jenkinson, Philip. "Hollywood Diary." *Film* (No. 52, Autumn 68) 14–18. A personal account of a visit to Hollywood and interviews with Hollywood personalities.

Tarratt, Margaret. "Reflections in a Golden Lens." *F&F* 16 (No. 4, Jan 70) 4–8; (No. 5, Feb 70) 14–18. Films about Hollywood itself; two articles.

Carson, L. M. K. "Phantom Empire." *Look* 34

(10 Feb 70) 13. Personal reflections on the Hollywood scene.

Mencken, H. L. "On Hollywood—and Valentino." *CJ* 9 (No. 2, Spring 70) 13–23. In an article reprinted from *Prejudices: Sixth Series* (1927) the essayist assails the dizzy editing of some movies, protests that he "saw no wildness among the movie-folk," who are basically romantic, and tells of Rudolph Valentino coming to him for advice.

7d(1). PRIVATE LIVES

Condon, Frank. "Where Beauty and Culture Reign Supreme." *SEP* 204 (8 Aug 31) 27+. Hollywood stars' homes.

Condon, Frank. ". . . Makes Jack a Bright Boy." SEP 204 (15 Aug 31) 33+. Spare time of Hollywood stars.

"Queer People." *Time* 18 (7 Sep 31) 29. Howard Hughes decides not to make film of that name about Hollywood depravity.

Gebhart, Myrtle. "This Man Spends $5,000,000 a Year of Other People's Money." *American* 112 (Dec 31) 76+. Profile of J. S. "Rex" Cole, financial and business manager for Hollywood stars.

"Death in Hollywood." *Time* 20 (19 Sep 32) 20–21. Suicide of MGM executive Paul Bern; speculation about his relationship with his wife, Jean Harlow, and his common-law wife, Dorothy Millette.

Shawell, J. "Hollywood Wives." *Pictorial Rev* 34 (Mar 33) 8–9+.

"Rags and Riches." *Time* 23 (2 Apr 34) 30–31. Actress Mary Astor's parents squander her money.

"Casting and Misconduct." *Time* 24 (2 July 34) 18. Head of Central Casting in court for immorality.

Deaner, F. "When Hollywood Stars Come Down to Earth." *Sunset* 73 (Aug 34) 9–11. A description of some of the gardens kept by Hollywood personalities.

"Hobbies of the Hollywood Stars." *Pop Mech* 63 (Mar 35) 372–374+.

"Churchgoing Hollywood." *Lit Dig* 121 (14 Mar 36) 18. Dr. J. George Dorn in *The Lutheran* reports church affiliations of stars.

Marshall, M. M. "Hollywood Babies." *Rdrs Dig* 28 (May 36) 58–60. It is easier to adopt them since actresses lose salary and shape when they have babies; condensed from *Liberty*.

Crichton, Kyle. "Star Straighteners: Hollywood Management." *Collier's* 100 (3 July 37) 18+. Hollywood Management, Inc., pampers the stars and handles their finances for them.

Orcutt, E. "Privacy on Parade." *SEP* 210 (7 Aug 37) 16–17+. Beverly Hills—its social life, tourism, lack of privacy.

"Being Homely in Hollywood." *SEP* 210 (18 Sep 37) 25+. An insight into Hollywood society life, with the thesis that homeliness wins more attention.

"Boy Almost Meets Girl." *SEP* 210 (22 Jan 38) 22–23. Hollywood's fickleness.

Peterson, E. T. "Human Side of Hollywood He-men." *Better Homes & Gardens* 17 (May 39) 22–23+. Hollywood tough guys puttering in the garden.

"New Hollywood: Stars Now Build Homes, Live Quietly and Raise Children." *Life* 9 (4 Nov 40) 65–71. A press agent's viewpoint of the life of a star at home; mostly pictures.

"Hollywood Party." *Life* 10 (17 Feb 41) 84–86. Pictures and stories of a Hollywood party.

"Star Boarders at Hollywood's Y." *American* 134 (Oct 42) 102–103. Photo tour of Studio Club, established by YWCA and MPPA for movie-struck girls.

Porter, A. "You'd Never Know." *Collier's* 113 (29 Jan 44) 16–17+. Hollywood stars welcome motherhood, yet retain their girlish figures.

"Children of the Stars." *Woman's Home Companion* 72 (Feb 45) 56–57.

"Art in Hollywood." *Life* 24 (1 Mar 48) 64–68+. Edward G. Robinson and other film stars as art collectors.

Slater, L. "Road to Rome." *Newswk* 33 (7 Feb 49) 85–86. Hollywood's growing colony in Rome and its possible effects on Italy's film industry.

"Hollywood in Italy." *NYTM* (25 Sep 49) 24–25. American film celebrities find Italy rewarding as a place to work and to relax.

"Hollywood Christians?" *Time* 56 (17 July 50) 72. "Born-again believers in Jesus," among them Jane Russell, as reported in *Christian Life* magazine.

English, R. "Man Who Worries for the Stars: Bö Roos." *SEP* 223 (24 Feb 51) 32–33+. He handles financial headaches and investments.

"Pets on Trial: Dogs of Hollywood Stars." *Coronet* 29 (Mar 51) 114–115.

"Movie Marriages." *Coronet* 30 (June 51) 118–119. Stills about stars whose happy married lives never make the headlines.

Bell, P. "How the Stars Stick to Their Diets." *Woman's Home Companion* 79 (Jan 52) 34–35. A picture essay.

"Life Goes to a Big Marion Davies Party." *Life* 33 (20 Oct 52) 132–134+.

Taylor, Frank J. "He Sells Houses to the Stars." *SEP* 226 (25 July 53) 32–33+. The star's whims in buying houses make big business for real-estate broker Al Herd.

Muir, Jean. "Boardinghouse of Broken Hearts." *SEP* 226 (19 Sep 53) 40–41+. The Hollywood Studio Club, for actors.

Parsons, Louella. "Lonely Glamour Girls of Hollywood." *Cosmopolitan* 135 (Nov 53) 10–11.

Wallace, Robert. "Stargazer for Stars." *Life* 36 (5 Apr 54) 143–144+. Astrologer Carroll Righter does horoscopes for such stars as Marlene Dietrich, Tyrone Power, and Lana Turner.

Lindsay, C. H. "The Lindsay Report." *Holiday* 15 (May 54) 48–53. The social behavior of Hollywood celebrities; with emphasis on the Hollywood party.

"Uncle Deductible." *Fortune* 50 (Aug 54) 124. Bö Roos—Los Angeles business manager for the stars—helps them keep some of their income, through advice and investments.

"Hollywood Mothers." *Look* 18 (24 Aug 54) 42–45. Picture essay.

Kuhn, Irene Corbally. "Hollywood, Unhitching Post." *Am Mercury* 80 (Jan 55) 7–11. A look at the on-again off-again marriages in Hollywood, with particular attention given to Marilyn Monroe and Joe DiMaggio.

"Hollywood Fathers." *Look* 19 (12 July 55) 38–41. Picture essay: stars and their children.

"Hollywood Hobbies." *McCall's* 83 (Oct 55) 16+. Picture essay: actors' spare-time talents.

Lindsay, C. H. "Those Gaudy Hollywood Weddings." *McCall's* 83 (Sep 56) 40–41+. Studio publicists, dress designers, coordinators, and other costly preparations.

Parton, Margaret. "Why Do So Many Hollywood Marriages Fail?" *Ladies' Home J* 74 (Jan 57) 40–41+.

Peck, Seymour. "New Dynasties Among Actors." *NYTM* (24 Mar 57) 30–31. Theatrical families, photographs; sons and daughters of famous actors and actresses of stage and screen.

Nunn, Richard. "Hollywood Handymen." *Better Homes & Gardens* 35 (Nov 57) 78–79+. Pictures of leading stars in their workshops at home.

Blatty, William P. "They Believed I Was an Arab Prince." *SEP* 230 (29 Mar 58) 28–29+. Blatty's adventures in Hollywood posing as visiting royalty.

"Grownup Movie Kids." *Life* 44 (31 Mar 58) 117–118+. A birthday party with children of Hollywood stars.

Lindsey, Cynthia. "Child Care in Hollywood." *McCall's* 85 (June 58) 48+. Showers for mothers-to-be; children's schooling; other examples from Hollywood families.

Christian, F. "Young Family in Hollywood: Don Murray and Hope Lange." *Cosmopolitan* 145 (Sep 58) 56–59.

Sheridan, Michael. "How the Stars Keep Fit." *Today's Health* 36 (Nov 58) 30–33+.

O'Neil, P. "Clan Is the Most." *Life* 45 (22 Dec 58) 116+. Social customs of Hollywood stars.

Slater, Leonard. "Disgrace of Hollywood: First Divorce Chart Ever Compiled." *McCall's* 86 (Mar 59) 50–52+. From 1934 to 1958.

"Wives of Western Stars." *Look* 23 (23 June 59) 92–99.

Tusher, Bill. "Do It Yourself; Hollywood Does." *Pop Mech* 112 (Aug 59) 125–129+. Hollywood stars in their home shops.

Norman, D. C. "Stars Who Do Their Own Hair." *Ladies' Home J* 76 (Dec 59) 78–79+.

"Shirley's Spoof Party." *Life* 47 (7 Dec 59) 167–169. Pictures taken at a charity party given by Shirley MacLaine.

Lemon, Richard. "Glamour Girls Off-Duty." *Newswk* 55 (4 Jan 60) 60–61. Leslie Caron, Joanne Woodward, Barrie Chase, and Joan Collins: what they do in New York during their spare time.

Hyams, Joe. "Should Movie Stars Marry?" *Ladies' Home J* 77 (May 60) 58–59+. Reasons for Hollywood divorces, with some psychological undertones.

"Musical Pairs." *Time* 75 (16 May 60) 59+. Some recent divorces among Hollywood stars.

Hyams, Joe. "Should Movie Stars Be Parents?" *Ladies' Home J* 77 (June 60) 72–73+. Problems in various homes.

Gehman, Richard. "Success Versus Marriage." *Cosmopolitan* 149 (Nov 1960) 86–93. A long study of the limelight tensions of Hollywood marriages.

Hart, B., and J. Anderson. "Hollywood News; How the Stars Eat and Exercise." *Ladies' Home J* 78 (July 61) 48–51+. Janet Leigh, Jack Lemmon, and Natalie Wood give advice.

Hecht, Ben. "Hollywood's Gift to America." *Sat Rev* 45 (13 Jan 62) 6–8. The town itself, a living contradiction of the "national sex phoniness" promulgated by its films, helped change the mores of America.

Hyams, Joe. "When Love Goes on Location." *McCall's* 90 (June 63) 88–93. Famous love affairs and divorces which began far from home; latest example: Taylor-Burton.

Taylor, Jeanette. "Sometimes the Dream Comes True." *Seventeen* 23 (Mar 64) 66–67. On the aspiring girls at the Hollywood Studio Club.

"Lawyer of the Big Deals." *Bus Wk* (8 Nov 69) 56. Hollywood attorney Gregson Bautzer.

"How Movies Break Up Marriages." *Ebony* 20 (Sep 65) 98–100+. Sidney Poitier as a case in point.

"Keeping the Stars in Fiscal Shape." *Bus Wk* (4 June 66) 160–162+. Report on A. Morgan Maree, business manager for notables in the film industry.

Joseph, J. "Cars of the Stars." *Motor T* 19 (July 67) 89–92.

"Where Traders Upstage the Stocks in Glamour." *Bus Wk* (9 Sep 67) 160–162. The brokerage firm of E. F. Hutton lures Hollywood stars with a dual office in MCA's Universal City.

"Mocking the Mockery." *Time* 95 (20 Apr 70) 72. Party held by producer Don Mitchell for stars to watch the Academy Awards on TV.

7d(2). PUBLIC AFFAIRS AND POLITICS

[See also 7c(2d).]

Steele, Walter S. "Radicals and Film Propaganda." *Nat Rep* 19 (Aug 31) 40. Formation and implications of American "Proletkino" in Hollywood.

McWilliams, Carey. "Hollywood Plays with Fascism." *Nation* 140 (29 May 35) 623–624. Organizations in Hollywood set up to "promote Americanism" claimed to be fascist.

Ryskind, Morrie. "No Soap Boxes in Hollywood." *Nation* 142 (4 Mar 36) 278. People in the film industry are uninformed about affairs of state and afraid to make a stand about their political beliefs. Discussion (1 Apr 36) 431; (13 May 36) 612–613.

Winter, E. "Hollywood Wakes Up." *New Rep* 95 (12 Jan 38) 276–278. Political activity among screenwriters and actors.

Ryskind, Morrie. "Move Over, Mr. Frankenstein." *Nation* 147 (10 Sep 38) 244–245. Author protests that he does not belong to the Hollywood Anti-Nazi League, but he does confess to being a liberal.

North, Joseph. "The New Hollywood." *New Masses* 32 (11 July 39) 14–16. The growing political awareness of Hollywood workers and organization of these workers has led and can lead to more and more progressive films.

"Hollywood Girds for War." *Life* 12 (19 Jan 42) 30+. Hollywood's first air-raid rehearsal brings a flurry of publicity.

"Hollywood in Uniform." *Fortune* 25 (Apr 42) 92–95+. The contributions, moods, and manners of wartime Hollywood.

"Hollywood Stars Hit Road for Army-Navy Relief." *Life* 12 (June 42) 32–33. Brief account of an early benefit show for troops.

Hirschfeld, Al. "On the Hollywood Front." *NYTM* (23 Aug 42) 16–17. Hollywood in wartime, with Hirschfeld drawings.

Rosten, Leo C. "Hollywood Goes to War." *Woman's Home Companion* 69 (Dec 42) 14–15+. Hollywood stars have enlisted, and films themselves are being used for military instruction and building morale.

Davis, Bette. "Hollywood Canteen." *Collier's* 111 (2 Jan 43) 10–11. Unions and guilds work together in providing servicemen with fun and entertainment.

Nugent, F. S. "Super Duper Epic: Hollywood Canteen." *NYTM* (17 Oct 43) 16–17. Hollywood entertains servicemen.

"Stars Cluster Again at Birthday Balls." *Life* 16 (14 Feb 44) 34. Franklin Roosevelt's sixty-second birthday party.

Hodson, J. L. "Hollywood Argument." *Spectator* 172 (26 May 44) 471. Political controversy and effect of the war on Hollywood;

formation of Motion Picture Alliance to prevent spread of subversive ideas.

Minton, Bruce. "Blackmailing Hollywood." *New Masses* 52 (15 Aug 44) 11–12. The forces of reaction are trying to take over the film industry in order to gain an irresistibly powerful tool in molding public opinion; "Hollywood is the scene of a major anti-fascist struggle."

Rice, Elmer. "Strictly Personal: The M.P.A. and American Ideals." *SRL* 27 (11 Nov 44) 18. The Motion Picture Alliance for the Preservation of American Ideals wants to counteract the public impression that Hollywood is run by radicals; is MPA isolationist and anti-union? Reply with rejoinder (23 Dec 44) 9–10.

"Hollywood and Vine." *New Rep* 114 (13 May 46) 697. Politics in Hollywood.

Hayes, Alfred. "Lyons Tale: A Report." *Screen Writer* 2 (Apr 47) 18–22. Criticizes Eugene Lyons, who addressed the Motion Picture Alliance (new right-wing political group) on the danger of Communists in the film business.

Pascal, Ernest. "Art, Business and the Liberals." *New Rep* (31 Jan 49) 21–23. The immaturity of the Hollywood liberal.

Shaw, Robert. "Hollywood Counts the Vote." *New Rep* 120 (31 Jan 49) 19–21. Hollywood's political attitudes of the day; responses to Committee on Un-American Activities.

"The Stars' Lament." *Newswk* 48 (24 Dec 56) 54. The Internal Revenue Service cracks down.

"Meanwhile, in Hollywood." *Time* 76 (25 July 60) 19. Frank Sinatra's Hollywood "clan" at the Democratic Convention.

"Happy as a Clan." *Time* 76 (5 Dec 60) 52+. Involvement of stars in the 1960 Presidential campaign.

Alexander, Shana. "My Technicolor Senator." *Life* 57 (4 Dec 64) 30. Reflections on film celebrities in public office.

"Activism, Hollywood Style." *Newswk* 70 (28 Aug 67) 74. Hollywood personalities in political activity.

7d(3). AROUND THE TOWN

Woodward, W. E. "Nine-O'Clock Town." *Collier's* 89 (30 Apr 32) 22+. Hollywood gone domestic and respectable.

Beatty, Jerome. "Hullabaloo Town." *American* 113 (May 32) 22–26+. Impressionistic journey through Hollywood.

Beebe, J. "Hollywood with a Pinch of Salt." *Scribner's* 102 (Oct 37) 84–88. Its restaurants.

Carson, Ruth. "Cock 'n' Bull." *Collier's* 108 (6 Dec 41) 14+. Hollywood restaurant.

Marshall, Jim. "Everybody's Night Club." *Collier's* 113 (13 May 44) 24. Hollywood's Palladium.

"Hollywood Gallery." *Life* 19 (15 Oct 45) 84–89. A painter's portfolio of impressions of movie city.

"Life Goes to Mike Romanoff's Restaurant." *Life* 19 (29 Oct 45) 141–145. Picture story of restaurant which Hollywood stars frequent.

Levine, J. "The Customer Is Always Wrong." *Collier's* 116 (22 Dec 45) 20–21+. Grocery store patronized by the stars.

"Life Goes to a Circus in Hollywood." *Life* 25 (27 Sep 48) 138–142+. The stars, including Burt Lancaster, put on a charity show for a hospital fund.

"Night over Hollywood." *Coronet* 31 (Jan 52) 115–130. Picture story about the city and its parties.

Marx, A. "Mink's-Eye View of Hollywood." *Collier's* 130 (13 Sep 52) 38–39+. Fur magnate Al Teitelbaum on the buying habits of film stars.

Marx, A. "Hollywood's Favorite Sweatshop." *Collier's* 130 (13 Dec 52) 56–58+. Inside comments from Terry Hunt, the owner of a Hollywood health club for movie stars.

McClung, Ahlean Masters. "Hollywood Glamorizes Itself." *FIR* 7 (Nov 56) 433–438. Hollywood as a tourist center; a report on the current project of relandscaping Hollywood Boulevard.

Marcorelles, Louis. "American Diary." *S&S* 32 (Winter 62–63). *See 4d.*

Zinsser, W. "*Quo* Hollywood?" *Look* 31 (11 July 67) 14. What a sightseer might see.

Hutchens, John K. "One Thing and Another." *Sat Rev* 51 (23 Mar 68) 37+. Recollections of a tourist in Hollywood.

Hamilton, J. "Hollywood: The Year You Almost Couldn't Find It." *Look* 34 (3 Nov 70) 27–33. A pictorial essay on filmland, yesterday and today.

7d(4). AT WORK

Condon, Frank. "They Shall Not Pass." *SEP* 204 (1 Aug 31) 29+. On Hollywood studio security.

Condon, Frank. "How Do You Address a Duke?" *SEP* 204 (29 Aug 31) 28+. On various duties of Hollywood personnel.

Packer, Eleanor. "Hollywood Goes to Lunch." *Ladies' Home J* 50 (Nov 33) 28–29+. Stars' eating habits at MGM commissary.

Morriss, Ruth Moore. "One-Piece Meals." *Collier's* 96 (5 Oct 35) 26+. Stars enjoy "eating on the run."

Walter, Eugene. "The Hardest Way." *Cinema Arts* 1 (No. 1, June 37) 37–39. One man's view of the power structure in Hollywood.

Macgowan, Kenneth. "I Went to College." *Cinema Arts* 1 (No 3, Sep 37) 36–38. A personal account by a producer of the disadvantages of a college degree in Hollywood.

Benham, L. "Food for Stars." *Woman's Home Companion* 65 (Apr 38) 17–18. A look at the commissary of Warner Brothers.

Rosten, Leo C. "Truth About Hollywood." *Sci Dig* 11 (June 42) 23–27. The legendary Hollywood is compared to the workaday reality.

"Actress Buff Cobb Parodies the Day of a Movie Star." *Life* 20 (8 Apr 46) 12–13+. Pictorial satire on movie life.

Zierer, C. M. "Hollywood—World Center of Motion Picture Production." *Annals of Am Acad of Polit and Soc Sci* (1947) 12–17. Early history of the city.

Manvell, Roger. "Revaluations: *Shooting Stars*, 1928." *S&S* 19 (June 50). *See 3c, Shooting Stars.*

Ace, Goodman. "Soothsaying for the Panic-Stricken." *SRL* 34 (9 June 51) 28. Humorous word of hope to those who are afraid of TV's replacing movies.

"Day with the Stars." *Look* 18 (13 July 54) 46–49+. Picture essay of stars at work.

McNulty, William. "Hollywood Ribbing." *FIR* 5 (Nov 54) 457–458. A fan-appeal article that cites some instances of self-satire by the film industry in films.

"New Hollywood." *Time* 69 (13 May 57) 44+. How television has come to dominate Hollywood production and society.

Ager, Cecelia. "Rip, Race, Rock: What's in a Name?" *NYTM* (16 Feb 58) 26+. How actors go about renaming themselves.

White, G. M., and H. Beaumont (eds.). "Between Jobs." *Ladies' Home J* 75 (June 58) 127–130+. In *How America Lives* series: Hollywood from a working actor's point of view—Hugh Beaumont and his family.

Meehan, Thomas. "Early Morning of a Motion-Picture Executive." *New Yorker* 37 (6 May 61) 39–40. Essay in Joycean style on hypothetical making of *Ulysses.*

Higham, Charles. "Hollywood Boulevard 1965." *S&S* 34 (Autumn 65). *See 4d.*

Crist, Judith. "Commercially Yours." *Ladies' Home J* 84 (Mar 67) 70. Stars who do TV commercials and other advertisements.

Knight, Arthur. "The Eucalyptic Dream." *Sat Rev* 50 (23 Sep 67) 70–71+. Hollywood as a state of mind which produces films with a distinctive look, a result of the production philosophy of film as entertainment; a short history of the development of Hollywood and as it is today.

Latham, A. "Day at the Studio." *Harper's* 241 (Nov 70) 38–50. An excerpt from the book *Crazy Sundays* (Viking, 1971) on Scott Fitzgerald in Hollywood.

7e. International Relations

[See also 6c(4), 7a(1).]

"Sensitive Europeans." *Time* 15 (10 Feb 30) 19. Protests about U.S. films.

"Talkies in Germany." *Living Age* 338 (1 May 30). *See 4e(4).*

"Lord Irwin and the Movies." *Chris Cent* 48 (29 July 31) 964–965. Viceroy of India charges movies with irresponsibility in international image making.

"Europe's Highbrows Hail Mickey Mouse." *Lit Dig* 110 (8 Aug 31). *See 2h(3).*

"Our Screen Fight with Russia." *Lit Dig* 113 (28 May 32) 16. German film critics pit Russian movies against Hollywood products.

Bryher. "West and East of the Atlantic." *Close Up* 9 (No. 2, June 32) 131–133. Problems in English and American coproduction.

Morkovin, Boris V. "Cinematograph as a Factor in International Life." *Proceed of Instit of World Aff* (Los Angeles) 10 (1933) 258. Report on informal group meeting at USC annual conference.

Weinberg, Herman G. "The Foreign Language Film in the United States." *Close Up* 10 (No. 2, June 33) 167–181.

Biery, Ruth, and Eleanor Packer. "England Challenges Hollywood." *SEP* 206 (29 July 33). *See 4e(1c).*

Grundy, J. B. C. "Language in Film." *S&S* 2 (No. 6, Summer 33) 45–46; (No. 7, Autumn 33) 85–86. Distortions that result from sound films being shown in different cultures; some suggestions.

Winter, Mrs. Thomas G. "Cinematography as an Agency for World Unity: Summary of Round Table." *Proceed of Inst of World Aff* (Los Angeles) 11 (1934) 245–247. Public-relations representative of Motion Picture Producers and Distributors summarizes proposals for improvement.

Kelley, J. D. "Cinema Overseas." *S&S* 3 (No. 10, Spring 34) 58–60. Notes on the films screened in Abadan and the nature of the audience there.

"Britain Invades U.S. Market with Improved Shows." *Newswk* 4 (18 Aug 34). *See 4e(1c).*

Clarrière, Georges. "The Western Peril." *S&S* 3 (No. 12, Winter 34–35) 153–156. The dominant role and influence of American films in France.

Cressey, Paul. "The Influence of Moving Pictures on Students in India." *Am J Sociology* 41 (Nov 35). *See 4f(2).*

Harvey, Jim. "The Presentation of Foreign Films." *Life & Letters Today* 15 (No. 5, Autumn 36) 166–170. The exhibition of foreign films in Great Britain: subtitles, dubbing, and censorship.

Holmes, Winifred. "British Films and the Empire." *S&S* 5 (No. 19, Autumn 36). *See 4e(1).*

"Italian Sailors Raid Isis Theatre, Burn *Abyssinia* Film." *China Weekly Rev* 79 (27 Feb 37) 438–439. This incident in China was followed by Russian protest; see 80 (6 Mar 37) 9.

Greene, Graham. "Ideas in the Cinema." *Spectator* 159 (19 Nov 37) 894–895. International films attempt to appeal to too large an audience; proposes development of cinemas for national publics in order to make screen ideas more direct and meaningful.

Phillips, Henry Albert. "Movies Move the World." *Rotarian* 52 (June 38) 23–26. The influences of films and stars all over the world; a trip through the sound stages of Hollywood.

Thomas, Yvonne. "The Foreign Films Return." *S&S* 8 (No. 29, Spring 39) 28–29. An overview of the past and the future of foreign films and their reception in other countries.

Weinberg, Herman G. "Happy Landings!" *S&S* 9 (No. 33, Spring 40) 8. America's positive reception to British films during wartime.

De Rochemont, Richard. "As America Sees It." *S&S* 10 (No. 37, Spring 41). *See 4e(1b).*

Lejeune, C. A. "Film: International Medium." *Th Arts* 26 (May 42) 336–343. The visual language in cross-cultural communication.

"Films Across the Sea." *New S&N* 27 (11 Mar 44). *See 4e(1d).*

Isaacs, H. R. "Two-Way Traffic." *Th Arts* 29 (Jan 45) 32–33. The "international" film after the war.

Joseph, Robert. "Cinema: Comment and Criticism." *Arts & Arch* 62 (May 45) 15+. Films to be shown to Nazi prisoners of war.

Buchman, Sidney. "A Writer in VIP's Clothing." *Screen Writer* 1 (Oct 45) 17–31. Buchman's impressions of what screenwriters should write after he has toured the European Theatre of Operations in World War II; the Germans have shaped men's minds all over Europe; can films help the children?

Seton, Marie. "British and Canadian Films in America's Middle West." *S&S* 14 (No. 55, Oct 45) 94–95.

Wollenberg, H. H. "Towards European Cooperation." *S&S* 14 (No. 55, Oct 45) 91–92. Signs of this in the film industry.

Carr, Philip. "One Hollyworld." *Spectator* 175 (30 Nov 45) 507. Because Hollywood corners the world film-distribution market, national individualism is declining.

"Thank You, Stars." *Time* 46 (31 Dec 45) 39. Canada expresses its thanks for good film relations with U.S. in wartime.

Joseph, Robert. "American Films in Germany —A Report." *Screen Writer* 1 (May 46). *See 4e(4e)*.

Jeanson, Henri. "Open Letter to Our Friends, the American Screen Writers." *Screen Writer* 2 (July 46) 19–25. French playwright complains about the unfair advantage in American films being shown widely in France, while French films are excluded from American theatres by government trade agreements; first printed in *Spectateur*.

Powell, Michael. "Your Questions Answered." *Penguin F Rev* 1 (Aug 46) 102–110. Roger Manvell asks this director whether a film maker should consciously try to be "international in appeal"; the negative answer ranges over the history of the silent film and early sound.

Inglis, R. A. "Freedom to See and Hear." *Survey* 35 (Dec 46) 477–481+. Possibilities of films for bringing mutual understanding to a world audience; aiming for "general appeal" in all films won't do it.

Huntley, John. "British Film Music and World Markets." *S&S* 15 (No. 60, Winter 46–47) 135. British film exports are received favorably because of their music.

Wollenberg, H. H. "British Films Overseas." *S&S* 15 (No. 60, Winter 46–47) 146–148. A summary of foreign opinions and reactions to British films.

Gordon, Jay E. "Operation Celluloid." *Hwd Q* 2 (No. 4, July 47). *See 7b(1)*.

Pudovkin, Vsevolod. "The Global Film." *Hwd Q* 2 (No. 4, July 47) 327–332. Like *Prelude to War,* which uses montage methods so well, the feature documentary may be able to cross international boundaries; other inventions are needed.

Weinberg, Herman G. "The Language Barrier." *Hwd Q* 2 (No. 4, July 47). *See 2d(5)*.

Meadow, Noel. "Evolution of the French Cinema in the U.S." *Screen Writer* 3 (Sep 47) 24–26.

Sharin, Eugen. "Disunion in Vienna." *Screen Writer* 3 (Oct 47) 10–14. American films shown to postwar Austrian audiences and what appealed to them; Hollywood's insufficient consideration of foreign sensibilities.

Harrison, Stella. "Letter from London." *Canad Forum* 28 (Apr 48). *See 4e(1c)*.

Weinberg, Herman G. "I Title Foreign Films." *Th Arts* (Apr 48). *See 2d(5)*.

Sutherland, Donald. "Bogus Ballyhoo." *S&S* 17 (No. 67, Autumn 48). *See 6d(3)*.

Borneman, Ernest. "Films for International Understanding." *Penguin F Rev* 7 (Sep 48) 97–106. UNESCO plans and purposes.

"Foreign Showcase: Paris Theatre." *Newswk* 32 (20 Sep 48). *See 4e(2c)*.

Slater, L. "Road to Rome." *Newswk* 33 (7 Feb 49). *See 7d(1)*.

Griffith, Richard. "Where Are the Dollars?" *S&S* 19 (Dec 49). *See 4e(1c)*.

"More Grief for Movie Exports." *Bus Wk* (15 July 50). *See 4e(1c)*.

Queval, Jean. "France Looks at British Films." *S&S* 19 (July 50). *See 4e(1)*.

Feldman, Joseph and Harry. "The D. W. Griffith Influence." *FIR* 1 (July–Aug 50). *See 5, D. W. Griffith*.

Cooke, Alan. "Free Cinema." *Sequence* (No. 13, 1951). *See 8d*.

Patterson, Richard. "The UN in Hollywood: A Lesson in Public Relations." *Hwd Q* 5 (No. 4, Summer 51) 326–333. Graduate student describes United Nations film unit and its work as well as the influence of such UN representatives as Benoit-Lévy, Skot-Hansen and others on issues presented in feature films.

McLean, Ross. "Notes in Passing." *Arts & Arch* 68 (Nov 51) 23. Head of Films and Visual Information Division, UNESCO, comments on the effectiveness and responsibility of film.

O'Shaughnessy, Marjorie. "Hands, or Something, Across the Sea." *S&S* 21 (Jan–Mar 52) 135–136. A humorous account of a fictional visit to an American theatre to see a British film.

Sprager, Harva Kaaren. "Hollywood's Foreign Correspondents." *QFRTV* 6 (No. 3, Spring 52) 274–282. Survey based on questionnaire includes income, education, and attitudes of Hollywood-based reporters from seventy countries.

Knight, Arthur. "Creativity in Film." *FIR* 3 (Mar 52) 125–131. Inherent national traits in film making can't be imitated elsewhere successfully.

Bray, Mary. "Interlingua." *FIR* 3 (Oct 52) 380–382. A proposal that Interlingua, the artificial language created by the International Auxiliary Language Association, be utilized by the different communications media, including films; following is a portion of an article translated into Interlingua.

"Cinematographic Exhibitions." *US Dept of State Bul* 29 (31 Aug 53) 292. An announcement that U.S. government will be represented at international exhibitions of films.

Loveman, Amy. "Unrealized Asset: Fostering of International Understanding." *Sat Rev* 36 (5 Sep 53) 22. Movies' potential in "bringing together all the ends of the earth" could be a foundation for future peace.

Everson, William K. "Movie Titles." *FIR* 4 (Dec 53) 516–518. Reasons the original titles of some films are changed for overseas distribution; examples.

"Hollywood: The Focus Is Overseas." *Bus Wk* (9 Oct 54) 158–160. Great Britain's protective barriers, German revival, and Italians in U.S. discussed.

"Contest in Damascus." *Collier's* 134 (12 Nov 54). *See 2m(3)*.

Welles, Orson. "For a Universal Cinema." *F Cult* 1 (No. 1, 1955) 31–32. Problems in completing *Mr. Arkadin;* Welles argues for the suppression of national censorship and freedom of communication for film makers in all countries.

Reisz, Karel. "Return Engagement." *S&S* 25 (Summer 55) 6–7. Note on visit by British film makers to informal film conference in Rome.

"Hands Across the Sea." *S&S* 25 (Winter 55–56) 116. Note on British films in America, especially on TV.

de Laurot, Edouard L., and Jonas Mekas. "Foreign Film Distribution in the U.S.A." *F Cult* 2 (No. 7, 1956) 15–17. An interview with distributor Thomas J. Brandon.

Dickinson, Thorold. "Conference in Paris." *S&S* 26 (Summer 56) 38–40. An account of the first international meeting of "Auteurs de Films," held in Paris: every nation has the right to see films of all nations; coproduction should be encouraged, film schools opened to all; other issues aired.

"Empty Cinemas." *Fortune* 54 (Nov 56). *See 4e(1c)*.

Dickinson, Thorold. "A Note on *Out*." *S&S* 26 (Spring 57) 174. Production story on UN film scripted by John Hersey, directed by Lionel Rogosin in five weeks, about Hungarian refugees.

Marcorelles, Louis. "Paris Notes." *S&S* 26 (Spring 57). *See 4e(2c)*.

Jones, Dorothy B. "Hollywood's International Relations." *QFRTV* 11 (No. 4, Summer 57) 362–374. Foreign reactions to American films; import-export problems.

Marcorelles, Louis. *"Cinémas d'Essai." S&S* 27 (Autumn 57). *See 6e(2b)*.

"In the Meantime." *Time* 70 (18 Nov 57) 112+. Some current foreign films that have found their way to non-art theatres.

"Old World Fans." *New Yorker* 34 (10 May 58) 29–30. A United Artists tour in Germany, accompanied by Richard Widmark.

Mayer, Arthur. "From Bernhardt to Bardot." *Sat Rev* 42 (27 June 59) 8–10+. The new popularity of foreign films; how film importing began.

Kozintsev, Gregory. "Deep Screen." *S&S* 28 (Nos. 3–4, Summer–Autumn 59). *See 3b(2)*.

Mayer, Arthur. "From Bernhardt to Bardot." *F&F* 6 (No. 5, Feb 60) 7–8+. History of American interest in foreign films.

Monaco, Eitel. "The Time Is Now—For a World Film Meeting." *JSPG* (Mar 60) 25–26. President of Italian Association of Producers and Distributors argues for central international organization for the motion-picture industry.

Nelson, C. M. "The United Nations in Films." *JSPG* (Sep 60) 25–26. UN public-information consultant discusses UN-made documentary and feature films.

"Film's Foreign Accent." *Economist* 198 (4 Feb 61) 453. American audience's increasing preference for foreign films.

Hull, David S. "International Delinquency." *Film* (No. 28, Mar–Apr 61). *See 4k(10)*.

Clarens, Carlos. "Among the Missing." *NY F Bul* 3 (No. 4, 1962) 3–6. An article regretting that more foreign films aren't released in the U.S., with special attention to the then unreleased films of Visconti and Antonioni.

"U.S. and Rumania Exchange Films." *US Dept of State Bul* 46 (11 Jan 62) 959. Notice of the agreement.

Zarecki, Yona. "Research in Content Structures and Techniques of Films for Heterogeneous Population." *JUFPA* 15 (No. 1, 1963) 14–17+. Tel Aviv educational film maker stresses problems of communication with population of widely varied educational and cultural backgrounds; emphasis on positive feelings and inclusion of a representative range of facial types help to make a film effective with this varied audience.

Renton, Bruce. "Letter from Italy." *Nation* 196 (2 Mar 63). *See 4e(3)*.

Leglise, Paul. "The Useless Barriers." *UNESCO Courier* 16 (May 63) 21–23+. On the international exchange of films and UNESCO's role in it.

Mayer, Arthur. "The New Film Frontier." *Sat Rev* 46 (5 Oct 63) 20–21+. Coproduction and other international projects.

Baker, Peter. "Foreign Papers." *F&F* 10 (No. 5, Feb 64) 41–61. Series of interviews on why so few foreign films get to the British public.

Schlesinger, Arthur, Jr. "A Life Line Thrown into Chaos." *Show* 4 (Apr 64) 72–73. Worldwide significance of the motion picture.

Salomon, Barbara Probst. "The Franglais Film." *Nation* 199 (10 Aug 64). *See 4e(2c)*.

"Mecca for Film Trade." *Bus Wk* (17 Apr 65) 80. Report on the Film Centrum in Brussels, a place for independent film makers to bargain for production money and distribution.

Weiss, Jiri. "Mixing It." *F&F* 11 (No. 9, June 65) 46–48. General reflections on the international film world.

Pearson, Wilbert H. "The Persistence of Visionaries." *JUFPA* 18 (No. 3, 1966) 16–21+. Address before the Columbus International Film Festival discusses necessity of film for worldwide communication and education—and some of its problems.

Sonnenfeld, Albert. "A Note on Linguistic Morality." *FQ* 19 (No. 4, Summer 66) 29–31. How the American film handles multilingual problems in *The Train* and *Von Ryan's Express*.

Levine, N. "Influence of the Kabuki Theater on the Films of Eisenstein." *Mod Drama* 12 (May 69) 18–29.

Williams, Don G. "Universities in Overseas Production." *JUFA* 22 (No. 4, 1970). *See 4f.*

"French Films on British Screens." *F&F* 16 (No. 9, June 70) 18–26. A survey of the independent British distributors to find out how foreign films get to the British audience.

7e(1). THE WORLD MARKET

[See also 2d(5), 2g(3).]

"Sound [and Fury] in Movie Export." *Bus Wk* (1 Jan 30) 31–32. Producers are turning to dubbing to increase badly sagging export market.

Kauffman, Reginald Wright. "War in the Film World." *North Am Rev* 229 (Mar 30) 351–356. Foreign correspondent summarizes Europe's campaign against American movies.

"Down with American Films!" *Rev of Reviews* 81 (Apr 30) 116–117. Surveys European "quota system" for importing American films.

"German Talkie War Comes Home to New York and May End There." *Bus Wk* (9 Apr 30) 8. Tobis-Klangfilm patent suit against Western Electric prohibits U.S. export to Germany.

"Talkies Abroad." *Outlook* 155 (28 May 30) 137. Europeans contemplate merging to combat American competition.

Johnston, William A. "The World War of Talking Pictures." *SEP* 203 (19 July 30) 31+. Hollywood talkies now being dubbed for international release.

"Talkie Patent Dispute Ends; Its Prize Big German Market." *Bus Wk* (23 July 30) 8. Agreement on interchangeability of sound-film patents.

"German-American Talkie Trust." *Rev of Reviews* 82 (Sep 30) 110–111. Sound-patent agreement between RCA, Fox, Pathé, Paramount, Metro-Goldwyn and others with German sound-film companies.

"Talkies in Foreign Languages Keep American Films on Top." *Bus Wk* (25 Feb 31) 22. European market for talkies helps industry during Depression.

"France May Open Door to American Talkies." *Bus Wk* (8 July 31) 22–23. Secret dealing with Minister of Art may remove French quota on American films.

"America's Film Monopoly." *Living Age* 341 (Dec 31) 373–374. European hostility toward U.S. films noted.

Chavance, Louis. "American Movies in France." *Canad Forum* 12 (Mar 32). *See 4e(2c).*

"Movie Amalgamation." *Bus Wk* (25 July 36) 24. Fox and MGM plan to make British

"quota pictures" as Schenck brothers buy into Gaumont-British.

"Hollywood Buys: MGM and Fox Strengthen Tie-Up with Gaumont-British Films." *Lit Dig* 122 (1 Aug 36) 39.

"Deal from Divan." *Time* 28 (3 Aug 36) 45. MGM buys into Gaumont-British.

"Anglo-U.S. Film Deal." *Bus Wk* (4 Dec 37) 30+. British money said to back Goldwyn-Korda bid for United Artists.

"Tokyo Goes Back to Hollywood—Orders 200 Pictures!" *China Weekly Rev* 85 (18 June 38) 73–74. Japan ends nine-month ban on exhibition of American films.

Deane, A. "Films Follow the Flag." *CSMM* (25 July 42) 4+. American-made films enjoy worldwide distribution and projection in spite of wartime difficulties.

"Mexican Movies Challenge Hollywood." *Scholastic* (4 Jan 43) 15. Mexican films in Latin America.

"New Film Deal? Department of Justice Watches for Worldwide Movie Cartel." *Bus Wk* (12 Aug 44) 75.

Grierson, John. "Hollywood International." *Nation* 160 (6 Jan 45) 12–14. Because of high costs in production, the U.S. and Great Britain will always need a world market.

Moley, Raymond. "Motion Picture's Critical Future." *Newswk* 26 (9 July 45) 108. The problem of maintaining a world market for U.S. films.

"World Pictures." *Bus Wk* (8 Dec 45) 44+. New movie organization set up by Rank, Universal, and International will compete with "Big 5" on a global scale.

"Glad Hands Across the Sea." *Time* 46 (10 Dec 45) 82. The deal between Universal International and England's J. Arthur Rank to distribute films in U.S. and England jointly.

"U.S. Films Face Fight Abroad." *Bus Wk* (29 Dec 45) 109–110. The reopening of world markets for American films exposes major impediments; a country-by-country examination of postwar changes in foreign markets.

"Railroad Movies: Eagle Lion Films." *Newswk* 27 (7 Jan 46) 54. Robert R. Young and J. Arthur Rank to distribute films in England and the U.S. jointly.

"Battle of the Screen." *Fortune* 33 (Mar 46) 200. Hollywood's export market, which accounted for one-third of the industry's annual prewar income, faces a partial embargo.

"Film Comeback: American Pictures Showing Again in Foreign Theatres." *Bus Wk* (6 July 46) 24+.

"Deal with Rank." *Newswk* 28 (12 Aug 46) 80. J. Cheever Cowdin's leadership of Universal Pictures and his ties with England's J. Arthur Rank to distribute films.

Vermorel, Claude. "Future of French Films." *Free World* 12 (Nov 46) 50–51. American and French agreement to remove import restrictions is harmful to both countries.

Manvell, Roger. "Clearing the Air." *Hwd Q* 2 (No. 2, Jan 47). *See 4e(1).*

Winston, A. "Movies; Hollywood Starts to Slip in International Battle." *UN World* 1 (Feb 47) 59–60. In the face of better foreign films and poorer U.S. ones, Hollywood no longer dominates filmdom.

"Hollywood's One World." *New Rep* 116 (31 Mar 47) 42–43. Why foreign markets for U.S. films are decreasing and what this does to Hollywood films.

"Movie Jitters: Foreign Business Is Slipping Away." *Bus Wk* (10 May 47) 70.

"British Squeeze on Movies: First Victim of Dollar Crisis." *US News & World Report* 23 (22 Aug 47) 20. Why Great Britain levied a film import tax and with what results.

"Pleasant Boomerang." *Nation* 165 (23 Aug 47) 176–177. The pros and cons of the British import tax on American films.

Moley, Raymond. "Hollywood's War with England." *Newswk* 30 (25 Aug 47) 84. Hollywood retaliates against England's film tax with an export ban.

Goldwyn, Samuel. "World Challenge to Hollywood." *NYTM* (31 Aug 47) 8+. Declining markets overseas threaten not only film profits but, more importantly, the potential of the American film as our ambassador.

"War with Britain." *Newswk* 32 (13 Sep 47) 66. U.S. industry retaliates.

"Panic in Paradise." *Time* 50 (22 Sep 47) 97. Occasioned by the British tax on U.S. films.

"New British Film Pact Cheers Hollywood." *Bus Wk* (20 Mar 48) 100.

Baker, S. *"Pax Britannica." Newswk* 31 (22 Mar 48) 96. Settlement of British-American tax row over movie imports.

"Compromise in London." *Time* 51 (22 Mar 48) 96. The British 75% tax on U.S. film profits is lifted.

"French Earn More from U.S. Movies, So They Turn Their Studios into Factories." *US News & World Report* 24 (2 Apr 48). *See 4e(2c).*

Wyatt, W. "Dollars and Films." *New S&N* 35 (8 May 48) 368. Hollywood's problem of regaining unremitted sterling may be solved by buying up western-hemisphere rights to distribute British productions.

"Bacon and Bogart Too." *Fortune* 37 (June 48) 122. The deal between Eric Johnston and the British government to abolish embargoes on films.

"Bad News." *Newswk* 31 (28 June 48) 69. Increased French taxes, Britain's cut-down on U.S. films, lower receipts.

"Johnson Socko." *Newswk* 32 (8 Nov 48) 73. MPAA president's world trip goes beyond the Iron Curtain.

Redmont, B. S. "New Issue in Brazil: Movie-Ticket Prices." *US News & World Report* 25 (26 Nov 48) 61. The troubles of U.S. movie distributors.

Jarrico, Paul. "They Are Not So Innocent Abroad." *New Rep* 120 (31 Jan 49) 17–19. The resistance in England, France, Italy to Hollywood film exporters.

Tavares de Sá, H. "Hollywood Needs Latin America." *Américas* 1 (Oct 49). *See 4h.*

"Hollywood's Exports Pay Off." *Bus Wk* (29 Apr 50) 113–114.

"Global Interest in Aid for Foreign Films." *CSMM* (23 Sep 50) 15. Discusses MPAA Unit of Foreign Films program of assistance.

"Help for Hollywood from Overseas." *Bus Wk* (14 Oct 50) 106–108. Korean and British impact on the industry.

Carroll, Ronald. "Which Films Should Go Abroad?" *FIR* 3 (Nov 52) 443–449. Classifying theatrical films into six divisions, ranging from musical to slapstick, he gives the order of preference for thirty-one foreign countries, Puerto Rico, and Hong Kong; condensed from *American Journal of Marketing.*

Loew, Arthur. "What They Like." *JSPG* (Nov 54) 13. Musicals and action dramas are the American films that do the best international business; survey with tabulations for MGM.

Pearse, B. "How the Movies Get Their Money out of Europe." *SEP* 227 (27 Nov 54) 43+.

"Deal with Japan." *Newswk* 46 (31 Oct 55) 90. America makes some film-distribution agreements with Japan.

"Yen for Hepburn." *Fortune* 52 (Dec 55) 78. Movie agreement concerning remittances between Tokyo and Hollywood.

"Agreement with Germany on Motion Picture Films." *US Dept of State Bul* 34 (14 May 56) 814–815. Changes in the German tariff concession affecting motion-picture films.

Daff, Al. "The Gravy Is Now Meat." *JSPG* (Dec 59) 34–36. The foreign market has become a major source of revenue.

Johnston, Eric. "Our Biggest Bargain in Foreign Policy." *JSPG* 6 (Dec 59). *See 6a(3).*

"Sexports." *Time* 76 (19 Sep 60) 61+. Reshooting scenes in U.S. films for foreign audiences.

MacCann, Richard Dyer. "Hollywood Faces the World." *Yale Rev* 51 (June 62) 593–608. The problems facing Hollywood in the foreign markets of the 1960s; trends in the international film industry.

Léglise, Paul. "Hidden Face of the Cinema: An Audience of 12,000,000,000." *UNESCO Courier* 16 (Feb 63) 26–31. On film exhibition around the world.

"Box Office Buzzes Overseas." *Bus Wk* (7 Nov 64) 64+. Report on Hollywood's overseas markets.

Thompson, Thomas. "Tuning U.S. Musicals to Overseas Box Office." *Life* 58 (12 Mar 65)

55+. How American musicals have fared abroad.

Fixx, J. F. "The Great Gallic Welcome; American Films and Film Makers Take Over Paris." *Sat Rev* 48 (25 Dec 65). See *4e(2c)*.

Guback, T. H. "American Interest in the British Film Industry." *Q Rev Econ and Bus* 7 (Summer 67) 7–21. Financially advantageous, it endangers cultural identity.

Berns, William A. "Where Film Buyers Meet Sellers." *Sat Rev* (23 Dec 67) 45. Film trade between U.S. and Socialist countries at the International Film Fair in Brno, Czechoslovakia. Part of *Saturday Review* report "Film-Making Behind the Iron Curtain."

Valenti, Jack. "The 'Foreign Service' of the Motion Picture Association of America." *JSPG* (Mar 68). See *6b(3)*.

Catalano, G. "*La Dolce Vita* Falls Prey to *Easy Rider*." *Atlas* 19 (June 70) 53–55. Reduction in Italian movies and cutbacks of American capital said to be due to impact on American market of youth-oriented American "new movie."

7e(2). FILMS AS CULTURAL AMBASSADORS

Ahern, Maurice L. "The World Gets an Earful." *Commonweal* 11 (22 Jan 30) 333–335. Surveys influence of talkies on American image abroad.

Eastman, Fred. "Ambassadors of Ill Will." *Chris Cent* 47 (29 Jan 30) 144–147. Part of series "The Menace of the Movies."

Seidenburg, Frederick. "Motion Pictures Abroad." *Commonweal* 12 (13 Aug 30) 381–383. They misrepresent American life.

Stewart, Maxwell S. "Deflating the Movies." *Chris Cent* 47 (13 Aug 30) 987–988. They present distorted image abroad.

Pickford, Mary. "Ambassadors." *SEP* 203 (23 Aug 30) 6–7. Actress describes recent overseas tour.

Williams, Chester S. "Wall Street and Hollywood Boulevard." *World Tomorrow* 13 (Dec 30) 501–503. Calls for action against "the whole world . . . being Americanized."

"Paris Raps Our Movie Methods." *Lit Dig* 109 (11 Apr 31) 17. Parisian critics accuse Hollywood of making vulgar films.

"Whistling Down the American Film in Germany." *Lit Dig* 113 (16 Apr 32) 20. German critics disillusioned by American talkies.

Valdes-Rodriguez, J. M. "Hollywood: Sales Agent of American Imperialism." *Experimental Cinema* 1 (No. 4, Feb 33) 18–20.

Brumbaugh, T. T. "American Films Breeding War: Pictures Shown in Japan." *Chris Cent* 50 (4 Oct 33) 1248. Tokyo correspondent sees U.S. war films such as *Men Must Fight* as representing a militaristic America to Japan.

Grierson, John. "Propaganda for Democracy." *Spectator* 161 (11 Nov 38) 799–800. Concern over impression of Great Britain to be presented at the New York World's Fair.

Wanger, Walter. "120,000 American Ambassadors." *Foreign Affairs* 18 (Oct 39) 45–59. The relation of the American motion picture to foreign markets.

Wright, Basil. "Films and the War." *Spectator* 163 (13 Oct 39) 498. Call for using film to present the British side of the war to "ordinary" men and women of other countries.

Sanderson, I. T. "Foreigners See Our Films." *Atlantic* 168 (Aug 41) 238–240. Assessment of effectiveness of American films in Africa and South America, based on interviews.

Goodman, Ezra. "Hollywood Belligerent." *Nation* 155 (12 Sep 42) 213–214. Hollywood begins to use film for international understanding and propaganda.

"Films About Americans for Other Peoples to See." *Asia* 42 (Nov 42) 658–659.

Cockerell, T. D. A. "Moving Pictures and International Good Will." *School and Society* 57 (6 Mar 43) 272–273. American films abroad sometimes confirm that we are a coarse and vulgar people.

Brogan, D. W. "Europe's Portrait of Uncle Sam." *NYTM* (21 Mar 43) 7+. Today it is built up by our movies.

Oppenheim, B. "Propaganda Puppets." *NYTM* (20 Feb 44) 43. Bill and Cora Baird create puppet movies for promoting U.S. agricultural methods in Latin America.

Anstey, Edgar. "Review of the Year." *Spectator* 173 (29 Dec 44) 598. Screen as important source for impressions of foreign peoples; war forced more favorable portrayal of allies.

Hansen, Harry L. "Hollywood and International Understanding." *Harvard Bus Rev* 25 (1945) 28–45.

Lowe, H. A. "Washington Discovers Hollywood." *Am Mercury* 60 (Apr 45) 407–414. Movies as ambassadors of goodwill abroad.

Kouwenhoven, John A. "Will We Lose Freedom of the Screen?" *Rdrs Dig* 47 (July 45) 59–61. Why American movies should be shown abroad and why the government should keep hands off.

Mayer, Arthur. "People to People." *Th Arts* 30 (June 46) 361–363.

Joseph, Robert, and Gladwin Hill. "Our Film Program in Germany." *Hwd Q* 2 (No. 2, Jan 47). See *4e(4c)*.

Bergman, Ingrid. "Films as Ambassadors." *Scholastic* 50 (14 Apr 47) 36. An actress discusses discrepancies between movies and real life.

"Movie Man's Burden." *New Rep* 117 (21 July 47) 37–38. Eric Johnston's "paradoxical" statements about Hollywood's mission in showing other countries our way of life.

Mayer, G. M. "American Motion Pictures in World Trade." *Annals of Am Acad of Polit and Soc Sci* 254 (Nov 47) 31–36. The extreme popularity American films enjoy abroad; the necessity and difficulty of giving a "balanced" view of American life; American films advertise American products abroad at no extra cost.

"Celluloid Ambassadors." *S&S* 17 (No. 65, Spring 48) 39–41. An account by an executive of Eagle-Lion Film Distributors, Ltd., of the present position of British films abroad.

Nathan, Paul S. "Books into Films." *Publishers Weekly* 154 (18 Sep 48) 1119. L.L.A. Vié, export manager of Dutch publishing house, answers the question: "What do Europeans really think of American movies?"

Garrett, Oliver H. P. "The Little Brown Men." *Screen Writer* 4 (Oct 48) 1–2. Offenses in U.S. pictures against Latin-American feelings.

Johnston, Eric. "Report from Europe." *Screen Writer* 4 (Oct 48) 4–6+. "America is like a great mosaic. . . . Our pictures tell the best and the worst about us." What happened in Warsaw when the audience got a Russian picture instead of *Random Harvest*.

Wanger, Walter F. "Donald Duck and Diplomacy." *Pub Opin Q* 14 (No. 3, 1950) 443–452. Hollywood popularizes American ideas and products.

Cousins, Norman. "The Free Ride." *SRL* 33 (21 Jan 50) 24–25; (28 Jan 50) 20–21; (4 Feb 50) 22; (11 Feb 50) 25. Analysis of bad effects of American films shown abroad. Responses to replies.

Johnston, Eric. "Messengers from a Free Country." *SRL* 33 (4 Mar 50) 9–13. A reply to Norman Cousins' editorial "The Free Ride," about American films abroad.

Seaton, George. "Reply to Norman Cousins." *SRL* 33 (25 Mar 50) 22+.

Johnston, Eric A., and Norman Cousins. "Do U.S. Films Abroad Speak for America?" *FIR* 1 (Mar 50) 8–10. Johnston maintains that these films speak for America, while Cousins claims that they defame American culture.

Goldwyn, Samuel. "Our Movies Speak for Us." *SRL* 33 (1 Apr 50) 10–12. Another reply to Norman Cousins' editorial; defense of American films abroad.

Cousins, Norman. "Our Films Speak for Hollywood." *SRL* 33 (1 Apr 50) 12–13+. Cousins' reply to Goldwyn, reaffirming his original editorial.

Canty, George R. "American Films Abroad." *FIR* 2 (May 51) 12–13+. Italian representative for Motion Picture Association says prestige of the American film throughout the world exceeds that of any other country.

"Hollywood's America: Real or Unreal?" *Scholastic* 61 (21 Jan 53) 7–8.

"U.S. Movie Ads in the Orient." *America* 93 (7 May 55). *See 6d(3)*.

Johnston, Eric. "Mirrors of Society." *Américas* 7 (July 55) 3–6. Motion Picture Association president examines movies' international role.

"After Hours: Big Splash." *Harper's* 211 (Sep 55) 87–88. In search of a movie that shows off America the way American movies show off other countries.

"The Image of the U.S." *Time* 66 (12 Sep 55) 26. The case of *Blackboard Jungle* at Venice Film Festival.

McIlvaine, Robinson. "Department Reply to Protest on *Blackboard Jungle* Incident." *US Dept of State Bul* 33 (3 Oct 55) 547. State Department denies there is any pre-censorship in favor of Ambassador Luce's objections.

De Mille, Cecil B. "A Man Is No Better Than What He Leaves Behind Him." *JSPG* 4 (No. 1, Feb 56). *See 7b(2a)*.

"How Others See Us on Film." *America* 95 (8 Sep 56) 516. Juvenile crime in Japan a result of violence in American movies?

Axelrod, Joseph. "German and Austrian Reaction to the *Blackboard Jungle*." *School and Society* 85 (Feb 57) 57–59.

"America in the Eyes of Foreign Teen-Agers." *Senior Scholastic* 70 (15 Feb 57) 5–6. Roundtable discussion; includes some talk about films.

Johnston, Eric. "Hollywood: America's Travelling Salesman." *Vital Speeches* 23 (1 July 57) 572–574. Hollywood's role abroad as seen by the president of the MPAA.

King, Henry. "Filmakers as Goodwill Ambassadors." *FIR* 9 (Oct 58) 425–427. American film makers on foreign locations can raise America's prestige by a little thoughtful help and friendliness.

Knopp, R. "How We Look to Latin Americans." *America* 100 (7 Mar 59) 662–664. Films are giving a false impression of America.

"Hollywood and the Face." *Times Lit Supplement* 3010 (6 Nov 59) xxi. Hollywood films are the visual Voice of America.

Johnston, Eric. "What *Is* the American Film Image Abroad?" *JSPG* (Mar 61) 3–6. MPA President says our motion pictures, more good than bad, "inescapably reflect our spirit of élan and compassion, our belief in the right of self-determination and individual liberty."

Cousins, Norman. "The Free Ride." *JSPG* (Mar 61) 7–8+. Excerpted from an editorial in *Saturday Review*: American film industry's image of America is a nation of gangsters, murderers, swindlers, and insensitively wealthy people.

Shelton, Turner B. "Impact of American Motion Pictures Overseas." *JSPG* (Mar 61) 9–12. Director of USIA's motion-picture service concludes that the overall effect of

American motion pictures on the U.S.'s image abroad is favorable.

Jones, Dorothy B. "Hollywood Faces Global Challenge." *JSPG* (Mar 61) 13–16+. The State Department could help by selecting some of Hollywood's best films and encouraging their distribution abroad.

Kennedy, Bishop Gerald. "Impressions of an Image." *JSPG* (Mar 61) 17–18+. American films give the U.S. an ugly image abroad; Hollywood should begin to "recognize the moral framework of all life."

Andrews, Robert Hardy. "Ourselves as Others See Us." *JSPG* (Mar 61) 19–20+. There are little things in U.S. films that "betray the carelessness of arrogance" to foreign nations.

Fitzgerald, John E. "Who's the Fairest? . . ." *JSPG* (Mar 61) 21–22+. Catholic columnist suggests foreign viewers can judge U.S. films for themselves.

Wolffers, Jules. "To Hold a Mirror . . ." *JSPG* (Mar 61) 23–24+. If we want films to represent the finest things in American life, we will have to support an organization whose object is to make fine films regardless of profit—a counterpart of the Bolshoi Ballet or the Stratford festival.

Dassin, Jules. "The European Image of the American Film." *JSPG* (Mar 61) 25–26+. Expatriate film maker discusses why certain American films fail in the European market—they are childish, Puritan, uncinematic, miscast, sentimental, overproduced, etc.

Ireton, Glenn F. "America's Film Image in the Far East." *JSPG* (Mar 61) 27–30. After ten years of living with the Japanese, writer discusses Japanese reactions to American films and argues for films genuinely representative of American character and problems.

Zanuck, Darryl F. "Hollywood vs. Communism." *F&F* 7 (No. 9, June 61) 10. Zanuck responds to March 1961 issue on Soviet film making by noting the value of films containing controversy as ambassadors for the U.S.

Fadiman, William. "Murrow Projects Tomorrow's Image." *F&F* 7 (No. 10, July 61) 30. Criticism of Edward R. Murrow, head of United States Information Agency, and his attempts to influence Hollywood film makers.

Luft, Herbert G. "Is Hollywood a Mirror of America?" *JSPG* (Sep 61) 31–33. No, American films tend to stress negative, violent images.

Gans, H. J. "Hollywood Films on British Screens: An Analysis of the Function of American Popular Culture Abroad." *Social Problems* 9 (1962) 324–328.

Tubby, Roger W. "Industry Communications Programs in Support of U.S. Foreign Policy." *US Dept of State Bul* 46 (5 Feb 62) 213–215.

How the film industry supports U.S. objectives.

Bernays, Edward L. "By Your Films Shall They Know You." *JSPG* (Mar 62) 23–24+. Export of American films injures U.S. prestige by predominant sex and sadism; eventually there will be government restraints.

"American Movies Abroad: A Hit or Miss in Diplomacy?" *Senior Scholastic* 81 (12 Sep 62) 12–13. Both sides of the question: Are European moviegoers being given a distorted view of America?

Gervasi, Frank. "Hollywood Exports: The Good Side of American Movies." *Show* 2 (Oct 62) 51+. Defense of Hollywood's image making overseas; the gospel of the good things of the American way of life.

Zanuck, Darryl F. "How to Be Self-Critical While World Popular." *Show* 4 (Apr 64) 77–78. Discussion of the Hollywood film on the international scene, reactions of foreign audiences, the image of America in Hollywood films, the industry and self-censorship, and comparative freedom from restraint in the U.S. industry.

Halliwell, Leslie. "America, the Celluloid Myth." *F&F* 14 (No. 1, Oct 67) 12–16; (No. 2, Nov 67) 10–14. Reality of America versus the view presented by films; two articles.

7e(3). INTERNATIONAL CENSORSHIP

[See also 7c(1).]

Whang, Paul K. "Boycotting of Harold Lloyd's *Welcome Danger*." *China Weekly Rev* 52 (8 Mar 30) 51. Protest against this film's misrepresentation of the Chinese people.

"Foreign vs. the Chinese Movie Censorship." *China Weekly Rev* 52 (5 Apr 30) 200–201. Shanghai International Settlement's reasons for censoring Lloyd's *Welcome Danger* and the Fox Movietone newsreel *The Ten Commandments*.

"American Films Too Filthy for Turkey." *Lit Dig* 108 (10 Jan 31) 21. Reviews speech by the Reverend Clifford Twombley on movie immorality.

"Hollywood's Contribution to International Good Will." *Chris Cent* 48 (11 Mar 31) 333–334. French soldiers seize "immoral" U.S. film in Peiping, China, theatre.

"China Sets an Example in Motion Picture Control." *Chris Cent* 48 (9 Sep 31) 1109. Chinese refuse American films without approval of national film-censorship board.

"Shanghai Becomes Graveyard for Better Feature Films." *China Weekly Rev* 66 (8 July 33) 214–215. Pressure groups cause Shanghai police to ban certain films, including MGM's *Rasputin and the Empress*.

"French Fans." *Commonweal* 18 (4 Aug 33)

337. On French restriction of American films.

"Bergner Banned." *Time* 23 (19 Mar 34) 21. Reich Film Chamber bans *Catherine the Great* after street riot because of Jewish actress Elisabeth Bergner.

"Rabid Film Censorship Opposed by Americans in Shanghai." *China Weekly Rev* 70 (17 Nov 34) 383–384.

"Celluloid Censorship." *Time* 27 (1 June 36) 40–42. President of Board of Film Censors in Great Britain censors political items in *March of Time*.

"Franco in Hollywood." *Nation* 155 (19 Dec 42) 668. International controversy over adaptation of *For Whom the Bell Tolls* for the screen.

"Local Censors in Shanghai Ban O'Neill's *Long Voyage Home*." *China Weekly Rev* 97 (2 Aug 44) 264.

"Twin Bed Trouble." *Life* 22 (19 May 47) 142–144. What happens when England censors a U.S. film.

"*Oliver Twist* in Berlin: Jewish D. P.'s as Critics of Dickens." *Illus London News* 214 (5 Mar 49) 297. Jewish demonstration against screening of *Oliver Twist* in British sector of Berlin.

"Hollywood's Wrong Whatever It Does." *Collier's* 123 (25 June 49) 78. On British censorship of *The Snake Pit*.

Volmar, Victor. "The Babel of Tongues." *FIR* 2 (Mar 51). *See 2g(3)*.

Mirams, Gordon. "Drop That Gun!" *QFRTV* 6 (No. 1, Fall 51) 1–19. New Zealand censor studies 100 features (seventy of them American), January–April 1950, with a statistical analysis of the types and intensity of violence, sex, and sadism.

Brill, H. "Will We Gag Italian Films?" *Nation* 175 (16 Aug 52) 132–133. Increased distribution of Italian films in the U.S. might lead Italian producers to impose indirect censorship.

"Quebec Censor Bans Luther Film." *Chris Cent* 71 (20 Jan 54) 69.

Geis, Gilbert. "Film Censorship in Norway." *QFRTV* 8 (No. 3, Spring 54) 290–301. Brief history of film making in Norway; how censorship laws evolved; kinds of content censored in both Norwegian and American films; tables of footage cut from films of various countries.

McCarthy, Frank. "What the Censors Don't Like." *JSPG* (Nov 54) 15–16. Director of public relations for 20th Century-Fox discusses foreign censorship of American films.

Halliwell, Leslie. "*The Wild One* at Cambridge." *S&S* 25 (Summer 55) 5. Note on wild response to Stanley Kramer picture about motorcycle gang banned by British Board of Film Censors but given an X by Cambridge justices.

"Plagued If We Do, Plagued If We Don't." *Chris Cent* 72 (5 Oct 55) 1133. International storm over *Blackboard Jungle* and *House of Bamboo* in Japan.

"A Little History of Banned Films." *S&S* 25 (Spring 56) 206–209. Chronological list by year and country of films forbidden.

"U.S. Movie in India." *Newswk* 47 (25 June 56) 96–97. India's severe censorship.

von Kuehnelt-Leddihn, E. "Rating Films in Europe." *America* 97 (28 Sep 57) 670–672. How Catholic organizations classify films; emphasis on Germany.

Gillett, John. "Cut and Come Again." *S&S* 27 (Summer 58). *See 2f*.

"The Lady's No Tramp." *Newswk* 54 (13 July 59) 88. Court case of French film version of *Lady Chatterley's Lover*.

"World-Wide Censorship Practices." *JSPG* (Sep 61) 20. Brief note reports Motion Picture Association survey: of sixty-three countries outside the U.S., sixty have government censorship of films and forty-three have a classification system.

"Luther Goes to Quebec." *Chris Cent* 79 (15 Aug 62) 977. The film *Martin Luther* meets obstacles abroad.

Léglise, Paul. "Censorship: A Double-Edged Weapon." *UNESCO Courier* 16 (Apr 63) 28–32. Censorship and the growing importance of films for young people.

Hunnings, Neville. "The Silence of *Fanny Hill*." *S&S* 35 (Summer 66) 134–138. Changes in attitudes on censorship; possible future developments in Great Britain; reports on U.S., Quebec, Denmark, New Zealand. See letters 36 (Winter 66–67) 52, suggesting New Zealand censorship practices are quite restrictive.

"Pasolini's *Teorema*." *America* 120 (3 May 69). *See 9, Teorema*.

7e(4). U.S.-SOVIET RELATIONS

"Russia in American Films." *Living Age* 343 (Sep 32). *See 3b(4)*.

"Soviet Government Requested to Cease Showing Unauthorized American Motion Picture Films." *US Dept of State Bul* 24 (5 Feb 51) 229. A request to return all prints of *Mr. Smith Goes to Washington* and *Mr. Deeds Goes to Town* to the American Embassy.

"Russia Scolds Tarzan." *Scholastic* 63 (13 Jan 54) 19. Newspaper *Pravda*'s view of "trashy American movies."

"Russia Takes an American Partner in Its Venture into Wide Screen." *Bus Wk* (12 May 56) 158. Announcement that Mike Todd and the Russians will coproduce five movies.

"U.S.-Soviet Negotiations for Exchange of Films." *US Dept of State Bul* 38 (7 Apr 58) 552. Report on the agreement reached.

"U.S.-Soviet Discussions on Exchange of Films." *US Dept of State Bul* 38 (19 May 58) 830. Further details of agreement between the U.S. and the USSR for the exchange of films.

"U.S.-U.S.S.R. Film Exchanges." *US Dept of State Bul* 39 (18 Aug 58) 289–290. Further developments in an exchange program.

"U.S. and U.S.S.R. Agree on Films to Be Exchanged; Department Announcement and Memorandum of Agreement." *US Dept of State Bul* 39 (3 Nov 58) 696–698.

"No Axes to Grind." *Newswk* 53 (26 Jan 59) 100. List of seven Russian films of a movie-swap plan between U.S. and USSR.

"U.S.S.R. Selects Final Four Films Under Exchange Agreement." *US Dept of State Bul* 40 (6 Apr 59) 483. A list of the ten films selected for exhibition in the USSR.

"Movies Downgrade the U.S. Again." *Chris Cent* 76 (7 Oct 59) 1140. Protest against showing *Can-Can* production number to Khrushchev while he was in Hollywood.

Clark, Roy. "Krushchev in Hollywood." *Dance Mag* 33 (Nov 59) 24–25+. A behind-the-scenes report.

Stanbrook, Alan. "The Legacy of the Thaw." *F&F* 6 (No. 2, Nov 59) 8+. Five years of Soviet film in the West (1954–1959).

"U.S. and U.S.S.R. Show First Films Under Exchange Agreement." *US Dept of State Bul* 41 (9 Nov 59) 671. Report on the premieres of the exchange films.

"First Flickers." *Newswk* 54 (23 Nov 59) 46. U.S.-Soviet exchange of movies.

Lyons, Warren. "A Cinemaddict in Moscow." *FIR* 11 (No. 4, Apr 60) 208–209+. Describes mutilation and bad showings U.S. films get in Russia, and the resulting bad impressions given about this country.

"U.S. and U.S.S.R. Review Motion Picture Exchanges." *US Dept of State Bul* 45 (6 Nov 61) 770–771. Report of the meeting and names of people attending.

Turner, Joseph. "Say, Comrade." *Science* 136 (15 June 62) 951. Editorial about an upcoming Russo-American coproduction from a novel called *Meeting at a Far Meridian*.

"The Russians . . . *Nyet*, Yet." *Action* 1 (No. 1, Sep–Oct 66) 16–17. Background information on an attempted relationship with the Russians for the filming of Norman Jewison's *The Russians Are Coming*.

Valenti, Jack. "The Motion Picture Bridge Between East and West." *Sat Rev* 50 (23 Dec 67) 8–9+. Part of *Saturday Review* report "Film-Making Behind the Iron Curtain."

7e(5). EXCHANGE OF PERSONNEL

Collins, F. L. "Will Hollywood Move to England?" *Rdrs Dig* 28 (Jan 36) 95–96. Actors are going back; condensed from *Liberty*.

Daugherty, F. "Hollywood's Foreign Colony." *CSMM* (3 June 36) 4–5.

Weinberg, Herman G. "Old Wine in a New Bottle." *S&S* 8 (No. 29, Spring 39) 21–22. Only three foreign directors have ever done well in Hollywood: Victor Seastrom, Ernst Lubitsch, and Fritz Lang.

Weinberg, Herman G. "Glory's End." *S&S* 8 (No. 31, Autumn 39) 97–98. Notes on the German film makers who took refuge in Hollywood and a postscript on censorship.

Arliss, George. "Londoner Looks at Hollywood." *Current His* 51 (Mar 40). See 7d.

Selfridge, J. "Hollywood Crown Colony: British Actors Organize Benefits for Britain." *Scribner's* 9 (Jan 41) 45–49.

"Latin Ladies: Hollywood Invaded by Talent from South of the Rio Grande." *Life* 10 (3 Feb 41) 50–52.

Dieterle, William. "Europeans in Hollywood." *S&S* 22 (July–Sep 52) 39–40. A director who left Europe for Hollywood gives the Hollywood side and how to make the most of the opportunities.

Houston, Penelope. "The Ambassadors: Americans in Europe." *S&S* 23 (Apr–June). See 2c.

"By Any Other Name." *Harper's* 210 (Mar 55) 80–81. Hollywood's tendency to abandon names connoting national origin: a list included of stars, with their real names.

Fadiman, William. "A Word to the Tax-Wise." *JSPG* (Sep 60) 11–12. Loose talk about how many Hollywood stars living abroad avoid paying income tax creates bad image of the industry.

Fadiman, William. "Taxiles." *F&F* 9 (No. 1, Oct 62) 56–57. Temporary "exiles" created by tax laws; advantages of foreign residence for Hollywood moneymakers.

"Some of the Worms Are Turning." *Time* 81 (11 Jan 63) 59. U.S. stars migrate to Europe.

Bocca, Geoffrey. "They Kept the Old Flag Flying." *Horizon* 5 (Sep 63) 74–81. The British colony in Hollywood.

Dewey, Lang. "Parthenogenesis Swedish Style." *Film* (No. 45, Spring 66) 11–15. Swedish cinema people working in other countries.

Braun, Eric. "A Code of Behaviour." *F&F* 16 (No. 7, Apr 70) 24–30. British actresses in Hollywood, especially Deborah Kerr. See also May and June issues.

Braun, Eric. "With Deep Sincerity." *F&F* 16 (No. 9, June 70) 108–112. Conclusion of series of articles on British actresses in Hollywood, especially Deborah Kerr; see also April and May.

7f. Films by Public Agencies

[*See also 4i, 3a(6), 6a(3).*]

"Annual Report, 1935–1936." *School and Society* 44 (21 Nov 36) 671. Summary of the annual report of the New York State Motion Pictures Division. See also 46 (13 Nov 37) 619.

"Films Aid in State and Local Traffic Control." *Am City* 54 (Oct 39) 64. Their use by police in California.

"Motion Pictures to Aid Law Enforcement." *Am City* 55 (Mar 40) 105. Emphasis on *Know Your Money,* typical of such current films.

Wright, Basil. "Five-Minute Films." *Spectator* 165 (16 Aug 40) 167. Shorts designed to point up the moral aspect of Great Britain's war activities.

Wright, Basil. "Disappointing Report." *Spectator* 165 (13 Sep 40) 267. Why the Films Division's first productions were unsuccessful.

Hobson, Harold. "Swords out of Celluloid." *CSMM* (20 June 42) 5. The value of Great Britain's Army Kinematograph Department in supporting morale and disseminating information.

Anstey, Edgar. "Ministry of Information Films." *Spectator* 169 (18 Dec 42) 575. Weekly distribution of five-minute propaganda films to be discontinued in favor of fewer but longer films.

Myers, Kurtz. "Foreign Film Omnibus." *Lib J* 73 (1 Oct 48) 1398–1401. A compilation of documentary films from foreign government sources; emphasis on the British and Canadian contributions.

Schulberg, Stuart. "For the Record: *Of All People.*" *Hwd Q* 4 (No. 2, Winter 49) 206–208. Responding to article by Egon Larsen on German film industry 3 (No. 4, Summer 48–Summer 49) 387–394. Head of documentary film unit for occupation government lists titles produced.

Gibbs, R. "Seattle Police Take a Tip from Hollywood." *Pop Mech* 112 (July 59) 130–132+. Police programs use film.

Vas, Robert. *"Power Among Men."* *S&S* 28 (Nos. 3–4, Summer–Autumn 59) 175. Review of the UN documentary feature and the problem of generalities in such films.

"Very Educational." *Nation* 196 (20 Apr 63) 319. Bonn government propaganda film.

Richter, Robert. "Freedom, Film, and Politics." *JUFPA* 16 (No. 2, 1964) 10–11+. A film maker who made films for a state government discusses the limitations of these films resulting from the state's censorship and public-relations approach to the subject matter; he concludes that if a state wants truth-ful films and good film makers, it should set up an independent unit, with a yearly budget that it can spend as it chooses.

Oettinger, Elmer. "The North Carolina Film Board: A Unique Program in Documentary and Educational Film Making." *J Soc Cin* 5 (1965) 55–65. The films and the political and administrative problems of the short-lived state production center directed by James Beveridge, supported by the Richardson Foundation and initiated by Governor Terry Sanford in 1962.

Gessner, Peter. "Films From the Vietcong." *Nation* 202 (24 Jan 66) 110–111. Reactions after seeing a half dozen films produced by the National Liberation Front.

Friedlander, Madeline S. "Challenge for Change: An American View." *F Lib Q* 2 (No. 4, Fall 69) 48–52. Parallels in the U.S. to Canada's Challenge for Change film program.

7f(1). U.S. GOVERNMENT FILMS

"Federal Movie Furor." *Bus Wk* (11 July 36) 14. Distributors refused *The Plow That Broke the Plains* as government competition but it is booked in 2,000 theatres.

"Educational Newsreels for WPA." *Lit Dig* 122 (8 Aug 36). See 8b.

"WPA: Pathé Wins Film Contract as New Deal Goes Hollywood." *Newswk* 8 (15 Aug 36) 18. The film "Information about the operations of WPA" to be made for state offices and one a month included in national theatrical newsreel.

"Real Life Drama Produced by Agriculture Department." *Sci Newsletter* (Mar 37) 196–197. Life history of the egg for the first time on film.

Hearon, Fanning. "Interior's Division of Motion Pictures." *School Life* (Sep 37) 6–7.

"Federal Film Hit." *Bus Wk* (19 Feb 38) 35–36. The wide showing accorded FSA's *The River* has implications for industrial movies.

Evans, Ernestine. "Much Could Be Done." *Virginia Q Rev* 14 (Oct 38) 491–501. A defense of U.S. government film units and of John Grierson and Pare Lorentz.

Hearon, Fanning. "The Motion Picture Program and Policy of the U.S. Government." *J Educ Soc* 12 (No. 3, Nov 38) 147–162.

Mercey, Arch. "Films by American Governments: The United States." *Films* 1 (No. 3, Summer 40) 5–20. Brief summary of work of Pare Lorentz and the U.S. Film Service by its assistant director; extracts from committee hearings and the *Congressional Rec-*

ord at the time of the termination of the USFS.

"Power and the Land: Stills from Film Made for Rural Electrification Administration by J. Ivens." *Mag of Art* 34 (Jan 41) 43.

Anderson, H. "Clearing House for War Films." *School Rev* 50 (Nov 42) 619.

Evans, Raymond. "USDA Motion Picture Service 1908–1943." *Bus Screen* 5 (No. 1, 1943). Early development of government films in Department of Agriculture.

"Distribution of War Films." *School and Society* 57 (30 Jan 43) 123. The National University Extension Association's plan to distribute government films through nonprofit film-lending libraries.

"As to the Disposition of the Government's Educational Films." *School and Society* 61 (23 June 45) 407. Resolution adopted at the thirtieth annual meeting of the National University Extension Association to preserve wartime, educational, and documentary films.

"Preservation of War Films: Resolution Adopted by the National University Extension Association." *School Rev* 53 (Dec 45). *See 4a(4b).*

"Visual Aids to Education: Government Films on Health and Agriculture Released." *School Life* 30 (June 48) 10–11.

Reid, S. "U.S. Government Film News." *School Life* 31 (May 49) 14.

Anderson, Robert, and Irving Jacoby. "Scenario for Psychiatry." *SRL* 32 (15 Oct 49) 32–33. Story on the new production program of the Mental Health Film Board.

Reid, S. "How to Obtain U.S. Government Motion Pictures." *School Life* 32 (May 50) 120–121.

Busch, Glen. "The Film Forum: Marshall Plan at Work." *Sat Rev* (17 Feb 51) 42. Films made in Europe about effects of U.S. aid.

Starr, Cecile. "Uncle Sam: Film Maker." *Sat Rev* 35 (12 July 52) 30+. Recent efforts at a system of unified distribution and information about government films.

"Mr. Brownwell's Headache." *Collier's* 131. (25 Apr 53) 78. Editorial on films made by the government which cannot be sold to TV.

Starr, Cecile. "Psychiatry Without Jargon." *Sat Rev* 37 (10 July 54) 32+. The history and work of the Mental Health Film Board compared to government units such as the wartime Office of War Information.

Greenberg, Stanley S. "Operation Persuasion." *JUFPA* 16 (No. 2, 1964). *See 7b(5).*

"Juiced for You." *New Rep* 155 (10 Sep 66) 7. Foreign film program of U.S. Department of Agriculture.

Morgenstern, Joseph. "50,000 Films for Sale." *Newswk* 69 (6 Mar 67) 90. The U.S. government sells films to the public.

7f(1a). Military

Miller, J. "Army's Animated Cartoons Make Better Soldiers." *Pop Sci* 126 (June 35). *See 2h.*

Grahame, A. "Army Movies Help Train Our Soldiers for War." *Pop Sci* 135 (Dec 39) 122–125.

"Movies Join the Army." *Pop Mech* 72 (Dec 39) 888–889+. The efforts of the Signal Corps in making army training films.

Thone, F. "Movies for Soldiers." *Sci Newsletter* 37 (3 Feb 40) 74–76. Training films.

"Army Makes Films at Its Own Hollywood." *Newswk* 18 (13 Oct 41) 56. Production of training films.

Crowther, Bosley. "Picture of the Year: The Making of a Soldier." *NYTM* (25 Oct 42) 18–19+. Production of army training films.

Furman, R. T. "They Fight with Films: Signal Corps Camera Crew." *Rdrs Dig* 42 (Feb 43) 132–134. Signal Corps cameras record the war.

"Enter Private Snafu." *NYTM* (25 July 43) 14–15. Sketches of newest army cartoon subject.

"Films Teach Soldiers Lessons of War." *Life* (26 July 43) 47–48+.

Manning, C. "Fighters with Film." *Am Photog* 37 (Aug 43) 20–21. Army Air Force's first motion-picture unit shows enemy's tactics and helps save U.S. lives.

Whittaker, L. I. "Army's Little Hollywood— Army's Movie Studio at Astoria." *Pop Mech* (Oct 43) 56–59.

Agee, J. "Army's Screen Magazine." *Nation* 158 (4 Mar 44) 288. Army newsreels—the problems of art under authoritarian auspices.

Nugent, F. "Film Men of the Air Force." *NYTM* (30 Apr 44) 14. Its first motion-picture unit in Hollywood.

Isaacs, H. R. "War Fronts and Film Fronts." *Th Arts* 28 (June 44) 343–349. The best Hollywood talent has been drawn off by the war, but some good documentaries have been made.

Cohen, Emanuel. "Film Is a Weapon." *Bus Screen* 7 (No. 1, 1945). Report on armed services' cameramen and films made for military uses.

O'Connor, R. "AAF Film Unit." *Flying* 36 (Apr 45) 54–55.

Goldner, Orville. "The Story of Navy Training Films." *Bus Screen* 8 (No. 5, June 45).

Medford, Harold. "Report from a GI Typewriter." *Screen Writer* 1 (June 45) 15–21. Writer for *Resisting Enemy Interrogation* reports on government documentaries by Capra, Huston, Kanin, and others.

Koenig, Lester. "Back from the Wars." *Screen Writer* 1 (Aug 45) 23–29. Screenwriter for *Memphis Belle*, William Wyler's Army Air Force film, writes about the feature documentaries made by Hollywood people in uniform.

Greenberg, Alex, and Malvin Wald. "Report to the Stockholders." *Hwd Q* 1 (No. 4, July 46) 410–415. Statistical summary of production by Army Air Force First Motion Picture Unit; 228 films, including an animation series with "Trigger Joe," who insisted on learning by trial and error.

Hubley, John, and Zachary Schwartz. "Animation Learns a New Language." *Hwd Q* 1 (No. 4, July 46). *See 2h(1).*

Roosevelt, James. "From 'Do It Now' to 'Well Done.'" *Screen Writer* 2 (July 46) 26–31. On the making of amphibious training films by the U.S. Navy.

Calhoun, John B. "Rats in Relationship to Man's Welfare." *Science* 114 (24 Aug 51) 214. U.S. Signal Corps biology films.

Gallez, Douglas W. "Patterns in Wartime Documentaries." *QFRTV* 10 (No. 2, Winter 55) 125–135. Themes of wartime films by De Rochemont, Ford, Wyler, Huston, and Capra.

Krasney, Phillip. "The Responsibility of the University to the Photographic Profession." *JUFPA* 16 (No. 4, 1964) 10–13+. Chief of the Air Photographic and Charting Service discusses what his service does and its need for trained photographers; he feels universities should place more emphasis on technical facility and less on aesthetics.

Commager, H. S. "On the Way to 1984: Analysis of Film *Why Vietnam,* and Arguments Against Carrying War Propaganda into the Classroom." *Sat Rev* 50 (15 Apr 67) 68–69+. About Defense Department film of this title. Discussion 50 (20 May 67) 72.

"U.S. Government Films on the Vietnamese War." *F Com* 5 (No. 2, Spring 69) 81–84. Annotated list, including staff film reports on individual units.

7f(1b). USIA and OWI

"Facts by OWI." *Newswk* 20 (2 Nov 42) 79. Office of War Information documentaries exemplify the screen's potentialities in educating and informing a nation.

Wanger, Walter. "OWI and Motion Pictures." *Pub Opin Q* 7 (Spring 43) 100–110. Criticism of the policies, personnel, and methods of the Motion Picture Bureau of U.S. Office of War Information by Hollywood producer, then president of Academy of Motion Picture Arts and Sciences.

Dunne, Philip. "The Documentary and Hollywood." *Hwd Q* 1 (No. 2, Jan 46) 166–172. How documentaries have been written and made for the overseas branch of the U.S. Office of War Information.

Larson, Cedric. "The Domestic Motion Picture Work of the Office of War Information."

Hwd Q 3 (No. 4, Summer 48–Summer 49). History, funds, duties, films, up to 1943; unhappy relations with Hollywood.

Katz, Robert. "Projecting America Through Films." *Hwd Q* 4 (No. 3, Spring 50) 298–308. International Motion Picture division of State Department, 1946–1949, attempts to continue documentary work of wartime OWI, counteracting Hollywood's "kiss-kiss-bang-bang" impression of America.

Pearson, Wilbert H. "The 1956 Kenneth M. Edwards Memorial Lecture." *JUFPA* 9 (No. 1, Fall 56) 4–9. A government official reports on U.S. Information Agency overseas film activities.

Hitchens, Gordon. "An Interview with George Stevens, Jr." *F Com* 1 (No. 3, 1962) 2–7. Broadcast interview covers U.S. Information Agency production program; Stevens expresses the hope that his film makers can be encouraged to express their talents.

Drukker, Leendert. "USIS Makes a Movie." *Pop Photog* 51 (Oct 62) 95+. Mrs. Kennedy's visits filmed as *Invitation to India* and *Invitation to Pakistan.*

Reynolds, C. "USIA Offers New Jobs for Apprentice Film-Makers." *Pop Photog* 51 (Dec 62) 111+. George Stevens, Jr., describes "intern" program.

Fiering, Alvin. "Reflections on Making *Sculptor.*" *F Com* 1 (No. 6, Fall 63) 48–50. Young director reports production of film for USIA.

Alpert, Hollis. "Movies that Carry the Freight." *Sat Rev* 47 (12 Dec 64) 69–70+. Motion pictures of the United States Information Agency.

"History and All that Jazz." *F Com* 3 (No. 2, Spring 65) 64–66. Background and quotations from news stories and editorials on the "fake" footage shot for U.S. Information Agency Vietnam documentary.

"American Films and Foreign Audiences." *F Com* 3 (No. 3, Summer 65) 50. Summary of U.S. Information Agency survey of Japanese reactions to American feature films, which are "favorable."

"Films from Uncle Sam." *Newswk* 67 (18 Apr 66) 109–110+. USIA films, including *John F. Kennedy: Years of Lightning, Day of Drums.*

Loeb, Anthony. "A Renaissance in Government Film-Making at USIA." *Action* 2 (No. 5, Sep–Oct 67) 16–19.

"*Years of Lightning, Day of Drums.*" *F Com* 4 (Nos. 1–2, Fall–Winter 67) 22–46. Transcript of sound track of U.S. Information Agency film on John F. Kennedy; background for release of film in U.S. by special resolution of Congress; biographies of Roger Stevens, Joseph Levine, Bruce Herschensohn, and George Stevens, Jr.; comment by

Martin Dworkin at seminar sponsored by American Council on Education.

"Use and Abuse of Stock Footage." *F Com* 4 (Nos. 1–2, Fall–Winter 67) 47–53. Material from film about privately sponsored group, *Crossroaders in Africa* (directed by Gordon Hitchens for USIA), was wrongly used to represent Peace Corps work in Kennedy film *Years of Lightning, Day of Drums.*

"Films in Vietnam." *F Com* 5 (No. 2, Spring 69) 46–80. Former film officer of U.S. Information Agency in South Vietnam anonymously tape-records his recollections of his own and others' films (North and South Vietnamese, network news work, USIA's *Night of the Dragon*) and gives an extended description of *The Leaflet,* with still photographs. See also followup letter by William Bayer and reply by editor 6 (No. 2, Summer 70) 56–58.

MacCann, Richard Dyer. "Film and Foreign Policy: The USIA, 1962–67." *CJ* 9 (No. 1, Fall 69) 23–42. The propaganda framework for a documentary revival which used the services of a number of new young film makers; the contract problem; the films, including *The March* and *The School at Rincon Santo.*

"USIA's Quickie." *Nation* 209 (8 Dec 69) 620–621. Editorial on recent USIA film *The Silent Majority.*

7f(2). FILMS BY POLITICAL PARTIES

Pringle, H. F. "Movies Swing an Election: Sinclair or Merriam?" *Rdrs Dig* 29 (Aug 36). See 8b.

"Republicans Make First Campaign Movie of 1940: *New Tomorrow.*" *Life* 8 (29 Aug 40) 36–37.

Perentesis, John L. "Effectiveness of a Motion Picture Trailer as Election Propaganda." *Pub Opin Q* 12 (No. 3, 1948) 465–469. In Detroit one candidate benefited.

"Morality Issue." *Newswk* 64 (2 Nov 64) 25–26. Republican campaign film called *Choice.*

"That Sinful Movie." *Reporter* 31 (5 Nov 64) 15. Troubles of Republican film on moral decay called *Choice.*

7f(3). UNIVERSITY FILMS

[See also 1a(3b).]

Falk, S. "Strength of a City: A University-Made Documentary Film for the Syracuse Community Chest." *Th Arts* 24 (July 40) 504–505+.

"First Annual Edwards Awards Presented." *Am Photog* 46 (Oct 52) 13. University Film Producers Association picks outstanding university-produced films.

Henry, Dr. David Dodds. "The 1954 Kenneth M. Edwards Memorial Lecture." *JUFPA* 7 (No. 1, Fall 54) 4–10. NYU vice-chancellor, since chosen president of University of Illinois, speaks to University Film Producers conference on the need for the university-produced film to have a "unique nature, a unique substance, an unusual excellence for educational use."

Starr, Cecile. "Campus Cinematics." *Sat Rev* 38 (13 Aug 55) 26. Film-making units on university and college campuses.

Wagner, Robert. "Film in American Education." *JUFPA* 8 (No. 4, Summer 56) 7–11. A report to Paris film students and teachers about the making and use of films in universities.

MacCann, Richard Dyer. "The Critic Looks at the Information Film." *JUFPA* 9 (No. 2, Winter 57) 4–7. *Christian Science Monitor* Hollywood correspondent encourages university film makers to give their viewers an experience, not just more information.

Bryan, Julien. "The 1958 Kenneth Edwards Memorial Address." *JUFPA* 11 (No. 1, Fall 58) 4–7. Reminiscing about his own career, this documentary and educational film maker urges university film producers to have "dreams that will really affect mankind."

Rose, Ernest D. "Screen Writing and the Delicate Art of Persuasion." *JUFPA* 14 (No. 2, 1962). *See 2d.*

Snyder, Luella. "Are Technical Advisors People?" *JUFPA* 14 (No. 2, 1962). *See 2d.*

Thoresby, Henry. "University Film-Making." *Motion* (No. 3, Spring 62) 41+. Problems and difficulties of university film units.

Lorentz, Pare. "The University, the Film, and the Community." *JUFPA* 15 (No. 2, 1963) 4–7+. Too many films are being turned out for the sake of turning out films; too many students are taught the technique of film making without the comprehension of their purpose; mechanical aptitude is not enough.

Smith, Myron P. "Competitive Comparison Pays Off." *JUFPA* 16 (No. 1, 1964) 12–14. Suggests that university film makers would benefit by occasional ventures into commercial film making, where competition provides impetus to produce more and compare results with other film makers.

Keehn, Neal. "Where Does the University Film Serve?" *JUFPA* 17 (No. 3, 1965) 18–21. According to this commercial-film professional, the university film should stick to educational films for campus use.

Elton, Sir Arthur. "Film Considered as Language." *JUFPA* 18 (No. 1, 1966) 3–6+. Some general observations about the importance of film for the sciences and the universities.

MacCann, Richard Dyer. "The NASA Project." *JUFPA* 18 (No. 4, 1966) 3–4. Coordinated activities of the UFPA, the University Film Foundation, and NASA in producing ten films at ten different universities, about scientific research.

McLean, Grant. "Film in Government and in the University—A Comparative View." *JUFPA* 18 (No. 4, 1966) 5–7+. Production manager of Canada's National Film Board points out parallels between the university-made film and the government-made film.

Ver Ploeg, Don. "The Next Ten Years." *JUFPA* 18 (No. 4, 1966) 9–10. Summary of statements of a panel of university film teachers on how university-made films have improved and what further improvements are needed.

Smith, Hubert. "The University Film Director and *Cinéma Vérité*." *JUFPA* 19 (No. 2, 1967) 58–62. If university directors more often involved themselves emotionally with their subjects, they would use *cinéma vérité* more than they do.

Glimcher, Sumner J. "Film as University Press." *JUFA* 22 (No. 1, 1970) 3–7. Productions and administration of the Center for Mass Communication of Columbia University Press.

Williams, Don G. "Universities in Overseas Production." *JUFA* 22 (No. 4, 1970). *See 4f.*

8. Nonfiction Films

8a. General

Chadwick, Mary. "Commission on Educational and Cultural Films." *Close Up* 8 (No. 1, Mar 31) 55–60. The report of the commission.

Grierson, John. "The Artist and the Teacher." *S&S* 1 (No. 2, Summer 32) 45–46. The film which actually teaches is different from one which serves as a background for teaching.

Herring, Robert. "The Experiment of Chesterfield." *Close Up* 9 (No. 3, Sep 32) 161–162. Comments on a film entitled *New Generation,* made by the town of Chesterfield about its schools.

Hutchins, Robert M. "New Tool." *Am Scholar* 2 (Mar 33) 241–243. University of Chicago plans basic films for survey courses in physical and biological sciences, social science, and the humanities.

"All-America Film Survey at Philadelphia." *Museum News* 19 (15 Dec 41) 2. Report on a film program entitled "Rediscovering America" at the Philadelphia Museum of Art.

"Films to Bring to Your Community." *Parents Mag* 17 (Apr 42) 116. Brief descriptions of religious and social films.

Goodman, Ezra. "Non-Theatrical in America." *S&S* 11 (No. 41, Summer 42) 21–23. An overview: creation, distribution, and exhibition.

Hartung, Philip T. "Short Now Raised to a Position of Some Respect." *Commonweal* 37 (20 Nov 42) 121–123. Documentary and instructional films from OWI, Grierson, *March of Time,* on various phases of the war.

"Schoolmaster M-G-M." *Newswk* 27 (20 May 46) 97. MGM plans to distribute classroom, documentary, and fact films throughout the world.

Benoit-Lévy, Jean, and H. Hansen. "Future of the Film." *Survey Graphic* 35 (Sep 46) 329–330. French author hopes for expanded use of the film as an educational and editorial tool.

Wadsworth, E. "Hollywood in School." *Scholastic* 50 (14 Apr 47) 19T. Details Hollywood's efforts in educational film through Teaching Film Custodians.

Blair, Patricia. "Which of the Free Films Really Offer Something for Nothing?" *Lib J* 72 (15 May 47) 791–793+. Cautions concerning "free" films offered to libraries.

Lyons, Sumner. "Other End of the Rainbow." *Screen Writer* 3 (June 47) 12–13. On the writing of the documentary and commercial nontheatrical film and the special talents it requires.

Kracauer, Siegfried. "Filming the Subconscious." *Th Arts* 32 (Feb 48) 36–44. What has been happening in experimental psychological films; what it takes to make a good film of this type.

Mayer, Arthur. "An Education in Educational Films." *Screen Writer* 3 (Mar 48) 18–22. Report by theatre operator and distributor on his experience with book publishers' group in preparing pilot films for education.

Maddison, John. "The Scientific Film." *Penguin F Rev* 7 (Sep 48) 117–124. The use of the camera for the recording and observation of movements in nature.

"Film Council to Survey All Phases of Film Handling." *Lib J* 73 (1 Nov 48) 1607–1608. Film Council of America has launched two surveys to find out what types of films are wanted and how informational films can be obtained.

Spottiswoode, Raymond. "16mm Comes of Age." *SRL* 31 (11 Dec 48) 32. As 16mm becomes more sophisticated, Hollywood award givers continue to ignore it.

Readers are advised to acquaint themselves with the range of categories throughout the bibliography in the search for specific subjects. In some cases, cross-categorical comparisons are directly suggested. In general, however, each article is placed under one category only. Cross-references on individual articles have been kept to a minimum.

Entries are in chronological order of publication under each category. Exceptions are: Part 5, Biography, in which the order is alphabetical by name; Part 9, Case Histories of Film Making, which is alphabetical by film title; and 3c and 8c(4), also alphabetical by title.

Robert Flaherty's *Nanook of the North.*

Evans, Ernestine. "New Jobs in New Films." *Independent Woman* 28 (Jan 49) 6–8+. College graduates urged to do documentary and educational films; introduction to John Grierson's work.

Painlevé, Jean. "The Documentary Film." *Penguin F Rev* 9 (May 49) 47–52. Scientific-film maker comments on several kinds of teaching films and the danger of making a subject so clear the class will not go through the effort of remembering it.

Spottiswoode, Raymond. "Ideas on Film." *SRL* 32 (14 May 49) 60. An optimistic look at decentralization of nontheatrical film production.

"Sixteen Millimeters at Lunch Hour." *Commonweal* 50 (15 Apr 49) 4. Lord and Taylor showings for employees.

Starr, Cecile. "Ideas on Film." *SRL* 32 (15 Oct 49) 31. Report on films dealing with mental health.

Rosenberg, John. "Want to Write a Movie Message?" *Coronet* 28 (Oct 50) 152–156. A man who gave his wife a film of himself explaining his side of an argument is now selling similar films, like "letters," to individuals.

Cummings, P. "And Now We Take You." *Collier's* 130 (18 Oct 52) 10. Ridicules movie shorts about "the great outdoors."

Schreiber, Flora Rheta. "New York—A Cinema Capital." *QFRTV* 7 (No. 3, Spring 53) 264–273. From Cinema 16 to the UN, there are many kinds of films made and distributed besides the theatrical kind.

Starr, Cecile. "Going Places." *Sat Rev* 36 (11 Apr 53) 69–70. A "hectic but refreshing" excursion into the world of 16mm travelogues.

Michaelis, Anthony R. "Cinematographic Evidence in Law." *QFRTV* 8 (No. 2, Winter 53) 186–193.

"Scientific Film Congress." *S&S* 23 (Jan–Mar 54) 116. Note on London meeting and films.

Legg, Stuart. "Shell Film Unit: 21 Years." *S&S* 23 (Apr–June 54) 209–212. The history and present organization of the Shell Film Unit and its distribution system.

Gerstlé, Ralph. "Non-Theatrical Films." *FIR* 5 (June–July 54) 292–294. A review of 16mm nonfiction films recently seen at the Museum of Modern Art and the American Film Assembly in Chicago.

Leyda, Jay. "Tolstoy on Film." *S&S* 24 (July–Sep 54) 18–20+. How Tolstoy, who hated to have photographs taken and usually refused, submitted to these rare films.

Hine, A. "Sports on Film." *Holiday* 16 (Sep 54) 11–12. Some short documentaries on sports.

Anstey, Edgar. "Sponsorship and the Art of the Film." *Film* 1 (Oct 54) 9–12. A positive view of industry-sponsored films.

Gerstlé, Ralph. "Non-Theatrical Films." *FIR* 5 (Dec 54) 530–532. Nonfiction seen at the American Film Assembly.

Crowther, Bosley, and James Card. "Perspectives and Prospects of 16mm Film." *F Cult* 1 (No. 3, 1955) 12–14. "The Role of 16mm Film in American Society," by Crowther; "16mm Film in Historical Perspective," by Card.

de Laurot, Edouard L. "Audio-Visualism versus Education." *F Cult* 1 (Nos. 5–6, 1955) 6–13. A critical assessment of the current theory and practice in the audiovisual field, suggesting some fundamental revisions of concepts and methods.

Gerstlé, Ralph. "2nd American Film Assembly." *FIR* 6 (May 55) 216–219. Film Council of America, sponsored by Ford Foundation Fund for Adult Education, shows nonfiction 16mm films and selects "Golden Reel Winners."

Starr, Cecile. "For the Public." *Sat Rev* 38 (9 July 55) 27. A review of some of the 16mm films to be seen at the seventy-fourth annual convention of the American Library Association.

Duncan, Catherine. "The World of Silence." *S&S* 26 (Summer 56) 36–37. *The Silent World* is an account of a voyage of the ship *Calypso* and of the underwater exploits of some of her crew; an essay on such films.

Michaelis, Anthony R. "Research Films." *JUFPA* 9 (No. 2, Winter 57) 11–13. Editor of British scientific journal *Discovery* lists uses of film for scientific inquiry.

Morley, Ronald. "Non-Theatrical Films." *FIR* 9 (May 58) 249–253. A review of some of the sponsored films and TV commercials presented at a recent meeting of the New York Film Council for its members and friends.

Healy, Paul F. "They Make the Strangest Movies." *SEP* 231 (7 Mar 59) 28–29+. The world of educational films in U.S.

Caplan, Ralph. "Industry on the Screen." *Industrial Design* 7 (Apr 60) 48–65. A survey of the industrial film.

Breitrose, Henry. "The Nontheatrical Film, 1960." *FQ* 14 (No. 3, Spring 61) 40–42. Recent activities and screenings at the Flaherty Seminar and the San Francisco Film Festival.

Glover, Guy, Francis Thompson, Lee R. Bobker, Peretz W. Johnnes. "Creative Film Making—A Symposium." *JUFPA* 15 (No. 2, 1963) 18–21. The participants criticize the staleness and the standardized approaches prevalent especially in the educational film and suggest the necessity of financial support of the experimenter, the man with a strong filmic sense; talks given at the Educational Film Library Association American Film Festival 1962.

Wagner, Robert W. "The Creative Educational Film." *JUFPA* 15 (No. 2, 1963) 21–23. Designing good films that teach requires experimentation and the development of talented people; a talk presented at Eastman House, Rochester, New York.

Holloway, George. "Controversy on Film." *Lib J* 88 (1 Feb 63) 513–515. Criteria for selection of political films for public film libraries.

Tourtelot, Madeline. "The New Non-Theatricals." *FIR* 14 (June–July 63) 346–348. Account of 1963 American Film Festival.

Gibson, George W. "More Return from Your Film Dollar." *Harvard Bus Rev* 41 (July 63) 162–163+. A review of the state of business film as it is and ought to be.

Ellis, Jack C. "Films for Education." *JUFPA* 16 (No. 4, 1964) 6–9+. Educational films suffer from attempting to cover all fields, even those which gain nothing from film as a medium; part of a paper presented to Society of Cinematologists.

Ellis, Jack C. "Film for Education: Considerations of Form." *J Soc Cin* 4 (1964) 31–36. Film should undertake subjects it "can handle uniquely well," and the educational film should experiment with form as a way of accomplishing new kinds of communication.

Drukker, L. "Film Festival." *Pop Photog* 55 (Aug 64) 97+. Brief report on nonfiction "film as art" category at American film festival.

Schwartz, Tony. "Steichen and His Sound." *Pop Photog* 55 (Sep 64) 18. The famous still photographer making a film of a shad-blow tree.

"Charity Plays the Lead in Reel Buffs' Movies." *Bus Wk* (22 Jan 66) 34–35. The Reel Fellows, a group of Los Angeles businessmen who formed a nonprofit, nonprofessional group for public-service film making.

Johnson, William. "Lively Arts." *Senior Scholastic* 91 (2 Nov 67) 22. Report on "historically based" films at the New York Film Festival.

Brody, Tom. "C. B. De Mille of the Pros." *Sports Illus* 27 (20 Nov 67) 74–76. On Ed Sabol, who films professional football games.

Smith, Clyde. "The Galapagos on Film." *JUFA* 20 (No. 2, 1968) 39–45. A project for filming flora and fauna of Galapagos Islands for scientific films about evolution.

"A Split-Screen Search into Troubled Minds." *Life* 64 (9 Feb 68) 68–70. Examples of patients watching movies of themselves for therapeutic purposes.

"Kaiser Aluminum Uncovers Money in Its PR Efforts." *Bus Wk* (12 July 69) 88–89. Information about short film, *Why Man Creates,* based on material in house organ; film has since won an Oscar.

Goldstein, Norman, *et al.* "Special Report: The Sponsored Film." *Action* 4 (No. 4, July–Aug 69) 19–31. A thorough report on the sponsored film in America, its history and present state.

Chittock, John, *et al.* "Sponsored Cinema." *Film* (No. 56, Autumn 69) 16–20. A critic, a sponsor, and a producer discuss various aspects of sponsored cinema.

Cantwell, R. "Sport Was Box Office." *Sports Illus* 31 (15 Sep 69) 108–116. Early history of movies about sports.

Little, Stuart W. "Sponsored Films Are Better Than Ever: Projecting the Corporate Image." *Sat Rev* 53 (12 Sep 70) 90–92. Report on recent films made by American industry on a variety of subjects.

8a(1). FILM AND ANTHROPOLOGY

Popkin, Zelda. "Camera Explorers of the New Russia." *Travel* 58 (Dec 31). See 4e(8).

"Ethnographical Films." *Science* 81 (15 Mar 35) 265. British Film Institute's desire to begin anthropological collection.

"News and Views: Films and Folk-Lore." *Nature* 141 (No. 3567, 12 Mar 38) 441–442. Proposal that ethnographic films be made to preserve the festivals and customs of Great Britain.

"Inter-Museum Conference on Anthropology Films." *Museum News* 18 (15 Feb 41) 5.

Bjerre, Jens. "Filming the African Native." *S&S* 16 (No. 64, Winter 47–48) 148–150.

Leacock, Richard. "To Far Places with Camera and Sound-Track." *FIR* 1 (Mar 50) 3–7. Robert Flaherty's cameraman on *The Louisiana Story* describes his experiences among the Berber tribe as cameraman for John Ferno on one of the geography films produced by Louis De Rochemont for Universal Pictures.

Sulistrowski, Zygmunt. "On Location in the Amazon." *Natural Hist* 62 (Mar 53) 130–136. Problems among a group of Brazilian Indians, told by a moviemaker.

"Safari in Color." *Time* 57 (11 June 51) 108. *Latuko,* a movie by an amateur photographer.

Nagrin, D. "American in the Fiji Islands." *Dance Mag* 28 (Feb 54). See 4k(6).

Tschopik, Harry, Jr. "Filming Jungle Fishermen." *Natural Hist* 64 (Jan 55) 8–19. Problems of filming a scientific picture of a tribe of forest Indians in Peru; film maker's own story.

Zebba, Sam. "Casting and Directing in Primitive Societies." *Hwd Q* 11 (No. 1, 1956). See 2c.

Gardner, Robert. "The Ethnographic Film." *FIR* 9 (Feb 58) 65–73+. Harvard's anthropologist-film maker reports on the sixth International Seminar on Ethnographic Film (Sep 57), which was sponsored by UNESCO and attended by the delegates of seventeen nations; films shown (by Jean Rouch, Vittorio De Seta, and others) are assessed and also the problems of art and science in this kind of film making.

Hitchcock, J. T., and P. J. Hitchcock. "Some Considerations for the Prospective Ethnographic Cinematographer." *Am Anthropologist* 62 (Aug 60) 656–674. Detailed advice: assessment of needs; choice of equipment; financing; technique.

Steele, Robert. "The Film-Maker's Approach to Aboriginal Peoples." *J Soc Cin* 2 (1962) 34–60.

Hitchens, Gordon. "The Festival of the People." *F Com* 2 (No. 1, Winter 64) 9–14. Reviews of ethnographic films shown in Florence; additional statements by Robert Gardner on the making of his film *Dead Birds* and by Margaret Mead reviewing it.

"Too Much Realism?" *Newswk* 65 (19 Apr 65) 48. Doubts about Jacopatti's *Africa Addio* as a documentary, along with *Mondo Cane*.

Adair, J., and S. Worth. "Navajo as Filmmaker: A Brief Report of Research in the Cross-Cultural Aspects of Film Communication." *Am Anthropologist* 69 (Feb 67) 76–78. Investigating value systems through the visual mode.

Eibl-Eibesfeldt, I., and H. Hass. "Film Studies in Human Ethnology." *Cultural Anthropologist* 8 (Dec 67) 477–479.

Sorenson, E. R. "Research Film Program in the Study of Changing Man." *Cultural Anthropologist* 8 (Dec 67) 443–469.

Desanti, D., and Decock, J. "Jean Rouch: *Cinéma et Ethnographie* (with English summary)." *African Arts* 2 (No. 1, Autumn 68) 36–39+.

Mead, Margaret. "Filming Life and Death in a New Guinea Village." *Redbook* 132 (Nov 68) 46+.

Ruby, Jay. "Visual Anthropology—Film as a Means of Presenting Man." *JUFA* 21 (No. 3, 1969) 68–71. Assistant professor of anthropology at Temple University points out pitfalls of separating scientists and artists: they must know about each other's approach.

MacDougall, David. "Prospects of the Ethnographic Film." *FQ* 23 (No. 2, Winter 69–70) 16–30. Seeking to "reveal one society to another," the ethnographic film maker follows in the footsteps of Flaherty, Cooper, Marshall, Gardner, Rouch; flat record making is useful but the humanistic goal is to give "a sense of the wholeness of other cultures."

Worth, S., and J. Adair. "Navajo Filmmakers." *Am Anthropologist* 72 (No. 1, Feb 70) 9–34. Six Navajo youths are given cameras, taught the basic elements of motion-picture technology, asked to make films, and then their films are analyzed for cross-cultural differences in perception.

8a(2). WILDLIFE FILMS

Woodard, Stacy. "Insect Warriors Battle for the Movies." *Sci Am* 150 (Apr 34) 178–179. Director tells about filming insects in natural locale and in studio.

Cockerell, T. D. A. "Zoology and the Moving Picture." *Science* 82 (18 Oct 35) 369–370. Reviews anthropologist Grey Owl's latest book and notes applicability of films to zoological study.

Woolfe, Bruce. "I Remember." *S&S* 10 (No. 37, Spring 41) 8–9. British short-film maker reminisces about earlier years.

Reynolds, Laurel. "American Continent Is Her Backyard." *Audubon Mag* (Mar 48) 108–109. Picture story on Laurel Reynolds, who makes films about birds for the Audubon Screen Tours.

Hugo, Ian. "Animal Close-Ups." *FIR* 1 (Nov 50) 13–15. Impressions of an informal Mexican zoo's activities.

Ganio, Alma. "Disney's Nature Films." *FIR* 2 (Nov 51). A brief appraisal of *Seal Island, Nature's Half Acre,* and *Beaver Valley.*

Downes, Elizabeth. "Screen." *Natural Hist* 61 (May 52) 236–237; (Dec 52) 740–742. Comments on films in the field of nature, geography, and exploration, including Jacques Yves Cousteau's *Danger Under the Sea.*

Fleay, David. "Movie-Making in Platypus-Land." *Natural Hist* 62 (Jan 53) 38+.

Disney, Walt. "What I've Learned from the Animals." *American* 155 (Feb 53) 22–23+. Walt Disney talks about his nature films.

Disney, Walt. "Why I Like Making Nature Films." *Woman's Home Companion* 81 (May 54) 38. A brief answer, plus lots of pictures.

Jamison, Barbara B. "Amazing Scripts by Animals." *NYTM* (18 July 54) 16–17+. Disney's "True-Life Adventures" series calls for a rare breed of photographer.

Disney, Walt. "Lurking Camera: Producing the True-Life Adventure Series." *Atlantic* 194 (Aug 54) 23–27.

McEvoy, J. P. "McEvoy in Disneyland." *Rdrs Dig* 66 (Feb 55) 19–26. Camera teams used for the True-Life Adventures.

"Walt Disney Receives Audubon Medal." *Audubon Mag* 58 (Jan 56) 25+. Presentation speech and Disney's reply.

Peterson, Roger. "Wildlife on Film." *Audubon Mag* 58 (May 56) 102–103+. Comments on wildlife films; technical intricacies and expenses. Reply (Sep 56) 194.

Petite, Irving. "They Know the Wild in Wildlife." *Audubon Mag* 66 (Jan 64) 20–25. On making films for Walt Disney.

Gimbel, Peter R. "Shark!" *Sports Illus* 25

(29 Aug 66) 68–76. On the making of *In the World of Sharks.*

8a(3). FILMS ABOUT ART

[See also 3f(3).]

Randall, Arne W. "16mm Motion Picture Art Films." *Design* 44 (Dec 42) 21–24. Remarks on the misuse of the motion picture as a visual aid in the teaching of art; list of major educational-film distributors; filmography for studies in architecture, design, history, artists, sculpture, commercial art.

McInnes, Graham. "Films on Painting." *Design* 46 (Nov 44) 30–31. Remarks on the importance of 16mm films about art, with comments on the National Film Board of Canada's Canadian Artists Series.

Krasne, Belle. "Sound Tracks to Art Appreciation." *Independent Woman* 27 (June 48) 176–178. Falcon Films and its three women managers introduce their first release, on a Henry Moore exhibition.

Queval, Jean. "Film and Fine Arts." *S&S* 19 (Jan 50) 33–36. *Le Monde de Paul Delvaux,* a film which found its subject in painting, yet experiments with film as a medium; also a film by Henri Storck and Paul Haesaerts, on Rubens.

Berkowitz, Sidney. "The Information Film in Art." *College Art J* 10 (No. 1, Fall 50) 44–49. Its use in the teaching of art.

Pichel, Irving. "Stills in Motion." *Hwd Q* 5 (No. 1, Fall 50) 8–13. *The Titan, 1848,* and *Images médiévales* as examples; the techniques used, and their limitations.

"Art Film Festival at Woodstock, N.Y." *Art Dig* 25 (Sep 51) 5.

Lewis, Stephan. "An Art Film Festival." *FIR* 2 (Oct 51) 11–13. Woodstock, New York, awards prizes for films about the arts.

Knight, Arthur. "Art Films Served Without Demi-Tasse." *Art Dig* 26 (1 Nov 51) 34. The rise in art-film production in the United States.

"Adventure in Art." *Th Arts* 36 (Feb 52) 90. Films about art.

Amberg, George. "Art, Films, and 'Art Films.'" *Mag of Art* 45 (Mar 52) 124–133. A survey of films about art and artists based on the critical premise that the less attempt at "objectivity" the better the film; Haesaerts and Resnais discussed.

"Mobiles, Schmobiles." *Harper's* 205 (Dec 52) 92–93. How pretentious "film artistry" can wreck the "art" film's subject matter.

Krasne, Belle. "Art of the Film Makers." *Art Dig* 27 (15 Dec 52) 5. Films on art, their functions and artistic merits.

Knight, Arthur. "Art Gallery for the Millions." *Th Arts* 37 (Jan 53) 74–77. The film about art as an educational device; the Film Advisory Center, which distributes foreign productions.

Venturi, Lauro. "Films on Art: An Attempt at Classification." *QFRTV* 7 (No. 4, Summer 53) 385–391.

North, Christopher. "The Second Art Film Festival." *FIR* 4 (Jan 53) 28–33. The 1952 festival of films on art held in New York City.

Pool, Brenda. "Paintings into Films." *F&F* 1 (No. 4, Jan 55) 13. A report on the meeting of the International Federation for Art Films.

Young, Vernon. "The Not-So-Innocent Eye." *Arts Mag* 30 (Dec 55) 35–37. Comparison of a number of films about art and artists.

Starr, Cecile. "Living Portraits of Contemporary Artists." *House Beautiful* 98 (Oct 56) 244+.

Read, John. "The Film on Art as Documentary." *F Cult* 3 (No. 13, 1957) 6–7. The author argues that films about art belong in the "documentary" category, and talks about the need for distribution outlets for these films.

Hayman, Patrick. "Art Films by John Read." *S&S* 26 (Spring 57) 217–218. John Read's documentary films about artists' lives and work were made for broadcast by BBC television.

"Screening Art." *Art News* 56 (May 57) 20. Comments on the Art Film Festival at the Metropolitan Museum, which includes documentary surveys of the work and lives of individual artists, such as *Goya;* studies of particular styles, such as *Prehistoric Images;* studies of works of art in special media; and animation, such as *The Adventures of Asterisk.*

Berger, John. "Clouzot as Delilah." *S&S* 27 (Spring 58) 196–197. A description of Clouzot's film *The Picasso Mystery;* Picasso's way of working is shown; he becomes merely "an entertainer."

"Films on the Fine Arts to See at Home." *Good Housekeeping* 150 (May 60) 174.

Seckler, D. G. "In the Movies." *Art in America* 50 (No. 1, 1962) 58–63. New conception of the artist in three short films, *A Bowl of Cherries, Day of the Painter, The Gift.*

Laurie, Edith. "Ottawa's UNESCO Seminar on Films on Art." *F Com* 1 (No. 5, Summer 63) 44–46. Art educators express dislike of films on art; film makers urge such films as a way of reaching the public, not the scholars.

Brown, Gordon. "Mixed Media Man." *Arts Mag* 41 (Apr 67) 51. A short interview with Jules Engel, sculptor who made a film of Paul Jenkins working on his paintings.

"Films on Ceramics." *Ceramics Monthly* 17 (Feb 69) 28–29+. Titles and sources.

Gilmour, P. "Art Films of James Scott." *Art and Artists* 4 (Mar 70) 16–19. Painting from the artist's point of view.

"Clark's Tour." *Time* 95 (9 Mar 70) 53. The beginnings of and response to Kenneth Clark's series *Civilization*.

Sheratsky, Rodney. "Atget, Lange, Picasso." *F Lib Q* 3 (No. 3, Summer 70) 23–26. A review of three films about the works of these artists.

8a(4). FILMS ABOUT DANCE

[See also 2b(8), 4k(6).]

Rosenheimer, Arthur. "Towards the Dance Film." *Th Arts* 26 (Jan 42) 57–63.

Knight, Arthur. "Dance in the Movies." *Dance Mag* 32 (June 58) 14–15. Short films at the U.S. exhibition hall at the Brussels World Fair.

Trexler, Larry. "*Dance Magazine*'s 1st Annual Directory of Dance Films." *Dance Mag* 34 (Feb 60) 32–34+. Covers ballet, modern dance, avant-garde, mime, ethnic and folk dance, and square dance.

Bacharach, Richard S. "Dance: A Movie Challenge." *Pop Photog* 51 (Nov 62) 92+. How to photograph it cinematically.

Hering, Doris. "A Sliver of Hope." *Dance Mag* 39 (Sep 65) 46–48. Jeri Salkin and Trudi Schoop's "body-ego technique" and the mentally retarded.

Livingston, D. D. "1965 Directory of Dance Films." *Dance Mag* 39 (Sep 65) 58–78+.

Covers features, experimental, avant-garde, ballet, ethnic, modern dance, children's dance, cartoons, ballroom, mime, and therapy.

Joel, Lydia. "George Balanchine at Work on a Permanent Record." *Dance Mag* 40 (Aug 66) 24–27. Production background of *A Midsummer Night's Dream*.

Knight, Arthur, Maya Deren, Parker Tyler, Sidney Peterson, Shirley Clarke, Ed Emshwiller, Stan Vanderbeek, Jonas Mekas, Stan Brakhage, Len Lye, Slavko Vorkapich, Hilary Harris, and Allegra Snyder. "Cine-Dance." *Dance Perspectives* (No. 30, Summer 67) 4–51. Each writes on some aspect of the relationship between film and dance.

Anderson, Jack. "A Film Not for Viewing." *Dance Mag* 42 (Apr 68) 52–57. Petit's two films of *Le Jeune Homme et la Mort*.

"Taylor & Co. on Film and Canvas." *Dance Mag* 42 (Nov 68) 24–25. Comments of choreographer Paul Taylor from a documentary on his work.

Harriton, Maria. "Film and Dance." *Dance Mag* 43 (Apr 69) 42. They share the immediacy that mirrors the subconscious.

Snyder, Allegra Fuller. "Who Can Make Them? How Can We Use Them?" *Dance Mag* 43 (Apr 69) 38–41. A report on the expanding dance-film scene.

Snyder, Allegra Fuller, and Monica Moseley. "Directory of 16mm Dance Films." *Dance Mag* 43 (Apr 69) 47–62.

8b. Newsreels

Murphy, Charles J. V. "In the Day's Grind." *American* 109 (Mar 30) 50–52+. Profile of Russell Muth, Fox Films newsreel cameraman who filmed Pancho Villa, the British fleet, and Mount Vesuvius.

Irwin, Theodore D. "Camera! Feeding the News Reels." *Pop Mech* 53 (May 30). See 2e(1).

Dodge, Natt N. "Adventures of a News Hound." *Sunset* 65 (July 30) 34–35. About Charles Perryman, Seattle newsreel man.

Beatty, Jerome. "Shooting the Big Shots." *American* 111 (Feb 31) 68–69+. Profile of Jack Connolly, Fox Movietone newsreel cameraman who filmed speeches by Coolidge, Mussolini, King George V, George Bernard Shaw, and others.

"Matinee Idols of the News Reels." *Lit Dig* 110 (5 Sep 31) 32–33. Public figures becoming proficient movie actors.

Schnurmacher, Emile C. "Get the Story! They Risk Their Lives to Live." *Pop Mech* 57 (Mar 32) 404–411. On newsreel cameramen.

"On the Jump with Newsreel Men." *Lit Dig* 112 (19 Mar 32) 36+. Roy Horn relates experiences with Royal Canadian Mounted Police,

in Parliament, with Pancho Villa, and on the Byrd North Pole expedition.

Smith, Alison. "The Town Crier Finds a Home." *Delineator* 121 (Sep 32) 20+. On popularity of newsreels.

Bishop, H. W. "Newsreel in the Making." *S&S* 3 (No. 11, Autumn 34) 150–152. Background of the making of one Gaumont British newsreel.

North, Anthony. "Let's Wait for the Newsreel." *New Outlook* 164 (Oct 34) 21–25. Newsreel, hurt by Depression and industry growth, now enters competitive field.

"Newsreels Seek Gains." *Newswk* 4 (6 Oct 34) 22. Use of announcers and "super-commentators."

Roberts, Glyn. "News-Reels." *New S&N* 10 (7 Sep 35) 304–305. Newsreels have become an important feature of cinema programs. Discussion (12 Sep 35) 372; (28 Sep 35) 407.

Menefee, Selden C. "The Movies Join Hearst." *New Rep* 84 (9 Oct 35) 241–242. Criticizes use of militarism and fascist propaganda in newsreels, especially by Hearst and Macfadden.

Pringle, H. F. "Movies Swing an Election: Sinclair or Merriam?" *Rdrs Dig* 29 (Aug 36) 4. From *The New Yorker*, brief report on newsreels that sought out nice-looking people who favored the Republican candidate for governor in California—and unkempt ones who favored Upton Sinclair.

"Educational Newsreels for WPA." *Lit Dig* 122 (8 Aug 36) 32. How Pathé makes newsreels; new contract with government for monthly reports on WPA.

Stallings, Laurence. "Words and Pictures." *SEP* 209 (21 Nov 36) 8–9+. Stories about newsreels and their cameramen.

"Hearst's News of the Day." *Time* 28 (23 Nov 36) 25. Audience booing in theatres causes name change for newsreels from *Hearst Metrotone* to *News of the Day*.

"Sound and Fury over Free Speech." *Lit Dig* 123 (1 May 37). *See 7c(1b)*.

Sharar, Dewan. "Twenty-two Soho Square: British Movietone News." *Great Britain and the East* 49 (29 July 37). *See 4e(1a)*.

Munro, W. C. "Cameras Don't Lie." *Current Hist* 46 (Aug 37). *See 7c(1d)*.

Sharar, Dewan. "Shanghai Massacre and the Films." *Great Britain and the East* 49 (14 Oct 37) 535. Controversy over showing of uncensored newsreels of the Sino-Japanese War.

Rose, Felix. *"Ciné Actualité."* *S&S* 1 (No. 26, Summer 38) 70–72. France's news cinemas are facing many difficulties.

Desmond, R. W. "News About the Newsreel." *CSMM* (28 Sep 38) 5+.

Blake, George. "Magna It Fama." *S&S* 8 (No. 29, Spring 39) 10–11. The nature of the rivalry between newsreels, newspapers, and television.

Sanger, Gerald. "A Newsreel Man's Conscience." *S&S* 10 (No. 38, Summer 41) 22–23. The virtues of the British newsreel, especially its independence from the government.

"Scenes from the Nazi Horror News-Film." *Illus London News* 99 (13 Sep 41). *See 4e(4b)*.

Williams, Michael. "Demoralizing Use of Musical Backgrounds with Newsreels of the War." *Commonweal* 35 (6 Mar 42). *See 2g(2a)*.

Genock, Ted. "Newsreel Man Shoots the War." *Am Mercury* 55 (Aug 42) 158–166. From the war notes of a Paramount cameraman—May 1940 to February 1942.

O'Brine, J. "Studios on the Battlefield." *Pop Sci* 142 (Mar 43) 108–113. Daredevil cameramen shoot "history's most photographed war."

Kracauer, Siegfried. "Conquest of Europe on the Screen: The Nazi Newsreel, 1939–1940." *Social Research* 10 (Sep 43). *See 4e(4b)*.

"Library of Congress Unearths First News-reels." *Life* 15 (20 Sep 43) 18–19+. Library discovery of 2,500,000 feet of paper film from 1897 to 1912—with frame enlargements.

Farber, M. "Russian Victory." *New Rep* 109 (11 Oct 43) 487. Examination of Russian war newsreel work.

"Axis Newsreels." *Life* 15 (13 Dec 43) 43–44+. Pictorial article with frame enlargements from OSS-edited versions of Axis newsreels.

Harris, James. "New Zealand Newsreels." *S&S* 13 (No. 50, July 44). *See 4j*.

"Newsreel Race; Advantages of 16mm Film Forecast Its Wide Adoption." *Bus Wk* (5 Jan 46) 41. The end of a newsreel pool established during the war promises keener competition for the future.

Davidson, Bill. "The Newsreel Business." *Cosmopolitan* (Sep 46) 149+.

"Victim." *New Yorker* 25 (26 Nov 49) 24–25. The world's first newsreel theatre, the Embassy, closes down.

"Newsreel Analysis." *CSMM* (26 Aug 50) 19. On MPAA study of newsreel content.

Fielding, Raymond. "The Nazi German Newsreel." *JUFPA* 12 (No. 3, Spring 60). *See 4e(4b)*.

Zavattini, Cesare. "The New *Free* Newsreels." *Cinéaste* 3 (No. 2, Fall 69) 17+. The theory behind the Italian free newsreel, Centro dei Cinegiornali Liberi.

Prottri, Danielle. "Letter from Italy." *Cinéaste* 3 (No. 3, Winter 69–70) 26+. A report on the activities of the Cinegiornali Liberi, the Italian newsreel.

8b(1). HISTORY AND THEORY

Bakshy, Alexander. "The News Reel." *Nation* 130 (8 Jan 30) 54. Asks whether the newsreel offers both entertainment and information.

"The Universal Spotlight." *New Rep* 63 (25 June 30) 139–140. Outlines effectiveness of the newsreel.

"Movie Business Started in 1895 in Japan." *Trans-Pacific* 18 (31 July 30) 19.

Fraser, Donald. "Newsreel: Reality or Entertainment?" *S&S* 2 (No. 7, Autumn 33) 89–90. The problems of depicting truth in the newsreel.

Littell, Robert. "A Glance at the Newsreels." *Am Mercury* 30 (Nov 33) 263–271. Declaration that newsreels are historically valuable and need not be trivial, lazy, or misleading.

Hulbert, Norman J. "News Films and Their Public." *S&S* 2 (No. 8, Winter 33–34) 132–133. They have influenced public attitudes.

Troy, William. "Journey to the End." *Nation* 138 (30 May 34) 630. Suggests newsreels produce catharsis lacking in features.

Ritchie, David. "That News-Reel Villainy." *S&S* 3 (No. 11, Autumn 34) 113–114.

Particular reference to newsreels of February 1933 and their use as historical record.

Markey, Morris. "A Reporter at Large: Newsreel." *New Yorker* (22 Sep 34) 68+.

"Filming of Tragedy in France Related." *Trans-Pacific* 22 (29 Nov 34) 15. Newsreel coverage of Marseilles assassination of Yugoslav king.

Erskine, John. "Newsreels Should Be Seen and Not Heard." *Am Mercury* 35 219–222. Critic assails newsreels' literary techniques and calls for reportage.

"Are Newsreels News?" *Nation* 141 (2 Oct 35) 369–370. Objects to moral editing of newsreels.

Mullen, S. M. "All That Flickers Is Not News." *Scholastic* 28 (23 May 36) 11+. It may be propaganda.

Littell, R. "Hard on Heroes." *Rdrs Dig* 29 (July 36) 89–90. Newsreel close-ups remove halos from statesmen.

"WPA: Pathé Wins Film Contract as New Deal Goes Hollywood." *Newswk* 8 (15 Aug 36). *See 7f(1).*

Sugrue, T. "Newsreels in America." *Scribner's* 101 (Apr 37) 9–18. Their origin, history, social function, and how they are made.

Seldes, Gilbert. "Screen and Radio." *Scribner's* 102 (July 37) 56–58. A counter to Will Hays' praise of the newsreel; history and current state of the newsreel detailed.

Pritt, Emile. "Trickery in Newsreels." *New Masses* 39 (6 May 41) 26–28. Feature films cannot speak directly to issues, but newsreels are slanted to be pro-British, pro-Washington, and anti-labor.

Anstey, Edgar. "Newsreels." *Spectator* 168 (9 Jan 42) 35. Annual review of newsreels points out enormous propaganda power in the film of "fact."

Farber, M. "Newsreels." *New Rep* 109 (22 Nov 43) 717–718. Ruthless criticism of insipid newsreels.

Ford, R. R. "Newsreel; Reply with Rejoinder." *New Rep* 110 (24 Jan 44) 119. A correspondence debate between Manny Farber and a British government film officer concerning newsreels.

Agee, James. "News Reels and War-Record Films." *Nation* 158 (24 June 44). *See 8c(2b).*

Farber, M. "More Notes on Newsreels." *New Rep* 111 (16 Oct 44) 495. Newsreel makers' apparent lack of interest in the unspectacular but filmic material of everyday life.

Woods, T. E. "Headlines in Celluloid." *SEP* 218 (11 Aug 45) 22–23. Why the newsreel, once zero box office, is coming out of the war with increased popularity.

Sanger, G. F. "Propaganda and the Newsreel." *S&S* 15 (No. 59, Autumn 46) 79–80.

Meltzer, Newton E. "Are Newsreels News?"

Hwd Q 2 (No. 3, Apr 47) 270–272. No, they are escapism.

Cave, G. Clement. "Newsreels Must Find a New Policy." *Penguin F Rev* 7 (Sep 48) 50–54. They are too inoffensive.

Crosby, John. "Newsreeland." *Atlantic* 182 (Dec 48) 126–127. The "beautiful life" of America which is seen in the typical newsreel.

Lyford, J., and Siegfried Kracauer. "Duck Crosses Main Street." *New Rep* 119 (13 Dec 48) 13–15. Why newsreels are so bland and light.

Bolton, Isabel. "At a Newsreel Theatre." *FIR* 2 (June–July 51) 15–17. Poetic responses as the "visual images jostled and pushed at each other"—monstrous crimes, miracles of nature.

Stone, Dorothy T. "The First Film Library." *FIR* 2 (Aug–Sep 51). *See 1b(3).*

"Pioneer Newsreels." *Image* 2 (No. 6, Sep 53) 39–40. Coronation of Czar Nicholas II (1896) and Vitagraph record of fighting in Cuba 1898.

Hochberg, Joel. "The Vanishing Newsreel." *FIR* 10 (June–July 59) 344–345+. Factors which have all but brought an end to the newsreel in theatres.

"A Change of Screen." *Time* 90 (29 Dec 67) 35. Newsreels are finished.

"Last Reel." *Newswk* 71 (1 Jan 68) 53. The end of the newsreel.

Goodman, Rhonna. "A 20th Century Visual Encyclopedia." *F Lib Q* 3 (No. 2, Spring 70) 30–31. Archives Unlimited set up by Mert Koplin is a storehouse for all types of newsreel footage.

8b(2). MAGAZINE FILMS AND *MARCH OF TIME*

Taylor, D. F. "Screen Magazines." *CQ* 2 (No. 2, Winter 33–34) 93–95. Andrew Buchanan's work is fresh and well cut, but the temptation in all these reels is to add an entertaining commentary.

"Re-enacted Events Make Bow." *Newswk* 5 (9 Feb 35) 38–39. *March of Time* series begins.

Troy, William. "Pictorial Journalism." *Nation* 140 (20 Feb 35) 232. Praises *March of Time* series.

Mabie, Janet. "Pictorial Journalism." *CSMM* (30 Oct 35) 3+. Profile of men behind *March of Time* series.

Greene, Graham. *"March of Time." Spectator* 155 (8 Nov 35) 774. Praise for innovative editing techniques used in *March of Time* series; problems of political freedom in newsfilms voiced by the British Board of Film Censors.

"Celluloid Censorship." *Time* 27 (1 June 36). *See 7e(3).*

Dangerfield, George. "Time Muddles On." *New Rep* 88 (19 Aug 36) 43–45. The *March of Time* is not so much fascist, as claimed by the *American Spectator* (March issue), but (1) simply a series of thrillers, (2) so passionately two-sided as to be irresponsible.

Van Doren, Mark. "What Pictures Mean." *Nation* 146 (29 Jan 38) 136–137. A review of the *March of Time*'s *Inside Nazi Germany: 1938.*

"Freedom of Film and Press." *Chris Cent* 55 (2 Feb 38). See 7c(1d).

Galway, Peter. *"Inside Nazi Germany, 1938: The March of Time." New S&N* 15 (30 Apr 38) 728. Effects of this film on British audiences.

Frakes, Margaret. "Time Marches Back: Propaganda for Defense." *Chris Cent* 57 (16 Oct 40) 1277–1278. A look at *The Ramparts We Watch,* a *March of Time* film, with comments on the documentary for propaganda purposes.

"New *March of Time* Program Features Books." *Publishers Weekly* 146 (28 Oct 44) 1756. And spurs book sales.

Anstey, Edgar. "The Magazine Film." *Penguin F Rev* 9 (May 49) 17–21. Documentary director recalls *World in Action, This Modern Age,* and De Rochemont's willingness to create characters in such *March of Time* films as *Father Divine* and *Fiorello LaGuardia.*

Fielding, Raymond. "Time Flickers Out: Notes on the Passing of the *March of Time.*" *QFRTV* 11 (No. 4, Summer 57) 354–361. "A critical autopsy" of the history and popularity of the theatre series of news documentaries which began in 1935 and ended in 1951.

Fielding, Raymond. "Mirror of Discontent: The *March of Time* and Its Politically Controversial Film Issues." *West Polit Q* 20 (Mar 59) 145–152. Analysis of one episode, *Inside Nazi Germany,* which reveals a strong visual-verbal contrast; critical reactions claimed it was both pro-Nazi and anti-Nazi.

8c. Documentary

Sharar, Dewan. "Educational and Documentary Films." *Great Britain and the East* 49 (1 July 37) 13–14. The British Film Institute's efforts to encourage use of cinema.

Ferguson, Otis. "Home Truths from Abroad." *New Rep* 93 (15 Dec 37) 171–172. Paul Rotha's visit to the U.S. stirs interest in the sponsored documentary.

Ivens, Joris. "Collaboration in Documentary." *Films* 1 (No. 2, Spring 40) 30–42. The sponsor, business manager, cameraman, writer, editor, audience, and especially the nonprofessional actor.

Kline, Herbert. "Extract from a Letter." *S&S* 9 (No. 35, Autumn 40) 44. Director's plan for a documentary in Mexico.

Maddow, Ben. "Reconstruction of the Truth." *Calif Arts and Arch* 61 (No. 1, Jan 44) 20+. A description of the functions of the writer in the documentary film.

Hutchins, Patricia. "Cine Camera in Gaeltacht." *S&S* 14 (No. 55, Oct 45) 86–87. An account of a film dealing with the entire life and history of a glen in Donegal, Ireland.

Barry, Iris. "The Film of Fact." *Town & Country* 100 (Sep 46) 142+.

"Sheep Come in a Flock." *Harper's* 197 (July 48) 118–120. Stuart Legg of World Today, Inc., a documentary company, discusses his films and the documentary in general.

Losey, Mary. "More Seeing, Less Selling." *SRL* 31 (9 Oct 48) 61–62. A plea for organized sponsorship for the documentary film; *Louisiana Story* an example.

Mayer, Arthur. "Documentary Film." *Sat Rev* 31 (13 Nov 48) 61–62. Plea for more organized sponsorship and distribution of documentary films.

Sternfeld, Frederick W. "Current Chronicle." *Musical Q* 35 (Jan 49). See 2g(2d).

Spottiswoode, Raymond. "Ideas on Film." *SRL* 32 (9 Apr 49) 32. A report on the return of the realistic, "eyewitness" type of film.

Van Dyke, Willard. "Director on Location." *SRL* 32 (10 Sep 49) 45–46. Using untrained actors in documentary educational films about marriage.

Wright, Basil. "The Documentary Dilemma." *Hwd Q* 5 (No. 4, Summer 51) 321–325. Director says production has become difficult (in government, much interference; in business, a lack of enlightened patronage), but UN agencies may offer new chances.

Balcon, Sir Michael. "The Feature Carries on the Documentary Tradition." *QFRTV* 6 (No. 4, Summer 52). See 4e(1b).

Trumbull, Robert. "Focus on the Future." *NYTM* (12 Oct 52). See 4f(2).

Rotha, Paul. "Television and the Future of Documentary." *QFRTV* 9 (No. 4, Summer 55) 366–373. Sponsorship has assisted documentary in the past, and TV offers wider distribution.

Marcussen, E. B. "Danish Film Production." *Am Scandinavian Rev* 43 (Dec 55). See 4e(5).

Starr, Cecile. "Men in Movement: Film Ideas." *Sat Rev* 39 (22 Sep 56) 34. Survey of prominent documentary-film makers, discussing ideas they would like to put to film.

Starr, Cecile. "Film Seminar in Vermont." *Sat Rev* 39 (13 Oct 56) 32–33. Report on a ten-day Flaherty seminar.

Mix, Hugh. "Telling the Story—On Film." *JUFPA* 9 (No. 3, 1957). *See 2d.*

Freed, Edward. "Pre-Planning the Documentary Film." *JUFPA* 9 (No. 3, Spring 57) 8–10.

"Rotha and the Abbey." *S&S* 28 (No. 2, Spring 59) 67. Paul Rotha makes a documentary about Dublin theatre group.

Young, Colin, and A. Martin Zweiback. "Going Out to the Subject." *FQ* 13 (No. 2, Winter 59) 39–49. Reports on documentaries at the Flaherty seminar held at Santa Barbara, California, including the work of Jean Rouch.

Rogosin, Lionel. "Interpreting Reality." *F Cult* (No. 21, 1960). *See 2b(1).*

Vas, Robert. "Short—or Documentary?" *S&S* 29 (Summer 60). *See 4a(5).*

"The Anatomy of a Documentary." *JUFPA* 14 (No. 2, 1962). *See 2d.*

Hitchens, Gordon. "The Eighth Flaherty Film Seminar." *F Com* 1 (No. 2, Summer 62) 16–17.

Fondiller, H. V. "Flaherty Seminar: Fresh Air for Film-Makers." *Pop Photog* 54 (Feb 64) 112–113. Films shown; comments by participants.

Osborn, Elodie. "New York on Screen." *Art in America* 52 (Oct 64). *See 4k.*

Conover, G. "God's Spies." *Nation* 199 (26 Oct 64) 283–285. A program of the new documentary at Gallery of Modern Art, New York.

Lipton, L. "Should You Go to the Flaherty Film Seminar?" *Pop Photog* 59 (July 66) 140+. Films shown the year before.

Arnold, J. W. "Robert Flaherty Film Seminar." *America* 119 (23 Nov 68) 519–521.

Fondiller, H. V. "Flaherty Film Seminar." *Pop Photog* 65 (Dec 69) 132–133+. Films shown.

8c(1). PURPOSES AND THEORIES OF THE DOCUMENTARY

[*See also 3a(2).*]

Saalschutz, L. "Mechanisms of Cinema." *Close Up* 6 (No. 4, 1930) 303–308. Theoretical notes on documentary and comedy.

Buchanan, Andrew. "Making a Documentary Film." *S&S* 1 (No. 2, Summer 32) 47–48.

Grierson, John. "Documentary." *CQ* 1 (No. 2, Winter 32) 67–72; (No. 3, Spring 33) 135–139. "As gravely distinct a choice as the choice of poetry instead of fiction." Second article expresses doubts about Walter Ruttman's *Berlin* and other "city-symphonies." Both reprinted in *Grierson on Documentary* (Praeger, 1972; F. Hardy, ed.).

"Embfu." "A Working Plan for Sub-Standard." *CQ* 2 (No. 1, Autumn 33) 19–25. Amateurs using 16mm film are advised to link their purposes with public needs and share in the documentary tradition. (Probably written by John Grierson.)

Blakeston, Oswell. "Manifesto on the Documentary Film." *Close Up* 10 (No. 4, Dec 33) 325–326. A plea for truth in the documentary.

Rotha, Paul. "The Documentary Director." *CQ* 2 (No. 2, Winter 33–34) 78–79. Documentary is an approach which stresses the significance of things; it has a purpose beyond itself.

Schrire, David. "The Psychology of Film Audiences." *S&S* 2 (No. 8, Winter 33–34) 122–123. The increased exhibition of documentaries is making the public more conscious of the world and critical of films in general.

Grierson, John. "The G.P.O. Gets Sound." *CQ* 2 (No. 4, Summer 34). *See 4c.*

Schrire, David, and John Grierson. "Evasive Documentary." *CQ* 3 (No. 1, Autumn 34) 7–11. Attack on Flaherty's escapism as "documentary in decay"; Grierson defends him.

Grierson, John. "Two Paths to Poetry." *CQ* 3 (No. 4, Summer 35) 194–196. Paul Rotha's *Shipyard* is the impressionist approach; Wright, Elton, and Legg come at it by analysis.

Leech, Clifford. "Definitions in Cinema." *CQ* 3 (No. 2, Winter 35) 79–80. Response to David Schrire article; definitions of documentary types.

Griffith, Richard. "Film Faces Facts." *Survey Graphic* 27 (Dec 38) 595–600. Documentary must be concerned with audience effects.

Hauser, Arnold. "The High or the Low Road?" *S&S* 7 (No. 28, Winter 38–39) 158–159. Art critic and historian discusses the documentary film, its merits and faults.

Baird, Thomas. "The Film and Society." *Life & Letters Today* 20 (No. 18, Feb 39) 87–95. Documentary films attempt to create new tastes.

Ferguson, Russell. "Bells *Et Cetera*." *S&S* 8 (No. 30, Summer 39) 52–54. Humorous comments on documentary-film making.

Grierson, John. "Story of the Documentary Film." *Fortnightly Rev* 152 (Aug 39) 121–130. A defense of the documentary film, with emphasis on history, concepts, and government use.

"Documentary Film, an Instrument of Propaganda and Morale." *Th Arts* 24 (Nov 40) 768.

Haggin, B. H. "Music for Documentary Films." *Nation* 152 (15 Feb 41). *See 2g(2a).*

Strauss, Theodore. "Documentaries at the Crossroads." *Th Arts* 25 (Sep 41) 683–689. Documentary-film producers should give up their intellectual isolation and assemble their energies to serve the public needs.

Whitebait, William. "Film and Reality." *New S&N* 23 (28 Feb 42). *See 8c(4)*.

Farber, Manny. "Memorandum to the Makers of Documentary War Movies." *New Rep* 107 (5 Oct 42) 414–415. A documentary should analyze the facts in visual images—narration should not be necessary.

Mayer, Arthur L. "Fact into Film." *Pub Opin Q* 8 (No. 2, 1944) 206–225. Significance of documentary films during war and peace.

Elvin, George H. "Planned Production." *S&S* 13 (No. 50, July 44) 30–31. The need after the war for government-sponsored documentary and educational films, in order to win the peace.

Mayer, Arthur L. "Films for Peace." *Th Arts* 28 (Nov 44) 642–647. A proposal for postwar documentary production.

Joseph, Robert. "Cinema: Comment and Criticism." *Arts & Arch* 62 (Mar 45) 17. Appraisal of the documentary film.

Mayer, Arthur L., and Richard Griffith. "The Shape of Films to Come: The Writer and the Documentary." *Th Arts* 29 (Nov 45) 647–649.

Grierson, John. "Postwar Patterns." *Hwd Q* 1 (No. 2, Jan 46) 159–165. The documentary "attempts to give form and pattern to the complex of direct observation"; it goes beyond the primitive innocence of Flaherty to do the jobs needed by government in war and peace.

Kline, Herbert. "Shape of Films to Come; Reply." *Th Arts* 30 (Jan 46) 58+. Another look at the future of the documentary, with a longing for more dialogue and color.

Van Dyke, Willard. "The Interpretive Camera in Documentary Films." *Hwd Q* 1 (No. 4, July 46) 405–409. It may be limited by training in still photography or it may be freely hand-held, but it is there to present an idea, as in *Library of Congress*.

Pratzner, Wesley F. "What Has Happened to the Documentary Film?" *Pub Opin Q* 11 (No. 3, 1947) 394–401. It has failed as a promoter for understanding and friendly attitudes among nations.

Wright, Basil. "Documentary To-Day." *Penguin F Rev* 2 (Jan 47) 37–44. As a method of approach to public information, it must be concerned with relationship to the public; its purposes and methods of production.

Pudovin, Vsevolod. "The Global Film." *Hwd Q* 2 (No. 4, July 47). *See 7e*.

Holmes, Winifred. "What's Wrong with Documentary?" *S&S* 17 (No. 65, Spring 48) 44–45. Several complaints, including lack of humanity and passion.

Grierson, John. "Prospect for Documentary." *S&S* 17 (No. 66, Summer 48) 55–59. What is wrong and why.

Read, John. "Is There a Documentary Art?" *S&S* 17 (No. 68, Winter 48–49) 156–158. Yes, if it doesn't confine itself to purely factual reports.

Bryan, Julien. "Face to Face; Documentaries Can Promote International Understanding." *SRL* 32 (9 Apr 49) 33–34.

Dobson, Quentin. "The Land of Pog." *S&S* 19 (Dec 49) 31. Documentary started as a reaction to the synthetic, celluloid world, a tool of liberals, reporters and evangelists, but it lost its force somehow and now seems more unreal than Hollywood products, intimidated by sponsors and more interested in technique than in ideas.

Siepmann, Charles A. "Documentary Redefined." *SRL* 32 (17 Dec 49) 34–36.

Mackie, Philip. "Documentary: One for the Road." *S&S* 19 (Jan 50) 43–44. A lightly written article about the problems of current documentarians involved with sponsors; the habit good directors have of migrating to feature production as soon as they get a name.

Strand, Paul. "Realism: A Personal View." *S&S* 19 (Jan 50). *See 3a(6)*.

Vardac, A. Nicholas. "The Documentary Film as an Art Form." *S&S* 19 (Apr 51) 477–479. His theory: Documentary structure occurs only when the agents of action are not capable of choice.

Rotha, Paul. "On Documentary." *Film* (No. 2, Dec 54) 12–16. The relationship between television and documentary, and the role of sponsorship.

Grierson, John. "A Review of Reviews." *S&S* 24 (Jan–Mar 55) 157–158. A few words to students of documentary film: The idea of documentary can be quickly learned but the style and the impetus for exploring cannot be taught; comments on the art of criticism.

Blanche, W. H. "Was This Picture Faked? How Documentary Picture Was Staged for *Our World* Magazine." *Pop Photog* 38 (Apr 56) 68–69+.

Dickinson, Thorold. "This Documentary Business." *F Cult* 3 (No. 13, 1957) 5–6. The author argues for a reassessment of the term "documentary."

Riley, Ronald H., and Philip Leacock. "Fact and . . . Fiction." *F&F* 3 (No. 7, Apr 57) 16–17. Documentary-film influences on entertainment film and vice versa.

Quigly, Isabel. "Relevant Documents." *Spectator* 199 (22 Nov 57) 689–690. Documentaries (i.e., informative films) are always dull.

Callenbach, Ernest. "The Understood Antagonist and Other Observations." *FQ* 12 (No. 4, Summer 59) 16–23. The British documentary depended too much on curiosity; others try to introduce "human interest"; Lorentz, Ivens, and Flaherty wisely depended on conflict; the new enemy, perhaps, is overorganization, as seen in British "free cinema."

Mercey, Arch A. "The 1960 Kenneth Edwards Address." *JUFPA* 12 (No. 4, Summer 60) 4–7+. Assistant director of the U.S. Film Service in the time of Pare Lorentz, the author proposes many "American heritage" subjects for university film makers: conservation, rivers, liberty, organizations, immigration, architecture, mobility.

Leacock, Richard. "For an Uncontrolled Cinema." *F Cult* (Nos. 22–23, 1961). *See 3a(2)*.

Rose, Ernest D. "What Is a 'Documentary'?" *JUFPA* 13 (No. 2, Winter 61) 7–8. Reprint from *UCLA Alumni Magazine* emphasizes controversy as a natural part of documentary tradition, which draws "out of life itself the drama that is already there."

Fuller, J. G. "Heyday of the Documentary." *Sat Rev* 47 (29 Aug 64) 172. Problems of technique and truth in the TV documentary series *20th Century*.

Jersey, William C. "Some Thoughts on Film Technique." *F Com* 2 (No. 1, Winter 64) 15–17. What is "legitimate" restructuring of reality in order to show truth in documentary?

Bluem, A. William. "Documentary in a Nuclear Age." *JUFPA* 17 (No. 4, 1965) 12–16. Elements necessary for documentary (technology, desire to persuade, dramatic narrative); its propaganda role in the Cold War; a talk before the Armed Forces TV Conference in Washington.

Currie, Hector, and Michael Porte. "Television: Escape or Encounter?" *JUFPA* 18 (No. 3, 1966) 22–24. Response to Bluem: TV, being primarily a sales medium, is currently most suitable for entertainment; yet documentary may be an esthetic rather than merely persuasive experience.

Sughrue, John F. "What's a Documentary?" *Action* 1 (No. 1, Sep–Oct 66) 6–7. Problems of making documentaries in foreign countries.

Sarton, Edgar. "The Documentary as Actuality, as Poetry, as Fake." *Take One* 1 (No. 3, 1967) 17–18. Impossibility of objectivity in any documentary.

Houston, Penelope. "The Nature of the Evidence." *S&S* 36 (Spring 67) 88–92. Reflections on the trustworthiness of compilation film documentaries.

Willis, Jack. "TV and the Social Documentary." *F Lib Q* 1 (No. 1, Winter 67–68) 50–54. Network documentaries are seldom done in human terms.

Russell, Robert. "The Next Medium: Superdoc." *Take One* 2 (No. 2, 1968) 10–11. A humorous attempt to predict the need for, and coming of, long documentaries.

Routt, William D. "One Man's Truth . . . Another Man's Poison." *FQ* 21 (No. 3,

Spring 68) 25–31. In three films—Robson's *Low Water,* Varda's *Elsa,* and Guillemot's *Dialectique*—questions are raised as to the nature of documentary.

Barron, Arthur. "Towards New Goals in Documentary." *F Lib Q* 2 (No. 1, Winter 68–69) 19–23. "I'd like a little less information and a lot more feeling."

Barron, Arthur. "Ken Edwards Memorial Address." *JUFA* 21 (No. 3, 1969) 77–80. Academic film teachers and producers focus on "reportage and instruction" rather than on the possibilities of film for "human revelation."

Dowd, Nancy Ellen. "Popular Conventions." *FQ* 22 (No. 3, Spring 69). *See 3a(2)*.

Graham, John. "How Far Can You Go: A Conversation with Fred Wiseman." *Contempora* 1 (No. 4, Oct–Nov 70) 30–33. Problems of the documentary.

8c(2). HISTORY OF DOCUMENTARY FILM

[*See 5, Biography: Georges Franju, Joris Ivens, Allan King, Jean Rouch, Walter Ruttmann, Dziga Vertov.*]

Buchanan, D. W. "Propaganda in Your Eye." *Canad Forum* 16 (Oct 36) 18. Social documentaries in Europe and U.S.

Rotha, Paul. "Making Facts Dramatic." *Scholastic* 31 (15 Jan 38) 25s–26s+. The "struggle for realism"—the documentary, with roots as far back as Lumière.

Rotha, Paul. "Films of Fact and Fiction." *Th Arts* 22 (Mar 38) 186–197. A general, worldwide survey of the documentary film, from *March of Time* to Pabst's *Kameradschaft*.

Griffith, Richard. "Films at the Fair." *Films* 1 (No. 1, Nov 39) 61–75. Critical survey of public-relations and documentary films shown at New York World's Fair of 1939, including *The City,* De Mille's *Land of Liberty,* Joseph Losey's *Pete Roleum and His Cousins,* and British films.

Rosenheimer, Arthur. "Documentary Film as a Living Art." *Design* 41 (Mar 40) 22. Comments on the genesis of documentary film as art as based on Flaherty's *Nanook of the North* and on Russian documentaries of the "epic cycle," such as *Potemkin*.

Strauss, Theodore. "Documentaries at the Crossroads." *Th Arts* 25 (Sep 41) 683–689.

Kline, Herbert. "Films Without Make-Believe." *Mag of Art* 35 (Feb 42) 58–63+. The author describes his work as a documentary-film maker.

Farber, Manny. "Wartime Documentaries." *New Rep* 108 (15 Feb 43) 211. Praises Stuart Legg's *World in Action* series for the

National Film Board of Canada; OWI films are "seldom spontaneous."

Hartung, Philip T. "Stay for the Shorts." *Commonweal* 37 (5 Mar 43) 496–497. Collective review of documentary shorts from OWI, *March of Time, World in Action, This Is America.*

"Partisans in Action: People's Avengers." *Newswk* 22 (30 Aug 43) 80+. Sixteen Russian cameramen were sent behind German lines and captured what must be called the ultimate in *cinéma vérité.*

Mayer, Arthur, and Richard Griffith. "Shape of Films to Come." *Th Arts* 29 (Nov 45) 647–649. How the war changed some concepts of the documentary and what the peacetime results in film making might be.

Barry, I. "Documentary Film: Prospect and Retrospect." *NY Mus of Mod Art Bul* 13 (Dec 45) 2–5.

"Film Foundation." *Museum News* 23 (15 Dec 45) 3. Information on International Film Associates and their promotion of documentary films.

Barry, Iris. "Challenge of the Documentary Film." *NYTM* (6 Jan 46) 16–17+. The Museum of Modern Art's review *Documentary: 1922–1945* spurs this look at types of documentary and their wartime applications.

"Documentary Film." *Social Service Rev* 20 (June 46) 263–267. Value of the documentary; review of series shown at Museum of Modern Art in New York.

Goodman, E., and J. Lyford. "These Movies Ring True." *New Rep* 118 (24 May 48) 18–20. Documentary-film makers face problems of sponsorship and distribution, but they do not have to worry about huge costs and box-office appeal.

Gerrard, John. "Ireland and the Documentary." *S&S* 17 (No. 68, Winter 48–49) 164–165.

Gerrard, John. "Irish Documentaries." *S&S* 18 (Spring 49) 34–36. Early history.

Katz, Robert, and Nancy Katz. "Documentary in Transition, Part II: The International Scene and the American Documentary." *Hwd Q* 4 (No. 1, Fall 49) 51–64. France, Italy, Canada, Great Britain, and other countries; the UN Film Board; many problems preventing production in U.S.

Starr, Cecile. "Looking Forward." *SRL* 33 (14 Jan 50) 37. Review of achievements in documentary production in 1949.

Knight, Arthur. "Ideas on Film." *SRL* 34 (17 Feb 51) 40–42. Documentary as major element in ferment of European film activity; U.S. Marshall Plan films.

Guitar, Mary A. "Facts on Films." *Nation* 172 (5 May 51) 429. UN documentaries.

Wald, Malvin. "1950's Best Short Documentaries." *FIR* 2 (June–July 51) 11–14. *Why Korea?* and *The Titan* won awards.

Broughton, James. "Ideas on Film." *SRL* 34 (13 Oct 51) 60–62. The author's impression of the Edinburgh Documentary Festival.

Wald, Malvin. "1952's Short Documentaries." *FIR* 4 (Apr 53) 168–170. Nominations for the 1952 Academy Award.

Smith, Janet Adam. "Filming Everest." *S&S* 23 (Jan–Mar 54) 138–139. A brief history of some earlier mountain-conquest pictures such as *Annapurna* and a review of *The Conquest of Everest,* filmed with the Hillary expedition by Tom Stobart and George Lowe.

Wald, Malvin. "1953's Short Documentaries." *FIR* 5 (Apr 54) 82–83.

Starr, Cecile. "Ideas on Film: Appraising the Prizes." *Sat Rev* 37 (19 June 54) 36–37. Festivals for documentary films at home and abroad; many titles discussed.

Wald, Malvin. "1954's Short Documentaries." *FIR* 6 (May 55) 230–231+. Critical review of some of the twenty-five films nominated for the 1954 Academy Award.

Wald, Malvin. "1955's Short Documentaries." *FIR* 7 (Apr 56) 152–156. Those submitted for Academy Award nomination.

Tanner, Alain. "Recording Africa." *S&S* 26 (Summer 56) 41–44. Three serious films which portray Africa, *Bororo, Les Fils de l'eau,* and *Les Maîtres fous,* the last two by Jean Rouch.

Gerstlé, Ralph. "Non-Theatrical Movies." *FIR* 7 (Aug–Sep 56) 334–335+. Critical reviews of ten documentaries.

Goretta, Claude. "Aspects of French Documentary." *S&S* 26 (Winter 56–57) 156–158+. Political and social criticism is difficult in France because of censorship; Georges Franju, who directed *Le Sang des bêtes* and *Hôtel des Invalides;* Rouquier's *Farrebique;* Alain Resnais, who directed *Van Gogh* and *Guernica.*

Gay, Ken. "Life's Joys and Horrors." *F&F* 3 (No. 6, Mar 57) 33. Review of French documentary series shown at National Film Theatre.

Wald, Malvin. "1956's Short Documentaries." *FIR* 8 (Apr 57) 167–170. Review of the five films nominated for the best short documentary of 1956.

Wald, Malvin. "1957's Short Documentaries." *FIR* 9 (Apr 58) 171–174. Those nominated for the Academy Award.

Vaughan, Dai. "Pre-History of Documentary." *F&F* 4 (No. 8, May 58) 8+. Documentaries in early 1900s.

Moore, David. "Short and Long." *Film* (No. 24, Mar–Apr 60) 25–28. Brief overview of recent documentaries of importance.

Wilenski, Stewart. "New Documentary Goal: The Revealed Situation." *F Com* 1 (No. 2, Summer 62) 63–66. Film maker comments on his ABC-TV *Close-Up* documentary on

Russian education, then sketches brief history of documentary film.

Knight, Arthur. "The Decline of Documentary." *Sat Rev* 46 (30 Mar 63) 35. Report on screening of the five contenders for Oscars.

Barnouw, Eric. "Films of Social Comment." *F Com* 2 (No. 1, Winter 64) 16–17. Brief statement on TV documentaries.

Sipherd, Ray. "The Long Courtship: Films of Social Inquiry for Television." *F Com* 2 (No. 1, Winter 64) 17–19. Brief statement on network documentaries.

Leiser, Erwin. "Notes on the Documentary Film Week in Mannheim." *F Com* 3 (No. 1, Winter 65) 50–51.

Davies, Brenda. "Pop Documentary." *S&S* 35 (Spring 66) 71. Objection offered to methods of Belgian-published poll of critics with "top twelve" documentaries (only two since 1929).

"Propaganda Films About the War in Vietnam." *F Com* 4 (No. 1, Fall 66). See *7b(5)*.

8c(2a). Great Britain

[*See also 4e(1).*

[*See 5, Biography: John Grierson, Humphrey Jennings, Paul Rotha.*]

Grierson, John. "The E. M. B. Film Unit." *CQ* 1 (No. 4, Summer 33) 203–208. Development of Grierson's group at government's Empire Marketing Board.

Furse, Sir William. "The Imperial Institute." *S&S* 2 (No. 7, Autumn 33) 78–79. A discussion of its history and goals and the contribution of the Empire Marketing Board.

Woolfe, H. Bruce. "Commercial Documentary." *CQ* 2 (No. 2, Winter 33–34) 96–100. Instances of distributor's opposition, followed by successful theatre showings; the author's new program, Gaumont-British Instructional.

Read, Herbert. "Experiments in Counterpoint." *CQ* 3 (No. 1, Autumn 34). See *2g*.

Alexander, Donald. "Documentary Films." *New S&N* 14 (14 Aug 37) 246–247. Difficulties of the documentary movement in England.

Tallents, Stephen. "British Documentary Films." *Spectator* 159 (19 Nov 37) 893–894. Brief history of the formation and operation of British documentary-film units; wide praise for British documentaries cannot aid feature films.

Grierson, John. "Projection of Scotland." *Spectator* 160 (6 May 38) 828+. Article covers cinema, theatre, broadcasting, etc.; cinema section discusses the beginning of campaign for production of Scottish films, with brief history and background comments on the movements.

Greene, Graham. "New Documentaries by the GPO Films Unit." *Spectator* 162 (26 May 39) 901. Remarks on Cavalcanti's *Men in Danger, Health of a Nation,* and Jennings' *Spare Time.*

Sauvage, Leo. "The Army Cinema Goes to War." *S&S* 8 (No. 32, Winter 39–40) 126–127. The sudden need for films to be shown to soldiers.

Bell, Oliver. "Wartime Uses of the Film; With Discussion." *Royal Soc of Arts J* 88 (5 Apr 40) 467–481. The possibility of using films to explain political and wartime situations to the common man.

Rotha, Paul. "British Documentary Films: 1930–1940." *Art and Industry* 28 (May 40) 134–139.

Holmes, Winifred. "Bill Smith and Mrs. Brown Like the Latest Documentaries." *S&S* 9 (No. 33, Spring 40) 10–11. A celebration of the virtues of the British documentary.

"Film at War." *New S&N* 20 (7 Sep 40). See *7b(5)*.

Devine, John. "Ministry of Information, Films Division." *Pub Opin Q* 4 (Dec 40) 684–685. Subcommittee report of British House of Commons recommending that the Ministry of Information abandon all film production.

Rotha, Paul. "Statesmanship in Celluloid." *New S&N* 21 (22 Mar 41) 208. Concern of the documentary group over the character of some of the British films designed for foreign dispatch. Reply (29 Mar) 325.

Devine, John. "British Wartime Shorts." *Pub Opin Q* 5 (June 41) 306–307.

Anstey, Edgar. "Outside the Theatres." *Spectator* 166 (13 June 41) 630. Report on Ministry of Information's distribution of public-information films through sixty-five mobile projection units.

Wright, Basil. "Realist Review." *S&S* 10 (No. 38, Summer 41) 20–21. The progress of the documentary film in Britain.

Fraser, G. Lovat. "New Romanticism." *Studio* 122 (Oct 41) 109–111. Romanticism in the films made for the Ministry of Information.

Kline, H. "Films Without Make-Believe." *Mag of Art* 35 (Feb 42) 58–63+. Interview with a documentary-film maker working in England during World War II.

Whitebait, William. "50 Below Zero." *New S&N* 23 (14 Feb 42) 108. Brief remarks on the making of *Behind the Line of the Enemy* and the Crown Film Unit's *Wavell's 30,000.*

Waley, H. D. "British Documentaries and the War Effort." *Pub Opin Q* 6 (Dec 42) 604–609. Advantages of film as propaganda; statistics on Ministry of Information's Central Film Library.

Williams, J. R. "Britain Makes the Movie a Weapon of War." *Am Federationist* 50 (May 43) 30–31. Films to glorify the war effort and inspire the common man.

"Documentaries Grow Up." *Time* 42 (13 Sep 43) 94–95. Some recent documentaries, particularly British, demonstrate the quality potential of this form.

Wright, Basil C. "New Vistas for the Film in Britain: Development of the Documentaries." *Pub Opin Q* 7 (No. 4, 1944) 544–550. British documentary film may contribute to UN effort to establish international understanding.

Tallents, Stephen. "Documentary Films; With Discussion." *Royal Soc of Arts J* 95 (20 Dec 46) 68–85. A history of the Empire Marketing Board, with remarks on the present state of the documentary.

Grierson, John. "The Film in British Colonial Development." *S&S* 17 (No. 65, Spring 48) 2–4.

Mathieson, Muir. "Music for Crown." *Hwd Q* 3 (No. 3, Spring 48). *See 2g(2).*

Schemke, Irmgard. "Documentary To-Day." *Sequence* (No. 3, Spring 48) 12–14. The British government's policies have become harmful to the documentary film.

Gardner, B. Bellamy. "Television Documentaries." *S&S* 18 (No. 68, Winter 48–49) 171–172. Why they are so few and so bad.

MacKenzie, N. "This Modern Age." *New S&N* 39 (29 Apr 50) 480–481. Documentary-film production hard-hit by financial crisis as short films rarely pay for costs. Reply (13 May) 546.

Grierson, John. "Public Relations." *S&S* 19 (July 50) 201–204. The British documentary-film units still surpass in the articulation of humanitarian progress, but there are few adventures into the life of people or communities and there is a lack of a sense of an event or forces in the making.

Wright, Basil, and Brian Smith. "Documentary: The Sulky Fire." *S&S* 21 (Jan–Mar 52) 128–129+. Wright says the British documentary has lost its life and originality, smothered by sponsors; Smith replies that sponsors during the time of the great documentaries were easy to please and wanted to be associated with the prestige concepts of the common man.

Anstey, Edgar, William Alwyn, Ian Dalrymple, James Beveridge, and Denis Forman. "The Living Story." *S&S* 21 (Apr–June 52) 176–179. Epitaphs for the Crown Film Unit and British government documentary.

Legg, Stuart. "The Sulky Fire." *S&S* 22 (July–Sep 52) 38+. A second article on the predicament of documentary-film making in England; Legg feels that the documentary has lost its strength because most of the issues it stood for have come to pass, and no new cause of equal vigor has been brought forward.

Price, Peter. "The Sulky Fire: The Light that Failed." *S&S* 22 (Jan–Mar 53) 139. Third article about the crisis in the British documentary film; Price feels that the older

leaders of the documentary school have become conservative and are unwilling to stop trying to educate for awhile and learn to understand.

Rotha, Paul. "Documentary at the B.B.C." *Film* (No. 3, Feb 55) 12–15. An outline of recent work in the field of television film.

Taylor, Brian. "Projecting Britain." *F&F* 1 (No. 8, May 55) 12. A review of the British documentary-film movement on the twenty-fifth anniversary of the first public screening of Grierson's *The Drifters.*

"Experiment." *S&S* 25 (Winter 55–56) 116. BFI-sponsored films, including *Mama Don't Allow,* to be shown.

Lambert, Gavin. "Free Cinema." *S&S* 25 (Spring 56) 173–177. The short British films *Together* (Lorenzo Mazzetti), *O Dreamland* (Lindsay Anderson), and *Mama Don't Allow* (Karel Reisz and Tony Richardson) have an "attitude in common," that of individual recognition versus urban mechanization and conformism, and a belief in the dignity and importance of the individual and in the recognition of the "significance of the everyday."

Gay, Ken. "This Way Back to War-Time Unity." *F&F* 2 (No. 6, Mar 56) 19. Current state of documentary production in England.

Rotha, Paul. "Presenting the World to the World." *F&F* 2 (No. 7, Apr 56) 8+. Reflections on the "World" social documentary series the author has been associated with off and on since 1942.

"Documentary Merger." *S&S* 26 (Autumn 56) 62. Note on companies under Ken Cameron and Basil Wright.

Robinson, David. "Looking for Documentary: The Background to Production." *S&S* 27 (Summer 57) 6–11. The state of the documentary in Great Britain: much sponsored film making but fewer imaginative demands.

Berger, John. "Look at Britain." *S&S* 27 (Summer 57) 12–14. English documentary, its present setting and its future possibilities; comments on Lindsay Anderson's *Every Day Except Christmas* and the Goretta-Tanner film *Nice Time.*

Robinson, David. "Looking for Documentary: The Ones That Got Away." *S&S* 27 (Autumn 57) 70–75. The expository film is useful, but documentaries about human relationships are rare; television is doing good work.

Hall, John, and Derrick Knight. "Look at Britain." *Film* (No. 13, Sep–Oct 57) 10–16. Two authors agree on the decline of British documentary but differ on whether or not "free cinema" offers any real new promise.

Houston, Penelope. "Captive or Free." *S&S* 27 (Winter 57–58) 116–120. A comparative discussion of film documentaries (free) and television documentaries (captive); television uses interviews, hastily shot footage which has a kind of realism that is unique.

Jacobs, Lewis. "Free Cinema I." *F Cult* 4 (No. 17, 1958) 9–11. Analysis of the British "free cinema" films—*Nice Time, Momma Don't Allow, Together, O Dreamland,* and *Every Day Except Christmas.*

Arnheim, Rudolf. "Free Cinema II." *F Cult* 4 (No. 17, 1958) 11. Comparisons of these British documentaries with various periods in art history.

Hopkinson, Peter. "Facts Out of Film." *F&F* 4 (No. 4, Jan 58) 13+. The decline of British documentaries.

McCarthy, Matt. "Free Cinema—in Chains." *F&F* 5 (No. 5, Feb 59) 10+. "Free cinema" must pay more attention to film techniques than political statements.

Gay, Ken. "Making Them Without Style." *F&F* 7 (No. 2, Nov 60) 39+. Documentary films in contemporary Britain.

"Facing the Facts." *F&F* 6 (No. 8, May 60) 11+. Questions on the future of British documentary movement asked of prominent documentarians.

Crick, Philip. "Michael Grigsby and Unit Five Seven." *Film* (No. 38, Winter 63) 8–9. One independent production unit in Great Britain is trying to make documentaries which comment on the current social scene.

Tallents, Stephen. "The Birth of British Documentary." *JUFA* 20 (No. 1, 1968) 15–21; (No. 2, 1968) 27–32; (No. 3, 1968) 61–66. Former head of Empire Marketing Board and of GPO information program recounts early film work supervised by John Grierson.

8c(2b). United States

[*See 5, Biography: Arthur Barron, Julian Bryan, Emile DeAntonio, Robert Flaherty, Richard Leacock, Pare Lorentz, Kent Mackenzie, Albert and David Maysles, Lionel Rogosin, Willard Van Dyke, Frederick Wiseman, David Wolper.*]

Belitt, B. "Camera Reconnoiters." *Nation* 145 (20 Nov 37) 557–558. The efforts of Paul Strand to make his documentaries outside of Hollywood through Frontier Films.

Goodman, Ezra. "The American Documentary." *S&S* 7 (No. 27, Autumn 38) 124.

Winge, John H. "In Defence of Liberty." *S&S* 8 (No. 29, Spring 39) 23–26. Some recent American documentaries reveal a new move toward realism.

Miller, J. "Unreeling History." *Current Hist* 50 (May 39) 39–42. The rise of the documentary.

Bryan, Julien. "Adventures of a Roving Cameraman." *Pop Mech* 71 (June 39) 840–843+; 72 (July 39) 72–75+. Story of a documentary-film maker who films the world over.

Beiswanger, G. "Camera Over the U.S.A." *Th Arts* 28 (Dec 39) 886–894. American documentary-film history, with emphasis on the 1939 World's Fair and recent efforts by the Association of Documentary Film Producers and United States Film Service.

Crowther, Bosley. "Realistic Stepchild of the Movies." *NYTM* (25 Aug 40) 12–13. A short history of the documentary, how one is filmed, and Hollywood's reaction; many recent ones cited.

Rosenheimer, Arthur, Jr. "American Documentary Films to the Fore." *Design* 42 (Nov 40) 20+. Discussion of shift in attention from British documentaries to American documentaries as seen in Pare Lorentz' films and others shown at the World's Fair.

"Fact-Film Futures." *Newswk* 19 (9 Feb 42) 66. Wartime demand for documentary film technicians.

Agee, James. "News Reels and War-Record Films." *Nation* 158 (24 June 44) 743. American war documentaries—preferable to fiction films about the war, but still lugubrious attempts at effective cinema.

Agee, James. "Seeing Terrible Records of War." *Nation* 160 (24 Mar 45) 392. Analysis of the Fox and Paramount versions of documentary footage from the battle of Iwo Jima.

Isaacs, Hermine R. "War and Love." *Th Arts* 29 (May 45) 273–274+. Why the wartime documentary fails to hold an audience.

"Books into Films." *Publishers Weekly* 147 (30 June 45) 2526. The influence of the documentary on the so-called entertainment film.

Grierson, John. "America's Most Vital Medium: The Documentary Film." *Lib J* 71 (1 May 46) 630–634.

Griffith, Richard. "Post-War American Documentaries." *Penguin F Rev* 8 (Jan 49) 92–102. A letdown after the wartime experience.

Katz, Robert, and Nancy Katz. "Documentary in Transition, Part I: The United States." *Hwd Q* 3 (No. 4, Summer 48–Summer 49) 425–433. Wartime films for the services; the OWI Overseas Branch; prewar government films; postwar activity in and out of government.

Hatch, Robert. "The New Realism." *New Rep* 118 (8 Mar 48) 27–28. The growth of the "documentary approach" to film making through World War II.

Nathan, Paul S. "Books into Films." *Publishers Weekly* 157 (18 Feb 50) 1019. Flaherty Films Inc.'s plan to film American states series; other books to be filmed.

Starr, Cecile. "American Scene." *Sat Rev* 37 (9 Jan 54) 44–46. The Museum's retrospective of American documentaries attempts to answer the question: To what extent has the documentary lived up to its potential since World War II?

Miller, Don. "The Visual Chronicle." *FIR* 8 (Dec 57). *See 2f.*

"Young King David." *Newswk* 64 (23 Nov 64) 111–112. David Wolper, producer of film documentaries.

Sloan, William J. "The Documentary Film and the Negro: The Evolution of the Integration Film." *J Soc Cin* 5 (1965) 66–69. Brief commentary on eighteen films from 1940 to 1964, including nontheatrical and TV films.

Braudy, Leo. "Newsreel: A Report." *FQ* 22 (No. 2, Winter 68–69). *See 3a(6).*

Fruchter, Norm, Robert Kramer, Marilyn Busk, and Karen Ross. "Newsreel." *FQ* 22 (No. 2, Winter 68–69). *See 3a(6).*

Rodakiewicz, Henwar. "Documentary: A Personal Retrospect." *F Lib Q* 2 (No. 3, Summer 69) 33–37. Reminiscences by a documentary-film maker about his films of the last thirty years.

8c(3). CINÉMA VÉRITÉ

Bachmann, Gideon. "The Frontiers of Realist Cinema: The Work of Ricky Leacock." *F Cult* (Nos. 22–23, 1961) 12–23. From a radio interview with Richard Leacock, Don Alan Pennebaker, and Robert Drew conducted by Gideon Bachmann; discussion of *Primary* and problems of *cinéma vérité.*

Callenbach, Ernest. "Going Out to the Subject: II." *FQ* 14 (No. 3, Spring 61) 38–40. Three TV films made by Richard Leacock and produced by Robert Drew for Time, Inc.: *Yanki No, Primary,* and *On the Pole.*

Shivas, Mark, *et al.* "Cinéma-Vérité." *Movie* (No. 8, Apr 63) 12–26. Comments on methods and goals; interviews with Richard Leacock, the Maysles brothers, William Klein, Jean Rouch, and Jacques Rozier.

Marcorelles, Louis. "Nothing But the Truth." *S&S* 32 (Summer 63) 114–117. A three-day conference in Lyons devoted to *cinéma vérité;* Richard Leacock criticizes Jean Rouch for trying to force interpretations; the author likes Albert and David Maysles' *Showman* and Michel Brault's *Pour la suite du monde.*

Lamont, Austin. "Cinéma Vérité at the Ninth Flaherty Seminar." *F Com* 1 (No. 6, Fall 63) 12–13.

Knight, Arthur. "Flip Side: *Cinéma Vérité.*" *Sat Rev* 46 (28 Dec 63) 20. Jean Rouch's films offer models for American documentary makers.

Cohen, Art, and Terry Hickey. "Al Maysles and *The Showman.*" *JUFPA* 16 (No. 2, 1964) 7–9+. Maysles explains his approach to film making (no preconceived opinions foisted on the material) and his technical procedures; from conversations at the Flaherty Seminar in 1963.

Booker, Christopher. "Back to Nature." *Spectator* 212 (20 Mar 64) 379. The development and nature of *cinéma vérité.*

Crawford, Stanley. "From Visionary Gleams to *Cinéma-Vérité.*" *Film* (No. 40, Summer 64) 34–38. How the documentaries of the 1940s and 1950s led to *cinéma vérité.*

Young, Colin. "Cinema of Common Sense." *FQ* 17 (No. 4, Summer 64) 26–29. The *cinéma vérité* of Drew and Leacock, Jean Rouch, Jean Herman, the Canadians; *On the Pole, Nehru, Crisis,* and others compared.

Graham, Peter. "Cinéma-Vérité in France." *FQ* 17 (No. 4, Summer 64) 30–36. Jean Rouch, Mario Ruspoli, Chris Marker in France; Drew, Leacock, and the Maysles brothers in America; none is "objective"; each has his own vision and makes his own choices with the camera and in the cutting room; some of Drew's work is more subject to uncontrollable events; Marker is passionate and personal.

Breitrose, Henry. "On the Search for the Real Nitty-Gritty: Problems and Possibilities of *Cinéma-Vérité.*" *FQ* 17 (No. 4, Summer 64) 36–40. *Nehru, On the Pole, David, Mooney vs. Fowle* reported; "living camera" subjects make good films if they have within them the prospect of a dramatic structure.

Lipscomb, James C. "Cinéma Vérité." *FQ* 18 (No. 2, Winter 64–65) 62–63. In a letter, one of the group that worked under Robert Drew responds to articles in the Summer 1964 issue; "talk about objectivity is beside the point," but fairness and "revealing a character through action" are both worth seeking.

Jaffe, Patricia. "Editing *Cinéma Vérité.*" *F Com* 3 (No. 3, Summer 65) 43–47. Some proposed principles based on personal experience of the author as editor for Drew, Leacock, and others; she is critical of Drew's tendency to put together the most exciting moments instead of leaving in the natural rhythms of life, as Maysles does.

Schroeder, Barbet. "Cinéma Vérité." *TDR* 11 (Fall 66) 130–132. Use of the actor in movies without stories.

Jersey, William. "Some Observations on *Cinéma Vérité.*" *Motive* 27 (No. 2, Nov 66) 11–12. "Setting things up" is not being true to the event or to the inner reaction of people, but on the other hand, it is not wrong to bring people "together in relationships which are catalytic."

"In Search of Realism—Symposium." *Pop Photog* 60 (Jan 67) 76–78. Staff members of magazine discuss recording versus re-creation with Al and David Maysles.

Dawson, Jan. "Warrendale." *S&S* 37 (Winter 67–68) 44–46. Some comments about the individual's right to privacy in *cinéma vérité* reportage, prompted by Allan King's film about emotionally disturbed children; should the camera be a mirror without explanation?

Zimmerman, Paul D. "Shooting It Like It Is." *Newswk* 73 (17 Mar 69) 134–135. New documentarians Albert and David Maysles, Frederick Wiseman, and D. A. Pennebaker introduced.

"Leacock-Pennebaker: The M-G-M of the Underground?" *Show* (Jan 70) 34–37+. Discussion of the filming of *Monterey Pop* and *Primary* and a brief attempt to define "direct cinema."

8c(4). CASE STUDIES

Hill, Jerome. "Making a Documentary—**Albert Schweitzer**." *F Cult* 3 (No. 12, 1957) 10–12.

Nicolson, Harold. "**Battle of Britain**, Film Version and Real Version." *Spectator* 171 (8 Oct 43) 334. Comparison of personal experiences of Nicolson and the filmic portrayal of *The Battle of Britain*.

Milburn, W. S. "Wild Stallions Make a Western!" *Am Photog* 43 (Dec 49) 766–769. Shooting of the two-reel documentary **The Battle of the Wild Stallions**.

Cowie, Peter. "Berlin." *F&F* 7 (No. 11, Aug 61) 10–12+. Analysis of the 1927 Ruttman film.

Kolaja, Jiri, and Arnold W. Foster. "**Berlin, the Symphony of a City** as a Theme of Visual Rhythm." *J Aesthetics and Art Criticism* 23 (No. 3, Spring 65) 353–358.

Ivens, Joris. "**Borinage**—A Documentary Experience." *F Cult* 2 (No. 7, 1956) 6–11. A personal account of the making of *Borinage* by the Dutch film maker.

Lardner, Ring, Jr. Maurice Rapf, John Hubley, and Phil Eastman. "**Brotherhood of Man**: A Script." *Hwd Q* 1 (July 46). *See 2d(4)*.

"**Brotherhood of Man**." *Arts & Arch* 63 (Dec 46). *See 2d(4)*.

Grierson, John. "The Symphonic Film." *CQ* 2 (No. 3, Spring 34) 155–160. Short piece in series on documentary; Basil Wright's **Cargo from Jamaica**.

"Compulsion." New Yorker 36 (18 June 60) 30–31. A chat with Lionel Rogosin, director of **Come Back, Africa**.

Williams, Elmo. "Chousing the Cowboy." *FIR* 5 (Aug–Sep 54) 347–349+. A case study of the feature documentary **The Cowboy**, made independently by the author and his wife.

Rotha, Paul. "Making **Contact**." *CQ* 1 (No. 3, Spring 33) 156–159. Imperial Airways documentary film called *Contact*.

Cameron, Ian. "Chris Marker: **Cuba, Si!** Censor, No!" *Movie* (No. 3, Oct 62) 14–21. A reprint of the script for *Cuba, Si!* and comments on Marker's work, especially the political aspects.

Bishop, Terry. "Film-Making in Udi." *Spectator* 182 (1 Apr 49) 443. The British Crown Film Unit in Nigeria shooting a film on education, **Daybreak in Udi**.

Gardner, Robert. "Chronicles of the Human Experience: **Dead Birds**." *F Lib Q* 2 (No. 4, Fall 69) 25–34. The film maker writes about the making of his film on a tribe in New Guinea.

Maddow, Ben. "**Death and Mathematics**: A Film on the Meaning of Science." *Hwd Q* 1 (No. 2, Jan 46). *See 2d(4)*.

Cameron, Evan. "An Analysis of **A Diary for Timothy**." *Cinema Studies* (Bridgewater, Mass.) (No. 2, Spring 67) 1–68. Detailed analysis of the British documentary film by Humphrey Jennings.

Grierson, John. "Making a Film of the Sea." *World Today* 55 (Mar 30) 350–356. Putting the drama of herring fishing on the screen in *Drifters*.

"**Every Seventh Child**." *F Com* 4 (No. 4, Summer 68) 62–79. Gordon Hitchens presides over panel at New York Film Festival on documentary about parochial schools shown on National Educational Television and made by Jack Willis, who was present.

Wald, Malvin. "Profile of a Filmmaker." *JUFPA* 16 (No. 2, 1964) 21–22+. Brief biographical sketch of USC film graduate Kent MacKenzie and his documentary **The Exiles**.

Whitebait, William. "Film and Reality." *New S&N* 23 (28 Feb 42) 140–141. Cavalcanti's **Film and Reality** hailed as one of the best pieces of film criticism (on film).

Strick, Philip. "**Fires Were Started**." *F&F* 7 (No. 8, May 61) 14–16+. Humphrey Jennings' 1942 documentary.

Duncan, Catharine. "**The First Years**." *S&S* 19 (Mar 50) 37–39. Report on Joris Ivens making a film about Poland, Czechoslovakia, and Bulgaria since the war.

Greaves, William. "Log: **In the Company of Men**." *F Lib Q* 3 (No. 1, Winter 69–70) 29–34. Record of the making of this film about foremen and the hard-core unemployed, written by its director.

Rosenthal, Alan. "Diary of a TV Documentary." *Screen* 11 (No. 1, Feb 70) 87–94. **It Happened to Me**, about safe driving in Israel.

Smith, Desmond. "On Location in Rostov: Filming the New Revolution." *Nation* 204 (27 Feb 67). *See 2k(4)*. About **Ivan Ivanovich**.

Herring, Robert. "**Jamaica Problem**." *Life & Letters Today* 57 (Apr 48) 81–82. *Jamaica Problem* as an honest film document when compared to Lowell Thomas' *Memories of Columbus*.

Tilton, Roger, *et al.* "**Jazz Dance**: Analysis of a Documentary." *F Cult* 1 (No. 1, 1955) 39–44. Analysis of Roger Tilton's *Jazz Dance* in three parts—the director's statement, the technical problems discussed by the cameraman and editor, and a critical evaluation of the film by John Gilchrist.

Peavy, Charles D. "Cinema from the Slums." *Cinéaste* 3 (No. 2, Fall 69) 11–12+. The 12th and Oxford Film-Makers Corporation in Philadelphia; the work of the Brooks Foundation; the film **The Jungle.**

Sammis, Edward. "Flaherty at Abbeville." *S&S* 21 (Oct–Dec 51) 68–70. On location for **Louisiana Story.**

Sadoul, Georges. "A Flaherty Mystery." *CdC in Eng* (No. 11, Sep 67) 46–51. The French critic comments on the studies for **Louisiana Story** as presented by Frances Flaherty and on Robert Flaherty's unique personality.

"March to Aldermaston." *Film* (No. 18, Nov–Dec 58) 18–20. An account of the attempt to film the anti-bomb campaign march from Trafalgar Square to Aldermaston.

Rosenthal, Alan. "The Fiction Documentary." *FQ* 23 (No. 4, Summer 70) 9–33. Interviews with Allan King, Canadian producer-director, and with the cameraman and editor of **A Married Couple,** which records daily life but is edited to show dramatic conflict.

Steele, Robert. "Meet Marlon Brando." *F Her* 2 (No. 1, Fall 66) 2–5. A long review of the Maysles brothers' film.

Nicholson, Irene. "Memoirs of a Mexican." *S&S* 23 (July–Sep 53) 13–15. Some comments on a remarkable historic film document, **Memorias de un mexicano,** made by Salvador Toscano between 1910 and 1924; the film maker's daughter, Señora Toscano, edited her father's footage; her finished film, previewed in Mexico City in 1950, met with critical and public success.

Marcorelles, Louis. "Nuit et brouillard." *S&S* 25 (Spring 56) 172. Note on Resnais and his new short documentary about concentration camps, *Night and Fog.*

"Moral Breach." *Time* 54 (31 Oct 49) 76. **On Polish Land,** documentary banned in Maryland as "Communist propaganda."

Sufrin, Mark. "Filming a Skid Row." *S&S* 25 (Winter 55–56) 133–139. An account of the problems involved in filming **On the Bowery** in New York.

Leiser, Erwin. "Ordinary Fascism." *F Com* 5 (No. 1, Fall 68). See *4e(8b).*

Bazelon, David T. "Background to **Point of Order.**" *F Com* 2 (No. 1, Winter 64) 33–35. Editorial consultant on film about Joseph McCarthy briefly traces history that led up to the hearings; preceded by review by Edward Crawford, pp. 31–33.

DeAntonio, Emile. "The Point of View in **Point of Order.**" *F Com* 2 (No. 1, Winter 64) 35–36. Editorial director and coproducer of film about Joseph McCarthy lists his assumptions: "The *vérité,* as well as the prejudice, is Talbot's and mine."

Kane, Bruce, and Joel Reisner. "**The Queen.**" *Cinema* (Calif) 4 (No. 3, Fall 68) 2–5. Producer Si Litvinoff and director Frank Simon interviewed about their documentary on the "enclosed world" of female impersonators.

DeMoraes, Vinicius. "The Making of a Document: **The Quiet One.**" *Hwd Q* 4 (No. 4, Summer 50) 375–384. Brazilian vice-consul, poet, and film-magazine editor describes in detail what happens in the film about a delinquent Negro boy.

"**Republic of Childhood** Documentary Based on Children's Books." *Publishers Weekly* 160 (27 Oct 51) 1716–1717. Filming of Peter Elger's documentary in the New York Public Library.

Bunting, Caroline K. "Filming Young Readers for Globe-Circling Picture." *Lib J* 76 (15 Dec 51) 2105–2106+. Filming of **The Republic of Childhood,** about the Children's Room of the New York Public Library.

"The Narration of **The River.**" *F Com* 3 (No. 2, Spring 65). See *2d(4).*

Van Dyke, Willard. "Letters From **The River.**" *F Com* 3 (No. 2, Spring 65) 38–56. One of four cinematographers for U.S. government documentary wrote letters to his wife about the scenes he was shooting, the confidential talks he had with Pare Lorentz (including what happened with the photographers on *The Plow That Broke the Plains*), and the climactic flood of January 1937.

Rotha, Paul. "Roads Across Britain." *Arch Rev* 85 (Mar 39) 133–134. Documentary films' supply and demand; special reference to a film made under author's supervision, *Roads Across Britain.*

Lane, Mark, and Emile DeAntonio. "Rush to Judgment." *F Com* 4 (Nos. 1–2, Fall–Winter 67) 2–18. Dialogue about the making of this film, based on Lane's book, which questions the decision of the Warren Commission on the Kennedy assassination; extensive description of eyewitness accounts not used by the Commission.

Craddock, John. "**Salesman.**" *F Lib Q* (No. 3, Summer 69) 8–12. Critique of this film by the Maysles brothers.

Gregory, James. "A Documentary Gets the Hard Sell." *FIR* 7 (Nov 56) See *6d(3).* About **The Silent World.**

Wright, Basil. "Filming in Ceylon." *CQ* 2 (No. 4, Summer 34) 231–232. Brief report on material shot for the documentary **Song of Ceylon.**

"**Spain in Flames:** Film Censorship." *Nation* 144 (27 Mar 37). See *7c(1d).*

Earle, G. H. "**Spain in Flames:** Reply with Rejoinder." *Nation* 144 (10 Apr 37). See *7c(1d).*

MacLeish, Archibald. "The Last Train from

Madrid: MacLeish on Spain. *Cinema Arts* 1 (No. 3, Sep 37) 59. About **Spanish Earth.**

Turner, Ann. "Working Title—**Sunday Night: Venice.**" *Studio Inter* 157 (Aug 66) 82–83. Director describes making of a BBC documentary on the five British artists chosen to exhibit in the British pavilion at the Venice Biennale.

"**Target for To-Night:** Filming of an R.A.F. Bombing Raid." *Illus London News* 96 (2 Aug 41) 153. Illustrated with synopsis of this documentary film.

Schecter, Leona. "War II on Japanese Screens." *FIR* 8 (Mar 57). See *4f(1).* About **Thus Fought Japan.**

Bradlow, Paul. "Two, But Not of a Kind." *F Com* 5 (No. 3, Fall 69) 60–61. Psychiatrist compares two documentaries about mental illness, *Warrendale* and **Titicut Follies.**

"**World Première of Troublemakers.**" *New Yorker* 43 (10 Dec 66) 47–48. Movie about Newark Community Union Project.

Hoggart, Richard. "**We Are the Lambeth Boys.**"

S&S 28 (Nos. 3–4, Summer–Autumn 59) 164–165. Sociologist urges Karel Reisz, director of this "free cinema" documentary, to go beyond an idealizing kind of sympathy to an imaginative probing more like Chekhov.

"Nobody Talked." *Newswk* 59 (25 June 62) 42. Danish Henning Carlsen's secret documentary **A World of Strangers,** dealing with racial discrimination in South Africa.

Rotha, Paul, and Basil Wright. "A UNESCO Film." *S&S* 23 (July–Sep 53) 16–17. Report from Mexico and Thailand, respectively, by directors of a new documentary about social and economic reforms, **World Without End.**

Modern, Klara. "**Young Workers Film Their Own Life.**" *Close Up* 9 (No. 1, Mar 32) 53–54. Comments on a film of that title made by the Young Socialists' Union in Vienna.

Holmes, Winifred. "**Your Freedom Is at Stake!**" *S&S* 15 (No. 60, Winter 46–47) 117–120. Title of Danish documentary begun after the occupation, finished after the liberation.

8d. Avant-Garde Films

[*See also 2h, 6c(3).*]

[*See 5, Biography: Kenneth Anger, Bruce Baillie, Jordan Belson, Charles Boultenhouse, Stan Brakhage, Robert Breer, James Broughton, L. M. Kit Carson, Bruce Conner, Carmen D'Avino, Storm De Hirsch, Maya Deren, Robert Downey, Charles Eames, Viking Eggeling, Ed Emshwiller, Curtis Harrington, Ian Hugo, Dimitri Kirsanov, Peter Kubelka, George Kuchar, Mike Kuchar, Fernand Léger, Carl Linder, Len Lye, Willard Maas, Gregory Markopoulos, Jonas Mekas, Sidney Peterson, Man Ray, Ron Rice, Hans Richter, Harry Smith, Frank Stauffacher, Stan Vanderbeek, Andy Warhol, John Whitney.*]

Stenhouse, Charles E. "And Thus It Goes On." *Close Up* 7 (No. 6, Dec 30) 393–397. Experimental cinema in Europe.

Potamkin, Harry Alan. "That Old Saw on the Weather Gets a New Meaning: Photographing the Seasons." *Am Photog* 26 (May 32) 264–268. On "weather films" such as Ivens' *Rain.*

Moore, John C. "The Experimental Film and Its Limitations." *Close Up* 9 (No. 4, Dec 32) 281–284. With particular reference to Vertov's *Enthusiasm.*

Moholy-Nagy, L. "An Open Letter to the Film Industry and All Who Are Interested in the Good Film." *S&S* 3 (No. 10, Summer 34) 56–57. A manifesto for the experimental, independent, personal film.

"Expanding Cinema's Synchromy 2." *Lit Dig* 122 (8 Aug 36) 20. Mary Ellen Bute and

Theodore J. Namath showed abstract images to Wagner music in Radio City Music Hall; their company, Expanding Cinema, Inc.

McKay, H. C. "Abstract Films: Mechanism of Perception, Association of Ideas, Abstract Motion." *Am Photog* 32 (Nov 38) 817–820. Some psychological association concepts applied to the abstract film, particularly animation.

Weinberg, Herman G. "Forward Glance at the Abstract Film." *Design* 42 (Feb 41) 24. Discussion of limited audience for "abstract" films because of commercial distribution in America; includes comments on nine films shown at the Museum of Modern Art.

Bute, Mary Ellen. "Light, Form, Movement, Sound: Absolute Film." *Design* 42 (Apr 41) 25. Comments on the "absolute" film as an art combining the interrelation of light, form, movement, and sound; *Synchromy #9* cited as example.

Farber, Manny. "Up from Slavery." *New Rep* 110 (17 Apr 44) 532–533. Suggestions for the first Hollywood film Dadaist.

Leyda, Jay. "Exploration of New Film Techniques." *Arts & Arch* 62 (Dec 45) 38–39+. Experimental films of John and James Whitney.

Willis, Eli. "Abstract Film Explorations." *Th Arts* 31 (Feb 47) 52–53. Whitney brothers search for new forms and sound.

Jacobs, Lewis. "Experimental Cinema in America (Part 1)." *Hwd Q* 3 (No. 2, Winter 47–48) 111–124. From 1921 to 1941, the films and the film makers.

"Experiment 16." *Newswk* 31 (23 Feb 48) 89. Cinema 16 and its efforts to make avant-garde 16mm films.

Jacobs, Lewis. "Experimental Cinema in America (Part 2)." *Hwd Q* 3 (No. 3, Spring 48) 278–292. After World War II: the San Francisco group, the "agony-and-experience school," the nonobjectivists, the realists.

Morrison, George. "The French Avant-Garde." *Sequence* (No. 4, Summer 48). *See 4e(2a).*

Agee, James. "Cinema 16: Film Society." *Nation* 167 (3 July 48) 24–25. The birth of a new film society in New York devoted to showing the best of documentary, pedagogical, experimental, and sometimes censorable films.

Tyler, Parker. "Experimental Film: A New Growth." *Kenyon Rev* 11 (No. 1, 1949) 141–144. The programs of Cinema 16 and the films of Maya Deren and Hans Richter as attempts to purify cinematic art.

Richter, Hans. "Experiments with Celluloid." *Penguin F Rev* 9 (May 49) 108–120. In a reprinted chapter from Roger Manvell's anthology *Experiment in the Film* (Macmillan, 1951), the maker of many films in Germany and the U.S. recounts his early explorations with Viking Eggeling, his competition with Ruttmann, and the advertising jobs which often resulted in new filmic ideas.

Tyler, Parker. "Experimental Film: Layman's Guide to Its Understanding and Enjoyment." *Th Arts* 33 (July 49) 46–48.

Harrington, Curtis. "Personal Chronicle: The Making of an Experimental Film." *Hwd Q* 4 (No. 1, Fall 49) 42–50. How the author made his film called *Picnic* with $159.45.

Richter, Hans. "The Avant-Garde Film Seen from Within." *Hwd Q* 4 (No. 1, Fall 49) 34–41. Painter and film maker offers four types: "orchestration of motion"; those which seek to "create the rhythm of common objects in space and time and present them in their plastic beauty"; the "distortion" or "dissection" of a movement or form; surrealism.

Knight, Arthur. "Self-Expression." *SRL* 33 (27 May 50) 38–40. A report on private film production.

Cooke, Alan. "Free Cinema." *Sequence* (No. 13, 1951) 11–12. A British response to screenings of films by Maya Deren, Norman McLaren, Curtis Harrington, Kenneth Anger, and others.

Markopoulos, Gregory J. "*L'Arbre aux champignons:* A Little Tragedy of the Avant Garde." *Sequence* (No. 13, 1951) 31–32. Director describes his attempt to make a film.

Weinberg, Herman G. "30 Years of Experimental Film." *FIR* 2 (Dec 51) 22–27. A brief summary of early abstract films, which the author considers pure cinema, and a survey of the present occupations of their creators; an account of the author's interview with Hans Richter, who made *Rhythm 21,* one of the first purely abstract films, and who calls Georges Méliès his master.

Broughton, James. "Odd Birds in the Aviary." *S&S* 21 (Jan–Mar 52). *See 3a.*

Richter, Hans. "Easel—Scroll—Film." *Mag of Art* 45 (Feb 52). *See 3f(3).*

"An Evening of Abstract Films." *FIR* 3 (Feb 52) 67–70. Titles of films shown and quotations of Edward Steichen's commentary upon them as master of ceremonies.

Starr, Cecile. "Dots and Dashes, Circles and Splashes." *Sat Rev* 35 (8 Mar 52) 64+. Study of several abstract, nonrepresentational films occasioned by a survey by the Museum of Modern Art in New York.

Rogers, Robert Bruce. "Cineplastics: The Fine Art of Motion Painting." *QFRTV* 6 (No. 4, Summer 52) 375–387. Painter and film maker includes in his new art form the works of Norman McLaren, John and James Whitney, Hans Richter, and others, calling it "an organized 'river' of light and form—more or less abstract."

Farber, Manny. "Films: Kinesis Films." *Nation* 175 (11 Oct 52). *See 2h(4).*

Coté, Guy L. "Cinema *sans* Sense." *QFRTV* 7 (No. 4, Summer 53) 335–340. Director at Canadian National Film Board attacks immaturity and banality of a current Dada-like movement in France typified by Jean Isodore Isou and his pupil, Maurice Lemaître, who say, "Commercial film must die."

Starr, Cecile. "Occasion for Cheers." *Sat Rev* 36 (19 Dec 53) 36–38. The history and development of Cinema 16, a film society in New York City founded by Amos and Marcia Vogel to show adult documentary, experimental, and special films.

Potter, Ralph. "Abstract Films." *FIR* 5 (Feb 54) 82–89. Innate technical and psychological problems; uses of sound.

Bute, Mary Ellen. "Abstronics." *FIR* 5 (June–July 54) 263–266. Author puts music into visual representation with an oscilloscope.

Young, Vernon. "Fantasies of Hans Richter." *Art Dig* 29 (1 Oct 54) 19. Discussion of Richter retrospective (1921–1954) at the Thalia Theatre in New York City; animation of nonobjective forms and blending of fantasy and reality.

Mekas, Jonas. "The Experimental Film in America." *F Cult* 1 (No. 3, 1955) 15–20. Negative critique: "adolescent" and "technically crude"; annotated list of "most representative American film poets."

Richter, Hans. "Eight Free Improvisations on the Game of Chess." *F Cult* 1 (No. 1, 1955) 36–38. Description of his upcoming film *8 × 8.*

Richter, Hans. "*8 × 8.*" *F Cult* 1 (Nos. 5–6,

1955) 17–19. A sequence from Richter's latest experimental film.

Moss, Diana. "Experimental Film." *Film* (No. 7, Jan–Feb 56) 23. Is there a letdown?

Bachmann, Gideon. "On the Nature and Function of the Experimental (Poetic) Film." *F Cult* 3 (No. 14, 1957) 12–15. Excerpts from a symposium conducted by Bachmann over radio station WFUV-FM, New York, with Amos Vogel, Parker Tyler, Ian Hugo, and Lewis Jacobs as panelists.

Tyler, Parker. "A Preface to the Problems of the Experimental Film." *F Cult* 4 (No. 17, 1958) 5–8. The chief problem is to find in ordinary behavior the sources of ritual and myth; after that, to show it through a personal message and a gift for inventing with images; mere mobility is hardly enough.

"Days of Experiment." *F&F* 4 (No. 9, June 58) 10. Short films at Brussels World Fair.

Reisz, Karel. "Experiment at Brussels." *S&S* 27 (Summer 58) 231–234. Festival report.

Jacobs, Lewis. "Morning for the Experimental Film." *F Cult* (No. 19, 1959) 6–9. Jacobs hails the International Experimental Film Competition at Brussels (27 April 1958) as a historic breakthrough for the experimental film.

Mekas, Jonas. "A Call for a New Generation of Film Makers." *F Cult* (No. 19, 1959). See 6c(3).

Thompson, Francis. "More Optic Nerve for the Film Maker." *Art in America* 47 (No. 4, Winter 59) 58–63. Plea for new kinds of control and manipulation of film through slow motion, distortion, cutting; stills from author's film *N.Y., N.Y.*

Bogdanovich, Peter. "The Ninth Wave." *NY F Bul* 1 (No. 9, 1960) 5–6. The new American cinema as seen through *Come Back, Africa* and *Pull My Daisy*.

Mekas, Jonas. "Cinema of the New Generation." *F Cult* (No. 21, 1960) 1–20. An article that attempts to link "free cinema" (of Great Britain), the *nouvelle vague,* and the "new American cinema" (*Shadows, Pull My Daisy,* etc.).

Stoller, James. "A Criticism and a Challenge." *NY F Bul* 1 (No. 20, 1960) 1–11. Showings at New York's Cinema 16; comments on such films as *Shadows*.

Tyler, Parker. "Harrington, Markopoulos and Boultenhouse: Two Down and One to Go?" *F Cult* (No. 21, 1960) 33–39. Article on the experimental-film makers; analysis of *Fragment of Seeking, Serenity,* and *Hand Written.*

Durgnat, Raymond. "Beat, Square and So Cool!" *F&F* 7 (No. 1, Oct 60) 36. American avant-garde and documentary films shown at National Film Theatre.

New American Cinema Group. "The First Statement of the Group." *F Cult* (Nos. 22–23, 1961). See 6c(3).

Rappaport, Mark. "New York Film Workshop: Projection One." *NY F Bul* 2 (No. 1, 1961) 4–5. Experimental screenings. See response 2 (No. 4, 1961) 8–9.

"Outside the Frame." *FQ* 14 (No. 3, Spring 61) 35–37. Jordan Belson contributes non-objective, patterned films to Vortex series— "a new form of theater based on the combination of electronics, optics, and architecture"; reviewed by Harriet Polt. Francis Thompson experiments with three screens in *Atom;* reviewed by Roger Sandall.

Thurston, Wallace. "Creative Film Award Winners: 1959 and 1960." *FQ* 14 (No. 3, Spring 61) 30–34. The winners in the Creative Film Foundation–Cinema 16 awards include work by Emshwiller, Conner, Shirley Clarke, Vanderbeek.

Vanderbeek, Stan. "The Cinema Delimina." *FQ* 14 (No. 4, Summer 61) 5–15. A collage of photos, poems, and statements of the "film experimenters."

Lane, John Francis. "The American Outsiders at Spoleto." *F&F* 7 (No. 12, Sep 61) 35. Brief analysis of the American independents' films of the late 1950s and early 1960s shown at this Italian festival.

Cameron, Ian. "Spare a Thought for the Entertainers." *FQ* 15 (No. 2, Winter 61–62) 63–64. Letter from British critic asks whether experimental-film makers given space in *Film Quarterly* (Summer 61, Stan Vanderbeek, "The Cinema Delimina") are any more creative than those who work within the commercial forms; rejoinder by Ernest Callenbach, editor.

Batten, Mary. "Ron Rice and His Work." *F Com* 1 (No. 3, 1962) 30–35. Descriptions and outline of *The Flower Thief;* interview with Rice, who talks about his use of sound and his later film, *Sense-Less.*

de Laurot, Edouard. "The Future of the New American Cinema." *F Cult* (No. 24, 1962) 20–22. "A singular lack of talent, technique, and significance"; a sarcastic glossary of cinematic terms the author believes is applicable to these films.

Marien, Marcel. "Another Kind of Cinema." *F Com* 1 (No. 3, 1962) 14–19. Critical of the romanticizing effect of most films, Belgian surrealist writer proposes using old stock and putting together surprises, sometimes dramatic, sometimes comic; in additional note, Gregory Markopoulos comments on Marien's film, *L'Imitation du cinéma.*

Mekas, Jonas. "Note on the New American Cinema." *F Cult* (No. 24, 1962) 6–16. "What the new artist feels, how his mind works, why he creates the way he does; why he chooses his particular style to express the physical and psychological realities of his life"; discussion of the work of Morris Engel, John Cassavetes, Sidney Meyers, Ricky Leacock, Stan Brakhage, Ron Rice, and others; excerpts reprinted in (No. 25) 68–70.

Preston, Richard. "The Deep-Frozen Eye of God." *F Cult* (No. 24, 1962) 17–18. Subtitled "Notes Towards a Social Surrealist Manifesto."

de Laurot, Edouard. "From Alienation to Cinema." *F Cult* (No. 25, 1962) 66–68. A critical attack upon "new American cinema"— Ron Rice's *Flower Thief* is an escape from life into "absurdity and feeble-mindedness."

Sitney, P. Adams, and Mary Batten. "A View of Burckhardt." *Vision [Film Comment]* 1 (No. 1, Spring 62) 13–16. Critical view of Rudolph Burckhardt's experimental films; separate comment on his biography and intentions by Mary Batten.

MacDonald, D. "Some Animadversions on the Art Film." *Esq* 57 (Apr 62) 13–14+. Survey of films shown in the last fifteen years by a New York film society, Cinema 16; the search for freer form needs also inspiration, reverence, and taste.

Ross, Walter. "*La Nouvelle Vague de* New York." *Esq* 57 (May 62) 35–36+. Underground cinema: Mekas, Vanderbeek.

"Private." *New Yorker* 38 (5 May 62) 35–36. The fifteenth anniversary of Cinema 16.

Dienstfrey, H. "The New American Cinema." *Commentary* 3 (No. 6, June 62) 494–504. A survey. Reply by William Kronick with author's rejoinder 34 (Sep 62) 256–257.

Batten, Mary. "Actuality and Abstraction." *F Com* 1 (No. 2, Summer 62) 55–59. Discussion with Mary Ellen Bute about her films based on mathematics, electronics, music, and beams of light.

Craddock, John. "Towards an Abstract Cinema?—Not Yet." *F Com* 1 (No. 2, Summer 62) 21–24. Critique of the underground.

Feldman, Harry. "Back to the Greeks." *F Com* 1 (No. 2, Summer 62) 13–15. A negative view of what Jonas Mekas, Stan Vanderbeek, and others said at a Museum of Modern Art symposium in New York.

Markopoulos, Gregory. "Beyond Audio-Visual Space." *F Com* 1 (No. 2, Summer 62) 52–54. Comments on films made by Mary Ellen Bute, with filmography.

Boultenhouse, Charles. "The Camera as a God." *F Cult* (No. 29, 1963) 20–22. Against Hollywood; for experiment.

Brakhage, Stan. "Metaphors on Vision." *F Cult* (No. 30, 1963) entire issue. A collection of writing (statements, letters, scripts) on the creative process of film making by one of the leading avant-garde film makers; introduction by P. Adams Sitney.

Maas, Willard. "The Gryphon Yaks." *F Cult* (No. 29, 1963) 46–54. The Gryphon Film Group was mostly Maas and Marie Menken

(whose filmographies are appended); this recorded monologue tells the story of their films and their friends—Norman McLaren, George Barker, Ben Moore, Charles Boultenhouse, *et al.*

Peterson, Sidney. "A Note on Comedy in Experimental Film." *F Cult* (No. 29, 1963) 27–29. Author's filmography included.

Amberg, George. "The Rationale of the Irrational." *Minnesota Rev* 3 (No. 3, Spring 63) 323–347. A chronicle and analysis of Dada and surrealist cinema, particularly in the works of Hans Richter, Man Ray, Marcel Duchamp, Fernand Léger, René Clair, Antonin Artaud, Luis Buñuel and Salvador Dali, Jean Cocteau.

Milne, Tom. "The Real Avant-Garde." *S&S* 32 (Summer 63). *See 4e(2a).*

"Cinema Underground." *New Yorker* 39 (13 July 63) 16–17. Film-Makers' Co-operative, Bleecker Street Cinema, and a chat with Jonas Mekas.

Johnson, Albert. "Experiment in San Francisco." *S&S* 32 (Autumn 63) 176. Note on Canyon Cinema group of film makers, including Bruce Baillie and Will Hindle.

Hamill, Pete. "Explosion in the Movie Underground." *SEP* 236 (28 Sep 53) 82–84. Includes quotations from film makers.

Knight, Arthur. "New American Cinema?" *Sat Rev* 46 (2 Nov 63) 41. "Rebels without cause or purpose, technically they may be accused of sheer incompetence, while thematically they seem to be leading to a blind alley of self-indulgence and self-satisfaction."

Brakhage, Jane. "The Birth Film." *F Cult* (No. 31, 1963–1964) 35–36. How it felt to be photographed by her husband during childbirth.

Kelly, Robert. "The Image of the Body." *F Cult* (No. 31, 1963–1964) 1–2. The author criticizes "the film's almost total inability to present the form and movement and weight of the human body."

Sitney, P. Adams. "Imagism in Four Avant-Garde Films." *F Cult* (No. 31, 1963–1964) 15–21. Maya Deren's *Choreography for Camera,* Kenneth Anger's *Eaux d'artifice,* Charles Boultenhouse's *Hand Written,* and Stan Brakhage's *Dog Star Man: Part 1.*

Gavronsky, Serge. "The Body as Will and Motion." *F Cult* (No. 32, 1964) 22–24. Written in response to Robert Kelly's article "The Image of the Body," *F Cult* (No. 31), the author discusses film's depiction of the human body.

Markopoulos, Gregory. "Projection of Thoughts." *F Cult* (No. 32, 1964) 3–5. Markopoulos discusses the work of the "new American cinema."

Kelman, Ken. "Death and Trancefiguration." *F Cult* (No. 34, 1964) 51–53. Kelman discusses Harry Smith's (then untitled) *Heaven-*

Hell film, the transformations within it, the projection devices.

King, Kenneth. "Plurality Pieces: Re: Experiences." *F Cult* (No. 34, 1964) 53–57. Subtitled: "Gregory Markopoulos / The New American Cinema / Dancefilm / John Cage and New Music / Computers / Some Words About Aesthetics Whatever That Is Now Etc."

Callenbach, Ernest. "Auguries?" *FQ* 17 (No. 3, Spring 64). *See 2h(4).*

Stein, Elliott. "Fog at Knokke." *S&S* 33 (Spring 64) 88–89. Avant-garde film festival in Belgium; the U.S. sent 143 films.

"In the Year of Our Ford." *Time* 83 (3 Apr 64) 96+. Experimental-film makers awarded Ford Foundation grants.

Kelman, Ken. "Anticipations of the Light." *Nation* 198 (11 May 64) 490–494. Playwright's view of "new American cinema," themes and styles.

Wagner, Geoffrey. "Muckmanship." *Nat Rep* 16 (16 June 64). *See 7b(6).*

Conover, Grandin. *"Laterna Magika." Nation* 199 (24 Aug 64) 79–80. Review of a Czechoslovakian event, a welding of music, theatre, dance, motion pictures.

Boultenhouse, Charles. "Film for the Time Being." *Kulchur* 4 (No. 15, Autumn 64) 41–47. On the plastic beauty of film.

Callenbach, Ernest. "The New Resistance." *FQ* 18 (No. 1, Fall 64) 28–32. Reviews of "poetic" films which, like the sit-in, resist modern life: Clement Perron's *Day After Day,* Stanton Kaye's *Georg,* Bruce Baillie's *Mass,* Carl Linder's *The Devil Is Dead.*

Sarris, Andrew. "Underground Movies." *Show* 4 (Nov 64) 44–49+. Who makes them and various reasons why; activities of Film-Makers' Cooperative.

Amberg, George. "Pop Avant-Garde." *Arts in Soc* 3 (No. 2, Fall–Winter 64–65) 256–261. This is what happens when mass audience meets art, especially in film.

Markopoulos, Gregory. "Three Film-Makers." *F Cult* (No. 35, 1964–1965) 23–24. Markopoulos briefly discusses the work of Andrew Meyer, Charles Boultenhouse, and Storm De Hirsch.

Bergé, Carol. "Dialogue Without Words: The Work of Harry Smith." *F Cult* (No. 37, 1965) 2–4. Content and audience for his *Heaven-Hell* film, said to have been made between 1940 and 1960.

Whitney, John H. "An Abstract Film-Maker's View of the Belgium Experimental Film Competition (1963) and All." *F Cult* (No. 37, 1965) 24–26.

Alexander, Shana. "Report from Underground." *Life* 58 (29 Jan 65) 23.

Belz, C. I. "Film Poetry of Man Ray." *Criticism* (Spring 65) 117–130. Serious experiments in visual perspective; a way of seeing

rather than a pointed statement about reality.

Markopoulos, Gregory J. "What Are You Ready For?" *December* 7 (No. 1, Spring 65) 147–151. Personal reflections on the development of New American Cinema.

Ewald, William. "A Report from Detroit on 16mm in '65." *F Com* 3 (No. 3, Summer 65) 48–49. Experimental films at the Art Institute festival.

Bachmann, Gideon. "The New American Cinema: Five Years Later." *F&F* 11 (No. 12, Sep 65) 54–56. On the last five years of New York City independents.

"Festival I." *New Yorker* 41 (4 Dec 65) 52–54. Report on experiments of film makers' cinemathèque.

Junker, Howard. "The Underground Renaissance." *Nation* 201 (27 Dec 65) 539–540.

Osborn, Elodie. "Young Film-Maker." *Art in America* 54 (Jan 66) 62–68. Abstract experiments and *cinéma vérité* by various directors.

Hatch, Robert. "Media-Mix." *Nation* 202 (31 Jan 66) 139. Avant-garde films; *Hubbub,* a multichannel show.

Vanderbeek, Stan. "Culture Intercom and Expanded Cinema: A Proposal and Manifesto." *F Cult* (No. 40, Spring 66) 15–18. For an international picture language.

"Up From Underground." *Newswk* 67 (25 Apr 66) 90+. Film makers' own distribution center; Jonas Mekas' comments.

Lash, Vivian. "Experimenting with Freedom in Mexico." *FQ* 19 (No. 4, Summer 66). *See 4h(1).*

Mussman. Toby. "Early Surrealist Expression in the Film." *F Cult* (No. 41, Summer 66) 8–17. Richter, Léger, Duchamp, Buñuel, Ray and their friends in the 1920s.

Mussman, Toby. "The Surrealist Film." *Artforum* 5 (No. 1, Sep 66) 26–31. Dada and surrealist experiments through the 1930s.

Mekas, Jonas (ed.). "Expanded Arts." *F Cult* (No. 43, Winter 66) 1–12. Various articles by and about experimental film makers and other artists in newspaper format.

Junker, Howard. "New Silver Screen." *Esq* 66 (Oct 66) 62+. Omnirama, art mix, "Rauschenberg-in-sync."

Vanderbeek, Stan. "Culture-Intercom and Expanding Cinema." *Motive* 27 (Nov 66) 13–23. An international picture language is urgently needed; a "movie-drome" can depict man's history.

Dworkin, Martin. "Avant-Garde Cinema: A Muted Fanfare." *Motive* 27 (Nov 66) 24–27. Its very faults are proclaimed as integral with its attack on conventional culture; the early roles of Richter, Dali, Cocteau.

Sarris, Andrew. "The Independent Cinema." *Motive* 27 (Nov 66) 29–31. Most underground-film makers "lack the humility to be great artists," but they express "the chaos and confusion of our time."

Cobbing, Bob. "London Co-op." *Film* (No. 47, Winter 66). *See 6c(3).*

Wilson, David. "London Film Cooperative." *S&S* 36 (Winter 66–67) 17. Branch of international association, like the New York underground group, will rent films and publish *Cinim* magazine.

Hofsess, John. "Towards a New Voluptuary." *Take One* 1 (No. 4, 1967) 8–10. The film maker (*Redpath 25* and *Black Zero*) discusses his theory of film as sensory exploration.

Cowan, Bob. "Donna Kerness Talks to Bob Cowan." *Take One* 1 (No. 8, 1967) 22–23. An interview with the American underground-film star.

Hofsess, John. "Film as Guerilla Warfare." *Take One* 1 (No. 6, 1967) 9–11. A theoretical discussion of the underground film points out its humane and imaginative importance.

Mancia, A., and W. Van Dyke. "Four Artists as Film-Makers." *Art in America* 55 (Jan 67) 64–73. The work of Robert Breer, Carmen D'Avino, Ed Emshwiller, Stan Vanderbeek.

Kroll, Jack. "Up from Underground." *Newswk* 69 (13 Feb 67) 117–119. Trends and leading figures in underground film.

"Art of Light and Lunacy." *Time* 89 (17 Feb 67) 94+. The new underground films; recent films and key figures.

Knight, Arthur, and Hollis Alpert. "The History of Sex in the Cinema—Part 15: The Experimental Films." *Playboy* 14 (No. 4, Apr 67). *See 4k(8).*

Vogel, Amos. "Thirteen Confusions." *Evergreen Rev* 11 (No. 47, June 67) 50–53+. A critique of the American Independent Cinema.

Talbot, Daniel, Gregory Markopoulos, Parker Tyler, Richard Schickel, and Annette Michelson. "The New American Cinema: Five Replies to Amos Vogel." *Evergreen Rev* 11 (No. 48, Aug 67) 54–56+.

Fothergill, R. "How Deep Is Underground?" *Arts Canada* 24 (Aug–Sep 67) (sup) 6. Brief report on symposium in Toronto seeking to define which underground films are "better"; but "why do you need to know?"

Shatnoff, Judith. "Expo '67—A Multiple Vision." *FQ* 21 (No. 1, Fall 67) 2–13. Reviews of some of the multiscreen experiences at the Montreal Fair, including the National Film Board's *Labyrinth,* Francis Thompson's *We Are Young,* and Christopher Chapman's *Ontario: A Place to Stand.*

Steele, Robert. "Japanese Underground Film." *F Com* 4 (Nos. 1–2, Fall–Winter 67). *See 4f(1).*

Gough-Yates, Kevin. "An Underground Movie Trip." *Studio Inter* 174 (Nov 67) 185.

Gray, C. "Rediscovery: Jim Davis." *Art in America* 55 (Nov–Dec 67) 64–69. Trying to paint with light and movement led this artist to make abstract films of light in movement.

Cobbing, Bob. "Underground Explosion." *Film* (No. 50, Winter 67) 15–17. Underground films in several countries, particularly America.

Battcock, G. "New Experiments in Cinema." *Art Ed* 20 (Dec 67) 12–17.

Durgnat, Raymond. "Underground Subversive." *F&F* 14 (No. 3, Dec 67) 4–8. The avant-garde of the 1960s and the films leading up to it.

Roud, Richard. "The Underground Surfaces." *S&S* 37 (Winter 67–68) 19–20. Features are now being shown in regular theatres in New York.

Dean, William. "Criticism and the Underground Film." *Take One* 1 (No. 9, 1968). *See 3b.*

Malanga, Gerard (ed.). "Interview with Jack Smith." *F Cult* (No. 45, 1967) 12–16. Entire issue edited by Malanga includes various pieces on New York underground-film makers.

Sitney, P. Adams (ed.). "New American Cinema." *F Cult* (No. 46, Autumn 67–Oct 68) 1–54. Various articles on New York underground-film makers.

Brakhage, Stan. "Closed-Eye Vision." *Caterpillar* 1 (No. 2, Jan 68) 26–37. On the "grain" in the picture image.

Hindle, Will. "About *Chinese Firedrill,*" *Cinéaste* 1 (No. 4, Spring 68) 19–20. Production notes on this prizewinner at the 1968 Ann Arbor Film Festival; sound recording for the film.

Marton, Patricia. "Nothing New at Knokke II." *FQ* 21 (No. 3, Spring 68) 32–34. Fourth International Experimental Film Festival in Belgium.

Stein, Elliott. "Dr. Ledoux's Torture Garden." *S&S* 37 (Spring 68) 72–73. Films shown at the Fourth Experimental Film Festival at Knokke-le-Zoute in Belgium.

Hitchens, Gordon. "The Need for Independence and Experimentation in the American Film." *F Soc Rev* (Apr 68) 32–35. A plea for understanding the attitudes and styles of the experimental-film artist.

Hitchens, Gordon. "Half a Dozen Avant-Gardes." *F Soc Rev* (May 68) 35–37+. Concluding section of article begun in April.

Pontell, Jonathan. "Open." *Cinéaste* 2 (No. 1, Summer 68) 18+. Brief article suggesting the independent film consists of four categories: man in his society, confusion, sex, and the war in Vietnam.

Weinberg, Herman. "A Statement on Experimental Work in Cinema." *F Com* 4 (No. 4, Summer 68) 22–23. Trying to put on the screen "imagery that is inevitable" (Proust).

Weightman, John. "Notes from the Underground." *Encounter* 31 (July 68) 54–55. The National Film Theatre presents a program of American underground films.

Burns, Dan. "Pixillation." *FQ* 22 (No. 1, Fall 68). *See 2h.*

Rayns, Tony. "The Underground Film." *Cinema* (Cambridge) (No. 1, Dec 68) 8–11. Comparison of directors.

Baker, Tom. "In an Above-Ground Society." *Cinema* (Calif) 5 (No. 4, 1969) 28–31. By the director of underground film *Bongo Wolf's Revenge;* about his film and working with Warhol and Mailer.

Cocking, Loren. "Francis Thompson's Optic Nerve." *JUFA* 21 (No. 1, 1969) 25–30. The use of multiple screens, distorted images, close-up photography, and subjective camera in motion by the director of *To Be Alive* and other prizewinning films.

Baker, E. C. "Secret Life of John Chamberlain." *Art News* 68 (Apr 69) 48–51+. Retrospective of lifetime of sculpture includes first two films, especially *Wide Point,* for which "everything went wrong"; therefore this beautiful "garbage" has been projected at random on seven screens simultaneously.

Weaver, M. "Concrete Films of Oskar Fischinger." *Art and Artists* 4 (May 69) 30–33. Visual motion with music.

Ford, Barbara. "Underground Movie Thing." *Sci Dig* 65 (June 69) 42–53. The interest of youth in film making; older "underground"-film figures.

Sitney P. Adams. "Structural Film." *F Cult* (No. 47, Summer 69) 1–10. Also various articles on "new American cinema."

Meyer, Richard J. "Television Station Breaks: A New Art Form?" *F Com* 5 (No. 3, Fall 69) 62–65. Director of school service for New York City educational TV describes brief films by Wayne Sourbeer of Denver.

Gordon, M. W. "What Film Making Is All About." *America* 121 (6 Dec 69). *See 3a.*

Johnston, Claire, and Jan Dawson. "Declarations of Independence." *S&S* 39 (Winter 69–70) 28–32. Development of the English "underground"-film movement; a note on the problems of criticizing such films.

Sitney, P. Adams. "Ideas Within the Avant-Garde." *F Lib Q* 3 (No. 1, Winter 69–70) 5–

15. Ideas and films at the International Experimental Film Festival in Belgium.

Sitney, P. Adams, ed. "Film Culture." *F Cult* (Nos. 48–49, Winter–Spring 70) 1–68. Various articles about or by members of "new American cinema" groups in New York.

Weiner, Peter. "New American Cinema." *Film* (No. 57, Winter 69–70) 4–6; (No. 58, Spring 70) 22–24. Development and origins of underground-film makers.

Vanderbeek, Stan. "New Talent—The Computer." *Art in America* 58 (Jan 70) 86–91. Designs achieved by computer-generated films.

Eliscu, Lita. "Hand-Held: Underground and College Films." *Show* (Jan 70) 27–28. Survey of films from 1969 of the "expansive cinema"; includes *Brigit's Dream* by Jim Tiroff, *Mondo Trasho* by John Water, *Unstrap Me* by George Kuchar, and Paul Morrissey's *Flesh.*

Johnston, Claire. "New Directions." *S&S* 39 (Spring 70) 74. Jimmy Vaughan distributes underground films in London in partnership with Lionel Rogosin in New York.

Youngblood, Gene. "*Expanded Cinema.*" *Show* (Mar 70) 34–38+. Excerpts from his book of the same title (Dutton, 1970); environment as intermedia network; the need for an expanded cinematic language; the possibility of feedback from cinema as the "synaesthetic."

Sarlin, Bob. "Robert Downey Goes to the Dogs." *Show* (June 70) 58–62. Comments on the filming of Downey's *Pound.*

Dawson, Jan, and Claire Johnston. "More British Sounds." *S&S* 39 (Summer 70) 144–147. A followup of a more general survey of avant-garde film making in England in (Winter 69–70); critical assessments of some of the films and directors.

Galluzzo, Tony. "Filmmakers of Tomorrow." *Mod Phot* 34 (Aug 70) 50+. A report on the Kinetic Art program of short films at Lincoln Center: such film makers as Yoji Kuri, Jan Svankamajer, Leonard Glassner.

Sitney, P. Adams. "The Avant-Garde Film." *Afterimage* (No. 2, Autumn 70) 9–28. An overview; also recent work of Stan Brakhage, Michael Snow, Ken Jacobs, Kenneth Anger, and George Landow.

8e. Religious Films

[See also 4k(5).]

Ford, James Tooker. "Motion Pictures and Foreign Missions." *Missionary Rev* 54 (Aug 31) 611–612. Suggests founding academy of Christian art to produce religious films.

Gregory, Benjamin. "Screen World: Religious Films." *Spectator* 160 (14 Jan 38) 46–47.

Recent experimentation with open-air Cinema Evangelism proves the gospel may be effectively presented through film.

"Religious Films." *Time* 31 (14 Feb 38) 22. Survey of films produced by religious organizations; history of the Religious Films Society.

"Religious Classes in Film." *Newswk* 16 (23 Dec 40) 44. Story of James K. Friedrich, his company, Cathedral Pictures, and the religious films he makes.

"The Africa Motion Picture Project." *S&S* 14 (No. 56, Winter 45–46) 130. Missionary films.

"Movies in Church." *Newswk* 27 (11 Feb 46) 74. The struggles of James K. Friedrich and his Cathedral Films, the biggest producer of religious shorts in America.

Buchanan, Andrew. "God and Film." *S&S* 15 (No. 57, Spring 46) 7–9. A request for a religious-film center.

"Protestant Cooperation Provides Films." *Chris Cent* 64 (19 Feb 47) 229. Report on the Religious Film Association, which provides visual-aid materials to local churches and church organizations.

Hession, Brian. "Religion in Films Versus Religious Films." *S&S* 16 (No. 62, Summer 47) 53–57.

Buchanan, Andrew. "Religious Rations." *S&S* 16 (No. 63, Autumn 47) 107–108. A plea for progressive religious-film production.

"Sermons in Films." *Newswk* 30 (10 Nov 47). See 7c(2c).

Robbins, Michela. "Films for the Church." *Hwd Q* 3 (No. 2, Winter 47–48) 178–184. Feature films briefly discussed; shorter films

by Moody Bible Institute and Cathedral Films.

"Shot in the Arm." *Time* 52 (6 Dec 48) 52. Cinemogul Rank's other side: a producer of religious films.

"Fox Consults Publishers on Short Religious Films." *Publishers Weekly* 159 (3 Feb 51) 797.

Starr, Cecile. "Ideas on Film." *Sat Rev* 35 (8 Nov 52) 46–48. Critical evaluation of 16mm religious films; cites scarcity of time, money, talent, and devotion.

Mack, S. F. "On the Movie Lot in Hollywood." *National Council* 3 (Mar 53) 10–11.

"Religious Film Boom." *Newswk* 41 (9 Mar 53) 54–55. The leading producers.

"Movies Go to Church." *American* 157 (Apr 54) 59. Brief history of Cathedral Films and its founder, the Reverend James K. Friedrich.

Ferguson, A. "Trials of a Producer." *National Council* 6 (Nov 56) 13–14.

Harrell, J. G. "Should We Abandon the Movies?" *Chris Cent* 76 (2 Sep 59) 993–994. Objections to church-sponsored "religious films." Discussion (30 Sep 59) 1122.

Larson, Lawrence A. "The Cinematic and the Biblical Points of View: A New Correlation." *Religion in Life* 35 (Summer 66). See 3f(2).

9. Case Histories of Film Making

[See also 2d(4), 2g(2d), 3c, 7c(1d), 8c(4).]

A

"Fun in Farouk's Palace." *Life* 36 (22 Mar 54) 89–90+. A preview of **Abdullah the Great**.

Taylor, John Russell. "Accident." *S&S* 35 (Autumn 66) 179–184. Work in process on Joseph Losey's film; talks with the director, designer, lighting cameraman, the stars, the writer, Harold Pinter.

"Putting Life into a Movie." *Life* 30 (19 Feb 51) 57–58+. Director Billy Wilder explains his editing choices in **Ace in the Hole**.

Schulberg, Stuart. "Filmaking." *FIR* 9 (May 59) 284–286. Production report in letter to editor by director on **Across the Everglades**.

"Act One in Action." *NYTM* (19 May 63) 62+. Production stills from the film of the book *Act One*.

Skow, John. "The Harold Robbins Co." *Playboy* 16 (No. 12, Dec 69) 231. Making **The Adventurers**.

Bean, Robin. "Adventures with Yurek." *F&F* 15 (No. 3, Dec 68) 56–60. On location with Yurek Skolimowski during shooting of **Adventures with Gerard**.

"Unanimous Consent." *Newswk* 58 (25 Sep 61) 29–30. The filming of **Advise and Consent**; cooperation by Washington people.

"Advise *und* Consent." *Time* 78 (29 Sep 61) 69. Otto Preminger making his latest picture, **Advise and Consent**.

Drury, A. "Based on the Novel, **Advise and Consent**." *McCall's* 89 (July 62) 12+. Diary of the film production of *Advise and Consent*.

Bunzel, P. "Patriotic Movie . . . Or Not." *Life* 53 (6 July 62) 73–75+. The controversy over **Advise and Consent**.

"An Affair of the Skin." *F Com* 1 (No. 4, 1963) 28–29. Brief production story about film being made by Ben Maddow starring Diana Sands.

"Life Goes on Location in Africa." *Life* 31 (17 Sep 51) 172–176+. Behind-the-scenes look at John Huston's **African Queen**.

Huston, John. "African Queen." *Th Arts* 36 (Feb 52) 48–49+.

"Agony and the Ecstasy of Michelangelo." *Look* (9 Mar 65) 41–48. Mostly color photographs.

Stone, Irving. "A Novelist Looks at His Movie." *F&F* 12 (No. 12, Sep 66) 53. His view of **The Agony and the Ecstasy**.

"Airport Becomes a Movie." *Good Housekeeping* 170 (Apr 70) 52+. A comparison of illustrations created for this magazine when the book originally appeared and the stars who were cast for the film.

James, T. F. "Man Who Talks Back to John Wayne." *Cosmopolitan* 149 (Aug 60). *See 2d*. About **The Alamo**.

Wald, Malvin. "The Making of a Bio-Pic." *FIR* 10 (Apr 59). *See 2d*. About **Al Capone**.

"Boy Who Took the World." *Life* 39 (14 Nov 55) 79–83+. Preview of Robert Rossen's **Alexander the Great**.

"Millions That Made Alexander Great." *F&F* 2 (No. 5, Feb 56) 8–9. Robert Rossen and preparations for **Alexander the Great**, starring Richard Burton.

"Teresa at Twilight." *Collier's* 137 (30 Mar 56) 24–25. Filming of **Alexander the Great**; stills of Teresa del Rio, Alexander's bride, ballet dancing between the takes.

"In Wonderland." *Time* 22 (25 Dec 33) 20–22. Production story on **Alice in Wonderland**, Paramount live-action film, with career of Charlotte Henry, actress.

Disney, Walt. "How I Cartooned 'Alice.'" *FIR* 2 (May 51). *See 2h(3)*. About **Alice in Wonderland**.

Medjuck, Joe. "Alice's Restaurant." *Take One* 2 (No. 1, 1968) 6–9. Interviews with Arthur

---

Readers are advised to acquaint themselves with the range of categories throughout the bibliography in the search for specific subjects. In some cases, cross-categorical comparisons are directly suggested. In general, however, each article is placed under one category only. Cross-references on individual articles have been kept to a minimum.

Entries are in chronological order of publication under each category. Exceptions are: Part 5, Biography, in which the order is alphabetical by name; Part 9, Case Histories of Film Making, which is alphabetical by film title; and 3c and 8c(4), also alphabetical by title.

From the David O. Selznick production, *Gone With the Wind.*

Penn, Alice Brock, and other principals involved in the film.

Miller, Edwin. "Spotlight: Hollywood Scene." *Seventeen* 28 (Feb 69) 42+. On the making of **Alice's Restaurant**.

Hedgepeth, William. "The Successful Anarchist." *Look* 33 (4 Feb 69) 60–62+. On the filming of **Alice's Restaurant**.

Berg, Lily Van Den. "Alice's Restaurant." *S&S* 38 (Spring 69) 67–69. On the set with director Arthur Penn, who also comments on some of his other films.

Stickney, John. "Alice's Family of Folk Song Fame Becomes a Movie." *Life* 66 (28 Mar 69) 43–45+. The filming of **Alice's Restaurant**.

Zimmerman, Paul D. "Alice's Restaurant's Children." *Newswk* 74 (29 Sep 69) 101–104+. Cover story on the making of **Alice's Restaurant**; biography of Arlo Guthrie; the "new, searching, restless breed of young Americans."

"America! America!" *Show* 3 (July 63) 62–63. On location with Elia Kazan; Stathis Giallelis' role in the film.

Silke, James R. "Three Directors in Danger: Kazan the Violent." *Cinema* (Calif) 1 (No. 6, Nov–Dec 63) 4. Report on Elia Kazan's **America! America!**

Klugman, Don, et al. "American Revolution 2." *Take One* 2 (No. 7, 1969) 7–10. Impressions, interviews, and statements concerning this film made in Chicago.

Daugherty, Frank. "Steel Comes to the Films." *CSMM* (8 May 43) 8–9+. King Vidor's *America* (later titled **American Romance**).

Milne, Tom. "L'Amour Fou." *S&S* 38 (Spring 69) 63–66. Plot, production, shooting, and review of new film done in *cinéma vérité* style by Jacques Rivette.

Weinberg, Herman. "Von Sternberg Films the Anatahan Story." *S&S* 22 (Apr–June 53) 152–153. Note on production in Japan.

Weinberg, Herman G. "Has Von Sternberg Discovered a 'Japanese Dietrich'?" *Th Arts* 37 (Aug 53) 26–29. Von Sternberg's **Anatahan**, why he made it, and to what effect.

Havemann, E. "Joe Welch in Juicy New Role." *Life* 46 (11 May 59) 116–118+. Attorney Welch plays a judge in **Anatomy of a Murder**.

Knight, A. "Wise in Hollywood." *Sat Rev* 53 (8 Aug 70) 22–25. Production notes on **The Andromeda Strain**; the necessity of major studio facilities for such an undertaking.

Kotlowitz, Richard. "Making of **The Angel Levine**." *Harper's* 239 (July 69) 98–100.

Guy, Rory. "Angels from Hell." *Cinema* (Calif) 4 (No. 1, Spring 68) 45. Article on Bruce Kessler's film of this title.

Martin, Geoffrey. "The Designer and the Cartoon Film." *Art and Industry* 55 (Sep 53). *See 2h(5).* About **Animal Farm**.

"The Making of a Movie." *Coronet* 38 (Aug 55) 41–48. Jeanmaire and Bing Crosby in **Anything Goes**; picture story.

"Wilder Touch." *Life* 48 (30 May 60) 41–42. Directing **The Apartment**.

"All Eyes on Doris Day." *Collier's* 130 (9 Aug 52) 10–12. Stills from the musical comedy **April in Paris**.

Ronan, M., and Stanley Donen. "Senior Scholastic Interview: Choreographing a Spy Thriller, **Arabesque**." *Senior Scholastic* 87 (2 Dec 65) 20.

Weinman, M. "Around the World in Eighty Days." *Collier's* 137 (17 Feb 56) 62–67. The filming of Mike Todd's movie; pictures of some fifty top stars.

"When This World Was Wider." *Life* 41 (22 Oct 56) 81–85+. A preview of Mike Todd's **Around the World in Eighty Days**.

Goodman, Ezra. "Rounding Up the Stars in 80 Ways." *Life* 41 (22 Oct 56) 87–88+. Mike Todd's successful effort to sign big names for cameo parts in **Around the World in Eighty Days**.

"On Everybody's Tongue." *Newswk* 48 (5 Nov 56) 114–115. Reactions to **Around the World in Eighty Days**.

"Talent." *New Yorker* 32 (24 Nov 56) 45–46. Mike Todd talks about his latest success, **Around the World in Eighty Days**.

"Watch the Bull Go." *Newswk* 49 (15 Apr 57) 113. Mike Todd's short commentary about a movie record of the actual making of **Around the World in Eighty Days**.

Levin, Bernard. "Night Out with Mr. Todd." *Spectator* 198 (10 May 57). *See 6d(2).* About **Around the World in Eighty Days**.

Anderson, Michael. "How Todd Made the 'World.'" *F&F* 3 (No. 12, Sep 57) 11+. Director comments on **Around the World in Eighty Days**.

Coonradt, Peter. "Boetticher Returns." *Cinema* (Calif) 4 (No. 4, 1968) 11–15. On Boetticher's film **Arruza**.

"Wajda's The Ashes." *F&F* 11 (No. 4, Jan 65) 24–25. On the making of the film.

Metzner, Ernö. "On the Sets of the Film **Atlantis**." *Close Up* 9 (No. 3, Sep 32) 153–159. Comments by the set designer for Pabst's film.

Da Costa, Morton. "Auntie and I." *F&F* 5 (No. 4, Jan 59) 11. On the making of **Auntie Mame**.

B

Grenier, C. "Bonjour, B. B." *Reporter* 20 (30 Apr 59) 34–35. On-set account of filming of **Babette Goes to War**.

"Baby Doll." *NYTM* (22 Apr 56) 47. A preview of the Elia Kazan film shot in Mississippi.

"Reflections on a Condemned Film: **Baby**

455

Doll." *America* 96 (5 Jan 57). *See 7b(6).*

"Bitter Dispute over **Baby Doll.**" *Life* 42 (7 Jan 57) 60–65.

"**Baby Doll.**" *Commonweal* 65 (11 Jan 57). *See 7c(2b).*

Cogley, John. "**Baby Doll** Controversy." *Commonweal* 65 (11 Jan 57). *See 7c.*

Scott, N. A., Jr. "**Baby Doll** Furor." *Chris Cent* 74 (23 Jan 57). *See 7b(6).*

Cogley, John. "More on **Baby Doll.**" *Commonweal* 65 (1 Feb 57). *See 7c(2b).*

Block, M. "Birth of a Film." *Wilson Lib Bul* 13 (Jan 39) 325+. On-the-set report of the filming of **Back Door to Heaven,** a story of hometown life outside of Cleveland, Ohio.

Winters, Shelley. "I Wish They'd Lose the Negative." *Cinema* (Calif) 1 (No. 4, June–July 63) 7–11+. Interview with star about **The Balcony.**

Graham, Peter. "Balthazar." *F&F* 12 (No. 4, Jan 66) 56–57. On location for the shooting of **Au Hasard Balthazar** and other current French films.

Peattie, Donald. "Nature of Things." *Audubon Mag* 44 (Sep 42). *See 7c(2).* About **Bambi.**

"Pistol-Toting Director." *Newswk* 56 (21 Nov 60) 108. Vittorio De Seta directing **Bandits of Orgosolo.**

De Sica, Vittorio. "Notes on **Banditi a Orgosolo.**" *F Cult* (No. 24, 1962) 36–41. The young Italian director on making his film.

"Production Notes on **Bandits of Orgosolo.**" *F Com* 2 (No. 2, 1964) 36. A few quotations from Vittorio De Seta; filmography.

Taylor, John Russell. "Script by Christopher Fry." *S&S* 31 (Spring 62) 65–66. Note on his preparation of **Barabbas.**

"Pictorial: The Bizarre Beauties of **Barbarella.**" *Playboy* 15 (No. 3, Mar 68) 108–117.

Beech, Keyes. "Hollywood's Oriental Fad." *SEP* 230 (10 May 58) 28–29+. On the filming of **The Barbarian and the Geisha.**

Harvey, E. "Ava Gardner Plays the Gypsy." *Collier's* 134 (23 July 54) 28–29. Filming of Joseph L. Mankiewicz' **The Barefoot Contessa.**

Weiss, Trude. "The First Opera-Film." *Close Up* 9 (No. 4, Dec 32). *See 4k(6).* About **The Bartered Bride.**

"Saga of Sam and a Colonel." *Life* 42 (25 Feb 57) 137–138. Report on the making of **Battle Hymn.**

Mussman, Toby. "Gillo Pontecorvo." *Medium* 1 (No. 2, Winter 67–68) 45–51. A summary of **Battle of Algiers** and an interview with its director; the politics of the film and the problems it caused.

Bogart, Humphrey. "Beat the Devil." *Look* 17 (22 Sep 53) 128–129+. Actor's own story about the filming.

"Movie Making Across the World." *Th Arts* 32 (Jan 48) 20–26; 32 (Feb 48) 51–53. Cocteau on the filming of **Beauty and the Beast.**

"Pictorial: In Bed with Becket." *Playboy* 11 (No. 2, Feb 64) 76–79. Richard Burton, Peter O'Toole, Veronique Verdell in candid photos of bedroom scene taken during filming of **Becket.**

Glenville, Peter. "Reflections on **Becket.**" *F&F* 10 (No. 7, Apr 64) 7–8. On his making of *Becket.*

Hanson, Curtis Lee. "**The Bedford Incident.**" *Cinema* (Calif) 3 (No. 1) 28. Interview with James B. Harris about this film.

Brooks, Louise. "On Location with Billy Wellman." *London Mag* new series 8 (No. 2, May 68) 32–45. The actress writes about working with this director on **Beggars of Life** in 1928.

Zinnemann, Fred. "Revelations." *F&F* 10 (No. 12, Sep 64) 5–6. On filming **Behold a Pale Horse.**

Jacob, Gilles. "Benjamin." *S&S* 37 (Spring 68) 74. Michel Deville directs, Nina Companeez writes; a new team?

"Movies in the Making: **Bells Are Ringing.**" *Dance Mag* 34 (July 60) 42–43. Charles O'Curran tells how he makes nondancers dance.

"So Big: Production of **Ben-Hur.**" *Newswk* 51 (5 May 58) 114.

Genêt. "Letters from Rome." *New Yorker* 34 (27 Sep 58) 96+. A location report of the filming of **Ben-Hur.**

"**Ben-Hur** Rides a Chariot Again." *Life* 46 (19 Jan 59) 70–73. Filming the chariot race.

Coughlan, Robert. "Generals' Mighty Chariots: **Ben-Hur.**" *Life* 47 (16 Nov 59) 118–120+. *See 4k(4).*

Whitcomb, Jon. "**Ben-Hur** Rides Again." *Cosmopolitan* 147 (Dec 59) 26–29. History of *Ben-Hur,* with location account.

Marton, Andrew. "**Ben-Hur's** Chariot Race." *FIR* 11 (No. 1, Jan 60) 27–32+. How the race was staged and filmed.

Heston, Charlton. "**Ben-Hur** Diaries." *Cinema* (Calif) 2 (No. 2, July 64) 10–13+. Star's daily diary during making of this film.

Brownlow, Kevin. "**Ben-Hur:** The Heroic Fiasco." *F&F* 16 (No. 4, Jan 70) 26–32+. Selection from his book *The Parade's Gone By* (Ballantine, 1969) on the making of the 1924 *Ben-Hur.*

Jones, Dorothy B. "Foreign Sensibilities." *FIR* 6 (Nov 55). *See 7a(1).* About **Bengal Brigade.**

"Benny Is Heard But Not Seen." *Life* 40 (13 Feb 56) 56. The jazz clarinetist plays his own music, as Steve Allen pantomimes, in Universal-International's **The Benny Goodman Story.**

Granet, Bert. "Berlin Express Diary." *Screen Writer* 3 (May 48) 12–13+. This film was the first to use American actors in occupied Germany.

Clayton, Jack. "Challenge from Short Story

Films." *F&F* 2 (No. 5, Feb 56) 10. About making **The Bespoke Overcoat.**

Wyler, William. "No Magic Wand." *Screen Writer* 2 (Feb 47) 1–14. Detailed history of the writing and preparation of **The Best Years of Our Lives.**

Lyon, Peter. "The Hollywood Picture." *Hwd Q* 3 (No. 4, Summer 48–Summer 49) 341–361. Script of CBS radio documentary attempting to reproduce roles of Robert Sherwood, William Wyler, Samuel Goldwyn, and others in making **The Best Years of Our Lives.**

Wald, Jerry. "Don't Pity the Working Girls." *F&F* 6 (No. 1, Oct 59) 6+. On **The Best of Everything.**

"Pictorial: The Dolls of Beyond the Valley." *Playboy* 17 (No. 7, July 70) 121–129. On-set shots of **Beyond the Valley of the Dolls.**

Robinson, David. "The Two Bezhin Meadows." *S&S* 37 (Winter 67–68) 33–37. A detailed history of Sergei Eisenstein's two versions of **Bezhin Meadow** and of the political pressures that surrounded the filming; a half-hour film based on single frames has been made.

Leyda, Jay. "Eisenstein's **Bezhin Meadow.**" *S&S* 28 (No. 2, Spring 59) 74–77. Extracts from author's production diary on the film, to be published in his book *Kino* (reprinted Macmillan, 1972).

La Barre, H. "Ava in Pakistan." *Cosmopolitan* 140 (Mar 56) 70–73. Filming **Bhowani Junction.**

Gray, Martin. "Must They Export Hollywood?" *F&F* 2 (No. 12, Sep 56) 8. Filming in Pakistan of George Cukor's **Bhowani Junction.**

Ardagh, John. "Huston in Eden." *S&S* 33 (Autumn 64) 173. John Huston comments on filming the American-Italian coproduction **The Bible** in Rome.

"Problems in Paradise." *Newswk* 64 (14 Sep 64) 90+. Huston's troubles making **The Bible.**

Pollock, Eileen, and Robert Mason Pollock. "The Making of Eve." *Show* 4 (Oct 64) 64–65+. Casting of Ulla Bergryd in the role of Eve for Huston's **The Bible.**

"Bible as Living Technicolor." *Time* 85 (15 Jan 65) 70. The filming of **The Bible.**

Sage, Tom. "Giraffe in Piazza del Popolo." *Nat Rev* 17 (9 Feb 65) 105–106. On the filming of **The Bible.**

"Noah: Literal View of the Bible in Huston's New Movie, **The Bible.**" *Look* 29 (27 July 65) 21–26.

"Ark That John Built." *Life* 59 (13 Aug 65) 43–44. Huston filming **The Bible.**

Ross, Lillian. "Our Far-Flung Correspondents, **The Bible** in Dinocitta." *New Yorker* 41 (25 Sep 65) 185–186+. On-set account of John Huston's *The Bible* made for Dino De Laurentiis; other productions in Italy.

Knight, Arthur. "The King John Version." *Sat Rev* 49 (1 Oct 66) 34. John Huston's **The Bible** in production.

Chiaromonte, Nicola. "Italian Movies." *Partisan Rev* 16 (June 49). See *4e(3b)*. About **The Bicycle Thief.**

"Banned Bicycle." *Newswk* 35 (13 Mar 50). See *7c(4)*. About **The Bicycle Thief.**

"Bicycle Thief Banned by Motion Picture Association of America." *New Rep* 122 (13 Mar 50). See *7c(4)*.

"Censor's Censor." *Time* 55 (13 Mar 50). See *7c(4)*. **The Bicycle Thief.**

Crichton, Kyle. "Soon I Am in Bellevue." *Collier's* 101 (9 Apr 38) 51+. An interview with motion-picture producer Harlan Thompson; production of **The Big Broadcast of 1938.**

"Peck, Incorporated." *Newswk* 50 (21 Oct 57) 114–115. Gregory Peck's first personal production, **The Big Country.**

"Hollywood Prefabs a Pioneer Boat." *Pop Mech* 97 (Apr 52) 146–148. Some technical information on the filming of Howard Hawks' **The Big Sky,** and on keelboats in general.

Johnson, Albert. "Echoes from **The Birds.**" *S&S* 32 (Spring 63) 65–66. Hitchcock on location in northern California for this film.

Hitchcock, Alfred. "**The Birds.**" *Take One* 1 (No. 10, 1968) 6–7. Hitchcock discusses special effects used in *The Birds.*

MacKaye, M. "**Birth of a Nation.**" *Scribner's* 102 (Nov 37). See *5, D. W. Griffith.*

Cripps, Thomas R. "The Reaction of the Negro to the Motion Picture **Birth of a Nation.**" *Historian* 25 (May 63) See *7a(3)*.

Stern, Seymour. "Griffith: 1—**The Birth of a Nation.**" *F Cult* (No. 36, 1965) 1–210. Entire issue devoted to encyclopedia of information on D. W. Griffith's *The Birth of a Nation:* production, exhibition, technique, musical score, impact; quotes from other authorities and newspaper clippings.

"The Image of the U.S." *Time* 66 (12 Sep 55). See *7e(2)*. About **Blackboard Jungle.**

Schary, Dore. "Hollywood's Public Relations." *FIR* 6 (Dec 55). See *6d*. About **Blackboard Jungle.**

"She Who Got Slapped." *Life* 46 (23 Feb 59) 73–74. The filming of **Black Orchid:** Ina Balin is slapped repeatedly for retakes.

Taylor, W. "Secret Movie Censors: Behind the Attack on **Blockade.**" *Nation* 147 (9 July 38). See *7c(2)*.

Dugan, James. "Movies." *New Masses* 28 (2 Aug 38) 30–31. Reports on support of the boycotted film **Blockade** by various organizations.

"Holdouts." *Time* 19 (9 May 32) 23. Sternberg and Dietrich refuse to work on revised script of **Blonde Venus;** Paramount threatens to sue them.

"Antonioni's Hypnotic Eye on a Frantic World."

Life 62 (27 Jan 67) 62B–65. Quotes from Antonioni, and the filming of **Blow-Up.**

Vidor, King. "Lillian Gish in Opera." *F&F* 1 (No. 4, Jan 55) 4–5. The story of the making of *La Bohème* (1926) excerpted from Vidor's autobiography, *A Tree Is a Tree* (Harcourt, 1953).

Knight, Arthur. "**Bolshoi Ballet:** How the Film Was Made." *Dance Mag* 32 (Jan 58) 38–43. An interview with Paul Czinner, director.

Whitcomb, John. "**Bonjour Tristesse** on Location." *Cosmopolitan* 144 (Mar 58) 76–77.

Penn, Arthur. "**Bonnie and Clyde:** Private Morality and Public Violence." *Take One* 1 (No. 6, 1967) 20–22. The director discusses various aspects of his film.

Towne, Robert. "A Trip with **Bonnie and Clyde.**" *Cinema* (Calif) 3 (No. 5, Summer 67) 4–7. On the making of this film.

Toland, John. "Sad Ballad of the Real **Bonnie and Clyde.**" *NYTM* (18 Feb 68) 26–29+. On the myth and the historical characters. Discussion (10 Mar 68) 16+.

Renoir, Jean. "How I Came to Film *Boudu.*" *F Soc Rev* (Feb 67) 23–24. Brief introductory remarks on his film **Boudu Sauvé des Eaux.**

Lassally, Walter. "Making **Bow Bells.**" *F&F* 1 (No. 3, Dec 54) 6. Production notes by the cameraman.

Rapper, Irving. "Bull Fervour." *F&F* 1 (No. 11, Aug 55) 11. Experiences in Mexico making **The Boy and the Bull,** by the director.

Star, Jack. "Faces of **The Boys in the Band.**" *Look* 33 (2 Dec 69) 62–67. Portraits of the cast.

"Making of a Movie Matador." *Life* 29 (10 July 50) 55–56+. Mel Ferrer and stand-in cope with **The Brave Bulls.**

"Meet Miss Miroslava." *Life* 29 (10 July 50) 58. Czechoslovakian actress in **The Brave Bulls.**

Brooks, Richard. "A Novel Isn't a Movie." *FIR* 3 (Feb 52). See *3f(2).* About **The Brick Foxhole.**

"Built to Be Destroyed: The Bridge of **The Bridge on the River Kwai.**" *Illus London News* 231 (9 Nov 57) 805.

"*Popular Photography* Analyzes an Outstanding New Film: **Bridge on the River Kwai.**" *Pop Photog* 42 (Apr 58). See *2e.*

Harvey, E. "Legs and a Legend." *Collier's* 133 (5 Mar 54) 24–27+. Cyd Charisse and Gene Kelly in **Brigadoon;** concentration on the dancing ability of the stars.

"Highland Flingding." *Life* 37 (9 Aug 54) 94–95+. Scottish moors are built indoors for MGM's film version of **Brigadoon.**

Robinson, David. "Around Angel Lane." *S&S* 39 (Summer 70). See *4e(1).* About **Bronco Bullfrog.**

Brooks, Richard. "On Filming Karamazov." *FIR* 9 (Feb 58). See *3f(2).* About **The Brothers Karamazov.**

Brooks, Richard. "Dostoievsky, Love—and American Cinema." *F&F* 4 (No. 7, Apr 58) 26. Director writes about **The Brothers Karamazov.**

Denton, J. F. "Red Man Plays Indian." *Collier's* 113 (18 Mar 44) 18–19. Navajos help the filming of **Buffalo Bill.**

Lane, John Francis. "Is Marlon Brando Really Necessary?" *Show* (Jan 70) 46–48+. Comments from Gillo Pontecorvo on disputes with Brando while filming *Quemada* (**Burn!**).

"Old Comic and Pupil." *Life* 42 (6 May 57) 91–92+. Keaton coaches Donald O'Connor for his role in **The Buster Keaton Story.**

C

French, Carl. "Hollywood Goes to Rome." *Collier's* 121 (6 Mar 48) 18–19. On Gregory Ratoff's filming of Orson Welles in **Cagliostro.**

Kracauer, Siegfried. "Caligari." *Partisan Rev* 14 (No. 2, Mar–Apr 47) 160–173. Chapter from author's book *From Caligari to Hitler* (Princeton University Press); how **The Cabinet of Dr. Caligari** came to be made.

Morgenstern, Joseph. "Letter from **Camelot.**" *Newswk* 69 (8 May 67) 100+. On the filming of the Warner Brothers musical.

Borgzinner, Jon. "Shining Pageant of **Camelot.**" *Life* 63 (22 Sep 67) 70–76+. The filming of *Camelot,* and story on Richard Harris.

"Pictorial: *Camille* Turns On." *Playboy* 16 (No. 5, May 69) 150–155. Scenes from film **Camille 2000,** an updating of *Camille.*

"Candy for Everybody." *Newswk* 71 (5 Feb 68) 76–76A. A short account of the production of the film *Candy.*

Shenker, Israel. "Good Grief, It's **Candy** on Film!" *NYTM* (11 Feb 68) 50–51+. Production story.

Hughes, Eileen. "**Candy.**" *Life* 64 (8 Mar 68) 43–44. The cast's short comments about *Candy* on the set in Rome.

"Everybody's Sweet Little Swede." *Look* 32 (14 May 68) 50–54+. Pictures of Ewa Aulin, star of **Candy.**

"Pictorial: **Can Hieronymus Merkin Ever Forget Mercy Humppe?**" *Playboy* 16 (No. 3, Mar 69) 130–139. Scenes of Anthony Newley, Joan Collins, *et al.* from the movie.

"Convicts See a Movie of Their Own Escape." *Life* 25 (2 Aug 48) 72–74+. An account of the participants' reactions to the film treatment of their prison break in **Canon City.**

Tracy, Spencer. "Log of We're Here." *Woman's Home Companion* 64 (Apr 37) 13–14+. Location work for **Captains Courageous.**

"John Huston, Actor." *Newswk* 61 (18 Mar 63) 102. Otto Preminger and Huston working on **The Cardinal.**

"Preminger & Company." *Show* 3 (Sep 63) 98–101. On location for the filming of **The Cardinal.**

Preminger, Otto. "**The Cardinal** and I." *F&F* 10 (No. 2, Nov 63) 11–12. On making of the film *The Cardinal.*

"John Cardinal Huston." *Life* 55 (22 Nov 63) 61–62+. Huston acts in **The Cardinal.**

Silke, James R. "Three Directors in Danger: Otto the Great." *Cinema* (Calif) 1 (No. 6, Nov–Dec 63) 4–9. Report on Preminger's **The Cardinal.**

Walsh, Moira. "Otto Preminger Looks at the Catholic Church." *Cath World* 198 (Mar 64) 365–371. *See 4k(5).* About **The Cardinal.**

"Little Cleopatra." *Time* 87 (6 May 66) 86. Filming **Casino Royale.**

Hamilton, J. "Who Is the Real James Bond Anyhow?" *Look* 30 (15 Nov 66) 50–54+. Various actors in **Casino Royale.**

Allen, Woody. "The Girls of **Casino Royale.**" *Playboy* 14 (No. 2, Feb 67) 109–121.

Heller, Joseph. "How I Found James Bond." *Holiday* 41 (June 67) *See 2d.* About **Casino Royale.**

Sokolov, Raymond A. "There's a Catch: **Catch-22.**" *Newswk* 73 (3 Mar 69) 52–55. The filming in Guaymas, Mexico.

Ephron, N. "Yossarian Is Alive and Well in the Mexican Desert: Production of **Catch-22.**" *NYTM* (16 Mar 69) 30–31+.

Arkin, Alan. "A **Catch-22** Family Album." *Show* (Mar 70) 39–48. Captioned photographs reporting filming in Mexico and Rome, with comments on the cast and crew.

Henry, B. "Frantic Filming of a Crazy Classic." *Life* 68 (12 June 70) 44–48. **Catch-22:** fragments of a diary kept by the screenwriter, Buck Henry.

"Some Are More Yossarian Than Others." *Time* 95 (15 June 70). *See 5, Mike Nichols.* About **Catch-22.**

Flagler, M. "Mike Nichols Tries the Impossible: A Movie of **Catch-22.**" *Look* 34 (30 June 70) 55–59. Production notes and Nichols' thoughts on the film.

Thegze, Chuck. " 'I See Everything Twice': An Examination of **Catch-22.**" *FQ* 24 (No. 1, Fall 70) 7–17. The problem of adaptation of the novel.

"Screen Morals." *New S&N* 8 (17 Nov 34). *See 7b(1a).* About **The Catspaw.**

Laing, Nora. "**Cavalcade** at Hollywood: The Casting of the Film." *Rev of Reviews* (London) 82 (No. 515, 10 Dec 32) 53–57.

Wallis, Hal. "Movies Stars You Never Saw." *Rdrs Dig* 75 (Nov 59) 122–124. Hollywood producer describes the filming of semidocumentary war story **Cease Fire.**

Frank, Robert. "Films: Entertainment Shacked Up with Art." *Arts Mag* 41 (Mar 67) 23. Cameraman on **Chappaqua** writes of the superiority of Conrad Rooks' first film to Antonioni's *Blow-Up.*

"*Tom Jones* Meets *Goldfinger.*" *Time* 90 (4 Aug 67) 57. On the filming of **The Charge of the Light Brigade.**

Ehrlich, Henry. "The Light Brigade Charges Again." *Look* 32 (6 Feb 68) 58–61. A picture essay and a short portrait of David Hemmings in **The Charge of the Light Brigade.**

Brown, Jeff. "Making of a Movie." *Holiday* 39 (Feb 66) 87–99. Daily and hourly notebook on the making of Arthur Penn's **The Chase.**

Leonard, John. "**Che!** The Making of a Movie Revolutionary." *NYTM* (8 Dec 68) 56–57+. On the filming of **Che!**

Morgenstern, Joseph. "Che Lives!" *Newswk* 72 (9 Dec 68) 110–111. An on-location account of the filming of **Che!**

Carey, E. Gilbreth. "**Cheaper by the Dozen** Goes to Hollywood." *Parents Mag* 25 (May 50) 34–35+. One of the Gilbreths recalls how their book *Cheaper by the Dozen* became a movie.

Warhol, A. "My Favorite Superstar, Notes on My Epic, **Chelsea Girls.**" *Arts Mag* 41 (Feb 67) 26. Warhol "interrogated" by Gerard Malanga.

Renoir, Jean. "La Chienne." *Film* (No. 9, Sep–Oct 56) 8–11. Renoir discusses his film and his own outlook toward realism.

Koval, Francis. "Benedek in Hamburg." *S&S* 24 (Jan–Mar 55) 118. Laslo Benedek is making **Children, Mothers, and a General** for Erich Pommer.

Billard, Pierre. "**Chimes at Midnight.**" *S&S* 34 (Spring 65) 64–65. For his Falstaff film, Welles intended to use many close-ups, but was tempted by his Spanish interior locations to use perspectives "which irresistibly recall Eisenstein."

Cobos, Juan, and Miguel Rubio. "Welles and Falstaff." *S&S* 35 (Autumn 66) 158–163. Edited version of interview conducted by Cobos, Welles' assistant during the shooting of **Chimes at Midnight** (*Falstaff*), and by his colleague on the Spanish magazine *Griffith,* where it was originally printed; mainly about Shakespeare adaptation and Falstaff.

Cobos, Juan, and Miguel Rubio. "Welles on *Falstaff.*" *CdC in Eng* (No. 11, Sep 67) 5–15. Orson Welles discusses his new film, also shown as **Chimes at Midnight**; reviews on pp. 19–23.

Simons, Mary. "**Chitty Chitty Bang Bang.**" *Look* 32 (24 Dec 68) 84–85+. Production stills.

Baker, Peter. "And Now—the Greatest Picture Since . . ." *F&F* 7 (No. 9, June 61) 14–15+. Visit to the set of **El Cid,** including a sample call sheet.

"Life of the Spanish Hero of the 11th Century, **El Cid,** Retold in the Original Country in a

Major Film." *Illus London News* 239 (18 Nov 61) 884–885. Seven photos with brief synopsis.

"Norman Jewison Discusses Thematic Action in **The Cincinnati Kid**." *Cinema* (Calif) 2 (No. 6, July–Aug 65) 4–6.

Ellison, Harlan. "Edward G. Robinson in **The Cincinnati Kid**." *Cinema* (Calif) 2 (No. 6, July–Aug 65) 12–13.

Pritt, Emile. "Orson Welles and **Citizen Kane**." *New Masses* 38 (4 Feb 41) 26–27. The attempt to suppress *Citizen Kane* shows the producers' regret that they brought to Hollywood a genuine antifascist.

Sage, M. "Hearst Over Hollywood: Matter of Orson Welles' Film, **Citizen Kane**." *New Rep* 104 (24 Feb 41) 270–271. This commentary on the Hearst-Welles feud is critical of the Hays office for its failure to support Welles.

Drake, Herbert. "**Citizen** (Orson Welles) **Kane**." *Calif Arts and Arch* 58 (No. 7, July 41) 16+. Orson Welles' struggle with the industry in making **Citizen Kane**.

Shaw, Robert. "Hearstian Criteria for Movie Critics." *Screen Writer* 1 (Sep 45). *See 3b.* About **Citizen Kane**.

"Alexandria Comes to Buckinghamshire." *Illus London News* 238 (14 Jan 61) 75. Two large stills of Alexandria set in Buckinghamshire for **Cleopatra**.

"Liz Is Back as Enchantress of Egypt." *Life* 51 (6 Oct 61) 93–98+. Elizabeth Taylor, after illness, returns to work in **Cleopatra**.

Capp, Al. "The Roman Spring of Al Capp." *Show* 2 (June 62) 52–55+. On location in Rome, with comments about the filming of **Cleopatra**; remarks from Federico Fellini.

Alpert, Hollis. "Joseph and **Cleopatra**." *Sat Rev* 45 (18 Aug 62) 20+. On-set account of *Cleopatra* and director Joseph L. Mankiewicz.

"Pictorial: Liz as Cleo." *Playboy* 10 (No. 1, Jan 63) 80–87. Pictures of Elizabeth Taylor taken during production of **Cleopatra**.

"Fortunes of **Cleopatra**." *Newswk* 61 (25 Mar 63) 63–66. Production from the beginning, reasons for rising costs, comments by many involved.

Mankiewicz, J. L. "**Cleopatra** Barges In—At Last." *Life* 54 (10 Apr 63) 72–81. The making of the disaster-ridden epic.

"**Cleopatra**'s Prospects." *Fortune* 67 (May 63). *See 6a(1).*

Hamilton, J. "Elizabeth Taylor Talks about **Cleopatra**." *Look* 27 (7 May 63) 41–47+. Taylor and Richard Burton give their opinions of each other and their experiences during filming.

Wanger, Walter, and Joe Hyams. "**Cleopatra**: Trials and Tribulations of an Epic Film." *SEP* 236 (1 June 63) 28–38+.

"Can Cleo Pay It Back?" *Bus Wk* (8 June 63). *See 6a(1).* About **Cleopatra**.

"**Cleopatra** Touch." *Economist* 207 (15 June 63). *See 6a(1).*

Price, James. "**Cleopatra** Revisited." *London Mag* new series 4 (No. 6, July 64) 73–79.

"A Day's Work for Gary Cooper." *Look* 10 (No. 21, 15 Oct 46) 70–71. Production stills of **Cloak and Dagger**, directed by Fritz Lang.

"Cold-Turkey Month." *Time* 94 (13 Sep 69) 76. On the filming of **Cold Turkey** in Greenfield, Iowa.

"Wyler's Wiles." *Time* 85 (18 June 65) 92. William Wyler and the making of **The Collector**.

Corbett, T. "Film and the Book: A Case Study of **The Collector**." *English J* 57 (Mar 68) 328–333.

"The Green Shills of Africa." *Time* 89 (3 Feb 67) 55. On the filming of **The Comedians**.

Rasponi, Lantranco. "Burtons in Dahomey." *Vogue* 149 (15 Apr 67) 92–93+. The making of **The Comedians**.

Garrison, Lloyd. "On location with Richard and Elizabeth (& 145 Friends)." *NYTM* (7 May 67) 30–31+. On the filming of **The Comedians** in Dahomey.

Brossard, Chandler. "On Location with Richard and Liz: Why They're Never Dull." *Look* 31 (27 June 67) 64–67. The filming of **The Comedians**.

"Famous Case Is Retried." *Life* 46 (13 Apr 59) 60+. The filming of **Compulsion**.

Murphy, Richard. ". . . And Why We Were Compelled to Put Frost on the Cake." *F&F* 5 (No. 8, May 59) 19+. The need to sell a story changes its original intent; on the film **Compulsion**.

"Horn-Happy: Filming **Confidential Squad**." *New Yorker* (31 Dec 49) 12. On location.

Oshlag, Dorothy. "Filming **The Connection**." *S&S* 30 (Spring 61) 69. Shirley Clarke experimenting with reality; her backers.

Whitcomb, Jon. "Jon Whitcomb Watches the Filming of the Fabulous Life of Genghis Khan." *Cosmopolitan* 137 (Nov 54) 74–77. Backstage look at **The Conqueror**.

Powell, Dick. "Sand, Sun, and History." *F&F* 1 (No. 6, Mar 55) 7+. Actor-director Powell describes the making of **The Conqueror**.

Oshlag, Dorothy. "**The Cool World**." *S&S* 32 (Summer 63) 121–122. With Shirley Clarke on location in Harlem for this film.

Chelminski, R. "Cotton Cashes In." *Life* 69 (28 Aug 70) 58–61. Comedy with black cast booms at the box office; literary history of the novelist who wrote **Cotton Comes to Harlem**.

Perlberg, William. "Searching Europe for Authenticity." *F&F* 7 (No. 5, Feb 61) 9. Locations for **The Counterfeit Traitor** discussed by the film's producer.

Baker, Peter. "The Tour of Babel." *F&F* 7 (No. 5, Feb 61) 10–11+. On location with **The Counterfeit Traitor.**

Brownlow, Kevin. "Watching Chaplin Direct **The Countess from Hong Kong.**" *F Cult* (No. 40, Spring 66) 2–4. Detailed dialogue and description of set visit.

Hamblin, Dora Jane. "Passionate Clown Comes Back." *Life* 60 (1 Apr 66) 80–86. Charles Chaplin directs **A Countess from Hong Kong.**

Hamilton, Jack. "Charlie and His Countess." *Look* 30 (19 Apr 66) 96–100. On the set of **A Countess from Hong Kong** with Charlie Chaplin.

"The Custard Pie of Creation." *Newswk* 67 (6 June 66). *See 5, Charlie Chaplin.* About **A Countess from Hong Kong.**

Gilliatt, Penelope. "The Genius of Chaplin." *Vogue* 148 (July 66) 94–97+. On the filming of **A Countess from Hong Kong.**

"Comic Knighthood for Kaye." *Life* 40 (30 Jan 56) 93–94+. Preview of Danny Kaye in **The Court Jester.**

Callenbach, Ernest, and Albert Johnson. "Feature Production in San Francisco: An Interview with John Korty." *FQ* 19 (No. 3, Spring 66). *See 5, John Korty.* About **Crazy Quilt.**

Cameron, Ian, V. F. Perkins, and Mark Shivas. "A Conversation about **The Criminal** with Joseph Losey." *NY F Bul,* Series 2 (Nos. 12, 13, 14, 1961) 14–21.

Cohen, Elliott. "Letter from a Movie Maker." *Commentary* 4 (1947). *See 7b(2a).* About **Crossfire.**

Scott, Adrian. "You Can't Do That!" *Screen Writer* 3 (Aug 47). *See 3a(6).* About **Crossfire.**

Mason, James. "The Man Who Wants Men of Steel." *F&F* 4 (No. 11, Aug 58) 6+. Actor writes about **Cry Terror,** directed by Andrew Stone.

"Cry the Beloved Country." *Our World* 6 (July 51) 34–36. Visiting actors taste South Africa's race hate while making movie.

Gries, Tom. "**Cyrano de Bergerac,** Stanley Kramer Production." *Th Arts* 34 (Nov 50) 32–35.

D

Clark, Roy. "Movies in the Making: **Darby O'Gill and the Little People.**" *Dance Mag* 33 (May 59) 18–19.

"Hard Way." *Time* 81 (25 Jan 63) 59+. How **David and Lisa** was made.

Trombley, W. "Small-Budget Triumph; **David and Lisa.**" *SEP* 236 (15 Mar 63) 56+.

Carson, L. M. Kit. "More Notes from the Underground." *Cinema* (Calif) 5 (No. 1, 1969) 20–22. On the making of **David Holzman's Diary.**

Adamson, Joseph. "The Seventeen Preliminary

Scripts of **A Day at the Races.**" *CJ* 8 (No. 2, Spring 69). *See 2d(1).*

"Just Like the Movies." *Lit Dig* 124 (11 Dec 37). *See 7b(3).* About **Dead End.**

Alpert, Hollis. "Visconti in Venice." *Sat Rev* 53 (8 Aug 70) 16–18. The making of **Death in Venice:** problems of actors, rights, setting; talk with Dirk Bogarde.

Hinxman, Margaret. "**Death in Venice.**" *S&S* 39 (Autumn 70) 198–200. Luchino Visconti works in Trieste.

Tynan, Kathleen. "**Death in Venice:** At the End of the Path of Beauty Lies Eros." *Vogue* 156 (Dec 70) 164–165+. The author talks with people concerned in the creation of Visconti's film.

Tellig, Jean. "A New Wave." *S&S* 29 (Autumn 60) 172. A short review of **Death of a Girl,** including comments by its twenty-four-year-old French director, Pierre Puerilescu.

Benedek, Laslo. "Directing **Death of a Salesman** for the Screen." *Th Arts* 36 (Jan 52) 36–37+. How the film form altered the stage play.

Benedek, Laslo. "Play into Picture." *S&S* 22 (Oct–Dec 52). *See 3f(1).* About **Death of a Salesman.**

Joel, Lydia. "**Les Demoiselles du Rochefort.**" *Dance Mag* 40 (Oct 66) 20–21+. Production background.

"Colossal Collision." *Time* 58 (30 July 51) 68. Train crash for **The Denver and Rio Grande.**

Clayton, George. "Contemporary Morality of the Marquis de Sade." *Cinema* (Calif) 4 (No. 4, 1968) 20–22. Comments on the film **De Sade** and on other film villains.

"Pictorial: De Sade." *Playboy* 16 (No. 6, June 69) 105–109. Scenes with Senta Berger, John Huston.

Joseph, Robert. "**De Sade.**" *F&F* 16 (No. 5, Feb 70) 63–66. On the predecessors of the 1967 film.

Harvey, E. "Napoleon Brando." *Collier's* 134 (29 Oct 54) 108–109. The efforts of Brando to look like Napoleon in **Desirée.**

Macgowan, Kenneth. "O'Neill and a Mature Hollywood Outlook." *Th Arts* 42 (Apr 58). *See 3f(1).* About **Desire Under the Elms.**

Ehrlich, Henry. "Sinatra's English Import." *Look* 32 (19 Mar 68) 71–75. On Jackie Bisset and filming of **The Detective.**

Whitcomb, J. "Red Coats Are Coming Again." *Cosmopolitan* 146 (Feb 59) 19–21. Filming of **The Devil's Disciple** plus the career of Burt Lancaster.

Stang, J. "Stevens Relives Anne Frank's Story." *NYTM* (3 Aug 58) 14+. **The Diary of Anne Frank.**

"Great Director, Great Story." *Life* 45 (22 Dec 58) 44–51. George Stevens directs **The Diary of Anne Frank.**

Johnson, Albert. "Sounds from the Westoren."

S&S 28 (No. 2, Spring 59) 79. Visit to the set for **The Diary of Anne Frank.**

Brusati, Franco. "Disorder." *Cinema* (Calif) 1 (No. 4, June–July 63) 14–15. Interview and summary of this film.

Sage, Tom. "Who's Afraid of **Dr. Faustus?**" *Nat Rev* 18 (27 Dec 66) 1319–1320. Production story of Richard Burton's own film for Oxford University.

Price, Stanley. "On the Spanish Steppes with **Dr. Zhivago.**" *Show* 5 (May 65) 36–41. Comments on the filming of *Dr. Zhivago,* with emphasis on locations (Spain, Finland), and remarks from David Lean about film as the great modern "near-art" form.

Stewart, R. S. "**Dr. Zhivago:** The Making of a Movie." *Atlantic* 216 (Aug 65) 58–64. On-location interviews with David Lean and Omar Sharif.

Leduc, Violette. "I Went on Location with Zhivago." *Vogue* 146 (15 Sep 65) 114–121+. Making the film of **Dr. Zhivago.**

Lawrenson, H. "Letter Home." *Esq* 64 (Dec 65) 132+. Filming of **Doctor Zhivago.**

"Oscarbound: **Doctor Zhivago.**" *Time* 86 (24 Dec 65) 44–45.

Martin, Harold H. "The Two Loves of **Doctor Zhivago.**" *SEP* 239 (15 Jan 66) 26–31. Comparison of Julie Christie and Geraldine Chaplin.

Macpherson, Kenneth. "A Night Prowl in La Mancha." *Close Up* 9 (No. 4, Dec 32) 225–230. Comments on Pabst's filming of **Don Quixote.**

"Filming **Don Quixote.**" *Living Age* 343 (Feb 33) 555. Details behind Charles Chaplin's backing of the Chaliapin film.

Buck, Tony. "Cherkassov's **Don Quixote.**" *S&S* 27 (Autumn 58). See 5, Nikolai Cherkassov.

Kozintsev, G. "Making of Russian Movies." (Tr. by G. Azrael.) *Atlantic* 205 (June 60) 87–91. The production and direction of **Don Quixote**—planning, rehearsals, stars.

Lowenstein, Harold. "I Filmed in Madrid." *S&S* 7 (No. 26, Summer 38) 60–61. Personal reactions to the country, political climate, and production of film, **Dona Francisquita.**

Cooper, Eunice, and Helen Dinerman. "Analysis of the Film **Don't Be a Sucker:** A Study in Communication." *Pub Opin Q* 14 (1951). See 7b(2b).

Barber, Rowland. "The Seven Days of Sam Katzman." *Show* 2 (June 62) 98–101. How Katzman makes "B" movies cheaper and faster; seven-day diary on the filming of **Don't Knock the Twist.**

"Movie Making." *Life* 18 (8 Jan 45) 69–77. Comprehensive report on the elaborate preparations necessitated by a brief interior one-line take in Warners' **The Doughboys.**

Jenkins, Dan. "How to Succeed at Racing Without Really Racing." *Sports Illus* 31 (24

Nov 69) 66. Robert Redford on **Downhill Racer.**

Probyn, Brian. "The Camera on Skis." *F&F* 16 (No. 6, Mar 70) 14–16. Filming the skiing sequences in **Downhill Racer.**

Fayard, J. "Happy Jack." *Life* 68 (27 Mar 70) 36A–36C. Interviews for a new film, **Drive He Said;** how Jack Nicholson asks a girl to take her clothes off.

"Censorship Shortened These *Duel* Scenes." *Look* 11 (No. 12, 10 June 47) 110. Producer David Selznick cut **Duel in the Sun** to get a favorable rating from the Legion of Decency.

E

Fonda, Peter, and Leslie Reyner. "Thoughts and Attitudes About **Easy Rider.**" *Film* (No. 56, Autumn 69) 24. Fonda comments about the goals of the film.

Lane, John Francis. "Antonioni Diary." *F&F* 8 (No. 6, Mar 62) 11–12+. Extracts from notebook kept during film of **L'Eclisse.**

"Dizzy Doings on a Set." *Life* 55 (19 July 63) 95–97. The making of **8½.**

Fellini, Federico. "Fellini **8½.**" *Cinema* (Calif) 1 (No. 5, Aug–Sep 63) 19–22. Comments from director and pictures from **8½.**

"**Éléna et les Hommes.**" *S&S* 25 (Spring 56) 192–193. Ingrid Bergman in a Jean Renoir film; photographs of production.

"Herd of Delicate Destroyers." *Life* 35 (12 Oct 53) 75+. Elephants destroy the interior of a Ceylon plantation house in a scene from **Elephant Walk.**

Whitcomb, Jon. "**Elmer Gantry** Comes to the Screen." *Cosmopolitan* 148 (Mar 60) 78–81. On location with Jean Simmons and Burt Lancaster.

Johnson, Albert. "*Studs Lonigan* and **Elmer Gantry.**" *S&S* 29 (Autumn 60). See 9, *Studs Lonigan.*

McBride, Joseph, and Michael Wilmington. "A Long Way from Home." *S&S* 39 (Winter 69–70) 39–43. The first Swedish film on location in the United States, **The Emigrants,** directed by Jan Troell; conversations with leading actors Liv Ullman and Max von Sydow, who mainly talk about Ingmar Bergman and his films.

"Bing Crosby in the 'Alps.'" *Look* 10 (No. 20, 1 Oct 46) 28–29. On location for Paramount's **Emperor Waltz,** directed by Billy Wilder.

Merryman, Richard. "Cinematic Assault." *Life* 67 (7 Nov 69) 64–72. On **End of the Road,** independent production, and its challenge to Hollywood's system.

Cahn, Robert. "Dance Is Born." *Collier's* 130 (12 July 52) 42–43+. A picture essay and a short account of the dance sequences from

MGM musical **Everything I Have Is Yours** starring Marge and Gower Champion.

Baker, Peter. "Exodus." *F&F* 6 (No. 12, Sep 60) 28–30. A visit to the set during filming.

Whitcomb, J. "The Sage of **Exodus,** Movie Version." *Cosmopolitan* 149 (Nov 60) 12–15. Location story.

F

"Transfer to the East." *New Yorker* 32 (1 Dec 56) 42. Movie makers in New York—on the set of **A Face in the Crowd.**

"Calamity Lucy." *Newswk* 56 (22 Aug 60) 86–87. On-set account of **The Facts of Life,** starring Lucille Ball.

Trauffaut, François. "Journal of **Fahrenheit 451.**" *CdC in Eng* (No. 5, 1966) 11–23; (No. 6, Dec 66) 10–23; (No. 7, Jan 67) 8–19. The making of the film as recorded by its director.

Robinson, David. "Two for the Sci-Fi." *S&S* 35 (Spring 66. *See 9, 2001: A Space Odyssey*. About **Fahrenheit 451.**

Mann, Anthony. "Empire Demolition." *F&F* 10 (No. 6, Mar 64) 7–8. On the making of **The Fall of the Roman Empire.**

"New Light on Roman History from **The Fall of the Roman Empire.**" *Illus London News* 244 (4 Apr 64) 541. Five photos with brief synopsis.

Logan, Joshua. "My Invasion of Marseilles." *Harper's* 223 (July 61) 14–16. Director's own account of making the motion picture **Fanny.**

Caron, Leslie. "Making the Mighty Three-in-One into Logan's **Fanny.**" *F&F* 7 (No. 10, July 61) 7–8. Interview with the star.

"Double Fanny." *Newswk* 63 (1 June 64) 83. Two productions of **Fanny Hill** in work.

"Pictorial Essay: The Unsinkable Fanny Hill." *Playboy* 12 (No. 3, Mar 65) 76–80. Scenes from the movie **Fanny Hill** illustrated in words and pictures.

Hicks, Jimmie. "Fantasia's Silver Anniversary." *FIR* 16 (No. 9, Nov 68) 529–535. History of Disney's film.

Miller, Edwin. "A Hip Trip." *Seventeen* 25 (Oct 66) 116–117. On the making of **Fantastic Voyage.**

Selznick, D. O. "Making a Movie." *Life* 44 (17 Mar 58) 92–94+. Memos from David O. Selznick to various associates during the production of **A Farewell to Arms.**

Flink, Stanley. "Lusty New Role for Julie Christie." *Look* 31 (21 Mar 67) 59–65. About **Far from the Madding Crowd.**

Kahan, Saul. "Transylvania, Polanski Style." *Cinema* (Calif) 3 (No. 4, Dec 66) 7–9. On **The Fearless Vampire Killers.**

Gilbert, Lewis. "**Ferry to Hong Kong** and Why We Went Around the World to Make *All* of It." *F&F* 5 (No. 10, July 59) 19.

Sansom, William. "The Making of **Fires Were Started.**" *FQ* 15 (No. 2, Winter 61–62). *See 5, Humphrey Jennings.*

"Tale of Five Little Shorn Lambs." *Life* 48 (11 Apr 60) 75–78. Actresses have their heads shaved for **Five Branded Women.**

Guerin, Ann. "Tormented Tale of an Innocent." *Life* 64 (16 Feb 68) 88–89+. The filming of **The Fixer** in Budapest.

Alpert, Hollis. "Hollywood in Budapest." *Sat Rev* 50 (23 Dec 67) 20–21+. On the filming of **The Fixer** in Hungary.

Markopoulos, Gregory. "Innocent Revels." *F Cult* (No. 33, 1964) 41–45. Method and purposes of Jack Smith's **Flaming Creatures.**

Conrad, Tony. "Tony Conrad on **The Flicker.**" *F Cult* (No. 41, Summer 66) 1–8. A letter about his film of black-and-white frames; interview by Toby Mussman; mathematical-musical note.

Nugent, Frank S. "**Forever Amber,** or Crime Doesn't Pay." *NYTM* (4 Aug 46) 12+. Only in Hollywood: $300,000 worth of film scrapped to start anew on this film; behind the scenes with scriptwriter and censor.

Kline, H. "**Forgotten Village.**" *Th Arts* 25 (May 41) 336–343. Film making in Mexico.

Jones, G. "How to Make a Movie." *SEP* 210 (9 Oct 37) 8–9; (6 Nov 37) 22–23. Detailed description of movie making from script to publicity using **52nd Street** as an example.

"Franco in Hollywood." *Nation* 155 (19 Dec 42). *See 7e(3)*. About **For Whom the Bell Tolls.**

Silke, James R. "Three Directors in Danger: Robert Aldrich on the Warpath." *Cinema* (Calif) 1 (No. 6, Nov–Dec 63) 4–9. Report on **Four for Texas.**

"No Method: Vincente Minnelli." *Movie* (No. 1, June 62). *See 5, Vincente Minnelli*. About **Four Horsemen of the Apocalypse.**

"Is Nothing Obscene?" *Time* 88 (4 Nov 66). *See 7b(6)*. About film called **491.**

"Pictorial: **The Fox.**" *Playboy* 14 (No. 10, Oct 67) 81–85. Sandy Dennis and Anne Heywood both on and off set.

"Assisi Revisited." *Time* 77 (6 Jan 61) 56. Making Francis of Assisi.

"Film of the Month: **French Can-Can.**" *F&F* 2 (No. 1, Oct 55) 16–17. Photo story of film by Jean Renoir.

"Treasure of the Madre." *Time* 76 (3 Oct 60) 66. Early plans for the making of **Freud.**

West, Jessamyn. "Hollywood Diary: Filming **Friendly Persuasion.**" *Ladies' Home J* 73 (Nov 56) 70–71+.

"Censored: **From Here to Eternity.**" *Look* 17 (25 Aug 53). *See 7c(4)*.

Wald, Jerry. "Screen Adaptation." *FIR* 5 (Feb 54). *See 3f(2)*. About **From Here to Eternity.**

Young, Terence. "Sadism for the Family." *Cinema* (Calif) 1 (No. 5, Aug–Sep 63) 32–

33. Interview about **From Russia with Love.**

Nugent, Frank S. "Hollywood Invades Mexico." *NYTM* (23 Mar 47) 17+. John Ford's **The Fugitive,** shot on location, provides this comparison between the Mexican and American film industries.

Cook, P. "Photographer and His Model Make a Pretty Movie." *Cosmopolitan* 142 (Feb 57) 50–53. Richard Avedon fashion stills from **Funny Face.**

"Fun, Fashions, Photographic Tricks." *Life* 42 (15 Apr 57) 88–91. Picture story on the making of **Funny Face.**

Knight, Arthur. "Choreography for Camera." *Dance Mag* 31 (May 57) 16–22. Production background for **Funny Face.**

"Pictorial: The Girls of **Funny Girl.**" *Playboy* 15 (No. 9, Sep 68) 144–153.

Mothner, I. "Barbra." *Look* 32 (15 Oct 68) 50–53. Streisand and **Funny Girl.**

G

Canham, Cleve. "A Day in the Life of **Gaily, Gaily.**" *Cinéaste* 2 (No. 3, Winter 68–69) 13–15. On-location notes; informal interview with the director, Norman Jewison.

Christopoulos, George. "Markopoulos **Galaxie.**" *F Cult* (No. 42, Fall 66) 2–4. Description of his latest film, which collects a series of motion photographs of people; on pp. 4–7, Gregory Markopoulos describes his own production and the negative reviews in Chicago.

"Technicolor Blossoms in Selznick's **Garden of Allah.**" *Newswk* 8 (21 Nov 36) 20–22. Production story on desert location; director Richard Boleslawski and color director interviewed.

Knight, Arthur. "Japan's Film Revolution." *Sat Rev* 37 (11 Dec 54) 26. Producer Masaichi Nagata talks of style and ritual in **Gate of Hell.**

Kaufman, Sidney. "Odets' First Film." *New Masses* 20 (28 July 36) 12–13. The screenplay for Clifford Odets' forthcoming first film, **The General Died at Dawn,** contains socially aware speeches within the framework of melodrama.

"Pictorial: Saturday Night with Genghis Khan." *Playboy* 12 (No. 9, Sep 65) 153–157. Scenes from movie **Genghis Khan,** with Telly Savalas and friends on set.

Rhode, Eric. "Dostoevsky and Bresson." *S&S* 39 (Spring 70). *See 3f(2).* About **A Gentle Creature.**

Middleton, Russell. "Ethnic Prejudice and Susceptibility to Persuasion." *Am Sociological Rev* 25 (Oct 60). *See 7b(2b).* About **Gentleman's Agreement.**

"Marilyn Takes Over as Lorelei." *Life* 34 (25 May 53) 79–80+. A preview of **Gentlemen Prefer Blondes.**

"A Day from **Gervaise.**" *S&S* 25 (Winter 55–56) 142–143. Photo-report on film by René Clement with Maria Schell.

Whitcomb, Jon. "Liz Taylor as Edna Ferber's Heroine." *Cosmopolitan* 141 (Aug 56) 44–47. On the set of Stevens' **Giant;** location shooting; James Dean.

"A Tale of a Rich Land and Its Lords." *Life* 41 (15 Oct 56) 68–70+. A preview of George Stevens' **Giant.**

Genêt. "Letter from Paris." *New Yorker* 33 (7 Sep 57) 76+. A note on filming of **Gigi.**

Whitcomb, Jon. "Leslie Caron as **Gigi.**" *Cosmopolitan* 144 (May 58) 76–79. Interview on location.

Beaton, Cecil. "On Making **Gigi.**" *Vogue* 131 (June 58). *See 2i(1).*

Beaton, Cecil. "Beaton's Guide to Hollywood." *F&F* 5 (No. 4, Jan 59) 9+. Working on **Gigi.**

"Magnificent Muttonhead." *Time* 77 (5 May 61) 52–53. The making of **Gigot.**

Lassally, Walter. "A Girl in Black." *S&S* 25 (Winter 55–56) 115. Brief production report on the Greek film.

MacMullan, Hugh. "Translating **The Glass Menagerie** to Film." *Hwd Q* 5 (No. 1, Fall 50) 14–32. Dialogue director reports on problems of writing, acting, staging, symbolism, dramatic intent, etc., in bringing the stage play to the screen.

"Mixed Emotions Promise a Box Office Hit at the Movies." *Life* 36 (1 Mar 54) 73+. Audience reaction to **The Glenn Miller Story.**

Taylor, John Russell. "The Go-Between." *S&S* 39 (Autumn 70) 202–203. Joseph Losey shooting this film in a seventeenth-century home.

"Film of the Month: **God's Little Acre.**" *F&F* 4 (No. 12, Sep 58) 18–19. Photo story of the film by Anthony Mann.

"Gone to Earth." *Time* 54 (14 Nov 49) 34+. Troubles in filming of *Gone to Earth* in Britain.

Watts, Richard. "Director's Dilemma." *Cinema Arts* 1 (No. 1, June 37) 21–23. Selznick's difficulties casting **Gone with the Wind.**

Pringle, H. F. "Finished at Last." *Ladies' Home J* 57 (Jan 40) 25+. The inside story of the filming of **Gone with the Wind.**

Dyer, Tom. "The Making of G-W-T-W." *FIR* 8 (May 57) 205–210. A case study of the creation of **Gone with the Wind,** which was planned, cast, made, and exhibited successfully by David O. Selznick without a finished shooting script.

"Box Office Movie Belle Makes Its Third Debut." *Bus Wk* (14 Oct 67) 40–41. The latest "premiere" of MGM's **Gone with the Wind,** a ploy to regain film's No. 1 box-office ranking.

de Havilland, Olivia. "Dream That Never Died:

Gone with the Wind." *Look* 31 (12 Dec 67) 113–114.

Pell, Mike. "Shooting China." *New Masses* 16 (13 Aug 35) 29–30. While shooting **The Good Earth** in China, MGM agreed with Chiang Kai-shek not to use any scenes of poverty and is acquiescing in the exploitation of native extras.

Noble, Lorraine. "**Goodbye, Mr. Chips.**" *S&S* 8 (No. 29, Spring 39) 27–28. One of the writers for the MGM film gives her impressions of the film and its making.

"First Steps Up a Familiar Ladder." *Life* 30 (8 Jan 51) 78–79. Janice Rule is the ingenue in new Warner Brothers film, **Goodbye, My Fancy.**

Surtees, Bob. "Using the Camera Emotionally." *Action* 2 (No. 5, Sep–Oct 67). *See 2e.* About **The Graduate.**

Surtees, Robert L. "**The Graduate's** Photography." *FIR* 19 (No. 2, Feb 68). *See 2e.*

Rollin, Betty. "Mike Nichols: Wizard of Wit." *Look* 32 (2 Apr 68) 71–74. On the filming of **The Graduate.**

Alpert, Hollis. "**The Graduate** Makes Out." *Sat Rev* 51 (6 July 68). *See 7b(1a).*

Macklin, F. Anthony. " '. . . Benjamin Will Survive . . .' Interview with Charles Webb." *F Her* 4 (No. 1, Fall 68). *See 3f(2).* About **The Graduate.**

Daley, Robert. "Race It Like It Was, Baby." *Vogue* 149 (15 Jan 67) 110–111+. On the filming of **Grand Prix.**

Mok, M. "Slumming with Zanuck." *Nation* 150 (3 Feb 40). *See 7a.* About **The Grapes of Wrath.**

Ludwig, William. "Caruso on the Movies." *S&S* 21 (Apr–June 52) 164–165. **The Great Caruso** was a success with audiences; the man who wrote the script answers the charges of critics.

Cooke, Alistair. "Charlie Chaplin." *Atlantic* (Aug 39) 176–185. Emphasis on production of **The Great Dictator.**

Todd, Daniel. "About Chaplin's Film." *New Masses* 37 (17 Dec 40) 30–31. Despite rumors to the contrary, the film industry is not trying to suppress **The Great Dictator**; reaction to the film.

Small, Collie. "Rock of Hollywood." *Collier's* 125 (25 Feb 50) 13–14; (4 Mar 50) 30–31. On Cecil B. De Mille and **The Greatest Show on Earth.**

"De Mille Films **The Greatest Show on Earth.**" *Look* 15 (No. 12, 5 June 51) 36–39. Production story.

"Stars on the Sawdust; **Greatest Show on Earth.**" *Life* 31 (2 July 51) 63–66.

"Cut!" *Newswk* 58 (18 Sep 61) 77–78. **The Greatest Story Ever Told** is indefinitely postponed; financial difficulties at 20th Century-Fox.

"Forget the Incense." *Time* 80 (28 Dec 62) 34. Filming **The Greatest Story Ever Told.**

Trombley, William. "**Greatest Story Ever Told.**" *SEP* 236 (19 Oct 63) 34–40+. Production in Utah desert.

Sayre, Joel. "The Biblical Then & Now—Or, George Stevens, C. B. De Mille and Jesus of Nazareth." *Show* 3 (Nov 63) 114–115+. Comments on the filming of Stevens' **The Greatest Story Ever Told,** director's techniques, casting, locations, etc.; with background comments on the Biblical epics of De Mille.

"**Greatest Story Ever Told.**" *Life* 56 (27 Mar 64) 54–67. A gallery of photographs by Eliot Elisofon from the film.

Knight, Arthur. "Showmanship." *Sat Rev* 48 (5 June 65). *See 6d(2).* About **The Great Race.**

Zeitlin, David. "Greatest Pie Fight Ever Creates a Horrendous Splaat." *Life* 59 (9 July 65) 84–85+. Blake Edwards filming the finale of **The Great Race.**

Daley, Robert. "**Great White Hope** Hits the Movies." *Vogue* 155 (1 Apr 70) 90–96. Production history.

Barthel, Joan. "John Wayne, Superhawk." *NYTM* (24 Dec 67) 4–5+. On the filming of **The Green Berets.** Reply with rejoinder (14 Jan 68) 4+.

"Glory." *New Yorker* 44 (29 June 68) 24–27. Reactions to John Wayne's film **The Green Berets.**

"Gamble on a Fantasy." *Newswk* 52 (24 Nov 58) 110+. Troubles of **Green Mansions**; Audrey Hepburn's and Mel Ferrer's comments.

"Movies in the Making: **Green Mansions.**" *Dance Mag* 33 (Feb 59) 22–23.

Willson, Dixie. "Making Heaven on Earth Was Only a Minor Achievement in Producing **Green Pastures.**" *Good Housekeeping* 103 (Aug 36) 28–29+. Production story.

Mothner, I. "Big Build-Up and a No-Name Cast for **The Group.**" *Look* 29 (7 Sep 65) 32–36. On-set account and closer look at Candice Bergen.

Bergen, Candice. "What I Did Last Summer." *Esq* 64 (Dec 65) 234–237+. Journal of acting in **The Group** and meeting seven other actresses of the movie.

Kael, Pauline. "An Eight-Sided Gambol by **The Group.**" *Life* 60 (8 Apr 66) 116–122. A study of the film's actresses and their roles.

Miller, E. "Kath and Her Aunt Kate." *Seventeen* 27 (Feb 68) 134–135+. Filming of **Guess Who's Coming to Dinner.**

Ronan, Margaret. "The Lively Arts." *Senior Scholastic* 92 (1 Feb 68) 16. Stanley Kramer on the making of **Guess Who's Coming to Dinner.**

Lane, John Francis. "Big Guns." *F&F* 6 (No.

11, Aug 60) 28–29+. On location with **The Guns of Navarone.**

Whitcomb, Jon. "Hollywood Colossus of Rhodes." *Cosmopolitan* 150 (Jan 61) 12–16. On location with **Guns of Navarone,** interviews with stars (Tony Quinn, Irene Papas).

"Realistic Storm: The Filming of a Dramatic Sequence." *Illus London News* 249 (31 Dec 66). 1198–1199. Special effects used in storm sequence of **The Guns of Navarone.**

Pryor, Thomas. "The Goldwyns—and **Guys and Dolls.**" *Collier's* 135 (29 Apr 55). *See 5, Samuel Goldwyn.*

"Gambler's Gambol." *Life* 38 (13 June 55) 164–168+. Producer Sam Goldwyn protected his investment in **Guys and Dolls** by acquiring proven talent—Frank Sinatra and Marlon Brando.

"*Guys* Dolled Up." *Life* 39 (19 Sep 55) 122–131. Preview of Sam Goldwyn's **Guys and Dolls.**

"Michael Kidd and **Guys and Dolls.**" *Dance Mag* 29 (Nov 55) 18–23.

H

Schulberg, B. "The Real Anger Was Backstage." *Life* 69 (21 Aug 70) 50–59. The shooting of **Halls of Anger.**

"Distinguished Decor for **Hamlet** on the Screen." *Illus London News* 212 (31 Jan 48) 136–137. Sets and costumes for Olivier's *Hamlet.*

"Russians Film **Hamlet.**" *Illus London News* 245 (26 Dec 64) 1026–1027.

Friedrichsen, Frank. "The New Goldwyn Girl." *Collier's* 129 (3 May 52) 22–23. Actress Renée Jeanmaire in the film **Hans Christian Andersen.**

"Hans Christian Andersen." *Life* 33 (3 Nov 52) 84–89. A preview of the film.

Hochman, L. "Gjon Mili Photographs **Hans Christian Andersen.**" *Photography* 32 (Jan 53) 44–49+.

"Sweet Tears for Lost Tresses." *Life* 43 (1 July 57) 59–60+. Ten-year-old French actress has her hair cut in **The Happy Road.**

"Rotten Business in the Ring." *Life* 40 (16 Apr 56) 103–104+. Preview of Columbia's **The Harder They Fall,** based on the career of boxer Primo Carnera.

Miller, Edwin. "What Are the Beatles Really Like?" *Seventeen* 23 (Aug 64) 236–237+. A report on the Beatles after finishing **A Hard Day's Night.**

Poppy, J. "Hawaii." *Look* 30 (6 Sep 66) 48–57. On-set account with Julie Andrews.

Tavel, Ronald. "The Banana Diary." *F Cult* (No. 40, Spring 66) 44–66. The making of Andy Warhol's **Harlot;** transcript of sound track; author was one of the actors.

Zeitlin, David. "A Big Bundle of Royalty."

Life 61 (14 Oct 66) 69–70+. The filming of **Hawaii.**

Harvey, E. "Greeks Had a Horse for It." *Collier's* 134 (17 Sep 54) 34–35. New film, **Helen of Troy.**

Castellani, Renato. "Putting Gloss on Prison." *F&F* 5 (No. 7, April 59) 9+. Director writes about his **Hell in the City.**

Kluge, P. F. "Old Foes with a New View of War." *Life* 65 (28 Sep 68) 52–53+. Lee Marvin and Toshiro Mifune recalling their own experiences in the war, while making **Hell in the Pacific.**

Kelly, Gene. "Directing *Dolly.*" *Action* 4 (No. 2, Mar-Apr 69) 8–10. American dancer-director and **Hello, Dolly!**

March, J. M. "About **Hell's Angels.**" *Look* 18 (23 Mar 54) 14. A letter concerning Howard Hughes and the author's part in making **Hell's Angels.**

Hall, Ben M. "Mr. Hughes' War." *Show* 5 (May 65) 69–71. Comments on Howard Hughes' **Hell's Angels;** production details; reshooting with the coming of sound; replacement of Greta Nissen by Jean Harlow; cost figures and audience reactions.

Hiller, Edwin. "On the Scene with the Beatles." *Seventeen* 24 (Aug 65) 230–231+. The filming of **Help!**

"**Herr Puntila and His Servant Matti.**" *S&S* 25 (Autumn 55) 63. Note on new Cavalcanti film based on the Brecht comedy.

Marcorelles, Louis, Henri Colpi, and Richard Roud. "Alain Resnais and **Hiroshima, Mon Amour.**" *S&S* 29 (Winter 59–60) 12–17. Marcorelles offers biographical notes and a survey of Resnais' other films, including his shorts; Henri Colpi, the editor of *Hiroshima,* reports that Resnais stayed close to the script; Roud adds a brief interview with Marguerite Duras on her script.

Lewis, R. W. "Paul Newman Makes a Western." *NYTM* (6 Nov 66) 38–39+. On the filming of **Hombre.**

"Pictorial: Wet and Wild." *Playboy* 15 (No. 8, Aug 68) 116–117. Carroll Baker in nude shower scene from **Honeymoon.**

"Talk with the Makers." *Newswk* 57 (6 Mar 61) 104–105. Don Murray, coproducer of **The Hoodlum Priest,** with former advertising man Walter Wood.

Murray, Don, and Walter Wood. "Conviction or Convention." *F&F* 7 (No. 12, Sep 61) 8+. Coproducers of **The Hoodlum Priest** talk about that film and their plans.

Tyler, Parker. "Has the Horse's Mouth a Golden Tooth?" *Art News* 57 (Jan 59) 38–39+. Discussion of the filmic interpretation of Joyce Cary's novel **The Horse's Mouth,** and John Bratby's painting for the film.

Rosen, Robert. "Enslaved by the Queen of the Night: The Relationship of Ingmar Bergman to E. T. A. Hoffman." *F Com* 6 (No. 1,

Spring 70). *See 3f(2)*. About **Hour of the Wolf.**

Hodge, P. G. "Tree of Liberty on Location." *Publishers Weekly* 137 (11 May 40) 1834–1835. Shooting scenes for the film to be called **The Howards of Virginia.**

Gross, L. "John Lennon: Beatle on His Own." *Look* 30 (13 Dec 66) 58–60+. Filming of **How I Won the War.**

"Wrap-Around Western." *Newswk* 57 (26 June 61) 94–95. The filming of **How the West Was Won.**

Leduc, Violette. "Steal-scening with Hepburn and O'Toole." *Vogue* 147 (1 Apr 66) 172–173. Filming of **How to Steal a Million.**

"The Hunt for Huck." *Newswk* 54 (3 Aug 59) 47–48. Talent hunt for Samuel Goldwyn, Jr.'s, **Huckleberry Finn** and an interview of fourteen applicants.

"Bright Debut of an Old Pro." *Life* 48 (27 June 60) 113–114. Boxer Archie Moore acts in **Huckleberry Finn.**

Crichton, Charles. "Children and Fantasy." *Penguin F Rev* 7 (Sep 48) 44–49. The director of **Hue and Cry** describes the production of his film.

Guerin, Ann. "After *Faces*." *Life* 66 (9 May 69) 53–56+. The filming of John Cassavetes' **Husbands.**

"New Hollywood Is the Old Hollywood." *Time* 96 (7 Dec 70). *See 6c(3)*. About **Husbands.**

"All About Hustlers." *Newswk* 57 (27 Mar 61) 100. Paul Newman and Jackie Gleason acting in a picture so far titled *Sin of Angels*, later called **The Hustler.**

I

Thompson, J. Lee. "I Aim at the Truth." *F&F* 7 (No. 3, Dec 60) 20. The British film director explains why he agreed to make the biography of German rocket scientist Wernher von Braun. **I Aim at the Stars.**

"Film of the Month: **I Am a Camera.**" *F&F* 2 (No. 2, Nov 55) 14–15. Photo story of film.

Atcheson, Richard. "I Was Curious About **I Am Curious (Yellow)** and Found out Why." *Holiday* 44 (Dec 68) 66–67+. A detailed report on Sweden's most controversial movie, banned in U.S. at that time.

Pyryev, Ivan. "From the Book." *F&F* 6 (No. 8, May 60) 29–30. On filming **The Idiot.**

Robinson, David. "Anderson Shooting **If**." *S&S* 37 (Summer 68) 130–131. On-location observations over a period of three months of the filming of three different scenes from Lindsay Anderson's first feature since *This Sporting Life*.

Gladwell, David. "Editing Anderson's **If . . .**" *Screen* 10 (No. 1, Jan–Feb 69). *See 2f*.

"Pictorial: The Reel McNair." *Playboy* 15 (No. 10, Oct 68) 143. Scenes of Barbara McNair in her first nude role, in **If He Hollers, Let Him Go** (with Raymond St. Jacques).

Margulies, Stan. "**If It's Tuesday, This Must Be Belgium.**" *Travel* 131 (June 69) 72–75. Production story on the film.

Whitcomb, Jon. "Songbird Susan." *Cosmopolitan* 140 (Feb 56) 60–63. **I'll Cry Tomorrow,** the story of Lillian Roth.

Björkman, Stig. "**I Love, You Love.**" *Movie* (No. 15, Spring 68) 20–21. The director of the Swedish film describes its making.

Howard, Jane. "Nightmare Lived Again." *Life* 62 (12 May 67) 98–101+. The filming of **In Cold Blood.**

"Strangers Stop Off in Holcomb Again." *Bus Wk* (15 Apr 67) 140–142. With the filming of **In Cold Blood,** Holcomb, Kansas, relives a savage murder.

Gordon, Stanley. "Two Unknowns Seek Movie Fame as Killers: **In Cold Blood.**" *Look* 31 (13 June 67) 114+.

Capote, Truman. "Truman Capote Reports on the Filming of **In Cold Blood.**" *SEP* 241 (13 June 68) 62–65.

Cosulich, Callisto. "Rossellini's India." *F&F* 5 (No. 7, Apr 59) 12. On Rossellini's **India—1958.**

Preminger, Otto. "Keeping Out of Harm's Way." *F&F* 11 (No. 9, June 65) 6. Interview on the making of **In Harm's Way.**

Houston, Penelope. "**The Innocents.**" *S&S* 30 (Summer 61) 114–115. On-set account of the film, with Deborah Kerr and the director, Jack Clayton.

Shaw, Irwin. "My Chancy Life as a Moviemaker." *Vogue* 142 (1 Sep 63) 162–163. On the making of **In the French Style.**

Nolan, William F. "Southern Pride." *F&F* 8 (No. 7, Apr 62) 21+. On the making of **The Intruder,** on Southern school integration.

Knight, Arthur. "Invitation to the Dance." *Dance Mag* 30 (June 56) 14–17. Gene Kelly's integration of dance and cinema in this film.

"**H.M.S. Torrin.**" *Newswk* 20 (21 Dec 42) 80–82. Story of torpedoed destroyer in Noël Coward film **In Which We Serve.**

Roddy, Joseph. "Shirley MacLaine: New Style Star Tries a Rough Role." *Look* 27 (29 Jan 63) 60–65. On-set account of **Irma La Douce.**

Mirisch, Harold. "Who Made Irma?" *Cinema* (Calif) 1 (No. 4, June–July 63) 12–14. Commentary on **Irma La Douce,** Billy Wilder, directors in general, by independent producer.

Krims, Milton. "Iron Curtain Diary." *Screen Writer* 4 (Sep 48). *See 2d*. About **The Iron Curtain.**

Maclain, Jon, and Kenneth Sylvia. "**Isadora.**" *Dance Mag* 42 (Feb 68) 43–47. Production background of this film.

Hamilton, Jack. "Immortal Isadore." *Look* 32 (10 Dec 68) 70–74. On the filming of Karel Reisz' **Isadora.**

"Island and Dissent." *Newswk* 50 (1 July 57) 77. Controversy over Darryl Zanuck's production of **Island in the Sun**.

Genêt. "Letter from Paris." *New Yorker* 41 (18 Sep 65) 142–43. Filming of **Is Paris Burning?**

Fixx, James F. "The Great Gallic Welcome." *Sat Rev* (25 Dec 65) 14–17. The Parisian production of **Is Paris Burning?** Part of *Saturday Review* report "Where the Action Is."

"Defeat of Hitler's Order to Burn Paris: Filming of **Is Paris Burning?**" *Look* 30 (25 Jan 66) 40–45.

Guy, Rory. "**Is Paris Burning?**" *Cinema* (Calif) 3 (No. 3, July 66) 4–7. Article on the movie and its director, René Clement.

Brownlow, Kevin. "**It Happened Here**." *Film* (No. 32, Summer 62) 27–30. An account of the making of the film.

"Doubles for Movie Stars Get Their Own Chance in a Movie." *Life* 3 (18 Oct 37) 78–80. In **It Happened in Hollywood**.

Higham, Charles. "**It's All True**." *S&S* 39 (Spring 70). *See 5, Orson Welles.*

Wilson, Richard. "**It's Not Quite All True**." *S&S* 39 (Autumn 70). *See 5, Orson Welles.* About **It's All True**.

"Ash Can School of Ballet." *Life* 39 (3 Oct 55) 75. Dancers in **It's Always Fair Weather** do an impromptu hoedown with ashcan lids on their feet.

Rose, William. "**It's a Mad, Mad, Mad, Mad World**." *Film* (No. 37, Autumn 63). *See 5, William Rose.*

Hamilton, Jack. "Faye Dunaway: The Farmer's Grand-Daughter." *Look* 30 (13 Dec 66) 108+. Filming of **It's What's Happening!**

Leyda, Jay. "Two-Thirds of a Trilogy." *FQ* 12 (No. 3, Spring 59). *See 4e(8a).* About **Ivan the Terrible**.

J

Treadway, Elizabeth. "**Joan of Arc**." *Collier's* 121 (26 June 48) 24–25. On production of Victor Fleming's film with Ingrid Bergman.

"Bergman as Joan." *Look* 12 (No. 15, 20 July 48) 34–39. Production stills of Ingrid Bergman in **Joan of Arc**; accompanied by brief story on her life and career.

"The Moonchild and the Fifth Beatle." *Time* 93 (7 Feb 69) 50–54. The new anti-star image—Mia Farrow and Dustin Hoffman as trend setters; a report on the filming of **John and Mary**.

Jenkins, Dan. "In an Epic Movie, One Dame Beats Another." *Sports Illus* 21 (20 July 64) 50–54+. On the making of **John Goldfarb, Please Come Home**.

"Notre Dame's Irish Dander Rises Over a Movie." *Life* 57 (18 Dec 64) 68+. Notre Dame president seeks injunction against **John Goldfarb, Please Come Home**.

Zinnamon, J. "Diary of a Dead Bavarian." *Esq* 74 (Dec 70) 68–78. An extra in **Johnny Got His Gun** writes of his experiences on the set.

Manvell, Roger. "End at Nuremburg." *F&F* 7 (No. 2, Nov 60) 10+. On the production of Stanley Kramer's **Judgment at Nuremburg**.

Liber, Nadine. "New Fantasy by the 8½ Man." *Life* 59 (27 Aug 65) 50–54. Fellini shoots **Juliet of the Spirits**.

Meehan, Thomas. "Fantasy, Flesh and Fellini." *SEP* 239 (1 Jan 66) 24–28+. On the filming of **Juliet of the Spirits**, and on Fellini's career.

Bradley, David. "Shooting Caesar." *Sequence* (No. 10, 1950) 171–173. An account by an American film maker of his work in progress, **Julius Caesar**.

Seton, Marie. "Ancient Rome in Gangster Town." *S&S* 19 (June 50) 176–177. About David Bradley's 16mm film, **Julius Caesar**, shot mainly on the steps of a Chicago building, at a cost of about $10,000.

"Speaking of Pictures . . ." *Life* 34 (2 Feb 53) 8–9. Preview of MGM's **Julius Caesar**.

Houseman, John. "On Filming **Julius Caesar**." *FIR* 4 (No. 4, Apr 53) 184–188. The problem was to present Shakespeare's words in a medium primarily visual; case-history account of the MGM 1953 production written by its producer.

Houseman, John. "Filming **Julius Caesar**." *S&S* 23 (July–Sep 53) 24–27. A compilation of two earlier articles (in *Theater Arts*, May 1953, and in *Films in Review*, April 1953), concerned with the film directed by Mr. Houseman.

"Pictorial: The Girls of **Julius Caesar**." *Playboy* 17 (No. 3, Mar 70) 91–95. The Peter Snell version, with John Gielgud and Charlton Heston.

"Even the Stagehands Have to Swim: Filming **Jupiter's Darling**." *Pop Mech* 103 (Jan 55) 93–96.

"Esther Williams' Underwater Industry." *Look* 19 (22 Feb 55) 70+. Filming of **Jupiter's Darling** underwater.

Clarens, Carlos. "Cukor and **Justine**." *S&S* 38 (Spring 69) 74. George Cukor takes over direction from Joseph Strick.

Durrell, Lawrence. "**Justine**: Behind the Novels and the Motion Picture." *Holiday* 45 (Apr 69) 74–77. About the city of Alexandria.

K

Metzner, Ernö. "A Mining Film." *Close Up* 9 (No. 1, Mar 32) 3–9. The set designer discusses the problems of design for Pabst's **Kameradschaft**.

Seton, Marie. "Satyajit Ray at Work on His Film Kanchenjunga." *S&S* 31 (Spring 62) 73–75.

"Pictorial: Susan and Kim." *Playboy* 10 (No. 12, Dec 63) 115–121. Kim Novak and Susan Strasberg in **Kapo.**

Taylor, John Russell. "The Kes Dossier." *S&S* 39 (Summer 70) 130–131. A case history of a boy-bird novel, **A Kestrel for a Knave,** made by Tony Garnett and Ken Loach, and the kind of problems film makers with "an off-beat property" have to face.

Schickel, Richard. "Shock of Seeing a Hidden World." *Life* 65 (1 Nov 68) 34–38. The filming of **The Killing of Sister George.**

"Small House of Uncle Thomas." *Dance Mag* 30 (July 56) 22–23. The painstaking filming of the ballet sequence in **The King and I.**

Lane, John Francis. "My Life as Chaplin's Leading Lady." *F&F* 3 (No. 11, Aug 57) 12–13+. Interview with Dawn Addams about her work in **A King in New York.**

"Unfunny Charlie Chaplin." *Newswk* 50 (9 Sep 57) 108+. Chaplin making **A King in New York.**

Baker, Peter. "Making It B-I-G." *F&F* 7 (No. 2, Nov 60) 14–15+. On location for **King of Kings.**

Carlson, Richard. "Diary of a Hollywood Safari." *Collier's* 126 (8 July 50) 22–24+; (15 July 50) 32–33+; (22 July 50) 20–21+. On **King Solomon's Mines.**

Johnson, Albert. "A Visit to Kismet." *S&S* 25 (Winter 55–56) 152–156. A day at MGM with Vincente Minnelli, director of **Kismet**; the studio setting, the stage, the rehearsal; Minnelli speaks of film making, dancing, set decoration.

Thompson, Thomas. "Wilder's Dirty-Joke Film Stirs a Furor." *Life* 58 (15 Jan 65). *See 7b(6).* About **Kiss Me, Stupid.**

Taylor, John Russell. "Two on the Set." *S&S* 30 (Spring 61). *See 9, The Roman Spring of Mrs. Stone.* About **The Kitchen.**

Lester, Richard. "In Search of the Right Knack." *F&F* 11 (No. 10, July 65) 14–16. Interview on the making of **The Knack.**

"Fun Can Be Work." *Dance Mag* 27 (Dec 53) 21–24. Filming a comic ballet sequence in **Knock on Wood.**

"Takes." *New Yorker* 45 (14 June 69) 31–33. Shooting scenes for **The Kremlin Letter**; an interview with John Huston, the director.

"Pictorial: Bibi and Barbara." *Playboy* 17 (No. 2, Feb 70) 83–85. Bibi Andersson and Barbara Parkins, co-stars of **Kremlin Letter** (off the set).

L

"Triple-Decker Bachelor's Paradise for Jerry Lewis." *Life* 50 (3 Mar 61) 12–13. On the set of **The Ladies' Man.**

Whitcomb, Jon. "Jon Whitcomb Visits Peggy Lee." *Cosmopolitan* 138 (Feb 55) 56–59. Production of **Lady and the Tramp.**

"Saying Something." *Newswk* 62 (5 Aug 63) 72. Frank Perry directs **Ladybug, Ladybug.**

de Havilland, Olivia. "Come Out Fighting." *F&F* 12 (No. 6, Mar 66) 19–21. Interview on her making **Lady in a Cage.**

Lightman, Herb A. "Revolution with a Camera." *Collier's* 118 (9 Nov 46) 22–23+. Robert Montgomery directs and acts in **Lady in the Lake** using subjective camera.

Salemson, Harold J. "The Camera as Narrator —Technique or Toy." *Screen Writer* 2 (Mar 47). *See 2e.* About **Lady in the Lake.**

"Film of the Month: The Ladykillers." *F&F* 2 (No. 4, Jan 56) 18–19. Photo story of film.

Fondiller, H. "Invitation to the Masquerade." *Pop Photog* 66 (Apr 70) 105–107. Production notes from the masquerade-ball sequence of **The Landlord.**

"Great Event Repeats Itself." *Life* 37 (20 Sep 54) 23–29. Preview of Howard Hawks' **Land of the Pharaohs.**

"Lassie, Come Home." *Scholastic* 43 (25 Oct 43) 17–19. Scenes from the MGM version of the book.

Darrach, Brad. "Easy Rider Runs Wild in the Andes." *Life* 68 (19 June 70) 48–50. Dennis Hopper making **The Last Movie**; biography.

Nolan, Tom. "You Can Bring Dennis Hopper to Hollywood But You Can't Take the Dodge City Out of Kansas." *Show* (23 July 70) 20–26. On location with Dennis Hopper and crew for shooting of **The Last Movie** in Peru.

Burke, T. "Dennis Hopper Saves the Movies." *Esq* 74 (Sep 70) 138–141+. Production notes on the making of **The Last Movie.**

"Take to Remember." *Time* 73 (15 June 59) 74+. Sinking a ship for **The Last Voyage.**

Campbell, Alexander. "Farcical Finish of a Famous Old Ship." *Life* 47 (7 Sep 59) 86–90+. The sinking of the *Ile de France* for **The Last Voyage.**

Robbe-Grillet, Alain. *"L'Année Dernière à Marienbad."* *S&S* 30 (Autumn 61) 176–179. How he worked with Resnais during the conception, writing, and making of **Last Year at Marienbad.**

Labarthe, Andre S., and Jacques Rivette. "A Conversation with Alain Resnais and Alain Robbe-Grillet." *NY F Bul* 3 (No. 2, 1962) 1–13. Director and scenarist on **Last Year at Marienbad.**

Colpi, Henri. "On Last Year at Marienbad." *NY F Bull* 3 (No. 2, 1962). *See 2f.*

Resnais, Alain. "Trying to Understand My Own Film." *F&F* 8 (No. 5, Feb 62) 9–10+. Discussion with Resnais about **Last Year at Marienbad.**

Resnais, Alain, and Alain Robbe-Grillet. "Last Words on *Last Year.*" *F&F* 8 (No. 6, Mar 62) 39–41. Discussion about **Last Year at Marienbad.**

Purdy, S. B. "Gertrude Stein at Marienbad." *Pubs Mod Lang Assoc* 85 (No. 5, Oct 70).

See 3f(2). About **Last Year at Marienbad.**

Bogdanovich, Peter. "Otto Preminger." *On Film* (1970). *See 5, Otto Preminger.* About the film **Laura.**

"Lawrence of Arabia." *Newswk* 58 (28 Apr 61) 79–80. In production; comments from David Lean comparing the picture with *Bridge on the River Kwai.*

Knowles, John. "All Out in the Desert." *Horizon* 4 (July 62) 108–111. The filming of **Lawrence of Arabia.**

Bowen, Elizabeth. "Lawrence of Arabia." *Show* 2 (Dec 62) 66–69+. Behind-the-scenes account on location in Seville; a brief excerpt (Lawrence meets Feisal) from Robert Bolt's script.

Fixx, James F. "The Spiegel Touch." *Sat Rev* (29 Dec 62) 13–15. On **Lawrence of Arabia;** part of *Saturday Review* report "The Lonely Art of Film-Making."

Moore, Gerald. "Return of the Prodigy." *Life* 65 (15 Nov 68) 116–124. Gordon Parks and the filming of **The Learning Tree.**

Freeman, Gillian. "On Location at the Ace." *New S&N* 67 (21 Feb 64) 288. The location filming of Sidney Furie's **The Leather Boys.**

Strick, Philip. "White Man's Burdens." *S&S* 38 (Summer 69) 121. John Boorman shooting **Leo the Last** in London.

Melville, Jean-Pierre. "Finding the Truth Without Faith." *F&F* 8 (No. 6, Mar 62) 9. On the new wave and his film **Leon Morin, Priest.**

Colquhoun, Archibald. "On Safari with Visconti." *F&F* 9 (No. 1, Oct 62) 10–11. On the filming of **The Leopard.**

Davies, Brenda. "Can The Leopard . . . ?" *S&S* 33 (Spring 64). *See 4a(4b).*

Zeitlin, David. "Marilyn's Movie Lover." *Life* 49 (15 Aug 60) 64–71. Monroe and Yves Montand rehearse **Let's Make Love.**

Marcorelles, Louis. "*L'Affaire* Vadim." *S&S* 29 (Winter 59–60). *See 4e(2d).* About **Les Liaisons Dangereuses.**

"Zen Commandments." *Time* 78 (11 Aug 61). *See 4f(1).* About **The Life of Buddha.**

"Under the Locusts." *New Yorker* 39 (17 Aug 63) 23. On-set account of **Lilith** and Jean Seberg.

Cohen, Saul B. "Robert Rossen and the Filming of **Lilith.**" *F Com* 3 (No. 2, Spring 65) 3–7. Filmography; description of setups and the director's work with actors; sketches of camera positions.

Seberg, Jean. "Lilith and I." *CdC in Eng* (No. 7, Jan 67) 34–37. The actress writes about Robert Rossen and her title role in his film *Lilith* (interview by Jean-André Fieschi).

Pryor, Thomas M. "How Mr. Chaplin Makes a Movie." *NYTM* (17 Feb 52) 18–19+. On the set of **Limelight.**

"Chaplin at Work." *Life* 32 (17 Mar 52) 117–127. Directing **Limelight.**

Panter-Downes, Mollie. "Letter from London." *New Yorker* 28 (1 Nov 52) 62. The world premiere of Chaplin's **Limelight.**

"The Process of Dissolution." *Commonweal* 57 (6 Feb 53). *See 7c(2d).* About **Limelight.**

"Limelight Out." *Time* 61 (9 Feb 53). *See 7c(1d).*

"Don't Tease the Lion!" *Newswk* 58 (11 Dec 61) 90+. Filming **The Lion** in Kenya.

Weinraub, Bernard. "Director Arthur Penn Takes on General Custer." *NYTM* (21 Dec 69) 10–11+. On the filming of **Little Big Man.**

Merryman, R. (ed.). "Old Age of D. Hoffman." *Life* 69 (20 Nov 70) 75–79. Makeup for 121-year-old character in **Little Big Man;** interview with Hoffman about portrayal.

Astor, G. "Good Guys Wear War Paint." *Look* 34 (1 Dec 70) 56–61. Hoffman and Penn talk about **Little Big Man.**

Hine, A. "Little Boy Lost." *Holiday* 14 (Oct 53) 26+. Interview with William Perlberg, producer of this film.

"Hard Way to Go." *Mech Illus* 66 (June 70) 72+. Motorcycle racing in **Little Fauss and Big Halsy.**

Cohen, Larry. "The Making of **Little Murders.**" *Sat Rev* 53 (8 Aug 70) 19–21. Coverage of the filming as well as background on the origin of the film: transformation from stage to screen.

Niebuhr, Reinhold. "Lolita." *Show* 2 (Aug 62) 63–69. Photographic impressions of Sue Lyon by Bert Stern; comments on Stanley Kubrick adaptation.

"Yes, They Did It: **Lolita** Is a Movie." *Life* 52 (25 May 62) 93–94+. How Kubrick did it.

"Shooting O'Neill." *Newswk* 58 (6 Nov 61) 102. Katharine Hepburn and Sidney Lumet talk about **Long Day's Journey into Night.**

"Economy-Class Journey." *Time* 79 (1 June 62) 50. The success of **Long Day's Journey into Night.**

"Dwight D. Zanuck." *Time* 78 (8 Sep 61) 74. Filming **The Longest Day.**

"Depending on History." *Newswk* 58 (18 Sep 61) 104. Darryl F. Zanuck and actors on set of **The Longest Day.**

Morgan, Thomas B. "Presenting Darryl F. Zanuck's War!" *Esq* 57 (Mar 62) 92–94+. Detailed story on the production of **The Longest Day,** interviews with the cast and Zanuck himself.

Oulahan, Richard, Jr. "The Longest Headache." *Life* 53 (12 Oct 62) 113–114+. Darryl F. Zanuck and the filming of **The Longest Day.**

Zanuck, Darryl F. "A Bank Cheque for the Real Thing." *F&F* 9 (No. 2, Nov 62) 10–11. On the making of **The Longest Day.**

"Return of Awesome Welles." *Life* 44 (24 Feb 58) 53–54+. Orson Welles directed by Martin Ritt: the making of **The Long, Hot Summer.**

Kaufman, Joseph. "Making **Long John Silver**." *F&F* 1 (No. 4, Jan 55) 6. Production notes by the producer.

"Hollywood Calls American Artists." *Art Dig* 14 (June 40) 17. Nine are commissioned ($50,000) to work on the screen version of **The Long Voyage Home**: Thomas Benton, Grant Wood, Ernest Fiene, Raphael Soyer, George Biddle, Robert Philipp, Luis Quintanilla, James Chaplin, and Georges Schreiber. See also *Art Dig* 14 (Aug 40) 10 and 14 (Sep 40) 34 for comments on completed work.

Miller, Edwin. "**Lord Jim** in a Jungle Paradise." *Seventeen* 23 (Nov 64) 132–133+. On the filming of *Lord Jim*.

Hamill, Pete. "**Lord Jim**." *SEP* 237 (21 Nov 64) 24–29. Production story.

"**Lord Jim**." *Life* 58 (22 Jan 65) 85–86. Troubles encountered by Peter O'Toole during production.

Brooks, Richard. "**Lord Jim**." *Cinema* (Calif) 2 (No. 5, Mar–Apr 65) 4–5. Interview with director of this film.

Oshlag, Dorothy. "**Lord of the Flies**." *S&S* 30 (Autumn 61) 175. Peter Brook filming William Golding's novel *Lord of the Flies* on an island near Puerto Rico.

Gutwillig, R. "**Lord of the Flies**." *Vogue* 141 (May 63) 154–157+. Production story.

Wallace, R. "Young Wild Pack in **Lord of the Flies**." *Life* 55 (25 Oct 63) 96–99+.

"Fadeout for Censors?" *Time* 54 (28 Nov 49). *See 7c.* About **Lost Boundaries**.

Weisman, A. "He Passed as a Negro." *Negro Dig* 9 (Oct 51) 16–20. Mel Ferrer's experiences with the public and with his acquaintances after playing a Negro in **Lost Boundaries**; some changes in the script that he and some black cast members requested.

Mitford, Jessica. "Something to Offend Everyone." *Show* 4 (Dec 64) 41–43+. Report on the filming of **The Loved One**; how scriptwriter Terry Southern adapted the Waugh story; denunciations from Forest Lawn, the D.A.R., and Los Angeles handled by MGM's legal department.

"Jonathan Winters." *Cinema* (Calif) 2 (No. 6, July–Aug 65) 9–11. Actor discusses principally **The Loved One**.

"Why Not Be in Paris?" *Newswk* 48 (26 Nov 56) 106+. Behind the scenes of Billy Wilder's **Love in the Afternoon**.

Gillett, John. "Wilder in Paris." *S&S* 26 (Winter 56–57) 142–143. Visit to the set on **Love in the Afternoon**.

"*McCall's* Visits." *McCall's* 84 (June 57) 22. On the set of **Love in the Afternoon** with Gary Cooper and Audrey Hepburn.

"Child Star, '56 Model." *Th Arts* 40 (June 56) 10. How stars were chosen for **Lovers and Lollipops**.

Joel, Lydia. "Ludmila Tcherina in **The Lovers of Teruel**." *Dance Mag* 37 (Jan 63) 32–35.

Mulligan, John. "Vincent van Gogh: The Big Picture." *Paris Rev* (No. 30, Summer–Fall 63) 12–62. Unfavorable account of location shooting and industry preview for **Lust for Life**.

M

Skow, John. "OK, Julie Is a Beautiful Mute, Nymphomaniac Indian Girl." *SEP* 241 (1 June 68) 71–75. Location account of **Mackenna's Gold**.

"Film Life of Friese-Greene, the English Inventor of the Cinematograph." *Illus London News* 219 (22 Sep 51) 454–455. Stills and comments about **The Magic Box**, directed by John Boulting.

Hicks, Jim. "Is That You in There, Ringo?" *Life* 66 (13 June 69) 59–60+. Ringo Starr stars in **The Magic Christian**.

Green, Guy. "**The Magus**." *F&F* 15 (No. 4, Jan 69) 59–61. Director writes about his filming of the book.

Silke, James R. "War." *Cinema* (Calif) 2 (No. 3) 6. Article on Charlton Heston and **Major Dundee**.

Adler, Dick. "New Partner for Dan Rowan, the Werewolf." *Life* 66 (23 May 69) 54–60. Rowan and Martin in film **The Maltese Bippy**.

Hannardt, John. "George Axelrod and **The Manchurian Candidate**." *F Com* 6 (No. 4, Winter 70–71). *See 5, George Axelrod.*

Miller, Edwin. "Peter Pan Is Out!" *Seventeen* 25 (Mar 66) 158–159+. On the filming of **A Man Could Get Killed**.

"We Four Teens in London Town." *Seventeen* 26 (Jan 67) 80–81+. Teenagers report on the filming of **A Man for All Seasons**.

"Suiting Up as a Suburbanite." *Life* 39 (7 Nov 55) 135–136. Gregory Peck visits Madison Avenue and rides a commuter train to prepare for his role in **The Man in the Gray Flannel Suit**.

"A Day in the Life of a Film: **The Man in the White Suit**." *S&S* 19 (Apr 51) 462–463. On the set with the director, Alexander Mackendrick, and Alec Guinness.

Grierson, John. "Making **Man of Africa**." *F&F* 1 (No. 1, Oct 54) 14. Production notes on story film about racial hatred between blacks and pygmies directed by Cyril Frankel, produced by Grierson for Group Three and the colonial office.

"Chaney Chills Them Again." *Life* 43 (2 Sep 57) 105–106+. Pictures from **Man of a Thousand Faces**, the movie biography of Lon Chaney.

"Gay Girl from Gaul." *Life* 28 (26 June 50) 56–58+. Cecile Aubrey, French actress, in **Manon Lescaut**.

Adler, Dick. "Zinnemann's Fate." *Show* (May

70) 40–45. Comments on the filming of Zinnemann's **Man's Fate** and why MGM canceled the production after $4 million of the budget had been expended; remarks on set construction, adaptation, actors, etc.

Knight, Arthur. "Filming **Marat/Sade**." *Sat Rev* 49 (30 July 66) 43. Peter Brook talks about his production in London.

Ronan, Margaret. "Lively Arts." *Senior Scholastic* 90 (31 Mar 67) 21. An interview with Peter Brook on the making of **Marat/Sade**.

Peaslee, Richard. "**Marat/Sade** Diary." *Take One* 2 (No. 8, 1969) 15. Notes on the Peter Brook film by the man who composed the music.

Billard, Ginette. "Richard Todd Tells Why Britain Should Film in France." *F&F* 2 (No. 5, Feb 56) 7. Production story on **Marie Antoinette**.

Joel, Lydia. "**Marjorie Morningstar** on Location." *Dance Mag* 31 (Nov 57) 24–25. Production background.

"Operation Morningstar." *McCall's* 85 (Mar 58) 8+. Interviews with the crew of **Marjorie Morningstar**.

"Stage Set: New York." *NYTM* (30 Sep 51) 48–49. **The Marrying Kind**, with Judy Holliday, is shot on location in Central Park and the Port Authority Bus Terminal in New York.

Klausler, Alfred P. "**Martin Luther**, the Story of a Film." *Chris Cent* 70 (21 Oct 53). *See 4k(5)*.

Pichel, Irving. "**Martin Luther**: The Problem of Documentation." *QFRTV* 8 (No. 2, Winter 53). *See 4k(7)*.

Lee, Robert E. A. "Censorship: A Case History." *Chris Cent* 74 (Feb 57). *See 7c(2b)*. About **Martin Luther**.

Welch, R. J. "**Martin Luther** Film." *America* 96 (23 Mar 57). *See 7c(2b)*.

"Marty in Movies." *NYTM* (20 Mar 55) 36. TV drama (in 1953) has been rewritten for the screen; stills from both versions.

Trutta, G. "**M*A*S*H**." *Harper's Bazaar* 103 (Mar 70) 200–201. A few words by Ingo Preminger on production of his film.

Preminger, Ingo. "**M*A*S*H** Notes." *Esq* 74 (Aug 70). *See 6c(1)*.

Graham, Frank. "Man Behind **M*A*S*H**." *Today's Health* 48 (Dec 70) 24–27. A talk with the doctor, H. Richard Hornberger, M.D., who wrote the novel under the pseudonym Richard Hooker, about the film and his experiences which led to his writing the novel.

Buckley, Jack. "An Ancient Woman." *Opera News* 34 (13 Dec 69) 8–13. About Maria Callas in Pasolini's **Medea**.

"Making of a Big Feature Film: An Artist's Impressions; Drawings by T. T. Cuneo, with Text." *Illus London News* 210 (11 Jan 47) 57. Impressionistic sketches from location

studio shooting of **Meet Me at Dawn**, with brief caption comments.

Hampton, William J. "Film-Making in Michigan." *FIR* 2 (Dec 51) 28–33. A case-history report on the production of a 16mm version of Kafka's **Metamorphosis** in Ann Arbor, Michigan, through the efforts of a collective semiprofessional crew, written by its elected producer-director.

Chapman, Daniel. "Graduate Turns Bum." *Look* 32 (17 Sep 68) 66–72. On the filming of John Schlesinger's **Midnight Cowboy**.

"Hollywood Discovers a Dramatist." *Lit Dig* 120 (14 Sep 35) 29–30. Production details on Reinhardt's **Midsummer Night's Dream** with reference to other studios' plans for Shakespeare.

Shuler, Marjorie. "The Bard of Hollywood." *CSMM* (2 Oct 35) 5. Production details of **Midsummer Night's Dream**.

Verley, Bernard. "Buñuel's Christ." *Film* (No. 56, Autumn 69) 23. A personal account by the actor who played Christ in Buñuel's **The Milky Way**.

Sheriff, Paul. "Designing for an Heiress." *F&F* 7 (No. 2, Nov 60) 16. The designer for **The Millionairess** discusses his job.

"Miracle on 58th Street." *Harper's* 202 (Apr 51). *See 7c(2b)*. About **The Miracle**.

"Another Miracle." *Newswk* 58 (24 July 61) 72. Anne Bancroft in **The Miracle Worker**.

Mathison, R. "Who's a Misfit?" *Newswk* 56 (12 Sep 60) 102–103. Filming of **The Misfits**.

"Famous Pair and a Finale." *Life* 50 (13 Jan 61) 53–54B. The making of **The Misfits**.

Weatherby, W. J. "**The Misfits**: Epic or Requiem?" *Sat Rev* 44 (4 Feb 61) 26–27. Study of the Huston film in production.

McIntyre, A. "Making **The Misfits**." *Esq* 55 (Mar 61) 74–81. Problems with Marilyn Monroe.

Bachmann, Gideon. "Eli Wallach on **The Misfits**." *Film* (No. 29, Summer 61) 13–15. The actor discusses the making of the film.

Koch, Howard. "The Historical Film—Fact and Fantasy." *Screen Writer* 1 (Jan 46). *See 4k(4)*. About **Mission to Moscow**.

"Action at Hell's Gate." *Newswk* 63 (16 Mar 64) 110+. **Mister Moses** shooting in Kenya.

"Carroll Cavorts in Kenya." *Life* 57 (17 July 64) 76–78. The filming of **Mister Moses**.

"Famous Tub Sails Again." *Life* 38 (6 June 55) 82–83+. Preview of Warners' **Mister Roberts**.

"First Christian Western." *Time* 58 (8 Oct 51). *See 4k(5)*. About **Mister Texas**.

"Foolproof." *New Yorker* 26 (13 May 50) 20–21. Shooting **Mister Universe**, a film about wrestling—and the discovery of Vince Edwards.

Henry, Marguerite. "Filming of **Misty of Chincoteague**." *Library J* 86 (15 May 61) 1945–

1946. Author Marguerite Henry watches her book become a film.

"Moby Dick." *NYTM* (8 Aug 54) 42–43. A preview of John Huston's film, on location in Youghal, Ireland.

"Filming in Colour the Hunting of **Moby Dick**." *Illus London News* 225 (9 Oct 54) 597. Location shooting aboard nineteenth-century whaling boat.

"Moby Dick Is Missing." *Life* 37 (22 Nov 54) 52–53. A life-sized model of the giant whale is lost in the North Atlantic.

"The New Captain Ahab." *F&F* 1 (No. 5, Feb 55), 4. Gregory Peck in John Huston's **Moby Dick**.

Harvey, E. "**Moby Dick**." *Collier's* 135 (4 Mar 55) 70–73. Production and direction difficulties of the John Huston picture.

Knight, Arthur. "Director of **Moby Dick**." *Sat Rev* 39 (9 June 56) 29–30. John Huston: his screenplay, locations, and photography.

"White Whale and Woeful Sea." *Life* 40 (25 June 56) 50–53. Preview of John Huston's **Moby Dick**.

de Laurot, Edouard. "John Huston on **Moby Dick**." *Film* (No. 10, Nov–Dec 56) 11–13.

Schwab, Mack. "Chaplin's New Film." *CQ* 3 (No. 2, Winter 35) 88–91. On the set with **Modern Times**.

"Monica Vitti: She's Not That Way at All." *Look* 30 (14 June 66) 83–85. Filming of **Modesty Blaise** and a short interview.

"Glamour in Africa." *Look* 17 (2 June 53) 41–44+. Filming **Mogambo**.

Lane, John Francis. "Moments of Truth." *F&F* 11 (No. 3, Dec 64) 5–10. On the set with Francesco Rosi during the shooting of **Moment of Truth**.

"Pictorial: 37-22-37 Meets 50-47-50." *Playboy* 16 (No. 9, Sep 69) 136–139. Julie Newmar and Zero Mostel in scenes from **Monsieur Le Coq**.

Burke, John A. V. "**Monsieur Vincent**." *S&S* 16 (No. 63, Autumn 47) 89–92. A film supported in part by subscriptions from the French parishes.

Moskowitz, Gene. "A Visit to Jacques Becker and Modigliani." *S&S* 27 (Winter 57–58) 112. Filming the artist's last year: **Montparnasse 19**.

Sheerin, John B. "**Moon Is Blue**." *Cath World* 177 (Aug 53). *See 7c(4)*.

"Movie Producers Stand by the Code." *America* 89 (19 Sep 53). *See 7c(4)*. About **The Moon Is Blue**.

Mage, David A. "The Way John Huston Works." *FIR* 3 (Oct 52) 393–398. A case-history account of the Paris location shooting of **Moulin Rouge** by the second assistant director.

Chassler, S. "Great Imitation; Designs for **Moulin Rouge**." *Collier's* 131 (21 Feb 53)

30–31. A short biography of Marcel Vertès who helped design sets and costumes for John Huston's **Moulin Rouge**.

Hine, A. "Paris in the 90's." *Holiday* 13 (Apr 53) 26–27. Interview with John Huston on location with **Moulin Rouge**.

"Pictorial: Solid Gould." *Playboy* 17 (No. 10, Oct 70) 99–103. Elliott Gould and Paula Prentiss in scenes from **Move**.

"American Queen." *Life* 29 (11 Sep 50) 81. Irene Dunne portrays Queen Victoria in **The Mudlark**.

Hanson, Curtis Lee. "The Mummy." *Cinema* (Calif) 2 (No. 5, Mar–Apr 65) 30–31. Article, credits, stills on the film by Karl Freund.

Jacob, Gilles. "True to Sartre." *S&S* 36 (Summer 67) 123–124. Note on Serge Roullet, who has made **Le Mur**, based on Sartre's Spanish Civil War story.

"Horror Comedy." *New Yorker* 72 (23 July 66) 23–25. Filming of Ken Burrow's **Murder à la Mod**.

Hoellering, George. "The Film of **Murder in the Cathedral**." *Film* (No. 7, Jan–Feb 56) 6–9. By the director of the film version of T. S. Eliot's work.

Joel, Lydia. "Music Man in Hollywood." *Dance Mag* 35 (July 61) 38–39.

"Under the Bam, the Boo." *Time* 77 (10 Feb 61) 45–46+. The making of **Mutiny on the Bounty**.

Zeitlin, David. "Calamity on the Bounty." *Life* 51 (27 Oct 61) 21. The technical and personnel problems encountered in the filming of **Mutiny on the Bounty**.

Davidson, Bill. "Mutiny of Marlon Brando." *SEP* 235 (16 June 62) 18–23. How Brando broke the budget of **Mutiny on the Bounty**.

Peck, Seymour. " 'Enry 'Iggins in 'Ollywood." *NYTM* (1 Sep 63) 20–21. Production stills of **My Fair Lady**.

Seidenbaum, A. "Why They Let George Do It." *McCall's* 92 (Oct 64). *See 5, George Cukor*. About **My Fair Lady**.

Weiss, Jiri. "My Friend the Gypsy." *F&F* 1 (No. 9, June 55) 13–14. The Czech film maker discusses his most recent film.

"East-West Twain Find a Meeting in MacLaine." *Life* 50 (17 Feb 61) 91–96. The actress practices her part in **My Geisha**.

Trillin, Calvin. "Through the Muck with Myra." *Life* 68 (6 Mar 70) 50–52. A day on the set of **Myra Breckinridge**.

Reed, Rex. "Myra Goes Hollywood." *Playboy* 13 (No. 8, Aug 70) 74–80. Off-camera intrigue between Mae West and Raquel Welch on set of **Myra Breckinridge**.

Mendoza, Joe. "Making Mystery at Monstein." *F&F* 1 (No. 2, Nov. 54) 12. Director and scriptwriter describes the making of this film.

N

Trexler, Larry. "Movies in the Making: **Naked Maja.**" *Dance Mag* 32 (Dec 58) 16–17.

Whitcomb, Jon. "Goya's Artistic Violence Makes an Exciting Movie." *Cosmopolitan* 146 (Jan 59) 68–71. Ava Gardner's on- and offscreen performance for **The Naked Maja.**

"Goya's Girl Goes Aloft." *Life* 46 (27 Apr 59). *See 6d(3).* About **The Naked Maja.**

Guy, Rory. "Africa Goes Wilde." *Cinema* (Calif) 3 (No. 1, Dec 65) 44–45. Making of **The Naked Prey,** directed by Cornel Wilde.

Flaherty, Frances. "Flaherty's Quest for Life." *F&F* 5 (No. 4, Jan 59) 8. About **Nanook of the North.**

Brownlow, Kevin. "The Making of a Masterpiece." *F&F* 16 (No. 3, Dec 69) 26–31+. Abel Gance's **Napoleon.**

"**Native Son** Filmed in Argentina." *Ebony* 6 (Jan 51) 84–85. Chicago slums recreated in Buenos Aires; Richard Wright explains ideas about movie making; Pierre Chenal directed author in title role.

Ptushko, A. "The Coming of a New Gulliver." *S&S* 4 (No. 14, Summer 35) 60–62. The Soviet author-director discusses his approach to the making of the film **The New Gulliver.**

Schary, Dore. "Case History of a Movie." *S&S* 19 (Apr 51) 466–471. The birth of a film, **The Next Voice You Hear,** from a producer's standpoint.

"Cast Menagerie." *Time* 82 (8 Nov 63) 69. Filming **The Night of the Iguana.**

"Stars Fell on Mismalaya." *Life* 55 (20 Dec 63) 69–74+. The making of **The Night of the Iguana.**

Lawrenson, Helen. "The Nightmare of the Iguana." *Show* 4 (Jan 64) 46–49+. On location near Puerto Vallarta for the filming of Huston's **The Night of the Iguana.**

Kerr, Deborah. "Days and Nights of the Iguana." *Esq* 61 (May 64) 128–130+. Journal by a co-star in **The Night of the Iguana.**

Davidson, Thelda. "Drama the Cameras Missed." *SEP* 237 (11 July 64) 24–28+. On the filming of **The Night of the Iguana.**

Ebert, Roger. "Just Another Horror Movie, or Is It?" *Rdrs Dig* 94 (June 69). *See 7b(3a).* About **The Night of the Living Dead.**

"Governor Does His Bit." *Life* 41 (22 Oct 56) 61. Colorado's Governor Ed Johnson plays a scene in Universal-International's **Night Passage** as a railroad telegrapher, a job he once held.

Harrington, Curtis. "Curtis Harrington on **Night Tide.**" *Cinema* (Calif) 1 (No. 2) 22. Director talks about his first film.

Robson, Mark. "Nine Hours of My Life." *F&F* 9 (No. 2, Nov 62) 47. On making **Nine Hours to Rama.**

Gidding, Nelson. "Interlude in India." *JSPG* (Mar 63) 27–28. Incidents while on location for **Nine Hours to Rama.**

"Doublethink." *S&S* 25 (Spring 56) 170. Hopeful (revised) ending for **1984** for British viewers.

"New Role for Sinatra-San." *Life* 57 (3 July 64) 80+. Frank Sinatra directs **None But the Brave.**

Bryant, Peter. "Making a Film in Bella Coola." *Take One* 2 (No. 7, 1969) 17–18. Diary of the making of **Noohalk** in Bella Coola, British Columbia.

Joseph, Robert. "Hollywood Discovers Russia." *Calif Arts and Arch* 60 (No. 2, Feb 43) 24+. Preparation for filming Samuel Goldwyn's **The North Star.**

Kramer, Stanley. "Into Surgery For: **Not as a Stranger.**" *Collier's* 135 (4 Feb 55) 78–81. How actors and crew absorb techniques of medical life from real-life hospitals.

Carey, Alida L. "Then and Now." *NYTM* (2 Dec 56) 94+. **The Notebooks of Major Thompson,** shot in Paris, marks the first film in six years by the American expatriate director Preston Sturges.

Cohen, Saul B. "Michael Roemer and Robert Young, Film Makers of **Nothing But a Man.**" *F Com* 3 (No. 2, Spring 65). *See 5, Michael Roemer.*

"Film Clips." *S&S* 33 (Autumn 64) 204. Hitchcock's story about the uranium "McGuffin" in **Notorious.**

Ellis, R. "Movie Star Who Hates His Job." *Negro Dig* 9 (Dec 50) 81–83. Richard Widmark's aversion to playing a bigot in the film **No Way Out.**

"The Wonderful Things." *Newswk* 50 (14 Oct 57) 121. Report on Fred Zinnemann's procedure on **The Nun's Story.**

"**Nun's Story**—Filmed." *America* 101 (23 May 59). *See 7c(2b).*

"Lovely Audrey in Religious Role." *Life* 46 (8 June 59) 141–144. The filming of **The Nun's Story.**

Zinnemann, F. "Director's View: **Nun's Story.**" *America* 101 (27 June 59) 469. Zinnemann tells why he made the film and the story's impact on him.

O

Johnson, Nunnally. "The Long and the Short of It." *F&F* 3 (No. 9, June 57) 10. On the making of **Oh Men! Oh Women!**

Powell, Michael. "Four Powers in Waltz Time." *F&F* 2 (No. 2, Nov 55) 5. Director writes production story on his modern adaptation of *Die Fledermaus,* to be called **Oh, Rosalinda!**

"**Oh, What a Lovely War!** Oh, What a Lovely Cast!" *Holiday* 45 (Jan 69) 70–71. Main characters in the film.

Harvey, E. "**Oklahoma!**" *Collier's* 134 (12

Nov 54) 30–33. Fred Zinnemann filming the stage musical in an Arizona valley.

Reed, A. C. "Oklahoma!, A Visit to the Motion Picture Location in Southern Arizona." *Ariz Highways* 31 (Apr 55) 8–15.

Rodgers, Richard, and Oscar Hammerstein 2nd. "Oklahoma! Revisited." *Good Housekeeping* 140 (June 55) 25+. The creators of *Oklahoma!* discuss its painstaking transcription to the screen.

Knight, Arthur. "Gene Nelson, Agnes De Mille and *Oklahoma!*" *Dance Mag* 29 (July 55) 28–31.

De Mille, Agnes. "Laurey Makes Up Her Mind." *Dance Mag* 37 (Mar 63) 34–35. Notes by choreographer of Oklahoma!

"Tardy Old Man." *Newswk* 49 (18 Mar 57) 117. Production of The Old Man and the Sea.

Hicks, Jim. "Hair-Raising Class of 1830." *Life* 64 (19 Jan 68) 72–76. On-location report of Oliver!

"Twist Twists." *Newswk* 36 (18 Dec 50). *See 7c(4)*. About Oliver Twist.

"Simulating Siberia." *Time* 95 (2 Mar 70) 77. Production notes: filming of One Day in the Life of Ivan Denisovich in Norway.

"Operatic Opener." *Time* 24 (17 Sep 34) 38. Ballyhoo by Columbia for opera star Grace Moore and One Night of Love.

Berchtold, William E. "Grand Opera Goes to Hollywood." *North Am Rev* 239 (Feb 35) 138–146. Reacts to Grace Moore's One Night of Love as setting new trend.

Roud, Richard. "One Plus One." *S&S* 37 (Autumn 68) 182. Note on origins of this film being made in London by Godard.

"One, Two, Three, Wilder." *Show* 1 (Dec 61) 78–79. Photographs by Gjon Mili of Billy Wilder on location in Berlin for the filming of One, Two, Three, with brief comments on the production.

Lane, John Francis. "One-Way Pendulum." *F&F* 11 (No. 2, Nov 64) 6–9. On the filming of One-Way Pendulum; extract from the screenplay included.

"Dire Drama on the Death of the World." *Life* 47 (30 Nov 59) 96. Stanley Kramer and On the Beach.

"Rush: Three Sailors in New York." *New Yorker* 25 (28 May 49) 22–23. Gene Kelly directing On the Town.

Harvey, E. "Saint on the Waterfront." *Collier's* 133 (19 Mar 54) 86–87. Eva Marie Saint in Elia Kazan's On the Waterfront, her film debut.

Massee, Paul. "What Asquith Did for Me." *F&F* 4 (No. 5, Feb 58) 11+. Star of Orders to Kill writes of his experiences with Asquith.

Fonns, Møgens. "Carl Dreyer's New Film." *FIR* 6 (Jan 55) 19–22. Ordet (The Word): the plot of the film, some notes on its history,

the filmic technique of "floating close-ups" used by Dreyer.

Dreyer, Carl. "Metaphysic of Ordet." *F Cult* 2 (No. 7, 1956) 24. Letter from the Danish director Carl Dreyer, concerning Ordet.

Yutkevitch, Sergei. "My Way with Shakespeare." *F&F* 4 (No. 1, Oct 57) 8+. Soviet director of Othello explains his approach.

"Our Town, From Stage to Screen." *Th Arts* 24 (Nov 40) 815–824. Correspondence between the writer, Thornton Wilder, and Sol Lesser, producer of the film.

Farson, Daniel, et al. "A Day in the Life of a Film." *S&S* 20 (June 51) 48–50. Carol Reed directing Outcast of the Islands.

Hubler, Richard G. "As I Remember Birdie." *Screen Writer* 3 (Sep 47). *See 6d(1)*. About The Outlaw.

"Out of the Clouds." *Royal Inst of Brit Arch J* 61 (No. 12, Oct 54) 480. A description of the set of this film.

Field, Sydney. "Outrage." *FQ* 18 (No. 3, Spring 65) 13–39. From script to screen: a blueprint on Hollywood film making. Writer Michael Kanin, producer Ronald Lubin, photographer James Wong Howe, editor Frank Santillo, composer Alex North, and director Martin Ritt discuss their various roles in *The Outrage*, a remake of *Rashomon*.

P

Lawrie, James, and Richard Mason. *"A Pattern of Islands." Film* (No. 7, Jan–Feb 56) 10–13. The producer and the scriptwriter discuss the making of this British film (later titled Pacific Destiny).

Rilla, Wolf, et al. "Pattern of a Film." *Film* (No. 8, Mar–Apr 56) 9–11+. Director, sound recordist, and photographer discuss their work on the British film A Pattern of Islands (Pacific Destiny).

"Pacific Destiny." *Film* (No. 9, Sep–Oct 56) 18–20. A summary of the responses to the British film, earlier entitled A Pattern of Islands, directed by Wolf Rilla and produced by James Lawrie.

"Fool's Gold." *Time* 94 (24 Oct 69) 100+. Lee Marvin on the road promoting Paint Your Wagon.

Brooks, Louise. "Pabst and Lulu." *S&S* 34 (Summer 65). *See 5, Louise Brooks*. About Pandora's Box.

Alda, R. "Why Am I Playing Quarterback for the Detroit Lions?" *SEP* 241 (16 Nov 68) 56–57+. On the filming of Paper Lion.

"Pictorial: Paradiso." *Playboy* 9 (No. 3, Mar 62) 89–93. The first nude film to "show the touch of the experienced director."

"Paris Blues." *Ebony* 16 (Aug 61) 46–50. Picture story of the film starring Sidney Poitier.

"Talk with the Director." *Newswk* 58 (2 Oct

61) 86–87. Martin Ritt's comments on **Paris Blues.**

Champlin, Charles. "Peter's $3 Million Party." *Life* 64 (15 Mar 68) 60A–60B+. The filming of **The Party,** with Peter Sellers.

Bean, Robin. "Passion of Love." *F&F* 11 (No. 12, Sep 65) 43–46. On making this film.

"Twenty-nine and Running." *Newswk* 50 (2 Dec 57) 96. Short interview with Stanley Kubrick while filming **Paths of Glory.**

Lumet, Sidney. "Keep Them on the Hook." *F&F* 11 (No. 1, Oct 64) 17–20. Interview about his making **The Pawnbroker.**

"They Dance on the Walls in Pepe." *Dance Mag* 34 (Dec 60) 34–35.

"The Perils of Betty Hutton." *Look* 11 (No. 11, 27 May 47) 96–98. The American actress in a new film version of **The Perils of Pauline;** also the original serial queen Pearl White, who starred in the series 1913–1924.

"A New Look at Neverland." *Life* 34 (16 Feb 53) 62–63. A preview of Disney's **Peter Pan.**

"Town Playing a Part." *Life* 43 (26 Aug 57) 97–101. Shooting scenes at Camden, Maine, for **Peyton Place.**

"Iron-Curtain Blockbuster." *Illus London News* 245 (24 Oct 64) 662–663. Polish film **The Pharoah.**

" 'Sin City' Sizzles Again, But on Film." *Life* 39 (26 Sep 55) 123–124+. Allied Artists makes a realistic thriller. **The Phenix City Story.**

"A Big Picnic for a Young Star." *Life* 39 (11 July 55) 128–130. Susan Strasberg makes her film debut in Columbia's **Picnic.**

Hamilton, Jack. "Faye & the Italian." *Look* 33 (21 Jan 69) 44–49. On the filming of **A Place for Lovers.**

"Planet Gone Ape." *Life* 63 (18 Aug 67). *See 2i(2).* About **Planet of the Apes.**

Nathan, P. S. "Books into Films: **Plymouth Adventure.**" *Publishers Weekly* 162 (25 Oct 52) 1808.

"Storm over *Mayflower.*" *Life* 33 (17 Nov 52) 122–124+. With miniatures MGM re-creates the Atlantic crossing in **Plymouth Adventure.**

"Capra's Capers." *Newswk* 57 (5 June 61) 93. Cast and their comments on Frank Capra's **Pocketful of Miracles.**

"Talk with the Director." *Newswk* 58 (18 Dec 61) 97–98. Frank Capra's comments on **Pocketful of Miracles.**

Peck, Seymour. "Porgy and Bess Is a Movie Now." *NYTM* (19 Oct 58) 34–35. Production stills.

Houston, Penelope. "Ermanno Olmi in London." *S&S* 31 (Winter 61–62) 16. Note on production details of **Il Posto:** The office building was the Edison Company in Milan; the boy was a young cousin's friend who now has a similar job.

"Finished Portrait." *New Yorker* 23 (26 July 47) 18–19. Brief glimpse behind the scenes

of the filming of **Portrait of Jennie** in Manhattan.

Eisenstein, Sergei. "The Birth of a Film." *Hudson Rev* 4 (No. 2, 1951) 208–221. The making of **Potemkin:** script, physical locale, other reminiscences.

Kurnitz, H. "Antic Arts." *Holiday* 19 (May 56) 85–86. An interview with Stanley Kramer on location with **The Pride and the Passion;** the problems of filming a spectacle.

"Film-Making for a Scene in **The Pride and the Passion.**" *Illus London News* 229 (15 Sep 56) 437.

Alpert, Hollis. "Hollywood in Spanish." *SRL* 39 (22 Sep 56) 32. Report on Stanley Kramer making **The Pride and the Passion** in Spain.

Joel, Lydia. "Movie Star as Flamenco Dancer." *Dance Mag* 31 (Jan 57) 10–11. Production background for **The Pride and the Passion.**

"Epic Tale of a Gun." *Life* 42 (4 Feb 57) 114–123. A gallery of sketches from production of Kramer's **The Pride and the Passion.**

"Scenes from Walt Disney's Adaptation of Mark Twain's **The Prince and the Pauper.**" *Illus London News* 239 (5 Aug 61) 222–223. Twelve photos with a brief synopsis.

Moffitt, Jack. "Intrusion Into the Past." *Collier's* 124 (31 Dec 49) 38–39. On Leon Shamroy's camerawork for **Prince of Foxes.**

Gillett, John. "In Search of Sherlock." *S&S* 39 (Winter 69–70) 26–27. On the set in Scotland and at Pinewood Studios with Billy Wilder; **The Private Life of Sherlock Holmes** marks Wilder's first encounter with British studios and the 128th film featuring Holmes.

"Shoestring." *Newswk* 55 (25 Apr 60) 114. Filming of **Private Property** by independents Leslie Stevens and Stanley Colbert.

Claunch, C. K. "Hollywood Re-Styling: St. Thomas." *Travel* 106 (Aug 56) 26–28. Lieutenant governor of the Virgin Islands tells what happens when Hollywood crew moves in to shoot **The Proud and Profane.**

"On Location with **PT-19.**" *Newswk* 60 (23 July 62) 72–73. Lewis Milestone's doubts about the script and other comments.

Davidson, Bill. "President Kennedy Casts a Movie." *SEP* 235 (8 Sep 62) 26–27. John Kennedy finally decided on Cliff Robertson to play him in **PT-109;** the troubles that beset the film.

"Twenty Years After: **PT-109.**" *Life* 54 (17 May 63) 98+. Choosing the actor to portray President Kennedy.

"New Twist." *Harper's* 207 (Aug 53) 95–97. A French company on location in New York shooting **Public Enemy Number One** with Fernandel.

Hancock, Tony. "Punch and Judy Man." *F&F* 8 (No. 11, Aug 62) 9–10. Comments on this film by the actor.

Condon, F. "Shaw Man." *Collier's* 103 (29

Apr 39) 48–50+. Producer-director Gabriel Pascal and the film version of George Bernard Shaw's **Pygmalion**.

Q

"Disquieted Americans." *Time* 69 (25 Feb 57) 34+. Joseph Mankiewicz in South Vietnam filming **The Quiet American**.

Genêt. "Letter from Rome: Filming of **Quo Vadis?**" *New Yorker* 26 (27 Oct 50) 116+.

Stevens, Edmund. "A New **Quo Vadis?**" *CSMM* (25 Nov 50) 13. Production details on MGM's film.

"**Quo Vadis?**, Colossal Epic." *Life* 30 (9 Apr 51) 52–53.

Surtees, Robert L. "On Filming **Quo Vadis?**" *FIR* 3 (Apr 52) 184–194. Its cinematographer describes the problems of the making of MGM film at the Cinecitta Studios in Rome.

Gray, Hugh. "When in Rome . . . (Part I)." *QFRTV* 10 (No. 3, Spring 56) 262–272. Description of production problems on **Quo Vadis?** by professor-screenwriter. Second article (Summer 1956).

R

Wilson, Jane. "Paul Newman: What If My Eyes Turn Brown?" *SEP* 241 (24 Feb 68). *See 5, Paul Newman.* About **Rachel, Rachel**.

"Joanne and Paul and Rachel." *Life* 65 (18 Oct 68) 46–51+. Joanne Woodward and Paul Newman preparing **Rachel, Rachel**.

"Pictorial: Elsa Martinelli." *Playboy* 10 (No. 10, Oct 63) 142–149. Her nude scenes from upcoming **Rampage** with Robert Mitchum.

Bean, Robin. "On Location with **Rapture**." *F&F* 11 (No. 5, Feb 65) 53–55.

Hitchcock, Alfred. "**Rear Window**." *Take One* 11 (No. 2, 1968) 18–20. The director discusses his film.

Ray, Nicholas. "Story into Script." *S&S* 26 (Autumn 56) 70–74. An abridged chapter from a proposed book; the search for a writer, the writer's place in the Hollywood scheme, and the scripting of the film **Rebel Without a Cause**.

Walters, R. "Enhancement of Punitive Behavior by Audio-Visual Displays." *Science* 136 (8 June 62). *See 7b(4).* About **Rebel Without a Cause**.

Ross, Lillian. "Onward and Upward with the Arts." *New Yorker* 28 (24 May 52) 32–36+; (31 May 52) 29–32+; (7 June 52) 32–34+; (14 June 52) 39–40+; (21 June 52) 31–32+. On-the-spot report of Huston's filming of **The Red Badge of Courage**; basis for her book, *Picture* (Reinhart, 1952).

Reinhardt, Gottfried. "Sound Track Narration." *FIR* 4 (Nov 53). *See 2d.* About **The Red Badge of Courage**.

Richie, Donald. "**Red Beard**." *FQ* 19 (No. 1, Fall 65) 14–25. Extract from Richie's book on Kurosawa (University of California, 1965). Detailed look at his latest film about two doctors: the story, characterizations, actors, sets, music.

Manceaux, Michele. "In the **Red Desert**." *S&S* 33 (Summer 64) 118–119. Short interview with Michelangelo Antonioni reprinted from *L'Express; Il Deserto Rosso* was shooting in Ravenna.

Jacob, Gilles. "**La Religieuse**." *S&S* 35 (Winter 65–66) 21. Note on preparations by Jacques Rivette for making this film.

Minnelli, Vincente. "So We Changed It." *F&F* 5 (No. 2, Nov 58) 7. On **The Reluctant Debutante**.

"Styles and Railings: Errors in the Properties of **Rembrandt**." *Antiques* 31 (No. 2, Feb 37). *See 2j(2).*

"**Requiem at Cohen's**." *Newswk* 58 (4 Dec 61) 88. Location story about **Requiem for a Heavyweight** with Anthony Quinn.

Zeitlin, D. "Good Drizzle After a Big Sizzle." *Life* 57 (26 Feb 65) 45–46+. The filming of **The Reward**.

Bourguignon, Serge. "**The Reward**." *Cinema* (Calif) 2 (No. 5, Mar Apr 65) 6–7. Interview with French director of this film.

"**Les Gangsters**." *NYTM* (20 May 56) 78. Preview of **Rififi**.

"Horse Opera." *Life* 21 (7 Oct 46) 93+. Making **Rio Grande Raiders** at Republic.

Graham, W. Gordon. "The Making of **The River**." *CSMM* (10 June 50) 5. Details of Jean Renoir film.

McEldowney, Melvina. "We Made a Movie Without Hollywood!" (Ed. by P. Martin.) *SEP* 224 (8 Sep 51) 22–23. Jean Renoir's **The River**.

"Pageant of India." *Life* 31 (5 Nov 51) 155–158. Preview of Renoir's **The River**.

Florea, J. "Marilyn on the Rocks." *Collier's* 132 (16 Oct 53) 54–56. Publicity gimmicks for **River of No Return**.

Plimpton, George. "A Block on the Road to Yaksville." *Show* 2 (Apr 62) 95–97+. Filming of **The Road to Hong Kong** with Bob Hope and Bing Crosby at Shepperton Studios in England.

Shamroy, Leon. "Shooting in CinemaScope." *FIR* 4 (May 53). *See 2e(1).* About **The Robe**.

"**The Robe**." *Collier's* 131 (23 May 53) 31–34. Movie version of Lloyd C. Douglas' best seller.

Lane, John Francis. "Pasolini's Road to Calvary." *F&F* 9 (No. 6, Mar 63) 68–70. On the filming of "La Ricotta" section of **Rogopag**.

Taylor, John Russell. "Two on the Set." *S&S* 30 (Spring 61) 72–75. **The Roman Spring of Mrs. Stone** with Vivian Leigh, Warren

Beatty, and director José Quintero; *The Kitchen,* with its director James Hill, writer Arnold Wesker, and producer Sidney Cole.

Quintero, José. "The Play's the Thing." *F&F* 8 (No. 1, Oct 61) 19+. Interview about his first film, **The Roman Spring of Mrs. Stone.**

Simons, Mary. "New **Romeo and Juliet.**" *Look* 31 (17 Oct 67) 52–55+. Preview story, with pictures of Leonard Whiting and Olivia Hussey.

Miller, E. (ed). "Love Is the Sweetest Thing." *Seventeen* 27 (Jan 68) 82–83+. Filming of **Romeo and Juliet.**

"De Sica Seeks a Star." *NYTM* (13 Nov 55) 40. Five hundred hopefuls turn up at his Roman studio when director Vittorio De Sica advertises for an unknown young girl to star in **The Roof.**

"John Huston's Big Stage." *Newswk* 52 (21 July 58) 87. Huston talks about his technique while filming **The Roots of Heaven** in Paris.

Grenier, Cynthia. "Huston at Fountainebleau." *S&S* 28 (Autumn 58) 280–285. Three days of production on **The Roots of Heaven** with the director and Darryl Zanuck.

Hamilton, Jack. "**Rosemary's Baby.**" *Look* 32 (25 June 68) 91–94. On-the-set account of the Roman Polanski film.

Baker, Peter. "Williams' Italian Rose." *F&F* 2 (No. 2, Nov 55) 6. Production story on **The Rose Tattoo.**

Budgen, Suzanne. "Some Notes on the Sources of *La Règle du Jeu.*" *Take One* 1 (No. 12, 1968) 10–12. Some of the literary sources for Renoir's film **Rules of the Game.**

S

McCarthy, Frank. "I Borrowed the British Navy." *Look* 17 (No. 17, 25 Aug 53) 74–77. Production story of **Sailor of the King.**

"Set Free." *New Yorker* 32 (22 Sep 56) 38–39. With Otto Preminger at auditions for the title role of **Saint Joan.**

"St. Joan Nearly Burnt in Earnest: Drama at a Film Studio." *Illus London News* 230 (2 Mar 57) 347. Stills from Preminger's **St. Joan;** one paragraph of production comments.

"Charmer on the Set." *Newswk* 49 (8 Apr 57) 113–114. Otto Preminger making **Saint Joan** with Jean Seberg.

"I.U.M.M.S.W. with Love." *Time* 61 (23 Feb 53) 102. Blacklisted film makers making semidocumentary of mining workers in New Mexico: **Salt of the Earth.**

"Silver City Troubles." *Newswk* 41 (16 Mar 53) 43. Troubles faced by the **Salt of the Earth** company while trying to make a political film about American persecution of Latin Americans.

Bloom, H. "Vigilantism Plays the Villain, Silver City, N. Mex." *Nation* 176 (9 May 53) inside cover. Shooting a film in New Mexico about strike conditions in a mining community: **Salt of the Earth.**

"Typhoons and Takes." *Newswk* 67 (9 May 66) 98+. **Sand Pebbles;** Taiwan location troubles.

Minnelli, Vincente. "**The Sandpiper.**" *Cinema* (Calif) 2 (No. 6, July–Aug 65) 7–8. Director discusses relationship of style to content in this film.

Munsan, F. "Movies and History." *Sat Rev* 24 (3 May 41). *See 4k(4).* About **Santa Fe Trail.**

Alpert, Hollis. "Fellini at Work." *Sat Rev* 52 (12 July 69) 14–17. An on-location account of the filming of **Satyricon.**

Hughes, Eileen. "Old Rome *alla* Fellini." *Life* 67 (15 Aug 69) 56–59+. Fellini's **Satyricon** in the making.

Fellini, Federico. "**Satyricon.**" *F&F* 16 (No. 2, Nov 69) 26–31. Comments on his film.

Langman, Betsy. "Working with Fellini." *Mlle* 70 (Jan 70) 74–75+. An actress recounts her experiences with Fellini in his **Satyricon.**

Rollin, B. "Fellini: He Shoots Dreams on Film." *Look* 34 (10 Mar 70) 48–53. Production notes on the filming of **Satyricon.**

Clark, Roy. "Production Notes on Sayonara." *Dance Mag* 31 (Dec 57) 81.

Wright, C. M. "Community Stands on Its Rights." *Chris Cent* 49 (3 Aug 32). *See 7c(2a).* About **Scarface.**

"Scarlet Street Banned." *Life* 20 (21 Jan 46) 72–74. New York state license denied; picture story of the movie.

"Man-Made Snow for the Studio Scenes in the Film **Scott of the Antarctic.**" *Illus London News* 213 (11 Dec 48) 675.

Balcon, Sir Michael. "The Technical Problems of **Scott of the Antarctic.**" *S&S* 17 (No. 68, Winter 48–49) 153–155.

Blanch, Lesley. "**Sea Gull** from the Wings." *Vogue* 153 (1 Apr 69) 216–217+. On the making of Sidney Lumet's *The Sea Gull.*

Zinnemann, Fred. "The Story of **The Search.**" *Screen Writer* 4 (Aug 48). *See 2d.*

Reed, Allen C. "John Ford Makes Another Movie Classic in Monument Valley." *Ariz Highways* 32 (Apr 56) 4–11. Filming of **The Searchers.**

"Seat in a River." *Life* 43 (16 Sep 57) 16–17. Brief look at the making of Cinerama's **Search for Paradise.**

"Goldwyn vs. Thurber." *Life* 23 (18 Aug 47) 19–20. Producer and author dispute over the transition from story to screen of **The Secret Life of Walter Mitty.**

Bean, Robin. "**The Secret of Santa Vittoria.**" *F&F* 15 (No. 2, Nov 68) 65–68. On location for the shooting of the Stanley Kramer film.

Hamblin, Dora Jane. "Pasta You Want? Pasta You Get!" *Life* 65 (6 Dec 68) 135–136+. The filming of Stanley Kramer's **Secret of Santa Vittoria**.

"A Day in the Life of a Film." *S&S* 21 (Aug–Sep 51) 24–26. On the set of **The Secret People**, directed by Thorold Dickinson.

Frankenheimer, John. "7 Days of 7 Days in May." *F&F* 10 (No. 9, June 64) 9–10. Interview on making of his **Seven Days in May**.

Knebel, Fletcher. "Seven Days in May: The Movie the Military Shunned." *Look* 27 (19 Nov 63) 90–95. Co-author gives his impression of the filming of his novel.

Enley, Frank. "In the Making: **Seven Days to Noon**." *S&S* 19 (Jan 50) 13–15.

"Pictorial: Oh Susannah!" *Playboy* 11 (No. 6, June 64) 75–77. Photos of Susannah York and William Holden in scenes from film **The Seventh Dawn**.

"Monroe Scene: New York's Disgrace." *America* 92 (2 Oct 54) 3. Shooting of a scene for **The Seven-Year Itch**.

"Marilyn on the Town." *Life* 37 (27 Sep 54) 71–72+. Monroe visits Manhattan for location shooting for **Seven-Year Itch**.

"Out of the Shadows." *Newswk* 56 (7 Nov 60) 120. Making of John Cassavetes' film **Shadows**.

Hoover, Clara. "An Interview with Hugh Hurd." *F Com* 1 (No. 4, 1963) 24–27. The Negro actor who played the older brother in **Shadows** comments on John Cassavetes' methods of improvisation and how volunteers sent in money to get the picture started.

Parajanov, Serge. "Shadows of Our Forgotten Ancestors." *F Com* 5 (No. 1, Fall 68) 38–48. Soviet director describes how he made this film in the Carpathian Mountains, describing in his own subjective monologue his avant-garde psychological approach to a romantic triangle; introduced by Steven Hill and translated from *Iskusstvo Kino* (1966, No. 1).

"Hollywood in Ireland; **Shake Hands with the Devil**." *Newswk* 52 (3 Nov 58) 104+. On location with James Cagney.

Bergman, Ingmar. "Moment of Agony." *F&F* 15 (No. 5, Feb 69) 4–6. Discussion of his work, especially **Shame**.

Lynes, Russell. "Never on Tuesday." *Harper's* 236 (Jan 68) 13–16. The filming of **She Let Him Continue** in Barrington, Illinois.

McGivern, William P. "Ship of Fools: Has Stanley Kramer Got a Tiger by the Tail?" *Show* 4 (Sep 64) 57. Difficulties of adapting Porter's novel for the screen; filming at Columbia studio.

Hosie, S. W. "Have You Seen *Shoes*?" *America* 120 (31 May 69). See *7b(1)*. About **The Shoes of the Fisherman**.

"The Director Points His Candid Camera at **Show Boat**." *Look* 15 (No. 11, 22 May 51) 123–127. Production stills from MGM's *Show Boat,* directed by George Sydney.

McCabe, Inger. "A Boy's First Film." *Show* (May 70) 74–77. The scripting and shooting of **Sidelong Glances of a Pigeon Kicker** with emphasis on the script by Ron Whyte.

Burke, P. E. "The Shock of Silence." *F&F* 10 (No. 3, Dec 63) 53–55. On Bergman's **The Silence** and Swedish censorship.

Miller, E. "You've Got to Shout to Make Yourself Heard." *Seventeen* 27 (June 68) 90–91+. Filming of **Sinful Davey**.

"Sink the Bismarck: The Film of the End of a Great German Warship." *Illus London News* 236 (23 Jan 60) 153.

Hulett, J. E., Jr. "Estimating the Net Effect of a Commercial Motion Picture on the Trend of Local Opinion." *Am Sociological Rev* 14 (1949). See *7b(2b)*. About **Sister Kenny**.

Wells, John. "The Mills Family Presents . . ." *F&F* 12 (No. 6, Mar 66) 31–33. Interview about the making of **Sky West and Crooked**.

"Lass in the Brass." *Life* 33 (27 Oct 52) 104. Extras have to stand for long hours during MGM's musical **Small-Town Girl** with Ann Miller.

Boone, A. R. "Snow White and the Seven Dwarfs: First Full-Length Cartoon Movie." *Pop Sci* 132 (Jan 38). See *2h(3)*.

Stillwell, M. "Walt Disney's $10,000,000 Surprise: Snow White and the Seven Dwarfs." *Rdrs Dig* 32 (June 38) 25–26.

Meehan, Thomas. "The Last Days of *The Last Days.*" *Show* 2 (May 62) 79+. On location in Italy for the filming of **The Last Days of Sodom and Gomorrah**.

Nelson, Ralph. "Massacre at Sand Creek." *F&F* 16 (No. 6, Mar 70) 26–27. Interview on **Soldier Blue**.

Whitcomb, J. "Gina as Sheba." *Cosmopolitan* 147 (Aug 59) 12–15. Lollobrigida in the film version of the Biblical love story **Solomon and Sheba**.

Vidor, King. "Me . . . and My Spectacle." *F&F* 6 (No. 1, Oct 59) 6. The making of **Solomon and Sheba**.

Whitcomb, Jon. "The New Monroe." *Cosmopolitan* 146 (Mar 59) 68–71. On the set of **Some Like It Hot** with Marilyn Monroe.

"Walk Like This, Marilyn." *Life* 46 (20 Apr 59) 101–104. Billy Wilder coaches Marilyn Monroe in **Some Like It Hot**.

"Practice for an Actress." *Life* 49 (28 Nov 60) 41–42+. Carroll Baker lives her part in **Something Wild**.

Robin, S. "On Location with Edvard Grieg." *Dance Mag* 44 (Jan 70). See *2b(8)*. About **Song of Norway**.

Lambert, Gavin. "Lawrence: The Script . . ." *F&F* 6 (No. 8, May 60) 9. Screenwriter on his adaptation of **Sons and Lovers**.

Cardiff, Jack. "Lawrence: . . . and the Camera." *F&F* 6 (No. 8, May 60) 9. Director discusses **Sons and Lovers.**

Wald, Jerry. "Scripting **Sons and Lovers.**" *S&S* 29 (Summer 60) 117. Correspondence with Mrs. D. H. Lawrence.

Knight, Arthur. "Dance in the Movies." *Dance Mag* (Feb 55) 9. Especially in **So This Is Paris.**

Poppy, John. "Julie Andrews' Star Rises Higher with **The Sound of Music.**" *Look* 29 (26 Jan 65) 38–42+.

"Gross Is Greener." *Time* 87 (14 Jan 66) 46. The financial success of **The Sound of Music.**

Barthel, Joan. "Biggest Money-Making Movie of All Time, How Come?" *NYTM* (20 Nov 66) 45–47+. On **The Sound of Music.**

Schoenfeld, Bernard C. "The Mistakes of David Loew." *Screen Writer* 1 (Oct 45). *See 5, David Loew.* About **The Southerner.**

Trexler, Larry. "Movies in the Making: **South Pacific.**" *Dance Mag* 32 (Feb 58) 42.

"Dream Coming True." *Newswk* 53 (9 Mar 59) 110–111. The **Spartacus** set in Hollywood, with reporters, Kirk Douglas, cameraman, etc.

"Stanley Kubrick: Thirty-two-Year-Old Director of a $12,000,000 Movie." *Look* 24 (22 Nov 60) 88. Filming of **Spartacus.**

"Reborn **Spirit of St. Louis.**" *Aviation Wkly* 63 (29 Aug 55) 33.

"Yockenee-Poo!" *Newswk* 66 (30 Aug 65) 79. **Stagecoach** is being remade.

Morrison, Chester. "Norman Rockwell: 'Silent' Film Star." *Look* 30 (8 Mar 66) 40+. Noted painter appears in new version of **Stagecoach.**

Davidson, Muriel, and Janet Rale. "**Stagecoach.**" *SEP* 239 (9 Apr 66) 30–33+. The *Stagecoach* remake.

Zill, Jo Ahern. "Julie Plays Gertie." *Look* 31 (19 Sep 67) 26–30+. The filming of **Star!**

Frankel, Haskel. "The Sound of More Music!" *SEP* 241 (29 June 68) 28–33. On the filming of **Star,** with drawings by Al Hirschfeld.

"In **A Star Is Born** Janet Gaynor Is a Star Reborn." *Life* 2 (No. 18, 3 May 37) 41–43.

Brownlow, Kevin. "**Stark Love.**" *Film* (No. 53, Winter 68–69) 15–18. Karl Brown's film, once thought lost and now rediscovered in the Czech archive, is discussed.

West, Stephen. "Sousa Marches On." *Etude* 71 (Jan 53) 10+. Production of **The Stars and Stripes Forever,** based on the life of America's famous bandleader.

"Film of the Month: **Storm over the Nile.**" *F&F* 2 (No. 3, Dec 55) 14–15. Photo story of the film.

"Pearl Harbor, Japanese View." *NYTM* (13 Nov 60) 53–54. Production stills from **Storm over the Pacific,** a Japanese film on Pearl Harbor and its aftermath.

"19 Century Fox." *Time* 88 (8 July 66) 28. Filming **The Story of Doctor Dolittle.**

"Muddle in Puddleby: Protests by Villagers in Castle Combe, England." *Newswk* 68 (11 July 66). *See 2k(4).* About **The Story of Dr. Dolittle.**

Hunt, George P. "Trouble in Puddleby-on-the-Marsh; Castle Combe, England." *Life* 61 (30 Sep 66) 7. A brief report on the filming of **The Story of Dr. Dolittle.**

"Debonair Rex Now a Celebrated Doctor." *Life* 61 (No. 14, 30 Sep 66) 122–124. Rex Harrison in **The Story of Dr. Dolittle.**

"Murder on the Merry-Go-Round: **Strangers on a Train.**" *Life* 31 (9 July 51) 70–72.

Palmer, Cap. "How a Movie Gets Made." *Collier's* 124 (17 Sep 49) 22–23; (24 Sep 49) 28–29. Production details of **The Stratton Story.**

Johnson, Albert. "**Studs Lonigan** and *Elmer Gantry.*" *S&S* 29 (Autumn 60) 173–175. Irving Lerner is interviewed about his first major directing job, *Studs Lonigan,* Richard Brooks about his problems in adapting and directing the Sinclair Lewis novel.

Lerner, Irving. "Breaking Down the Conventional Barriers." *F&F* 7 (No. 7, Apr 61) 18–19+. Director discusses his production of **Studs Lonigan.**

Whitcomb, Jon. "The Subterranean Miss Caron." *Cosmopolitan* 148 (Jan 60) 18–19. Visit to the studio set of **The Subterraneans.**

Alpert, Hollis. "In a Messel Garden." *F&F* 6 (No. 4, Jan 60) 8+. Messel's sets for **Suddenly Last Summer.**

Prouse, Derek. "**Summer Fires.**" *S&S* 34 (Autumn 65) 173–174. Note on French location for this Jean Genet story with Jeanne Moreau directed by Tony Richardson.

"Hepburn in Venice." *NYTM* (19 Sep 54) 66–67. Actress Katharine Hepburn shooting **Summertime** on location.

"Hemingway's Lost Souls." *Life* 43 (16 Sep 57) 61–62+. Descriptions of characters and settings in **The Sun Also Rises.**

Drasin, Dan. "On Making **Sunday.**" *Vision* [*Film Comment*] 1 (No. 1, Spring 62) 20–21. Young director's problems with this film.

Taylor, John Russell. "**Bloody Sunday.**" *S&S* 39 (Autumn 70) 200–201. John Schlesinger shooting **Sunday, Bloody Sunday** at the Café Royal ballroom.

"Forever Gloria." *Life* 28 (5 June 50). *See 5, Gloria Swanson.* About **Sunset Boulevard.**

"**Sunset Boulevard:** Hollywood Tale That Gloria Swanson Makes Great." *Newswk* 35 (26 June 50) 82–84. Production story and Gloria Swanson.

Levin, Meyer. "Writing and Realization." *Screen Writer* 3 (July 47). *See 2d.* About **The Survivors.**

Swisher, Viola H. "Bob Fosse Translates **Sweet Charity** from Stage to Screen." *Dance Mag* 43 (Feb 69) 22–25. Production background.

"Pictorial: Sweet Paula." *Playboy* 16 (No. 8,

19 Aug 69) 82–85. Photos of Paula Kelly in her role in **Sweet Charity.**

"O.K., Everybody Out of the Pool." *Time* 88 (19 Aug 66) 64. Filming **The Swimmer.**

Gowland, T. "Letter from the Set." *Pop Photog* 58 (May 66) 42. Author plays role of magazine photographer in **The Swinger.**

"Pictorial: Ann-Margret as Art." *Playboy* 13 (No. 10, Oct 66) 86–91. Scene from **The Swinger**; she is smeared with paint and rolled on a canvas to make "abstract art."

Whitcomb, Jon. "Swiss Family in Disney's Zoo." *Cosmopolitan* 148 (May 60) 12–15. Filming **Swiss Family Robinson.**

Martin, Pete. "Walt Disney Shoots the Works." *SEP* 233 (10 Dec 60) 38–39+. On the filming of **Swiss Family Robinson.**

T

Griffith, Richard. "Flaherty and **Tabu.**" *F Cult* (No. 20, 1959) 13–14. The second half of **Tabu,** about the collision of two cultures, was Flaherty's special interest in the film he helped F. W. Murnau make.

Flaherty, David. "A Few Reminiscences." *F Cult* (No. 20, 1959) 14–16. How F. W. Murnau and David and Robert Flaherty began the making of **Tabu.**

Clarke, T. E. B. "Every Word in Its Place." *F&F* 4 (No. 5, Feb 58) 10+. Screenwriter approaches adapting **A Tale of Two Cities.**

"The Bawd of Avon." *Time* 87 (3 June 66) 58. Brief reports on the making of **The Taming of the Shrew.**

Lane, John Francis. "**The Taming of the Shrew.**" *F&F* 13 (No. 1, Oct 66) 52–54. On the filming.

"This Time They're Taming the Shrew." *Look* 30 (4 Oct 66) 58–63. The Burton and Taylor version of Shakespeare's **The Taming of the Shrew.**

Braddon, Russell. "Richard Burton to Liz: I Love Thee Not . . ." *SEP* 239 (3 Dec 66) 88–91. On the filming of **The Taming of the Shrew.**

"Charge!" *Show* 2 (Apr 62) 66–69. Photographs by Ernst Haas/Magnum of the filming of **Taras Bulba.**

"Russian Ruckus on the Pampas." *Life* 52 (18 May 62) 66–75. Filming **Taras Bulba** in Argentina.

Miller. Edwin. "Tony Curtis and Yul Brynner Among the Cossacks." *Seventeen* 21 (Oct 62) 92–93+. On the filming of **Taras Bulba.**

"Pall of the Wild." *Time* 86 (29 Oct 65) 60. Filming **Tarzan and the Big River.**

Rothwell, John. "*Rashomon* Girl Tries Western Comedy." *F&F* 3 (No. 6, Mar 57) 6. Machiko Kyo in **Teahouse of the August Moon.**

"Stars in the Soup." *Life* 27 (11 July 49) 61–62+. Rosalind Russell and Robert Cum-

mings spend a day treading water for a scene in **Tell It to the Judge.**

"Violent Spectacle in Battle." *Life* 46 (30 Mar 59) 40–45. The production of **The Tempest** in Yugoslavia.

Lattuada, Alberto. "We Take the Actors into the Streets." *F&F* 5 (No. 7, April 59) 8+. Shooting on location for **The Tempest.**

"De Mille Directs His Biggest Spectacle." *Life* 39 (24 Oct 55) 142–149. **The Ten Commandments** in Egypt.

Harbert, Ruth. "How They Filmed the Movies' Biggest Scene." *Good Housekeeping* 142 (Apr 56) 103–104+. The Exodus sequence in De Mille's **The Ten Commandments.**

Hill, Gladwin. "Most Colossal of All." *NYTM* (12 Aug 56). See 5, Cecil B. De Mille. About **The Ten Commandments.**

Maas, P. "Yul Brynner's Candid Camera Covers **The Ten Commandments.**" *Collier's* 138 (14 Sep 56) 90–93.

Gray, Martin. "New Treatment for the Old Testament." *F&F* 3 (No. 1, Oct 56) 8. **The Ten Commandments** is reviewed, with emphasis on how it was made and the relationship of the Old Testament story to the final script.

De Mille's Greatest." *Life* 41 (12 Nov 56) 115–118. A preview of **The Ten Commandments.**

"Fitzgerald on Film: **Tender Is the Night.**" *Newswk* 58 (17 July 61) 83–84.

"Pasolini's **Teorema.**" *America* 120 (3 May 69) 518. Review of censorship tribulations of this film.

Walsh, Moira. "**Teorema.**" *America* 120 (10 May 69). See 7c(2b).

"New Star from Italy." *Life* 30 (19 Mar 51) 77–78+. Picture story about Italian actress Pier Angeli in new film, **Teresa.**

"Temperament at a Terminal." *Life* (9 Mar 53) 135–136. David Selznick and Vittorio De Sica make **Terminal Station** together in Rome.

Prouse, Derek. "Le Testament d'Orphée." *S&S* 29 (Winter 59–60) 18–19. Jean Cocteau acting in and directing his last film on location.

Grenier, Cynthia. "Film of the Mad." *S&S* 27 (Autumn 58) 276. Production note on Franju's first feature, **La Tête Contre les Murs.**

Riley, Philip. "That Uncertain Feeling." *London Mag* new series 1 (No. 5, Aug 61) 74–78. Filming the British adaptation of the Kingsley Amis novel; a talk with Peter Sellers.

Mankiewicz, Joseph L. "Cocking a Snook." *F&F* 16 (No. 2, Nov 70) 18–22. On his filming of **There Was a Crooked Man.**

Adler, Dick. "They Danced Till They Dropped." *Life* 67 (25 July 69) 58–61. The making of **They Shoot Horses, Don't They?**

Dempsey, Michael. "They Shaft Writers, Don't They?—James Poe Interviewed." *F Com* 6

(No. 4, Winter 70–71). *See 2d.* About **They Shoot Horses, Don't They?**

Greene, C., and R. Rouse. "It Had to Be Told Without Dialogue." *Th Arts* 36 (Oct 52) 74–75+. Producers' conception of **The Thief,** which uses sound effects but otherwise is "purely visual."

Boone, Andrew R. "Hollywood Planets Wage Space War." *Pop Sci* 165 (Nov 54) 768–769. Filming of **This Island Earth.**

"Filming Finale of **This Is the Army.**" *Life* 15 (12 July 43) 84–85. Technical procedures involved in filming a complicated scene.

Milne, Tom. "**This Sporting Life.**" *S&S* 31 (Summer 62) 113–115. Production story and interview with director Lindsay Anderson.

Lipscomb, James. "Improvise! Films Are Made of Whimsy." *Life* 63 (10 Nov 67) 86–88+. On the Set with Norman Jewison on **Thomas Crown Affair.**

Hamilton, John. "When the 20th Century Got Off the Ground." *Look* 29 (12 Jan 65) 44–49. Production of **Those Magnificent Men in Their Flying Machines.**

Schoenbaum, David. "The Threepenny Opera." *S&S* 33 (Winter 63–64) 22–23. Wolfgang Staudte's remake stirs little political excitement in Munich.

"The Good Sergeant's Return." *Life* 39 (31 Oct 55) 101–102+. A U.S. soldier returns to Japan to be technical advisor for a film, **Three Stripes in the Sun,** about his construction of an orphanage during the occupation.

"Film of the Month: **Throne of Blood.**" *F&F* 4 (No. 9, June 58) 20–21. Photo story of Kurosawa's *Macbeth* film.

Maibaum, Richard. "My Word Is His Bond." *Esq* 63 (June 65) 73+. A view from the back room: writing and producing **Thunderball.** Detailed descriptions of machinery and guns used (pp. 62–72).

Zimmermann, Gereon. "James Bond Conquers All in **Thunderball.**" *Look* 29 (13 July 65) 45–50+. Shooting in Nassau; talk with Sean Connery.

Zinsser, William K. "The Big Bond Bonanza." *SEP* 238 (17 July 65) 76–81. On the filming of **Thunderball.**

Allen, Betty. "Sean Connery Takes Over Rock Point." *Mlle* 62 (Dec 65) 127+. Shooting of **Thunderball:** a poolside view.

Stern, Seymour. "*Que Viva Mexico!*" *CQ* 1 (No. 2, Winter 32) 73–80. "The fate of Eisenstein's American Film" (**Thunder over Mexico**); readers urged to send protest letters to Upton Sinclair.

"Manifesto on Eisenstein's Mexican Film." *Close Up* 10 (No. 2, June 33) 210–212; (No. 3 Sep 33) 248–254. Originally prepared by *Experimental Cinema,* this manifesto called for Eisenstein to be allowed to

edit the Mexican footage and to stop distribution of **Thunder over Mexico;** a second manifesto was issued later.

Bond, Kirk. "Destruction of a Masterpiece." *Adelphi* 6 (Aug 33) 372–374. The end of Eisenstein's *Que Viva Mexico!* (**Thunder Over Mexico**): the value of the work.

Bond, Kirk. "Spoliation of *Que Viva Mexico!*" *Hound & Horn* 7 (No. 1, Oct–Dec 33) 144. An attack on Upton Sinclair's reediting of Eisenstein's film and the upcoming release of it as **Thunder over Mexico.**

Sinclair, Upton. "**Thunder over Mexico.**" *Close Up* 10 (No. 4, Dec 33) 361–363. A letter to the magazine, defending his actions concerning *Que Viva Mexico!*

Montagu, Ivor. "Sinclair Tragedy: Eisenstein's **Thunder over Mexico.**" *New S&N* 7 (20 Jan 34) 85–86. Upton Sinclair's version of difficulties with Eisenstein's *Que Viva Mexico!*

Seton, Marie. "Treasure Trove." *S&S* 8 (No. 31, Autumn 39) 89–92. The recovery and some description of the lost 100,000 feet of Eisenstein's *Que Viva Mexico!* (**Thunder Over Mexico**).

Leyda, Jay. "Eisenstein's Mexican Tragedy." *S&S* 27 (Autumn 58) 305–308. Author describes his attempts to recatalogue *Que Viva Mexico!* (**Thunder Over Mexico**); director's sketches and outline of epilogue reproduced.

Erdman, R. "Time of My Life: Making a Motion Picture of William Saroyan's Play, **The Time of Your Life.**" *Th Arts* 32 (Apr 48) 47–48.

Sanders, Denis, and Terry Sanders. "Small Films Can Have Big Themes." *F&F* 2 (No. 9, June 56) 13. Production notes for **Time Out of War.**

Cutts, John. "**Time Without Pity.**" *S&S* 26 (Autumn 56) 61. Note on Joseph Losey's new film in production in London.

Murphy, Audie. "Soldier Relives Anzio." *Collier's* 136 (2 Sep 55) 72–73. Audie Murphy's notes on what he felt while repeating before the cameras his own battle actions for **To Hell and Back.**

"Triumph in Cannes." *Sports Illus* 22 (31 May 65) 17. Response to Ichikawa's **Tokyo Olympiad.**

LaBadie, Donald W. "Albert Finney & Tom Jones." *Show* 3 (June 63) 64–65+. Remarks on the acting career of Albert Finney, with comments on location shooting of *Tom Jones* and on Richardson's directing technique.

"From Script to Screen." *Scholastic* 31 (15 Jan 38) 30–31. Behind the scenes of **Tom Sawyer** from book to film.

"Classic into Movie." *Publishers Weekly* 33 (5 Feb 38). *See 7c(1d).* About **Tom Sawyer.**

"Cast of Directors." *Time* 92 (20 Dec 68) 78. Finding Japanese businessmen for roles in **Tora! Tora! Tora!**

"Filming a Day That Will Live in Infamy." *Bus Wk* (28 June 69) 68–70. The filming of **Tora! Tora! Tora!**

Ehrlich, H. "**Tora! Tora! Tora!**" *Look* 34 (22 Sep 70) 27–32. Factual background.

Nugent, John. "Hitchcock's Three Nightmares." *Newswk* 67 (24 Jan 66) 89–89A+. Interview at the time of production of **Torn Curtain**.

Ronan, Margaret. "Teacher in Slum School." *Senior Scholastic* 90 (7 Apr 67) sup 6. Interview with Edward Braithwaite, author of **To Sir with Love.**

Riggan, Byron. "Damn the Crocodiles, Keep the Cameras Rolling!" *Am Heritage* 19 (June 68) 38–45+. The filming of **Trader Horn,** Hollywood's first jungle spectacular.

"Big-Bang Bagatelle." *Newswk* 60 (20 Apr 64) 112. John Frankenheimer's costly troubles with **The Train.**

"Leapin' Gina." *Life* 39 (24 Oct 55) 173–174. Gina Lollobrigida practices on trampoline for her acrobatic role in **Trapeze.**

"This Daring Young Man." *Newswk* 47 (4 June 56) 94+. Inside look at the filming of **Trapeze.**

Guerin, Ann. "A Traveling Executioner in Heaven." *Show* (25 June 70) 36–38. Comments on the filming of **The Traveling Executioner** (MGM, Jack Smight), at Kilby Prison near Montgomery, Alabama.

"Prodigal Revived." *Time* 79 (29 June 62) 30. Orson Welles back at work, filming **The Trial.**

Martinez, Enrique. "**The Trial** of Orson Welles." *F&F* 9 (No. 1, Oct 62) 12–15. French critic on the filming of **The Trial.**

"Pictorial: **The Trip.**" *Playboy* 14 (No. 10, Oct 67) 106–109. Peter Fonda and Susan Strasberg on camera.

Lewis, Marshall. "**Triumph of the Will.**" *NY F Bul* (Nos. 12–14, 1960) 7–8. Its propaganda background and physical planning.

Miller, Henry. "**Tropic of Cancer** Revisited." *Playboy* 17 (No. 6, June 70). See 3f(2).

"Good Men and True and All Angry." *Life* 42 (22 Apr 57) 137–138. Sidney Lumet makes **Twelve Angry Men.**

"A Weird New Film World." *Life* 36 (22 Feb 54) 111–117. Scenes under water in Disney's **20,000 Leagues Under the Sea.**

Harbert, R. "Assignment in Hollywood: Under the Sea." *Good Housekeeping* 139 (Nov 54) 114+. Filming the attack of the giant squid in **20,000 Leagues Under the Sea.**

"Plush Parlor for Captain Nemo." *Life* 38 (10 Jan 55) 42–43. A lavish Victorian salon is built inside the submarine *Nautilus* for Disney's **20,000 Leagues Under the Sea.**

"Visualizing." *Times Lit Supplement* 3,405 (1 June 67). See 2d. About **Two for the Road.**

"Beyond the Stars." *New Yorker* 41 (24 Apr 65) 38–39. Session with Stanley Kubrick and Arthur C. Clarke about their science-fiction movie to be called *Journey Beyond the Stars* (subsequently **2001: A Space Odyssey**).

Robinson, David. "Two for the Sci-Fi." *S&S* 35 (Spring 66) 75–81. A report on two films in production in England, Stanley Kubrick's **2001: A Space Odyssey** and François Truffaut's *Fahrenheit 451.*

"Kubrick, Farther Out." *Newswk* 68 (12 Sep 66) 106+. Filming of **2001: A Space Odyssey.**

Spinrad, Norman. "Stanley Kubrick in the 21st Century." *Cinema* (Calif) 3 (No. 4, Dec 66) 4–6+. A prerelease analysis of **2001: A Space Odyssey,** and a theory of its relationship to science-fiction films.

Dempewolff, R.F. "**2001:** Backstage Magic for a Trip to Saturn." *Pop Mech* 127 (Apr 67) 106–109+.

"Inside *2001.*" *Take One* 1 (No. 11, 1968) 18–22. Interview with Wally Gentleman, director of special effects for Kubrick's **2001: A Space Odyssey.**

Rosenfeld, Albert. "Fanciful Leap Across the Ages." *Life* 64 (5 Apr 68) 24–35. Planning session for **2001: A Space Odyssey.**

Dempewolff, Richard. "How They Made **2001.**" *Sci Dig* 63 (May 68) 34–39. Reprinted from *Popular Mechanics* (1967).

Clark, Paul Sargent. "*2001:* A Design Preview." *Industrial Design* 15 (May 68) 34–41. A review of the technology displayed in Stanley Kubrick's **2001: A Space Odyssey,** the agencies and corporations that supplied designs and data, and an appraisal of the future of technology.

Shuldiner, Herbert. "How They Filmed **2001: A Space Odyssey.**" *Pop Sci* 192 (June 68) 62–79.

James, Clive. "**2001:** Kubrick vs. Clarke." *Cinema* (Cambridge) (No. 2, Mar 69) 18–21. Differences and similarities between the director and the author of the story.

McKee, Mel. "**2001:** Out of the Silent Planet." *S&S* 38 (Autumn 69) 204–207. Parallels between C. S. Lewis' science-fiction novel *The Ransom Trilogy* and Stanley Kubrick's film of Arthur C. Clarke's novel; "one could almost argue that *2001* is *The Ransom Trilogy* visualised."

James, Clive. "**2001:** Kubrick vs. Clarke." *F Soc Rev* 5 (No. 5, Jan 70) 27–35. Kubrick's concern for formal beauty and lack of interest in a strictly narrative science-fiction film versus Clarke's contribution—the maintenance of thematic and linear continuity.

U

"Joycensors Beware." *Newswk* 69 (19 Sep 66) 110+. Making a movie out of James Joyce's **Ulysses.**

"Ulysses." *Life* 62 (31 Mar 67) 54–58. Making the film.

"Not the Best, Not the Worst." *Time* 89 (31

Mar 67) 92+. On the making of **Ulysses**.

Wiser, William. "**Ulysses** at Cannes." *Playboy* 15 (No. 5, May 68) 101. Negative reception given *Ulysses* at Cannes Film Festival described; also recounts the fight over censoring the film.

McVay, Douglas. "The Music in *Les Parapluies*." Film (No. 42, Winter 64) 31–32. An analysis and appreciation of Michel Legrand's score for the film **The Umbrellas of Cherbourg**.

Demy, Jacques. "I Prefer the Sun to the Rain." *F Com* 3 (No. 2, Spring 65) 61. Director comments on his film **The Umbrellas of Cherbourg**.

Patrick, Nigel. "Directing My First Film." *F&F* 3 (No. 8, May 57) 7+. On directing **Uncle George**.

"Cinema Chekhov." *NYTM* (24 June 56) 34. **Uncle Vanya** is brought to the screen by an American company.

"Epic in Durango." *Time* 73 (23 Mar 59) 70. Trouble while filming **The Unforgiven**.

Percey, H. G. "Union Pacific: Use of Western History in Creative Work." *Ore His Q* 41 (June 40). *See 2j(4)*.

Miller, Edwin. "Anyone You Know?" *Seventeen* 26 (June 67) 118–119+. On the making of **Up the Down Staircase**.

"Uptight." *Ebony* 24 (Nov 68) 46–48+. Production story of this film.

Skow, John. "Uptight!" *SEP* 242 (25 Jan 69) 36–39+. On the filming of *Uptight*, about black revolution.

V

Rollin, Betty. "Dames in the **Valley of the Dolls**." *Look* 31 (5 Sep 67) 53–56+. Pictures of the female stars.

Weinberg, Herman G., and Gretchen Weinberg. "Vampyr—An Interview with Baron de Gunzburg." *F Cult* (No. 32, 1964) 57–59. Personal account of the filming of Carl Dreyer's *Vampyr*.

Harvey, E. "Coop Gets Girl, Burt Gets Bullet." *Collier's* 134 (6 Aug 54) 72–73. **Vera Cruz**, starring Gary Cooper and Burt Lancaster.

"Set 'Em Up in the Other Valley." *Life* 37 (20 Dec 54) 80–82. A preview of **Vera Cruz**.

James, Howard. "To the Spoils Go the Victors." *Cinema* (Calif) 1 (No. 5, Aug–Sep 63) 9–11. Pictures of actresses in Carl Foreman's film **The Victors**, and article.

Foreman, Carl. "The Road to **The Victors**." *F&F* 9 (No. 12, Sep 63) 11–12. On the filming of *The Victors*.

Bruner, J., and G. Fowler. "The Strategy of Terror: Audience Response to *Blitzkrieg im Western*." *J of Abnormal and Social Psych* 36 (1941). *See 7b(5)*. About **Victory in the West**.

"Why Am I Happy?" *Newswk* 57 (12 June 61) 94. On-set account of Sidney Lumet's **A View from the Bridge** in Paris.

"Massing the Vikings." *Newswk* 50 (26 Aug 57) 96. Production of **The Vikings** in Norway, with Kirk Douglas' comments.

Whitcomb, Jon. "Kirk Douglas Makes a Violent Movie." *Cosmopolitan* 144 (June 58) 16–19. On location with **The Vikings**.

Nichols, M. "Little Viking on Location." *Coronet* 44 (July 58) 26–33. Filming of **The Vikings**.

Buñuel, Luis. "On Viridiana." *F Cult* (No. 24, 1962) 74–75. The Spanish director comments on his film.

"Sight and Sound." *McCall's* 91 (Nov 63) 12+. On location of **Viva Las Vegas** with Elvis Presley and Ann-Margret.

Brossard, Chandler. "On the Set with Moreau and Bardot." *Look* 29 (4 May 65) 64–66+. Filming of **Viva Maria**.

"New Star over Hollywood." *Coronet* 31 (Apr 52) 14–15. Jean Peters in **Viva Zapata**.

Maben, Adrian. "Le Voleur." *S&S* 36 (Winter 66–67) 16. Louis Malle making this film with Jean-Paul Belmondo as the thief.

W

Ehrlich, Henry. "Anjelica." *Look* 32 (12 Nov 68) 66–71. The filming of John Huston's **A Walk with Love and Death**.

Koningsberger, Hans. "From Book to Film—via John Huston." *FQ* 22 (No. 3, Spring 69). *See 3f(2)*. About **A Walk with Love and Death**.

Mayer, Arthur. "War and Peace." *FIR* 7 (Aug–Sep 56) 314–316. A case history of the film version of Tolstoy's *War and Peace*, produced by Dino De Laurentiis and directed by King Vidor; others planning to make it were MGM, David Selznick, and Michael Todd.

Miller, Edwin. "A Budding Ballet Dancer Becomes the Greatest Heroine of All Russia." *Seventeen* 27 (Aug 68) 270–271+. On Russia's film **War and Peace** and its star, Ludmila Savelyeva.

Guralnik, Vran. "Vast as an Ocean." *F&F* 15 (No. 8, May 69) 60–63. On Bondarchuk's **War and Peace**.

Blue, James, and Michael Gill. "Peter Watkins Discusses His Suppressed Nuclear Film, **The War Game**." *F Com* 3 (No. 4, Fall 65) 4–19. How the director got the hypothetical situation of a nuclear attack on Great Britain to "look real" on the screen; amateur actors and nonactors; pp. 4–12 consist of responses to the film by various critics and observers, some of whom agree with the BBC-TV decision not to show it.

Brossard, Owen B. "Step Right This Way to Movieland: Studio Tour of Universal and

Visit to **Warlord Set**." *Senior Scholastic* 86 (13 May 65) 34.

"Hollywood Builds Flying Saucers." *Pop Sci* 161 (Nov 52) 132–134. Filming of **War of the Worlds**.

Kocian, E. "Smile, Comrade Napoleon . . . Ah *Molto Bene*." *Atlas* 19 (Jan 70) 53–55. The trials of making an Italian-Russian-Rod Steiger collaboration film (**Waterloo**) in the Soviet Union.

Dunbar, Ernest. "Godfrey Cambridge Turns White." *Look* 33 (30 Dec 69) 57+. On the filming of **Watermelon Man**.

Fondiller, H. V. "Starting at the Top." *Pop Photog* 67 (Apr 70) 117–118. The career of Barry Brown, producer-director of **The Way We Live Now**.

Alpert, Hollis. "**West Side Story**." *Dance Mag* 34 (Oct 60) 36–39.

Alpert, Hollis. "Getting the Boys on Their Toes." *F&F* 7 (No. 5, Feb 61) 20–21+. Choreography in **West Side Story** on location.

Allen, Woody. "What's Nude, Pussycat?" *Playboy* 12 (No. 8, Aug 65) 99–107. Scenes from **What's New, Pussycat?** with accompanying text by actor and screenwriter Allen.

"Faith Domergue." *Life* 29 (17 July 50) 79. Picture story of actress in **Where Danger Lies**.

MacDonough, Scott. "Oh Momma! Poor Momma! Where's Poppa?" *Show* (17 Sep 70) 20–25. Filming of **Where's Poppa?** with emphasis on George Segal's role in the film.

MacCann, Richard Dyer. "Louis De Rochemont Turns Facts into Fiction, with Care." *CSMM* (30 Dec 50) 14. **The Whistle at Eaton Falls** on location in New Hampshire.

Kahan, Saul. "Who Is Polly?" *F&F* 14 (No. 5, Feb 68) 47. On the making of **Who Are You, Polly Maggoo?**

"Call Me Elizabeth." *Newswk* 66 (13 Sep 65) 86. Filming **Who's Afraid of Virginia Woolf?**

Jennings, C. Robert. "All for the Love of Mike." *SEP* 238 (9 Oct 65) 83–87. On the filming of **Who's Afraid of Virginia Woolf?**

Roddy, J. "Elizabeth Taylor and Richard Burton: The Night of the Brawl." *Look* 30 (8 Feb 66) 42–48. Filming of **Who's Afraid of Virginia Woolf?**

Newquist, R. "Behind the Scenes of a Shocking Movie." *McCall's* 93 (June 66) 86–89. **Who's Afraid of Virginia Woolf?**

Thompson, Thomas. "Surprising Liz in a Film Shocker." *Life* 60 (10 June 66). *See* 7b(6). About **Who's Afraid of Virginia Woolf?**

Mailer, Norman. "Some Dirt in the Talk: A Candid History of an Existential Movie Called **Wild 90**." *Esq* 68 (Dec 67) 190–194+. Writer-director on his own film.

Lardner, Ring, Jr. "**Wilson** and the Boxoffice." *New Masses* 52 (5 Sep 44) 27–28. Because it is so expensive, *Wilson* will lose money,

and this will hurt those trying to get backing for other "significant" pictures.

Sjöman, S. "From L 136: A Diary of Ingmar Bergman's **Winter Light**." (Tr. by K. Grimstad.) *Lit Rev* 9 (Winter 65–66) 257–265.

Dent, Alan. " 'Tis Music Makes the World Go Round." *Illus London News* 220 (3 May 52) 756. The sentimentality of **With a Song in My Heart**.

Hall, J. "**Wizard of Oz**." *Good Housekeeping* 109 (Aug 39) 40–41. Behind the scenes and on the sets of the motion-picture production: whimsical interviews and pictures.

Whitcomb, Jon. "On Location with the Opposite Sex." *Cosmopolitan* 141 (Oct 56) 68–71. Remake of Cukor's **The Women** (1939); differences of stars then and now.

Oares, Phillip. "Ken & Glenda & Peter & Nina." *Show* (Mar 70) 56–59+. Report on the filming of **Women in Love** with supplementary comments from Glenda Jackson and Ken Russell.

Kobal, John. "Al Jolson and Wonder-bar." *Film* (No. 59, Summer 70) 21–23. Jolson's film, **Wonderbar**, is seen as a paradigm of failures by theatrical personalities to make films.

"A Cinerama Battle: Who's Being Shot?" *Show* 2 (2 Feb 62) 95–97. Photographs with brief comments on the filming of **The Wonderful World of the Brothers Grimm**.

"Toy." *New Yorker* 37 (9 Sep 61) 34–37. The filming of **Wondrous Troy**, a movie shot completely on location in New York.

Miller, Edwin. "New Faces in a Smash New Movie." *Seventeen* 23 (June 64) 132–133+. On the making of **The World of Henry Orient**.

"Hong Kong *Wong*." *Newswk* 55 (8 Feb 60) 102. On location with **The World of Suzie Wong**.

Whitcomb, Jon. "New Suzie Wong." *Cosmopolitan* 148 (June 60) 10–13. Nancy Kwan during filming of **The World of Suzie Wong**.

Innes, Hammond. "A Film That Put Me All to Sea." *F&F* 6 (No. 6, Mar 60) 27–28. Background and filming of **The Wreck of the Mary Deare**.

Havener, H. "Reader Interest Stimulated." *Lib J* 64 (15 May 39). *See* 3f(2). About **Wuthering Heights**.

Y

Maerka, Christa. "**Years of the Cuckoo**—A Success in Europe." *Cinema* (Calif) 3 (No. 6, Winter 67) 39. *The Years of the Cuckoo* and its director, George Moorse.

Chamberlin, Jo Hubbard. "Motion Picture Making Isn't All Glamour." *Nation's Business* 26 (Oct 38) 20–22+. Behind the scenes of **You Can't Take It with You**; detailed look at budget, sets, etc.

Gogen, William. "Jottings from a Dublin Journal." *Show* 5 (Jan 65) 46–49. Observations on the filming of **Young Cassidy**, based on Sean O'Casey's boyhood; emphasis on actors (Julie Christie, Maggie Smith, and Rod Taylor) and locations.

Duncan, Douglas. "Hollywood Goes to a Hospital." *Today's Health* 39 (July 61) 19–23. On the filming of **The Young Doctors.**

Dahl, Roald. "007's Oriental Eyefuls." *Playboy* 14 (No. 6, June 67) 86–91. Girls from **You Only Live Twice.**

Golden, David. "Praise Be the Mayor." *Action* 2 (No. 3, May–June 67). *See 2k(4).* About **You're a Big Boy Now.**

Z

Joseph, Robert. "Billboards, Beards, and Beads." *Cinema* (Calif) 4 (No. 4, 1968) 2–6. On Antonioni and the making of **Zabriskie Point.**

Kinder, Marsha. "*Zabriskie Point.*" *S&S* 38 (Winter 68–69) 26–30. An interview conducted with Antonioni in Death Valley, where he was shooting his first American film; his intentions, his young actors, union and budget problems.

Bosworth, Patricia. "Antonioni Discovers America." *Holiday* 45 (Mar 69) 64–65+. Italian director preparing **Zabriskie Point.**

Hamilton, Jack. "Antonioni's America." *Look* 33 (18 Nov 69) 36–40. On the filming of **Zabriskie Point.**

Antonioni, M. "Let's Talk about **Zabriskie Point.**" *Esq* 74 (Aug 70) 69+. The director writes about his film.

Gindoff, Bryan. "Thalberg Didn't Look Happy; Or, With Antonioni at **Zabriskie Point.**" *FQ* 24 (No. 1, Fall 70) 3–6. How the pairs of lovers were rehearsed for the scene in Death Valley.

Index

Rubenstein, Leonard, 229
Rubin, D., 104
Rubin, Joan Alleman, 12, 349
Rubio, Miguel, 323, 459
Rubsamen, Walter H., 17, 64, 67
Ruby, Jay, 429
Rukeyser, Muriel, 54
Rule, John T., 333
Rush, Barbara, 250
Russel, Bob, 327
Russell, Evelyn, 106, 115
Russell, Ken, 48, 311
Russell, Lee, 101, 249, 271, 272, 279, 281, 288, 294, 307, 310, 320
Russell, Robert, 122, 437
Russell, Rosalind, 404
Rutherford, Eldred, 69, 378
Ryall, Tom, 220
Ryan, Terry, 218
Ryskind, M., 33, 397, 408
Ryu, Ohishu, 300

Saalschutz, L., 89, 220, 435
Sachs, Charles, 138
Sachs, Hanns, 95, 99
Sadleir, Michael, 194
Sadoul, Georges, 151, 169, 172, 186, 187, 188, 293, 301, 444
Safilios-Rothschild, C., 199, 363
Sagan, Leontine, 26, 41
Sagar, Isobel C., 72
Sage, M., 390, 460
Sage, Tom, 457, 462
Sahl, Mort, 121
Sainsburgy, Peter, 189
St. John, Earl, 25
Saisselin, Remy G., 224
Saks, Gene, 311
Sale, Richard, 77
Salemson, Harold J., 57, 189, 254, 399, 469
Salomon, Barbara, 189, 412
Salomon, G., 374
Saltzman, Harry, 174, 311
Sammis, Edward, 444
Samuels, C. T., 244, 282
Samuels, Gertrude, 42
Sancton, Thomas, 362
Sanders, Charles L., 252
Sanders, Denis, 482
Sanders, Terry B., 332, 347, 482
Sanderson, I. T., 415
Sandler, C., 78
Sanford, John, 324
Sanger, Gerald, 432, 433
Sanjines, Jorge, 106
Sansom, William, 285, 463
Santar, Karel, 206
Santelli, Cesar, 239, 374
Sargeant, Winthrop, 263
Sarha, Kolita, 212
Sarlin, Bob, 451
Sarne, Mike, 34, 43
Saroyan, William, 49, 54, 159, 296
Sarris, Andrew, 19, 30, 43, 98, 99, 104, 109, 110, 113, 117, 124, 125, 129, 130, 134, 135, 155, 165, 166, 224, 274, 275, 279, 283, 291, 294, 300, 304, 306, 310, 349, 383, 387, 449
Sarthe, Jean, 26
Sarton, Edgar, 437
Sasaki, Norio, 91

Sauvage, Leo, 107, 185, 366, 439
Sayers, Dorothy L., 237
Sayers, Frances, 71, 148, 264
Sayers, Jack, 329
Sayre, Gertrude, 404
Sayre, Joel, 40, 87, 317, 404, 465
Sazonov, Alexei, 207
Schaffner, Franklin, 311
Schallert, Edwin, 112, 330
Scharper, Phillip J., 228
Schary, Dore, 25, 136, 330, 332, 344, 351, 363, 368, 400, 457, 474
Schauder, Leon, 213
Schecter, Leona Protas, 208, 445
Schein, Harry, 14, 198, 221, 223, 265, 335
Schemke, Irmgard, 440
Schenck, Aubrey, 344
Schenk, Rolf, 194
Scher, Saul N., 249
Scherer, Maurice, 310
Scherk, Alfred, 190
Scherman, D., 148
Scheuer, Dick Richards, 110
Scheuer, Philip K., 225, 246, 259, 262, 279, 330
Scheufele, Kirk, 16
Schickel, R., 71, 111, 117, 148, 167, 197, 199, 225, 235, 297, 304, 326, 379, 384, 403, 450, 469
Schiffer, George, 65, 348, 402
Schillaci, Anthony, 167, 369
Schindel, M., 236
Schire, David, 372
Schlanger, Ben, 358
Schleifer, Marc, 97
Schlesinger, Arthur, Jr., 137, 166, 412
Schlesinger, John, 312
Schlichter, Karl, 372
Schnee, Charles, 32, 350, 402
Schnitzler, Peter, 12
Schnurmacher, Emile C., 58, 431
Schoenbaum, David, 197, 482
Schoenberg, Arnold, 100
Schoenfeld, Bernard C., 292, 480
Schoeni, Helen, 200
Schoenstein, Ralph, 359
Schofield, Stanley, 98
Schonert, Vernon L., 289, 298
Schooling, Patricia, 235
Schorer, Mark, 208, 237
Schrader, C. N., 372
Schrader, Leonard, 300
Schrader, Paul, 238, 249, 258, 266, 302
Schreiber, Flora Rheta, 427
Schrire, David, 102, 269, 435
Schroeder, Barbet, 442
Schulberg, B., 50, 56, 146, 151, 153, 154, 166, 195, 227, 329, 404, 405, 466
Schulberg, Stuart, 193, 196, 324, 420, 453
Schuldenfrei, Robert, 307
Schumach, M., 324, 385
Schuster, Mel, 289
Schuth, H. Wayne, 12
Schwab, Mack W., 71, 473
Schwartz, Allen K., 126
Schwartz, Delmore, 334
Schwartz, J., 365
Schwartz, Tony, 428
Schwartz, Zachary, 69
Schwegler, Edward S., 391
Schwerin, Jules, 69, 320
Scott, Adrian, 103, 125, 461
Scott, Barbara, 386